International Directory of

COMPANY HISTORIES

International Directory of COMPANY HISTORIES

VOLUME 41

Editor
Tina Grant

ST. JAMES PRESS
AN IMPRINT OF THE GALE GROUP
DETROIT • NEW YORK • SAN FRANCISCO
LONDON • BOSTON • WOODBRIDGE, CT

STAFF

Tina Grant, *Editor*

Miranda H. Ferrara, *Project Manager*

Erin Bealmear, Christa Brelin, Joann Cerrito, Steve Cusack, Kristin Hart, Melissa Hill, Margaret Mazurkiewicz, Carol Schwartz, Christine Tomassini, Michael J. Tyrkus, *St. James Press Editorial Staff*

Peter M. Gareffa, *Managing Editor, St. James Press*

Library of Congress Catalog Number: 89-190943

British Library Cataloguing in Publication Data

International directory of company histories. Vol. 41
I. Tina Grant
338.7409

ISBN 1-55862-446-5

Printed in the United States of America
Published simultaneously in the United Kingdom

St. James Press is an imprint of The Gale Group

Cover photograph: Istanbul Stock Exchange
(courtesy: Istanbul Stock Exchange)

10 9 8 7 6 5 4 3 2 1

CONTENTS

Company Histories

PREFACE

The St. James Press series *The International Directory of Company Histories (IDCH)* is intended for reference use by students, business people, librarians, historians, economists, investors, job candidates, and others who seek to learn more about the historical development of the world's most important companies. To date, *IDCH* has covered over 5,125 companies in 41 volumes.

Inclusion Criteria

Most companies chosen for inclusion in *IDCH* have achieved a minimum of US$25 million in annual sales and are leading influences in their industries or geographical locations. Companies may be publicly held, private, or nonprofit. State-owned companies that are important in their industries and that may operate much like public or private companies also are included. Wholly owned subsidiaries and divisions are profiled if they meet the requirements for inclusion. Entries on companies that have had major changes since they were last profiled may be selected for updating.

The *IDCH* series highlights 10% private and nonprofit companies, and features updated entries on approximately 45 companies per volume.

Entry Format

Each entry begins with the company's legal name, the address of its headquarters, its telephone, toll-free, and fax numbers, and its web site. A statement of public, private, state, or parent ownership follows. A company with a legal name in both English and the language of its headquarters country is listed by the English name, with the native-language name in parentheses.

The company's founding or earliest incorporation date, the number of employees, and the most recent available sales figures follow. Sales figures are given in local currencies with equivalents in U.S. dollars. For some private companies, sales figures are estimates and indicated by the abbreviation *est.* The entry lists the exchanges on which a company's stock is traded and its ticker symbol, as well as the company's NAIC codes.

Entries generally contain a *Company Perspectives* box which provides a short summary of the company's mission, goals, and ideals, a *Key Dates* box highlighting milestones in the company's history, lists of *Principal Subsidiaries, Principal Divisions, Principal Operating Units, Principal Competitors,* and articles for *Further Reading.*

American spelling is used throughout *IDCH*, and the word "billion" is used in its U.S. sense of one thousand million.

Sources

Entries have been compiled from publicly accessible sources both in print and on the Internet such as general and academic periodicals, books, annual reports, and material supplied by the companies themselves.

Cumulative Indexes

IDCH contains three indexes: the **Index to Companies**, which provides an alphabetical index to companies discussed in the text as well as to companies profiled, the **Index to Industries**, which allows researchers to locate companies by their principal industry, and the **Geographic Index**, which lists companies alphabetically by the country of their headquarters. The indexes are cumulative and specific instructions for using them are found immediately preceding each index.

Suggestions Welcome

Comments and suggestions from users of *IDCH* on any aspect of the product as well as suggestions for companies to be included or updated are cordially invited. Please write:

The Editor
International Directory of Company Histories
St. James Press
27500 Drake Rd.
Farmington Hills, Michigan 48331-3535

ABBREVIATIONS FOR FORMS OF COMPANY INCORPORATION

A.B.	Aktiebolaget (Sweden)
A.G.	Aktiengesellschaft (Germany, Switzerland)
A.S.	Aksjeselskap (Denmark, Norway)
A.S.	Atieselskab (Denmark)
A.Ş.	Anomin Şirket (Turkey)
B.V.	Besloten Vennootschap met beperkte, Aansprakelijkheid (The Netherlands)
Co.	Company (United Kingdom, United States)
Corp.	Corporation (United States)
G.I.E.	Groupement d'Intérêt Economique (France)
GmbH	Gesellschaft mit beschränkter Haftung (Germany)
H.B.	Handelsbolaget (Sweden)
Inc.	Incorporated (United States)
KGaA	Kommanditgesellschaft auf Aktien (Germany)
K.K.	Kabushiki Kaisha (Japan)
LLC	Limited Liability Company (Middle East)
Ltd.	Limited (Canada, Japan, United Kingdom, United States)
N.V.	Naamloze Vennootschap (The Netherlands)
OY	Osakeyhtiöt (Finland)
PLC	Public Limited Company (United Kingdom)
PTY.	Proprietary (Australia, Hong Kong, South Africa)
S.A.	Société Anonyme (Belgium, France, Switzerland)
SpA	Società per Azioni (Italy)

ABBREVIATIONS FOR CURRENCY

$	United States dollar
£	United Kingdom pound
¥	Japanese yen
A$	Australian dollar
AED	United Arab Emirates dirham
B	Thai baht
B	Venezuelan bolivar
BFr	Belgian franc
C$	Canadian dollar
CHF	Switzerland franc
COL	Colombian peso
Cr	Brazilian cruzado
CZK	Czech Republic koruny
DA	Algerian dinar
Dfl	Netherlands florin
DKr	Danish krone
DM	German mark
E£	Egyptian pound
Esc	Portuguese escudo
EUR	Euro dollars
FFr	French franc
Fmk	Finnish markka
GRD	Greek drachma
HK$	Hong Kong dollar
HUF	Hungarian forint
IR£	Irish pound
K	Zambian kwacha
KD	Kuwaiti dinar
L	Italian lira
LuxFr	Luxembourgian franc
M$	Malaysian ringgit
N	Nigerian naira
Nfl	Netherlands florin
NIS	Israeli new shekel
NKr	Norwegian krone
NT$	Taiwanese dollar
NZ$	New Zealand dollar
P	Philippine peso
PLN	Polish zloty
Pta	Spanish peseta
R	Brazilian real
R	South African rand
RMB	Chinese renminbi
RO	Omani rial
Rp	Indonesian rupiah
Rs	Indian rupee
Ru	Russian ruble
S$	Singapore dollar
Sch	Austrian schilling
SFr	Swiss franc
SKr	Swedish krona
SRls	Saudi Arabian riyal
W	Korean won
W	South Korean won

International Directory of

COMPANY HISTORIES

AK Steel Holding Corporation

703 Curtis Street
Middletown, Ohio 45043
U.S.A.
Telephone: (513) 425-5000
Fax: (513) 425-2676
Web site: http://www.aksteel.com

Public Company
Incorporated: 1899 as The American Rolling Mill Company
Employees: 11,500
Sales: $4.6 billion (2000)
Stock Exchanges: New York
Ticker Symbol: AKS
NAIC: 331221 Rolled Steel Shape Manufacturing; 324199 All Other Petroleum and Coal Products Manufacturing; 551112 Offices of Other Holding Companies

AK Steel Holding Corporation is the controlling body for numerous steel production companies throughout the United States, including its own namesake, AK Steel Corporation. AK Steel manufactures and sells value-added hot-rolled and cold-rolled steel, flat carbon steel, stainless steel, and specialty electrical steels. AK then sells its product to other manufacturers, such as the construction, automotive, and appliance industries. AK Steel Holding Corp. also owns Sawhill Tubular Products, a steel pipe and tubing manufacturer; Douglas Dynamics L.L.C., the largest producer of snowplows and ice control products in North America; and the Greens Port Industrial Park in Texas. AK Steel Holding acquired steel producer Armco Inc. in 1999, a purchase that secured the firm as a leader in the carbon, stainless, and electrical steel markets.

The Early Years

The history of AK Steel Holding Corporation itself (incorporated in 1994) is extremely short, yet the company's roots actually date back to the late 1800s. In 1899, the American Rolling Mill Company was created to engage in the production of rolled steel, mainly for other manufacturers to use in their own products. After 20 years of successful production, the company had laid plans for and broken ground at the site of a new manufacturing facility at Middletown, Ohio. The facility, dubbed Middletown Works, remained in operation into the 1990s as one of AK Steel's two principal production plants.

The company's second production plant was erected in Ashland, Kentucky, 11 years later. The facility was named Ashland Works and joined Middletown in the production of both coated and uncoated rolled steel. The plants produced the company's custom-engineered, low-carbon steel products through two different processes. Both hot and cold flat rolling procedures were used to create the company's high-strength steel sheets.

The American Rolling Mill Company continued to operate its steel mills under that name for almost 30 years after Ashland was constructed. Then in 1948, the company adopted the acronym ''ARMCO,'' and soon thereafter, changed its formal name to Armco Steel Corporation.

Acquisitions in the 1950s–70s

After realizing a decent amount of success with the Middletown and Ashland production centers, Armco began to purchase additional steel facilities in the 1950s. These purchases were added to the company's existing holdings, subsequently adopting both the Armco name and business procedures. This practice continued for two decades, as Armco expanded its operational base both geographically and throughout the steel industry itself. Geographic expansion enabled the company to distribute its finished product to a wider base of customers more easily, while expansion in the steel industry gave the company more market share.

In 1978, Armco Steel Corporation changed its name to Armco Inc., which more accurately reflected the company's few nonsteel holdings that had been added during Armco's acquisition phase. The original steel mill holdings, Middletown and Ashland Works, were placed in a newly formed group called the

Company Perspectives:

AK Steel offers a diverse product line unmatched by any other competitor in the market. Our flat-rolled carbon, stainless and electrical steels meet and exceed specifications of the world's most demanding customers in the automotive, appliance, construction and manufacturing markets.

Eastern Steel Division. The company then left its Ohio-based headquarters location and moved to New Jersey in 1985, believing that the new location was better suited to serve the majority of its holdings' and customers' needs.

By the end of the 1980s, Armco Inc. was continuing to gain market share and increase annual sales, in an industry that many felt was prone to low profitability. Sales figures were hovering near the $1 billion mark, and the company began exploring options for future growth. In 1989, Armco entered into a limited partnership with the Kawasaki Steel Corporation of Japan, merging portions of each company to form the Armco Steel Company, L.P. Another partnership formed by Armco was with the Japanese steel maker Itochu Corporation, a deal that gave Armco an almost 50 percent share of Nova Steel Processing, one of the company's present-day operating divisions.

The Early 1990s: Birth of AK Steel Holding Corporation

Entering the 1990s, Armco's annual sales had surpassed the $1 billion mark, with 1991 sales reaching $1.3 billion. Unfortunately, however, the company was not as profitable as its sales figures might indicate. Armco was realizing firsthand what analysts had been preaching for years, which was that the steel industry required such a large output of operating expenses that achieving a high profit was incredibly difficult. Armco had found itself with approximately $600 million in debt and negative equity, and made the decision that it was time to make moves to turn its situation around.

Armco began searching for a new management head to give the company some direction and build a new era of profitability in the 1990s. The company finally persuaded Tom Graham to come out of retirement and lead Armco Steel Company's redirection efforts. In 1992, at the age of 65, Graham had spent almost 45 years working in the management of different steel companies around the United States. Earlier in his life, Graham had spent substantial time at J & L Steel, U.S. Steel, and Washington Steel. When he came to Armco, he brought with him another ex-U.S. Steel and Washington Steel coworker, Richard M. Wardrop, Jr.

Graham and Wardrop immediately set about the task of turning Armco's financial situation around. First came an extensive evaluation of the company's holdings, which resulted in the divestiture of more than ten of the company's subsidiaries and operating divisions. These operations either lacked efficiency in production or profit potential and were relinquished in an effort to lower Armco's operating costs and subsequently boost earnings. Another notable change that occurred within the first year of Graham's tenure was the replacement of a whopping 75 of the company's top executives and managers.

Next, the newly restructured Armco worked on improving its actual operations and service. The quality of the company's finished steel product was improved upon first, in order to increase its ability to market and sell the steel to its customers, such as the construction, automotive, and large appliance industries. Then came an improvement in Armco's service, with an emphasis on increasing the company's ability to deliver its products to buyers on time.

Meanwhile, Armco had acquired a new subsidiary, Cyclops Industries, a producer of specialty steel products. In 1993, Armco again moved its corporate executive offices, this time from New Jersey to Pittsburgh, Pennsylvania. The following year, the limited partnership between Armco and Kawasaki was altered slightly and AK Steel Holding Corporation was finally born. Its main operating division became AK Steel Corp., at which steel production continued as normal. AK Steel Holding Corporation was then taken public later that same year, and the sale of common and preferred shares of its stock helped the company earn $654 million. The money was used to pay off AK's debt, leaving the company's balance sheet clear and in excellent financial condition.

Success in the Middle to Late 1990s

After relocating its corporate offices again—this time from Pittsburgh back to Middletown, Ohio—AK Steel entered 1995 with high hopes for strong financial success. Profits throughout the entire steel industry dropped, however, which briefly signaled problems through a turn of events. But despite difficulties in the industry, AK Steel still managed to achieve an estimated $146 million on sales of $2.26 billion. As a result of this success, the Regis ICM Small Company Mutual Fund increased its holdings in AK Steel, noting the fact that the company was averaging annual growth rates in the realm of 15 percent and above.

Graham then made the risk-laden decision to forge ahead with plans to construct a brand new, state-of-the-art steel production facility in Rockport, Indiana. The cost of building the new manufacturing site was estimated at $1.1 billion. Right away, many analysts and industry experts criticized the decision, some in awe of the fact that a company that had just rescued itself from massive debt would choose to put itself back into that position again. Immediately, comparisons were drawn between AK Steel and competitor Inland Steel, who had built its own $1 billion steel facility in a joint venture with Nippon Steel in the beginning of the 1990s. Inland's complex was completed in 1993, and four years later had still not earned a good return on its cost. Some thought that AK Steel should take a hint from Inland's situation and reconsider its plan.

But Graham insisted that the addition of a newer and more efficient production facility was important to AK Steel's future. He cited increased efficiency and lower energy consumption as factors that would aid in lowering AK Steel's operating costs if the new Rockport site was erected. In addition, the new facility would be equipped to produce 80-inch-wide rolls of carbon steel, whereas all existing mills were capable only of producing

Key Dates:

1899: American Rolling Mill Company is established.
1910: Another product plant is opened under the name Ashland Works.
1948: The company adopts the acronym ARMCO.
1978: The firm changes its name to Armco Inc.
1985: Headquarters is moved to New Jersey.
1989: The company enters into a limited partnership with Kawasaki Steel Corporation of Japan.
1994: AK Steel Holding Corporation is established.
1995: Headquarters is moved back to Ohio.
1996: The company announces plans to construct a $1.1 billion manufacturing plant in Rockport, Indiana.
1998: Production begins ahead of schedule at the new Rockport facility.
1999: The company acquires Armco for $1.3 billion.
2001: The company begins construction on the first antimicrobial home in the United States.

rolls with a width of 72 inches. Graham believed that this would increase the demand for AK Steel's finished product, because it would allow auto makers to save money through elimination of the necessity to weld together two pieces of steel.

In 1997, Graham retired once again at the age of 70. Wardrop took his place at the head of the company as chairman and CEO with the intent to continue not only Graham's plans for the new facility, but also the business practices that had helped AK Steel recover in the beginning of the decade. James Wareham, former president of Wheeling-Pittsburgh Steel Corp., was elected president of AK Steel.

Although the company appeared to be financially back on track—sales in 1996 reached $2.3 billion—safety problems and rifts with its unions were casting a shadow upon its successes. The company had one of the worst safety records in the U.S. industry in 1996 with ten fatalities since 1993 and nearly $2 million in fines paid out to the Occupational Safety and Health Administration (OSHA).

By 1998, however, management was able to turn the safety issues around by focusing on eliminating workplace injuries, revamping its safety and health programs, and getting employees as well as contractors involved in safety awareness. Its positive safety performance was rated by OSHA and the American Iron and Steel Institute, and the company claimed that it had the best performance out of the eight largest integrated steel firms in the United States.

Along with its turnaround concerning safety issues, AK Steel was securing positive operating results and in November 1998 its Rockport facility began production nearly three months ahead of schedule. While many of its competitors fell victim to falling prices in hot-rolled steel due to overcapacity in foreign markets, AK Steel's stock rose by 50 percent from August 1998 to January 1999. The firm's focus on cold-rolled steel and coated steel in its Rockport facility gave it an edge over competitors and left it nearly untouched by the hot-rolled steel crisis, squashing analyst speculation that constructing the plant would have devastating effects on the firm.

In 1999, AK Steel announced plans to acquire Armco Inc. in a $1.3 billion deal that would secure its position as the fourth largest steelmaker in the United States. The deal would give AK Steel access to Armco's specialty steel products including Series 400 stainless steel, a market in which the firm controlled an 80 percent share. Later that year, however, the firm was once again plagued with labor issues when labor negotiations failed with about 650 United Steelworkers of America hourly employees at its Mansfield Works plant. AK Steel replaced the workers with temporary help and salaried employees, but the problems cost the firm nearly $21 million in profits that year. Nevertheless, the firm secured record revenues of $4.6 billion and earnings of $132.4 million.

Focus on Safety, Service, and Quality in the New Millennium

AK Steel entered the millennium dealing with labor issues, rising energy costs, and weakening market conditions. At the same time, Wardrop was awarded the Green Cross for Safety medal by the National Safety Council for the company's turnaround in safety issues related to employees and contractors—the United Steelworkers of America raised issue with the council for praising Wardrop, claiming it was undeserved.

To combat the issues plaguing the industry, AK Steel focused on quality and service as well as safety. It also continued to focus on cold-rolled steel due to the ongoing problems in the hot-rolled market. In 2000, hot-rolled steel accounted for just 5 percent of total shipments.

The company also began an innovative project with AgION Technologies in which the first antimicrobial home would be built in the United States utilizing AK Steel's carbon and stainless steels coated with AgION's antimicrobial compound, a product that reduced the growth of bacteria, mold, and fungus. The 11,000-square-foot home on 130 acres in California was entitled Camino de Robles—path of oaks. Management felt confident that it would continue to successfully battle negative market conditions and, by focusing on innovation, safety, service, and quality, it would continue to remain a leader in the industry for years to come.

Principal Divisions

AK Steel Corporation; Sawhill Tubular Products; Douglas Dynamics L.L.C.; Greens Port Industrial Park.

Principal Competitors

Bethlehem Steel Corp.; The LTV Corporation; USX-U.S. Steel Group.

Further Reading

''AK Steel's Rockport Works Launches Early Start-Up,'' *Appliance Manufacturer,* November 1998, p. 20.

Frazier, Mya, ''Raw Material Prices Auger Hard Year at AK Steel,'' *Business Courier Serving Cincinnati,* April 7, 2000, p. 27.

Nelson, Brett, ''The Cortez of Steel Doesn't Look Back,'' *Forbes,* January 11, 1999, p. 192.

Robertson, Scott, ''AK Steel Chairman Is Hailed, Assailed,'' *American Metal Market,* July 18, 2000, p. 5.

——, ''AK Steel, Once Under Fire, Shows Safety Success,'' *American Metal Market,* March 10, 1998, p. 8.

——, ''The Country's Sixth-Largest Steelmaker, AK Is Poised to Move into Fourth Place,'' *American Metal Market,* May 24, 1999, p. 1.

Rudnitsky, Howard, ''A Throw of the Dice,'' *Forbes,* February 10, 1997, p. 47.

Sekhri, Rajiv, ''AK Steel Delivered Year of Record Performance,'' *Business Courier Serving Cincinnati,* February 5, 1999, p. 3.

——, ''AK Steel Turns Around Its Financial Performance,'' *Business Courier Serving Cincinnati,* May 30, 1997, p. 30.

—Laura E. Whiteley
—update: Christina M. Stansell

Akzo Nobel N.V.

Velperweg 76
NL-6800 SB Arnhem
The Netherlands
Telephone: (31) 26 366-4433
Fax: (31) 26 366-3250
Web site: http://www.akzonobel.com

Public Company
Incorporated: 1969 as Akzo N.V.
Employees: 85,000
Sales: $13.1 billion (2000)
Stock Exchanges: Amsterdam
Ticker Symbol: AKZ
NAIC: 212393 Other Chemical and Fertilizer Mineral Mining; 325181 Alkalies and Chlorine Manufacturing; 325412 Pharmaceutical Preparation Manufacturing; 325611 Soap and Other Detergent Manufacturing; 32551 Paint and Coating Manufacturing; 325188 All Other Basic Inorganic Chemical Manufacturing

The Dutch company Akzo Nobel N.V. is a highly diversified conglomerate that conducts business in more than 75 countries. In 2000, the company ranked as world's largest paint manufacturer, as well as a top chemical manufacturer. Akzo Nobel business operations are organized into three major divisions: Pharma, which manufactures contraceptives, fertility drugs, antidepressants, over-the-counter drugs, and veterinary drugs; Coatings, which produces paint, printing inks, and automotive and marine finishes; and Chemicals, the division responsible for producing functional chemicals, pulp and paper chemicals, polymer chemicals, resins, salt, and plastic additives. Akzo Nobel was formed in 1994, by the merger of Akzo N.V. of the Netherlands, and Nobel Industries of Sweden. Its operations are located in the Netherlands, Germany, and the United States.

Akzo's Early History

The merger of Akzo and Nobel represented the culmination of more than a century of acquisitions and mergers between two companies with long histories. Some of the companies that Akzo acquired can be traced as far back as the 18th century. For example, one of the coating units that it acquired, Sikkens, was formed in 1792. Another subsidiary, a food company named Duyvis, was founded in 1806. Akzo's chemical interests in the United States were tied to Armour & Company, a leading meat-packing firm that began operating in the 1860s.

Akzo's foundation, however, was based on Vereinigte Glanzstoff-Fabriken, a German chemical company formed in 1899. In the early decades of the 20th century, Vereinigte established itself in the chemical industry as a leading producer of rayon and various paints and coatings. In 1929, Vereinigte merged with Nederlandsche Kunstzijdebariek (NK), a competing Dutch manufacturer of rayon. The resulting organization was named AKU.

From the 1930s to the 1960s, AKU became a solid market leader in the development and manufacture of synthetic fibers. In addition to rayon, AKU began producing such breakthrough synthetics as nylon and polyester. Chief among the company's significant innovations was the invention of a material called aramid, a derivative of nylon. AKU experimented with this synthetic fiber in the late 1960s.

Indeed, AKU had enjoyed generous profits from its core synthetic fiber products during the 1960s, and its corporate strategy looked sound for the 1970s. AKU joined forces with KZO—a major Dutch producer of chemicals, drugs, detergents, and cosmetics—in 1969, and the resultant organization became Akzo. Further expansion plans on the part of Akzo were thwarted in the early 1970s, however, when actions by the OPEC oil cartel wreaked havoc with petrochemical markets. Akzo's businesses, particularly those related to synthetic fibers, suffered. In addition to these oil-related problems, the fibers market was affected by turbulence from other quarters. During this period, many synthetic fibers became a commodity product, and low-cost Far Eastern manufacturers took control of many industry segments. Burdened by weak demand and manufacturing overcapacity, Akzo's profits plunged. By the late 1970s, some analysts speculated that Akzo was headed for bankruptcy.

Another setback came when in the 1980s, when the company was selling its new synthetic fiber under the name of Twaron. Unfortunately for AKU, the fiber industry leader du Pont, headquartered in the United States, was simultaneously

Company Perspectives:

Akzo Nobel is a multicultural company. We are market-driven and technology-based, serving customers throughout the world with healthcare products, coatings, and chemicals. Akzo Nobel conducts its diversified activities through Business Units, which report directly to the Board of Management. We maintain a product portfolio with leading positions in important market segments.

developing the fabric under the name of Kevlar, and du Pont began selling its product first. As a result, AKU was both shut out of the lucrative U.S. market for the product and also faced stiff competition in its home market of Europe. AKU's failure to carve out a market for Twaron proved to be the culmination of the setbacks that adversely affected its synthetic fibers operations throughout the 1970s.

Reorganization Strategies

Throughout this turbulent period, Akzo executives scrambled to overcome adversity. They reduced the percentage of revenues attributable to synthetic fibers from more than 50 percent in the early 1970s to less than 30 percent going into the 1980s. At the same time, they tried to supplant income from the struggling fiber division with higher margin products such as paint coatings, noncommodity chemicals, and pharmaceuticals. Akzo executives made another significant move toward reorganizing their operations in 1982, when they appointed Arnout A. Loudon as chief executive of the company. Loudon, a 46-year-old attorney turned executive, had demonstrated an impressive financial acumen in turning around Akzo subsidiaries in France and Brazil. Upon assuming leadership of the company, Loudon initiated an aggressive restructuring strategy designed to stabilize Akzo's unwieldy balance sheet and to ensure the company's long-term profitability.

Among other maneuvers, Loudon further reduced Akzo's emphasis on synthetic fibers to only 20 percent of corporate revenues and boosted its position in coatings and industries related to healthcare. He also decentralized decision-making and eliminated management layers. At the same time, Loudon launched an ambitious acquisition drive in 1984 chiefly designed to increase Akzo's presence in the important U.S. market and to diversify into higher profit-margin chemical businesses. Between 1984 and 1990, Akzo purchased more than 30 companies, most in the United States, at a cost of about $1.8 billion. The units were primarily involved in the production of salt, chemicals, and pharmaceuticals. To fund these purchases, Loudon simultaneously jettisoned poorly performing assets that were worth more than $1.5 billion. By the end of the acquisition campaign, Akzo had emerged as the leading global producer of salt and peroxides and one of the top 20 chemical companies in the world. 1990 sales approached $10 billion as profits surged.

Streamlining for Greater Efficiency

During the early 1990s, Akzo concentrated on improving efficiency. Indeed, compared to chemical companies in Japan and the United States, its operations were bloated, chiefly due to restrictive government and organized-labor regulations in Europe. Gradual improvements in efficiency led to marked success in important divisions such as pharmaceuticals, which captured a key position in the reproductive medicine market. Its most notable product was Desogen, the top-selling birth control formula in the world. Similarly, Akzo enjoyed steady market share gains in some of its paints and coatings divisions. The net result was that Akzo sustained steady sales and profits throughout the early 1990s, despite a global economic downturn.

Going into the mid-1990s, Akzo continued to reduce its emphasis on such low-profit commodities as salt and fibers and to boost its dependence on coatings and specialty chemicals. To that end, Akzo consummated a pivotal merger early in 1994 with Nobel Industries of Sweden. Nobel was a major contender in global paint, coatings, and specialty chemical industries. It operated subsidiaries worldwide and enjoyed a relatively strong position in U.S. markets. The company that resulted—Akzo Nobel N.V.—elevated Akzo's revenue figure by more than 25 percent, gave the new company a leadership role in the global paints and coatings industry, and bolstered the former Akzo's stance in the European and U.S. markets. The former Nobel Industries also was able to reduce costs because it could obtain needed materials more cheaply from Akzo, such as inexpensive access to such raw materials as salt and chlorates.

Nobel Industries's Early History: 1864–1984

Akzo's merger partner was originally founded in 1864 by Alfred Nobel, the progenitor of the Nobel Peace prize. Nobel was born in 1833 into a Swedish family that claimed heritage to the 17th-century Swedish prodigy Olaf Rudbeck. Alfred Nobel's father, Immanuel, was a self-educated inventor with an interest in explosives. An unsuccessful businessman, Immanuel was forced to file for bankruptcy in 1832 after the family's home burned down. In 1837, Immanuel moved to Russia, leaving his family behind, to start a new business. There, he invented an explosive device for which demand gradually increased. By 1842, Immanuel had achieved modest success with his invention, and he sent for his family. Alfred's exposure to that environment, combined with his natural interest in chemistry, prompted him to form his own company in 1864 called Nitroglycerin AB.

Alfred's key invention was a process of making nitroglycerin that did not explode during production and handling. However, the perfection of this technique came at a great personal cost for Nobel in that an explosion killed Alfred's brother and four other workers during the testing process. This breakthrough led to Nobel's development of dynamite in 1866, which combined nitroglycerin and an absorbent earthy substance. Nobel went on to create blasting gelatin and smokeless powder, and eventually claimed 350 patents. In an effort to overcome opposition from established gunpowder manufacturers and other competitors, Nobel and several associates formed the Nobel Dynamite Trust in 1886. This cartel eventually dominated five continents and Nobel dynamite factories dotted the globe.

A surprising turn of events occurred for Nobel in 1888 when his brother, Ludwig, died and a local French newspaper accidentally reported Alfred's death instead. To his dismay, Alfred

Key Dates:

1929: Vereinigte Glanzstoff-Fabriken, a German manufacturer of paint and rayon, merges with the Dutch company Nederlandsche Kunstzijdebariek, a competing rayon producer, and forms Algemene unstzijde Unie (AKU).
1969: AKU merges with Koninklijke Zout Organon (KZO) to form Akzo.
1979: Akzo profits continue falling due to weak demand and overcapacity.
1982: Arnout A. Loudon is named CEO.
1984: Nobel Industries is created by the merger of KemaNobel and Bofors.
1990: Following the merger, Akzo acquires more than 30 firms and sales reach $10 billion.
1994: Akzo completes the merger of Nobel's six business groups, and Akzo Nobel becomes one of the ten largest chemical companies in the world.
1996: The firm's finances suffer due to flat markets and falling prices.
1998: The firm acquires Courtaulds, a coatings a fiber manufacturer.
1999: The firm purchases Hoechst Roussel Vet, a unit of Hoechst AG, and divests its Fibers unit.
2000: Akzo Nobel achieves record earnings and growth.

read his own obituary, in which he was described as the inventor of dynamite and the ''merchant of death,'' even though most of his explosives were used in nonmilitary applications. This experience motivated Nobel to demonstrate his true intent. Thus, when he died in 1896, Alfred directed that his entire fortune be entrusted to the Norwegian parliament and distributed annually as a reward to individuals who ''shall have conferred the greatest benefit on mankind.'' Subsequently, the Nobel Foundation was established and the first prize was awarded in 1901.

After his death, Nobel's conglomeration of businesses was divided into various corporations. Nobel's Swedish companies evolved into two separate organizations. His original company, Nitroglycerin AB, continued to make explosives. Its name was changed to Nitro Nobel in 1965 before it was bought out by a chemical group controlled by the prominent Wallenberg family in 1978. The resultant organization was called KemaNobel. The other segment of the Swedish Nobel operations became Bofors, a manufacturer of munitions. In 1982, Erik Penser, a young Swedish stockbroker, engineered the purchase of Bofors. Two years later, he purchased KemaNobel, reuniting the two divisions in a company he called Nobel Industries.

In 1986, Penser's company won a five-year, $1.2 billion contract to supply field artillery to the Indian government. Business analysts lauded the deal as one of the largest orders ever secured by a Swedish company until it was discovered that Penser may have made illegal, covert payments of $4.5 million into a secret Swiss bank account to get the contract. To make matters worse, it was discovered in 1987 that Nobel Industries had illegally shipped arms to Iran, Iraq, and other countries not sanctioned for arms trade by the Swedish government. Meanwhile, Nobel's U.S. chemical subsidiary, Bofors Nobel, Inc., filed for bankruptcy in 1985, largely because the U.S. Department of Natural Resources had sued the division for $15 million in environmental clean-up costs. Initially, Bofors Nobel had agreed to pay the clean-up expenses, but once the higher-than-expected costs accrued, the division elected to file for bankruptcy instead.

The Merger: 1994

Despite Nobel Industries's setbacks, Akzo executives viewed the company as a potential asset to their organization. In 1994, Akzo completed the merger of Nobel's six business groups, making Akzo Nobel one of the ten largest chemical companies in the world. Shortly before the merger, Akzo had implemented a sweeping reorganization drive to dismantle the company's five major business divisions and recreate them in four new groups—chemical, fibers, coatings, and pharmaceuticals. Akzo continued to develop its U.S. markets aggressively, while it worked simultaneously to penetrate Asian and South American markets. By this time, Akzo had invested about 33 percent of its resources in the Netherlands, 20 percent in Germany, and 22 percent in the United States, with many of its remaining investments scattered throughout Europe. Akzo Nobel's 1994 sales rose slightly to about $11.5 billion, roughly 5 percent of which was netted as income.

Challenges, Restructuring, and Growth

Akzo Nobel faced several challenges as it entered the mid-1990s. In 1995, its pharmaceutical unit, Organon, lost revenues following a scare that its Marvelon and Mercilon oral contraceptive pills were linked to increased risk of thrombosis (abnormal blood clotting). Falling fiber prices, stagnant markets, and declining sales in the coating division also led to a mere 0.3 percent increase in profits in 1996. The firm did make some key partnerships, however, including a joint venture with Courtaulds to develop and market NewCell, a cellulosic filament yarn. The company also spent $240 million to expand its fluidized catalytic cracking (FCC) catalysts and hydroprocessing catalysts (HPC) capacity. The capital investment was made to attract partners to its FCC and HPC business. The firm also began restructuring its specialty surfactants business, which had been dealing with overcapacity as well as a stagnant market. As a result, the unit began cutting costs and consolidating production. Akzo also sold its subsidiary Akzo Nobel Salt, Inc. in 1997 as part of its effort to focus on its core operations.

Akzo's restructuring of its pharmaceutical, coatings, and chemical businesses, began to pay off, and the balance sheet in 1997 reflected this. Akzo recorded a 7 percent increase in sales, and operating profits in its pharmaceutical interests climbed by 17 percent. Its coatings and chemicals divisions secured a 27 percent increase in operating profits. In 1998, the firm focused on making key alliances and acquisitions as well as paring back less profitable operations. An agreement with Bayer AG was formed in which the German-based firm would produce ethylene amines exclusively for Akzo. Three printing ink companies—Louis O. Werneke, Werneke & Mulheran, and Label Inks—were purchased to secure Akzo's position as a leading supplier of printing inks in the U.S. market. The company also acquired Courtaulds plc in July 1998 in a deal that created the world's largest coating company. The firm merged its fiber business into a newly created company, Acordis. At the same time, because of poor growth and overcapacity, the firm continued to consolidate its surfactants operations. The company also sold its plastic packaging and laminate and aluminum tubes interests.

A disappointing 1 percent increase in net profits in 1998 led to a renewed focus on integrating its newly acquired firms into its current businesses. The firm's pharmaceutical operations—growing twice as fast as other companies in the industry—also became a major focus. The division had a strong position in the women's healthcare market, and its Organon business operated as the world's fourth largest producer of oral contraceptives. Akzo also strengthened its Intervet division with the purchase of Hoechst Roussel Vet, a deal that doubled the size of its animal healthcare interest. Perhaps the most important move in 1999 was the sale of Acordis to CVC Capital Partners. The deal marked Akzo's exit from the synthetic fiber business and solidified the company's intent to focus on its core divisions—Pharma, Coatings, and Chemicals.

Positive Advances in the New Millennium

As Akzo entered the new millennium, its Pharma division was the fasting-growing pharmaceutical company in Europe. The unit accounted for 47 percent of Akzo's total profits, and its core operations focused on human and animal healthcare. The company's other divisions also fared well in 2000 despite weakening market conditions. The Coatings division acquired the aerospace and specialty coatings business of Dexter Corporation, which strengthened its position in the global market and significantly increased the size of its aerospace coating operations. The Chemicals division also acquired Hopton Technologies, which was purchased to boost the paper chemicals business in the United States.

Although 2000 was the company's best year in its history, Akzo did have to face an antitrust investigation concerning some of its chemical products. While the company took a charge of $136 million in 2000 for anticipated legal fees and fines, net income increased 25 percent over the previous year. Akzo's strategy for the future included securing leadership positions in its markets, with a continuing focus on its Pharma, Coatings, and Chemicals business units. According to a January 2001 company press release, the firm was, "sticking to our basic themes of coherence and value. We have created expectations both internally and externally. We now have to live up to them."

Principal Subsidiaries

Advanced BioScience Laboratories Inc.; Akzo Nobel Coatings Inc.; Akzo Nobel Resins and Vehicles; Akzo Noble Resins Inc.; Akzo Nobel Rheology Additives Inc.; Colbond Geosynthetics; Diosynth Inc.; Eka Chemicals Inc.; Intervet Inc.; Organon Inc.; Organon Teknika N.V.; Rosemont Pharmaceutical Corporation.

Principal Operating Units

Pharma; Coatings; Chemical.

Principal Competitors

PPG Industries Inc.; Imperial Chemicals Industries plc; Dow Chemical Co.; BASF AG.

Further Reading

"Akzo Nobel Buys Coatings," *Chemical Market Reporter,* August 7, 2000, p. 3.

"Akzo Nobel's CEO Cees Van Lede in New Year's Address," *Business Wire,* January 11, 2001.

"Akzo Nobel Combination Look Like a Perfect Fit," *Chemical Marketing Reporter,* April 18, 1994, p. 8.

"Akzo Nobel Offers Premium for Courtaulds," *Chemical Market Reporter,* April 27, 1998, p. 8.

"Akzo Nobel Trims Surfactants Unit," *Chemical Market Reporter,* October 26, 1998, p. 8.

"Akzo Nobel 2000: Best Year Ever," *Business Wire,* February 23, 2001.

Alerowicz, Natasha, "Akzo Nobel to Grow Drugs and Coating Sectors," *Chemical Week,* March 4, 1998, p. 15.

——, "Akzo's Prescription Pharma Moves to Center Stage," *Chemical Week,* June 9, 1999, p. 26.

Fallon, James, "Acordis Fibers Sold to London-Based Consortium," *Daily News Record,* December 3, 1999, p. 21.

Fattah, Hassan, "Akzo Sees Promise in Alliances," *Chemical Week,* June 5, 1996, p. 36.

Gain, Bruce, "Akzo Noble Buys Werneke Businesses," *Chemical Week,* June 17, 1998, p. 8.

Hunter, David, and Lyn Tattum, "Akzo Shapes Up with a New Organization," *Chemical Week,* October 27, 1993, p. 26.

Lawton, Graham, "Happier Times Ahead?," *Chemistry and Industry,* March 17, 1997, p. 203.

Mendes, Joshua, "A New, Improved Chemical Stock at Half-Price," *Fortune,* July 2, 1990, p. 28.

Moskowitz, Milton, *The Global Marketplace,* New York: Macmillan, 1987.

Reier, Sharon, "Master of the Hunt: While Most of Europe's Chemical Industry is Hurting, Akzo Surges Ahead," *Financial World,* January 5, 1993, p. 26.

Sommers, Nick, "Akzo Nobel Launches New Generic Pharmaceutical Firm," *Business Wire,* September 6, 1994.

Srodes, James, "Dutch Treat," *Financial World,* January 9, 1990, p. 32.

—Dave Mote
—update: Christina M. Stansell

The Albert Fisher Group plc

'C' Sefton Park, Bells Hill
Stoke Poges
Buckinghamshire SL2 4FG
United Kingdom
Telephone: (+44) 1753-677-877
Fax: (+44) 1753-664-481
Web site: http://www.albertfisher.com

Public Company
Incorporated: 1920 as Albert Fisher & Son Limited
Employees: 5,871
Sales: £612.4 million ($1.03 billion) (2000)
Stock Exchanges: London
Ticker Symbol: FSH
NAIC: 311712 Fresh and Frozen Seafood Processing; 311421 Fruit and Vegetable Canning; 311991 Perishable Prepared Food Manufacturing

The Albert Fisher Group plc is one of the United Kingdom's leading fresh, chilled, and frozen foods groups, operating within the fruits and vegetables and seafood markets. The company is the leading supplier of frozen vegetables in the United Kingdom and also processes and distributes a wide range of foods, from frozen fruits to rice and pasta to precooked meals. In the United States, the company is also a leading supplier of fresh packaged salads. Albert Fisher Group, which has undergone a thorough reorganization through the 1990s, now operates through three primary divisions: Fisher Foods (U.K.); River Ranch Fresh Foods (U.S.A.); and produce distribution and trading. The company markets its own brands of frozen and chilled products, such as Fisher in the United Kingdom and River Ranch in the United States, and is a major supplier to the private label market. Albert Fisher Group, which trades on the London stock exchange, is led by chairman Hugh Ashton and CEO T.J. Robinson. The company's streamlining effort has cut its sales by more than half since the early 1990s, to £612.4 million.

Overnight Conglomerate in the 1980s

Albert Fisher Group posted just £6.7 million for its fiscal year 1982. By 1992, the company's sales neared £1.2 billion. At the company's height in the mid-1990s, revenues had swelled to more than £1.6 billion, before unraveling at the end of the century.

The company origins traced back to 1920, when Albert Fisher incorporated his wholesale fruit and vegetable business as Albert Fisher & Son. The company changed its name to Albert Fisher Group after adding a number of other companies operating in its Lancashire region. The company extended its wholesale activity into the north and Midlands regions of England in the early 1960s, then took a listing on the Liverpool stock exchange in 1964. Albert Fisher moved its listing to the London stock exchange in 1973. By the beginning of the 1980s, the company's operations had grown to include several wholesale fruit and vegetable depots as well as distribution activities in potatoes and onions. The company also operated a fleet servicing business for its own fleet of vehicles. The small company, which posted just £6.7 million in turnover in 1982, was losing money—£29,000 for that year.

The arrival of Tony Millar as chief executive of the company in 1982 marked the beginning of a vast change in the modest Albert Fisher Group. Millar became caught up in the spirit of the times, which saw the growth of new large-scale, often globally operating conglomerate companies. The company raised £385,000 in a rights issue in 1982 and in 1983 made its first acquisition, that of Wentworth Import & Export Limited. By the end of that year, the company had more than doubled sales, while returning a profit of £327,000 for the year.

Albert Fisher followed the Wentworth acquisition with that of FJ Need (Foods) Limited, which brought the company a cheese wholesaling business. The company next added the Henry Long Group, which operated warehousing and distribution facilities, as well as a Mercedes-Benz commercial vehicle franchise. The addition of Stokes Bomford Limited, in 1984, extended the company's fruit and potatoes operations and helped boost revenues past £44 million. That same year, Albert

> **Company Perspectives:**
>
> *With the objective to be a leading customer branded food company through commitment to quality, service and value for money, we aim to exploit our sourcing and processing expertise and work closely with customers to continually enhance the quality of our products and services.*

Fisher moved into the United States, acquiring Miami-based Carnival Fruit company.

In 1985, Albert Fisher began to drift farther from its core fruits and vegetables buying, selling, processing, and distribution business. The company acquired Plane Tracking, giving it that company's Manchester-based international transport operations. The company also acquired Charles Sidney, based in Bradford, a franchise for Mercedes-Benz automobiles. Still farther afield was the company's acquisition of Ziff Company, based in Massachusetts, which brought the company into paper products marketing and distribution.

Closer to its original focus, the company acquired Curtis, Knee & Co., a frozen fruits and vegetables producer and distributor located in Hertfordshire, and Los Angeles' Coast Produce, specialized in fresh fruits and vegetables. Albert Fisher's Stokes Bomford subsidiary opened a new processing facility as the company expanded its offering of packaged fruits to the United Kingdom's supermarket chains as well as to other food processing companies.

The company's revenues topped the £100 million mark in 1986 as the company stepped up its acquisition fervor. After acquiring Apex Wholesale Produce of Los Angeles, then Tavilla Group, based in Florida, Albert Fisher's U.S. interests continued to grow, with new acquisitions including Red's Market Group and Cape Coral Produce, both in Florida. The following year, Albert Fisher added Lee Ray-Tarantino Co. of San Francisco, Scalisi Produce Company of West Palm Beach, Florida, and Pacific Produce Group, based in British Columbia.

Back in the United Kingdom, the company's acquisition of Sea Products added that company's wholesale fish and fish products distribution activity, a new area for Albert Fisher. Albert Fisher moved onto the European continent in 1987 with the purchase of Reingold, based in Rotterdam. This move was quickly complemented by the addition of Citronas Group, a Rotterdam-based fresh produce distributor, and its Pakomi onion subsidiary, and Limax, which distributed mushrooms, also in The Netherlands.

Unravelling in the 1990s

Albert Fisher continued on its aggressive acquisition drive, raising financing in part through a series of stock splits and rights issues, but also by taking on a fast-growing debt burden. Nonetheless, the company's expansion was bearing fruit, as turnover topped £248 million for 1987 and then jumped to £831 million by 1989. Among the company's acquisitions was that of State Paper, based in Maine, which was added to the Ziff Company subsidiary. Ziff Company also added Grossman Paper Company, based in New Jersey, in 1988.

Yet the majority of Albert Fisher's acquisitions remained centered around its growing foods businesses. A major acquisition came in April of 1988, when Albert Fisher acquired Mondi Foods BV, based in The Netherlands and with operations in Belgium, Germany, and Switzerland, giving it one of the largest fruit processing groups in Europe. The company's growing size placed larger and larger targets in its reach, such as its acquisition of JJM Theeuwen Beheer BV, which became known as Holco BV, of The Netherlands, in 1990, adding that leading European mushroom processor and distributor.

The company continued to extend its range of foods, adding companies such as Rowats Food Limited, a Glasgow-based processor of pickles and sauces, and then Beswicks Limited, based in Lancashire, which produced dressings and sauces. In August 1990, Albert Fisher moved into Spain and Portugal through the joint venture Albert Fisher Larios SA, working with Larios to acquire and build food products processing operations through those two countries. In December, the acquisition of Campbell's UK Vegetable Division and UK Seafood Division boosted the company's operations in both the frozen vegetable and frozen and specialty fish segments. By then, the company had exited the paper business with the sale of Ziff Company.

By 1991, Albert Fisher's sales had swelled past the £1 billion mark. Millar's leadership had led the once-tiny company to a position in the prestigious FTSE 100 list and a market capitalization of nearly £800 million. The first signs of trouble were beginning to appear, however. The company's huge debt burden, and a policy of deferring its acquisitions fees, soon caught up to its balance sheet. As the *Financial Times* wrote, Albert Fisher ''was a classic 1980s conglomerate, built on hot air and a chain of unrelated acquisitions. Nobody had time to integrate businesses or devise a strategy.''

Millar left the company and was replaced by Stephen Walls in 1992. Walls led the company on ''a strategic repositioning'' designed to trim the bloat from the company's heavily expanded list of operations. Albert Fisher now sought to transition from its low-margin production, commodity, and wholesaling businesses to more profitable value-added processing activities.

The company disposed of its trucking companies and sold off some of its other operations, such as Holco BV, in 1992. The company also spun off its Charles Sidney franchise in a public listing. Yet Albert Fisher remained locked on the acquisition trail, continuing to take on debt while adding to its list of subsidiaries. Some effort, however, was made to integrate its operations, such as the establishment of a new European Seafood Division in 1992. That same year, the company created its Fisher Quality Foods division through the merger of a number of subsidiary operations.

Focusing on the 21st Century

Further acquisitions helped the company extend its U.S. presence, including Reddi-Made Foods Inc., of Florida; Imperial Produce Company Inc., of Washington, DC; Fresh Western Marketing Inc., of California; and the assets, including the trademarks and customer lists, of Dallas's American Produce

Key Dates:

1920: Albert Fisher incorporates Albert Fisher & Son Limited.
1961: Company reincorporates as Albert Fisher Group.
1964: The Group goes public on Liverpool stock exchange.
1973: Company gains listing on London stock exchange.
1982: Tony Millar becomes CEO.
1984: Company acquires Stokes Bomford Ltd. Carnival Fruit Company (U.S.A.).
1985: Company acquires Plane Trucking; Coast Produce (U.S.A.); and Ziff Company (U.S.A.).
1989: Company acquires Guanaria & Sons Ltd; sells Henry Long Transport Ltd.
1990: Company acquires Holco BV (Netherlands); sells Ziff Company.
1992: Stephen Walls joins as non-executive chairman.
1996: Company sells North American distribution business; Neil England becomes CEO.
1998: Market capitalization slumps to £38 million; Walls and England resign.
1999: Company begins disposal program and restructuring.
2001: Company consolidates its frozen vegetable processing operations.

and Vegetable Company Inc. In 1994, Albert Fisher added the Rahbek Group, giving it operations in Denmark, as well as that company's Scotland and England fish fillet processing facilities. By 1995, the company had begun to cast its net still farther abroad, taking a 20 percent interest in Buenos Aires-based SA San Miquel, a world-leading lemon grower and processor. The company's sales reached their peak in that year, topping £1.6 billion.

Charges following the disposal of a number of businesses, including the company's North American produce distribution operation and the sale of its German and Netherlands wholesaling operations, led to Walls being replaced as chief executive by Neil England in 1996; Walls remained as chairman. The company then began talks with Chiquita Brands to be acquired by that company. The company's disappointed shareholders, who had seen the company's market capitalization enter a long downslide during the decade—bottoming out at just £38 million in 1998—now insisted on a new course of action. Both Walls and England resigned in 1998. Terry Robinson took over the CEO spot, and Hugh Ashton became chairman.

Albert Fisher now embarked on a new program of slashing its debt and reducing its number of businesses to focus exclusively on its value-added operations. The company began a long series of disposals, the proceeds of which were used to pay down the company's debt burden. One of the first businesses to go was its Fisher Quality Foods division, which gained the company £43 million from Unigate PLC. Other disposals included its River Ranch Los Angeles subsidiary, which netted close to £2 million in a management buyout, and the purchase by Carl Kuhne GmbH & Co. of Fisher Quality Foods Uyttewaal BV for £4.4 million.

By the end of the company's fiscal year 2000, Albert Fisher's sales, excluding discontinued operations, had been cut back to just £612 million. The company's newly refocused operations now emphasized its U.K. business, whereas both North American and Continental Europe operations had been cut in half in terms of sales volume. Albert Fisher had reorganized itself around three core activities, those of its U.K. value-added foods group Fisher Foods, the River Ranch Salinas U.S.A. fresh salads distributor, and a produce distribution and trading arm. Albert Fisher had, in large part, completed its disposal program by the end of 2000, and it began to look forward to rebuilding its profitability while consolidating its position as a leading U.K. and North American value-added food processing group. The company now began to look for ways to increase its operational efficiency. A step toward streamlining its ongoing operations was taken in early 2001, when the company announced its was combining its frozen vegetable processing activities into a single plant.

Principal Subsidiaries

Aartsenfruit Breda BV (Netherlands); Agricommerce SA (France); Fisher Chilled Foods Limited; Fisher Foods Ltd; Fisher Fresh Vegetables Ltd.; Fresh Western International Inc. (U.S.A.); Fresh Western Marketing Inc. (U.S.A.); Mondi Foods Belgium NV; River Ranch Fresh Foods—Salinas, Inc. (U.S.A.); SPI plc; Westminster Produce Pty (South Africa).

Principal Competitors

Chiquita Brands International Inc.; CHR CH Robinson Worldwide Inc.; Danone S.A.; Dole Food Company; Fresh Del Monte Produce Inc.; Geest Plc; Hibernia Foods; Nestlé S.A.; Northern Foods plc; S.A.; Savia, S.A. de C.V.; Sunkist Growers, Inc.; Unigate plc; Unilever; U.S.A. Floral Products, Inc.

Further Reading

''Albert Fisher to Shut Grimsby Plant,'' *Independent,* February 21, 2001, p. 19.
Gimbel, Florian, ''Competition Hits Albert Fisher,'' *Financial Times,* April 27, 2001.
Hall, Amanda, ''When Will Walls Bear Fruit?,'' *Daily Telegraph,* August 22, 1997.
Haughton, Andrew, ''Recovery Strategy at Albert Fisher Is Starting to Bear Fruit,'' *Financial Times,* May 3, 2000.
''The History of the Albert Fisher Group,'' Stoke Poges: Albert Fisher Group, 1999.
Urry, Maggie, ''Albert Fisher Hints at Recovery,'' *Financial Times,* October 20, 2000.

—M.L. Cohen

Amer Group plc

Makelankatu 91
Helsinki FIN-00601
Finland
Telephone: (+358) 9-725-7800
Fax: (+358) 9-7257-8200
Web site: http://www.amer.fi

Public Company
Incorporated: 1950 as Amer-Tupakka Oy; 1973 as Amer-yhtyma
Employees: 4,327
Sales: EUR 1.09 billion ($1 billion) (2000)
Stock Exchanges: Helsinki London
Ticker Symbol: AGPDY
NAIC: 339920 Sporting and Athletic Goods Manufacturing; 3122 Tobacco Manufacturing; 312229 Other Tobacco Product Manufacturing

Finland's Amer Group plc is building a world-leading portfolio of sporting goods companies. The company owns Chicago-based Wilson Sporting Goods; Austria's Atomic, producer of ski and snowboarding equipment under the Oxygen and Dynamic brand names; and, since 1999, fellow Finn Suunto, a maker of high-performance wristwatches (the company prefers "wrist computers") and other accessories for the sports and outdoors markets. Amer is also Finland's leading manufacturer and distributor of cigarettes, cigars, and other tobacco products, the company's historic activity, which accounts for 9 percent of its annual sales. Yet sporting goods has become the company's strategic focus. The company groups its operations into the Golf, Racquet, Team Sports, Winter Sports, and Outdoor and Sports Instruments divisions. Wilson, which manufactures equipment for the first three divisions, is also the company's largest subsidiary, accounting for some two-thirds of annual sales. The United States is also Amer's primary market, representing more than half of the company's sales. Europe, excluding Finland, adds another 25 percent of sales, while Finland, incorporating the company's tobacco sales, accounts for 11 percent of the company's sales. Amer's shares are traded on the Helsinki and London stock exchanges and through the United States' OTC market through an ADR facility. The company posted sales of more than EUR 1 billion in 2000.

Smoking Start in the 1950s

Amer was founded in 1950 as Amer-Tupakka Oy, or Amer Tobacco, in order to manufacture and distribute American-style tobacco products in Finland. The company's founders were four education-oriented organizations: the Finnish Association of Graduate Engineers, the Finnish Association of Graduates in Economics and Business Administration, the Land and Water Technology Foundation, and the Student Union of the Helsinki School of Economics and Business Administration. The four organizations launched Amer with the intention of using the company's sales to fund educational and research programs in Finland.

One of Amer-Tupakka's first business successes was its introduction of the Boston brand of American-style, Virginia-blended tobacco cigarettes. By the end of the 1950s, the company already had established itself as one of the country's major tobacco companies. A licensing agreement to manufacture and distribute Philip Morris's cigarette brands in Finland boosted the company's sales even higher, enabling it to establish itself as the country's dominant tobacco company.

By the mid-1960s, Amer's tobacco profits had outpaced the needs of its education and research programs. The company decided to invest its profits in other activities, taking the first step toward becoming somewhat of an industrial conglomerate. The company purchased three ships, forming a shipping company to manage its small fleet. Its new activity gave the company a new source of profits. Yet the rise of air cargo activity began to cut into the worldwide shipping market. The company decided to divest its shipping interests, a process begun during the 1970s and completed with the sale of its last ship in 1981.

By then, the company already had begun to pursue other interests. In 1970 Amer acquired Finnish encyclopedia and textbook publishing company Weilin + Göös, establishing its Printing and Publishing division. Amer, which restructured as Amer-yhtyma Oy (Amer Group Ltd.) in 1973, began adding to its new division with a number of acquisitions, culminating in

Company Perspectives:

Amer Group's target is to become the undisputed leader in the global sports equipment market.

the purchase of Time/System International, a maker of personal agendas and the like in 1987. Amer also formed a Paper division, after acquiring Hyppöla in 1979. Later known as Amerpap, the acquisition marked the first of several, including that of Chicago's Hobart/McIntosh Paper Company, and other acquisitions in Belgium and The Netherlands. The company maintained its Printing and Publishing division until the late 1990s, selling off Weilin + Göös in 1995 and shutting down the division altogether with the sale of Time/System International in 1997. By then, Amer had exited the paper business as well, selling off its holdings in this division by 1994.

Yet the 1970s also had marked the beginning of Amer's interests in sporting goods. The company's first purchase in this area was the acquisition of hockey equipment manufacturer Koho-Tuote Oy in 1974. Amer then boosted its youngest division with the purchase of the Koho brand's U.S. distributor in 1978, followed by the acquisitions of HockeyCanadien Inc., and that Quebec, Canada company's ''Canadien'' brand hockey sticks in 1979. Amer added another Quebec company, Sherbrooke Sports Division, which manufactured protective equipment for ice hockey players. Although its interest in sporting goods later came to define the company, Amer's involvement in ice hockey came to a close in 1986, when it sold off all of its ice hockey operations.

By then, Amer had gone public, listing on the Helsinki stock exchange in 1977 and becoming the second Finnish company to obtain a listing on the London stock exchange in 1984. The company also began selling its shares through an ADR facility on the U.S. OTC market. Amer continued to display a taste for diversified activities. In the late 1970s the company had built up a domestic distribution business, obtaining licenses to import and market such brands as Zebra, Montblanc, Seiko, Casio, and others. In 1984, the company also entered the automobile business, buying up the country's largest automobile importer, Korpivaara. That company also brought Amer operations in plastics manufacturing, notably the Terhi brand of plastic boats. The company formed a Plastics Division in 1987 after acquiring a majority share of Denmark-based plastics distribution company, Rias A/S. The company dropped its plastics operations in 1990, selling off Korpivaara.

In 1985, Amer turned to the textiles industry, acquiring Marimekko. That company had shot to fame at the beginning of the 1960s when then First Lady Jacqueline Kennedy bought a number of Marimekko's maternity dresses. Yet Amer's ownership of Marimekko accompanied a decline in its fortunes. After Marimekko posted losses through the end of the decade, Amer divested the company and exited the textile industry.

Sporting Focus in the 1990s

Despite exiting the ice hockey arena, Amer remained interested in the sporting goods field. In 1986 the company acquired Jack Nicklaus's MacGregor Golf Company, which became the centerpiece of its new Sports Division. That division took on new weight in 1989 when Amer paid $200 million to acquire Chicago's Wilson Sporting Goods, instantly transforming the Finnish company into one of the world's sporting goods leaders.

Wilson had been at the center of the sports world since its founding in 1916. Originally known as Ashland Manufacturing Co., the company had been formed to make use of animal byproducts left over from its parent company's meat-packing and slaughterhouse activities. The company began marketing a range of products, ranging from surgical sutures to tennis racquets and racquet strings to shoes for baseball players. When Thomas Wilson took over as president of Ashland, the company, renamed Thomas E Wilson Co., moved to its own manufacturing facilities and began its focus on sports products.

Wilson especially became known for its commitment to developing high-performance products for a wide variety of sports fields. From the outset, the company grew through a long line of innovative products and a number of acquisitions, from that of Hetzinger Knitting Mills, its first purchase in 1916, through to the acquisition of DeMarini Sports Inc., made in 2000. Along the way, Wilson also had established a reputation for its products in a variety of sports fields, from baseball, football, and basketball to tennis and golf. Wilson was also a pioneer in cooperating with noted sports personalities, such as its long-standing association with coaching great Knute Rockne.

Wilson became known as Wilson Sporting Goods Co. in 1931. The company remained a part of its original meat-packing owner—which adopted the Wilson name for itself—until their acquisition by Dallas aerospace group Ling-Temco-Voughtin 1967. Wilson came under PepsiCo's control in 1970. Under PepsiCo, Wilson was split up into its main product categories, which became more or less independently operated divisions with their own marketing and distribution departments. Wilson was sold to Wesray Capital Corporation in 1985 before finding a new parent in Amer in 1989.

Streamlined for the New Century

Amer began steamlining its diversified operations in the 1990s. By the end of the decade, the company had pared down its activities to just its Amer Tobacco unit and its growing sporting goods unit. Wilson now formed the centerpiece of this latter division; throughout the end of the 1980s and the early 1990s, the company's MacGregor Golf Company operations had suffered from the extended economic recession, slipping into losses. With its products overlapped by those of Wilson, MacGregor was sold off to British company Masters International Ltd. in 1996.

Amer continued to pursue the reorganization of its other operations, ceding its plastics, distribution, paper, printing, and publishing businesses as the company redefined its core activities. The acquisition of Austrian winter sports equipment manufacturer Atomic, and its Oxygen and Dynamic brands, in 1994, helped Amer move closer to a new definition for its future. Meanwhile, the company, which was posting losses at middecade, announced a three-year restructuring of its operations,

Key Dates:

1916: Ashland Manufacturing Co. is founded.
1917: Ashland becomes Thomas E. Wilson Co.
1931: Wilson becomes Wilson Sporting Goods Co.
1950: Amer-Tupakka Oy is started.
1961: Amer receives Finnish Philip Morris license.
1965: Amer begins shipping division.
1970: Amer acquires Weilin + Göös; PepsiCo acquires Wilson.
1973: Amer changes name to Amer-yhtyma (Amer Group).
1974: The company acquires Koho-Tuote Oy.
1977: The company is listed on the Helsinki Exchange.
1979: The company establishes Paper Division.
1984: The company is listed on the London stock exchange; Korpivaara is acquired.
1986: The company acquires MacGregor Golf Company.
1989: The company acquires Wilson Sporting Goods Co. (U.S.A.).
1994: The company acquires Atomic (Austria).
1997: The company is restructured as sporting goods manufacturer.
1999: The company acquires Suunto.
2000: The company acquires DeMarini Inc.

regrouping its sporting goods activities around the new Golf, Racquet, Team Sports, and Winter Sports divisions.

Amer made a firm commitment to its sporting goods interests in 1997. Declaring its intention to becoming the world's leading sporting goods company, Amer divested the rest of its noncore operations, keeping only its highly profitable Amer Tobacco unit. That division was comforted by the renewal of the company's long-term Philip Morris license, and the award of a manufacturing and distribution contract from Swedish Match, both in 2000.

In 1998, Amer pursued the next phase of its restructuring, streamlining the somewhat unwieldy distribution system inherited through the Wilson acquisition. Both Wilson and Atomic were reorganized as Amer put into place a true worldwide distribution system. The result was a return to profitability—and strong profit growth—throughout the sporting goods divisions.

Amer promised not only a streamlined organization, but a renewed commitment to technological innovation throughout its sports products categories, particularly in what the company called ''game improvement products.'' Among those introduced at the turn of the century were the Rollers tennis racquets, the first to feature moving parts; the Reaction volleyball, featuring ''Floating Cover Technology''; the Deep Red Driver; and the Device Step In System snowboard binding.

Rounding out the company's product categories was the acquisition of fellow Finnish company Suunto, a maker of high-performance sports and outdoors instruments, including wristwatches and ''wrist computers'' and gauges and instruments for the diving market. The December 1999 purchase created a new division in the company. The year 2000 saw another acquisition, that of Chicago's DeMarini Inc., a maker of bats for softball and baseball, which was placed under the Wilson Sports Co.

By the beginning of its 2001 fiscal year, Amer was posting strong profits, among the best in its industry. The company then confirmed its strategy of continuing to build sales by as much as 10 percent per year through the year 2004, toward claiming the global leadership position as a sports equipment manufacturer. Celebrating its 50th year in business, Amer marked the turn of the century with a more unusual honor. A volleyball dubbed ''Wilson'' was featured in the hit film *Cast Away*—and went on to win the award for Best Inanimate Object in a Motion Picture, a category specifically created for the Wilson company product and its role as sole companion to a stranded Tom Hanks by the Broadcast Film Critics Association for the Critics Choice Awards.

Principal Subsidiaries

Amer Holding Company (U.S.A.); Amer Sport AG (Switzerland); Amer Sport Oy; Amer Tobacco Ltd.; Amera Oy; Amernet Holding BV (Netherlands); Atomic Austria GmbH (95%); Konemuovi Oy; Suunto Oy; Wilson Sporting Goods Co. (U.S.A.).

Principal Competitors

adidas-Salomon AG; Callaway Golf Company; Fortune Brands, Inc.; Head N.V.; K2 Inc.; Nike Inc.; Northwestern Golf Company; Pacific Dunlop Limited; Rawlings Sporting Goods Company, Inc.; Skis Rossignol S.A.; Spalding Holdings Corporation; TaylorMade Golf Company, Inc.

Further Reading

''Amer 2000 Results Meet Expectations,'' *Reuters,* February 27, 2001.
Grady, Barbara, ''Amer to Divest MacGregor Golf Company,'' *Reuters Business Report,* October 14, 1996.
Peltola, Anna, ''Amer Sees Flat 2001 as US Market Loses Its Bounce,'' *Reuters,* March 5, 2001.

—M.L. Cohen

American Homestar Corporation

2450 South Shore Boulevard
Suite 300
League City, Texas 77573
U.S.A.
Telephone: (281) 334-9700
Fax: (281) 334-9737
Web site: http://www.americanhomestar.com

Public Company
Incorporated: 1971 as Mobile America Housing Corporation
Employees: 3,934
Sales: $574 million (2000)
Stock Exchanges: NASDAQ
Ticker Symbol: HSTR
NAIC: 321991 Manufactured Home (Mobile Home) Manufacturing; 45393 Manufactured (Mobile) Home Dealers; 52421 Insurance Agencies and Brokerages; 524126 Direct Property and Casualty Insurance Carriers; 52413 Reinsurance Carriers

American Homestar Corporation, one of the leading producers of site-assembled manufactured housing in the United States, was forced to declare Chapter 11 bankruptcy in early 2001, due to an industry-wide slump. Reorganization ensues, and the company hopes to resume its design, construction, and marketing of pre-constructed homes.

Manufactured homes are complete single-family housing units fabricated in sections, or ''floors.'' Constructed in a factory and then trailered to a site of their owner's choosing, they offer amenities comparable with those of site-built homes. Although manufactured homes were once the focus of ridicule within the housing construction industry, in the 1990s they managed to shed their association with the tacky, disordered trailer parks of the 1960s and 1970s. In fact, the quality and design of manufactured (as opposed to mobile) homes improved to such an extent that the more upscale models have became almost indistinguishable from homes being constructed in newer, moderate-cost, single-family subdivisions in many parts of the country. The growing popularity of the manufactured housing trend came to an abrupt halt at the end of the 1990s, however. Whereas in the mid-1990s, manufactured homes made up the fastest-growing segment of home sales in the United States—accounting for 33 percent of all single-family home sales in 1996—by the late 1990s the industry began to experience a sharp decline; sales at American Homestar dropped 24 percent between 1999 and 2000, and the company floundered.

Answering the Need for Affordable Housing Since 1971

Responding to the changing requirements of U.S. homebuyers, American Homestar Corporation was founded in 1971 as Mobile America Housing Corporation. Company founder and Texas native Finis Teeter, who had been selling manufactured housing since hiring on at Mobile Home Industries in 1969, decided to focus his area of operations in the southwest region. Establishing a 137,000-square-foot manufacturing facility in Fort Worth, Teeter began marketing middle-priced homes within the five-state area that has remained the company's core market. Teeter responded to the obviously unsatisfied need for affordable housing by setting up a retail network throughout the Southwest. The year 1971 proved to be a banner one for both Teeter and the manufactured housing industry as a whole as unit sales peaked throughout the nation.

The company reincorporated as American Homestar Corporation in 1983. Whereas the next few years would be rocky, indeed—the industry as a whole saw shipments of manufactured homes drop nationwide from 295,079 in 1983 to only 179,713 in 1991—Teeter and his company kept their footing until economic conditions across the nation began to stabilize.

It was not only a national recession, however, that affected the company. During the late 1980s, Texas experienced a dramatic decline in its own economic fortunes as the state's oil industry went through the ''bust'' cycle after its earlier boom years. Within American Homestar's core market area, the number of manufactured home-makers shrank from 54 in 1984 to six by the

Company Perspectives:

American Homestar Corporation is one of the nation's leading, vertically integrated manufactured housing companies. The company designs, produces, and retails manufactured homes. Through its subsidiaries, the firm provides installment financing, insurance, and transportation services.

early 1990s. The state began a financial comeback, however; along with other southern states, which have traditionally served as the manufactured home industry's strongest sales territory, Texas returned to its former glory, once again providing American Homestar with a lucrative market for its product.

Early 1990s: Developing Manufacturing and Sales Networks and Achieving Vertical Integration

By 1994, despite the setbacks caused by the local Texas economy, American Homestar ran three manufacturing plants located throughout the Dallas/Fort Worth area. Under the umbrella of National Housing Systems, Inc., the company retailed its homes in Arkansas, Colorado, Kansas, Louisiana, Missouri, New Mexico, Oklahoma, and Texas via 34 company-owned retail centers. These company-owned centers were supplemented by 103 independent retailers in the same core market area.

Due to the high cost of materials and storage, as well as the cyclical nature of the construction industry, factory-built homes were usually not manufactured until an order had been received, either from an independent retailer or one of American Homestar's own sales centers. The average rate of production in the company was 23 floors per day; the decline in orders experienced by the slump in housing demand over the winter months was balanced by a corresponding increase in production during warmer weather. Sixty percent of total sales was generated by company-owned retailers, with the remainder written by its network of independents. New company-manufactured homes—medium- to upper-priced houses that vary in features and design—comprised more than 60 percent of the homes sold by American Homestar, which also sold used homes and homes from other manufacturers. In the early 1990s, company goals continued to focus on increasing this percentage to 80 percent through enlargement of American Homestar's own manufacturing facilities.

The implementation of a management strategy known as vertical integration—the ability to design, manufacture, market, deliver, and finance its product—was the key to the success of several competitors in the manufactured home industry, notably the Knoxville, Tennessee-based Clayton Homes. Teeter also recognized the benefits of this means of developing structural efficiency early on, and he guided American Homestar in the direction of vertical integration. In light of Teeter's success in this area, analysts praised American Homestar as possessing one of the best-managed corporate organizations in the manufactured housing industry.

The company obtained a controlling interest in the newly formed Roadmaster Transport Company in 1992 as its first step toward vertical integration. Because of the specialized trucking needs of the manufactured home industry, Roadmaster was organized as a means of providing transit from factory to homesite. Deriving only a small percentage of its revenue from American Homestar—26 percent in 1996—Roadmaster generated most of its income by servicing other home manufacturers within its transit area. Under efficient management, it had become one of the largest transporters of manufactured homes in the southwest region.

1992: Merger with Oak Creek Homes

The year 1992 was significant, not only for the company's diversification into the transport business, but also for its timely merger with another home manufacturer. Recognizing the increased potential for profits with an increase in production and retail size, CEO Teeter formed a joint venture with Oak Creek Homes, a major supplier of homes to American Homestar retailers. Under the joint name of American Homestar, Oak Creek CEO and primary shareholder Laurence A. Dawson, Jr., worked with Teeter to open two new manufacturing plants to capture the still-increasing demand for manufactured homes. The Lancaster manufacturing facility was opened in December 1992 to produce lower-priced homes; upper medium- and higher-priced homes would be constructed at the 94,000-square-foot Burleson plant beginning in May 1993. Oak Creek Homes was acquired by American Homestar in August 1993. Under the acquisition, all corporate operations were combined; Dawson was named co-CEO and director alongside Chairman and CEO Teeter.

Providing its customers with adequate long-term financing for home purchases also contributed to American Homestar's goal of vertical integration. Through its 50 percent ownership of 21st Century Mortgage, which was formed in early 1996, the company reaped the profits of $47 million in home mortgages by the end of its first fiscal year. Approximately half of the homes purchased through American Homestar retailers would eventually be financed by 21st Century. Through its ownership of Western Insurance Agency and Lifestar Reinsurance Ltd., the company was able to service its customers' property/casualty and credit life insurance needs and profit from yet another financial transaction on the way to owning a home.

Going Public in 1994

Company management's efforts toward vertical integration paid off. Although sales in 1992 had contributed only $27 million to revenues of $28.7 million, by 1994 they had reached $109 million, an increase of more than 400 percent. Such rapid growth enabled American Homestar to consider an expansion of its sales territory through the acquisition of smaller manufactured home producers. Expansion into these new markets, however, would necessitate an influx of capital. Accordingly, in July 1994 the company went public, offering two million shares on the New York over-the-counter market. While Teeter and Dawson retained 45 percent of the company stock, the sale of the remaining 1.1 million shares generated sufficient revenues to continue the implementation of their acquisition plans.

Formulating reorganization strategies was only a means to an end. American Homestar approached the year 2000 with several strategic goals, which included opening new retail cen-

Key Dates:

1971: Mobile America Housing Corp. is established.
1983: The firm reincorporates as American Homestar Corporation.
1992: American Homestar Corporation gains controlling interest in Roadmaster Transport Company and merges with Oak Creek Homes.
1994: The company goes public.
1996: The company purchases a 50 percent stake in 21st Century Mortgage and acquires three firms.
1999: The company begins joint venture with HomeMax Inc. and purchases R-Anell Homes.
2000: Due to a decline in the industry, the firm begins restructuring operations.
2001: American Homestar Corporation declares Chapter 11 bankruptcy.

ters, expanding its current network of independent retailers and strengthening retailer loyalties to its product, and further expanding its manufacturing capacity. The company also focused on maximizing the profit opportunities inherent in its vertical structure through earning manufacturing, retailing, and financial service profits on every home sold. Management felt that the company's continued policy of aggressive acquisitions would ensure ever-increasing market opportunities for both its mortgage and insurance sectors.

By the mid-1990s, American Homestar was reporting annual average growth rates of between 15 and 18 percent, with 1995 revenues of $187 million and sales in its core market area cresting between 35 and 45 percent. Sales of new homes for 1995 were reported at 3,127 units, evenly distributed between single- and multifloored home models. Branching out into its first retail sales location in the state of Louisiana, the company worked toward its goal of establishing 40 new retail centers by 1997. The September 1995 investment of $2.5 million in 21st Century Life, a venture with partners Vanderbilt Mortgage & Finance and Clayton Homes, reaped $22,000 in net income by the following year.

Reaping Rewards Through Aggressive Expansion in the Mid-1990s

In 1996, American Homestar more than doubled the size of its manufacturing capacity through the acquisition of three firms: Guerdon Homes, Inc., which sells and produces manufactured homes within a 13-state region; Henderson, North Carolina's Heartland Homes, Inc.; and the 15-member Manu-Fac, Inc., retailer network, also located in North Carolina. This expansion made the company a major industry presence in 24 states through the addition of 215 new independent retailers and five additional manufacturing locations to its operations. Guerdon and Heartland, both manufacturers of upscale double-section homes, were predicted to especially enhance the company's overall sales figures. The trend within the manufactured home industry had been toward such larger, multisection homes, which accounted for almost half of the industry's 1996 sales. These more upscale homes—sometimes boasting three bedrooms, luxury amenities, or innovative architectural elements—had become an increasingly attractive alternative to buyers considering more expensive site-built homes. With American Homestar's traditional mid-priced homes serving both ends of the country's new homebuyer demographic profile (first-time homebuyers and retirees), the addition of multisection homes was seen to be an effective way to expand company market share.

Reflecting an industrywide trend toward consolidation, the acquisitions of Guerdon and Heartland made American Homestar an industry leader, not only in its core southwest and south central regions, but in the Pacific Northwest, Rocky Mountain area, and the southeastern United States as well. By the second quarter of fiscal 1997, with the multistage acquisition of Guerdon Homes completed, the company had diversified its geographical base to the point where it could boast 48 company-owned retail centers and 300 independent dealerships servicing customers in 24 states, with eight manufacturing plants at their disposal. Through this dramatic increase in its sales base, coupled with a 100 percent increase in its manufacturing capabilities, American Homestar seemed poised on the brink of rapid financial growth.

In both 1996 and 1997, American Homestar announced a five-for-four split of its stock, increasing its common shares outstanding and generating new funds for the continued implementation of its plan for aggressive expansion. Praising the company's stock—one of the lowest-valued stocks in the industry—as one of the best picks of 1997, industry analysts expected the company's earnings to rise at an annual rate of 20 percent into the next century. Company goals for fiscal 1997, which included the addition of ten new retail facilities, reflected such an optimistic outlook. By the first quarter of fiscal 1997, three new retail outlets already had been established; by the second quarter American Homestar had reported record gains as revenues rose 76 percent from 1996 levels to $89.3 million.

According to the industry's Manufactured Housing Institute, the 370,000 manufactured homes shipped in 1996—a 9 percent increase over the previous year and a 37 percent increase over the previous decade—generated $14 billion in sales for the industry. American Homestar's piece of this growing pie was $208 million, generated through the manufacture and sale of 3,593 new homes. Housing analysts noted, however, that fluctuations in the interest rate, as well as excess inventories caused by slow orders, would begin to affect the manufactured home industry as it began its process of maturation.

Nevertheless, American Homestar continued to introduce new manufactured home models in 1997, including the Celebration Model 487 and the Galaxy Model 694. By 1998, the company's revenues had grown to $514 million, an increase of 26 percent over the previous year. The firm operated 86 retail centers and served 40 franchisees and 300 independent retailers in 28 states.

Continuing with its acquisition strategy, American Homestar purchased R-Anell Custom Homes Inc.—known for its manufactured and modular homes—in January 1999. Included in the deal were Gold Medal Homes Inc. and Gold Medal Homes of North Carolina Inc. The company also began a joint venture with HomeMax, Inc., a subsidiary of Zaring National Corporation. HomeMax operated 12 retail sales centers, called model home villages, in North and South Carolina and in Kentucky. As part of the venture, American Homestar homes would be sold in the model home villages.

Industry Decline in the New Millennium

Although the company had pursued an aggressive acquisition strategy, it entered the new millennium with an uncertain future. Housing analysts' predictions rang true as the manufactured housing industry, which had grown quickly in the 1990s, began to experience sharp declines in demand. American Homestar was forced to take action. Production in its Alabama and North Carolina plants was consolidated in an effort to improve profits. At the same time, the company sold its interest in 21st Century Mortgage and instead began a joint venture with the firm. The new entity, Homestar 21 LLC, operated as a loan originator for American Homestar customers, franchisees, and dealers.

Revenue for fiscal 2000 dropped to $574 million from $654 million recorded in the previous year. In August 2000, Dawson, Jr., resigned as CEO, president, and director of the company. Teeter remained chairman but relinquished his operating responsibilities. The company continued to consolidate operations as means of controlling costs. The decline in the industry continued with nearly 40,000 unsold mobile homes left on dealer lots in 2000. Many independent dealers were forced to go out of business, and American Homestar was left having to repurchase the unsold homes. In December 2000, retail sales in the industry declined by 32 percent over the previous year and shipments fell by 47.1 percent.

By early 2001, almost 80 manufacturing housing factories had been shut down throughout the industry. Despite the company's efforts at cutting costs, American Homestar, was forced to declare Chapter 11 bankruptcy in January. The firm, stating that the decline was the worst it had seen in two decades, was left with few options and felt that Chapter 11 was the best solution. Craig Reynolds, American Homestar's executive vice-president and chief financial officer, stated in a company press release, ''If we're going to have the opportunity to reorganize at all, we have to resort to this measure; otherwise we would just sit and run right out of cash.'' At the time of the filing, the company had $363 million in assets and nearly $280 million in debt. Management planned to file a reorganization plan to restructure operations in early summer 2001 and remained optimistic that the industry would bounce back, as it had in the past.

Principal Subsidiaries

First Value Homes Inc.; R-Anell Custom Homes Inc.; Associated Retailers Group Inc.; Nationwide Housing Systems; Oak Creek Homes Inc.; Roadmaster Transport Company.

Principal Competitors

Champion Enterprises Inc.; Fleetwood Enterprises Inc.; Oakwood Homes Corporation.

Further Reading

''American Homestar Corporation Announces Results for Fiscal 2000,'' *Business Wire,* August 15, 2000.

''American Homestar Corporation Further Expands Its Retailing Operations Through a Joint Venture with HomeMax Inc.,'' *Business Wire,* February 25, 1999.

''American Homestar to Consolidate Production in Alabama,'' *Business Wire,* March 15, 2000.

''American Homestar to Consolidate Production in North Carolina,'' *Business Wire,* May 26, 2000.

Apte, Angela, ''King of the Doublewide,'' *Houston Business Journal,* January 22, 1999, p. 14A.

''Bankruptcy Filing,'' *Houston Business Journal,* January 19, 2001, p. 22.

Byrne, Harlan S., ''Once a Joke, Manufactured Housing Has Gained Respect,'' *DowVision,* January 6, 1997.

Fowler, Tom, ''Sales Slump Leads Texas-Based Mobile Home Firm into Bankruptcy,'' *Knight-Ridder/Tribune Business News,* January 12, 2001.

''Mobile Home Company's Revenue Up 26%,'' *American Banker,* June 29, 1998, p. 17.

''Spring Festival of Homes,'' *Manufactured Home Merchandiser,* March 1997, p. 34.

Timmons, Heather, ''Home Manufacturer with Finance Affiliate Seeks Wider Horizons,'' *American Banker,* March 11, 1996, p. 10.

Trager, Cara S., ''Mobile Houses Provide Path to Affordability,'' *Newsday,* November 22, 1996.

—Pamela L. Shelton
—update: Christina M. Stansell

ARAMARK Corporation

ARAMARK Tower
1101 Market Street
Philadelphia, Pennsylvania 19107
U.S.A.
Telephone: (215) 238-3000
Fax: (215) 238-3333
Web site: http://www.aramark.com

Private Company
Incorporated: 1959 as Automatic Retailers of America, Inc.
Employees: 139,000
Sales: $7.2 billion (2000)
NAIC: 42232 Men's and Boys' Clothing and Furnishings Wholesalers; 72231 Food Service Contractors; 812332 Industrial Launderers; 62441 Child Day Care Services

ARAMARK Corporation is a diversified service company whose operations include the ARAMARK Food and Support Services Group, the ARAMARK Uniforms and Career Apparel Group, and the ARAMARK Educational Resources Group. Its food service and support operations provide food, refreshments, facilities, and various other services to corporations, health care systems, schools, colleges, convention centers, national parks, sporting venues, and correctional institutions. ARAMARK's uniform operations—the second largest in the United States—provide workplace clothing services through ARAMARK Uniform Services, WearGuard-Crest, and Gall's Inc. The firm's educational services provide child care and education programs through its Children's World Learning Centers. The division also provides private education programs. In 2000, ARAMARK—owned mainly by its employee managers—was ranked as one of the top 100 ''Most Admired Companies'' by *Fortune* magazine.

Company Origins

ARAMARK was founded by Davre Davidson and Bill Fishman, both owners of peanut-vending businesses. The two had never met when they started expanding the boundaries of the traditional vending industry in the early 1940s. In Los Angeles, Davidson began moving his machines from traditional outlets like drug stores, bowling alleys, and restaurants to factories and offices. In Chicago, Fishman was attempting to transform his vending operation from a ''fringe benefit'' into a bona fide food service operation. The two met when each won a contract to serve Douglas Aircraft plants in Santa Monica and Chicago. In the following years, they frequently discussed their desire to provide food service along with their vending operations. Finally, after a number of unsuccessful attempts to subcontract to catering companies, the two decided to merge their operations in 1959. Their company was incorporated under the name Automatic Retailers of America, Inc. (ARA), and earned $24 million in its first year.

A Period of Expansion: 1959–69

Almost immediately, the company began expanding through acquisitions. Between 1959 and 1964, ARA merged with or acquired more than 150 smaller vending companies. Its largest acquisition (and one that fulfilled a dream for both Fishman and Davidson) was the 1961 purchase of Slater Company, the largest food service business in the United States, for $15 million. The purchase made ARA a diversified food service company, and gave it a strong foothold in institutional markets such as colleges and universities. During the early 1960s, ARA led the trend among vending companies to expand into the food service industry. ''We recognized that vending was moving into food service and that this more sophisticated business would require skills we couldn't attain individually,'' Davidson told *Business Week* in 1964. By 1964, ARA operated 95,000 vending machines, offering freshly brewed coffee, hot soup, sandwiches, and other items. It had 750 cafeterias or other ''manual food service'' outlets, and total revenues of $200.6 million.

The company's dominance of the vending industry grew so quickly that in 1964 the Federal Trade Commission (FTC) required ARA to divest itself of a number of vending companies, worth about $7.6 million in annual sales. The company complied, selling one-third of the required portion by 1965 and the remainder in the following year. Fishman and Davidson had other plans for their company's growth. ''We're in the service

Company Perspectives:

Because we value relationships, we treat customers as long-term partners, and each other with candor and respect. Because we succeed through performance, we encourage the entrepreneur in each of us, and work always to improve our service. Because we thrive on growth, we seek new markets and new opportunities, and we innovate to get and keep customers. And because we're ARAMARK, we do everything with integrity.

business,'' ARA vice-president Harry Stephens told *Business Week,* ''and food is only one of the services necessary to keep an institution operating. There's janitorial services, cleaning, lawn care, security, laundry, accounting, many things.'' This concept became the cornerstone of ARA's expansion. The company established a division to run resorts, sports parks, and amusement parks; acquired Air La Carte Inc., a private company that provided in-flight meals for more than 20 domestic and international airlines; and ventured into periodicals distribution, purchasing 39 local distributorships over a period of about four years.

Problems Arise: 1970s through the early 1980s

In 1972, the FTC again charged ARA with anticompetitive practices. The first complaint stated that its recent purchase of 39 distributorships posed a potential monopolistic threat. The second charged the company, which by then had grown to be the nation's largest vending machine company, with anticompetitive practices through the purchase of 97 separate vending companies. ARA vigorously defended itself against the charges, stating that ''approximately 80 percent'' of ARA's revenues were not earned by the segments under question. In 1973, the court ordered ARA to cease purchasing ''certain types of wholesale operations in the paperback books and periodicals field'' and to divest itself of a portion of its vending business. The company's image suffered again in 1973 when a federal grand jury indicted ARA, Western Vending, and AAV Cos. of Cleveland with colluding to fix prices and illegally control the customers and locations of cigarette vending machines. ARA filed a ''no contest'' plea, stating that the charges dealt with a market segment that was too small to warrant the cost of defending them in court.

ARA's earnings grew at a compound annual rate of 10 percent from 1970 to 1975, fueled primarily by internal expansion. In addition to its food and distribution services, ARA had branched into student bus services, maintenance and housekeeping, and merchandising. The majority of the company's income, however, came from food service. According to analysts, its growth was remarkable given the rising foods costs that had adversely affected many companies in the food service industry. ''We try to manage our services like an investment portfolio,'' Fishman told *Financial World* in 1975. ''While one area may be down another is up. That's why we've been able to hold our margins.'' During this time, the company also ventured into the somewhat unpopular nursing home management field, purchasing National Living Centers in 1973 and Geriatrics Inc. in 1974. Although many in the investment community questioned the move (leading to a drop in stock prices), Fishman defended it, stating, ''We've been in the medical market for over thirty years, so it was just a natural transition.''

By 1977, the company had divested almost all of its vending operations. That year, the FTC asked the federal Justice Department to force ARA to further divest itself of four periodicals distribution companies in the South and Midwest, stating that the purchases were in violation of its 1973 order. ARA complied with the order, paid a $300,000 fine, and continued to grow through the purchase of several service-oriented companies, including Aratex Inc., a uniform laundry and delivery service, Daybridge Learning Centers, a chain of day care centers, Smith Transfer Corp., a trucking company, and Physicians Placement, a management support and physician service for hospital emergency rooms. As it had with its other operations, ARA expanded each new division by purchasing other small companies and consolidating them.

The company also continued to develop internally. By 1979, ARA operated more than 6,000 food service establishments in the United Kingdom, Belgium, France, and Germany. In Canada, ARA purchased VS Services, a food service operation which quickly grew to become the largest food service operation in that country. Its student transport division, which operated school bus fleets throughout the United States, also grew at a rapid rate during the last half of the 1970s, providing 9.5 percent of revenues by 1979. ARA president and chief operating officer Marvin Heaps attributed the company's success during difficult economic times to its effective management of three factors: food costs, energy costs, and labor costs. Sales for the first six months of 1979 topped $1 billion. Earnings per share rose to $2.80, ten cents below the hourly wage the company paid a large number of its employees.

ARA's reputation was tarnished once again in 1981 as a federal grand jury began investigating the company's student transport division to determine whether it engaged in a bid-rigging strategy designed to squeeze out local competition. ARA management maintained that the company was a victim of a ''smear campaign'' started by disgruntled former employees and local transport companies angry that ARA had won certain bids. ARA's earnings dropped from $63 million in 1980, to $39 million in 1982, and share prices steadily declined although sales had risen to $3 billion by fiscal 1983. Many investors believed that ''the company's many divisions had gotten out of control from too much growth too fast.'' Although profits in its geriatrics, health care, textile service, and distribution divisions were strong, profits in its trucking and food service divisions were severely affected by recessions, and its European food service operations also posted heavy losses.

New Management: Mid-1980s

Led by the newly appointed president and chief executive Joseph Neubauer, ARA management responded to the company's uneven results by reorganizing its divisions by geography as well as type of operation. Its acquisition program slowed slightly, focusing on companies in profitable markets such as geriatrics and distribution. The company also embarked on a major public relations campaign with two specific goals: to

Key Dates:

1959: Automatic Retailers of America, Inc. (ARA) is established.
1961: ARA acquires the Slater Company, the largest food service business in the United States.
1964: Revenues exceed $200 million.
1968: ARA acquires the District News Company.
1972: ARA faces FTC charges due to its monopolistic control of the vending machine market.
1977: The company divests nearly all of its vending machine operations.
1981: A federal grand jury begins investigating the company's student transport division; sales begin to drop off.
1984: The company restructures and executes a leveraged management buyout.
1992: ARA provides international food service at the 1992 Barcelona Olympics.
1994: The company changes its name to ARAMARK Corporation.
1997: ARAMARK enters the hospital food services market.
1999: ARAMARK acquires the Restaura dining operations from Viad Corp.
2000: ARAMARK purchases Odgen Corp.'s Entertainment division and secures a $700 million food service contract with Boeing Company.

make ARA a respected household word, and to generate a sense of corporate identity among its 112,000 employees. ''Originally the strategy was 'we are servants in other people's homes and ought to be invisible,' '' Neubauer told the *Wall Street Journal* in 1984. ''But now we are going to stand for something.'' Advertising expenditures jumped to around $2 million as the company took out ads in major weekly magazines such as *Time* and *Newsweek.* Employees began wearing company uniforms embroidered with the ARA logo, and managers began receiving incentives, worth up to 45 percent of their annual salaries, as rewards for work well done.

Perhaps the largest change that year was an unexpected $850 million leveraged buyout, which was orchestrated by ARA management in the surprisingly short time span of 99 days from start to finish. Deemed an ''absolute necessity'' by management to prevent undesired investors from bidding for control of the company (although the only known bid was for $720 million from former food service division president William Siegel), the buyout was financed by borrowing from Chemical Bank and Morgan Guaranty Trust Co. After the buyout, ARA neither cut its operating expenditures nor, with the exception of its unprofitable Smith Transfer division, sold any major assets to pay down the debt. ARA actually acquired three companies within its first three years of going private, while paying $100 million on its debt.

Success Under a New Corporate Identity: The 1990s

In the early 1990s, the company began selling assets, including its Ground Services Inc., which cleaned aircraft and handled cargo and baggage at airports. And in 1992, ARA spun off a portion of its geriatrics division in an initial public offering that raised $112.7 million. ARA held a 10 percent interest in the new company, which took the name Living Centers of America, and used $76 million of the money raised in the IPO to pay ''certain intercompany indebtedness.'' By 1992, ARA's annual revenues totaled $4.8 billion. Its image was greatly improved, especially in its food service and leisure service divisions, where ''customized service'' allowed the company to expand throughout Europe and into Japan, and even serve Olympic athletes their native foods at the 1992 Barcelona Olympics. Its day care division was growing more slowly than desired, as corporations and government cut back on expenditures, but the rest of its operations remained relatively healthy. Having transformed itself from a collection of vending machines into a mature, $5 billion corporation, ARA developed a new logo and changed its name to ARAMARK Corporation in 1994, reflecting the changes that it had undergone during its 36-year history.

Organized under a new corporate identity, ARAMARK experienced success and growth in the mid-1990s. The company continued its tradition of serving Olympic athletes in Atlanta, Georgia, during the 1996 Summer Games, having served all but one of the events in the last 28 years. The firm also teamed up with renowned chef Charlie Trotter to design menus and wine lists, and to implement chef training programs for its executive and corporate dining division. Under the leadership of Neubauer, the company's focus remained on securing strong and strategic relationships with its customers. By 1997, ARAMARK recorded $6 billion in sales.

As the firm's food service business prospered, the company's other business segments continued to grow as well. Its child care business, through its Children's World Learning Centers, was second behind Kinder-Care in terms of students in 1997, and served over 80,000 children. The firm's uniform business also fared well with large customers like McDonald's Corp. Along with strengthening business operations, management also sought to solidify its ownership in the company and announced a $440 million stock buy-back plan of its entitled ''Share 100'' in 1997. According to ARAMARK management, the buy-back of the 20 percent owned by outside investors was necessary to thwart any future takeover attempts. CEO Neubauer was quoted in an *Amusement Business* article stating, ''This marks the successful conclusion of a buy-out process that started in 1984. Over the past 13 years, we've proven we can generate enough cash to fuel continuing growth and increase our ownership of the company.''

In 1998, ARAMARK secured a ten-year contract with Sprint Corp. to manage food service operations at its world headquarters. The company also continued developing its PanGeos and Fresh World Flavors food concepts, debuting those as well as new ideas at the Goldman, Sachs' Manhattan headquarters cafeteria. With nearly 65 percent of company revenue's stemming from its food services and support services division, management continued to focus heavily on that area. In early 1999, the firm announced plans to acquire the Restaura dining operations of Viad Corp. The deal was anticipated to boost corporate food service revenues by 18 percent. By continuing to land new customers, ARAMARK secured $750 million in revenues from new business in 1999.

Continued Growth in the New Millennium

ARAMARK's growth strategy continued into the new millennium. While facing increased competition, tight labor markets, and rising costs, the company continued to look for strategic partnerships and alliances. In March 2000, the firm acquired the food and concession services of the Ogden Corp., which would make it the largest sports and entertainment concessions provider in the United States. ARAMARK also contracted with Boeing Corp. to provide food services to its locations across the country. The $700 million deal was the largest competitively-bid contract for food service in the industry. Other contracts for the year included deals with Wal-Mart and CitiGroup. The company also partnered with Einstein/Noah Bagel Corp. and Ben & Jerry's Homemade Inc. to open licensed stores on college campuses. ARAMARK expanded globally as well with a joint venture with Campbell Bewley Group, the largest food service company in Ireland.

According to the Outsourcing Institute, U.S.-based companies spent over $200 billion in outsourcing noncore operations and were predicted to spend over $300 billion in 2001. ARAMARK continued to focus on being the first choice among these businesses for providing managed services in its core areas of operation. By serving 15 million people on a daily basis at 500,000 locations in 15 countries, ARAMARK was poised to remain an industry leader in the years to come.

Principal Subsidiaries

ARAMARK Business Dining Services; ARAMARK Correctional Services; ARAMARK Refreshment Services; ARAMARK Campus Services; ARAMARK School Nutrition Services; ARAMARK Health Care Support Services; Gall's Inc.; GMARA; ARAMARK Leisure Services; ARAMARK International Services; ARAMARK Uniform Services; WearGuard-Crest; Spectrum Health Care Services; Children's World Learning Centers; ARAMARK Magazine and Book Services.

Principal Competitors

Cintas Corp.; Compass Group; Sodexho Marriott Services Inc.

Further Reading

Allen, Frank, "ARA, Betting on Pride, Approves Plan to Give Its Managers Voting Control," *Wall Street Journal,* March 16, 1988, p. 25.

"ARAMARK Adds Restaura to Mix," *Restaurants & Institutions,* February 1, 1999, p. 20.

"ARAMARK to Expand Ben & Jerry's at College Sites," *Nation's Restaurant News,* September 25, 2000, p. 4.

"ARAMARK Wins World's Largest Foodservice Contract in Deal With Boeing," *Business Wire,* June 20, 2000.

"Bagel Company Partners With ARAMARK," *The Food Institute Report,* September 11, 2000, p. 2.

Engelmayer, Paul A., "ARA Attempts Revival Using a High Profile," *Wall Street Journal,* June 8, 1984, p. 1.

Evans, Rob, "Management Buyback Proposed at ARAMARK," *Amusement Business,* November 17, 1997, p. 15.

"Has ARA Misstepped?" *Financial World,* February 5, 1975, p. 12.

King, Paul, "ARAMARK Hits Mark with Latest Goldman, Sachs Cafeteria," *Nation's Restaurant News,* August 10, 1998, p. 73.

——, "That's Entertainment: ARAMARK Buys Ogden Arm," *Nation's Restaurant News,* April 10, 2000, p. 1.

"Trotter to Take ARAMARK 'To the Next Level'," *Nation's Restaurant News,* April 21, 1997, p. 27.

"Vendors Outgrow Machines," *Business Week,* October 10, 1964, p. 136.

Vogl, A.J., "The Extended Corporation," *Across the Board,* June, 1997, p. 37.

Weber, Joseph, "Catering to the Olympics: A Gold Medal—But Not Much Gold," *Business Week,* July 27, 1992, p. 38.

—Maura Troester
—update: Christina M. Stansell

ARD

Bertramstrasse 8
D-60320 Frankfurt am Main
Germany
Telephone: (49) (69) 590-607
Fax: (49) (69) 155-2075
Web site: http://www.ard.de

Federation of Public Nonprofit Companies
Incorporated: 1950 as Arbeitsgemeinschaft der öffentlich-rechtlichen Rundfunkanstalten der Bundesrepublik Deutschland
Employees: 24,600
Operating Budget: DM 11.4 billion ($5.82 billion) (1999)
NAIC: 51312 Television Broadcasting; 513112 Radio Stations

ARD (Arbeitsgemeinschaft der öffentlich-rechtlichen Rundfunkanstalten der Bundesrepublik Deutschland) is a federation of one national and ten regional public broadcasting stations that reach over 72 million people in about 34 million German households. In a cooperative effort, these stations produce the content for the national ''First German Television'' channel, eight regional TV channels, and over 50 national and regional radio channels, including radio programs in 12 different languages for foreigners. The national TV and radio network, Deutsche Welle, is government-owned and financed by taxes. ARD has a 30 percent share in German satellite channel 3sat, a 25 percent stake in European culture channel ARTE, a 50 percent interest in the children's channel KI.KA and the news-oriented PHOENIX channel, and runs a joint national video-text service and an Internet portal. To maintain its leading position in Germany's TV news market, ARD employs a network of roughly 100 foreign correspondents in 30 cities around the world.

ARD's communications infrastructure is provided mainly by Deutsche Telekom. Its central dispatching office, located in Cologne, manages the use of mobile TV broadcasting equipment. About 83 percent of ARD's funding is derived from a fee that every German household with radio receivers or TV sets, except low-income households and hospitals, are required to pay monthly. The fees are collected by Cologne-based Gebühreneinzugszentrale der öffentlich rechtlichen Rundfunkanstalten (GEZ). Approximately 14 percent of ARD's funds come from licensing, co-productions, and merchandising. ARD's third source of funding is advertising, which contributes about three percent of the total; the amount of advertising is strictly limited by law. ARD's advertising time is sold through ARD-Werbung SALES & Services GmbH (AS&S) while licensing for sports events is overseen by Sportrechte- und Marketing-Agentur GmbH (SportA), a joint venture of ARD and Germany's second public TV broadcaster ZDF. The federation is not a legally liable entity. ARD member stations take turns chairing the network's management board, while the managing station is elected by the general assembly. The managing station is legally liable for the federation during its one-year term, which can be extended for an additional year, and its director becomes ARD chairman during that period. ARD's various functions are supported by several subsidiaries, including Frankfurt-based management office ARD-Büro, the central program coordination office in Munich, its news headquarters located in Hamburg, the Frankfurt-based movie acquisition and production arm Degeto Film GmbH, and a central archive with locations in Frankfurt and Berlin.

German Radio: From Monopoly to Federation after World War II

When Germany entered the age of radio broadcasting in 1923, the government decided to raise the funds necessary for technical infrastructure and programming by imposing a general fee on every household that owned a receiver. The fee, in German the *Rundfunkgebühr*, was determined by the government-owned post office, the German Reichspost, and collected from German households by the mailman. The Reichspost also established the technical backbones of German broadcasting, including mid-, long-, and shortwave radio broadcasting stations. In 1925 the Reichs-Rundfunk-Gesellschaft (RRG) was founded as an umbrella organization for German radio broadcasting. First in the Weimar Republic, and then especially after the Nazis came to power in 1933, radio broadcasting in Germany was increasingly

Company Perspectives:

As institutions under public law, ARD's state-owned broadcasting stations are independent of government control; their sole obligation is to serve the public. Within the dual broadcasting system (nonprofit public and commercial private broadcasting), their task is providing the German public with information, education and entertainment.

centralized. It became a propaganda vehicle of the Nazi government before and during World War II.

After Nazi Germany was defeated in 1949, the Western Allies started rebuilding a radio broadcasting infrastructure in West Germany. To prevent the formation of a new centralized system that could be misused again by political parties, they sought an appropriate organizational structure. After several abandoned proposals, the Arbeitsgemeinschaft der öffentlich-rechtlichen Rundfunkanstalten der Bundesrepublik Deutschland (ARD), that is the federation of public broadcasters of the Federal Republic of Germany, was formed in June 1950. The legal form of the new entity was Anstalt des öffentlichen Rechts, a nongovernment and nonprofit organization with its own administration under the control of two commissions, the Rundfunkrat and the Verwaltungsrat, in which different stakeholders from German public life were represented. ARD's founding members were six German broadcasting stations, the successors to the Allied Forces radio stations: Nordwestdeutscher Rundfunk (NWDR), the broadcasting station in the former British zone; Südwestfunk (SWF), the station in the French zone; and four stations located in the former part of Germany that was occupied by the Americans, Bayerischer Rundfunk (BR), Süddeutscher Rundfunk (SDR), Hessicher Rundfunk (HR) and Radio Bremen (RB). The new entity was financed by an obligatory fee which every German household with at least one radio receiver paid. Each station received the money collected in its state. However, larger ARD members subsidized smaller ones to a certain extent.

Between its foundation and 1962, the number of ARD members increased to ten. First, between 1953 and 1955, the new station Sender Freies Berlin (SFB)—literally translated Station Free Berlin—was founded in West Berlin, in the heart of the Soviet zone. NWDR dissolved during this time, and two new stations took its place, Norddeutscher Rundfunk (NDR) in the northern and Westdeutscher Rundfunk (WDR) in the western part of West Germany. After the French-occupied Saarland voted to join West Germany, the newly founded Saarländische Rundfunk (SR) joined ARD in 1959. Finally, in 1960 the international German radio station Deutsche Welle (DW) was founded and became ARD's tenth member two years afterwards. Every member of the federation remained independent, and decisions were made by the directors of all member stations.

The Age of German Television Begins in 1950

During the Nazi years, radio broadcasting was equivalent to the voice of the political power, and thus the German public was not accustomed to a plurality of ideas. Therefore, the Western Allies and the Americans in particular put a high emphasis on airing discussions and shows that invited different opinions. The year 1950 marked the beginning of the postwar radio broadcasting age for Germany. On November 27 of that year, ARD member NWDR began broadcasting three times a week from its studio in an old bunker on Hamburg's Heiligengeistfeld. Two years later, on Christmas Day 1952, German television was officially launched. On the following day, ARD's flagship daily news program "Tagesschau" aired for the first time and found a permanent home in ARD's news headquarters in Hamburg Lokstedt in 1955. Broadcast three times a week at first, the show later switched to a daily schedule and became a hallmark of German public television. Two of the first TV events of the time were the live broadcasts of the crowning of the English Queen Elizabeth II in June 1953 and the soccer world championship games in Switzerland in summer 1954 at which Germany won the title. ARD's first U.S. correspondent, Peter von Zahn, informed German TV viewers about life in the United States in his monthly show *Bilder aus der neuen Welt*—Pictures From The New World.

In the summer of 1954, SWF, BR, and NDR started their own regional TV programs. On November first of the same year, ARD's joint channel, Deutsches Fernsehen, which later became Erstes Deutsches Fernsehen (First German Television), went on air. The new channel consisted of jointly-produced shows such as *Tagesschau* as well as broadcasts produced individually by ARD member stations. The programs were coordinated by the *Programmdirektion* based in Munich. Besides several entertaining shows, ARD went political in 1957 when it launched its first political TV magazine, *Panorama*. Germany's first political TV show adopted the slogan "What is being talked about and what should be talked about" and pictured all aspects of postwar West German society—including conflict-laden topics, scandals, and other taboo topics, such as former Nazis who then held high positions in the political and legal systems. Embraced by the German public, *Panorama* became the instant enemy of the German federal government. One of the first moderators of the show, Gert von Paczensky, greeted his viewers with: "And now let's pick a little bit on the federal government." The leading party at that time, the Christian Democrats, objected to the critical tone of the TV journalism, and Paczensky lost his position in 1963. By the end of the 1950s the number of German TV viewers had exploded. While only about 1,500 TV sets in private households, public halls, and shopping windows had shown queen Elizabeth's crowning in 1953, the German post office reported the one millionth TV consumer in October 1957. Only one year later that number had doubled; it would reach roughly 3.4 million by 1960.

Reoganization and Private Competition in the 1960s, 1970s and 1980s

The success of NDR's *Panorama* inspired ARD to launch two more political shows. The first one, *Report,* was introduced in 1960 and broadcast by BR and SWR. WDR-produced *Monitor* followed five years later. ARD's political shows were enormously popular and reached up to 40 percent of TV viewers during the 1960s. Beginning in March 1960, *Tagesschau* viewers were presented with "Tomorrow's Weather" after the

Key Dates:

1950: Company is founded by six German broadcasting stations.
1952: ARD's flagship daily news program *Tagesschau* airs for the first time.
1967: The era of color television begins at the international broadcasting trade show Funkausstellung in Berlin.
1978: ARD's moderated late-night news show *Tagesthemen* is launched.
1984: The first commercial TV broadcasting stations go on air.
1989: ARD reports live about the fall of the Berlin Wall.
1992: The new ARD stations MDR and ORB begin serving the eastern German states.
1993: ARD programs are broadcast via satellite.
1995: ARD closes the ''night gap'' and broadcasts around the clock.
1998: Former ARD stations SDR and SWF merge to form SWR.
1999: ARD's new capital broadcasting studio opens in Berlin.

news of the day. In the following two decades ARD consistently expanded its information and news reporting capabilities and broadcasts. In 1963 *Bericht aus Bonn*, a weekly news show covering the major events in West Germany's new capital, Bonn, premiered. Based on the reports of ARD correspondents in London, Paris, Rome, Belgrade, New Delhi, Tokyo, New York, and Washington D.C., the international news show *Weltspiegel* was launched at the same time. ARD presented an election prognosis for the first time during the 1965 governmental elections.

The era of color television officially began in Germany when West Berlin mayor Willy Brandt pushed a button at the international broadcasting trade show Funkausstellung in Berlin in August 1967. Other TV events of the 1960s included U.S. President John F. Kennedy's visit in West Germany in 1963 and the live broadcast of U.S. astronaut Neil Armstrong's landing on the moon on July 21, 1969, at four o'clock in the morning for German viewers.

In 1975 ARD opened a studio in East Berlin, and three years later its half-hour moderated late-night news show *Tagesthemen* was launched. In addition to its information arm that also produced documentaries such as *The Third Reich*, ARD developed a diverse set of entertaining broadcasts, including quiz-shows, TV series, programming for kids, and music shows.

During the 1960s and 1970s, the ARD organization itself also changed significantly. In June 1961 all German states signed the ''*Staatsvertrag über das Zweite Deutsche Fernsehen*,'' a law that created the second German public broadcaster (ZDF) owned by the states. The new station became ARD's first competitor for TV viewer's attention. In 1964 ARD member station BR launched its own TV programming, and other ARD member stations followed suit. These programs ultimately became Germany's so-called ''third channels.'' They were free of advertising and focused on regional news, information, and entertainment with a regional touch. After a 1968 ruling of the *Bundesverwaltungsgericht*, Germany's highest administrative court, the responsibility for setting the *Rundfunkgebühr* was transferred from the post office to the German states. In 1976 the *Gebühreneinzugszentrale* (GEZ) was founded by ARD and ZDF and took over the collection of the fee. However, the change with the most fundamental impact on ARD occurred in 1984 when the first commercial TV channels ended the public broadcaster's monopoly of the German market. Beginning in 1986, an ever growing competition from private radio stations challenged their public counterparts. However, while the new private competitors sharpened their weapons, a historical surprise created a TV spectacle for ARD and new challenges for German politics.

The Effects of German Reunification in 1990

On November 9, 1989, ARD's *Tagesschau* reported that GDR-government official Günter Schabowski had proclaimed freedom to travel to the West for GDR citizens. On the same evening the first openings of the Berlin Wall were covered live in special broadcasts. Pictures of East Berliners celebrating with their Western countrymen took the world by storm—and by complete surprise as well. The reunification of Germany in October 1990 resulted in a major challenge for ARD since its mission had to be expanded to include the new German states. In December 1990 ARD started broadcasting in former East Germany. While East Germany's central TV channel DFF was shut down, some of its most popular shows were integrated into ARD's programming.

On August 31, 1991, the Minister Presidents of all German states signed an agreement that became the new legal basis of the so-called ''dual radio broadcasting system,'' the ''*Staatsvertrag über den Rundfunk im vereinten Deutschland*.'' This agreement regulated the rights and responsibilities of the public broadcasting sector, including its financing, and contained guidelines for commercial broadcasters as well. The treaty guaranteed the existence of public broadcasting and its financing through the *Rundfunkgebühr*. Among other things, it regulated the quality and quantity of advertising among public and commercial radio and TV stations. The new law also abandoned the 50-percent discount that hotels had received on the TV-fee for some of their TV sets, which resulted in about DM 33 million in additional revenues for public broadcasters—and an equal amount in additional costs for Germany's hotels.

In 1992 two new ARD stations started broadcasting in the eastern German states. Mitteldeutscher Rundfunk (MDR) served the states of Saxony, Saxony-Anhalt, and Thuringia in the south; Ostdeutscher Rundfunk Brandenburg (ORB) covered Brandenburg and Berlin in the east; NDR served Mecklenburg-Vorpommern in the north. Beginning in 1992, GEZ started collecting the *Rundfunkgebühr* in the eastern German states and in the eastern part of Berlin. Another agreement between all public broadcasters enabled GEZ to function as their central data processing center administering the data of all ''radio broadcasting participants,'' or every household that owned at least on radio receiver or TV.

In July 1990 Germany's Minister Presidents also decided to merge the national radio channel Deutschlandfunk with the former West Berlin-based station of the American Allied Forces, Rundfunk im Amerikanischen Sektor (in short, RIAS 1), to form the new national radio channel DeutschlandRadio. The new channel, launched in 1994, was a cooperative venture of ARD and ZDF and not an ARD member.

Threats from Politicians and Private Media Giants in the 1990s

Since the beginning of commercial radio and TV broadcasting in Germany, ARD had two major adversaries: the commercial broadcasters and the federal government. The main criticism ARD had faced since the beginning involved two of its income sources, the obligatory *Rundfunkgebühr* and advertising. In the late 1950s, ARD had voluntarily limited the amount of its advertising. To avoid confrontations with newspaper publishers who accused ARD of taking away business, its directors opted not to broadcast any commercials after 8 p.m. However, with the emergence of private TV stations solely financed by advertising, ARD became commercial TV's permanent target of criticism. Their argument was that the public broadcaster should rely solely on the fee collected from German ''TV-households,'' which private stations had no share in. Public broadcasters, the private stations argued, should abandon the advertising business altogether. ARD and its political backers maintained that advertising revenues ensured the federation's political independence and that the *Rundfunkgebühr* would have to be raised by 36 to 84 German Marks, about $18 to $42, per household per year, to make up for the financial losses. However, after Germany's reunification, ARD and ZDF had already instituted an increase of the monthly TV-fee by 25 percent to finance their expansion into the new east German states, specifically its satellite and cable programming and technical infrastructure.

Germany's commercial TV broadcasters actually had little reason to complain. After 1984, they were able to continually command a larger market share, while ARD suffered significant losses in advertising revenues. By the 1990s, ARD's losses in advertising revenues were reaching up to 22 percent annually. The permission for public broadcasters to use program sponsoring after the 8 p.m. limit, which was part of the new law, brought only a meager relief. By 1991, private TV-stations RTLplus and SAT1 had surpassed ARD in revenues. In 1994 ARD's advertising losses were about $25 million with a total of $227 million in advertising revenues remaining.

German politicians had watched ARD suspiciously since its inception. As early as 1961, the Christian Democrat chancellor, the conservative Konrad Adenauer, had tried to create a central TV channel, the Bundes-Fernsehen, which was ultimately stopped by the *Bundesverfassungsgericht*. With the arrival of commercial TV, politician interest in ARD faded for a period of time. Private TV was being explored as a new medium of political mass communication, offering a broader variety of avenues in which leading party figures could spread their news.

In 1993, Christian Democrat Chancellor Helmut Kohl signed a contract for six appearances on SAT1, one of Germany's largest private TV channels, owned by movie mogul Leo Kirch, to be interviewed by ''friendly'' journalists from newspapers owned by the same conglomerate. Some commentators speculated that this was the result of a close friendship between Kohl and Kirch. At the same time, Kohl and his finance minister, Wolfgang Schäuble, started a debate questioning Germany's existing public broadcasting system. Two years later the conflict climaxed. In February 1995, the London-based newspaper *The Guardian* reported that in an unusually emotional reaction to a snide attack on an ARD show, Kohl complained that ARD had ''lost all sense of decency and dignity'' and threatened the federation's funding and structure. He suggested reducing the number of ARD member stations from 11 to around seven as a way of cutting costs and TV-fees. ARD and the opposition party, the Social Democrats, regarded this as the start of a campaign aimed at abolishing independent public broadcasting. Thus they threatened to use their majority in the *Bundesrat*, the assembly of German states, to block the further development of private TV in Germany. While the conflict lost steam, ARD was still plagued by the second means of influence of major politics: the political party membership of the directors of ARD's member stations, which often guaranteed a certain degree of compliance.

Strengthening Position in the New Millennium

ARD had lost no less than two-thirds of its advertising revenues, but this accounted for only a minority of its funding, the bulk being generated from the *Rundfunkgebühr* fees. Several lawsuits brought by organizations as well as individuals attacking ARD's funding privilege failed. The *Bundesverfassungsgericht* (BVG), Germany's Supreme Court, consistently decided in ARD's favor, willing to protect its political and financial independence. In 1994 BVG ruled that the commission that calculated the fee, KEF, had to be independent of state and federal politics. However, when commercial TV broadcasting stations SAT1, RTL, and other private cable TV channels were gaining momentum—and viewers—in the early 1990s, ARD felt pressed to adjust its programming to stay competitive. More and more entertainment formats used by private TV channels (talk shows and daily soap operas for example) made their way into ARD's programming, a trend which was harshly criticized by ARD backers as well as opponents.

Its 50th anniversary in 2000 fueled new public discussions about the legitimacy of ARD's existence. Besides being under attack for the diminishing quality of its programming, ARD also struggled with its image as an inflated bureaucracy. For example, each of the 11 regional ARD members maintained its own studios and editorial departments. Moreover, the already large group of stations sought to secure its place in the emerging markets of pay TV, digital radio and TV, and the Internet. While first signs of willingness to streamline its operations had been visible since 1998 when former ARD member stations SDR and SWF merged to form SWR, the battle against the interests of ever stronger private media networks showed no signs of abating. In the 1990s, ARD had lost to its rivals several radio and TV frequencies, high-profile staff, major movie rights, and licenses for broadcasting the most popular sports. A scandal caused by ARD member MDR provoked additional criticism. When it became known in the fall of 2000 that MDR had lost about DM 2.6 million in TV license fees in a currency speculation deal, Saxony's state assembly at first refused to approve the suggested increase in the *Rundfunkgebühr* of almost 12 percent.

Nevertheless, ARD remained a fierce competitor, and by its 50th anniversary year (2000) ARD had regained its place as Germany's top TV channel in the number of overall viewers as well as in popularity, beating its public rival ZDF as well as commercial channel RTL to which it had earlier lost this leading position.

Principal Subsidiaries

3sat (30%); ARTE (25%); KI.KA (50%); PHOENIX (50%); GEZ (50%); ARD-Werbung SALES & Services GmbH; Sportrechte- und Marketing-Agentur GmbH; Degeto Film GmbH.

Principal Members

Westdeutscher Rundfunk; Südwestrundfunk; Norddeutscher Rundfunk; Bayerischer Rundfunk; Mitteldeutscher Rundfunk; Hessicher Rundfunk; Deutsche Welle; Sender Freies Berlin; Ostdeutscher Rundfunk Brandenburg; DeutschlandRadio; Saarländischer Rundfunk; Radio Bremen.

Principal Competitors

RTL Group; KirchHolding GmbH & Co. KG; ZDF; n-tv.

Further Reading

ARD 50 Jahre Erste Reihe, Stuttgart, Germany: ARD-Pressestelle Südwestrundfunk, 2000, 18 p.

''ARD Takes Number One Spot in Germany,'' *Television Europe,* October 2000, p. 9.

Bolesch, Cornelia, ''Der 'Sündenfall' der falschen Fronten; Über die Werbung bei ARD und ZDF sollte mit den richtigen Argumenten diskutiert werden,'' *Süddeutsche Zeitung*, June 11, 1991.

——, ''Gerangel um das nationale Radio,'' *Süddeutsche Zeitung*, December 2, 1991.

Brühl, Kirsten, ''Düstere Aussichten für ARD und ZDF,'' *HORIZONT,* December 11, 1992, p. 33.

Christie, Alix, et. al., ''Power Games on the Channels of Influence,'' *Guardian,* February 11, 1995, p. 39.

Dempsey, Judy, ''Interference on the TV,'' *Financial Times,* February 3, 1995, p. 14.

Games, Stephen, ''Europe: Hard Arte of the Possible,'' *Guardian,* January 21, 1993, p.8.

Gross, Laurence H., ''Private TV Cutting into Pubcasters,'' *Variety,* September 9, 1991, p. 59.

Hanfeld, Michael, ''Interview mit dem ZDF-Intendanten Dieter Stolte und dem ARD-Vorsitzenden Peter Voss,'' *Frankfurter Allgemeine Zeitung*, October 31, 2000, p. 60.

Hils, Miriam, ''Pub Clones Crowd German Air,'' *Variety,* January 27, 1997, p. 25.

Kurz, Harald, ''Widerstand gegen TV-Gebühren,'' *HORIZONT*, August 21, 1992, p. 25.

Lieb, Rebecca, ''Pubcasters are Reeling; Private Webs Appealing,'' *Variety,* September 14, 1992, p. 37.

——, ''Static From Eastern Shake-Up Clouds Broadcast,'' *Variety,* September 9, 1991, p. 46.

Maier, Thomas, ''Die 'alte Tante ist quicklebendig': Die ARD wird 50,'' *dpa,* July 31, 2000.

Molner, David, ''Teutonic Pubcasters Falling on Hard Times,'' *Variety,* November 5, 1995, p. 169.

Neumann, Edgar, ''Amerikaner brachten Disput ins Radio,'' *dpa*, July 31, 2000.

Plewe, Heidrun, ''Mit Sport-Sponsoring über die 20-Uhr Grenze,'' *HORIZONT,* February 14, 1992.

Riehl-Heyse, Herbert, ''Öffentlich-rechtliche Rundfunkanstalten: Der schier aussichtslose Kampf um jedermanns Gunst,'' *Süddeutsche Zeitung*, January 28, 1993, p. 3.

Timm, Roland, ''Nun wollen wir uns mit der Regierung anlegen,'' *Süddeutsche Zeitung*, December 24, 1992.

Tritschler, Patrik, ''Geburtstag der 'alten Tante','' *Werben und Verkaufen*, October 6, 2000, p. 148.

Weber, Lukas, ''Das Oligopol der Anspruchslosen,'' *Frankfurter Allgemeine Zeitung*, August 5, 1993, p. 9.

—Evelyn Hauser

Associated British Foods plc

Weston Centre
Bowater House
68 Knightsbridge
London, SW1X 7LQ
United Kingdom
Telephone: (44) 207 589-6363
Fax: (44) 207 584-8560
Web site: http://www.abf.co.uk

Public Company
Incorporated: 1935 as Food Investments Ltd.
Employees: 34,372
Sales: £4.4 billion ($6.17 billion) (2000)
Stock Exchanges: London
Ticker Symbol: ABF
NAIC: 311812 Commercial Bakeries; 311211 Flour Milling; 311999 All Other Miscellaneous Food Manufacturing; 45299 All Other General Merchandise Stores; 551112 Offices of Other Holding Companies; 42241 General Line Grocery Wholesalers

With high-ranking positions in several categories of foodstuffs, Associated British Foods plc (ABF) stands as one of the United Kingdom's top producers of consumables. From its roots as a Canadian bakery, the company grew and evolved to become Britain's top manufacturer of bread, with more than one-third of the U.K. market. By the early 1990s, the company had diversified within the food business into tea and coffee (sold under the Twinings and Jackson brands), biscuits and crispbread (marketed under the Burtons and Ryvita names, respectively), as well as frozen foods and edible oils. Its British Sugar subsidiary ranked as the country's dominant producer of sugar. The company's activities throughout the United Kingdom, Australia, and the United States encompassed grocery product manufacturing, milling and baking, and soft goods retailing. Notwithstanding its geographic diversity, the vast majority of its revenues continued to be generated in the United Kingdom and Ireland into the new millennium. In 2001, AFB was the largest customer in the U.K. agriculture industry.

ABF, operating as a multibillion dollar international conglomerate, characterizes itself as a ''family of businesses.'' ABF subsidiaries, whether self-developed or acquired through merger or acquisition, retain their individuality in name, operations, and clientele, yet maintain strong connections with the parent's central management core. The company's major business divisions include Primary Food and Agriculture, Ingredients and Oils, Grocery, Retail and Packaging, and Australia and New Zealand, which focuses on George Weston Foods. For more than half a century, one family has controlled ABF: the Westons. In 2001, the Westons owned slightly more than half of ABF's equity through Wittington Investments Ltd. In May 2000, Garry Weston retired as chairman of the company due to poor health.

Early History

The family saga began in Toronto, Canada, in 1882, when George Weston, then 18, bought a bread-delivery route. During the following 36 years, he built a number of successful bakeries in that area. George Weston Ltd., the Toronto-based chain of bakeries and supermarkets that resulted from that growth, consistently ranked among North America's top businesses throughout the 20th century.

When George Weston's son Garfield took over the bakery business at his father's death in 1924, he had much more in mind than simply maintaining or building up the chain of local bakeries his father had founded; he was determined that it grow into an international business. Eleven years later, in November 1935, he took a giant step toward that goal by purchasing seven bakeries in England, Scotland, and Wales and adding them to his newly formed Food Investments Ltd., which was promptly renamed Allied Bakeries Limited. All seven bakeries remained in operation throughout the 20th century, three under their original names.

Within four years, Garfield had 18 bakeries and four biscuit factories throughout the British Isles, beginning decades of expansion into Europe, Africa, Australia, Asia, and North America. The expansion went beyond food products to encompass seed production, milling, canning, retail grocery and clothing outlets, restaurants, vehicle parts, fuel, and basic research.

The expansion was not always steady, however. At the onset of World War II, wartime restrictions and shortages of supplies

> **Company Perspectives:**
>
> *Associated British Foods plc is dedicated to making key investments for the future. In order to remain a market leader, the company strives to focus on investments in research and development, capital expenditure, its employees, and environmental policy.*

began to slow production, while high taxes and voluntary defense contributions reduced profits. But expansion picked up again in the postwar period. A postwar excess-profits tax refund was wholly invested in expansion and equipment. In 1948, Garfield's son Garry joined the board of directors. The following year, the company purchased two Australian firms: Gold Crust Bakeries in Adelaide and Gartrell White in Sydney. By the end of the decade, profits had surpassed £2 million a year.

A growth spurt in the 1950s added dozens of new bakeries, teashops, restaurants, and catering businesses, many of them in newly constructed shopping centers, which provided one-stop convenience for consumers. Food stores purchased by the company were refashioned into supermarkets to suit new shopping habits. This diversification led to a name change in 1960, to Associated British Foods. By 1964, the company claimed to be the largest baker in the world and one of the largest millers, in addition to being one of the largest grocers in the United Kingdom.

Rapid growth continued during the 1960s, with the acquisition of A.B. Hemmings, Ltd., a chain of 230 bakery shops in the London area, the entire chain of Fine Fare food shops, and a 51 percent interest in the South African Premier Milling Company.

In 1970, ABF also opened the largest bakery in Western Europe, in Glasgow, Scotland. A year later, ABF's Fine Fare opened its first two ''superstores.'' As the 1970s progressed, the Stewart Cash Stores in Ireland, which ABF had acquired some 20 years before, followed suit, opening their first hypermarket. In 1978, ABF expanded into a new market—frozen foods—by buying an ice cream factory and a pizza bakery.

Garfield died in October 1978 and Garry advanced to the chairmanship of ABF. The family no longer sought the public eye, keeping a low profile since 1983, when an attempt by six Irish Republican gunmen to kidnap a family member was foiled.

Despite difficulties such as fluctuation of the pound and climatic conditions affecting crops, ABF continued to expand and prosper. In 1980, a subsidiary, Twinings Tea, opened its first North American factory, in Greensboro, North Carolina, and also opened the Grosvenor Marketing Company in Paramus, New Jersey. Additional bakeries and other businesses were acquired, and ABF's continual program of monitoring and modernizing kept products and services up to date and operations efficient.

Growth of Major ABF Subsidiaries in the 20th Century

Some of ABF's subsidiaries are much older than their parent. The Twining Crosfield Group, for example, dates back to a coffee shop purchased by Thomas Twining in 1706, when coffee was the fashionable drink for men. Tea, introduced early in the 17th century, had been popularized as a drink for ladies by Queen Catherine, the wife of Charles II, at midcentury. But men usually drank it for medicinal purposes only (it was widely regarded as a remedy for headaches). When Twining introduced tea as a sideline, he found it was so popular that in 1717 he converted Tom's Coffee House into the Golden Lyon, London's first tea shop.

Twinings Tea, exported to nearly 100 countries in 2000, may be ABF's most widely known brand name. It has won the Queen's Award for export achievement, and it consistently dominated its market. In 2000, Twinings acquired a Sweden-based food distributor, introduced four new organic teas, and introduced new packaging to the Australian market.

The Ryvita Company, purchased by ABF in 1949, also won the Queen's Award for export with the crispbread that has long been its principal product and probably ABF's second best-known brand name. Increasing interest in health foods made Ryvita and the company's other main product, Crackerbread, popular in many countries in the 1980s. By the early 1990s, Ryvita eclipsed its competition with an 80 percent share of the market. ABF hoped to parlay the brand's strength into increased sales with the late 1988 introduction of a crossover product. Ryvita High Fibre Corn Flakes coupled the original product's reputation as a health food with a marketing emphasis on environmentalism; the product came in recycled packaging. Demand for high-fiber foods and the availability of new extrusion technology resulted in the development of Allinson's branded products, Croustipain, as well as other extruded breakfast cereals and cereal products. In 1998, Ryvita entered the Russian market and also introduced Ryvita Currant Crunch. Rising popularity of organic products also led to new product launches, including the Organic Allinson crackerbread.

Allied Bakeries, the group of bakeries Weston purchased at the time of its incorporation, continued to function as part of ABF's largest subsidiary. Over the course of the company's history, this segment grew to include some 40 wholesale bakeries and close to 1,200 retail bakery shops and restaurants throughout the British Isles. When the addition of in-house bakeries in many supermarkets put a slight crimp in the wholesale baked-goods business, Allied Bakeries countered this trend with a line of partially baked goods and a line of frozen bakery products, both of which could be completed at an in-house bakery or by the retail consumer at home. But by mid-1994, a string of losses in the Baker's Oven retail chain led to that operation's divestment. The sale, which encompassed two bakeries and more than 400 retail locations, generated £8.95 million. Allied Bakeries restructured itself into four operating units in 1998. Its Kingsmill brand continued to be a leader in the late 1990s.

Other subsidiaries included Cereal Industries and Fishers Agricultural Holdings, which supplied animal feeds and livestock marketing services, and Fishers Seed and Grain, which produced agricultural seeds. The Allied Grain Group marketed seeds and fertilizers and was the United Kingdom's largest grain trader at the start of the new millennium. ABR Foods supplied wheat by-products to several types of industry: baking and brewing, food and pharmaceutical manufacturers, animal

Key Dates:

1882: George Weston begins his career in the bakery industry.
1924: Weston's son, Garfield, takes over the bakery business.
1935: Seven bakeries are acquired and operate under the name Allied Bakeries Limited.
1948: Garry Weston joins the firm.
1949: The firm enters the Australian market with the purchase of two companies.
1960: The firm changes its name to Associated British Foods.
1964: The company operates as one of the largest bakers in the world.
1970: ABF opens the largest bakery in Western Europe.
1978: The company expands into the frozen food industry.
1980: Subsidiary Twinings Tea opens a factory in North America.
1982: AB Ingredients is formed.
1987: AB Technology is created to develop new technology.
1991: British Sugar plc is acquired.
1992: The company begins a corporate restructuring due to falling profits.
1994: Financial performance improves.
1995: The company acquires two U.S. firms, Abitec Corp. and AC Humko Corp.
1996: The company begins a joint venture with China-based Lianua Gourmet Powder Company.
1997: The company sells its retail food businesses to Tesco.
1998: Profits fall again due to U.K. market conditions.
2000: ABF expands through several acquisitions; Garry Weston retires.

feed, and packaging products. Poor market conditions, however, led to its sale in September 2000 to Roquette Freres. Allied Mills produced more than one million tons of flour each year, making it one of the leading flour mills in the United Kingdom. British Sugar processed 1.55 million tons of sugar in 2000, the second largest crop in its history.

ABF's Burton's Gold Medal Biscuits long ranked as one of the largest biscuit manufacturers in the United Kingdom. As consolidation swept through the biscuit market in the late 1990s, Burton's stood as the second largest in the industry. The business unit faltered in the late 1990s, however, as competition increased and as the Russian economy experienced a severe decline. Famous for its Jammie Dodgers and Wagon Wheel products, the subsidiary was sold to Hicks, Muse, Tate & Furst in October 2000, as a result of continued poor performance.

The firm's Irish retail group operated as the largest supermarket chain in Ireland (Quinnsworth stores in the Irish Republic and Stewarts and Crazy Prices in Northern Ireland) throughout much of its history. This group also included retail clothing stores—Penneys in Ireland and Primark in the United Kingdom—focusing on fashions for young people. Many of these stores opened in the 1960s; although they continued to do a thriving business through the 1980s, they were battered by cutthroat price wars in the early 1990s. ABF sold its retail food business to Tesco in 1997, which included Quinssworth, Crazy Prices, and Stewarts, in order to focus on its other retail ventures.

AB Ingredients, formed in 1982, and AB Technology, formed in 1987, constituted new directions for ABF. AB Ingredients developed and manufactured new ingredients and additives for Allied Bakeries and for other independent companies. It also developed improved bakery processes. AB Technology specialized in high-tech improvements for several types of industry, including food production. The company continued to focus on research and development through its Ingredients and Oils business segment.

Lagging Profits and Expansion: Early to Mid-1990s

It took a strong central management, an efficient reporting system, and vigilant personnel and investment programs to hold together so many relatively independent companies of disparate size and design, in widely separated geographic locations. ABF's continual expansion testified to its strength, but its structure, marked by an intricate system of holding companies and representation, was difficult to penetrate and analyze.

An early 1990s recession put ABF in what an anonymous analyst with Charles Stanley & Co., Ltd. called ''an unenviable situation.'' Cautious consumers and ready-to-please retailers squeezed profit margins on virtually all of the company's products. Sales declined from £4.81 billion in 1991 to £3.95 billion in 1992, and pre-tax profits dropped from £332.3 million to £267 million during the same period. The company responded with a major reorganization encompassing the core bakery division as well as the British Sugar plc operations acquired in 1991, closing factories and eliminating a net of nearly 1,500 jobs from 1992 to 1994. Net results rebounded in 1993, when the company recorded £4.39 billion in revenues and £338 million in pre-tax profits. Financial performance continued to improve in 1994, as sales increased to £4.48 billion and pre-tax profits increased to £360 million.

As finances appeared to be back on track, ABF made two key acquisitions in 1995. United States-based Abitec Corporation and AC Humko Corporation, specialty oils and cheese analogs businesses, were purchased as part of the company's efforts to penetrate that market. The next year, the firm began a joint venture with the Lianhua Gourmet Powder Company of Henan Province, China, and with Henan Lianhua BSO Pharmaceutical Company Ltd. Both ventures were related to its glucose and dextrose operations. Profits increased nearly 15 percent in 1996, due to U.K. flour milling and baking operations as well as the company's expansion into the United States. Positive growth in ABF's animal feed subsidiaries, the Twining companies, Burton's Biscuit operations, and the retail grocery and textile units also had a positive effect on the year's earnings. ABF's stock ended the year at an all-time high, the only U.K. food manufacturer to do so.

Declining Market Conditions: Late 1990s

In 1997, ABF purchased the One-UP chain of stores as part of its effort to focus on its clothing retail operations. Having sold its retail food interests in Ireland, the firm's Penneys and

Primark units continued to grow. The company's milling and baking operations, however, suffered in 1997, due to a poor harvest caused by bad weather and a surplus in the plant baking market. A drop in sugar prices also began to affect British Sugar's operations despite record production levels.

The following year was a tough one for the firm. Profits declined and market conditions continued to deteriorate due to the adverse effect the strengthening of the sterling had on sales. British Sugar also came under fire by the European Commission when it was fined for price fixing in the late 1980s—ABF appealed the fine. George Weston Foods also recorded a decline in profits.

In 1999, profits continued to fall while sales rose a modest 3 percent. Sugar prices plummeted and subsidiary ABR was negatively affected by a surplus in Europe in the wheat starch and glucose industry. Flour prices also fell, forcing Allied Mills to introduce new products such as organic flours. The firm's United Kingdom-based grocery units faced increased competition as well as George Weston Foods, and the glass packaging unit also experienced hardship as the U.K. market declined.

Some of ABF's subsidiaries did see positive growth, however. ABN and Fishers, animal feeds subsidiaries, acquired six mills from Dalgety Feed Ltd. and continued forging relationships in Asia. Allied Grain maintained profits as well as Germains seed coating operations. ABF's retail unit recorded a 23 percent increase in sales due in part to its expansion. The firm's United States interests, Abitec Corp. and AC Humko, also saw positive results in 1999. With the acquisition of German-based Rohm Enzymes, a leading enzyme producer catering to the food, industrial, and animal feed markets, ABF strengthened its food ingredients businesses. That division also acquired SPI, a U.S.-based ingredients company.

Restructuring in the New Millennium

The U.K. agriculture industry continued to decline into the new millennium. ABF also had to deal with flat and declining prices and margins in the food retailing and manufacturing industries. Despite these setbacks, the firm recorded a 4 percent increase in profits in 2000. To remain competitive in adverse market conditions, the company underwent a series of restructuring events in 2000, including the sale of its Allied Frozen Food and ABR Foods units. In addition, Burton's was sold due to increasing competition in the biscuit market and the firm's industrial fats business was divested.

Management also focused on strengthening its core operations by implementing an aggressive acquisition strategy. In an April 2000 *Grocer* article, CEO Peter Jackson stated, "There is no bigger priority than looking for the right acquisition." In keeping with the new strategy, ABF acquired four beet sugar plants in Poland, securing its position as the largest foreign investor in the Polish sugar industry. The firm also purchased the polyols business of Lonza Inc., a U.S. subsidiary of the Swiss Lonza Group. As management remained uncertain about future economic conditions in many of its core markets, it continued to restructure traditional business units. The company also sought international growth through acquisition and focused on the development of new technologies.

Principal Subsidiaries

AB Ingredients Limited (95%); Abitec Corporation; ABN Limited; AB Technology Limited; ACH Food Companies, Inc.; Allied Bakeries Limited; Allied Foods Co. Limited (78%); Allied Grain Limited; Allied Mills Limited; Barcroft Company; British Sugar plc; British Sugar (Overseas) Limited; Carl Lange AS; Cereal Industries Limited; Curkrownia Glinojeck SA (53%); Eastbow Securities Ltd; Eric Haugen SA; Fishers Agricultural Holdings Limited; Foods International S.A.; George Weston Foods Limited (78%); Germain's (U.K.) Limited; Germain's (Ireland) Limited; Germain's Sp zoo (65%); Gregg & Company (Knottingley) Limited; Grosvenor Marketing Limited; Guangxi Bo Hua Food Company (71%); Guangxi Bo Hua Food Co. Limited (60%); Henan Lianhua-BSO Pharmaceutical Co. Limited (57%); Jacksons of Piccadilly Limited; Jordan's (NI) Limited; Lax & Shaw Limited; Liaoning Liaohe Ai Min Feed Company Limited (55%); Liaoning Liaohe Yingpeng Feed Company Limited (55%); Nambarrie Tea Company Limited; Primark (Ireland); Primark Stores Limited; Rohm Enzyme GmbH; Rohm Enzyme OY; The Ryvita Company Limited; Seed Systems Inc.; Serpentine Securities Limited; Shanghai ABN (60%); SPCA Barcroft SA; SPI Polyols Inc.; Sugarpol (Poland); Trident Feeds; R Twining & Company Limited; R Twining & Co. Ltd (U.S.A.); Westmill Foods Limited; Weston Research Laboratories Ltd.

Principal Competitors

Hillsdown Holdings Ltd.; Tate & Lyle PLC; United Biscuits Holdings plc.

Further Reading

"ABF Acquires Lonza Polyols," *Food Trade Review,* August 2000, p. 506.

"ABF Again Stands Out in Share Performance Among Foreign Firms," *Milling and Baking News,* January 14, 1997, p. 14.

"ABF Hit by Tough Market," *Grocer,* April 22, 2000, p. 8.

"ABF Profits Rise 15%, Boosted by Gains in UK Milling, Baking," *Milling and Baking News,* November 19, 1996, p. 19.

"ABF Suffering Supermarket Price Pressure," *Eurofood,* November 18, 1999, p. 13.

"Associated British Foods," *Pensions & Investments,* May 25, 1992, p. 32.

"Associated British Foods: Company Report," Charles Stanley & Co., Ltd., November 16, 1994.

"British Deal with Kraft," *New York Times,* July 12, 1995, p. C4.

Davies, Charles, *Bread Men: How the Westons Built an International Empire,* Toronto: Key Porter Books, 1987.

"Fiscal '98 Tough for ABF," *Eurofood,* November 5, 1998, p. 14.

"Further Polish Sugar Acquisitions for ABF," *Food Trade Review,* August 2000, p. 566.

"Hicks Muse Takes the Biscuit-Again," *European Venture Capital Journal,* December 2000, p. 72.

Hoggan, Karen, "Ryvita Cereal Shows Its Fibre," *Marketing,* January 11, 1990, p. 2.

"Tesco," *Supermarket News,* March 31, 1997, p. 2.

Tigert, D., *George Weston Limited: A Corporate Background Report,* Toronto: Royal Commission on Corporate Concentration, 1977.

"UK-Based Associated British Foods," *Food Institute Report,* April 24, 2000.

—April Dougal Gasbarre
—update: Christina M. Stansell

Aston Villa plc

Villa Park
Trinity Road
Birmingham B6 6HE
United Kingdom
Telephone: +44 121-327-2299
Fax: +44 121-322-2107
Web site: http://www.astonvilla-fc.co.uk

Public Company
Incorporated: 1997
Employees: 223
Sales: £35.85 million ($57.4 million) (1999)
Stock Exchanges: London
Ticker Symbol: ASV
NAIC: 711211 Sports Teams and Clubs; 711310 Promoters of Performing Arts, Sports, and Similar Events with Facilities

Aston Villa plc is the publicly listed company governing the activities of England's Aston Villa Football Club and the Villa Park stadium in the city of Birmingham. A founding member of the Football League's Premier Division, Aston Villa is also among the first football (soccer) teams to become listed on the London Stock Exchange, joining such renowned teams as Manchester United and Arsenal in a run-up to what many consider will be a new era in sports marketing, when barriers to sports team ownership, notably by media corporations, are expected to fall. As such, Aston Villa has already entered a relationship with American cable television company NTL Inc., which has been building up its shareholding position in the more than 125-year-old team. The majority of Aston Villa's revenues, which neared £36 million in 2000, come from gate receipts. Broadcasting fees provide another 20 percent of annual sales, while merchandising and royalty receipts add 14 percent of the company's revenues. Aston Villa also operates conference and convention services, and expects to open its own hotel in the future. The company is also renovating its aging stadium, built in 1924, boosting the number of seats to 51,000. Aston Villa is led by chairman and CEO Herbert Douglas Ellis, who also owns some 33 percent of the company's stock.

Soccer Pioneers at the Turn of the Century

The history of Aston Villa began in the post-cricket season in Birmingham in 1874, when four players on the Villa Cross team sought a means to keep the team together during the winter off-season. Soccer had begun to make its appearance in England in the later part of the 19th century, swiftly gaining popularity and later replacing cricket itself as the United Kingdom's most popular sport. The Villa Cross team decided to take up the newly organized Football Association (FA) rules—which differed from the so-called Rugby Union rules of a rival form of football—and by 1875 had organized their first team of 15 players. The team played their first—and only—game of the year against a local Rugby Union team. In order to accommodate both sets of rules, the two sides agreed to play the first half of the game according the Rugby Union rules and using the oblong rugby ball. The second half of the game was played using the round ball and following Football Association rules. The future Aston Villa went on to win its first of many games.

The group stepped up its playing schedule the following winter, including a number of matches played on the playing field of its future permanent home. The arrival of Scot George Ramsay in 1876, and then fellow Scotsman Archie Hunter, sparked the beginning of Aston Villa's professional era. By then, the growing popularity of soccer in the area had enabled the team to beginning charging at the gate; in its first paying game, the team netted more than five shillings. The playing prowess of captains Ramsay and Hunter helped the team attract growing numbers of spectators. The team itself was gaining strength and by the end of the decade was confident enough to enter the FA Cup.

Association soccer had taken the United Kingdom by storm, prompting legislation to codify the growing numbers of professional teams and players. Toward the turn of the century, FA teams were required to distribute shares to investors, a means to enable trading among the teams without implicating the FA itself. The popularity of the sport was also seen in the rise of the

Key Dates:

1874: Founding of Aston Villa soccer team.
1887: Team wins the Football Association Cup.
1924: Inauguration of Villa Park stadium.
1968: Douglas Ellis becomes team chairman.
1982: Ellis becomes majority shareholder.
1997: Aston Villa lists on London stock exchange.
2001: Company begins a stadium expansion.

FA Cup; by the mid-1880s, more than 130 football clubs were vying for FA Cup positions. Aston Villa's own breakthrough came in the 1886–1887 FA Cup competition, when the young team captured the title before a crowd of 15,000.

For the next season, Aston Villa became one of the founding members of the new Football League. Designed to provide a more regular playing schedule among a limited number of more evenly matched teams, the Football League eventually developed into several divisions, with top ranking teams competing in the Premier Division. The formation of the Football League also helped to ensure rising numbers of spectators—and gate receipts—as competitions reached new levels of professionalism.

In 1892, Frederick Rinder, originally from Liverpool, joined Aston Villa as the team's financial secretary. Rinder was to introduce a number of standard business practices to the team's financial structure. Rinder also installed the first turnstiles at the entrance to the team's playing field, bringing in more revenues to the team. The importance of these were growing as the popularity of football grew. When Aston Villa played—and won—its third FA Cup final match in 1894, it was before a crowd of more than 42,000, establishing a new attendance record.

At the turn of the century, Aston Villa established a more lasting record—that of winning the mythical double, that is, the FA Cup and Football League championship in the same year. The double win in 1897 was to remain the only double achieved by any team for more than 60 years. The team also officially opened its home field, which was still to known as Aston Lower Grounds before taking the Villa Park name itself. The team's new home seemed to inspire Aston Villa on a new string of victories that was to last until the outbreak of the World War I.

Wartime Disruptions in the 20th Century

Yet the years leading up to World War I were to prove one of the few highlights for the team over the next several decades, culminating with the league championship in 1910. This was, however, to be the team's last league championship trophy until the end of the century. Three years later, the team won their fifth FA Cup.

The mobilization for the British war effort devastated the ranks of its soccer teams, and the Football League disbanded for the duration. League play only resumed in 1919. Aston Villa scored an early success, taking the FA Cup trophy in 1922. By then, the team was pulling down attendance figures of an average of 35,000 spectators per game, and as much as 66,000 for games against sworn rival teams such as West Brom. Yet Aston Villa's fortunes on the playing field were now set to go into a long decline; nearly 40 years were to pass before the team saw a new FA Cup trophy.

Nonetheless, the team was to continue to provide some of the great names in U.K. soccer history. And at the dawn of World War II, Aston Villa became an international name when the team, touring German, refused to present the Nazi salute before Hitler, the only British team that had refused to do so. During the war, however, league play was once again suspended, and Villa Park was taken over by the military; part of the stadium was even used as an air raid shelter. While the team continued to play—filling in its side with servicemen as guest players—full competitive play did not return to England until 1946.

Aston Villa's recovery proved extremely long. By the mid-1950s, the team's continued losses placed it under threat of relegation to the Football League's Second Division. Despite a losing record in league play, the team did manage to pull out a victory in the FA Cup in 1956. That victory was not enough to sustain the team, and by the end of the decade, Aston Villa faced a brief relegation to the Second Division.

By the beginning of the 1970s, even Second Division seemed too much for the flagging team, and Aston Villa found itself relegated to the Third Division. The team's finances were also in disarray, as attendance rates plummeted with the team's on-field losses, at one point dropping down to just 12,000 spectators. Slumping gate receipts led the team into losses of £200,000 by 1968. Meanwhile, the Villa Park stadium was in need of repairs.

New directors were brought in to help steer the club out of its financial troubles. Among them was Herbert Douglas Ellis, who had built up a successful travel agency business in the region and had been one of the pioneers of the packaged holidays in the Birmingham market. Ellis took over as chairman of Aston Villa. Ellis also slowly took over ownership of the club, buying up shares from a number of original shareholders. In this, Ellis became part of a larger industry trend, as a number of other businessmen quietly bought up the shares in a number of the United Kingdom's football teams. Ellis reportedly acquired his controlling share of Aston Villa for an estimated £500,000. While never confirmed, this figure paled in comparison to the team's valuation of more than £64 million at the time of its flotation in 1997.

Under Ellis, Aston Villa quickly regained its momentum. By 1975, the team had recaptured a place in the Premier Division and had also gained a spot in the UEFA Cup, the first time the team had entered European competition. In that year, however, Ellis resigned his position and his shareholding after a boardroom fight. Seven years later, Ellis was called back in to lead the team, which revealed a debt of more than £2 million. By then, however, Aston Villa had taken its first league championship in 71 years and was on its way to scoring its first win in Europe, capturing the European Super Cup in 1982.

Public Corporation for the 21st Century

The mid-1980s marked yet another low point for the team, as continuing losses saw its average attendance rates drop to just 15,000, the lowest since the beginning of the World War I. The team was also entering into an extended period of personnel problems, as Aston Villa became something of a revolving door for team managers; in just ten years, the team had hired and sacked six managers. The team also temporarily slipped out of First Division play at the start of the 1990s.

Throughout the 1990s, Aston Villa continued to display substantial evidence that it remained among the United Kingdom's top teams. In the 1993–94 season, the team took the league championship, its first trophy win in more than 12 years. Aston Villa was also becoming a fixture in European play, earning places in the UEFA throughout much of the second half of the decade.

Ellis became a still richer man when Aston Villa joined the wave of soccer clubs becoming publicly listed companies in the mid-1990s. Aston Villa's own public listing came in 1997, giving the company—called Aston Villa Plc—a market valuation of £64 million. Part of the interest in the new corporations was the growing marketing success of U.K. soccer, where teams such as Manchester United were becoming among the best known soccer teams worldwide. Still more interesting, however, was the potential for cross-ownership as teams and media companies began to woo each other for potential future marriages, expected to come early in the new century as rules changes were expected to allow cross-ownership for the first time. Aston Villa found its own suitor in U.S. cable company NTL Inc., which began building its shareholding at the turn of the century.

As Ellis approached his 80s, his grip on the club began to raise questions about his successor. These were heightened when, after a personal dispute, Ellis' son Peter was ousted from the company's board of directors. Yet father and son patched things up, and by 2001 the younger Ellis had regained a seat on the board. By then, Aston Villa had launched new plans to extend beyond its sport team. After the winning approval for a revamping of its Villa Park stadium—boosting seating to more than 51,000—the company, which had a strong real-estate portfolio in the Birmingham area, and particularly in areas adjacent to the stadium, unveiled plans to build a 150-bed hotel and conference center and a 160,000 square-foot shopping center.

These activities were expected to help cushion the variability of the company's gate receipts and other team-centered revenues. Particularly as player salaries had begun to skyrocket—jumping by some 24 percent in 2000 alone—and as teams found themselves increasingly competing on an international scale for broadcasting coverage, Aston Villa's own profitability had come under pressure. Despite rising revenues, which topped £35 million at the end of the company's 2000 fiscal year, Aston Villa was forced to post a loss in early 2001. Nonetheless, the company was widely regarded as one of the best run among the top U.K. teams, and a strong field at the turn of the century—including a second-place finish in the FA Cup final in 2000—gave Aston Villa reason for cheer as well as cheers from its fans.

Principal Subsidiaries

Aston Villa FC Ltd.; Aston Villa Football Club Ltd.; Aston Villa Indoor Cricket Centres Ltd.

Principal Competitors

Arsenal Football Club plc; Chelsea Village plc; Leeds Sporting plc; Leicester City plc; Liverpool Football Club plc; Manchester United plc; Tottenham Hotspur plc.

Further Reading

"Aston Villa Wins OK for Stadium Expansion," *Reuters*, January 7, 2000.

Cope, Nigel, "The Monday Interview: Doug Ellis," *Independent*, April 30, 2001, p. 15.

"Ellis Happy Families Amid Villa Rejig," *Birmingham Post*, June 1, 2000, p. 32.

"The History of Aston Villa," Birmingham: Aston Villa, June 2001.

Horrie, Chris, "They Saw an Open Goal and Directors Scored a Million," *Independent on Sunday*, August 1, 1999, p. 3.

Wall, Barbara, "At Play in the Uneven Fields of the Market," *International Herald Tribune*, September 26, 1998.

—M.L. Cohen

Aviation Sales Company

3701 Flamingo Road
Miramar, Florida 33027
U.S.A.
Telephone: (954) 538-8900
Fax: (954) 538-6626
Web site: http://www.avsales.com

Public Company
Incorporated: 1996
Employees: 4,300
Sales: $671.5 million (1999)
Stock Exchanges: New York
Ticker Symbol: AVS
NAIC: 421830 Industrial Machinery and Equipment Wholesalers; 421840 Industrial Supplies Wholesalers

Based in Miramar, Florida, Aviation Sales Company (ASC) is the product of a 1993 spin-off of the aviation services unit of Ryder Systems. Through the 1990s, ASC has expanded beyond the business of supplying parts to aircraft manufacturers and the airlines to also providing maintenance, repair, and overhaul services, as well as some parts manufacturing. Acquisitions have fueled growth but also led to crippling debt. Faced with a sluggish industry, ASC has been forced to shed assets to pare down debt and to restructure its business as it enters a new century.

Company Origins

When the company was originally founded in Miami in 1972, the business of ASC was to purchase aircraft and disassemble them in order to sell the component parts to airlines and independent repair aircraft operations. ASC was generating some $12 million in revenues by 1983 when it was acquired by Ryder Systems, Inc., a company best known for its consumer truck rental business. Ryder also had Miami roots. Its founder, James A. Ryder, worked as a truck driver during the early 1930s, hauling materials that were used to build up Miami Beach. He bought his own truck and began a truck-leasing business that would became Ryder Systems, Inc. and make a public stock offering in 1955. In 1968 Ryder launched its one-way nationwide consumer truck businesses. It also ran a number of other businesses, including an oil refinery, a truck-driving school, and a credit card operation. When the U.S. economy suffered a downturn in the early 1970s, however, Ryder Systems found itself on the verge of bankruptcy. The company was forced to sell off assets, and soon James Ryder was forced out. His successor, M. Anthony Burns, former head of Allegheny Airlines, began to revitalize the fortunes of Ryder Systems, which was healthy enough by the early 1980s to enter the aviation services business.

In addition to buying ASC, Ryder Systems made a number of other acquisitions as it assembled an aviation group that in 1987 would post almost $1 billion in sales and become the largest nonairline provider of aviation maintenance and parts. It contributed about 20 percent, or some $60 million, to Ryder's record 1987 pretax profits of $302 million. Aviation was also Ryder's fastest growing group, leading management to plan for even further expansion. Because Ryder had enjoyed 11 straight years of record earnings, the company's optimism seemed justified. When the U.S. economy stalled, however, Ryder saw its pretax profits fall to $180 million. The aviation group was hurt by low aircraft sales as well as a depressed market for used parts. Ryder began a restructuring effort that would result in the sell-off of almost $2 billion in assets and the termination of 9,000 employees. The aviation group would rebound but prove inconsistent. It posted earnings of $46.5 million in 1991, only to see a drop-off of 46 percent to $25.1 million the following year. In many ways Ryder's aviation group reflected the turbulence in an airline industry that suffered from overcapacity, which led to fare wars and massive losses to the bottom line.

A culmination of its restructuring efforts would come in 1993 when Ryder announced that it would spin off its aviation business. For every four shares of Ryder stock that investors owned, they received one share of the new company, which assumed the name of one of Ryder's major mid-1980s acquisitions, Aviall. Based in Dallas, Texas, it consisted of three units: Ryder Aviall, Ryder Airline Services, and the Inventory Locator Service. Other units, including ASC, were expected to be sold off by the new Aviall, Inc.

Company Perspectives:

Since our initial public offering we have acquired seven companies and have increased the scope of our products and services to include airframe, engine and component maintenance and airframe, jet engine parts manufacturing and new parts distribution.

Acquisition by Aerospace International in 1993

After being put on the market in July 1993, ASC would be acquired by Aerospace International Services (AIS) for $50 million in a transaction that was not completed until December 1994. AIS was created in February 1992 by Houston investor Robert Alpert and two Japanese firms (Japan Fleet Services and Toman), with Alpert holding a controlling interest of 52 percent. The sole purpose of the enterprise was the $55.2 million purchase of the spare parts inventory of bankrupt Eastern Airlines, amounting to some 27 million aircraft parts that were worth an estimated $700 million. AIS originally turned to GE Capital to fund the transaction, but the application was turned down. GE's 34-year-old senior vice-president in charge of mergers and acquisitions, Dale S. Baker, found alternative funding for AIS from a syndication of banks. He was then asked to become the new company's president. After some research into the aircraft parts redistribution market, he accepted the post. For the next two years AIS documented its Eastern Airlines inventory, reselling some of the parts to pay off $42 million of the $57 million debt the company had incurred. It was at the end of 1993 that Baker offered AIS investors the choice of completing the sell-off of the inventory, realizing a 40 to 50 percent profit, and shutting down the company, or using the parts to build an aviation service company. ASC, in the meantime, was put up for sale and Baker saw an opportunity to gain entry into the service business. Although AIS did not make the winning bid for ASC, Baker's belief that the winning bidder might not be able to raise the necessary funds was borne out. Thus, after the passage of several months, AIS finally purchased ASC. Because ASC was a known name in the air industry, the Aviation Sales name was retained. Baker moved to Miami to take over the company with the intention of changing ASC from a parts distribution company to a service company. The combined company boasted a parts inventory with a value in excess of $1.1 billion.

Baker saw the changing airline industry as an opportunity for the new ASC. Airlines were beginning to shy away from keeping a large supply of spare parts, which required an investment as large as $500 million that would not be generating any revenue. On the one hand, ASC would serve as a buyer for airlines that wanted to sell some of their parts' inventories to realize cash; and on the other hand, ASC would sell parts to the airlines and provide all of the necessary inventory management services, including the documentation to show regulators that the parts complied with airworthiness directives or engineering changes. By serving a large number of customers, ASC was banking on the economies of scale to allow it to do a better job with parts than the airlines could do themselves and thereby build a profitable business. In addition, ASC would serve freighter and military aircraft. Moreover, the prospects for ASC looked promising because of two salient facts: the average age of the world's aircraft fleet was almost 15 years and the number of air miles flown was continuing to climb. The need for maintenance and parts would surely keep pace. ASC wanted to position itself to be able to offer a package of inventory and maintenance services, a total solution that would drastically reduce the number of vendors for airlines, who at that time might be dealing with some 200 to 300 suppliers and service providers.

ASC revenues jumped from $28 million in 1994 to $113 million in 1995. To fuel external growth the company made a public offering of stock at $19 a share on June 30, 1996. By August ASC had made its first acquisition, Dixie Bearings, for approximately $9 million. Dixie would generate $7 million in revenues for ASC in the remainder of the year. In December 1996 the company also acquired AvEng Trading Partners, an Oklahoma aircraft engine parts redistributor, at a cost of approximately $8 million in stock. For the year, ASC would generate revenues of nearly $170 million.

Because its customers wanted parts that were overhauled and repaired, and freshly tagged, ASC looked to expand into the $27 billion a year maintenance, repair, and overhaul business (MRO). A major step in this direction was taken in September 1997 when the company bought Aerocell Structures of Hot Springs, Arkansas, an airframe component-overhaul company. ASC paid approximately $18 million in stock for Aerocell. A week later it moved into the business of manufacturing of parts by acquiring the Cincinnati-based Kratz-Wilde Machine Company, subcontract makers of jet engine components, at a cost of approximately $42.5 million in cash and notes and the assumption of some $2.5 million in liabilities. In December 1997, ASC added another subcontract parts maker, Apex Manufacturing of West Chester, Ohio, for $8.4 million in stock. Not only did these acquisitions broaden ASC's business, they helped to boast revenues to $257 million for 1997.

Setting a Goal of $1 Billion in Annual Sales by 2001

ASC continued its aggressive pattern of growth in 1998, as it endeavored to become what its CEO called a total service provider, with the goal of reaching $1 billion in sales by 2001. In March it acquired Caribe Aviation and Caribe's wholly owned subsidiary, Aircraft Interior Design, for cash, notes, and stock at a cost of nearly $25 million. Caribe provided repair and overhaul services, while Aircraft Interior Design manufactured such aircraft cabin parts as overhead bins and seat arms. In July 1998, ASC made its most significant transaction when it acquired Whitehall Corporation for $142 million, in what would be accounted for as a pooling of interests. Whitehall brought with it two FAA-licensed repair stations, specializing in heavy maintenance in narrowbody aircraft. In October ASC then acquired at the cost of $70 million Triad International Maintenance Co., a Greensboro, North Carolina company that specialized in widebody maintenance and modification. In essence, ASC was now able to offer ''nose to tail'' maintenance and repair, as well as parts inventory management. It was composed of nine companies divided into three groups: distribution service; manufacturing; and maintenance, repair, and overhaul. For the year ASC saw its earnings jump from $4.8 million in

Key Dates:

1972: Original business is founded in Miami.
1983: The company is acquired by Ryder Systems.
1993: Ryder spins off aviation businesses; Aviation Sales is acquired by Aerospace International Services.
1996: The company acquires Dixie Bearings.
1997: The company acquires Aerocell Structures.
1998: The company acquires Caribe Aviation and Aircraft Interior Design.
1999: The company acquires Whitehall Corporation.

1997 to $25.5 million in 1998. The next step for the company appeared to be the establishment of a global presence.

In 1999 ASC would move to Miramar, Florida, where it was able to secure 41 acres of land to build offices and warehouse space. Although the company's biggest customer, the Boeing Company, experienced a drop in production, ASC appeared quite healthy. While the stock of its competitors suffered, ASC continued to rise, approaching the $50 per share mark early in the year. In August the company acquired for $21.4 million the jet engine and Boeing 727 aircraft maintenance operations located in Oscoda, Michigan, from Kitty Hawk, a Texas air cargo company that decided to outsource its airframe and engine maintenance work. As part of the transaction, ASC would maintain Kitty Hawk's fleet of more than 100 aircraft.

ASC management continued to express optimism about the company's prospects, but in September the company was forced to announce that it would not meet its third quarter estimates. ASC stock lost more than a third of its value in a single day, prompting some shareholders to file a class action suit that alleged that some of the company's "officers and directors issued a series of materially false and misleading statements regarding the growing demand for the company's services, its operations and earnings." Between September 30 and October 5, officers, directors, and their affiliates bought more than 200,000 shares of ASC common stock in the open market. A company press release maintained that this action demonstrated confidence in the financial strength of ASC, but outside investors were not convinced. The price of ASC stock continued to slide. The company began talks of a possible merger with BFGoodrich, which already boasted the world's largest third-party-only MRO operation, but talks eventually broke off.

ASC failed to comply with December 31, 1999 obligations to lenders and was granted an extension until March 31, 2000. The company would announce that for the year it lost almost $22 million on sales of $672 million. As the price of ASC stock continued to fall, the prospects for the company appeared bleak. Unable to meet the March 31 deadline, ASC asked for more time from lenders, but by late April the company expressed "substantial doubt" about its ability to continue in business. With debt that amounted to more than $400 million, ASC had little choice but to sell off some of the assets it had assembled. Manufacturing operations were the obvious targets, as were three A-300 jets that the company owned. The jets would eventually fetch $36 million. In August ASC sold Kratz-Wilde Machine Co. and Apex Manufacturing to Barnes Group Inc. for $41 million. The price of ASC stock rebounded slightly, rising to $6. In September ASC then sold its used parts division to Kellstrom Industries Inc. for approximately $145 million, leaving ASC with a core maintenance and repair business. For used parts, the company would now rely on Kellstrom.

As ASC tried to reduce debt and refocus its business, it continued to report huge losses during the course of 2000. Its stock reached its lowest point when it fell to $1.63. Less than two years earlier, management was projecting that it would reach $54. In late December 2000, ASC sold its Dixie Aerospace Bearings unit for $17.7 million to Wencor West. By now the company's debt was reduced to approximately $50 million. A Texas investor named Lacy Harbor, in the meantime, began to buy up depressed ASC stock. The company granted him approval to increase his stake in the company to 30 percent. ASC went into 2001 with a great deal of unanswered questions. Would it be able to find a repair and maintenance niche in the aircraft services industry, and would control of the company change hands?

Principal Subsidiaries

Aviation Sales Distribution Services Company; Aviation Sales Manufacturing Company; Aviation Sales Maintenance, Repair & Overhaul Company; Aerocell Structures; Aircraft Interior Design, Inc.; Whitehall Corporation.

Principal Competitors

AAR Corporation; Aviation Distributors Inc.; Aviall Inc.; HEICO Corporaiton; First Aviation Services Inc.

Further Reading

Cordle, Ina Paiva, "Miami-Based Aviation Sales Uses Acquisitions to Expand Services," *Knight-Ridder/Tribune Business News,* July 13, 1998.

Deogun, Nikhil, "Ryder System Plans to Spin Off Aviation Lines," *Wall Street Journal,* July 1, 1993, p. A4.

Leder, Michelle, "In Aviation, the Bargains May Be in the Hangars," *New York Times,* February 28, 1999, p. 8.

Nelms, Douglas W., "Inventory Managers, Not Parts Salesmen," *Air Transport World,* March 1998, p. 78.

——, "One-Stop Shopping," *Air Transport World,* November 1998, pp. 89–95.

Zisser, Melinda, "Miami to Be Base for Parts Distributor," *South Florida Business Journal,* December 23, 1994, p. 3.

—Ed Dinger

Avondale Industries

5100 River Road
Avondale, Louisiana 70094
U.S.A.
Telephone: (504) 436-2121
Fax: (504) 436-5010
Web site: http://www.avondale.com

Wholly Owned Division of Northrup Grumman Ship Systems
Incorporated: 1938 as Avondale Marine Ways, Inc.
Employees: 6,000
Sales: $500 million (2000 est.)
NAIC: 336611 Ship Building and Repairing; 332312 Fabricated Structural Metal Manufacturing

The primary business of Avondale Industries is the construction, repair, conversion, and "jumboization" of ships, barges, tugboats, and other vessels. The company is a major supplier of vessels to the U.S. Navy, constructing a full range of destroyer escorts, frigates, cutters, fleet oilers, landing ship docks, and landing craft air cushion (LCAC) at shipyards and repair and manufacturing facilities in Louisiana and Mississippi. In addition, the company is a major manufacturer of double-hulled tankers, barges, and other commercial ships. Briefly under the parentage of Litton (and known then as Litton Avondale Industries), the company was sold to the defense powerhouse Northrup Grumman in 2000 and became a part of that company's ship systems unit.

River Boats and Navy Ships: 1938–59

Avondale grew out of a small barge repair business, Avondale Marine Ways, Inc., which was founded in 1938 by James G. Viavant, Harry Koch, and Perry N. Ellis about 12 miles up river from New Orleans on the Mississippi River. Almost immediately it began building river boats and barges, at first as a way of keeping employees busy between repair jobs, which were much more profitable. By 1941 the company employed about 200 workers.

With the United States gearing up for World War II, the government took control of the flow of metals and other raw materials. In 1941 James Viavant flew to Washington to find out from the Maritime Commission whether there were any small vessels on which Avondale could bid. The result was a contract to manufacture four tugboats, the company's first major building contract. This was followed by a contract to construct 14 M3 coastal cargo ships, 300-foot shallow draft vessels. Avondale continued to build ships including tankers, tugs, and other coastal vessels for the government for the duration of the war, which required expansion of the original shipyard facilities.

After the war, the company continued to grow as the oil industry in southern Louisiana expanded during the 1940s and 1950s. Avondale began building drilling barges and work boats and built its first submersible drilling barge in 1951. As river and intercoastal traffic grew, there was increasing need for repair facilities. Avondale purchased a major new site in 1946 at Harvey Canal and continued to expand its repair facilities throughout the period. The company's name was changed to Avondale Shipyards, Inc., in 1960.

In 1959 Avondale was sold to the Ogden Corporation of New York for $14 million. The company remained a subsidiary of Ogden until 1985, building guided missile destroyers, destroyer escorts, auxiliary oilers, and other vessels for the U.S. Navy; various types of commercial vessels, including cargo vessels, off-shore drilling rigs, tugs, oil tankers, LASH cargo vessels, dredges, tug/supply vessels, product tankers, container vessels, and miscellaneous barges; and Coast Guard cutters. In 1985 Ogden sold seven companies, including Avondale Shipyards, to the employees, and these became Avondale Corporation under an Employee Stock Ownership Plan (ESOP). The ESOP, one of the largest ever formed, was 70 percent employee owned, with Ogden retaining a 30 percent share. Ogden continued to have a minor interest in the company, but concentrated on its food service, building maintenance, waste recovery and management, and allied businesses. In 1987 Avondale Industries divested itself of six of those companies. The shipyard, with its various divisions centered around New Orleans, continued as Avondale Industries, Inc. In 1988 the company was taken public; the employees owned approximately 44 percent of the

Company Perspectives:

Northrup Grumman Avondale Industries is a manufacturer of sea-going vessels. We serve marine, transportation, energy, defense and industrial customers. Our products are made to customer specifications and are supported with superior engineering and service. We strive to be the leading supplier in every market we serve by adding significant value to our products; by providing outstanding quality at the lowest possible cost; by honoring our pledges to on-time delivery; and by forging true partnerships with our customers. Only in this way can we continue to compete in such challenging industries.

common stock in 1989. In 1991 that figure was about 54 percent.

The Transition to Modular Construction: The 1970s and 1980s

After World War II Japan became the leader in innovative methods of building high-quality ships utilizing modular construction, also known as "zone outfitting." In this mode of construction, large projects are broken up into manageable modules, which are worked on simultaneously in different workshops or facilities, sometimes many miles apart. The modules are then transported to the ship site. This method results in tremendous cost savings, although it requires complex planning, logistics, and engineering to maintain tight tolerances between the modules. In the late 1970s Avondale made the decision to study and adapt the Japanese system. To this end, Avondale management, under Chief Executive Albert L. Bossier, entered into a unique technology transfer agreement with Ishikawajima Harima Heavy Industries (IHI) of Japan in 1981. It took the company approximately five years to retrain and retool, but modular construction eventually gave Avondale a decisive competitive advantage in the shipbuilding industry. While Avondale thrived, other shipbuilders such as General Dynamics and Lockheed closed shipyards, and Todd Shipyards and MorrisonKnudsen experienced severe losses. The relationship with IHI has continued, but on a case-by-case consulting basis. In addition to its changeover to modular construction, Avondale also invested heavily in facility improvements and expansion. Between 1970 and 1992, the company poured more than $258 million into new manufacturing shops, modular assembly buildings, and state of the art equipment. In 1992 its lifting equipment included a 600-ton floating crane, seven cranes with capacity greater than 130 tons, and 29 cranes with capacity greater than 50 tons. Avondale also had an 81,000-ton dry dock measuring 900′ x 220′ and a 20,000-ton Panama dry dock measuring 705′ x 118′. Equipment of this size has enabled Avondale to specialize in "jumboization," a process whereby a ship is cut in half and a matching section is inserted to lengthen the vessel.

The company has used modular construction in some industrial nonmarine projects as well. These have included a 192-megawatt hydroelectric plant in Vidalia, Louisiana, four hazardous waste treatment plants for Ogden, compressor and pump modules for the oil industry, sulfur recovery units, cryogenic gas separation systems, sub-sea oil treatment units for oil companies, and a floating detention center for New York City capable of housing 800 inmates delivered in 1992.

Military Downsizing in the Early 1990s

By 1989 defense-related contracts, mainly with the U.S. Navy, accounted for as much as 85 percent of Avondale's business. In 1991 the Secretary of the Navy advised Congress that by 1995 the Navy's fleet would be pared from about 550 to 600 ships to 450, and the actual number might drop even lower. In terms of expenditures, this meant that the Navy's annual budget for shipbuilding would be reduced from $12–$14 billion in the 1980s to $6–$8 billion in the 1990s. In addition, because the Navy planned to concentrate on combat ships and submarines, vessels that Avondale had not previously produced, the effect of the cutbacks on Avondale would be that much greater.

In 1990 Avondale reported a net loss of $25.8 million and then a loss of $140.9 million in 1991. These losses were, however, not attributable to military downsizing, but rather to cost overruns on seven TAO (auxiliary oil tanker) and three LSD-CV (landing ship dock-cargo variant) contracts due to be completed in 1994 and 1995. In early 1992 the company applied for requests for equitable adjustments (REAs) of $300 to $340 million from the Navy. As Albert L. Bossier, Jr., Avondale's chairman, president, and CEO, stated at the time, "The REAs we are pursuing with the Navy are intended to seek reimbursement for the portion of our cost overruns resulting from disruption of work caused by contract delays and changes initiated by the Navy." To help alleviate a cash shortfall for 1992, the Navy released $15 million of earned retentions from previous contracts, and in December 1995 the two parties finally reached a settlement.

In 1992 Avondale learned that a competitor had been awarded a contract to build as many as seven MHC-51 minehunters, despite the fact that Avondale was already building four such vessels. On the other hand, the Navy changed its contract on three of the TAOs already being built by Avondale to make them double-hulled. The company also was awarded a $1.2 million contract to design ships for "Sealift," the ocean transport of weapons and supplies for ground troops. The company also launched the T-AGS 45 oceanographic survey ship for the Navy as well as several other ships in that year. In spite of the drop-off in Navy contracts, Avondale did show a small second quarter profit and a third quarter profit of about $280,000, although revenues declined for the sixth straight quarter from $205 million in the first quarter of 1991 to $139 million in the third quarter of 1992.

The combination of the Navy's cutbacks, the economic recession, and factors peculiar to the industry and/or Avondale hit the company particularly hard in its efforts to diversify. Congress passed the Oil Pollution Act of 1990 in the aftermath of the Exxon Valdez disaster. The Act mandated that all oil tankers entering U.S. ports after January 1, 2000 be double-hulled. Although this created some immediate opportunities for Avondale, the company found that the physical capacity of its main shipyard, the draft of the river, and the height of bridges spanning the Mississippi precluded it from making bids to retrofit or build ultra-large oil tankers.

Key Dates:

1938: Avondale Marine Ways, Inc. is formed.
1941: Avondale wins first contract with U.S. Navy.
1959: Ogden Corporation acquires Avondale Marine Ways.
1960: Avondale Marine Ways becomes Avondale Shipyards, Inc.
1981: Avondale enters into technology transfer agreement with Ishikawajima Harima Heavy Industries of Japan.
1985: Ogden Corporation sells majority stake in Avondale Shipyards to the employees.
1990: Oil Pollution Act is passed.
1991: Avondale enters into joint venture with Peter Gast Shipping GmbH.
1999: Avondale is acquired by Litton Industries, becoming Litton Avondale Industries.
2000: Litton is acquired by Northrop Grumman Corp.; Avondale Industries becomes a division of Northrop Grumman's Ship Systems unit.

In addition, although international demand for the replacement of large commercial ships was projected to be above average in the 1990s, most of Avondale's foreign competitors were subsidized by their governments, placing Avondale at a competitive disadvantage. In response to this, Avondale entered into a unique joint venture with Peter Gast Shipping GmbH, of Hamburg, Germany, and Wilhelm Wilhelmsen Ltd., of Oslo, Norway, in January 1991. Avgain Marine A/S, based in Oslo, was created to be an international broker of ship components, allowing Avondale to cut materials expenses by pooling purchasing power, and to boost Gast's efforts to market Avondale-built ships in Europe and elsewhere. It was thought that the lower value of the dollar would partially offset the disadvantage posed by European government subsidization. As Gast put it, ''Avondale's ship prices are now more competitive.''

Avondale's attempts to transfer its shipbuilding and managerial skills to nonmarine projects met with only limited success during this period. One bright spot during 1991, however, was a five-year contract worth approximately $63 million obtained by Avondale Technical Services, a subsidiary, to operate and maintain specialized commuter services for the handicapped and elderly in Dallas, Texas. The company also was looking into the possibility of getting back into the offshore construction business, principally offshore oil platforms for the international market.

Modernization and Mergers: Heading into the 21st Century

After losing out on a number of important bids in the early 1990s, it became clear that Avondale needed to improve its shipbuilding capacity to remain competitive. To this end, the company embarked on a major modernization project in 1994. This ambitious undertaking, focused primarily on Avondale's steel manufacturing capabilities, was aided in large part by a federal loan policy enacted by the Transportation Department the previous year. The new policy, designed to rejuvenate the slumping shipbuilding industry, was intended to spur comprehensive renovations of the nation's shipyards. With $15.9 million in federal assistance, the company was able to devote a total of more than $20 million to upgrading its operations. At the heart of Avondale's construction plan was an enclosed steel processing shed. The structure, along with a number of smaller manufacturing buildings, was completed in the fall of 1995, and expanded the total area of the company's shipyard to 500,000 square feet.

These improvements went far to revitalize Avondale's business. By June 1995 the company had a contract with Ingram Ohio to build river hopper barges, and in the fall it reached an agreement with American Heavy Lift Shipping Company (AHL) to construct four double-hulled product/chemical tankers. The keel for the first vessel, the Captain A.H. Downing, was laid in October; when the ship was completed in May 1996, it became the first commercial double-hulled tanker launched in the United States. It was also the company's first commercial ship since 1984.

The increased capacity also enabled Avondale to make successful bids on new projects for the U.S. Navy. In December 1996 the company was named prime contractor in the design and construction of the first vessel in the LPD-17 program, the Navy's newest line of amphibious assault ships. The contract included options for two additional ships, and had a value of $1.5 billion. The company was also able to get back on schedule with its outstanding Naval projects, including the Strategic Sealift program. In January 1997 Avondale delivered its fourth MHC-51 coastal minehunter, and in March it launched the USNS Bob Hope, the first of five Strategic Sealift deployment ships. This brisk production delivered record revenues to the company, with net sales reaching $625 million in 1996, up from $576 million in 1995. Avondale's sagging share value also got a significant boost, rising from a low of $6⅛ in early 1995 to $22¾ by January 1997.

With business booming, Avondale began looking for ways to expand its presence in the commercial vessel industry. In June 1997 it closed a $332 million deal with ARCO Marine to build two crude carriers, with an option for three additional ships. In September it formed a strategic alliance with rival Ingalls Shipbuilding to bid jointly on a number of commercial projects, including oil tankers. Hoping to further strengthen its bidding power, Avondale announced its intention to merge with Newport News Shipbuilding in January 1999, a move that would combine Avondale's expertise with naval and commercial surface ships with Newport's extensive experience building aircraft carriers and submarines. In May, however, Avondale received a far more lucrative offer from Litton Industries, owner of Ingalls Shipbuilding; in June the two companies reached an agreement, and Avondale became Litton Avondale Industries.

In addition to providing Avondale with the opportunity to become involved in a wider range of projects—including the burgeoning U.S. cruise vessel building business—the merger with Litton also turned out to be the unexpected solution to a lengthy battle between Avondale and its employees. The troubles began in 1993, when Avondale employees voted to join the New Orleans Metal Trades Union. Company executives, however, questioned the validity of the election procedures and refused to recognize the union. The National Labor Relations

Board ruled to uphold the elections, and a lengthy legal fight ensued. Avondale's troubles were compounded in January 1999, when an OSHA investigation revealed that the company had deliberately falsified employee injury reports, resulting in safety citations exceeding $500,000. The company was vindicated in July, however, when a U.S. circuit court ruled that the 1993 union election was ''fatally flawed.'' The merger with Litton, whose employees were already unionized, helped ease the tension, however, and in December Avondale's steel workers were officially unionized.

Throughout this transition period the company remained extremely active. It remained on schedule with the LPD-17 project; in July 2000, after three years of design and engineering work, construction began on the first vessel, the USS San Antonio. The company also continued work on its Bob Hope class Strategic Sealift ships, as well as a series of ''Millennium Class'' tankers for Polar Tankers, Inc.

If the announcement in December 2000 of Northrop Grumman's acquisition of Litton Industries cast a small shadow of uncertainty on the future makeup of Avondale, fears were allayed by March 2001, when the Department of Defense announced that it was awarding an $11.3 million contract to Avondale for engineering services needed to support the Department's program for modifying its LPD 17 Class of ships. Moreover, by June 2001, Northrop Grumman had completed the integration of its Litton properties; Avondale found a home as a division of Northrop Grumman's Ship Systems. It seemed likely that the company would remain one of the nation's major shipbuilders for years to come.

Principal Operating Units

Shipyards; Modular Construction; Steel Sales; Gulfport Facility; Tallulah Facility; Integrated Product Development Environment; Repair Services.

Principal Competitors

General Dynamics Corporation; Newport News Shipbuilding Inc.; Todd Shipyards Corporation.

Further Reading

''Avondale Industries Posts Net Loss, Cites Cost Overruns on Navy Pacts,'' *Journal of Commerce,* April 20, 1992.

Biers, John M., ''Merger Helps Avondale Union: Newport News Steelworkers Lend Clout,'' *Times-Picayune* (La.), January 21, 1999.

''Big Easy Survivor,'' *Forbes,* January 9, 1989.

Bonney, Joseph, ''Ogden Sells Avondale to Workers,'' *Journal of Commerce,* July 19, 1985.

Darce, Keith, ''Avondale Loses Cruise Ship Contract: Miss. Company Bids Better Price, Earlier Delivery,'' *Times-Picayune* (La.), October 7, 1998.

——, ''Litton Avondale Shares Cruise Ship Pact; Design Contract Could Lead to Building Deal,'' *Times-Picayune* (La.), March 28, 2000.

Hall, John, ''Avondale Begins Modernizing Yard,'' *Times-Picayune* (La.), February 11, 1995.

''Litton Avondale Industries,'' *Department of Defense News Release,* March 28, 2001.

''Northrop Grumman Announces Completion of Merger with Litton Industries Inc.,'' *PR Newswire,* May 20, 2001.

Pollack, Andrew, ''A Military Contractor Aims to Raise Its Profile Quickly,'' *New York Times,* May 8, 1999.

Porter, Janet, ''US Yards: Good Ships Are Stitch in Time for Owners,'' *Journal of Commerce,* May 29, 1997.

Swoboda, Frank, ''Avondale Faces Fine of $537,000 by OSHA; La. Shipyard Says It Will Contest Findings,'' *Washington Post,* April 6, 1999.

Toll, Erich E., ''US Shipbuilder to Join Norwegians, Germans in Unusual Partnership,'' *Journal of Commerce,* January 10, 1991.

—Kenneth F. Kronenberg
—update: Stephen Meyer

Bayer A.G.

Werk Leverkusen
51368 Leverkusen
Germany
Telephone: (49) 214 305-8992
Fax: (49) 214 307-1985
Web site: http://www.bayer-ag.de

Public Company
Incorporated: 1881 as Farbenfabriken vorm. Friedr. Bayer & Co.
Employees: 120,400
Sales: $29.1 billion (2000)
Stock Exchange: Munich Bonn Hamburg Frankfurt Paris Luxembourg Vienna Zurich Basle Geneva London Brussels Antwerp
Ticker Symbol: BAYZY
NAIC: 325412 Pharmaceutical Preparation Manufacturing; 32551 Paint and Coating Manufacturing; 551112 Offices of Other Holding Companies

Comprised of over 350 companies, Bayer A.G. operates as one of the world's largest chemical manufacturers. Its four main business segments include Health Care, Agricultural, Polymers, and Chemicals. Within the Health Care division are the Pharmaceutical, Consumer Care, and Diagnostics business groups. The Agriculture division operates the Crop Protection and Animal Health groups. The Polymers division is made up of five segments including Plastics, Rubber, Polyurethanes, Coatings, and Colorants, and also includes fiber subsidiary Bayer Faser GmbH. The Chemicals division operates the Basic and Fine Chemicals unit, Specialty Products, and subsidiaries Haarmann & Reimer, H.C. Stark, and Wolff Walsrode. Bayer has operations in nearly every country in the world with a majority of its business in Europe, the Far East, and North America. The firm is among industry leaders in research and development, spending nearly 12 percent of its revenues on this segment.

1860s Origins

Bayer traces its history to the 1863 founding of a dyestuffs factory in Barmen, Germany, a region that later became part of the industrial city of Wuppertal on the Rhine river in West Germany. The factory was set up by Friedrich Bayer and Johan Friedrich Weskott, a master dyer. Only two years later, the men commenced global operations of sorts, acquiring a share in a U.S. coal tar dye factory and exporting the product. Subsequent expansion included a new factory in Moscow. By 1881, the growing company was being run by heirs of Bayer and Weskott, and they reorganized the concern as Farbenfabriken vorm. Friedr. Bayer & Co., a joint-stock company. A plant in northern France was established in 1883 and others throughout the homeland of Germany followed.

In 1884, chemist Carl Duisberg joined the company; he would oversee a period of remarkable innovation at Bayer. Expanding beyond the development and manufacture of dyestuffs, the company established a pharmaceutical department in 1888. Although Bayer became a world leader in dyestuffs, its place in the history of early 20th-century chemistry was secured by its contributions to pharmacology. Specifically, at the turn of the century a Bayer chemist, Felix Hoffman, became the first to synthesize acetylsalicylic acid into a usable form. The result, aspirin, was patented in 1899 and went on to become the most popular pain reliever worldwide.

Moreover, in 1908, the basic compound for sulfa drugs was synthesized in Bayer laboratories. The immediate application of the compound was a reddish orange dye, which was soon discovered to be effective against pneumonia, a major health hazard of the early 20th century. Despite the lives that could have been saved if the sulfa drug had been released throughout Europe immediately, Bayer held onto the formula. Frustrated French chemists were forced to duplicate the drug in their own laboratories in order to introduce it to the market. In 1912, Bayer moved its headquarters to Leverkusan, where they would remain into the 21st century.

Unifying Under the German Government: 1920s–40s

Bayer chemists regularly tested dye compounds for their effectiveness against bacteria. In 1921, they discovered a cure for African sleeping sickness, an infectious disease that had made parts of Africa uninhabitable. Aware of the political as well as

Company Perspectives:

Our aim is to be the world's leading integrated chemical and pharmaceutical company, with core competencies in health care, agriculture, plastics, and specialty chemicals. Our aim is that our products should benefit humankind. We are committed to the principals of the international Responsible Care initiative in our research and development, manufacturing, marketing, and information policy.

pharmacological implications of its compound, Bayer offered the British the formula to the drug, known as Germanin, in exchange for African colonies. Britain declined the offer. Non-cooperation continued as during World War I Bayer deprived the Allies of drugs and anesthetics whenever possible. In 1925, Duisberg, who had become president of Bayer, organized a merger of the major German chemical companies into a single entity known as the Interessen Gemeinschaft Farbenwerke, or I.G. Farben. From their inception, the German chemical companies had been organized into a series of progressively more powerful trusts, but with I.G. Farben, the last vestiges of competition in the chemical industry were extinguished. Other industries, such as steel, were undergoing a similar process in Germany.

In addition to setting quotas and pooling profits, I.G. Farben pursued political aims, working to prevent any possibility of a leftist uprising that would establish worker control over industry. In order to prevent such an uprising, I.G. Farben financed right-wing politicians and attempted to influence domestic policy in secret meetings with German leaders. The trust also exercised its influence abroad, with Bayer and other companies contributing an estimated ten million marks to Nazi Party associations in other countries. Money was also designated for propaganda. In 1938, Bayer forced a U.S. affiliate, Sterling Drug, to write its advertising contracts in such a way that they would be immediately canceled if the publication in which the advertising appeared presented Germany in an unflattering light.

Bayer and I.G. Farben profited handsomely from their support of Adolf Hitler. By 1942, I.G. Farben was making a yearly profit of 800 million marks more than its entire combined capitalization in 1925, the year the cartel was formalized. Not only was I.G. Farben given possession of chemical companies in foreign lands (it had control of Czechoslovakian dye works a week after the Nazi invasion), but the captured lands provided its factories in Germany with slave labor. In order to take full advantage of slave labor, I.G. Farben plants were built next to Maidanek and Auschwitz.

Many of the I.G. Farben plants contracted during the war were built in remote areas, often with camouflage. Thus, these factories did not sustain much physical damage, in contrast to the many German cities that were completely destroyed. By I.G. Farben's account, only 15 percent of its productive capacity was destroyed by the Allies. The worst damage was sustained by the extensive BASF works and factories in eastern Germany, which were destroyed by I.G. Farben employees so that the buildings would not fall under Russian control.

Immediately after the war many members of I.G. Farben's Vorstand, or board of directors, were arrested and indicted for war crimes. I.G. Farben executives were in the habit of keeping copious records, not only of meetings and phone calls, but also of their private thoughts on I.G. Farben's dealings with the government; as a result, there was extensive written evidence incriminating the Vorstand. Despite this evidence and testimony from concentration camp survivors, the Vorstand was dealt with leniently by the judges at Nuremberg. Journalists covering the 1947 proceedings attributed the light sentences, none of which was longer than four years, to the fact that all the sentences handed down at the end of the trials tended to be less severe, as well as to the judges' unwillingness to expand their definition of war criminals to include businessmen.

Bayer Independence from I.G Farben: 1950s

I.G. Farben plants operated under Allied supervision from 1947 until 1951, when the organization was dismantled in the interests of "peace and democracy." The division of I.G. Farben generally adhered to the boundaries of the original companies; for example, the works at Leverkusen and Elberfield reverted to Bayer. Bayer also received the AGFA photographic works.

In the first five years of its independence from I.G. Farben, Bayer concentrated on replacing outdated equipment and on supplying Germany's need for chemicals. By 1957, Bayer had developed new insecticides and fibers, as well as new raw and plastic finished materials. Bayer's resiliency in recovering from the war impressed U.S. investors, who held 12 percent of the company's stock.

During the late 1950s, Bayer began to expand overseas and by 1962 was manufacturing chemicals in eight countries, including India and Pakistan. Most of the work done abroad was "final stage processing," whereby active ingredients were sent from Germany and mixed with locally obtained inert ingredients that would be expensive to transport overseas. Final stage processing arrangements allowed Bayer to manufacture products, mostly farm chemicals and drugs, in developing countries more profitably.

High tariffs in the United States and high labor costs in Germany also provided incentives for Bayer to acquire production facilities in America. In 1954, Bayer and Monsanto formed a chemical company known as Mobay to manufacture engineering plastics and dyestuffs. Because Bayer did not have sufficient funds to build a plant in the United States, it provided technical expertise while Monsanto provided financial resources. Although Bayer had part and eventually full interest in Mobay, its promotional material was never allowed to mention Bayer's name, because the American rights to the Bayer trademark had been given to Sterling Drug after World War I in retaliation for Bayer's suppression of U.S. dye companies during the early years of the 20th century.

Realizing that West Germany offered only limited opportunity for growth, Bayer worked to develop products for the U.S. chemical market, emphasizing value-added products for which Bayer held the patents, including pesticides, polyurethane, dye stuffs, and engineering plastics. Technical innovations that allowed Bayer to penetrate the U.S. market included the urethane compound that forms the familiar "crust" on urethane used in auto dashboards; before Bayer's discovery, the porous quality of urethane limited its usefulness. During this period Bayer

Key Dates:

1863: Friedrich Bayer establishes a dyestuffs factory.
1888: The pharmaceutical department of the firm is created.
1899: The Aspirin trademark is registered.
1912: Company headquarters are moved to Leverkusen.
1925: Merger of the major German chemical companies results in the Interessen Gemeinschaft Farbenwerke, or I.G. Farben.
1951: Following postwar breakup, I.G. Farben is reformed as Farbenfabriken Bayer A.G.
1972: The firm officially adopts the name Bayer A.G.
1978: Miles Laboratories is acquired.
1982: The firm restructures, creating a third tier below the management board.
1993: Pharmaceutical sales in Germany fall by 20 percent as a result of government efforts to cut expenditures on pharmaceuticals.
1994: Bayer purchases Sterling Drug for $1 billion.
1997: Company begins restructuring its chemical operations.
1998: Bayer purchases Chiron Diagnostics, becoming one of the world's largest diagnostic system suppliers, and initiates plans to spin-off its Agfa subsidiary.
1999: Company celebrates the centennial of Aspirin.
2001: A $1.64 billion alliance with CuraGen Corporation is forged.

consolidated and slowly expanded its international operations, especially in the United States. Overall, the 1960s was a good decade for Bayer as domestic production increased 350 percent while foreign production increased 700 percent.

U.S. Expansion in the 1970s

In the early 1970s, Bayer began to increase its already substantial investment in the United States. Between 1973 and 1977, its investment rose from $300 to $500 million, which went to expand production capacity and develop its product line, which included dyes, drugs, plastics, and synthetic rubber. Although all patents held by Bayer before 1952 had been taken away as war retribution, by the mid-1970s Bayer had expanded its product line to include 6,000 items, many of them patented by the company.

Bayer increased its capacity by expanding existing plants and purchasing new ones. In 1974, Bayer purchased Cutter Laboratories, a manufacturer of nutritional products and ethical drugs, which had financial difficulties until 1977. Later, Allied Chemical sold its organic pigments division to Bayer. In 1977, a U.S. antitrust suit forced Bayer to buy Monsanto's share of Mobay, which generated $540 million in sales. The following year Bayer purchased Miles Laboratories, manufacturers of Alka-Seltzer antacid and Flintstones vitamins.

Bayer had strong incentives to expand its U.S. operations. Due to the prevalence of strikes in Europe, which interrupted product shipments, U.S. retailers were wary of contracting with European suppliers who did not have large stockpiles of their products in the United States. Lower energy and labor costs made the United States even more attractive to Bayer. U.S. holdings also cushioned the negative effects of the strong deutsche mark on imports into the United States. By the mid-1970s, 65 percent of Bayer's sales came from outside of Germany, making it critical that Bayer protect itself against currency fluctuations.

Restructuring and Cost-Cutting During the 1980s and 1990s

In the early 1980s, Bayer's worldwide holdings had expanded such that its corporate structure needed streamlining. German law mandated a two-tier structure for corporations, with a management board similar in function to the board of directors of a U.S. corporation reporting to a supervisory board made up of major stockholders, labor representatives, and outside interests. This board served in a supervisory capacity, approved major decisions, and appointed board members. In 1982, Bayer created a third tier below the management board. This board consisted of senior managers and corporate staff members who took over management of specific product lines that had previously been the responsibility of board members.

The late 1980s and early 1990s were a time of stagnant revenues, cost containment efforts, and an increasing emphasis on non-European markets for Bayer. From 1988 through 1993, sales fluctuated between DM 40 billion and DM 43.3 billion, while profits leveled off. Business was affected by a serious recession in Western Europe, political changes in Eastern Europe, a cyclical downturn in the chemical industry, and government reforms in health care and agriculture. In 1993, Bayer's sales of pharmaceuticals in Germany fell 20 percent as a result of government efforts to cut expenditures on pharmaceuticals; doctors, facing reduced drug budgets, began to prescribe more generic drugs in place of the expensive, proprietary drugs developed by Bayer. Agrochemical sales were dampened by the Common Agricultural Policy reform effort that reduced the amount of farmland in Europe and the amount of chemicals used in farming.

Part of Bayer's response to this crisis was to drastically cut costs—$1.6 billion in expenditures were eliminated between 1991 and early 1995. Its worldwide workforce was slashed by 14 percent, and unprofitable operations were shed, including its polyphenylene sulfide unit. In 1992, Bayer integrated all of its U.S. holdings under its Miles Inc. subsidiary, based in Pittsburgh. The following year, under the leadership of a new chairman of the board of management, Manfred Schneider, Bayer committed to enlarging its Asian and North American operations in order to reduce its dependence on the European market. In Asia, Bayer focused its expansion efforts on joint ventures with firms in Japan, Hong Kong, Taiwan, and China. In 1993, Bayer signed an agreement with the Eisai Company of Japan to sell nonprescription drugs, and the following year several joint ventures were signed in China to set up Bayer and Agfa Gevaert production operations there.

In North America, Bayer began a drive not only to bolster its operations but also to fully regain the use of its name. After securing the rights to the Bayer name in the United States after

World War I, Sterling Drugs went on to establish Bayer aspirin as a household name. In 1986, for $25 million, Bayer secured from Sterling partial rights to use its name in North America outside the pharmaceutical area. In 1994, Eastman Kodak sold Sterling to the British firm SmithKline Beecham PLC, and only a few weeks later SmithKline sold the North American side of Sterling to Bayer for $1 billion. With the purchase, Bayer not only won back the full rights to its name in North America, but also gained Sterling's $366 million North American over-the-counter (OTC) drug business. In addition to the Bayer aspirin line, the Sterling acquisition included such familiar products as Midol analgesics and NeoSynephrine decongestant. The acquisition pushed Bayer into the top five producers of OTC products worldwide.

After the purchase of Sterling, Bayer changed the name of its Miles Inc. subsidiary to Bayer Corporation. The OTC operations of Miles and Sterling were then integrated into a single Bayer Corporation consumer care division. Another strategic step in North America, and one that brought added diversification to Bayer's health care operations, was the 1994 purchase of a 29.3 percent stake in Denver-based Schein Pharmaceutical Inc., a maker of generic drugs. Bayer planned to expand Schein's operations outside North America.

Bayer also beefed up its research and development (R&D) budget, particularly in health care. Its drug research efforts were already beginning to pay off in the mid-1990s, especially in North America. Bayer's anti-infective drug Ciprobay had generated $1.3 billion in sales by early 1995, with the firm's patent in effect until 2002. In 1993, Bayer introduced a hemophilia treatment called Kogenate, the company's first genetically engineered drug. Other major drugs under development included a cholesterol reducer and treatments for asthma and Alzheimer's disease.

As a result of its increasing diversification within its core businesses and its aggressive program of worldwide expansion, Bayer operated as a leading chemical and pharmaceutical company in the mid-1990s. Net income increased by 20 percent to DM 2.4 billion in 1995, the highest level the company had recorded in its history. The company's chemical business played a large role in securing such an increase. However, results for the firm's healthcare interests and its Agfa group were dim in comparison due to exchange rates, a decrease in demand, and increased pressure on prices.

The firm once again looked to restructure and control costs in order to maintain income levels. The financial success in 1995 was overshadowed by 3,800 job cuts and additional cuts were expected into the late 1990s. Underperforming assets and non-core assets were divested including the dental care and consumer businesses. As the German economy faltered, Bayer management continued to focus on cost-efficient operations. Chairman Schneider stated in an April 1996 *Chemistry and Industry* article, ''if our German operations are to remain competitive, we must at least stop costs rising any further and actually start to reduce them again.'' In order to do just that, the firm's bulk chemical plants in Leverkusen, Dormagen, and Uerdingen, underwent a major restructuring in 1997 after recording a 79 percent decline in operating profits.

At the same time, Bayer looked for strategic alliances to secure top positions in niches of the industry. In March 1996, the firm acquired the styrenics business of Monsanto Co. for $580 million. The deal doubled Bayer's North American plastics operations and secured its position as the second largest producer of engineering resins just behind GE Plastics. The firm also pledged to increase Asian business, which in 1996 secured 14 percent of company sales. Moreover, in September 1998, Bayer acquired U.S.-based Chiron Corp's Diagnostics business for DM 1.9 billion. The deal gave Bayer the number one spot in the diagnostic systems industry and also increased its international customer base as well as its research operations.

Bayer teamed with Millennium Pharmaceuticals Inc., a genome research company, to form a discovery alliance related to drug testing for cardiovascular disease, cancer, osteoporosis, liver fibrosis, and viral infections. Bayer also teamed up with General Electric to form GE Bayer Silicones GmbH & Co. KG, a unit dedicated to developing the silicon business. The firm also partnered with Japanese firm Fujisawa to prevent worms in pets and livestock, and also began work in China on crop protection and household insecticides.

Aspirin celebrated its centennial in March 1999. Bayer celebrated by tenting its corporate headquarters in an Aspirin box while 50,000 spectators looked on. Amid the festivities, the firm continued to strengthen its core businesses and spun off 70 million shares of its Agfa-Gevaert business in order to raise capital for other operations. At the same time, the firm continued to face increased competition, consolidation in the pharmaceutical industry, and difficult market conditions in the agrochemical field as well as in the chemicals segment. Strategic alliances remained a focus, and deals for the year included the purchase of the polycarbonate and polyester sheet business of Dutch-based DSM; the acquisition of Laserlite, an Australian plastic sheeting company; and Home & Garden Ltd, a plant protection and fertilizer manufacturer. Having spent the 1990s restructuring and selling off non core assets, Bayer's key business segments included Health Care, Agriculture, Polymers, and Chemicals at the close of the 20th century.

Alliances for the New Millennium

Bayer entered the new millennium on solid ground, despite weakening market conditions in several of its business segments. The company's strategy of strengthening its portfolio continued, and in April 2000 the firm acquired the polyols business of U.S.-based Lyondell Chemical Company for $2.5 billion. Bayer stood as the world's largest polyurethane raw materials supplier after the deal.

Bayer also forged several key partnerships that were related to the firm's drive for research and development as well as product innovation. A deal with Incyte Pharmaceuticals gave Bayer access to the U.S.-based company's database of over 480 patented human genes that could be used for research. The company also partnered with LION Bioscience AG to do research in the life sciences including pharmaceuticals and diagnostics. In February 2001, Bayer teamed up with CuraGen Corporation to research, develop, and market pharmaceuticals related to metabolic disease. Bayer received the ''President's Service Award'' and the ''Presidential Green Chemistry Challenge Award'' in 2000 due to its long-standing commitment to research and development.

Though overall sales for 2000 were impressive, the Chemicals segment of the business continued to struggle, and restructuring continued. Bayer's focus on the future included expanding its research and technology operations, as well as continuing to shed unprofitable business. For example, in May 2001 the company ceded its 50 percent interest in EC Erdoelchemie to BP Energy in a deal valued at $500 million. During this time, Tweedy Browne & Co., a large shareholder, called for Bayer to split into three segments: chemicals, pharmaceuticals, and agchems. In response to the proposed split, chairman Schneider stated in a *Chemical Week* article, "we are sure such a move would not increase Bayer's value in the long term. Our current structure facilitates the running of the business, enables us to capitalize on existing synergies, and gives us scope to respond swiftly should acquisition opportunities arise in the life science sector." Indeed, shareholders voted down the proposal overwhelmingly, trusting management and the current structure to see the company to ever more profitable decades ahead.

Principal Subsidiaries

Bayer Vital GmbH & Co. KG; Wolff Walsrode AG; Haarmann & Reimer GmbH; Bayer Faser GmbH; Rhein Chemie Rheinau GmbH; Bayer Corporation (U.S.); Bayer Inc. (Canada); Bayer Antwerpen N.V. (Belgium); Bayer Rubber N.V. (Belgium); Bayer A/S (Denmark); Bayer plc (U.K.); Bayer S.p.A. (Italy); Bayer International S.A. (Switzerland); Bayer Hispania, S.A. (Spain); Quimica Farmaceutica Bayer, S.A. (Spain); Bayer de Mexico, S.A. de C.V.; Bayer Ltd. (Japan); Bayer (Singapore) Pte. Ltd.; Bayer (Proprietary) Ltd. (South Africa); DyStar Group (50%); H.C. Starck GmbH & Co KG (99.9%); PolymerLatex GmbH & Co. KG (50%).

Principal Operating Units

Health Care; Chemicals; Polymers; Agriculture.

Principal Competitors

E.I. du Pont de Nemours and Co.; BASF A.G.; Novartis A.G.

Further Reading

"Bayer AG Announces US$100 Million Alliance in Life Science Research," *PR Newswire*, June 24, 1999.

"Bayer Bids to Be No. 1 in Polycarbonate," *Plastics Technology*, February 2000, p. 69.

"Bayer Buys Lyondell's Global Polyols for US$ 2.5 Billion," *Polymers Paint Colour Journal*, December 1999, p. 8.

"Bayer Continues Restructuring Plans," *Chemical Week*, January 13, 1999, p. 6.

"Bayer, CuraGen Alliance," *Chemical Market Reporter*, February 26, 2001, p. 7.

"Bayer Playing Catch-Up," *Med Ad News*, March 2001.

"Bayer Prepares Bulk Chemicals Restructuring," *Chemical Market Reporter*, March 24, 1997, p. 8.

"Bayer Regains U.S. Rights to Name with OTC Buy," *Chemical Marketing Reporter*, September 19, 1994, p. 3.

"Bayer to Sell Agfa-Gevaert Stock," *Chemical Market Reporter*, May 24, 1999, p. 7.

Brierley, David, "Bayer Finds Breaking Up Is Hard to Do," *European*, August 7, 1997, p. 24.

Hasell, Nick, "The View from Bayer," *Management Today*, November 1993, pp. 60–64.

Hayes, Peter, *Industry and Ideology: IG Farben in the Nazi Era*, New York: Cambridge University Press, 1987, 411 p.

Hume Claudia, "Bayer Rejects Call for Split," *Chemical Week*, March 21, 2001, p. 7.

Jackson, Debbie, and Emma Chynoweth, "Recession Reaches German Majors: Turnaround in 1991 Is Still Elusive," *Chemical Week*, April 15, 1992, pp. 22–23.

Jackson, Debbie, "Bayer: Deals in the Pipeline as Decline Continues," *Chemical Week*, December 8, 1993, p. 18.

——, "Bayer Mobilizes Resources to Counter Crisis at Home," *Chemical Week*, April 21, 1993, pp. 24–31.

——, "Bayer under Pressure," *Chemical Week*, March 24, 1993, p. 19.

"Job Losses Follow Best Year Ever," *Chemistry and Industry*, April 1, 1996, p. 237.

Keenan, Tim, "Bayer Pumps Up Plastics Division," *Ward's Auto World*, March 1996, p. 133.

Kuntz, Mary, "Extra-Strength Aspiration: Can Bayer's New Owners Expand the Market?," *Business Week*, May 1, 1995, p. 46.

Mann, Charles C., and Mark L. Plummer, *The Aspirin Wars: Money, Medicine, and 100 Years of Rampant Competition*, New York: Alfred A. Knopf, 1991, 420 p.

Miller, Karen Lowry, and Joseph Weber, "Bayer Group Eyes a Lost Continent: America," *Business Week International Editions*, June 6, 1994.

Reier, Sharon, "Elephant Walk," *Financial World*, February 28, 1995, pp. 38–39.

Rosendahl, Iris, "Out Miles, in Bayer," *Drug Topics*, February 6, 1995, p. 54.

—David E. Salamie
—update: Christina M. Stansell

Bed Bath & Beyond Inc.

650 Liberty Avenue
Union, New Jersey 07083
U.S.A.
Telephone: (908) 688-0888
Fax: (908) 688-6483
Web site: http://www.bedbath.com

Public Company
Incorporated: 1971 as Bed 'n Bath Inc.
Employees: 12,000
Sales: $2.2 billion (2000)
Stock Exchanges: NASDAQ
Ticker Symbol: BBBY
NAIC: 442299 All Other Home Furnishings Stores; 442291 Window Treatment Stores

Bed Bath & Beyond Inc. operates the largest houseware goods specialty stores in the United States. The company has a chain of over 300 stores that sell such domestic merchandise as bed linens, bath accessories, kitchen textiles, cookware, dinnerware, kitchen utensils, small electric appliances, and basic home furnishings. Throughout the company's short history, bigger has proven to be better. In the mid-1980s, Bed Bath & Beyond was a pioneer in the concept of superstores: large, well-stocked specialty shops with prices allegedly comparable to, or lower than, department store sale prices. Some Bed Bath & Beyond stores have over 80,000 square feet—the average is 45,000 square feet—of selling floor and offer more than 300,000 different items, stacked literally from floor to ceiling. The company expanded rapidly in the early 1990s on the strength of the superstore concept. Store count continues to grow at a rapid clip and in 2000, the company recorded its eighth consecutive year of record earnings. The $1.8 billion company has operations throughout the United States and plans to continue opening new stores to support its goal of doubling its earnings every three years.

1970s Origins

The driving force behind Bed Bath & Beyond was the partnership between founders Leonard Feinstein and Warren Eisenberg. Both men possessed over a decade of retail experience in 1971 when they formed Bed 'n Bath, a small chain of specialty linen and bath shops in suburban New York. As employees in management positions at Arlan's, a discount chain that fell on hard times during the early 1970s, the two sensed an essential change in retailing trends. ''We had witnessed the department store shakeout, and knew that specialty stores were going to be the next wave of retailing,'' Feinstein told *Chain Store Executive* in 1993. He added, ''It was the beginning of the designer approach to linens and housewares and we saw a real window of opportunity.'' Bed 'n Bath's first two 2,000-square-foot stores were located in high-traffic strip malls and carried such brand names as Cannon, Wamsutta, and Fieldcrest, as well as a line of lower-priced linens and bath towels.

During the 1970s, Bed 'n Bath expanded at a healthy pace, and by 1985 the chain had grown to 17 stores located in New York, New Jersey, Connecticut, and California. During this time, however, a number of similar bath and bed specialty shops had opened. What had begun as a niche market was growing increasingly competitive as retailers sensed a ''cocooning trend'' among baby boomers. Specialty chains such as Linens 'n Things, Pacific Linens, and Luxury Linens sprang up to tap into this new market. Feinstein and Eisenberg opened their first superstore in 1985, in an effort to set themselves apart from the sudden wave of competition that had appeared.

The new superstore was revolutionary in a number of ways. Over ten times the size of Bed 'n Bath's original shop, this 20,000-square-foot outlet offered a comprehensive line of home furnishings in addition to Bed 'n Bath's traditional linens and bath products. While most department stores and specialty shops offered only a few select brands, Bed 'n Bath's superstore offered seemingly every possible color, style, and size of each product. Until this time, most independent home textile retailers either copied department store merchandising techniques or followed the mundane merchandising style used by discount retailers. Eisenberg and Feinstein did neither. Bed 'n Bath, along with chains such as Toys 'R' Us and Blockbuster Video, became pioneering ''category killers'': large specialty retail outlets that beat their competition by offering virtually every possible product in their specific category at everyday low prices. Other than semiannual clearances to reduce inventory,

Company Perspectives:

Bed Bath & Beyond strives to provide a large selection of items and superior service at everyday low prices within a constantly evolving shopping environment that is both fun and exciting for customers.

the company never held sales. They claimed that their prices were already lower than other stores' sale prices.

Expansion Under a New Name: Late 1980s and early 1990s

In 1987, Eisenberg and Feinstein changed the name of their organization to Bed Bath & Beyond in order to more accurately reflect their superstore format. By 1991, Bed Bath & Beyond had opened seven new superstores in New Jersey, California, Virginia, Illinois, Maryland, and Florida, and expanded two existing stores into the superstore format. Sales reached $134 million that year, generating earnings of $10.4 million. Eisenberg and Feinstein funneled the revenue back into the company.

The company's success was considered unusual for the home products industry. As one analyst said, Bed Bath & Beyond "took a less than strong category and made it important." It did so by making ordinary household products seem exciting, even romantic. Customer service was an essential part of this marketing strategy. The company strove to build word-of-mouth by advertising through a unique combination of family atmosphere and attentive customer service. Both management and sales personnel worked the floor, arranging merchandise displays, helping shoppers carry products, and otherwise making themselves useful. According to *Fortune*, even Feinstein and Eisenberg would gather on the floor on Saturday, to "tidy merchandise and . . . pick up bits of litter." Check-out waiting time was reduced by increasing the number of cash registers, and the company developed a policy wherein, if the store was out of a desired product, Bed Bath & Beyond would deliver it to the customer's home, free of charge. Due to this strategy, Bed Bath & Beyond was able to keep paid advertising to a minimum. The company often saturated the market with advertising when a new store opened, then successfully relied on word-of-mouth to keep customers coming in.

Another important aspect of Bed Bath & Beyond's success was its merchandise layout. Related product lines were grouped together, giving the impression that the store was "comprised of several individual specialty stores for different product lines," according to company literature. To encourage impulse buying, seasonal products and other impulse items were arranged up front; further back, products were grouped on enormous vertical displays that reached to the ceiling. Such arrangements were designed to make it easier for customers to locate product and also to reinforce the perception that Bed Bath & Beyond offered an enormous assortment of goods.

Feinstein and Eisenberg also took an unusual hands-off approach to management. Bed Bath & Beyond employed no vice-presidents. Instead, store managers were given autonomy to cut prices to meet local competition or to try new marketing plans with the consent of the district manager. Within each store, new departments could be created and existing departments could be expanded or reduced as needed to respond to marketing trends.

This decentralization approach permeated all aspects of Bed Bath & Beyond's management. The company had no central warehouses. Goods were delivered directly to stores, where they either entered on-site inventory areas or went directly to the floor. This greatly reduced inventory costs and also gave store managers greater control over the flow of goods through the store.

These management strategies provided Bed Bath & Beyond with one of the retail trade's strongest return on sales during the early 1990s. Out of every $100 in sales, Bed Bath & Beyond retained $7.36. The company's growth soared in the early 1990s, fueled by its ability to tap into hot marketing trends. Between 1989 and 1993, Bed Bath & Beyond increased its number of stores from 24 to 38 in 11 states.

Going Public in the Early 1990s

Bed Bath & Beyond went public on the NASDAQ exchange in June 1992, trading at $17 per share. The company immediately became a Wall Street favorite, fueled by a rush of media coverage and the successful launch of a new Manhattan store. Analysts noted that, given the popularity of the merchandising concept that the company was championing, the timing to go public was ideal. By May 1993, shares were trading around $32 as the company announced record sales for the year: $216.7 million in sales, with earnings of $15.9 million.

As proof of Bed Bath & Beyond's status as a trendsetter, one needed only to examine the success of its Manhattan store. The store opened in November 1992, in what had been an abandoned, graffiti-covered department store at the heart of a dismal section of the city known as Ladies Mile. At the beginning of the 20th century, Ladies Mile had been a booming retail center, revered as the place where upscale, fashionable ladies bought their clothing. By 1990, despite its desirable location in the center of Manhattan, the district was a mess. When Bed Bath & Beyond opened, however, it kindled a renaissance of the neighborhood. Within a year, a number of other superstores, including Barnes & Noble books, Today's Man menswear, and Staples, a discount office supply chain, had also renovated boarded-up old emporiums. Bed Bath & Beyond added 30,000 more square feet to the store and it became the company's flagship store, a site where new merchandising concepts (such as a café and the introduction of gourmet food products) were given trial runs.

While Bed Bath & Beyond enjoyed tremendous success during this period in the home furnishings business, competitors sought to erode the company's standing. In the early 1990s, its primary rival, Linens 'n Things, began blatantly imitating its merchandising format. Supported by Melville Corp., a large conglomerate whose financial resources far outstripped Bed Bath & Beyond's, Linens 'n Things operated a chain of 144 stores by 1993 with annual sales around $290 million.

Linens 'n Things, which had utilized an integrated computer system since the late 1980s, enjoyed a tremendous advantage

Key Dates:

1971: Feinstein and Eisenberg establish Bed 'n Bath.
1985: Seventeen stores operate in New York, New Jersey, Connecticut, and California, and the first superstore is opened.
1987: The company's name is changed to Bed Bath & Beyond.
1991: Sales reach $134 million.
1992: The firm goes public.
1994: Electric appliances are added the store's product offerings.
1999: Sales exceed $1 billion.
2000: The firm grows to 311 stores in 43 states.

over Bed Bath & Beyond in the inventory management area. In 1993, however, Bed Bath & Beyond installed integrated computer systems in all stores that allowed managers to track inventory, sales, and receivables more efficiently. The new automated system also enabled the company to develop a chainwide bridal registry that analysts estimated would add another 15 percent to annual sales.

Luxury Linens and Pacific Linens also posed a threat to Bed Bath & Beyond's attempts to venture into new markets. Still, the company enjoyed a 37 percent increase in sales in 1992 as it continued to grow without benefit of acquisitions. Most competitors, on the other hand, relied on expansion through acquisitions to a much greater degree. Sales in the first six months of 1993, increased 43 percent and earnings improved by 47 percent, garnering Bed Bath & Beyond first place recognition in the *Chain Store Executive* survey of high performance retailers.

In 1994, the company began offering such small electric appliances as coffee makers, hair dryers, toaster ovens, and vacuum cleaners. Other home accessories like gourmet foods, clocks, and lamps were added to the product line as well. This further broadened its customer base and fortified the chain's edge in the retail market.

Continued Success the Mid- to Late 1990s

Entering the mid-1990s, Bed Bath & Beyond noted that none of its competition offered the diversity of products it sold. Moreover, no competitors were able to achieve the profit margins registered by Bed Bath & Beyond. By 1997, Bed Bath & Beyond planned to have approximately 100 stores across the United States, and Feinstein predicted that company sales would rise by 30 to 35 percent by that time.

The proliferating number of imitators, however, had created what *Barron's* called ''a treacherous environment requiring astute management.'' Analysts feared that the market would be saturated by the year 2000 and that perhaps Bed Bath & Beyond's impressive earnings had already peaked. They noted that by 1994, Feinstein, Eisenberg, and members of their respective families had sold almost five million shares of the firm—in 2000, they each both owned 5.1 percent of the firm. Nevertheless, Feinstein and Eisenberg remained the driving force behind the company.

As Bed Bath & Beyond entered the late 1990s, speculation that the company's earnings would suffer was brought to rest. Despite analyst's fears, the firm recorded record profits and earnings. In 1997 and 1998, 61 new stores were opened, exceeding company goals set in the mid-1990s. Bed Bath & Beyond also purchased an interest in Internet Gift Registries and began e-commerce on its web site.

In 1999, the company surpassed the $1 billion mark, recording its eighth consecutive year of record earnings. Growth also continued, as 45 new stores were opened that year. During this period of rapid expansion, 85 percent of a store's square footage was dedicated to selling space. The continued practice of eschewing a centralized warehouse enabled the company to open stores in any area it wished. As it had in the past, inventory was shipped directly to the store and piled from the floor to the ceiling. Utilizing this method in the late 1990s, the company was able to secure some $208, per square foot, per store, a rate 17 percent higher than that realized by competitor Linens 'n Things.

Positive Outlook in the New Millennium

As Bed Bath & Beyond entered the new millennium, it operated over 250 stores and had expanded into Rhode Island, Idaho, Maine, Mississippi, and North Dakota. With no debt—the company utilized cash flow for expansion—the firm's stock consistently grew since its launch in 1992 and analysts predicted its growth would continue. In July 2000, the company announced a two-for-one stock split. Bed Bath & Beyond's success was apparent as the firm ended the year with over $2 billion in sales and a store count of over 300 in 43 states.

Its discount prices, warehouse merchandising style, conservative advertising budgets, and highly successful web site helped secure record earnings and profits for the company, and management anticipated similar results in the future. The firm planned to open 80 new stores in 2001, a total of 2.4 million square feet. With co-CEOs Feinstein and Eisenberg—the pair reportedly spoke on a daily basis and were the executors of each other's estates—at the helm of the 30-year old company, Bed Bath & Beyond's continued success in the future seemed evident. Feinstein commented on the strong relationship with his co-founder in a 2000 *Forbes* article stating, ''there aren't many good marriages out there, but when you've got one of the great ones, it's wonderful.''

Principal Competitors

Linens 'n Things Inc.; Target Corp.; J.C. Penney Company, Inc.

Further Reading

''Bigger Stores, Bigger Profits Boost Bed Bath & Beyond,'' *Chain Store Executive*, November 1993, p. 21.

Kroll, Luisa, ''Bed Bath & Beyond Happy Together,'' *Forbes*, January 10, 2000, p. 156.

Lieber, Ed, ''Warren Eisenberg, Leonard Feinstein; Bed Bath & Beyond,'' *HFN—The Weekly Newspaper for the Home Furnishing Network*, November 27, 2000, p. 42.

Munarriz, Rick A., ''To Infinity and Bed, Bath & Beyond,'' *Motley Fool*, February 22, 2001.

Norton, Leslie P., ''One Step Beyond,'' *Barron's*, August 8, 1994, p. 17.

''A Retail Odyssey,'' *HFN—The Weekly Newspaper for the Home Furnishing Network*, January 1, 2001, p. 10.

Shoulberg, Warren, ''Way Beyond,'' *Home Textiles Today*, September 6, 1993, p. 1.

Slesin, Suzanne, ''It's Fun. It's Romantic. It's Soap and Dish Towels,'' *New York Times*, November 16, 1992, p. C1.

Zaczkiewicz, Arthur, ''Bed Bath & Beyond Beats the Odds in Q3,'' *HFN—The Weekly Newspaper for the Home Furnishing Network*, December 18, 2000, p. 4.

—Maura Troester
—update: Christina M. Stansell

BILL & MELINDA GATES *foundation*

Bill & Melinda Gates Foundation

P.O. Box 23350
Seattle, Washington 98102
U.S.A.
Telephone: (206) 709-3100
Fax: (206) 709-3252
Web site: http://www.gatesfoundation.org

Non-Profit Foundation
Incorporated: 1994 as the William H. Gates Foundation
Employees: 200
Total Assets: $21.8 billion (2000)
NAIC: 813211 Grantmaking Foundations

The Bill & Melinda Gates Foundation is the world's largest charitable foundation. Its assets of approximately $22 billion dwarf most other foundations, including such well-known giants as the Ford Foundation, the Carnegie Corp., and the Rockefeller Foundation. The Gates Foundation gives away approximately $1 billion annually. Its overarching philanthropic goals are to promote education and health for the world's underprivileged. The Gates Foundation funds a variety of health initiatives in the developing world, such as the search for vaccines for AIDS and malaria. Its educational initiatives include a minority scholarship program and a campaign to provide computers to needy public libraries across the United States and Canada. The Gates Foundation's assets are provided by Bill Gates, founder of the computer software firm Microsoft, and his wife Melinda French Gates. Top executives at the Gates Foundation include Bill Gates's father, William H. Gates, Sr., and Patty Stonesifer, formerly the top female executive at Microsoft.

Funding a Foundation with the Microsoft Fortune in 1994

The enormous endowment of the Bill & Melinda Gates Foundation springs from the fortune of the computer magnate Bill Gates, Harvard University's most successful dropout. Gates left Harvard when he was still only 19 and founded a computer software company in 1975 with a longtime friend, Paul Allen. Their company, Microsoft, was chosen by IBM in 1980 to write the operating system for the computer maker's new personal computers. Microsoft's operating system, called MS-DOS, became the standard operating system used on all IBM-compatible personal computers. Microsoft reaped vast amounts of money from the licensing of its system. In 1986, Microsoft went public. Gates's stake in the hugely profitable company made him a billionaire, and he was soon touted as the world's richest man. His fortune was estimated at around $65 billion at the end of the century. The company continued to grow and expand into the 1990s, as it developed or acquired many new software products. Microsoft was the world's leading software company, an indomitable competitor in the booming software industry.

Microsoft generated great wealth, not only for Gates and cofounder Allen, but for scores of executives whose stock in the company made them rich. Many Microsoft executives were young, and they found themselves able to retire comfortably by age 40. According to a July 24, 2000 article in *Time,* dozens of Microsoft millionaires set up charitable foundations in the 1990s. ''The status symbol of the '80s was a BMW. The status symbol of this decade is having your own foundation named after you,'' claimed a Microsoft employee quoted in the article.

Gates himself became one of the richest men on the planet while he was still in his 30s. Gates was instrumental to the running of his company and seemed to have no plans to step back from the extraordinary business he had founded in his teens. Yet Microsoft's competitive clout in the 1990s won it much criticism. Antitrust allegations soured a major acquisition the company planned to make in 1995, and in 1998 the United States Justice Department filed a far-reaching antitrust suit against Microsoft. The perpetually boyish, bespectacled Gates was also at times reviled as the personification of a company perceived by some as greedy and rapacious. He was called a miser, for holding on to his personal fortune. Microsoft had initiated a giving program as early as 1983, which at first focused on funding computer and science education scholarships. Gates arranged for charitable giving of his own wealth in the mid-1990s, when he announced that he intended to give away most of his money before his death.

Gates established a foundation for the charitable disbursement of much of his wealth in 1994, shortly after his marriage to

Company Perspectives:

The Bill & Melinda Gates Foundation places a major focus on helping to improve people's lives through health and learning. We will continue to look for strategic opportunities to extend the benefits of modern science and technology to people around the world, especially where poverty serves as an obstacle to participating in these benefits. As in the past, we will invest in partnerships with individuals and organizations that bring experience, expertise and commitment to their own efforts to help people through better health and learning.

Melinda French. This was known as the William H. Gates Foundation, and it was run by Gates's father, a Seattle lawyer, initially from the basement of his home. Apparently, Gates's marriage to Melinda French spurred the billionaire to find a way to give back some of his money. French grew up in Texas and studied computer science, engineering, and business at Duke University before joining Microsoft in 1987. While working as project manager at Microsoft, she also volunteered her time at a Seattle high school. On the eve of French and Gates's marriage, Gates's mother read the couple a letter that seemed to prod them to consider what to do with their plenty. As paraphrased in an article in the *New York Times Magazine* (April 16, 2000), it read, ''From those who are given great resources, great things are expected.'' The magazine also went on to claim that French was the instigator in the move toward building the Gates Foundation.

Administering Several Foundations in the Middle to Late 1990s

The William H. Gates Foundation began with an endowment of $106 million. Gates's father, who had retired from his law firm, volunteered to run the organization. Though active in local charity works, Gates, Sr., had no actual background in running a foundation. Although Gates was urged to hire someone with a professional background in charitable giving, the Gates Foundation continued to be overseen by Gates, Sr., Bill, and Melinda, and since 1997, former Microsoft executive Patty Stonesifer. Over its first several years, Bill and Melinda Gates added about $2 billion to the foundation. Some of its first projects were oriented to the Seattle and Pacific Northwest area. The Gates Foundation contributed $2 million to the Seattle Area YMCA, $20 million to the Seattle Public Library, and $1 million to the Tacoma Art Museum. Aside from programs that benefited the Northwest, the Gates Foundation also began to target educational programs and issues of global health.

In 1997 the Gateses endowed a separate charitable program, targeting $200 million for the Gates Library Foundation. The object of this charity was to overcome the so-called digital divide, where wealthier people had access to technology and information and poorer people did not. The Library Foundation planned to bring computers to poor and underserved public libraries across the country. The Library Foundation not only provided the computers, but also furnished Internet access and gave training and technical support to librarians. While both Gates Foundations were run by a very small staff, the library initiative required a flock of hundreds of paid technicians to do the installation and training across the United States and Canada. Patty Stonesifer, an old friend and coworker of Bill and Melinda, ran the library program. Over the next three years, the library initiative installed more than 22,000 computers in roughly 4,500 libraries in the United States. An additional 1,400 libraries in Canada were provided with some 4,000 computers total. The library program was expected to take until 2005 to serve all the needy North American libraries. After that, the foundation expected to expand the program to libraries worldwide.

Gates and his wife both had a consuming interest in computers and technology, given their work for Microsoft. A program like the library initiative seemed a natural place to spend a fortune made in software. But the Gateses became aware that simply giving people technology was not always effective charity. Gates recounted to the *New York Times Magazine* a trip he took to South Africa in the mid-1990s. Inhabitants of a poor ghetto eagerly showed the Microsoft billionaire the town's only computer. Gates noticed that the town also had only a single electrical outlet. Gates told the magazine, ''I looked around and thought, Hmmm, computers may not be the highest priority in this particular place.'' Gates and his family members began researching other areas where the Gates Foundation might make a difference. In the late 1990s, the Gates Foundation began funding a variety of healthcare programs designed to improve conditions in the developing world. This was an area where money was sadly lacking, due to market forces. Pharmaceutical companies had little incentive to spend research and development funds on Third World diseases such as malaria. Despite the vast numbers of people affected by malaria (about 200 million yearly), drug companies could not expect to make a profit from customers in the world's poorest nations. Thus the amount spent on vaccine development was fairly low. Worldwide spending on malaria vaccine research in the mid-1990s was about $60 million. In 1999 the Gates Foundation funded a $50 million Malaria Vaccine Initiative, making it the single biggest backer of malaria research. The Gates Foundation also funded a $100 million Children's Vaccine Program. This was to distribute vaccines in the Third World that were already commonly in use in the developed world. The vaccine program would buy and distribute vaccines for common childhood diseases such as tetanus, polio, whooping cough, diptheria, and measles in countries where existing healthcare programs were inadequate.

The Gates Foundation also funded research on a vaccine for AIDS. Seventy percent of AIDS sufferers were in sub-Saharan Africa, in poor countries where drug companies did not expect much return on their research investment. At the international AIDS conference in 1998, the Gates Foundation announced an initial gift of $1.5 million for its International AIDS Vaccine Initiative. The Gates gift promptly attracted other donations, one from the British government and one from the Elton John Foundation. The Gates Foundation increased its AIDS vaccine funding to $25 million the next year. The AIDS initiative targeted promising research, and helped drug manufacturers speed the work to clinical trials. In exchange for funding research, the Gates Foundation expected the pharmaceutical companies to provide resulting drugs or vaccine at low cost to developing countries. The AIDS Vaccine Initiative left the drug companies free to charge what they wanted for their new

Key Dates:

1994: William H. Gates Foundation is founded.
1997: Gates Library Foundation is founded.
1999: All Gates foundations are folded into one organization.
2000: First Millennium Scholars are chosen.

products in the United States, where there was some hope of profit. AIDS researchers agreed that the search for a vaccine seemed very difficult because of the peculiar nature of the AIDS virus. The Gates Foundation was able to provide money to researchers much more quickly than other organizations like the National Institutes of Health, and so gave needed momentum to a difficult project. The Gates Foundation gave money to other, similar healthcare projects as well. It funded work to detect and cure cervical cancer in 1999, giving $50 million to an existing network of care providers in Africa. The foundation's total spending on global health initiatives was estimated at around $400 million annually by 2000.

The Gates Foundation also was interested in helping disadvantaged students in the United States and elsewhere get access to quality education. In February 1999 the Gateses endowed a new foundation, the Gates Learning Foundation. Like the Gates Library Foundation, the Learning Foundation aimed to bridge the digital divide, providing access to technology for people who otherwise might not be exposed to it. With $1 billion, the foundation announced that it would provide college scholarships to 20,000 minority students over the next two decades. The foundation ran its Millennium Scholars Program through the United Negro College Fund, the Hispanic Scholarship Fund, and the American Indian College Fund. To be eligible, students had to be enrolled in a four-year college program and studying within certain specified fields. The winners received a grant to cover the difference between their financial aid package and the actual cost of their college education, including housing and books. The first winners for the program were picked in 2000. That year, the foundation also announced a similar scholarship program, to pay for graduate study at the University of Cambridge in England. The $210 million fund was intended primarily for students from developing countries.

Consolidation into One Foundation in 1999

By 1999, the Gates fortune was spread between three foundations: the William H. Gates Foundation, begun in 1994, the Gates Library Foundation, and the Gates Learning Foundation. These three had overlapping goals of providing opportunities for healthcare and education. In August 1999, the three foundations were folded into one, under the name the Bill & Melinda Gates Foundation. The foundation moved into a new building in Seattle, leaving the elder Mr. Gates's basement at last. Gates and his wife also stepped up the rate they gave to their foundation, infusing quarterly chunks of $5 billion and $6 billion at a time. In October 1999 it had assets of $17.1 billion, which made it the richest endowed foundation in the world. A year later, its endowment had reached $21.8 billion. According to *Time* magazine (July 24, 2000), Bill Gates had given "more money away faster than anyone else in history." Its largest programs were the $1 billion Millennium Scholarship Program, the $750 million grant to the Global Alliance for Vaccines and Immunization, and $350 million earmarked for teachers and schools in the United States for a variety of educational improvements. Even its smaller grants were huge, such as the $50 million for malaria vaccine research, another $50 million for groups working for the worldwide eradication of polio, and $25 million for a group fighting tuberculosis worldwide. Most of the Gates Foundation's projects were long-term, with results not expected for years, or even decades. So by 2001 it was still too early to see concrete results, such as the actual development of a successful AIDS vaccine. Yet in the few short years of its existence, the Gates Foundation had already had a marked impact, putting millions of dollars into areas that might otherwise have received little attention.

Principal Competitors

The Wellcome Trust; David and Lucile Packard Foundation; Carnegie Corp. of New York.

Further Reading

"The Art of Giving," *Business Week,* October 25, 1999, p. 80.
Cantrell, John, "Father Gives Best," *Town & Country,* December 1999, p. 210.
"Giving Billions Isn't Easy," *Time,* July 24, 2000, pp. 52–53.
Hardy, Quentin, "The World's Richest Donors," *Forbes,* May 1, 2000, p. 114.
Lewin, Tamar, "Gates Foundation Names 4,100 Minority Scholarships in 2-Decade Program," *New York Times,* June 9, 2000, p. C10.
Reis, George R., "U.S. Philanthropy Boosted by High-Tech Billions," *Fund Raising Management,* August 1999, p. 5.
Strouse, Jean, "How to Give Away $21.8 Billion," *New York Times Magazine,* April 16, 2000, pp. 56+.
Tice, Carol, "Gates Fund Earning Nonprofits' Respect," *Puget Sound Business Journal,* February 16, 2001, p. 13.
Waldhole, Michael, "Group Pledges $150 Million in Bid to Boost Children's Vaccinations," *Wall Street Journal,* September 21, 2000, p. B2.

—A. Woodward

Blue Square Israel Ltd.

2 Amal Street
Afek ind, zone
Rosh Haayin 48092
Israel
Telephone: (+972) 3-9282222
Fax: (+972) 3-9282999
Web site: http://www.coop.co.il

Public Subsidiary of Co-Op Blue Square Consumer Cooperative Society
Incorporated: 1991
Employees: 7,400
Sales: NIS 5.2 billion ($1.29 billion) (2000)
Stock Exchanges: Tel Aviv New York
Ticker Symbol: BSI
NAIC: 44511 Supermarkets and Other Grocery (Except Convenience) Stores

Israeli retail leader Blue Square Israel Ltd. is helping to change the way Israel shops. The publicly listed company on both New York and Tel Aviv stock exchanges is a subsidiary of Co-Op Blue Square Consumer Cooperative Society, which owns 80 percent of Blue Square Israel and is itself preparing to convert from its cooperative status into that of a publicly listed corporation. After selling off a number of diversified interests, including department stores, furniture centers, DIY stores, and retail franchises for such international brands as Zara and HM, much of which were sold back to its Co-Op parent, Blue Square Israel is concentrating on building its nationally operating network of more than 170 supermarkets. Since the late 1990s, Blue Square has been consolidating its supermarket operations into several supermarket formats to position itself within each of Israel's varied consumer segments. The company's youngest is the low-priced Mega Outlet, featuring selling floor space of more than 5,000 square meters, launched in 1999. At the end of 2000, there were seven Mega Outlets operating in Jerusalem, Holon, outside of Tel Aviv, Beer Sheva, Hadera, and Netanya, and two stores in Haifa. The company's primary retail chains operate under the Super Center, Super Co-Op, and Hyper Co-Op banners, accounting for the bulk of the company's retail portfolio and sales. More specialized formats include Pharm Store, a pharmacy chain located primarily as in-store shops in the company's larger supermarkets; and Shefa Mehadrin, a supermarket chain catering to the specific demands of Israel's large ultra-orthodox population. The company is phasing out its small-format, discount Zil v'Zol, in favor of the new Super Center City store format meant to compete with the country's open-air markets and traditional small grocer shops. Blue Square also has targeted Israel's Arab citizens, adapting its stores for these customers as well. In addition, Blue Square Israel has launched an on-line shopping site. The company has more than 250,000 square meters of total selling space. With sales of NIS 5.2 billion ($1.29 billion), Blue Square retains the leading share as the country's largest retailer, ahead of rival Super Sol Ltd. Yet the relatively low supermarket penetration in the country, where open-air markets and small stores still account for more than half of all food and clothing purchases, gives Blue Square plenty of room for future growth.

Cooperative Pioneers in the 1930s

Blue Square traced its origins to the pre-Israel 1920s, when a group of workers in the town of Givatayim set up their own cooperative grocery business. Inspired in part by the socialist idealism that formed the backbone of the growing Zionist movement and based on a model already prevalent in Europe, the cooperative was also a means for its members to make their food purchases at lower prices than they could find otherwise. Operated by workers for workers, this first cooperative proved to be the first of many similar cooperative ventures across the then-British colony.

Blue Square's oldest direct predecessor was the labor federation Histadrut's cooperative set up on Tel Aviv's Reines Street in 1937. This and the many other cooperatives formed during the prewar years bore little resemblance to supermarkets. Often operated from their members' homes, the cooperatives' products were available only to members, who each paid annual fees and often provided manpower as well. By the mid-1940s, there were more than 26,000 cooperative members throughout Israel, and their purchase power already represented some 3 percent of

Company Perspectives:

We know the Israeli population very well and have a clear vision of how the Israeli retail scene will look in the future. Ten years ago, it was difficult to imagine that shopping in Israel could change so completely in such a short time. We foresaw the process, and are now moving to the next stage. Our expansion plan is the key to spreading our retailing vision to every corner of Israel and every Israeli shopper.

the near-nation's total retail activity. The cooperatives remained small, independent operations, linked together in a more or less informal affiliation.

The end of the first Arab-Israeli war in 1948 and the creation of the state of Israel that same year gave new impetus to the cooperative movement. The cooperative movement fitted in well with the spirit of the times, as the Socialist-led country, together with the strong kibbutz and related moshav movements, set about building the nation. The food cooperatives were able to offer products at fair prices despite a long period of food shortages and rationing.

The rise of Tel Aviv as Israel's financial and business center helped the Reines Street cooperative grow strongly through the 1950s. Leading the cooperative then was Yehoshua Rabinowitz, who also served as the city's deputy mayor. Rabinowitz began a policy of purchasing properties with the cooperative's profits, thereby acquiring a number of prime real estate plots. The cooperative's strong real estate portfolio formed the foundation for its future growth, as well as later subsidiary Blue Square Properties.

Rabinowitz was also behind the process that slowly brought Israel's many independent cooperatives together. By the end of the 1950s, Rabinowitz had helped put into place a centralized wholesale buying operation from which Tel Aviv's many cooperatives could do their purchase. Their combined purchase power also enabled the cooperatives to demand lower prices from often unscrupulous suppliers. Combining purchasing activities proved a first step toward the consolidation of the cooperative market. Toward the beginning of the 1960s, cooperatives in each of the country's major cities began to join together before starting a long process of local mergers that took off toward the end of the decade.

Merging Toward Retail Dominance in the 1970s

The 1960s marked the beginning of a different revolution for the young country. The first supermarket appeared, opened by longtime Blue Square rival Super Sol Ltd. The Tel Aviv cooperative, which had by then grown to include most of the city's formerly independent cooperatives, opened its own supermarket, Shefa Chen, on Tel Aviv's Dizengoff Square in 1962.

During the 1960s, the Tel Aviv and other Histadrut-related cooperatives became affiliated under the Hevrat Ovdim holding company. The cooperatives were then operated under the Israeli branch of the 28-nation international cooperatives organization Consumers Cooperative Union-Central Cooperative Society (CCUCCS). The Histadrut cooperatives were granted permission to use the CCUCCS's Co-Op name. The Tel Aviv group was now known as Co-Op Tel Aviv Consumer's Society.

Co-Op Tel Aviv Consumer's Society joined in the consolidation of the country's cooperative market, merging with the cooperative groups in the cities of Bat Yam, Holon, Eilat, and others at the end of the 1960s before turning to larger-scale mergers in the 1970s. The cooperative launched that decade with the merger agreement with the Dan Hasharon Consumer's Society in 1972, which already had taken over the Haifa and Hadera cooperatives, among others.

Impetus toward consolidation was provided by the growing strength of Super Sol and other supermarkets in Israel. Nonetheless, Israel's retail climate remained dominated by more traditional open-air markets and small, so-called "mom-and-pop" corner shops. Throughout the 1980s, these sectors remained the largest sources of food, clothing, and other household good sales. During that decade, however, the growing Co-Op Tel Aviv group began adopting a more modern format, helping to transform the Israeli retail map.

Modern Supermarket Culture for the New Century

Much of the cooperative's modernization was credited to Benny Gaon, who served as the cooperative's president and CEO throughout most of the 1980s and later became Blue Square's chairman. Gaon instituted many of the changes that later enabled Blue Square to capture the leading share of Israel's retail market. An important change was the conversion of the group's grocery store format into the more modern supermarket format. The company also adopted new marketing techniques, and, significantly, moved toward a more traditional corporate culture.

An important move came when the cooperative created a limited company, Blue Square Israel, for its retail holdings, and formed a subsidiary under Blue Square Israel, called Blue Square Property and Investments, which then began issuing bonds on the Tel Aviv stock exchange in 1988. These moves enabled parent company Co-Op Blue Square, which adopted the name of Co-Op Blue Square Consumer Cooperative Society in 1992, to skirt restrictions that prevented it from raising capital through public placements. Until then, when the society had needed investment funding, it had been forced to seek capital from its own members.

When Gaon stepped down from the CEO spot in 1988, replaced by Yoseph Rosen, Blue Square was poised to enter a new growth phase. In 1991, Blue Square Property and Investments took a listing on the Tel Aviv stock exchange, selling some NIS 37 million in shares and options, approximately 10 percent of which had been bought by cooperative members. The following year, Blue Square merged with Jerusalem's co-op. At the same time, Blue Square acquired another cooperative, Hamashbir Central Cooperative Society for Supply, adding a department store component under the Hamashbir Lazarchan name.

Rosen left Blue Square in 1993, replaced by Ya'acov Gelbard. The company began expanding beyond supermarkets into other retail sectors, including a licensing agreement with

Key Dates:

1937: Tel Aviv co-op is founded.
1962: Shefa Chen supermarket is opened.
1972: The company takes the name of Co-Op Tel Aviv Consumer's Society; merges with the Dan Hasharon Consumer's Society.
1991: The company creates and floats Blue Square Property and Investments on Tel Aviv exchange.
1993: The company acquires Hamashbir Central Cooperative Society for Supply.
1996: The company is listed on the New York Stock Exchange.
1998: The company begins divesting nonsupermarket operations.
1999: The Mega Outlet format is launched.
2001: The company agrees to carry Leader Price private label products.

the United Kingdom's Marks & Spencer, and franchises of other retail brands, including Bon Mart, Pull & Bear, Mango, Guess, Mothercare, ID Design, and Zara, while building up DIY retail chain Home Center with partner Bilu Enterprise HC Ltd. By 1995, the group's total sales had topped $700 million.

Blue Square went public a second time in 1996, as Blue Square Israel itself took a listing on the New York stock exchange, selling some 19 percent of its shares, with the remainder held by parent Co-Op Blue Square Consumer Cooperative Society. The company continued to expand through the country, acquiring a number of other as-yet unconsolidated cooperatives. Blue Square also began adopting cutting-edge supermarket techniques and methods pioneered in the United States and Europe, such as the creation of ''Buy and Bonus'' customer fidelity program; the opening of a centralized distribution center; and the development of a state-of-the-art computerized information system.

In 1997, Blue Square took another initiative aimed at increasing its margins while lowering prices for its customers. The company unveiled its own private label brand, Select, for a variety of products including frozen foods, housecleaning supplies, and cosmetics. Meanwhile, Blue Square continued to grow, acquiring the six-store chain of Co-Op Ra'anana. The company also continued to develop and refine its grocery store and supermarket formats. By 1998, the company operated more than 150 stores under five store formats targeted at specific customer sectors, reflecting the diversity of Israel's population. The company's embrace expanded for the first time to Israel's Arab population, when the company opened its first store in Shfar'AM with a product range catering to that population.

Blue Square's operations at the time included another 44 specialty and department stores, as well as a new franchise to develop IKEA stores in Israel. Yet at the end of 1998, Blue Square had decided to divest its nonsupermarket holdings. The company already had abandoned its Marks & Spencer franchise in 1997, converting those locations to other brands. Blue Square sold its Hamashbir Lezarchan department store group to its parent at the end of 1998. That deal included most of Blue Square's other specialty retail holdings as well. The divestment coincided with a stepping up of Blue Square's supermarket openings—the end of 1998 saw 11 new stores open in just four months.

Helping guide the company's refocus was Yoram Dar, then in grooming to take over the president and CEO position as Ya'akov Gelbard prepared to retire in 1999. Dar, a 20-year veteran of the company, continued Blue Square's supermarket expansion, launching a new store format, the 5,000-square-meter Mega Outlet store, designed as a ''one-stop shopping'' environment with groceries, restaurants, and other retail goods and services. The discount Mega formula was a hit with Israeli consumers, and by 2001 the company prepared to open its ninth Mega Outlet store.

As parent Co-Op prepared for its own conversion from cooperative society to public company, Blue Square Israel enjoyed steady sales increases. The company also was working hard to improve its margins, including a stepping up of the number of private label goods present on its stores' shelves. Blue Square hoped to build private label scales to more than 10 percent of total sales by 2002, in part by boosting the number of SKUs to as many as 2,500 products. In 2001, Blue Square took a major step toward that goal when it reached an agreement with number-two French hypermarket group Casino to bring that company's Leader Price private label brand into the Blue Star retail network. The agreement, made in February 2001, also called for Blue Square to drop its own and other private labels currently in its stores. Meanwhile, Blue Square continued to seek expansion in Israel. Whereas Blue Square had been an important force beyond the shifting consumer trends, nearly doubling the supermarket sector's percentage of total sales since the early 1990s, some 50 percent of Israel's population had not yet converted to the call of Blue Square's modern supermarkets.

Principal Subsidiaries

Blue Square Properties & Investments Ltd. (80%); The Blue Square Chain (Hyper Hyper Ltd.); Pharam Blue Square Ltd.; Radio Non-stop Ltd. (35.8%).

Principal Competitors

Super Sol Ltd.

Further Reading

''Blue Square Israel in Talks with French Retailer Casino,'' *Jerusalem Post,* January 23, 2001, p. 12.
Gerstenfeld, Dan, ''Blue Square to Sell Hamashbir Stake,'' *Jerusalem Post,* July 22, 1998, p. 13.
Lipkis Beck, Galit, ''Co-Op to Raise $100m on Wall St.,'' *Jerusalem Post,* July 5, 1997, p. 15.
Neiman, Rachel, ''Sixty Years of Store-Hood,'' *Jerusalem Post,* September 16,1997, p. 11.

—M.L. Cohen

BOOKS-A-MILLION

Books-A-Million, Inc.

402 Industrial Lane
Birmingham, Alabama 35211
P.O. Box 19768
Birmingham, Alabama 36219
U.S.A.
Telephone: (205) 942-3737
Fax: (205) 942-6601
Web site: http://www.booksamillion.com

Public Company
Incorporated: 1964 as Bookland
Employees: 4,900
Sales: $418.6 million (2001)
Stock Exchanges: NASDAQ
Ticker Symbol: BAMM
NAIC: 451211 Book Stores

Books-A-Million, Inc. is the third-largest book retailer in the United States, ranking behind Barnes & Noble and the Borders Group. Based in Birmingham, Alabama, the company operates 202 stores in a total of 18 states, ranging from Texas to the mid-Atlantic region. The majority of these are Books-A-Million discount superstores. Others are more traditional Bookland stores, some of which (combination stores) offer gifts and greeting cards in addition to books and periodicals. Additionally, Books-A-Million operates Joe Muggs Newsstands. Also, apart from its primary retail components, the corporation has a book wholesale and distribution subsidiary, American Wholesale Book Company; an e-commerce division operating as booksamillion.com; and an Internet development and services company, NetCentral, in Nashville, Tennessee. Books-A-Million, as booksamillion.com, sells a range of products online via its wholly owned subsidiary, AIS (AmericanInternetServices). Booksamillion.com also runs an online café, Joemuggs.com, which offers a wide selection of whole bean coffee, confections, and related gift items.

Newspaper Stand Becomes a Bona Fide Bookshop

Books-A-Million's roots go back to a humble newspaper stand constructed in 1917 by 14-year-old Clyde W. Anderson, who had dropped out of school to support his family upon the death of his father. The young man's first job was delivering newspapers in his hometown of Florence, Alabama. Shortly after he began selling newspapers, a large group of construction workers from the North came to town to build the Wilson Dam. When they mentioned to the young newspaper boy that they missed reading their hometown newspapers, Anderson contacted northern newspaper publishers and made a deal with the railroad to have the papers delivered to Florence. Using old piano crates, Anderson built a newsstand, and business was soon booming. Within a few years, he and his brother were able to invest their profits in a bona fide book shop.

In 1950 Anderson's son, Charles C. Anderson, inherited the book store and expanded it into a chain of stores called Bookland, which were incorporated under that name in 1964. During the 1970s, Bookland expanded rapidly as shopping malls sprang up across the American landscape, and by 1980 Anderson operated 50 stores located primarily in shopping malls throughout the Southeast. Charles C. also established a book and periodical distribution business. When his sons, Charles, Jr., and Clyde B., were old enough, they began working in the wholesale business and book store, respectively.

In 1988, Bookland doubled its size when it bought Gateway Books, a chain of stores based in Knoxville, Tennessee. According to the young Clyde B. (who had moved into senior management after graduating from the University of Alabama), many Gateway stores were poor performers. Within two years, Bookland had closed 27 of 50 Gateway stores, a move that left the company with many excess books and store fixtures. These three factors—excess books, excess fixtures, and a young executive with big plans—combined to become the driving forces behind the company's move into superstores.

In 1988 the youngest Anderson led the company to open an 8,000-square-foot store in a shopping center in Huntsville, Alabama. By his own account, the store—furnished in part with

Company Perspectives:

The Company's growth strategy is focused on opening superstores in new and existing markets, particularly in the Southeast. In addition to opening new stores, management intends to continue its practice of reviewing the profitability trends and prospects of existing stores and closing or relocating underperforming stores or converting stores to different formats.

fixtures and stock from the abandoned Gateway stores—was a flop. "It was one of my early learning experiences," he reported in an interview with *Birmingham* magazine. Shortly afterward, however, the company opened a second superstore under the name Books-A-Million. The new superstore was located just down the street from the first one, but this time with 30,000 square feet of selling space, as opposed to 8,000. "We did very successfully from day one," Anderson told *Birmingham* magazine.

1989–91: Expanding the Superstore Format as Competition Stiffens

The company made the decision to expand into the superstore format at the right time. In other regions of the United States, larger book retailers, such as Barnes & Noble and Crown Books, had already begun to switch to the superstore format and were beginning to squeeze out smaller stores. The concept behind superstores was to establish specialty shops with an enormous selection of goods and prices comparable to, or lower than, department store sale prices. Bookstores were not the only retail businesses to explore this concept. Instituted by Toys 'R' Us in the early 1980s, the formula quickly spread into home furnishings (with Bed Bath 'N Beyond), electronics (with Circuit City), and do-it-yourself home improvement (with Builders Square).

Books-A-Million superstores sought to purchase books at high volume and pass the savings on to customers. To draw customers, bargain books—sold at 40 to 90 percent of publisher's suggested retail prices—were placed prominently in the front of the stores and updated weekly to keep bargain hunters coming back. In addition, the weekly top ten best sellers were offered for up to 40 percent off the publishers' suggested retail price, while paperbacks were offered at up to 25 percent off suggested retail prices.

Books-A-Million distinguished itself from its competitors by maintaining a regional focus at a time when national chains threatened to homogenize book selling. Individual Books-A-Million stores were given the freedom to launch marketing campaigns for books of particular interest to customers in their own markets. For example, books published by the *Birmingham News* on such topics as the University of Alabama's successful football season or the death of a local race-car celebrity, received special campaigns, as did *The Firm,* a first novel by Mississippi author John Grisham, which became a national bestseller and feature film. Books-A-Million was also one of the few book superstores to target medium-sized cities; its competitors most often chose to open new stores in larger metropolitan areas.

Bookland began opening new superstores at a rate of about ten per year while continuing to operate its smaller stores. Most of the company's 50 Bookland stores were located in shopping malls with department store anchors such as Sears and J.C. Penney's, or discounters like Wal-Mart or Kmart. Some of these were maintained according to their original format; others were converted to combination stores.

In a 1994 interview with *Retailing Today,* Anderson explained the reasons behind the decision to develop combination stores: "We're from a small town and we wanted a concept that would work in a small town. We found that some of these small towns couldn't support just a book store. But if you could have a combination book and something else—we developed a combination books and cards—that the economies of that may work."

1992–97: Going Public and Refining the Superstore Concept

In 1992 the company changed its name to Books-A-Million, Inc. and went public on the NASDAQ exchange, selling 2.6 million shares at $13 per share. (A secondary stock offering in October 1993 sold 1.25 million shares at $23 per share.) That year, Clyde B. Anderson became CEO. His father remained chairman, and Charles Anderson, Clyde's brother, took over the family's wholesale book and periodical distributorship.

The Anderson brothers proved to have a knack for marketing. "Get to know your customers and give 'em what they want," was Clyde's philosophy as told to *Forbes.* A prime example of his strategy occurred in 1993, the year the University of Alabama upset Miami in the Sugar Bowl. Although *Sports Illustrated* had decided not to feature the event as its cover story, the Anderson brothers convinced the magazine's editors to print 200,000 special editions of the magazine, put Alabama running back Derrick Lassic on the cover, and add additional stories about the Alabama victory. Books-A-Million bought all 200,000 copies of the special commemorative edition and within a month sold all of them, bringing in $900,000 and an estimated profit of $200,000.

By 1993 Books-A-Million operated 113 stores in cities and small towns across the southeastern Unites States. As the company grew, Anderson continued to expand the concept of a superstore. In addition to positioning itself as a bargain book outlet, Books-A-Million began developing the concept of bookstore-as-entertainment. Events such as book signings and readings (especially by Southern authors) became regular features, along with book-buying clubs and special discount cards. The company also strove to develop its customer service: book searches, special orders, and free gift wrapping encouraged customer loyalty. In 1993 about ten Books-A-Million stores contained espresso bars, which contributed to the store's image as a place to sit and enjoy books. Even the stores' hours of operation, from 9 a.m. to 11 p.m., encouraged visiting the store and browsing. "It's a very exciting place to be in our superstores," Anderson boasted to *Forbes.*

Books-A-Million also instituted a number of programs aimed at encouraging reading among children. By 1994 many stores

Key Dates:

1917: 14-year-old Clyde Anderson opens a newspaper stand in Florence, Alabama.
1950: Clyde Anderson's son, Charles, expands business into a bookstore chain called Bookland.
1988: Company buys Gateway Books and opens first book superstore.
1992: Bookland changes its name to Books-A-Million and goes public.
1994: Company purchases Books & Company of Dayton, Ohio.
1998: Books-A-Million launches its web site.
1999: Company acquires NetCentral.
2000: Charles Anderson retires, ceding company chairmanship to Clyde B. Anderson, the founder's grandson.

contained separate Kids-A-Million departments, colorful sections that offered a large selection of gifts, books, and videos for children. Weekly story hours were held, and the company supported local schools by offering discounts on library material and ordering bulk shipments of books on classroom reading lists.

In fiscal 1994 Books-A-Million had a profit margin of .046, the highest in the book superstore business, on net sales of $123.3 million. The company operated 84 Bookland stores and 29 superstores and was continuing to expand rapidly. By December 1994, the company operated 43 superstores across the southern United States. New stores were reported to cost $825,000 to build, but in 1994 start-up costs were recouped in less than one year.

Twenty more superstores were opened in fiscal 1995. Books-A-Million preferred to build its new superstores in regional shopping centers that had anchor tenants such as Toys 'R' Us or discount clothing chains like Marshalls and T.J. Maxx. Less desirable locations were shopping centers with upscale neighboring tenants such as the Talbot's clothing chain, or, on the opposite end, bargain factory outlets. In 70 percent of Books-A-Million's markets the company had no strong competitors; in the remaining 30 percent, its main competitor was Barnes & Noble. Some analysts feared that Books-A-Million superstores were pulling customers from its own Bookland stores, but Anderson told a group of investors in 1995 that sales erosion was minor and was ''more than offset by efficiencies in advertising and transportation costs.'' Sales in fiscal 1995 grew to $172.4 million, and net income grew to $8.1 million from $5.6 million in 1994. Same-store sales increased 13.8 percent for superstores and 6.4 percent for all stores.

Over the next two years, Books-A-Million continued to fare very well. Although its net income dropped off somewhat, its total sales grew to $229.8 million in 1996 and to $278.6 million in 1997. Over the same period, the total number of stores increased from 124 to 151. Significantly, the number of superstores grew from 45 to 91, while the number of traditional bookstores fell from 45 to 38 and combination stores from 34 to 30. The numbers reflected the company's determination to meet its chief competitor, Barnes & Noble, head-to-head in the discount marketplace. Books-A-Million was also looking for new marketing avenues, including those offered through computers and the World Wide Web.

1998–2001: Growth and Diversification through E-Commerce and Acquisitions

In the final years of the century, with its typical market savvy and flexibility, Books-A-Million entered the burgeoning world of e-commerce. In 1998, it put its own web site on the Internet. Later in the same year, after enhancing its original site, the company acquired NetCentral, the Nashville, Tennessee-based Internet development and services firm that specialized in design and e-commerce solutions. It was NetCentral that had designed and developed the newly refurbished web site for booksamillion.com.

On its booksamillion.com site, the company used some of the same marketing strategies that it employed in its superstores, including, for example, allowing Millionaire's Club Discount Card holders the same purchasing discounts that they enjoyed in company superstores: up to 46 percent off on best sellers, 37 percent off on all other in-stock hard covers, and 28 percent off on all in-stock paperbacks. Customers were given the option of joining the club online. The electronic shopping cart helped net sales, which in 1998 reached $327.8 million.

The company got another boost in 1999 when it arranged a deal with Wal-Mart whereby Books-A-Million would provide wal-mart.com customers with access to hundreds of thousands of book titles as well as provide the mass merchandiser with the services of the company's distribution center in Florence, Alabama.

Expanding its e-commerce ventures, in September 2000, Books-A-Million also negotiated a revenue-sharing contract with MediaBay, one of the world's largest purveyors of audio media, including audio books, old time radio shows, and classic videos, selling them as hard goods, including CDS and cassettes, or in downloadable formats via their web site at www.mediabay.com. Under the agreement, MediaBay became the exclusive provider of spoken audio products available to Books-A-Million customers at booksamillion.com. The two companies agreed to promote each other as ''trusted'' and ''preferred'' partners.

In January 2001, Books-A-Million announced a partnership agreement with Alibris, an international supplier of difficult-to-find books, including out-of-print and rare titles. Effective immediately, customers would gain access to over 14 million such titles, both at retail superstores and over the Internet. Next, in March, Books-A-Million made a significant expansion move, buying the Washington, D. C., area operation of Crown Books Corp., which, on February 12, 2001, had filed for Chapter 11 bankruptcy protection. Books-A-Million took over the operation of nine of the 14 Crown stores in northern Virginia. The company also agreed to buy the complete inventories of 19 Crown Books stores in the metropolitan Washington, D.C., and Chicago areas. The remaining inventory of Crown Books was sold off in liquidation sales and their stores were closed.

Plans announced in the company's fiscal 2001 Annual Report called for additional expansion as well as the integration of the Crown Book Stores it had just purchased. Books-A-Million indicated that it would open 4 or 5 new superstores in the next fiscal year and would expand its new and highly successful Joe Muggs newsstand concept. It also indicated that the e-commerce part of the business had continued to surpass expectations and had delivered major benefits to the company, suggesting that it would consider additional commitments to Internet marketing in the new century.

Principal Subsidiaries

AIS (AmericanInternetServices); American Wholesale Book Co.; Book$mart; NetCentral, Inc.

Principal Competitors

Barnes & Noble, Inc.; Borders Group, Inc.; Half Price Books, Records, Magazines Inc.; Amazon.com, Inc.; MTS, Inc.

Further Reading

''Borders, BAM Plan Many New Superstores,'' *Publishers Weekly*, May 11, 1998, p. 14.

McGaham, Jason, ''Crown Books' Woes Open Door to National Discounter,'' *Washington Post*, March 29, 2001, p. T06.

''MediaBay, Inc. and Books-A-Million, Inc. Announce Broad Marketing and Digital Distribution Alliance,'' *Business Wire*, September 12, 2000.

Mutter, John, ''Firings, Lie Detectors, Drug Tests Part of New Look at Books & Co.,'' *Publishers Weekly*, March 14, 1994, p. 11.

Nawotka, Edward, ''BAM to Buy Crown Stores in D.C. and Chicago,'' *Publishers Weekly*, March 12, 2001, p. 14.

Nelson, Emily, ''Wal-Mart Turns to Books-A-Million to Supply, Deliver Books for Web Store,'' *Wall Street Journal*, July 2, 1999, p. A3.

Stern, William M., ''Southern Fried Reading,'' *Forbes*, June 20, 1994, p. 91.

Teitelbaum, Richard S., ''Companies to Watch: Books-A-Million,'' *Fortune*, January 25, 1993, p. 105.

Williams, Roy, and Mick Normington, ''Anderson Family Values,'' *Birmingham News*, February 26, 1995, p. 1D.

—Maura Troester
—update: Jane W. Fiero

Brown & Brown, Inc.

220 South Ridgewood Avenue
Daytona Beach, Florida 32114
U.S.A.
Telephone: (904) 252-9601
Toll Free: (800) 877-2769
Fax: (904) 239-7252
Web site: http://www.brown-n-brown.com

Public Company
Incorporated: 1958 as Poe & Associates
Employees: 1,614
Sales: $209.7 million (2000)
Stock Exchanges: New York
Ticker Symbol: BRO
NAIC: 524210 Insurance Agencies and Brokerages

With offices in 24 states, Brown & Brown, Inc. is the ninth largest insurance brokerage in America. Although its agents also sell property/casualty, life, and health insurance to its mostly commercial clients, the company is best known for its customized package of insurance policies designed for proprietors of specific small businesses, such as dentists, architects, lawyers, funeral-home directors, and auto dealers. Brown & Brown maintains dual corporate headquarters in Tampa, Florida, and Daytona Beach, Florida—the result of a 1993 merger between Poe and Associates and Brown & Brown. That merger initiated a period of rapid growth, which was later fueled by a spate of acquisitions. Brown & Brown has a distinct corporate culture, and employs the cheetah as an unofficial mascot to emphasize a sense of urgency and the need to adapt to fast-changing business conditions.

Two Companies' Beginnings: 1939–93

The original Brown & Brown was started in Daytona Beach in 1939 by J. Adrian Brown, the father of the man who assumed control of the family business as chief executive in 1961. The younger Brown was also involved in Florida politics. He was elected to the Florida State House of Representatives in 1972, and served as speaker of the house in 1978–1980 before retiring from public service to concentrate solely on his insurance business. In those 12 years before merging with Poe & Associates in 1993, he increased Brown & Brown's annual revenues from less than $2 million to more than $33 million.

Poe & Associates, Inc. was founded by William F. Poe in 1956 as a one-man operation in Tampa, Florida. With $6,000 of his own money and $14,000 from his family, Poe teamed up with V.C. Jordan to form Poe & Associates. In 1969, Jordan created the company's first standardized policy for small businessmen. Designed for dentists, it packaged malpractice insurance along with other necessary office coverage. Poe and Jordan soon applied the package concept to a number of other businesses, and quickly developed a thriving business of their own. The company made an initial public offering of stock in 1973 and began branching outside of Florida. By the time it merged with Brown & Brown in 1993, Poe & Associates was selling its policies through a network of 130 independent insurance agents and was generating $50 million in annual revenues. The company also had grown to include 26 agencies in nine states: Florida, Georgia, Texas, Arizona, California, North Carolina, Pennsylvania, New Jersey, and Connecticut.

Poe & Brown is Formed Through Merger in 1993

Although they had been competitors for years, Poe and Brown had much in common. Although Poe was several years ahead of Brown, both men had graduated from the University of Florida and had been members of the same fraternity. Poe had also become involved in politics, leaving his business from 1974 to 1979 to serve as the mayor of Tampa, Florida. It was Poe who approached Brown about a possible merger in September 1992. Both he and his partner, Jordan, were looking to cut down on their responsibilities in order to spend more time with their families. For Brown, whose business was limited almost entirely to retail insurance in Florida, the merger was an opportunity to expand his product offerings and extend his reach to new regions. Taking advantage of being a public company he would also have greater potential for making acquisitions by issuing stock.

Company Perspectives:

Brown & Brown is a lean, decentralized, highly competitive, profit-oriented sales and service organization comprised of people of the highest integrity and quality, bound together by clearly defined goals and prideful relationships.

Poe and Brown met secretly in a small hotel between Tampa and Daytona to work out the details of what would become Poe & Brown. They agreed that Brown would serve as president and CEO and make the day-to-day business decisions. Poe would serve as chairman and Jordan as vice-chairman of the new company, and both would report to Brown. When the merger was finalized in 1993, Poe & Brown, Inc. became the largest insurance brokerage firm based in the Southeast.

William Poe Leaves Company in 1994

Although Poe and Brown had much in common, and expressed great respect for each other's abilities and accomplishments, they differed greatly in leadership style. ''He's a decentralist and I'm a centralist,'' Poe told the *St. Petersburg Times* in the paper's August 4, 1994 edition. ''He's more of a bottom-line-oriented manager, I'm more of a people-oriented manager. He's the hardest worker you've ever seen. He works about 70 hours a week.'' After the first year under Brown's leadership, however, Poe was pleased with the company's results. Revenues had jumped from $83 million combined for the two separate companies in 1992 to $95.6 million after the merger, making Poe & Brown the 19th largest insurance broker in the world. Nevertheless, Poe was unhappy in his new role. By August 1994 he decided to resign as chairman of the board, explaining that he wasn't comfortable serving in a subordinate position to Brown. ''I've always been the one who called the shots,'' he said. ''I asked him to do it, so it's only reasonable that he do it. I'm not sure that I like not doing it, but that decision is a little late.''

Poe & Brown's results were even more impressive when compared to the rest of the insurance industry. With a soft economy in the early 1990s, brokers were unable to raise rates, resulting in sluggish growth. But by 1995, unlike other brokers, Poe & Brown was poised to expand. In that year, the company acquired six other insurance agencies, adding to its Arizona and Pennsylvania subsidiaries as well as its Florida operations. The business climate was becoming so difficult for smaller insurance agencies and brokers that many actually approached Poe & Brown about being acquired.

Interestingly, during that time the price of the company's stock, although not depressed, did not really reflect the potential of Poe & Brown, due in great part to the limited number of shares available on the market. The company was reluctant to issue new shares because Poe was considering selling his 13 percent stake in the company, which amounted to more than one million shares. Eventually Poe did cash in his stock to start a new venture. His son, who had continued to work for Poe & Brown up to that point, joined him, thus cutting most of the family's ties to the company.

Growth and Expansion in the Late 1990s

What Poe did leave behind was the standardized policy business, which Brown continued to expand upon. In 1997 Poe & Brown introduced a liability package for small to medium-sized architectural and engineering firms, rolling it out initially in Illinois, Massachusetts, New Jersey, Ohio, and Texas. The following year, the company joined forces with the Hartford Financial Services Group to offer the Manufacturers Protector Plan (MPP), which included coverage for workers' compensation, property, crime, and general liability. For industrial manufacturers the package also provided coverage on worldwide product liability, product recall expense, and design errors and omissions.

With future plans to expand MPP to cover a number of niche manufacturing industries, the program initially targeted makers of all sizes of metalworking machinery, textile machinery, printing trade machinery, and food products machinery. Other than Hawaii and Alaska, MPP was available in every state. Later in 1998, Hartford and Poe & Brown introduced the Short Line Railroad Protector Plan, offering package coverage for rail lines designated as Class III. These so-called ''short lines''—ranging in length from 25 to 300 miles—included tourist, excursion, and dinner trains. With short lines growing, research indicated that the niche held great potential for Poe & Brown.

Most of Poe & Brown's growth was internal in 1996 and 1997, with the company acquiring just four independent insurance agencies in that period. Revenues reached $118.7 million in 1996, with a net income of $16.5 million. The following year, revenues exceeded $129 million, generating a 17.5 percent increase in net income, totaling $19.4 million.

The company's shareholders then approved an increase of the amount of company stock from 18 million shares to 70 million shares, and Poe & Brown was ready in 1998 to make a concerted push for more external growth. Unlike its larger publicly traded competitors, Poe & Brown targeted firms that serviced small and midsize businesses, which on average paid less than $50,000 in yearly premiums. In 1998 the company brought 26 agencies and three new product lines into its fold. One of the largest acquisitions that year, of the Daniel James Insurance Group, significantly enhanced Poe & Brown's Midwest presence—adding offices in Toledo, Ohio, and Indianapolis, Indiana. Bolstered by contributions from its acquisitions, Poe & Brown saw its revenues increase to $153.8 million in 1998 and its profits soar by 23.5 percent, reaching $23.1 million.

1999: A Return to the Brown & Brown Name

In April 1999, the company's shareholders voted to return to the ''Brown & Brown'' name. Although Poe & Associates had provided major assets in the 1993 merger, the Poe family now had no direct connection to Poe & Brown, and given J. Hyatt Brown's success at the helm, it seemed appropriate to revert to the corporate name that he felt paid tribute to his father and brother.

The new Brown & Brown continued its aggressive expansion program in 1999, acquiring 10 more independent insurance agencies and brokerages. For the seventh consecutive year the

Key Dates:

1939: Brown & Brown is established.
1956: Poe & Associates is established.
1969: Poe & Associates create first standardized policy for small businessmen.
1973: Poe & Associates makes its first public offering of stock.
1993: Poe & Associates and Brown & Brown merge, forming Poe & Brown, Inc.
1994: William Poe resigns as chairman of the board.
1999: Company name changed from Poe & Brown to Brown & Brown.
2000: The acquisition of Reidman Corporation greatly extends the company's reach.

company posted record results: net income increased 16.4 percent to $27.2 million, and revenues rose 11 percent to $176.4 million. For 28 consecutive quarters, Brown & Brown achieved a 15 percent increase in earnings over the same period in the previous year. The number that Brown focused on, however, was pre-tax profit margin. He instituted what he called ''Project 28'', an effort to boost Brown & Brown's pre-tax profit margin to 28 percent within three years, and an eventual goal of 30 percent. To foster a sense of competition within the company, the results of each profit center in each office were published in a book, with the office producing the highest profit margin ranked first. For 1999 Brown & Brown saw it pre-tax margin increase from 24 percent to 25.1 percent. Its top competitors, meanwhile, languished in the 15 percent range.

Dawn of the 21st Century

Brown & Brown continued to offer new products and make further acquisitions in the year 2000. The company teamed with Atlantic Mutual to offer an insurance package for the food processing industry called the Food Processors Preferred Program. It provided coverage for loss of income caused by adulteration and spoilage, transit mishap, equipment breakdown, and product recall. Brown & Brown also introduced insurance coverage for the fast-growing technology business segment. The High-Tech Target Program, with the appropriate acronym of HTTP, targeted a wide range of businesses, from hardware manufacturers to web site developers. Standard HTTP coverage included property, business income, general liability, crime, and workers' compensation. Customized packages could also be designed to include international coverage, media and internet liability, and network security coverage.

The most important of the several firms that Brown & Brown acquired in 2000 was the Reidman Corporation, based in Rochester, New York. Run by three generations of the Reidman family since 1938, the company was the 26th largest insurance broker in the country in 1999, and the ninth largest privately held firm, generating some $50 million in annual revenues. Reidman operated more than 60 offices in thirteen states, and other than its offices in Florida, Reidman's territory did not overlap with Brown & Brown. This allowed Brown & Brown to double the number of states in which it had offices to 24, and greatly widen the market for its products. Investors reacted positively to the news, bidding up the price of Brown & Brown stock. Despite the size of the Reidman deal, Brown & Brown continued to acquire other independents during the rest of 2000 as well, picking up new offices in California and Georgia.

Brown & Brown's acquisition spree continued into 2001, as Brown & Brown added to its already dominant presence in Florida, as well as buying The Harris Agency of Manassas, Virginia, which added the Washington, D.C., metropolitan area. The company announced its 2000 financial numbers, which again reflected record results. Revenues increased 11.3 percent to nearly $210 million, and net income jumped 23.9 percent to $33.2 million. With the addition of the Reidman offices, Brown & Brown was poised for even greater growth. Its size allowed it to negotiate exclusive contracts to sell a number of policies from the major insurers, thus making it tougher for independents to survive and making it more likely that Brown & Brown would continue to find agencies eager to be acquired.

Furthermore, the company's decentralized organization—which granted sales managers a great deal of power in running their offices—allowed Brown & Brown to recruit entrepreneurs as aggressive as its chief executive. J. Hyatt Brown was a man who expected results, and who made it clear that only employees who could thrive would survive at Brown & Brown. At annual sales meetings, each of the company's sales managers were made to stand before an audience in excess of 1,000 and detail their results for the year. The lowest earners were spotlighted by going first, accompanied by somber music. The top performers were given the coveted final slots in the program, where they are rewarded with applause and gifts, as well as cold hard cash. The fittest of the fit received Hawaiian leis made of $100 bills instead of flowers. Brown was unapologetic about what he expected from his people. As one executive vice president told the *Orlando Sentinel* in April 2001, ''You are either producing revenue for the company or you are overhead. It's that simple.'' In a business world that J. Hyatt Brown likened to a jungle, Brown & Brown was structured to flourish under any conditions, ready to adapt and survive if necessary, but more likely to thrive in the foreseeable future.

Principal Divisions

Retail; National Programs; Service; Brokerage.

Principal Competitors

Acordia Inc.; Arthur J. Gallagher & Co.; Marsh & McLennan Companies Inc.; Hilb, Rogal and Hamilton Company.

Further Reading

Bowers, Barbara, ''The M&A Way,'' *Best's Review,* April 1999, p. 81.
Brown, Thomas S., ''Poe & Brown Grows Into Old Name, Brown & Brown,'' *Daytona Beach News-Journal,* April 29, 1999, p. 13A.
Geer, Carolyn T., ''One-Stop Policy Shopping,'' *Forbes,* May 25, 1992, p. 94.
Goch, Lynna, ''Q&A: On the Prowl,'' *Best's Review,* September 2000, pp. 37–38.
Groeller, Greg, ''Eat or be Eaten Ethic Boosts Bottom Line,'' *Orlando Sentinel,* April 30, 2001.

Harrington, Jeff, "Buyout Expands Brown's Reach," *St. Petersburg Times,* September 12, 2000, p. 1E.

Huntley, Helen, "Founder of Agency Bows Out," *St. Petersburg Times,* August 4, 1994, p. 1E.

Ibold, Ken, "Survival of the Fittest: An Insurance Company Hunts New Business," *Florida Trend,* May 1999, p. 28.

Johnson, Robert, "Poe & Brown Stock May Finally Stir if Former Chairman Sells His Stake," *Wall Street Journal,* April 19, 1995, p. F2.

Roberts, Sally, "Acquisitions Changing Face of Brokerage Industry," *Business Insurance,* February 17, 1997, pp. 2, 69.

Souter, Gavin, "Spotlight Report: Poe & Brown Inc.," *Business Insurance,* July 18, 1994, p. 54.

Stengle, Bernice, "Insurance Firms Merge," *St. Petersburg Times,* December 1, 1992, p. 1E.

Tippett, Karen L., "Poe & Brown's Acquisitions Put Analysts in a 'Buy' Mood, as Well," *Wall Street Journal,* April 22, 1998, p. F2.

—Ed Dinger

Buhrmann NV

Hoogoorddreef 62
1101 BE Amsterdam
The Netherlands
Telephone: +31-20-651-1111
Fax: +31-20-651-1000
Web site: http://www.buhrmann.com

Public Company
Incorporated: 1993 as NV Koninklijke KNP BT
Employees: 26,296
Sales: EUR 9.60 billion ($9,042) (2000)
Stock Exchanges: Euronext Amsterdam
Ticker Symbol: BUHR
NAIC: 42211 Printing and Writing Paper Wholesalers; 42213 Industrial and Personal Service Paper Wholesalers; 322299 All Other Converted Paper Product Manufacturing

Buhrmann NV is the world's largest business-to-business provider of office products, paper, and graphics systems. From its headquarters in Amsterdam, Buhrmann oversees a globally operating network with offices in 30 countries and 26,000 employees, generating sales of more than EUR 9.6 billion in 2000. Buhrmann, claiming market leadership positions in North America, Europe, and Australia and New Zealand, has grown especially through acquisitions. The purchase of Corporate Express, based in Colorado, in 1999, has helped the company double its total office products sales. At more than EUR 6 billion in annual sales, Office Products is the company's largest business segment, divided into three geographic divisions: OP North America, OP Europe, and OP Australia. Buhrmann has kept the Corporate Express brand name, merging its former BT Office operations into the newly enlarged subsidiary. Buhrmann's Paper Merchanting division, which generated EUR 3.0 billion in revenues in 2000, is the leading paper products distributor in Europe, with three strong brands: Hello, Motif, and IBM. Paper Merchanting is also active in the North American, Southeast Asian, and South African markets. The third Buhrmann division, Graphics Systems, accounts for an additional EUR 556 million in revenues and is the European market leader in the distribution of graphics machines, materials, and services, including a long history as a distributor of Heidelberg printing presses. Buhrmann, formerly known as KNP BT, itself a result of a merger in 1993, traces parts of its history back to the mid-19th century. Traded on the Euronext Amsterdam stock exchange, Buhrmann is led by chairman and CEO Frans H.J. Koffrie.

Packaging Acquisitions in the 20th Century

A long list of acquisitions went into the formation of the Buhrmann NV entering the 21st century, with roots stretching back to the mid-19th century—and beyond. Indeed, one of the company subsidiaries, the Robert Horne Group, which remained the United Kingdom's leading paper products distributor, traced its own history back to around the late 16th century.

The company's core business was first established, however, in Maastricht, in 1850, as Lhoest Weustenraad & Cie. That company later took the name of KNP, for Koninklijke Nederlandsche Papierfabrieken, after being granted royal status as a national paper manufacturer in The Netherlands in 1875. KNP established paper mills in Belgium and Germany, in addition to its domestic manufacturing operations, and opened offices in the United Kingdom, Italy, Spain, and France. KNP also entered the North American market, before listing on the Amsterdam stock exchange in 1938.

Other members of the later KNP BT merger were also in the process of formation. Buhrmann-Ubbens Papierengroothandel was set up in 1866 by GH Buhrmann as a wholesale paper products distributor serving The Netherlands' printing industry. In 1963, that company joined with NV Lettergieterij, which had been founded as Tetterode in 1851 as a distributor of printing equipment, to form Buhrmann-Tetterode NV.

The third and youngest part of the KNP BT merger was the VRG Groep, which had been formed in 1950 through the merger of two companies, Van Reekum Papier, which had been founded in 1917, and NV Gepacy, founded after the end of World War II. VRG Groep grew quickly, and by the beginning of the 1990s had joined Buhrmann-Tetterode and KNP in the top three in The Netherlands' paper and office products market.

Company Perspectives:

Our Strategic Vision: As an international business services and distribution group, our focus is exclusively on the marketing and distribution of products and services to business customers. Currently we are the world's leading distributor of office products and the European leading distributor of paper, other related graphic-art products and graphic systems. This success is based on leveraging our core competencies, which include: superior customer service and orientation; a world-class distribution infrastructure with excellent geographic coverage; leading technology, including significant eCommerce capabilities; and dedicated, experienced management and staff.

While its competitors concentrated on the paper and printing industries, Buhrmann-Tetterode branched out in the mid-1970s to enter related activities such as flexible packaging. That product group was added in 1975 with the purchase of Germany's Kobush Packaging. Buhrmann-Tetterode continued making acquisitions to expand its packaging division, including the 1988 acquisition of Sengewald and Nordwest Packaging in 1990, both of which were also located in Germany. Buhrmann-Tetterode also had opened a U.S. packaging arm, through its Sengawald subsidiary, in 1989.

Buhrmann-Tetterode had by then already taken steps to restructure its U.S. paper, packaging, and office products interests into a new subsidiary, BT Office Products International, which was established in 1984 and listed on the New York stock exchange in 1995. A strategic review of the U.S. market led Buhrmann-Tetterode into a related direction, that of contract stationery. Buhrmann's first major activity in this area came in 1987 when BT Office Products acquired 70 percent of Summit Office Supply Inc., based in New York. More acquisitions followed, including that of MS Ginn Company, based in Washington, DC, and Publix Office Supply, based in Chicago, both made in 1987. Buhrmann also increased its holding in Summit to 100 percent that year.

BT Office Products' expansion across the United States proceeded steadily during the 1990s as the company joined in a consolidation of the fragmented office supply and contract stationers markets. The company acquired Buschart Office Products of St. Louis, Missouri and EW Curry Company of Pittsburgh in 1990, and California's Redwood Office Products the following year. A second office was opened in Amsterdam to handle BT Office Products' growing European activity as well. Shortly before the public floatation of BT Office Products, the two offices were consolidated at the subsidiary's Chicago headquarters.

In 1993, Buhrmann-Tetterode, VRG Groep, and KNP announced their intention to merge their operations to become not only the dominant office products and paper distribution company in The Netherlands, but among the top companies in the industry in the world. Listed on the Amsterdam stock exchange, the company, now named NV Koninklijke KNP BT, quickly launched an aggressive acquisition drive to build up its market positions. Among the most significant of this new round of acquisitions was its merger with Austria's Leykam in 1994. Leykam had been founded in 1870 as Leykam-Josephtal near Graz, one of the centers of the Austria-Hapsburg papermaking industry. Leykam-Josephtal became the empire's largest paper producer, then survived the empire's collapse in World War I only to see the bulk of its operations destroyed during World War II. Leykam later merged with nearby paper mill Murztaler, creating Leykam Murztaler in 1974.

The merger with Leykam created a new subsidiary for KNP BT's paper manufacturing operations, KNP Leykam. The newly merged company became the European leader in its wood-free coated paper specialty. The parent company meanwhile continued its expansion, targeting in particular the U.S. market, with acquisitions such as that of Northwest Stationers and Supply and Far West Office Systems. As the company developed its office products and contract stationers operations, KNP BT targeted primarily large-sized companies.

Streamlined for the 21st Century

Moving toward the close of the century, however, KNP BT was also closer to a major restructuring of its operations—and the company's identity. A massive drop in paper prices in the mid-1990s had brought its KNP Leykam subsidiary into losses. By 1996, the company announced that it would no longer make new investments in the subsidiary. KNP BT soon began looking to exit the paper manufacturing market altogether, putting an end to what had long been KNP's core activity. The company sold its paper manufacturing division in 1997 to Sappi Ltd., of South Africa.

KNP BT soon announced its intention to exit manufacturing altogether. The announcement came upon a failed attempt to merge the entire company with fellow Dutch company Hagemeyer, which was in the process of redefining itself as a business-to-business services provider. KNP BT began looking for a buyer for its packaging arm, promising that, should no buyer be found, the packaging arm would be spun off as a separate, publicly listed company, Kappa Packaging. Instead, Kappa Packaging found a buyer in venture capital firm CVC Capital Partners/Cinven Ltd., which paid NFL 3.4 billion ($1.7 billion), in 1998.

KNP BT now restructured its operations around a new core of business-to-business distribution, particularly the office products market. The company bought back all of the shares of BT Office Products, removing it from the New York stock exchange. At the same time KNP BT changed its name, in part to reflect its new focus, but in part as a result of a lawsuit it had filed—and lost—against similarly named KPN, the name of the recently privatized Dutch post office service.

The company chose the name Buhrmann NV to take it into the new century. Almost immediately, Buhrmann made a name for itself—in 1999, the company announced that it had acquired Corporate Express, based in Colorado, thereby becoming the world's leading office products supplier. The deal was worth $2.3 billion, including a cash price of $9.70 per share and the assumption of some $1.2 billion in debt.

Corporate Express had been established in 1986 by Jirka Rysavy, who had immigrated to the United States from his native Czechoslovakia at the beginning of the decade. Rysavy

Key Dates:

1850: Lhoest Weustenraad & Cie (LWC) is established.
1866: Buhrmann-Ubbens Papierengroothandel is founded.
1875: LWC changes its name to Koninklijke Nederlandsche Papierfabrieken (KNP).
1917: Van Reekum Papier is founded.
1938: KNP lists on Amsterdam stock exchange.
1947: NV Gepacy is founded.
1950: Gepacy and Van Reekum form VRG Groep.
1963: Buhrmann merges with NV Lettergieterij to form Buhrmann-Tetterode (BT).
1975: BT enters packaging industry.
1988: Corporate Express is founded.
1993: BT, KNP, and VRG merge to form KNP BT.
1994: KNP BT merges paper division with Leykam to form KNP Leykam.
1997: KNP BT sells KNP Leykam to Sappi Ltd.
1998: KNP BT sells packaging division to CVC/Cinven; changes name to Buhrmann.
1999: Corporate Express is acquired.
2001: U.S. Office Products is acquired.

reportedly had spent his last year in Czechoslovakia meditating in a shed in an isolated area near the Polish border, telling the *Boulder County Business Report,* ''I wanted to experience seeing myself through my own eyes.'' Arriving with little money in the United States, Rysavy quickly displayed a talent as an entrepreneur, opening a health food store, Crystal Market, in downtown Boulder. The store soon was turning over some $3 million per year. Yet Rysavy had been developing a new vision of building a corporate supplier of environmentally friendly products. Instead of developing the Crystal Market concept, Rysavy sold the store to Mike and Libby Gilliland, who transformed it into the $400 million-per-year Wild Oats Market retail chain.

Rysavy's new opportunity came with the purchase of an office supply store for just $100. Rysavy next used the $300,000 he had made with the sale of the Crystal Market to help him raise the funding for a takeover of the stationery division of Denver's NBI in 1988. That acquisition, which cost Rysavy $7.8 million, was just the first of more than 150 acquisitions made by the middle of the 1990s. By 1990, Rysavy's new company, called Corporate Express, was posting revenues of $70 million. Just four years later, the company's sales neared $700 million.

Not all of Corporate Express's fast growth was from acquisitions. The launch of the company's environmentally friendly EarthSaver line in 1991 proved immensely successful. By 1999, Corporate Express's sales had topped $4.5 billion. As the company's stock price proved highly volatile, Rysavy ceded his CEO position to company President Robert King, and then, at the urging of shareholders, abandoned his chairman position as well. When Corporate Express announced that it had agreed to be acquired by Buhrmann, Rysavy left the company altogether, concentrating instead on developing a third company, Gaiam, established in 1988. Buhrmann folded its BT Office Products operations into the new subsidiary in 2000, adopting the Corporate Express name for the company's worldwide office products operations.

Entering the 21st century, Buhrmann had successfully achieved a new identity for itself as the world's leading office products supplier. The company also was nearing the EUR 10 billion mark, posting EUR 9.6 billion in sales in 2000. Buhrmann was certain to reach EUR 10 billion in sales by the end of 2001: in March of that year, the company announced its intention to pay $250 million to acquire the office supply operations of failing U.S. Office Products, which also was selling off its Mail Boxes Etc. division to United Parcel Service. That company, which had filed for Chapter 11 bankruptcy protection in 2000 after posting losses of nearly $200 million, was expected to add approximately $1 billion in sales through its office products division. The two companies also were seen as highly complementary, as Corporate Express customers were primarily among large-sized companies, while U.S. Office Products' customer base was primarily among midsized companies.

Principal Subsidiaries

Adria Paper d.o.o (Croatia); Bratislavska Papierenska Spolocnostspol s.r.o. (Slovakia); Buhrmann France Image SAS; Caledonia Srl (Italy; 60%); Christian Christensen & Co. A/S (Denmark); Contact Papers Ltd (Ireland); Corporate Express Australia Ltd.; Corporate Express Austria; Corporate Express Belgium NV; Corporate Express Canada Inc.; Corporate Express Deutschland GmbH; Corporate Express, Inc.; Corporate Express Nederland BV; Corporate Express New Zealand Ltd.; Corporate Express Spa (Italy); Corporate Express UK Ltd.; Deutsche Papier GmbH; Epcar NV (Belgium); Grafiskt Papper Norden AB (Sweden); Howard Smith Paper Group Ltd (U.K.); Papelco SA (Spain; 76%); Plantin NV; Robert Horne Group Plc; Winpac Pte Ltd. (Singapore; 50%).

Principal Competitors

Arjo Wiggins Appleton p.l.c.; Boise Cascade Office Products Corporation; David S. Smith (Holdings) PLC; Guilbert S.A.; IKON Office Solutions, Inc.; International Paper Company; Manutan International S.A.; Moore Corporation Limited; Office Depot, Inc.; OfficeMax, Inc.; Online Office Supplies Company; Grupo Picking Pack, S.A.; Quill Corp.; United Stationers Inc.

Further Reading

De Marco, Donna, ''Rival to Buy U.S. Office Products,'' *Washington Times,* March 6, 2001, p. B8.

Frey, Eric, ''KNP Paper Arm Back in Black,'' *Financial Times,* February 12, 1997.

Greim, Lisa, ''Buyout Targets Corporate Express,'' *Denver Rocky Mountain News,* July 14, 1999, p. 1B.

''KNP BT to Split After Merger Failure,'' *Financial Times,* February 12, 1998.

''KNP Sidelines Core Operation to Refocus,'' *Financial Times,* September 27, 1996.

Lewis, Jerry W., ''Gaiam Third Child of Entrepreneur,'' *Boulder County Business Report,* November 1998.

Onstad, Eric, ''Burhmann Profits Jump, Outlook Surprises,'' *Reuters,* February 15, 2001.

—M.L. Cohen

BULOVA

Bulova Corporation

One Bulova Avenue
Woodside, New York 11377-7874
U.S.A.
Telephone: (718) 204-3300
Fax: (718) 204-3546
Web site: http://www.bulova.com

Wholly Owned Subsidiary of Loews Corporation
Incorporated: 1911 as J. Bulova Co.
Employees: 450
Sales: $134 million (1999)
NAIC: 42194 Jewelry, Watch, Precious Stone, and Precious Metal Wholesalers; 335313 Switchgear and Switchboard Apparatus Manufacturing; 334419 Other Electronic Component Manufacturing

Bulova Corporation is one of the largest and most venerable watch companies in the world. Among the most widely recognized brand names in its industry, Bulova produces watches in a wide variety of styles and is represented in every price range. At the upper end, the company's offerings include the Bulova gold and diamond watches and the famous Accutron line of luxury watches. In the lower price bracket, Bulova is represented by the Caravelle, a popular line originally introduced in the early 1960s, and Sportstime watches. The company also makes classic and contemporary clocks, has a Miniature Collectible Clocks product line, and offers a wide variety of licensed products through its Licensed Product Collection, which includes Royal Doulton, Frank Lloyd Wright, and Pfaltzgraff. Loews Corporation, which has holdings in the hotel, tobacco, and insurance industries, owns 97 percent of Bulova Corporation's stock.

Company Origins

Joseph Bulova, a Czech immigrant, founded the company that bears his name in 1875. Only 23 years old at the time, Bulova opened a modest jewelry shop in New York City. Initially, Bulova sold mainly pocket watches and other jewelry, but over time he expanded his line of products. He was manufacturing and selling his own desk clocks and other timepieces by 1911, the year he incorporated the operation as J. Bulova Company. By that time, Bulova's pocket watches already had attained a reputation for excellence, and New Yorkers bought them as fast as he could make them.

Although wristwatches existed before World War I, it was returning veterans who made them fashionable. Once Americans became aware of their convenience, the market for wristwatches in the United States expanded quickly. In 1919, Bulova introduced the first full line of jeweled wristwatches for men. Over the next several years, Bulova added several other industry firsts, including the first ladies wristwatch line and the first line of diamond wristwatches. In 1926, the company sponsored the first nationally broadcast radio spot commercials, featuring the immortal "At the tone, it's 8 p.m., B-U-L-O-V-A Bulova watch time" tag line. Bulova began selling the world's first clock radio two years later. Meanwhile, the company's name was changed to Bulova Watch Company, Inc., reflecting the growing role of Arde Bulova, Joseph's son, in the firm's management.

Innovative Advertising and Growth: 1930s–50s

Bulova continued to innovate in the areas of marketing and advertising over the decades that followed. The company launched the first million dollar advertising campaign the watch industry had seen in 1931. Ten years later, Bulova aired the world's first television commercial. Broadcast just before a 1941 Brooklyn Dodgers baseball game, the advertisement showed a simple picture of a clock superimposed on a map of the United States. The message was simply "America runs on Bulova time."

The entry of the United States into World War II led to Bulova's large-scale involvement in military manufacturing. In addition to producing precision timepieces for military equipment, Bulova's mass production facilities also began turning out fuses, aircraft instruments, and other mechanisms for use in the war effort. Toward the end of the war, Bulova opened the Joseph Bulova School of Watchmaking. Its main mission was to help disabled veterans learn a trade upon their return from the war.

Company Perspectives:

Today, one of the world's most recognized brands, and still wholly U.S. owned and operated, Bulova is dedicated to upholding its legacy of creativity and excellence, forging new directions in a classic American tradition.

By this time, Arde Bulova was firmly in charge of the company, and he ran it very much as a one-man show. Under Arde, Bulova grew to become one of the market leaders among U.S. watchmakers. By the mid-1950s, the company's annual sales had reached $80 million. In 1954, Arde Bulova hired General Omar Bradley, a World War II hero, as chairman of Bulova Research & Development Labs, Inc., a wholly owned subsidiary involved in developing the company's defense product business. Bradley was a close wartime friend of Harry D. Henshel, Arde Bulova's brother-in-law and one of the company's largest shareholders. When Arde Bulova died in 1958, Bradley was the logical choice to take over the chairmanship of Bulova, although it took a committee of 14 department heads to cover the huge range of responsibilities that Arde had refused to delegate in the past.

Meanwhile, a new contender had risen to challenge Bulova's dominant position in the watch industry. Throughout the second half of the 1950s, Bulova faced stiff competition from the Timex watch, made by U.S. Time Corporation. Priced far lower than Bulova products, Timex eroded Bulova's market share enough to cause the company's revenue to slip to $62.8 million by 1961. Under Bradley and CEO Harry B. Henshel, Bulova began to fight back. First, they began to institute modern management practices, replacing the old-fashioned methods of the autocratic Arde Bulova. More important, the company developed Accutron, the world's first electronic watch.

Key Developments and New Product Offerings: 1960s

Accutron represented the first major revolution in clock technology in three centuries. Before it was available in commercial products, the Accutron timer mechanism saw important action in the space program. When the Accutron watch finally became available to consumers in late 1960, it was a huge success. Far more accurate than any other watch commercially available, the Accutron was the first to be sold with a written guarantee of accuracy to within one minute a month. Accutron technology became the standard for the next decade both on human wrists and in orbiting satellites.

In 1963, Bulova introduced another line of watches, the Caravelle. The Caravelle was the company's answer to Timex and the other cheaper watch lines that had been eating away at Bulova's customer base for several years. Caravelle was priced much lower than the company's other watches, and it was hoped that the line would catch on among younger buyers who would later graduate to more expensive models. With the addition of Accutron and Caravelle, Bulova was able to regain much of the momentum it had lost to Timex and the many nameless brands of cheap watches that had hit the market over the previous decade. The company also eliminated outlets that were selling Bulova watches at discount prices, a practice company officials felt tarnished the Bulova name and reputation for excellence. By fiscal 1964, the year the company shipped its 250,000th Accutron watch, Bulova's revenue finally surpassed its pre-slump level, reaching a new high of $73 million.

The next several years were good ones for Bulova. By 1965, sales had grown to $84 million, about 20 percent of which was generated by defense and industrial products, including timing mechanisms and fuses. There were 58 different Accutron models for the wrist and 11 Accutron desk and table clocks by that time. Bulova controlled an estimated 15 percent of the market for high-priced men's watches. Throughout this period, the company also worked hard to increase its sales abroad. By 1967, 20 percent of Bulova's sales were generated in foreign lands. Bulova watches were being sold in 89 countries by that year, up from 19 in 1961. The fact that most of Bulova's watch movements were assembled in Switzerland added to its international flavor, and in 1967 the company acquired Universal Genève, a Swiss manufacturer of upper-end clocks and watches. Company sales leaped to $124 million for that year. Meanwhile, Bulova remained NASA's timekeeper of choice. Timing devices built by Bulova saw action during the first moon walk in 1969, as well as on subsequent missions.

By the beginning of the 1970s, Bulova had sold nearly 1.5 million Accutrons, and the company's watches could be bought in 110 markets around the world. The company was operating 20 plants, 12 of them in the United States. Even at that time, Bulova was still the only manufacturer of jeweled-movement watches in the United States. In 1971, the company launched a joint venture with a Japanese outfit, Citizen Watch Co., to make Accutrons for sale in Asia. Bulova was offering four basic lines of watches by 1973, covering every price range: the low-priced Caravelle, starting at $10.95; the Bulova line, which cost $35 and up; the still booming Accutron, whose bottom price had dropped to $95; and the Accuquartz, introduced in 1970 as the first quartz watch sold in the United States.

Changes in Ownership: Middle to Late 1970s

In 1973, Bulova's status as a fiercely independent company came to an end when Gulf & Western Industries, Inc. bought a stake in the company. That interest eventually grew to 29 percent ownership. Bulova's hot streak began to run out about the same time. One reason for the turnaround was that the company seemed to have miscalculated the popularity of digital watches. Bulova stood by idly while competitors were churning out and selling new quartz digital models in huge numbers. The company eventually started selling solid-state digital watches under the name Computron, but not before falling far behind in the battle for that market. Another problem was a dramatic inflation of the Swiss franc in relation to the U.S. dollar. This development made it difficult for Bulova to compete cost-wise, since so much of its manufacturing was done in Switzerland. For 1975, the company lost $25 million on sales of $204 million. With losses mounting in 1976, Gulf & Western sold its 26.8 percent interest in Bulova to Stelux Manufacturing Company, a watch components maker based in Hong Kong. With Stelux in control of the company, Henshel was replaced as chief executive by C.P. Wong, managing director of Stelux. It was hoped that Bulova would give Stelux a U.S. outlet for its goods,

Key Dates:

1875: Joseph Bulova opens a jewelry shop in New York City.
1911: The firm incorporates as J. Bulova Company.
1919: A line of men's jeweled wristwatches is introduced.
1923: The company changes its name to the Bulova Watch Company.
1926: The company launches the first ever radio spot commercial.
1931: The company begins the watch industry's first million dollar advertising campaign.
1941: The first television commercial in the world is aired—a Bulova watch commercial.
1952: The development of Accutron begins.
1960: Accutron watches become part of Bulova's product line and Accutron technology becomes part of NASA computers.
1963: The Caravelle line of watches is introduced.
1970: Accuquartz is the first quartz watch sold in the United States.
1979: After years of unstable ownership, Bulova becomes part of Loews Corporation.
1986: Miniature clocks are introduced.
1990: Bulova faces fierce competition from large, international firms.
1993: Bulova launches a highly publicized advertising campaign featuring nude celebrities wearing its watches.
2000: Bulova begins an Internet partnership with Polygon Networks Inc.

and Stelux would provide the impetus for Bulova's full-scale assault on the digital market. Unfortunately, the purchase of controlling interest by a foreign-owned company made Bulova ineligible for defense contracts, which had accounted for about 10 percent of sales the year before and was one of its few profitable areas. To circumvent those regulations, the company formed a subsidiary, Bulova Systems & Instruments Corporation, to perform its defense work under the management of a team of trustees.

The relationship with Stelux did not prove to be as mutually beneficial as had been hoped, and by 1977, Wong had resigned as CEO of Bulova. He gave up his spot as a director the following year. Between fiscal years 1976 and 1978, Bulova's losses totaled $48 million. In 1979, the 30 percent of Bulova's stock owned by Stelux was bought by Loews Corporation, the holding company run by Laurence Tisch, a close friend of Henshel's. Andrew Tisch, Laurence's 30-year-old son, was named president of Bulova, and Henshel stayed on as chairman.

Financial Hardships and Restructuring in the 1980s

Under the influence of Loews, Bulova gradually began to claw its way back into competitive form. The transition was not seamless, however. In 1982, the company spent $36 million to take some of its less viable watches off the market, and this move contributed to a $27 million loss for the year. Realizing that the company had cut back on quality control, many retailers had given up on Bulova by this time. Under Loews's management, renewed emphasis was placed on quality inspection. Loews also sold off a number of Bulova's assets between 1981 and 1987, including its electronics division, its main building in Queens, and facilities in Italy and Switzerland. By 1984, Loews owned 95 percent of Bulova's common stock, and Bulova turned an operating profit of more than $7 million.

During the late 1980s, Bulova worked hard to revamp its image and regain the respect its name once commanded. To attract younger customers, the company began making watches under licensing agreements with such firms as Benetton and Harley-Davidson, and with the National Football League. To appeal to the more highbrow market, Bulova began offering watches based on famous works of art. In 1986, the firm also began offering miniature clocks. In 1989, Andrew Tisch took over the leadership of another Loews subsidiary and was replaced at Bulova by Herbert Hofmann. That year, sales of fuses to the government generated 30 percent of the company's revenue.

By 1990, Bulova was the only major U.S.-owned watchmaker left in the business, and its $182 million in sales was dwarfed by the $2.6 billion in revenue generated by industry leader Seiko of Japan. Remaining in the black continued to be a struggle for the company. Bulova posted net losses in 1989 and 1990, as trendy watches such as the popular Swatch stole more market share from old-timers like Bulova. Convinced that classic models were finding their way back into fashion, Bulova reintroduced the Accutron in 1991, after seven years out of circulation. The new Accutron line included 26 different styles and ranged in price from $395 to $1,095.

As the 1990s progressed, the company continued to seek ways to restore its former luster through daring marketing and advertising initiatives, though its budget could not match those of its giant foreign competitors Citizen and Seiko. In 1993, Bulova launched a highly publicized advertising campaign featuring nude celebrities wearing Bulova watches. The theme of the campaign was ''I'd feel naked without my Bulova.'' Meanwhile, the company's defense-oriented subsidiary, now called Bulova Technologies, Inc., began diversifying into commercial areas in the face of shrinking military spending—this subsidiary eventually was sold in the mid-1990s.

Financial Gains: Middle to Late 1990s

For some time, Bulova had relied on an inflow of capital from its parent Loews Corporation to meet its annual financial needs. Nevertheless, going into the mid-1990s, the Bulova name and reputation continued to hold sway with a significant number of consumers. In 1996, the firm became part of Royal Doulton's licensing program and it began producing a line of glass, wood, and brass clocks, which was incorporated into Royal Doulton's china patterns. The Royal Doulton by Bulova products became available to consumers the following year.

In 1995, Bulova recorded increased profits and would continue doing so into the late 1990s. With its financials back on track, the firm began marketing its products on television again. In 1997, Bulova contracted with Burkhardt & Hillman to develop an ad campaign—the first in five years—that would emphasize the company's history and its large product line with 370 different designs.

The firm also continued to introduce new products. In 1998, the Millennia Collection was launched and featured watches with innovative technological designs. Included were solar watches, motion quartz, and vibra-alarm, which catered to the hearing-impaired market. The World Timer and Perpetual Calendar watches were added to the line one year later.

As Bulova closed out the century, revenues and profits continued to climb. In 1999, profits increased from $10.5 million in 1998, to $14.1 million. Management attributed the company's success to its aggressive marketing campaign. The firm's expenditures in network and cable television, radio, magazines, and catalogs increased and resulted in significant sales growth in many of its product lines. The Accutron brand secured a 16 percent increase in sales in 1999, and the Caravelle line saw a 21 percent climb. The Bulova Clock collection also experienced an 8 percent sales increase.

Along with its marketing campaign, the firm added additional strength to its sales force and also began its foray into e-commerce by introducing a company web site. Bulova also was recognized by Sears for the second straight year and was named the Sears Partner in Progress, an award symbolizing quality and service. The firm also was elected the best company in the industry by *Incentive Magazine* for the fifth consecutive year.

Growth in the New Millennium

Bulova entered the new millennium with a positive outlook despite increased competition. In early 2000, the company launched the second part to its e-commerce phase by forming a partnership with Polygon Networks Inc., a designer and maintainer of retail and supplier web sites. According to a *Daily News Record* article, "Polygon and Bulova can create sites for stores that don't already have them. For those already up and running, Bulova will provide product images and corresponding content that the watch firm will also update." The deal also allowed Bulova to support its retail customers rather than compete with them on the Internet.

As part of its 125th anniversary year celebration, the company also announced a sweepstakes with a grand prize of a Lincoln Navigator SUV in 2000. Management hoped the drawing would garnish attention and increase foot traffic in Bulova retailers such as Macy's, Fred Meyer, Sears, and other independent retail outlets.

In 2001, Bulova continued expanding its product lines. Indoor/outdoor clocks were introduced and new tabletop and desk clocks also were offered. The firm's licensed collections grew along with the miniatures collections. Having increased profits over the past five years, Bulova remained confident that the firm would continue securing positive results—even in the face of increased competition. Watch fashions come and go quickly, but there always seems to be at least a little room in the market for the company that put the first timepiece on the moon.

Principal Competitors

Citizen Watch Co. Ltd.; LVMH SA; Seiko Corporation.

Further Reading

Barmash, Isadore, "Bulova Seeking to Take the Watch Beyond Time," *New York Times,* October 5, 1989, p. D1.

——, "Bulova Tries to Make Up Lost Time," *New York Times,* June 13, 1976, p. F3.

"Bring on the Revolution," *Forbes,* December 1, 1972, p. 72.

"Bulova Adding a Variety of Tabletop, Wall Clocks to Its Line," *HFN—The Weekly Newspaper for the Home Furnishing Network,* January 15, 2001, p. 99.

"Bulova Earnings Likely to Wind Up at New Peak," *Barron's,* October 30, 1967, p. 38.

"Bulova Fights for Its Contracts," *Business Week,* August 30, 1976, p. 2.

"Bulova—Industry Leader," *Financial World,* August 9, 1967, p. 5.

"Bulova Watch Gets a Hong Kong Partner," *Business Week,* June 14, 1976, p. 29.

"Bulova Watch Gets a Tisch as President," *New York Times,* October 18, 1979, p. D2.

"Bulova Watch Ticks Off Smart Advance in Profits," *Barron's,* March 1, 1965, p. 20.

"Bulova's Henshel Goes Against the Trend," *Business Week,* July 14, 1973, p. 60.

"Crucial Hours for the Swiss Watch Industry," *Fortune,* August 15, 1969, p. 116.

Dolbow, Sandra, "Bulova's in Playful Mood for 125th," *Brandweek,* July 10, 2000, p. 4.

Finch, Camilla, "Traditional Watch May Wind Bulova into Better Future," *Crain's New York Business,* December 24, 1990, p. 13.

Flamer, Keith, "Bulova: Quiescent No Longer," *Jewelers Circular Keystone,* August 1998, p. 48.

"Good Time," *Time,* June 16, 1967, p. 85.

Hessen, Wendy, "Bulova Enters into Internet Partnership," *Daily News Record,* February 4, 2000, p. 33.

"Multinational Approach Helps Bulova Beat Competitors' Time," *Industry Week,* March 22, 1971, p. 19.

Rasmusson, Erika, "Big Advertising, Small Budget," *Sales & Marketing Management,* December 1999, p. 17.

"Sears Honors Bulova," *Gifts & Decorative Accessories,* August 1999, p. 170.

"Successor to a One-Man Regime," *Business Week,* November 21, 1959, p. 104.

Surman, Matt, "Burkhardt & Hillman Return Bulova to TV," *Adweek,* July 14, 1997, p. 40.

Tisch, Andrew H., "Why Marketing Ticks at Bulova," *Marketing Communications,* June 1982, p. 26.

"A Troubled Bulova Bides Its Time," *Business Week,* June 16, 1975, p. 22.

Underwood, Elaine, "Bulova 'Buffs' Up Its Image," *Brandweek,* November 29, 1993, p. 6.

"The Watch That Saved Bulova," *Forbes,* November 15, 1964, p. 42.

"Wong Moves in at Bulova," *Business Week,* June 28, 1976, p. 98.

—Robert R. Jacobson
—update: Christina M. Stansell

Burberry Ltd.

29-53 Chatham Place, Hackney
London, E9 6LP
United Kingdom
Telephone: (44) 208 985 3344
Fax: (44) 208 985 2636
Web site: http://www.gusplc.co.uk/burberry.html

Division of Great Universal Stores plc
Founded: 1856
Employees: 2,500
Sales: £230 million ($366.1 million) (2000)
NAIC: 31523 Women's and Girls' Cut and Sew Apparel Manufacturing; 31522 Men's and Boys' Cut and Sew Apparel Manufacturing; 44814 Family Clothing Stores

Burberry Ltd. is a manufacturer and marketer of men's, women's, and children's apparel, as well as accessories and fragrances. The Burberry name is virtually synonymous with the tan gabardine raincoat pioneered by the company more than 145 years ago. Writing for *WWD* (*Women's Wear Daily*) in 1989, Andrew Collier described the garment as ''a mainstay in outerwear worldwide, that symbolizes all that is Britain: sturdy and unassuming, equally at home in fine hotels and muddy lanes.'' In 2000, Burberry operated 58 company-owned stores, and its products were also found in department and specialty stores around the world. In 1999, the firm launched the Prorsum designer collection as part of its efforts to reinvent Burberry's luxury brand status. An icon of classic clothing, Burberry has utilized licensing and brand extensions to appeal to a younger generation of fashion-conscious customers. The company is a subsidiary of the United Kingdom's Great Universal Stores plc, the very closely held $9 billion credit reporting, mail-order, and retail apparel conglomerate.

19th-Century Origins

Founder Thomas Burberry was born in 1835 and apprenticed in the drapery trade, establishing his own drapery business in Basingstoke, Hampshire, in 1856. A sportsman, Burberry was dissatisfied with the then-popular rubberized mackintosh raincoat, which was heavy, restricting, and stifling, and thus unsuitable for extended outings. Inspired by country folk's loose ''smocks,'' Burberry designed a tightly woven fabric made from water-repellent linen or cotton yarn. Although sturdy and tear-resistant, this ''Burberry-proofed'' cloth was lightweight and allowed air to circulate, making it considerably more comfortable than the heavy mackintosh. The tailor trademarked his cloth ''Gabardine,'' a Shakespearean term that referred to shelter from inclement weather. Burberry developed five different weights of gabardine: ''Airylight,'' ''Double-Weave,'' ''Karoo,'' ''Wait-a-bit,'' and ''Tropical.'' He even patented ''Burberry-proofed'' linings made from silk and wool.

Burberry was a shrewd marketer, employing trademarking and advertising to great benefit. Illustrated advertisements touting the clothing ''designed by sportsmen for sportsmen'' drew customers to Burberry's retail outlet, which was established in London's Haymarket section in 1891. Having used a variety of labels to distinguish its garments from imitations, the company registered the ''Equestrian Knight'' trademark in 1909, an insignia used continuously through the mid-1990s. Also employed in the corporate logo, this image represents several Burberry ideals. The armor signifies the protection afforded by the outerwear, the ''Chivalry of Knighthood'' reflects the company's own standards of integrity, and the Latin adverb ''prorsum'' (''forward'') referred to Burberry's innovative fabrics and styles.

Although the gabardine name was used under exclusive trademark by Burberry until 1917, Britain's King Edward, one of the first members of the royal family to don the gabardine coat, has been credited with popularizing the Burberry name by requesting the garment by name. Burberry garments have enjoyed a loyal following among royalty and celebrities around the world ever since. The company's clientele has included Winston Churchill, Gary Cooper, Joan Crawford, Humphrey Bogart, George Bernard Shaw, Al Jolson, Peter Falk, Ronald Reagan, George Bush, Norman Schwarzkopf, and Paul Newman. The company also boasts warrants (endorsements of quality) from Her Majesty Queen Elizabeth II and H.R.H. The Prince of Wales. Considered a ''rite of passage'' by some commoners, a Burberry coat was a prerequisite to a first job interview.

Company Perspectives:

Burberry is an international luxury brand. Its globally recognized name, trademark, and signature trenchcoat have been synonymous with quality and enduring style for over 150 years.

New Products for the New Century

By the turn of the century, Burberry offered an extensive line of outerwear for both men and women. The company designed hats, jackets, pants, and gaiters especially for hunting, fishing, golf, tennis, skiing, archery, and mountaineering. The garments' time- and weather-tested reputation for durability helped make them the gear of choice for adventurers of the late 19th and early 20th century. Balloonists and early aviators wore specially made Burberry garments that let neither wind nor rain penetrate. Captain Roald Amundsen, Captain R.F. Scott, and Sir Ernest Shackleton wore Burberry clothing and took shelter in Burberry tents on their expeditions to the South Pole in the 1910s.

Burberry established its first foreign outlet in Paris in 1910 and soon had retail establishments in the United States and South America. It exported its first shipment of raincoats to Japan in 1915. It was World War I, however, that brought widespread acclamation and fame to Burberry. First worn by high-ranking generals during the turn of the century Boer War in South Africa, the Burberry coat soon was adopted as standard issue for all British officers. With the addition of epaulets and other military trappings, the garments came to be known as ''Trench Coats,'' so named for their ubiquity and durability through trench warfare. One Royal Flying Corps veteran wrote a testimonial noting, ''During the War, I crashed in the (English) Channel when wearing a Burberry trench coat and had to discard it. It was returned to me a week later, having been in the sea for five days. I have worn it ever since and it is still going strong.'' The company estimated that 500,000 Burberrys were worn and, perhaps more important, brought home, by veterans.

Rainwear became so important to Burberry that the company soon whittled its lines down to little more than trench coats and tailored menswear for much of the 20th century. The notoriously conservative manufacturer stuck primarily to its well-known raincoats until the 1960s, when a fluke led Burberry to capitalize on the garments' trademark tan, black, red, and white plaid lining. It all started with a window display at the company's Paris store. The shop's manager spiced up her arrangement of trench coats by turning up the hem of one coat to show off its checked lining, then repeated the check on an array of umbrellas. The clamor for the umbrellas was so immediate and compelling that Burberry's made and quickly sold hundreds. This experiment eventually led to the introduction of the cashmere scarf, also a perennial best-seller. By the 1990s, Burberry offered six different umbrella models and scarves in eight color schemes. This turning point in the company's merchandising scheme notwithstanding, rainwear remained Burberry's single largest line into the late 1970s and early 1980s, and menswear continued to dominate.

Emphasis on Exports and Women's and Children's Apparel in the 1980s and 1990s

Burberry's export business increased dramatically during the 1980s, fueled primarily by Japanese and American craving for prestigious designer goods. By mid-decade, exports constituted two-thirds of the British company's sales, with more than one-fourth of exports headed to Japan and another 15 percent sold in the United States. By 1996, Burberry had accumulated a record six Queen's Awards for Export Achievement and ranked among Great Britain's leading clothing exporters. Overseas sales continued to grow by double-digit percentages in the early 1990s.

Realizing that ''A fine tradition is not in itself sufficient today,'' Burberry sought to broaden its appeal to a younger, more fashion-conscious female clientele. Acknowledging that ''The first thing people think of when they hear Burberry is a man's trench coat,'' U.S. Managing Director Barry Goldsmith asserted in a 1994 *WWD* article, ''That's the image we're up against.'' One result was the Thomas Burberry collection, first introduced in Great Britain in 1988 and extended to the United States two years later. The new merchandise was priced 15 percent to 30 percent less than Burberry's designer lines, bringing a blouse down to $90 versus the normal $150 to $225, for example. Yet it was not just the price tags that set this ''bridge line'' apart from the brand's more traditional garb. The collection emphasized more casual sportswear, as opposed to career wear. ''Updated classics'' included youthful plaid mini kilts, jumpers, and snug ''jean fit'' slacks. U.S. advertising executive David Lipman called the line and its model, Christy Turlington, ''modernly relevant, yet classically beautiful.'' At the upper end of the scale, Burberry launched a personal tailoring service for the ladies. The company's women's division grew 30 percent from 1994 to early 1996 and was expected not only to overtake menswear, but to constitute more than 70 percent of total annual sales by 1999.

Although it continued to manufacture 90 percent of its merchandise in British factories, Burberry also started licensing its name, plaid, and knight logo to other manufacturers. By the mid-1990s, the Burberry name added panache to handbags and belts, throw pillows and boxer shorts, cookies and crackers, and fragrances and liquor. Childrenswear, stuffed toys, watches, handbags, golf bags, and even a co-branded VISA credit card sported the Burberry check.

Burberry's efforts at product and geographic diversification appeared to be paying off in the mid-1990s. Sales (including a small sister subsidiary, Scotch House) increased by more than one-third, from £200.9 million in fiscal 1994 (ended March 31) to £267.8 million in 1996. Net income before taxes grew twice as fast, from £41.1 million to £70 million, during the same period.

Focus on Strengthening the Burberry Brand in the Late 1990s

Despite diversification efforts, it became clear to company management that the Burberry brand did not have the spark it once claimed. In 1997, Rose Marie Bravo was elected CEO of Burberry. Her expertise in brand management fit in with company plans to strengthen the Burberry brand throughout the United States and Europe. Bravo began focusing on product and

Key Dates:

1856: Thomas Burberry establishes his first shop.
1891: Burberry begins selling clothing under the Burberry name in London's Haymarket section.
1909: The firm registers the "Equestrian Knight" trademark.
1915: Burberry ships its raincoats to Japan.
1966: The firm becomes a wholly owned subsidiary of Great Universal Stores.
1994: The company begins using well-known model Christy Turlington in its ad campaigns.
1996: By now, Burberry has accumulated a record six Queen's Awards for Export Achievement and ranks among Great Britain's leading clothing exporters.
1997: Rose Marie Bravo is hired as CEO.
1998: The Asian economic crisis causes financial problems for the firm.
1999: Burberry launches the Prorsum collection.
2000: Burberry breaks ground on a new flagship store in London.

design development and hired creative director Roberto Menichetti to head up this initiative.

While the company focused on positioning itself among leaders in the fashion industry, it began facing problems caused by its over-dependence on Asian customers. Sales decreased by 7 percent in 1998 and profits tumbled in its retail and wholesale sectors due to the Asian economic crisis. As a major exporter, Burberry also was hurt by the strength of the pound. The company also began to slow down its shipments to the Asian grey market—a market in which its products were sold cheaply or re-imported back to Europe and sold at a discount—and shut down three production facilities in the United Kingdom. Whereas this decision hurt the firm's profits in 1998, management felt it would, in the long run, protect the Burberry image.

In 1999, the company profits continued to falter. Sales decreased by 19 percent as the firm battled its Asian-related problems. Amidst its financial struggles, however, the company continued to focus on brand development and aggressive marketing. Under the leadership of Bravo, Burberry was once again re-emerging as an international luxury brand. The company launched its Prorsum collections in 1999, a new designer line that was part of Bravo's strategy. According to a June 1999 *Daily News Record* article, the launch was, "The latest step in the Bravo-directed makeover of the brand. Over the last 18 months, she's trimmed its distribution, cut the number of licensees, and ramped up marketing and advertising. The goal is to turn the Burberry name into a brand as hip as Gucci, Louis Vuitton, or Prada."

Success in the New Millennium

As Burberry entered the new millennium, its financial results improved dramatically. The Asian market recovered, its European and American markets grew, and its new brand strategy began to pay off. Trading profits increased 103 percent over the previous year and sales rose by 11 percent. The company also closed nonprofitable stores and opened new stores in Las Vegas, Nevada and in Tokyo. Burberry also opened a new three-floor flagship store in London that was 16,000 square feet in size and featured new product lines including lingerie and swimwear. A new licensing agreement was signed with Mitsui in Japan, securing a greater share of profits from that region, and the firm acquired its Spain-based licensee—Spain was the firm's second largest market after Japan.

Burberry's parent announced in late 2000 that it was planning an initial public offering (IPO) of the company's stock. Great Universal Stores did not consider the company one of its core businesses, and in light of Burberry's recent successes, it considered an IPO much more lucrative than selling the firm. In 2001, Burberry management continued its aggressive brand strategy and focus on its potential in the United States and in European markets such as France and Italy. Burberry's repositioning as a leading luxury brand left its management confident that it would remain successful in the future.

Principal Competitors

House of Fraser plc; Polo Ralph Lauren Corporation.

Further Reading

"Burberrys Goes Casual," *WWD,* December 21, 1993, p. 8.
Burberrys of London: An Elementary History of a Great Tradition, London: Burberry Ltd., 1987.
"Burberry's Women's Lines Thriving," *WWD,* May 15, 1996, p. 7.
Collier, Andrew, "Burberry Toasts Its History with Museum Exhibit," *WWD,* February 14, 1989, p. 10.
Emert, Carol, "Plaid in Dispute Concerning Sale of Burberry's Items," *Daily News Record,* August 8, 1995, p. 5.
Fallon, James, "Bravo on Burberry's Luxe New Digs: 'A Big Strategic Move,' " *Daily News Record,* August 23, 2000, p. 1.
——, "Burberry Considers Offering," *WWD,* November 17, 2000, p. 2.
——, "Burberry Profits More Than Double in Year," *Daily News Record,* June 9, 2000, p. 1B.
——, "Burberrys in U.S. to Get New Line," *Daily News Record,* August 23, 1990, p. 3.
——, "Burberrys' Next Generation; Company Revamps Thomas Burberry Line to Appeal to Younger Customer," *Daily News Record,* November 26, 1996, p. 3.
——, "Prorsum From Burberry: More Revolution Than Evolution," *Daily News Record,* June 21, 1999, p. 5.
Gray, Robert, "A Green and Pleasant Brand," *Marketing,* July 20, 1995, pp. 22–23.
Gray, Robert, and Arthur Friedman, "Finally, Some Sunshine for Rainwear," *WWD,* April 16, 1996, pp. 7-8.
Heller, Richard, "A British Gucci," *Forbes,* April 3, 2000, p. 84.
Pogoda, Dianne M., "Tipping the Sales," *WWD,* May 4, 1994, pp. 8–9.
Porter, Janet, "Burberrys Weathers Dollar Fall," *Journal of Commerce and Commercial,* February 26, 1987, pp. 1A, 6A.
"Stretching the Plaid," *Economist,* February 3, 2001, p. 7.
The Story of the Trenchcoat, London: Burberry of London, 1993.
Underwood, Elaine, "Check-ing Out," *Brandweek,* December 11, 1995, p. 32.
Woolcock, Keith, "The Great Universal Mystery," *Management Today,* November 1994, pp. 48–52.

—April Dougal Gasbarre
—update: Christina M. Stansell

Burns International Services Corporation

2 Campus Drive
Parsippany, New Jersey 07054
U.S.A.
Telephone: (973) 397-2000
Web site: http://www.burnsinternational.com

Wholly Owned Subsidiary of Securitas AB
Incorporated: 1909
Employees: 75,000
Sales: $1.3 billion (1999)
NAIC: 561611 Investigation Services; 561612 Security Guards and Patrol Services; 561613 Armored Car Services

A provider of investigative services, security guard staff, and other related services, Burns International Services Corporation, formerly operating as a division of the Borg-Warner Security Corporation, was purchased by the Swedish company Securitas AB in August 2000. Before its purchase, Burns operated over 320 offices in the United States, Canada, Columbia, Mexico, and the United Kingdom, and its services included providing security guards, background and drug screening, armored transport services, and investigation. It had a client base of over 14,000 commercial, financial, industrial, residential, and government customers and sales of $1.3 billion. After the Securitas purchase, Burns teamed up with Pinkerton's Inc.—another well-known U.S.-based security firm purchased by Securitas in March 1999; together, the firms operate over 600 U.S. offices, have 125,000 employees, and realize revenues of $2.5 billion.

Early 20th Century Origins

The company from which Burns International Services Corporation evolved, the William J. Burns National Detective Agency, was established in New York in 1909 by the son of Irish immigrant parents. Burns was born in Baltimore, Maryland, in 1861 and raised in Columbus, Ohio. He attended business college, and then joined his father in a tailoring enterprise, but became an amateur sleuth when, in 1878, his father began serving as police commissioner in Columbus. Although he had no official position with the police department, young William earned a reputation for detective work in forgery cases. For a brief period he worked for the Furlong Detective Agency in St. Louis, Missouri, then, in 1889, entered the U.S. Secret Service, where he had considerable success in tracking down counterfeiting operations, both in the United States and Costa Rica. He also uncovered bribery and land fraud by government employees, leading to the conviction of several federal, state, and municipal officials.

Burns left government service in 1906, with a growing reputation for incorruptibility and excellent detective work. For a time he continued to track down dishonest administrators, including the entire board of supervisors of San Francisco, California, and that city's political boss, Abraham Ruef. Burns and his associates had tough going, having to fight corrupt money interests, including, among others, a national trolley car trust and newspaper magnate William Randolph Hearst, who employed the cartoonist Ed Fisher to caricature them in what would later develop into the ''Mutt and Jeff'' comic strip.

In 1909, the by then celebrated detective organized the William J. Burns National Detective Agency, and within a year convinced the American Bankers' Association to terminate its association with the agency's chief competitor, the long established and renowned Pinkerton Agency. The move gave the new Burns agency the job of protecting the 12,000 member banks. Somewhat later the agency also gained the responsibility of protecting the holdings of the American Hotel Association. Initially, however, the agency was engaged as much in detective and investigative work as in protection services.

William Burns, from time to time returning to government service, left interim control of the agency to his two sons, Raymond J. Burns, president, and William Sherman Burns, secretary and treasurer. In 1913, the agency changed its name to the Burns International Detective Agency. By this time, the company was becoming famous for innovative detective methods, which, in 1916, involved Burns himself in something of a scandal and began the tarnishing of his image. Hired by the millionaire, J.P. Morgan, Burns led a midnight raid on the law offices of Seymour and Seymour, a firm that, like Morgan, was

Company Perspectives:

The company strives to be a world leader in security solutions, market by market; and pledges to offer the best security solutions, adapted to specific customer needs, precise in delivery, and cost efficient.

handling the sale of munitions to France and Great Britain, soon to be the allies of the United States in World War I. The firm was suspected of stealing trade secrets from Morgan, and Burns was trying to obtain evidence of its crime. Burns installed a Detectophone in the offices, a primitive listening device and the ancestor of the modern day ''bug.'' Also, with the aid of New York City police, he wire tapped the firm's telephones. The operation came to light when a disgruntled former employee of the Burns Agency disclosed it to the authorities. When the smoke created by newspaper coverage cleared, Burns was fined $100 for illegal entry.

In 1921, William J. Burns took the directorship of the Justice Department's Bureau of Investigation, the forerunner of the FBI. However, his three-year service in that office did nothing to enhance his reputation, since during that time the Bureau became involved in the scandals that plagued the administration of President Warren G. Harding. Burns resigned in 1924, leaving the directorship to his chief assistant, J. Edgar Hoover. By that time he was a fallen idol, a ''distinguished sinner,'' under virulent attack as an agent provocateur whose anti-union and anti-Communist crime-fighting methods played havoc with civil liberties. Burns went into full retirement, moving to Sarasota, Florida, where he died on April 14, 1932.

When Burns died, his agency was the second largest such business in the United States. His sons, Raymond J. and W. Sherman, always more cautious than their controversial father, began the process of transforming the business from a general detective firm to one specializing in guard services. During the Great Depression the agency's guards were used by industrialists, several of whom were under siege by desperate strikers. Some were also used to infiltrate unions as labor spies. In addition, Pinkerton and Burns both provided scabs during strikes, as a subcommittee of the Senate Committee on Education and Labor, chaired by Robert M. LaFollette, Jr., revealed in its investigations. When the practice came to public notice, both agencies ended it. Pinkerton even went so far as to refuse industrial guard services during strikes, but not Burns, which filled the need for some of Pinkerton's former clients. Between 1933 and 1936, the company made almost $330,000 from providing security guards, and in 1936 alone netted close to $156,000 from the operation, an increase of 266 percent over the previous year. However, the notoriety surrounding labor espionage and charges of civil liberty abuse lodged against both Pinkerton and Burns left both companies publicity shy and much more circumspect in their policies.

Growth and Expansion: 1950s–60s

Raymond J. and W. Sherman Burns remained at the company's helm through the Great Depression, World War II, and into the 1960s. In fact, the agency remained under direct family control into the late 1970s, when George E.B. King, the grandson of William J. Burns, became CEO. During that time the company had shifted its focus from crime investigation to protection service and continued to expand. By the end of the 1950s, Burns was grossing more than $20 million. Among its clients were General Motors, General Electric, Standard Oil of New Jersey, du Pont, A&P, and the American Bankers Association, the organization that had given the agency its first big contract back in 1909.

In 1959, in its 50th year, the company had 30 regional offices and close to 12,000 employees, about one-fourth of whom were either former FBI agents or policemen. Although it took on most protection and detective jobs, except divorce investigations, Burns declined to engage in labor espionage and cases involving politics, the areas in which it had previously been publicly embarrassed. The agency continued to use infiltration methods, and its Undercover Department remained at the core of the organization. Claiming to have the personnel and resources to take on an assignment ''of any size, any time and place a client wants it,'' Burns employees masqueraded undercover as everything from janitors to college professors, at rates of up to $25 per hour, depending on the assignment. Moreover, the company maintained enviable crime analysis laboratories and massive identification files, using an impressive array of state-of-the-art scientific equipment. By that time, supported by these resources, Burns was taking on about 5,000 assignments per year, some with considerable public fanfare, as when, in 1959, it was hired by the former Soviet Union to protect visiting Russian dignitaries, including Premier Khrushchev, and provide security at the Soviet trade fair in New York.

The business of Burns often necessitated clandestine or covert operations, which, as in the 1930s, subjected it to exposure and negative publicity. For example, in 1961, the agency went head to head with the American Association of University Professors (AAUP) when it circulated a letter indicating that it was ready to provide agents to infiltrate college student bodies in order to spy on faculty members. Burns apologized for what it maintained was the misguided scheme of a single operative in Houston and promised that academic espionage would be added to its list of taboo assignments.

As Burns continued to change its essential focus from criminal investigation to protection services, it led the way in what was a rapidly expanding industry. Undertaking some unique assignments, the agency agreed to protect the canine guards of the Dog Owners Guidance Service of New York against dognappers. That company's watchdogs came equipped with collars announcing that they were under the protection of Burns. It was that sort of service that helped Burns improve its sometimes tarnished image.

Competition Arises in the 1970s

In the 1970s, Pinkerton's and Burns International Security Services were the two largest contract security companies in the United States but were being pushed hard by the Wackenhut Corporation, a relatively new player in the security service game. There was undoubtedly room for competition, though, for it was in that decade, fired by drug trafficking, that the crime

Key Dates:

1909: The William J. Burns National Detective Agency is established.
1913: The firm changes its name to the Burns International Detective Agency.
1932: Burns dies and his sons take over what is now the second largest detective firm in the industry.
1959: The firm has grown to over 30 regional offices and 12,000 employees.
1981: Net earnings drop to $4 million due to increased competition.
1982: The firm becomes a subsidiary of Baker Industries, a division of Borg-Warner Security Corporation.
1987: Parent Borg-Warner is taken private.
1993: Borg-Warner enters the public arena for the second time under the name Borg-Warner Security; Burns operates as a division of this firm.
1997: Burns becomes part of Borg-Warner's Total Security Solutions unit.
1999: Borg-Warner unites its security operations under the name Burns International Security Services and adopts the corporate name Burns International Services Corporation.
2000: Burns is purchased by Securitas AB.

rate began a rapid upwards spiral. In 1974, analysts estimated that a full two percent of the GNP was being lost to crime.

By 1978, Burns had 99 branch offices in North and South America. Both Pinkerton and Burns were grossing about $200 million in business, and both employed about 40,000 people. With emphasis on security rather than detective work, Burns and Pinkerton became known colloquially as rent-a-cop businesses. Although Burns continued to provide alarm installation and monitoring systems, by 1979 about 86 percent of its total sales came from its guard services.

Despite the industry's growth, even the 1970s proved challenging for Burns. In 1971, a New York detective was convicted of selling police records to private businesses, including Pinkerton, Wackenhut, and Burns, and the security firms were fined for ''giving unlawful gratuities'' and ''rewarding official misconduct.'' Burns also came under scrutiny for its practice of hiring ex-FBI agents, although it was hardly alone in doing so. Competition was also growing, and Burns, Pinkerton, and Wackenhut, saw their combined share of the guard-service market drop from 39 percent in 1972 to about 23 percent by 1982. Of the three giants, Burns reportedly fared the worst. Still under the nominal control of the Burns family, its high net earning mark of about $8 million dropped to about $4 million in 1981. It then altered its market strategy somewhat, going after the business of large national and international firms, even using the equipment of its rivals to meet its customers' demands.

Burns Joins Borg-Warner in the 1980s

In 1982, Burns International Security Services became a subsidiary of Baker Industries and moved its operation from its Briar Cliff Manor headquarters in Westchester County, New York, to Parsippany, New Jersey. Baker had itself been acquired by the Borg-Warner Security Corporation in 1978, a division of Borg-Warner that was originally created as part of a continuing diversification and expansion program begun in the 1950s. Baker, operating under the Wells Fargo name, was a provider of armored car services, and Burns added new investigative and security services, providing additional diversification within the security service arena.

The security business, still dominated by Burns, Pinkerton's, and Wackenhut, picked up and boomed throughout the 1980s. By 1982, it had become a $3.3 billion industry, of which Burns had a $250 million share, second only to Pinkerton's $300 million. With crime rapidly becoming the number one problem in the United States, the number of persons employed by private security firms grew from about 1.05 million in 1980 to 1.6 million by 1993. Many companies that had formerly hired their own security guards changed to using services that Burns and other firms offered.

However, the period proved difficult for Burns's parent company. Straddled with a large debt, Borg-Warner had to take steps to downsize and restrict its operations. In 1986, it spun off York, one of its holdings, to its shareholders. The next year it was threatened with a hostile takeover from corporate raiders Irwin Jacobs and Samuel Heyman. It was saved when Merrill Lynch Capital Partners organized a leveraged buyout and converted Borg-Warner to a private company. Burdened with a $4.5 billion debt, Borg-Warner sold off all its holdings except its automotive and security divisions, including Burns. The company went public again in 1993, as Borg-Warner Security, and spun off Borg-Warner Automotive to its shareholders. With the restructuring, Burns initially remained a publicly traded subsidiary but was later converted to a division within the corporate infrastructure of Borg-Warner.

According to a 1993 study by industry analyst William Cunningham, growth in protection and security services was projected to continue into the 21st century. In fact, in the mid-1990s, there were over twice as many private-sector security personnel as there were public-sector law enforcement agents, and with a relative decline in public law enforcement funding, the demand on the private sector continued to increase.

Borg-Warner Adopts the Burns Name in the Late 1990s

Borg-Warner's focus on its security operations continued into the late 1990s. In 1997, the firm created its ''Total Security Solutions'' division by integrating its electronic, physical, and armored services, into one unit. CEO J. Joe Adorjan applauded the new business unit in a company press release stating, ''we created Borg-Warner Total Security Solutions to meet our customers' growing demand for an integrated, comprehensive security package. As the largest security company in the nation, we believe the time is right to offer customers the ultimate total security service.''

In another move to strengthen its brand recognition and unify its operations, Borg-Warner announced in May 1999 that it would officially adopt the name Burns International Services

Corporation and that its security operations would become Burns International Security Services. At the time of the change, business done under the Burns name was accounting for 60 percent of company revenues. Also during this time, the firm landed a large security services contract with the Immigration Service of the United Kingdom that year.

Amidst the changing corporate environment, Burns continued to secure large contracts including a deal with Motorola Inc. to provide security services. The firm also partnered with Cap Index Inc. in a deal that would allow Burns to access Cap's crime risk database. In order to strengthen the company's reach in Canada, Burns acquired Alberta-based Danfield Security Services Ltd.

Strategic Alliances in the New Millennium

The Burns corporate structure continued to change into the new millennium. Lackluster financial performance in its U.K. operations, slow growth expectations, and consolidation in the industry, were factors in its faltering $10 stock price. Management continued to aggressively pursue national clients, and talks of strategic alliances began. Then, in September 2000, Securitas AB, the largest security firm in Europe, announced that it had acquired Burns for $650 million and the assumption of $193 million of debt.

In March 1999, Securitas had purchased Pinkerton's Inc., the long-time Burns competitor. After the Burns purchase, Securitas integrated the two firms under their Security Services USA business unit. According to a *Mergers & Acquisitions* article, ''Securitas has said it believes that no other security company can match its global reach. It offers security officer services, systems integration, consulting, and investigations. As corporations expand around the world, the Swedish company is betting that its size and reach will make it the first choice for many multinational clients.''

The strategic positioning of Burns and Pinkerton left only one other major competitor in the U.S. security market—Wackenhut Corporation. Although industry analysts predicted little growth in the market for security services, particularly with U.S. crime rates realizing a slight decline, Burns's new alignment with Pinkerton's under the Securitas banner helped establish it as a market leader and began yet another chapter in its lively history.

Principal Competitors

Wackenhut Corporation; Chubb plc; Pittston Company.

Further Reading

''Borg-Warner Security Announces Brand Unification Strategy and Intent to Change Corporate Name,'' *PR Newswire*, May 4, 1999.

''Burns International Services Corporation Announces Acquisition of Danfield Security Services Ltd.,'' *PR Newswire*, February 1, 2000.

''Burns International Services Corporation CEO John Edwardson Talks to the Wall Street Transcript,'' *PR Newswire*, April 7, 2000.

Caesar, Gene, *The Incredible Detective: The Biography of William J. Burns*, Englewood Cliffs, N.J.: Prentice-Hall, 1968.

''Crime: The Super Sleuths,'' *Newsweek*, August 31, 1959, pp. 67–68.

''The Dog Watch,'' *Newsweek*, September 12, 1962, p. 104.

Donley, Michele, ''Burns International Services Corp.,'' *Crain's Chicago Business*, June 7, 2000, p. 44.

Dorfman, John R., ''Caught Flat-Footed,'' *Forbes*, April 12, 1982, pp. 74, 78.

''George E.B. King Elected Top Executive of Burns International,'' *Wall Street Journal*, May 4, 1979.

''The History of William J. Burns,'' *Nation*, November 23, 1927, p. 561.

''Junior Burns Man,'' *Newsweek*, May 22, 1961, p. 60.

Kerber, Ross, ''Policing the Growing Security Business,'' *Washington Post*, September 6, 1993, p. 5E.

Lipson, Milton, *On Guard: The Business of Private Security*, New York: Quadrangle/New York Times Book Co., 1975.

''Notes from the Capital: W.J. Burns,'' *Nation*, July 13, 1916, p. 32.

O'Toole, George, *The Private Sector: Private Spies, Rent-a-Cops, and the Police-Industrial Complex*, New York: W.W. Norton, 1978.

Rackham, Anne, ''Bad Times Mean Good Times for Security Guard Firms,'' *Los Angeles Business Journal*, February 15, 1993, p. 23.

''Securitas Buys Top U.S. Security Firms,'' *Mergers & Acquisitions*, October 2000, p. 17.

Youmans, Sabrina, ''Private Security Firms Locking Up Varied Services,'' *San Diego Business Journal*, October 11, 1993, p. 21.

—John W. Fiero
—update: Christina M. Stansell

CANDLEWOOD®
HOTEL COMPANY

Candlewood Hotel Company, Inc.

8621 East 21st Street North, Suite 200
Wichita, Kansas 67206
U.S.A.
Telephone: (316) 631-1300
Fax: (316) 631-1333
Web site: http://www.candlewoodsuites.com

Public Company
Incorporated: 1995
Employees: 1,123
Sales: $131.2 million (2000)
Stock Exchanges: NASDAQ
Ticker Symbol: CNDL
NAIC: 72111 Hotels (Except Casino Hotels) and Motels

Candlewood Hotel Company, Inc. is a leader in the extended-stay segment of the American hotel industry. Its hotels resemble apartment complexes, and guests, most of them business travelers, typically stay for two weeks or more. Candlewood hotels offer studio or one-bedroom suites, each equipped with a kitchen and a large work table, two-line phone, and many other amenities. Unlike other hotels, Candlewood Suites have no attached bar or restaurant, and do not have a front desk staffed all night. Candlewood hotels also operate with a far lower staff-to-guest ratio than most other hotels. The company leases hotels to franchisees and also directly owns and operates facilities. As of 2001 there were close to 90 Candlewood Suites hotels, spread across 30 states, with one under construction in Berlin. Candlewood Hotel Company also runs a sister brand, Cambridge Suites, for the upscale end of the market. Candlewood Hotel Company was founded by Jack DeBoer, recognized in the hotel industry as the father of the extended-stay concept. An approximately 27 percent share in the publicly traded company is owned by hotel company Doubletree Corp.

The Reluctant Hotelier in the 1970s

Candlewood Hotel Company, Inc. was founded by Jack DeBoer, who had made his name in the hotel industry in the 1970s with the Residence Inn chain. DeBoer was raised in Kalamazoo, Michigan, and he earned a business degree from Michigan State University. His family ran a business developing apartments. With a background in apartments, DeBoer got into the hotel business with trepidation. What became the first extended-stay hotel began as a short-term apartment complex, designed for business travelers who would lease a small apartment for a month. DeBoer built the complex in Wichita, Kansas, going into business with a partner, Rolf E. Ruhfus. It opened in 1975. Called the Residence Inn, DeBoer recalled for *Hotel & Motel Management* (October 2, 2000): ''When we built it, I didn't have a clue what it was.'' DeBoer's building did not include many traditional hotel trappings, such as a laundry operation, because he did not think of it as a hotel. The people who stayed at the Residence Inn were not called ''guests,'' and they did not ''check in.'' They were simply tenants who would stay for a minimum of 30 days. DeBoer himself had traveled for his family business for years, and he thought he had an idea what professional people wanted in terms of comfort and privacy. Still, he had only a hazy idea of who his tenants would be and what exactly they needed. He imagined they would be businessmen relocating, who had to have a place to stay until they rented a longer-term apartment or bought a house. So Residence Inn offered televisions, dishes, and other furnishings as extras, for a price. But DeBoer quickly found that his tenants always wanted these things, and the Residence Inn began providing them automatically, folding the cost into the room rate. Residence Inn also soon dispensed with the 30-day minimum stay. DeBoer had rented some rooms to the Boeing Co. for some traveling executives. Boeing liked the Residence Inn, but wanted to bring in other executives for less than the minimum 30 days. So the Residence Inn became a by-the-night arrangement.

DeBoer gradually abandoned the idea that he had a short-term apartment complex on his hands and embraced the extended-stay hotel idea. With the first Wichita hotel, DeBoer's goal was to charge $17 a night, a fee he at first thought was enormous. But he discovered that he could charge much more than that. The Residence Inn had landscaped walkways, gardens, and a basketball court, and looked more like a group of townhouses than a hotel. He explained to *Hotel & Motel Management* that no matter how nice the apartments were, ''I tell

Company Perspectives:

Candlewood Suites Mission Statement:

To create and operate a national brand of value-oriented, business-travel hotels that deliver exceptional value to customers and superior profits to franchisees and investors.

you the rent is $1,800 a month, you would say, 'You can't get $1,800 a month for this.' " Rent at a comparable apartment complex would have been a fraction of that. But asking $60 a night still struck travelers as a moderate price, compared with what other hotels were charging. So the hybrid apartment-hotel was much more profitable if clearly run as a hotel. When DeBoer realized this, he hung up a sign on the Wichita property that read, "Yes, we are a hotel."

DeBoer developed the Residence Inn into a small chain of hotels, even though experienced hoteliers told him he could not succeed. DeBoer sought out the founder of the Holiday Inn chain, Kemmons Wilson, who told him every hotel had to have a bar. DeBoer was adamant in building his hotels without bars or restaurants, despite Wilson's advice. DeBoer also dispensed with another hotel staple, service. Although other hotels might offer great customer service by staffing the desk 24 hours, doing daily laundry, and generally being conspicuous and available, the Residence Inn went the opposite route. It offered minimal service, arguing that what the guests really wanted was to be left alone. The Residence Inn in Denver began offering guests a free breakfast buffet, something that soon became standard in other hotels. But eventually the Residence Inn stopped serving breakfast. Guests had to alter their schedules to get to the lobby in time to eat. DeBoer reasoned that stopping the free breakfast was actually restoring peace of mind to the Residence Inn's guests. Now they would not have to bother with it. Less service was actually more of what customers in the extended-stay niche wanted. As a result, Residence Inns were able to operate with far fewer staff than traditional hotels. This increased their profitability.

Extended-Stay Niche Growing in the 1980s

The Residence Inn chain had only six hotels by 1981. DeBoer sold off the franchising rights that year, only to buy the company back in 1985. By that time, there were 44 Residence Inns in 23 states, with many more under construction. The extended-stay concept had been honed. Although service was minimal, personal touches prevailed. The guest suites had not only a full-service kitchen but a popcorn popper, and holidays were celebrated with parties in the lobby. The extended-stay niche was proven profitable—much more profitable than the hotel industry as a whole. More than half the Residence Inn guests stayed for two weeks or more, with an average stay of more than seven days. The occupancy rate was also high, about 75 percent, compared with about 65 percent for conventional hotels at that time. In addition, although traditional hotels had on average one staff member for every guest, Residence Inn had only one employee per five guests. Revenue for the chain was estimated at near $80 million in the mid-1980s. Although other hotels had copied the Residence Inn's extended-stay idea, DeBoer's chain was the market leader. In late 1985, DeBoer told *Industry Week* (August 5, 1985), a hospitality industry journal, that he planned to add one new property a week to the chain over the next few years and grow by $100 million annually. Yet in 1986 he sold the chain to Marriott Corporation, and ceased running it.

DeBoer had entered into a noncompete agreement with Marriott. But he was not ready to leave the market segment in which he had done so well. In 1988 he and his former business partner Ruhfus launched a new hotel chain, first called Neighborhood Inn. Its difference from Marriott's Residence Inn was a stringent requirement of a 30-day minimum stay. The first Neighborhood Inn property opened in 1989. But the name was soon changed to Summerfield Suites, for its more dignified sound, and the 30-day minimum stay was dropped. Summerfield offered two-bedroom suites, described by one Summerfield executive to *Travel Weekly* (June 10, 1993) as "a kind of upscale college dormitory suite." The two rooms could be billed separately, and the combined price was less than that of two single rooms. Like Residence Inn, Summerfield catered to business travelers. By 1991, Summerfield had sales of around $25 million, with 12 properties across the country. Many other companies had begun building extended-stay hotels. Already in the late 1980s the market niche included Hawthorn Suites, Quality Suites, Homewood Suites, and City Suites of America as major competitors, aside from Summerfield and Marriott's Residence Inns. These extended-stay hotels represented only 1 percent of the hotel industry, yet the market segment accounted for more than 30 percent of hotel industry revenue.

Moving on to Candlewood in the 1990s

Jack DeBoer sold his stake in Summerfield to the Summerfield Hotel Corp. in 1992. Summerfield eventually was bought and run by the giant Wyndham International, Inc., one of the largest hotel companies in the world. DeBoer was well-off financially after the sale of his share of Summerfield. He was an avid pilot and, in fact, held a world jet speed record. He and his wife set off on a three-and-a-half-month trip around the world in his own plane. It was this trip that inspired DeBoer's next venture, Candlewood. Impressed by the poverty they saw on their travels, DeBoer, at his wife's urging, went back into the hotel business, with the aim of contributing profits to the charitable DeBoer Family Foundation. The foundation gave loans and support to people and businesses in Burma (now Myanmar). In 1995, DeBoer began approaching possible partners for Candlewood, his new extended-stay hotel chain. He gathered executives from Residence Inns and Summerfield Suites, and got backing from the Doubletree Corp., a Phoenix-based company that ran hotels and resorts. Candlewood Hotel Co. aimed to build a brand of mid-priced extended-stay hotels that would put together everything DeBoer had learned about the industry over the past 20 years. The first hotel opened in May 1996, and in November that year, the firm went public, listing its shares on Nasdaq. Doubletree had invested $15 million in Candlewood and also arranged generous financing to spur the growth of the new venture. By 1997, Candlewood already had about 45 hotels. On average they had 122 rooms, which leased for around $50–$80 a night for a studio and up to

Key Dates:

1975: First Residence Inn debuts in Wichita.
1988: Summerfield chain starts, under the name Neighborhood Inn.
1995: DeBoer begins third hotel venture, Candlewood.
2000: Candlewood goes to Europe.

$100 a night for a one-bedroom suite. Candlewood continued the less-is-more concept of service that had proved popular with the Residence Inns, and added many special touches to the rooms. Each contained a small kitchen, complete with coffee maker, dishwasher, microwave, and full-sized refrigerator. The living room/office space included a television with a VCR, a desk, clock-radio, CD player, and two phone lines, all designed for the convenience of a traveler spending at least five days. Candlewood built its own properties for the most part, and each cost roughly $5 million to $7 million to construct. The firm saved on operating costs where possible, not using maintenance-heavy features such as exterior paint or landscape shrubbery. Like DeBoer's earlier Residence Inns, the Candlewood Suites had no bar or restaurant on site.

Extended-stay remained a hot growth area in the hotel industry overall. By the late 1990s, extended-stay had grown slightly as a percentage of available rooms, from around 1 percent a decade earlier to 1.4 percent. Yet extended-stay rooms accounted for some 12 to 14 percent of demand, and Candlewood Suites for the most part had a high occupancy rate. The average Candlewood customer booked a room for 14 days. As Candlewood extended its chain coast to coast, other hotels hoped to get a piece of the profitable niche. When Candlewood moved into key markets like Dallas/Fort Worth, it often found itself flanked by competitors such as Hampton Suites and Inn, Homestead Village, Fairfield Suites, Intown Suites, and even its own cousins Summerfield Suites and Residence Inn. By the late 1990s, Candlewood was opening around 20 hotels a year. Most of them were corporate-owned, but the company hoped to move to a mix of half-owned, half-franchised in coming years. By 1999 the company owned about 85 percent of its hotels.

The growing company did not turn a quarterly profit until 1999. It came up with losses as it continued to invest heavily in building and expansion. But by 2000, the company claimed its finances were healthy. It had about 85 hotels opened, 14 of which were run by franchisees. Five more were joint ventures. In terms of revenue per room, the company was growing in double digits, and Candlewood's occupancy rate remained much higher than the industry average. In 2000 Candlewood Hotel Co. began promoting a new brand of extended-stay hotels, called Cambridge Suites. Cambridge Suites was meant to capture a more upscale market than the emphatically mid-priced Candlewood. Cambridge offered more amenities than its sister brand, including a continental breakfast and a recreation room. The company also began piloting a smaller Candlewood, meant for smaller markets. Whereas the traditional Candlewood Suites had more than 120 rooms, the small-market hotel was designed with just 60 rooms.

In 2000 Candlewood Hotel Co. also began its first venture abroad, developing a Candlewood Suites hotel in Berlin with the Irish firm Midlantic Hotels Ltd. The agreement with Midlantic, which was ultimately owned by the Swiss conglomerate ERB Group, gave the hotel company exclusive rights to develop Candlewood Suites in Germany and Switzerland. Although the extended-stay concept was booming in the United States, such hotels were rare in Europe. Midlantic planned to build five Candlewood Suites in Europe over the next several years.

Principal Divisions

Candlewood Suites; Cambridge Suites.

Principal Competitors

Extended Stay America; Marriott International, Inc.; Hilton Hotels Corp.

Further Reading

Belden, Tom, "Four Philadelphia-Area Extended–Stay Hotels Planned," *Knight-Ridder/Tribune Business News,* May 14, 1997.

"Candlewood Hotel Co., LLC," *Hotel & Motel Management,* August 14, 2000, p. 52.

"Candlewood Suites," *Hotel & Motel Management,* February 15, 1999, p. 45.

Deady, Tom, "Marriott to Buy Residence Inns," *Travel Weekly,* May 7, 1987, p. 1.

"Doubletree to Be Partner in New Long-Stay Brand," *Travel Weekly,* October 26, 1995, p. 6.

Fisher, Michelle, "Extended Stay: DeBoer Starting Chain with 30-Day Minimum," *Hotel & Motel Management,* April 18, 1988, pp. 1, 102.

Gillette, Bill, "Summerfield Springing into Prominence," *Hotel & Motel Management,* September 6, 1993, pp. 4, 7.

Golden, Fran, "Summerfield Markets Its Roomy, Two-Bedroom Alternative," *Travel Weekly,* June 10, 1993, p. 21.

Higley, Jeff, "Candlewood Pursues More Partners," *Hotel & Motel Management,* June 3, 1999, p. 3.

——, "Newsmaker Jack DeBoer," *Hotel & Motel Management,* October 2, 2000, pp. 80–82.

Humphrey, Linda, "Candlewood Brand Appoints Roos Chief Operating Officer," *Travel Weekly,* June 23, 1997, p. 45.

Mathis, Karen Brune, "Wichita, Kan., Hotel Venture May Add to Jacksonville, Fla., Room Boom," *Knight-Ridder/Tribune Business News,* March 20, 1997.

McLinden, Mike, "Candlewood Plans Arlington, Texas, Hotel," *Knight-Ridder/Tribune Business News,* September 30, 1997.

Nelson, Eric, "Summerfield Opens Suites Hotel That Seeks Longer Stays," *San Francisco Business Times,* October 26, 1990, p. 12.

Pearce, Dennis, "Wichita, Kan.-Based Business-Hotel Firm Reports First-Ever Profit," *Knight-Ridder/Tribune Business News,* November 2, 1999.

——, "Wichita, Kan., Hotel Company Profits Continue to Increase," *Knight-Ridder/Tribune Business News,* August 4, 2000.

Verespej, Michael A., "Jack DeBoer's Sweet Suite Idea," *Industry Week,* August 5, 1985, p. 56.

Wolff, Carlo, "Flying the Contrarian Flag," *Lodging Hospitality,* November 1998, p. 42.

—A. Woodward

Chicago Board of Trade

Chicago Board of Trade

141 West Jackson Boulevard
Chicago, Illinois 60604
U.S.A.
Telephone: (312) 435-3500
Fax: (312) 341-3392
Web site: http://www.cbot.com

Non-Profit Company
Incorporated: 1848
Employees: 800
Operating Revenues: $184.7 million (1999)
NAIC: 52321 Securities and Commodity Exchanges

Chicago Board of Trade (CBOT) is one of the busiest commodities exchanges in the world. The Board of Trade has more than 3,600 members, who trade almost 50 different futures and options products, including U.S. Treasury bonds, silver, soy beans, wheat, and Dow Jones Industrial Average futures. Annual trading volume is more than 200 million contracts. The CBOT operates as a not-for-profit corporation run by its members and a Board of Directors. Trades are accomplished through a so-called open outcry system, where traders meet face-to-face to make transactions in trading rooms known as pits. The CBOT adopted a computerized trading system for some trades in the late 1990s. Open outcry trading fell out of use at other leading exchanges in the 1990s, and the future of CBOT's trading pits was increasingly called into question. By the early 2000s, the future direction of the CBOT was still under consideration. The CBOT announced a decision to transform itself into a for-profit corporation with two separate trading areas, one electronic and one open outcry. This restructuring was bogged down by negotiation and litigation between the CBOT and the other Chicago exchanges, the Chicago Board Option Exchange and the Chicago Mercantile Exchange, and by indecision on the part of CBOT members and executives. As of March 2001, the CBOT planned to move ahead with restructuring and to form an alliance with the electronic German/Swiss exchange Eurex.

Early History

The Chicago Board of Trade was formed in that city in 1848 by a group of businessmen who wanted to bring order to the Midwest's chaotic grain market. Farm prices were ruled by boom and bust cycles. In the winter, when grain was scarce, the price was high. At harvest time, Chicago was inundated with grain, and farmers had to accept extremely low prices. Some farmers kept their grain back from market, preferring to burn it for fuel rather than waste money shipping it when prices were low. Other farmers found that they could not get a fair price for their corn or wheat, and they ended up dumping it into Lake Michigan rather than pay to haul or store it. The Board of Trade offered farmers a way to get a guaranteed price for their goods ahead of time by offering ''to arrive'' contracts, or futures. At planting time, a farmer could negotiate the price he would get at harvest time. Big buyers of grain benefited by assuring themselves in advance a specific supply.

The Chicago Board of Trade first consisted of 25 directors who met in a space above a feed store on Water Street. The directors were not all grain merchants. The founding group also included a grocer, a tanner, a hardware merchant, a banker, a bookseller, and a druggist. The Board standardized bushel sizes and established ways of identifying different grades of grain.

Trading was not extremely active in the beginning, and the Board tried to lure business by offering free lunches. But Chicago was on its way to becoming the predominant grain market in the Midwest. Chicago's first railroad link was being laid the year the exchange began. Soon Chicago was a rail hub for ten major railroads, and more than a hundred trains came in and out of the city every day. A new canal linked the city to river traffic leading to the Mississippi. Its logistical convenience helped make the city a center for meat packing. Chicago became a national and even international center for agricultural commodities in the 1850s. In 1855 the French government abandoned its practice of buying grain in New York and came to Chicago instead. By 1856, the CBOT had about 150 members, and it moved to new quarters on the corner of South Water and LaSalle Streets. In 1859 the Illinois legislature granted the CBOT a charter, which allowed it authority to govern itself. The CBOT found itself a very popular institution by the end of the 1850s. It had established a new system of

Company Perspectives:

The CBOT's principal role is to provide contract markets for its members and customers and to oversee the integrity and cultivation of those markets. Its markets provide prices that result from trading in open auction or electronic platforms. The marketplace assimilates new information throughout the trading day, and through trading it translates this information into benchmark prices agreed upon by buyers and sellers.

grading grain that helped the market run more smoothly. Under the old system, a farmer's lot of grain had to be inspected at many points in the selling process, to make sure it was of the quality and cleanliness it was supposed to be. If a farmer stored his grain with other farmers' lots, grains of differing qualities might get mixed, affecting the price later. The Board of Trade instituted a new system where grain was graded before storage and dumped in a bin only with grain of the same quality. The farmer received a receipt for x amount of grain of x quality. Thus the farmer did not have to retrieve his individual bags of grain for resale, or trust that his grain's quality had not been downgraded by promiscuous storage. Use of the receipts made it easier to trade large volumes of grain. Instead of buying and selling actual bags of wheat or corn, brokers could trade the receipts. Soon they began vigorously trading grain futures. For the farmer, the futures contract guaranteed a certain price in a distant month. Speculators also could buy a futures contract, gambling that they could make money off it by selling it later if the price changed.

While Chicago became an agricultural center, the Board of Trade ensured that the city also became a financial center, with a huge liquid market in agricultural commodities futures. The CBOT standardized its futures contracts in 1865, and moved to its first permanent facility, in the Chicago Chamber of Commerce Building.

In the early years of the CBOT, many disreputable traders tarnished its reputation. Some traders tried to ''corner'' a market, that is, buy up most of the available corn or wheat to drive the price up. The Board acted to expel traders who cornered, but it was not successful in abolishing the practice. Another blemish on the CBOT was the existence of illegal outfits known as bucket shops. The bucket shops presented themselves as legitimate commodities brokers, but customer orders were not actually traded on the CBOT floor. In fact the bucket shops ran a numbers game using Board of Trade market figures. In the 1880s the CBOT worked hard to drive the bucket shops out of business.

The CBOT tried to keep its market information inside the building, banning telegraph employees, cutting telegraph lines, and even soaping its windows so bucket shop clerks could not see in and read the latest figures off the chalkboard. Fraud and manipulation of the market caused public outcry against futures trading. When the CBOT moved again in 1885, this time to its own building on LaSalle Street and Jackson Boulevard, protesters called the organization the ''board of thieves.'' Nevertheless, the CBOT continued to grow and prosper. Spectacular attempts to corner grain markets continued. In 1897 Joseph Leiter, 28-year-old son of one of the founders of Chicago's famed Marshall Field department store, attempted to corner the wheat market, driving the price per bushel up from 67 cents in April 1897 to $1.85 a bushel a year later. Leiter's corner broke down in May 1898, reputedly at the same time his father returned to Chicago and found out what he was doing. Leiter lost an estimated $20 million on this escapade. Despite Leiter's dramatic failure, another trader, James Patten, attempted a wheat corner in 1908. Because of Patten's hoarding, the price of wheat went up, though the supply of wheat was plentiful. Chicago newspapers speculated that the rising cost of bread might spark riots. Patten's corner was successful: his personal profit was estimated at more than $1 million. But Patten was vilified in the press, and the U.S. Congress contemplated a bill to ban futures trading altogether.

During World War I, the CBOT attempted to set reasonable prices for grain so that the price would not rise and fall continuously. Then the federal government asked the Board of Trade to stop trading wheat futures. The ban lasted almost three years. At the war's end, wheat prices plummeted. It was not clear that the resumption of wheat trading had anything to do with the slump, but enraged Midwestern legislators claimed that unregulated futures trading was behind the price fluctuations. President Wilson ordered an inquiry into the grain market. Eventually, the investigation led to the Grain Futures Act of 1922, establishing the first federal control over futures trading. Even after the new law's enactment, CBOT traders tried cornering the wheat market. Arthur Cutten tried to corner wheat in 1924, driving prices up more than a dollar per bushel. The CBOT formed its own regulatory body, the Business Conduct Committee, to investigate Cutten. The committee urged Cutten to stop buying up wheat, and he did, for the time being. But Cutten returned to futures trading in the 1930s, until the Grain Futures Administration, the government regulatory body, banned him from the market. Other cornering incidents in the 1930s, which sparked great fluctuations in wheat prices, led to increasing oversight of the CBOT from Washington. The 1922 Grain Futures Act was replaced in 1936 with the Commodity Exchange Act. This placed explicit limits on the number of contracts individual traders could hold, so that speculators like Arthur Cutten could not corner, and outlawed other practices as well. The new act still left the CBOT with many self-regulatory powers.

Changes After World War II

During World War II, trading at the CBOT came to a virtual standstill. The corn and wheat crops were under government control. CBOT traders had to content themselves with trading in rye and soybeans. Soybean futures trading had come to the CBOT in 1936. Eventually, this became one of the Board's most active commodities. After the war, the CBOT continued to trade an array of agricultural commodities. The CBOT added trading in soybean oil and soy meal in the early 1950s. The Board's first nongrain commodity was added in 1968, when the meat product known as Iced Broilers began trading. Then in 1969, the CBOT added two more significant commodities: plywood and silver. Silver was the first precious metal on the Chicago exchange.

In the 1970s, the CBOT began to move out of exclusively agricultural commodities and deal in financial instruments. In 1975, the CBOT began trading in futures on Government Na-

Key Dates:

1848: The company is founded by 25 Chicago businessmen.
1859: A charter is granted by the Illinois legislature.
1922: Grain Futures Act of 1922 establishes first federal control over futures trading.
1973: Chicago Board Options Exchange is founded.
1977: CBOT begins trading in U.S. Treasury bonds, which become the exchange's most active item.
1996: Project A is launched.
2001: New CEO reaffirms plans to restructure CBOT as for-profit company, with electronic trading component.

tional Mortgage Association certificates, called GNMAs, or Ginnie Maes. Like corn or wheat, the price of GNMAs fluctuated over time, and they could be bought or sold by traders speculating on future price changes. Then in 1977, CBOT began offering trading on U.S. Treasury bonds. Treasury bonds became the CBOT's most actively traded product.

Other changes came to the CBOT as well. The Board founded a sister entity in 1973, the Chicago Board Options Exchange (CBOE). This was established specifically to trade securities options. Options trading is governed by complex mathematical rules, where traders have the option, but not the obligation, to buy a futures contract at a specified price before a specified expiration time. The CBOT had been trading securities options since 1970, but by setting up a separate facility, the Board's traders were insulated from the risks of options trading. But CBOT members could exercise trading privileges at the CBOE as well. The CBOT also began to introduce more computers into its trading system in the 1970s. Financial data was tracked by computer at a separate facility starting in 1970. In other ways, though, trading at the CBOT continued as it had in the 19th century. Many traders were the sons and even grandsons of traders, keeping the skill in the family. The open outcry practice continued, where traders shouted out their orders to the entire trading pit. Traders at the CBOT had developed a complex system of hand signals, since it was often so loud in the pit that voices could not be heard across the room. Even as computers replaced Morse code and chalkboards, traders bought and sold by flashing fingers at each other. Orders were written on pocket-sized cards and conveyed here and there by a bevy of runners. The CBOT had admitted its first women traders in 1969. But the CBOT remained a mostly male world of shouting, jostling traders. No specific educational background was needed to become a trader. The CBOT was by most accounts a unique financial institution, where people with only a high school education could rise to prominence.

The CBOT did not leave cornering scandals behind in the 1970s. One of the most remarkable incidents of market manipulation came in 1979, when two wealthy Texas brothers, William Herbert Hunt and Nelson Bunker Hunt began buying up silver. The Hunts began buying and stockpiling silver in 1979, causing the price to rise. It was evident what they were up to early on, and the CBOT's president urged them to stop. By early 1980, the Hunts controlled 70 percent of the silver traded on the CBOT, and half the silver traded on the rival Commodity Exchange of New York (Comex). The regulatory Commodity Futures Trading Commission (CFTC) was empowered to act in case of a ''market emergency,'' but the commission's board could not agree that the silver corner was an emergency. Finally, the CBOT and Comex put limits on how much silver could be traded in each month, and then issued orders that silver trading was for ''liquidation only,'' meaning it could be sold, but not bought. Silver had climbed from under $9 an ounce to more than $50 because of the Hunt brothers' actions. Yet the collapse of the corner bankrupted the Hunts. The incident showed how vulnerable the commodities market still was to manipulation. However, the CBOT acted successfully to put a stop to the illegal activity.

Growth and Problems in the 1980s and 1990s

The CBOT had grown from a trading center for the Midwest grain market to a national financial center in the 1970s, especially because of its active market in U.S. Treasury bonds. By 1981, Treasury bonds were the most actively traded commodity contract in the United States. The growing activity of the Board led to more physical expansion. Since 1930 the CBOT had been housed in an impressive 45-story building at LaSalle and Jackson Streets, a landmark Chicago structure. The Board began a 23-story addition in 1980, to provide for more offices and more trading space. The new 32,000-square-foot trading floor opened in 1982. The CBOT introduced new options trading that year, beginning to trade options on Treasury bond futures. In 1984 it introduced options on soybean futures. The CBOT also had put together an energy complex, with trading on futures contracts in heating oil and crude oil. The cost of membership in the CBOT swung higher and higher, reaching $550,000 in 1987. Despite the stock market crash of October 1987, the CBOT remained open. It was the only major exchange in the world not shut down by the crisis. Trading volume also grew in the 1980s. By 1990, the CBOT traded 154 million contracts annually, making it the busiest exchange in the world.

Despite its increasing importance as a world financial market, the CBOT could not escape its reputation as a somewhat lawless, arcane place rife with market manipulators. In 1989 the CBOT suffered one of its worst embarrassments when dozens of traders there and at the Chicago Mercantile Exchange (CME) were arrested after an undercover FBI investigation. The FBI had put its agents into CBOT trading pits beginning in 1987. There the agents made trades while watching and recording the actions of their fellows. Many traders were charged with defrauding customers and were hauled in under federal racketeering laws. The traders were charged with illegal practices like trading ahead of a customer order. That is, when a trader knew he was going to execute a trade for a customer that might cause prices to go up or down, he would trade first on his own account, to his own advantage. Traders also were charged with completing trades after hours and with destroying evidence of losing trades. The resulting trials were long and drawn out, but in 1991 eight CBOT soybean traders were convicted and sentenced to prison terms. The Board of Trade upped its own surveillance of its members and increased the amount of fines it could levy.

The public scrutiny of the CBOT resulting from the FBI sting led to calls to update its operations. Trades made by a flash of fingers and recorded in pencil on a note card seemed to outsiders to invite confusion, if not fraud. But the CBOT was resistant to change. In the early 1990s, the CBOT began exploring different merger and joint venture options. The Board negotiated with the Chicago Mercantile Exchange to develop a new trading system, when in 1993 the CME suddenly announced it would work on its new system with the New York Mercantile Exchange instead. The CBOT also negotiated to buy the New York Commodity Exchange, but the deal fell through in mid-1993. The CBOT set a new record for number of contracts traded in 1994, and began construction of a huge new trading floor in 1995. The new floor would be for face-to-face trading, the same system that had been in place since the CBOT's founding. At the same time, the Board began an Internet-based market information service. In 1996 it introduced an electronic trading platform it called ''Project A.''

Open Outcry Versus Electronic Trading in the Late 1990s

By the mid-1990s, it was clear that the CBOT's open outcry trading system would have to make concessions to the march of technology. The Internet had opened the door to a variety of new electronic trading systems, which matched trades virtually instantaneously. Traders insisted that their face-to-face system worked well and should persist. Meanwhile, other exchanges were abandoning open outcry. In 1998, a German/Swiss all-electronic exchange called Eurex opened for business. Within a year, it had surpassed the CBOT for the title of world's busiest commodities exchange. It also put pressure on the London exchange LIFFE, which had traded currency futures using open outcry. LIFFE adopted an electronic trading platform in order to survive. The French commodities exchange, MATIF, decided to experiment. It opened side-by-side trading floors, one open outcry, one electronic. Within only weeks, the open outcry system at MATIF was dead. The CBOT moved to expand use of its Project A electronic system. It had been designed for after-hours use, but in September 1998, Project A became available for daytime trades as well. Onetime CBOT Chairman Patrick Arbor proposed another solution: an alliance with the upstart Eurex, to build a new electronic trading platform the two exchanges would share. In January 1999, CBOT members voted down the Eurex alliance. A mere six months later, the members reversed their position and voted to go ahead with the plan, which would replace Project A. Meanwhile, the Board suffered a decline in trading volume and began trimming its budget and cutting staff. Total trade volume was 254 million contracts for 1999, down from 280 million in 1998. Eurex racked up 379 million contracts traded for 1999, passing the CBOT by a wide margin.

The situation was probably not helped by much acrimonious jockeying for the chairmanship of the CBOT. While the negotiations with Eurex were playing out, the CBOT also had to work out an arrangement with the Chicago Board Options Exchange, which it had created in 1973. The two planned to merge and, together, transform into a for-profit company with both electronic and open outcry trading platforms. The CBOE objected to the form of the restructuring and threatened to cut off CBOT traders' rights at the CBOE. In December 2000, Nickolas Neubauer was elected chairman of the CBOT, upsetting the incumbent chairman by 7⅚ votes (the fraction occurred because some members only had ⅙ voting privileges). Neubauer wasted no time in hiring a CEO for the board. This crucial post had been open for months. When the new president and CEO, David Vitale, took over in March 2001, he announced that converting the CBOT to a for-profit company was his top priority. He resolved to work out a restructuring that would satisfy the fractious CBOE. As for moving to an electronic format, Vitale claimed to believe that it could co-exist with the open outcry system. ''Competition is going to drive the exchange to the most efficient format,'' he told *Futures,* an industry journal, in April 2001. The CBOT faced declining volume, budget cuts, and an uncertain path as it entered the new millennium.

Principal Competitors

Chicago Board Options Exchange; Chicago Mercantile Exchange.

Further Reading

Abbott, Susan, ''Traders Sentenced,'' *Futures,* July 1991, p. 50B.

Allison, Melissa, ''Chicago Board of Trade Surprised by Incumbent Chairman's Upset,'' *Knight-Ridder/Tribune Business News,* December 8, 2000.

——, ''Chicago Mercantile Exchange to Become a For-Profit Firm on Monday,'' *Knight-Ridder/Tribune Business News,* November 8, 2000.

Barboza, David, ''In Chicago's Trading Pits, This May Be the Final Generation,'' *New York Times,* August 6, 2000, pp. BU1, BU12.

''CBOT Agrees to Pay $300,000 to Settle Charges over Stotler,'' *Wall Street Journal,* April 19, 1994, p. C14.

''CBOT Hires New CEO,'' *Futures,* April 2001, p. 12.

''CBOT Up in Arms,'' *Futures,* February 2000, p. 10.

''Days of Futures Past,'' *American Heritage,* April 1998, p. 112.

DeCola, Dyanna, ''Head of CBOT Says Finances Remain Sound,'' *Wall Street Journal,* January 26, 2001, p. C15.

Greising, David, ''This Time, the Feds' Case May Not Be the Pits,'' *Business Week,* September 24, 1990, p. 48.

Greising, David, and Laurie Morse, *Brokers, Bagmen & Moles,* New York: John Wiley & Sons, 1991.

Hafeez, Zahda, ''Arcades Ease Pain of Waning Pit Volume,'' *Wall Street Journal,* November 15, 2000, p. C19.

''High Stakes for CBOT's Dow Index,'' *Futures,* September 1997, p. 12.

Julavits, Robert, ''Here We Go Again: Chi Board Builds Mortgage Trade Mart,'' *American Banker,* March 19, 2001, p. 11.

Mahoney, Dennis, ''Mergeless in Chicago,'' *Futures,* October 2000, p. 10.

''The Main Event: Trading Pits vs. Cyberspace,'' *Business Week,* February 15, 1999, p. 16.

McMurray, Scott, ''Chicago Futures Pit Trader Goes to Trial,'' *Wall Street Journal,* May 8, 1990, pp. C1, C21.

——, ''Futures' Past,'' *Wall Street Journal,* October 19, 1990, p. R7.

Mosser, Mike, ''CBOT Sees Edge with Eurex,'' *Futures,* August 1999, p. 13.

''Roiled: American Futures Markets,'' *Economist,* May 29, 1993, p. 85.

Rosenberg, Daniel, ''CBOT Backs Down in CBOE Fight, Decides to Revamp Restructuring Plan,'' *Wall Street Journal,* September 5, 2000, p. C18.

Rynecki, David, ''CBOT Gazes into the Pit,'' *Fortune,* May 15, 2000, pp. 278–97.

Sears, Steven M., ''Merger Statement from Eurex Official Adds Bizarre Twist to Talks Between CBOT, CBOE,'' *Wall Street Journal,* August 16, 2000, p. C17.

''Snakes in the Pits: The FBI Busts 46 Commodities Traders in Chicago,'' *Time,* August 14, 1989, p. 52.

Tamarkin, Bob, *The New Gatsbys,* New York: William Morrow and Company, 1985.

—A. Woodward

Chisholm-Mingo Group, Inc.

228 East 45th Street
New York, New York 10017
U.S.A.
Telephone: (212) 697-4515
Fax: (212) 661-7729
Web site: http://www.chisholm-mingo.com

Private Company
Incorporated: 1977 as Mingo Jones & Guilmenot Inc.
Employees: 52
Sales: $100 million (2000 est.)
NAIC: 54181 Advertising Agencies; 54182 Public Relations Agencies; 61143 Professional and Management Development

Chisholm-Mingo Group, Inc. is one of the largest advertising agencies owned and operated by African Americans. Its clients include the U.S. Army, General Motors Corp., Denny's Inc., Metropolitan Life Insurance Co. Inc., Joseph E. Seagram & Sons Inc., and Time Warner Inc. Divisions of Chisholm-Mingo also are engaged in public relations and crisis management, executive training in race relations, and account planning and research.

Mingo Plus Jones: 1977–86

The agency, based in New York City, was founded in 1977 as Mingo, Jones & Guilmenot. Frank L. Mingo, Jr., the president, left a $75,000 job at McCann-Erickson Inc., where he managed the Miller Brewing Co. account. Mingo brought to the partnership its first customer, Miller's, which entrusted to the fledgling agency its advertising campaign aimed specifically at African Americans. Caroline R. Jones and Richard A. Guilmenot III were former vice-presidents at another Madison Avenue agency, Batten, Barton, Durstine and Osborn (BBDO). The Interpublic Group of Companies provided the firm, for a fee, with critical support services such as media payments, accounting, and customer billings. The agency started out with a staff of four, two clients, and about $500,000 in billings during its initial year.

Another of the firm's earliest clients was Heublein Corp.'s KFC Corp. subsidiary, which fielded many Kentucky Fried Chicken outlets in African American and Hispanic neighborhoods. ''They were looking for a turnaround in their business, which was declining because of the intense fast-food competition in New York,'' an agency executive told Stephen Gayle for *Black Enterprise* in 1981. ''They had been running 'It's so nice to feel good about a meal,' but our research led us to the conclusion that we needed to get back to promoting the product itself.'' The agency decided to use billboards and radio commercials to disseminate its message, replaced the slogan with ''We do chicken right,'' and hired Gladys Knight to appear on the billboards and to sing the theme containing the new slogan. Between 1979 and 1981 sales in Kentucky Fried Chicken's New York outlets increased by 70 percent. KFC adopted the theme song for its nationwide campaign, which also proved successful.

Mingo, Jones and Guilmenot had annual billings of $3.5 million in 1979, when its accounts also included L'Oréal and Uncle Ben's Rice. By the end of 1981 Guilmenot was no longer with the firm, which was now named Mingo-Jones Advertising and listed Jones as executive vice-president and creative director. Mingo and Jones were the principal owners, and a majority of the 37 employees were African Americans. Mingo-Jones was the second largest African American advertising agency in the United States in late 1981, with annual billings of $12 million. Clients, aside from Kentucky Fried Chicken and Miller Brewing, included, in 1982, Philip Morris Cos. Inc., Liggett & Myers Tobacco Co., Seagram, Goodyear Tire and Rubber Co., and Westinghouse Electric Corp. For Liggett & Myers, Mingo-Jones handled Omni cigarettes, a low-tar mentholated brand that was being test-marketed primarily for African Americans. General assignments included Jeffrey Martin's Porcelana spotting cream and Cuticera soap.

Mingo estimated at this time that about 60 percent of the firm's current $20 million in annual billings consisted of African American-oriented business, ten percent was Hispanic-oriented, and the remaining 30 percent consisted of general accounts. Although he recognized that the African American consumer market was a natural starting point for the agency, Mingo told Shirley

Company Perspectives:

The company's mission is to leverage our roots and ethnic expertise into public relations, marketing and advertising to all consumers driven by an ethnic sensibility, by creating a pre-emptive emotional bond between the consumer and our client products and services.

James Longshore for an *Advertising Age* article that from the beginning the firm was ''not going to engage in tokenism. We position ourselves as a first-class agency—as professionals, not as black. . . . We are now in the enviable position where our work speaks for us.'' Realistically, however, the company was dependent on clients seeking to reach African American consumers. Interviewed by Cara S. Trager in 1985 for *Advertising Age,* Jones said, with regard to the agency's black-oriented marketing, ''We try to protect clients from themselves, because if an ad gets ghetto-ized, the consumer will be offended. . . . It's all right to show blacks living in houses and buying cars, and yet we know some don't live like that, but aspirations are what advertising can be about.''

At the end of 1985 Mingo-Jones Advertising still retained many of the preceding accounts—including Miller, KFC, Seagram, and Westinghouse (which was seeking to attract minority engineering students). It also had gained a number of others, including Walt Disney Productions, Pacific Bell Inc., and Pepsi-Cola Co. For Disney amusement park ads, the agency recruited African American celebrities such as Los Angeles Mayor Tom Bradley and author Alex Haley. For Pepsi, Diet Pepsi, and Mountain Dew, the campaign featured African Americans from all walks of life and economic levels. But Mingo chafed at the barriers that continued to restrict his business. KFC, for example, had made Mingo-Jones its agency nationwide for black consumers but had no plans to give the firm its general market business, which belonged to Young & Rubicam Inc. Similarly, the Pepsi-Cola account's ads for Mountain Dew featured Janet Jackson, but the firm retained BBDO for the drink's general market. His agency's clients, Mingo told Trager, have ''pigeon-holed us and some still pigeon-hole us. It's a real struggle and seems to be mainly a cultural thing and not something people overtly want to do,'' he added. ''They believe that if they are advertising to white, WASPy consumers, they need white, WASPy people to talk to them.''

Making the best of the situation, Mingo-Jones often contacted a company and suggested that it direct ads to African American consumers, particularly if research indicated that it had a product with overlooked strong sales potential among minorities. An agency team cited the travel, credit card, and clothing industries as among those remiss in this regard. Mingo-Jones had acquired a Hispanic subsidiary, Mingo-Jones/Garrido, Miami. After this arrangement ended, in 1986 the agency acquired four California minority-owned agencies—three headed by Hispanics and the fourth by an Asian—and combined them into a new, Los Angeles-based agency called Muse-Cordero-Chen & Beca Advertising (later Muse, Cordero, Chen). Mingo felt that the current political climate, however, was not encouraging companies to consider minority advertising. ''There's no pressure for people to do what they don't want to,'' he told Trager. ''In 1977 we had a lot more people looking for black or Hispanic agencies, and today we don't hear about people looking for them.'' (Mingo was active in the presidential campaigns of Democratic candidates Walter Mondale and Michael Dukakis and also was an adviser to Jesse Jackson's bid for the 1984 nomination.)

Mingo Group Inc.: 1987–96

Mingo-Jones Advertising's billing reached almost $50 million in 1986. Late that year, Jones left the firm to form her own agency. The lesser of the two partners, she said she felt she was working too hard for too little money. A 1987 *Advertising Age* article also cited a source claiming that she—and other women at the agency—were victimized by male chauvinism. Renamed the Mingo Group Inc., the agency continued to grow, winning accounts from General Motors and Sony Corp. and becoming the first African American agency to handle U.S. Army advertising (as subcontractor for Young & Rubicam). It ended its relationship with Muse, Cordero, Chen, however, because of a client conflict and closed branch offices established in Chicago and Denver. In the fall of 1989 Mingo died of heart failure at the age of only 49. (He was, in 1996, the first African American installed in the Advertising Hall of Fame.) Direction of the company now passed to Samuel J. Chisholm, a former marketing executive at Continental Can Co. who had become chief operating officer of the Mingo Group in 1987. Mingo's widow inherited a majority stake in the business.

Chisholm sought to lift the Mingo Group out of the minority ghetto by positioning the agency as a specialist in what he called ''urban marketing.'' Speaking to Randall Rothenberg of the *New York Times* shortly after Mingo's death, Chisholm said, ''People in Chicago, New York, Philadelphia live differently than they do elsewhere in America.'' He cited Spandex-clad bicycle messengers as an example of the African American community's influence on urban fashion. The following year he established a division called Mingo Group/Plus to undertake public relations, community relations, sales production, and product publicity. The firm was asked to do a television commercial for Miller for the first time since 1988. It also was hired by the National Basketball Association to publicize ex-players who had become successful businessmen and by W.K. Buckley Ltd. to market Buckley's Mixture, a Canadian cold remedy. By 1991 the Mingo Group had survived damaging rumors that it was unable to pay its bills, although revenues dropped from the 1989 peak of $62 million.

Mingo's death took a heavy personal, as well as economic, toll on his agency. ''There was a tremendous amount of hurt,'' Chisholm recalled in late 1990 to Kim Foltz of the *New York Times.* ''There has been a lot of tears and a lot of handholding. . . . I didn't feel prepared to run the agency. He'd always been there to talk to if you weren't sure you were making the right decision. Frank was the ringmaster; he taught us all how to fly.'' Chisholm reorganized the staff into several profit-oriented team groups, explaining to Foltz, ''We had been set up as a family, but that way of doing business wasn't going to work with Frank gone.'' Some longtime employees left on their own, others were dismissed, and a new group of senior account management executives was brought into the firm.

Key Dates:

1977: The agency is founded, originally as Mingo Jones & Guilmenot.
1981: Now Mingo-Jones Advertising, it is the second largest U.S. African American-owned agency.
1989: Billings peak at $62 million in the year in which Mingo dies.
1990: Samuel Chisholm, Mingo's successor, establishes three new divisions.
1996: The agency is renamed the Chisholm-Mingo Group and garners record revenues.

Chisholm-Mingo Group: 1996–2000

The Mingo Group was renamed the Chisholm-Mingo Group in 1996. That year it lost the Miller account when the company—like such earlier clients as Liggett & Myers, Goodyear, and Hanes Corp.—decided to stop aiming ads specifically to African American consumers. The agency gained lucrative accounts from Texaco Inc. and Denny's Inc., however, and ended the year with $73.7 million in billings, a 36 percent increase over the previous year and the best for the firm since Mingo's death. In addition to the advertising operation, its divisions included Chisholm-Mingo Plus, for public relations and crisis management; CMG Consulting, which trained top management on race relations issues; and CMG Account Planning and Research.

Texaco and Denny's turned to Chisholm-Mingo because of damaging incidents that made it a necessity to repair their relations with the African American community. Texaco, already facing sanctions from a federal commission for alleged discrimination in employment, suffered embarrassment when one executive recorded his colleagues speaking of ''black jellybeans.'' Denny's had just settled a lawsuit in which some of its fast-food outlets were cited for ignoring African American customers while white ones received prompt service. Chisholm-Mingo stepped in where other African American-owned advertising agencies feared to tread, according to a *Crain's New York Business* story that reported several such agencies had declined to compete for the Denny's account. Interviewed for the magazine by Chris Isidore, a market research executive observed, ''You don't want to become the halfway-house type of agency for clients that screw up their relationship with black consumers, only to have them leave you when the crisis is over.''

Reviewing Chisholm-Mingo's image-repair work, *Advertising Age* columnist Bob Garfield was caustic in his criticism of both the agency and its tainted clients. Writing about a Texaco commercial that celebrated the African American experience in what he called ''a beautifully rendered expression of unassailable sentiments,'' he concluded, ''Pandering isn't the right word. It's more like groveling.'' Garfield dismissed a ''Welcome back to Denny's'' spot featuring a low-cost breakfast promotion in which an African American architect, real estate agent, and designer were successively greeted by an African American hostess as ''a parade of the Afro-affluent.'' The agency's Denny's effort also included a campaign, mostly in print, that promoted what the company called its improved record of franchising restaurants to minorities, using minority suppliers, and in hiring and promoting African American executives.

With annual billings at an estimated $100 million, Chisholm-Mingo Group was the fourth largest African American-owned advertising agency in 2000, when it was contracted by Royal Caribbean Cruises Ltd. to help the company break into the African American travel market. The agency was to be responsible for strategic planning, creative media planning, promotions, and other services to support the expansion of Royal Caribbean's multicultural marketing efforts. Chisholm-Mingo was expecting the Royal Caribbean account to help boost its revenues by 20 percent in 2001. The agency also had received a portion of Young & Rubicam's $100 million Census 2000 account from the U.S. Department of Commerce.

Principal Operating Units

Chisholm-Mingo Advertising; Chisholm-Mingo Plus; CMG Account Planning and Research; CMG Consulting.

Principal Competitors

Burrell Communications Group Inc.; Omnicom Group Inc.; UniWorld Group Inc.

Further Reading

Dougherty, Philip H., ''Minority Marketing,'' *New York Times,* June 28, 1982, p. D6.

Foltz, Kim, ''Mingo Doing Well Despite a Tough Year,'' *New York Times,* January 2, 1991, p. D15.

Garfield, Bob, ''Class Consciousness Hurts Denny's Ads,'' *Advertising Age,* June 2, 1997, p. 49.

——, ''Texaco Spot Tainted by Suspicion of Intent,'' *Advertising Age,* May 17, 1999, p. 67.

Gayle, Stephen, ''Mingo-Jones: Doing the Colonel Right,'' *Black Enterprise,* December 1981, p. 56.

Isidore, Chris, ''Chisholm-Mingo Comeback,'' *Crain's New York Business,* July 27, 1998, pp. 15, 19.

Lafayette, Jon, ''Mingo Refocuses, Fights Rumors,'' *Advertising Age,* May 14, 1990, p. 17.

Longshore, Shirley James, ''Their Marketing Homework Rates an A+,'' *Advertising Age,* November 29, 1982, pp. M-14, M-16, M-17.

''Mingo Aims to Build First-Class Agency,'' *Advertising Age,* February 23, 1987, p. 89.

Mitchell, Grayson, ''. . . And Then There Were 13,'' *Black Enterprise,* September 1979, pp. 46, 49.

Richardson, Nicole Marie, ''Better Late Than Never,'' *Black Enterprise,* October 2000, p. 22.

Rothenberg, Randall, ''Shift Sought from 'Black' to 'Urban',' *New York Times,* November 30, 1989, p. D19.

Trager, Cara S., ''Mingo-Jones Builds Long-Term Relationships,'' *Advertising Age,* December 19, 1985, pp. 18, 20.

—Robert Halasz

Collins & Aikman Corporation

5755 New King Court
Troy, Michigan 48098-2396
U.S.A.
Telephone: (248) 824-2500
Fax: (248) 824-1614
Web site: http://www.collinsaikman.com

Public Company
Incorporated: 1988
Employees: 14,300
Sales: $1.9 billion (2000)
Stock Exchanges: New York
Ticker Symbol: CKC
NAIC: 31321 Broadwoven Fabric Mills; 336339 All Other Motor Vehicle Parts Manufacturing; 326199 All Other Plastics Product Manufacturing

Founded as a supplier of window shades in the mid-19th century, Collins & Aikman Corporation has survived a century and a half of corporate maneuvering to become a leading supplier of floor systems, fabric, interior trim, and convertible top systems to the automotive industry. Its acoustic component operations provide Noise/Vibration/Harshness (NVH) solutions to its clients. Collins & Aikman operates in 13 countries and its customer base includes General Motors, DaimlerChrysler, Ford, Honda, Nissan, and Toyota. In 2000, the company moved its headquarters from North Carolina to Troy, Michigan, a suburb of Detroit, in order to be closer to its major clients.

19th Century Origins

The business that was to become Collins & Aikman was founded in 1843, on the Lower East Side of New York. Sensing that the rapid growth of the increasingly crowded city would spur the market for privacy products, 21-year-old Gibbons L. Kelty opened a window shade shop on Catherine Street. Kelty's business prospered, and he gradually added various home furnishings lines and began to import upholstery fabrics. Kelty also opened a textile factory across the East River in Astoria.

By 1870, G.L. Kelty & Co. was operating several downtown stores, selling furniture, curtains, and upholstery. That year, Gibbons Kelty admitted his nephew, Charles M. Aikman, into partnership, and in 1871, they were joined by Gibbons's son, William Kelty. A year later Kelty became the first U.S. weaver of satin damask, and it won a gold medal for these fabrics at an American Centennial exhibition a few years later.

After Gibbons Kelty died in 1889, Charles Aikman formed C.M. Aikman & Co. and bought out the principal Kelty interests. The Kelty holdings included a half interest in a weave plant in the Manayunk section of Philadelphia. The other half was owned by William G. Collins. In 1891, they incorporated Collins & Aikman (C&A), with Aikman as president and Collins as secretary and treasurer. C&A continued its expansion as a specialist in heavy, upholstery-type fabrics. In 1898, it became the first American producer of jacquard velvet. About the same time the company got out of its original window shade business.

Charles Aikman retired in 1909, and sold his C.M. Aikman & Co. (which he may have used primarily as a holding company for his C&A and other interests) to C&A. A few years later, William Collins also retired, turning the presidency over to his son Kenneth. Tragically, Kenneth Collins was killed in early 1916 in a fire, after he had rescued two women who were trapped. His cousin, Dr. William M. Collins, who had held the title of treasurer in the company, took over as interim president, but by July 1916, the Collins family sold its holdings to Thomas Doody and Melville Curtis, who had first bought a stake in the firm in 1911, and had been directors and assistant treasurers.

Early in their tenure, Doody and Curtis brought in Willis G. McCullough, whose family was to play a major role in C&A for 70 years. Hired as a salesman, McCullough was promoted to sales manager within a year and also named treasurer and elected to the board. By 1929, he was president (with Melville Curtis stepping up to chairman), a job he held until his death in 1948.

In the early 1920s, McCullough was instrumental in steering C&A into what was quickly to become its largest business—and has remained so much of the time since. For a producer of upholstery fabrics, auto seat materials seemed a natural outlet,

Company Perspectives:

Our mission is to be recognized as a leading-edge automotive interior systems supplier and an innovator of world-class NVH and acoustic technologies. Our goal is to continually find ways to integrate our unparalleled styling and innovative acoustics technologies into all of our interior products.

and soon C&A also provided fabrics for headlining, sidewalls, and other automotive uses. McCullough persuaded the company to build a new plant for auto and furniture fabrics in West Philadelphia.

Going Public: 1926

In 1926, Collins & Aikman Company went public and was listed on the New York Stock Exchange. The next year it reincorporated as Collins & Aikman Corp. while absorbing three other companies, including its long-time mohair yarn supplier, Cranston Mills of Rhode Island, and a velvet weaver, which gave it a plant in North Carolina. More plants were built over the years. In 1929, C&A established a Canadian subsidiary with a plant in Farnham, Quebec, to supply the auto and furniture industries. By 1937, C&A moved into supplying the infant airline industry with specially developed fabrics that were light and durable. The company later supplied fabric for President Roosevelt's plane.

C&A managed to stay in the black for all but one year during the Depression. With the advent of World War II, civilian auto production, which by then accounted for about 75 percent of C&A's volume, came to a halt. The company switched to duck, alpaca linings, and upholstery fabrics for war uses, but it took time to adapt to new machinery, techniques, and employees. Profits collapsed from $3.1 million in the February 1941 fiscal year to $123,000 in fiscal 1943 before rebounding partway to $2 million in fiscal 1945.

Throughout his presidency, Willis McCullough emphasized C&A's tradition of research and development. For instance, the company developed techniques for back-coating auto and furniture fabrics and for large-scale range dyeing of pile fabrics. Even during the war, research efforts continued. In 1943, C&A patented a double-faced thermal cloth, initially used for cold-weather uniforms, and it worked with nylon originator duPont to adapt this first synthetic ''miracle fiber'' for upholstery fabrics. Also during the war, C&A expanded its presence in North Carolina by acquiring Norwood Company, a cotton spinner, in 1943, then modernizing its plant with the C&A-developed Bird spinning system.

McCullough also made C&A an early provider of health insurance and the 40-hour week. McCullough himself was very reticent. He kept published information about the company at a minimum and never permitted his photo to be released to the press. Fortune, with its army of indefatigable researchers, long tried to gather enough material for an article on C&A, but finally gave up in frustration.

Postwar Challenges

After McCullough's death in 1948, general counsel Albert Jube stepped in as what a company history describes as ''caretaker president.'' Whitworth Bird, who had developed the Bird spinning system for the company, took over in 1953. But despite the general economic prosperity in the United States, the first decade after the war was difficult for many textile companies, including C&A. It was saddled with many obsolete, high-cost plants in the Northeast and undertook a painful process of relocating to the South, especially North Carolina. C&A continued as a major supplier to the auto companies, but the shift away from pile and plush upholstery and greater use of plastics in seats and body linings cut C&A's contribution per car. C&A's efforts to compete with large, mass-volume textilers in ''flat fabrics'' for men's and women's clothing incurred substantial losses, until the Rhode Island plant producing them was finally closed in 1956. C&A ran three deficits in the four years ending February 1957.

In December 1956, C&A hired 49-year-old textile veteran Ellis Leach as president. With automotive products dropping as a percentage of C&A's sales, Leach stressed flexibility and emphasis on more specialized and stylish products. A prime goal was ''getting away from staple items'' where fierce competition permitted little if any profit, while ''putting emphasis on style'' where ''our forte lies in the finish of a product.'' Aided by Stead & Miller, a subsidiary acquired in 1952 that emphasized furniture damasks and novelty weaves, C&A increased furniture upholstery fabrics to a quarter of total business by the late 1950s, much of it to better-quality furniture makers. For the apparel market, C&A developed synthetic fur-like fabrics, mainly for use as liners that could also be reversed for use as outerwear, and trim. It also came out with periodic novelty items like Bear Hug shaggy-pile coats, and supplied plush ''fur'' for the toy market.

In 1961, Leach stepped up to the position of chairman and the presidency was assumed by 36-year-old Donald McCullough, the younger son of Willis, a Yale-trained engineer who had been persuaded by his father to turn down a job at Republic Steel to start as a C&A trainee in 1946. When Leach retired in 1966, Don McCullough also became chairman and CEO. Don McCullough shared Leach's faith in ''mobility and flexibility.'' Their policy was not only to replace plants and machinery as they became outmoded, but also to replace products that had outworn their welcome with new, market-pleasing varieties. They also believed in frequent acquisitions to expand C&A's market niches.

Expansion in the 1960s and 1970s

The 1960 acquisition of Pennsylvania-based Bangor Mills gave C&A an entry into tricot knitting. In less than a decade C&A tripled its tricot capacity and developed Certifab tricot for bonding to other fabrics. Another new field was entered in 1965 through Painter Carpet Mills, a specialist in commercial and institutional carpeting. C&A acquired wall coverings producer Imperial Paper in 1971, and Tennessee Trifting, which made scatter rugs, in 1972. By then, 42 percent of C&A's business was in apparel fabrics, while the home furnishing market (which comprised both furniture fabrics and wallpaper) ac-

Key Dates:

1843: Gibbons L. Kelty opens a window shade shop.
1870: Charles M. Aikman joins the business, by now a retailer of a wide variety of home furnishings.
1891: Kelty's interests are sold, Aikman partners with William Collins, and Collins & Aikman (C&A) is formed.
1916: The Collins family sells its holdings to Thomas Doody and Melville Curtis, and the company goes public.
1937: Company begins supplying the airline industry.
1943: A double-faced thermal cloth, initially used for cold-weather uniforms, is patented.
1960: Company acquires Pennsylvania-based Bangor Mills.
1971: Wall coverings producer Imperial Paper is acquired.
1987: The Wickes Companies purchase C&A for $1.16 billion.
1988: Blackstone Group and Wasserstein Perella purchase the firm and reorganize it as WCI Holdings Corp.
1992: WCI changes its name to Collins & Aikman and moves corporate headquarters from Southern California to Charlotte, North Carolina.
1994: Automotive products account for 59 percent of $1.5 billion in sales, and the firm initiates a public offering.
1997: Restructuring begins as C&A divests some holdings in order to focus on the automotive industry.
2000: Company headquarters are moved to Troy, Michigan.
2001: Heartland Industrial Partners L.P. purchases a 60 percent stake in the firm.

counted for 36 percent. Although the auto business was bringing in more revenues than it had in the past and was extended to such important new products as molded carpet flooring, C&A's transportation business (which also included airline sales) was down to about 20 percent of its revenues.

Leach and McCullough's policies paid off financially, with C&A returning to the black in Leach's first year and growing steadily for the next quarter century. Acquisitions and internal growth increased sales from $45 million in the year ending February 1959, to more than $200 million in 1969, and $1 billion in 1985. Earnings over the same period rose from $1.7 million (which was still below the nearly $2 million netted in mid-Depression 1937) to more than $60 million in 1985. Five stock splits between 1961 and 1985 turned each pre-1961 share into 24 new shares. Thus, the $22 market price of the stock in June 1985 compared with a split-adjusted trading range of $.50 to $1 during most of the 1950s and a 1937 high of $2.60.

The price nearly doubled again over the next twelve months, but by then C&A was beginning to get caught up in the market excitement that made most any company, whether ill or well managed, small or large, a potential buyout target. In particular, C&A attracted the attention of Sanford Sigoloff, CEO of The Wickes Companies.

Like C&A, Wickes traced its origin to family businesses started in the mid-1800s. By the 1960s, it was an important supplier of building materials and operated the Builders Emporium chain and other outlets. In 1980, it merged with Gamble-Skogmo, which operated a variety of merchandising units. However, the resultant Wickes Companies was burdened by $2 billion in debt and many run-down operating units. In March 1982, it turned for help to Sigoloff, who had a reputation as a turnaround specialist. Sigoloff, whose self-adopted nickname was ''Ming the Merciless,'' derived from a villain in Flash Gordon comic strips, prided himself on ruthless cost-cutting and efficiency. He promptly threw Wickes into Chapter 11 bankruptcy and managed to bring the reorganized company out again by January 1985, winning wide admiration for the speed and effectiveness of his moves.

Wickes was barely four months out of bankruptcy when Sigoloff announced his intention of making a $1 billion acquisition within a year. He handily beat that timetable when in September 1985, he completed the $1 billion purchase of Gulf & Western's Consumer and Industrial Products Group, doubling Wickes's size.

Changes in Ownership: Late 1980s

He amassed a new $1.2 billion war chest in 1986, but hostile efforts to capture National Gypsum and Owens-Corning Fiberglas both failed. He was more successful in quiet negotiations with C&A, and won the board's assent in November with a ''can't-refuse'' offer of $1.16 billion. That meant $53 a C&A share, a 50 percent premium over the market price two days earlier and double the price 12 months before. At almost the same time Wickes struck a $1.62 billion deal for Lear Siegler, but the takeover market had peaked and Wickes's investment bank Drexel Burnham Lambert was beginning to have problems of its own. The Lear deal was dropped by ''mutual consent'' in December, but the C&A transaction was pushed through. It formally took effect in January 1987.

In April came a shocker. It was discovered that for nearly a decade C&A had produced $360 million in carpeting that didn't meet flammability tests, although Wickes noted that it thought the products were safe. In early May the head of the Floor Coverings division was removed. Then the news improved. Government-ordered tests indicated the problem might not be as severe as first feared. That summer Wickes established an $11.2 million after-tax reserve, which, as the Wall Street Journal noted, ''surprised analysts who initially estimated liability in the hundreds of millions.'' For the year ended January 1988, C&A contributed $83 million in operating profits to the Wickes total.

Even so, Wickes, again burdened with heavy debt, never managed to gain momentum. Corporate-wide profits were down substantially for the year ending January 1988, and the company was in the red for the next two quarters, burdened by losses from units slated for disposal. In August 1988, Sigoloff tried a new tack. He proposed a buyout by his management team at $12 a Wickes share, well below what stockholders had been led to believe was the company's true value (the theoretical and admittedly unrealistic book value had been $25). Many Wall Street analysts reasoned that ''Ming'' really wanted to put the company ''in play,'' hoping to attract higher bids by outsiders. But with Wickes having to admit that earnings would be below projections (a falloff in C&A results was given much of the blame), no other bids were generated, and Sigoloff himself was unable to get the needed financing.

In November, Wickes settled for a buyout offer by prominent Wall Street investors Blackstone Group and Wasserstein Perella at $11.25 a share through a newly formed company named WCI Holdings Corp. The transaction, through which WCI also inherited some $2 billion of Wickes debt, was completed in December 1988. Representatives of Blackstone and Wasserstein took over as the 58-year-old Sigoloff departed.

In contrast to the highly centralized, detailed control practiced by Sigoloff, the new group allowed considerable operational autonomy, stating, ''We plan to establish a sense of ownership among the executives at each of the businesses.'' But by then the former senior executives at C&A were gone. Don McCullough retired at the end of 1987. He was succeeded as the unit's CEO by Alfred Crimmins, who had been president since 1984, but within five months Crimmins and a score of other executives also departed and Sigoloff had divisional C&A executives report directly to him.

In February 1989, the new owners brought in Thomas Hannah, an executive from the Milliken textile firm, to head C&A. In 1994, he was also named chief executive officer of the restructured parent corporation.

Restructuring and Continued Growth in the 1990s

WCI was determined to quickly implement a restructuring plan that slashed corporate overhead and focused on ''businesses in which it enjoyed a competitive advantage''—which turned out to be primarily the old C&A activities. This was emphasized by the 1992 name change from WCI to Collins & Aikman, as well as the move of corporate headquarters from Southern California to Charlotte, North Carolina, in the heartland of C&A operations.

During the restructuring process, some 27 business units, which had contributed 73 percent of 1988 sales, were divested (some to groups headed by division management). When no buyers could be found, some units were closed, as was the case with the Builders Emporium chain. One unit from the Wickes Manufacturing side originally slated for divesting—Dura Convertible Systems, the largest producer of top systems for convertibles—won a last-minute reprieve and was shifted to the C&A automotive group.

In the new C&A, automotive products were once again the dominant segment, accounting for 59 percent of the $1.5 billion in sales for fiscal 1994, with at least some C&A product in 86 percent of all North American cars. Customers included not only the Big Three but also U.S. plants of foreign producers. C&A claimed to be the largest supplier of seat fabrics, floor mats, and convertible tops, and ranked number two in molded floor carpets and luggage compartment trim. C&A moved abroad with plants in Mexico and Austria, primarily to serve local Chrysler plants. The company's other market segments included interior furnishings (27 percent), in which the company ranked first in both flat-woven upholstery fabric and commercial-type carpets, and wallcoverings (14 percent) in which C&A also claimed first place with its Imperial label.

By July 1994, C&A was ready to go public again, with an offering of 15 million shares at $10.50 each, followed by listing on the New York Stock Exchange. However, Blackstone and Wasserstein Perella still retained 76 percent of outstanding stock. Proceeds of the offering permitted substantial lowering of outstanding debt and refinancing of much of the rest on more favorable terms. CEO Tom Hannah noted that C&A was prepared ''to grow in businesses we know and understand. . . . We will invest in [our] existing businesses and [also] seek to expand into related product lines and in international markets to service our customers.''

In the mid-1990s, C&A continued to strategically position itself as a leading automotive supplier. In 1995, the firm purchased AMCO, a convertible top producer. One year later, the company made several key acquisitions including Manchester Plastics, BTR Fatati, and JPS Automotive—both manufacturers of automotive floor carpet—and Perstorp, an acoustics technologies firm. The shopping spree left C&A remained debt laden—some $1.2 billion in 1995—and strikes at General Motors plants cost the firm nearly $30 in revenues in 1996. Still, the company's products were found in 85 percent of the cars produced in North America, and revenues increased 28 percent to $1.1 billion, securing its position as the third-largest public auto supplier.

In 1997, C&A divested a number of its holdings to further strengthen its portfolio. Among those divested were the Collins & Aikman Floorcoverings unit, JPS Air Restraint & Technological Products, and the Mastercraft Decorative Fabrics Group. The following year, it also sold its Imperial Wallcoverings unit for $72 million. The firm also sought to beef up its international presence, entering into an alliance with Courtaulds Textiles, a European firm. It also acquired full interest in C&A Plastics UK and C&A Floormats Europe, as well as Enjema, a Mexico-based carpet systems manufacturer.

Thomas E. Evans joined the firm in 1999, after Hannah announced his retirement. The new chairman and CEO, formerly the president of Tenneco Automotive, immediately began a new restructuring plan and brought several top executives in the industry to the firm to aid in his strategic effort. Part of the new plan included the reorganization of the firm's global automotive carpet, acoustics, plastics, and accessory floormats businesses, into two major divisions: North America Automotive Interior Systems and Europe Automotive Interior Systems, with headquarters in Michigan and Germany. The company also formed the Specialty Automotive Products division, which operated the automotive fabrics and convertible tops business.

Alliances for the New Millennium

As C&A entered the new millennium, company headquarters were moved to Troy, Michigan, in order to be closer to the heart of the automotive industry and its customers. The firm continued its focus on its key business segments and purchased Comet, an acoustic software developer focused on NVH.

In 2001, Heartland Industrial Partners L.P., a private equity firm that invested in certain industrial companies and positioned them for growth, purchased a 60 percent stake in the firm for $260 million. CEO Evans elaborated on the deal: ''I believe that with this infusion of new capital from Heartland, we should be able to significantly enhance the growth opportunities for our global business, subsequently maximizing value for our organization and, as evidenced by their significant investment in the automotive industry, we couldn't ask for a more supportive and strategically aligned partner. This transaction should position Collins & Aikman to be an even stronger player in our sector.'' Shortly after receiving the cash infusion, C&A announced the acquisition of Becker Group LLC, an injection molder, for $60 million in cash, $2.5 million in stock options, and a $18 million non-competition agreement.

By this time, the company was the market leader in flooring and acoustic systems, convertible tops, floormats, and body cloth. With management strongly focused on its role in the automotive supply industry, and establishing a global presence, Collins & Aikman seemed assured of its strong market share in the future.

Principal Subsidiaries

Collins & Aikman Products Co.; The Akro Corporation; Carcorp Inc.; Cepco Incorporated; Collins & Aikman Asset Services; CW Management Corp.; Hopkins Services Inc.; SAF Services Corp.; Collins & Aikman Automotive International, Inc.; Collins & Aikman Carpet & Acoustics Inc.; Collins & Aikman Export Corp.; Collins & Aikman Holdings Canada, Inc.; Collins & Aikman Luxembourg SA; Collins & Aikman Europe Inc.; Collins & Aikman Products GmbH (Austria); Collins & Aikman International Corp.; Dura Convertible Systems GmbH; Collins & Aikman de Mexico, S.A. de C.V.

Principal Competitors

Lear Corporation; Johnson Controls Inc.; Magna International Inc.

Further Reading

''At 150, Collins & Aikman Is Dedicated to Its Markets,'' *Textile World,* June 1993, pp. 38–47.

''C&A Set to Spin Off Imperial Wallcoverings,'' *HFN—The Weekly Newspaper for the Home Furnishing Network*, April 15, 1996, p. 96.

Collins & Aikman: A Continuing Story, Charlotte, North Carolina: Collins & Aikman Corp., 1995.

McCurray, John, ''C&A Sells Carpet Biz,'' *Textile World*, January 1997, p. 23.

Miel, Rhoda, ''Collins & Aikman Set to Buy Becker Group in Cash, Stock Deal,'' *Crain's Detroit Business*, March 26, 2001, p. 4.

Sanger, Elizabeth, ''Snappy Threads: Textile Maker Collins & Aikman Thrives,'' *Barron's*, July 7, 1986, pp. 35–36.

Sansweet, Stephen J., ''Investment Firms Agree to Buy Wickes,'' *Wall Street Journal*, October 27, 1988.

Strong, Michael, ''Collins & Aikman to Seek Deal Soon as Part of its New Owner's Strategy,'' *Crain's Detroit Business*, February 26, 2001, p. 31.

''Textile Specialist Collins & Aikman,'' *Investor's Reader*, September 16, 1959, pp. 19–21.

''Textiles: Collins & Aikman's Specialty Fabrics Find More Market Areas,'' *Investor's Reader*, June 2, 1971, pp. 6–9.

Williams, Christopher C., ''Collins & Aikman Want Cars to Drive its Business,'' *Business North Carolina*, September 1997, p. 24.

—Henry R. Hecht
—update: Christina M. Stansell

COLT Telecom Group plc

15 Marleybone Road
London NW1 5JD
United Kingdom
Telephone: (44) 20-7863-5000
Fax: (44) 20-7863-3701
Web site: http://www.colt-telecom.com

Public Company
Incorporated: 1992 as City of London Telecommunications
Employees: 2,210
Sales: £687 million (2000)
Stock Exchanges: London NASDAQ
Ticker Symbols: CTM.L COLT
NAIC: 513310 Wired Telecommunications Carriers

Since it was founded in 1992 in the City of London, COLT Telecom Group plc has grown from a local fiber-optic network provider into a leading pan-European telecommunications company. During the latter half of the 1990s COLT built fiber-optic networks in 27 European cities in 11 countries. The company plans to provide an IP-based European network, COLT EuroLAN, that would link Europe's major business buildings into an effective single local area network across Europe. COLT also offers digital subscriber line-based (DSL) services in France, Germany, and the Netherlands, and plans to expand DSL service to nine European countries by 2001. COLT also operates 10 Internet Solution Centres (ISCs) that serve companies that want to outsource their Web hosting and other Internet-based services. COLT plans to have 20 to 24 ISCs in operation by early 2002. By late 2000, COLT had installed 2,676 route kilometers of fiber-optic cable in its city networks and had 5,277 buildings connected to its networks. COLT EuroLAN, the company's 15,000 route kilometer pan-European intercity network, was under construction, with a 3,000 kilometer intercity network in Germany coming online in July 2000.

London Telecommunications Service: 1992–94

COLT Telecom Group was formed in London, England, in 1992 by the venture capital arm of Fidelity Investments, the largest privately held mutual fund and investment company in the United States. COLT was an acronym for City of London Telecommunications. Fidelity persuaded an AT&T executive, Paul Chisholm, to relocate from Boston to London to be COLT's president and CEO, a position he retained until 2001.

In 1993 COLT obtained a PTO (telecommunications) license and completed the first 15 kilometers of its fiber-optic network in the City of London. COLT gained its first customer and received a ''considerate contractor'' award from the Corporation of London. The news service Reuters chose COLT's plan to link its television studios to video cameras on London's stock exchanges over those submitted by British Telecommunications plc and Cable & Wireless plc. For the rest of the decade COLT enjoyed a good reputation for service as it deployed its fiber-optic network in cities throughout Europe. In 1994 the company signed interconnect agreements with British Telecom and Energis plc and became Energis's preferred local supplier.

Expanding into Europe: 1995–97

In 1995 COLT was granted a U.K. Telecommunications Operators license from the Department of Trade and Industry, which allowed COLT to expand beyond London. The company completed the initial phase of its fiber-optic network in London's West End. A telecommunications license for Frankfurt, Germany, allowed COLT to begin its European expansion.

In 1996 COLT Telecom GmbH was established in Frankfurt, Germany, with more than 50 kilometers of network. COLT France was awarded a license to operate in Paris. COLT Telecom Group plc became a public company, with stock trading on the London Stock Exchange in the United Kingdom and NASDAQ in the United States.

In 1997 COLT accelerated its growth in Europe, bringing new networks online in Munich, Hamburg, and Berlin in Germany, for a total of six city networks. The company received

Company Perspectives:

COLT is one of the new competitive telecommunications companies operating in Europe. Founded in 1992, COLT operates an integrated IP-based (Internet protocol) pan-European network linking the financial and business centers of Europe, providing the full range of telecommunications services to high value corporate and carrier customers. COLT operates in 25 European cities in nine countries and plans to provide service in 30–32 European cities by the end of 2001. COLT is currently interlinking its city-based networks to create a truly pan-European network. COLT has established a reputation for first-class service and is increasingly regarded as the preferred supplier of high bandwidth telecommunication services. The COLT brand is synonymous with quality, reliability, and value.

more awards, including the FX award as the best telecommunications supplier in the City of London. COLT received approval to construct networks in Zurich, Switzerland, and Brussels, Belgium. During the year, it signed interconnect agreements with France Telecom and Deutsche Telekom AG. In the United Kingdom, COLT launched its first Internet services.

More Internet Services: 1998–2000

In 1998 COLT made two important acquisitions: France's leading independent corporate Internet service provider (ISP) ImagiNet, and Telecom Noord West N.V. in Amsterdam, which was renamed COLT Telecom N.V. New licenses obtained during the year included a switched voice license in Spain, and a license for Milan, Italy. By the end of 1998 COLT was operating networks in 12 European cities, having added Dusselforf, Germany, and Zurich, Switzerland, during the year.

For 1998 COLT reported revenue of £215 million, a 164 percent increase over its 1997 revenue. COLT's strong financial performance in 1998 helped get it listed on London's exclusive list of blue chip stocks, known as the FTSE-100 Index, or ''Footsie.'' COLT also benefitted from the telecommunications deregulation taking place in Europe, which allowed other companies to compete with established telecommunications monopolies. COLT was gaining market share in Europe by offering a high level of customer service. Its own dedicated fiber-optic network offered better service, in most cases, than the older networks of the established telecommunications giants.

COLT reduced the risk involved in building new fiber-optic networks by first obtaining commitments from a core group of large corporate customers. It then built fiber-optic networks, or ''backbone,'' just for those customers. New capacity to the network would be added only if COLT expected to get its money back within 24 months.

In 1999 Peter Manning joined COLT as chief operating officer. During that same year, the company COLT expanded its European network by bringing Stuttgart, Germany; Geneva, Switzerland; Barcelona, Spain; Cologne, Germany; Vienna, Austria; and Lyon, France, online. In December, COLT also began providing this service in Rotterdam, Netherlands, and Marseilles, France. In Germany COLT began constructing an intercity network.

The awards that the company received in 1999 included the U.K. carrier of the year and an accolade from CIGREF, the primary French corporate telecommunications user group. Reuters selected COLT as its pan-European service provider. An interconnect agreement was signed with Spain's Telefonica in October. COLT announced plans for four new city networks in Hanover, Germany; Rome, Italy; Turin, Italy; and Stockholm, Sweden. The company also announced plans to offer Web hosting capabilities in four Internet Solution Centres (ISCs) in Amsterdam, Frankfurt, London, and Paris. By the end of the year COLT Internet was available in Belgium, France, Germany, Italy, The Netherlands, Spain, Switzerland, and the United Kingdom. COLT planned to have more than 10 ISCs in service by the end of 2000.

During 1999 COLT raised £1.2 billion and planned to spend some £2.5 billion over the next four years. At the end of the year the company operated 1,892 route kilometers (1,175 route miles) of local digital fiber-optic network and was providing service to customers in more than 3,700 buildings.

During the first quarter of 2000 COLT gained 762 new customer accounts for a total of more than 5,000. The company enjoyed strong demand for high bandwidth service as well as for data and Internet-related services. In London the company had more than 230 corporate Internet customers, nearly double that of the previous year. LANLink 1000 was a recently launched service for corporate customers that featured a fully managed Gigabit Ethernet service for Local Area Networks (LANs). Plans for new networks in Birmingham, England, and Dublin, Ireland, were in advanced stages. COLT expected to complete construction of its intercity network in the United Kingdom by the end of 2000, with the network becoming operational during the first quarter of 2001. Germany was COLT's second most significant source of revenue after the United Kingdom. Revenue in France increased 78 percent over the same quarter of 1999, and the company launched its first commercial service that used digital subscriber line (DSL) technology in Paris and Lyon. COLT's DSL service in France utilized France Telecom's wholesale service offering. During the quarter Microsoft France began contributing to the COLT Internet Start Up Program, which was designed to help start-up Internet companies become established.

In January 2000 COLT announced that it had completed construction of its Internet Solution Centres (ISCs) in Amsterdam, Frankfurt, Paris, and London, giving the company about 120,000 square feet of Web hosting capacity in the four European cities. By the end of 2000 the company planned to have 500,000 square feet of hosting capacity in ten to 12 centers, with further expansion planned for 2001. COLT's goal was to become the premier web hosting enabler of e-business across Europe. COLT's ISCs would serve the need of companies wanting to outsource their e-services or Web hosting.

To finance the further expansion of its Internet services, including content distribution and the development of its Application Service Provider (ASP) enabling capacity, COLT placed nearly 13 million ordinary shares on the London Stock Ex-

Key Dates:

1992: COLT is formed in London, England, by the U.S. mutual fund and investment company Fidelity Investments.
1995: COLT is granted a U.K. Telecommunications Operators license, allowing it to expand beyond London. A telecommunications license for Frankfurt, Germany, allows COLT to expand into Europe.
1996: COLT Telecom GmbH is established in Frankfurt, Germany, and COLT France is awarded a license to operate in Paris. COLT Telecom Group plc becomes a public company, with stock trading on the London Stock Exchange in the United Kingdom and NASDAQ in the United States.
1998: COLT makes two important acquisitions: France's leading independent corporate Internet service provider (ISP) ImagiNet, and Telecom Noord West N.V. in Amsterdam, which is renamed COLT Telecom N.V.
1999: Peter Manning joins COLT as chief operating officer.
2001: Peter Manning is named president and CEO of COLT.

change in March and April at £38.52 per share. Together with a placing of convertible notes, COLT expected to raise about £600 million. The proceeds would also be used to finance the wider deployment of DSL-based services across Europe, the further expansion of the company's intercity network infrastructure in France, and its extension to Spain and Scandinavia. At the end of March 2000 COLT announced that its 20 route kilometer network in Turin, Italy, was operational; it was COLT's 21st fiber-optic city network in Europe.

By May 2000 COLT's stock had increased 30 times in value since it began trading in 1996. Stock options issued to COLT executives had made 150 of them millionaires. Although capital spending had kept COLT from reporting a profit, the company expected to become profitable in 2003. Also in May COLT launched its fiber-optic city network in Hanover, Germany. Hanover was COLT's 22nd European city network and its eighth in Germany.

COLT accelerated the development of its pan-European network, called COLT EuroLAN, by striking development deals with other network and infrastructure providers. In April it purchased 4,500 route kilometers of network from Louis Dreyfus Communications in exchange for 2,900 route kilometers of duct network in Germany. The agreement gave COLT additional infrastructure connections between its city networks in Paris, Lyon, Marseilles, Turin, Milan, Geneva, and Zurich. In June COLT announced a pan-European agreement with Telia, whereby COLT would acquire 3,600 route kilometers of network in Scandinavia and Austria in exchange for some 3,000 route kilometers in Germany.

In April COLT expanded its alliance with Cisco Systems, Inc., making Cisco its preferred IP equipment supplier. Cisco would develop applications for new business areas and address systems integration, support, and network management. COLT would gain access to Cisco's advanced IP technologies for voice and data convergence, worldwide IP-VPN (virtual private network) services, web hosting, ASP enabling capabilities, e-commerce solutions, and Internet billing.

In June COLT and Inktomi Corporation announced plans to enhance COLT's Internet network with Inktomi's network infrastructure technology. The Inktomi Traffic Server would provide core technology for COLT's network of Internet Solution Centres (ISCs), while Inktomi's Content Delivery Suite would allow COLT to deliver on-demand broadband service to its customers. COLT planned to have a network of 20 ISC's in place by the end of 2001. In June COLT opened ISCs in Madrid, Spain, and Milan, Italy. In July 2000 the first phase of COLT's 14,000 route kilometer pan-European network (COLT EuroLAN) began operating with the opening of its 3,000 kilometer German intercity network.

In August 2000 COLT announced that Peter Chisholm, president and CEO, planned to return to the United States in 2001. The company initiated a search for his successor. In January 2001 COO Peter Manning was named to succeed Chisholm as president and CEO of COLT. Under Chisholm's leadership, COLT had grown from little more than an idea to a leading pan-European communications company.

In September 2000 COLT launched its fiber-optic city network in Rome with an initial 20 route kilometers. It was COLT's 23rd European city network. Also in September COLT announced a strategic partnership with the Hewlett-Packard Company to rollout a comprehensive suite of online computing and services capabilities across Europe. HP would provide the "always-on" computing infrastructure and full range of e-services solutions for COLT's European network of ISCs. Other developments in September included the launching of COLT's DSL-based service in Germany, the opening of an ISC in Berlin, and the launch of COLT's 24th city network in Antwerp, Belgium. In October, the company launched DSL-based service in the Netherlands, added an ISC in Vienna, Austria, and launched its 25th city network in Stockholm, Sweden. In November COLT opened its tenth ISC—and the third in four weeks—in Zurich, Switzerland. The company also launched city networks in Birmingham, England, and Dublin, Ireland, before the end of the year, giving COLT high bandwidth fiber-optic networks in 27 cities in 11 countries.

With COLT quickly and successfully deploying fiber-optic networks and establishing Internet Solution Centres in leading cities throughout Western Europe, the company was carrying out its plan to provide an IP-based European network that linked Europe's major business buildings into an effective single local area network across Europe. It also planned to launch DSL-based services in nine European countries. COLT had signed supplier agreements with Siemens, Alcatel, and Convergys for the necessary equipment and support services. The DSL-based services would complement COLT's already significant local fiber access services. The company's vision was to become the leading content delivery network in Europe, and COLT appeared able to raise the funds to finance that vision and execute its plans.

Principal Subsidiaries

COLT Telecom GmbH (Germany); COLT France; COLT Telecom N.V. (Netherlands).

Principal Competitors

British Telecommunications plc; Cable & Wireless plc; Energis plc; Deutsche Telekom AG; WorldComm, Inc.; KPN Telecom Broadcast (Netherlands); France Telecom.

Further Reading

''COLT Expands UK Network,'' *Communicate,* May 2000, p. 13.

Egan, Jack, ''The $13 Billion Honey Pot,'' *Forbes,* May 15, 2000, p. 64.

Grimond, Magnus, ''British Telecommunications Firm Announces Plans for Fundraising Effort,'' *Knight-Ridder/Tribune Business News,* December 10, 1999.

Grose, Thomas K., et al., ''The Dinosaurs Dance: Deutsche Telekom and Telecom Italia Plan an Alliance, but Are Mergers Any Way to Run a Telecoms Business?,'' *Time International,* May 3, 1999, p. 80.

Guyon, ''Dialing for Euros: COLT's Winning Idea,'' *Fortune,* May 10, 1999, p. 26.

London Daily Mail, ''British Telecommunications Firm Ionica Suspends Trading,'' *Knight-Ridder/Tribune Business News,* October 26, 1998.

London, The European, ''New Names Added to London Stock Market's Blue-Chip List,'' *Knight-Ridder/Tribune Business News,* September 15, 1998.

O'Connor, Brian, ''British Telecommunications Firm Grows,'' *Knight-Ridder/Tribune Business News,* August 11, 1999.

——, ''British Telecommunications Firm Making Executives Rich,'' *Knight-Ridder/Tribune Business News,* April 15, 1999.

Oldroyd, Rachel, ''German Telecom Giant Showed Skill in Takeover of British Cell-Phone Firm,'' *Knight-Ridder/Tribune Business News,* October 24, 1999.

Oldroyd, Rachel, and Simon Fluendy, ''Opinion: Is it Time for Britons to Hang up on Their Telecom Shares?,'' *Knight-Ridder/Tribune Business News,* March 29, 1999.

''Peter Manning,'' *The Wall Street Transcript,* July 31, 2000.

Skeel, Shirley, ''Quarterly Sales Rise for British Telecommunications Firm,'' *Knight-Ridder/Tribune Business News,* May 6, 1999.

''Tracker,'' *New Media Investor,* May 31, 2000, p. 16.

—David P. Bianco

Columbia Sportswear Company

6600 North Baltimore
Portland, Oregon 97203
U.S.A.
Telephone: (503) 286-3676
Fax: (503) 289-6602
Web site: http://www.columbia.com

Public Company
Incorporated: 1938 as Columbia Hat Company
Employees: 1,450
Sales: $614.8 million (2000)
Stock Exchanges: NASDAQ
Ticker Symbol: COLM
NAIC: 315228 Men's and Boys' Cut and Sew Other Outerwear Manufacturer; 315239 Women's and Girls' Cut and Sew Other Outerwear Manufacturer; 316219 Other Footwear Manufacturing

One of the largest outerwear manufacturer in the world, Columbia Sportswear Company designs, manufactures, and markets outdoor apparel and footwear, distributing its merchandise to more than 10,000 retailers in North America, South America, Europe, Asia, and Australia-New Zealand. It is the leading skiwear manufacturer in the United States and also sells lines of snowboard apparel, hunting and fishing clothing, casual sportswear, and accessories such as mittens, hats, scarves, sunglasses, and ski goggles. Columbia's rise to the top began during the 1980s, when Gertrude Boyle and her son, Tim, orchestrated the remarkable growth of their family-owned business nearly 50 years after the company began doing business as Columbia Hat Company. With mother and son at the helm, Columbia's sales grew quickly after the company entered the skiwear market in 1986 with its trademarked Interchange System of layered outerwear. The company made a reputation for itself in part through an eye-catching advertising campaign featuring the chairwoman as hard-driven "Mother Boyle." The company is a global supplier of high-quality outerwear, with distribution in over 30 countries. The company operates a few of its own retail outlets, with stores in Portland, Oregon, Nagoya, Japan, and in Sydney, Australia. Columbia also sells discounted goods through its own outlet stores, with eight in the United States. The company went public in 1998. About two-thirds of the stock remains in the hands of the Boyle family.

1930s Origins

The Lanfrom family escaped from Nazi-controlled Germany before the start of World War II, resettling in Portland, Oregon, in 1937. The following year, the family, headed by Paul Lanfrom, purchased a small hat distributorship named Rosenfeld Hat Company and renamed it Columbia Hat Company. Such were the origins of Columbia Sportswear, a small, unknown hat company tucked away in a corner of the United States, one that half a century later would hold sway as a national leader in the sportswear market. Aside from the company's headquarters location in Portland, however, few vestiges of Columbia Sportswear's past remained by the 1990s. The transition from a small, locally oriented hat distributorship into a corporation with a global reach took decades to complete, but it began early, starting a few short years after Paul Lanfrom took control of the company.

The first of the many changes that shaped Columbia Hat Company into Columbia Sportswear occurred when Paul Lanfrom encountered problems with his vendors. The solution, as Lanfrom perceived it, was to begin manufacturing his products on his own. Though the move into manufacturing represented a signal milestone in Columbia Sportswear's development, it did not ignite the prolific growth that would later characterize the company. Rather, the company maintained a minor presence in the Portland area, operating as a small manufacturing concern capable of supporting Paul Lanfrom, his wife Marie, and their daughters in their new life in America.

A decade after Paul Lanfrom acquired Rosenfeld Hat Company, his daughter, Gertrude, married Neal Boyle, who subsequently joined the family business. Neal Boyle's ascendancy to control over the family business occurred in 1963 when Paul Lanfrom died and Boyle became president. By the time Boyle took charge, Columbia had begun to carve a niche for itself in the hunting and fishing apparel market, thanks in large part to

Company Perspectives:

Columbia Sportswear Company is a global leader in the design, sourcing, marketing and distribution of active outdoor apparel and footwear. As one of the largest outerwear manufacturers in the world and the leading seller of skiwear in the United States, the company has developed an international reputation for quality, performance, functionality and value. Outdoor Active Authentic American Value.

his wife's contributions. Three years before her father died, Gertrude Boyle designed and made a fishing vest jacket on her home sewing machine that paved the way for the company's future. The bolero-style vest, which was outfitted with numerous pockets, was revolutionary in concept and moved the company headlong into the market for fishing and hunting apparel. Neal Boyle expanded his company's presence into this market once he took control. His era as company president, however, was unexpectedly brief. In 1970, at age 47, Neal Boyle died of a heart attack, leaving Columbia in the hands of his wife, Gertrude Boyle.

1970s: Mother and Son Take Charge

At the time of Neal Boyle's death, Columbia was generating $650,000 a year in sales, but was teetering on the brink of insolvency. Although the company had made headway into the market for fishing and hunting apparel, profitability in this line of business had been a problem for years, leaving Gertrude Boyle in the unenviable position of inheriting a floundering business. To make matters worse, Neal Boyle had offered three family-owned homes and his life insurance policy as collateral for a Small Business Administration loan several months before his death, which exacerbated the financial pressures Gertrude Boyle inherited in 1970. Despite the bleak prospects Columbia faced and despite her lack of any managerial experience, Gertrude Boyle showed up at the company's headquarters the day after her husband's funeral ready to take charge, vowing to keep the three-decade-old family business running under her command.

In the months that followed Neal Boyle's death, Columbia's financial health went from bad to worse. Bankers were reluctant to provide credit, some stores refused to stock Columbia's merchandise, and others experienced delivery problems. By the end of Gertrude Boyle's first year of leadership, the situation was grave, prompting the mother of three to sit down and negotiate for the sale of the company her family had owned since she was a child. From across the table came an offer of $1,400, which Boyle flatly refused, reportedly telling Columbia's prospective buyer, ''For a lousy $1,400, I'll run the company into the ground myself.'' Boyle nearly did.

Gertrude Boyle's son, Tim, who had been working part-time at the company, left his final semester at the University of Oregon to join Columbia full-time after his mother balked at what she perceived to be an insulting bid for her family's apparel manufacturing business. Two years later, mother and son could not point to anything positive. Columbia had a negative net worth of $300,000, and as Tim Boyle later remembered, both he and his mother were at fault. ''We really blew it,'' the younger Boyle admitted to *Sporting Goods Business* 20 years later. ''You name it, we did it wrong. We went in and fired everyone. We just didn't know what in the world we were doing.''

Gradually, however, Columbia's anemic financial health began to improve under the determined control of Gertrude and Tim Boyle. The mother and son team were given credit after pledging Columbia's $200,000 manufacturing facility. Subsequently, they dramatically reduced the company's involvement in the wholesaling side of the apparel business, which had been stifling profits for years. Once this was done, the company was able to scrape by during the mid-1970s by targeting specialty catalog operators. In 1976, however, Tim Boyle made a decision about Columbia's future course that put an end to the years of merely striving to eke out an existence in the sportswear apparel market. Boyle resolved to concentrate on building a brand-label presence in Columbia's markets. From 1976 forward, marketing the Columbia label represented the number one priority and, as a consequence, nearly every available dollar was earmarked for advertising.

Columbia reached the $1 million mark in sales in 1978, as the company earned a reputation in specialized circles as a hunting and fishing apparel resource. The explosive growth that would catapult the company and the Columbia label toward global prominence was still several years away, but one of the key individuals for engendering such growth joined the Portland apparel manufacturer before the 1970s came to an end. In 1979, Don Santorufo began superintending all the purchasing of materials and the manufacturing of merchandise at Columbia's manufacturing facility in Portland and then quickly expanded production by contracting out work to several independent Pacific Northwest contractors. It was a definitive move that marked the gradual decline of production activities in Portland and set the stage for years of exponential sales growth. Within ten years, all production in Portland would come to an end.

Explosive 1980s Growth

Columbia's annual sales climbed robustly as production expanded, rising from the $1 million recorded in 1978 to $12 million by 1983, when Santorufo hired Korean nationals to oversee manufacturing overseas. The decision to manufacture overseas proved to be instrumental in Columbia's resolute rise during the 1980s because offshore production enabled the company to make its apparel items at a significantly lower price. ''What we did was lower the price of quality,'' Boyle explained years later. ''There was no need for performance apparel to cost what most manufacturers were charging for it. We were able to source better-made goods off-shore and offer them to consumers at a reasonable price.'' Santorufo's deal with the Koreans was pivotal, but equally important was the development of what Columbia designers christened the Interchange System. Introduced the year before Columbia began manufacturing overseas, the trademarked Interchange System consisted of a lightweight shell jacket and a warm liner that zipped together, giving the wearer three jackets for different weather conditions.

Together, the decision to manufacture offshore and the development of the Interchange System provided two key ingredients for the success Columbia achieved during the late 1980s

Key Dates:

1938: Lanfrom family buys Rosenfeld Hat Company and renames it Columbia Hat Co.
1948: Lanfrom's daughter Gertrude marries Neal Boyle.
1960: Gertrude Boyle designs a multi-pocketed hunting/fishing vest for the company to manufacture.
1963: Neal Boyle becomes president of the company.
1970: Neal Boyle dies, and control of company goes to Gertrude and their son, Tim.
1976: After near bankruptcy, company refocuses on promoting the Columbia brand name of sportswear.
1978: Sales pass $1 million mark.
1983: Company moves its manufacturing overseas.
1989: Columbia becomes leading U.S. skiwear manufacturer.
1998: Company goes public.

and into the 1990s. One other decisive move spurred the exponential growth to follow: in 1986 Columbia entered the skiwear market with a parka called the ''Bugaboo,'' featuring the company's Interchange System of layered outerwear. The Bugaboo, which ranked as the greatest selling parka at its price point in the industry by the end of its debut year, put the company on the map, touching off prodigious growth that elevated Columbia into the elite of nationally recognized contenders. In the decade that followed the introduction of the Bugaboo, annual sales soared 1,600 percent as the Boyles inundated the skiwear market with their highly popular Interchange System products.

By 1989, after sales had swelled from $18 million the year before the Bugaboo entered the market to nearly $80 million two years later, Columbia's ski sales outstripped all other competitors in the United States. It was a remarkable rise underpinned by aggressive and creative advertising that transformed the Columbia name into a widely recognized apparel label. The Boyles set aside large sums of cash for advertising, spending twice as much as their nearest competitor, and starred in their own humorous advertisements. In the series of commercials, which debuted in 1983, Gertrude Boyle put her son, Tim, through a series of tests designed to illustrate the durability of Columbia's garments. The humorous advertising campaign featured Tim Boyle as the test dummy and Gertrude Boyle as ''One Tough Mother'' and proved to be highly effective. By the beginning of the 1990s, Columbia had eclipsed the $100 million sales mark and the Boyles were mapping ambitious plans for the future.

In 1991, Tim Boyle announced his intention to reach $1 billion in sales by the year 2000, informing a reporter from *Sporting Goods Business,* ''I'm very serious about that figure. We have the management team in place and the product development to do it.'' To achieve this formidable objective, Boyle expanded the company's product lines during the first half of the 1990s, adding several different lines of apparel and accessories that contributed significantly to the company's revenue volume. In 1993, a line of denim apparel was introduced, featuring jeans, vests, and shirts marketed under the ''Tough Mother'' name. That same year, the company started a footwear division that manufactured the ''Bugaboot,'' a rugged, outdoor shoe worn by Gertrude Boyle in advertisements featuring the tag line, ''My Mother Wears Combat Boots.'' As the company moved into the mainstream of the apparel market with its line of denim wear, the awareness of the Columbia label grew significantly, aided by the perennially popular image of ''Mother Boyle,'' by then in her 70s, in print and television advertisements.

1990s Diversification

In response to the growing, broad-based appeal of the Columbia label, sales surged ahead. Record sales were recorded in 1991 and again in 1992, when the one millionth Bugaboo parka was sold, making it the best-selling parka in ski apparel history. Following the introduction of Tough Mother denim wear and footwear in 1993, record sales were once again recorded, fueling confidence at the company's Portland headquarters that the strength of the Columbia label could indeed carry the outerwear manufacturer toward $1 billion in sales by the end of the decade. In 1994, when Columbia was named the official supplier to CBS Sports for the Winter Olympic Games in Lillehammer, Norway, the company entered the burgeoning market for snowboard apparel by introducing its Convert line of loose-fitting, insulated outerwear, which helped make 1994 a record year in sales.

By the mid-1990s, Columbia was growing by leaps and bounds, particularly overseas, where the company's revenue volume tripled between 1993 and 1995. At the end of 1995, President and Chief Executive Officer Tim Boyle made a move to steer Columbia in a new direction when he acquired retail space for the company's flagship store in Portland. The store opened the following year, showcasing the full range of Columbia apparel, footwear, and accessories. Next, Boyle sought to extend Columbia's retail presence overseas by opening a retail store in Seoul, South Korea, where 14 years earlier Santorufo had negotiated the first deal that inaugurated Columbia's offshore manufacturing.

The first Seoul store opened in 1997, with another 16 retail outlets slated for grand openings in Seoul by the end of 1997, giving Columbia a powerful new engine for sales growth as the late 1990s began and the company pursued its goal of $1 billion in sales by the decade's conclusion. Although not halfway toward its lofty sales objective by the late 1990s, the company was nevertheless performing admirably as it neared its 60th year of business. With Gertrude and Tim Boyle still at the helm, it was expected that Columbia would continue to flourish into its seventh decade of business.

Going Public: The Late 1990s and After

The company had been controlled by family since its inception in 1938. By the late 1990s, Gertrude Boyle was in her 70s, and Columbia had become a huge firm with distribution all over the world. In 1998, the company decided to sell a portion of its shares to the public, on the NASDAQ stock exchange. The initial public offering (IPO) was conceived as a way of compensating the Boyle family and chief operating officer Santorufo, and Columbia would not receive proceeds from the offering. Yet Wall Street was apparently anxious for a bite of the thriving company. The shares sold well above the starting price and brought the Columbia executives over $100 million. Though many fashion and apparel IPOs had not done as well as expected around the time Columbia went public, the company presented itself as a solid outdoor brand, and investors snapped it up. Its competitor, North Face Inc., had also had a successful IPO recently, and analysts seemed to think Columbia was in the same mold. In fact, Columbia continued to prosper over the next few years, building its tough and functional image by not bending to fashion. The company did try to expand its apparel lines into some more year-round products. Columbia began selling men's, women's, and children's socks in 1999, through a licensing agreement with the Tennessee firm Crescent Hosiery Mills. It also spent money on a new distribution center, investing $33 million in 1999. The company continued to expand in overseas markets, and made inroads in the department store market in the United States. It made an agreement with the midwestern regional department store Kohl's in 1999. Columbia also grew through expanding the number of in-store ''concept shops'' it sold through. These were store-within-a-store areas that displayed a complete line of Columbia goods. Columbia had about 350 concept shops in 1998, and increased this by about 200 shops by 2000.

Columbia went briefly into the red in 1999 because of the expense of its new distribution center. However, by 2000, the company looked strong all around. Its international sales were on the way up, with sharp gains in Japan and Europe. Domestic sales too continued to climb, even though the retail market overall was not in good shape. The outerwear category was flat in general, yet Columbia posted sales growth of close to 30 percent for 2000. Net income went up around 70 percent for that year. The company seemed to do well by giving value—its prices were significantly lower than its competitors, such as North Face. And Columbia did not try to be fashionable. A writer for *Forbes* (December 25, 2000) noted that Columbia had ''barely tweaked its popular Bugaboo coat in 17 years.'' By not trying to be trendy, Columbia reinforced its image of authenticity and practicality. An industry analyst who followed the company told *WWD* (*Women's Wear Daily*) in July 2000 that she believed ''they're like Nike was ten years ago. . . . They have a technically advanced product line with something for everyone.'' The company increased its footwear offerings by buying up the trademark rights to bankrupt Canadian boot maker Sorel in late 2000. It continued to concentrate on making inroads into year-round products, for instance signing a licensing agreement in 2001 to sell both sunglasses and ski goggles through a leading French eyewear manufacturer. With low debt, growing international and domestic sales, and a well-respected core brand, the company seemed in good shape to reach the financial goal Tim Boyle had set for it.

Principal Competitors

North Face, Inc.; The Timberland Co.; Lost Arrow Corporation.

Further Reading

Barron, Kelly, ''Tough Mama,'' *Forbes*, December 25, 2000, p. 232.

Black, Jeff, ''3 Hot Houses in a Cool Retail Climate,'' *Daily News Record,* May 28, 1990, p. 16.

Black, Jennifer, ''Columbia Returns to Black in Quarter,'' *WWD*, July 27, 2000, p. 9.

Caminiti, Susan, ''When Your Back Is Against the Wall,'' *Fortune,* March 7, 1994, p. 139.

Carpenter, Kristin, ''So Big, So Fast,'' *STN*, December 1997, p. 1.

''Columbia Sportswear Files IPO to Raise $92 Million,'' *Daily News Record*, January 2, 1998, p. 1.

Gruner, Stephanie, ''Our Company, Ourselves,'' *Inc.*, April 1998, p. 127.

Hill, Luana Hellmann, ''Hot Flashes from a Hot Company,'' *Oregon Business,* October 1988, p. 34.

Leand, Judy, ''Columbia Sportswear 'Pacs' Up Sorel,'' *Sporting Goods Business*, October 11, 2000, p. 10.

Kletter, Melanie, ''Columbia Sportswear Loses $238,000 in Second Quarter,'' *WWD*, July 29, 1999, p. 30.

Marks, Anita, ''Columbia Hopes Korean Climate Spells Hot Sales,'' *Business Journal-Portland,* May 31, 1996, p. 1.

Moffatt, Terrence, ''Hail Columbia,'' *Sporting Goods Business,* March 1991, p. 40.

Ryan, Thomas J., ''Columbia Sportswear IPO Opens at 36.1% Above Offering Price,'' *Daily News Record*, March 30, 1998, p. 1B.

Slovak, Julianne, ''Columbia Sportswear,'' *Fortune,* April 24, 1989, p. 188.

Spector, Robert, ''Columbia Gets Street-Smart,'' *WWD,* March 16, 1995, p. 10.

Weitzman, Jennifer, ''Temperature Drop Boosts Columbia's Net,'' *Daily News Record*, February 14, 2001, p. 16.

Yang, Dori Jones, ''This Grandma Wants to Keep You Warm,'' *Business Week,* December 5, 1994, p. 111.

—Jeffrey L. Covell
—update: A. Woodward

Concord Camera Corporation

4000 Hollywood Boulevard, Suite 650N
Hollywood, Florida 33021
U.S.A.
Telephone: (954) 331-4200
Fax: (954) 981-3055
Web site: http://www.concordcam.com

Public Company
Incorporated: 1982
Employees: 218
Sales: $173.2 million (2000)
Stock Exchanges: NASDAQ
Ticker Symbol: LENS
NAIC: 333315 Photographic and Photocopying Equipment Manufacturing

With low-cost manufacturing facilities operating in the People's Republic of China, Concord Camera Corporation manufactures single-use and conventional cameras for its own labels, as well as for private labels and such major cameramakers as Polaroid, Eastman Kodak, and Agfa-Gevaert. Concord Camera's entry into digital cameras and development of wireless picture delivery systems holds great promise for the company. A decade-long conflict, however, with its founder and long-time chief executive, punctuated by occasional charges and countercharges of fraud and fiscal irresponsibility, has been both a source of distraction and embarrassment.

Establishing Concord Camera in 1982

Jack C. Benun started Concord Camera in Rahway, New Jersey, in 1982. He told the *Wall Street Journal* that he got his start in the business as a teenager when he resold pawn shop cameras out of a car on the streets of Manhattan. He claimed to later make $3 million as a minority partner in a Taiwanese camera business. Benun told *Business Week* that he made $1.8 million by the age of 30, decided to retire, but that within several weeks he was restless and returned to business by starting up Concord Camera. He turned to the People's Republic of China, which was beginning to open its doors to foreign businessmen, and in 1983 began operating a camera manufacturing plant in Baoan, 15 miles north of Hong Kong, where he had a design team in place. Skilled labor was both plentiful and cheap in China, allowing Benun to make cameras that were extremely price competitive. He concentrated on the low-end camera market, building cheap but reliable models. By 1988 Concord Camera was generating almost $20 million in annual sales, and Benun was looking to take the company public. What followed would begin a series of investigations and lawsuits that would haunt both Benun and Concord Camera well into a new century.

Roland W. Kohl was a senior executive of Concord Camera's Hong Kong affiliate, Dialbright Company. He and Benun were both directors of the company and stockholders. As part of taking Concord Camera public, Benun wanted to make Dialbright a fully owned subsidiary. The two men agreed to exchange their Dialbright shares for Concord Camera stock, with Benun further agreeing to buy 240,032 shares from Kohl to be paid for in six installments. In July 1988 Concord Camera completed its initial stock offering, selling 1.15 million shares at $5 each, and then consummated the acquisition of Dialbright, renaming it Concord Camera HK Limited, with Kohl serving as general manager. In 1989 the company used the funds its IPO raised to acquire the German company Peter Bauser GmbH, renaming it Concord Camera Gmbh, for approximately $1.6 million. Then in February 1990 Concord Camera formed a subsidiary in Canada, followed in June by another acquisition, the $2.2 million purchase of the Angus and Safari camera businesses from Optex, Inc. After the close of its fiscal year, which ended on June 30, Concord Camera reported a 1990 net loss of $3.2 million on $28.4 million in sales. The company attributed the loss in part to a poor U.S. economy, but in September it issued a statement that alleged its performance also was hurt by the wrongful acts of certain Hong Kong employees, in particular Kohl, all of whom had been subsequently terminated. The company said that legal proceedings against the employees also had been initiated in Hong Kong.

In the lawsuit Benun filed, he claimed that Kohl and his subordinates conspired to cripple the unit's business in order to

Company Perspectives:

Concord's mission is to be a world class, high quality, low cost designer, developer and manufacturer of popularly priced, easy-to-use cameras and consumer products with performance results and appropriate equity returns for shareholders.

induce Concord Camera to sell a major interest in the subsidiary to them. Asking for $3.6 million in losses and unspecified damages, the suit contended that Kohl fired nine supervisors and almost 500 factory workers between March 1989 and March 1990, a period in which production orders were backing up. The suit further contended that Kohl used up Concord Camera's line of credit by buying an excessively high number of camera parts. Publicly, Benun claimed that he had been preoccupied with the IPO and assured the press that he would never again let down his guard.

1992 Charges and SEC Investigation of CEO

Kohl would have his own grievances, which he would lay out when he sued Benun in 1992, but by that time Benun was already being sued by Concord Camera's former chief financial officer, Michael J. Rea, who was suddenly terminated in January 1991. A month later he sued Benun and Concord Camera, alleging that he discovered Benun had been embezzling company funds and was wrongfully dismissed when he refused to cover up the matter. Rea claimed that on a trip to the Hong Kong unit he asked a production manager named Eli Shoer about a $150,000 bonus he had been paid after being hired, only to discover that Shoer said he never received the money, but that he had signed the check over to Benun, who when later confronted would deny the matter. Finally, according to Rea, Benun said, ''Don't worry; no one will ever find out. Nobody could ever trace it.'' Rea further alleged that in November 1990 the Hong Kong subsidiary had arranged to buy equipment from a company owned by Shoer for $135,000 but actually paid $170,000. Confronted with this discrepancy, according to Rea, Benun replied, ''Don't be stupid. I need the money.'' Rea further charged that he discovered checks worth $250,000 from Shoer's company had been deposited in one of Benun's personal bank accounts. Although the suit would be settled out of court, Rea's charges prompted the Securities Exchange Commission to begin investigating Benun and Concord Camera. The company's board also announced that it would launch an internal investigation, and as a result of this unwanted publicity the price of Concord Camera stock lost almost a third of its value in one day.

Aside from Rea's allegations, Benun's general conduct as an executive caused some concern. He typically drew his entire annual salary of $375,000 on the first day of the fiscal year, thereby hurting cash flow. Although he occasionally lent money to Concord Camera, he borrowed large sums as well, including $1.4 million in fiscal 1990 and close to $1.1 million in 1991. Nevertheless, Benun was cleared by his board, the company's stock rebounded, and Concord Camera continued to grow. Amid the turmoil of 1991, the company created a British subsidiary, as well as acquiring Keystone Camera for $6.6 million. It also entered the single-use camera business, which would become a company mainstay.

Early in 1992 Kohl sued Benun in the U.S. District Court of New Jersey. His major charge was that Benun failed to pay the sixth installment on the Dialbright stock that Kohl had sold him in 1988, amounting to more than $140,000. Kohl also alleged that in June 1988 Benun borrowed $6,000, which he never repaid, and that later in the year Benun asked Kohl to lend $1,500 to Carla Drummond, described in the suit as Benun's ''friend and travelling companion.'' That money as well, Kohl alleged, was never repaid. Speaking on behalf of the company, William Pearson, Concord Camera's executive vice-president and a close associate of Benun, dismissed Kohl's charges as retaliation over Concord Camera's suit of Kohl in Hong Kong. Later in 1992 Pearson would leave the company, purchasing the Argus brand name and starting Argus Industries. By the end of the year, he would be suing Benun and Concord Camera as well, charging breach of contract, wrongful and malicious conduct, fraudulent practices, and violation of the New Jersey racketeering statute. In essence, Pearson alleged that Concord Camera tried to destroy his business. The attorney representing Concord Camera called the allegations ''absolutely untrue.''

Concord Camera also was experiencing problems with its primary lender, Midlantic National Bank, after receiving a number of extensions on a deadline to repay a $15 million loan. The company found new funds when New York investor Ira J. Hechler provided some $3 million. Despite its debt and posting a $2.7 million loss for fiscal 1992, Concord Camera was still looking to expand. It announced in September an agreement to purchase the Vivitar and Hanimex businesses from British competitor Gestetner Holdings PLC for $50.6 million. Benun also announced that he would step down as CEO when the transaction was complete. Only a few months earlier, when Benun's contract was set to expire and Concord Camera's board of directors had the chance to ease out their controversial chief executive, he received a new three-year deal that increased his salary to $600,000 (albeit it stipulated that he was to be paid in biweekly installments instead of a lump sum). Under the terms of the contract, if Benun was asked to leave his job without cause he would be entitled to full salary and benefits for the entire three years of the deal. In the press there was speculation that funding for the acquisition was contingent upon Benun stepping down, thus raising the possibility that he might be able to collect on his contract even though he resigned.

Discharge of Concord Camera's Founder and CEO in 1994

The Vivitar and Hanimex deal fell through, however, and Benun continued as CEO in 1993, as did the SEC investigation about him. Hechler, in the meantime, was purchasing more stock and gaining control of the company. On the other hand, Benun, who had owned 60 percent of Concord Camera stock after the IPO, had been selling off his interest and now held just 25 percent, according to published reports. Although the company announced a return to profitability in fiscal 1993, industry insiders were reported to claim that Concord Camera was dumping product in the market to gin up its numbers. In October 1993 the new investors, according to newspaper accounts, pushed for a renewed investigation of Benun, apparently re-

Key Dates:

1982: The company is created in New Jersey.
1988: The company goes public.
1991: The company acquires Keystone Camera.
1994: Founder and CEO Jack C. Benun is terminated for cause.
1998: Headquarters is moved to Florida.

sponding to pressure from the SEC. Rather than reforming an internal committee, which critics claimed had not interviewed key witnesses the first time, the board of directors hired the New York City law firm of Kramer, Levin, Naftalis, Nessen, Kamin & Frankel to conduct the inquiry, led by the head of the firm's white-collar crime department, Gary Naftalis. By July 1994 a confidential report was submitted, Benun was promptly fired, and the company then settled with the SEC. Although not admitting any wrongdoing, Concord Camera agreed to ''cease and desist from filing false reports and proxy statements and keeping inaccurate books and records.'' In September 1994 the SEC charged Benun with misappropriating $150,000 from Concord Camera. Without admitting or denying the allegations, Benun settled the complaint by agreeing to repay the embezzled funds plus interest, for a total of $215,000. In addition, he paid a $150,000 fine to the SEC.

At Concord Camera Benun was replaced by Ira Lampert, an investment banker with little experience in the camera industry who had served originally as a consultant in 1992 and then became the company's president in July 1993. He soon found himself the subject of criticism by Benun, and the company the subject of litigation. At the company's annual meeting in January 1995, Benun and his allies on the board charged Lampert with nepotism, demanding that Lampert's son, who worked at the Hong Kong subsidiary, be fired. They also alleged that Lampert had bribed Chinese officials with $1,250 in connection with a land contract. In the coming months Benun would elaborate on the bribery charge in letters to the company's board and to the SEC. Lawyers for Concord Camera would admit that certain Chinese officials were paid for travel and incidental expenses, but denied that the money was a bribe for signing a contract. Furthermore, Benun sued Concord Camera for $6.7 million over lost wages and benefits, claiming that he had been wrongfully terminated. The company then sued him, asking for damages of $2 million caused by ''his frauds and embezzlements.'' Separately, disgruntled shareholders also sued Benun.

Early in 1995, with all the controversy surrounding the company, Concord Camera stock dropped to $2 a share. Lampert brought in a new management team that shed nonessential businesses to cut costs, bolstered its design staff, and began investing in technology. After years of rushing out products to dress up its sales numbers, only to have a large number returned and see its retail reputation tarnished, Concord Camera decided to concentrate on doing one category well, the single-use camera, and rely on its low-cost China facility to give it a competitive edge. It landed a deal with 3M to manufacture its single-use cameras and other companies soon followed. Overall, the single-use camera category was experiencing robust growth. Concord Camera further capitalized on the trend by introducing a line of single-use cameras targeted at the under-12 market. Moreover, the outsourcing movement of the 1990s now extended to the camera industry, as both Kodak and Polaroid farmed out manufacturing work to Concord Camera and its low-cost China facilities. The company's commitment to research and development also was beginning to pay off. Its Keystone brand introduced a patented system that could automatically imprint on pictures such messages as ''Happy Birthday,'' ''Vacation Fun,'' and ''Stay in Touch.''

In December 1998 Concord Camera moved its headquarters from New Jersey to Hollywood, Florida. Its business now had a solid footing. It was producing point and shoot cameras for its own labels, as well as supplying private label cameras to major retailers such as Wal-Mart, Kmart, and Sears. It was a major supplier of single-use cameras for its own labels and major camera makers as well as toymakers Fisher-Price and Crayola. It also was working with Hewlett-Packard to develop a digital camera, as well as developing a digital image-capture device that could transmit pictures to a cell phone. In effect, Concord Camera was transforming itself into a technology company. By 1999 it generated $118.4 million in sales, after posting just $40 million four years earlier. By December 1999 Concord Camera stock was trading at more than $15, after a low of $3.50 in the previous 52 weeks. A few months later it introduced its first digital camera, ''eye Q,'' a low-cost product that it planned to sell on a private label basis to retailers and that industry analysts predicted would become a major success. The company's stock soared past $45 in March 2000. For fiscal 2000, Concord Camera would generate $173.2 million in revenues and $19.6 million in net income, which represented a 154.5 percent increase over the previous year. It reached #20 in *Fortune's* list of the fastest-growing companies and was listed #25 in *Forbes* 200 Best Small Companies.

Despite moving to Florida and establishing a solid reputation with customers and investors alike, Concord Camera was not free of Jack Benun. In September 1999 an arbitrator ruled that the company had just cause for firing him. Nonetheless, in December 2000 he was trying to stop the company's annual meeting scheduled for January 18, 2001, contending that his six-year-old employment agreement entitled him to nominate six of nine directors. He and Concord Camera would turn to arbitration and, again, Benun would lose. He maintained that he would continue to explore his options. The company, in the meantime, was experiencing continued growth, although poor earnings forecasts from Polaroid and Kodak had an adverse impact on Concord Camera stock. Prospects appeared promising, but Concord Camera faced competition in its outsourcing business from Asian competitors. Its move into high-tech products was also risky, as digital technology evolved far more rapidly than film. Although Concord Camera clearly had reached a new level in its business, in many ways it was now performing on a high wire and would not be afforded the luxury of too many missteps.

Principal Subsidiaries

Concord-Keystone Sales Corp.; Concord Camera Gmbh; Concord Camera France S.A.R.L.; Concord Camera HK Limited; Concord Camera (Europe) Limited; Goldline (Europe) Limited.

Principal Competitors

Fuji Photo Film Co., Ltd.; Vivitar; W. Haking Enterprises; Konica Corporation.

Further Reading

''Auditors Halt Work on Concord Camera Pending Investigation,'' *Wall Street Journal,* August 12, 1991, p. A3.

''Concord Camera Ousts Chief and Settles with S.E.C.,'' *New York Times,* July 15, 1994, p. D3.

Eichenwald, Kurt, ''Concord Camera's Hefty Pay Deal,'' *New York Times,* October 23, 1992, p. D6.

Henriques, Diana B., ''What's Keeping Concord on a Roll?,'' *New York Times,* December 8, 1991, p. F19.

Laderman, Jeffrey M., ''Smile—If You're onto Concord Camera,'' *Business Week,* October 10, 1988, p. 126.

Pandya, Mukul, ''A Former CEO Battles Concord Camera,'' *New Jersey Business News,* June 12, 1996.

——, ''The Inside Story of How Concord Camera Lost Its Chief Executive Officer,'' *New Jersey Business News,* July 27, 1994.

——, ''The Picture at Concord Camera Keeps Getting More and More Fuzzy,'' *New Jersey Business News,* April 1, 1992.

Pollock, Michael A., ''Small Firms Face Big Headaches in Far-Flung Places,'' *Wall Street Journal,* July 1, 1991, p. B2.

Rejtman, Jack, ''Hollywood, Florida-Based Disposable-Camera Maker Comes Back Strong,'' *Miami Herald,* December 6, 1999.

—Ed Dinger

Courier

Courier Corporation

15 Wellman Avenue
North Chelmsford, Massachusetts 01863
U.S.A.
Telephone: (978) 251-6000
Fax: (978) 251-8228
Web site: http://www.courier.com

Public Company
Incorporated: 1894 as Courier-Citizen Company
Employees: 1,535
Sales: $188.32 million (2000)
Stock Exchanges: NASDAQ
Ticker Symbol: CRRC
NAIC: 323113 Commercial Screen Printing; 323117 Books Printing; 323121 Tradebinding and Related Work; 511199 Miscellaneous Printing; 551112 Offices of Other Holding Companies.

Courier Corporation is the largest book manufacturer in the Northeast, the fifth largest in the nation, and a full-service publisher, printer, distributor, and marketer of a wide variety of books. The company focuses on streamlining and enhancing the process by which printed books and digital content reach end-user markets; services include prepress and production through storage and distribution. Courier has three business segments: book manufacturing, customized education, and specialized book publishing. Five of the company's subsidiaries focus on such specialties as short-run book manufacturing, printing on light-weight paper, and four-color manufacturing. This latter segment serves more than 650 book-manufacturing customers. Sales to one customer, The Gideons International (distributor of bibles), generated about 26 percent of fiscal 2000 consolidated sales, and Pearson plc (world's leading education business and international media company) accounted for about 17 percent of fiscal 2000 consolidated sales. Customized education is the specialty of Courier subsidiary Copyright Management Services (CMS), which provides Internet-based solutions to educators wanting to combine materials from multiple publishers into customized books and coursepacks. At the heart of the specialized book publishing segment is Dover Publications, Inc. (Dover), one of the world's most successful niche publishers. Dover sells books worldwide and mails its proprietary catalogs to over 500,00 consumers. Dover publishes books, including Dover Thrift editions that usually sell for $1.00, in more than 40 specialty categories ranging from military history to paper dolls, and from musical scores, typographic fonts, and Egyptian hieroglyphics to CD-ROMs. In fiscal 2000, Courier produced over 300 million books. *Forbes* magazine, in its October 30, 2000 issue, recognized Courier as one of ''The Best 200 Small Companies in America'' and rated Courier as one of 11 companies to watch.

1800–1940: The Forerunners

Long before the Industrial Revolution got underway, English-speaking settlers had been drawn to New England's surging waterways. Francis Cabot Lowell, an early settler, was a key player in the industrial development of that region. In 1814, after touring several English textile mills, he wanted to bring textile machinery back to the United States but British law prohibited its export to the United States. Upon his return home, Lowell ''built from memory the first power loom in the United States, set it up in Waltham, Massachusetts, and in 1815 began textile production,'' wrote John A. Conway in *The Citizens of Courier*, a history of the early years of Courier Corporation. The success of Lowell's venture led to a search for a site having enough water to expand the Waltham Experiment. Lowell died in 1817, but his dream of producing textiles became a reality when friends from Boston searched for a good source of hydraulic power to run a textile operation (steam power did not become available until the 1850s and electricity until the end of the 19th century).

After traveling to East Chelmsford and inspecting the so-called ''raging rapids of the Merrimack River,'' several of Lowell's admiring friends and entrepreneurs banded together ''to form a new company, the Merrimack Manufacturing Co., . . . which was to develop the finest textile mills in the world,'' wrote Conway. Ingenious engineering of the Merrimack enabled mills to garner the energy needed to support many mills on the river's banks, thereby fostering the development of bustling factory villages, such as Lowell and Chelmsford.

Company Perspectives:

Courier's mission is to enhance and accelerate the process of getting books and information from the point of creation to the point of use.

William Baldwin was the first journalist to comment on these new communities when—on June 25, 1824—he began publishing the *Chelmsford Journal*, the predecessor of Courier Corporation. In every issue, the *Journal* ran an ad for itself under the headline: ''Book and job printing . . . in all branches, executed on new type, with neatness and expedition, at this office.'' Conway commented that, like other newspapers of this period, the *Journal* was ''well written, political, candid and, at times,'' quite humorous. As the textile mills prospered, the population increased and so did the number of newspapers. By 1840 Lowell had more than 20,000 residents and newspapers for about every political viewpoint. After various name changes and mergers, the *Chelmsford Journal* became the *Lowell Courier*. Then, in 1856, three other newspapers merged with the *Chelmsford Journal* to form the *Lowell Daily Citizen* , which in 1882 was known as the *Citizen Newspaper Co.*

Meanwhile, Alexander Graham Bell had invented the telephone (1876) and created a singular marketing opportunity for the *Lowell Daily Citizen*. In 1878, that newspaper company printed the first issue of the *Boston Telephone Directory*—a one-page broadside containing 67 listings.

By 1890, however, the town's more than 11 newspaper publishers offered Lowell's 95,000 residents more newspapers than they wanted. In 1894, to counter the diminishing profitability of newspaper publishing, the *Lowell Daily Citizen* and the *Citizen Newspaper* Company. merged into one company, to be known as the Courier-Citizen Company (Courier). The new company was to publish, print and sell newspapers, periodicals, and books as well as develop a general job printing and bookbinding business, Conway reported in *The Citizens of Courier*. By 1900, Courier was one of the largest printing firms north of Boston; printing was the company's most profitable sector.

As New England towns and cities prospered, telephones and the need for local telephone directories increased. New England Telephone's widespread operation called for centralized records. To this end, the telephone company developed business forms for various activities, especially for billing, purchasing, and requisitions. Courier, the telephone company's long-time printer of choice for directories, picked up a contract for printing these business forms. This was Courier's first stationery contract; it was soon followed by a contract to meet the printing needs of New York's Waldorf-Astoria Hotel. In 1920, Courier agreed to produce forms and to print all of Western Union's telegrams as well as meet all the telephone company's printing needs east of the Mississippi River. For the first time, Courier also included warehousing and distribution services in this contract. During the 1930s, Courier became one of America's premier printers of business forms by servicing accounts for other large corporations; for example, American Cyanamid, Atlantic Refining, Uniroyal, United Fruit, and General Motors.

Forms, War, Recession, Computers: 1940–72

Courier further committed itself to printing forms when it sold the newspaper side of its business to the *Lowell Sun*. The company's next move was to buy the Chicago-based Uniform Printing and Supply Company, which printed and distributed ''standardized [insurance] policy forms from a central location,'' according to *The Citizens of Courier*. The acquisition included control of two plants—one in Chicago and the other in Brooklyn, New York—marking the first time Courier operated printing operations outside of its home base in Lowell. Courier gained the unofficial title of Printer by Appointment to the Insurance Industry.

During the two decades following World War II, the insurance industry grew at a record pace—and so did Courier's coast-to-coast market, which had more than 300,000 agents to whom it sent documents. Courier set up new systems for printing, distributing, and warehousing forms and manuals as well as for maintaining mailing lists and inventories. To assure an effective operation and to keep customers abreast of changes in state laws affecting the insurance industry, Courier also established central clearinghouses for each state.

By the early 1950s, Courier was prospering from its work with insurance companies. At about this time, James F. Conway, Jr. joined Courier as general manager. A lengthy study convinced him that moving most of the distribution out of Brooklyn to strategically placed locations would ''minimize shipping time and reduce expenses for delivering forms to insurance agents,'' according to *The Citizens of Courier*. Conway set up 15 distribution outlets, for which start-up costs were met within six months of operation.

Courier acquired the San Francisco-based Bosqui Printing Company in 1956 and became a truly nationwide manufacturing operation with a lucrative forms business. In 1966, James F. Conway, Jr.—newly named as Courier's president—authorized a $4.5 million bank loan to acquire the Westford, Massachusetts-based Murray Printing Company, one of the world's finest black and white printers. Murray had more than 500 employees working on college textbooks, dictionaries, and scientific books.

In the 1960s, however, a general shift in the insurance industry had a negative impact on Courier's Forms Division. Tough economic times and the introduction of business computers diminished the need for forms used by individual insurance agents; there was a trend to consolidate the writing of policies in regional offices. This shift in operation, ''pushed Courier's profits in the Forms Division to a low in 1968 and forced the company to adopt a new approach to the business,'' John Conway wrote in *The Citizens of Courier*.

To distinguish itself from the typical operation of other printing companies operating in 1970, Courier targeted some of the biggest companies in America by focusing on ''a full-service approach.'' Conway illustrated this new approach by quoting part of a Forms Division manager's sales pitch: ''We tell a customer we can do two things, affect an economy and improve efficiency. . . . We are attempting to provide a wider range of products and services, taking ourselves out of the arena of the traditional neighborhood printer. We will accomplish for

Key Dates:

1824: William Baldwin publishes the *Chelmsford Journal*, predecessor of Courier Corporation.
1835: After being acquired by several new owners, *Chelmsford Journal* is sold to the *Lowell Courier*.
1878: *Lowell Daily Citizen* prints the first Boston Telephone Directory.
1894: *Lowell Courier* and the *Lowell Daily Citizen*/Citizen Newspaper Company merge to form Courier-Citizen Company (Courier).
1920: Courier, in its first stationery contract, prints business forms for New England Telephone Company.
1930s: Courier becomes one of America's premier printers of business forms.
1941: The newspaper side of Courier business is sold to *The Lowell Sun*.
1950s: James F. Conway, Jr., joins Courier as general manager and leads the company to open distribution outlets across the country.
1966: Conway is named president of Courier.
1972: Courier-Citizen goes public under the name of Courier.
1978: Conway is named Courier chairman of the board; Alden French, Jr. becomes president.
1990: Courier launches Courier Connection and moves into electronic publishing.
1996: Courier moves its corporate headquarters to North Chelmsford.
2000: Courier acquires Dover Publications, Inc.; reports third consecutive year of record-breaking financial results; earns The Printing Industry Association's "Best Workplace in America" award.

you something you probably don't even appreciate you are paying for right now." The new marketing strategy paid off. By 1972 the forms business was at the top of Courier's divisions, accounting for more than $20 million of the company's total gross of approximately $53.8 million. However, severe price cutting throughout the business forms industry kept the division's profits on the 1971 level.

Going Public, Technology and Unions, a Joint Venture:1972–89

The next question that the company faced was whether the forms business would assure Courier's profitable longevity. Courier President and CEO Conway was well aware of the company's assets (printing equipment, various contracts, land, and little long-term debt) but equally attuned to a trend toward consolidation: large printing firms were buying relatively small printing companies. With funds generated from a public offering, he believed, the company would be positioned to grow while maintaining its reputation for product quality, competitive prices, and technology support. To go public, the Courier-Citizen Company created a holding company, called Courier Corporation; stock was offered for $15 a share on November 16, 1972 and more than $2.6 million was raised. The company planned to use the new funds to finance plant and equipment expansion.

Within a year of its public offering, Courier Corporation recorded its fifth consecutive annual increase in sales and earnings; in 1973 sales topped $60 million for the first time. The company was making good its promise of expansion and continued growth. In 1975, Courier acquired Philadelphia-based National Publishing Company, considered to be "the finest printer of light-weight papers in the nation . . . and specializing in reference texts, bibles and other religious products" according to the company's history in *The Citizens of Courier*. "National was able to handle the demanding binding assignments related to these high-quality books, making it a printer of unique capabilities and skill." Courier's new subsidiary spearheaded Courier's international expansion and reputation for excellence. National moved to a modern facility in Philadelphia in 1997.

In 1978 Conway was named chairman of the board and Alden French, Jr., became Courier's president. During the 1980s, Conway noted that the demand for forms was in steady decline, possibly because computers were making many business forms obsolete. In 1984, the company sold its Forms Division to a private investor. At the same time, Conway began to question the future profitability of printing telephone directories. This industry was changing from hand-laid, hot-metal type to a business based on new technology. The phone companies, with eyes on their bottom line, were pushing for change, and there was stiff competition for contracts. In 1985 Conway and French set up Courier in a joint venture—called North American Directory Corporation (NADCO)—with Toronto-based Bell Canada Enterprises, Inc. (BCE). That same year, Courier acquired Stoughton, Massachusetts-based Alpine Press Inc., a leading manufacturer of hard cover and softbound books serving educational, trade, and high technology markets. Alpine was later renamed Courier Stoughton.

NADCO sales grew quickly: the venture was well positioned to win the top position for publishing telephone directories in the United States. However, due in part to the rising cost of paper and to unrest resulting from jobs lost because of computers and other new equipment, there was growing unhappiness in both the workforce and management. Although sales increased, net income remained flat from year to year and in 1988 Courier sold its 50 percent interest in NADCO. That same year Alden French was succeeded as president by James F. Conway III.

Going Digital, Defining Growth Markets, E-Commerce, Consolidation:1990–2000

During the 1980s, the technological revolution that swept American businesses had a very powerful impact on the traditional American printing industry in general and on Courier Corporation in particular. Electronic prepress and desktop publishing were the first signs that printing and publishing workflow were going digital. In 1990, Courier became a pioneer in the book industry when it established Courier Connection, designed as "an electronic, integrated publishing service bureau . . . to provide the widest possible range of services using desktop publishing technology," according to newswriter Sally Taylor's story in the August 2, 1991 issue of *Publishers Weekly*. Customers gained instant online access to the company's prepress services—and Courier positioned itself as a full-service printer. This innovation notwithstanding, however, 1992 was the worst year in Courier's history.

The toll on sales came from the company's shift of focus from commodity-like business, the addition of new services to enable growth in higher value-added turnkey relationships, and the training of service teams to deliver these new services. The company revised its operating and marketing strategies; it began to regain its leadership position by forming an Electronic Publishing Innovations Center (EPIC), which in 1993 offered on-demand, technology-based publishing services ranging from processing electronic files through reproduction and end-user distribution; products for the growing software market included kitting, fulfillment manuals, and floppy disks. The quarterly dividend was restored. In a rapid turnaround, Courier reaped the benefit of the 1993 decision to focus on three specific markets—religion, education, and specialized publishing—where it could be the best and find customers who would place the most value on the company's services. Sales of software documentation and educational publishers' materials were particularly strong for fiscal 1994 and rose to $122.73 million. Sales dipped by about $2 million in 1995 but in 1996 Courier again reported a profit.

In December 1994, the company formed Courier New Media, Inc. (CNM), an information-management services company that worked with publishers, software developers, and other information providers to create products from new and existing intellectual properties. CNM included two operating units, Courier EPIC and Copyright Management Services (CMS), a new division established in December 1994, to help publishers and college bookstores obtain copyright permissions for products such as multiple-publisher college coursepacks. Courier EPIC conducted an electronic publishing service, including customized, on-demand printing and binding services. CMS specialized in helping publishers and college bookstores to obtain copyright permissions for educational products, such as multiple-publisher college coursepacks.

In 1996 Courier moved its corporate headquarters to North Chelmsford. In 1997, the company acquired Book-Mart Press, Inc., a book manufacturer specializing in short to medium runs of softcover and hardcover books. Book-Mart offered high-quality offset printing and binding for orders as low as 300 copies. This acquisition allowed Courier to complement its existing range of services by enabling its customers to shop for full-service book production of any run length. The company also acquired The Home School, Inc., a direct marketer (through retail, catalog and e-commerce) of educational materials to families who were educating their children at home.

By 1998 Courier was the largest book manufacturer in the Northeast. Over and above the manufacture of books and manuals, the company replicated diskettes and CD-ROMs for publishers, software developers, and other information providers—and managed the creation and distribution of these products. The company consolidated the kitting, assembly, inventory management, and related services of Courier New Media with those of Courier Stoughton's. North Chelmsford's end-user fulfillment operation was expanded to handle The Home School's national catalog roll-out and other end-user fulfillment business.

In 1999, Courier launched an e-commerce business—bookhound.com—for out-of-print books that it offered as replica books manufactured from an original; copyright permission was obtained from either publishers or authors. During the last quarter of fiscal 1999—for $39 million in cash—Courier acquired Mineola, New York-based Dover Publications, Inc., a consistently successful company that, in 1951, broke new ground with the introduction of the first trade paperbacks; Courier was the manufacturer of these high-quality books.

Dover sold its products through catalogs and a diverse range of wholesalers and booksellers, children's stores, craft stores, and gift shops in museums and historic sites—to name but a few of its outlets. In an interview in the September 2000 issue of *Graphic Arts Monthly*, Courier's president and CEO, James Conway III, commented on Dover's ''unique process of identifying pockets of demand and its track record of bringing more than 400 new specialized publications to market each year.'' He went on to say that ''The combination of Dover's publishing, sales, and distribution skills with Courier's book manufacturing, digital-content conversion, and e-commerce skills'' would ''produce a powerful end-to end solution for Dover,'' and that Courier would ''capture revenue and profits from every step of the process.''

In fiscal 1999 Courier's net income rose to $8.38 million, or $2.52 per diluted share, and sales peaked at $163.99 million—compared to 1997 net income of $4.32 million in fiscal 1997, or $1.41 per diluted share, and sales of $131.43 million.

2000 and Beyond

Within its chosen markets—religion, education, and specialized printing—Courier was agile at anticipating customer needs. In early fiscal 2000 the company invested $16 million in new technology, printing presses, and bindery lines. In 2000, the company reported that it was the only major book manufacturer to respond as quickly to what it described as ''an industry-wide capacity shortage.''

In March 2000, Dover—operating as an autonomous subsidiary—brought its list of more than 7,500 books directly to consumers through a brand-new web site, doverpublications.com. Customers could buy books in more than 40 categories, including more than 2,000 children's books, some priced as low as $1.00. Additionally, Dover offered sticker books, gift wrap, tattoo books, card, and paper-doll books—including ones on both Princess Diana and the Queen Mother. Among the new books selling for $1.00 each was *Wit and Wisdom of the American Presidents,* which contained over 400 *bon mots* by presidents from George Washington to Bill Clinton.

Having launched the Dover web site, Courier sold The Home School, Inc. to privately held Christian Book Distributors, Inc. of Peabody, Massachusetts. James Conway III, president and CEO, pointed out that this sale would allow Courier to focus more of its time and energy on Dover, a much larger business that offered far greater opportunity for development. Courier reported fiscal 2000 as another year of record growth, bringing the company's five-year compound annual growth rate to 9.3 percent for revenue and 15.3 percent for net income. Net sales for the year reached $188.32 million, and net income rose to $10.64 million, or $3.15 per diluted share. Book manufacturing accounted for 98 percent of fiscal 2000 revenues, and customized education accounted for 2 percent.

Building on three consecutive best-ever years, Courier management had reason to be optimistic about continuously profitable growth in fiscal 2001, and beyond.

Principal Subsidiaries

Book-Mart Press, Inc.; Courier-Citizen Company; Courier Foreign Sales Corporation Ltd. (Jamaica; 99 %); Courier Kendallville, Inc.; Courier New Media, Inc.; Courier Stoughton, Inc.; Courier Westford, Inc.; Dover Publications, Inc.; National Publishing Company.

Principal Competitors

Banta Corporation; Dai Nippon Printing Co., Ltd.; Hart Graphics, Inc.; Quad Graphics, Inc.; Quebecor World Inc.; R.R. Donnelley & Sons Company.

Further Reading

''The Best 200 Small Companies in America,'' *Forbes Magazine*, August 30, 2000.

Conway, John A., *The Citizens of Courier*, Lowell, Mass.: Courier Corporation, 1994.

Cross, Linda, ''Official 2000 Ranking of the Industry's Top Printing Firms,'' *Graphic Arts Monthly*, November 1, 2000.

''Inside Business: Book Printer Agrees to Buy Specialty Publisher,'' *Graphic Arts Monthly*, September 2000, p. 32.

Mason, Dennis E., ''Integrated Print Manufacturing: What's Next?,'' *Graphic Arts Technical Foundation*, May 1, 1999, pp. 9+.

Taylor, Sally, ''Courier Leaps Into Electronic Technology,'' *Publishers Weekly*, August 2, 1991, pp. 50–51.

Warsh, David, ''Lowell's Courier Corp. Prefers to Specialize,'' *Boston Globe*, December 20, 1979.

—Gloria A. Lemieux

The Daiei, Inc.

4-1-1, Minatojima Nakamachi
Chuo-ku, Kobe 650-0046
Japan
Telephone: (81) 78 302-5001
Fax: (81) 78 302-5572
Web site: http://www.daiei.co.jp

Public Company
Incorporated: 1957
Employees: 13,776
Sales: $25.8 billion (2000)
Stock Exchanges: Tokyo Osaka NASDAQ Brussels American
Ticker Symbol: DAIEY
NAIC: 45211 Department Stores; 45299 All Other General Merchandise Stores; 44512 Convenience Stores; 42241 General Line Grocery Wholesalers; 42231 Piece Goods, Notions, and Other Dry Goods Wholesalers; 42199 Other Miscellaneous Durable Goods Wholesalers

The Daiei, Inc. operates as one of Japan's largest retailers and was ranked 20th among the world's leading retailers at the end of the 20th century. Daiei founder and former chairman and CEO—Isao Nakauchi—once boasted that his company sells ''everything except ladies and opium.'' Indeed, the group operates many outlets, from supermarkets to department stores to warehouse clubs and convenience stores. Not limited to retailing, Daiei also owns and operates the Fukuoka Dome and Fukuoka Daiei Hawks—a major league baseball team—as well as Western-style fast food restaurants, a financial services network, and other real estate ventures. The Asian economic crisis of the late 1990s, however, forced Daiei to restructure its operations, close some stores, sell off other subsidiaries, and sell a portion of its interest in Lawson convenience stores.

1950s Origins

Isao Nakauchi founded Daiei in his hometown of Osaka in 1957; the company's name is a complicated play on words that means both prosperity of Osaka and big prosperity. A pharmacist's son, Nakauchi had made a small fortune in the years after World War II by participating in a venture that sold penicillin at above the legal price. His brother and some associates were arrested for their roles in the scheme, but the experience taught Nakauchi that risk taking and making money were inseparable.

His first Daiei store was a pharmacy called Housewives' Store Daiei. He gave its parent company the name Daiei Pharmaceutical Company. Japan's post-Korean War depression was then reaching its lowest point, and Osaka shoppers appreciated Daiei's discount pricing policy. Its initial success soon inspired him to open more stores in the Osaka area.

The poor economic conditions of the time also proved fortuitous for Daiei at the wholesale level. Manufacturers were grateful for the fact that Nakauchi always paid cash for their goods. He also bought whatever surpluses overextended manufacturers may have accumulated, and passed on the savings to consumers. Thus, Daiei quickly ceased to be merely a drug store chain; as Nakauchi would recall years later, ''We soon moved from drugs into candies and other foods and from cosmetics and toiletries into hard goods.'' In 1970, the company dropped the focus on specialized retailing and shortened its name to its current form.

Daiei Achieves National Dominance in 1970s

Daiei soon expanded to become a nationwide chain in Japan. By the time it celebrated its fifteenth anniversary in 1972, the company was operating 75 superstores and had become Japan's largest supermarket operator and second largest retailer. It had achieved this rapid and overwhelming success by breaking many of Japanese retailing's time-honored rules. In a nation where small shops often banded together in cartels to keep prices artificially high, Daiei was a high-volume, low-price retailer. ''Even our barbers and laundries have self-protective cartels,'' Nakauchi once complained. Nakauchi, an unlikely but

Company Perspectives:

''For our Customers—Good Products at Lower Prices for a More Bountiful Society.'' With this as our motto, we will continue to implement sound measures to realize our goal of Everyday Low Prices.

open admirer of Mao Tse-tung's strategic wisdom, cast Daiei in such a mold to draw on the strength of ''the masses,'' offering quality goods at the lowest possible prices.

In 1970, when outraged consumers realized that Japanese television sets were being sold for less in the United States than at home, Daiei leapt into the breach, signing a marketing deal with Crown Radio and selling Crown sets under their own name for less than half the going rate. Daiei was a pioneer in introducing the concept of house brands to Japanese consumers, who were used to paying higher prices for recognized brand names. In 1971, Daiei actually acquired Crown and added more electronics goods and household appliances to the Daiei name. Nakauchi kept his overhead low by opening stores in the suburbs, rather than the densely populated, high-rent urban areas favored by Japanese department stores. For his iconoclasm in a consensus-oriented society, he was reviled by ex-friends, threatened by irate competitors, and ostracized by the business establishment. This treatment, however, did not deter him from his vision of revolutionizing Japanese retailing, an arduous process he once compared to Mao's travails.

In the 1970s, the company began to internationalize, diversifying its range of goods and services even further. In 1972, it created Daiei U.S.A. as a wholly owned subsidiary and opened a branch in a Honolulu shopping center. Taking advantage of the liberalization of Japanese laws regarding the presence of foreign retailers, Daiei entered into joint ventures to open branches of U.S. department store Joseph Magnin and Swift & Company's Dipper Dan Ice Cream Shoppe chain in Japan.

In 1974, Daiei surpassed the sales of department store giant Mitsukoshi to become Japan's largest retailer. Once again, though, Nakauchi's ambitions were scarcely satisfied. In the spring of that year, Daiei began selling J.C. Penney merchandise as part of an arrangement with the U.S. retailer to test its popularity in Japan. The venture proved successful, and several months later, Daiei and J.C. Penney entered into a joint venture to open stores in Japan under the Penney name, beginning in 1976. Under the agreement, Daiei and Penney each owned 47.5 percent, with the remaining 5 percent going to trading company C. Itoh.

In 1978, Daiei continued to capitalize on the popularity of Western goods in Japan when it became the sole Japanese agent for British department store Marks and Spencer. Daiei chose Marks and Spencer merchandise because of its reputation for price competitiveness, especially in food and clothing. For its part, Marks and Spencer, which already had a substantial presence in Hong Kong, saw Japan as its largest remaining potential export market.

Diversification into Fast Food in the 1980s

In 1979, Daiei joined with Wendy's International to open Wendy's fast-food restaurants and Victoria Station steak houses in Japan. Wendy's Japanese rollout did not progress as quickly as had been hoped, however, because of the inflexibility of the American parent organization. Portions and stores, for example, were too big for Japanese tastes. And although the chain expanded too fast early on, it had fewer than 30 restaurants by 1988, when the operation still had yet to earn a profit.

Other cross-cultural ventures undertaken during the decade were more successful. In 1980, Daiei made its first serious incursion into the U.S. market when it acquired in its entirety Holiday Mart, a three-store discount chain in Honolulu, Hawaii. It also opened its first U.S. purchasing office. Not least of all, it joined with Au Printemps to open branches of that venerable French department store in Japan; the first Au Printemps Japan opened in Kobe in 1981, followed by stores in Sapporo in 1982, and in Tokyo the year after that.

Meanwhile, Daiei's supermarket operations continued to flourish. At the outset of the 1980s, Daiei controlled one-fifth of the entire Japanese food retail market. In 1981, it reorganized that side of its business somewhat when it merged its Sanko affiliate with food store chain Maruetsu. Daiei and Maruetsu each owned 50 percent of the new company, which immediately became the nation's ninth largest retailer, boasting 140 branches. Also in 1981, Daiei acquired a 10.5 percent stake in Takashimaya, another department store chain, making it that company's principal shareholder.

In 1984, Daiei's sales reached ¥1.4 trillion, and its chain of superstores had grown to 160. Daiei continued to expand at a breakneck pace, opening a branch in Tokyo's expensive Ginza district during this same period. Nakauchi financed this continuous augmentation with heavy borrowing, and the cost of financing this debt forced the company to post a ¥11.9 billion loss in 1984, despite its massive sales. The next year, Daiei lost ¥8.8 billion, spurring speculation among some analysts that Daiei's 60-something year-old founder and CEO had lost his Midas touch.

Nakauchi insisted all along that these deficits were part of his plan and that continued expansion would pay off in the long run. Daiei had cleverly spread its borrowing among four different banks—contrary to the usual Japanese corporate practice of borrowing from one bank, which then allowed that bank to become the company's principal stockholder. This wise move enabled Daiei to preserve its independence. In 1986, the company returned to profitability, earning ¥1.1 billion, and by 1987, it was healthy enough to acquire bankrupt sewing machine manufacturer Riccar at the request of the Ministry of International Trade and Industry. In that same year, it announced a five-year plan to install an electronic information network to link all of its branches, offices, and affiliates, starting with an ¥11 billion point-of-sale (POS) system for its superstores. POS systems give retailers quick and accurate information on sales and inventories—information that can be used to improve inventory control.

Key Dates:

1957: Isao Nakauchi establishes Daiei as a pharmacy called Housewives' Store Daiei.
1970: The company expands its focus and adopts its present name.
1972: By now, the firm operates 75 superstores and subsidiary Daiei U.S.A. is formed.
1974: The company becomes Japan's largest retailer.
1976: Daiei partners with J.C. Penney to open stores in Japan under the Penney name.
1980: The Holiday Mart chain is acquired in Honolulu, Hawaii.
1981: Company reorganizes its food retail operations.
1984: The firm records losses due to expenses related to its aggressive expansion.
1987: Profitability is restored and a plan to install an electronic information network within its branches, offices, and stores is developed.
1992: Nakauchi creates Japan's first wholesale membership club.
1995: Daiei enters the Chinese market; an earthquake demolishes eight superstores in the Kobe area.
1997: The company begins to falter as economic conditions worsen in Asia.
1998: The firm begins to restructure itself and sells off unprofitable assets.
2000: Daiei loses its top retailing position in Japan to Seven-Eleven Japan Co.

Retail Powerhouse Rolls on in the 1990s

Although some Japanese retailers began to follow Isao Nakauchi's price-slashing lead in the 1990s, none could keep up with his pace. He created Japan's first wholesale membership club in 1992. Like Sam Walton's groundbreaking ''Wal-Mart'' and ''Sam's Club'' stores, the new chain operated under the name Kuo's, an alternate pronunciation of Nakauchi's given name. In 1992, he brought ''everyday low pricing'' to the country, even abbreviating the concept as ''EDLP'' in Roman letters for advertisements. Meanwhile, Daiei's Big-A Co. box stores hoped to mimic ALDI's international success with limited lines of nonperishable staples in bare-bones stores. But even this was not enough for Nakauchi; in 1995, he announced his goal to slash consumer goods prices in half by 2010. This strategy continued to enjoy success: in the mid-1990s, Daiei accounted for 13 percent of Japan's grocery sales.

Nakauchi formed a Chinese joint venture and opened his first supermarket there in 1995. He also continued to invest in his Hawaiian operations, acquiring a supermarket in 1994, and expanding his shopping center there two years later. In 1993, the company opened the first phase of its Fukuoka Dome in Japan, home of the Fukuoka Daiei Hawks baseball team. By 1998, this twin-domed retail and entertainment complex was expected to also incorporate a 1,000-room hotel, amusement rides, and shopping.

Daiei's revenues increased to more than ¥3 trillion in fiscal 1995, but its net income had slid dramatically, from ¥10 billion in 1992 to ¥5.4 billion in 1994. Nature conspired to inflict a ¥50.7 billion loss on the group in 1995, when a January earthquake demolished eight superstores in the Kobe area. Daiei experienced a partial rebound in fiscal 1996, though, when it recorded a ¥5 billion profit.

The Daiei's erratic fiscal performance in the mid-1990s again raised a question about its future leadership. Although septuagenarian founder and CEO Isao Nakauchi appeared unmotivated to relinquish control of the company, he had been preparing for that eventuality by grooming son Jun Nakauchi as the company's executive vice-president.

Daiei Falters Along with the Asian Economy in the Late 1990s

In 1997, Japan lifted its long-standing ban on the formation of holding companies and Daiei formed K.K. Daiei Holding Corporation to control its non-retail business interests. Its expansion efforts were put on hold, however, as sales and net income fell once again due to the economic crisis sweeping through Asia in late 1997. The unstable economy caused consumer spending to fall and spelled disaster for the firm as most of its sales stemmed from domestic operations.

As the crisis continued into 1998, Daiei began to sell its real estate assets, restructure its operations, and sell off its unprofitable stores. Sales continued to fall and it was not Nakauchi's son, but instead Tadasu Toba, who took over the presidency of the ailing firm. Working along with chairman Nakauchi, Toba initiated a major restructuring effort in 1999, which included the sale of Recruit Co. and the Ala Moana Center shopping mall in Hawaii. Sales climbed slightly over the previous year, but net income still fell dramatically.

A Rocky Entrance Into the New Millennium

Daiei entered the 21st century battered and bruised from a continued lack of consumer spending. The firm initiated an IPO of its subsidiary Lawson Inc., but failed to raise the funds it had anticipated from the public offering. At the same time, tension between Toba and Nakauchi began to grow as the founder disagreed with the new president's plan to sell off more of the company's assets. At the same time, the Daiei's long-standing position as Japan's leading retailer—held since 1972—was suddenly taken over by convenience store operator 7-Eleven Japan Co. in 2000.

In October of that year, an insider trading scandal related to the purchase of consumer finance unit Daiei OMC Inc.'s stock became public. As a result, Toba relinquished the presidency, remaining a director of the firm. Nakauchi also resigned, but remained an advisor to the firm. Kunio Takagi, a Daiei executive, assumed the presidency.

The following month, Takagi outlined a restructuring plan designed to restore the company to its former glory. Included in the plan was the consolidation of the non-profitable assets of the Daiei Holding Corp. and the issuance of ¥120 billion in new shares. It also called for the closure of 32 outlets and 4,000 job cuts over a three-year period, and the sale of most of its interest in Lawson.

The company continued to focus on relieving its debt load in 2001 by selling off many of its subsidiaries. Under the leadership of Takagi, management aimed to reduce the number of its business units to 112 by February 2002. The firm's rocky past and the country's uncertain economic future, however, were sure to be major factors in determining whether or not Takagi would succeed in pulling Daiei out of financial straits.

Principal Operating Units

Beijing Liaison Office (China); Seoul Liaison Office (Korea); Shanghai Liaison Office (China); Taipei Liaison Office (Taiwan, R.O.C.); Hong Kong Liaison Office; Bangkok Liaison Office (Thailand); Hi-Daiei Trading Co., Ltd. (Philippines); Jakarta Liaison Office (Indonesia); Sydney Liaison Office (Australia); D International, Inc. (U.S.); Los Angeles Liaison Office (U.S.); New York Liaison Office (U.S.); Amsterdam Liaison Office (Netherlands); Milano Liaison Office (Italy); Printemps Ginza S.A., Paris Office (France); London Liaison Office (U.K.); Kaheka Office (U.S.).

Principal Competitors

Ito-Yokado Co. Ltd.; JUSCO Co. Ltd.; Mycal Corporation.

Further Reading

Belson, Ken, ''Japan: This Time, It Could Get Nasty,'' *Business Week,* January 15, 2001.

Bulman, Robin, ''Price-Cutting Effort by Store Group in Japan May Help U.S. Exporters,'' *Journal of Commerce and Commercial,* April 18, 1994, p. 3A.

Butterfield, Fox, ''Japan's Retailing Colossus,'' *New York Times,* November 3, 1974.

''Daiei Founder Steps Down As Chairman,'' *AsiaPulse News,* October 11, 2000.

''Daiei Hopes to Earn 20 Billion Yen in FY02,'' *Daily Yomiuri,* November 23, 2000.

''Daiei President Denies Insider Trading,'' *Daily Yomiuri,* October 4, 2000.

''Daiei's Discount Empire Prospers,'' *World Business Weekly,* January 12, 1981.

''Daiei to Cut Subsidiaries,'' *Daily Yomiuri,* December 1, 2000.

''Daiei to Issue New Shares for Restructuring,'' *Mainichi Daily,* November 28, 2000.

''Economic Forum Daiei Rift Shows Company Owners No Longer Have Free Rein,'' *Daily Yomiuri,* October 18, 2000.

Holden, Ted, ''A Retail Rebel Has the Establishment Quaking,'' *Business Week,* April 1, 1991, pp. 39–40.

''Japan: Mao in the Supermarket,'' *Time,* June 28, 1971.

''Japan's Daiei Group to Sell Lawson Shares to Mitsubishi Group,'' *AsiaPulse News,* February 22, 2001.

''Japan Showing the Strain,'' *Grocer,* July 29, 2000.

Markowitz, Arthur, ''Daiei Opens Kuo's, Japan's First Club,'' *Discount Store News,* October 5, 1992, pp. 1–2.

Merrefield, David, ''Big-A Powers Growth at Daiei,'' *Supermarket News,* October 5, 1992, pp. 11–15.

——, ''Japan's Pricing Pioneer,'' *Supermarket News,* October 5, 1992, pp. 11–15.

O'Brien, Tim, ''Japan's Fukuoka Dome Set To Open in March,'' *Amusement Business,* September 28, 1992, pp. 1–2.

''The Perils of Popularity,'' *Economist,* August 24, 1996, p. 53.

''Retailers Get Ready To Move into the U.S.,'' *Business Week,* August 4, 1980.

''Seven-Eleven Japan to Overtake Daiei As Top Retailer,'' *AsiaPulse News,* April 24, 2000.

Sherrid, Pamela, ''What Barriers?'' *Forbes,* October 10, 1983, p. 180.

Simmons, Tim, ''Big Business,'' *Supermarket News,* October 5, 1992, p. 2.

Smith, Lee, and Philip Jones Griffiths, ''Japan's Autocratic Managers,'' *Fortune,* January 7, 1985, pp. 56–65.

Zwiebach, Elliot, ''Daiei Net Tumbles in Quake Wake,'' *Supermarket News,* May 22, 1995, p. 23.

—Douglas Sun
—updates: April Dougal Gasbarre,
Christina M. Stansell

The David and Lucile Packard Foundation

300 Second Street, Suite 200
Los Altos, California 94022
U.S.A.
Telephone: (650) 948-7658
Fax: (650) 941-0205
Web site: http://www.packfound.org

Nonprofit Foundation
Incorporated: 1964
Employees: 113
Total Assets: $9.8 billion (2001)
NAIC: 813211 Grantmaking Foundations

The David and Lucile Packard Foundation is one of the world's largest charitable foundations, with assets of close to $10 billion. Its endowment comes from stock in the Hewlett-Packard Company bequeathed by the company's co-founder, David Packard, and his wife Lucile. Packard was at one time one of the five richest men in America. He gave away an estimated two-thirds of his fortune to his family foundation before his death, and then gave billions of dollars more in the form of Hewlett-Packard stock to the foundation when he died in 1996. The Packard Foundation is the largest shareholder in the Hewlett-Packard Company. The Packard Foundation operates primarily by making grants to educational and charitable organizations. By law, the foundation is required to give away at least five percent of its assets annually. For 2000, the foundation granted approximately $500 million to a variety of organizations in six main areas of interest. These are: conservation; population; science; children, families, and communities; arts, and a sixth category called organizational effectiveness and philanthropy. The foundation is headquartered in Los Altos, California, near San Francisco and the high-technology corridor known as Silicon Valley. Many of the Packard Foundation's grants go to area organizations, such as arts programs in Northern California. The Packard Foundation supports scientific research, with particular interest in ocean science, engineering, and sustainable living. The foundation makes grants to minority scholars to study advanced science and mathematics, and supports science programs at the nation's historically black colleges and Native American tribal colleges. The Packard Foundation also has a key interest in population control and makes grants to family planning organizations in the United States and abroad. The foundation is run by David and Lucile Packard's four children, and the diversity of its interests reflects the varied outlooks of the family.

The Hewlett-Packard Story

The David and Lucile Packard Foundation owes its huge assets to the success of what was perhaps the nation's first high-technology firm in what became known as Silicon Valley. David Packard, raised in Pueblo, Colorado, studied electrical engineering at Stanford University. When he graduated in 1934, in the midst of the Great Depression, it wasn't clear that his new field would yield him a job. Accordingly, he decided to create his own job. He went into business with a friend and fellow Stanford graduate, William Hewlett. The two friends began their business with slightly more than $500 and some tools in Packard's one-car garage. Their equipment included little more than a soldering iron and a drill press, but the two men had many ideas. Some of their first, and unsuccessful, products were a harmonica tuner and a foot-fault indicator for bowling alleys. In 1939 Hewlett-Packard had its first winner with an electronic tester for sound equipment, called an oscillator. This found buyers in the film industry. The firm also developed products for the military. By the late 1950s, Hewlett-Packard had sales of more than $30 million annually, and its almost 2,000 employees manufactured hundreds of different products. During the next decade, sales vaulted to more than $300 million. Packard left the company briefly in the 1960s to work as deputy secretary of defense in the Nixon administration, at the height of the Vietnam War. He later returned to the company, which continued to boom. Two landmark products were the Hewlett-Packard hand-held calculator in 1972, and the LaserJet printer in 1984.

A Family Foundation

The Packard family started the David and Lucile Packard Foundation in 1964. Because of the huge success of Hewlett-Packard, the family was becoming increasingly wealthy. The foundation offered a reasonable format for putting some of their

Company Perspectives:

The David and Lucile Packard Foundation was created in 1964 by David Packard (1912–1996), co-founder of the Hewlett-Packard Company, and Lucile Salter Packard (1914–1987). They believed the United States to be the home of a unique type of organization dependent upon private funding and volunteer leadership. Together, universities, national institutions, community groups, youth agencies, family planning centers, and hospitals constitute a great U.S. tradition that complements government efforts to focus on society's needs. In many ways, private programs are more effective than those of government. By using private funds for public purposes, programs of this type channel the personal commitment of millions of individuals who participate as volunteers or donors. The David and Lucile Packard Foundation, now in its 37th year, will continue to support these organizations with the hope and expectation that we can strengthen them and, thereby, conserve and enhance resources and improve the quality of life in our community, the nation, and the world.

money toward charitable ends. In its early years, the foundation was overseen chiefly by Lucile Packard, who not only handled grant-making decisions but oversaw the design of its modest headquarters building. Grants followed family interests. The foundation gave lavishly to Stanford University, Packard's alma mater, and financed research and scholarship in the sciences. David Packard gave to Republican causes, having served in the Republican Nixon administration, while Lucile Packard wished to focus on children and the poor. She gave her husband photographs of poverty-stricken Native American reservations, which were then hung on the wall of the foundation's headquarters. These served to remind the foundation of the lacks and inequalities its money could address. Under her direction, the foundation supported community programs in Northern California that helped children and families. The foundation also gave more than $100 million to build a pediatric hospital at Stanford, which was named the Lucile Salter Packard Children's Hospital. Lucile Packard was deeply involved in the day-to-day operation of the foundation. She met personally with prospective grantees, visited sites, and evaluated proposals.

Lucile Packard died in 1987. At that time, the David and Lucile Packard Foundation was relatively small, with assets of around $145 million. It made yearly grants of about $10 million. David Packard was one of the richest men in America, worth some $3 billion. A year after his wife's death, Packard announced a huge gift to the Packard Foundation. In 1988 he declared that he would give over $2 billion to the charity, making it suddenly one of the largest private foundations in the country. From a little-known regional organization, the Packard Foundation suddenly ranked number 11 nationwide, in the company of better-known foundations such as the Andrew W. Mellon Foundation, the Rockefeller Foundation, and the Pew Charitable Trusts. The Packard Foundation continued to give grants in areas of which the late Lucile Packard would have approved, with children's health continuing to be a major focus. The foundation also increasingly reflected the interests of the Packard's four children, Nancy, Julie, David, Jr., and Susan. Both Nancy and Julie Packard were marine biologists, and Julie was director of the Monterey Bay Aquarium. The aquarium was built with a donation from the foundation, and the foundation also funded programs to conserve fisheries and promote ocean science. David, Jr., worked in theater, and he was said to be behind the foundation's support of art and archaeology programs.

Becoming a Philanthropy Powerhouse

Although the gift that Packard made to the foundation after his wife's death suddenly made it one of the top-ranked philanthropies in the nation, it remained small in other ways. By the mid-1990s, it still had a staff of only about 50 people. It gave out grants worth about $100 million total annually in the mid-1990s, continuing to follow family interests. Its guidelines remained somewhat general and broad. A foundation publication from 1996 quoted in the *New York Times* (May 6, 1996) stated that the organization hoped to ''help people through the improvement of scientific knowledge, education, health, culture, employment, the environment, and quality of life.'' When David Packard died in March 1996, the foundation found itself for the second time suddenly bestowed with an astonishing amount of money (in the form of Hewlett-Packard stock). It had gone from having assets of around $100 million in the mid-1980s to over $1.5 billion a decade later, due to the infusion of Hewlett-Packard stock after Lucile Packard's death. David Packard left the bulk of his estate to the foundation, adding another $4 billion to its assets. This catapulted the foundation from its ranking as number 11 to one of the top three or four philanthropies in the United States. The well-known Ford Foundation had an endowment of around $7.4 billion in the mid-1990s, followed by the Kellogg Foundation, with assets around $7 billion. The Packard Foundation's assets rose to more than $6 billion and continued to rise as the value of its Hewlett-Packard shares increased.

The Packard family reacted cautiously to the new infusion of wealth into the foundation. The foundation's president was Susan Packard Orr, and the other Packard children had long been active in running the organization. After their father's death, the Packards spent several months developing a strategy for the foundation and making open-ended plans for dispensing funds. The Packards wanted to keep to their earlier goals, working on such issues as overpopulation, science education, and preservation of the environment. But with greater assets than before, it was possible to make bigger grants or approach issues in a more global way.

In 1997, the Packard Foundation gave to large number of groups, many of them active in environmental protection and population control. The foundation funded the World Wildlife Fund, the Environmental Defense Fund, the World Resources Institute, the Reproductive Rights Action League, Planned Parenthood, the National Abortion Rights Action League, and others, all of which reflected the long-term concerns of the Packard children. However, the right-leaning political commentary magazine *National Review* ran an article (March 23, 1998) claiming that the foundation's backing of these predominantly liberal causes flew in the face of the values of David Packard. Packard's wishes for his foundation had been expressed in a private letter to his children in 1987, apparently in very general

Key Dates:

1934: David Packard co-founds Hewlett-Packard.
1964: David and Lucile Packard establish the foundation, with Lucile taking primary responsibility for its structure and focus.
1987: Lucile Packard dies.
1996: David Packard dies and bequeaths billions of dollars to the foundation in the form of Hewlett-Packard stock.

terms. After his death, the foundation continued to back projects that he had begun in his lifetime, such as grants to historically black colleges to fund science education. The foundation also continued along lines that Lucile Packard had mapped out decades earlier. It gave heavily to groups that encouraged child welfare, funding area after-school daycare programs, giving $1 million in 1998 to build a new Child Development Center at San Jose State University, and making many smaller donations to child advocacy groups. The foundation also made special note of David Packard's hometown of Pueblo, Colorado. Beginning in 1999, the foundation gave several grants to Pueblo organizations, funding an aircraft museum, a health center, a school, and a Jewish temple, among others. Support for regional art centers continued as well. The Packard Foundation backed many Northern California arts institutions, giving grants to the San Jose ballet company, and helping rebuild a civic theater in Santa Cruz, among other projects. The foundation gave out 1,155 grants in 1998, totaling about $3.5 million. About 40 percent of these funds went to groups in the four counties surrounding the foundation's headquarters. Another 57 percent went to domestic organizations, and only 3 percent went to organizations abroad. In 1999 grants increased to over $4 million, with a slightly larger percentage going to international groups.

In 1999, the foundation's total endowment increased to around $13 billion, buoyed by the rising worth of Hewlett-Packard stock. The Packard Foundation became one of the wealthiest in the world, surpassed only by Britain's Wellcome Trust, and the rapidly growing Bill and Melinda Gates Foundation. Like the Gates Foundation, which got its funds from the family of Microsoft chairman Bill Gates, the Packard Foundation represented a new era in U.S. philanthropy. Older philanthropies such as the Carnegie Corporation and the Rockefeller Foundation depended on money earned in industry in the early part of the 20th century. The Packard Foundation represented a fortune made in high technology, which had boomed extraordinarily at the very end of the century. Except for the overshadowing presence of the Gates Foundation, its wealth was almost unprecedented. Grants made in 2000 totaled approximately $614 million. Even as its assets shrank to $9.8 billion as of December 31, 2000, it remained far larger than many older philanthropies. The foundation expected grants for 2001 to total around $550 million.

Principal Competitors

Bill and Melinda Gates Foundation; Wellcome Trust; Ford Foundation.

Further Reading

''$2 Billion Poorer,'' *Economist,* May 7, 1988, p. 26.

Freeman, Neal B., ''Shaky Foundation,'' *National Review,* March 23, 1998, pp. 38–40.

Geier, Thom, ''The Visionary in a Palo Alto Garage,'' *U.S. News & World Report,* April 8, 1996, p. 13.

Goldberg, Carey, ''With Fortune Built, Packard Heirs Look to Build a Legacy,'' *New York Times,* May 6, 1996, pp. A1, B9.

Gomes, Lee, ''Packard's Expected Bequest Would Put Foundation into Stratosphere,'' Knight-Ridder/Tribune News Service, March 27, 1996.

Mercer, Joyce, ''As It Joins Nation's Richest Philanthropies, Packard Foundation Considers Its Options,'' *Chronicle of Higher Education,* August 9, 1996, pp. A29–31.

''Packard's Big Giveaway,'' *Time,* May 9, 1988, p. 70.

Reis, George R., ''U.S. Philanthropy Boosted by High-Tech Billions,'' *Fund Raising Management,* August 1999, p. 5.

—A. Woodward

DAY RUNNER®

Day Runner, Inc.

2750 West Moore Avenue
Fullerton, California 92833
U.S.A.
Telephone: (714) 680-3500
Toll Free: (800) 232-9786
Fax: (714) 680-0538
Web site: http://www.dayrunner.com

Public Company
Incorporated: 1980 as Harper House, Inc.
Employees: 841
Sales: $171.5 million (2000)
Stock Exchanges: OTC Bulletin Board
Ticker Symbol: DAYR
NAIC: 323118 Blankbook, Loose-leaf Binder and Device Manufacturing

Day Runner, Inc., headquartered in Fullerton, California, is a major developer and manufacturer of and paper- and computer-based personal organizers. The company produces and markets a wide variety of such aids, as well as refills and other accessories, ranging from student planners to sophisticated systems for busy executives. Included are desk and wall calendars, combination telephone and address books, wall organizers, and dated appointment books. The company's line of products is available in more than 20,000 stores, including office supply superstores and mass merchandising outlets. Office Depot, Staples, OfficeMax, and Wal-Mart account for almost half of the company's sales. In addition, its products are sold in approximately 6,000 international retail outlets. In April 2001, the financially troubled company sold off Filofax Inc., which produced a line of products popular in Europe but which had become a financial burden for the parent company because of its increased debt service. The company's financial straits were also exacerbated by stiffening competition from such electronic organizer systems as those produced by Palm Pilots and other software and hardware makers.

1980–89: Novelty Day Runner Personal Organizers Develop into a Big Business

Day Runner was established as Harper House, Inc., in 1980. The personal organizer that became the company's flagship product was conceived by Boyd and Felice Willat, film production coordinators in Hollywood. The Willats discovered that the simple planners on the market at that time were not up to the task of organizing the frantic schedules they kept in both their work and social lives. To meet their own needs, they designed an organizer that combined the functions of calendar, address and telephone book, and personal planner. Reasoning that other people were probably having similar problems managing their hectic lives, Harper House put its first generation of Day Runner personal organizers, called the Day Runner System, on the market in 1982, targeting the growing numbers of young, ambitious professionals and entrepreneurs with family responsibilities and numerous outside interests.

Initially, Day Runner organizers were marketed mainly in gift stores, as something of a novelty item for executives. It quickly became clear, however, that the Day Runner had market potential far beyond what could be called a novelty. A key shift in strategy came in the mid-1980s, when Harper House began emphasizing "productivity" in its promotion of the Day Runner line, and the organizers began appearing in office supply stores rather than gift shops. Soon Day Runner organizers were being purchased by a much broader range of people, including executives, blue-collar workers, and students.

By 1987 Harper House had annual sales of $11 million. As the decade rolled on, consumers continued to flock to office supply stores to buy Day Runners. Over the years, the Day Runner System was offered in a growing array of styles. Users could choose between loose-leaf and spiral formats; vinyl and leather; and snap, Velcro, and zipper closures. The systems could also be personalized by choosing from a variety of refills, calendar formats, and accessories. All versions of the system shared Day Runner's trademark burgundy and gray page design, and featured the company's characteristic colored tabs.

As the name Day Runner began to achieve a high degree of recognition in the growing personal organizer market, Harper

Company Perspectives:

The Company's near and long-term operating strategies are focused on stabilizing profitable sales volume in its retail markets, exploiting product innovation and promotions where appropriate profitability is achieved, and aggressively reducing costs to better position the Company to compete under current market conditions. The Company remains highly focused on providing products to the consumer of recognizable value, while removing any product and service costs not recognized or valued by the ultimate consumer.

House made the decision to adopt it as its corporate name in 1988. Company revenues continued to soar over the next few years. By 1989 Day Runner's sales had grown to $26 million, with net income reaching $2.3 million. The impressive increase in the company's sales during this period was fueled in part by its appearance in low-cost office product superstores, such as Office Depot and Staples. Around this time, competition began to emerge from electronic organizers, like Sharp Co.'s Wizard. Although electronic gizmos like the Wizard and similar products made by Casio and other companies sold reasonably well, they did not make much of a dent in the market for paper-based planning systems at the time.

1990–92: Company Develops New Products and Goes Public

Day Runner entered the 1990s on a strong note. By early in the decade, the personal organizer market had blossomed into a $500 million business, with Day Runner in the lead among companies doing primarily retail business. Since the other leading planner companies sold their wares through different channels—Franklin Quest Co. at its own time management seminars and Day-Timers by direct mail—competition was relatively scarce. By 1991 Day Runner's sales had grown to $53 million, a 500 percent jump over a period of just four years. That year the company rolled out a new line of products, called the FactCentre. First introduced as one model, the FactCentre was essentially a more economical version of the original Day Runner System, with sections for calendars, addresses, and notes. The line was eventually expanded to include specialized models for business people (Personal Organizer), purse carriers (Compact Organizer & Memo Planner), home planning (Home Manager), and school (Student Organizer & Planner). Suggested prices for the various FactCentres ranged from $10 to $65.

The year 1992 was particularly eventful at Day Runner. In March the company went public, with an initial offering of 1.4 million shares. By this time, there were about 80 different Day Runner organizers for customers to choose from, and about 6,000 stores from which those organizers could be bought. At the root of the company's ongoing growth was the idea that each individual had different planning needs, and these differences could be translated into subtly different organizer products. In order to assess exactly what these differing needs were, the company sought out feedback from customers. As its base of potential customers broadened, Day Runner began selling its goods in large discount chains, such as Fred Meyer, Inc., and Wal-Mart. The target market throughout these mass marketing efforts was usually the 25 to 49 age group with better-than-average incomes and busy lifestyles.

Day Runner also introduced its first organizer computer software, Time Plus, in 1992. Designed to be used in conjunction with a paper-based personal organizer, Time Plus duplicated the most worthwhile features of existing planner software in a more user-friendly format. Day Runner's system, for DOS-based IBM-compatible computers, offered automatically updated to-do lists, special abbreviations to ease database manipulation, and the ability to print out updated address book entries, project notes, and other features on sheets that could then be popped into a conventional Day Runner organizer.

In spite of a fourth-quarter slump that saw Day Runner's newly offered stock sink to around $8 a share (from a high of $21.75 shortly after it began trading), company sales soared again in 1992, reaching $71 million for the year. Day Runner Chairman Mark Vidovich attributed the slump to poor sales at smaller independent dealers. Large wholesalers, the company's bread and butter, continued to sell Day Runner products at a brisk pace. By this time Day Runner controlled at least half of the retail market for personal organizers.

1993–95: New Product Development Continues

Day Runner emphasized mass market channels even more as the 1990s continued. New outlets for Day Runner products in 1993 included Payless Drug Stores, Revco, and Kmart. During 1993 the company sold over three million organizers and planners and about 12.5 million refills. Two new products were introduced during the year. The PRO Business System, designed for business managers, took the standard Day Runner concept to new levels of sophistication. New wrinkles offered by the PRO Business System included a seven-ring format, graphics for locating specific sections more easily, a built-in solar-powered calculator, and, in some models, a slide-out panel that turned the organizer into a miniature desk top.

The other new Day Runner product launched in 1993 was the d'Affaires, a line of organizers with an elegant look. The d'Affaires was designed to be sold in departments stores, luggage shops, leather goods stores, and other specialty retailers. This new look featured beige pages and brown ink in a soft leather binder. Like the classic Day Runner organizer, the d'Affaires was offered in a variety of page sizes and book thicknesses. Along with the addition of the PRO Business System and d'Affaires lines, the company also expanded the FactCentre line.

For 1993 Day Runner reported sales of nearly $82 million, about one-fourth of which came from mass market sources. That figure was held down somewhat by a wave of closings and consolidations among independent office supply dealers. Nevertheless, net income took a healthy jump to $5.6 million, a company record. A number of other developments took place during 1993. James E. Freeman, formerly president and chief operating officer of Stuart Hall Co., was named to the newly created position of chief operating officer at Day Runner. An

Key Dates:

1980: Company is founded as Harper House.
1982: Harper House puts Day Runner System on market.
1987: Company's sales reach $11 million.
1988: Harper House changes name to Day Runner.
1989: Day Runner's sales climb to $26 million.
1991: Company introduces new product line called Fact-Centre.
1992: Day Runner goes public.
1995: Company markets a Day Runner Planner for Windows.
1998: Company acquires Filofax.
1999: Day Runner begins selling product line on the Internet; losses lead to 20 percent cut in workforce.
2000: A consortium of banks attempt to bail out the struggling company; NASDAQ delists Day Runner when stock remained under $5 per share.
2001: Unable to meet its debt obligations, Day Runner sells Filofax operation for $30 million debt reduction.

East Coast distribution facility was opened as well. Perhaps more importantly, the company increased its focus on operations outside North America by creating Day Runner International Ltd., a wholly owned subsidiary based in the United Kingdom. Sales to foreign customers during the year amounted to $3.5 million.

As the 1990s progressed, more new products were unveiled. The 4-1-1 line of student planners, first introduced for the 1994 back-to-school season, was aimed at the student market from junior high through college. Available in both loose-leaf and wire-bound formats with youthful styling, the 4-1-1 line included places for phone numbers, class notes, class schedules, and personal information. Day Runner was recognized by the Calendar Marketing Association for its innovative design work on the 4-1-1 system. Fueled by the company's success at seeking out new market segments and targeting new products accordingly, Day Runner's sales reached $97 million in 1994. As Day Runner continued to parlay its dominance in the personal organizer market—which it had largely created—into profits, the business media began to take notice. Both *Forbes* and *Business Week* included Day Runner on their lists of the United States' best small companies in 1994.

In 1995 Day Runner introduced a Day Runner Planner for Windows. The new Planner software combined all of the most popular Day Runner functions, including calendars, phone books, to-do lists, project planners, and expense reports into an easy-to-use system whose graphics resembled the classic look of the paper-based Day Runner organizer. Other features made possible by the software included auto-dialing and audible alarms. Pre-formatted, hole-punched paper for printing out sheets generated by the software were also made available. For those customers who did not already use Day Runner organizers, a special package that included both the Planner software and a paper-based organizer was offered at a bargain price.

For the fiscal year ending in June 1995, Day Runner's sales increased by 26 percent to $121.8 million. During 1995 Freeman was given the additional title of president in addition to his role as chief operating officer. Day Runner was also cited again by the Calendar Marketing Association, this time receiving that organization's Gold Award for the page design of its PRO Business System.

1996–98: Sales Stagnate in Light of Electronic Organizers

In 1996, Day Runner began construction of a new warehouse in La Vergne, Tennessee. Located across the street from its existing eastern operations facility, the new building was slated to increase its area distribution capacity by nearly 300 percent. Also that year, continuing its commitment to introducing of new products, Day Runner began marketing a new line of diaries and planners decorated with licensed cartoon characters, and in 1997 came out with a line of organizers featuring *Dilbert* and *The Far Side* illustrations. In the same year, the company purchased Ram Manufacturing, a privately-owned, Arkansas-based producer of erasable wallboards and other bulletin and activity boards.

Despite its aggressive growth and product development, Day Runner experienced stagnating sales between 1995 and 1997. Although still maintaining a healthy profit margin, the company's revenues, which in 1995 had reached $121.8 million, grew to only $127.4 million in 1997. Several factors contributed to the stagnating sales, including the growing competition from producers of electronic (as opposed to paper) organizers and, specifically, Wal-Mart's decision, later revoked, to replace Day Runner's product line with cheaper imitations.

In 1998, Day Runner paid $85.8 to acquire Filofax Group PLC, a British competitor. This turned out to be costly move. For one thing, as many analysts believed, the company probably paid too much. Also, the timing was bad; the popularity of Filofax's product line was in decline. Moreover, the domestic market for Day Runner's paper-based organizer systems suffered because of increasing popularity of the electronic versions of such accessories. As a result, the company's biggest customers, including Wal-Mart, Office Depot, and Staples, began reducing their Day Runner paper product inventories. Nevertheless, the Filofax acquisition sent Day Runner's sales up to $167.8 million in 1998, producing a net income of $15.9 million. It turned out to be Day Runner's last profitable year.

1999–2001: Challenges and an Uncertain Future

By 1999, Day Runner went in the red to the tune of $4 million, despite the fact that its Filofax acquisition helped drive the company's sales up to $196.2 million, an increase of about 17 percent over the previous year and its all-time high. Very early in the year, Day Runner had laid off 20 percent of its workforce, a belt-tightening move designed to offset its increased operating costs. To enhance its sales, the company also began e-commerce marketing, selling its products online at its dayrunner.com web site. These measures were not enough to keep the company profitable, however.

Day Runner also faced other difficulties, including a class action suit filed on behalf of the company's common stock holders who purchased shares from October 20, 1998 through August 31, 1999. The suit charged that the company violated federal security laws by misrepresenting or omitting information about Day Runner's revenue, thereby artificially inflating the value of the company's stock. The suit named both the company and certain of its officers and directors. Defections, firings, and resignations ensued, starting in December with Dennis K. Marquardt, who resigned as CFO and executive vice-president and was replaced by David A. Werner.

By the end of 1999, the company was openly seeking a buyer as a way of extricating itself from its difficulties. None was forthcoming, and in 2000 the company's problems worsened. In an attempt to stem further losses, early in the year Day Runner closed its European plants as well as its Irvine, California, administrative offices. It also reduced its workforce, trimming it from 1,620 in 1999 to 841 in 2000.

Still, troubles continued to mount. A major problem was that the value of the company's stock had dropped by over 98 percent in one year. The decline of its stock value forced Day Runner into an agreement with NASDAQ that required Day Runner to achieve and maintain a stock value of at least $5 per share. In April 2000, the company attempted to boost its stock value through a five-for-one reverse stock split, but the move failed, and in May the exchange delisted Day Runner's stock and forced the company into over-the-counter trading. The upshot was that James Freeman, Day Runner's CEO, resigned and was replaced by an interim CEO provided by a crisis-management firm.

The move did little to help. Sales were dropping alarmingly as the company's principal customers continued to tighten their inventories. Badly reeling, in July the company began reorganizing, replacing key officers, including the company's chairman, Mark A. Vidovich, as well as other members of the company's board of directors: Jill T. Higgins, James P. Higgins, and Boyd I. Willat.

All of its strategies failed to keep Day Runner from financial disaster in 2000. Its total revenues dropped off to a $171.5 million from its 1999 historic peak of $196.2 million with the devastating result that it recorded a net loss of $106.6 million. The picture improved slightly in 2001, although Day Runner was still struggling just to stay afloat. On March 31, at the end of the third quarter of its fiscal year, its net loss on revenues of $110.7 million had reached almost $22.9 million. Failing to fulfill the obligations of its debt service, in April it sold off Filofax, its London-based wholly-owned subsidiary. Under the sale agreement, Day Runner offset its $30 million debt. It remained to be seen whether the strategy would be adequate to restore the company to financial stability.

Principal Subsidiaries

Day Runner Direct Inc.

Principal Competitors

Franklin Covey Co.; The Mead Corporation; Palm, Inc.

Further Reading

Battle, Bob, ''Day Runner, Ingram Periodicals Build New Warehouses in La Vergne, Tenn.,'' *Knight Ridder/Tribune Business News*, September 10, 1996.

Bluth, Andrew, ''CEO Out at California-Based Day Runner Inc.,'' *Knight Ridder/Tribune Business News*, May 16, 2000.

''Chairman Resigns from Fullerton, Calif.-Based Maker of Paper Organizers,'' *Knight Ridder/Tribune Business News*, July 14, 2000.

O'Brien, Timothy L., ''Day Runner Stock Falls 28% as Sales Slip Below Forecast,'' *Wall Street Journal,* December 23, 1992, p. C11.

——, ''Fast Track: Personal Organizer Firm's Days Are Full—Of Cash,'' *Wall Street Journal,* October 14, 1992, p. B2.

Petruno, Tom, ''A Stock Offering That Should Fit in Your Schedule,'' *Los Angeles Times,* February 28, 1992, p. D3.

Rapoza, Jim, ''Day Runner Looks Good on Paper, But . . . ,'' *PC Week*, November 27, 1995, p. 91.

Teitelbaum, Richard S., ''Companies to Watch: Day Runner,'' *Fortune,* June 15, 1992, p. 123.

Whitmyer, Claude F., ''Discovered: A Time Manager That Works,'' *Office,* October 1992, p. 26.

—Robert R. Jacobson
—update: Jane W. Fiero

The Detroit Pistons Basketball Company

2 Championship Drive
The Palace of Auburn Hills
Auburn Hills, Michigan 48326
U.S.A.
Telephone (248) 377-0100
Fax: (248) 377-4262
Web site: http://www.pistons.com

Private Company
Founded: 1941
Employees: 300
Sales: $90.6 million (2000)
NAIC: 711211 sports Teams and Clubs

The Detroit Pistons Basketball Company is a member of the National Basketball Association (NBA), operating under an umbrella corporation, Palace Sports & Entertainment, Inc., which was created to build the team's arena, The Palace of Auburn Hills.

Founded in 1941 as the Fort Wayne Zollner Pistons, the team has had only two owners: the millionaire Fred Zollner and the billionaire William Davidson. During those same years of stable ownership, however, the team had a succession of coaches. It was during the Pistons' one period of coaching stability, when Chuck Daly led the team for nine straight seasons, that the franchise enjoyed it greatest success in Detroit, winning back-to-back NBA championships in the 1980s. Since then, due in large part to shrewd management of its arena, the Pistons have become one of the most profitable franchises in all of professional sports.

Zollner Sponsored both Softball and Basketball in the 1930s

Fred Zollner inherited his father's business, Zollner Machine Works, which was founded in 1912. He moved the company to Fort Wayne, Indiana, in 1931 and changed the name to Zollner Pistons. Initially, he had little luck in attracting business from the major Detroit automakers. His big break came when he landed an exclusive contract to supply engine parts for a company that wanted to cut up old Packards, then fit them together like contemporary stretch limousines to haul interstate passengers. Several years later that fledgling bus company became known as the Greyhound Corporation. With his piston business established, Zollner sponsored a company fast-pitch softball team. He recruited top players to work at his factory and play on the team, eventually assembling a powerhouse club that would win three consecutive world championships in 1945, 1946, and 1947.

In 1939 Zollner began to sponsor a company basketball team, which played in the Fort Wayne YMCA Industrial League. After the Zollner Pistons won the league title in 1941, Zollner was eager for stiffer competition. He sent one of his star players, Carl Bennett, to Chicago, the home of the fledgling National Basketball League, to line up exhibition matches with some of the professional clubs. Soon, however, Zollner decided to turn his team professional and simply join the NBL, entering play for the 1941–42 season. His players continued to work in Zollner's factory for a weekly wage. It was only at the end of the season that they would be paid for playing in the NBL, splitting among them whatever profits were generated, which in the first year came to some $2,500.

The National Basketball League was not the first professional basketball league in America. As far back as 1898, a mere seven years after James A. Naismith invented the game in Springfield, Massachusetts, an organization called the National League played for pay, but lasted only five seasons. Other short-lived leagues that hired players on a per-game basis followed. Touring professional clubs also barnstormed the country, one of which called itself the Harlem Globetrotters, even though the club originated in Chicago. In 1925 the owners of the Chicago Bears and Washington Redskins of the National Football League established the first true national league for professional basketball teams. The American Basketball League standardized the rules of the game and also signed players to exclusive contracts. Crippled by the Depression, the league essentially folded in 1933, although regional versions of it occasionally arose and played into the 1940s. The NBL, originally called the Midwest Basketball Conference, started in 1937 with 10 owner-operated teams, plus 3 company teams of the Midwest Industrial League: Goodyear, Firestone, and General Electric. By

Key Dates:

1941: The Fort Wayne Zollner Pistons begin play in the National Basketball League.
1948: Fort Wayne joins the National Basketball Association.
1957: The franchise relocates to Detroit.
1961: The team moves into Cobo Arena.
1974: The William Davidson-led investor group purchases the team from Fred Zollner.
1978: The team leaves Cobo Arena for Pontiac Silverdome.
1988: The Palace of Auburn Hills opens.
1989: The Pistons win first NBA championship.
1990: The Pistons win second NBA championship.

1940 the league was reduced to 8 teams, and World War II further affected the organization.

The Fort Wayne Zollner Pistons finished second in its first NBL season, prompting Zollner to recruit more top-notch players for his club. Not only did the Pistons win league championships in 1944 and 1945, they won three consecutive titles at the annual Chicago World Tournament, between 1944 and 1946. After the war ended, and more players became available, the NBL added new teams. It also faced new competition in 1946 in the form of a rival professional league, the Basketball Association of America. The BAA was organized by the Arena Managers Association of America, all of whose members owned hockey teams and were looking for new ways to utilize their buildings. The hockey connection influenced the new basketball league to adopt the playoff system of series, as opposed to elimination tournaments. The league also hired the commissioner of the American Hockey League, Maurice Podoloff, to serve as the commissioner of the BAA.

The Fort Wayne Pistons Switch Leagues in 1949

The NBL and BAA co-existed at first, with neither raiding the other for players. In fact, they relied on a uniform contract and traded players between the two leagues. After two dismal seasons at the gate, however, Podoloff decided to take drastic measures. He telephoned Bennett, Zollner's former plant employee and company team player and now the NBL commissioner, about a possible merger. Zollner, as well as the Indianapolis and Rochester owners, agreed to switch leagues. Minneapolis and star player George Mikan, the biggest draw in basketball, soon followed. After the Toledo and Flint franchises folded, the days were numbered for the NBL. The league played one more season, after which its remaining six teams joined the BAA. On August 3, 1949, the BAA also merged its name with the NBL, becoming officially known as the National Basketball Association. The NBA, with its 17 teams, was far too large for the time, and following the 1949–50 season most of the smaller cities dropped out: Anderson, Indiana; Sheboygan, Wisconsin; and Waterloo, Iowa.

Because Fort Wayne, the smallest remaining city in the league, boasted one of the richest owners in the league, the Pistons were able to maintain a place in the NBA, although their first playing venue was a high school gym that seated only 3,800. Eventually the team moved into the Allen County War Memorial Coliseum that seated 10,000 and hosted the 1953 NBA All-Star Game. The Fort Wayne Pistons enjoyed limited success in the NBA. The team received a great deal of notoriety in 1950 when it won a 19–18 game against the Minneapolis Lakers, employing a stalling tactic to negate the Lakers' decided advantage in talent, in particular Mikan. In the fourth quarter of the game, in fact, the score was just Fort Wayne 3, Minneapolis 1. Although the 24-second shot clock was not instituted for another four seasons, the 1950 game was generally considered to be a major reason that the NBA began to look for a way to eliminate delaying tactics.

The Fort Wayne Pistons also raised some eyebrows following the 1953–54 season when Zollner hired a league referee, Charley Eckman, to coach his team. Jovial, colorful, and not one to mince words, Eckman was a shocking choice, especially to anyone who knew him well. He expressed obvious contempt for even the rudiments of coaching. Asked by a reporter what was his favorite play, he replied, "*South Pacific.*"

Nevertheless, with Eckman cheering on the players from the bench, the Pistons reached the NBA finals in 1955. Perhaps more surprised than anyone with the team's success was the management of the Allen County War Memorial Coliseum, which had scheduled a bowling tournament for the week of the NBA finals. The Pistons were forced to play their home games in Indianapolis and lost the championship to Syracuse in seven games. The team again made the finals the following season, losing out in five to the Philadelphia Warriors.

For several years rumors circulated that the Pistons were about to leave Fort Wayne. As the NBA began to expand the number of games that its teams played, from 60 in its first season to 72 in 1953–54, it was becoming clear that Fort Wayne was simply too small a market to support that many dates. Because the major customers for Zollner Pistons were the big automakers, it made sense for Zollner to move both himself and his basketball team to Detroit. On April 17, 1957 the NBA's Board of Governors approved the request to relocate the Pistons from Fort Wayne to Detroit, which was hardly clamoring for an NBA team. The city had been represented by teams in both the NBL and BAA, neither of which enjoyed a long tenure. Many years later, Eckman told a reporter, "We had no place to practice. We were the last kid on the block. They had the Tigers, Lions, and Red Wings. The first time I saw our home floor was the night we played our opening game on it." After 25 games as the Detroit Pistons, the team had won just nine games, and attendance was lower than it had been in Fort Wayne. Depending upon which version of the story is told, Zollner either telephoned Eckman or summoned him to his office to announce, "We're going to be making a change in your department." Because he was the only one in his department, Eckman surmised that he had been fired.

Over the next dozen years the Detroit Pistons employed seven different coaches and fail to post a winning record. At first they played their home games at both Olympia Stadium, home of the Red Wings of the National Hockey League, and at the University of Detroit, but when neither facility was available during the 1960 playoffs, they were forced to play one game at the Grosse Pointe High School gym. In 1961 the Pistons moved into 9,500-seat Cobo Arena in downtown Detroit, which during the 1960s experienced race riots and a mass flight to the suburbs of middle-class people that should have formed the team's fan base. Attendance was dismal, yet the team hung on. The Detroit Pistons finally posted their first winning record in 1970–71, yet failed to make the playoffs. After the team won 52 games in 1973–74, Zollner decided to sell the franchise to one of his rich neighbors, William Davidson.

Pistons Start Over With New Ownership in the 1970s

Davidson was born in Detroit and indulged his interest in sports by running track and cross country in high school and playing freshman football at the University of Michigan. He earned a law degree at Wayne State University and practiced law for a short time before going to work for himself in the early 1950s. After saving two troubled businesses, he turned his attention in 1957 to a bankrupt maker of car windshields called Guardian Glass that an uncle of his had founded in 1932. By 1968 he took the company public and changed its name to Guardian Industries. He then decided to indulge his passion in sports by becoming a team owner. "I was looking at both football and basketball at first," he told a reporter in 1988. "At the time, they were bringing out the Tampa franchise for pro football, and I was friendly with Joe Schmidt, who played for the Lions. We talked about buying in. Then, the prices escalated, and that took care of that. But, I also had gotten to know Fred Zollner, because he lived three doors down from me. We started talking. Next thing I knew, I'd bought the team."

Davidson was technically the managing partner of an ownership group that included 11 others, who in July 1975 paid Zollner $8.1 million for the Detroit Pistons. At first, under Davidson, the Pistons reverted to their losing ways and changed coaches on a consistent basis. One notable hire was Dick Vitale, who after leaving the Pistons gained popularity as a color analyst for college basketball telecasts and become a major personality. As a coach of the Pistons, however, he lasted little more than a season. It was also during Vitale's brief tenure that the team left Cobo Arena for the suburbs, opting to play games in the indoor home of the Detroit Lions football team, the Pontiac Silverdome. The team was simply following its fans, and although the Pistons would on occasion record incredible attendance figures for a basketball game, including an NBA record crowd of 61,983 for a game against Boston, playing in the Silverdome was far from ideal. The lights were not conducive to basketball, and in the winter it was still cold enough inside the dome to require fans to keep their coats on.

Davidson finally began to turn around the fortunes of the Pistons in 1979 when he hired Jack McCloskey as the team's general manager. Through wise drafting of college players and other transactions that earned him the moniker of "Trader Jack," McCloskey slowly began to assemble the pieces of a championship club. In 1983 he hired Chuck Daly to coach the Pistons. By 1986–87 the team was strong enough to take the Boston Celtics to seven games before losing in the Eastern Conference finals. The Pistons became known as "The Bad Boys" for their hard-nosed style of play that troubled many in the league but was embraced by the Detroit fans. The 1987–88 team was on the verge of an NBA championship in its last season playing in the Silverdome, but lost to the Los Angeles Lakers in seven games after leading the series three games to two.

After the 1986 seasons the Pistons announced that they would leave the Silverdome when their contract ran out after the 1987–88 season. Davidson and a group of investors formed Palace Sports and Entertainment, Inc. to build the $70 million Palace of Auburn Hills (costing $30 million more than budgeted), which would establish a trend for every arena that followed it. Instead of simply adding in luxury boxes, a major source of team revenue, the Palace was designed around its three tiers of 180 suites. During their first year at the 21,454-seat Palace, the Pistons won the NBA championship, defeating the Lakers. The following season the team again won the championship, beating Michael Jordan and the Chicago Bulls along the way.

With success came the spoils. For five straight seasons the Pistons sold out every home game, a consecutive sell-out streak that reached 245 games. The Pistons also ranked high in merchandise sales in the NBA, which reached $1.1 billion in 1990–91. Four years later that league-wide figure grew to $2.65 million. Not only did the team make money selling the broadcast rights of some of their games to PASS, Detroit's regional cable sports network, it was able to use its own production facilities at the Palace to produce telecasts of the remaining games, a practice the team started in 1979. By buying air time from WKBD-TV, the Pistons were able to sell advertising themselves. Davidson even talked about the possibility of the Pistons launching a sports network to challenge PASS, but lack of channel capacity on local cable systems scotched the idea.

The glory days of the Bad Boys were brief, however. Two years after winning back-to-back NBA championships, the Pistons lost more games than they won. Daly left the team, as did McKloskey. In the 1993–94 season the Pistons won only 20 games, and their consecutive sell-out streak came to an end. Excitement over well-publicized rookie Grant Hill boosted ticket sales the following season, and once again it appeared that the Pistons were building a championship-caliber club. Within two seasons the team posted a 54-win season, only to again drop off. Grant Hill left the club for free agency, and once again the Pistons began changing coaches each year. Former Pistons player Joe Dumars was hired in June 2000 to head the front office, but during his first year, the team missed the playoffs and once again fired its coach.

Despite poor results in the ten years since its NBA championships, the Detroit Pistons remained one of the most valuable franchises in the league and one of the most profitable in all of sports. According to *Financial World,* the team was the second most profitable sports franchise for a three-year period ending in 1997, besting such large market clubs as the Chicago Bulls and New York Yankees. According to *Forbes* in December 2000, the Pistons were the sixth most valuable franchise in the NBA. Purchased for $8.1 million 25 years earlier, the Pistons were now estimated to be worth $236 million. Although average game attendance for the club dipped to 14,000 per game in 2000, all of the corporate suites remained booked. The team's greatest asset was the Palace of Auburn Hills and its marketing operation. From another perspective, however, the Pistons had simply become a valuable asset of the Palace, which posted the fourth highest amount of revenue among all indoor arenas in 2000. It ranked only second to New York City's Madison Square Garden in the number of concert tickets sold. The Pistons continued to try to win basketball games and NBA championships, but, as was the case with most basketball and hockey franchises, it was the arena business that increasingly mattered more and more.

Principal Competitors

Chicago Bulls; Cleveland Cavaliers; Milwaukee Bucks; Toronto Raptors.

Further Reading

Addy, Steve, *The Detroit Pistons: Four Decades of Motor City Memories,* Champaign, Ill.: Sports Publishing, 1997.

Asp, Karen, ''Zollner Pistons,'' *Indiana Business Magazine,* December 1995, p. 54.

Barkholz, David, ''Palace Ushered in the Reign of Modern Arenas,'' *Crain's Detroit Business,* February 26, 1996.

——, ''Pistons Revived in Grant's Boom: Season Ticket Sales Revived by Hope Aroused by Rookie,'' *Crain's Detroit Business,* October 24, 1994.

Downey, Mike, ''Party Time for Bill Davidson, Pistons,'' *Los Angeles Times,* June 5, 1988, p. 3.

——, ''With Detroit Pistons, It's Often Hard to Tell Fact From Fiction,'' *Los Angeles Times,* June 6, 1988, p. 3.

Falls, Joe, ''Perennial Losers Have Turned the Tide,'' *USA Today,* June 14, 1989, p. 3C.

Ham, Eldon, *The Playmasters,* Lincolnwood, Ill.: Contemporary Books, 2000.

''Pistons Shakeup Isn't Slowing Suite, Ad Sales,'' *Crain's Detroit Business,* August 29, 2000.

Pluto, Terry, *Tall Tales,* New York: Simon & Schuster, 1994.

Sharp, Drew, ''Dumars Must Clean Up Mess Left by Pistons Management,'' *Detroit Free Press,* June 6, 2000.

Stauth, Cameron, *The Franchise,* New York: William Morrow, 1990.

Vincent, Charlie, ''Davidson's Pistons: Up From Scrap Pile,'' *Detroit Free Press,* March 25, 1984, p. 8D.

Wyman, Thomas P., ''Pistons Got Their Start in Indiana,'' *Los Angeles Times,* June 19, 1988, p. 10.

—Ed Dinger

Deveaux S.A.

Le Pont de la Cote
F-69240 Saint-Vincent-de-Reins
France
Telephone: +33 4 7489 6969
Fax: +33 4 7489 6970

Public Company
Incorporated: 1922 as Gouttenoire et Deveaux
Employees: 700
Sales: EUR 199 million ($169 million) (2000)
Stock Exchanges: Euronext Paris
Ticker Symbol: DEV
NAIC: 313111 Yarn Spinning Mills; 31321 Broadwoven Fabric Mills; 422310 Piece Goods, Notions, and Other Dry Goods Wholesalers

Deveaux S.A. is Europe's number three leading manufacturer of textiles. The company manufactures nearly all of the major categories of textiles, from its core dyed-weaving fabrics to printed and plain fabrics, knitwear, toweling fabrics, and woven fabrics. The company also has access to the silk fabrics produced by Ercea, a separate company held personally by CEO Lucien Deveaux and expected to be merged into Deveaux early in the new century. Deveaux has pursued a strong diversification and internationalization through the 1990s that has made it one of the healthiest of an otherwise troubled French textile industry. One of the few remaining companies manufacturing all of its textiles in France, Deveaux has, nevertheless, built its international sales to account for more than 70 percent of its annual sales of nearly EUR 200 million. The company produces textiles for such major brand names as Naf Naf, Gap, Camaieu, Zannier, Zaro, Marks & Spencer, Pimkie, and others.

Transforming a Family Business in the 1960s

When Lucien Deveaux, age 27, took over his family's textile company in 1967, the operation remained a small, Rhône Valley-based concern with just FFr 3 million in sales per year and 90 employees. In just 30 years, Lucien Deveaux was able to boost the company to the ranks of the top three textile manufacturer in Europe, while at the same time controlling a ''side'' business in clothing manufacture and retail stores to place him at the head of an empire worth some EUR 400 million per year.

Deveaux's origins trace back to the early 19th century, when the Deveaux family purchased its first weaving looms and set up a weaving mill in the village of Montagny, near the town of Roanne, one of the centers of France's textile industry. Early on the family specialized in producing dyed-weaving fabrics, a specialty Deveaux was to maintain into the 1970s. Within its specialty, however, Deveaux quickly covered a wide range of fabric types, from gingham checks to tartans and plaids.

Led by Ernest Deveaux, the company began to expand its operations in the 1870s. One of Deveaux's earliest acquisitions, made in 1874, was that of a weaving mill situated in the nearby village of Saint-Vincent-de-Reins. The company continued to expand through the 20th century, all the while maintaining the Roanne area as its center of operations. The growing use of industrial production techniques and a concurrent rise of new retail formats not only helped step up the demand for textiles and clothing, but also helped the company achieve higher production levels. Reflecting its growth, the company formally incorporated in 1922 as Gouttenoire et Deveaux.

A recession in the 1950s cut Deveaux's growth short when demand for its textile products dropped sharply. The company languished into the 1960s, until a new generation of the family stepped up to the company's helm. In 1962, Lucien Deveaux joined the family company and began acquiring control of the company, which had had its shares diluted among the various Deveaux family members. By 1967, Lucien Deveaux had been placed in charge of Deveaux.

Deveaux's first move to restore the company's growth track was to embark on an ambitious expansion program to increase the company's production capacity. Deveaux began buying up a number of nearby—and struggling—rivals, such as the 1972 acquisition of Cergne-based Bertaud. Deveaux continued to make a number of key acquisitions during the 1970s, boosting its park of manufacturing facilities, while remaining true to its core dyed-weaving fabrics market. In 1975, Deveaux acquired

Company Perspectives:

In order to meet its own challenges, over the years the Deveaux group has embarked on a rigorous selection of its partners. Whether they are forwarders, weavers, spinners, manufacturers of part for weaving looms, professionals in sizing or suppliers of IT solutions, they are honored for their dynamic collaboration and team spirit.

Tissages Dechelette Frères, located at Montagny. Then in 1979, the company bought up Tissage du Ronzy. This acquisition marked one of the company's earliest moves to diversify its product range, as it brought the company manufacturing facilities for the production of toweling fabrics.

By the beginning of the 1980s, Deveaux's annual sales had topped FFr 150 million. Nearly 80 percent of the company's sales remained in France; however, that situation saw some dramatic changes during the 1980s. By the end of that decade, the company's revenues had swelled to nearly FFr 500. Nearly half of its sales now came from beyond France, with western Europe representing the overwhelming majority of Deveaux's international activity.

Expansion for the 21st Century

Diversification became a central part of Deveaux's growth during the 1980s. The company sought to transform itself from a single-product enterprise into a major textile producer operating in nearly all of the various textile categories—and in this way become one of the rare textile companies capable of supplying the wide range of its customer's needs. Helping to fuel Deveaux's expansion was a two-prong opening of its capital: the first came with the purchase of Deveaux shares by French banks BNP and Credit Lyonnais in 1986. The second came that same year when Deveaux took a listing on the Bourse de Lyon's secondary market. In order to achieve this step, Deveaux reorganized its operations, formally merging its various acquisitions—including Bertaud, Tissages Dechelette Frères and Tissage du Ronzy—under the single Deveaux S.A. name. Despite the opening of its shareholding, Lucien Deveaux remained in solid control of the company he had built over the past 20 years.

Deveaux continued to build up its newly acquired towel fabrics operations during the 1980s, establishing that market as one of its core specialty areas. In 1987, Deveaux's toweling activities were boosted by the acquisition of the license to produce Cacherel branded towel products. This division also later added another important label when it began producing towel products for the Pierre Cardin label. By the 1990s, Deveaux had boosted itself to the ranks of the third largest European producer of towel fabrics. In 1988, the company added another subsidiary, under its Société Tissage du Ronzy subsidiary, when it acquired 100 percent of Ateliers Deveaux et Groebli.

Deveaux also stepped up its expansion by investing in enhancing its park of production facilities and then expanding its competence to include other areas of textile manufacture. The company capped its strong expansion during the 1980s with a series of strategic acquisitions, starting in 1988 and extending into the mid-1990s. After the acquisition of Ateliers Deveaux and Groebli in 1988, the company continued its expansion drive, forming a partnership to establish Sprintex in nearby Villefranche sur Saône in 1990. The Sprintex subsidiary, held at 70 percent by Deveaux (boosted to 100 percent in 1997) confirmed Deveaux's diversification strategy with the addition of new production facilities operating into the plain and printed fabrics textiles categories. Moving into the 1990s, the company's acquisition program included the purchases of Teinture et Apprêts de la Trembouze (TAT) and Teintures de Ronzy, made in 1992; the dyed-woven fabrics division of rival French textiles and accessories group DMC; and, adding another new product group, the company Xémard, a manufacturer of knitted fabrics in 1993. In 1994, the company added another important part of its growing textiles empire when it acquired Teintures et Impressions de Lyon in 1994. This acquisition, together with the earlier acquisitions of TAT and Teintures de Ronzy were part of the company's strategy towards greater vertical integration, giving it significant dyeing facilities.

Rather than place Deveaux itself at risk, Lucien Deveaux engaged in a policy of acquiring new—and especially struggling—companies in his own name. Once he had succeeded in returning the new acquisitions to profitability, at the same time gradually installing his own personnel to lead the acquired operations, the companies were then merged into Deveaux S.A. Deveaux continued to pursue this strategy into the mid-1990s with two new acquisitions in 1995. The first was the relatively modest, yet significant, purchase of Ercea, which gave the company not only a new product category, that of printed silks, but also a position in the famed Parisian garment district, the Sentier. The second acquisition was more substantial and marked a new road for the company.

If the company had successfully diversified to cover nearly all the manufactured textile categories, it remained absent from the clothing manufacture and retail clothing fields. Yet in 1995, Lucien Deveaux joined with a partner—who left after only a few months due to a disagreement over strategy—to acquire the European holdings of the shattered Bidermann International clothing and retail group headed by Maurice Bidermann. Deveaux promptly changed the company's name to Ecce (Entreprise de confection et de commercialization européenne) and concentrated on restoring the new company's diverse operations—which ranged from clothing manufacture for such high-end labels as Givenchy Men and Yves Saint Laurent pour Homme to retail sales through its Armand Thierry and Classe Affairs retail chains and the Arrow clothing label—to profitability. By the late 1990s, Deveaux had successfully turned around both Ercea, which was slated to join the Deveaux S.A. group at the turn of the century, and Ecce. Nevertheless, Deveaux suggested that he would not combine his textile operations with his clothing activities.

After boosting its knitted fabrics production with the acquisition of 48.95 percent of Teintures et Apprêts de Roanne in 1996, Deveaux turned its attention to boosting its international profile. By the mid-1990s, Deveaux had achieved a new transformation, becoming a diversified textile products group with more than FFr 1 billion in sales in 1996. Yet France continued

Key Dates:

1830: The Deveaux family opens a weaving mill.
1874: A weaving mill in Saint-Vincent-de-Reins is added to the business.
1922: Company incorporates as Gouttenoire et Deveaux.
1967: Lucien Deveaux takes company lead.
1986: Company is listed on Bourse du Lyon's secondary market; company reorganizes as Deveaux S.A.
1990: Deveaux forms Sprintex.
1991: Deveaux acquires license for Naf Naf.
1992: Company acquires Teinture et Apprêts de la Trembouze (TAT) and Teinture de Ronzy.
1996: Company acquires 48.95 percent of Teintures et Apprêts de Roanne.
1997: Deveaux takes full control of Sprintex; company joins Paris Bourse main board.
2001: Deveaux begins FFr 15 million expansion of TAT.

to represent a large part of Deveaux's sales—more than 45 percent in 1995. Deveaux began to eye entry into the vast North American market, as well as the developing South American and Asian markets, announcing its intention to build sales to those markets to represent as much as 20 percent of its annual sales, while at the same time boosting its total exports to more than 85 percent of its sales in the early years of the 21st century.

Indeed, by the late 1990s, Deveaux had successfully boosted the part of international sales in its total sales to more than 70 percent. Deveaux also capped its strong growth with a conversion of its stock listing to the Paris Bourse's main board in 1997. Yet the company was soon hit hard by a number of factors at the end of the decade that saw its revenues slip backward for the first time since the mid-1980s. A large part of the company's problems stemmed from the economic crisis that had rocked the Asian economies in the late 1990s, when Asian textile manufacturers, faced with oversupplies, slashed their prices by as much as 50 percent and cut into European textiles makers' sales.

Adding to Deveaux's difficulties was a trend in fashions toward plain fabrics—textiles produced much more cheaply by the company's foreign competitors and which represented lower margins than the higher value-added printed fabrics segment. As such, the company worked on reducing its activities in plain fabrics at the start of the year 2000. At the same time, the company continued to boost its dyeing facilities, supplying not only its own needs, but also dyes and printed fabrics to a wide range of textile and clothing manufacturers. In January 2001, the company announced a FFr 15 million expansion and modernization of its TAT dye production facility. While many of its competitors continued to struggle, Deveaux's diversified operations enabled it once again to renew its revenue growth by the end of 2000, when its annual sales topped EUR 199 million.

Principal Subsidiaries

S.A. Sprintex; SARL Tissage de Montagny; SA Teinture et Apprêts de la Trambouze-TAT; SA Teinture du Ronzy; SA Teintures et Impressions de Lyon; SA Teintures et Apprêts de Roanne (48.95%) .

Principal Competitors

Bassetti S.p.A.; Burlington Industries, Inc.; Coats Viyella Plc; Concord Fabrics Inc.; Cotonificio Olcese Veneziano S.p.A.; Filatura di Pollone S.p.A.; Guilford Mills, Inc.; Manifattura Lane G. Marzotto & Figli S.p.A.; Milliken & Company Inc.; Ratti S.p.A.; Vincenzo Zucchi S.p.A.; WestPoint Stevens Inc.

Further Reading

''Deveaux: l'exercise 2000 a effacé les conséquences de la crise asiatique,'' *Les Echos*, January 17, 2001, p. 14.

''Le groupe Deveaux confirme ses objectifs pour 2000,'' *Les Echos*, June 19, 2000, p. 23.

Marcellin, Valérie, ''Rencontre avec Lucien Deveaux,'' *Usine Nouvelle*, January 7, 1999.

Meunier, Arthur, ''TAT modernise et agrandit son unité de production,'' *La Tribune*, January 11, 2001.

—M. L. Cohen

The Drees Company, Inc.

211 Grandview Drive, Suite 300
Fort Mitchell, Kentucky 41017
U.S.A.
Telephone: (606) 578-4200
Fax: (606) 341-5854
Web site: http://www.dreeshomes.com

Private Company
Incorporated: 1928
Employees: 650
Sales: $515 million (2000)
NAIC: 23321 Single Family Housing Construction; 23322 Multifamily Housing Construction; 23332 Commercial and Institutional Building Construction

The Drees Company, Inc. is one of the largest home builders in the United States. In an industry made up principally of small local companies, Drees is one of several dozen big firms with operations in many markets. The company began as a modest home builder in northern Kentucky, then spread across the Ohio River to the Cincinnati metropolitan area. It became the biggest builder in Cincinnati while moving into other more distant geographical markets. It now builds homes or develops land in Dallas and Austin, Texas; Washington, D.C., Maryland, and Virginia; Raleigh, North Carolina; and in and around the Ohio cities of Cincinnati, Cleveland, and Dayton. Although most of its work is in residential building on land it owns, the company also builds and manages apartments and town homes, builds commercial property, and undertakes commercial renovation. Drees maintains its own architects and runs a computerized design center for its customers. Homes the company builds run the gamut from cheaply priced starter homes to luxurious upscale dwellings. The company is privately owned, with most of the stock in the hands of the Drees family. The CEO of the company is David Drees, grandson of founder Theodore Drees and eldest son of former CEO Ralph Drees.

Modest Beginnings

Theodore Drees emigrated from his native Germany as a young man, leaving in 1925 and settling at first in Brazil. A carpenter by trade, Drees was unmarried, and apparently left his homeland with only vague plans. He went to Brazil because of its lenient immigration laws and worked in the construction business there. But after three years he moved on to the United States. Drees had a friend who had friends in the Cincinnati area, and the two set off together on a six-week sea voyage to reach America. Drees settled in northern Kentucky, across the bordering Ohio River from Cincinnati. In 1928 he founded The Drees Co., a home-building company. The company built five homes its first year, and ten the second. The Drees Co. remained small under Theodore, building only about a dozen houses a year. Drees had married and had children, and the company did enough business to support the family. Drees also built up a reputation for quality work and meticulous craftsmanship.

It was not until the next generation of Dreeses entered the business that the company began to grow substantially. In 1958, The Drees Co. became a partnership between Theodore and his two sons, Richard and Ralph. The name of the company at that time changed to Drees Builders and Developers. Richard eventually left the business, but Ralph showed a great proclivity for building from the first. He joined the company full time in 1959, after he got out of the army. His father gave him a lot of autonomy, starting Ralph off with an 80-acre plot of land to develop on his own. With five employees, Ralph made plans, bought materials, supervised the building, and sold the resulting homes. In his first year, Ralph built and sold five houses, rivaling his father's start. But within only a few years, he had far surpassed his father, building hundreds of units in a new subdivision. They were modest homes, selling for between $16,000 and $25,000. But sales were slower than Ralph would have liked. The reason turned out to be that school buses did not serve the subdivision, making it difficult for families to get their kids to school. Ralph's remedy was to buy a bus and drive it himself. He moonlighted as a bus driver for more than three years, while Drees Builders continued to grow.

Ralph Drees clearly had the drive and ingenuity needed to expand the company. In 1967 his brother Richard left the partnership, and Ralph acquired 100 percent of the company. His father retired in 1968, and the company incorporated as The Drees Builders and Developers Inc. It was a private company, with stock going to Ralph Drees and his family, and to top

Company Perspectives:

Drees Mission Statement: To create superior homes and communities that provide our customers with choice, value and satisfaction. To conduct all activities with honesty, integrity and fairness. To keep a long term perspective, emphasizing business opportunities that provide personal pride and corporate growth. To demand continual improvement of ourselves and our processes.

executives. Under Ralph Drees's management, the company grew at an impressive rate. Its annual sales passed $1 million in 1970, and by 1974 had reached $4.5 million. In 1975 the company changed its name to simply The Drees Company, Inc.

The Drees Co. was willing to diversify its product. After at first focusing on building single-family homes, the firm started an Investment Properties Division in 1972, later renamed the Commercial Division. This division built office buildings, apartment houses, banks, condominiums, strip malls, and restaurants. The company eventually owned and managed more than 1,500 rental apartments. In 1973 the firm began its first geographic expansion, seeking work in Cincinnati. Although only a river separated Drees's northern Kentucky territory from urban Cincinnati, it was not easy to break into that market. Cincinnati builders had different ways of working, and Cincinnati customers wanted a different product. Drees finally split into North (Ohio) and South (Kentucky) divisions, because the two territories demanded different business practices. But the firm was ultimately successful in penetrating Cincinnati. By the end of the 1970s, sales stood at more than $20 million, and Drees was the fourth largest builder in the Cincinnati area.

Geographic Diversity on a Bigger Scale in the 1980s

Breaking into the Cincinnati market had been difficult for Drees. But the first serious obstacle to the company's success came with a dire housing slump in the early 1980s. Housing starts declined dismally in the Cincinnati area, dropping as much as 70 percent for 1982. That year, Drees brought in only $15 million, and ended up in the red for the first time since the company's founding. The next year was better. Drees built 254 houses around Cincinnati and brought in $22.5 million. But the housing market continued depressed through 1984. Drees struggled. Eventually, the company came up with a two-pronged plan. It increased its presence in its home market, continuing to buy, build, and advertise even as its competitors cut back and lay low. Then Drees began to build in a new and distant market: Dallas, Texas.

Ralph Drees prided himself on conservative fiscal management, yet he was not afraid to move boldly in other ways. With conditions so bad in Cincinnati, it looked like the firm would have to lay off valued workers. Rather than curtail the business, Drees decided to look for a more promising market. Drees told *Business First-Louisville* (July 9, 1990) that his thinking at the time was that ''If we're going to fail, let's fail in a good market.'' Ralph Drees and a trusted top executive took several trips to Dallas to make sure it was a good decision. The company began building homes there in 1984. The Dallas market was more upscale than Cincinnati and northern Kentucky. The homes Drees built there were larger and more complex, with many customized features, such as luxurious baths. Drees managed to do well in Dallas from the start, and by the early 1990s, it had become the firm's biggest market.

The company learned a lot from its first geographical move, from northern Kentucky to Ohio, and then prospered in Texas. Further geographical expansion drove the company's growth in the 1980s into the 1990s. After Dallas, Drees decided to move into the Washington, D.C. area. When that proved difficult at first, the company instead chose Atlanta, beginning work there in 1987. Within a year, Drees was building homes at six different developments around Atlanta. The next year, the company proceeded to Washington, D.C. The early 1980s housing slump seemed far behind as Drees built rapidly at the end of the decade. Sales for 1989 were around $135 million, compared with less than $23 million in 1984, the start of the company's geographic expansion. It sold 950 single-family homes in 1989, almost a third of them in the Dallas market. The company also sold more than 450 apartment units and a small number of commercial buildings. Drees was the biggest home-builder in the Cincinnati area, with a market share of around 12 percent. This was twice the market share of its nearest competitor. The company also was becoming one of the bigger builders nationwide. By 1990 there were roughly 100,000 home builders in the United States, most of them small local companies. Drees was in the top 100 builders by sales by 1990, ranking 71st that year. The company retained a tight central management system, even though it moved into other distant markets. The firm's headquarters remained in Fort Mitchell, Kentucky. Drees also kept its finances under control, always maintaining a low debt-to-equity ratio.

A National Presence in the 1990s

By the early 1990s, four of the five Drees children were working for their father's company. The eldest son, David, became president of The Drees Co. in 1993. Ralph Drees retired in 1995. The company continued to expand into new markets when the opportunity arose. It moved into the Dayton, Ohio area in 1995. The company had been investigating the Raleigh-Durham, North Carolina market since the mid-1990s, and in 1997 Drees acquired North Carolina builder Charter Homes. The Dallas market continued to be its most successful, contributing a large percentage of the company's sales. In 1997, which proved a record year for the firm, sales topped $300 million, a 20 percent increase over the previous year.

Not only had the company diversified geographically, but it built a wide variety of products. Especially in Cincinnati, Drees made a broad range of dwellings. At first it had made, principally, so-called starter homes, designed for people buying their first house. Increasingly, Drees built more upscale houses, meant as ''move-up'' homes for people with growing budgets. The company also built town homes designed for empty-nesters—couples who no longer needed a large house once their children were grown. Drees ran a realty company in Cincinnati and managed more than 1,500 apartments. Drees's hallmark in Cincinnati was customization. It offered around 40 different floor plans, which could be customized with thousands of options.

Key Dates:

1928: Theodore Drees founds company.
1959: Ralph Drees joins firm.
1968: Ralph takes over top management spot.
1984: Drees expands into Dallas market.
1993: David Drees becomes president.
1998: The company acquires Palmer Homes in Austin, Texas.
2000: The company acquires Zaring National Corp.

Drees had grown mostly by diversifying its product and moving into new markets. In the late 1990s, it began to make key acquisitions of other builders. In 1998 Drees bought an Austin, Texas building company called Palmer Homes. Drees already had a strong presence in Dallas, where it had been entrenched since the mid-1980s. Buying Palmer gave Drees automatic entry into Austin, saving the many start-up costs associated with moving into a new market. Taking on Palmer caused overall sales to balloon. Drees brought in about $400 million in 1998, again almost a 20 percent increase over the year before. By 1999, Drees ranked as the 40th largest builder in the United States, according to statistics compiled by *Professional Builder,* an industry journal.

Over the next two years, Drees worked to accomplish two things. It focused on its Dayton, Ohio market, and it set up a new division to market specifically to first-time home buyers. The first-time buyers unit was called Marquis Homes. It designed homes that sold for between $120,000 and $160,000. The company had marketed more aggressively to first-time home buyers earlier in its history, but by the late 1990s it had seen some of its market share slip. By 2000, the company was selling more homes than ever. It closed on 2,036 homes that year, up from 1,734 the previous year. Despite the new division's focus on cheaper houses, the average sale price of a Drees home rose from $218,000 in 1999 to $237,000 in 2000. Total sales in 2000 were at $515 million.

In 2000 the firm made another major acquisition. It bought substantial assets of Zaring National Corp., another builder with a national presence. Zaring, based in Cincinnati, ranked 48th on the *Professional Builders* list of top companies. Its sales for 1999 were slightly more than $314 million. It built homes in Cincinnati and Dayton, Ohio, where Drees already operated, as well as in Raleigh and Charlotte, North Carolina, and in Indianapolis, Indiana; Louisville, Kentucky; and Nashville, Tennessee. The deal was a complicated one, since Drees did not want all of Zaring. Drees first acquired Zaring's business in Raleigh, paying around $12 million for the division. The deal was completed some months later, when Drees acquired Zaring's business in Nashville, Indianapolis, and Cincinnati. What was left of Zaring changed its name to First Cincinnati, Inc., while the Zaring units operated as a subsidiary of Drees, under the name Zaring Premier Homes. Drees estimated that its total sales would go up considerably after it swallowed Zaring, hoping to increase from around $515 million in 2000 to about $800 million in coming years.

Principal Subsidiaries

Zaring Premier Homes.

Principal Competitors

Hovnanian Enterprises, Inc.; Crossmann Communities, Inc.; NVR, Inc.

Further Reading

Donahue, Gerry, ''Ralph Drees: CEO, the Drees Company, Fort Mitchell, Ky.,'' *Builder,* January 1994, p. 312.
''Drees Co.,'' *Cincinnati Business Courier,* February 14, 1994, p. 12.
''The Drees Company,'' *Builder,* January 1998, p. 264.
''The Drees Company,'' *Business First-Louisville,* July 9, 1990, p. S13.
''Drees Proves Multiple Profit Centers Can, Do Work,'' *Professional Builder and Remodeler,* October 1, 1990, p. 47.
Fowler, Wayne, ''The Drees Co.,'' *Cincinnati Business Courier,* June 20, 1988, p. 6C.
Hemmer, Andy, ''Drees Buys Palmer; Expands in Lone Star State,'' *Business Courier,* August 6, 1999, p. 19.
''Home Builder Reaches Pact to Be Acquired by Drees,'' *Wall Street Journal,* August 18, 2000, p. A6.
Lawley, Lauren, ''Drees Chief Ready—Almost—for New Generation,'' *Business Courier,* December 4, 1998, p. 17.
Lurz, Bill, ''Is Builder Merger Mania Returning?,'' *Professional Builder,* September 2000, p. 22.
Lurz, William H., ''1991 Builder of the Year: Ralph Drees,'' *Professional Builder and Remodeler,* January 1992, p. 160.
——, ''Smoothing the Transition,'' *Professional Builder,* August 1994, p. 44.
May, Lucy, ''Drees Looking Beyond Zaring Merger,'' *Business Courier,* December 8, 2000, p. 19.

—A. Woodward

Edmark Corporation

6727 185th Avenue Northeast
Redmond, Washington 98052
U.S.A
Telephone: (425) 556-8400
Fax: (425) 861-8998
Web site: http://www.edmark.com

Wholly Owned Subsidiary of Riverdeep Group plc
Incorporated: 1970
Employees: 150
Sales: $32 million (1996)
NAIC: 51121 Software Publishers

Edmark Corporation is a developer and publisher of educational software for the consumer and education markets. Engaged in the development of multimedia educational software since 1992, Edmark has garnered over 340 important industry design awards heralding the company's innovative approach and its software's educational value. Edmark's software products, targeting students in grades K-12, are sold to a customer base largely made up of software distributors and retailers and educational institutions. Along with more than 50 software titles, the firm manufactures hardware and software products for children with special needs, as well as products that restrict access to certain web sites. Edmark's products are found in 46,000 schools throughout the United States.

Origins and Expansion

Edmark was founded in 1970 as a developer and publisher of school print materials and established its headquarters in Redmond, Washington. During its first 15 years, Edmark focused its operations on print materials for the special education market, and became well regarded within its niche despite its slow sales growth, which did not break the $1 million mark until 1985.

During the latter half of the 1980s, Edmark made several moves to diversify its product line and enhance its revenues. In 1985, the company began developing and publishing Apple II software programs for special education students, and soon afterwards the company entered the preschool market. In 1986, with the company expanding its product range, Edmark went public. As part of the company's expansion into computer-based educational materials, Edmark's chief executive, Tom Korten, orchestrated the acquisition of the TouchWindow product line in 1988. Often referred to as the "Touchscreen," the product sat atop a computer monitor and for all practical purposes replaced a computer's keyboard, making it much easier for students who could not use the keyboard to use a computer. Having acquired the TouchWindow from the Personal Touch Corporation for $126,500, Edmark expanded on its new product by developing TouchWindow software for Apple computers.

In 1988, Edmark hired Sally G. Narodick to serve as a consultant and help develop a new strategic plan for the company. Narodick, who had started her own consulting firm a year earlier after relinquishing a senior vice-president's post at Seattle's largest bank, Seafirst, held advanced degrees in both business and education. She suggested that Edmark become an educational technology business that made learning fun and embark on a gradual entrance into the consumer software market. She based her recommendation on three trends: a rising birth rate (due to baby boomers having babies), increasing numbers of home computers, and a slow-growing special education market in which sales to schools would not support substantial company growth.

With multimedia software as its targeted product of the future, between 1989 and 1991, Edmark made several moves to finance its entrance into the preschool and early childhood consumer and education markets and to build a software development team that could produce quality products. At Narodick's suggestion, Edmark restructured its corporate board to bring on Seattle investor W. Hunter Simpson, and in early 1989, both Simpson and Narodick became directors. After serving as a consultant for Edmark for less than two years and a director for six months, Narodick was named chairman and chief executive of Edmark in October 1989, signaling the beginning of the company's transformation from a special education print materials publisher to a multimedia educational software publisher.

A New Strategic Plan: Early 1990s

Narodick took over the helm of Edmark at a time when its revenues were $2.5 million, and the company was principally a

> **Company Perspectives:**
>
> *Edmark's goal is to develop products that encourage children to discover and believe in the power of their own minds.*

publisher of special education workbooks for schools. In 1990, Edmark began expanding its management and development teams in order to initiate a new strategic plan centered around multimedia software. To that end, in October 1991, Narodick hired a Minnesota educator and award-winning software developer, Donna Stanger, as vice-president of product development. Stanger brought to Edmark 20 years of experience as a teacher and more than a dozen years as a developer of computer-based curriculum materials and educational software. She placed Edmark in the fairly rare position as a software company with two females in lead executive roles. The Minnesota teacher insisted that she be accompanied by a team of three younger male programmers—with whom she had worked since those programmers were in high school. (Stanger referred to herself as the team's ''den mother.'') Although Edmark's balance sheet included $1.9 million in recently generated equity capital, only a year earlier the company had been forced to reduce staff and salaries because of a cash shortage. Nonetheless, Narodick took the financial risk and hired the four-person team, although they had never developed a consumer product before, and their salaries increased Edmark's 25-person payroll by 20 percent.

For the 1992 fiscal year (ending June 30, 1992, and thus including the previous 1991 holiday season), Edmark earned $364,000 on sales of $6 million, compared to earnings of $265,000 a year earlier on sales of $4.3 million. As Edmark was closing its books on its 1992 fiscal year, the company debuted two consumer demonstration products: Millie's Math House, a preschool numbers and math program targeting a market niche with little competition, and KidsDesk, a desktop utility program that safeguarded the files of parents (making them feel more secure about investing in children's software) and allowed children to open their own setup folder and files.

In 1992, Edmark secured distribution or sales arrangements for its new products with Egghead Software, Ingram Micro (the industry's largest distributor), and a handful of other computer software retailers and catalogs. In October 1992, Edmark released KidsDesk and Millie's Math House, the two of which, combined, received 29 important industry design awards during the next three years and an initial highly favorable review from the *Wall Street Journal* prior to the 1992 holiday season.

For the 1993 fiscal year ending in June of that year, Edmark earned $125,000 on sales of $8.7 million. To enhance sales and distribution efforts, in 1993 Narodick hired Daniel Vetras as vice-president of consumer sales and Paul Bialek as vice-president of finance and administration. Vetras was a native of the same Massachusetts town as Narodick and a sales veteran who had worked for both Digital Equipment and Lotus Development Corporation. Bialek's experience included work as a senior audit manager for the international accounting firm KPMG Peat Marwick, which served as Edmark's independent auditors.

For the 1993 holiday season, Edmark doubled its software product line with the release of Bailey's Book House, a reading skills program, and Thinkin' Things Collection 1, which introduced a critical thinking product line. The company also released an updated version of KidsDesk. However, Edmark entered the 1993 holiday season with several factors working against it: a limited marketing budget, only four software products appearing in fewer than than 2,000 outlets, and an insufficient sales tracking system that resulted in sold-out shelves in some retail outlets and products stuck in storerooms in other outlets.

Expanding Distribution Channels and Brand Recognition: 1994–95

Edmark entered 1994 seeking additional financing to expand distribution channels and gain a presence in superstores and mass-merchandising outlets, as well as to fund stepped-up product development. As a result, in February 1994 Edmark—for the third consecutive year—returned to investors for capital. Narodick courted Doug Mackenzie, a partner in the venture capital firm Kleiner Perkins Caufield & Byres, who agreed to lead an equity investment of $5.5 million, paying the going market price of $10 a share. (Mackenzie later joined the company's board.) Despite the increased funding, the company braced for an annual loss stemming from increased development and marketing expenses, and it lost $1.9 million on sales of $11.6 million in the 1994 fiscal year.

For the 1994 holiday season Edmark doubled its product line for the second straight year. The company's four new releases included Sammy's Science House, a program designed to build fundamental science skills and the third program in the company's early-learning family, and Thinkin' Things Collection 2. Edmark also expanded its age market through the debut of a new family of interactive story-writing programs for 6-to-12-year-olds, the Imagination Express Series. That year the company released the first two titles in the series, Destination: Neighborhood and Destination: Castle. Destination: Neighborhood featured materials for children to create interactive stores, poems, and journals describing their real and make-believe experiences; Destination: Castle provided children with a medieval kingdom setting for the same.

To enhance name recognition of Edmark products, in mid-1994 Narodick hired Mark McNeely—a former chairman of a leading Seattle advertising agency that was known for building brand names—to lead an expanded marketing program. Entering the 1994 holiday season, Edmark's distribution channel had more than doubled, having expanded to 5,000 outlets that included book stores, toy stores, office superstores, and mass-merchandisers, such as Wal-Mart and the Price Club. Edmark also added a much-coveted distributor, CompUSA, the computer superstore chain, which signed a purchase order for Edmark's entire line and agreed to fund jointly marketing programs and Edmark's presence at industry expositions.

In 1994, Edmark also took steps to improve its product visibility in stores and to address stock outages. A new tracking system was initiated, and Vetras hired part-time field merchandisers, mothers with young children, in ten major metropolitan areas to help with in-store demonstrations. Edmark also initiated a holiday promotion in which KidsDesk was packaged as a

Key Dates:

1970: Edmark is founded as a developer and publisher of school print materials.
1985: The company begins developing Apple II software programs.
1986: Edmark goes public.
1988: The firm acquires the TouchWindow product line; Sally G. Narodick is hired and begins developing a new strategic plan for the company.
1991: Donna Stanger is hired to lead multimedia software product development.
1994: Edmark forms a partnership with the publisher Harcourt Brace & Company.
1995: The company doubles it workforce and its product offerings and secures record earnings of $2 million.
1996: The IBM Corporation purchases Edmark for $80 million.
2000: Edmark is sold to Riverdeep Group plc for $85 million.

free bonus with all other Edmark products. The package contained registration cards for a $10,000 savings bond contest that expanded the company's customer mailing list to more than 150,000 user names.

In December 1994, Edmark entered into a strategic alliance with Harcourt Brace School Publishers, a division of Harcourt Brace & Company. The publisher of educational materials agreed to collaborate on the development of educational software and to develop new lines of multimedia software, including products based in part on technology used in Edmark's Imagination Express software. Harcourt agreed to pay Edmark a one-time $1 million licensing fee as well annually co-fund research and development costs, beginning with a $347,500 contribution in 1994.

During the 1995 fiscal year Edmark doubled its work force and its number of software titles (after more than doubling its development funding to $4.6 million, up from $2.1 million in 1994 and $450,000 in 1993), in addition to nearly doubling its distribution outlets to 9,000. These efforts translated into sales that also nearly doubled, rising 95 percent to $22.7 million and generating record earnings of $2 million. The largest jump in Edmark's revenues came from multimedia software, with sales to the consumer market growing from $3.3 million in 1994 (and $1.5 million in 1993) to $10.9 million in 1995. Slightly more than half of all consumer sales were of CD-ROM products, with the majority of those released just prior to the 1994 holiday season. Sales of multimedia software to the education market also rose dramatically, from $934,000 in 1994 (and $130,000 in 1993) to $3.4 million in 1995. Sales of special education products for 1995 were $7.1 million, a slight decrease from the previous year and nearly the same as 1993 sales.

Edmark attributed much of its increasing success to a healthy market for its products and that the company was well positioned to capitalize on a growing industry. In 1995, Edmark qualified for listing on the NASDAQ National Market, and between mid-1994 and mid-1995 the company's stock value mushroomed 800 percent from a first quarter 1994 low of $6.50 to more than $50 a year later. The value in Edmark's stock signaled Wall Street's increasing interest in companies producing CD-ROM software, particularly children's educational programs. Edmark's success did not go unnoticed in business publications; between May and August 1995 the small but growing company was the subject of feature articles in *Business Week, Inc.,* and the *Wall Street Journal.* With its stock value rising, in August 1995 Edmark split its common stock three-for-two and completed a secondary public offering of 1.1 million shares (639,000 of which were sold by the company), generating $22.5 million in proceeds. Following the offering Edmark's management and board members owned approximately 36 percent of the company. The proceeds from the public offering, along with a $2 million line of available credit, were expected to be sufficient to meet the company's financial outlays through fiscal 1996.

For the 1995 holiday season, Edmark released new versions of most of its multimedia titles for Microsoft Corporation's Windows 95 operating system. Edmark also planned to have products from its collaboration with Harcourt released before the close of 1995 and a total of 13 titles on retail shelves. New offerings anticipated to make their first holiday season appearance included Trudy's Time & Place House, a new early learning series program to build time-telling, mapping, and direction skills; Thinkin' Things Collection 3, the third in Edmark's critical thinking skills series of programs; and two new interactive story-making programs offering new landscapes, Destination: Rain Forest and Destination: Ocean.

As it moved through the 1996 fiscal year, Edmark management hoped to add 5,000 new outlets for its software (including more book stores, mass-merchandisers, and toy stores) and to expand its work force by about one-third. With only 3 percent of the $600 million educational software market in 1995, the company recognized it had room to grow, and analysts were suggesting sales could reach $40 million for the 1996 fiscal year.

The market for educational software also held potential for significant growth, with home computer ownership expected to continue to increase for the foreseeable future. Edmark anticipated that its partnership with Harcourt would generate an expanded share of the educational software market, which was growing increasingly competitive with such companies as Microsoft and Disney moving into the field. That field's landscape was also being modified in the mid-1990s with new exclusive distribution agreements that were placing distribution firms in a position to dictate what chains would pay for products and how products would be displayed, with larger players able to exert more leverage than smaller ones.

As it entered 1996, Edmark maintained its goal of publishing high-quality educational products and was banking on distinguishing itself from larger competitors through its award-winning products. Given that repeat business in the educational software market required upgrading software and expanding product lines, Edmark continued its strategy of introducing consumers to its families of software at a young age in hopes that customers would progress from one title and one product series to the next.

Edmark Is Acquired by IBM: 1996

In the mid-1990s, however, a shakeout in the growing industry appeared inevitable, and Edmark recognized it was increasingly being viewed as an attractive acquisition target. Although entertainment and education software titles accounted for a large portion of software sold at retailers, the average price had fallen from $60 in 1995, to $40 in 1996. There was also an increasing number of titles competing for shelf space, and the cost related to product development and marketing was rising dramatically. By the fall of 1996, Edmark stock had fallen to $12 per share as competition increased throughout the industry. Its sales were unremarkable, and it had recorded losses in the previous two quarters. Its competitors were being acquired left and right by larger firms, leaving the smaller Edmark in an unfavorable position when competing for shelf space. In September of that year, Narodick left the firm suddenly due to stress-related health problems. Stanger was elected to act as interim CEO.

Edmark, like many others in the industry, was left with few options. In December 1996, the firm agreed to be acquired by IBM Corporation for $80 million. Stanger stated in a December 1996 *PC Week* article that, ''we had to decide if we were going to stay an independent company and do acquisitions ourselves to grow, or if we were going to be a part of a larger entity. Since our stock was declining steadily, unfortunately, we decided to look for a partner.'' IBM, looking to break into the consumer market, planned to market Edmark's educational software products to PC buyers.

Under the leadership of IBM, Edmark continued to see falling sales in the retail sector, but sales to educational institutions increased. Although the education software market grew by 50 percent in 1994, its growth was slowing to an average rate of around 4 percent by 1997. In response, the firm focused heavily on customer research, began to repackage its product line, and forged ahead in creating a new brand image with hopes that it would secure new customers.

In 1998, Edmark's parent decided to exit both the consumer and publishing business and focus on selling computers to educational institutions. IBM targeted the marketing of Edmark's products to K-12 schools, and its sales to schools increased to $20 million by 1999.

Edmark Is Sold to Riverdeep: 2000

Edmark's relationship with IBM lasted only four years. As part of the IBM's exit from the consumer business, it decided to sell Edmark to Riverdeep Group plc in 2000 for $85 million. As part of the deal, IBM took a 14 percent stake in Riverdeep, a growing curriculum-based Internet and CD-ROM software company. According to a *Puget Sound Business Journal* article, ''the deal boosts Riverdeep's sales considerably and gives the company many products aimed at younger children.''

After the deal was completed, Riverdeep began to reorganize Edmark's product offerings, planning to compile them into a comprehensive courseware package available on the Internet by subscription. Edmark's product line included critical thinking, early learning, language arts, math, science, social studies, and desktop security categories. Under new ownership once again, Edmark was poised to remain a player in the ever-changing software industry.

Principal Competitors

Renaissance Learning Inc.; Scholastic Corporation; Vivendi Universal Publishing.

Further Reading

Baker, M. Sharon, ''Edmark Has High Hopes for New Holiday-Season Offerings,'' *Puget Sound Business Journal,* November 4, 1994, p. 6.

——, ''Edmark Pressured as CEO Quits,'' *Puget Sound Business Journal*, September 13, 1996, p. 1.

——, ''Edmark Ready for Reawakening,'' *Puget Sound Business Journal*, August 29, 1997, p. 1.

——, ''IBM Sells Edmark to Irish Firm for $85 M,'' *Puget Sound Business Journal*, August 4, 2000, p. 4.

Baker, Molly, ''Edmark Charms the Kids and the Street,'' *Wall Street Journal,* May 30, 1995, pp. C1, C7.

Browder, Seanna, ''The Disappearing CD-ROM Players,'' *Business Week*, December 16, 1996.

Erickson, Jim, ''Edmark's Earnings Up but Stock Goes Down,'' *Seattle Post-Intelligencer,* October 20, 1995, pp. D1, D5.

Geballe, Bob, ''Edmark: Software Killer with a Woman's Touch,'' *Seattle Weekly,* October 18, 1995, pp. 23–27.

Guglielmo, Carrie, ''Romping Room,'' *PC Week*, December 23, 1996, p. 1.

''IBM Buys Troubled Edmark,'' *Software Industry Report*, November 18, 1996, p. 3.

Murphy, Anne, ''The Link,'' *Inc.*, June 1995, pp. 58–66.

Yang, Dori Jones, ''The Pied Piper of Kids' Software,'' *Business Week,* August 7, 1995. pp. 70–71.

—Roger W. Rouland
—update: Christina M. Stansell

Electricité de France

2 rue Louis Murat
75384 Paris
Cedex 08
France
Telephone: (331) 4042-5430
Fax: (331) 4042-7940
Web site: http://www.edf.fr

State-Owned Company
Incorporated: 1946
Employees: 132,550
Sales: $32.268 billion (1999)
NAIC: 221122 Electric Power Distribution

France's second largest company, Electricité de France (EDF), is a state-owned utility involved in all phases of electricity: generation, transmission, and distribution. The bulk of EDF's immense generating system is dependent on the world's largest nuclear power program. As the European Union opens borders to competition for electricity, EDF has increased its efforts to become a global provider of power, even as it tries to free itself from 50 years of entrenched monopolistic attitudes and political entanglements.

1946 Origins

EDF was formed in 1946 when the French government decided to nationalize the production and distribution of electricity. This was part of a general wave of nationalizations of key industries in France and elsewhere in Europe following the end of World War II.

Before 1946, the French electrical industry was in the hands of a large number of private companies, providing production, distribution, and other services connected with the industry under a variety of agreements with local authorities and regional administrations. The system had developed with no centralized planning following the appearance of the first distribution networks in 1884. By the outbreak of World War II, electricity was provided by about 200 companies engaged in production, another 100 in transport, and about 1,150 involved in distribution. An estimated 20,000 concession-holders provided equipment and other services to these companies. The system was irrational and inefficient, going as far as having two companies providing electricity to the same place, such as in the Lyon region, where two companies competed directly, one selling alternating current from its hydroelectric plant, the other offering direct current produced at a coal-fired thermal station.

The main reason for the government's decision to consolidate the electrical industry into a single nationalized utility was its determination to speed up industrialization and urbanization after World War II. Defeat by the German forces had revealed the weaknesses of the French economy, and there was a widespread agreement on the need to modernize what was still a largely rural, agricultural society. The electric industry was central to these plans for industrialization, and the government regarded a single utility as the best way of providing the resources for the swift increase in productive capacity that would be needed, as well as overcoming the inefficiencies of the old system.

The decision to establish a nationalized utility, rather than a private one, was largely due to the influence of Marcel Paul, a Communist, who, in November 1945, seven months after being freed from the Nazi concentration camp at Buchenwald, was appointed minister for industrial production by the head of the government, Charles De Gaulle. Besides strong technical arguments for nationalization as the most efficient means of rationalizing the industry, Paul brought a firm ideological commitment to nationalization, as well as the bitter enmity of the French political left toward the private electricity owners, who had often funded right-wing political organizations and were widely suspected of collaborating with the Nazi occupiers during the war. Paul's work toward nationalization paid off on April 8, 1946, when the National Assembly voted almost unanimously in favor of the law nationalizing electricity and gas.

Given the task of dramatically increasing France's output of electricity, the new organization immediately began work on a massive program of hydroelectric plant construction, which was the method favored by Marcel Paul and by Pierre Simon, whom Paul appointed as first president and director general of EDF. Simon was the former director of hydroelectric energy at the Ministry of Public Works. The dam-building program domi-

Company Perspectives:

Globalization, the fast growth of energy needs, the opening of the markets, the change in the needs of customers: the power industry has entered an era of far-reaching change. The EDF Group has taken an active part in these changes through its industrial investments in the emerging countries, by extending its range of energy and service offers via specialised subsidiaries and by means of rapid development within its new internal market, Europe.

nated EDF's activities throughout the late 1940s and 1950s. Although generally well received by the public, the program gave the utility its first encounter with public opposition, when its first dam, which required the flooding of the village of Tignes in the Alps, met strong local resistance, including the bombing of a crane at the building site in 1946. Nevertheless, EDF pressed on with the program.

Seven new hydroelectric installations were delivered in 1949, ten more in 1950, eight in 1951, and another eight in 1952. By 1957, a further 15 hydroelectric facilities were brought into service, turning the French Alps into the heart of the French electrical industry. The dam-building program culminated in the largest project, the redirection of the Durance river inland from Marseille, a project that created one of the largest lakes in France when it began operating in 1960.

This vast hydroelectric expansion increased EDF's production by two-and-a-half times, and made water power the most important part of the French electrical system. Until 1961, hydroelectric installations provided at least half of EDF's total production every year except in two years of drought. In 1960, the dams and their associated plants produced over 37.1 billion kilowatt hours of electricity, representing 71.5 percent of EDF's total production, compared with 18 percent provided by coal-fired thermal stations and only 3 percent by oil-burning stations.

The hydroelectric program had succeeded in providing France with a solid electrical supply. In the 1960s, however, as demand for electricity continued to increase in response to the rapid growth of the French economy, EDF turned away from its hydroelectric policy in the search for more highly productive capacity. Urbanization and general prosperity had caused a sharp increase in the use of domestic electrical appliances, creating much greater variation in the seasonal and daily demand for electricity. To cater for these changes, EDF turned to oil-fired thermal power stations, which burned a cheap fuel and were capable of providing a flexible output of current in accordance with the demand for energy. By 1973, EDF's oil-fired power stations were producing 59.7 billion kilowatt hours of power, providing 43 percent of EDF's total output compared with only 3 percent 13 years before. Over the same period, hydroelectricity had dropped to only 32 percent of EDF's output compared with 71.5 percent in 1960.

EDF Concentrates on Nuclear Power in the 1970s

Although oil had come to dominate EDF's activities, the company had also begun relatively small-scale developments in producing electricity from nuclear fission. Closely connected with the French military's development of its own arsenal of nuclear weapons, a civil nuclear project was begun in the late 1940s. In 1957 EDF decided to build its first nuclear power station at Chinon in the Loire valley, using technology developed by the French Atomic Energy Commissariat (CEA). Compared with later projects, the Chinon plant was fairly small, using natural uranium as fuel, graphite as a moderator, and carbon gas as a refrigerant. The first phase of the project, with a capacity of just 68 megawatts (MW), came into service in 1962; the second 200MW stage in 1965; and the third in 1967, with capacity of 500MW. Research and development programs were launched on Heavy Water Reactors and Pressurized Water Reactors (PWR). It was determined that PWR was the more efficient technology, and a the government began work on a 1300MW system. As nuclear power gradually increased in importance within EDF during the 1960s, the utility commissioned more plants, turning from gas-graphite technology to the more efficient PWR. By 1973, nuclear stations were producing 14 million kilowatt hours of electricity a year, representing 8 percent of EDF's output.

Despite this development, nuclear power remained the poor relation of the French electrical family, dominated by oil and hydroelectricity, until oil was delivered a devastating blow in 1973. When the Organization of Petroleum Exporting Countries (OPEC) decided to increase oil prices sharply in that year, the importance of oil to the industrialized West was crudely illustrated. In France, the prospect of a huge increase in the oil bill for the electrical industry prompted the government to swing strongly in favor of rapid nuclear development, which had previously been considered too expensive compared to oil. Now, as oil prices shot up, the slogan of French independence, which had prompted the postwar hydroelectric projects, reemerged as the rationale for a massive nuclear power project to ensure that France would never again depend on other countries' whims for its energy.

The French prime minister, Pierre Messmer, outlined the pro-nuclear case in a speech on national television on March 6, 1974: "France has not been favored by nature in energy resources. There is almost no petrol on our territory, we have less coal than England and Germany and much less gas than Holland . . . our great chance is electrical energy of nuclear origin because we have had good experience with it since the end of World War II . . . In this effort that we will make to acquire a certain independence, or at least reduced dependence in energy, we will give priority to electricity and in electricity to nuclear electricity." The Messmer Plan, as it became known, involved a huge and sudden swing toward nuclear dependence, foreseeing the launch of 13 nuclear power plants, each with a capacity of 1,000MW, within two years.

In 1974 alone, three new plants—Tricastin, Gravelines, and Dampierre, with a combined capacity of nearly 11,000MW—were begun. By 1977 work had begun on another five stations, all using PWR, with a total capacity of 13,000MW. As part of a consortium of European utilities, in which it holds a 51 percent stake, EDF also began building the most ambitious of all its nuclear installations—the FFr27 billion Superphenix fast-breeder reactor at Creys-Malville on the banks of the Rhone, the world's only commercial fast-breeder reactor, using enriched uranium and plutonium and capable of generating 12,000MW.

Key Dates:

1946: The French government nationalizes its electrical industry, bringing about the creation of Electricité de France.
1962: The company's first nuclear power plants goes into service.
1986: An undersea electrical cable between France and England is completed.
1990: Nuclear power supplies 75 percent of France's electricity.
1996: The European Union decides to open all markets to competition for electricity.

The Messmer plan succeeded in turning France into a nuclear-powered country. In the six years to 1979, nuclear energy's share of EDF's total output rose from 8 percent to 20 percent. By 1983 it had jumped to 49 percent, and by 1990 nuclear plants were providing 75 percent of EDF's electricity. By contrast, the share produced by stations burning oil or coal fell from 53 percent in 1973 to 24 percent in 1983, and down to just 11 percent in 1990. The importance of hydroelectricity also continued to decline, although less sharply, dropping from 32 percent in 1973 to 14 percent in 1990. EDF's total nuclear capacity had reached 54,000MW by the end of 1990, with another 6,800MW under construction, giving France a nuclear capacity greater than those of West Germany, the United Kingdom, Spain, and Sweden combined.

EDF's nuclear buildup faced opposition from anti-nuclear groups, but the utility and the government refused to yield to any pressure to moderate their ambitious nuclear plans, or even to accept a public debate on the issue. When huge demonstrations took place at the building site for the Superphenix plant in 1977, the authorities relied on firm police action to disperse the protesters. One demonstrator was killed in the violent clashes that followed. The unimpeded nuclear program finally slowed in 1981, when the newly elected Socialist government of François Mitterrand froze reactor construction. However, the government soon changed its position and allowed construction to continue, but at a greatly reduced rate.

In the mid-1980s it gradually became clear that the frenzied rush towards nuclear dependence had been overambitious. The construction program had compelled EDF to borrow heavily and, although building a standardized reactor had allowed the company to streamline the construction process and thus cut costs, this saving would only be realized if the plants were operating at full capacity. The sheer size of the nuclear build-up, caused by incorrect energy demand forecasts made in the late 1970s and by the obsession with energy independence, had, however, left EDF with an immense overcapacity. By 1988, EDF's nuclear units were operating at an average load factor of 61 percent, compared with West Germany's 74 percent, and the much more efficient systems of smaller nuclear operators like Switzerland, at 84 percent, and Finland, at 92 percent.

During this period EDF began to sell its expertise and its product in foreign markets. The utility became closely involved in power projects in French-speaking countries in Africa and in 1985 began a series of projects in China, working on thermal, hydroelectric, and nuclear generation, distribution networks, maintenance, and training. By 1990, EDF had signed 20 contracts in China, had become project consultant for a controversial 1,800MW sea-water-cooled nuclear plant at Daya Bay and on the construction of a 1,200MW pumped storage power station.

EDF also began a concerted campaign to export its electricity to neighboring countries. In 1986, after six years of building, an undersea electrical cable was completed between France and Britain. Although this was theoretically to allow each country to draw on the other's power grid in times of shortage, it effectively became a one-way cable for the export of electricity from France to Britain. By 1990, France was exporting 11.9 billion kilowatt hours of power a year to Britain, close behind its two biggest customers: Italy, with 12.9 billion kilowatt hours, and Switzerland, with 13.6 billion kilowatt hours. EDF also exported large bands of power to Germany, the Netherlands, Belgium, and Luxembourg and in 1990 signed an agreement worth $4 million to supply the Spanish electrical grid with 1,000MW of capacity beginning in the mid-1990s.

The utility was also quick to take advantage of the dramatic changes in eastern Europe following the collapse of Communism in 1989 and 1990. In 1991, EDF was on the verge of joining a German-led consortium to modernize East Germany's power network, and was leading an international team providing technical and management advice to Bulgaria's troubled nuclear industry. EDF was also broadening its activities in more developed markets. In July 1991, the utility became a key part of a consortium with Britain's East Midlands Electricity and several other companies to build a £400 million, 800 MW gas-fired power station in Lincolnshire, in a direct challenge to the two main British power companies, National Power and PowerGen, on their own territory. The consortium, Independent Power Generators, planned to invest in private power projects around the world.

While these foreign moves went ahead, EDF was also trying to stimulate demand for electricity within France to soak up its spare capacity. EDF also set out to encourage industrial companies to build power-consuming plants in France. However, large companies would only do this if EDF offered them power at a heavily subsidized rate, which the utility agreed to do when the aluminum producer Pechiney threatened to move its production to Venezuela because French power was too expensive. Instead, Pechiney, in partnership with EDF, built a new plant at Dunkirk in 1988, to which EDF agreed to provide electricity at half the production cost per kilowatt hour for the first six years, with the price rising gradually over subsequent years. The European Commission (EC) regarded the deal as nothing less than anti-competitive electricity dumping and forced EDF to renegotiate it on more competitive grounds, but EDF received EC approval in 1990 for similar cheap power deals with the Exxon Chemicals and Allied Signal, two U.S. companies.

EDF Reaches a Turning Point in the 1990s

The problems confronting EDF crystallized in 1989, when the utility reported an annual loss of FFr4 billion, a result that EDF's president, Pierre Delaporte, described in the *Financial Times* of January 31, 1990, as ''catastrophic, though mainly due to unforeseen problems, such as the mild winter, drought, and reduced availability of the PWR 1300MW series.'' In 1990, it received a further blow when the overseer of nuclear technology in France, EDF's former partner, the CEA, released a report sharply criticizing EDF's overinvestment in nuclear capacity and calling for urgent solutions to unresolved problems of nuclear waste disposal. By 1990, EDF had begun looking for ways to diversify its power sources.

Although EDF returned a small profit in 1990, a nuclear program costing FFr800 billion had left the utility with long-term debt of FFr226 billion. The long-term problems of waste disposal needed to be dealt with, while many of EDF's older reactors would soon be due for decommissioning, an operation whose cost, although unknown, was expected to be very high and would provide no financial return. However, the problem of overcapacity had been reduced, owing to the development of exports and increasing demand from French heavy industries. EDF ordered a new nuclear plant in 1991 and anticipated further investment in peak facilities and nuclear plants. From 1990 onward, debt was also decreasing. By 1990 repayment exceeded borrowing by FFr 3 billion, with a provisional figure of FFr 13 billion for 1991. EDF's rates, meanwhile, though already among the lowest in Europe, continued to decrease at 1.5 percent per year in real terms.

A new vision took shape for EDF in the early 1990s. With limited potential for growth on the domestic front, the company expanded its international efforts. Spending abroad increased from FFr300 million to FFr3 billion in 1994. The company purchased stakes in Sweden's Sydkaft and Italy's Ilva SE. In 1996 EDF joined a consortium of companies to buy a major Brazilian electric company. A year later it purchased 55 percent of a Polish power station. On the distribution side, EDF invested in Massachusetts-based American Superconductor Corporation to develop new technology that would permit 5 to 10 times more electric power to be conveyed over the same size cable or conduit. EDF also joined forces with Texaco, Inc. to build an integrated gasification/combine-cycle plant in Normandy, France, despite the company's general reluctance to add to its already high electric power capacity. The new plant would allow EDF to offer process steam and industrial gases to industrial clients, thus providing a competitive edge when the European Union (EU) allowed open competition in the electricity market.

In 1996, the EU energy ministers met to discuss the opening of its markets to allow consumers to choose among competing suppliers of electricity. France was reluctant to agree to the proposal, afraid of the effects on its state-run monopoly, in particular the loss of jobs. It was estimated that as much as 30 percent of the workforce would have to be trimmed if EDF lost its privileged status in France. EDF workers were members of a strong union, and it was certain that they would rally in the streets of Paris, much to the discomfort of the politicians. Jobs were also the payoff to local communities for accepting reactors in their backyards. As *The Economist* noted in a 1996 article: ''If EDF loses its reputation as a creator of jobs, public support for its nuclear programme may begin to ebb. Meanwhile, competition would certainly encourage suppliers in other countries to question whether EDF had incorporated all the costs of decommissioning reactors in its tariffs; they would also demand that EDF be financed at market rates. EDF is a mighty edifice which has so far been supported by powerful union, political and industrial interests. Take one leg away, however, and the whole structure could collapse.''

Only after a meeting between the French president, Jacques Chirac, and German chancellor, Helmut Kohl, did France finally agree to European deregulation of electricity. The plan was to be phased in over several years beginning on February 19, 1999, when high-volume customers would be allowed to choose suppliers, with a minimum market opening of 25 percent. When that date arrived, however, legislation had still not been completed to provide for France's participation. In the meantime, EDF completed its most ambitious acquisition when, for $2.3 billion, it purchased London Electricity. France's subsequent failure to comply with EU deregulation sparked outrage from many governments, whose own companies were barred from competing in the French market.

Ironically, its was the lobbying of EDF itself that would finally lead to France opening its markets to a minimum level of compliance. Francois Roussely, who had become chairman and chief executive of EDF in July 1998, was convinced that the utility could prosper under the new conditions. He set a goal of EDF realizing half its revenues from business other than electricity in France by 2005. That portion in 1999 stood at just 18 percent of revenues. Roussely also set an ambitious target for a return on capital, growing it from 7.4 percent to 10 percent. Despite Roussely's belief that EDF was destined to play a major role in Europe and the world in general, he still had to contend with the nature of the utility's ownership. To prosper, EDF had to act like a private-sector company, yet it remained caught in a political thicket. Privatization, even partial, would seem a likely step for EDF, but political considerations may very well trump economics ones, at least in the short term.

Principal Operating Units

London Electricity; Atel; ASA; Clemessy; Graninge.

Principal Competitors

Suez Lyonnaise des Eaux; E.ON AG.

Further Reading

''A Giant Awakes,'' *Economist,* November 4, 2000, pp. 71–72.

George, Gerry, ''The Global Giants,'' *Transmission & Distribution World,* 2000, pp. 30–50.

Holmes, A., *Electricity in Europe: Power and Profit,* London: Financial Times Business Information Ltd., 1990.

''How the French Get Power,'' *Economist,* May 11, 1996, p. 62.

Picard, J.-F., A. Beltran, and M. Bungener, *Histoires de l'EDF,* Paris, Dunod, 1985.

—Richard Brass
—update: Ed Dinger

Ellerbe Becket

800 LaSalle Avenue
Minneapolis, Minnesota 55402-2014
U.S.A.
Telephone: (612) 376-2000
Fax: (612) 376-2271
Web site: http://www.ellerbebecket.com

Private Company
Incorporated: 1909 as Ellerbe Architects
Employees: 800
Sales: $118 million
NAIC: 54131 Architectural Services; 54133 Engineering Services; 23332 Commercial and Institutional Building Construction

Ellerbe Becket is one of the leading architecture and design firms in the United States. The company provides integrated services that begin with an initial design concept, continue on through the engineering process, and end with management of a building's construction. The firm's many successes include the unique, round Capitol Records tower in Los Angeles, the retractable-roofed Bank One Ballpark in Arizona, and the Kingdom Centre in Riyadh, Saudi Arabia, a multipurpose facility that is the tallest structure in the Middle East or Europe. Ellerbe Becket has long specialized in designing a variety of institutional and healthcare facilities, including many built over an 80-year relationship with the Mayo Clinic. A stadium design group, started in 1988, also has become a major source of revenue. Ellerbe Becket has 12 offices around the United States and in England, South Korea, the United Arab Emirates, Russia, and Egypt. The company has been employee-owned since the late 1960s, when Thomas Ellerbe, the founder's son, retired.

Early Years

Ellerbe Becket began life as Ellerbe Architects in 1909, when the design firm was founded by Franklin Ellerbe. One of the St. Paul, Minnesota-based company's first projects was the Old Fireside Inn, a combined dance hall, retail store, and apartment complex. The Mayo Clinic, based in Rochester, Minnesota, soon contracted with Ellerbe for the design of its first group practice building, and the Minnesota Mining and Manufacturing Company (later known as 3M) called on the architect for its first structure as well. In 1911 Ellerbe took a partner, Olin Round, and the growing firm counted 18 employees by the end of the following year. Round left in 1914, but Ellerbe's son Thomas signed on following service in World War I. When Franklin Ellerbe died in 1921, Thomas Ellerbe took control of the company.

A creative architect in his own right, Thomas Ellerbe presided over the firm's growth for the next several decades. During these years Ellerbe Architects came to specialize in designing healthcare facilities. In 1922 Thomas Ellerbe proposed the then-new idea of adding a private bathroom to each hospital room, and the firm later developed a number of new floor plans for hospitals in the 1940s including the cross, radial, cloverleaf, Y-plan, penta, and others. World War II saw the company working with Northwest Airlines at St. Paul Municipal Airport to build new hangars, which featured the largest laminated pine-arch trusses used to that time. The 170-foot-wide structures these helped support were built without metal components because of wartime steel rationing.

Thomas Ellerbe was a strong believer in cooperative values, both in regard to his staff and in the design process. His firm was the first of its size to pay salaries and offer benefits to its employees, and the first to experiment with a four-day workweek. The company's approach to design was also a cooperative one, featuring an integrated set of services that offered design, engineering, and construction management, with the client given significant input into the process.

By 1966, when Thomas Ellerbe decided to retire, the firm he had run for nearly half a century had more than 300 employees. At this time Ellerbe, who already had shown considerable concern for his staff's welfare, gave ownership of the company to his employees. He remained involved as a consultant until his death at 94 some 20 years later.

In 1971 the firm formed a subsidiary to provide construction management, facility maintenance, and other building services. The 1970s and 1980s saw continuing growth for the company,

Company Perspectives:

Philosophy: To work for our clients' success in an environment that DEMANDS worldwide collaboration, creativity and innovation: Continual investment in process and knowledge allows us to offer our customers superior solutions; the delivery of architecture, engineering and construction services is an integrated process; our integrity and dependability make us a firm of breadth, depth and history. Values by which the firm operates: We focus on our clients and endeavor to be their trusted advisors; we are innovative and creative problem solvers.

but also a series of internal power struggles, which one former executive attributed to the employee-ownership structure and its lack of an ultimate controlling hand. In 1983 the firm hit an especially low point, losing $3.6 million. Within a year it had experienced a complete change in top management and layoffs of a third of its staff. Despite these troubles, Ellerbe Associates (as the firm was now known) was ranked among the top ten design firms in the country and was still receiving important commissions, such as the renovation of Mount Sinai Hospital in New York in collaboration with I.M. Pei Architects. In 1986 a new CEO, John Labosky, began to more aggressively expand the company's operations. He sought to improve profitability by better managing the hours staff worked on each project, automating various functions of the process, and by merging with complementary firms to offer a more complete range of services.

Merger with Welton Becket in 1988

In July 1987 Labosky proved true to his word and announced plans to merge with Welton Becket of Los Angeles, the 13th-ranked U.S. architecture and design firm. Welton Becket had a storied history of its own, having been formed in 1933 in Los Angeles by its namesake, with major projects over the years, including the Moscow World Trade Center, Los Angeles International Airport, and the Capitol Records building, a round tower that looked like a stack of record discs. Welton Becket also designed some residential structures, including the home of movie star James Cagney. The company specialized in high-rise offices and hotels, as well as corporate facilities.

The merger was finalized early in 1988 with an exchange of stock. The firm would henceforth be known as Ellerbe Becket, Inc., while formally remaining a subsidiary of parent entity The Ellerbe Group. John Labosky was named CEO of both. Offices were located in the Minneapolis–St. Paul area, and in Los Angeles, New York, Washington, D.C., Chicago, and Tampa, Florida. Following the merger the combined firm became one of the top three companies of its kind in the United States, with a total of 800 employees and revenues of more than $70 million. During this period the company also acquired the design firm SGE West of Los Angeles.

Ellerbe Becket continued to grow following the merger, with a new sports facility design office opened in Kansas City, Missouri during the summer of 1988. It was formed by several defectors from Kansas City-based Howard Needles Tammen & Bergendoff. The new unit soon won a major commission to renovate New York's famed Madison Square Garden. In August of 1988 Ellerbe Becket's board decided to oust CEO Labosky, whose program of rapid change had clashed with the company's more conservative corporate culture. He was replaced by a five-member executive committee, headed by President John Gaunt.

The late 1980s saw the company receive numerous high-profile commissions, including the interior of the plush Star Princess cruise ship, twin 20-story office towers in Toronto, Canada, and the $665 million International Cultural and Trade Center and Federal Office Complex in Washington, D.C., which was that city's biggest project since the 1930s. For the latter, Ellerbe Becket would work with lead designer Pei Cobb Freed & Partners to prepare construction documents and engineer the heating, cooling, and plumbing systems. In 1990 the firm opened its first overseas office, in Tokyo, Japan, where work already had begun on designing an 800-room hospital and a resort hotel.

After just a short time in operation, Ellerbe Becket's sports facility design group was blossoming into a major success story, and it grew to employ 100 by the early 1990s. In 1991 a merger with Kansas City-based Jaramillo and Associates further enlarged the office. Its projects now included the design of the New Boston Garden, renovations of several existing stadiums, and the Minnesota Twins' spring training center in Fort Myers, Florida. In 1992 a major commission was won for a new stadium to be built in Atlanta for the 1996 Olympic Games. The 85,000-seat arena would be converted into a 48,000-seat baseball stadium following the two-week games, and would then become the new home of the Atlanta Braves.

Downsizing in the Early 1990s

At the same time that it was enjoying these successes, the weakening U.S. economy and fierce competition for work among architecture firms were putting the squeeze on Ellerbe Becket. The company, which had hit peaks of 1,100 employees and revenues of $114 million in 1991, began to downsize once again, letting nearly 250 of its workers go by 1993. John Gaunt, who was now serving as CEO, was reassigned in the late fall of the year by the company's board. Refusing to accept a reduced role at the firm he had led for four years, he quit. His replacement was President Robert Degenhardt, who had been with the company since 1978.

In 1994 Ellerbe Becket's Kansas City office won a commission for a new major league baseball stadium to be built in Arizona. The 46,350-seat ballpark would feature a retractable roof that could open or close in just five minutes. This permitted use of air conditioning during events, but also would allow the growth of natural turf on the field by admitting sunshine when the field was not occupied.

Restructuring continued into 1995, when further staff reductions brought the company's total number of employees down to 669. The Los Angeles office was particularly hard hit, dropping in size from 50 to ten. It was later closed. During the spring of the year an attempt by a group of Kansas City staffers to buy

Key Dates:

1909: Ellerbe Architects is founded in St. Paul, Minnesota by Franklin Ellerbe.
1921: Thomas Ellerbe assumes control of company upon his father's death.
1940s: A steel-conserving, pine-trussed hangar is developed for Northwest Airlines.
1966: Thomas Ellerbe retires and gives ownership of company to his employees.
1971: Construction services subsidiary is formed.
1983–84: Mounting losses lead to management changes and layoffs of one-third of staff.
1988: The company merges with Welton Becket of Los Angeles; a sports facility design group is formed.
1992: The company wins competition to design an 85,000-seat stadium for the 1996 Olympics.
1994: The firm is chosen to design retractable-roofed baseball stadium in Phoenix, the first in the United States.
1997: The commission for 983 feet tall Kingdom Centre in Saudi Arabia is won.

out the firm's lucrative sports design practice was rejected, leading to the departure of three of those involved. The three, all shareholders in Ellerbe Becket, subsequently were sued by the company for violating the terms of their shareholder agreement. They had quickly joined competing sports design firms, and the company alleged that they were trying to recruit other key staffers. The suit was later dropped. The company also was involved in litigation with the Atlanta Committee for the Olympic Games, which allegedly had refused to pay the firm and its three design partners for some 46,700 hours of overtime work.

Despite these problems and the ongoing downsizing, the company was working at expanding its overseas business. An office was opened in Russia to facilitate the construction of a new headquarters for the Bank of Moscow. This project was particularly complicated, given the often chaotic and corruption-rife conditions of post-Communist Russia. Other offices were opened in the Middle East, where a major commission had been won in early 1997 for the Kingdom Center in Riyadh, Saudi Arabia. The structure, estimated to cost $500 million, would be a twin-towered multipurpose facility that incorporated a luxury hotel and conference center, offices, condominiums, and retail space. The 983-foot building, dubbed ''The Eiffel Tower of the Middle East'' by observers, would be the tallest structure in the region or in Europe when finished.

In April of 1998 a lawsuit that had been brought against Ellerbe Becket for alleged violations of the Americans with Disabilities Act in its stadium designs was settled. The firm, which was not penalized, agreed to design future projects so that wheelchair-bound spectators could see the action even when those standing in front of them stood up, as often happened during exciting moments in games. Ellerbe Becket claimed that the government's overly vague original guidelines led to the problem and that the revised designs would need to be modified only slightly from the ones cited in the suit.

A Growing Demand for High-Tech Buildings in the Late 1990s

During the summer of 1998 a major new commission was received from State Farm Mutual Automobile Insurance Company for a 900,000-square-foot building in Bloomington, Illinois. The $200 million project would feature a special electrical service and extra structural strength to enable it to withstand severe weather conditions. The facility would be in use 24 hours a day, seven days a week, and would house 2,400 employees charged with responding quickly to insurance claims. Ellerbe Becket, which had enjoyed a long-standing relationship with State Farm, had become known for its expertise in designing high-tech facilities, including a number built for Internet companies. These buildings typically required extra security features and redundant power systems to minimize the possibility of a blackout. The company also was making use of the Internet for its own purposes, in particular for improving staff access to information by putting a project's technical drawings and specifications online. This enabled the firm to maintain a single central office for generating blueprint drawings, which could then be distributed electronically to its offices around the world.

Ellerbe Becket also was strengthening its focus on providing a ''turnkey'' service for clients. This was a consciously integrated approach to design that began with a concept and carried it through the engineering process, then ended with overseeing the actual construction. It contrasted with the less seamless path often encountered by clients who had to deal with separate companies for each of these steps. Ellerbe Becket customers reportedly found the integrated approach to be much less complicated and one that gave them more input into the end result.

At this time new stadium projects were continuing to come in steadily, with such work now accounting for 20 percent of Ellerbe Becket's billings. Healthcare design was the top revenue generator with 30 percent, and college building projects brought in a quarter and government and corporate designs made up the rest. In 2000 the firm received a commission to renovate and expand the Green Bay Packers' historic Lambeau Field. The $296 million project would add 20,000 seats and many amenities. The Packers had been impressed by the firm's renovation of the stadium at Notre Dame University, which was another longtime Ellerbe client. Other stadium projects were also under way in China, Japan, and South America.

In early 2001 Robert Degenhardt stepped back from his CEO duties, retaining the job of president while company veteran Rick Lincicome took over the top role. The firm had recently opened a new office in Greenville, South Carolina, bringing its total to 12 worldwide. These included locations in Cairo, Egypt; Dubai, United Arab Emirates; Moscow, Russia; Seoul, South Korea; Wakefield, England (as a joint venture with David Lyons Associates); and U.S. offices in Phoenix, San Francisco, Washington, D.C., Seattle, Kansas City, and Greenville. The company's headquarters remained in Minneapolis, in a 30-floor building of its own design.

After more than 90 years, Ellerbe Becket had grown to become one of the leading architectural firms in the United States. Its reputation for well-designed structures and its established specializations in healthcare facility, stadium, college, hotel, and office design were well known. It would no doubt continue creating well-built, innovative new structures around the world for many years to come.

Principal Subsidiaries

Ellerbe Becket Construction Services, Inc.

Principal Competitors

Hellmuth, Obata & Kassabaum, Inc.; The HNTB Companies; Pei Cobb Freed & Partners Architects LLP; Skidmore Owings & Merrill LLP; URS Corp.

Further Reading

Apgar, Sally, "Minneapolis Company Ellerbe Becket Announces New Leadership Structure," *Star-Tribune Newspaper of the Twin Cities Minneapolis-St. Paul,* December 10, 1993, p. 1D.

Blade, Joe, "Acquisition to Make Ellerbe Nation's No. 2 Design Firm," *Star-Tribune Newspaper of the Twin Cities Minneapolis-St. Paul,* July 28, 1987, p. 7B.

Bormann, Joan, "Ellerbe Inc. Builds National Network to Stay Competitive," *HealthWeek,* January 1, 1988, p. 14.

Cookson, Brian, "Local Sports Architecture Firms Start Playing International Game," *Kansas City Business Journal,* June 2, 2000, p. 8.

Daniels, Stephen, "Designer Sues Defectors," *Engineering News-Record,* November 6, 1995, p. 21.

"Firm Agrees to Design New Arenas to Allow Wheelchair Views," *Washington Post,* April 28, 1998, p. C4.

Fisher, Thomas, "Ellerbe Becket (Firm's Architects Explore Leading Edge of Modernism)," *Progressive Architecture,* October 1, 1991, p. 102.

Gose, Joe, "KC Architects Help with Conversion—Ellerbe Becket Worked on Plans to Provide a New Home for Atlanta Braves," *Kansas City Star,* July 31, 1996, p. B1.

Jones, Syl, "Self-Redesign at Ellerbe Falls Short," *Star-Tribune Newspaper of the Twin Cities Minneapolis-St. Paul,* December 10, 1993, p. 23A.

Lester, Chris, "Ellerbe Becket Cuts Staff by 15, Citing Stoppage of Two Big Jobs," *Kansas City Star,* December 3, 1993, p. B3.

Mack, Linda, "Architects' Hands Design 14 Very Classy Decks in the New Star Princess," *Star-Tribune Newspaper of the Twin Cities Minneapolis-St. Paul,* April 16, 1989, p. 1G.

Marcotty, Josephine, "Ellerbe Becket Busy Building Bank, Toehold in Moscow," *Star-Tribune Newspaper of the Twin Cities Minneapolis-St. Paul,* November 5, 1993, p. 1A.

Menninger, Bonnar, "Stadium Designers Go from Dining Room to the Big Time," *Kansas City Business Journal,* August 20, 1999, p. 12.

Moore, Janet, "Ellerbe Becket's Princely Project," *Star-Tribune Newspaper of the Twin Cities Minneapolis-St. Paul,* September 24, 1997, p. 1D.

Olson, Chris, "From the Top: CEO Moves to Blend Design, Construction," *Omaha World-Herald,* October 31, 1998, p. 54.

Peterson, Susan E., "Ellerbe Group Chief Labosky Ousted," *Star-Tribune Newspaper of the Twin Cities Minneapolis-St. Paul,* August 12, 1988, p. 1D.

Roe, Andrew G., "A Firm Strives to Integrate Mice and Models in Design—Ellerbe Becket Melds New Technology with Old Methods," *Engineering News-Record,* September 25, 2000, p. 68.

Rosenberg, Martin, "KC Blazes Path in Arena Design—Ellerbe Becket Is Doing the Portland Sports Complex," *Kansas City Star,* June 21, 1992, p. E1.

——, "Officers' Buyout Bid Fails," *Kansas City Star,* May 4, 1995, p. B1.

Schwartz, David, "Through the Roof—'Simple' Plan Wins Ballpark-Design Derby," *Arizona Republic,* June 17, 1994, p. A1.

"Settlement Defines Stadium ADA Requirements," *Civil Engineering,* July 1, 1998, p. 18.

"Stadium Designers Seek Business from Colleges, Overseas," *Journal Record,* December 4, 1998.

Whiteson, Leon, "Ellerbe Becket President Sees Need for U.S. Architects to Become Bigger," *Los Angeles Times,* June 19, 1988, p. 2.

—Frank Uhle

Empresas ICA Sociedad Controladora, S.A. de C.V.

Mineria 145
Mexico City, D.F. 11800
Mexico
Telephone: (525) 272-9991
Fax: (525) 277-1428
Web site: http://www.ica.com.mx

Public Company
Incorporated: 1947 as Ingenieros Civiles Asociados, S.A.
Employees: 21,873
Sales: 11.49 billion pesos ($1.21 billion) (2000)
Stock Exchanges: Mexico City New York
Ticker Symbol: ICA
NAIC: 23311 Land Subdivision and Land Development; 23331 Manufacturing and Industrial Building Construction; 23321 Single Family Housing Construction; 23322 Multifamily Housing Construction; 23332 Commercial and Institutional Building Construction; 23411 Highway and Street Construction; 23412 Bridge and Tunnel Construction; 23491 Water, Sewer and Pipeline Construction; 23492 Power and Communication Transmission Line Construction; 339999 All Other Miscellaneous Manufacturing; 54133 Engineering Services; 551112 Offices of Other Holding Companies

Empresas ICA Sociedad Controladora, S.A. de C.V. is a holding company that, through its subsidiaries, is the largest construction and engineering firm in Mexico. The company is also active in eight other Latin American countries, Spain, and Puerto Rico, constructing highways, bridges, wharves, public transit lines, hydroelectric projects and electrical and gas lines, dams, water and sewage tunnels, chemical and petrochemical plants, factories, mining complexes, commercial developments, sports stadiums, hotels, dwellings, and parking lots. In addition, it conducts small-scale manufacturing of products for use in the oil exploration, petrochemical, power generation, and transportation industries, and it develops, arranges finances for, and invests in real estate development.

30 Eventful Years: 1947–77

Bernard Quintana Arrioja was educated to be a civil engineer at the National Autonomous University of Mexico (UNAM) in Mexico City, receiving a degree in 1947. That year he founded, with 17 others, Ingenieros Civiles Asociados, S.A. (ICA), an association of young civil engineers, with initial capital of 100,000 pesos (about $20,000). Quintana took the helm of this company as its *gerente* (director general). Most heavy construction in Mexico was being conducted by U.S. or European contractors, and ICA benefited from the government's desire to Mexicanize the industry.

ICA's first jobs included collaboration in the construction of the National Conservatory of Music and the Escuela Normal Superior (National Teacher-Training School). Another was the President Aleman housing project—the first of its kind in Mexico—a 13-story building. All of these buildings were in Mexico City. A 1950 commission to build a 16-story science building for UNAM was followed by the contract for other UNAM structures. Between 1948 and 1952 ICA completed dams on Rio Tepalcatepec in the state of Jalisco, its first heavy construction job. The company soon had eight subsidiaries for such purposes as obtaining bricks, gravel, sand, concrete, and machinery, and for the transport of materials. In 1956 ICA founded Laboratorios Solum, the first Mexican enterprise dedicated to the mechanics of soil. It also founded a subsidiary specializing in building houses and industrial plants.

ICA remained extremely active throughout the 1950s. One of its biggest projects was Ciudad Satelite (1956–58), a Mexico City housing project of about 220 acres that accommodated an estimated population of 200,000 on 233 blocks and seven superblocks. The construction of a 40-mile stretch of the Chihuahua-Pacific railway line included a number of bridges. The La Soledad hydroelectric works and dam in the state of Puebla, begun in 1954, was the equivalent in height of a 40-story building. Other works completed included the Chinonautla aqueduct in the state of Mexico (1955–56) and a terminal for trams in

Company Perspectives:

ICA's mission is to be the foremost Mexican company in the development, construction and operation of basic infrastructure projects, with focus on service to clients, state of the art technical capabilities, professional ethics and uncompromising quality carrying out commitments.

Tetepilco (1957). "For most of its 51 years," Joel Millman of the *Wall Street Journal* wrote in 1998, ICA "served almost as an adjunct to Mexico's public-works bureaucracy. It was so dominant in projects like dams and bridges, it rarely deigned to enter competitive bids for private-sector jobs. Even when times were tough at home, ICA managed to thrive by exporting its expertise, usually with the help of Mexico's state export bank. . . . Engineering, procurement and financing were handled through the bureaucracy, where ICA lobbyists had an inside track."

ICA established a profit-sharing plan for its employees in 1959 and updated its name to Grupo ICA in 1962. The Infiernillo dam it built on the river Belsas (1960–66) was 485 feet high, the fifth highest in the world in its category. This was a turnkey project, meaning ICA was responsible for all phases up to actual operation. The company built the Electrometro industrial park in Queretaro in 1963, a highway between Tijuana and Ensenada that year, and another between Mexico City and Queretaro. ICA built the peripheral ring of highways around Mexico City (1960–67). It undertook, in 1965, the largest share of the 870-mile Baja California highway linking Ensenada and Cabo San Lucas, a project not completed until 1973. Of great importance was its completion (1967–77) of a group of deep-drainage tunnels ten to 40 feet below ground to carry wastewater from Mexico City to a point 50 miles northeast, where they emptied into the Tula River. This project had been started by eight other firms but was assumed by ICA after a personal appeal to Quintana by President Luis Echeverria.

Grupo ICA's highest profile project in the 1960s was its construction of the Metro, Mexico City's rapid transit system, much of it a subway. Work on the first line began in 1967 and on two others the following year. The first phase, with more than 25 miles of track, was completed on time in November 1970. For the 1968 Olympic Games held in Mexico City, ICA built a 17-story telecommunications tower for the Palace of Sports, and the Villa Olimpica, a housing project consisting of 13 ten-story buildings and 16 six-story ones. It built eight offshore oil drilling platforms for Petroleos Mexicanos (Pemex), the nation's state-owned oil monopoly, between 1966 and 1973. The company began its first projects outside Mexico in this decade, including roadwork in Nicaragua (1966), a building for thermoelectric machinery in Guatemala (1968), and roads in Guatemala and Honduras (1969). By 1970 it had done work in ten Latin American countries. Among these, Grupo ICA especially was active in Colombia, where it eventually built nearly half of the country's hydroelectric capacity. It also left its stamp on that country in the form of thermoelectric plants, highways, bridges, tunnels, ports, industrial plants, commercial centers, public and private buildings, hotels, schools, and above all, in underground and elevated systems of transport.

Grupo ICA had 41 subsidiaries in 1972 and was participating in many joint ventures, plus holding minority shares in other enterprises. During the 1970s the firm prepared many areas for cultivation with dams and irrigation projects. Among its projects was a six-mile channel diverting the waters of the Tijuana River from the city and the construction of a thermoelectric plant in Altamira, Tamaulipas. ICA constructed a number of petrochemical plants and similar works for Pemex, extended the Mexico City deep-drainage system further, and built more Metro lines as well as extensions of existing ones. The company, which had constructed the Maria Isabel luxury hotel in Mexico City (1962), completed several others in the booming late 1970s, including two in Acapulco, two in Cancun, and one each in Ixtapa and La Paz. One of its most noted commissions was the construction of the new Basilica of Guadelupe in Mexico City, on the site of the holiest Catholic shrine in Latin America. Projects outside Mexico included a convention center and airport in Panama City.

Slowdown in the 1980s

By the time the company was reorganized as Empresas ICA Sociedad Controladora in 1979, it was a behemoth with more than 90 subsidiaries and a workforce of 95,000, which reached 115,000 in 1981. This included 11 companies making construction equipment, structures for oil drilling platforms, sugar mill equipment, hydraulic turbines, and piping. Normally ICA, as a private company, did not disclose its finances, but the Mexican business magazine *Expansion* classified it as the eighth largest reporting company in the nation in 1980, with revenues of 26.19 billion pesos ($1.15 billion).

The 1980s was a more difficult decade for Mexico, but Empresas ICA remained active. In 1981 it completed a 53-story tower for Pemex in Mexico City. Among other buildings were hotels for the Sheraton and Radisson chains and Cancun Towers as part of a joint venture with American Express Bank. Water supply works were constructed in Mexico City, Guadalajara, and Tijuana. An Olympic stadium was built in Zacatecas in 1984 and an old cigarette factory was remodeled to form Mexico City's public library in 1989. ICA also constructed three airports during the decade. After Mexico City was struck by a destructive earthquake in 1985, ICA rushed the greater part of its 50,000 remaining employees to help rescue people trapped in the rubble, then donated 622 million pesos (about $2 million) and installed a network of 32 seismographs to analyze further tremors to determine whether they presented further dangers. Gilberto Borja, a veteran ICA executive, was now at the helm, having succeeded Quintana on his death in 1984.

Empresas ICA also branched out into other fields. In 1979 it acquired a stake in Automanufacturas S.A., a producer of auto parts, gradually increasing its investment until it became the majority holder in 1985. It shed this business in the early 1990s. A joint venture with Vulcan Materials Co. was established in 1987 to extract, process, transport, and sell limestone from the state of Quintana Roo to the United States. This required the construction of a port named Sectun in Quintana Roo. ICA also had taken a 26 percent share in the largest cement complex in Mexico, Cementos Tolteca, S.A. de C.V., a subsidiary of British-owned Blue Circle Industries plc, in the 1970s, but this was sold to Cemex, S.A. de C.V. in 1989. Typically, about 60

Key Dates:

1947: ICA is founded by 18 young Mexican civil engineers.
1958: ICA completes Ciudad Satelite, a big Mexico City housing project.
1967: ICA begins work on the Metro, Mexico City's subway system.
1981: The company reaches its greatest extent, with 115,000 employees.
1992: Empresas ICA makes its initial public offering of common stock.
2001: ICA announces that it will continue to downsize to pay down its debt.

percent of ICA's business had come from the public sector and 40 percent from the private sector, but by 1985 the ratio was 20:80 because of constraints on spending by the Mexican government.

During the presidency of Carlos Salinas de Gortari (1988–94) Empresas ICA was invited to participate in a program establishing privately run highways, with the constructor to take profits in the form of tolls for as long as 20 years before ownership reverted to the government. ICA participated in the construction of seven of these roads, including the one between Guadalajara and Tepic, Nayarit. In 1991 work on toll roads accounted for about one-quarter of ICA's revenues of $1.37 billion, but costs were high and the program proved to be a financial disaster. ICA lost some $500 million on the scheme. In 1998 the company received 2.8 billion pesos (about $330 million) as the first installment of a government bailout. Another 1.5 million pesos was received in 1999. In 2000 bondholders threatened legal action to stop Empresas ICA from collecting a further $230 million in reimbursements.

Scrambling in the 1990s

In need of more funds to finance road construction, Empresas ICA became a public company in 1992, raising about $450 million by selling 25 percent of its common stock on the Mexico City exchange and American Depositary Receipts on the New York Stock Exchange. The company also stepped up its participation in foreign projects. In 1991 it earned about $90 million in 11 Latin American countries and the United States, where, based in Miami, a subsidiary formed in 1988 had constructed five schools and two real estate developments and, with a U.S. company, collaborated in the building of six metro stations. In 1993 ICA formed a partnership with the U.S. company Fluor Daniel Inc. Their first project was the construction of a thermoelectric plant in Chihuahua, the first of its kind in Mexico totally privately financed.

Beginning in 1992, ICA participated in the installation of a national network of fiber-optic cable for Telefonos de Mexico (Telmex). Avantel, another telephone company, then hired ICA Fluor Daniel to do the same. Other projects that occupied ICA in this period included continued extension of the Metro. By 1999 it had built 110 miles of rail rapid transit in Mexico City, Monterrey, Miami, and in Santiago, Chile and San Juan, Puerto Rico; participated in the construction of government offices in San Salvador, El Salvador; and constructed, with two other companies, a nine-mile Chicago water tunnel to capture and disperse wastewater. Other foreign projects included oil pipelines and coal mines in Colombia, a major highway in Guatemala, a reservoir in the Dominican Republic, and a petrochemicals plant in Louisiana. In 1996 the company won a piece of a $6 billion hydroelectric project in Malaysia scheduled for completion in 2003.

Within Mexico, Empresas ICA's hotel division contributed 257 million new pesos ($79 million) to the company's 1992 revenues of 5.59 billion new pesos ($1.7 billion). ICA and Banco Nacional de Mexico, S.A. owned and operated the Radisson hotels in Mexico through a franchise agreement with Carlson Hospitality Group Inc. and owned and operated five Sheraton hotels in the resort destinations of Acapulco, Cancun, Huatulco, Ixtapa, and Puerto Vallerta in association with Sheraton International and American Express Co. In 1994, as Mexico plunged into a currency crisis and economic recession, ICA announced that it would sell the hotel division in order to focus on its core construction business. By the end of 1999 the company was completely out of the hotel business.

Borja resigned as chief executive of Empresas ICA in 1994 and was succeeded by Bernardo Quintana Isaac, the eldest of the founder's six children and a company executive since 1963. Revenues dropped—in dollar terms—by almost half in 1995, mainly because of the devaluation of the peso. The price of company shares sold in New York fell from $30 to $4. Nevertheless, ICA continued to turn a profit, in part because it slashed its payroll from 42,000 to 19,000. With the national economy paralyzed, ICA turned increasingly to foreign projects, including a toll highway connecting downtown Panama City with the international airport. But the company also purchased a number of privatized government-run facilities, including a railroad, seaport terminals, pipelines, and warehouses. For example, a 20-year operating concession for one of Veracruz's container terminals was sold in 1995 to ICA and a Filipino company, International Container Terminal Services, Inc., for 531 million pesos ($88.5 million) in 1995.

Empresas ICA continued to downsize in the late 1990s, choosing to pay down debt by shedding businesses and assets it considered not to be strategic. In 1999, for example, it announced plans to reduce expenses by more than $25 million and to reduce personnel by 20 percent. It sold its 13 percent share of Mexico's longest railway, privatized in 1997, to Union Pacific Corp. for $87 million. Its 10 percent share of the Chihuahua thermoelectric plant went to El Paso Energy Corp. for $21.6 million. ICA's stake in the Hotel Paraiso Radisson Perisur was purchased by Grupo Carso, S.A. de C.V. for $18 million. The company then made early debt payments of 1.32 billion pesos (about $137 million) and refinanced its credit lines. One of its problems was a $67 million loss on a public works contract in Bogota, Colombia, during 1998–99.

ICA announced in early 2001 that it planned further disinvestments during the year amounting to $260 million and a reduction of $300 million in its debt, which had reached $756 million in the fall of 2000. Accordingly, it sold its shares in three joint ventures with Vulcan Materials for $121 million. The company announced that it would invest $100 million in home-building and municipal services, including, in partnership with Canada's Reichmann International, a long-planned Mexico City high-rise called Torre Mayor. ICA planned to become a major player in housing construction by competing for credits granted by the government for housing programs. The company also invested $100 million to build a complex of commercial buildings, offices, and residential areas on artificial islands in the Bay of Panama, and ICA Fluor Daniel won a $140 million contract for a power generation plant in the Dominican Republic.

Much of this foreign activity was meant to compensate for the loss of contracts in Mexico to foreign firms. Even when ICA won a government contract, it now tended to be a turnkey project that required company financing so that state agencies could avoid costly overruns. But when ICA won contracts abroad, the projects often proved more costly than expected. In 2000, the company was seeking $45 million, which it claimed was owed for street repairs in Bogota, and $25 million to build a natural gas pipeline in the Brazilian jungle. It also was considering withdrawing from its part in a $2 billion Venezuelan hydroelectric dam project because of a series of labor disputes.

In large part because of downsizing, ICA's net sales fell from 15.52 billion pesos (about $1.64 billion) in 1999 to 11.49 billion pesos (about $1.21 billion) in 2000. This reduced its operating loss from 966.67 million pesos ($101.97 million) to 279.92 million pesos ($29.59 million). The net loss was scarcely reduced, however—from 1.66 billion pesos ($175.11 million) to 1.55 billion pesos ($163.85 million). The long-term debt was $627 million at the end of 1999. Of ICA's 1999 revenues, construction accounted for 79 percent; aggregates and ports, 7 percent; concessions, 6 percent; manufacturing, 4 percent; and real estate, 3 percent. Mexico accounted for 71 percent of 1999 revenue; other Latin American countries, 15 percent; the United States, 8 percent; and Spain, 6 percent. Directors and executive officers owned 44 percent of the stock.

Principal Subsidiaries

Concesionarias ICA, S.A. de C.V.; Constructoras ICA, S.A. de C.V.; ICA Fluor Daniel, S. de R.L. de C.V. (51%); ICA Inmobiliaria, S.A. de C.V.; ICA Reichmann, A. en P. (50%); Ingenieros Civiles Asociados, S.A. de C.V.; Internacional de Contenedores Asociados de Veracruz, S.A. de C.V. (50%); Operacion y Mantenimiento de Sistemas de Agua, S.A. de C.V. (50%); Perini-ICA-O&G.J.V. (25%); Reichmann Chapultepec A. en P. (50%).

Principal Competitors

Bufete Industrial, S.A.; Grupo Tribasa, S.A.

Further Reading

''Empresas ICA S.A.: Construction Concern Plans to Sell Its Hotel Division,'' *Wall Street Journal,* March 7, 1994.

ICA: Hacemos realidad grandes ideas, Mexico City: Empresas ICA Sociedad Controladora, S.A. de C.V., 1997.

Martinez Staines, Javier, ''Grupo ICA: Manual de sobrevivencia,'' *Expansion,* August 4, 1999, pp. 31–33, 35–36, 38–39.

''Mexico's ICA Group at Crossroads,'' *ENR/Engineering News Record,* June 9, 1983, pp. 22–24.

Millman, Joel, ''ICA's Collection of Payments Will Aid Profit,'' *Wall Street Journal,* October 9, 2000, p. B28.

——, ''Mexico's Empresas ICA Copes with New Times—Construction Firm Seeks Foreign Jobs,'' *Wall Street Journal,* July 10, 1998, p. A12.

——, ''Ministry of Public Works, Inc.,'' *Forbes,* April 26, 1993, pp. 104, 106–07.

Moffett, Matt, ''ICA, Mexico's Major Construction Company, to Offer a Way to Play the Country's Growth,'' *Wall Street Journal,* April 1, 1992, p. C2.

Nahoul, Vanessa, and Javier Martinez Staines, ''ICA se diversifica,'' *Expansion,* April 29, 1992, pp. 58–59.

Norris, Floyd, ''Mexican Stock's Underpinnings,'' *New York Times,* April 10, 1992, p. D6.

Testimonios sobre Bernardo Quintana Arrioja, Mexico City: Fundacion ICA, 1996.

Torres, Craig, ''Empresas ICA Wins Admirers as Mexican Firm Seeks to Broaden Scope Beyond Construction,'' *Wall Street Journal,* August 18, 1995, p. C2.

Yamashiro Arcos, Celina, ''Vende ICA 3 subsidiarias a Vulcan Materials por 121 mdd,'' *El Financiero,* January 12, 2001, p. 17.

—Robert Halasz

Entravision Communications Corporation

2425 Olympic Boulevard
Suite 6000 West
Santa Monica, California 90404
U.S.A.
Telephone: (310) 447-3870
Fax: (310) 447-3899
Web site: http://www.entravision.com

Public Company
Incorporated: 1996
Employees: 1,000
Sales: $154.02 million (2000)
Stock Exchanges: New York
Ticker Symbol: EVC
NAIC: 51111 Newspaper Publishers; 513111 Radio Networks; 51312 Television Broadcasting; 54185 Display Advertising

Entravision Communications Corporation is a diversified media company utilizing a combination of television, radio, outdoor-advertising, and publishing operations to reach the rapidly growing number of Hispanic customers in the United States. At the end of 2000, Entravision owns and operates television stations in 22 U.S. markets and is the largest station group in the United States affiliated with the Univision network. It also owns and/or operates 58 radio stations. In addition, the company is the owner of El Diario/La Prensa, a Spanish-language daily newspaper in New York City that is the oldest major such newspaper in the country, and about 11,200 outdoor billboards, primarily in Hispanic communities around Los Angeles and New York.

The Early Years: 1996–99

Entravision was formed in 1996 as a limited partnership by Walter F. Ulloa and Philip C. Wilkinson. Ulloa became the company's chairman and chief executive officer, and Wilkinson became its president and chief operating officer. Ulloa had an interesting background; he was a lawyer who had then entered the Spanish-language television industry as a part-time broadcaster for Los Angeles station KMEX-TV. He rose to the position of sales manager before leaving in 1989 to build other properties for Univision Communications Inc., a dominant Spanish-language television broadcasting network in the United States. Wilkinson, on the other hand, had started out selling radio time for three FM-radio stations in the San Diego metropolitan area, one of them a Spanish-language station. After nearly four years as an account executive, he became Univision's sales manager for all of the network's stations outside the Los Angeles area. Later he was named West Coast sales manager.

After Ulloa and Wilkinson developed a friendship, ''We began to share leads,'' Wilkinson recalled to Alan Singer of the *Public Record* (Palm Springs, California) in 1997. ''This developed into a style [of marketing] and continued discussions.'' According to Ulloa, the founding of Entravision began ''in kind of an ad hoc way. We really started to think seriously of bringing everything under one company. It was complicated—the transfer applications, waiting for the FCC—but we did it.''

Their first acquisition was KVER-TV in California's Coachella Valley, which Ulloa called ''a growing market, an important market adjacent to Los Angeles . . . outdelivering CBS, Fox, NBC and ABC, combined.'' Ulloa told Singer that, among Hispanics, ''Buying decisions are created by an almost three times greater awareness by advertising in Spanish.'' Wilkinson added, ''The Hispanic market is growing in size, income, and political clout. An advertiser who ignores this segment of the market will not be competitive if the Hispanic market is not pursued. It will be a missed opportunity.''

There were also three other original investors, who were all TV station owners who decided in 1995 to roll all of their interests into one company. Univision invested about $10 million into the project, in return for the option of converting this investment into a 25 percent equity interest in Entravision. This was part of its corporate strategy to own or control stations in the top 15 Hispanic markets in the United States. Outside of Univision's owned-and-operated group of stations, plans called for Entravision to own the largest Univision affiliate group in the nation.

Entravision, by the spring of 1997, also owned and operated television and radio stations in San Diego, Denver, Las Vegas, the California metropolitan area that included Monterey and

Key Dates:

1996: Entravision is founded by Walter Ulloa and Philip Wilkinson.
1997: Entravision owns several radio and television stations in the western United States.
1999: Entravision ends the year with 25 television and radio stations.
2000: Entravision raises $814 million in its initial public offering of stock; two acquisitions add 50 more radio stations and 10,000 billboards.

Salinas, and the metropolitan area including Yuma, Arizona, and El Centro, California. Soon after, it acquired Univision-affiliated TV stations in McAllen and El Paso, Texas. The $65 million needed to buy these last two stations and restructure debt was provided by Union Bank of California, which soon expanded Entravision's credit to $150 million so that it could purchase more stations.

By the fall of 1998, Entravision owned 11 Univision-affiliated television stations and three radio stations, all with Spanish-language programming. Of the TV stations, four were in California, four along the Texas border with Mexico, two in Colorado, and one in Nevada. Entravision's 12th television station, WBSV-Channel 62 in Sarasota, Florida, aired English-language syndicated reruns and movies to an audience of about 300,000. It was purchased for $17 million in cash, although only 2.8 percent of the population of Sarasota County was Hispanic. The station's real appeal for Entravision was its UHF antenna, which the company sought to move to a much taller tower in another county so that the WBSV antenna signal would reach the Tampa-St. Petersburg-Clearwater area.

Entravision owned 16 television stations and 9 radio stations at the end of 1999. Its net revenue increased from $12.07 million in 1996 to $59 million in 1999. After earning $137,000 in net revenue in 1996 and $2.84 million in 1997 (when an income tax benefit of $7.53 million more than compensated for net interest expense of $5.11 million), in 1998 the company lost $3.7 million. That year, a net interest expense of $8.24 million outstripped operating income. The following year, in 1999, Entravision lost $39.96 million, including an operating loss of $27.99 million. Most of this loss resulted from compensation issued to one company executive in the form of stock.

An Acquisition-Fueled Public Company: 2000–01

The red ink at the end of the 1990s did not keep Entravision from stepping up its expansion plans. In early 2000, the firm acquired Latin Communications Group Inc. for $256 million. The purchase included 17 Spanish-language radio stations in 9 markets, including Los Angeles and San Francisco. It also consisted of Latin Communications' publishing operations. Chief of these was El Diario/La Prensa, the largest Spanish-language newspaper serving the New York metropolitan area, with circulation of 68,000. It was also the oldest major Spanish-language daily newspaper in the United States. The other publishing operation was a Spanish-language New York City tourist guide that was soon discontinued. El Diario/La Prensa, though, had been formed in 1968 by the merger of the city's original Spanish-language newspapers. La Prensa began publication in 1913, serving Spanish immigrants. El Diario first appeared in 1948, catering to the city's growing Puerto Rican population. Circulation fell from a peak of more than 100,000 in the 1960s to less than 40,000 in 1989, when a partnership purchased it for about $20 million from the Gannett Co. This partnership, El Diario Associates, became part of Latin Communications Group in 1995.

Just prior to its initial public offering of stock in August 2000, Entravision reorganized itself and went from being a limited-liability company to a corporation. Ulloa, Wilkinson, and Paul A. Zevnik (a Washington, D.C.-based lawyer who had served as secretary of Entravision since its inception), along with each of their trusts and other controlled entities, exchanged ownership interests in the predecessor company for newly issued shares of Class B common stock. Meanwhile, other individuals, trusts, and entities exchanged their shares and interests for newly issued shares of Class A common stock. Univision exchanged its subordinated note and option in the predecessor—amounting to an estimated $120 million—for shares of Class C common stock. Entravision then sold 46.44 million shares of Class A stock to underwriters at $16.50 a share, and 6.46 million shares of this stock to Univision for $15.47 a share. Total realized net proceeds were $814 million.

A week after raising this money, Entravision completed the previously-announced acquisition of Z-Spanish Media Corp. for about $462 million, including the assumption of about $110 million in debt. Z-Spanish owned and operated 33 radio stations in 13 markets, including stations in Dallas, Fort Worth, Houston, Phoenix, and Sacramento. As a result of this purchase, Entravision had become the owner of the largest group of Spanish-language radio stations in the United States, and the largest centrally programmed radio network in the country who primarily targeted Hispanic listeners. The purchase also included about 10,000 billboards in the Los Angeles and New York metropolitan areas. Two months later, Entravision bought about 1,200 more billboards from Infinity Broadcasting Corp. for about $168 million—primarily in high-density Hispanic neighborhoods in New York.

These acquisitions did not end Entravision's spending spree, though. The company also acquired radio stations in Newport Beach and Santa Monica (site of corporate headquarters), California, from Citicasters Co. for $85 million. Also acquired were four radio stations in the McAllen, Texas, market from Sunburst Media, LP for $55 million. In the early days of 2001, the company also announced that it had completed the acquisitions of WUNI-TV, Channel 27, serving Boston, from Jasas Corp. for $47.5 million; and WHCT-TV, Channel 18, serving Hartford, Connecticut, from Astroline Communications Co. and Two If By Sea Broadcasting Corp. for $18 million. This raised the number of Univision-affiliated television stations owned and operated by Entravision to 18.

In March 2001, the launching by Entravision of Spanish-language TV stations in Santa Barbara, California, and Tampa, Florida (the latter replacing an Entravision low-power station)–plus new ones in Odessa and Amarillo, Texas–brought the number of Univision-affiliated television stations owned and operated by Entravision to 22.

Entravision in the New Millennium

The Entravision television station available to the largest number of Hispanic households as of March 2001 was KNVO-TV, a UHF station serving southern Texas, including the communities of Brownsville, Harlingen, McAllen, and Weslaco. The company either owned or held large interests in four San Diego UHF stations, but all were low-power. Among the top-15 Hispanic markets, it also owned two UHF stations serving the Albuquerque and Santa Fe markets in New Mexico, and KINT-TV, a UHF station in El Paso, Texas. The other Entravision stations were in California, Colorado, Connecticut, Florida, Nevada, Texas, and the District of Columbia, and the company held minority interests in UHF stations in Tecate and Tijuana, Mexico.

Entravision's television stations were enhanced by the availability around the clock of Spanish-language programming from Univision, the leading Spanish-language broadcaster in the United States. Univision's broadcast coverage was reaching more than 92 percent of all Hispanic households, and represented about an 84 percent market share of the U.S. Spanish-language network television prime-time audience as of December 2000. All but two of Entravision's television stations were affiliated with Univision by means of agreements that provided each station with the exclusive right to broadcast Univision network programming in its respective market. This programming began in the morning with talk and information shows, followed by telenovelas, a talk show, a game show, a news magazine and national news, and local news. During prime time, Univision was airing telenovelas, variety shows, a talk show, comedies, news magazines, and lifestyle shows. Also aired were specials and movies, followed by late news and a late-night talk show. Entravision's local news was rated first in nine markets in any language among viewers 18 to 34 years of age.

Furthermore, radio stations owned and/or operated by Entravision formed the single largest U.S. Hispanic radio market, with more than 17 million potential listeners. They were available to about 58 percent of the Hispanic population, and all but two were located in the top-50 Hispanic markets. The company was also providing programming to 39 affiliated stations in 38 markets. Five stations (three AM, two FM) were in the Los Angeles metropolitan area (including the Riverside-San Bernardino area), the largest in the United States in terms of Hispanic households. The company had a radio presence in all other top-5 Hispanic markets except the New York City metropolitan area. States represented in addition to California were Arizona, Colorado, Florida, Illinois, New Mexico, Nevada, and Texas.

Entravision's radio operations combined network programming with local time slots available for advertising, news, traffic, weather, promotions, and community events. Affiliates received Entravision programming in exchange for two minutes per hour for network commercials. Entravision was producing programming in a variety of music formats simultaneously distributed via satellite with a digital CD-quality sound. The four primary formats offered were Romantica (adult contemporary, romantic ballads/current hits, primarily for females); Tricolor (Mexican country, primarily for males); Super Estrella (pop and alternative Spanish-language rock); and La Zeta (top Spanish-language hits, primarily Mexican, with recognizable radio personalities, primarily for males).

Entravision's net revenue almost tripled in 2000, reaching $154.02 million, of which television accounted for 54 percent. Radio accounted for 28 percent; publishing accounted for 10 percent; and outdoor advertising accounted for 8 percent of revenues. The company's expenses also rose, however, resulting in an operating loss of $31.37 million. While television operations were solidly profitable and publishing and outdoor advertising marginally so, the radio sector lost nearly $26 million. General corporate expenses and stock-based compensation accounted for another $18.5 million in expenses. Combined with net interest expense of $23.92 million and a special interest expense of $39.68 million (relating to the conversion of stock options and subordinated notes mainly arising from acquisitions), the company incurred a net loss of $92.24 million. Entravision's long-term debt was $255.15 million at the end of 2000. Univision owned 13 percent of the company's Class A common stock and 19 percent of its Class C common stock in early 2001.

Principal Subsidiaries

Entravision, L.L.C.; Entravision Communications Company, L.L.C.; Entravision Holdings, LLC; Entravision 27, L.L.C.; Latin Communications Inc.; Latin Communications EXCL Inc.; Latin Communications Group Inc.; LCG Holdings, L.L.C.; Z-Spanish Media Corporation; Z-Spanish Media licensing Company, LLC; Z-Spanish Radio Network, Inc.

Principal Competitors

Hispanic Broadcasting Corp.; Outdoor Systems Inc.; Spanish Broadcasting System Inc.; Telemundo Group Inc.

Further Reading

Consoli, John, "Latin Acquisition Creates Spanish-Language Giant," *Mediaweek,* January 3, 2000, p. 2.

"Entravision Communications Completes Acquisitions of WUNI-TV Serving Boston Massachusetts and WHCT-TV Serving Hartford Connecticut," *PR Newswire,* January 4, 2001.

"Entravision Finalizes Z-Spanish Media Buy, Posts 2nd-Period Loss," *Wall Street Journal,* August 17, 2000, p. C13.

"Hispanic Paper Defies the Ad Slump," *New York Times,* April 22, 1991, pp. D1, D10.

Lane, Cherie Jacobs, "California Company to Buy WBSV-TV," *Sarasota Herald Tribune,* October 30, 1998, p. D1.

Mendosa, Rick, "The Quiet Network Player," *Hispanic Business,* December 1997, p. 66.

Mirabella, Alan, "Latin Media Group Is Ready to Tango," *Crain's New York Business,* April 17, 1995, pp. 1, 57.

Perez, Janet, "A Capital Idea," *Hispanic Business,* October 1999, p. 14.

Ramirez, Anthony, "Carlos D. Ramirez, 52, Publisher of El Diario," *New York Times,* July 13, 1999, p. A15.

Romney, Lee, "Entravision Launches 2 Spanish TV Stations," *Los Angeles Times,* March 30, 2001, p. C2.

Singer, Alan, "Coachella Valley Market a Key Ingredient in Broadcast Plan," *Public Record (Palm Springs, Ca.),* March 14, 1997, p. 4.

Vrana, Deborah, "Hispanic TV, Radio Firm Entravision Plans IPO," *Los Angeles Times,* April 22, 2000, pp. C1, C4.

—Robert Halasz

Enzo Biochem, Inc.

60 Executive Boulevard
Farmingdale, New York 11735
U.S.A.
Telephone: (631) 755-5500
Fax: (631) 755-5561
Web site: http://www.enzo.com

Public Company
Incorporated: 1976 in New York
Employees: 220
Sales: $50 million (2000)
Stock Exchanges: New York
Ticker Symbol: ENZ
NAIC: 621511 Medical Laboratories

The first biotechnology company to go public, Enzo Biochem, Inc., located in Farmingdale, New York, consists of three wholly owned subsidiaries. Enzo Clinical Labs, Inc. offers diagnostic testing at laboratories in the New York metropolitan area and provides a steady income to support the company's research efforts. Enzo Diagnostics develops and markets DNA probe-based tests to detect viral and bacterial diseases, including cancer and sexually transmitted diseases. (DNA probes operate at the genetic level, providing a faster and more definitive diagnosis.) Potentially the company's most lucrative business, Enzo Therapeutics applies exclusively licensed antisense nucleic acid technology to find cures to cancer, viral, and other diseases by altering the generic makeup of cells and, in effect, ''turning off'' the traits of particular genes. Over the years, Enzo has been something of a cipher, riding on more than two decades of unrealized potential. Periodically, Wall Street bids up the company's stock in anticipation of Enzo producing a scientific breakthrough, only to be persistently disappointed. In addition to research, Enzo has spent a great deal of time in the courtroom, involved in a series of patent disputes with rivals and broken contracts with allies.

Establishing Enzo in 1976

In 1953 Alan Watson and Francis Crick set the stage for biotechnology by revealing the shape of DNA and explaining how genetic information was passed from one generation to the next. Scientists rapidly began to search for ways to manipulate nature at the molecular level through genes, leading to such discoveries as cloning. Like the personal computer and Internet revolutions that would follow, biotechnology was based on publicly supported research that was then commercially exploited by individual entrepreneurs in small start-up companies. Genentech is generally regarded as the company that launched the biotechnology industry, founded in April 1976 by Herb Boyer, co-inventor of gene-splicing, and a young venture capitalist named Robert Swanson. Only a few months later, in August 1976, Enzo Biochem would become another early biotechnology pioneer.

The scientist behind Enzo was Elazar Rabbani. Born in Iran from a long line of Sephardic rabbis, including a grandfather who was the chief rabbi of Isfahan, Rabbani broke from family tradition, traveling to the United States to study science. After receiving a B.A. degree in chemistry from New York University, he earned a Ph.D. in biochemistry from Columbia University. Rabbani was completing his dissertation when he started Enzo with his brother Shahram, who also earned a chemistry degree, and their brother-in-law Barry Weiner, who held an M.B.A. from Boston University and was working for Colgate-Palmolive. Enzo started business in space located in Manhattan, just north of the Wall Street area, but eventually moved its headquarters and research operations to Long Island. Whereas the company began to conduct research, its primary business at first was the production of enzymes that it sold to research laboratories. Although the company would lose $3,400 on just $133,000 in revenues in 1979, Enzo became the first of the biotechnology companies to go public when it made an initial offering of stock in June 1980. The company sold 700,000 shares of stock at $6 per share, setting the stage for other biotech start-ups that would become hot Wall Street offerings during the next few years. Within a month Enzo was trading higher than $10. By 1983, following several splits, it would be trading in the low $30s.

Like other new biotech companies, Enzo did not lack in confidence or lofty ambitions. In its 1980 annual report, the company indicated that it was conducting wide-ranging research: from developing vaccines to creating microorganisms that could eat oil spills, and even to the creation of synthetic

Company Perspectives:

Enzo Biochem is positioning itself for a fundamental role in the evolution towards biological medicines in clinical treatment.

fuels. Soon, however, Enzo elected to focus its resources on nonradioactive DNA probes, making use of a patent awarded to a Yale University scientist on its advisory board named David Ward. In 1983 the company signed a major joint venture agreement with Johnson & Johnson to develop and market products based on DNA technology.

Enzo was perceived as a company on the verge of greatness, yet it never seemed to deliver. At the same time, it was beginning to gain unwanted notoriety. When Ward left the advisory board to work for Integrated Genetics in 1985, Enzo sued him, claiming that he disclosed trade secrets. The case was settled out of court, with the company agreeing to make royalty payments and provide shares of stock that it promised Ward before he resigned. Enzo also sued two other members of its six-member advisory board, including Robert Prensky of the Sloan-Kettering Institute, who established the board. More important, Enzo failed to bring products to the market, a situation not uncommon for biotechs, which require long lead time and enough cash to sustain research and development that in the end could still be leapfrogged by newer technologies. To generate revenues, in much the same way that it sold enzymes in its early days, Enzo acquired Lattingtown Cytology Center in January 1985 in order to offer testing services for New York doctors.

By 1986 the state of Enzo could be described as uncertain. Minus research money, most of which came from Johnson & Johnson, revenues amounted to just $6.8 million. Its earnings essentially came from interest income and the Lattingtown lab business. Nevertheless, the company was valued at more than 110 times its earnings, and although a number of investors lost faith in the company, whenever its stock dipped below $9 per share, the price rebounded. A July 1986 *Financial World* article written by Ellen Benoit offers a somewhat critical portrayal of the company, maintaining, ''Enzo's promise and promises have frustrated many for six years. Take, for instance, those squabbles with prominent scientists. A rule of thumb for investors in gauging a high-tech company's prospects is to assess the quality of its board of advisers; in this case, some of the advisers turned their own thumbs down.'' While noting that Enzo had husbanded its money well, Benoit also quoted an analyst who called the company ''stingy.'' Overall, Benoit depicted Enzo as a company that was perceived to have failed to back up its hype, and one that would no longer be given the benefit of the doubt.

Filing Suit Against Johnson & Johnson in 1987

In January 1987 Johnson & Johnson expressed concerns about Enzo's performance and asked for information and assurances that it was complying with its obligations before it would release $3 million in promised funds. In August 1987 Enzo sued Johnson & Johnson, alleging unfair competition, as well as failure to market some of the genetic diagnostic tests that Enzo had developed. The suit called for $100 million in damages and $500 million in punitive damages. While the suit made its torturous journey through the legal system, Enzo carried on, adding to its laboratory testing business and taking a major step on the research side by signing an exclusive licensing agreement with the Research Foundation of the State University of New York, located at Long Island's Stony Brook, on its patents regarding antisense technology. A 1988 *Wall Street Journal* article on the promise of antisense provides a succinct overview of the method: ''In its simplicity and specificity, antisense is utterly unlike mainstream biotechnology, which involves splicing a new gene into a medium such as bacteria to produce a desired protein that will combat a disease. Nor is it like 'gene therapy,' which aims to splice in a good gene to compensate for a defective one. The new science looks to target and block bad genes—such as cancer-causing oncogenes—much as correcting tape blocks out a typographic error.'' To be sure, antisense held out great promise, but cures, and profits for the companies like Enzo that sought to develop commercial products, were admittedly many years away.

In the meantime, Enzo found itself burdened with $30 million of junk bond debt and losing significant amounts of money, especially to debt service. In fiscal 1991 the company generated revenues of just $19.8 million and posted a $10.8 million loss, after losing $2.5 million the year before. In May 1991 it failed to make a semiannual interest payment of approximately $1.4 million, prompting First National Bank of Boston, trustee of the debenture holders, to demand immediate repayment of the entire debt. The parties worked out a prepackaged bankruptcy plan that would allow Enzo to make interest payments using stock instead of cash for three years. When the price of the stock suddenly took off, however, Enzo was able to exchange its bonds for shares of stock, as a vast majority of bondholders elected to convert their holdings at $5 per share, thus freeing the company of its onerous debt.

The run-up on Enzo stock was apparently precipitated by new-product announcements by the company. With its shares trading at just $1.12 in early December, Enzo announced that it had developed a test to detect the AIDS virus, claiming that it was more effective than what was currently in use. In less than a day of trading, Enzo's stock soared 400 percent, eventually climbing as high as $8.50 per share. Some analysts were puzzled by the excitement generated by Enzo's announcement, given that the new AIDS test would require the use of three patents held by other companies and for which Enzo was not licensed. This fact was made clear in an earlier press release to the research community but not mentioned in the general announcement. Enzo's stock soon settled to the $3 level, then took off again in January 1992 when the company announced eight new tests to detect cancer. This time the stock surged to $7.50, at which point many of Enzo's bondholders decided to convert to stock. What the second press release did not note was that seven of the eight cancer tests were not proprietary, nor did any have FDA approval. Enzo denied that its announcements were misleading, maintaining that the dramatic increase in the price of its stock was simply investor reaction to company progress.

Later in 1992, Enzo's stock took off again, this time when the company announced that it would receive a patent on antisense technology, originally filed nine years earlier. Al-

Key Dates:

1976: The company is established.
1980: Initial public offering of stock is made.
1983: Joint agreement is made with Johnson & Johnson.
1987: The company sues Johnson & Johnson.
1994: The Johnson & Johnson suit is settled out of court.
2000: Stock price peaks at $139.

though the technology held potential benefits for humans, its most immediate application would be in agriculture. Indeed, a biotech company named Calgene only a few months earlier had received an antisense patent for tomatoes and other plants and was preparing to market its extended shelf-life Flavr Savr tomato. With Enzo believing that its patent should supersede all other existing antisense patents, it was inevitable that Enzo and Calgene would skirmish. Calgene went to court first, hoping to invalidate Enzo's patent. A month later, in March 1993, Enzo sued Calgene, charging patent infringement.

Settling the Johnson & Johnson Suit in 1994

While Enzo and Calgene engaged in a protracted court battle, Enzo finally settled its case with Johnson & Johnson in October 1994. Johnson & Johnson agreed to pay Enzo $35 million. At the same time, Enzo announced that it would post a profit for fiscal 1994, its first since 1986. On revenues of $22.8 million, the company made $5.3 million. Its entry into the clinical laboratory business appeared to be paying off, supplying steady cash flow. At the same time, Enzo Diagnostics also was beginning to generate significant sales, accounting for about 30 percent of the company's revenues. Only a year earlier the laboratories supplied 90 percent of all revenues. Enzo Therapeutics remained the business with the greatest possible payoff in the future. Overall the game plan was clear: diversify, maintain a positive cash flow, invest in research, and wait for the scientific breakthrough that would launch Enzo to another level.

The company suffered some setbacks in the next couple of years. The courts ruled in February 1996 that Calgene had not infringed on Enzo's patents. The clinical laboratory business was hurt by reductions in reimbursements for Medicare services, leading to a loss of $7.7 million in net income for 1996. Nevertheless, the company recovered and was profitable again in 1997. It followed with a steady increase in both revenues and profits in 1998 and 1999. Annual sales grew from $40.4 million in 1998 to $44.3 million in 1999, with net income of $3.4 million and $6.5 million.

After the price of Enzo stock dipped to the $6 range in the summer of 1998, it began a steady rise that eventually would reach a fever pitch. Encouraging test results of a new treatment employing antisense technology for people with HIV appeared to be behind the enthusiasm for the company's prospects. In July 1999 Enzo's stock traded at $14 per share. By November it reached $25, then following a move from the NASDAQ to the New York Stock Exchange in January 2000, it soared past $75, eventually topping out at an incredible $139. The roller coaster ride continued for the next several months, before the price settled to a more sustainable level in the $20 range.

Enzo reached $50 million in annual sales in 2000 and posted a record profit of $6.6 million. Although exhibiting steady growth, Enzo remained a small company with big hopes. In contrast, its fellow pioneering biotech company, Genentech, was generating more than $1.6 billion in sales in 2000. In December 2000 Enzo entered a second phase of testing for its new AIDS drugs. It also had two hepatitis drugs in early phases of tests. The company clearly had taken positive steps, but the ultimate goal of producing commercial products remained in the uncertain future. Enzo, with its clinical laboratory business and income from its diagnostics subsidiary, was financially stable enough after 25 years of existence to at least stay the course.

Principal Subsidiaries

Enzo Clinical Labs, Inc.; Enzo Diagnostics, Inc.; Enzo Therapeutics, Inc.

Principal Competitors

Abbott Laboratories; Biogen Inc.; Bristol-Myers Squibb Company; Calgene, Inc.; Chiron Corporation; E.I. du Pont de Nemours & Company; Eli Lilly & Company; Johnson & Johnson; Merck & Co., Inc.; Schering-Plough Corporation; Certex Pharmaceuticals.

Further Reading

Benoit, Ellen, ''Promises, Promises, Promises,'' *Financial World,* July 8, 1986, pp. 102–07.

Chase, Marilyn, ''Promise Seen in 'Anti-Sense' Medicine—Approach Aims at Neutralizing Harmful Genes,'' *Wall Street Journal,* August 22, 1988, p. 1.

''Enzo Biochem, Inc.,'' *Wall Street Transcript,* April 17, 1995, pp. 1–4.

Hardy, Eric S., ''Technobubble,'' *Forbes,* September 25, 1995, p. 206.

''The Hunt for Plays in Biotechnology,'' *Business Week,* July 28, 1980, p. 71.

Kadlec, Daniel, ''Patent Heals Bruised Enzo Biochem,'' *USA Today,* August 20, 1992, p. 3B.

Power, William, ''Johnson & Johnson Is Sued by Enzo for Breach of Pacts,'' *Wall Street Journal,* August 25, 1987, p. 1.

Spalding, B.J., ''Engineering Cells to Destroy Viruses,'' *Chemical Week,* July 29, 1987, p. 27.

Unger, Michael, ''Enzo Takes Investors on Wild Ride,'' *New York Newsday,* January 31, 1992, p. 35.

——, ''Separated at Birth,'' *New York Newsday,* September 23, 1996, p. C1.

—Ed Dinger

Extended Stay America, Inc.

450 E. Las Olas Boulevard, Suite 1100
Fort Lauderdale, Florida 33301
U.S.A.
Telephone: (954) 713-1600
Fax: (954) 713-1660
Web site: http://www.exstay.com

Public Company
Incorporated: 1995
Employees: 6,100
Sales: $518 million (2000)
Stock Exchanges: New York
Ticker Symbol: ESA
NAIC: 721110 Hotels (Except Casino Hotels) and Motels

Established in 1995, Extended Stay America, Inc. (ESA) operates some 400 extended-stay hotels in 38 states. The facilities, which are a cross between a hotel room and an apartment, cater to business travelers on assignment as well as people who simply need long-term accommodations for other reasons. ESA has three brands of lodging that are generally priced by the week but are also available on a nightly basis. Crossland Economy Studios range in price from $169 to $199 per week, offering a double bed, limited kitchen facilities and utensils, cable television, a table and chairs, voice mail with free local calls, and a computer data port. Extended StayAmerica Efficiency Studios, priced between $199 and $299 per week, offer larger rooms and a recliner. StudioPLUS Deluxe Studios, which cost as much as $399 per week, offers such amenities as a fitness center and an outdoor pool or spa, and features a separate living area and kitchen. Based in Fort Lauderdale, Florida, ESA is chaired by businessman Wayne Huizenga, best known for his success in building Blockbuster Video and his ownership of the Miami Dolphins, Florida Panthers, and Florida Marlins professional sports teams. Huizenga turned to ESA and several other ventures after the 1995 merger of Blockbuster Video and Viacom left him without active control of his former business.

The Extended-Stay Concept: Dating Back to 1975

The explosive growth in the mid-1990s in the extended-stay segment of the lodging industry hearkened back to the 1950s when Kemmon Wilson took advantage of the post-World War II interstate highway system to create the Holiday Inn chain, resulting in a vast number of motor lodges springing up across the country. In that same period, another man who would have a tremendous influence on lodging got his start in the business. Kansas native David L. Brock cofounded a hotel company in 1956. He and Wichita developer Jack DeBoer coined the term "extended stay" and opened the first extended-stay hotel for business travelers in 1975. They called it Residence Inn, which grew into a chain of 96 hotels before being purchased and expanded upon by Marriott International. An Atlanta company named Suburban Lodge developed the economy segment in the extended-stay business in 1987, and other local developers also built similar facilities, but no one was in a position to attract the necessary capital to attempt a national rollout of an economy version of Residence Inn. Moreover, the lodging business in general was overbuilt in the 1980s, further dampening investor interest in the concept.

By the mid-1990s, however, a number of factors changed the viability of the extended-stay economy segment. Looking to cut costs, businesses were more receptive now to the idea of cheaper extended-stay lodgings, and the increasing dependence on high technology required many employees to travel for long-term training. Businesses also saved money by downsizing staff in favor of bringing in contractors on a project basis, people who would also need affordable accommodations for weeks at a time. Added to this rising tide of business customers were other potential guests that could help keep vacancy rates low: military personnel; construction workers; people relocating or looking for a new apartment or home; and people looking for long-term lodging for personal reasons, such as divorce, or simply to visit family members. Industry statistics also made a compelling case for investing in extended-stay hotels. Out of America's 3.1 million hotel rooms, less than 10,000 were in the economy end of the extended-stay market. Extended-stay hotels in general enjoyed a higher occupancy rate than standard hotels and with much less turnover. Expensive frills were not expected by

Company Perspectives:

Three brands, one mission: deliver the finest in extended-stay lodging at the best possible price.

guests, saving both on construction and the cost of paying personnel to provide services. Moreover, developers could choose secondary sites. There was no real need to acquire expensive property near highways to attract an ever-changing supply of overnight guests. Less expensive land located near industrial parks was actually more desirable. As a result of all these factors, extended-stay hotels were much cheaper to build and operate and generated a high profit margin. Because the demand for such accommodations far exceeded the available supply of rooms, the stage was set for economy extended-stay hotel chains to finally roll out on a national basis.

Wayne Huizenga had never been involved in the hotel business, but he had experience in consolidating a fragmented industry and taking a concept nationwide—and his name attached to any venture was certain to attract a great deal of attention. Huizenga started out in waste management. After his father's construction business failed, Huizenga ran a family friend's garbage business until 1962 when at the age of 25 he borrowed $5,000 from his father-in-law to buy a truck and a garbage route. The business, Southern Sanitation Service, would evolve into Waste Management Inc. With $2 billion in sales it would become the world's largest waste handler. Huizenga left Waste Management in 1983 and became involved with several other businesses before buying into Blockbuster Video. As he had done in waste management, Huizenga quickly bought up smaller operations and opened new outlets at a breakneck pace until he had created yet another financial behemoth. In just seven years the Blockbuster chain grew from a $7 million business with 19 stores to a $4 billion business with more than 3,700 stores in 11 countries. Blockbuster merged with media giant Viacom Inc. in 1994 and Huizenga ceded control to Viacom's chairman of the board, Sumner Redstone. Huizenga was still the owner of three south Florida professional sports teams, but soon after the Viacom merger he and his longtime lieutenants were looking at a number of business opportunities.

Establishing Extended Stay America in 1995

Huizenga had several guidelines for selecting a new venture: it had to be able to be run from south Florida; it should be a service business as well as a repeatable business, like renting videotapes or leasing garbage containers; and it had to be a concept that could be rolled out nationwide. Longtime friend and executive at both Waste Management and Blockbuster, George Johnson, Jr., approached Huizenga with an idea in early 1995. As a business traveler himself, Johnson recognized the need for moderately priced hotels for stays of a week or longer. Extended-stay hotel rooms were growing at only 3.3 percent a year, with very few rooms in the economy price range, thus leaving an open niche in the business that could be exploited. Huizenga was persuaded, and in January 1995 he and Johnson invested $56 million to start Extended Stay America, which they incorporated in Delaware. Johnson would serve as president and chief executive officer, with Huizenga as chairman of the board. In August of that year, ESA opened its first Extended StayAmerica Efficiency Studios property in Spartanburg, South Carolina, Johnson's home state, where in the early 1970s he served in the House of Representatives. In that same month, ESA would acquire an existing extended-stay property in Marietta, Georgia.

With just two hotels in operation and nine others under construction, ESA made an initial public offering of its stock in December 1995. On the strength of Huizenga's name, ESA stock more than doubled in price on the first day, opening at $13 per share and closing at $27.50. Vowing to become the Wal-Mart of lodging, Huizenga and Johnson quickly moved to justify investor confidence in ESA. They opened newly constructed hotels and acquired existing facilities in Georgia, Kansas, and Las Vegas, and a traditional hotel in Colorado that was converted to an extended-stay format. By the end of 1996 ESA would be operating 40 Extended StayAmerica Efficiency Studio brand hotels, far more than originally projected, with 50 additional properties under construction and the land for another 106 under option. For the year, ESA would generate $38.9 million and post $7.7 million in earnings.

ESA was not alone, however, in recognizing the potential in extended-stay lodging. Studio Plus Hotels went public a year before ESA and was expanding quickly, as was Sierra Suites by Summerfield Hotel Corporation. Traditional hotel chains also looked to enter the market. Doubletree launched Candlewood Hotels. Choice Hotels International—which boasted such brands as Comfort, Quality, Econo Lodge, and Rodeway—introduced MainStay Suites, and Marriott International broke ground on its first TownePlace Suites property. Furthermore, Prime Hospitality announced plans for a chain of AmeriSuites and Wyndham was developing a concept.

In January 1997 ESA opened its first Crossland Economy Studios brand hotel in Independence, Missouri. Crossland was ESA's entry in the ''budget'' category of extended-stay lodging. Also in January, ESA acquired Studio Plus Hotels in a stock swap worth approximately $290 million. Studio Plus had 35 hotels in operation and another 11 facilities under construction. By May, ESA would open its 100th hotel, and in June it would move its stock from the Nasdaq to the New York Stock Exchange. The company negotiated a $500 million line of credit to fuel its continued growth. By the end of 1997 ESA would have 185 hotels in operation under its three brands, with another 84 properties under construction and 146 sites under option. Management was now projecting that by 2000 it would have 540 hotels in operation. Revenues for 1997 increased to $130 million, although rapid expansion resulted in lower earnings, which fell to $2.6 million.

Slowing the Pace in 1999

In 1998 ESA opened its 200th property, prompting management to boast that it was the fastest-growing hotel chain in American history. According to Bear, Stearns & Co., Best Western required 29 years to reach the 200 mark, La Quinta Inns 21 years, and Holiday Inns nine years. Sluggish stock prices in the hotel industry, however, would curtail ESA's rapid growth. Investors were concerned that overbuilding would lead to lower profits. Although continued expansion could increase

Key Dates:

1995: Extended Stay (ESA) is incorporated and makes initial public offering of stock.
1997: ESA acquires Studio Plus Hotel, Inc.
1998: ESA opens its 200th hotel.
2000: Company reaches $500 million in annual revenues.

revenues to the point where its stock would follow suit, by the end of 1998 ESA decided to cut back on the number of hotels it would roll out in 1999. Instead of 120 new properties it decided to open between 50 and 70. Despite tepid support from Wall Street, ESA posted healthy results for 1998: earnings of $28 million on revenues of $283 million.

Aside from investor caution, the economy extended-stay lodging business was becoming the object of social criticism. In addition to business travelers, economy hotels were attracting families but lacked the recreational areas necessary for children. Zoning laws that would require such facilities were skirted by building in commercial areas. Furthermore, the low-end segment of extended-stay hotels were hardly selective in clientele and saw a high incidence of crime. Add these factors to the cheap construction of the buildings, and critics warned that some extended-stay hotels were simply slums in waiting. On the other hand, extended-stay hotels were not intended for families and communities themselves would have to bear responsibility for not providing adequate low-cost housing for its residents.

As ESA scaled back construction in 1999, it concentrated on sites where there was an opening in the market while giving up options in areas that already had strong competition in extended-stay lodging. Overall, the industry experienced a slowdown in construction despite no real evidence that demand had fallen. While the stock market, enamored with tech stocks, rose significantly in 1998, lodging stocks actually lost value. Publicly trade companies now shied away from rapid expansion, fearing that earnings would be hurt. ESA faced a further problem in 1999 when some of Huizenga's other business ventures stumbled, in particular AutoNation, a ''cradle-to-grave'' business that was intended to combine new and used car dealerships with car rental agencies and repair shops, as well as auto financing and insurance operations. In the four companies he chaired, Huizenga saw the value of his stock fall from an earlier peak of $3.2 billion to less than $700 million. ESA continued to generate cash, earning more than $47 million on revenues of $417 million in 1999, but just as the company's stock initially had benefited by its association with Huizenga it now suffered when his magic touch was being questioned by investors. ESA now planned to build just 30 hotels in 2000, compared with 57 the company opened in 1999 and 120 in 1998.

ESA stock rebounded somewhat in the first few months of 2000, but because of the company's large amount of free-cash flow it was in a position to continue to grow without resorting excessively to the capital markets. Only Marriott among ESA's competitors was able to continue opening new extended-stay hotels. ESA ended 2000 with 392 hotels in operation, 19 properties under construction, and another 58 sites under option. Overall in 2001 it looked to open 28 additional hotels. Financially, the company again showed significant gains over the previous year, posting $518 million in revenues and more than $70 million in earnings. Its stock also showed marked improvement, more than tripling during the period of March 2000 to February 2001. Nevertheless, ESA had its share of skeptics who questioned if it could continue to fill rooms at a high rate given a slowing national economy and the price cutting of competing chains. There were also concerns about how well older ESA properties were performing. Company policy, unlike others in the industry, was not to report results of hotels open more than one year. Management insisted that properties showed tremendous growth when they first opened and that comparing numbers to subsequent years would give a false impression of weakness. Critics countered that the only way to determine a company's long-term prospects was to gauge how established properties were performing. The fear was that older properties had declining revenues and that the hot flash of profits derived from newly opened hotels were simply masking the reality of ESA's situation. Only time would reveal the truth, as was the case for the extended-stay hotel business in general. With economic conditions far less rosy than those of the late 1990s when the segment show such dramatic gains, it remained to be seen if consumers would continue to spend their money on extended-stay hotels or simply choose to sleep on a friend's couch.

Principal Operating Units

Crossland Economy Studios; Extended StayAmerica Efficiency Studios; StudioPLUS Deluxe Studios.

Principal Competitors

Candlewood Hotel Company, Inc.; Choice Hotels International Inc.; Equity Inns; Marriott International, Inc.; Suburban Lodges of America.

Further Reading

Alpert, Bill, ''Express Check-Out,'' *Barron's,* February 12, 1996, p. 17.
Brack, Elliott, ''Let's Keep 'Extended Stay' at Bay,'' *Atlanta Journal-Constitution,* December 16, 1996.
DeGeorge, Gail, *The Making of a Blockbuster: How Wayne Huizenga Built a Sports and Entertainment Empire from Trash, Grit, and Videotape,* New York: John Wiley, 1995.
Evans, Judith, ''Extended-Stay Hospitality Sector Has Room to Grow,'' *Washington Post,* July 21, 1997, p. 27.
Hutt, Katherine, ''Extended Stay America Hopes Growth Will Polish Lackluster Stock Price,'' *Sun Sentinel,* May 21, 1998.
Levy, Adam, ''Trouble in Wayne's World,'' *Houston Chronicle,* December 19, 1999, p. 4.
Richards, Rhonda, ''Midprice Hotels Becoming Mainstay of Travel,'' *USA Today,* January 26, 1996, p. B1.
Rosato, Donna, ''Investors Welcome Extended Stay,'' *USA Today,* December 15, 1995, p. B3.
Selz, Michael, ''Extended Stay's Rapid Development Concerns Analysts,'' *Wall Street Journal,* February 20, 1991, p. B2.
Terhune, Chad, ''Hoteliers Remain Bullish Even as Demand Flattens,'' *Wall Street Journal,* December 23, 1998, p. F1.

—Ed Dinger

Flexsteel Industries Inc.

3200 Jackson Street
P.O. Box 877
Dubuque, Iowa 52004-0877
U.S.A.
Telephone: (319) 556-7730
Fax: (319) 556-8345
Web site: http://www.flexsteel.com

Public Company
Incorporated: 1918 as Sanitas Spring Company
Employees: 2,600
Sales: $286.9 million (2000)
Stock Exchanges: NASDAQ
Ticker Symbol: FLXS
NAIC: 337121 Upholstered Household Furniture Manufacturing; 33636 Motor Vehicle Seating and Interior Trim Manufacturing; 337125 Household Furniture (Except Wood and Metal) Manufacturing; 337214 Office Furniture (Except Wood) Manufacturing

Flexsteel Industries Inc. is a leading manufacturer of furniture seating for the home and office, the hospitality and healthcare industry, and the recreational and marine vehicle markets. Flexsteel's Home Furniture line, which ranges from upholstered chairs, recliners, sofas and sectionals, and convertible sofa beds to seating and sofa bed units for vans, mobile homes, and marine vehicles, features the company's patented Flexsteel spring, a uniquely flexible and durable design backed by a lifetime guarantee. The company's collections—Metropolitan, Big Horn, Timeless Traditions, and Casual Classics—can be found in 259 Flexsteel Galleries located in retail stores across the United States. Flexsteel operates nine factories that utilize state-of-the-art computer technology and a large fleet of delivery trucks to ensure quick delivery time to its dealers. In fiscal 2000, Flexsteel's nine manufacturing plants, 21 Comfort Seating Showrooms, and 259 retailer-positioned gallery showrooms combined to produce more than $286 million in revenues for a net income of $11.9 million.

Company Beginnings: Early to Mid-20th Century

Flexsteel's origins may be traced to Frank Bertsch, an upholstery apprentice born in Wurttenberg, Germany, who immigrated to the United States in 1881. Arriving with just 50 cents in his pocket, Bertsch traveled first to Dubuque, Iowa, then to Chicago, and finally to Minneapolis in search of work. By 1893, Bertsch had found employment with the McCloud & Smith Furniture Company. In that same year, a new company was founded in Minneapolis, called the Rolph & Ball Furniture Co., which manufactured upholstery. In 1901, Bertsch, together with three employees from McCloud & Smith, bought Rolph & Ball, and renamed it Grau & Curtis Co., after two of the partners. Bertsch initially functioned as the company's director of upholstery. The company's first catalog was sent out in 1902; by the following year the catalog's 64 pages offered furniture not only for the home but also for commercial use in hotels, lounges, and churches. Already, however, the company's focus was on seating. By the end of its first decade, the company employed 22 people, who crafted and assembled its furniture by hand.

Frank Bertsch bought out his partners in 1917 and brought his son, Herbert T. Bertsch, into the company. The Grau & Curtis Co. next attempted to move into other areas of the furniture industry, purchasing a dining room and bedroom furniture maker during the 1920s. Although the company lost that plant during the 1929 stock market crash, the rest of the Bertsch business survived and, under the new name of Northome Furniture Industries in 1929, actually grew during the Great Depression. Part of the reason for this was its introduction of the ''flexsteel'' spring in its furniture designs.

The flexsteel spring was conceived initially by E. Werner Schlaprittzi while studying at the University of Zurich early in the 20th century. Schlaprittzi modeled it after the springs found in clocks, while also incorporating the springlike action of tree branches. He was able to sell the spring design for use in the seats of European railroad cars, and upon immigrating to the United States in 1918, he founded the Sanitas Spring Company in Minneapolis.

Nearby manufacturer Northome added the spring to its furniture designs in 1927, and soon purchased a 50 percent stake in

Company Perspectives:

Flexsteel Industries Inc. is committed to building its brand as a successful seating specialist. The company is committed to exceeding customer expectations. With emphasis on high quality Home Seating, Recreational Vehicle Seating, and Commercial Seating, Flexsteel will remain focused upon strengthening its product integrity and customer service programs, expanding its customer base, and profitably growing our business in order to increase shareholder value.

Sanitas Spring, which was renamed the Flexsteel Spring Corporation in 1934. From the beginning, Northome products featuring the Flexsteel spring carried an extended guarantee, initially for 25 years, and later for the lifetime of the product. In the 1990s, the company could boast that they still received trade-ins of furniture from this era.

Northome furniture continued to be built by hand until 1936. In that year, attempts at unionizing the company's workers led the Bertsches to relocate their operations to Dubuque, Iowa, where they purchased the former Brunswick Victrola plant, a 480,000-square-foot facility. For the new plant, the Bertsches decided to incorporate the line production techniques developed by the Ford Motor Company. Northome, which had to replace and retrain its entire production staff, was among the first in the furniture industry to incorporate the moving assembly line in their manufacturing process. Over the next decade, production jumped from one million to four million units per year. In 1946, the first company-owned trucks began delivering its furniture; by the 1990s, the Flexsteel fleet would grow to 350 trucks traveling ten million miles per year. In 1948, Frank Bertsch died, and Herbert Bertsch took over the company.

Company Expansion: 1950s–80s

Northome moved toward national distribution and greater expansion during the 1950s. The company built a second, 220,000-square-foot plant in Lancaster, Pennsylvania, in 1955. During that decade, Northome also initiated separate departments for design and development and for central engineering and rolled out its first national advertising campaign. By 1958, the Flexsteel spring had become so well known that the company renamed itself Flexsteel Industries Inc.

The company also kept up with the changes in furniture styles of the era. Through the 1920s and 1930s, mass market furniture styles had seen little change from the standard overstuffed Victorian design, but as the country emerged from World War II, furniture styles underwent dramatic and more frequent changes, from the simple look of the 1940s to the more dramatic styles of the 1950s.

By the mid-1960s, Flexsteel's revenues had topped $15 million per year. That decade saw the rise of the recliner, and Flexsteel began producing its own ''Flex-o-Lounger'' recliners and reclining mechanisms. During this time, the company also bought its first aircraft—turboprops, which it used to fly dealers to the company's factories. In 1965, Flexsteel created the Brunswick Converting Division for production and printing of its own ''space age'' nylon fabrics. The company also opened several more manufacturing plants and by the end of the decade expanded its line to include seating for the growing recreational vehicle (RV) market. The company went public in 1969, after posting a net income of $1.17 million on revenues of $25 million.

The company made a cash purchase of the National Furniture Manufacturing Co. in Evansville, Indiana, in 1970, and entered the exposed-wood furniture market with the introduction of its Charisma chair division. Flexsteel moved forward in RV seating, developing its own line of sofa sleepers specially scaled for the limited space requirements of mobile homes and other vehicles. By the end of the decade, the company had gained the entire seating and sleeping business for General Motors Corp. RVs. Flexsteel also brought in computerized automation to its production line, beginning in 1974 with the introduction of Gerber fabric cutting machines. These machines allowed far more precise cutting of fabrics, reducing waste while allowing more precise pattern matching. Sales climbed steadily through the decade, from $38.5 million in 1972 to more than $96 million in 1979. In that year, Flexsteel's net income reached nearly $4.5 million.

By then the third generation of Flexsteel's founders was leading the company, and the fourth generation was entering the business. The company opened a new plant in New Paris, Indiana, in 1982, moving part of its RV seating capacity closer to the van conversion center of Indiana. Flexsteel also opened showrooms, called Flexsteel Total Concept Galleries, the first of which was called Furniture Manor in Osseo, Minnesota; the company opened two factory showrooms as well. Recliner sales became a more important part of the business, particularly with Flexsteel's invention of an adjustable lumbar support mechanism. Then the company moved into a new market in 1984, creating its commercial seating division with a separate sales force and a product line for healthcare and other institutional settings. Sales increased throughout the 1980s, reaching $130 million in 1984, and $173 million in 1990.

Adapting to Recession Key to Continuing Success and Expansion in the 1990s

The onset of the recession of the early 1990s saw Flexsteel's revenues drop in 1991, to $145 million, and the company was forced to write off some $1.6 million in uncollectible accounts receivable, while downsizing reduced its employee rolls by more than 300 people. The following year, the company also took restructuring charges of approximately $2.6 million in connection with the closing of its Evansville plant, and the consolidation of its recliner and motion furniture production at its Dublin, Georgia plant. By 1992, however, Flexsteel was growing again, outpacing the furniture industry as a whole. Motion—or modular—furniture was helped by the company's newly designed latching mechanism. In 1992, Flexsteel rolled out its moderate-priced Grand Haven line of sofas, which hit the midrange price point of $599 to $699, compared with the typical Flexsteel sofa range of $799 to $999. Costs were trimmed for the new line not by skimping on scale, but rather by limiting the range; the Grand Haven line featured only two sofa styles available in 14 fabrics, compared with the 1,000 fabric choices available for the Flexsteel line.

Key Dates:

1893: The Rolph & Ball Furniture Company is founded.
1901: The company is renamed Grau & Curtis Co.
1902: The firm's first catalog is introduced.
1917: Bertsch buys out his partners and brings his son into the business.
1927: Flexsteel spring is added to furniture designs.
1929: The company is renamed Northome Furniture Industries.
1934: Sanitas Spring Company is renamed Flexsteel Spring Corporation.
1946: Company-owned trucks begin delivering furniture.
1955: A plant is established in Lancaster, Pennsylvania.
1958: The firm is renamed Flexsteel Industries Inc.
1965: The Brunswick Converting Division is created.
1970: National Furniture Manufacturing Co. is acquired.
1982: A plant begins operations in New Paris, Indiana.
1984: The Commercial Seating Division is established.
1991: Revenues drop due to a recession.
1993: The company celebrates its centennial and launches the Centennial Royale Collection.
1996: The Comfort Seating program is introduced.
1999: The company enters the Western U.S. market by opening a Comfort Seating Showroom in Arizona.
2000: The company is named one of *Forbes* ''200 Best Small Companies.''

Leather furniture was another growing part of Flexsteel's business, doubling in size through the early 1990s and accounting for more than 10 percent of its revenues. RV products were particularly strong, growing at 10 to 18 percent through 1994, and making up as much as 35 percent of total revenues. By 1993—the year the company celebrated its centennial—these had climbed again to $177 million, and reached $195 million in 1994. In addition, from a low of $1.2 million in 1991, net income rose to $6.8 million in 1994. International sales also began to play a stronger role for the company.

By 1995, Flexsteel had rebuilt its employee levels to nearly 2,400 workers. Revenues grew a modest 6.7 percent, however, to $208 million, as RV sales suffered from an economic slowdown. Flexsteel closed its Sweetwater, Tennessee plant and consolidated its Charisma contract line at the Starkville plant. Yet Flexsteel continued to invest in new technologies, including dealer-friendly video cataloguing and automated sales inquiry systems and computer-assisted design manufacturing techniques. The firm also spent $3.5 million for the expansion of its Starkville plant and a 20,000-square-foot addition to its Dubuque facility.

In 1996, Flexsteel launched its Comfort Seating program, a furniture display system based in a retail setting. These new showrooms displayed company furniture exclusively and allowed dealers an option to the traditional Flexsteel Gallery concept. The company also created the industry's first ready-to-assemble recliner and featured it at the year's North Carolina International Home Furnishings Market. Flexsteel ended 1996 with a 9 percent sales gain.

Flexsteel began aggressively pursuing its options in the recreational seating industry, specifically the marine segment, in the middle to late 1990s. In 1997, Flexsteel began supplying Carver Yachts with captain's chairs, sofas, and dinette chairs, for its motor yachts that were between 27 and 50 feet in length. As below-deck floorplans became more standardized in this segment, management felt that Flexsteel products would take hold in this industry as they had with RVs.

The company also was expanding with the continued growth of its showrooms. By February 1999, there were 14 Flexsteel Comfort Seating galleries in operation, primarily in the Midwest. Just seven months later, the largest store to date was opened in Scottsdale, Arizona. This move marked the firm's expansion into the Southwest; it also began marketing the Comfort Seating concept to dealers in the West Coast and Southeast areas. Flexsteel began expanding into the bedding industry as well. Restonic—the firm's long-time partner that produced mattresses for its sleeper sofa line—began to utilize the well-known Flexsteel steel support system in its box spring and marketed the line under the Legacy brand name.

Maintaining Stability in the New Millennium

The company entered the new millennium on steady ground. With no long-term debt and positive sales figures, Flexsteel remained ahead of many of its competitors with an average five-year growth rate of 7 percent. In the October 30, 2000 issue of *Forbes* magazine, the company was named one of the ''200 Best Small Companies'' for the first time in its history. The firm also remained on top of ever-changing consumer trends. For example, it shifted its merchandising techniques with its recliners to offer more fabrics, colors, and a variety of styles. John St. John, Flexsteel's merchandise manager for recliners, stated in a May 2000 *HFN* article that the company is ''growing the business to sell a more fashionable product because we're selling consumers who would not have ever bought a recliner before.''

By early 2001, however, a slowdown in spending due to faltering consumer confidence and a weakening economy began to slightly impact Flexsteel's revenue levels. Management believed the slowdown would be short-lived and planned to remain focused on growth opportunities in the retail furniture dealer market, recreational seating, and the hospitality and healthcare industries.

Principal Divisions

New Design; Flexsteel Commercial Seating; Flexsteel Home Furniture; Flexsteel Recreational Vehicle & Marine Seating.

Principal Competitors

Furniture Brands International Inc.; La-Z-Boy Inc.; LifeStyle Furnishings International Ltd.

Further Reading

''Beating the Traffic; Attendance May Have Been Down, But Vendors Said High Point Had the Write Stuff,'' *HFN-The Weekly Newspaper for the Home Furnishings Network,* October 30, 2000, p. 30.

Brin, Geri, ''Flexible Flexsteel,'' *HFD-The Weekly Home Furnishings Newspaper,* April 6, 1992, p. 28.

Buchanan, Lee, ''Flexsteel Goes West with Retail Rollout,'' *HFN-The Weekly Newspaper for the Home Furnishings Network,* September 13, 1999, p. 22.

A Century of Seating Craftsmanship, Dubuque, Ia.: Flexsteel Industries, Inc., 1993.

''Corporate Profile for Flexsteel Industries Inc.,'' *Business Wire,* December 15, 2000.

''Flexsteel Industries,'' *Hospitality Design,* March 2000, p. 200.

Flexsteel Industries Inc., ''America's Seating Specialist: Our History,'' Dubuque, Ia.: Flexsteel Industries Inc., 2000.

Kunkel, Karl, ''Flexsteel Gets into Bedding,'' *HFN-The Weekly Newspaper for the Home Furnishings Network,* April 24, 2000, p. 28.

——, ''Flexsteel Rolls Out Comfort Seating Stores,'' *HFN-The Weekly Newspaper for the Home Furnishings Network,* February 1, 1999, p. 31.

Kurowski, Jeff, ''Flexsteel Looking for More Marine Industry Customers,'' *Boating Industry,* February 1998, p. 13.

Levine, Charlotte, ''Flexsteel Celebrates 100th Anniversary,'' *Central Penn Business Journal,* May 5, 1993, p. 12.

Schroeder, Angel, ''Designer Recliners; Fashionable Recliners Are Broadening the Category and Expanding Price Points,'' *HFN-The Weekly Newspaper for the Home Furnishings Network,* May 22, 2000, p. 24.

—M.L. Cohen
—update: Christina M. Stansell

Flint Ink Corporation

4600 Arrowhead Drive
Ann Arbor, Michigan 48105
U.S.A.
Telephone: (734) 622-6000
Fax: (734) 622-6060
Web site: http://www.flintink.com

Private Company
Incorporated: 1920 as Howard Flint Ink Company
Employees: 3,500
Sales: $1.2 billion (1999 est.)
NAIC: 32591 Printing Ink Manufacturing

Flint Ink Corporation is the largest American-owned manufacturer of printing inks, inkjet inks, and toners, for newspaper, directory, magazine, packaging, commercial, and digital printing applications. Moreover, the company is the second-largest ink producer in the world and among the top ten privately held corporations in Michigan. Flint Ink operates 100 facilities worldwide. CDR Pigments & Dispersions—owned and operated by Flint Ink—is an industry leader in colorants manufacturing, while CDR International serves the European flushed color market. The Flint Ink Research Center in Ann Arbor, Michigan, provides state-of-the-art product research, environmental testing, and support.

Early History and Expansion

Flint Ink was founded in 1920 in Detroit, Michigan, by H. Howard Flint as the Howard Flint Ink Company. Initially a one-man operation supplying ink to local newspapers, the company grew quickly and steadily, with Flint's sons Edgar and Robert eventually joining the enterprise. From its earliest years, the Flint sought to develop new technologies and utilized quality control methods to test raw materials and finished products; his was the first ink company to do so. The year 1922 saw the company's first tanker truck delivery of letterpress news ink. In 1926, Flint Ink opened its first branch in Indianapolis, which was followed by the opening of four additional branches over the next decade. The company acquired Temple Inks Company of Denver in 1936—the same year its sales hit the $1 million mark.

By the 1940s, Flint Ink had equipped all of its branches with full quality control and formulation labs and established rigid product specifications. One of its subsidiaries, California Ink Company (Cal/Ink), became the first U.S. company to make and market lithol red pigments. Cal/Ink over the next decade would develop the nation's first magnetic inks for check imprinting.

During this time, leadership of Flint Ink was gradually ceded to the second generation of Flints; Robert Flint was named secretary/treasurer of the company after his service during World War II, and by 1950 he was named vice-president of operations. Founder H. Howard Flint remained chief operating officer (COO), while eldest son Edgar was company president. With its holdings increasing and its role in the industry becoming more prominent, the company changed its name to Flint Ink Corporation in 1957. Within three years, the company had expanded into the publication gravure business, a process used by publishers desiring the highest quality color reproductions for long run applications.

In 1966, Edgar Flint succeeded his father as COO. Two years later, Flint Ink made the first tanker delivery of offset news ink, and in 1969, the company introduced the use of alkaline fountain solutions for newspaper printing. In 1975, Flint Ink acquired Cal/Ink and opened a state-of-the-art gravure facility in New Albany, Indiana. A joint venture between Flint Ink and Sun-Fast Color in 1977 made Flint Mexicana, S.A., de C.V. the second-largest ink manufacturer in Mexico. The next year Flint Ink pioneered the use of conductivity to monitor the concentration of fountain solution, and in 1979, the company made its first tanker delivery of offset color news inks.

Chromatic Color, another subsidiary, was incorporated in 1980 and began producing dry and flushed color. Two years later, Robert H. Flint succeeded his brother Edgar as president and CEO. Flint Ink acquired Drew Graphics, Inc., a manufacturer of water dispersions for the ink, paper, paint, and coatings industries in 1984. The following year marked the completion of the company's second varnish plant, furthering Flint Ink's

Company Perspectives:

Our mission is to be a leader in global manufacturing and distribution of quality inks, colorants, supplies, and expert support services to the graphic arts industry and other color consumers.

move toward vertical integration. Flint Ink acquired Capitol Printing Ink Company in 1986, providing a larger presence on the East Coast.

Late 1980s Focus on Research and Quality

In 1987, Robert H. Flint was elected chairman and CEO, while the founder's grandson, H. Howard Flint II, was elected president and COO, ushering in the third generation of managerial Flints. That same year Flint Ink was a majority participant in a leveraged buyout of the Sinclair & Valentine Division of Allied-Signal. The acquisition provided Flint Ink with ownership of the fourth-largest manufacturer in the commercial and packaging printing ink segments. The Sinclair & Valentine Division included David M, Ridgway Color, the S & V Canadian unit, and S & V Screen Inks.

Another important milestone reached in 1987 was the completion of the Flint Ink Research Center, a 72,000-square-foot research facility in Ann Arbor, Michigan. The research center was established to develop new technology to confront the challenges faced by the printing industry, including the availability and cost of raw materials, environmental protection, and the computerization of press-side and pre-press operations. Researchers sought to develop proprietary raw materials that offered greater performance as well as environmental and economic value. Chemists at the center investigated new inks with the characteristics necessary for optimum performance on new substrates, on higher-speed computerized presses, and with developing press and plate chemistry. Extensive research led to ''environmentally friendly'' alternatives in ink technology, utilizing vegetable oils or water in place of traditional petroleum or solvent ingredients.

Building upon the company's history of quality control and quality assurance methods, Flint Ink embarked on ''The Flint Ink Quality Journey'' in 1987. The journey employed the principles and techniques of continuous quality improvement, and re-emphasized long-term quality partnerships with customers and suppliers. A comprehensive training program began to provide managers and employees alike with problem-solving techniques, testing procedures, and statistical methods. Milestones along the journey included the following: statistical methods were used to monitor ink batch specifications; product quality certification procedures were put in place; computerized color matching in branch sites insured that every custom match was completed quickly and accurately; improvements in delivery methods and scheduling permitted just-in-time delivery to minimize inventories; and quality partnerships were established with both customers and suppliers to increase awareness of needs, define common goals, set specifications, improve communications, and resolve problems.

Continued Growth in the 1990s

Flint Ink was reorganized in 1991, consolidating several subsidiary firms under the Flint Ink umbrella. S & V Printing Ink, Capitol Printing Ink, and Cal/Ink began operating under the Flint Ink Corporation name. Chromatic Color, Ridgway Color, and Drew Graphics began operating as CDR Pigments & Dispersions. S & V Screen of Canada became Flint Ink Corporation of Canada, and S & V Screen Inks became Summit Screen Inks. In addition, LeMaster Litho Supply was acquired.

Flint Ink continued to be a leader in the area of environmentally friendly products, including low-rub, soy oil-based newspaper inks. In 1991, the firm introduced AGRI-TEK vegetable-oil based inks for commercial sheetfed and folding carton applications. The company by that time had a fully staffed Environmental Services Department that evaluated and addressed regulatory issues as they affected Flint Ink products and customer applications. A 1992 article in Crain's Detroit Business, ''Flint Ink's Future Is Printed in Soybeans,'' reported that the company was producing soy- and water-based inks in anticipation that the use of traditional petroleum-based inks would diminish under environmental pressures. Chairman/CEO Robert Flint predicted that mounting environmental regulations for air quality, pollution, and hazardous waste would spur the shift away from petroleum toward alternative materials, noting, ''I think, maybe, by the turn of the century, we're going to see the end of petroleum inks.''

Robert Flint retired his positions as chairman and CEO in 1992, but continued to serve as chairman of the executive board, which now was comprised of four directors from outside the Flint family. Two years later a fifth non-family member was elected to the board, bringing the membership to 11. In 1994, Flint Ink opened its first offices overseas, including a sales office in Singapore to explore entry into Pacific Rim markets. CDR Pigments & Dispersions established CDR International and opened a sales office in Brussels to expand into the European market. The company also acquired outstanding shares of Flint Mexicana, assuming full ownership.

In 1994, the corporation also acquired Rendic International, a Miami-based distributor of graphic arts supplies, in order to strengthen the ink manufacturer's position in South America and the Far East. Rendic International had marketed printing inks, blankets, and printing presses outside of the United States for Flint Ink Corporation and Rockwell International for more than a decade. The company's president, Jerko E. Rendik, was asked to stay on to help Flint Ink continue to expand its export business. Rendic noted that he believed his company's familiarity with South America and the Pacific Rim made it a good fit with Flint Ink's plan for growth in the world market.

In another major initiative, Flint Ink completed the purchase of North American Printing Ink Company, with plants in Elgin and Salem, Illinois. According to Chairman Howard Flint II, the move was expected to enhance the company's ability to service large heatset publication printers. NAPIC had specialized in the manufacture of heatset inks for use in magazine printing. Since its founding in 1978, the company had achieved a major position as a supplier to publication printing plants throughout the United States. Under the terms of the agreement, NAPIC re-

Key Dates:

1920: H. Howard Flint sets up the Howard Flint Ink Company in Detroit.
1926: The firm opens a branch in Indianapolis.
1936: Sales reach $1 million and the company acquires the Temple Inks Company.
1957: The firm changes its name to Flint Ink Corporation.
1969: Company introduces alkaline fountains solutions for newspaper printing.
1975: Flint Ink acquires the California Ink Company.
1987: Construction on the research center in Ann Arbor, Michigan, is completed.
1991: The firm restructures operations, and CDR Pigments & Dispersions is created.
1997: Flint Ink North America and Flint Ink Latin America are created.
1998: Flint Ink Europe is established with the purchase of Manders Premier in the United Kingdom.

mained a separate business unit, operating within Flint Ink's Publication Ink Group.

Flint Ink of Canada purchased Lester Ink and Coatings Company in 1994 to provide Flint Ink with much-needed sheetfed manufacturing capacity. Flint Ink of Canada president Dan Keough stated that Lester's well-established reputation for excellent quality in the products it manufactures and the company's leadership in the commercial sheetfed market will give Flint Ink added presence in that important market segment. Lester Inks and Coatings had sales offices in Montreal, Vancouver, and Calgary, in addition to its 60,000-square-foot manufacturing site in Toronto.

Flint Ink was named the winner of the 1994 Distribution/ Nasstrac LTL Shipper of the Year Award, according to an article in Distribution magazine. ''By helping its more than 70 LTL carriers improve their operations, the Detroit-based manufacturer of printing inks has actively spread the quality message among carrier and shipper channels,'' the article stated. ''Flint Ink has simplified its shipping process for field supervisors by creating a routing software package; centralized its traffic function to coordinate transportation operations for its manufacturing locations; hired certified hazardous materials instructors to train staff; developed its own rate base to insure fair bidding; implemented contracts with all its TL and LTL carriers; and developed quality programs that are compatible with ISO 9000 standards.''

In the company's ongoing quest to develop environmentally friendly processes, Flint Ink announced in 1995 an exclusive distribution agreement with Unichema International to market Unichema's PRIFER 3303+ low-VOC, non-volatile roller and blanket wash for sheetfed lithographic inks. The agreement was reached after testing by Flint Ink showed the vegetable-based wash to combine environmental benefits, commercial practicality, and effective cleaning capabilities. According to Leonard Walle, Flint Ink's director of marketing, pressure has increased to reduce emissions in order to avoid operating permit requirements. ''One of the most significant areas for potential reduction is the chemicals used for cleaning press rollers and blankets—chemicals which have traditionally been petroleum-based and very high in VOCs,'' he stated. Walle noted that control technique guidelines for offset lithographic printers set forth by the EPA in September 1993 recommended the use of cleaning solutions that do not contain any hazardous air pollutants and have less than 30 percent VOC by weight in their useable form.

In an effort to help customers achieve lower emissions, Flint Ink tested a number of environmentally friendly press washes to determine which offered reduced VOCs while at the same time giving cleaning results comparable to conventional cleaners. Extensive testing settled upon a product that was cost-effective, safe, and non-volatile.

Despite an increase in paper prices that negatively affected the ink industry in 1995, and a patent infringement suit concerning the firm's use of soy ink, Flint Ink recorded increased sales in 1996. Flint Ink's continued leadership in promoting environmental awareness, investment in research, commitment to quality, and steady growth, had it well positioned for continued growth. Dedicated to European expansion, the firm began a joint venture with Coates Lorilleux in Spain to manufacture flush color. It also acquired certain units of BASF Corporation's North American Graphics Group, and sold its David M division and its Summit Screen business during this time period.

The company continued to restructure itself in 1997 in a manner conducive to international growth. Its Commercial/ Packaging Ink operations, its Publication Ink Group, and Flint Ink of Canada, became Flint Ink North America, and Flint Ink Latin America was created and included the businesses of Rendic International and Flint Ink Mexicana Srl de CV.

International Development: Late 1990s and Beyond

In 1998, the firm acquired Manders Premier, a leading manufacturer of inks based in the United Kingdom. The deal, which marked an important push into the European inks market, resulted in the establishment of Flint Ink Europe division, to oversee operations in that geographic area. The company also launched Flint Ink Asia/Pacific to cover business dealings in that region. Sales for the year topped $1 billion.

Flint Ink continued its growth by acquisition strategy in 1999. Standing as the second largest ink producer—behind Sun Chemical Corporation—and controlling 9 percent of the market, Flint Ink successfully faced the problems plaguing the global inks industry. Low profitability, increased competition, and overcapacity had been causing consolidation throughout the industry, and Flint Ink was positioned to take advantage of the situation. It purchased The Ink Company based in West Sacramento, California, in order to gain increased market share in the United States. The firm also beefed up its Latin American operations with the acquisition of Polychem SA, a packaging ink manufacturer based in Argentina, and Companhia Quimica Industrial Brasiliera, an ink manufacturer based in Brazil. During this purchasing spree, Flint Ink moved its world headquarters from Detroit to Ann Arbor, Michigan, presumably to be closer to its state-of-the-art Technology Park research facility.

The company continued its expansion into the new millennium. Alper Ink Group L.L.C. was acquired and secured Flint Ink's leading position in the North American ink market. The company also purchased Creanova Ink Pty Ltd. of Australia. The deal made Flink Ink Asia/Pacific the second-largest ink manufacturer in Australia.

Along with its focus on acquisitions, the firm's management team also concentrated on new product development. Michael Gannon, Flint Ink CFO and senior vice-president, stated in a *Crain's Detroit Business* article that, ''all of these acquisitions are really good stuff, but at the same time, we need to grow internally and come up with new products that add value and are competitive in the marketplace.'' Doing just that, the firm launched GlobaLink, a color replication system, and SFI, a single fluid ink technology concept that allowed offset printing without the use of fountain solution. The company also introduced the Gemini Ultraviolet Ink system, which enabled printers to produce UV-quality print.

In January 2000, Robert Flint, son of the company's founder and an influential leader at Flint Ink throughout most of the century's expansion, died. Remarking on his uncle's role at Flint Ink, chairman and CEO H. Howard Flint II observed: ''In some ways, Bob's passing marks the end of an era for Flint Ink Corporation. In other ways his influence be felt for many years to come. He had the respect and admiration of his family, his employees, and the industry as a whole, and he will be missed.''

Growth at Flint Ink continued apace. In 2001, INKS-Chemicals B&T SA, a Venezuelan paste ink manufacturer, was purchased. Management continued to actively seek out acquisition opportunities and focus on product and technology innovation as a means of remaining competitive in the consolidating ink industry. As part of the *Forbes* top 220 Private Companies in the United States, Flint Ink was well positioned for future growth.

Principal Divisions

Flint Ink America; Flint Ink Europe; Flint Ink Latin America.

Principal Operating Units

CDR Pigments & Dispersions.

Principal Competitors

Sun Chemical Corporation; Toyo Ink Manufacturing Co. Ltd.; Nazdar.

Further Reading

''Flint Ink Corporation,'' *Canadian Packaging*, May 2000, p. 9.
''Flint Ink Expands in Latin America,'' *Paper, Film & Foil Converter*, March 2000, p. 46B.
Green, Leslie, ''Flint Ink Absorbs Rival, Adds Market Share,'' *Crain's Detroit Business*, November 1, 1999, p. 3.
——, ''Flint Ink Solidifies its No. 2 Spot; Purchase of Pair of Ink Companies Adds to Market Share,'' *Crain's Detroit Business*, June 5, 2000, p. 3.
''Ink Expansion,'' *Graphic Arts Monthly,* December 1999, p. 31.
King, Angela, ''Flint Ink's Future Is Printed in Soybeans,'' *Crain's Detroit Business*, August 31, 1992, p. 3.
''New Offices,'' *Paperboard Packaging*, March 1999, p. 54.
''Printing Inks Market Consolidates,'' *Chemical Market Reporter*, September 20, 1999, p. 17.
Savastano, David, ''Building a Successful Legacy,'' *Ink World,* August 1992.
——, ''Flint Ink Acquires The Ink Company,'' *Ink World,* November 1999.
Schmitt, Ben, ''Robert Flint: Led Ink Firm into Global Marketplace,'' *Detroit Free Press,* January 11, 2000.
Serwach, Joseph, ''Flint Ink Appealing Patent Ruling,'' *Crain's Detroit Business*, June 17, 1996, p. 3.
Thomas, Jim, ''The Color of Excellence,'' *Distribution*, September 1994, pp. 42+.
''UV Ink System,'' *American Printer*, December 2000, p. 82.
Walsh, Kerri, ''Flint Acquires Manders,'' *Chemical Week*, January 7, 1998, p. 45.

—Pamela Berry
—update: Christina M. Stansell

FRENCH CONNECTION

French Connection Group plc

60 Great Portland Street
London W1N 5AJ
United Kingdom
Telephone: (44) 20 7399 7200
Fax: (44) 20 7399 7201
Web site: http://www.frenchconnection.com

Public Company
Incorporated: 1969 as Mark Stephens London Ltd.
Employees: 1,718
Sales: £193.6 million ($309.76 million)(2001)
Stock Exchanges: London
Ticker Symbol: FCCN
NAIC: 422330 Women's, Children's, and Infants' Clothing and Accessories Wholesalers; 448150 Clothing Accessories Stores

French Connection Group plc is a leading retailer and wholesaler of its own in-house clothing and accessories designs. Led by its founder, Stephen Marks, French Connection has made waves—and profits—with its controversial advertising campaigns built on its French Connection U.K. acronym. The company backs the edginess of its advertising with trendy and trendsetting high-end clothing designs, and since the late 1990s has extended placed its brand name on products ranging from grooming products created by Boots to watches by Timex. French Connection is the holding company for two strong brands—the youth-oriented FCUK and the high-end Nicole Farhi brand, targeting an older, more affluent, yet still fashion-conscious market. Both FCUK and Nicole Farhi are supported by company-owned retail networks, totaling some 100 stores in the United Kingdom, the United States, and Canada. The company also manages a wider franchise and concessions network bringing its fashions into more than 1,500 venues worldwide. At the beginning of the new century, French Connection has targeted especially the North American and Japanese markets for future growth. The company acquired full control of its U.S.-based joint venture, the Best of All Clothing (BOAC), in 2001 and had already established some 20 retail shops in that country, including a new flagship stores in San Francisco. French Connection expected to open as many as 300 retail stores in the United States in the early years of the new century. The company is also joining with a Japanese partner to expand into the Japanese market and opened a flagship store in Tokyo in 2001. Back home, the company unveiled its largest store, on London's Oxford Street, featuring 14,000 square feet of selling space. Wholesale accounts for slightly more than half of the company's £193 million in 2001 revenue. The company has been traded on the London Stock Exchange since 1986.

Hairdresser's Son to Hotpants King in the 1970s

Stephen Marks grew up in the Harrow area of north London, helping out his father in his hairdresser's shop and leaving school at the age of 16. Marks's initial interest was in playing tennis—in 1964, at the age of 18, he won the junior's title at Wimbledon. Tennis back then was still an amateur sport, however, and Marks looked about for ways to earn a living. Having seen how hard his father had to work, Marks sought a different career direction. As Marks told the *Independent:* ''My father used to leave home at 6:30 a.m. and get back at 9 p.m., 11 p.m. on Saturdays,'' earning ''enough to give us a comfortable life, but not that comfortable.''

Marks went to work for a clothing manufacturer run by a family friend. There, as Marks told the *Guardian*, ''they gave me the most wonderful training, although I didn't realise it at the time, learning about everything from cloth buying to designing.'' Toward the end of the 1960s, Marks left the coat manufacturer for clothing designer and manufacturer Louis Feraud. Marks was behind the successful launch of the company's Miss Feraud label. That success led Feraud's management to offer Marks a position as a director of the company. Marks described the appointment to the *Guardian:* ''I asked if that meant I got a share of the company and they said: 'No, you just get called a director.' That made me very depressed, because I wanted to get on in life. I didn't care what I was called.''

A friend came to the aid of the depressed Marks, suggesting that he go into business for himself and promised financial backing for Marks's new venture. In 1969, Marks struck out on his

Company Perpectives:

Whether it shocks you or amuses you, fcuk certainly makes you think.

own, establishing Stephen Marks London Ltd. with just £17,000. The clothing was designed by Marks, who was joined in the business by a pattern cutter and an accountant. Marks described his own role in the new company to the *Independent on Sunday* as that of "a salesman who 'had a sense of what was right and what was wrong,' who used to 'botch a collection together and sell it.' " Marks quickly displayed a flair for fashion—or at least a commercially successful fashion trend. On a trip to Paris, he discovered the newest French fashion phenomenon, hotpants. "I came back to London, had some run up and showed them to a buyer at Miss Selfridge," Marks told the *Guardian*, "She took 36 pairs and sold them all in a day. She came back for 2,000 pairs, and I became the Hotpants King." By the end of its first year, the company had posted sales of £180,000.

Marks launched his own label, designing a line of suits and coats, although he was to become especially known for his youth-oriented fashions. By 1972, Marks's designs were generating £700,000 in revenues. In that year, Marks traveled to Hong Kong. "Once I saw Hong Kong I realised the potential of the Far East," Marks told the *Guardian*, It was like a shining light in terms of price and quality. And so French Connection was born."

Marks then entered the retail arena, opening a furniture and clothing shop, called Cane, then a second store, also in London, called Friends. The French Connection brand name came in the 1970s as Marks contracted to sell his designs through the Top Shop retail chain. Joining Marks was a freelance designer, Nicole Farhi, who became his companion and mother of his first child—and then the company's chief designer. "She was always criticizing my designs and saying she could do better. So in the end I said 'bloody get on with it then,' and she did," Marks told the *Guardian*. Farhi not only handled the youth-oriented designs for the French Connection label, she also began to produce designs under her own name for an older, wealthier women's market.

French Connection soon became the company's retail store brand, as Marks began to open new stores in London and then throughout the United Kingdom. The Nicole Farhi brand was also transformed into its own retail format, yet French Connection remained the company's flagship brand. In 1984, the company turned toward the United States, partnering with American Michael Axelrod in a 50–50 joint venture Best of All Clothes (BOAC). The joint venture's role leaned especially toward wholesale sales of the French Connection brand, rather than a retail expansion of the company's store format. Two years later, as French Connection prepared to boost its expansion in the United Kingdom, the company listed on the London Stock Exchange.

Controversial Success for the New Century

At the end of the decade, however, French Connection appeared to be on the brink of disaster. The company had been caught up short by the beginning of a new recession that affected not only the United Kingdom, but also the company's growing activities in the United States. Despite holding two-thirds of the company's shares, Marks resigned from the CEO chair in 1989, a position taken up by Michael Shen. By then too, Marks's personal relationship with Farhi had ended, although they remained business partners. Threatened with the loss of his majority share and in order to rescue the company of he had founded from collapse, Marks lent French Connection more than £3.5 million.

Arguments with Shen led Marks to take back the CEO position in 1991. Marks set to work rebuilding the company, bringing it back into renewed profit growth by mid-decade. Marks's personal fortunes also received a boost, when Hard Rock Café, in which he had been one of the original financial backers and retained the second-largest holding of shares, was sold to the Rank Organization, allowing Marks to pocket a strong share of the £300 million purchase price. By 1996, his company's operations were also growing, now reaching 30 retail stores in the United Kingdom—primarily under the French Connection name, but also under the Nicole Farhi signage—and 11 stores in the United States. That year the company was also able to pay out its first stock dividends since 1991. Yet the company's strongest expansion was still ahead.

Until the mid-1990s, French Connection had operated more or less without an advertising budget. In 1997, the company turned to the then independent Trevor Beattie (who was shortly to form his own TBWA advertising agency) for assistance. Beattie quickly spotted opportunity in the company's own name. French Connection's United Kingdom office had long been addressing its correspondence with its Hong Kong office using the acronyms from FCUK to FCHK. The FCUK acronym had also been used in the company's stores. But Beattie took the acronym and turned it into a U.K. sensation.

After an initial series of deliberately provocative ads, featuring models wearing "fcuk fashion," the company rolled out a new and more playful billboard and press campaign, playing on the garbled appeal of the FCUK logo with such taglines as "I you want," and "night all long." Complaints from, among others, the Church of England (for the company's "fcuk Christmas" campaign), brought the company under investigation from the U.K.'s Advertising Standards Association.

The controversy surrounding French Connections new advertising campaign helped put the company into high gear. Backed by a string of strong clothing designs, French Connection's sales took off, reaching £83 million in 1997 and topping £117 million by 1999. The company quickly added new stores, boosting its total number of French Connection and Nicole Farhi stores to more than 100 by the end of the decade. The company's wholesale arm was also performing strongly, adding a number of foreign concessions in countries such as Australia, Holland, the Scandinavian market, Singapore and Hong Kong, and Saudi Arabia and Dubai.

Until then, French Connection had built a strong, albeit niche, position in the United States. The success of the FCUK campaign gave the company a new base from which to attack the U.S. market—traditionally resistant to foreign retailers. By

Key Dates:

1969: Mark Stephens launches Mark Stephens London Ltd.
1972: Stephens opens his first retail store.
1984: The company launches the French Connection label in the United States through joint venture with Best of all Clothing (BOAC).
1986: The company is listed on the London Stock Exchange.
1989: Mark Stephens gives up the position of CEO.
1991: Mark Stephens becomes the CEO again.
1997: The company launches the of first FCUK campaign.
2000: The company signs a partnership agreement with D'Urban Inc. in Japan.
2001: The company acquires 100 percent of BOAC and opens the first store in Tokyo.

the end of 2000, the company's expansion in the United States led it to forecast growing to as many as 300 retail stores in that country—with immediate plans to expand to nearly 60 stores there by 2004. To consolidate its growth in the United States, the company acquired the 50 percent of the BOAC joint venture it did not own in 2001. As Stephen Marks told the press, ''Acquiring 100 percent ownership of our US business is an important milestone for our global brand strategy. We believe that complete ownership will enable us to maximise French Connection's potential as it enters the next stage of its development in the US.''

Meanwhile, French Connection had for some time been eyeing the Japanese market. In 2001, the company opened its first store in that market in Tokyo, teaming up with a local partner, D'Urban, Inc., for a three-year partnership. The company expected to open up two more Japanese stores before the end of the year and use that country as a springboard for expansion throughout the Far East.

French Connection made no secret of its plans to develop into a globally operating retailer, raising its French Connection and Nicole Farhi brands to true international status. The company's advertisements continued to draw criticism and complaints—and customers. By the end of its 2001 fiscal year, the company's sales had topped £193 million. In early 2001, the company was delighted to discover that its latest campaign, dubbed 'fcukinkybugger' had been banned from the British national television—the company immediately launched a web site featuring the full-length advertisement. The hundreds of thousands of teenagers sporting the company's ''FCUK ME'' tee shirts gave Mark Stephens and French Connection a strong base on which to bet its future growth.

Principal Subsidiaries

French Connection Retail Ltd.; French Connection Ltd.; NF Restaurants Ltd.; French Connection (Hong Kong) Ltd.; Toast (Mail Order) Ltd. (75%); Stephen Marks (London) Ltd.; French Connection 2000 Sarl (France); French Connection No.2 Pour Hommes Sarl (France); French Connection (Canada) Ltd. (75%); Stephen Marks (New York) Inc.; Nicoles Café LLC (U.S.); PreTex Textilhandels GmbH (Germany); Best of All Clothing Ltd. (U.S.); BOAC Ltd. (U.S.); Lousiana Connection Ltd. (U.S.; 50%); Roosevelt Connection Ltd. (U.S.; 50%); Soho Connection Ltd. (U.S.; 50%); Westwood Connection Ltd. (U.S.; 50%).

Principal Competitors

Abercrombie & Fitch Company; Arcadia Group plc; Benetton Group S.p.A.; Diesel SpA; Esprit Holdings Limited; Guess?, Inc.; H&M Hennes & Mauritz AB; Hot Topic, Inc.; Marks and Spencer plc; New Look Group plc; NEXT plc; The Gap, Inc.

Further Reading

Benady, David, ''FCUK America,'' *Marketing*, March 22, 2001.
D'Silva, Beverley, ''Stephen Marks: No Marks for Subtlety,'' *Independent*, August 8, 1998, p. 16.
Finch, Julia, ''Oh So Pretty Blatant,'' *Guardian*, March 31, 2001 .
''Four-Letter Fashion,'' *Independent on Sunday*, April 4, 1999, p. 3.
''French Connection Buys Rest of US Business,'' *Reuters*, February 20, 2001.
Garrett, Jade, ''Sold on Bare-Faced Chic,'' *Independent*, March 20, 2001, p. 8.
Jardine, Alexandra, ''Style Offensive,'' *Marketing*, April 5, 2001.
Rankine, Kate, ''Cool, Calm and Connected,'' *Daily Telegraph*, October 31, 1998, p. 33.

—M.L. Cohen

Freudenberg

Freudenberg & Co.

D-69465 Weinheim
Germany
Telephone: +49 6201-805808
Fax: +49 6201-883430
Web site: http://www.freudenberg.com

Private Company
Incorporated: 1849 as Carl Freudenberg, Weinheim
Employees: 29,667
Sales: DM 7.08 billion ($3.5 billion) (1999)
NAIC: 316999 All Other Leather Good Manufacturing; 332999 All Other Miscellaneous Fabricated Metal Product Manufacturing; 3363 Motor Vehicle Parts Manufacturing

Weinheim, Germany's Freudenberg & Co. is a private partnership owned by the nearly 300 members of the founding Freudenberg family and acting as a holding company for a vast and diversified manufacturing and engineering company with global operations ranging from high-quality leather to nonwoven textiles to seals for the automotive and other industries. Freudenberg oversees a network of nearly 200 German and international companies, many of which are operated as joint ventures, including long-standing partnerships such as Freudenberg-NOK and its United States branch Freudenberg NOK GP, in partnership with Japan's NOK Corporation (in which Freudenberg holds a significant minority share as well). Another longtime partnership is the Freudenberg & Vilene Nonwovens joint venture with Japan Vilene Company Ltd. Freudenberg's operations are grouped under several business groups: Seals and Vibration Control Technology Europe and Seals and Vibration Control Technology North America; Nonwovens; Freudenberg Politex Nonwovens; Specialty Lubricants, notably through Klüber Lubrication; Building Systems; Household Products, including Vileda, Enka, and Wettex-branded products; and Technical Distributors. Business groups handle global responsibility for their operations. In addition, Freudenberg operates a number of divisions, which report directly to the parent company: Flexible PCBs, through Freudenberg Mektec; Soft-Running Rolls; Industrial Procurement; Leather, the company's founding activity; and Jela children's shoes. The company sold its Elefant children's shoes business to Clarks Shoes of England in 2001. The Seals and Vibration Control business groups combine to provide more than DM 3.4 billion of the company's DM 7.08 billion in sales in 1999. The next-largest business sector is Nonwovens, which added DM 1.44 billion. Europe, including primary market Germany, accounts for some 61 percent of sales, with North America adding nearly 31 percent of sales. The company's operations are guided by "spokesman" Peter Bettermann.

Leather Innovator in the 19th Century

Carl Johann Freudenberg joined with Heinrich Christian Heintze to take over a tannery in Weinheim, Germany. Freudenberg gave the company his name in 1849 and led the company in the development of a variety of leather products, especially patent and satin leathers. Freudenberg's son Hermann Ernst Freudenberg joined the family business and, at the turn of the century, began experimenting with a newly discovered tanning process, using chrome liquor instead of traditional plant-based dyes. The chrome tanning process offered much greater speed in what had been a long and tedious business, and Freudenberg became the first company in Europe to introduce the new technology.

The company quickly became the leading tanner in Europe, with exports to other countries topping two-thirds of the company's total production. Yet the outbreak of World War I and the subsequent economic upheavals not only eliminated the company's export markets but forced a near-collapse of the leather industry. By then led by the third generation, Freudenberg determined to branch out into a new direction, wagering on a new product line while waiting for the leather market to return to health.

The company focused on its readily available supply of scrap leather and other by-products, seeking new uses for these materials. The development of industrial machinery and the internal combustion and other engine types, and their need for sealing systems, gave Freudenberg a new market in the 1920s.

Company Perspectives:

1. The Freudenberg Group must remain broadly diversified; it is this structure which lends it its valuable stability. In belonging to the group as a whole, the various business operations gain a special, shared identity and a support permitting them to gear their strategy to long-term planning. 2. The Freudenberg Group must remain a 100 percent family enterprise. This means a high equity capitalization of at least 40 percent is essential. This in turn necessitates not only adequate profitability, but also a proper balance between capital investments and cash flow. 3. The group is open to joint ventures with other companies, if these will usefully complement or further strengthen our business operations. Relationships with our associates in these ventures must be based on fairness and personal trust. 4. The Freudenberg Group has its headquarters at the original Weinheim location, which forms part of its identity, and where substantial resources of knowledge, tradition and infrastructure are gathered in one place. Weinheim is to remain a significant production location in the future as well. This requires that the Weinheim-based facilities, like all the others at home and abroad, hold their own against their competitors in terms of performance and costs.

Until then, most seals found in Europe came from the United States and made use of leather skirts to form the packing for the seal. Freudenberg began producing its own version of the seal. Freudenberg, with Walter Simmer as head of this project, also worked on perfecting the design of the seal. By packing the leather bushing inside a metal housing, adding a spring to maintain tension, the company had created a mechanical breakthrough.

The company debuted its patented Simmerring radial shaft ring in 1929, setting an industry standard. The original leather used proved too fragile for the intense demands placed on the seal and in 1936 the company developed a synthetic rubber replacement. The new version of the Simmerring became an indispensable component used across a wide range of industries and products. During this time, the company incorporated as a family-owned partnership to accommodate the growing number of Freudenberg family members. The Simmerring and the company's leather products once again brought Freudenberg to the international market, and the company opened production facilities in Switzerland, France, Austria, and Great Britain. Much of the company's foreign operations were to be shut down by the outbreak of World War II, however.

Freudenberg's successful diversification encouraged the company to extend its operations into other new directions. One of the company's biggest successes came when its engineers, including Ludwig Nottebohm, developed the so-called staple-fiber nonwovens, a new method of creating high-resistant fabrics and materials without using traditional weaving techniques. The nonwovens proved useful for such applications as clothing, handbag, and luggage linings and interlinings; industrial applications such as filters and insulation; protective coverings for plants; and medical uses, such as bandages, and personal hygiene—most famously, disposable diapers. Freudenberg introduced its first staple-fiber nonwovens in 1948, marketing the Vileda Window Cloth and other household products using the Vileda brand name and interlinings under the Vlieseline brand name.

The company's growing expertise in a wide range of materials was extended again in 1949 when the company turned its production of rubber used in its Simmerring operations to a new sector, that of floor-coverings. This activity, later placed under Freudenberg's Building Systems business group, targeted especially the industrial market, with such products as high-resistance pastille-type floor-coverings.

International Activities in the 1950s

Freudenberg returned to the international scene in the 1950s. The company came to the United States in 1951, forming a partnership to produce nonwovens in that country. Freudenberg also opened production facilities in a number of markets, including the United Kingdom, France, Spain, Italy, and The Netherlands. The European countries soon came to represent more than a third of the company's total sales. Toward the end of the 1950s, the company extended its sealing systems production to include the related vibration controls systems, a market the company entered in 1957.

Freudenberg found a new international market and new and lasting international partnerships in 1960. In that year, the company and Japan Reichold Chemical formed a joint venture company, Japan Vilene Company Ltd., to manufacture nonwovens for that and other Asian markets. That same year saw the debut of a still more important joint venture for Freudenberg, the formation of Freudenberg NOK with Nippon Oil Seal Company. The joint venture agreement also gave Freudenberg a 25 percent share of its Japanese counterpart.

In 1965, Freudenberg developed a new nonwovens production process, called Spunbonded, allowing the continuous production of nonwoven materials, binding threads formed from a molten plastic solution. The highly resistant and flexible material represented a new textiles industry breakthrough and formed the backbone of the new Freudenberg Spunbonded subsidiary.

In 1966, Freudenberg's acquisition of Klüber Lubrication, based in Munich, gave it a position in the specialty lubricants market. Founded in 1929, Klüber Lubrication produced special purpose lubricants such as extreme temperature lubricants and ultra-pure lubricants for ultra-small ball bearings.

During the 1970s, Freudenberg concentrated on expanding its production and distribution networks. The company opened facilities throughout North, Central, and South America. Australia, South Africa, and Central Asia were also part of the company's international growth. Much of its international expansion came through its increasingly close NOK partnership. In 1976, the two companies founded NOK Klüber Co. Ltd. to produce specialty lubricants for the Japanese markets. That same year saw the founding of another joint venture with NOK, that of Simrax GmbH, for the production of axial face seals in Weinheim. NOK's acquisition of Rubrasil S.A of Brazil opened the way for the later Freudenberg NOK Componentes Brasil

Key Dates:

1849: Carl Freudenberg takes over tannery.
1900: Freudenberg introduces chrome tanning process in Europe.
1929: The company begins seal manufacturing.
1936: The company introduces synthetic rubber-based seals.
1948: The company launches first nonwoven products.
1949: The company begins manufacturing rubber floor-coverings.
1951: The company enters the U.S. market.
1956: The company begins production of vibration control systems.
1960: The company forms joint ventures with NOK and Vilene.
1965: Spunbonded nonwovens are introduced.
1966: The company acquires Klüber Lubrication.
1976: NOK Klüber Co. Ltd joint venture is founded.
1981: The company founds Freudenberg Mektec GmbH & Co. KG.
1989: Freudenberg NOK GP (U.S.A.) is created.
1995: The company is reorganized as Freudenberg & Co.
1997: Freudenberg Politex Nonwovens joint venture is formed.
1999: The company acquires Meillor SA (France) and Xerex Corp. (Korea).
2001: Elefant shoe subsidiary is sold.

Ltda. Freudenberg also bought a share of NOK's Singapore Oil Seal Co. Ltd. at the end of the decade.

The partners joined together at the beginning of the 1980s to launch an entirely new operation. In 1981 the companies, together with Mekton, of Japan, inaugurated Simflex, in Weinheim, for the production of flexible printed circuit boards. These components were to become an essential element in the development of a variety of technologies and industries, found in products ranging from calculator and mobile telephones to the companies' car seals and vibration control systems. Simflex became known as Freudenberg Mektec GmbH & Co. KG in 1996.

Freudenberg's Japanese partners not only became part of the company's organization growth, they formed a primary influence on its industrial operations. Adopting elements of the Japanese kaizen corporate culture, Freudenberg began introducing a variety of quality and process improvement programs, culminating in what the company called its GROWTTH (''Get Rid of Waste Through Team Harmony'') program.

The end of the 1980s saw the formation of what was to become Freudenberg's single largest operation. In 1989, NOK and Freudenberg combined their U.S. seals and vibration controls operations into a single body, Freudenberg NOK General Partners. Over the next decade, the company built up a strong market, especially among Japanese car makers producing in North America. By the end of the 1990s, the partnership also was attracting important orders from the Big Three U.S. automakers, such as a $1 billion order from Ford to supply engine sealing packages.

New Organization for a New Century

Freudenberg continued to seek new product categories. A new market was found in 1991 when the company began producing and marketing MicronAir filters, using the company's nonwoven materials, for automotive air intake systems. The reunification of Germany, meanwhile, enabled the company to expand its park of production facilities, when it acquired two plants in the former East Germany.

By 1995, Freudenberg had developed a large and complex network of business operations and subsidiaries. In that year, the company restructured its organization, splitting off its primary business units into fully independent limited partnership companies granted global responsibilities for their operations—and giving these units the ability to respond more quickly to changes in their specific industries. At the same time, Carl Freudenberg, Weinheim was transformed into the smaller Freudenberg & Co. holding company. The partnership agreement that had kept the Freudenberg company solidly under the family's control remained relatively unchanged.

Freudenberg and partners NOK and Vilene took the leap into the Chinese market, forming joint venture production and distribution companies for both seal and nonwovens in 1996. A year later, Freudenberg found a new partner in longtime Italian rival Politex, when that company agreed to merge its spunbond nonwoven operations into the Freudenberg Politex Nonwovens joint venture. The company also acquired Marelli & Berta SpA, a manufacturer of nonwoven linings based in Italy; Meillor SA, a France-based manufacturer of flat gaskets; and Xerex Corp, a producer of fleece based in South Korea, in 1999. Meanwhile, Freudenberg was preparing to introduce its Vileda brand to the United States, through the acquisition of that country's MB Walton. Freudenberg also hoped to extend the Vileda brand throughout Eastern Europe, South America, and China.

Although its industrial operations were proceeding smoothly, the labor costs and other issues forced the company to reexamine its position in the leather market. In 1996, Freudenberg decided to concentrate its leather production on the high-end sector, producing for such luxury products company as Hermès, Gucci, Cartier, and others. The company's footwear subsidiary, Freudenberg Schuh KG, was preparing to cut back on its range of shoe brands. After building its Elefant brand into one of Western Europe's leading children shoe makers, the company sold that subsidiary to Clarks Shoes, based in Somerset, England, in 2001. Freudenberg retained its Jela, Freewalk, and Nora brands and its Tack chain of retail footwear stores.

Freudenberg celebrated not only its 150th anniversary at the turn of the century but also its 40th anniversary in close partnership with NOK Corporation. Freudenberg remained a representative of a rare breed of company at the beginning of the 21st century: highly diversified, family-owned—and highly successful.

Principal Subsidiaries

Freudenberg Haushaltsproduktie KG; Freudenberg Mektec GmbH & Co. KG (50%); Freudenberg-NOK (50%); Freudenberg NOK Componentes Brasil Ltda (50%); Freudenberg-NOK

General Partnership (U.S.A.; 50%); Freudenberg Politex Nonwovens SA (50%); Freudenberg Schuh KG; Klüber Lubrication München KG.

Principal Competitors

Amcast Industrial Corporation; BBA Group plc; Edelbrock Corporation; E.I. du Pont de Nemours and Company; GKN plc; Intertape Polymer Group Inc.; Kolbenschmidt Pierburg AG; Nippon Piston Ring Co., Ltd; Rheinmetall AG; Robert Bosch GmbH; Valeo S.A; ZF Friedrichshafen AG.

Further Reading

"Freudenberg bezahlt das Wachstum mit Gewinnruckgang," *Frankfurter Allgemeine Zeitung,* June 4, 1999.

"A Hidden Champion of Europe," *Financial Times,* September 16, 1999.

"Mit Vileda auf den US-Markt," *Handelsblatt,* May 27, 1998.

"Nonwovens Manufacturers Form Joint Venture in China," *Textile World,* May 1, 1995, p. 24.

—M.L. Cohen

GAIAM®

A LIFESTYLE COMPANY

Gaiam, Inc.

360 Interlocken Boulevard, Suite 300
Broomfield, Colorado 80021
U.S.A.
Telephone: (303) 464-3600
Fax: (303) 464-3700
Web site: http://www.gaiam.com

Public Company
Incorporated: 1988
Employees: 295
Sales: $60.6 million (2000)
Stock Exchanges: NASDAQ
Ticker Symbol: GAIA
NAIC: 454110 Electronic Shopping and Mail-order Houses; 512110 Motion Picture and Video Production

Gaiam, Inc. markets products designed for ecological sustainability, holistic well being, and personal growth. The product line includes energy-efficient light bulbs, solar panels. gardening products, alternative healthcare and fitness products, apparel, and household products. Proprietary products include a line of organic cotton clothing and bedding, under the Gaiam Organix brand, and health and fitness videos, produced by its subsidiary, Living Arts, Inc. Gaiam markets through mail-order catalog, its web site, through wholesale distribution to 17,000 mainstream retail outlets, including Borders, Target, and Discovery Channel Stores, and through retail boutiques within larger stores such as Whole Food Markets. Gaiam also provides consulting services to businesses interested in reducing their negative impact on the environment. Gaiam takes its name from ''Gaia,'' the ancient Greek goddess of the earth who represented the idea of the earth as a living system, and from ''I am,'' evoking a sense of human interconnectedness with the earth.

Gaiam Founder a Czech Horatio Alger

Gaiam's founder, Jirka Rysavy, traveled to the United States with a vision of starting a business offering products for the consumer interested in natural health and ecological sustainability. With very little money in his pocket, Rysavy left Czechoslovakia in 1984 and never returned. He chose to live in Boulder, Colorado, a community known for being socially progressive, and took a job at a print shop for $3.35 per hour. After three months, Rysavy had saved $600, which he used to start Transformational Economy, or Transecon, a recycled paper distribution company. In its first year the company earned $100,000 in pretax profits.

In 1985 Rysavy invested $30,000 to start Crystal Market, a natural foods store, earning $2.5 million the first year. Rysavy intended the store as a prototype for a multiunit chain, but he was sidetracked by the opportunity to purchase an office supply store in downtown Boulder. Seeing the possibility to have a greater impact on the environment by providing ecologically sound products to businesses, Rysavy purchased the store and assumed $15,000 in accounts payable liabilities. He discovered the strength of the company to be in serving corporate customers who purchased large quantities of supplies. He sold Crystal Market (which became the first store in the Wild Oats chain of natural food grocers) and transformed Corporate Express into a worldwide corporate supplier of office goods. In keeping with Rysavy's vision, Corporate Express initiated the Earth Saver line of more than 1,000 products made from recycled or renewable resources.

While Corporate Express grew at a phenomenal rate, becoming a Fortune 500 public corporation, Rysavy maintained an interest in healthful lifestyles and providing products for that market. He started Gaiam, a direct mail catalog company offering recycled paper products, as an affiliate to Transecon in 1988. Transecon took its first step toward significant growth in 1995 when the company acquired the catalog business from Seventh Generation.

Seventh Generation produced and sold its own brand of ecologically sustainable products, such as recycled paper products for the home, nontoxic household cleaning products, and recycled plastic bags. Published four times per year and distributed nationwide, the Seventh Generation catalog offered more than 300 products, including energy-efficient light bulbs, solar-powered radios, recycling bins, gardening tools, games, books, and organic cotton linens and clothing produced without the use

Company Perspectives:

Gaiam was created as a multichannel lifestyle company to provide choices that allow people to live a more natural and healthy life with respect for the environment. Our vision was inspired by the growing number of people who make purchasing decisions based on personal values. We believe that it is through the simple choices we make every day that we can transform the world in which we live.

of chemical dyes or preservatives. With the acquisition of the Seventh Generation direct mail business, Gaiam became the main source of revenue at Transecon, growing from $229,000 in sales in 1991 to $8.4 million in 1995. The following year Transecon ranked 34th in *Inc.* magazine's list of the Fastest Growing Private Companies with sales at $14.5 million.

Rapid growth required investment in the infrastructure at Transecon, including new operating systems. In conjunction with Corporate Express, Transecon relocated from the back room of the original office supply store in downtown Boulder to the Interlocken Business Park in nearby Broomfield. Construction of the building involved the use of renewable materials, energy-efficiency lighting and cooling, nontoxic paints, and untreated wool carpet. The company also opened a 64,000 square foot order-processing and fulfillment center in Cincinnati. They chose that location because that city was at the crossroads of major highways and within 30 minutes of Airborne and United Parcel Service airport hubs. Overall labor and facilities overhead made Cincinnati a low-cost base for shipping customer orders.

1996 Study of "Cultural Creatives" Defines Future Growth

In 1996 two events occurred that had an impact on Gaiam at a crucial period of its growth. The first event was a chance meeting between Rysavy and Lynn Powers on an airplane. A common interest in the convergence of business and alternative lifestyles led to a meeting of the minds between Rysavy and Powers, who became CEO and president of Gaiam in 1996. Powers had served as senior vice-president of strategic planning, marketing, and merchandising at Miller Outpost, transforming that company from a 24-store company to a 335-unit chain with $575 million in annual revenues.

Also in 1996, the sociologist Paul Ray published his groundbreaking research in which he identified a new American demographic called the "Cultural Creatives." Cultural Creatives matched the profile of Gaiam's customers, educated consumers who based their purchasing decisions on certain values, either concern for the environment, holistic health and well being, a personal philosophy, or a mix of the three. Ray estimated the growing market at 44 million people and more than $200 billion annual revenues in 1996.

This market was also known as the Lifestyles of Health and Sustainability (LOHAS). The LOHAS market consisted of five segments of interest: (1) Sustainable Economy, (2) Healthy Living, (3) Alternative Health, (4) Personal Development, and (5) Ecological Living. Rysavy determined to focus Gaiam's growth on this market by consolidating various segments of the LOHAS market to create a unified, identifiable brand, trusted by the customer for the credibility of its information and the quality of its products and services. Gaiam identified its customer base as 80 percent female, 20 percent male, with a median age of 42, earning a median annual income of $52,000, with more than one-third earning more than $75,000 per year.

In pursuing the goal of serving all facets of the LOHAS market, Gaiam acquired two catalog companies in early 1998 that complemented or overlapped with existing businesses. For $25 million in cash, Gaiam acquired a 67 percent interest in Healing Arts Publishing, LLC, doing business as Living Arts. Based in California since 1987, Living Arts produced and distributed yoga and meditation videos, which it sold through 15,000 retail outlets, including Target, Borders, and Musicland. Living Arts published a catalog through which the company sold its videos, and related products, as well as ecologically sound products. An existing order fulfillment service agreement with InnerBalance Health, based in Colorado, evolved into Gaiam ownership of that company. InnerBalance sold vitamins, herbal supplements, and fitness equipment by direct mail. Gaiam also renamed the Seventh Generation catalog, selling environmental products under the catalog brand Harmony.

As Gaiam grew, its place on the *Inc.* list rose to 11th in 1997 with $19.7 million in sales and to 10th in 1998 with $30 million in sales. The customer base grew from 300,000 in 1996 to 685,000 in 1998. The company operated at a loss in 1996 and 1997, but marketable securities contributed by Rysavy and sold by Gaiam countered losses. The company also supported growth with private placements of stock and subordinated debentures. Moe Siegel, founder of Celestial Seasonings, and Michael Gilliland, founder of Wild Oats Markets, known leaders in LOHAS markets, became investors during this time. In 1998 a private placement of stock and debentures raised $2.65 million for operating capital and acquisitions.

By the fall of 1998, Rysavy decided to resign his position as CEO at Corporate Express to dedicate himself to Gaiam's future, specifically an initial public offering of stock. Rysavy's resignation became official in February 1999, when he took the position of CEO; Powers became COO and retained the position of president. Gaiam went public in October. The company first offered stock to its 800,000 customers at $4.50 per share for up to 200 shares, a 10 percent discount off the public price of $5.00 per share. On the public offering Gaiam net $6.1 million on 1.7 million shares sold at $5.00. Rysavy retained a 77 percent ownership in the company.

Funds from the public offering provided capital for further expansion. The company relocated its fulfillment center in Cincinnati to a larger, 208,000-square-foot space only two miles from the original site. In July the company acquired complete ownership of Living Arts as well as a 50 percent stake in a company that supplied environmental products to Living Arts.

Much of the Gaiam's growth in 1999 stemmed from acquisitions. In 1999 Gaiam ranked fourth on *Inc.*'s list of the fastest growing private companies, with $45.7 million in revenue, while net income nearly doubled to $1.8 million. Increased

Key Dates:

1995: The company's growth phase begins with the acquisition of the catalog business Seventh Generation, Inc.
1996: Paul Ray identifies the $200 billion Cultural Creatives market.
1998: The company acquires Healing Arts Publishing and InnerBalance Health.
1999: The company is ranked fourth on *Inc.* magazine's list of Fastest Growing Private Companies, the fourth consecutive year that it is listed.
2000: The firm forms Gaiam Organix division for organic cotton clothing and linens.
2001: The merger with Real Goods Trading Corporation is completed.

profit margin to 60.2 percent in 1999, largely due to an increase in proprietary products, such as, mind-body-spirit videos that garnered a 70 percent gross profit margin, selling for $10.00 to $14.00 each. Gaiam's web site, launched in late 1998, contributed to the company's success with a 50 percent gross profit margin and an average order of $100, more than double industry averages at 17 percent to 20 percent and $40, respectively. Gaiam attributed the high average order to the high annual income of its customers.

Business-to-business revenues grew by 49.4 percent in 1999 to $11.2 million, accounting for 24 percent of revenues, compared to 13 percent in 1998. Businesses that used Gaiam products included spas and resorts and health care providers, while wholesale business included lifestyle stores, bookstores, sporting goods stores, and national and regional mass merchandisers. Gaiam planned to expand its consulting business, providing other businesses with a ''green audit,'' a sort of environmental impact statement, advising companies on how to improve resource usage. Services included the design and installation of renewable energy systems. Gaiam initiated an Internet site specifically for access by its business customers.

Multichannel Growth at Turn of the 21st Century

In September 2000 Gaiam launched an upgraded Internet site at www.gaiam.com, expanding the line of products for sale at the site and powering the site with a stronger engine. One of a few profitable e-commerce sites, Gaiam's success stemmed from low advertising overhead, avoiding online advertising and expensive advertising campaigns. Instead, Gaiam promoted its web site on yoga videos and DVDs and in its catalogs, resulting in a $20 per customer advertising expense. As the site developed, Gaiam attained gross profit margin of 55 percent and an average of $106 per order, higher than the company's cataog order average of $90.

Gaiam and Whole Foods Market merged web sites in June 2000. By merging with WholePeople.com, Gaiam eliminated a competitor and gained exposure to customers of Whole Foods Market. Since WholePeople.com suffered losses of over $5 million, the partnership benefitted Whole Foods with a financial cushion and shared data on a common customer base. Gaiam owned 50.1 percent, of the venture, Gaiam.com, Inc., while Whole Foods' vitamin subsidiary, Amiron, maintained a 49.9 percent stake. Wholepeople.com deactivated its web site and entered a direct link to gaiam.com in its place. Gaiam then upgraded the web site with a stronger engine and a new look. The site offered more than 10,000 stock keeping units, including over 2,000 proprietary products.

The media became an important new avenue of growth for Gaiam as Living Arts began to produce yoga and health programs for cable television. The company provided 13 programs for broadcast on the Discovery Health Channel in the fall of 2000. International distribution involved productions for networks in Italy, Germany, Brazil, Canada, and Australia. Living Arts produced 16 new video/DVD titles, including the popular *Pilates* and *Yoga Conditioning for Weight Loss*, the latter selling 250,000 copies. A series of massage videos included *Accupressure Massage*, *Reflexology*, and *Couples Massage*. With On Command, which provides in-room entertainment to hotels, Gaiam arranged for two *Yoga for Beginners* shows to be available to travelers at more than 500,000 hotel rooms. Participating chains included the Hyatt, Four Seasons, Marriott, Radisson, and Inter-Continental. Living Arts gained exposure on mainstream television as well, including yoga instructor Rodney Yee's guest appearance on *The Oprah Winfrey Show* in April 2001. Gaiam also introduced the *Gaiam Lifestyle* magazine/catalog, featuring articles and information on personal well being and ecological sustainaibility.

The company expanded its reach into retail stores, providing products to retailers that few competitors could duplicate. New retail customers included Store of Knowledge, Discovery Channel stores, and regional Canadian retailers. Gaiam experimented with the store-within-a-store concept in 2000, developing Gaiam Natural Living Centers in such national chains as Borders Books, Whole Foods Markets, Gaylans (sporting goods), Dick's Sporting Goods, Target, and Ulta (skin care products). The company planned to expand product lines offered within these branded retail boutiques and to expand the number of stores involved in the program. Toward that end, Gaiam introduced a line of organic cotton clothing and bedding, using the brand name Gaiam Organix. Gaiam signed an agreement to obtain exclusive rights to North American distribution of organic cotton products from the leading producer in Europe.

Gaiam's business consulting continued to be a focus of growth in 2000. Gaiam began consultation with Hilton Hotels on providing hypoallergenic products for the chain's specialty rooms as well as for Hilton's ''stress-less'' rooms. Gaiam assisted in the energy and ecological efficiency of several large corporations, such as Disney, Sony, and AT&T, and several government agencies, including the White House, NASA, the Department of Defense, and the Department of Energy.

Sales for 2000 reached $60.6 million, a 33 percent increase over 1999, while net income increased to $2.65 million, nearly double profits of the previous year. Gaiam attributed the increase on an internal growth rate on proprietary products of 37 percent. Business-to-business revenues increased 50.3 percent to $16.8 million in 2000. Gaiam.com continued to be profitable.

The next step on Gaiam path of growth and industry consolidation involved a merger with Real Goods Trading Company. In business since 1978, Real Goods complimented Gaiam's existing products with renewable energy products, such as solar panels and energy efficient lighting, and books and information on ecologically sustainable living. Through its two catalog businesses, Real Goods and Jade Mountain, and corresponding web sites, as well as five retail centers in Hopland, Berkeley, Los Gatos, Santa Rosa, and West Los Angeles, California, Real Goods offered a variety of environmentally positive products. These included clothing from hemp and organic cotton, gardening tools, recycled glass products, and other household items, as well as information on alternative home building and materials, such as straw bale houses. The Solar Living Center, a 12-acre demonstration facility at the Hopland, California, store provided consulting on renewable energy for commercial applications, a program compatible with Gaiam's green audit.

In January 2001 Gaiam and Real Goods completed the merger through a stock swap valued at $8.7 million. Real Goods shareholders received one share of Gaiam for ten shares of Real Goods stock. All accounting responsibilities were consolidated at Gaiam's offices in Colorado, while graphics merged with Gaiam in Santa Monica, California/Real Goods, and Gaiam also merged order processing and distribution centers in Cincinnati, implementing a new supply-chain management information system. Real Goods added approximately $19 million in annual revenues as well as thousands of customers to Gaiam.

Principal Subsidiaries

Gaiam.com, Inc.; InnerBalance Health; Healing Arts Publishing, Inc.; Real Goods Trading Company.

Principal Competitors

Foster & Gallagher, Inc.; General Nutritional Companies, Inc.; Seventh Generation, Inc.

Further Reading

Beauprez, Jennifer, "Gaiam Banks on Bottom Line Profitable E-Tailer Expects to Lure Investors Despite Cold IPO Market," *Denver Post,* April 28, 2000, p. C2.

Branaugh, Matt, "Broomfield, Colo., 'Lifestyle' Products Company Makes Foray into Canada," *Knight-Ridder/Tribune Business News,* November 2, 2000.

Cohen, Barbara, "Gaiam: Making of *The* Lifestyle Company for Cultural Creatives," *Natural Business LOHAS Journal,* September/October 2000.

"Gaiam Helps Bring Yoga to the Masses," *Internet Wire,* April 24, 2001.

"Gaiam Offering Customers First Chance at IPO Stock," *Boulder County Business Report,* August 1, 1999, p. 7A.

"Gaiam Third Child of Entrepreneur Rysavy," *Boulder County Business Report,* November 1, 1998, p. 1.

"Gaiam.com Bucks Trend of Internet Companies and Shows Profit," *Business Wire,* April 27, 2000.

Glarian, Susan, "Broomfield, Colo.-Based E-Commerce Firm to Merge with California Company," *Knight-Ridder/Tribune Business News,* October 16, 2000.

Gonzalez, Erika, "Gaiam Gets *Inc.* Recognition," *Denver Rocky Mountain News,* October 14, 1999, p. 3B.

Hemmer, Andy, "Gaiam Inc. Makes Move to Union Center," *Business Courier Serving Cincinnati-Northern Kentucky,* October 27, 2000, p. 5.

Lilson, Marianne, "It's Easy Being 'Green' for Real Goods," *Chain Store Age Executive with Shopping Center Age,* May 2000, p. 240.

Locke, Tom, "Fast-Growing Transecon Moves to Broomfield Park; Catalog Sales Company is Keeping a Small Office on Pearl Street," *Boulder Daily Camera,* November 12, 1996, p. 5D.

Pate, Kelly, "Whole Foods, Gaiam Merge Online Ventures," *Denver Post,* June 21, 2000, p. C1.

Raabe, Steve, "Company Founder Steps Aside Corporate Express Seeks Investors, Tries to Refocus," *Denver Post,* February 9, 1999, p. C1.

——, "Gaiam, Real Goods to Merge," *Denver Post,* October 17, 2000, p. C2.

Smith, Jerd, "Gaiam Seeks $10 Million in Offering Broomfield Natural Products Company Honored by Magazine," *Denver Rocky Mountain News,* July 22, 1999, p. 3B.

Solomon, Stephen D., "New World, Ordered," *Inc.,* December 1995, p. 68.

Watkins, Steve, "Hugging the Green: Gaiam Goes to Mother Earth for Source of Income, Light," *Investor's Business Daily,* June 20, 2000, p. A14.

—Mary Tradii

German American Bancorp
Strong Ties. Strong Solutions.

German American Bancorp

711 Main Street
P.O. Box 810
Jasper, Indiana 47546
U.S.A.
Telephone: (812) 482-1314
Fax: (812) 482-0758
Web site: http://www.germanamericanbancorp.com

Public Company
Incorporated: 1910
Employees: 407
Total Assets: $1.07 billion (2000)
Stock Exchanges: NASDAQ
Ticker Symbol: GABC
NAIC: 551111 Offices of Bank Holding Companies

German American Bancorp (GAB) is a Jasper, Indiana-based multibank holding company. The company consists of five affiliate banks, which serve more than 60,000 individuals and businesses. These affiliate banks—which include Citizens State Bank, First American Bank, First State Bank Southwest Indiana, German American Bank, and Peoples National Bank—operate in 27 locations throughout eight southwestern Indiana counties. GAB's banking services include a full line of checking and savings accounts, as well as mortgages and consumer and commercial loans. German American Bancorp also owns five full-service independent insurance agencies: German American Insurance, Doty Agency, Inc., First Financial Insurance, Smith and Bell Insurance, and Knox County Insurance. The company has total assets of more than $1 billion.

1910–50s: The Beginnings of a Community Staple

The flagship bank in German American Bancorp's collection is German American Bank. German American was organized on November 2, 1910 in Jasper, Indiana—a small town in the southwestern part of the state, less than an hour from the Kentucky border. The town of Jasper was less than a century old at the time and was populated predominantly by German immigrants recruited to the area by a German-speaking priest who owned several acres in the county. It was the community's German heritage that prompted the new bank's name.

The bank, which was the 353rd bank chartered in Indiana, was organized by William F. Beckman, a native of the area who had just completed a term as the county's treasurer. German American's original 57 shareholders—who included several of the town's prominent citizens along with some of the wealthiest farmers in the region—subscribed to capital stock of $40,000. These shareholders elected seven local men as directors, and the bank opened for business on December 19, 1910 with two employees: a cashier and an assistant cashier. Its offices consisted of one-half of the first floor of a commercial building owned by William Wilson, one of the bank's directors. The other half of the building was occupied by Wilson's own real estate and insurance offices.

The Indiana constitution at that time limited the corporate existence of state banks to 20 years. This meant that in 1930, German American had to apply for a second charter. In the process of so doing, the organizers increased the bank's capital stock from $40,000 to $50,000. A change in leadership also accompanied the re-chartering; Winfield Hunter, who had served as the bank's president since its inception, retired. He was replaced by Louis Eckstein, a local businessman.

By the mid-1940s, German American was ready to expand and modernize its facilities a bit. It purchased the building in which it was located and enlarged its offices, remodeling the interior and adding new equipment at the same time.

1960s–70s: Changes in Leadership and Branching Out

Louis Eckstein held the office of bank president until his death in 1962, when he was succeeded by his brother Clem Eckstein. That same year German American opened its first branch location, in the neighboring town of Dubois, Indiana.

Clem Eckstein headed the bank for only two years, and upon his death in 1964, O. Leo Beckman became German American's fourth president. Beckman was the son of William Beck-

Company Perspectives:

Taking a personal interest in ensuring generations to come will enjoy Southwestern Indiana as home, German American Bancorp is putting money to work for clients, building for today and for the future.

man, the bank's founder. Two years into the younger Beckman's tenure, German American outgrew its original offices. The bank razed the building it had occupied and built a new, larger two-story office on the same site. By that time, the bank employed 27 people and had capital accounts of more than $1.4 million and deposits of more than $17 million.

As the bank's business grew, it began to expand its geographic reach. In 1973, two German American branches were opened in Jasper, to provide customers with more convenient, easy-to-access banking services. In 1980, the bank established a branch in Ferdinand, Indiana, a small town to the south of Jasper. The Ferdinand office, which opened for business on March 17, 1980, was housed in a newly built two-story structure.

1980s to Mid-1990s: Growth Through Acquisition

In 1983, the owners of German American Bank formed a holding company—German American Bancorp (GAB)—as preparation for taking advantage of merger opportunities. For three years, however, the German American Bank remained the sole bank held by the company. In May 1986, GAB made its first acquisition when it purchased the Bank of Ireland. This new bank, which was located just a few miles from Jasper, in the town of Ireland, was converted into a German American branch. In the early part of 1987, the company opened still another office, in the community of Huntingburg, Indiana. This branch was German American's seventh location.

Meanwhile, remodeling was under way at the bank's main office. In June 1986, German American completely modernized its downtown headquarters, providing customers with more than 33,000 square feet of space, plenty of parking, covered drive-through units, and access to a 24-hour automatic teller machine. The mid-1980s also saw GAB offer a form of branch banking that was entirely new to the area. The bank opened offices inside two Jasper supermarkets, making it easy for customers to consolidate their grocery shopping and banking into a single stop.

The 1990s ushered in changes in federal and state banking laws that were to dramatically change the face of the industry. With the loosening of regulations governing bank ownership, an immense wave of mergers and acquisitions swept the United States. Large banks that had been pillars of the financial world—like Chase Manhattan, Chemical Bank, CitiCorp, NBD, and Bank One—began to merge and meld into a seemingly ever-fluctuating series of new institutions. Smaller banks were, perhaps, even more affected. As the large banks grew even larger and more powerful, they began absorbing the smaller ones at an astonishing rate. According to Robert DeYoung, the Federal Reserve Bank of Chicago's senior economist and economic advisor, mergers and acquisitions began to reduce the number of commercial banks in the United States by between 4 and 6 percent annually starting in the mid-1980s and continuing into the 1990s; most of the banks absorbed were small (as cited in the September 1999 edition of the *Chicago Fed Letter*).

German American Bancorp entered the new decade faced with the same choice as many other small and mid-sized banks: ''Eat or be eaten.'' The company chose the first option, deciding to establish its own collection of local banks. GAB's plan was to grow its assets from the $200 million it then held to approximately $1 billion. The goal of $1 billion in assets was chosen to afford the bank the efficiencies associated with size, while still keeping it small enough to stay focused on the communities it served.

The notion of community was, in fact, to play a significant role in GAB's choice of acquisitions. Rather than looking far afield for candidates, the company chose instead to stay close to home, solidifying its position as a local institution. In a May 1998 interview with the *Evansville Courier,* GAB's president and COO Mark Schroeder explained: ''We're very active in putting together a community bank holding company. We truly are a family of community banks.'' In keeping with its focus on community, GAB decided that each of its acquisitions would retain its local leadership and policies, in order to more effectively serve the specific needs of its customers and community.

Preparing to launch its expansion campaign, GAB began listing its stock on the NASDAQ exchange in 1993. It hoped that the enhanced stock liquidity resulting from this listing would serve as an enticement to the banks it planned to court, many of whom had trouble selling their thinly traded stock.

In 1993, GAB began taking serious steps toward realizing its expansion goal. In March, the company acquired Union Bank, a single-branch bank in Loogootee, Indiana, some 30 miles to the north of Jasper. Union Bank had been in existence since 1929. The following month, GAB purchased Winslow Bancorporation of Winslow, Indiana, and its subsidiary Southwestern Indiana Bank.

More acquisitions followed. In April 1994, the company acquired Otwell State Bank of Otwell, Indiana, for approximately $3.7 million. Otwell State had total assets of $15.6 million. This new bank, along with the previously acquired Southwestern Indiana Bank, was merged into Community Trust Bank, a combined banking institution operating in Otwell, Petersburg, and Winslow, Indiana. In October 1994, GAB acquired three branches of Regional Federal Savings Bank in the towns of Huntingburg, Rockport, and Tell City, Indiana, adding approximately $25 million in assets. The company then converted Regional Federal's Huntingburg office into a German American branch. Regional Federal's other two locations—in Tell City and Rockport—were combined into a newly formed subsidiary of GAB: First State Bank Southwest Indiana.

Late 1990s: Further Expansion

After a two and one-half year lull, GAB got back into the acquisition game in 1997. In March of that year, the company acquired the 109-year-old Peoples National Bank for approximately $21.1 million in GAB stock. Peoples' main office was

Key Dates:

1910: German American Bank is established in Jasper, Indiana.
1930: German American is rechartered.
1962: The first branch office, in Dubois, Indiana, is opened.
1973: Two additional branch offices are opened in Jasper.
1983: The German American Bancorp holding company is established.
1986: The Bank of Ireland is merged with German American Bank.
1993: Bancorp goes public on NASDAQ.
1994: An aggressive acquisition program is initiated.
1999: First American Bank and The Doty Agency join German American.

located in Washington, Indiana, and it had five branches in two southwestern Indiana counties. At the time of the acquisition, GAB merged its Loogootee office—Union Bank—into Peoples National. Once the Peoples acquisition was completed, German American Bancorp had total assets of $475 million.

In the summer of 1998, German American Bancorp made two more acquisitions: FSB Bank of Francisco, Indiana, and Citizens State Bank of Petersburg, Indiana. Formed in 1874, Citizens State Bank held the oldest banking charter in the state. GAB consolidated its two new acquisitions, rolling FSB into Citizens. At the same time, the company also merged Community Trust into Citizens, considerably expanding the historic Petersburg bank.

Early 1999 also saw acquisitions for GAB. In January, the company paid $57.1 million in stock to purchase the Vincennes, Indiana-based 1st Bancorp. 1st Bancorp's subsidiaries included a three-location bank and two insurance agencies, doing business in Vincennes and Princeton, Indiana. The 1st Bancorp acquisition pushed GAB considerably closer to its goal of $1 billion in assets; with the addition of the new business, the bancorp held total assets of $850 million. The early part of 1999 also marked the acquisition of two more insurance agencies: The Doty Agency, Inc., of Petersburg, Indiana, and Smith and Bell, of Vincennes, Indiana.

In 1999, Mark Schroeder became German American Bancorp's new CEO. Schroeder had been with the German American Bank for 25 years and had served as head of lending operations, chief financial officer, president, and chief operating officer before becoming the holding company's CEO. It was under Schroeder's watch that GAB met its asset level goal. In July of 2000, the company announced that it had, for the first time in its history, exceeded $1 billion in assets.

Even so, GAB was not quite finished expanding. In October 2000, the company acquired Holland Bancorp, the parent company of Holland National Bank for approximately $14 million in stock. Holland National's four branches, which were located in the same county as GAB's headquarters, were converted to German American branches. This merger, therefore, served both to eliminate a rival bank and to expand GAB's presence in the area. The company also acquired its fifth insurance agency—the Fleck Insurance Agency, of Jasper. Fleck was merged into GAB's recently acquired Doty Agency.

Outlook for the 21st Century

In his 2000 letter to shareholders, German American Bancorp's president and CEO Mark Schroeder wrote, "Throughout the previous decade, our Company's strategic focus was one of growth through acquisition. . . . Now, as with any organization that has experienced significant growth, we have reached the point at which management's focus has turned to maximizing the value of this expanded franchise." A bit further in his letter, Schroeder continued, "As we enter the new decade, century, and millennium, German American Bancorp also enters a new era, one in which management of your Company concentrates its strategic focus, attention, and energy on leveraging the potential of our existing operations."

From the tone of Schroeder's letter, it appeared that GAB was wrapping up its decade-long phase of expansion and turning its focus to improving and strengthening its operations and service offerings within existing markets. Toward that end, the company planned to continue its strategy of establishing an insurance presence in each of its banking markets. It also was striving to grow its brokerage, trust, and financial planning services groups by adding more financial advisors.

Principal Subsidiaries

German American Bank; First American Bank; First State Bank Southwest Indiana; German American Holdings Corporation; GAB Mortgage Corporation; German American Reinsurance Co., Ltd.; Peoples National Bank; Citizens State Bank; The Doty Agency, Inc.; First Title Insurance Company.

Principal Competitors

Fifth Third Bancorp; First Indiana Corporation; Home Building Bancorp, Inc.; Home Federal Bancorp; Home Financial Bancorp; Indiana United Bancorp; Integra Bank Corporation; Norwood Financial Corp.; Old National Bancorp; Union Planters Corporation.

Further Reading

DeWitte, Dave, "Local Banks Remain Strong, Independent," *Evansville Courier,* June 5, 1994, p. E1.
Ferdinand, Indiana: A Sesquicentennial History, Ferdinand, Ind.: Ferdinand Historical Society, 1990.
Raithel, Tom, "German American Bancorp in Jasper Expands in Seven Nearby Counties," *Evansville Courier,* May 31, 1998, p. E1.
Smith, Bruce C., "Jasper Banks Taking Separate Paths," *Indianapolis Star,* March 7, 1993, p. C7.

—Shawna Brynildssen

Group Health Cooperative

521 Wall Street
Seattle, Washington 98121
U.S.A.
Telephone: (206) 326-3000
Toll Free: (888) 901-4636
Fax: (206) 448-5963
Web site: http://www.ghc.org

Nonprofit Organization
Incorporated: 1945 as Group Health Cooperative of Puget Sound
Employees: 9,800
Sales: $1.4 billion (1999)
NAIC: 621491 HMO Medical Centers; 62211 General Medical and Surgical Hospitals

Group Health Cooperative (GHC) is a health maintenance organization (HMO) serving nearly 600,000 enrollees in Washington State and Idaho. Of these, 30,500 voting members select a panel of 11 trustees to represent consumers. Although part of its founding mission was ''to serve the greatest number,'' CEO Cheryl Scott stresses that neither GHC nor HMOs in general are the best choice in medical care for everyone. Group Health has cut back unprofitable services and limited enrollments to balance its budget.

Cooperative Origins

The inspiration for Group Health Cooperative came from Dr. Michael Shadid, who is credited with starting America's first cooperatively owned and managed hospital. Shadid left his native Lebanon in 1898 at the age of 16 and later, horrified by the high toll of medical costs on Oklahoma farmers and also by the plight of the poor in his homeland, he set up the first cooperative hospital in the nation in Elk City, Oklahoma, in 1931.

A crusader against traditional fee-for-service medicine, Shadid lectured in Seattle in August 1945, where the idea of a medical services cooperative began to take root. Farmers had used co-ops to finance machinery and farm supplies and markets; extending the concept to a hospital seemed a logical progression.

According to the historian Walt Crowley, Group Health's founding members were farmers, workers, and political activists who believed consumer-owned cooperatives represented a safe middle ground between the extremes of capitalism and socialism.

Led by attorney Jack Cluck, Group Health Cooperative of Puget Sound incorporated as a nonprofit organization in 1945. It began operating, so to speak, on January 1, 1947, when it took over a Medical Security Clinic (MSC) and St. Luke's Hospital. The Medical Security Clinic was a local prepaid group health practice of 16 physicians led by Dr. Sandy MacColl. It paid $200,000 for MSC and assumed a mortgage of $50,000 on St. Luke's Hospital, which was renamed Group Health Hospital in 1948. Four hundred of the original clientele were GHC enrollees; Medical Security brought another 8,000 from its industrial contracts.

At the time, prepayment of medical services was rare, but not completely novel. The Virginia Mason Clinic was another local group practice; the Mayo Clinic had become internationally famous. Still, the American Medical Association (AMA) denounced the group's leftist leanings even as Congress debated the issues of universal access and affordable healthcare.

Group Health's other main priority was preventative medicine. This concept might seem to be a matter of common sense and would become commonplace within a couple of decades, but it was treated by the medical profession with suspicion at the time, says Crowley.

Despite opposition from the medical establishment, Group Health was clearly an idea whose time had come. Its hospital was able to add another 30-bed wing in August 1950. In 1951, Group Health contracted to provide medical care to 2,200 members of the International Longshoremen and Warehousemen's Union. Coverage was extended to dependents within a few years.

Group Health was staffed with contract doctors and demobilized Army doctors. In 1951, after a two-year legal battle, the

Company Perspectives:

The company's purpose is to transform healthcare, working together every day to improve the care and well-being of our consumers and communities. Our mission, as a consumer-governed organization, is to design, finance, and deliver high-quality healthcare. Our guiding principles are respect, integrity, scientific discipline, a pioneering spirit, and stewardship.

Washington State Supreme Court determined the King County Medical Society had conspired against Group Health by blacklisting its doctors. Medical Society doctors continued to quip about ''Group Death'' after the ruling.

In the summer of 1953, Group Health created an independent co-op to provide dental services. Enrollment for medical services approached 36,000 by the end of 1953. Group Health only had 17 doctors at the time, and with the aggressive membership drive, they were swamped with bodies in need of repair.

In 1952, with the controversial departure of general manager Don Northrop impending, the board decided to appoint a single leader ultimately in charge of both medical and administrative staff. Dr. Sandy MacColl, who had been with the organization from the beginning, was the first to take this position of executive director. He was succeeded in 1955 by Dr. John A. Kahl (pronounced ''kale''), formerly head of the state department of health. The chain-smoking Dr. Kahl headed the group for ten years.

Clinics in Renton and North Seattle opened in the mid-1950s. Plans were underway for a new $2.5 million, 150-bed hospital to replace the existing one. To finance it, Group Health levied an additional $100 in addition to the $75 one-time capital dues paid by each member (who also paid in addition an average of $54 per year).

Growing in the 1960s and 1970s

In spite of its success in raising funds for its new hospital, in the late 1950s GHC was logging annual deficits in the range of $250,000 to $350,000, due largely to rising medical costs. Dues were raised in 1960 (to $8.00 a month for men and $8.50 for women) in an attempt to cap a projected $500,000 deficit. Enrollment began to slow. By the end of 1960, Group Health had 65 physicians and 60,000 members.

In 1961, representatives of Kaiser Permanente, a prepaid medical services firm based in Portland, Oregon, intimated they would pursue group contracts within Washington State if Group Health did not. In 1963, Group Health signed an agreement with the Seattle Professional Engineering Employees Association, its first inroad among Boeing employees since it supported the machinists' union in a 1948 strike at the aircraft manufacturer.

Clinics were added or expanded in the mid-1960s to support a recovered rate of growth (8,000 new members signed up in 1964 alone). Mental health was a new area of service being introduced.

Dr. H. Frank Newman took over Group Health after Dr. Kahl died of a stroke in 1965, the same year the Medicare program was created. As it was first set up, Medicare gave pay-for-fee providers little incentive to control costs. As a prepaid provider, Group Health had to create some mechanism for billing the government for specific procedures.

In the last half of the decade, several new building projects were started. The most critical need, however, was for more doctors. By 1968, Group Health had 100,000 members and a physician-to-patient ratio of 1:1,800.

Seattle's 1970s began with an ominous sign: Boeing laid off nearly 60,000 workers. Group Health was not hit as hard as rival King County Medical, as many members continued to pay for their own coverage themselves. In fact, Group Health's enrollment actually increased.

Group Health's popularity and reputation grew as then President Richard Nixon championed the creation of ''health maintenance organizations''—HMOs—as the saviors of the American medical system. (However, it was not until 1975 that Group Health was conditionally recognized by Medicare as an HMO, due to its prepayment methodology.) Amid a period of intense media scrutiny, Group Health's enrollment grew to 149,000 in 1971 and 173,000 at the end of 1973—far greater numbers than anticipated or desired by the board of directors. The building of new medical centers and the recruiting of doctors continued at full pace. Hospital costs and doctors' fees grew too during the decade's inflationary periods—about 20 percent in 1974 alone.

Group Health had more than 200,000 enrollees in 1975; many of them complained—publicly—about problems booking appointments. One TV journalist reported having to make 78 phone calls to schedule a visit with his Group Health physician.

Workers, having recently won the right to strike, were also voicing their discontent. X-ray technicians walked off the job for ten days in 1975, and nurses staged a 28-day strike the following year.

''Controlled growth'' became the policy for the rest of the decade. In 1976, Group Health chose a new leader, Don Brennan, formerly vice-president for finance and administration. In late 1978, GHC took over a Tacoma medical center operated by the nation's first federally recognized HMO, Sound Health Association.

Reagan Era Competition

Brennan resigned in 1980; Gail Warden, who had formerly led Chicago's Rush-Presbyterian-St. Luke's Medical System, became CEO the next year. Crowley's history notes that in 1981, while President Ronald Reagan taunted the Soviets, Group Health members inclined to political activism in a variety of causes voted to further the cause of nuclear disarmament, hoping to prevent ''this final epidemic.'' (The cooperative's Nuclear Awareness Group would be nullified by trustees in 1987.) Another sign of the Reagan era was the termination of a rural healthcare program that Group Health administered, which affected 6,000 beneficiaries.

Key Dates:

1947: Group Health begins providing prepaid medical care.
1967: The organization's enrollment exceeds 100,000.
1987: Group Health Northwest is created.
1993: GHC enters an alliance with Virginia Mason Medical Center.
1997: GHC enters an alliance with Kaiser Permanente.

At the same time, many more new HMOs were federally sanctioned across the country, giving Group Health its first taste of direct, prepaid competition. By 1984, the Puget Sound area had four other HMOs vying for business. A restructuring ensued at Group Health to keep it lean enough to survive.

In November 1981, Group Health began leasing a new administrative center, giving the organization more of the appearance of a corporation than the grass roots cooperative it had once been. Many on the board and the staff were becoming more willing separate the organization from nonmedical causes; however activists continued to protest GHC's coverage of abortions. In 1983, Group Health officials created a credibility crisis when they suppressed an article on noxious arsenic emissions from the American Smelting and Refining Company, with whom Group Health had a contract, set to run in the cooperative's *View* magazine.

Also in 1983, Group Health took over a Spokane-area managed-care operation set up by the California-based Insurance Companies of North America, which was itself merging with CIGNA Healthplan, Inc. There followed inconsequential talks about creating a national network with other HMOs. Group Health also served customers in some outlying areas with outside physicians.

Enrollment growth failed to meet projections in 1985. In fact, it was the first year enrollment had suffered a net loss. Nevertheless, GHC was able to open or buy several new medical centers in the 1980s. Administrative offices were moved to the old *Seattle Post-Intelligencer* headquarters in 1987. Warden stepped down as CEO, to be succeeded by Aubrey Davis in February 1988. When Davis took over, Group Health had 325,000 enrollees and 9,000 employees; its annual budget was $325 million.

Enrollment increased 40 percent between 1987 and 1989, fueled by new programs to extend service to new populations, such as a state-sponsored one to help the working poor called the Basic Health Plan. However, Security Care, which aimed at long-term care for senior citizens, was cancelled after state insurance regulators blocked Aetna from taking over a partnership role.

Joining Forces, Cutting Programs in the 1990s

Group Health's 1990 operating budget was $555 million. In 1990, Group Health incorporated a for-profit affiliate, Options Health Care. A major source of pride for the organization was its role in providing medical services for the Goodwill Games in Seattle in 1990. This made Group Health even more visible nationally; it would also be praised by the *New England Journal of Medicine* and *U.S. News and World Report* as a paradigm for successful health care.

Phil Nudelman, executive vice-president for operations, replaced Aubrey Davis as president and CEO in January 1991. He embraced the philosophies of Total Quality Management.

Among new facilities opened in the early 1990s was the $55 million Central South Specialty Center, which opened in November 1991, just as Group Health was laying off about a hundred nurses.

Group Health unsuccessfully bid for a CHAMPUS contract to provide service to 250,000 military dependents and retirees, but was hired by the winner (Foundation Health of California) as a subcontractor.

In November 1993, Group Health announced a comprehensive alliance with the Virginia Mason Medical Center, a nonprofit system that had 300 physicians at 13 medical centers in addition to its teaching hospital, and 41,000 subscribers. The two soon began marketing an insurance product allowing consumers to have access to doctors in both systems.

One of the nurses' unions feared that restructuring would jeopardize its members' career prospects. After months of tense negotiations and a one-day strike, Group Health agreed to provide a fund for their retraining.

Group Health launched ''The Partnership Program'' in February 1993. This was a comprehensive initiative to address all areas of employee health on behalf of client companies. The goal was to stabilize healthcare costs by raising the level of health of the employee population. Expected side benefits for employers included a reduced number of workmen's compensation claims, fewer absences, and greater productivity. Services offered ranged from counseling to quit smoking to onsite medical care. GHC also sponsored four programs to help rebuild communities affected by violence. Annual revenues exceeded $1 billion for the first time in 1994. Group Health had more than 500,000 participants.

Talks with an Oregon-based unit of Kaiser Permanente, a similar HMO, began in 1996. The ensuing alliance gradually extended into areas such as joint purchasing, marketing, and reciprocity in medical care. Wider geographic reach made GHC more attractive to national and regional employers.

In 1997, the rapidly expanding GHC had more than 700,000 members. Still, it was a bad year. Nudelman's claimed educational achievements featured in the ''Dubious Credentials'' episode of the tabloid television show *American Journal*. Administrator Cheryl Scott later became the new president and CEO. Group Health also lost $10.4 million on revenues of $1 billion in 1997, due to vigorous price competition.

Scott reduced costs, increased premiums, abandoned more than a dozen counties, and dropped out of low-income programs. GHC also closed enrollment in individual plans. GHC logged a profit of $3 million in 1999 after losing $68 million in the previous two years. As the patients' rights movement built momentum, in 2000 GHC joined 21 other health plans in a series of voluntary reforms.

In another change designed to encourage more member participation, GHC dropped the requirement to pay an additional $25 annual dues to become a voting member of the cooperative. However, the hectic pace of modern living, rather than the fee, was what kept most from attending meetings.

In the late 1990s, GHC (along with two other carriers, Premera Blue Cross and Regence BlueShield) began offering insurance to individuals, yielding to political pressure to help the state's uninsured residents (although those with the worst health problems were referred to the state's high risk pool).

In 1999, Group Health cut Medicare service in some areas after pulling out of most remaining rural counties the previous year. GHC's Medicare unit was the subject of numerous complaints. In 1999, the state ombudsman took the unprecedented step of referring one complainant to an administrative law judge at the Social Security Administration. Soon after, the federal government stopped funding Medicare and Medicaid admissions at Group Health's Bellevue nursing home (Kelsey Creek), citing violations with federal law.

Principal Subsidiaries

Center for Health Studies; Center for Health Promotion; Group Health Community Foundation; Group Health Enterprises; Group Health Options, Inc.; Kaiser/Group Health.

Principal Competitors

Adventist Health; Health Net, Inc.; PacifiCare Health Systems, Inc.

Further Reading

Anders, George, ''For a Shangri-La of HMOs, a Dose of Modern Reality,'' *Wall Street Journal,* August 4, 1998, p. B1.

Barker, Kim, ''Two HMOs to Drop Medicare Customers,'' *Seattle Times,* July 1, 1999.

Beason, Tyrone, ''Group Health Pulls Out of Most Rural Areas,'' *Seattle Times,* May 27, 1999.

——, ''Two More Insurers Won't Sell Health Policies,'' *Seattle Times,* December 25, 1998.

Bernstein, Sharon, ''HMOs, Under Political Pressure, Offer Package of Patient-Friendly Policies,'' *Seattle Times,* July 19, 2000.

Cimini, Michael H., ''Training Featured in Group Health Settlement,'' *Monthly Labor Review,* December 1995, p. 47.

Crowley, Walt, *To Serve the Greatest Number: A History of Group Health Cooperative of Puget Sound,* Seattle: Group Health Cooperative of Puget Sound/University of Washington Press, 1996.

Egan, Timothy, ''Seattle Showpiece of Health Care by Democracy,'' *New York Times,* May 2, 1991.

Frabotta, David, ''Up in Smoke,'' *Managed Healthcare,* September 1999, p. 42.

Fryer, Alex, ''Nudelman Smarts Over Focus on His Degrees,'' *Seattle Times,* June 1, 1997.

Gilje, Shelby, ''For this Health Insurance, a Mere 272 Questions,'' *Seattle Times,* November 1, 2000.

Gould, Bob, Ted Nolan, and Robert C. Schuweiler, ''An Experiment in Risk Sharing,'' *Health Forum Journal,* September/October 1999, pp. 19, 26+.

Hagland, Mark, ''Synergy in Seattle,'' *Hospitals & Health Networks,* June 20, 1996, p. 55.

——, ''Two HMOs Play 'Let's Make a Deal','' *Hospitals & Health Networks,* November 5, 1996, p. 64.

King, Marsha, ''HMO Under Fire: State Backs Woman in Dispute with Group Health,'' *Seattle Times,* October 4, 1999.

Kokmen, Leyla, ''Old Health Groups Eye Benefits of New Alliances,'' *Seattle Times,* September 14, 1996.

Lee, John Y., and Pauline Nefcy, ''The Anatomy of an Effective HMO Cost Management System,'' *Management Accounting,* January 1997, pp. 49–54.

Levine, Ruth, ''Group Health Searches for Solutions in Tough Market,'' *Puget Sound Business Journal,* June 23, 2000.

Lumsdon, Kevin, ''Hospitals, Suppliers Put TQM to the Test,'' *Hospitals,* March 20, 1993, p. 58.

McCue, Michael T., ''Consumer Governed, Patient Focused,'' *Managed Healthcare Executive,* January 2001, pp. 14–26.

''New Buildings for a New Era Can Look Very Different,'' *Medical Economics,* February 9, 1998, pp. 90–91.

Nudelman, Phillip M., ''Stop Violence Now,'' *Hospitals & Health Networks,* July 20, 1995, p. 62.

——, ''The Partnership Prescription,'' *Chief Executive,* January/February 1994, p. 57.

Walker, Tracey, ''Three HMOs Ask for Regulation,'' *Managed Healthcare,* November 1997, pp. 10–11.

Winslow, Ron, ''Kaiser Permanente Unit, Group Health Enter Talks That Could Lead to Merger,'' *Wall Street Journal,* September 16, 1996, p. B6.

—Frederick C. Ingram

Gruppo Coin S.p.A.

Via Terraglio, 17
30174 Mestre
Venezia
Italy
Telephone: (+39) 41-239-8000
Fax: (+39) 41-982-722
Web site: http://www.gruppocoin.com

Public Company
Incorporated: 1934 as SACMA SpA
Sales: L 2.36 trillion ($1.18 billion)
Stock Exchanges: Italy
Ticker Symbol: GC
NAIC: 452110 Department Stores

Based in Italy, Gruppo Coin S.p.A. is buying its way into the top ten of European department store retailers. At the beginning of the 21st century, the company claimed the leading share—5.65 percent—of Italy's highly competitive and highly fragmented retail department store market. Coin operates department stores and specialty stores throughout Italy under several brand names, each targeting a specific market. The company's flagship ''Coin'' department store chain targets the Italian upscale market with more than 80 company-owned and franchised stores. The company's discount clothing and home furnishing chain, ''Oviesse,'' is located throughout Italy with nearly 130 stores and is being developed by Gruppo Coin into the company's international spearhead. Gruppo Coin also operates a 129-store chain of mid-priced department stores under the ''La Standa'' name, which were acquired in 1998. Coin, however, is making steady inroads toward converting the La Standa stores into the Odiesse and Coin formats, while also selling off some other properties, including 12 stores to the Benetton group in 2000. At the same time, the company is also building two other brands, ''Bimbus'' and ''Kids Planet,'' both of which target the children's market. In 1999, Gruppo Coin also joined with France's Pinault-Printemps-Redoute to open ''Fnac'' book, record and electronics stores in Italy. Listed since 1999 on the Italian stock exchange, Gruppo Coin continues to be controlled at more than 74 percent by the founding Coin family, now in its third generation under the leadership of Piergiorgio Coin.

Pushcarts in World War I Times

Gruppo Coin developed an international retail empire from a single pushcart in less than a century. In 1916, patriarch Vittoria Coin was granted an itinerant merchant's license and began selling clothing and other apparel (such as hats and traditional head-coverings) from a pushcart in the countryside around his home in the Pianiga, Venice region. Coin quickly showed a flair for more modern sales techniques, and was soon joined by his sons Alfonso, Aristide, and Gionvanni in opening his first retail store in Mirano in 1926.

The new Coin family store not only featured clothing and other apparel, but also offered home furnishings. Over the next decade, Coin developed his retail format into a broader department store concept, while also retaining an upscale, high-quality reputation. Coin and his sons soon began opening new retail stores; the second Coin store opened in Dolo in 1929, and a third in Venezia-Mestre in 1933.

In 1934, Coin and his sons incorporated their growing business under the name of SACMA SpA—for the Societa Associativa Commercio Manifatture e Affini—highlighting not only the company's growing retail network, but also its entry into the manufacturing of clothing and other goods for its stores. By the outbreak of World War II, the company operated seven stores in the Venice region.

Trying Times and Expansion Following World War II

At the end of World War II, all of the Coin family's stores had been destroyed. Leadership of the company was turned over to Alfonso, who, with brothers Giovanni and Aristide, began rebuilding the company's stores. After reopening its Venice store first, and then its store in San Giovanni Grisotomo, the company slowly opened stores in Mirano, Dolo, Mestre and Padova by 1947. Alfonso also helped steer the family's operations in a new direction, adding ready-to-wear fashions to the stores. In 1950, the company adopted a new name, Coin SpA,

Key Dates:

1916: Vittoria Coin gains license as a pushcart vendor.
1926: Coin opens first retail store.
1929: Second store opened in Dolo.
1933: Store opened in Venezia-Mestre.
1934: Company is incorporated as SACMA SpA.
1946: Alfonso Coin becomes president.
1950: Company changes name to Coin SpA, and moves headquarters to Trieste.
1957: Company acquires Ohler department stores.
1965: 5,000-square-meter flagship built in Milan.
1972: Odiesse brand is launched.
1980: Headquarters transferred to Venice.
1986: New Coin flagship is established in Venice.
1995: Coin and Odiesse are combined into Gruppo Coin SPCA.
1998: La Standa department store division is acquired.
1999: Company is listed on Italian stock exchange; joint-venture agreement created with Pinault-Printemps-Redoute.
2000: Franchise agreement created with Magazine zum Globus (Switzerland).
2001: Kaufhalle department stores (Germany) are taken over.

and opened a new warehouse and shifted its headquarters to Trieste.

1957 marked the company's first step toward building a full-fledged retail empire, when it acquired the Italian stores of Austrian retail chain Ohler. A year later, Coin expanded beyond its Venice province home base to establish a new 1,400-square-meter flagship store in Bologna.

Diversification in the 1960s and 1970s

The next generation of Coins joined the company at the beginning of the 1960s, as Aristide Coin's sons Piergiorgio and Vittorio Coin prepared to take over the family company's lead. The company now began to expand its retail format into a larger department store format, adding departments for items such as sporting goods, luggage, appliances, and the like. The company opened six new stores in the early 1960s, culminating with the opening of a new 5,000-square-meter flagship store in Milan. In 1966 Alfonso Coin died, and his brother Aristide took on the company presidency.

Coin then entered into a new expansionist period, opening ''Grandi Magazzini Coin'' stores in Brescia, Vicenza, Varese, Pordenone, Vigevano, Mantova, Genova, Livorno, Udine, Piacenza, Napoli, Taranto and Ferrara between 1966 and 1974. In 1974, Aristide turned over the company's presidency to Piergiorgio Coin, who was aided by brother Vitorrio.

By then, the company had also begun developing a second retail store format, Odiesse, which had been introduced as a subsidiary operation in 1972. The Odiesse brand, offering a discount pricing formula, was first opened in Padova and grew quickly, operating branches in Milan, Carpi, Valdagn, Villafranca and Legnago by 1974. The chain continued to grow through the end of the century, later totaling nearly 130 branches in Italy before becoming the company's spearhead brand for its international growth.

International Expansion at the End of the 20th Century

By the 1980s, Coin was fast on its way to becoming one of Italy's leading department store groups. In the early 1980s the company returned to Venice when it transferred its headquarters to that city. The company also opened a new Venice flagship store in 1986. At the same time, Coin began to adopt the ''store-in-store'' concept that had become fashionable among the world's department stores, adding branded in-store boutiques to its floors.

The 1990s marked a period of transition for the company, which had grown not only into one of Italy's top retail companies, but which was also quickly climbing the ranks of European leaders as well. Coin had long been operated as a typical family-owned company, but began to restructure and streamline its management and organization into a single chain of command. The company also restructured its operations, combining Coin SPCA and Odiesse SPCA into a single entity, Gruppo Coin SPCA.

The reorganization of the company resulted in clearly defined brand and market concepts, with the Coin department stores dedicated to the upscale market, and the fast-growing Odiesse brand committed to the discount-price market. Coin also began rolling out a new flagship store concept for the Coin brand, opening new stores in Milan and Genoa in 1998, and in Catania and Rome in 1999.

By then, the company had taken on an entirely new size when it completed a L 9 billion acquisition of the department store division of rival Italian company La Standa. Coin then began a program to convert the 129 La Standa stores into the Coin and Odiesse concepts. When the conversion program proved successful—with both the Odiesse and Coin brands boosting the new stores' per-square-meter sales—Coin stepped up its conversion drive. At the same time, Coin also sought to sell off a number of the less profitable La Standa properties. This move was completed in November 2000 when Coin agreed to sell 12 stores to Gescom, which was part of the Benetton group. Meanwhile, Coin was also introducing new retail store concepts, including two children's formats—Bimbus and Kid's Planet.

Coin Enters the New Millennium as a Public Entity

The now streamlined and growing Coin group went public in 1999, listing slightly more than 25 percent of its shares on the Italian stock exchange. The Coin family's nearly 75 percent of shares kept the retail empire firm in their hands, however. Soon after the public offering, Coin announced it had signed an agreement with French retail and luxury goods group Pinault-Printemps-Redoute to form a joint venture in order to introduce the Fnac retail store brand to the Italian market. As part of the agreement, Coin agreed to turn over 12 of its La Standa stores to be converted into Fnac's book, music and electronics formula.

The first Coin/Fnac stores were expected to open soon after the turn of the century.

Having established a strong national presence—Coin claimed nearly 6 percent of the total Italian retail market, which was enough to give it the leading position—Coin now looked forward to developing an international presence for the 21st century. The company, now led by President Vittorio Coin, made a bold move to establish itself on the international scene. In January 2001, the company announced that it had acquired Germany's Kaufhalle department store chain, giving it nearly 100 stores in Europe's largest single retail market. Coin immediately began converting the Kaufhalle stores to its Odiesse format, chosen as the company's international spearhead. Coin pledged an investment of some L 300 million toward the conversion effort, which was expected to take some three years to complete.

The Kaufhalle acquisition helped propel Coin into the European big leagues, where it now claimed the number nine spot among leading retailers. Coin's move into Germany was also expected to be accompanied by an extension into Switzerland. In September 2000, the company reached an agreement with Swiss group Magazine zum Globus—which operated stores under the names Au Bon Marché, Globus and Heren Globus, Interio, Office World, Globe and other names—to introduce an Odiesse franchise concept in Switzerland. The initial agreement called for two stores to open in Zug and Lancy by the end of 2000, and for two new stores to be opened in the first half of 2001, with an extension to as many as 40 stores throughout the Swiss market starting from 2002. Given Coin's success at empire-building in its Italian home, the company looked forward to developing a truly international presence before the end of its first century in existence.

Principal Subsidiaries

Manifatture di Fara; Sirema.

Principal Competitors

La Rinascenta S.p.A.; Benetton Group S.p.A.; Metro AG; Rinascente S.p.A.

Further Reading

''Coin spinge sulla conversione Standa,'' *Il Sole 24 Ore,* December 3, 1999.

''Il prossimo traguardo fissato e quello di superare I 3 mila miliardi di fatturato,'' *La Repubblica,* February 26, 2001.

''Vola dopo il blitz tedesco,'' *Il Sole 24 Ore,* August 30, 2000.

—M.L. Cohen

Guillemot Corporation

Place de L'Etoile
56910 Carentoir
France
Telephone: (+33) 2 99 08 08 80
Fax: (+33) 2 99 08
Web site: http://www.guillemot.com

Public Company
Incorporated: 1984 as Guillemot Informatique
Employees: 1,500
Sales: EUR 222.31 million ($205 million)(2000)
Stock Exchanges: Euronext Paris
Ticker Symbol: 6672
NAIC: 334119 Other Computer Peripheral Equipment Manufacturing

Brittany, France-based, Guillemot Corporation has taken the fast track toward becoming one of the world's premier producers of peripherals, hardware, and other accessories for the computer and console gaming markets. The company produces graphics cards and graphics accelerators, sound cards, DVD and CD-ROM drives, television acquisition cards, joysticks, gamepads, steering wheels, and other devices under the Guillemot, Maxi Sound, Thrustmaster, and Hercules brand names. Led by the five Guillemot brothers—Claude, Christian, Yves, Michel, and Gerard—who also founded and continue to operate video game specialist Ubi Soft Entertainment S.A., Guillemot Corporation has grown quickly at the turn of the century through its often innovative, feature-packed, and aggressively priced products. Although the Guillemot name has become well-known in France and the rest of Europe, Guillemot is known to North Americans especially through its acquisitions of well-respected brand names Thrustmaster and Hercules, both acquired in 1999. The company operates sales and marketing subsidiaries in 14 countries worldwide, two research and development centers in Canada and France, and six logistics facilities supporting its core European, Asian, and North American markets. The company's North American headquarters are located in Montreal. Guillemot has been traded on the Euronext Paris fast-growth Nouveau Marché since its initial public offering was made in 1998. The company topped the FFr 1 billion mark in 2000—worth more than EUR 220 million. Guillemot has its goals set on gaining a position among the top five gaming hardware and accessories companies by the year 2003.

Startup in the Family Barn in the 1980s

The Guillemot family's origins in commerce traced back to the beginning of the 20th century, when the family operated a cider distillery in its Carentoir, Brittany home. The family's cider sales led the Guillemot into wholesale sales of apples, and by the 1930s, the family had built up a strong export trade in Germany. Later, in 1958, Yvette and Marcel Guillemot set up a new business as a wholesale agricultural products distributor, while raising their children, including their five sons, Michel, Claude, Yves, Christian, and Gerard, all of whom worked part-time in the family business while completing their studies.

By the early 1980s, the Guillemot brothers were graduating from school and beginning to look forward to establishing their own professional careers. The family's agricultural products business had been successful, producing sales of some FFr 17 million per year, and the Guillemot's parents agreed to provide backing for their sons to begin their own business.

By then, Michel Guillemot, who had completed his university studies in Lille, had already led his brothers into an interest in a still-emerging new industry, computers. Michel had already been behind the founding of the Microtel computer clubs that for a time helped introduce much of France to the new technology. Back at Carentoir, Michel, joined by brother Claude and then the remaining three Guillemot brothers, was given the go-ahead from father Marcel to launch the family into the computer industry.

The Guillemots started out in retail, opening their first Guillemot Informatique store near their home in 1984, but quickly focused on mail-order and wholesale distribution wing as well. The company's early arrival gave Guillemot a head start and by their second year of business, the company had won contracts to supply computers and equipment throughout much of the French national school system. Although the growing

Company Perspectives:

Guillemot is committed to being the top producer of exciting accessories and hardware for gamers and to be among the top five gaming hardware and accessories manufacturers worldwide by 2003.

company remained interested in the general computer market, the young Guillemot brothers were quickly captivated by the new and growing market for video computer games, which itself had only recently come into being with the launch of the Commodore and Atari computer-based gaming systems. Meanwhile, its growing success caused it to drop its mail-order component and focus on its blossoming wholesale distribution operations.

Yet many of the new games proved impossible to find in France. The Guillemots recognized the opportunity and began importing the elusive titles, including such early hits as ''SOS Ghosts'' and others. The company now featured strong software and hardware distribution, which, by 1986, was producing FFr 40 million in sales. An important breakthrough for the Guillemots came with contracts from French retail leaders Auchan, Carrefour, and others to supply these nationally operating chains of hypermarkets with computer hardware and software products. At the point, the company changed its name to Guillemot International.

The ''international'' part of its name was quickly developed as the company extended its distribution activities into other parts of Europe. The company expanded rapidly and in 1986 separated its two lines of activities, hardware and software, into two companies with the creation of Ubi Soft Entertainment SA. While that company was headquartered in Paris, Guillemot International itself remained in the family's native Carentoir.

Ubi Soft quickly imposed itself as a major distributor of computer and video games and later as one of the world's leading developers and publishers of video games. In 1988, the Guillemot brothers sought to make their mark on the hardware side of things as well and began to introduce the company's own computer peripheral designs. In 1990, the company launched its first line of products bearing the Guillemot brand name. At the same time, Guillemot began acting as exclusive French distributor for Soundblaster—which was quickly establishing itself as the computer industry standard in sound cards—and Thrustmaster, the first company to create joysticks for the computer game market.

Soundblaster, Thrustmaster, and other companies, such as graphics-card maker Hercules, were in the process of transforming the computer from a silent, sober, work-oriented piece of equipment into a full-fledged entertainment center—where one just happened to work sometimes. Although the computer gaming market remained somewhat restrained through the first half of the decade, the arrival of new technologies, such as CD-ROM drives, 3D graphics accelerators, 16-bit stereo sound cards and other peripherals, as well as the launch of new generations of video gaming consoles from Sega and Nintendo were set to launch the gaming segment into a full-fledged entertainment industry and rival to the television and motion picture industries. Guillemot positioned itself to be at the forefront of this development, extending the company's operations beyond France by opening a series of foreign sales offices. Between 1994 and 1996, Guillemot opened offices in Belgium, Germany, United Kingdom, Switzerland, the United States, Canada, and Hong Kong.

The company's interests were also turning more and more toward the development of its own hardware. By the mid-1990s, the company's brands included its Fun Access and Access Line accessories products, and also the Maxi brand of hardware and peripherals, including gamepads and other devices. Among the early Maxi products were the first of the company's Maxi Sound line of sound cards. The development of these cards caused the company to end its distribution arrangement with Soundblaster—and Guillemot proceeded to become one of Soundblaster's strongest competitors.

Gunning for the Top in the 21st Century

If Guillemot's early products had often seemed little more than clones of rival products, in the mid-1990s the company stepped up its research and development and determined to make establish its name as a product innovator. A breakthrough for Guillemot came in 1996 with its release of the Maxi Sound 64 sound card, the first card on the market featuring 64-voiced polyphony. The following year, the company extended the Maxi Sound 64 range with the release of the Home Studio Pro version, the first all-in-one computer-based solution for music creation and recording accessible to a large public. At the same time, the Home Studio Pro offered cutting-edge technologies for the gaming market, including one of the first attempts at introducing 3D positional sound to computer games.

Through the middle years of the decade, Guillemot extended its range to include a wide variety of peripherals for both the computer and console markets. The company was now placing its various brand names on steering wheels, joystick and game pads, CD-ROM drives, digital video acquisition boards, speaker systems, and other products.

With Ubi Soft making steady games in the ranks of games developers—driven by the worldwide success of the Rayman games series—the Guillemot brothers sought to raise their hardware operations to its own leadership positions. The company restructured in 1997, then renamed itself Guillemot Corporation in 1998, when it took a listing on the Paris Stock Exchange high-growth Nouveau Marché. The company now began to phase out the Maxi and Maxi Sound and other brand names in favor of the Guillemot name itself.

After establishing itself as a major player in the worldwide soundcard market, Guillemot also extended itself into the booming—and still more competitive—market for graphics cards, releasing its own board designs based on technologies developed by 3DFX, NVIDIA, and others. Until its public offering, Guillemot had focused on its European community market, where it succeeded in boosting itself to one of the top hardware and peripherals manufacturers.

In 1998, Guillemot Corporation determined to take on the far larger North American market. The company opened its

Key Dates:

1984: Guillemot Informatique is founded.
1986: The company name changes to Guillemot International.
1988: Guillemot begins manufacturing hardware and accessories.
1994: The company begins international expansion and launches the Maxi brand name.
1997: The company Releases Maxi Sound 64 sound card.
1998: The company changes its name to Guillemot Corporation, with a public listing on Paris stock exchange.
1999: Guillemot acquires Thrustmaster and Hercules.
2000: The company opens new subsidiaries in Japan, Australia, the Czech Republic, and Italy.
2001: Guillemot signs a licensing agreement for Microsoft Xbox.

headquarters on that continent in bilingual Montreal, where it also established a second research and development facility. That unit, opened in 1999, was also slated to become the growing group's principal R&D center as Guillemot poised to begin a new and more aggressive expansion phase. Yet Guillemot's North American expansion seemed hampered by its lack of a strong brand name in that market—and even the difficulty many English speakers experienced when trying to pronounce the company's name.

Guillemot (pronounced as ''gee-ye-moe'') raised new capital in 1999 and quite a few eyebrows when, within the space of five months, it made two important acquisitions. The first of these came in July 1999, when Guillemot paid $15 million to acquire the gaming peripherals operations and brand name from Thrustmaster, of Oregon (the remaining operation subsequently renamed itself).

One of the leading names in gaming and simulation hardware, Thrustmaster had been founded in 1990 and had been the first company to produce a realistic joystick, the Mark I Weapons Control System, released in 1991. Thrustmaster continued to improve its technology, releasing its Pro Flight Control System in 1992, the F-16 and F-22 joystick—foot pedal units. In the mid-1990s, Thrustmaster turned its simulation expertise to the popular racing game market, releasing Formula T1 Driving Controls. Thrustmaster quickly became a leading name in game controls, and the company's sales grew to $15 million by 1995 and then to $25 million by 1998.

Guillemot began phasing out its own branded line of controls in favor of the Thrustmaster name. The company next began looking for an acquisition to help it gain similar recognition among the intensely competitive graphics market. A new opportunity presented itself in August 1999 when Hercules Computer Technology filed for bankruptcy protection.

The company had been a pioneer in the computer graphics market. At the beginning of the 1980s, Van Suwannukul, a native of Thailand and then resident of the town of Hercules, California, had been preparing his doctoral thesis but was unable to display the Thai alphabet on the text-based, monochrome displays available at the time. Suwannukul developed his own display system, an add-on board that allowed for both graphics and text to be displayed. In 1982, Suwannukul formed Hercules Computer Technology in his garage and launched the first Hercules graphics display board.

The launch of the Hercules coincided with the release of the first version of the popular spreadsheet program Lotus 1-2-3. Built for the IBM PC platform, the Hercules card quickly established itself as an industry standard—and in turn helped the IBM platform replace all but the Apple as a computer standard. Throughout the 1980s and early 1990s, Hercules was able to command high prices for its graphics cards. Yet by the mid-1990s, the increasing power of CPUs and the appearance of faster rival technologies, doomed Hercules to a steady decline. Nonetheless, the Hercules brand name remained one of the industry's best known and most highly respected.

Guillemot acquired the Hercules brand name and quickly added it to its own line of graphics cards, themselves now based around the cutting-edge graphics processors developed by NVIDIA. Guillemot and NVIDIA had signed a strategic partnership agreement early in 1999. Other partnerships followed, including an agreement with Ferrari to add the famed carmaker's name and logo to the company's driving simulators. The following year, the company launched its own investment vehicle, Guillemot Ventures, and joined with the newly formed Ubi Ventures subsidiary of Ubi Soft to begin making venture capital investments. The two companies joined in the creation of the online gaming start-up www.Gameloft.com, and also in the creation of Ludi Wap, a company dedicated to providing online gaming content for the new generation of Internet-capable mobile phones.

Guillemot continued extending its infrastructure, opening new subsidiaries in Japan, Italy, Australia, and the Czech Republic into 2001. Guillemot also stepped up its product development, releasing new and highly acclaimed Hercules-branded graphics cards and signing a licensing agreement with Microsoft to develop peripheral products for the highly awaited Xbox gaming console to be launched in 2001. As Guillemot's sales topped the FFr 1 billion mark in its 2000 year, the company now set its sights on taking a spot in the top five gaming hardware and accessories companies by the year 2003. With its strong Thrustmaster and Hercules brand names, as well as the continuing growth of the Guillemot name, the company seemed likely to remain in high gear for a long time to come.

Principal Subsidiaries

Guillemot BV (Netherlands); Guillemot Conditionnement SARL; Guillemot Conditionnement France SARL; Guillemot Participations SA; Guillemot France SA; Guillemot GmbH (Germany); Guillemot Logistique SARL; Guillemot Logistique Inc. (Canada); Guillemot Logistik GmbH (Germany); Guillemot Logistique France; Guillemot Logistics Ltd (Hong Kong); Guillemot Logistica SL (Spain); Guillemot Logistic Ltd (U.K.); Guillemot Ltd (U.K.); Guillemot Ltd (Hong Kong); Guillemot Manufacturing Ltd (U.K.); Guillemot SA (Spain); Guillemot SA (Belgium); Guillemot Online.com, Inc. (U.S.); Guillemot, Inc. (U.S.); Guillemot, Inc. (Canada); Guillemot Recherche et Développement SARL; Guillemot Recherche et

Développement, Inc.; Guillemot Studio Graphique SARL; Guillemot Support Technique SARL (Canada); Hercules Technologies SA; Hercules Technologies, Inc.; (U.S.); Logicosoftware SA (Switzerland); Thrustmaster SA; Thrustmaster, Inc. (U.S.).

Principal Competitors

ATI Technologies, Inc.; Creative Technology Ltd.; Diamond Multimedia Inc.; Elsa AG; Hauppauge Inc.; Logitech SA; Matrox Graphics; Terratec AG; Trust SA.

Further Reading

''Guillemot Corporation Entre Dans le Grand Jeu Bien Réel de la Bourse,'' *Le Télégramme*, October 13, 1998.

Kern, Josh, ''Guillemot Builds Brand Name in North America,'' *Computer Dealer News*, January 28, 2000.

Peterson, Thane, ''France's Guillemot May Be Rural, But It Sure Isn't Backward,'' *Business Week Online*, July 29, 2000.

Romaine, Garrett, ''Paid to Play,'' *Computer Bits*, May 1997.

Spring, Tom, ''Graphics Board Maker Hercules Folds,'' *PC World*, August 31, 1999.

—M.L. Cohen

Hanger Orthopedic Group, Inc.

Two Bethesda Metro Center, Suite 1200
Bethesda, Maryland 20814
U.S.A.
Telephone: (301) 986-0701
Fax: (301) 986-0702
Web site: http://www.hanger.com

Public Company
Incorporated: 1988 as Sequel Corporation
Employees: 3,531
Sales: $486 mil (2000)
Stock Exchanges: New York
Ticker Symbols: HGR
NAIC: 62149 Other Outpatient Care Centers; 33911 Surgical Appliance and Supplies Manufacturing; 55111 Offices of Other Holding Companies

Hanger Orthopedic Group, Inc. is the oldest and one of the largest prosthetics and orthotics (O&P) companies in the world. At the end of 2000, its patient care division, Hanger Prosthetics & Orthotics Inc., owned and operated 620 centers in 45 states and the District of Columbia and provided O&P services to more than 1,100 managed care programs through its OPNET program. Its manufacturing division, Seattle Orthopedic Group, Inc., made custom and prefabricated orthotics (braces) and prosthetics (artificial limbs) under brand names such as Seattle Limb Systems and Lenox Hill. Southern Prosthetic Supply, Inc., the company's distribution division, was the largest distributor of O&P products in the country.

An Amputee's Invention: 1861–1919

James Edward Hanger's life changed in 1861. A college sophomore from Churchville, Virginia, Hanger left school to join the Confederate cavalry. Before he even formally enlisted, his leg was shattered by a ricocheting cannonball fired by Union troops during the battle of Philippi, Virginia. Operated on by a Yankee surgeon, who took his leg off above the knee, Hanger became the first amputee of the Civil War. Shortly afterwards he was sent home in a prisoner-of-war exchange.

Unhappy with the wooden peg he had been given, Hanger locked himself in his upstairs room, vowing not to come out until he could walk down. During the next several months, he designed an artificial leg with the first hinged knee and hinged foot, forming it out of whittled barrel staves, rubber, wood, and metal components. According to a history of prosthetics from Northwestern University Medical School, Hanger ''replaced the catgut tendons of the American leg [an earlier prostheses named in 1856] with rubber bumpers to control dorsiflexion and plantarflexion and he used plug fit wood socket.''

Other Confederate amputees quickly created a demand for the realistic ''Hanger limb,'' and Hanger established his business, J.E. Hanger, Inc., in Richmond, Virginia. He patented his limb in 1871.

The Civil War also generated the first government commitment to provide veterans with prostheses. The ''Great Civil War Benefaction'' was the forerunner of the federal support that played a major role in assisting war veteran amputees to the present time.

In 1915 Hanger went to Europe to help World War I amputees and to learn from European prosthetists. Because the number of American casualties was much smaller than that of British and European troops, Europe was where prosthetic advances were being made. Considered by many to be the father of modern prosthetics, Hanger died in 1919.

A Family Tradition: 1915–1960s

Interest in the prosthetic business ran throughout the Hanger family. During the second decade of the century, Hanger's five sons split the original company, and they began operating unaffiliated Hanger offices in Atlanta, Georgia; Philadelphia, Pennsylvania; St. Louis, Missouri; and the District of Columbia. Their offspring, along with associates and various Hanger in-laws and cousins, continued the Hanger dynasty, moving their artificial limb businesses into Canada and Europe.

The company's primary business, prosthetics, covered the fitting, design, and building of artificial limbs (prostheses) for people who had lost an arm or leg, through illness, such as

Company Perspectives:

The company strives to be the best in providing the most advanced orthotic and prosthetic services and products available, and provide orthotic and prosthetic services in a timely and professional manner, in a pleasant atmosphere, at a reasonable cost to our patients, and continually strive to improve our services and facilities, while maintaining a rewarding atmosphere for our associates and investors.

cancer, or more usually in an accident or from a war injury. The industry in the United States did not change much from the technology used in the 1800s until World War II. In 1946, with veterans demanding better prosthetics, the federal government, in the form of the surgeon general and the Veterans Administration, supported research and development to improve on the wooden artificial limbs that were belted on to a leg or arm.

Several federal agencies, along with the armed services, established research laboratories. From these came new socket designs and improved materials, including thermosetting resins, used to form structural components. During this period, orthotists, who made external braces and support devices, joined those who created the artificial limbs, forming the American Orthotics and Prosthetics Association in 1950.

The 1950s also saw a tremendous increase in educational courses and certification for prosthetists, culminating in the establishment of postgraduate programs in the late 1950s.

By the mid-1950s, there were 50 Hanger offices in North America and 25 in Europe.

Changes in the Field: the 1970s

Technological developments continued to influence the industry during the 1960s and 1970s, as did the Vietnam war. The passage of Medicare and Medicaid contributed to rehabilitation support for the aging and the poor. One of the important developments was a 1965 prosthetic dubbed "the Seattle foot." This innovation, which made it possible for amputees to be more active, was based on putting a spring in the false foot. The foot also looked more real, with toenails and veins.

With funding from Liberty Mutual Insurance Company, the Massachusetts Institute for Technology developed a bionic arm that used the body's own muscle signals for control. But it was during the 1980s that technology development became "truly fantastic," as an October 1980 *Business Week* article claimed, as scientists and engineers explored how to link prosthetic devices directly to the brain.

At the same time, the entire health care industry was undergoing changes, including consolidation and for-profit managed care, that would soon become factors in the O&P industry.

From Cell Phones to Artificial Limbs: 1986–89

Orthotics and prosthetics was highly fragmented industry, consisting primarily of individual offices or small franchise chains of care centers. Its potential for consolidation attracted a variety of companies. One that saw opportunities in the field was Sequel Corporation, a communications company that abruptly changed its focus in 1986 from owning and operating radio stations to running patient care centers.

Colorado-based Sequel had already been through one major corporate change. It began life in 1983 as Celltech Communications Inc., with plans to gain licenses for cellular phone systems and eventually to establish cellular phone service around the country. This strategy was disrupted when the Federal Communications Commission changed its licensing process to a lottery system, which Celltech indicated made it hard for small companies to compete. In 1985, Celltech moved into a different area of the communications field, buying three radio stations, in Lincoln, Nebraska and Brainerd, Minnesota. When these continued to lose money, Celltech changed its name to Sequel, sold off its cellular phone interests and radio stations, and hired a new president, Robert Fine, with experience in the health industry.

Sequel's first acquisitions, in 1987, were Capital Orthopedics of Bethesda, Maryland, for which it paid an estimated $1.5 million, and Greiner and Saur Orthopedic Appliances Corporation of Philadelphia, paying $680,262. During its first year of existence, Sequel moved its headquarters east to Philadelphia and then to Connecticut. In 1988, the company named the founder and head of its Capital subsidiary, Ivan Sabel, president and chief operating officer. Sabel was particularly interested in centralizing the design and manufacturing of devices and distributing them nationwide. "Sequel will be the first publicly held company whose sole business will be the manufacturing of these devices on a national basis," he told *The Denver Business Journal* when his business became part of Sequel.

The company continued making acquisitions, and in 1989, bought J.E. Hanger, Inc. of Washington, D.C., one of the surviving branches of the business started by the Civil War amputee. At the time of purchase, J.E. Hanger was an $8 million business, with offices in 11 cities and eight states.

The $14.25 million purchase was a complicated stock exchange transition, with two venture capital firms and a bank providing the financing and ending up with 69 percent of the stock. Chemical Venture Capital Associates, the major financier and an affiliate of Chemical Bank, appointed the majority of seats on Sequel's board. Chemical also controlled major policies, such as the payment of dividends, and established performance requirements for management, to make ensure an acceptable return on its investment. For example, according to a 1991 *Washington Post* article, when Sequel did not meet agreed upon "internal rates of return," its top managers had to turn over shares of their personal stock in the company to Chemical.

Soon after the acquisition, Sequel, which was the smaller company, changed its name to Hanger Orthopedic Group.

Continued Consolidation: 1990–94

In 1990, the orthotics and prosthetics industry did $700 million in business a year, providing patient care as well as manufacturing and distributing braces and artificial limbs. Unlike the earlier years of the industry, when wars provided most of the business, now it was the growing elderly population and

Key Dates:

1861: James Edward Hanger develops a wooden artificial leg for himself and Confederate amputees. He establishes J.E. Hanger, Inc. in Richmond, Virginia.
1915: Hanger's five sons split J.E. Hanger, Inc. into four separate companies, each based in a different region.
1919: James Edward Hanger dies.
1986: Sequel Corporation switches from cellular phones to orthotics and prosthetics with purchases of Capital Orthopedics and Greiner and Saur Orthopedic Appliances Corporation.
1989: Sequel acquires Washington, D.C.-based J.E. Hanger, Inc. and becomes the Hanger Orthopedic Group.
1991: Hanger Orthopedic goes public.
1995: Hanger forms OPNET, its managed-care division.
1996: Hanger Orthopedic Group buys Georgia-based J.E. Hanger, Inc.
1999: Hanger buys NovaCare O&P.

people suffering injuries while playing sports or from physical fitness activities who were being referred to O&P offices.

Hanger continued to buy up family-owned firms, mostly along the East Coast. Between 1989 and 1991, it purchased 13 companies, borrowing more than $23 million to pay for them. As a result, although the company brought in nearly $20 million in revenue in 1990, its long-term debt and hefty interest payments left it in the red, with a loss of $1.5 million. To help pay down the debt, Hanger created and issued new shares of common stock through public offerings. In 1994, it went through a major restructuring.

Hanger's Competition

Hanger's major competitor, and the largest of the O&P companies, was Orthopedic Services, Inc. (OSI) of King of Prussia, Pennsylvania. Started in 1987, OSI quickly bought up practices around the country, particularly on the West Coast. It went public in 1990, and in 1992 merged with NovaCare, Inc., the country's largest provider of contract rehabilitation therapy services, for the price of $248 million. At the time OSI provided services through 104 patient care centers in 20 states and was the largest operation in the O&P industry.

The two companies were controlled by the same man, John Foster. A venture capitalist, in 1985, Foster began focusing on consolidating companies in the rehabilitation field. His first purchase was InSpeech, a speech pathology business. Within three years he had diversified into occupational and physical therapy, and in 1989, he renamed his company NovaCare to reflect its broader scope.

The OPNET Network in the mid-1990s

In February 1996, with record revenues for the previous year of $52.5 million and record profits of $2.1 million, Hanger made a big move in response to the managed care phenomenon. It created OPNET, a national network of O&P providers, that negotiated contracts to provide O&P services to health maintenance organizations, major insurance companies, employers, and other health care payers. In addition to working through existing Hanger offices, OPNET also contracted with independent O&P practices, which paid an annual membership fee and received discounts on Hanger products.

Through OPNET, members received the rights to all managed-care contracts in an exclusive territory, but did not have to do all the negotiating; Hanger handled that aspect. Hanger worked closely with the U.S. Department of Justice in designing this network to avoid antitrust problems.

Family Reunion

By 1996, the O&P industry was generating $2 billion in sales. New technology, much of it developed by the National Aeronautics and Space Administration (NASA), enabled the industry to incorporate telemetry, ultralight plastics and polyesters, and small motors into its products. Computers also influenced the business, making it possible to scan casts into a computer to create digitized, 3-D designs.

That year Hanger Orthopedic continued to reunite the original Hanger companies when it spent $49 million to buy J.E. Hanger, Inc. of Georgia. In the process, it doubled its size, with a total of 175 patient care centers, six distribution sites, four manufacturing plants and 1,000 employees in 30 states.

One of the purchases, in 1998, was the Seattle Orthopedic Group, Inc. (SOGI). Unlike Hanger's other acquisitions, SOGI was a manufacturing company, producing artificial limbs and custom braces for practices within the United States and internationally. Part of SOGI was the company that manufactured the first Seattle foot; another, Lenox Hill Brace Company, developed the first custom knee brace in 1968, for NFL quarterback Joe Namath. SOGI's products and services were available under three trade names: Seattle Limb Systems, Lenox Hill orthotics, and Sea Fab central fabrication services.

NovaCare Merger: 1999–2000

Hanger kept buying up small companies, and by the end of 1998 it was operating 256 centers. Then, in 1999, it bought its bigger competitor, NovaCare's O&P division, for $420 million in cash and assumed debt. Adding NovaCare's nearly 400 patient care centers made Hanger the 500 pound gorilla of the U.S. orthotics and prosthetics industry and a national player. In addition to holding 25 percent of the U.S. market, the company was able to negotiate more favorable prices with its suppliers and to sign national distribution and service contracts.

But Hanger had trouble digesting the NovaCare division. As Hanger CEO Ivan Sabel told *Fortune* in a September 4, 2000 article, "We may have been more optimistic than we should have been." Part of the problem arose from integrating NovaCare's billing, collection, and payroll systems. While that was solvable, it proved more difficult to mesh different corporate structures. Dozens of NovaCare's specialists left when faced with Hanger's more entrepreneurial style.

Hanger considered various cost-savings measures. It briefly put its manufacturing division, Seattle Orthopedic Group, Inc. (SOGI), up for sale to help reduce debts. But the potential buyer, Otto Bock Orthopedic Industry, Inc., was not able to get financing terms that were acceptable to Hanger for the $75 million purchase.

As the sale was being considered, Hanger announced that SOGI and Sandia National Laboratories had signed an agreement on the development of the Smart Integrated Lower Limb. This advanced prostheses would be a complete system rather than an assemblage of components and make it possible to simulate the human walk. An interesting aspect of the project, which was funded in part by a $1.5 million grant from the U.S. Department of Energy, was that some of the research was subcontracted to a former Soviet nuclear weapons laboratory to help Russian scientists shift to nonmilitary research and development.

2000 and Beyond

Despite growing business at its local patient care centers, Hanger's sagging stock prices, the big interest payments on its debt and costs associated with integrating the NovaCare O&P division resulted in a 2001 restructuring plan aimed at cutting costs and increasing marketing efforts. The plan included halting acquisitions and concentrating on existing operations.

J.E. Hanger would hardly recognize the industry he contributed to so significantly. While Hanger wanted an artificial limb that made it possible for him to walk down a flight of stairs, today's strong, light-weight, custom fitted prostheses enabled amputees to ski, climb mountains, and run or walk normally. With an electrically powered artificial arm, an amputee could easily grasp a water bottle or a car steering wheel.

As the largest O&P provider in the country, and one of the biggest in the world, Hanger Orthopedic Group expected to weather its financial difficulties and maintain its dominance in the years to come.

Principal Subsidiaries

Hanger Prosthetics and Orthotics Inc.; OPNET; Seattle Orthopedic Group, Inc.; Southern Prosthetic Supply, Inc.

Principal Competitors

Biomet Inc.; Smith & Nephew plc; Stryker Corporation.

Further Reading

Amos, Denise Smith, ''H.O.P.E.-Ful; Prosthetist Carries on Work His Ancestor Started During the Civil War,'' *St. Louis Dispatch*, February 19, 1996, Bus. Sec., p. 3.

Anason, Dean, ''Reunited After 80 Years,'' *Atlanta Business Chronicle*, October 4, 1996.

Bulkley, Kate, ''Sequel Alters Course, Acquires Orthotics Firms,'' *Denver Business Journal*, November 3, 1986, p. 11.

Carson, Rob, ''A Revolution in Sports for Disabled People,'' *News Tribune* (Tacoma, Washington), June 9, 1999, p. A1.

''Expansion in Orthopedics,'' *Mergers & Acquisitions*, September 1991/October 1991, p. 162.

''Facing Acquisition Woes, Hanger Tries to Cut Costs,'' *Washington Business Journal*, March 2, 2001, p. 7.

''Hanger Forms National Orthotic, Prosthetic Provider Network,'' *Medical Industry Today*, September 21, 1995.

''Hanger Orthopedic Buys NovaCare Subsidiary,'' *Medical Industry Today*, April 6, 1999.

Henry, Kristine, ''Hanger Profit Takes a Hit,'' *Baltimore Sun*, July 15, 2000, p.C11.

Hinden, Stan, ''New Bethesda Health Services Firm Readies Stock Offering,'' *Washington Post*, November 26, 1990, p. F41.

Kahn, Jeremy, ''Growth Elixirs May Be Risky,'' *Fortune*, September 9, 2000, p. 164.

Knight, Jerry, ''Hanger Orthopedic to Acquire Ga. Firm,'' *Washington Post*, July 30, 1996, p. C1.

Myers, Randy, ''Consolidation in Ortho Industry Sets Hanger Orthopedic on Track for 30 Percent Growth,'' *Warfield's Business Record*, February 5, 1993, p. 5.

''Sandia, Seattle Group Employ Ex-Soviets in Prosthetics Work,'' *Federal Technology Report*, September 21, 2000, p. 7.

''Sequel Corp. Acquires J.E. Hanger, Inc.,'' *PR Newswire*, May 19, 1989.

''Sequel Corp. to Acquire J.E. Hanger, Inc.,'' *PR Newswire*, March 2, 1989.

''Sequel Corporation Names Ivan Sabel President and COO,'' *PR Businesswire*, January 19, 1988.

Swardson, Anne, ''Hanger Orthopedic's High-Stakes Gamble,'' *Washington Post*, April 22, 1991, p. F1.

''Technology's New Promise for the Handicapped,'' *Business Week*, October 13, 1980, p. 54 B-I.

Zimm, Angela, ''Cannonball Run: Company Launched by Civil War Amputee Mounts Recovery,'' *Warfield's Business Record*, June 3, 1996, p. 13.

——, ''Fake Limb Sellers Reattached,'' *Daily Record* (Baltimore, Maryland), July 30, 1996, p. 1.

—Ellen D. Wernick

Harris Interactive Inc.

135 Corporate Woods
Rochester, New York 14623
U.S.A.
Telephone: (716) 272-8400
Toll Free: (877) 919-4765
Fax: (716) 272-8680
Web site: http://www.harrisinteractive.com

Public Company
Founded: 1956 as Louis Harris and Associates
Employees: 1,262
Sales: $51.3 million (2000)
Stock Exchanges: NASDAQ
Ticker Symbol: HPOL
NAIC: 541613 Marketing Consulting Services

Harris Interactive Inc. combines the capabilities of the Internet with the name recognition of renown opinion pollster Louis Harris, and has become one of the world's fastest growing Internet-based market research companies. After Louis Harris and Associates was purchased in 1996 by a Rochester, New York market research company—Gordon S. Black Corporation—it de-emphasized the telephone as a primary means to conduct its surveys, opting instead for the Internet. After being briefly known as Harris Black International, the combined company changed its name to Harris Interactive in 1998 to better reflect its changing business and focus. Although the transition led to losses to the bottom line, the company remains well funded and expects to return to profitability soon and begin a prosperous future. Most of its revenues are drawn from commercial clients, yet it continues to conduct the Harris Poll—which for 40 years has tracked public opinion on political and societal issues. In reality, the Harris Poll has always served more as a way to maintain a brand name than to turn a large profit.

Public Opinion Polling Comes of Age in the 20th Century

Political polls in the 1800s were conducted by newspapers and magazines by means of a straw vote. Ballots were printed within the publication, and readers then mailed in or hand delivered their votes. This method was susceptible to ballot box stuffing, however; in fact, the practice was actually encouraged by the publishers, who were more interested in greater sales than greater accuracy. To offset this obvious defect, the idea of the ''sample'' was developed to create a random group of votes from which to derive more accurate results. Early pollsters then tried to achieve a cross section of voters by creating quotas of respondents—for example, people of differing incomes. This intuitive concept eventually led to the scientific polling methods pioneered by George Gallup in the 1930s. During the 1932 presidential election, he upstaged the best known straw poll of the day—sponsored by the *Literary Digest*—and ushered in the modern age of public opinion polling, as well as the image of the pollster as a wizard.

One of Gallup's early rivals was Elmo Roper, who drifted into market research after failing in the jewelry business. His attempts to sell stock to other jewelers involved conducting some market research, and in 1934 he and two partners started their own market research firm and began printing the results of its surveys in *Fortune* magazine. Questions about the 1936 presidential election were also asked, resulting in an accurate prediction that helped Roper to launch his own marketing firm. Several years later he looked for someone to write up his material. He hired a young World War II veteran named Louis Harris.

Born in 1921, Harris joined the Navy soon after graduating from the University of North Carolina at Chapel Hill. After World War II, he went to work for the American Veterans Committee and in 1947 met Roper, who at the time was conducting research on veterans. Roper offered Harris a job writing his radio spots, as well as his regular column on veterans. Harris turned down the offer, however, because he did not want to write for someone else. Roper hired him anyway, putting him to work instead on commercial projects. Following the 1948 presidential election, though, when the polls inaccurately predicted that Truman would be defeated by Dewey (which led to many years of public distrust of pollsters), Roper put Harris in charge of political polling.

In 1954 Harris published a seminal book on political polling, *Is There a Republican Majority? Political Trends, 1952–1956.* He argued that polls were more important in explaining elec-

> **Company Perspectives:**
>
> *We are dedicated to delivering global research products and services that meet or exceed client requirements, to creating a client-focused culture that excites and motivates our people, to sustaining our leadership in Internet-based research and technology, and to providing superior value to our shareholders.*

tions than predicting them. Having established his own reputation, and becoming dissatisfied with a meager partnership offer from Roper, Harris left in 1956 to form his own company—Louis Harris and Associates—in New York City. He took with him three major clients, which infuriated Roper. For the rest of his life, Roper would condemn his former protégé as a ''crook.'' In his defense, Harris insisted that it was the clients themselves who convinced him to break away from Roper.

Kennedy's 1960 Presidential Campaign Makes Louis Harris the Top Political Pollster

Harris served on a number of political campaigns, but it was his work for John Kennedy in the presidential election of 1960 that elevated him to a stature close to that of Gallup. Until then, no presidential candidate had ever hired a personal pollster. Although valuable to the campaign, especially given the wafer-thin margin of victory, Harris made a number of mistakes that have since been glossed over. Kennedy himself noted that ''a pollster's desire to please a client and influence strategy sometimes unintentionally colored his analyses.'' Moreover, Nixon had a pollster of his own—Claude Robinson. If Nixon had prevailed in 1960, Robinson would have likely eclipsed Harris in reputation.

Considered the top in his field but exhausted after working on more than 240 campaigns, Harris decided to discontinue private political polling and challenge Gallup and his long-running syndicated newspaper column ''American Speaks.'' Indeed, if Harris were to publish national public opinion polls, he had to give up private political work, to avoid any appearance of a conflict of interest. The Harris Poll began running in newspapers in 1963. Over the years to come, he provided political polling for two of the three major television networks, as well as for *Newsweek, Time, Life, Business Week,* the Associated Press (AP), and National Public Radio (NPR). At the same time, his firm also began to attract lucrative commercial work.

In 1969 Harris sold his company to a brokerage firm, Donaldson, Lufkin & Jenrette, staying on as the head of the polling organization. Louis Harris and Associates was then sold in 1975 to the *Gannett* newspaper chain, with Harris agreeing to serve as chief executive officer of the new subsidiary. The focus of his work was very much commercial by that point. He created the Harris Perspective, a public opinion service that cost subscribers—mainly corporations—$25,000 a year.

Founder Leaves Company in Early 1990s

By the early 1990s, Louis Harris and Associates was generating approximately $7 million in annual revenues. At the age of 71, Harris announced in January 1992 that he had decided to leave the firm that bore his name in order to start a new public opinion and market research company that would concentrate on international issues. He and Gannett management maintained that his departure was amicable and, in fact, they hoped to work together on future projects. They also agreed to share the Harris name.

While his former company retained the Harris Poll, Harris was still able to publish his new works as ''surveys by Louis Harris.'' Meanwhile, taking over for Harris as the CEO of his old company was Humphrey Taylor. Taylor's UK polling firm had been acquired by Harris in 1970, at which point Taylor took charge of the company's expanding international business. He moved to New York in 1976 and had become president of Harris in 1981.

Although considered a prestigious acquisition some 20 years earlier, Louis Harris and Associates was just a small part of Gannett's media by the mid-1990s. Even Gannett's flagship publication, *USA Today,* relied on the Gallup Organization for its polling. The syndicated weekly Harris Poll was relegated to medium and smaller-sized newspapers. Roughly half of the company's work was now in the public policy field, providing research in health care, aging, education, and race relations. Only 3 percent of revenues were derived from political polling. The company also engaged in strategic research for commercial clients such as banks, insurers, and telecommunications companies. Overall, Gannett was disappointed in the financial performance of Harris and no longer felt that the company fit in with its future plans.

Gordon S. Black Corporation Buys Harris in 1996

In 1994 Gannett sold off the Harris European subsidiaries located in London and Paris. Then in 1996, the company sold Louis Harris & Associates itself to the market research firm Gordon S. Black Corporation for an undisclosed amount. Analysts estimated the cost to be between $14 and $20 million. The plan was to operate separately under a holding company, Harris Black International. The CEO and chairman of the company—Gordon Black—had earned a doctorate in political science from Stanford, and had then began teaching political science at the University of Rochester in 1968. He was soon doing consulting work on the side, with his first assignment coming in 1969 when he was hired by a group of local Republican officials to determine the chances of them being unseated from office. When Black's study indicated that they would lose, his results were readily dismissed. Every one of the officials, however, was subsequently voted out.

Black's first major client was Xerox Corporation, which commissioned a study from him in 1973. That job would lead to others, and several years later, in 1978, Xerox would save Black from bankruptcy. While working on a project for the city of Troy, New York, Black was caught up in a political imbroglio that resulted in the city refusing to pay his bill and leaving him responsible for $35,000 in expenses. With the young professor on the edge of financial ruin, Xerox asked him to bid on two projects for a total of $80,000. The company also paid Black up-front, allowing him to pay off his debt. Years later, he would learn that the Xerox management knew of his difficulties. Their unsolicited help earned Black's lifelong loyalty.

Key Dates:

1956: Louis Harris and Associates founded in New York City.
1963: Syndicated Harris Poll is launched.
1969: Harris acquired by Donaldson, Lufkin & Jenrette, Inc.
1975: Gordon S. Black Corporation founded in Rochester, New York; Harris sold to Gannett Corporation.
1992: Louis Harris leaves company.
1996: Gordon S. Black acquires Louis Harris and Associates to become Harris Black International.
1999: Company changes name to Harris Interactive Inc.

Although a tenured professor, Black resigned from his teaching post in 1978 to run his company full-time. Within a few years he was generating $1.5 million in annual revenues and serving other well-known clients such as Eastman Kodak and Gannett. By the time he bought Louis Harris and Associates from Gannett, his firm was posting $12 million in annual revenues, which ironically was double what his better-known acquisition was producing.

The Late 1990s and A New Focus on Internet Polling

Black began to recognize the possibilities of using the Internet for market research in the late 1980s when his company began working for the Media Advertising Partnership for a Drug Free America. Rather than contact a set number of households for their study, Black's people conducted interviews in central locations around the country, such as shopping malls, then used a non-probability model to account for differences in the population to arrive at their data. They found that the results matched perfectly with those obtained by telephone interviews. Black became convinced that they could perform projectable research if they had a large enough database. Later work done for *Business Week* on Internet penetration revealed how rapidly the population was getting online and how the demographics were converging with the general population.

Moreover, an increasing number of people were refusing to participate in telephone or in-person surveys. By receiving surveys via e-mail, however, participants could respond at their own pace and convenience. The Internet also allowed pollsters to conduct surveys at a much faster pace than could be done using traditional methods. Aside from speed, the Internet held the promise of lower costs and the ability to reach desired pools of people. Web capabilities also allowed marketers to test out ad concepts or movie trailers.

Black was convinced that the Internet was going to revolutionize polling, and felt that if his company failed to embrace the new technology it would only be a matter of time before it simply failed to exist. In January 1998 his management team met and decided to change the direction of the company. At a time when Harris Black was worth just $18 million, it began looking for $15 million in funding in order to buy the necessary hardware and establish a large enough polling panel of respondents. The Chicago venture capital firm of Brinson Partners Inc. provided $14.7 million in funding, and Black signed a deal with MatchLogic, Inc., a company also looking to develop a database for advertising. They agreed to co-finance a 5 million-name database for $15 million.

By July 1998 Harris Black had developed a panel of 700,000 online respondents, but the company had yet to generate any revenues using its new capabilities. Customers were cautious, and internally at Harris Black there were signs of discontent. Nevertheless, Black and his chief financial officer, David Clemm, pressed on. In 1999 the company finally began to generate Internet revenues. Also in that year, Black changed the name of the company to Harris Interactive to better reflect the changing nature of its business.

In December 1999 Black took Harris Interactive public. The company offered 5.8 million shares of common stock, initially priced at $14 per share, and raised $81.2 million. By this point, the size of its online panel had surpassed 4 million. The company also entered into a significant alliance with the advertising agency of Young & Rubicam, which invested in Harris Interactive as part of the deal between them.

In 2000 the company focused more on international business, signing an agreement with Blauw Research of the Netherlands to expand its panel of European respondents. This move was followed by a deal with Le Vote, a Honduras firm, to expand its presence in Latin America; and also by a deal with MASMI Research, a Russian company, to expand into Russia and Eastern Europe. By July 2000, Harris Interactive had more than 6.5 million online panelists in its database. It had also increased its Internet-based clients from 261 to 363 over the previous quarter.

As was expected, however, the transition to an Internet-based business was expensive. Revenues, which jumped to $37.3 million in 1999—a 34.2 percent increase over the previous year—simply could not match the transition costs. The company posted a loss of $1.9 million in fiscal 1998, followed by a loss of $8.8 million in 1999, and $20.9 million in 2000. During those three years, Harris Interactive spent almost $13 million to develop its Internet panel and approximately $21.6 million on infrastructure. As a result of these high losses, the company soon began instituting some cost saving measures.

In the summer of 2000, Harris Interactive faced a major problem in how it conducted its business: a large number of its e-mail surveys were blocked by efforts to prevent ''spamming'' (unsolicited mass e-mailings), affecting approximately 2.7 million of its 6.6 million panelists. Harris Interactive quickly filed suit, contending that a nonprofit organization, Mail Abuse Prevention System, had wrongfully identified Harris as a ''spammer,'' a matter they alleged was instigated by an executive of a competing research firm, Incon Research Inc. Named in the suit were America Online, Microsoft, and a dozen Internet companies that Harris Interactive accused of blocking e-mail to its users. By October the company had dropped its suit, though, after agreements had already restored connections to 98 percent of its panelists.

In November 2000, Harris Interactive put its methods to the test by predicting national election results, which according to

Black was the industry's gold standard. Harris correctly predicted 36 out of the 38 states it polled for the presidential race, as well as 27 senatorial and 7 governors' races. It was the only organization to correctly forecast the nationwide presidential race as a dead heat, estimating 47.4 percent of the popular vote for Gore and 47.2 percent for Bush. While telephone polling methods had produced results that were generally within normal sampling error, Harris Interactive's online model, according to Black, "succeeded on a scale that cannot be explained by luck, statistical accident or any false claim about what we do."

Harris Interactive cut 12 percent of its workforce—about 70 workers—in response to a slowing U.S. economy in 2001. Nevertheless, the company hoped to return to profitability within the first year or two of the new millennium. The company had a significant amount of cash and securities in hand—some $60 million—so that it was well positioned to ride out both a downturn in the economy and the completion of its transition to an Internet-based business. Although a number of high-profile Internet companies had gone out of business, there was no doubt that the Internet itself would continue to grow and become an even more prevalent part of daily existence. Other market research firms followed the lead of Harris Interactive, and also began to develop Internet-based polling systems. Harris Interactive, combining an old brand name with new technology, had a significant head start over its competitors, however, and appeared well positioned for the dawning of a new era in market research.

Principal Divisions

Health Care and Clinical Trials; Emerging Markets; Business and Consumer Research; Brands and Consulting; International Research; Harris Interactive Service Bureau.

Principal Competitors

The Gallup Organization; Greenfield Online Inc.; Incon Research Inc.; Information Resources; Knowledge Network; Media Metrix; NFO Worldwide Inc.; Nielsen Media Research; Roper Starch Worldwide Inc.

Further Reading

Dickson, Mike, "Forging a New Direction for His Industry," *Rochester Business Journal,* February 25, 2000.

Farhi, Paul, "Gannett Sells Harris Survey Research Firm," *Washington Post,* February 13, 1996, p. D2.

Flynn, Laurie J., "Harris Files Suit Against AOL Over Blocking of E-Mail," *New York Times,* August 3, 2000, p. C7.

"Gannett to Sell Its Polling Unit to Competitor," *New York Times,* February 13, 1996, p. D8.

"Gordon S. Black Corp.: Market-research Company Buys Gannett Polling Firm," *Wall Street Journal,* February 13, 1996, p. B7.

"Harris Interactive Uses Election 2000 to Prove its Online MR Efficacy and Accuracy," *Research Business Report,* November 2000.

Krauss, Michael, "Research and the Web: Eyeballs or Smiles?," *Marketing News,* December 7, 1998, p. 18.

Lipke, David J., "You've Got Surveys," *American Demographics,* November 2000, pp. 42–45.

"Louis Harris Leaves Firm He Started to Begin Other," *Wall Street Journal,* January 10, 1992, p. B4.

Moore, David W., *The Superpollsters,* New York: Four Walls Eight Windows, 1992, 338 p.

Nasar, Sylvia, "Louis Harris Forms New Polling Company," *New York Times,* January 15, 1992, p. D2.

Sandlund, Chris, "A History on its Side; Harris Interactive Inc.," *Crain's New York Business,* November 27, 2000, p. 64.

Wheeler, Michael, *Lies, Damn Lies, and Statistics,* New York: Liveright, 1976, 300 p.

—Ed Dinger

Heller, Ehrman, White & McAuliffe

333 Bush Street, Suite 3000
San Francisco, California 94104-2878
U.S.A.
Telephone: (415) 772-6000
Fax: (415) 772-6268
Web site: http://www.hewm.com

Partnership
Founded: 1890
Employees: 1,400+
Sales: $196.5 million (1999)
NAIC: 54111 Offices of Lawyers

Heller, Ehrman, White & McAuliffe is one of America's top 100 law firms. The San Francisco-based firm is recognized for its key role in developing the West, having helped found Wells Fargo Bank and arrange for financing of the Golden Gate Bridge. In the late twentieth century the firm has become a leader in providing legal services to new high technology and biotechnology industries. Its corporate clients include VISA, Bank of America, Symantec Corporation, Philip Morris, Pacific Gas & Electric, ALZA Corporation, Raychem, and Ernst & Young. The firm also ranks as one of the nation's leaders in providing pro bono services.

Origins and Early Practice: 1890–1945

Emanuel S. Heller (1865–1926) graduated from the University of California at Berkeley and the Hastings College of the Law before passing the California bar in 1889 and then starting his solo law practice in 1890 in the heart of San Francisco's financial center. In 1896 Heller and Francis H. Powers created the partnership of Heller & Powers. When Sidney M. Ehrman (1873–1974) joined the young partnership, it changed its name to Heller, Powers & Ehrman. A native of San Francisco, Ehrman graduated from the University of California at Berkeley in 1896 and earned his LL.B. at the Hastings College of the Law in 1898.

The firm's most important early clients were Isaias W. Hellman and his two institutions, the Nevada Bank and the Union Trust Company. When the Nevada Bank merged with the Wells Fargo Bank in 1905, the Heller firm moved its offices to its client's headquarters of the new Wells Fargo Nevada National Bank. After many records were destroyed in the famous 1906 San Francisco earthquake, the Heller law firm kept busy filing land ownership papers in addition to its typical workload. Meanwhile, the Heller firm represented the San Francisco Stock and Bond Exchange, the Bankers Investment Company, the Spring Valley Water Company, Pabst Brewery, Pacific Coast Shredded Wheat Company, Guggenhime & Company, and various prominent families.

Following the death of Francis Powers and the addition of Jerome White (1883–1972) and Florence McAuliffe (1886–1957) as new partners, the firm's name became Heller, Ehrman, White & McAuliffe in 1921. In the 1920s the firm's lawyers helped completely revise California's Uniform Corporation Code. When the Union Trust Company merged with the Wells Fargo Nevada National Bank, the firm represented both of its clients and then continued to serve the merged entity as its largest client. Other companies served at the time were Proctor & Gamble Company, Federal Construction Company, the Patterson Ranch, the Italian-American Bank, National Surety Company, Sacramento Northern Railroad Company, and United States Rubber Company.

In 1930 the firm's offices in the Nevada Bank Building housed 12 lawyers. After President Franklin D. Roosevelt was inaugurated in 1933, his New Deal legislation had a major influence on how lawyers dealt with their corporate clients. For example, Heller Ehrman helped its clients develop fair competition codes to comply with the National Recovery Administration. When the Wells Fargo Bank resisted closing during the 1933 ''bank holiday,'' the firm persuaded the bank's leaders to go along with the rest of the nation.

Also in 1930 a group of contractors called Six Companies, Inc., formed with the help of Heller Ehrman, began construction of the Hoover Dam. In the next few years the firm also helped win several lawsuits filed against Six Companies. About the same time, the firm worked with the federal Reconstruction Finance Corporation, Congress, and the California legislature to gain the financing for the Golden Gate Bridge between San

Company Perspectives:

What continues to distinguish Heller Ehrman from competitors is not only the quality and breadth of our practice and client base, but also our commitment to certain core values—to excellence, to our people, to teamwork, to our communities and to our concept of ''one firm.'' We believe these values matter to the people who come to work at Heller Ehrman and we believe they matter to our clients.

Francisco and Oakland. During World War II, many attorneys at the firm enlisted for service. On the homefront, the firm began focusing on its tax practice.

The Firm after World War II

Specialization increased after World War II as the economy grew in leaps and bounds. Some Heller Ehrman lawyers for the first time devoted their entire practice to one legal specialty. Labor law and tax law were the firm's first two specialty practices, although they did start a probate practice in the 1950s. It was not until the 1960s that some of the firm's lawyers began specializing as litigators.

Heller Ehrman has a long history of serving technology clients. According to Carole Hicke in her firm history, ''Heller, Ehrman pioneered in the field of large equipment leasing in the United States'' in 1954. First, they represented Boothe Leasing Company, which leased heavy equipment, and later Boothe Computer Corporation, which leased costly computers. In 1959 Heller Ehrman handled the initial public offering for Ampex, a client since about 1947 that provided the technology for the first recorded radio and television programs. The firm participated in many more IPOs after 1959, including Portland's Big C Stores and Salt Lake City's Bancorporation.

Consolidated Foods Corporation became a new client in 1948. By the 1960s, after having helped the corporation on tax and other issues, Heller Ehrman helped it acquire Abbey Rents, Aris Gloves, Shasta Water Company, and Sara Lee bakery products, and also successfully defended Consolidated Foods subsidiary Chicken Delight in the antitrust lawsuit *Siegal* v. *Chicken Delight.*

As Southern California's population boomed after World War II, the state needed much more water. After voters in 1960 approved the Feather River Project, Heller Ehrman represented Wells Fargo and other banks that provided the equipment financing for the various construction companies.

The firm also played a role in the counterculture centered in San Francisco. For example, in 1969 it helped negotiate an end to a student boycott and faculty strike at San Francisco State College, where the protestors wanted an ethnic studies department. One of the law firm's best-known pro bono cases occurred in *Trafficante* v. *Metropolitan Life Insurance Company*, in which the firm represented white plaintiffs who sued the insurance company because of its discrimination against minorities in a San Francisco apartment. Both the U.S. District Court and the Ninth Circuit Court of Appeals said the plaintiffs had no standing to sue because they were not facing discrimination, but the U.S. Supreme Court in 1972 unanimously agreed they could sue. Meanwhile, new apartment owners made a favorable settlement that led to integration.

In the post-World War II period, Heller Ehrman played a significant role in the origins of some key firms in the computer, biomedical, and biotechnology industries. First, it helped create and set up financing for Fairchild SemiConductor Company, the first company to make semiconductors. Second, in 1968 Heller Ehrman helped begin ALZA Corporation, a pioneer in producing certain drug delivery methods. ALZA remained a long-term client. Third, in 1972 it assisted in the organization of Cetus Corporation. Martin Kenney noted in his book on the history of biotechnology that for a time Cetus was ''the only operating biotechnology company'' in the 1970s.

Meanwhile, Heller Ehrman opened new offices along the Pacific Coast in the 1970s and 1980s. In 1974 it opened a small office in Palo Alto to serve high-tech companies that already were clients. That was expanded in 1985 to become a full-service office with expertise in labor, tax, and litigation. Heller Ehrman also opened a Hong Kong office in 1978, and within a few years began operating out of a Beijing hotel suite. However, both Chinese operations ended in 1987 when the firm decided it could more efficiently serve its Asian clients from its West Coast offices.

The firm in 1983 established offices in Seattle and Portland due to its representation of Alcoa in *Alcoa* v. *Central Lincoln*, a case won in the U.S. Supreme Court. In 1988 the Seattle office merged with two small Seattle firms. The firm's Los Angeles office, which opened in 1987, expanded rapidly to have almost 50 lawyers by 1991. To relieve the Seattle office of its growing work for clients in Alaska, the firm opened its Anchorage office in July 1989.

Not surprisingly, the firm's growth led to new facilities. In 1986 the San Francisco headquarters was moved to a new skyscraper at 333 Bush Street. By 1991 the firm had 370 lawyers, over 3.5 times what it had employed just ten years earlier. To celebrate its achievements and heritage, it hired Carole Hicke, a University of California historian at the Bancroft Library's Regional Oral History office, to write a centennial history.

Practice in the 1990s and Beyond

In the late 1990s Heller Ehrman gained an important client when it defended Visa against antitrust allegations. In 1996 Wal-Mart, Sears, and Safeway filed a lawsuit against Visa USA and MasterCard International to protest the two associations requiring retailers to accept their debit cards if they also accepted their credit cards. In 1998 the U.S. Department of Justice filed a lawsuit against Visa USA, Visa International, and MasterCard International over alleged lack of competition in the credit card industry.

In 1999 Heller Ehrman merged with Werbel & Carnelutti, described in a March 22, 1999 *PR Newswire* as ''a highly regarded New York City corporate finance, securities and litigation boutique.'' The addition of Werbel & Carnelutti's 18 lawyers resulted in Heller Ehrman's total of 450 lawyers. Robert H.

Key Dates:

1890: Emanuel S. Heller begins his solo law practice in San Francisco.
1896: The partnership of Heller & Powers is formed.
1905: The firm is renamed Heller, Powers & Ehrman.
1921: The firm adopts its permanent name of Heller, Ehrman, White & McAuliffe.
1974: A Palo Alto office is established.
1978: A Hong Kong office is started, but is closed in 1987.
1983: The firm opens its Seattle and Portland offices.
1987: The Los Angeles office is opened.
1989: The Anchorage office is opened.
1993: The firm reestablishes an office in Hong Kong.
1994: The Singapore office is opened.
1998: A second Silicon Valley office is opened in Menlo Park.
1998: The San Diego office is started.
1999: The firm opens its New York office by merging with Werbel & Carnelutti.
2000: The firm starts an office in Madison, Wisconsin.

Werbel had founded what became Werbel & Carnelutti in 1981 when he and another lawyer began serving the investment banking firm of Allen & Company as their major client. The Werbel firm merged in 1989 with Carnelutti & Downs, the New York City branch of the Italian law firm Carnelutti. The union with Heller Ehrman maintained the affiliation with Carnelutti's offices in Milan, Rome, Paris, and Naples, thus helping the merged firm develop international capabilities to better serve its clients.

Heller Ehrman represented Symantec Corporation in 2000 when it announced an agreement to acquire Axent Technologies in a stock transaction worth about $975 million. Based in Cupertino, California, Symantec operated in 33 countries to provide computer security systems, as did Axent, headquartered in Rockville, Maryland.

Based on its 1998 gross revenue of $169 million, *The American Lawyer* ranked Heller Ehrman as the nation's 61st largest law firm in July 1999. The firm also ranked number 11 for its pro bono work. When Heller Ehrman brought in $196.5 million in gross revenue in 1999, it was once again ranked the 61st largest law firm.

In October 2000 Heller Ehrman opened a Madison, Wisconsin, office when it hired two biotechnology partners from the law firm of Foley & Lardner. David Harth, one of the two partners, said in the *Madison Capital Times* that Heller was ''if not the premier, one of the premier, law firms in the country in life sciences and biotechnology.'' At least 40 biotechnology firms were based in the Madison area, mainly because of research programs at the University of Wisconsin in Madison.

Heller Ehrman also supported the biotechnology/biomedical industry when it participated in the Southern California Biomedical Council's planning of the second annual conference on Investment and Strategic Partnering Opportunities in Southern California.

At the dawn of the new millennium Heller Ehrman faced great challenges and opportunities. Some critics were concerned about the possible dangers of biotechnology or genetic engineering, a major practice area for the firm. New coinage, such as the Euro, and new trade agreements impacted the firm's international practice. Larger law firms had more resources, an important aspect since consolidation created larger and larger multinational corporations. How the law firm responded to these developments remained to be seen.

Principal Competitors

Baker & McKenzie; Gibson, Dunn & Crutcher; Skadden, Arps, Slate, Meagher & Flom.

Further Reading

Beckett, Paul, ''Wal-Mart Can Stay in Debit-Card Suit, U.S. Judge Rules,'' *The Wall Street Journal,* November 20, 2000, p. B12.
Hicke, Carole, *Heller Ehrman White & McAuliffe: A Century of Service to Clients and Community,* San Francisco: Heller Ehrman White & McAuliffe, 1991.
''Justice Fires Its Opening Volley,'' *Credit Card Management,* July 2000, pp. 6–8.
Kenney, Martin, *Biotechnology: The University-Industrial Complex,* New Haven: Yale University Press, 1986.
Richgels, Jeff, ''Biotech Law Practice Opens Here Major Firm Adds Local Attorneys,'' *Madison Capital Times,* October 14, 2000, p. 12D.
''The Southern California Biomedical Council Announces Selection of Companies to be Featured During Its 2000 Investor Conference,'' *PR Nerwswire,* September 27, 1999, p.1.
''Symantec: Symantec Strengthens Security Leadership with Acquisition of Axent; Accelerates Symantec's Strategic Shift Towards the Fast Growing Enterprise,'' *M2 Presswire,* July 31, 2000, p. 1.
Timmerman, Luke, ''Spotlight Still Aimed at Insider Trading,'' *Seattle Times,* August 6, 2000, p. F6.
''West Coast's Heller Ehrman White & McAuliffe Combines with New York's Werbel & Carnelutti in East Coast/International Expansion,'' *PR Newswire,* March 22, 1999, p. 1.

—David M. Walden

Herbalife International, Inc.

1800 Century Park East
Los Angeles, California 90067
U.S.A.
Telephone: (310) 410-9600
Fax: (310) 216-5169
Web site: http://www.herbalife.com

Public Company
Incorporated: 1979
Employees: 2,391
Sales: $944 million (2000)
Stock Exchanges: NASDAQ
Ticker Symbol: HERBA
NAIC: 45439 Other Direct Selling Establishments; 445299 All Other Specialty Food Stores; 325412 Pharmaceutical Preparation Manufacturing

Herbalife International, Inc. markets and distributes a broad spectrum of more than 150 herb- and botanicals-based weight management and dieting products, cosmetics, and general health and nutrition products, through a worldwide network of more than one million independent distributors in 50 countries. Herbalife products, sold under a variety of brand names, include the Thermojetics Weight-Management Program, the Health & Fitness Bulk & Muscle Program, the Dermojetics herbal and botanical skin care products, the Cell-U-Loss cellulite-attacking supplement, Colour cosmetic products, as well as perfumes for men and women under the Vitessence brand name. Herbalife has thrived despite negative claims against its marketing schemes, product ingredients, and distribution methods.

''Herbalife uses 'network marketing' as a way to describe its marketing and sales programs as opposed to multi-level marketing,'' according to the company's 1995 annual report, ''because multi-level marketing has had a negative connotation in certain countries in which Herbalife does business.'' Nevertheless, Herbalife's distribution network closely resembles the typical multilevel marketing approach—sometimes referred to as a pyramid scheme—and has been accused of crossing the line into the illegal endless-chain marketing. Multilevel marketing remains legal in most states in the United States, with the condition that the company's sales force of distributors actually receive earnings by selling products to people not related to the company. In an illegal endless-chain scheme, earnings are achieved primarily through recruiting new salespeople into the pyramid.

In the Herbalife network marketing plan, potential distributors buy into the network by purchasing Herbalife products, generally at a 25 percent discount off the retail price, which they may then in turn sell to others. Once they place orders above a certain amount—ranging from $2,000 to $4,000—a distributor may become supervisor, at which point they receive a 50 percent discount on Herbalife products. Distributors also become supervisors by recruiting new distributors into the network. They then receive a percentage of each recruit's sales—usually about 8 percent. As supervisors rise higher in the pyramid, their earnings have the potential of rising dramatically, depending on the number of supervisors below them.

Herbalife distributors are supported by a range of company career and training programs. Among these are the company's annual distributor convention, called the Herbalife Extravaganza, which features five-day intensive training; HBN, a private satellite broadcasting network that provides training in recruitment and retention techniques, as well as marketing support and training; bonus vacation programs for top-selling distributors; and the company's own magazine, featuring testimonials of success stories by Herbalife distributors and customers. Top distributors may earn $250,000 per year and more; nonetheless, the average annual earnings among all Herbalife distributors has been estimated at $1,500. As independent contractors, distributors receive no salary or benefits from the company.

Company founder and CEO Mark Hughes, owner of more than 60 percent of the company, died unexpectedly in 2000, just after failed attempts to take his company private.

American Success Story Beginning in 1980

Master salesman Mark Hughes began Herbalife in a Beverly Hills warehouse in 1980, selling the new company's dieting aids from his car. Hughes, whose parents were divorced soon after his

Company Perspectives:

Herbalife is united with a single purpose—to capitalize on the core strengths that have raised Herbalife to the worldwide status it enjoys today and, through strategic decision-making, to lead Herbalife toward greater success in the future.

birth in 1956, was raised in Lynwood, California, outside of Hollywood. By ninth grade, Hughes had dropped out of high school. He became involved in drug use and by the age of 16 was sent to the Cedu School, a private residential home for emotionally disturbed and troubled teenagers. It was there that Hughes developed a knack for salesmanship, rehabilitating himself by selling door-to-door raffle tickets in support of the school. By the end of his tenure, Hughes had joined the school's staff.

Another turning point for Hughes came at the age of 18, when his mother died due to an overdose of diet pills. As Hughes would tell it, according to *Inc.* magazine: "My mom was always going out and trying some kind of funny fad diet as I was growing up. Eventually, she went to a doctor to get some help, and he prescribed . . . a form of speed, or amphetamine. . . . After several years of using it, she ended up having to eat sleeping pills for her to sleep at night. And after several years of doing that, her body basically began to deteriorate." The death of his mother stimulated Hughes's interest in herbs and botanicals, the use of which had become popular during the 1960s. Hughes set out to develop a dieting program based on herbal and botanical products that would enable people to lose weight safely.

Before founding Herbalife, Hughes the salesman received another kind of training when, in 1976, he began selling the Slender Now diet plan from multilevel marketer Seyforth Laboratories. Hughes quickly rose to become one of the pyramid's top earners. When that operation collapsed, Hughes joined another multilevel marketer, selling Golden Youth diet products and exercise equipment. By 1979, however, Hughes, then 23 years old, decided to form his own company.

Together with Richard Marconi, former manufacturer of the Slender Now products, Hughes developed the first Herbalife line of diet aids. Marconi, who claimed to hold a Ph.D. in nutrition, would later admit that his doctorate was a mail-order certificate from a correspondence school; nevertheless, Marconi would remain an officer at D&F Industries, Inc., which would continue to manufacture much of the Herbalife line throughout the company's history. Also joining Hughes in the new venture was Lawrence Thompson, formerly of Golden Youth, and earlier, Bestline Products, which in 1973 was fined $1.5 million for violating California's pyramid scheme laws. At both Bestline and Golden Youth, Thompson worked with Larry Stephen Huff—later to become a Herbalife distributor—who was involved in what *Forbes* labeled the "father of all pyramid schemes," Holiday Magic, Inc., a multilevel marketer charged by the Securities and Exchange Commission (SEC) in 1973 with defrauding its distributors of $250 million.

The Herbalife plan involved limiting meals to one per day and supplementing the diet with protein powders and a regimen of as many as 20 pills per day. According to the company, Herbalife was an instant success, selling $23,000 in its first month and $2 million by the end of its first year. Hughes, described by *Inc.* as "a honey-tongued spellbinder" and "a tanned and blow-dried California swashbuckler," and by *Forbes* as a "firebrand preacher," brought multilevel marketing to a new height, by taking the Herbalife message to television. Booking two- to three-hour slots on cable television, including the USA Cable Network, Herbalife was an early purveyor of the so-called "infomercial." The Herbalife television programs, led by Hughes himself, were, as described by *Forbes,* "full of inspiring testimonials from common people and resemble[d] old-style revival meetings in their fervor." At the same time, Herbalife published its own magazine, *Herbalife Journal,* equally filled with testimonials, for which the company reportedly paid $200 each, from distributor success stories to weight-loss victories of Herbalife customers. Within a short time, the Herbalife slogan, "Lose Weight Now—Ask Me How," began appearing on buttons and bumper stickers everywhere.

Legal Challenges in the Mid-1980s

Herbalife grew rapidly. By 1985, the company appeared on *Inc.* magazine's list of fastest-growing private companies. (That magazine labeled Herbalife's five-year growth "from $386,000 to $423 million, an increase of more than 100,000 percent, [as] by far the highest growth rate in the history of INC. 500 listings.") In that year, the company claimed more than 700,000 distributors in the United States, Canada, the United Kingdom, and Australia, bringing annual (gross) revenues of nearly $500 million. Yet, as early as January 1981, the Food and Drug Administration (FDA) began receiving complaints of nausea, diarrhea, headaches, and constipation, which were attributed to the use of Herbalife products. Herbalife distributors reportedly were instructed to assure customers that these side effects were the result of the body purging itself of toxins. By 1982, when the company published that year's edition of the Herbalife Official Career Book—a guide given to distributors that contained a full product list and descriptions of the uses and benefits for each product, as well as advice on building their Herbalife sales—the FDA took action against the company.

Among the complaints leveled against the company was a number of the claims Herbalife made for its products in the Career Book. The Herbal-Aloe drink, for example, was said to help treat kidney, stomach, and bowel "ulcerations"; and Herbalife Formula #2 was said to be a treatment for 75 conditions ranging from age spots to bursitis to cancer, herpes, and impotence. In the summer of 1982, the FDA sent Herbalife a "Notice of Adverse Findings" requiring the company to remove the mandrake and poke root ingredients—both considered unsafe for food use—of Slim and Trim Formula #2, while finding questionable the existence of "food-grade" linseed oil also in the product. In response, Herbalife removed the mandrake and poke root and promised to modify the product claims found in the 1982 Career Book.

Herbalife was well into its surging growth—and Hughes was riding high himself, purchasing for $7 million the former Bel-Air mansion of singer Kenny Rogers, and marrying Angela Mack, a former Swedish beauty queen—when the FDA released a "Talk Paper" on its complaints against Herbalife to the press and public in August 1984. The company's troubles increased several months later when Canada's Department of Justice filed 24 criminal charges for false medical claims and misleading adver-

Key Dates:

1980: Mark Hughes establishes Herbalife and begins selling diet aids out of the trunk of his car.
1982: The FDA sends a "Notice of Adverse Findings" to the company.
1985: Herbalife is labeled one of the fastest-growing companies in the United States by *Inc.* magazine amidst negative publicity.
1986: The company officially takes on the name Herbalife International and goes public.
1988: The company continues aggressive international expansion into Japan, Spain, New Zealand, Israel, and Mexico.
1991: With the help of international business, sales reach $191 million.
1993: Sales reach $700 million.
1995: The company introduces a line of personal care products.
1997: The firm again becomes subject to negative publicity when Clint Fallows, a former distributor, files suit against Herbalife.
1999: Hughes attempts to take the firm private.
2000: The buyout attempt falls short and, in May, Hughes dies unexpectedly.

tising practices against Herbalife. In December of that year, Hughes went on the attack, filing a suit against both the FDA and the U.S. Secretary of Health and Human Services, accusing them of "grossly exceeding their authority by issuing false and defamatory statements and by engaging in a corrupt trial-by-publicity campaign against the company." In a press release, Hughes said: "[We're] not about to stand around and let this agency or anyone else issue blatant lies about us or our products, or to lie down and roll over while they take pot shots at us. In the five years we've been in business, literally billions of portions of Herbalife products have been consumed by millions of people. And we have never been sued or subjected to any formal proceedings by the FDA." In the same press release, Hughes also suggested that the FDA "attack" on Herbalife was inspired by legislation pending in Congress that sought to regulate the rapidly expanding dietary supplement market.

Although Hughes would withdraw the lawsuit the following year, Herbalife began to suffer from the negative publicity surrounding not only its products, but also its marketing tactics. After a still-strong first quarter, the company ended 1985 with only $250 million in retail sales. In March 1985, Herbalife itself was charged in a civil suit brought against it by the California attorney general, the California Department of Health, and the FDA. That suit, which included Hughes as a defendant, charged Herbalife with making false product claims, misleading consumers, and with operating an illegal endless-chain scheme. At the same time, both the U.S. Senate and U.S. Congress began investigations into the company, during which time the investigating subcommittees pursued allegations that Herbalife products had been responsible for as many as five deaths. While the civil suit was based in California, the Washington investigations brought the negative publicity surrounding the company nationwide.

With sales stalling, the company cut its workforce—which had reached approximately 2,000 people—laying off 270 in April 1985, and nearly 600 more the following month. Herbalife distributors were also hard hit, leaving many with unsalable inventories of Herbalife products and many others seeing their income drop to nothing overnight. Sales dropped even more precipitously the following year. Despite repeated vows to fight the charges against his company, Hughes reached an out-of-court settlement with the California attorney general's office. Under terms of the settlement, Herbalife paid $850,000 in civil penalties, investigation costs, and attorneys' fees. Herbalife also agreed to discontinue two of its products, Tang Quei Plus and K-8 at FDA insistence that, although the products posed no safety risks, the claims made for them by the company would require them to be considered as drugs under the Food, Drug and Cosmetic Act. In addition, the company agreed to make further changes to its Career Book, including dropping claims for its Cell-U-Loss product as a natural eliminator of cellulite. By the end of 1986, Herbalife posted a $3 million loss.

Going Overseas and Back Again in the 1990s

Herbalife's domestic sales were at a standstill, so Hughes took the company overseas to expand its international markets. To finance the expansion, the company went public in December 1986, merging with a public Utah-based shell company, which allowed the company to go public much faster than if it had been required to file an initial public offering. Hughes became chairman of the new company, now called Herbalife International, taking 14.8 million of 16.8 million shares of outstanding common stock. The remaining two million shares went to newly named director and executive vice-president, Lawrence Thompson.

By 1988, Herbalife had moved into Japan, Spain, New Zealand, and Israel, and soon added Mexico as well. The company's aggressive expansion forced it to take a loss of nearly $7 million that year, but international sales built quickly, raising worldwide sales to $191 million in 1991. Meanwhile, domestic sales continued their slide, reaching a low of $42 million that year. At the same time, critics of the company pointed to an emerging pattern: that in many of the countries Herbalife entered, sales would surge initially, then plunge, often in the face of government scrutiny.

Nonetheless, Herbalife continued to grow strongly through the first half of the 1990s. Retail sales doubled to $405 million in 1992 and jumped again to nearly $700 million in 1993. Although 80 percent of sales still came from international markets, Herbalife's U.S. sales began to climb, reaching $85 million. Buoyed by this growth, Herbalife filed for a secondary offering of five million shares in 1993.

The company came under attack again, however. An Herbalife program introduced in 1992 called Wealth Building—in which newly recruited distributors could achieve supervisor status, with an immediate discount of 50 percent, if they made a first purchase of $500—was seen as skirting the edge of an illegal endless-chain scheme. The company's newly introduced Thermojetics Program of products also was criticized by the FDA and others for containing the Chinese herb ma huang, which contains ephedrine. In response to a Canadian threat to ban Thermojetics, the company agreed to reformulate the product. Despite this publicity, sales of Thermojetics were credited with raising Herbalife's retail sales still higher, to $884 million in 1994 and to $923 million in 1995, for net earnings of $46 million and $19.7 million, respectively.

The company's international operations also was faced with problems. In France, claims that a group of Herbalife's distributors were part of an unpopular religious group led to falling sales in that region. In 1995, the firm suspended the sale of Thermojetics Instant Herbal Beverage in Germany after receiving complaints from government agencies about the product. The suspension led to a sharp increase in product returns and distributor resignations as well as a decline in sales of related products.

The firm continued to thrive, however, despite the conflicts in which it was involved. In 1994, the company began developing a new line entitled Personal Care, which focused on health awareness. The products were launched in 1995 and included The Skin Survival Kit, Parfum Vitessence fragrances, and Nature's Mirror, a line of facial products. Herbalife also entered the catalog sales market in 1994 and developed ''The Art of Promotion'' catalog that was used by distributors and complemented existing product lines.

Continued Growth in the Mid-1990s

The company entered the mid-1990s focused on international expansion as well as continuing its growth in existing markets. By 1996, Herbalife was operating in 32 countries and international sales accounted for more than 70 percent of total sales—sales in the United States, however, declined by 16.2 percent to $279.6 million. The firm also began restructuring its European distribution system. It closed four warehouse facilities, leaving five in operation, and established new sales centers for distributor meetings. The company also opened a main sales office in the United Kingdom that could process telephone orders from European distributors.

The firm came under fire once again in 1997 when Clint Fallow, a former distributor, filed suit against Herbalife claiming that the firm withheld earned income. The suit, which Fallow detailed on a public web site, garnered negative attention and was the first of many filed against the company by disgruntled distributors.

Nevertheless, the company forged ahead, securing $54.7 million in net income in 1997, a 22.2 percent increase over the previous year. By 1998, the firm had expanded into Turkey, Botswana, Lesotho, Namibia, Swaziland, and Indonesia. The next year, Hughes set plans in motion to take the company private in a $17 per share buyout plan after claiming that Wall Street was undervaluing his firm. Although the Herbalife board approved the offer, many shareholders claimed that the offer was not fair and filed suit against the firm.

Problems Continuing into the New Millennium

Herbalife continued to battle problems into the new millennium. The use of ephedrine in its products raised issues as the FDA linked heart attacks and strokes and even death to its use. Then in April, Hughes abandoned his buyout efforts when he was unable to raise enough capital to fund the deal. The firm settled the suit with shareholders and stock price faltered, trading around $10 per share after the announcement—in spring 1998 the stock had traded at $27 per share.

The company was again faced with hardship when in May 2000, Hughes died unexpectedly. Rumors spread about his death claiming that Hughes himself had not been a picture of health and had died of an alcohol and antidepressant overdose. The MLM Watch, a group that investigates marketing schemes, also claimed that the story about Hughes's mother dying of an overdose of diet pills was false and that newly elected Chairman John Reynolds was not really Hughes's father, as the company claimed. For the first time in five years, sales declined and the firm recorded a 35.1 percent decrease in net income over the previous year.

The company moved forward as it had done in the past when faced with adversity. In 2001, Herbalife expanded into Morocco. Newly elected President and CEO Christopher Pair stated in a company press release, ''The addition of Morocco as our 50th market represents an important milestone for Herbalife. We are committed to strengthening our global presence by making our products available around the world and extending new business opportunities for our distributors.'' Despite continuing negative publicity surrounding the company, management continued to focus its future efforts on growth markets.

Principal Competitors

Alticor Inc.; GNC Inc.; Nu Skin Enterprises Inc.

Further Reading

Barrett, Amy, ''A Wonder Offer from Herbalife,'' *Business Week,* September 13, 1993, p. 34.

Belgum, Deborah, ''Herbalife Stock Ailing After Unsuccessful Buyout Effort,'' *Los Angeles Business Journal,* April 24. 2000, p. 42.

Cole, Benjamin Mark, ''Herbalife Plans Share Offering of $101 Million,'' *Los Angeles Business Journal,* August 23, 1993, p. 1.

Day, Kathleen, ''Herbalife Lays off 573, Blames Slowing Sales,'' *Los Angeles Times,* May 29, 1985, p. D1.

Evans, David, ''Herbalife Faced Struggle After Death of Founder Mark Hughes,'' *MLM Watch,* August 11, 2000.

Evans, Heidi, ''Agencies Sue Herbalife, Alleging False Claims,'' *Los Angeles Times,* March 7, 1985, p. D1.

Hartman, Curtis, ''Unbridled Growth,'' *Inc.,* December 1985, p. 100.

''Herbalife Founder Dies,'' *Los Angeles Business Journal,* May 29, 2000, p. 49.

Kravetz, Stacy, ''Bitter Herb Distributor Hopes,'' *Wall Street Journal,* November 12, 1997.

Linden, Dana Wechsler, and William Stern, ''Betcherlife Herbalife,'' *Forbes,* March 15, 1993, p. 46.

Lubove, Seth, ''But Where Are the Directors' Yachts?,'' *Forbes,* October 20, 1997, p.43.

Paris, Ellen, ''Herbalife, Anyone?,'' *Forbes,* February 25, 1985, p. 46.

''Self-Healing,'' *Forbes,* November 17, 1986, p. 14.

Shiver, Jube, Jr., ''Herbalife Says All Queries into Tactics Now Resolved,'' *Los Angeles Times,* October 17, 1996, p. D4.

Svetich, Kim, ''Herbalife Seeking to Rebuild Its Domestic Market,'' *California Business,* February 1990, p. 18.

Yoshihashi, Pauline, ''The Questions on Herbalife,'' *New York Times,* April 5, 1985, p. D1.

—M. L. Cohen
—update: Christina M. Stansell

Hoenig Group Inc.

Reckson Executive Park
4 International Drive
Rye Brook, New York 10573
U.S.A.
Telephone: (914) 935-9000
Toll Free: (800) 999-9558
Fax: (914) 935-9146
Web site: http://www.hoenig.com

Public Company
Incorporated: 1970 as Hoenig & Strock Inc.
Employees: 104
Sales: $100.11 million (2000)
Stock Exchanges: NASDAQ
Ticker Symbol: HOEN
NAIC: 52131 Investment Banking and Securities Dealing; 52132 Securities Brokerage; 52392 Portfolio Management; 52393 Investment Advice; 551112 Offices of Other Holding Companies

Hoenig Group Inc., through its brokerage subsidiaries, provides global securities brokerage, marketing and distribution of proprietary and independent research, and other services to institutional investors. Through its asset management subsidiary, the company provides professional investment management services to public and corporate employee benefit plans, investment partnerships, and other institutional clients. Its customers are mainly investment advisers, hedge funds, investment partnerships, banks, insurance companies, corporations, employee benefit plans, mutual funds, and other investment professionals. The Hoenig Group conducts business from its headquarters in Rye Brook, New York—a suburb of New York City—its international offices in London and Hong Kong, and its branch offices in Boston and New York. Through its subsidiaries, the group is a member of the New York Stock Exchange, all major regional U.S. exchanges, the London Stock Exchange, and the Stock Exchange of Hong Kong. The company was executing trades in equity securities in 34 countries.

Soft-Dollar Specialist: 1970–92

The firm was founded in 1970 as Hoenig & Strock Inc. by Ronald H. Hoenig, Max H. Levine, and Paul Strock, but Strock soon left the firm. Hoenig functioned as chief executive officer, and Levine was head of trading. Its first home was a single-room Manhattan office near Wall Street. The company found its niche in soft-dollar brokerage, which involves the acquisition of independent third-party research by a brokerage firm and the delivery of this research to a client. In return for this research, the client consents to conduct an agreed-upon amount of securities trading through the brokerage firm. According to industry analysts, in the early 1990s nearly 40 percent of all U.S. institutional trading was being done on a soft-dollar basis.

Hoenig Group's revenues increased from $26.87 million in 1987 to $48.65 million in 1991, the year the company made its initial public offering of stock, netting $15 million. Shortly before this offering, Hoenig Group was incorporated as a holding company operating through three wholly owned subsidiaries: Hoenig & Co., Inc., Hoenig & Company, Limited, and Vortex Management, Inc. It had about 500 institutional clients and offices in Boston; Denver; Greenwich, Connecticut; Hong Kong; London; and Tokyo, in addition to its New York headquarters. It was a member of all of the major U.S. stock exchanges as well as the London Stock Exchange.

Soft-dollar brokerage accounted for about 75 percent of Hoenig's commission revenues in 1991. The firm declared in its first annual filing with the U.S. Securities and Exchange Commission that "research prepared in a conventional manner by brokerage firms is often imitative and redundant. Therefore, the range of opinions among Wall Street analysts can tend to be narrow." Rather than build an in-house staff of research analysts, the company was meeting its clients' particular portfolio needs for focused data from more than 200 vendors, including private research groups, computer service organizations, and other business entities. Its general practice was to require $2 in commissions for every $1 in research services provided under a soft-dollar arrangement. The remainder of its business came from trades on a competitive commission-rate basis. About 95 percent of its income was coming from commissions and the rest from asset management.

Company Perspectives:

For thirty years, Hoenig Group Inc. has provided high quality trade execution, independent research and premier client service to professional money managers and alternative investment funds throughout the world. Hoenig Group Inc. operates through its brokerage subsidiaries in the United States, the United Kingdom and Hong Kong. Hoenig Group's U.S. asset management subsidiary, Axe-Houghton Associates, Inc., provides investment management services to public and corporate employee benefit plans, investment partnerships and other institutional investors.

Hoenig Group moved its headquarters from downtown Manhattan to the Westchester County suburb of Rye Brook in 1992, taking a ten-year lease in an office park. It maintained a presence in the city through a much smaller office. The company closed its Denver and Greenwich offices that year. (In 1993 it opened another one in Woodland Hills, California, but closed it in 1995.) Hoenig introduced, in 1992, an institutional bond capability to go along with its equities brokering. It also established an independent research summary service available by means of Bloomberg Inc.'s Bloomberg Financial Markets, a provider of computerized financial information and securities quotations. This service allowed Bloomberg's 20,000 worldwide clients access to research reports and updates at no cost.

Growing Revenue: 1993–99

Hoenig's net income reached a peak of $5.35 million in 1993 on revenues of $58.37 million. That year, the company purchased Axe-Houghton Associates Inc. of Tarrytown, New York, a money management firm with about $1.4 billion under management. This firm, which replaced Vortex, specialized in active equity and fixed income management, indexing, and international investment with American Depositary Receipts. Axe-Houghton's investment team remained in place with five-year employment contracts. Hoenig's clients at this time included Aetna Life Insurance & Annuity Co., Bank of Bermuda Ltd., Bankers Trust Co., Dreyfus Corp., General Electric Co., Tokyo Fire & Life Insurance Co., UBS Asset Management, and Value Line Inc. The firm now was employing 300 global research vendors and, through its domestic and international markets, executing trading orders on a worldwide basis around the clock in any currency. Global equities now accounted for about 18 percent of the firm's business.

The soft-dollar share of Hoenig Group's commission revenues rose to 83 percent in 1993 and reached a peak of 87 percent in 1994 and 1995. Hoenig's net income slumped to $2.6 million in 1994 on revenues of $59.91 million. The following year its revenues dropped to $53.53 million, and it lost money during the first quarter of the year for its first quarterly loss since going public. It attributed the loss to lagging global finance markets and a decline in commissions following the departure of six brokers. The company ended the year, however, by posting net income of $4.92 million. Axe-Houghton, whose clients included AT&T Corp. and the state of Arizona, increased the amount of assets under its management to some $3.5 billion by the end of the year.

Ronald Hoenig died in 1995 and was succeeded as chief executive officer by Joseph A. D'Andrea, an investment banker who had overseen oil and gas real estate investment activities at Lazard Freres & Co. and its partners. He was succeeded the following year by Frederic P. Sapirstein, an investment banker who had been overseeing trading in Asian equities for Bear, Stearns & Co., Inc.

The firm hired its own four-member proprietary research team in 1996. Among them was Robert J. Barbera, formerly an analyst for Lehman Brothers Holdings Inc., who became chief economist for the U.S. subsidiary, Hoenig & Co. "I get paid for looking out for what might change the conventional view," Barbera told Jonathan Fuerbringer of the *New York Times* in 1999. "There is a small list of portfolio managers who think I have something to deliver, and we talk." Barbera correctly forecast that the Asian financial crisis of 1998 would result in lower inflation, lower interest rates, and greater growth in the United States—a contrarian view at the time.

Hoenig had net income of $2.89 million on revenues of $70.43 million in 1996. Its revenues and net income continued to grow in every remaining year of the decade, with the 1993 record for net income surpassed in 1999.

Hoenig Group in 2000

Hoenig Group again set records for revenues and net income in 2000, earning $11.43 million on operating revenues of $100.11 million. Some 76 percent of its brokerage commissions came through soft-dollar arrangements, with the rest from execution-only brokerage and in-house research—Hoenig's most profitable brokerage activities. Domestic brokerage comprised 85 percent of the company's brokerage revenues. Asset management accounted for 12 percent of the company's revenues.

Hoenig's principal activity continued to be that of providing high-quality trade execution services in global equities and domestic fixed income securities to institutional customers. It also earned commissions by providing independent research and other services (such as proprietary research) to investment managers; providing execution-only services; and paying expenses of, or commission refunds to, customers under directed-brokerage or commission-recapture arrangements.

Hoenig Group now was obtaining research products and services from more than 400 independent sources. These products and services included fundamental research, economic research and forecasting, quantitative analysis, global research, quotation, news and database systems, fixed income research, software for securities analysis, portfolio management, and performance measurement services. Almost all of the company's research relationships were nonexclusive.

Hoenig Group's Axe-Houghton subsidiary was providing professional investment management for employee benefit plans, investment partnerships, and other institutional clients in the United States and also was acting as the general partner of two investment limited partnerships. It was specializing in active small-capitalization growth equity management, small- and mid-capitalization value management, and international indexing using American Depositary Receipts. Axe-Houghton had $4.43 billion in assets under management at the end of the

Key Dates:

1970: The firm is founded by Ronald H. Hoenig, Max H. Levine, and Paul Strock.
1991: Hoenig Group makes its initial public offering of common stock.
1993: Hoenig purchases Axe-Houghton Associates Inc., an asset management firm.
1995: Ronald Hoenig, chairman, president, and chief executive officer of the firm, dies.
1999: Hoenig Group breaks a six-year-old record for annual net income.

year. This was, however, below the figure of $4.96 billion at the end of 1999, which the company attributed primarily to decreased investment performance. Particularly hard hit were the Focused Growth and Technology Growth disciplines, with assets under management decreasing from $181.1 million to $103.4 million during the year. The Technology Growth discipline ceased to have any assets under management at year's end. Revenue from asset management came to $12 million.

Hoenig (Far East) Limited closed its Tokyo office in 2000. Hoenig Group invested $7.5 million during the year in InstiPro Group, Inc., the parent company of a new business-to-business on-line brokerage firm. Hoenig Group's ten executive officers and directors collectively owned about 52 percent of the company's common stock in early 2001. The company had no long-term debt.

Principal Subsidiaries

Axe-Houghton Associates Inc.; Hoenig & Co., Inc.; Hoenig & Company Limited (U.K.); Hoenig (Far East) Limited (Hong Kong).

Principal Competitors

Bear Stearns Cos. Inc.; Lehman Brothers Holdings Inc.; Merrill Lynch & Co. Inc.

Further Reading

''Axe-Houghton Purchased by Brokerage Firm,'' *Pensions & Investments,* March 22, 1993, p. 37.
Fuerbringer, Jonathan, ''When Being Wrong Won't Hurt,'' *New York Times,* October 15, 1999, pp. C1, C7.
Jordan, John, ''Hoenig Group Leases 15,000 Square Feet of Office Space in Rye Brook,'' *Westchester County Business Journal,* January 6, 1992, p. 8.
McBride, Caryn A., ''Soft-Dollar Expertise Makes Hoenig a Tough, Well-Respected Competitor,'' *Fairfield County Business Journal,* April 19, 1993, p. 8.
Philippidis, Alex, ''Hoenig Group's New Chief Sets Ambitious Goals for 1996,'' *Westchester County Business Journal,* January 22, 1996, p. 10.

—Robert Halasz

Hudson River Bancorp, Inc.

One Hudson City Centre
Hudson, New York
U.S.A.
Telephone: (518) 828-4600
Fax: (518) 828-0082
Web site: http://www.hudsonriverbank.com

Public Company
Incorporated: 1998
Employees: 333
Sales: $79 million (2000)
Stock Exchanges: NASDAQ
Ticker Symbol: HRBT
NAICs: 522120 Savings Institutions; 551112 Offices of Other Holding Companies

Hudson River Bancorp, Inc. is the holding company for Hudson River Bank & Trust, formed in 1998 as part of a plan to convert from a mutual savings bank owned by depositors to a stock savings bank owned by shareholders. With its headquarters located in Hudson, New York, Hudson River Bancorp serves a limited area of the upstate region. Since receiving a large amount of money following its public offering of stock, the bank has acquired major stakes in an insurance agency and mortgage company, as well as acquiring two other area banks, one of which precipitated an expensive and drawn-out contest with two other area rivals. As a result of these additions, Hudson River Bancorp now boasts approximately $1.8 billion in assets, making it large enough to compete against major regional financial institutions that in recent years have threatened the existence of small community banks.

Origins in the Mid-1800s

The original entity that led to Hudson River Bancorp was the Hudson City Savings Institution, which grew out of the savings bank movement that began in Europe in the second half of the 18th century. Small savings organizations were formed in Germany and Switzerland to benefit members of the working class, who pooled their small deposits in order to earn a higher return. Because subscribers could only withdraw their money upon reaching a prescribed age, these early mutuals were similar to contemporary retirement plans. British progressives latched onto the idea as a way to eliminate poverty. They thought that by setting up savings and annuity plans, rather than giving alms that they believed would reward idleness, they could instill the virtues of thrift, industry, and sobriety in the poor. In 1810 the first self-sustaining savings bank was founded in Scotland. Very quickly the concept spread throughout the British Isles, so that by 1818 the United Kingdom boasted 465 savings banks.

The mutual savings movement spread to the United States, with the first New York City institution opening in 1819. Again, the emphasis was on promoting thrift among the laboring class, a panacea that was believed to cure any manner of social problems. These early savings banks were generally only opened a few hours a week and often shared offices with commercial banks where the mutuals deposited their money. As the funds in these so-called ''thrifts'' increased, however, the ties to charity were gradually loosened. They became full-fledged businesses, housed in their own impressive buildings, run by full-time managers. The Civil War helped to accelerate this transition, and soon there was little to separate savings institutions from other community banks. Thrifts were just as willing to accept deposits from middle-class businessmen as they were from laborers.

Hudson City Savings, one of a number of mutuals formed in New York State before the Civil War, received its charter on April 4, 1850, when Governor Hamilton Fish signed a special act of the New York State Legislature. The bank's first president was Robert A. Barnard, who was very active in the community, serving as postmaster and judge, as well as alderman and state senator. At first the bank operated out of the insurance office of one of its trustees, Josiah W. Fairfield. It was only open on Mondays and Saturdays, from 10 a.m. until 8 p.m. The bank's first deposit, in the amount of $80, was made on October 7, 1850. By the end of that year, Hudson City Savings had 20 accounts, with a total of $2,184 in deposits.

By 1866 the bank was prosperous enough to build its own headquarters, a modest three-story attached structure. In 1910

Company Perspectives:

As we move forward and look ahead at the changes that are sure to come, we believe it is important to look back and draw from the core values that have guided our institution over the last 150 years. We believe our commitment to our communities and response to the needs of our customers has been the basis of our longevity and our success. These will continue to be our guiding principles.

Hudson City Savings constructed a much larger and imposing neo-classical building, the entrance flanked by matching pairs of imposing columns. Over the years, the building would be remodeled and enlarged as the bank grew. By 1875 the bank accumulated more than $1 million in assets. By 1900 that amount increased to $2.65 million. When the new building opened in 1910, assets reached $5.1 million. In 1940 the bank topped $12 million, and by 1950, following a post-war boom, it reached $25.8 million. By 1970 the assets of the Hudson City Savings Institution stood at $80.4 million.

Expanding Beyond the Home Base in 1970

Until this point, Hudson City Savings operated solely out of its Hudson bank building, then in 1970 began to branch out to other locations in Columbia County, starting with an office in Chatham. Two years later the bank opened a branch in Valatie. In 1974 Hudson City Savings added a branch in Copake and extended the back of its main building to add more office space and provide drive-up teller lanes. The bank moved beyond Columbia County in 1975 when it opened a branch office in Nassau, Rensselaer County. In 1989 Hudson City Savings acquired a Dime Savings Bank branch and established a presence in downtown Albany. The bank opened its first supermarket branch in Greenport in 1994.

Hudson City Savings was now headed by Edward A. Brablc, who joined the bank in 1990 as executive vice-president, then became president and chief executive officer a year later. In five years under Brablc, the bank grew from seven branches and $450 million in assets to 11 branches with $600 million in assets. In March 1996 he gained unwanted notoriety for himself and the bank when he became involved in a domestic dispute with his pregnant wife. He was charged by the State Police with third-degree assault after his wife, Susan Brablc, was treated in an area hospital for two broken bones under her left eye. The incident, which took place on March 10, was not made public until March 30, at which time the 43-year old Brablc was placed on indefinite leave by the bank's board. Little more than a week later he resigned. Despite protests from his wife, who did not want her husband prosecuted, Brablc would eventually be sentenced to 30 days in a county jail and fined $1,000.

Brablc was replaced on a interim basis by Carl A. Florio, the chief financial officer who had been with the bank since 1993. He grew up in Columbia County, graduated from the University of Albany, and was a partner of an accounting firm before joining Hudson City Savings. The bank's board formed a search committee in late April to hire a replacement for Brablc, but two months later decided to name Florio as the new president and chief executive officer.

Under Florio the bank created a subsidiary, Hudson River Mortgage Corporation, to provide residential mortgages in the Albany area. It also opened a 12th branch location. The bank was growing, but not at a pace to compete with other financial institutions that had access to capital in the stock market. In general, mutuals had begun to suffer in the 1970s from rising interest rates. Committed to long-term, low-yielding mortgages, many of these thrifts lacked the flexibility to adapt to adverse economic conditions. By the mid-1990s, mutual savings banks were becoming a dying breed. At the end of 1972 there had been 1,817 federally chartered mutual savings banks; by the end of 1996 there were only 653. Hudson City Savings was one of 28 New York State chartered mutuals, but by 1997, when it announced its intention to covert to stock ownership, only a handful of state mutuals remained.

A mutual converts to stock ownership by creating a holding company, then making a subscription offering to allow depositors, employees, officers, and directors to buy shares in the new corporation at a set price. Half the proceeds are used to acquire the bank, while the rest is available for use in expanding the institution. Depositors of the mutual stand to gain because the stock of the new holding company is likely to rise substantially, generally spiking 15 percent to 20 percent on the first day of public trading. Management of the mutual usually receive stock options that are potentially lucrative. Furthermore, executives of public companies are also paid better. Through the holding company the bank can also expand into complementary businesses such as insurance, real estate, and financial planning. On the other hand, instead of being owned by the community through its depositors, converted mutuals now have to answer to shareholders, with the result that a longer-term outlook may give way to a quarterly results-oriented approach and that the interests of depositors and shareholders may conflict.

As part of its conversion Hudson City Savings changed its name to Hudson River Bank & Trust Company. Its holding company, Hudson River Bancorp, planned to raised $150 million by selling 15 million shares of common stock at $10 a share. The demand for the offering, however, was nearly triple that amount, due in large part to syndicates that used depositors to buy shares. Limited to a maximum of 17 million shares, Hudson River allocated no more than 100 shares to each depositor who had been with the bank as of September 30, 1996. The offering raised $170.3 million after expenses, approximately half of which went to the bank for its purchase and would then be available for use in generating new loans or acquiring other institutions. The holding company would also be able to invest its remaining money. Furthermore, as part of the conversion plan, 520,000 shares of stock were contributed to establish the Hudson River Bank & Trust Company Foundation, devoted to supporting charitable causes and community development activities in the upstate New York counties that the bank served.

Conversion and Further Expansion in 1998

Soon after completing its stock offering, Hudson River began to expand its holding. In October 1998 it bought an Albany-based mortgage company, Homestead Funding Corporation, which sold

Key Dates:

1850: Hudson City Savings Institution is chartered by New York State.
1910: The company's current headquarters is constructed.
1950: The bank tops $25 million in assets.
1970: The bank's first branch office is opened.
1975: The first branch office is opened outside the bank's home county.
1998: Hudson River Bancorp is formed to convert the bank from mutual to stock ownership.
1999: Total assets exceed $1 billion.
2001: The bank completes acquisition of Cohoes Bancorp.

and serviced multifamily residential and construction loans. Homestead was licensed to do business in most of the country and provided Hudson River with offices in Florida and Pennsylvania, as well as several branches in New York State. In May 1999, Hudson River announced it would acquire SFS BAncorp Inc., the holding company for Schenectady Federal Savings Bank. The $32 million transaction expanded Hudson River's reach to the Schenectady market, adding four branches and no overlap with current operations. SFS also added $176 million in assets, making Hudson River a $1 billion bank. Later in 1999, Hudson River also entered the commercial and residential insurance market when it acquired an equity interest in the Bostwick Group. Based in Hudson with offices in five other upstate New York counties, Bostwick generated more than $2.5 million in revenues in 1998, offering commercial and personal property and casualty insurance; life, health, and employee benefits; plus bonding, risk management, and pension services.

To compete against giant regional banks, such as Key Corporation, FleetBoston, and Charter One, which dominated banking in upstate New York, Hudson River needed to grow at a much faster clip. In May 2000 it announced a merger with Cohoes Bancorp Inc., another area converted-mutual holding company, that would greatly enhance it stature. The combined institutions, with 38 branches, would boast assets of $1.8 billion and a market capitalization of $230 million. Not only were there only two overlapping branches, located in downtown Albany, the bank's operations dovetailed nicely. Hudson River had a trust department that Cohoes lacked, and Cohoes brought with it a brokerage subsidiary that Hudson River lacked. Moreover, once the merger was completed, Hudson River would be positioned to acquire smaller banks, possibly expanding into Connecticut and Massachusetts. Under the terms of the deal, Cohoes shareholders would receive 1.185 shares of Hudson River stock, or roughly $11 per share, which amounted to an $87 million deal. For the first three years, Cohoes's CEO, Harry Robinson, would serve as CEO with Florio acting as president. The two executives would then share the CEO position for six months, at which point Florio would take over, and Robinson would become chairman for another three years.

As promising as this friendly merger of two equals appeared on the surface, however, analysts and shareholders of Cohoes questioned whether the price was right. They speculated that a larger bank might offer substantially more money, especially when there were so few community banks available to acquire. Within days there were two other suitors for Cohoes, followed by a shareholder suit that attempted to prevent the merger with Hudson River. The main threat was TrustCo Bank Corporation NY of Schenectady, which proposed buying both institutions. It offered an exchange of TrustCo shares, valued at $16 each for Cohoes shareholders and $14 each for Hudson River shareholders. Ambanc Holding Company, owner of Mohawk Community Bank based in Amsterdam, New York, then offered $15.25 a share in cash for Cohoes. Both Florio and Robinson dismissed the offers, contending that TrustCo was simply looking to scuttle the merger between Cohoes and Hudson River because it feared competition from the proposed combination. Located in an economically distressed area, Ambanc was seen as looking to inflate its value in order to then sell itself at a high premium, thus satisfying disgruntled shareholders and directors. Robinson even claimed that Ambanc, which had been on the market for two years, was actually trying to be purchased by Cohoes.

Florio and Robinson remained committed to the merger, which would be decided by two separate shareholders' meetings in August 2000. TrustCo, meanwhile, took out full-page newspaper ads in local publications criticizing the deal, claiming that insiders like Florio and Robinson stood to make out better than shareholders. TrustCo then took a formal step to prevent the merger by filing SEC documents in order to launch its own tender offers for both Cohoes and Hudson River. To remain in the hunt, Ambanc increased its bid for Cohoes to $16.50 per share. As the voting date neared, TrustCo produced a study that blasted the proposed merger between Cohoes and Hudson River. The two banks answered these assertions with a study of their own that supported the deal. Shareholders of the two banks were then besieged by professional firms hired to convince them which to accept or reject the proxy offers.

A *Times Union* article encapsulated the effort, quoting one investor who owned stock in both banks as saying, " 'There are the phone calls urging me to send in the white (tear up the gold or green if you have any proxy, or to send in the green or gold (and tear up the white) proxy,' she related in an email. One call, even, from a TrustCo vice president. Another, long distance from Illinois. I have never before felt loved by so many people'. . . . It runs beyond phone calls. Shareholders, and their mail carriers, may welcome the end of the paper dump that the various companies have unleashed. Altogether, an investor with shares in Cohoes would have received seven proxy statements by now. Investors with shares in both receive more."

In the end, Hudson River shareholders approved the merger, Cohoes shareholders rejected it. Cohoes then hired a New York City Investment firm to help it consider its options, as the names of other possible suitors also began to surface. TrustCo then sweetened its bid, while Ambanc's offer lapsed. Hudson River's largest shareholder, Florida-based Private Capital Management, with an 8.4 percent stake, urged Hudson River to accept TrustCo's offer. Because PCM could nominate its own slate of board members or simply dump its shares of Hudson River, Florio had little choice but to at least announce that he would consider the offer. Eventually he urged shareholders to reject the deal, even though the bid had been bumped to $17 per share.

In late November 2000, after months inactivity, Hudson River and Cohoes announced a new merger agreement. Hudson River increased its offer to $19.50 in cash for each share of Cohoes stock, for a total of $158 million. A few days later TrustCo decided to withdraw its offers for the two banks. Hudson River's new price was simply too rich for TrustCo. Under the new terms, Florio would continue to serve as president and CEO, and Robinson would retire. In a special meeting held in January 2001, Cohoes shareholders approved the deal, and following federal regulatory approval, the merger became official in April 2001. With assets approaching $2 billion, Hudson River was now in a position to grow into an even larger bank, although some analysts were not yet ready to write off TrustCo, which boasted $2.3 billion in assets. Although losing a major battle, TrustCo might still wish to continue the bank war and pick off Hudson River, now an even more inviting target.

Principal Subsidiaries

Hudson River Bank & Trust Company; Hudson City Associates, Inc.; Hudson River Mortgage Corp.; Hudson River Funding Corp.; Hudson City Centre, Inc.; SSLA Services Corporation.

Principal Competitors

Green County Bancorp; M&T Bank; Trustco Bank Corp NY.

Further Reading

Aaron, Kenneth, ''Shareholders Targeted on Vote,'' *Times Union,* August 17, 2000, p. E4.

——, ''TrustCo Slams Targets of Buyout Bids in Ads,'' *Times Union,* July 11, 2000, p. E1.

Agosta, Veronica, ''Two N.Y. Thrifts Wish Trustco Would Go Away,'' *American Banker,* July 26, 2000, p. 1.

DerGurahian, Jean, ''Cohoes Savings Sale Set, *Times Union,* November 25, 2000, p. E1.

Feldstein, Betsy, ''Merger Creates $1B Bank,'' *Times Union,* August 28, 1999, p. B8.

Johnston, Jo-Ann, ''Friendly Merger Helps Banks' Survival,'' *Times Union,* April 27, 2000, p. E1.

——, ''3 Now Courting Cohoes Savings, *Times Union,* June 28, 200, p. E1.

Leuchter, Miriam, ''Drums Along the Mohawk,'' *US Banker,* August 2000, p. 64.

Olmstead, Alan L., *New York City Mutual Savings Banks, 1819–1861,* Chapel Hill: The University of North Carolina Press, 1976.

Pinckney, Barbara, ''Bank Has More Buyers Than Stock for Initial Offering,'' *Capital District Business Review,* June 29, 1998.

——, ''Cohoes-Hudson River Deal a Quiet End to Region's Bank War,'' *Capital District Business Review,* December 4, 2000, p.6.

——, ''Thrift Conversions Mean Money,'' *Capital District Business Review,* May 11, 1998.

——, ''Thrift Projects $150M Offering,'' *Capital District Business Review,* March 23, 1998.

—Ed Dinger

International Game Technology

International Game Technology

9295 Prototype Drive
Reno, Nevada 89511
U.S.A.
Telephone: (775) 448-7777
Toll Free: (800) 688-7890
Fax: (775) 448-0719
Web Site: http://www.igt.com

Public Company
Incorporated: 1980
Employees: 3,600
Sales: $1 billion (2000)
Stock Exchanges: NASDAQ
Ticker Symbol: IGT
NAIC: 713290 Other Gambling Industries

International Game Technology (IGT) is the world's leading designer and manufacturer of slot machines and video gaming machines, controlling approximately two-thirds of the market. IGT sells wide area progressive systems that allow slot machines from a number of locations to pool massive payouts that can total tens of millions of dollars. IGT also manufactures video gaming terminals for state-run lotteries and accompanying monitoring systems. IGT software systems that allow casinos to monitor play and to track player activity have become the target of antitrust litigation. Competitors contend that rival machines are not compatible with the IGT system, thus making it difficult to sell non-IGT equipment to casinos.

Slot Machine Technology Dates Back to the 1800s

In the 19th century any machine that took a coin, whether it was for gambling or vending, was called a slot machine. The early gambling devices, such as a mechanical horse race, were penny machines that provided an opportunity for barroom wagering. Machines that dispensed a small payout of coins arrived in the early 1890s. These were crude devices that anticipated the spinning reels and symbols used in later slot machines. The basic mechanics of slot machines would remain unchanged through most of the 20th century. Spring-driven reels, generally three but as many as five, would portray an assortment of symbols, such as playing card suits, bells, bars, cherries, lemons, and JACKPOT. When the reels were sent spinning by a pull of the handle, the machine would pay out if the symbols lined up in a winning combination. It was the number of reels and the number of symbols that determined the odds of winning, a method that would change with the rise of technology in the 1990s when computer chips would select the random winners. Slot machines were popular in the 1920s and 1930s, especially in resort areas, but, because of suspected links to organized crime by the 1950s, they were prohibited everywhere but Nevada. In the early 1960s Bally developed a machine with electromechanical circuitry and motorized hopper pay that opened up design variations. For the next 20 years Bally would be the dominant manufacturer of casino slot machines.

IGT was founded by William S.(''Si'') Redd, the son of a Mississippi sharecropper. He began his career in the gaming industry at age 18, when he bought a used pinball machine and convinced a hamburger stand operator to keep the game in his establishment in exchange for 50 percent of its revenues. After working as a distributor for Wurlitzer jukeboxes in New England, Redd was hired by Bally Manufacturing in 1967 to distribute slot machines in Nevada. He founded his own affiliate, Bally Distribution, and became known throughout the state as ''The Slot Machine King.'' In 1975 Redd created A-1 Supply and a year later entered into a deal with Bally Manufacturing through which he acquired sole rights to the company's burgeoning video business.

Redd devoted a large amount of resources to research and development. As a result, A-1 Supply became a pioneer in the video gaming industry, developing a line of video poker, blackjack, keno, as well as slot machines, which Redd sold to casino operators throughout Nevada and Atlantic City. Redd changed the name of his company to SIRCOMA (from ''SI Redd COin MAchines'') in 1979. In 1980, through an exchange of stock, SIRCOMA changed its name to International Game Technology and went public on NASDAQ in October 1981. Annual sales had grown from less than $3 million in 1975 to over $61 million in 1982. By 1982, approximately 9 percent of gambling

Company Perspectives:

As a recognized leader in slot machine and video gaming machine design and production, IGT is committed to providing our customers with the quality products at a competitive price which, together with excellent service and support, will assist them in maximizing their profitability.

machines in Nevada were video machines, and IGT held 90 percent of that market. More importantly the casino business was entering a major shift in emphasis. In Nevada in 1983 machines surpassed table games in revenues for the first time, ushering in a period of great opportunity for the makers of slot machines and video games. After twenty years of industry dominance, Bally Gaming had grown stale. The company's new slot machines were deemed bland by customers who simply refused to play them. Bally quickly lost market share and was overtaken by Universal, with IGT and Sigma looking to make inroads as well.

IGT also began developing its lottery game technology and by 1986 was one of the top six players in the $1 billion business. That year it purchased a 36 percent stake in Syntech International, Inc., a rival manufacturer of lottery ticket vending machines and manager of several state lottery games. IGT's total revenues dropped precipitously in 1986, however, due to a slump in the Nevada gaming industry and growing competition from Japanese manufacturers. To help revive his struggling company, Redd hired Charles W. Mathewson, a retired executive from the investment firm of Jefferies & Co., to take over as chairman.

IGT Controls Top Market Share by 1987

When Mathewson was subsequently named president in 1986, he boasted that IGT stock prices (then trading at 11 cents a share) would double within two years. The company's heavy R&D spending paid off in 1987 when it introduced Megabucks, a computerized slot machine network that allowed any number of participants across the state to play for the same progressive jackpot. Within a year, IGT had sold Megabucks to over 30 casinos throughout Nevada and had obtained rights to sell the system in New Jersey. Mathewson's boasting had been proven correct. Fueled by strong sales of Megabucks, IGT's sales hit $81 million in 1987, and earnings rose to 71 cents a share. In addition, IGT surpassed Universal as the top gaming manufacturer.

By 1988, IGT's Megabucks and other newly developed progressive jackpot systems had captured 60 percent of the Nevada slot machine market. IGT had also secured 25 percent of the international gaming market, with machines in Australia, Portugal, the Netherlands, Turkey, and Monte Carlo. Sales in 1988 were $95 million, 25 to 30 percent of which came from international markets. The following year, revenues soared 50 percent to $151 million as earnings jumped to $1.73 a share.

By 1991 IGT controlled almost 54 percent of the North American market. Its management team was seasoned and stable, and its rivals were being relegated to also-ran status. Whereas the U.S. gaming market had been limited to Nevada, Atlantic City, and Florida cruise ships, the early 1990s would see a growth spurt that sent IGT sales soaring. The federal government passed a law permitting Native Americans to own and operate casinos on Indian reservations. Many other states, particularly those along the Mississippi River, began permitting riverboat gambling. In all, some 60 new casinos opened between 1991 and 1995, and IGT was well positioned to serve these emerging markets. Over half the river casinos built in the early 1990s were stocked solely with IGT machines. The nation's largest Indian reservation casino purchased 80 percent of its machines from IGT, and the new Luxor, Treasure Island, and MGM Grand casinos in Las Vegas purchased a minimum of 70 percent of their machines from IGT.

European gaming markets also expanded, and in 1991 IGT opened a European division, with plans to establish an assembly factory, a product distribution center, and a direct factory sales center in Europe. After a long and arduous effort to break into the Japanese gambling market that took six years, IGT finally received approval to sell slot and paschisuro machines in April of 1993.

In 1993, IGT reorganized its corporate structure, establishing IGT-International to oversee manufacturing and sales outside of North America, and creating the corporate "Office of the President" to direct strategic planning worldwide. Sales in 1993 were $478 million, with earnings over $100 million. Stock prices continued to climb, peaking just above $41. IGT became the darling of many investors on Wall Street. However, a backlash against gambling set in as voters turned against gambling initiatives, government tightened regulations, and new casino building stopped dead. Moreover, foreign expansion at the time was equally uncertain. By 1995, when new domestic gambling markets bottomed out, IGT held 78 percent market share of the slot machine and video game business, but its stock was being battered. It dropped off 70 percent from its high in 1993.

David Hanlon took over for Mathewson in 1995, a move that would produce disappointing results. Several top executives left IGT, reportedly because of Hanlon's abrasive management style. Mathewson returned to replace Hanlon in 1996, and quickly brought back many of the people who had defected. Despite IGT's dominant market share, Mathewson knew that the company remained vulnerable to competition, just as Bally had been in the 1980s. IGT's new challengers in the business—Casino Data Systems, WMS Industries, Alliance Gaming, and Sega Gaming Technology—embraced the possibilities of high tech, believing that younger gamblers, raised on computer games, would be attracted to better sound and graphics and interactivity. Mathewson maintained that the average player was a 55-year-old woman who couldn't even program a VCR. Nevertheless, in August 1996 IGT formed a new division to develop interactive casino games.

In other areas Mathewson was more open-minded. He established joint venture alliances to develop games, sometimes with rivals. When IGT acquired a license from Sony to develop a Wheel of Fortune game, he joined forces with Anchor Gaming which already had a popular game, Wheel of Gold, on casino floors. The two companies agreed to split the profits generated by the hybrid-design slot machine. IGT also teamed with Gtech to develop and market video-lottery games. Mathewson was

Key Dates:

1975: Original company is founded as A-1 Supply by William S. (''Si'') Redd.
1979: A-1 Supply changes name to SIRCOMA.
1980: International Game Technology is incorporated.
1981: SIRCOMA merger with IGT in a tax-free exchange is complete.
1986: Charles W. Mathewson is named president of IGT.
2000: Company reaches $1 billion in annual sales.
2001: Company announces intentions to merge with Anchor Gaming.

also willing to continue spending significantly more on R&D than IGT's competitors. In addition, the company invested some $30 million overseas where markets appeared to be opening up, in particular Greece, Mexico, and South Africa where 40 casino licenses had been allocated. New majors casinos scheduled to open in Atlantic City and Las Vegas also promised to boost IGT sales.

IGT Rebounds in the Late 1990s

IGT's business was again thriving in the late 1990s. In 1997 it introduced MegaSports, a betting system that allowed players to make specialized wagers on sporting events. It developed computerized casino management systems to keep real-time records of activity on every gaming machine and table in a casino, as well as player tracking and the ability to award the best customers with specialized bonuses. IGT continued to outspend its rivals in R&D, investing more than $30 million annually while Anchor, Alliance, and Silicon Gaming spent less than $20 million combined. IGT, following its success with Wheel of Fortune, adapted other well-known pop culture icons and products, including The Addams Family, I Dream of Jeannie, Elvis, and The Munsters. In 1999 IGT purchased Sodak Gaming, a primary distributor to Native American casinos, for $230 million. The following year, the company purchased one of its rivals, Silicon Gaming, maker of a number of innovative games. In 2000 IGT debuted its EZ Pay paper voucher system that enabled slot machines to pay off in tickets that could be reinserted into machines for further play or redeemed for cash.

In 2000 not only did IGT manufacture its one millionth slot machine, it topped the $1 billion mark in annual sales. Its share of the U.S. market was still a robust 68 percent. And although IGT was doing well overseas, it suffered a setback in Australia when a Japanese newcomer, Konami, moved ahead of IGT to second place in sales. The 1998 purchase of Australian slotsmaker Olympic Amusements proved to be a financial loss. Konami also made plans to enter the U.S. market, especially targeting the California Native American tribes who were unhappy that IGT had spent money along with Nevada casinos to oppose a ballot initiate to allow expanded gaming in California. Furthermore the gambling market had clearly matured. State governments, enjoying the positive effects of a strong economy, felt little need to legalize gambling to augment revenues. The real market for slot machine makers was in replacing the games already on the casino floor, and that decision was in large part made by the customers. Many of the newer interactive games that IGT had once eschewed began to replace its reliable money-makers.

Potentially more troubling for IGT was an antitrust suit filed against it by WMS Gaming in 2000. WMS essentially compared IGT to Microsoft, claiming that it offered its computerized management programs for free to casinos in exchange for a promise to buy 75 percent of their gaming machines from IGT. Because WMS and other competitors were denied the protocol to the IGT system until after casino orders were made, they were placed at a competitive disadvantage. As with Microsoft, IGT was gaining a reputation for arrogance in its dealings.

IGT's stock soared despite the litigation. How the suit was resolved and IGT's response to the changing gaming culture would go a long way to determine if the company would continue as the Goliath of slot machines or the Bally of a new century. Its position certainly seemed fortified when, in July 2001, IGT announced plans to merge with its Nevada-based rival Anchor Gaming. Whether such a merger would pass scrutiny from antitrust regulators remained to be seen.

Principal Subsidiaries

IGT; IGT-Europe B.V.; IGT Japan, K.K.; IGT-UK Limited; Sodak Gaming.

Principal Competitors

Alliance Gaming; Anchor Gaming; GTECH Holdings; WMS Industries Inc.

Further Reading

Alm, Rich, ''Gaming Industry Betting on Risky Business' Future Boom,'' *Houston Chronicle,* October 22, 2000, p. 2.

Clements, Jonathan, ''IGT Stock Is Riding High on Gambling Boom, and the Bells Could Keep Ringing for A While,'' *Wall Street Journal,* September 20, 1993, p. C2.

Hackney, Holt, ''IGT: Rolling Again,'' *Financial World,* April 22, 1996, p. 18.

Lane, Randall, ''Back into the Breach,'' *Forbes,* November 9, 1992, p. 96.

Marriott, Michel, ''Luck, Be a Microchip Tonight,'' *Denver Post,* December 21, 1998, p. E-07.

Paris, Ellen, ''Call and Raise,'' *Forbes,* August 30, 1982, p. 50.

Pomerantz, Dorothy, ''High Stakes,'' *Forbes,* July 3, 2000, p. 74.

Rasmusson, Erika, ''Hitting the Jackpot,'' *Sales & Marketing Management,* June 1998, p. 34.

Schlesinger, Jacob M., ''Tough Gamble: A Slot-Machine Maker Trying to Sell in Japan Hits Countless Barriers,'' *Wall Street Journal,* May 11, 1993, p. A1.

Slavin, Al, ''Slot Machine Supplier's Patent Lawsuit Turns into Antitrust Case,'' *Crain's Detroit Business,* June 5, 2000, p. 48.

Weinberg, Neil, ''A Run of Bad Luck,'' *Forbes,* May 22, 1995, p. 12.

—Maura Troester
—update: Ed Dinger

Isle of Capri Casinos, Inc.

1641 Popps Ferry Road
Biloxi, Mississippi 39532
U.S.A.
Telephone: (228) 436-7000
Toll Free: (800) 843-4753
Fax: (228) 435-5998
Web sites: http://www.theislecorp.com; http://isleofcapricasino.com

Public Company
Incorporated: 1990
Employees: 10,000
Sales: $684.9 million (2000)
Stock Exchanges: NASDAQ
Ticker Symbol: ISLE
NAIC: 72112 Casino Hotels; 71329 Other Gambling Industries; 711212 Racetracks

Isle of Capri Casinos, Inc., only a decade old in 2000, had by then already grown into one of the ten largest, publicly-held gaming corporations in the nation. By 2001, it ranked seventh and was still growing. The company owns and operates 11 riverboat and dockside casinos in Louisiana, Mississippi, and Missouri, plus a riverboat casino in Davenport, Iowa, that runs under the name Rhythm City Casino. In addition, the company owns or has an interest in two land-based casinos: the Isle of Capri Casino in Black Hawk, Colorado; and the Lady Luck Casino in Las Vegas, Nevada. The company also owns and operates Pompano Park Racing, a parimutuel, harness track in Pompano Beach, Florida, and, in partnership with Commodore Cruise Lines, runs the *Enchanted Capri*, a fully-appointed gaming cruise ship berthed in New Orleans. In 2001, the company also had two more casinos under construction in Missouri. Although Isle of Capri Casinos, Inc. is a public corporation, a 57 percent controlling share of it is owned by the family of the company's principal founder, chairman, and CEO, Bernard Goldstein.

1990–91: Bernard Goldstein founds Kana Corporation

In 1990, Bernard Goldstein combined two of his privately owned businesses—Riverboat Corporation of Mississippi and Riverboat Services—into Kana Corporation. The resulting company, incorporated in Delaware, was designed as a vehicle to raise sufficient capital for the acquisition of or investment in other businesses. Of Goldstein's two merged companies, the one, Riverboat Services, was a casino consulting firm; while the other, Riverboat Corporation of Mississippi, was a Biloxi gaming enterprise. Goldstein, a gaming-industry entrepreneur and attorney, had been involved in developing gaming in a number of states and had been actively engaged in lobbying for riverboat gaming in Iowa, where he had helped establish the industry. In the early 1990s, among other posts, he held the chairmanship of the steamboat companies which operated the Emerald Lady and Diamond Lady casino riverboats and served as president of Casino Cruises, Inc., which managed gaming on the Par-A-Dice Riverboat Casino in Peoria, Illinois. Goldstein also had behind him a long career in businesses totally unrelated to gaming. He had joined the Alter Companies in 1950 and served in various executive posts before becoming the group's chairman in 1980. The Alter Companies include affiliates in the scrap metal recycling, trucking, and barge-line transportation industries.

With Goldstein at its helm, Kana immediately acquired the Casino Career Training Center, then owned by James Ernst and Allan B. Solomon. Along with Goldstein, Ernst and Solomon made up Kana's top management, although Ernst resigned in 1995. Solomon, like Goldstein, was also trained in law and, prior to becoming a director of Kana Corp., had been a partner in Broad and Cassel, a Florida-based law firm.

1992–94: Reorganization and Expansion

In April 1992, Goldstein changed the name of Kana to Anubis II Corporation and in June of that year reorganized the company. The Riverboat Corporation of Mississippi, Riverboat Services, Inc., and the Casino Career Training Center, Inc., through stock-for-stock exchanges, became wholly-owned subsidiaries of Anubis, or, as it was quickly renamed, Casino

Company Perspectives:

The Isle of Capri Casinos' Mission is to be the Best Gaming Entertainment Company . . . Best for its Guests . . . Best for its Employees . . . Best for its Communities . . . Best for its Investors. . . . Not the Biggest—But the Best!

America, Inc., The newly reorganized corporation then went public, trading on Nasdaq under the symbol CSNO.

It was also in 1992, on August 1, that Casino America opened the Isle of Capri, Biloxi, Mississippi's first gaming facility, under the operational control of the Riverboat Corporation of Mississippi, alternatively known as the Biloxi Gaming Subsidiary. Through various stages in its development, the 50,000 square-foot dockside casino would become a major complex, boasting a 32,500 square feet gaming area accommodating 1,149 slot machines and 42 table games, with an adjacent land-based pavilion, a hotel, and parking for over 1,100 vehicles.

In the next year, 1993, Casino America opened the Isle Capri-Vicksburg, which began operations on August 9. It was the first of four casinos to open in the Vicksburg, Mississippi, area. Located on an 18-acre site adjacent to the Mississippi River, the facility originally started as a riverboat and barge casino with 21,000 square feet of gaming space. The operation's temporary facilities were replaced in 1994 with a 32,000 square-foot dockside casino and a land-based pavilion housing administrative offices and various non-gaming conveniences.

It was also in 1993 that Casino America entered a 50–50 partnership arrangement with Edward J. DeBartolo, a successful mall developer and owner and operator of Louisiana Downs, a horse racetrack in Shreveport, Louisiana. Because he had a 20-year record of running a profitable, untainted gambling operation in the state, DeBartolo seemed a certain bet to get one of the 15 casino gaming licenses to be granted by Louisiana. The plan was to open a new riverboat casino in Bossier City, just 5 miles from Louisiana Downs. Casino America put up $35 million in cash, and the partnership borrowed another $25 million to build the boat. Under the terms of the joint venture, styled the Louisiana Riverboat Gaming Partnership, DeBartolo put up no capital but had to wait for Casino America to recoup its investment before he could take a share of the profits. The new Isle of Capri Carribean-themed casino opened in May 1994 and was an instant success, partly because it had been heavily promoted in the Dallas area, just a three-hour drive away, and from which it drew a steady stream of customers.

1995–96: Casino America Improves and Acquires

The following year, 1995, Casino America began buying DeBartolo's share in the Bossier City riverboat casino. It also bought a half interest in a casino that opened in Lake Charles, Louisiana, in the summer of the same year. At that time, besides its Isle of Capri Casino in Biloxi, Casino America also owned the casino in Vicksburg, Mississippi.

On June 30, 1995, branching out in the gaming industry, Casino America acquired Pompano Park, a harness racing track situated in Pompano Beach, Florida, about half way between West Palm Beach and Miami. The only licensed harness racing track in the state, Pompano Park consisted of approximately 180 acres of owned land used for the racing operations. In addition, Casino America bought a lease-purchase agreement for an additional 143 acres that were used for training operations. Speculating that Florida would eventually legalize casino gambling, the company purchased the extra acreage for $12 million but later sold it to developers. Competition for Pompano Park came primarily from other south Florida parimutuel enterprises, including thoroughbred and greyhound racing tracks and jai alai frontons.

In August of the same year, as part of its Biloxi Improvement Program, Casino America held the grand opening of new facilities featuring an array of non-gaming amenities designed to make the Isle of Capri-Biloxi into a more customer-friendly vacation spot. Included were a 367-room, 15-story hotel tower—the Isle of Capri Casino Crowne Plaza—and the 32,000 square foot pavilion, which housed three restaurants and offered such entertainment as Las Vegas-style revues. Other improvements included the addition of new island-theme decor designed to enhance the casino's distinct image. By the time its Biloxi Improvement Program was completed in 1996, Casino America had spent about $50 million on its additions and renovations.

It was also in 1995 that Casino America applied to the Securities Exchange Commission for approval to trade on the New York Stock Exchange, switching from Nasdaq. It also filed a registration statement planning an offering of three million shares of common stock plus 664,167 shares owned by certain sellers. However, the change did not materialize, and Casino America remained on Nasdaq.

1997–2001: Millennium Expansion Plan

In June 1997, Casino America announced its joint venture plans to open a new casino in Black Hawk, Colorado in a partnership with Nevada Gold & Casinos. Land for the new Isle of Capri-style operation, 45 minutes away from downtown Denver, was bought from a Caesars World affiliate. It was a carefully selected site, chosen because the Denver metropolitan area was one of the fastest growing areas in the country and offered Casino America a new, very strong market. However, it was not wide-open; Colorado law limited gamblers to slot machines, poker, and blackjack, with a bet limit of $5.

By September 1998, the month and year in which Casino America officially changed its name to Isle of Capri Casinos, Inc., the company owned and had in operation four island-themed casinos under the Isle of Capri name—the two in Mississippi and the two in Louisiana—plus its parimutuel track in Florida. In addition, the Black Hawk casino, which it owned in an even partnership with Nevada Gold, opened in December. That same September, Isle of Capri had begun negotiations with Harrah's in an attempt to purchase one of that competitor's gaming properties in Tunica County, Mississippi. The facility, closed at the time, was known as ''little Harrah's'' and had first opened in 1993 and remained in operation until 1997.

Isle of Capri completed the purchase of the Harrah facility early in 1999, paying a reported $9.5 million for the 62,100-

Key Dates:

1990: Isle of Capri Casino founded as Kana Corporation.
1992: Kana Corp. becomes Casino America and opens Isle of Capri-Biloxi.
1993: Casino America opens casino in Vicksburg, Mississippi.
1994: Company opens casino in Bossier City, Louisiana.
1995: Casino America purchases Pompano Park Racing in Florida and opens a new casino in Lake Charles, Louisiana.
1998: Company changes name to Isle of Capri Casinos; *Enchanted Capri* makes maiden voyage; company opens Isle of Capri-Black Hawk in Colorado.
1999: Isle of Capri opens a new casino in Tunica, Mississippi.
2000: Company acquires five Lady Luck Gaming casinos, the Kansas City Flamingo Hilton Riverboat Casino, and President Casino and Hotel in Davenport, Iowa.

square-foot casino. Although considerably smaller than other facilities built or purchased by the company, the casino gave the company a presence in the northwest corner of Mississippi. Drawing customers from Memphis, Tennessee, and Little Rock, Arkansas, Tunica County had become the fasting growing gambling area in the state.

Because revised gaming regulations in Mississippi required that licensees spend an amount equal to 100 percent of what they spent on the gaming facility on land-based improvements, Isle of Capri immediately began making additions, including two theaters and a hotel. In March 1999, the company entered into a joint venture with singer-showman Wayne Newton to develop theaters at Isle of Capri sites, setting up a Wayne Newton Theatre complex in Tunica as the partnership's venue.

As part of its ''Millennium Expansion Plan,'' in 2000 the company purchased and converted four Lady Luck properties into Isle of Capri Casinos. These properties, located in Lula and Natchez, Mississippi, and Betterndorf and Marquette, Iowa, were refurbished and decorated in accordance with the Isle of Capri's signature Carribean theme. Somewhat later, the company purchased another Lady Luck Casino, located in the nation's gambling epicenter, Las Vegas. The company also purchased the Kansas City, Missouri, Flamingo Casino, which it also converted into an Isle of Capri-themed casino in early 2001. Earlier, in May 1999, also as part of the its Millennium Plan, the company entered a partnering arrangement with Bally Gaming and Systems, a business unit of Alliance Gaming Corporation, and SystemSource to co-develop a casino marketing and management system under the name Gold Casino System. Over the next two years, the new system was to be implemented at all of the company's casinos, providing information enhancement and data collection as well as better service for the casinos' customers.

Additional changes came in early 2001. Notably, in its first departure from its standard policy of acquiring gaming emporia and converting them into Isle of Capri styled casinos, the company purchased the President Casino in Davenport, Iowa, with plans to turn it into the company's first ''Rhythm City'' branded casino. It completed the conversion of that property in February 2001.

So far luck has been with Isle of Capri, despite ammunition fed to the anti-gambling movement by strong evidence of graft and corruption in states like Louisiana. Gaming has become a major means of raising revenue in the poorer southern states, where legislators are loathe to add new taxes by doing away with homestead exemptions or increasing income taxes. As long as the legal door remained open and the popularity of gaming stays strong, Isle of Capri would likely prosper. It had shown an enviable record of being in the right places at the right times.

Principal Competitors

Alliance Gaming Corporation; Ameristar Casinos, Inc.; Casino Magic Corp.; Harrah's Entertainment, Inc.; Park Place Entertainment Corporation; President Casinos, Inc.

Further Reading

Adderton, Donald V., ''Robert F. Boone, Top Black in Casino Industry,'' *Jet*, October 9, 1995, p. 12.

Bechard, Theresa, ''Isle of Capri Says Old Harrah's Is a Perfect Gamble,'' *Memphis Business Journal*, February 12, 1999, p. 3.

Eichenwald, Kurt, ''A Big Gamble on Mississippi Casinos,'' *New York Times*, January 31, 1993, p. F15.

Elliott, Suzanne, ''Casino America, DeBartolo Seek Strip Gaming Site,'' *Pittsburgh Business Times*, August 1, 1994, p. 1.

''Isle of Capri Casinos, Inc. Announces Systems Portion of the Millennium Expansion Program,'' *PR Newsletter*, May 24, 1999.

Lunsford, Darcie, ''Pompano Races Ahead; Developer Plans Class A, Retail Space for Broward's Last Frontier,'' *South Florida Business Journal*, April 30. 1999, p. 1A.

Monti, Lisa, ''Casino America Enters Joint Venture to Build in Colorado,'' *Knight-Ridder/Tribune Business News*, June 19, 1997.

Palmeri, Christopher, ''Horse Sense,'' *Forbes*, October 24, 1994, p. 19.

Taylor, Louise, ''Casino America Applies to Switch Trading from Nasdaq to New York Exchange,'' *Knight-Ridder/Tribune Business News*, August 21, 1995.

—John W. Fiero

Karlsberg Brauerei GmbH & Co KG

Karlsbergstrasse 62
D-66424 Homburg
Germany
Telephone: (49) (6841) 105-0
Fax: (49) (6841) 105-269
Web site: http://www.karlsberg.de

Private Company
Incorporated: 1878 as Bayerische Bierbrauerei zum Karlsberg
Employees: 2,353
Sales: DM 1.1 billion ($562 million) (2000)
NAIC: 31212 Breweries; 312111 Soft Drink Manufacturing; 312112 Bottled Water Manufacturing

Karlsberg Brauerei GmbH & Co KG is one of Germany's top ten beer and beverage producers. The Homburg-based company has a century-long brewing tradition and has developed into a beverage concern with 16 subsidiaries involved in beer and nonalcoholic beverage production, services, and logistics in Germany and France. Karlsberg Brauerei's core brand "Karlsberg Ur-Pils" and other specialty beers are mainly sold in the westernmost German states. Its export beer brand "Karlsbräu" is shipped to France, Italy, England, and eastern Europe. The company owns the Koblenz-based brewing group Königsbacher Brauerei, Coca-Cola licensee OKKO-GmbH, nonalcoholic beverage producers Merziger, Klindworth, Lindavia, and Dietz. In the services sector, Tiefkühlkost-Zentrale (TKZ) supplies restaurants with frozen produce and ServiPlus stocks food and beverage vending machines. Karlsberg Brauerei also owns a brewery and a fruit juice producer in France, Brasserie de Saverne and Cidou. Karlsberg Brauerei is majority owned by the Weber family.

New Owner for Old Brewery in 1878

In 1878 the biggest brewery in Homburg, a town in the German Saar region with a long beer-brewing tradition, was up for sale. The brewery was built by the Jacoby brothers at the foot of the Karlsberg mountain in 1858 and 1859. On top of the mountain in the Karlsberg castle lived the noble Pfalz-Zweibrückische family, which since the middle of the 18th century had operated the predecessor of the Jacoby brothers' brewery. Limited raw material and food supplies in the years after the German-French War led to extraordinarily high prices and caused many small businesses to declare bankruptcy. One of them was the Jacoby brothers' Bayerische Bierbrauerei zum Karlsberg.

On May 28, 1878, the Karlsberg brewery was auctioned off in Carl Cappel's restaurant. After being outbid a few times in the course of the auction, import goods wholesaler Christian Weber finally won the bidding. The son of a family of farmers from Altstadt-Limbach, Weber had taken over an import goods retail business in Homburg that he had entered as an apprentice ten years earlier. He eventually expanded the store into a wholesale food business. By the age of 38 Weber had accumulated 57,000 Marks, sufficient capital to purchase the brewery. However, that didn't mean that the new brewer knew anything about brewing beer. And, as the story goes, his master brewer didn't either! The malt facility was at a different location from the brewery and so the wort, an unfermented mixture of ingredients, had to be transported to the brewing tanks in a bin by oxcart. The contents of the first bin had to be discarded because the master brewer forgot to add hops to the mixture. Despite this early mishap, things went very well after this "dress rehearsal."

As a result of its rapidly developing reputation for high-quality beer, the Karlsberg Brauerei was soon the most important supplier of beer to Homburg and its environs. While smaller local breweries were struggling and one after the other ceased production, rising demand forced Christian Weber to expand his production facilities. In 1884 the brewery was relocated to a new property with a great deal of cellar and warehouse space. It was renamed the company Bayerische Bierbrauerei zum Karlsberg, von Christian Weber, because it was brewed in a style popular in Bavaria (Bayerische). A new brewhouse was erected between 1883 and 1886, an office building was acquired, and a new machine house was built in 1896. The invention of the "ice machine" solved the main problem facing beer producers—how to keep their product cool during warmer seasons.

Company Perspectives:

The steady expansion of Karlsberg's product range is an important part of the company's corporate strategy. Its goal is to provide a unique beverage for every taste through a decisive strategic development of a variety of different brands.

From Local Brewery to Regional Brewery After 1897

By the end of the 19th century Karlsberg Brauerei was established locally and ready to expand into bordering territories. These included the industrial centers in the Saar basin, Luxembourg and Lorraine. To finance the expansion of the brewery's capacity, Christian Weber decided to transform the family business into the then-popular form of an Aktiengesellschaft. The transformation went into effect on January 19, 1897. The company's name was changed to Bayerische Bierbrauerei zum Karlsberg, vormals Christian Weber Aktiengesellschaft. Nonetheless, although the brewery was a share company, all but 14 of the 1,100 shares were held by Christian Weber. The rest were held by other family members and a few strangers. So in essence, nothing had really changed in terms of who controlled the Karlsberg Brauerei. The single change made was to introduce a new position, commercial director, who dealt with the other shareholders, mainly banks that had given the brewery long-term loans to finance further expansion.

The extension of the brewery's market was a challenge to its distribution network. Transportation posed a major problem. At the time horse-drawn coaches were the normal means of transportation. However, the brewery only owned 30 horses, not enough for transporting beer longer distances. Transportation by rail provided the solution. Karlsberg Brauerei acquired their own rail coaches to ship its beer to Luxembourg and Lorraine. Another significant investment was the erection of an new steam-powered brewing facility that doubled the brewery's capacity.

At first, all these investments resulted in increased sales figures. However, the first decade of the 20th century brought change and new challenges. The brewery's profits were hurt by steel crises in 1901 and 1902, by rising prices for coal, rising wages for brewery workers, increased taxes, and falling beer prices. Commercial director Louis Göhring was highly successful in expanding Karlsberg Brauerei's reach; he organized the Vereinigung der pfälzischen Brauereien, a regional trade organization for beer brewers. However, one day Göhring failed to return from a business trip and was never seen again. It was speculated that his mysterious disappearance was connected with irregularities in his sales work.

On December 20, 1912, Christian Weber announced at a company meeting that because of his age—he was 72 years old at that time—he was resigning from the business. His oldest son, Richard Weber, who had studied beer brewing at the Königlich Brautechnische Fakultät in Weihenstephan, became president and technical director. Richard had been involved in the daily business as vice-president since the time he had finished his brewing studies. One of the first changes he made was to purchase a second truck, a decision that was finally approved by the management board after his father had left.

Shaken by Two World Wars

After only two years, Christian Weber returned from retirement at the outbreak of World War I. The war caused shortages in raw material supplies and decreased consumer demand. Most beer consumers and brewery workers were fighting at the front, and barley was being rationed to make solid food, instead of beer. When the war ended, Germany had lost some of its western areas, specifically Luxemburg and Lorraine, which interrupted Karlsberg Brauerei's westward expansion and cut the brewery off from half of its market in the Pfalz. Despite these obstacles the company turned out growing sales and profits. According to the 1927 edition of the *Handbuch der Deutschen Aktiengesellschaften*, a handbook of German companies, Karlsberg Brauerei owned 20 automobiles, 25 horses, and three railway wagons and employed 22 white collar and 100 blue collar workers. The upswing lasted until the worldwide economic depression hit the Saar in 1931. The downswing was followed by another temporary economic upturn under the new Nazi regime that promoted new job creation in Germany.

On June 29, 1937, the company was transformed into a Kommanditgesellschaft. This corporate form, which was officially supported by the Nazis, put a higher emphasis on the personal reliability of the owners. The following year the brewery achieved a new production record of about 150,000 hectoliters and installed a modern bottling plant. In September 1939 World War II broke out. Just two months later, while being evacuated, Christian Weber died two and a half months before his 100th birthday.

During the war the entire German economy was administered by the government. For German beer brewers this meant they were required to brew a low-quality beer. At first the basic ingredients were limited to 6 percent, then temporarily raised again after the successful invasion of France, but repeatedly lowered afterwards. At the same time the Nazis massively propagandized the new ''light beer'' as the new beverage of the German people. Karlsberg Brauerei's trucks were confiscated and most of its employees were called to the front. Many of them did not return—including the founder's grandson Richard Weber who was killed at age 30 on November 4, 1941, in the Crimea near Sevastopol, Russia. The young brewing engineer had been actively involved in the company's top management since 1936. In addition to these losses, the company's facilities suffered severe damage.

After repairs to the facilities began, the Karlsberg Brauerei started brewing a 1-percent ''near beer.'' It was delivered to what customers were left with some old trucks and seven horse- or ox-drawn carts. Malt shortages after the war limited beer brewing again, and eventually a temporary prohibition on brewing was imposed. On November 20, 1947, the Saar basin became part of France. It was cut off from its traditional German customers, but the brewery was at least able to purchase raw materials freely, to replace run-down machinery, and to enjoy the relatively stable French currency. In 1948 the company was allowed to brew beer again and the situation gradually nor-

Key Dates:

1878: Wholesaler Christian Weber acquires Bayerische Bierbrauerei zum Karlsberg.
1912: Richard Weber takes over as president and technical director.
1937: The company is transformed into a Kommanditgesellschaft (KG).
1947: The Saar basin, where the brewery is located, becomes part of France.
1953: Karlsberg Brauerei starts selling beer in cans.
1959: Saarland joins the Federal Republic of Germany.
1962: Dr. Paul Weber takes over as CEO.
1979: Karlsberg Brauerei acquires majority share in Saarfürst-Brauerei AG.
1983: The company buys a 60 percent share in OKKO Getränke GmbH.
1984: Karlsberg Brauerei takes over Merziger Süßmosterei and founds Tiefkühlkost-Zentrale (TKZ).
1989: The brewery takes over Becker Brauerei, including French brewery Brasserie de Saverne.
1992: The company takes over Königsbacher Brauerei AG.
1996: Karlsberg Brauerei GmbH & Co KG becomes management holding.
1999: Karlsberg Brauerei introduces beer in plastic bottles.

malized. In 1953, on the occasion of the company's 75th anniversary, Karlsberg Brauerei brewed 200,000 hectoliters of beer—more than ever before.

From Regional Brewery to National Brewery After 1953

At the end of the postwar years of reconstruction, Karlsberg Brauerei entered a period of dynamic growth. As the demand for beer rose, the company initiated several improvements in its technological base between 1953 and 1956. Warehouse and cellar space was extended, the power station modernized, and new brewing equipment installed. Another novelty Karlsberg introduced was beer in cans. Karlsberg Brauerei had started putting beer in bottles before the Second World War, and, by the early 1950s, 60 percent of beer being produced was in bottles. When a new bottling plant was built to replace the old one, the company decided to transform the older plant into a canning facility. The company started selling canned beer in 1953.

Major changes also occurred in the brewery's distribution network in the 1950s. An influential distribution partner was found in Hofbräubierzentrale GmbH Saarbrücken. Karlsberg Brauerei signed a 20-year contract with the distributor who guaranteed to buy at least 20,000 hectoliters of beer annually. The brewery's own distribution center in Saarlouis was closed down and another exclusive contract signed with a local distributor for that area. When another regional brewery, Walsheimbrauerei AG, was liquidated, its major shareholder, French bank Credit Commercial de France, contracted with Karlsberg Brauerei to deliver beer for export to France under the "Walsheim" brand. The export of canned beer to France and its colonies in Africa and Indochina contributed significantly to the brewery's total output growth to 420,000 hectoliters by 1958.

When the Saarland joined the Federal Republic of Germany in July 1959, Karlsberg Brauerei was the leading beer brewer of the state. The sudden exposure to the tough German competition resulted in Karlsberg's beer output dropping by 12 percent. However, an agreement with France guaranteed the toll-free export of as much beer as the brewery had exported in 1955. To make the state's integration into the German economy easier, businesses in the Saarland were also subsidized with 5 percent of their products' sales price and through special tax breaks.

In April 1962 Richard Weber's son, Dr. Paul Weber, became Karlsberg Brauerei's new CEO and a young management team replaced the old one. In the early 1960s larger breweries in the Saarland began buying up smaller ones that were struggling to stay in business. In this way, Karlsberg Brauerei acquired Ottweiler-based Simon AG and a 10-percent stake in Saarfürst-Brauerei AG based in Merzig. It acquired the sport hotel at the foot of the hill in its hometown Homburg, which had replaced a restaurant in 1971. In business year 1972–73 the company passed the one-million hectoliter mark in production for the first time in its history.

From Family Business to Family of Businesses After 1974

By 1975 Karlsberg Brauerei was among Germany's leading breweries and the fourth largest private beer brewer of the country with a total annual output of 1.37 million hectoliters. The company exported about 8 percent of its total production to France, Austria, Switzerland, and Italy. Dr. Paul Weber's son Richard entered the company at the end of 1974, at a time when the beer and beverage markets were experiencing a downturn. However, Karlsberg Brauerei went on expanding and modernizing its production facilities. Brewing capacity was doubled once again and the entire brewing process, from the mixture of the first ingredients until the final brew was completed, was fully automated. Under director for exports Richard Weber, the brewery expanded its reach throughout Germany, as well as into 24 countries around the world.

Besides expanding internationally Karlsberg Brauerei utilized two other strategies to establish a basis for future growth: acquisitions of other breweries and expansion into new markets, mainly alcohol-free beverages, services, and logistics. In 1979 Karlsberg Brauerei increased its share in Saarfürst-Brauerei to 81 percent. Between 1986 and 1989 the company acquired four more breweries, in Riegelsberg, Neunkirchen, and Metz, France, and acquired shares in Löwenbrauerei Trier J. Mendgen GmbH & Co. The largest among them was Saarland's second biggest brewery Becker GmbH & Co KG based in St. Ingbert, which also owned Brasserie de Saverne, a brewery in France. The largest deal of that period followed in 1992 when Karlsberg Brauerei took over 85 percent of Königsbacher Brauerei AG after two years of working together. This Koblenz-based regional brewing operation owned several breweries in big cities such as Cologne, Dusseldorf, Nassau, and Eisenach, as well as produced bottled water, and also owned advertising companies and distribution firms.

Karlsberg Brauerei's massive venture into alcohol-free beverages started in 1983 when it bought a 60 percent share in OKKO Getränke GmbH, one of Germany's largest Coca-Cola licensees. A year later the brewery purchased a majority share in alcohol-free fruit beverage maker Merziger Süßmosterei GmbH & Co KG. In 1992 Karlsberg Brauerei acquired Saar-Pfalz-Erfrischungsgetränke GmbH, a regional producer of soft drinks, to which all of the company's alcohol-free beverage production was transferred. The brewery took its first steps into services and logistics in 1975 when it founded a company that provided a rental service for tents and other large-scale party and catering equipment and supplies. In 1984 the company set up a new subsidiary, Tiefkuhlkost-Zentrale GmbH, St. Ingbert (TKZ), which supplied regional restaurants with frozen produce. In 1990 Saarbrücken-based ServiPlus GmbH was set up along with a French subsidiary to market food and beverage vending machines and their goods. In 1991 Karlsberg Brauerei acquired French carrier Saverne Transports S.à.r.l. to expand its distribution network for French customers.

From Brewery Concern to Beverage Concern After 1995

After an unprecedented shopping spree, in the second half of the 1990s Karlsberg Brauerei focused on reorganizing its business and integrating its new companies into the group. In 1996 the brewery Karlsberg Brauerei KG Weber became the core operating company of the conglomerate's beer business division run by an independent management team. All subsidiaries were made part of the Karlsberg-Verbund, which was managed by the holding company Karlsberg Brauerei GmbH & Co KG.

For most of the 1990s the German economy was sluggish, unemployment rose, consumers became more conscious of their spending, and the overall beer market stagnated. Karlsberg Brauerei strengthened its brands, introduced new products and expanded its nonalcoholic beverage division. Production of Karlsberg Brauerei's major domestic brand ''Karlsberg Ur-Pils'' passed the 1 million hectoliter mark for the first time in 1994. That same year the company also introduced ''Karlsbräu,'' its successful export brand, to the German market. By then, exports accounted for about 15 percent of the company's total sales; its foreign markets extended beyond France as far as Italy, England, and eastern Europe. To combat the declining beer market, the company introduced new beer beverages for younger target groups, including ''Mixery,'' a mixture of beer and Cola, ''Desperados,'' a beer with tequila aroma, and ''Joy's,'' a mixture of beer and apple juice. Other innovations included the two heavy beer brands ''Ballermann'' and ''8,8.''

In addition to these product innovations, in the fall of 1999 Karlsberg Brauerei became the first German brewery to fill beer into plastic (PET) bottles. Although at first considered unusual and the target of criticism in the media, the company saw several advantages in this approach. PET bottles are ultralight weighing only 30 grams; they hardly ever break, which made it possible to sell bottled beer in stadiums where glass bottles were banned for security reasons; beer in PET bottles holds its carbonation longer, and the beer stays fresh and cool longer, according to the brewery.

In 1998 and 1999 Karlsberg Brauerei acquired three more fruit juice producers, one of which was located in France. The group's fruit juice businesses were organized under the Merziger Fruchtsaftverbund in 1999. By 1994 alcohol-free beverages represented 28 percent of Karlsberg Brauerei's total output. In 1999 they reached 40 percent and the company aimed at a long-term boost to 60 percent. Ultimately, the company's vision was to be able to supply its customers with whatever beverage they wanted.

Principal Subsidiaries

Karlsberg Brauerei KG Weber (Germany); Königsbacher Brauerei AG (Germany); Brauerei Becker GmbH & Co. KG (Germany); Löwenbrauerei Trier GmbH & Co. (Germany); Brasserie de Saverne S.A. (France); OKKO Getränke GmbH (Germany); Merziger Fruchtsaftgetränke GmbH & Co. KG (Germany); Danuer Sprudel GmbH (Germany); TKZ Tiefkuhlkostzentrale GmbH (Germany); ServiPlus - Getränke und Versorgungsautomatenservice GmbH (Germany); St. Ingberter Transport - und Speditionsgesellschaft mbH (Germany); Karlsberg Freizeitservice GmbH (Germany); SWG Südwest Getränke Plus GmbH (Germany); Saverne Transports S.à.r.l. (France).

Principal Competitors

Dortmunder Actien-Brauerei AG; Warsteiner Brauerei Haus Cramer GmbH & Co. KG; Brauerei VELTINS; Binding Brauerei AG; Brauerei Beck & Co.

Further Reading

Dietz, Dirk, ''Für jede Gelegenheit das passende Getränk,'' *Lebensmittel Zeitung,* February 4, 2000, p. 56.

''Karlsberg-Umsätze klettern über 1 Milliarde,'' *OTS Originaltextservice*, September 21, 2000.

''Karlsberg-Verbund kann den Absatz ausbauen,'' *Lebensmittel Zeitung,* February 3, 1995, p. 20.

''Karlsberg will seine Marken staerken,'' *Frankfurter Allgemeine Zeitung*, September 29, 1995, p. 24.

Schleiden, Karl August, *Zur Geschichte der Karlsberg-Brauerei,* Homburg, Germany: Karlsberg Brauerei GmbH & Co KG, 1978, p. 177.

—Evelyn Hauser

LaBarge Inc.

9900A Clayton Road
Post Office Box 14499
St. Louis, Missouri 63178
U.S.A.
Telephone: (314) 997-0800
Fax: (314) 812-9438
Web site: http://www.labarge.com

Public Company
Incorporated: 1953 as LaBarge Pipe and Steel Company
Employees: 800
Sales: $79.61 million (2000)
Stock Exchanges: American
Ticker Symbol: LB
NAIC: 33429 Other Communications Equipment Manufacturing; 334417 Electronic Connector Manufacturing; 334418 Printed Circuit Assembly (Electronic Assembly) Manufacturing; 335999 All Other Miscellaneous Electrical Equipment and Component Manufacturing

LaBarge Inc. manufactures electronic components and systems for specialized applications, such as environments with high levels of vibration and heat. Defense-related contracting provided slightly less than half the company's revenues in the late 1990s. The company has gone to a great deal of expense trying to enter rising new markets. Only the traditional Manufacturing Services Group was profitable in 2000, however.

Origins

LaBarge Inc. began its existence in 1953 as a St. Louis steel pipe distributor called LaBarge Pipe and Steel Company. The firm formed a separate tubing division in 1966 and entered the electronics business in late 1967, merging with Tulsa-based Dorsett Electronics Inc. Dorsett's primary markets were the aerospace, communications, and medical industries. LaBarge Steel and Pipe was renamed simply LaBarge Inc. after the merger.

Nelson Concrete was acquired in 1969 and the next year LaBarge entered the medical electronics field. Soon, the company introduced a prosthetic voice box called the VoiceBak. The 3 oz. plastic device was worn outside the patient's neck and was operated manually, unlike electronic neck resonators. At the same time, the Dorsett Electronics subsidiary was introducing a new system of aircraft escape seats.

Nevertheless, LaBarge's greatest growth was coming from its more traditional lines of business. The company continued to expand its tubular steel business throughout the 1970s. Tubular steel accounted for 80 percent of LaBarge's 1974 earnings of $6.5 million. LaBarge Tubular was formed in Canada in 1976. The company also expanded its wire and cable offerings. In 1975, it announced a new 50,000-square-foot wire and cable plant in California. Pretax income rose 40 percent in 1978 alone; sales of tubular steel were up 23 percent. In 1980, LaBarge announced plans to open a $1.6 million steel tube distribution center near Birmingham, Alabama.

LaBarge acquired Omni Duralite Co. in 1982, entering the furniture business. Another 1982 acquisition, A. Baldwin & Co., was a New Orleans-based distributor of tubular steel pipe with sales of about $12 million a year.

Restructuring in the 1980s

In 1984, LaBarge sold its steel business at a $12 million loss to a management group led by Pierre LaBarge III, son of the founder. (In 1992, LaBarge Inc. agreed to pay $300,000 to settle an antitrust case related to alleged price-fixing by this unit in the late 1970s and early 1980s.) In 1986, LaBarge sold its furniture company, also at a loss. After defaulting on the debt it had taken on to acquire that company in October 1986, LaBarge exchanged its debentures for shares of preferred stock.

Soon, Cincinnati investment firm Pacholder Associates, owning a significant minority of both preferred and common stock, tried to force founder Pierre L. LaBarge, Jr., and two other directors out of the board. A complicated stock buyback scheme deflected this threat.

LaBarge undertook a partial restructuring in the late 1980s. Japan's Sanwa Bank provided $18 million of credit to finance

Company Perspectives:

LaBarge's operating philosophy is to build close relationships with our customers, working to provide them total solutions rather than just selling them products or services. Our objective is to work in tandem with our customers to create the results they need to achieve their goals. To accomplish this, we often participate at the concept stage of a project's development, providing input on design, engineering, cost and "manufacturability." Later, project management teams oversee the manufacturing process from prototype through full-scale manufacturing.

this after the company bought back millions of dollars in preferred stock. By 1989, the three-year-long restructuring process was beginning to show some results in terms of increased sales and profits, thanks to a new emphasis on low-cost production and a focus on electronics. Sales reached $69 million in fiscal 1989; profits of $4.4 million were double those of the year before. The company had also cut its debt from $57 million in 1987 to $28 million, not including $8 million in preferred stock.

Defense work accounted for about 80 percent of LaBarge's revenues in the late 1980s. The company also supplied the aerospace, computer, and medical diagnostic equipment industries. Net earnings rose slightly to $502,000 in 1990, although sales slipped a bit to $17.7 million. Net earnings for the fiscal year ended June 30, 1991 were $2.5 million—up 50 percent from the previous year, as sales reached $73 million.

Expanding in the 1990s

In 1991, LaBarge signed a five-year, $2 million contract to have a unit of McDonnell Douglas Inc. electronically link LaBarge's six factories with its headquarters. Unfortunately, McAuto (which McDonnell soon sold to EDS) consistently failed to meet price objectives, and LaBarge transferred the work to May & Speh, Inc. of Illinois.

Craig E. LaBarge succeeded his father, Pierre L. LaBarge, Jr., as CEO in August 1991. Pierre LaBarge retained the title of chairman. Craig LaBarge had been company president since 1986; he also had been president of the LaBarge Electronics unit for several years prior to that.

The company refinanced its debt again in 1992, giving it the ability to pursue potential acquisitions or expansions. The refinancing eliminated the company's most expensive class of debt-convertible preferred stock.

At first, LaBarge seemed to benefit from the post-Glasnost cuts in military spending that had major defense contractors downsizing throughout the early 1990s. The company subcontracted to make electrical cables, wiring harnesses, printed circuits, and other electronic parts. In 1991, the company employed more than 1,200 people at factories in Missouri, Oklahoma, and Arkansas.

By the mid-1990s, it had become apparent that its defense electronics business was facing dwindling prospects. In 1994, LaBarge agreed to sell its Arkansas operations to Avnet Inc. The plant there, which manufactured cable assemblies, had accounted for a quarter of LaBarge's revenues. Avnet paid LaBarge $10.5 million in cash and assumed $3 million of liabilities.

LaBarge employed 650 people in Arkansas, Missouri, and Oklahoma in 1995. It had net sales of $61.7 million, down from $73.1 million in 1994 and $81.6 million in 1993. Profits fell to $1.3 million from $2.4 million in 1994 and $1.9 million in 1993.

In 1996, LaBarge acquired SOREP Technology Corporation, a Houston firm that manufactured high temperature electronic assemblies used in the oil business. Its revenues were about $6 million a year. The subsidiary was renamed LaBarge/STC, Inc.; its acquisition cost LaBarge $3.1 million.

LaBarge Clayco Wireless L.L.C., a 1996 joint venture with Clayco Construction Company, provided interconnection systems and cell site services to major infrastructure vendors and telecom service providers. The focus on high-growth industries paid off handsomely in 1996, when LaBarge experienced a 408 percent profit surge, reported the *St. Louis Post-Dispatch.* In January of the year, newly licensed mobile phone service providers began flocking to LaBarge Clayco.

In 1993, LaBarge contracted to manufacture a small medical laser that could collect blood samples without the risk of handling needles or lancets. FDA approval for the Laser Lancet finally came in 1997. These blood laser perforators had been developed by Venisect Inc. of Little Rock, Arkansas (soon renamed Transmedica International, Inc.). The company claimed that 3,000 medical workers in the United States every year were accidentally pricked by sharps contaminated with the HIV virus; deadly hepatitis B could be spread the same way.

Also in October 1997, LaBarge acquired 10 percent of one-year-old Open Cellular Systems, Inc., a St. Louis-based provider of telecom products. (LaBarge would buy the remaining shares for $5.8 million in March 1999.)

By the end of 1997, it appeared that LaBarge would meet its ambitious goal to raise annual revenues to $200 million by 2000. Yet, a lack of visibility among analysts kept its stock price from rebounding in the bull market of the late 1990s, noted the *Post-Dispatch.*

The company continued to pick up lucrative defense orders in the late 1990s despite its focus on more rapidly growing markets. Lockheed Martin contracted it to produce electronic assemblies for the U.S. Navy's AEGIS Weapons System. (Lockheed Martin sales accounted for nearly a quarter of LaBarge's total revenues.) The company also was supplying cable assemblies for the Space Shuttle and printed circuit board assemblies for military radar systems. In 1997, LaBarge had a 52/48 percent ratio of commercial sales to defense sales.

LaBarge invested in Transmedica, formerly Venisect, its medical laser partner. By 1998, LaBarge owned 9.5 percent of its common stock. In June 1999, Transmedica defaulted on payment of a $2 million note due LaBarge, which had yet to make a profit on this relationship. In December 1999, LaBarge settled litigation pending with Transmedica, taking $2.2 million

Key Dates:

1953: LaBarge Pipe and Steel Company is founded.
1967: LaBarge merges with Dorsett Electronics.
1975: A big new wire and cable plant is built in California.
1982: LaBarge enters furniture business.
1984: LaBarge sells steel business at a loss.
1986: LaBarge sells furniture business at a loss.
1993: LaBarge contracts to develop Laser Lancet blood-collecting device.
1994: Arkansas cable manufacturing operations are sold.
1996: LaBarge buys SOREP Technology Corporation, forms Clayco Wireless joint venture.
1999: Remainder of Open Cellular Systems is acquired.
2000: LaBarge Clayco Wireless is sold.
2001: LaBarge writes off its Noticom investment.

and shares in Norwood Abbey, an Australian medical device manufacturer that acquired Transmedica.

Open Cellular Systems, Inc. (OCS) was acquired in March 1999, forming the basis of LaBarge's Network Technologies Group. LaBarge had bought a 10 percent share of OCS for $500,000 in October 1997; it paid $5.6 million for the remainder of shares.

Slimming Down Again in 1999

LaBarge reorganized into three groups in August 1999: Manufacturing Services, LaBarge Clayco Wireless, and Network Technologies. Electronics manufacturing remained LaBarge's core line of business. Network Technologies Group's ScadaNET Network for remotely monitoring rail crossings was gaining acceptance in the railroad industry, however.

In fiscal 1999, LaBarge bought an additional 39 percent of the LaBarge Clayco Wireless joint venture from Clayco Construction Company for $300,000, bringing its ownership to 90 percent. In June 2000, LaBarge sold its 90 percent interest in LaBarge Clayco Wireless to Phoenix-based Evolution Holdings, Inc. for $4.7 million.

Energy companies reduced their capital expenditures in the late 1990s, resulting in a sales decline at LaBarge's related units. LaBarge posted loss of $3.9 million and $1.9 million in 1999 and 2000 as annual revenues approached $80 million—down from 1998's $95.6 million.

One enterprise that LaBarge would not focus on was its short-lived joint venture with Global Research Systems, Inc. called Noticom L.L.C. Its BusCall service electronically informed parents when their children's school buses would be late. Although installed in a number of school districts beginning in 1998, LaBarge exited the venture early in 2001, taking a $2.6 million write-off.

Principal Divisions

Manufacturing Services; Network Technologies.

Principal Operating Units

Telecommunications; Geophysical; Aerospace and Defense; Network Technologies Group—ScadaNET Network.

Principal Competitors

General Cable Corporation; Raytheon Company; Schlumberger Limited.

Further Reading

Allen, Leslie J., ''Bouncing Back: Regrouping Boosts LaBarge's Sales,'' *St. Louis Post-Dispatch,* Business Plus, September 18, 1989, p. 1.

——, ''Japanese Firm to Lend to LaBarge,'' *St. Louis Post-Dispatch,* April 4, 1989, p. 9B.

——, ''LaBarge Sees Growth Ahead,'' *St. Louis Post-Dispatch,* November 1, 1989, p. 7B.

Carey, Christopher, ''LaBarge Agrees to Sell Operation in Arkansas,'' *St. Louis Post-Dispatch,* November 9, 1994, p. 9D.

——, ''LaBarge Seeks Bigger Share of Spotlight,'' *St. Louis Post-Dispatch,* October 22, 1997, p. 8C.

——, ''LaBarge to Make Medical Lasers,'' *St. Louis Post-Dispatch,* October 8, 1993, p. 1F.

Goodman, Adam, ''LaBarge Refinances Debt to Gain Flexibility,'' *St. Louis Post-Dispatch,* June 9, 1992, p. 6C.

——, ''LaBarge Says Defense Cuts Working to Its Advantage,'' *St. Louis Post-Dispatch,* October 30, 1991, p. 5B.

——, ''LaBarge Settles Antitrust Case,'' *St. Louis Post-Dispatch,* August 8, 1992, p. 9C.

——, ''Write-Offs Give LaBarge $1.58 Million of Red Ink,'' *St. Louis Post-Dispatch,* August 25, 1992, p. 12C.

''LaBarge Credits New Orders, Sales as Earnings Skyrocket,'' *St. Louis Post-Dispatch,* January 31, 1992, p. 3B.

''Laryngectomee Sings Praises of New Device That Restores Voice,'' *Wall Street Journal,* March 8, 1973, p. 8.

Luna, Lynnette, ''LaBarge Studies Wireless Buildout from Manufacturing Stance,'' *RCR: Radio Communications Report,* March 3, 1997, p. 56.

Schatz, Willie, ''Get Ready for Bailoutsourcing,'' *Computerworld,* Manager's Journal, January 25, 1993, p. 57.

Stroud, Jerri, ''Profit Pie: LaBarge Eats Large in Hot Growth Fields,'' *St. Louis Post-Dispatch,* Business Plus, May 19, 1997, p. 13.

''Testing the School Market,'' *Advanced Transportation Technology News,* February 2001.

—Frederick C. Ingram

LAMAUR

The Lamaur Corporation

5601 East River Road
Minneapolis, Minnesota 55432
U.S.A.
Telephone: (763) 571-1234
Fax: (763) 572-2781
Web site: http://www.lamaur.com

Public Company
Incorporated: 1936 as La Maur Inc.
Employees: 21
Sales: $24.8 million (2000)
Stock Exchanges: OTC
Ticker Symbol: LMAR
NAIC: 32562 Toilet Preparation Manufacturing

The Lamaur Corporation, headquartered in Minneapolis, is a producer and marketer of personal hair care products, including shampoos, conditioners, hair sprays, and assorted hair styling preparations. Its line includes products marketed under a variety of names, including B in10se and Willow Lake brands, the mid-priced Salon Style, and the value-priced Style brands. Since 1998, the company has revised its production and marketing strategies. Until that year, it operated a salon division, which developed, formulated, and marketed custom hair-care products for professional salons and specialty shops; but in July 1998 it sold the division to Zotos International, Inc., a subsidiary of the large, Tokyo-based cosmetics firm, Shiseido Co., Ltd. Until the end of 1999, in its custom manufacturing division, Lamaur also developed, manufactured, and marketed hair care, personal care, and household products for third parties. Late in 2000, however, the company sold its custom manufacturing division to Tiro Industries, which, under a contractual agreement, continued making Lamaur's products. Lamaur itself then reorganized, cutting its workforce down to just 20 core employees and refocusing its business on product development, brand management, marketing, and distribution. The company, with over 300 active customer accounts, primarily sells its products to mass merchandisers, supermarket chains, drugstores, and other retail outlets, combining a direct sales force and an independent brokerage network. In its customer base it has over 100 major retail accounts. In 2000, its biggest customer was Wal-Mart, which accounted for 27 percent of its sales. However, none of its other customers accounted for more than 10 percent. The heirs of Don Hoff, Lamaur's former chairman and CEO, own approximately 28 percent of the company.

1930–78: Origins and Evolution into National Brand Name

In 1930, two brothers, Larry and Maurice Spiegel began manufacturing hair-care products for other companies. They dubbed their own firm La Maur, an acronym made up their first names. A graduate of the University of Minnesota Business School, Larry Spiegel took care of the production and packaging end of the business. Brother Maurice, a graduate in pharmaceutical chemistry, also from the University of Minnesota, set up the company's first laboratory in his garage and developed the formulas for the fledgling firm's products.

In its formative years, most of the company's business consisted of formulating and producing products for the beauty salon trade. The Spiegels made privately-labeled hair-care items for a variety of companies. In addition to these products, they developed their own brands primarily for distribution in the upper midwestern states.

First incorporated as a private company in 1936, La Maur initially went public in 1962. It was first listed on the American Stock Exchange in 1964, but eventually would move to the New York Stock Exchange in 1984, three years before it became part of the Dow Chemical Company. The company made considerable progress in developing an industry name in the 50-odd years that it was an independent firm. In fact, the Spiegels proved themselves to be hair-care industry innovators of note.

Among other innovations, in 1950, they began marketing STYLE, the first water-soluble hair spray. Initially, they distributed it primarily to the professional beauty-salon trade. However, during the 1960s, when aerosol hair sprays gained popularity in both the consumer retail and salon hair-care industries, La Maur established its own consumer division. Initially called the House of Style, the division had a retail sales organization

Company Perspectives:

2000 is . . . Ground Zero. New Ideas. New Direction. New Products. New Vision for the Future. It's The New Lamaur.

formed to call on retailers. The Spiegels renamed the House of Style the Consumer Division in 1978, by which time they had also renamed their company. For the next twenty years, under the new name, the Lamaur Company, the firm produced popular salon products including such brands as Vita/E, Apple Pectin, Nucleic A, and Pativa.

1979–87: Continued Growth Amidst a Hostile Takeover

Throughout the late 1970s and into the 1980s, Lamaur Inc. continued on its successful course. Between 1978 and 1983, when its revenues hit close to $82 million, its sales grew at an average annual rate of 21 percent. Still, Lamaur's brands only commanded a minuscule share of its massive markets, encouraging the company to undertake some bold risks. One of these involved the 1983, $15 million launching of Perma Soft, a new line of shampoos and conditioners for women with permanent waves. The company, then headed by Maurice Spiegel's son Richard, hoped to garner $30 million in annual sales, or nearly 2.5 percent of the nation's very fragmented and highly competitive shampoo business. It was a bigger gamble than the company had ever taken but one that panned out well enough.

In 1987, Alberto-Culver Company, maker of VO5 hair care products, attempted a hostile take-over of Lamaur. Its efforts were thwarted only by the intervention of the Dow Chemical Company, which purchased Lamaur and made it part of its subsidiary, DowBrands, which already manufactured and marketed household cleaning products and plastic bags and wrappings for food protection and storage. Lamaur then became known as the DowBrands Personal Care Division.

1987–98: Another Acquisition and Some Marketing Problems

In November 1995, under the guiding hand of Don G. Hoff., Electronic Hair Styling, Inc. (EHS), a private company, purchased the DowBrands Personal Care Division from Dow. EHS, incorporated in 1993, merged with the Personal Care Division to reincorporate in Delaware as a single entity. In 1997, with Hoff as chairman and CEO, EHS changed its name to The Lamaur Corporation to take advantage of the long-established reputation and name recognition of Lamaur.

The later 1990s proved difficult, however. Between 1995 and 1997, Lamaur's sales basically stagnated, and the company had net losses in both 1995 and 1997. Particularly discouraging was the $19.4 million loss in 1997, by far the worst in the company's history. Company executives blamed the loss on increased marketing costs. In any case, it was clear that some draconian measures were needed to reverse the firm's fortunes.

Lamaur's strategic choice was to downsize. It started retrenchment in 1997, when it eliminated about 90 jobs, delayed planned product development, and reduced its leased space. Then, in July 1998, Lamaur sold its professional salon brands to Zotos International, Inc., a subsidiary of the mammoth Shiseido Co., Ltd., a manufacturer and distributor of cosmetics. The proceeds of the sale, approximately $10 million net, were basically utilized to pay off its debt under a credit agreement with Norwest Business Credit, Inc. and for ongoing operations, which, later in the year, Lamaur extensively restructured. The changes were necessitated by the selloff to Zotos of Lamaur's professional salon brands, the decline in the company's retail sales, and the 1997 expiration of a manufacturing agreement with former owner, DowBrands. The move did produce some stockholder disgruntlement and claims that the sale was made, not to benefit the company, but to benefit only the directors through inflating their potential severance agreement payouts.

1999–2001: Retrenching and Struggling to Regain Profitability

In July 1999, Don Hoff suddenly died. After a half-year transition period, in which Joseph F. Stiley served as acting CEO, a national search led to the election of Lawrence Pesin to the posts of CEO, CFO, and chairman. Stiley, one of the founding members of EHS in 1991, had been Lamaur's vice-president and chief scientist. Pesin, when he assumed executive control of the company in December 1999, had behind him over 30 years of senior management in the personal care industry, including 16 years in which he had held positions on the top rung of corporate executive ladders, including a three-year stint as president of Helena Rubinstein, USA. Among other things, he had managed bottom-line turnarounds for five different enterprises. He also brought international trade experience to the job. Just prior to taking on the Lamaur positions, he had been general manager of the Americas, Concord Camera Corp.

A major realignment of Lamaur's operations took place under Pesin. In 2000, Lamaur began re-keying its marketing efforts on its already established retail brands, using magazine advertising, nationally distributed coupons, and trade promotions. Also, early in 2000, the company sold its custom manufacturing division, including its facility in Fridley, Minnesota and to Tiro Industries, Inc. for $13.25 million in cash plus the assumption of capital leases totaling $765,000. Tiro then commenced making Lamaur's products under a manufacturing agreement scheduled to expire at the end of 2002. Additionally, Lamaur began renting office space in Fridley from Tiro under a lease due to expire at the end of 2001.

With the sale of its manufacturing plant to Tiro completed, Lamaur underwent a complete reorganization. It reduced its personnel from 220 to a core of only 20 employees, with cutbacks made primarily in production, purchasing, administration, and research and development. Its principal focus shifted almost entirely to marketing.

The results were disappointing, however. The 2000 sales produced by some brands declined as much as 80 percent over the previous year, and the total revenue dropped from $50.2 million to $24.8 million, over a 50 percent decline. The only bright performers were the Salon Style branded products, which, reintroduced in 1999, had a 41% increase in sales. Although $20 million of the net sales decline in 2000 was

Key Dates:

1930: Larry and Maurice Spiegel form La Maur.
1936: La Maur is incorporated in Minnesota.
1962: La Maur goes public.
1978: Lamaur's House of Style is renamed Consumer Products Division.
1983: Company introduces Perma Soft Shampoo and Conditioner.
1987: The Dow Chemical Company purchases Lamaur, making it part of DowBrands, a Dow subsidiary, and renaming it DowBrands Personal Care Division.
1995: Electronic Hair Styling, Inc. (EHS), a private company headed by Don Hoff, purchases Personal Care Division from Dow Chemical.
1996: EHS goes public.
1997: EHS changes its name to The Lamaur Corporation.
1998: Lamaur sells its Salon Division to Zotos International, a subsidiary of Shiseido, a Japanese cosmetics corporation.
2001: Lamaur launches new B in10se line.

attributed to the sale of the company's custom manufacturing division, Lamaur took steps to reduce losses by discontinuing some of its unprofitable product lines, including Perma Soft, Color Soft, and Style Natural Reflections brands.

The company also expected a further decline in sales of its Willow Lake product line, but it anticipated increasing sales for its Style and Salon Style lines. It was banking on the impact of new customer programs and new product plans introduced in 2000. In July of that year, the company aggressively positioned its Style brand in the rapidly growing dollar-store market, pricing some Style-brand hair spray products within that market's narrow pricing range. Although producing lower than average margin on sales in that market, the Style hair sprays achieved wide distribution and major sales, and it was projected that the dollar-store customer program would grow in 2001. In the third quarter of 2000, the company also introduced new products in its Salon Style line and planned to introduce additional items in 2001.

Meanwhile, the company's problems mounted. Because of its tepid sales in the late 1990s and the new century's start, Lamaur was basically unable to pay its vendors at the scheduled payment dates agreed to in their contracts. In its first fiscal quarter of 2001, the company negotiated a forbearance agreement with its vendors whereby no legal action would be taken in return for assurances that Lamaur would pay all of its past due vendor debts by the end of December 2001.

Meanwhile, the company continued to work on finding the right formula for a revitalized financial health. In February 2001, Lamaur introduced B in10se, its newest hair care brand. The 13-piece line consisted of a daily shampoo and conditioner, plus a weekly stripper shampoo, a deep conditioner, a curl control gel, creme gelee, pomade, two waxes, and four gels. The line went into the mass merchandising market in March. The products, designed for customers in the 20–30 age bracket, were line priced at $6.99 per item and were designed to attract a larger customer base. Also in February, Lamaur brought suit against Fridley-based Big Values Inc., which conducted its retail business as The Big Dollar Store. Lamaur's complaint was that Big Values marketed a line of hair products under the name Willow Creek, which, because of its confusing similarity to Lamaur's Willow Lake line, infringed on that brand's trademark. No settlement had been reached by the summer of 2001.

Principal Competitors

Alberto-Culver Company; Bristol-Myers Squibb Company; L'Oréal SA; The Procter & Gamble Company; Unilever.

Further Reading

Anreder, Steven S., "Shampoos, Conditioners: They're Adding Luster to Results of La Maur," *Barron's*, April 19, 1982, p. 52.
Ettore, Barbara, " 'We Don't Think We're Foolish People,' " *Forbes*, December 19, 1983, p. 96.
Grossman, Andrea M., "Brand Trend Shakes Up Hair Care," *WWD*, August 4, 2000, p. 10.
——, "Lamaur Is Intense About Hair Care," *WWD*, December 15, 2000, p.12.
Hahn, Shannon, "Lamaur Divests Facility, Operations to Tiro," *Minneapolis-St. Paul City Business*, January 21, 2000, p. 4.
"Lamaur Elects Lawrence Pesin New CEO and Chairman; Personal Care Industry Leader in Profitable Turnarounds," *Business Wire*, February 9, 2000.
"Lamaur Leverages Salon Experience," *Chain Drug Review*, June 7, 1999, p. 319.
"Lamaur Line Positioned in Middle of Hair Care Market," *Chain Drug Review*, June 23, 1997, p. 226.
Schechter, Dara, "Alberto Is Rebuffed, Lamar Inks Dow Pact," *WWD*, September 25, 1987, p. 27.
Tellijohn, Andrew, "Lamaur, Big Values Clash over Products," *Minneapolis-St. Paul City Business*, February 16, 2001, p. 6.
"Zotos Announces Purchase of Lamaur Professional Salon Products," *PR Newswire*, July 16, 1998.

—John W. Fiero

Lance, Inc.

8600 South Boulevard
Charlotte, North Carolina 28273
U.S.A.
Telephone: (704) 554-1421
Fax: (704) 554-5562
Web site: http://www.lance.com

Public Company
Incorporated: 1926 as Lance Packing Company
Employees: 4,623
Sales: $576.3 million (2000)
Stock Exchanges: NASDAQ
Ticker Symbol: LNCE
NAIC: 311821 Cookie and Cracker Manufacturing; 311911 Roasted Nuts and Peanut Butter Manufacturing; 311919 Other Snack Food Manufacturing

Lance, Inc., headquartered in Charlotte, North Carolina, is one of the most profitable snack food makers in the United States. The company manufactures, markets, and distributes a variety of snack foods, including sandwich crackers, cookies, restaurant crackers and bread basket items, candy, chips, meat snacks, nuts, and cake items. These are packaged and sold in single, larger, and multi-pack servings under such brand names as Captain's Wafers and Toastchee. In addition to marketing products under its own brand names, Lance sells some of its snacks under private and third-party labels. The company makes about three-fourths of its products and purchases the remaining fourth from other manufacturers. It distributes its product line through a direct-store-delivery (DSD) system, third party carriers, and direct shipments via its own carriers. The company's larger customers include grocery chains and mass merchants, drug and convenience stores, food service brokers and institutions, vending operations, and government and military facilities. Lance markets its products across the United States as well as in Europe and parts of Canada. Although Lance is a public company, descendants of the founders hold about a 40 percent share of the business.

1913–25: Origins

In 1913 Philip L. Lance and his son-in-law, Salem A. Van Every, founded the Lance Packing Company. They offered roasted peanuts to Charlotte, North Carolina, area merchants, as well as peanut butter, which they packed by hand. The business began when a customer asked Philip Lance, primarily a coffee dealer, to obtain 500 pounds of Virginia peanuts. The customer soon withdrew from the deal, but Lance was unwilling to disappoint the farmer who sold them to him. He roasted small quantities of the nuts himself on his kitchen stove and packaged them in brown paper bags which he sold for five cents a bag to passersby in downtown Charlotte.

Confident of providing a nutritious, profitable food, Lance bought a mechanical roaster and moved the business out of his home. A mill allowed him to supply merchants with both peanuts and peanut butter, which he spread on crackers for customers to sample. This led to an innovation: the first packaged peanut butter cracker sandwiches, reportedly invented by Lance's wife and his daughter, using Lance peanut butter and saltine crackers. At first the company sold their product door-to-door, but soon it gained an important client, a local grocery store. Demand steadily increased, necessitating a move to larger facilities in Charlotte. Soon the company's predilection for peanuts and for single-serving packages was well established. A soldier stationed at a nearby World War I training base provided the recipe for Lance's next snack food: peanut brittle.

1926–59: The Depression, World War II, and the Postwar Boom

After Philip Lance's death in an auto accident in 1926, Salem Van Every assumed control of the company and incorporated it. The company grew dramatically during this period, earning its first $1 million in sales in 1935 and the first $2 million in 1939. It began baking its own crackers in 1938, a change reflecting the increased scale of operations. Salem Van Every died that same year, and his son Phil became president.

While candy came to dominate the company's product line before World War II, wartime sugar rationing swayed Lance towards baked goods, specifically peanut butter sandwiches and

Company Perspectives:

Fresh, great-tasting snacks that are convenient to buy and easy to carry—these have been the keys to Lance's success since Philip Lance began the Company over eight decades ago. Now, with a renewed company-wide mission based on these founding principles, Lance continues to research and introduce new products, packaging, and distribution to make certain that customers are getting snacks that are always fresh, fast, filling, and satisfying. Today, whether you're at a grocery store or a downtown corner superette, you can enjoy the fresh taste of Lance, just as Philip Lance had intended back in 1913.

cookies. The company's maintenance shop also helped the war effort by making certain tools, such as a wrench for attaching warheads to bombs. Phil Van Every's successor, his son, Philip Lance Van Every, brought a new management style to the company, hiring consultants and implementing a unique administration style called multiple management. However, the company reached a rare landmark in 1944, Lance's only year to date in which annual sales volume did not increase. This was undoubtedly precipitated by the austerity of wartime; postwar fortunes would rise again as new sales districts were organized and many operations were automated. Lance achieved an annual sales volume of $14 million in 1950, and the decade ended with annual sales at Lance of $26.5 million. A new line of packaged saltine crackers for institutional use introduced in 1953 proved an enduring success.

1960–80: Sustaining Growth and Diversification Despite Price Controls and Higher Operating Costs

The 1960s brought many changes. The company, which had been 80 percent owned by the Van Every family, made a large public share offering on December 7, 1961. In order to further diversify, a committee was formed to locate potential acquisitions, and Bullock Manufacturing Company in Conyers, Georgia, was acquired to produce potato chips. Although the unit posted a loss that year, it offered Lance an entrance into the chip business. A record 87,000 accounts were opened in 1962 through 96 sales headquarters. Lance operated in 23 states at this point and was prompted to move its plant to a new 231-acre site. The next year, Lance set its record for lowest cost of delivery.

The last half of the 1960s was particularly productive for Lance, as the company spent $2.5 million to expand its Charlotte plant. After Bullock Manufacturing became profitable in 1968, Lance acquired Food Processors, Inc., a Wilson, North Carolina, sweet potato plant. The next year a distribution center in Greenville, Texas, was completed to facilitate service to the southwestern sales territories. Revenues in 1969 were $57.8 million, up from $26.5 million in 1960, while earnings per share increased from $0.72 to $1.81.

Since the company's beginning, all of its individually-packaged products, including the very first roasted peanuts, had sold for five cents each. On March 6, 1970, the last of the nickel merchandise was produced, and henceforth the snacks would sell for a dime apiece. Nevertheless, the company continued to add new sales territories, totaling 1,111 in 1970.

The following year, a new vending machine was developed capable of carrying any item in the company's line of snacks. To meet the increase in demand, the manufacturing area of the company's plants was increased to 485,000 square feet with the addition of a 15,000-square-foot candy department. Plans were drawn for a new potato chip plant and a new baking plant in 1971. Over the next two years, the company sold Food Processors, Inc., and replaced the Georgia chip plant with a new 60,000-square-foot facility in Charlotte. Another 25,000 square feet of space was added for truck maintenance and shipping functions. The same year, Board Chairman Phil Van Every retired and was replaced by Glenn Rhodes.

The company was shaken in 1973 by high materials costs and federal price controls. Newly acquired Tri-Plas, Inc., a plastic food container manufacturer, performed poorly at first. Another major cost was the energy required by the new factory space. In 1974, federal price controls were removed and the escalation in raw materials prices slowed. The company acquired more manufacturing capabilities: a 23,600 square foot plant in Arlington, Texas, for potato chip production and Hancock's Old Fashion Country Ham of Franklinville, North Carolina. Although demand was so high that sales expansion was limited for part of the year, 75 new territories were created, down from 125 the previous year. This came in spite of a price increase of the snack line from ten cents to 15 cents, which also required retooling of the vending machines.

In the mid-1970s, concerns over energy availability prompted Lance to install propane gas storage in its plants, providing increased energy sources. In 1976, a development and exploration partnership was formed with C&K Petroleum Co., Inc. of Houston, Texas, in order to deal with the extreme shortage of natural gas that had developed by that time. The company also made efforts to conserve as much as possible. Although unprecedented pork prices hurt Hancock Ham, the Tri-Plas subsidiary continued to grow. A.F. "Pete" Sloan succeeded the retiring Glenn Rhodes as chairman of the board.

Sales territory continued to grow in the late 1970s, expanding into New England and the Great Lakes region. The company bought a 44,431-square-foot factory 25 miles from Charlotte for its Tri-Plas subsidiary. Although rising energy costs remained a prime concern, increasingly expensive packing materials also spawned a major conservation effort. However, sales and earnings continued to rise, perhaps reflecting a new 20 cent snack price. Lance's Charlotte plant was expanded yet again, adding high-speed wrapping machines, and the Midwest Biscuit Company of Burlington, Iowa, was purchased. The new subsidiary supplied midwestern grocery stores with crackers and cookies, mostly under private labels. Lance also created an audiovisual studio dedicated to the production of training materials in 1979, and bought a new site for its Tri-Plas west coast operations in 1980.

1980–89: Facing Challenges

The 1980s proved a challenging period from the beginning. Due to a dismal domestic harvest, peanuts had to be imported

Key Dates:

1915: Lance and his son-in-law, Salem A. Van Every, found Lance Packing Company.
1916: Mrs. Lance and daughter create peanut butter cracker sandwiches.
1926: Founder Lance dies in auto accident, and Van Every assumes control of the company; enterprise is incorporated as Lance Packing Company.
1935: Company reaches annual sales of $1 million.
1938: Lance begins baking its own crackers.
1943: Salem Van Every dies, and his son Philip takes over leadership of the company.
1953: Company introduces packaged saltine crackers for institutional use.
1954: The first Lance vending machine is placed on site.
1960: Annual sales reach $26 million.
1961: Company goes public.
1971: A new Lance vending machine accommodates entire line of Lance snacks.
1973: Philip Van Every retires as president and CEO and is succeeded by Glenn Rhodes, the first company head outside the family.
1988: Lance replaces the saturated fats in its products with vegetable oils.
1990: CEO Pete Sloan retires and is succeeded by J.W. ''Bill'' Disher as chairman and president.
1999: Lance acquires Tamming Foods and Cape Cod Potato Chips.

for the first time. In response to the shortage, the company's packaged salted peanuts were diluted with sesame sticks, and its Peanut Bar and Redskins snacks were temporarily dropped from the product line. Even after the next year's improved harvest, government price supports kept prices high. In March 1980 the suggested retail price of Lance snack increased a nickel to 25 cents. However, the combination of all these factors resulted in net sales of $249.3 million for 1980.

The company concentrated on construction in 1981, completing or starting a vending machine repair shop, an efficient peanut roaster room, and 52,000 additional square feet of shipping space in Greenville, Texas. Lance modernized its fleet with more efficient tractors and larger (45 foot) trailers. A new convenience pack of ''Captain's Wafers,'' salted crackers commonly found at restaurant salad bars, helped Lance break into supermarket sales. Soon the snacks were packaged in groups of eight, which became known as Home Paks, for this market, in spite of some reluctance by Pete Sloan, who believed ''a supermarket sale takes away a vending machine sale.'' (In the 1990s, ''Club Paks'' containing 18 snacks would be offered through mass merchandisers.) In spite of a lackluster economy, 1982 proved successful, owing partly to the sale of Hancock's Old Fashion Country Ham to Smithfield Packing Company.

In spite of increased competition, Lance continued to prosper for the rest of the 1980s. Net annual sales increased 9.4 percent in 1984 to $337.4 million, spurred by more generous incentives. New sales districts continued to be added, and several new snacks were developed. Lance did acquire a Melbane, North Carolina, granola producer, Nutrition-Pak Corporation, but by this time the market for granola bars had peaked, and the unit was closed in 1988. However, a taste for healthier snacks remained. A launch of reformulated snacks dubbed the ''Snack Right'' program coincided, more or less, with Lance's 75th anniversary. Saturated fats and cholesterol were the targets of this campaign. The company even changed the way it labeled nutritional information to specify the different types of fat (saturated, polyunsaturated, etc.) that were included. Manufacturing capacity continued to be increased in the areas of peanuts and potato chips, which also began to be packaged in ''family size'' bags.

1990–97: New Challenges and Opportunities

Like the preceding decade, the 1990s began with serious challenges which Lance met successfully. Its large number of customers provided some protection from the economic recession. Company social concerns were focused on recycling programs throughout its facilities and offices. After his retirement in April 1990, Chairman and CEO Pete Sloan was succeeded by J.W. ''Bill'' Disher, who was elected chairman and president. Technological advances during this time included the successful implementation of automated route accounting, which, with the aid of hand-held computers, enhanced the productivity of sales representatives. Regional offices were consolidated into the central accounting department, and to remain competitive, new attention was given to marketing research and Leslie Advertising of Greenville, South Carolina, was retained to develop a new marketing plan. In 1990, chocolate bars, including some Mars brand products, were successfully tested in vending machines, and Lance began producing its own. Production capacity was increased with the purchase of a Columbia, South Carolina, plant, which began operations as Vista Bakery late in 1992.

Even with the employment of new marketing techniques, the individual serving sector of the market, Lance's home ground since the beginning, continued to enable the company to keep operations simple and provide a diversified clientele, tempering economic fluctuations. Moreover, the company managed to keep costs down, earning the loyalty of its many blue-collar consumers, in part by usually only introducing new products when similar ones proved successful for competitors. Although the company traditionally relied on availability, not advertising, as a main marketing tool, it rediscovered television and radio advertising in the mid-1990s and used these media to support its expansion into supermarkets.

The company also undertook some other promotional initiatives. For example, in the mid-1990s it began sponsoring race car drivers in the Busch Grand National Series, first sponsoring Bobby Hillin, Jr. Then, in 1996, along with stock-car racing great Richard Petty, Lance co-sponsored Rodney Combs in the same series. Later it would sponsor yet another driver, Shane Hall. Also in 1996, it sent some of its products (Toastchee and Van-O-Lunch) into the stratosphere aboard the space shuttle Columbia in a 6.5 million mile journey, orbiting the earth 252 times. Finally, Lance redesigned its logo and packaging, adding its tradition of ''freshness'' motto to these items.

Despite all these measures, Lance had to weather a slump that had hit it fairly hard in 1995, when it ended the year with a decline in revenue from $488 million in 1994 to $477.5 million and reported a $6.9 million net income loss. In 1996, the company took some severe steps to correct the problem, shuttering two plants and laying off workers for the first time in its history. It also reshuffled its management. For the first time, in hiring Scott Lea as chairman, Lance employed an outsider to preside over the board. It also acquired new executives from Coca-Cola, Pepperidge Farms, Nabisco, and Tropicana. The strategy proved successful; in 1996 the company returned to profitability, which it maintained for the rest of the decade, despite the fact that sales remained sluggish through 1998.

Lance, in an effort to increase its sales, also looked to new markets. Notably, in 1997, it expanded its territory, extending its presence to the western United States as well as abroad—to Puerto Rico, Aruba, Jamaica, Dominican Republic, England, China, and Western Europe. It also looked to increase sales by introducing new products, some of which were extensions or repackaging of existing lines.

1998 and Beyond: Continued Innovation and Expansion

In 1998, Lance, to achieve greater efficiency, implemented a new route management information system for its direct-store-delivery (DSD) operations. It also completed the distribution of new hand-held computers used by the DSD field sales personnel. Additional improvements were made to these systems in 1999. In that year, the company also streamlined the DSD organization by employing a segmented route structure, using metro distribution centers, and setting up a route alignment information system. These measures were undertaken in support of Lance's plan for increasing sales and profits.

Also in 1999, Lance made some significant purchases. First it acquired Tamming Foods Ltd., a Canadian sugar water manufacturer headquartered in Waterloo, Ontario. Tamming, selling its products in Canada, Mexico, and the United States, had reported annual sales of $20 million in 1998. Next, Lance acquired Cape Cod Potato Chip Company, Inc., based in Hyannis, Massachusetts. Lance bought Cape Cod, which specialized in making salty snacks, from SMS Brands LLC, a food product holding company. Cape Cod had generated about $30 million in sales in 1998. Additionally, Lance negotiated an agreement with China Peregrine (renamed China Premium Food Corp.) whereby Lance would export its private label snacks to China.

In addition to making acquisitions, Lance continued to seek ways of extending its business operations and thereby increasing its sales. For example, in 2000, it signed an agreement with Proctor & Gamble under which Lance became the distributor of P&G's Pringles brand potato chips in Lance's core market areas. By allowing P&G to utilize Lance's efficient DSD system, the arrangement benefitted both companies.

Although Lance would continue to face competition from industry heavies like Frito-Lay, Keebler, and Nabisco—and even makers of its signature sandwich crackers, Austin and Tom's—its main problem was actually tied to its long-standing success. A historically debt-free company, through the 1990s Lance was seen as an alluring buyout target, and would likely remain so in the first decade of the 21st century.

Principal Subsidiaries

Cape Cod Potato Chip Co.; Vista Bakery, Inc.

Principal Competitors

Frito-Lay, Inc.; Golden Enterprises, Inc.; Keebler Foods Company; Kraft Foods Inc.; Proctor & Gamble Company.

Further Reading

Anderson, Dick, "Getting There Second," *Southpoint,* June 1989, pp. 18–20.

Bary, Andrew, "Fresh Growth in Store," *Barron's,* February 16, 1992, pp. 23–24.

Hannon, Kerry, "Why Steal Your Own Sales?," *Forbes,* May 18, 1987, pp. 208–210.

Hiestand, Michael, "Lance Inc: 'We're Not in the Junk Food Business'," *Adweek's Marketing Week,* May 9, 1988, pp. 26–30.

"The History of Lance," Charlotte, N.C.: Lance, Inc., 1992.

Hopkins, Stella M., "Lance of Charlotte, N.C., Reorganizes, Looks for Sales Growth," *Knight-Ridder/Tribune Business News*, April 30, 1998.

James, Frank E., and Alix M. Freedman, "Lance Cuts Fat From Junk Foods to Sell Snacks as Healthier Fare," *Wall Street Journal,* March 29, 1988, p. 36.

Kimbrell, Wendy, "Southern Powerhouse," *Snack Food,* February 1994, pp. 26–41.

Lahvic, Ray, "Snack Baker Captures Impulse Sales," *Bakery,* April 1988, pp. 70–78.

"Lance Announces Top Management Changes," *PR Newswire*, March 1, 1999.

"Lance to Also Sell Procter & Gambles Pringles," *PR Newswire*, February 15, 2000.

Martin, Edward, "The Snack Attack," *Business North Carolina*, July 1996, p. 26.

Mildenberg, David, "Snack-Maker Lance to Cut 507 Jobs in South Carolina, Texas," *Knight-Ridder/Tribune Business News*, December 14, 1995.

Price, Scott, "Lance's Big Cheese," *Business Journal,* December 5, 1988, pp. 8–9.

Rickard, Al, "Lance Labels Tell It All," *Snack World,* April 1988, pp. 39–40.

Robinson, Russ, "Snack Maker Replaces Fat, Oils with Low-Cholesterol Substitute," *Greensboro, NC News & Record,* March 12, 1988, p. 4.

Sigo, Shelly, "To Deliver Goods, Lance Moves Closer to Customers," *Tampa Bay Business Journal*, February 11, 2000, p. 16.

Smith, Doug, "Counter Attack," *Snack Food,* October 1991, pp. 38–44.

——, "Lance's Anti-Recession Recipe," *Charlotte Observer,* July 29, 1991, pp. I1–I2.

Tippett, Karen, "The Conservative Flavor of Lance," *FW,* June 26, 1990, pp. 49–51.

"To Win Hearty Market Share, Lance Gets the Lard Out," *Business North Carolina,* October 988.

"Value Added: Baking's Key to Prosperity," *Milling & Baking News,* November 29, 1988, pp. 24–35.

Van Every, Philip Lance, *The History of Lance,* New York: The Newcomen Society in North America, 1974.

—Frederick C. Ingram
—update: Jane W. Fiero

LeCroy Corporation

700 Chestnut Ridge Road
Chestnut Ridge, New York 10977
U.S.A.
Telephone: (845) 425-2000
Fax: (845) 425-8967
Web site: http://www.lecroy.com

Public Company
Incorporated: 1964 as LeCroy Research Systems
Employees: 424
Sales: $121.4 million (2000)
Stock Exchanges: NASDAQ
Ticker Symbol: LCRY
NAIC: 334515 Instrument Manufacturing for Measuring and Testing Electricity and Electrical Signals

LeCroy Corporation is a world leader in the development, manufacture, and distribution of mid- to high-end digital oscilloscopes, used primarily by electronic engineers involved in the research and development of new products or upgrades to existing products in the communications, automotive, computer, and electronics industries. Oscilloscopes help to detect problems by allowing engineers to compare the actual shape of a signal within an electronic circuit to its ideal. Because it originally served a highly specialized scientific market, LeCroy emphasized digital technology well before its much larger competitors, all of whom were analog-based. As design engineers work with faster and more complex electronic signals, LeCroy is well positioned to achieve significant future gains in the high-end digital oscilloscope market, despite a lean period for the company in the late 1990s.

Walter LeCroy Starts his Business in 1964

The company's founder, Walter LeCroy, received an undergraduate degree in physics from Columbia University, then worked as the chief electronics engineer in the school's physics department. A number of people recognized his talent for developing instrumentation and encouraged him to start his own business. In 1964 LeCroy set up shop in a former Irvington, New York, Laundromat, naming his new company LeCroy Research Systems. Focused on high-energy physics instrumentation, LeCroy was an innovator in capturing and analyzing the signatures of transitory subatomic particles traveling close to the speed of light. It was a highly specialized market, limited to nuclear and particle-physics laboratories, yet the small company prospered. By 1965 LeCroy was able to leave the former Laundromat for larger facilities in Elmsford, New York, followed by another upgrade to West Nyack, New York, two years later. In 1972 LeCroy took a major step forward when it opened an instrument design and production facility in Geneva, Switzerland, near one of its most important customers, CERN (Centre European Recherche Nucleaire), which operated a giant accelerator for high-energy physics. The company then established sales and service operations in the United States, Europe, and Asia. In 1976, the company moved its headquarters to its present location in Chestnut Ridge, New York.

By the early 1980s LeCroy controlled an 80 percent share of a narrow market that not only was not growing, but was beginning to contract. The company decided to change its name to LeCroy Corporation and transfer its expertise to electronics to design more general purpose instrumentation. Management settled on oscilloscopes and by 1983 began to apply high-energy physics technology to its new product line, as well as conduct extensive market research. In 1985 LeCroy introduced its first digital oscilloscope, finding a niche in the fast-growing commercial test and measurement market. And just as high-speed electronics was beginning to take off, government funding for high-energy physics was being cut, thus confirming the wisdom of LeCroy's shift in business.

Branching into oscilloscopes required changes in LeCroy's approach to sales and marketing. For 20 years the company had sold to a very small number of customers, mostly heads of university physics and research laboratories. With technical backgrounds, LeCroy's 46 salespeople were well suited to this environment. According to one LeCroy executive, ''Our salespeople were used to visiting 'Herr Professor' or 'Herr Doktor' at the lab.

Company Perspectives:

LeCroy Corporation, headquartered in Chestnut Ridge, New York, develops, manufactures, and markets electronic signal acquisition and analysis products and services. The company's core business is the production of high-performance digital oscilloscopes, which are used by design engineers and researchers in a broad range of industries, including electronics, computers, and communications.

They would talk to them about the instruments and projects and when it came time, the customers would buy from us. But that doesn't work in business. Business works at a much faster pace.'' LeCroy conducted a number of seminars to both prepare and motivate the sales force before it began to sell to corporations. Although most embraced the change, a number of salespeople left the company. The focus of the sales call remained the engineer, but now LeCroy's representatives also had to cater to less knowledgeable executives who, although they wouldn't be using the instruments, were key in the buying process. The sales force had a further problem: convincing engineers that they should buy from a company unknown in their field, instead of the well-established Hewlett-Packard or Tektronix. The fact that LeCroy was well respected by physicists and that the company offered a superior product was simply not enough. LeCroy had to convince its new customers that it could deliver on service and, in short, make their lives easier.

LeCroy posted oscilloscope revenues of $20 million in 1985. Five years later annual sales increased to $55 million, enough to show up on the radar screens of its larger competitors. By the end of 1993 digital oscilloscopes would account for 70 percent of corporate revenues, then increase to 75 percent the following year, and 80 percent the year after that. At the same time, sales of instrumentation for high-energy physics research steadily eroded.

Challenges By a Rival in 1992

Not only did industry-leader Tektoronix notice LeCroy, in 1992 it sued the company, alleging patent infringement. LeCroy vowed to vigorously contest the charges, and the case made its way through the legal system for almost two years before the parties reached an out-of-court settlement. In the end, LeCroy signed a license agreement with Tektronix regarding four patents. It paid $1.5 million up front and agreed to pay royalties of at least $3.5 million over the ensuing ten years and up to an additional $3.5 million, depending on sales. Tektronix could also terminate the agreement should LeCroy acquire 20 percent or a controlling interest in any rival company on a restricted list. Likewise, if any company on the list acquired 20 percent or a controlling interest in LeCroy, or LeCroy attempted to transfer its Tektronix license to a restricted company, Tektronix could terminate the agreement. In essence, Tektronix looked to solidify its dominant position in the oscilloscope industry.

At the time, Tektronix generated $1.3 billion in annual revenues. With sales of only $63.4 million in 1994, LeCroy was simply looking to solidify its revamped business. The company had been barely profitable in 1992, earning $200,000 on revenues of $59.9 million, followed by a loss of $200,000 in 1993 on revenues of $61.2 million. The company lost an additional $1 million in 1994. Nevertheless, with the Tektronix litigation settled, LeCroy was positioned to take its business public. The process began in 1993 when Walter LeCroy decided to bring in more seasoned management to replace technically knowledgeable but less commercially aware officers. He remained chairman of the board and named Lutz P. Henckels to serve as chief executive officer. According to Henckels, his predecessors ''wouldn't even have known what matters to a Wall Street audience. When our underwriter asked us all those probing questions, they would have said, 'Why does that matter?' '' Born in Germany, Henckels moved to the United States after high school, earning undergraduate and master's degrees in electrical engineering and a Ph.D. in computer science from the Massachusetts Institute of Technology. He gained business experience by founding HHB Systems, Inc., a computer-aided design and test company. As CEO he took the company public in 1987. He also served as the president of U.S. operations for Racal-Redac, Inc., an electronic design automation company, from 1989 until January 1993, when he began a short stint as a consultant at LeCroy before taking the reins.

Under Henckel, LeCroy cut back further on its high-energy physics products and phased out older oscilloscopes, narrowing its offerings to the high-performance 9300 series, which accounted for the lion's share of company revenues. LeCroy also began efforts to develop oscilloscopes better suited for use in testing in such growth areas as computer equipment, LANs (Local Area Network), and communications. Although these changes would cause short-term pain, reflected in the $1 million net loss for 1994, the company was better positioned for the future. For the fiscal year ending June 30, 1995, LeCroy's revenues rose significantly, topping $82 million and resulting in a net profit of $2.6 million. In November 1995 the company was ready to make an initial public offering of stock, selling 2.1 million shares at $12 each. Of the $16.1 million raised, $14.7 million was spent to pay off debt. By the end of 1995, LeCroy maintained a 10 percent share of the digital oscilloscope market, trailing only Tektronix with 44.5 percent and Hewlett-Packard with 17.8 percent.

LeCroy introduced the 9384 family of mid-range oscilloscopes in 1996 to compete with Tektronix and its 50 percent share of a $250 million market. Prices for the units ranged from $19,490 to $28,990. The company also signed a technology licensing deal with Fluke, a maker of handheld signal instruments, which ranked fourth behind LeCroy in digital oscilloscope sales with a 5.8 percent market share. In exchange for royalties, Fluke would gain access to the technologies that LeCroy developed for its bench-top oscilloscopes. In turn, LeCroy was able to participate in a growing market segment. For fiscal 1996, revenues grew to $101.5 million and net profits to $4.3 million. The following year, revenues jumped to $117.1 million, and the company posted a net profit of $7 million.

In general, LeCroy continued to evolve into a large company with far-flung operations. With its engineers split between Switzerland and New York, weekly video conferencing became

Key Dates:

1964: Walter LeCroy starts the company.
1972: After several moves within the United States, the company opens a second facility in Geneva, Switzerland.
1976: The company moves to Chestnut Ridge, New York.
1985: The company introduces the digital oscilloscope.
1993: Lutz P. Hickels becomes president and CEO.
1995: The company makes an initial public offering of stock.
2000: The company acquires Lightspeed Electronics.

necessary. The Swiss proved to be more detail oriented and thorough, while the Americans were more innovative and willing to take risks. They worked well together, and LeCroy continued to push the envelope on high-performance oscilloscopes. As computer processing speeds expanded rapidly, and the signals to be tested grew longer and more complex, the market for oscilloscopes was clearly moving in the direction of LeCroy's expertise and boded well for the company's future.

In October 1997 LeCroy made its first stab at external growth, acquiring Preamble Instruments, Inc. of Beaverton, Oregon, for stock and $411,000 in cash. Preamble manufactured stand-alone differential amplifiers and probes. After introducing a LAN analyzer called NEWSLine, LeCroy supported the new product offering by acquiring Digitech Industries, Inc. and its LAN and WAN (Wide Area Network) protocol analysis technology used in data communication and telecommunications. LeCroy then aligned itself with Anixter, Inc., a $2.8 billion network and cable solutions company. During fiscal 1999 LeCroy formed a subsidiary called Vigilant Networks, Inc. for its network analysis business, into which it folded Digitech.

LeCroy moved next into Asian markets. In 1998 LeCroy acquired Woojoo Hi-Tech Corporation, its Korean distributor since 1991, and formed a wholly owned subsidiary, LeCroy Korea Ltd. LeCroy also made a $7 million equity investment in Japan's Iwatsu Electric Company, Ltd., which along with its subsidiary, LeCroy Japan, had been distributing the company's digital oscilloscopes. An expanded partnership deal included a technology transfer agreement, as well as granting LeCroy sole distribution rights to North America and Europe for complementary Iwatsu products, to be marketed under the LeCroy logo. It was the Far East and its economic woes, however, that hindered LeCroy's growth in the late 1990s and lead to falling revenues and net losses.

Asian Economic Woes in the Late 1990s

Although revenues grew to $131 million in 1998, LeCroy posted a loss of nearly $2 million. The following year, revenues dropped to $126.2 million, despite increases in sales in the United States and Europe. In the rest of the world, in particular Asia, revenues fell off by 30 percent. The result for 1999 was a net loss of $6.8 million. Customers in the Far East simply weren't able to buy products, so that LeCroy had no choice but to retrench and wait out the downturn. It slashed its work force and closed down its Swiss manufacturing operations, electing to shift the work to its New York facilities. Sales continued to slide in 2000, coming in at $121.4 million, and restructuring costs resulted in a net loss of $3.4 million. In August 2000, LeCroy agreed to sell Vigilant Networks to GenTek Inc. for $12 million. The company had tried to develop a new product and deliver it to an unfamiliar market, but learned that it lacked the necessary expertise and resources. In the future, Henckels vowed to find partners and to design its technologies so that they were easy for others to deploy. In fact, the Vigilant sale created something of a partnership with GenTek, which as part of the transaction agreed to source Vigilant products from LeCroy.

LeCroy continued to spend money on research and development. In 1997 the company had combined its high-energy physics operations with the oscilloscope group to form a team to develop technologies, as well as to take advantage of the technologies acquired from Iwatsu and Fluke. In 1999 LeCroy increased its R&D spending by some $4 million, up from 13 percent of sales to 15 percent. Over a three-year span the company also spent more than $11 million to upgrade its facilities and management systems. It was also willing to make strategic acquisitions. In July 2000 LeCroy purchased Lightspeed Electronics, which provided microwave communication analysis technology for high-speed communications components and systems. With an increasing demand for broadband Internet access, this area was poised for tremendous growth.

During the first three quarters of 2001, LeCroy experienced a turnaround in its business and reported strong financial results. The past three years had been difficult, but management was optimistic about the future. Although the low-end part of the oscilloscope market appeared to be declining, the high-performance end was growing. Signals continued to gain in complexity, and design engineers needed analysis in real time, a level of sophistication that LeCroy, with its high-energy physics heritage, was well suited to meet. Instead of accommodating their high-performance technology to commercial needs, after 20 years LeCroy saw the market growing in its direction. It had a number of products waiting in the wings to meet the demand for high-end products. Within five years management expected the company to be generating $500 million in annual revenues. LeCroy's R&D had also made a software technology breakthrough that would bear watching in the years to come. Called MAUI (Massive Advance in User Interface), the software technology held the potential, according to management at least, to do to oscilloscopes and electronic instruments what Windows did to the personal computer. This advantage in signal analysis would, he hoped, provide LeCroy with the competitive advantage needed to make it the leader in the high-end oscilloscope market.

Principal Subsidiaries

Digital Industries, Inc.; LeCroy, Ltd.; LeCroy GmbH (Germany); LeCroy, S.A.R.L.; LeCroy, S.R.L.; LeCroy Japan Corporation, K.K.; LeCroy Korea, Ltd.; Preamble Instruments, Inc.; LeCroy Lightspeed Corporation.

Principal Competitors

Tektronix Inc.; Acterna Corporation; Agilent Technologies, Inc.; Danaher Corporation; Keithley Instruments, Inc.

Further Reading

Kelley, Bill, ''When Your Customer Base Changes,'' *Sales and Marketing Management,* February 1990, pp. 72–74.

''LeCroy,'' *Wall Street Reporter,* December 8, 2000, p. 1.

Lium, Alice Fussell, ''R&D is the Key,'' *Design News,* December 7, 1998, pp. 82–83.

Mulqueen, John T., ''LeCroy's New Line's a Big Seller,'' *Communications Week,* October 30, 1995, p. 75.

Neale, Ron, ''On the Shoulders of a Giant,'' *Electronic Engineering,* January 1999, p. 7.

Runyon, Stan, ''Scopes Fight it Out on High-end Turf,'' *Electronic Engineering Times,* March 3, 1997, p. 43.

—Ed Dinger

Lithia Motors, Inc.

360 East Jackson Avenue
Medford, Oregon 97501-5892
U.S.A.
Telephone: (541) 776-6591
Fax: (541) 858-3279
Web site: http://www.lithia.com

Public Company
Incorporated: 1946
Employees: 3,400
Sales: $ 24.3 million (2000)
Stock Exchanges: New York
Ticker Symbol: LAD
NAIC: 441110 New Only or New and Used Cars

Lithia Motors, Inc. is one of the largest full-service new vehicle retailers in the United States with 56 stores and 114 franchises in California, Oregon, Washington, Nevada, Colorado, Idaho, South Dakota, and Alaska. Lithia sells 26 brands of new, domestic, and imported vehicles and all makes of used vehicles; it arranges finance, warranty, and credit insurance contracts and provides vehicle parts, maintenance, and repair services at all of its locations. Internet sales are centralized at Lithia.com, ''America's Car & Truck Store.'' Since going public, Lithia has grown by purchasing underperforming family-owned dealerships in smaller cities.

The Early Years: 1946–68

Walter DeBoer started Lithia Motors as a single store on ''The Plaza'' in Ashland, Oregon, in 1946. The company, which took its name from nearby springs containing lithium, had five employees. During its first year in business, the sales staff sold 14 vehicles, totaling sales of fewer than $100,000. DeBoer continued to operate Lithia as a small family business for the next 24 years, bringing in less than $1 million in sales per year. His son, Sid DeBoer, the oldest child of DeBoer's six, joined Lithia in 1964 at the age of 21 to become its bookkeeper.

In 1968, Walter DeBoer was killed in a car-pedestrian accident, and Sid DeBoer assumed control of the small Chrysler-Dodge store. The small business sold 30 to 40 cars a month. That year, the younger DeBoer was issued a nonrenewable two-year franchise from Chrysler Corporation for the Ashland facility. In May 1970, Sid DeBoer purchased the Dodge Center in Medford and closed the Ashland business. At the same time, DeBoer convinced Dick Heimann to leave his position with Chrysler and become a partner at Lithia Motors.

First Steps Toward Growth: 1970–90

Together DeBoer and Heimann, the company's new operating officer, slowly turned the single store into a very large and successful chain of franchised auto retail stores. From 1970 to 1990, Lithia bought three dealerships encompassing five auto franchises and grew, in the process, to include five stores and 19 franchises in southern Oregon.

But by 1987, DeBoer began to sour on acquisitions. Each one took months to complete and involved assuming substantial, if manageable, debt. He began to look for other means of raising growth capital and, at last, made the unprecedented decision to take Lithia Motors public. It was not until December 18, 1996, however, that the company's $31 million NASDAQ offering finally occurred, and by then Lithia was the third auto dealership to go public. During the intervening nine years, big companies began to jockey for car franchise ownership with the traditional family-owned dealership.

Several trends drove the move away from small ownership: the maturation of the automotive industry and consequent tightening of profit margins; fewer dealers passing their business on to their children; and the automakers' desire to deal with fewer, stronger retail outlets. The growth of Internet buying services had begun to force dealers to compete on price with dealers in other cities. The big companies, which had the capacity to borrow money at lower interest rates than independent dealers, had the advantage in both purchasing cars from the manufacturers and in buying advertising in bulk at a discount. They thus moved in to purchase the many dealerships up for sale as thousands of owners neared retirement. Automotive manufacturers, however, did not yet trust public ownership of dealerships.

DeBoer and associates worked to develop a proven operating model that investors would trust and that some analysts

Company Perspectives:

The mission of Lithia Automotive Group is to be the best provider of cars and trucks and related services in North America. Utilizing a common language, we believe in developing motivated people who are committed to our goals and mission. We are a team. As a team we come together to create and execute the best buying and owning experience that exceeds our customers' expectations while maintaining our integrity with our customers, our vendors, and with each other. We develop our people, procedures and financial plans today, with a focus on ensuring a successful and stable future. We are never satisfied with ''good enough.'' By being committed to our jobs and constantly seeking to better ourselves, we will find our motivation. We are aggressive in our approach to our jobs, ensuring that each of our departments, stores, and areas are growing and improving to their full potential. We are always committed to each team member to see that they each excel in their respective jobs.

credit with making Lithia the most successful public offering in the automotive sales field. This model consisted of four elements. First, DeBoer instituted public audits of Lithia Motors' books by Peat Marwick in preparation for its initial public offering. Second, he standardized Lithia's management information systems to be able to track sales, inventories, and profit performance on a daily basis. Third, DeBoer and Heimann held meetings with employees to craft a mission statement for the company as a whole and statements of purpose for each individual department—sales, parts, service, and administration—''missions for each that could integrate into the whole,'' according to DeBoer in a 1997 *Oregon Business* article. Fourth, Lithia instituted its ''Priority You'' marketing program, a customer pledge intended to simplify car buying.

Lithia also hired a new financial officer, Brian Neill, a former banker whose father was a Cadillac dealer, whose job was to spearhead the public offering. Neill, who joined the company in 1995 and spent his first six months on the job selling cars, ran the search for an underwriter and chose the San Francisco brokerage firm of Furman Selz.

While Neill drafted the prospectus to meet the requirements of both the brokers and the Securities Exchange Commission, DeBoer met with the major automakers, who had actively opposed most public offerings in the dealer sector, preferring to hold individuals rather than corporations accountable for the performance of their stores. DeBoer gained their acceptance of his plan by virtue of his reputation and by catering to their concerns, assuring them that he and not shareholders would control the fate of his company. To do so, he designed Lithia's initial public offering to feature two classes of stock. Of the first class, he offered 46 percent for public ownership; of the second, operating stock, DeBoer retained ownership of 92 percent.

Rapid Growth as a Public Company: 1996–2000

After a two-week, 22-city, 54-presentation road show to win over investors, and a last-minute decision to lower Lithia's initial share price, Lithia held its initial public offering, raising approximately $27 million, which it put toward paying down its debt with manufacturers and bankers and financing the purchase of more than ten dealerships in a matter of months. Most of these were in California, although subsequent acquisitions focused on the intermountain west. The company made a practice of clustering its franchises in areas with strong regional economies and ''livable'' cities. Many of the dealerships Lithia purchased had a history of underperforming and thus were available for less than top dollar. According to DeBoer in the 1997 *Oregon Business* article, his strategy for managing a successful public company was to ''lower the real multiple in purchasing'' car dealerships while relying upon his operating model and structure to boost underperformers' growth and profitability. At each newly incorporated dealership, the staff of each department sat down and hashed out the local meaning of Lithia's mission statements. They had to adopt Lithia's ''Priority You'' program, including its ten-minute credit check, 30-minute trade-in appraisal, 90-minute sales transaction, and 60-day or 3,000-mile used car warranty, and institute its management information systems before reopening as part of Lithia Motors.

Key Dates:

1946: Walter DeBoer starts Lithia Motors.
1968: Sid DeBoer takes over the business after Walter dies.
1970: Lithia purchases the Dodge Center in Medford and closes its Ashland facility.
1996: Lithia Motors begins trading on NASDAQ.
1999: Lithia moves to the NYSE as LAD and opens Lithia.com.

From 1997 to 1999, Lithia increased its sales volume more than eight times and added 34 stores and numerous franchises to its fold. Still far behind the No. 1 ranked auto retailer in sheer number of transactions, Lithia sold 17,708 cars in 1998, compared with AutoNation's 286,179. Lithia reported impressive profits, however, of $6.0 million in 1997 on revenues of $319.9 million, up from profits of $2.6 million on revenues of $142.8 million. By 1998, both profits and revenues had just about doubled again, totaling $10.8 million and $714.7 million, respectively. In 1999, the company ranked first in the *Seattle Times* annual ranking of the Northwest's fastest growing publicly held companies. It also ranked as the tenth largest auto retailer in the country by the *Automotive News Survey* and was included in *Fortune*'s list of the 1,000 largest companies in the nation.

Lithia moved to the New York Stock Exchange under the ticker symbol LAD in 1999 and opened Lithia.com, which it dubbed ''America's Car & Truck Store.'' The site aimed to forge a relationship with consumers as opposed solely to facilitating an on-line purchase. The company's profits and revenues continued on their steeply upward trend, almost doubling again, with profits of $19.1 million and revenues of $12.4 billion. Lithia added 13 new dealerships in 1999 to bring its total to 41 dealerships in six states.

By the end of 2000, Lithia's operations included 52 stores, 111 franchises, and 26 brands in seven states: Oregon, California, Nevada, Washington, Colorado, Idaho, and South Dakota.

Although new vehicle sales had begun to slow in 2000, its revenues that year increased by 33 percent to $1.66 billion and its net profits rose by 27 percent to $24.3 million. *Fortune* added the company to its Fortune 1000 list and ranked it first among America's most admired publicly traded automotive retailers. Whereas many of the publicly traded auto retailers forecast few to no acquisitions during the next couple of years, Lithia planned an aggressive growth plan, focusing on markets west of the Mississippi. In an industry ripe for consolidation because of its size and fragmented nature—the sector as a whole totaled $700 billion in new and used sales—Lithia continued to manifest impressive growth.

Principal Subsidiaries

Lithia Properties, LLC.

Principal Competitors

AutoNation USA; CarMax; Cross-Continent Auto Retailers; Prospect Motors; Republic Industries, Inc.; Sonic Automotive; United Auto Group, Inc.

Further Reading

Bjorhus, Jennifer, ''Medford, Oregon-Based Car Dealer's Earnings Hit High Speed,'' *Oregonian,* October 28, 1999.

Bradsher, Keith, ''Car Dealerships Are Facing Consolidation and Change,'' *New York Times,* January 15, 1997, p. D1.

''Consolidator and Operator,'' *WSCR.com,* March 13–19, 2000.

Medina, Hildy, ''Road Warrior,'' *Forbes,* November 30, 1998, p. 136.

Wojahn, Ellen, ''An IPO Nine Years in the Making,'' *Oregon Business,* October 1997, p. 103.

—Carrie Rothburd

MagneTek, Inc.

26 Century Boulevard, Suite 600
Nashville, Tennessee 37214
U.S.A.
Telephone: (615) 316-5100
Fax: (615) 316-5158
Web site: http://www.magnetek.com

Public Company
Incorporated: 1984
Employees: 2,000
Sales: $294 million (2000)
Stock Exchanges: New York
Ticker Symbol: MAG
NAIC: 333612 Speed Changer, Industrial High-Speed Drive, and Gear Manufacturing; 335311 Power, Distribution, and Specialty Transformer Manufacturing; 335312 Motor and Generator Manufacturing; 335999 All Other Miscellaneous Electrical Equipment and Component Manufacturing

MagneTek, Inc. supplies digital power products for communications, industrial and building systems, data processing, imaging, and various other applications that require precision power. The company is distinguished as the world's leading independent manufacturer of elevator drives and drive systems for cranes and hoists. MagneTek operates as an electronics products company with five research and manufacturing centers in North America, two in Europe, and one in China.

Early Beginnings with Litton Industries Inc.

MagneTek was created in July 1984 when Litton Industries, Inc. spun off its Magnetics Group. Litton Industries was a diversified conglomerate with an emphasis on high-tech industries. Founded in 1954 by Charles ''Tex'' Thornton, Litton had expanded rapidly during the 1960s and 1970s by developing its own technologies and by acquiring numerous companies. Among the ventures in which it became involved were various electric equipment businesses. For example, in 1967, Litton purchased Louis Allis, a leading manufacturer of specialty electrical motors, condensers, and generators. Litton assembled several of its electric products companies into the Magnetics Group.

Litton fostered growth and success at many of its subsidiaries by providing investment capital and allowing them to cooperate with other Litton companies. In fact, engineers in Litton's electric products companies achieved a number of notable technological breakthroughs. In the mid-1970s, for example, they developed the first high-efficiency electric motor. Dubbed the E-plus, the device set the energy-saving standard in the industry for the next decade. Despite successes in the Magnetics Group, by the early 1980s Litton was ready to jettison the division as part of its ongoing effort to streamline operations and focus on key industries and technologies. Litton sold its Magnetics Group by way of a leveraged buyout, and MagneTek was incorporated on June 1, 1984 to purchase the assets of the Magnetics Group in July of that year.

At the time of the purchase, the Magnetics Group was generating close to $200 million in annual sales from four primary product lines: integral horsepower motors; drives and controls; lighting ballasts; and small transformers. Integral horsepower motors are used to power commercial mechanisms like heating and air-conditioning systems, mining and petrochemical equipment, and commercial laundry machines. Integral horsepower drives and drive systems are mechanisms used to adjust and control the speed and output of electric motors. They typically drive motors in applications like air-conditioning systems, elevators, and machine tools. Lighting ballasts are used in both residential and commercial fluorescent lighting fixtures. The ballast controls the power going to the light bulbs and can have a significant impact on the amount of energy consumed by the lighting fixture. Finally, MagneTek's small transformers were used as power conversion devices in a range of electronic equipment.

Expansion in the late 1980s and early 1990s

MagneTek posted a net loss of $501,000 in 1985 from sales of $195 million. After reorganizing the former Magnetics

Company Perspectives:

MagneTek now operates as a smaller but stronger company fixed on products that process power for the digital economy including broadband, wireless and optical wireline communications infrastructure, mass data processing and storage, high-tech manufacturing, distributing power generation, and specialized industrial controls.

Group during that first full year of business, however, MagneTek began posting consistently rising profits and sales. Indeed, revenues bolted to $273 million in 1986, $608 million in 1987, and then to more than $900 million in 1988. Those gains were primarily the result of an aggressive acquisition strategy adopted by MagneTek's management team. In February 1986, MagneTek purchased Universal Manufacturing Corp. for $71 million, the first in a string of buyouts. In October, the company bought motor manufacturer Century Electric, Inc. for $76 million, and in December of that year MagneTek paid $108 million for Cooper Service, Inc., Cooper Controls, Inc., and Universal Electric Co. Six months later, MagneTek also snared ALS Corp. for about $50 million.

MagneTek's expansion strategy during the late 1980s and into the early 1990s was devised by Frank Perna, Jr., the chief executive hired in 1985 to head MagneTek. Perna was a veteran of the electric products industry. He had earned a master's degree in management from the Massachusetts Institute of Technology, as well as a master's degree in electrical engineering from Wayne State University. Perna spent 17 years with General Motors, after which he served as president of Sun Electric and as head of the Instrumentation Group at the venerable Bell & Howell Co. Prior to joining MagneTek, he was serving as the chief executive of a subsidiary of Whittaker Corp.

Perna had witnessed firsthand the evolution of the electrical equipment industry during the late 1970s and 1980s. Among the dominant trends were increasing foreign competition and a rising emphasis on advanced technology, particularly related to energy efficiency. Perna believed that for MagneTek to compete in the widely diverse electric products industry, the company would have to become big enough to overcome barriers such as low-cost foreign manufacturers and high capital requirements for product development and manufacturing. His plan was to purchase other companies and integrate them into a cohesive whole, thus achieving economies of scales related to product development, production, marketing, and distribution. To that end, during the late 1980s and early 1990s, MagneTek made the six major acquisitions described above, added numerous product lines, and purchased various manufacturing operations, including several in Europe.

By 1990, MagneTek was operating 50 manufacturing and service facilities throughout North America and overseas and employing roughly 15,000 workers. Revenues had risen to $961 million in 1989 before cruising past the $1 billion mark in 1990. Furthermore, the company had managed to post steady profit growth, culminating in a $33 million net income for 1990. MagneTek then ceased its acquisition efforts during the early 1990s, concentrating instead on whipping its existing operations into shape. Sales rose about 8 percent in 1991 to $1.13 billion and then to $1.23 billion in 1992. Those sales gains were achieved despite an economic recession that reduced orders from many market segments, particularly those related to defense and new construction.

MagneTek had started out as a private venture. The leveraged buyout was funded heavily by two investment partnerships, Magtek Partners and Champlain Associates, which provided seed money for MagneTek's start-up and acquisition drive. The partnerships were created by colleagues of the infamous Michael Milken at investment firm Drexel Burnham Lambert. In 1989, the owners of MagneTek decided to take the venture public to help pay down the company's debt and to provide more growth capital. MagneTek made its initial public stock offering in July 1989 at a price of $12 per share. Unfortunately, the stock price languished during the early 1990s and provided little opportunity for the company to benefit greatly from subsequent stock sales.

Part of the reason that MagneTek's stock stagnated was that investors were concerned about the Milken-related investment groups, which still owned about one-third of the company by the early 1990s. More importantly, Wall Street was concerned about the massive liabilities that MagneTek had assumed when it was created and during its buyout blitz of the late 1980s. Indeed, by the end of the 1980s MagneTek was staggering under a hefty debt load that was eating into profits and cash flow. The stock sale had helped to reduce that debt, and MagneTek went a long way toward improving its equity position between 1990 and 1992. But weak sales gains during the recession pressured the company and began to take a toll. Although sales rose to a peak of $1.5 million in 1993, profits slipped for the first time in the company's short history in 1992 and stood still in 1993.

Although MagneTek's financial performance waned, the company claimed victories in other arenas. For example, in 1992 MagneTek introduced an ultraefficient light bulb designed to operate for 20,000 hours (compared to about 750 hours for the typical incandescent light bulb). The new bulb, dubbed the E-Lamp and priced at $10 to $20, operated without a filament. Instead, a signal generated by an electronic circuit excited a phosphor coating inside the bulb that produced a glow similar in intensity to a traditional filament bulb. The breakthrough device reflected MagneTek's marketing strategy of emphasizing energy-efficient products. ''We've been pursuing this energy-engineered strategy for three and one-half years,'' Perna said in the *Los Angeles Business Journal.* ''And I think it was finally recognized as a good strategy,'' he added.

Restructuring in the Mid-1990s

Despite some engineering and marketing successes, MagneTek's balance sheet at the end of 1993 demanded that the company adopt a new strategy. Perna exited his post and was replaced as chief executive by Andrew G. Galef. The 60-year-old Galef had served as chairman of the company since its inception and had broad experience in investment and management consulting. Galef steered MagneTek on a new course. Rather than try to compete in the increasingly diverse electrical

Key Dates:

1984: MagneTek is incorporated.
1986: MagneTek acquires Universal Manufacturing Corp., Century Electric, Inc., Cooper Service, Inc., Cooper Controls, Inc., and Universal Electric Co.
1989: Company goes public.
1990: Revenues exceed $1 billion.
1993: Andrew G. Galef takes over as CEO.
1994: The firm begins a major restructuring effort.
1997: MagneTek forms a partnership with GE Lighting.
1998: Company acquires Omega Power Systems.
1999: The firm's generator business and electric motor business is sold.
2000: MagneTek announces plans to divest all remaining electrical component operations.

equipment industry, the company would eliminate noncore business and focus on product segments in which it was most competitive: ballasts, transformers, motors, and generators. Importantly, the move would allow MagneTek to sell off many of the assets that it had accrued during the late 1980s and early 1990s. The company hoped to use that cash to reduce its $530-million debt burden.

By the end of 1993, the sprawling MagneTek organization had grown to encompass 79 production and support facilities in North America, Europe, Japan, and the Far East. Early in 1994, MagneTek announced a restructuring plan that entailed the divestment of six business groups that accounted for roughly 30 percent of the company's annual revenues. Those groups encompassed certain noncore product lines related to electrical services, utility and power products, component transformers and converters, and controls. Among the businesses sold, for example, was the Louis Allis subsidiary, which by 1994 had become a relatively meager part of MagneTek's holdings. (Louis Allis was sold to managers at the subsidiary, making it independent for the first time since Litton bought it in 1967.) Also part of the restructuring was a move of the company headquarters from Los Angeles to Nashville, Tennessee.

MagneTek completed its restructuring and divestment plan by mid-1995. The effort reduced the number of production and support facilities by more than half, to 38, and generated about $200 million in cash. Similarly, MagneTek's 42 business units were consolidated into three groups: lighting products, motors and controls, and power electronics. Company revenues dipped to $1.13 billion in 1994 but rose to $1.2 billion in 1995, and net income recovered to $21.5 million. Meanwhile, MagneTek sustained its energy-engineering strategy, as evidenced by its introduction of the E-plus III in 1995. That motor, a successor to the E-plus motor that Litton had introduced in the 1970s, set a new standard for efficiency in the industry.

Renewed from its recent restructuring effort, MagneTek continued to develop products related to its newly aligned groups. Along with the release of a new line of motors, the firm also purchased a stake in Automation Systems and Products Inc., a factory automation software developer. The firm's lighting products division also beefed up its offerings and a new line of lighting controls was introduced to compliment its electronic ballast products. In October 1997, MagneTek teamed up with GE Lighting to develop and market energy-efficient lighting systems.

The company's power electronics group, based in Valdarno, Italy, made a key acquisition in July 1998. Omega Power Systems, an electronic power supplies manufacturer, was purchased to diversify the firm's product line and solidify its stance in the North American market. By the end of the year, MagneTek's product lines included electronic power supplies, motor drives, electric motors and generators, and lighting ballasts. Sixteen factories were in operation in North America, seven were functional in Europe, and one operated in Asia. Revenues for the year reached $1.2 billion.

MagneTek began once again to restructure itself in 1999 in an effort to gain financial strength and remain competitive. The firm began to sell off major business operations, including its European ballast operations, its generator business, which was sold to Emerson Electric Co. for $115 million, and its electric motor interests, purchased by A.O. Smith Corp. for $253 million. Management used the cash generated by these sales to pay off debt, repurchase stock, and make strategic acquisitions. One such acquisition occurred in July 1999, when MagneTek acquired EMS Inc., an electronic drives manufacturer, as part of a new company focus on growth in the programmable power supplies industry.

New Focus in the New Millennium

Management's plan to divest certain business units continued into the new millennium. The company decided to focus solely on its power electronics interests, which meant the discontinuation of its lighting ballasts, magnet wire, capacitors, and small transformers. According to a company press release, CEO Galef stated, ''All of these actions are aimed at creating a pure power electronics company that is financially strong and focused on markets that offer double-digit margins and double-digit growth.'' Galef also stated that the company made the decision to focus on its power electronic business due to the increased demand for electric power sparked by the burgeoning telecommunications industry. This new focus led to the November 2000 acquisition of J-Tec Inc., a power systems integrator catering to the telecommunications industry.

MagneTek continued with plans to divest the remainder of its electrical components. In early 2001, the firm sold its Drive Products division to Yaskawa Electric America for nearly $30 million. Management remained focused on research and development in power electronics technology and becoming debt-free. By catering to the digital power marketplace, MagneTek appeared on track to remain a strong leader in the industry with its strategic focus on products that processed power for the digital economy.

Principal Subsidiaries

A.O. Smith Electrical Products Co.; MagneTek Drives & Systems; MagneTek Lighting Products; MagneTek Power Electronics Group of North America.

Principal Competitors

Aerovox Inc.; Artesyn Technologies Inc.; Insilco Holding Co.

Further Reading

''A.O. Smith Completes MagneTek Acquisition,'' *Appliance,* October 1999, p. 13.

Deady, Tim, ''Restructuring Plan to Create Slimmer MagneTek,'' *Los Angeles Business Journal,* January 17, 1994, p. 28.

''GE and MagneTek Form Joint Lighting Systems Venture,'' *Energy User News,* September 1997, p. 1.

''How MagneTek Views Reliability,'' *Industry Week,* October 21, 1996, p. 97.

Kirchen, Rich, ''MagneTek Future Upbeat As It Awaits New Owner,'' *Business Journal-Milwaukee,* July 1, 1995, p. 7.

''MagneTek,'' *Pulp & Paper,* February 1997, p. 122.

''MagneTek Acquires Omega,'' *Electronic News,* July 6, 1998, p. 56.

''MagneTek Completes Acquisition of Telecom Power Company,'' *PR Newswire,* November 13, 2000.

''MagneTek Compliments Dimming Ballast Line,'' *Energy User News,* September 1997, p. 53.

''MagneTek to Divest Remaining Electrical Component Operations,'' *PR Newswire,* July 27, 2000.

''MagneTek, Inc.,'' *Machine Design,* November 26, 1992, p. 119.

''MagneTek Inc. Provides Additional Insights into Its Business and Market Opportunities,'' *PR Newswire,* November 2, 2000.

''MagneTek Inc. Sees Great Market Opportunities Ahead,'' *PR Newswire,* October 5, 2000.

Mullins, Robert, ''From 'Round Error' to 'The Whole Enchilada','' *Business Journal-Milwaukee,* August 27, 1994, p. A2.

Murray, Robert, ''MagneTek Announces Fiscal 1994 Results,'' *Business Wire,* August 22, 1994.

——, ''MagneTek Announces Restructuring Plan,'' *Business Wire,* January 6, 1994.

——, ''Ronald W. Mathewson Named President of MagneTek's Lighting Group,'' *Business Wire,* May 18, 1994.

Stoll, Otto G., ''Perna Elected Chief Executive Officer of MangeTek,'' *Business Wire,* September 17, 1990.

Vrana, Debora, and Todd White, ''MagneTek Stock Jumps on News of Product Sales Rise,'' *Los Angeles Business Journal,* January 18, 1993, p. 31.

White, Todd, ''MagneTek Lights Up Over Electronic Lamp,'' *Los Angeles Business Journal,* June 8, 1992, p. 5.

—Dave Mote
—update: Christina M. Stansell

Mail Boxes Etc.

6060 Cornerstone Court West
San Diego, California 92121-3795
U.S.A.
Telephone: (858) 455-8800
Fax: (858) 455-8961
Web site: http://www.mbe.com

Wholly Owned Subsidiary of U.S. Office Products Company
Incorporated: 1980
Employees: 300
Sales: $81.1 million (2000)
NAIC: 488991 Packing and Crating; 561431 Private Mail Centers

Mail Boxes Etc. is the world's largest franchise network of postal, business, and communications retail service centers. Nearly eight times larger than its nearest competitor, the Mail Boxes Etc. (MBE) system consists of about 4,300 franchise locations worldwide. The chain continues to grow at the brisk pace it established almost from its birth in 1980 and has master licenses for international franchise locations in 70 countries. From its origins as an alternative to the U.S. postal system for both sending and receiving, MBE has expanded its line of services to include mailbox rentals, packaging, shipping, copying, faxing, passport photos, office supplies, money transfers, computer workstation rental, and a wide range of other conveniences. The company's on-line business—www.mbebiz .com—caters to the small and home office market and offers an array of business services.

Company Origins

MBE was founded in 1980 by Herb Goffstein and Pat and Mimi Senn. The group was later joined by Anthony DeSio, a former aerospace executive whose resume included stints with Lockheed, General Electric, and Western Union. DeSio and his three partners envisioned an establishment at which people could conduct their postal business in an environment somewhat more agreeable than that of the typical U.S. Post Office—for a premium price, of course. They opened the first MBE store in Carlsbad, California, with an initial investment of $25,000 from each partner. Initially, the company's core business was mail box rental with 24-hour access. Among the other services offered were sales of postage stamps and wrapping and shipping of packages via independent delivery services such as Federal Express and United Parcel Service (UPS).

Franchising Sparks Growth in Early 1980s

Within a short time, there were three MBE outlets in operation. Funds for further expansion proved hard to come by, however. Since banks and venture capitalists failed to grasp the potential of the concept, DeSio and his partners turned to franchising to finance their company's expansion. The first MBE franchises were sold during the company's first year of operation and, by 1982, MBE was selling area franchises for multiple outlets. Despite the company's quick growth, squabbles arose between the partners. DeSio mortgaged his house and used his wife's engagement ring as collateral to secure nearly $900,000 in funds used to purchase controlling interest in the company in 1983.

It was not long before MBE began to evolve from a chain of surrogate post offices into a chain of surrogate offices for small business operators. Early on, DeSio realized that mail boxes and shipping made a pretty small hook on which to hang an entire franchise network. One of the first new services he added was sending and receiving faxes. From the beginning, an individual could pass an MBE postal box off as an office suite number on a business card or letterhead. Now that person was able to list the fax number of an MBE location as his or her own number. In addition, MBE could provide the cards, stationery, rubber stamps, and other business identification items that contained those numbers.

As the 1980s continued, MBE was able to take advantage of the explosion of home-based businesses in the United States. MBE outlets were able to provide tiny firms that could not afford their own support staffs or equipment with the kinds of services that larger companies had in-house. In 1984, the company formed a key partnership with the United Parcel Service (UPS). In 1986, DeSio took the company public, selling most of

Company Perspectives:

Mail Boxes Etc. strives to make business easier worldwide through its service and distribution network and by delivering personalized and convenient business solutions with world-class customer service. The company's core values include caring, honesty, fairness, integrity, trust, respect, commitment, and accountability.

the 51 percent of company stock he then owned and raising about $5 million in capital to fuel further expansion. That year, MBE earned $900,000 on sales of $4.6 million.

By 1987, there were more than 400 MBE franchise locations in 37 states. Service continued to be the company's main competitive edge over the U.S. Post Office. For one thing, MBE could receive packages for rental box customers, a service regular post office boxes did not provide. In addition to simply providing a wider array of services, MBE outlets were likely to be staffed by the franchiser, whose very livelihood depended on getting customers to come back. To do that, many operators offered such conveniences as allowing customers to check on their rental boxes by telephone. By 1988, MBE stores were in 43 states and numbered more than 700. It was one of the fastest-growing franchisors in the United States and nearing the head of the pack among nonfood franchisors. Company revenue had grown to $12.4 million by this time, with after-tax earnings reaching $1.85 million.

International Expansion in the Late 1980s

MBE began to foray into international markets in 1988. This was done by selling a master franchise for all of Canada to a company called Can-Mail Inc. for a licensing fee of $500,000, plus a share of the royalties it received from its Canadian franchisees. MBE was not the first American mail center chain to cross the border, however. A year earlier, Colorado-based Pak Mail Centers had opened a store in Canada. The fact that MBE was beaten into Canada by Pak Mail—a chain a fraction of MBE's size—reflected DeSio's conservative approach to financing. His aim was to expand quickly without sinking deeply into debt and without overburdening the parent company's management or corporate structure.

By 1990, the MBE chain was more than 1,200 outlets strong, compared with only about 230 for its nearest competitor, Pak Mail. Stores were located in Mexico and Japan by this time. The company continued to add new services to its line, including electronic tax filing at many locations. As the popularity of MBE and other retail postal centers grew, the company began to agitate for a better deal from the Postal Service and private carriers such as UPS and Federal Express based on the volume of business the centers were generating for the carriers. MBE finally broke through in 1990 with an overnight carrier called DHL Worldwide. In exchange for a discount that allowed MBE to charge customers the same rate as if they had gone to DHL directly, MBE began serving as official drop-off sites for DHL.

The addition of secretarial, answering, and other services made MBE even more of a one-stop business services center by the early 1990s. The company's success spawned a wave of new competitors, with names like Postal Annex Plus, The Packaging Store, and Mail 'N More, but MBE remained the clear leader in this emerging industry, with several times as many outlets as the next largest chain. As the national ''downsizing'' trend among corporations heated up, MBE was able to take advantage of the growing SOHO (small office/home office) market, which was composed to a large extent of former professional employees of shrinking companies.

Despite the growing range of services being offered at MBE stores, shipping services remained the company's core business. Whereas each outlet was able to emphasize its own strengths, it was its connection to the big shippers, especially UPS, that made MBE attractive to many potential franchisees, and franchise fees remained by far the most important source of revenue for the company. In 1991, franchise fees made up 27 percent of MBE's $25.7 million in revenue. That year the company's ongoing alliance with UPS was cemented when UPS purchased 9.5 percent of MBE's stock, with warrants that gave UPS the option of increasing its holdings to more than 17 percent over the following three years. The transaction was mutually beneficial. For MBE, it ensured that UPS would not set up its own retail network, as Federal Express had done, thereby depriving the chain of one of its biggest revenue sources. For UPS it provided a low-cost, wide-ranging distribution system that was already intact and fully operational.

As the 1990s continued, MBE took on even more roles in its attempt to become a provider of every business service imaginable. The MBE network soon began functioning as customer service or distribution centers for a wide variety of business equipment companies, which found it more economical to use MBE than to set up their own outlet systems. Among the companies that used the MBE chain in this way were Nintendo, Acer Computers, Xerox, Panasonic, Toshiba, and Hewlett-Packard. Another service the company began to experiment with around this time was airline ticket distribution. For fiscal 1992, MBE's revenue grew to $36 million, with the majority again coming from franchise fees, royalties, and the sale of supplies and equipment to franchisees. The franchises themselves, by this time numbering nearly 2,000, were generating a total of about $570 million in sales.

Continuing Growth in the Mid-1990s

By 1993, MBE was well-enough established on both the national and international levels that it was able to introduce its ''Big or Small. We Ship It All'' program, in which participating MBE stores had the capacity to ship just about any item to just about any destination in the world. MBE also forged an alliance with the Staples chain of office supply superstores, giving rise to the appearance of MBE ''boutique'' stores inside Staples outlets. Before the end of that year, there were more than 2,100 MBE Centers throughout the world, with more than 130 of them outside the United States. The chain was growing at the rate of about one store a day. Italy, France, the United Kingdom, Spain, Greece, and Turkey, to name just a few, were all home to MBE stores by the mid-1990s. MBE's international expansion was accomplished through the sale of master licenses, which gave a company the rights to subfranchise MBE stores for a whole country. The MBE concept was particularly appealing in

Key Dates:

1980: Mail Boxes Etc. is established and the first store opens in Carlsbad, California.
1982: The first area franchise is sold.
1983: Founder DeSio gains controlling interest in the firm.
1984: The company becomes partners with the United Parcel Service.
1986: The company goes public.
1988: MBE opens its first international outlet in Canada.
1990: More than 1,000 franchise locations operate worldwide.
1992: Revenues reach $36 million.
1993: The company launches ''Big or Small. We Ship it All'' shipping program.
1995: The company introduces first-ever national ad campaign, ''It's not what we do, it's how we do it.''
1997: U.S. Office Products acquires MBE.
1998: The company opens the 3,000th outlet in the United States.
1999: The company's on-line business center is launched.
2000: More than 4,000 outlets operate worldwide.

countries with historically poor mail service, since customers there were generally eager to skirt the existing national postal monopolies.

MBE reported revenue of $43.7 million for fiscal 1994, a moderate increase over the previous year. Around that time, the company launched its first-ever national advertising campaign, ''It's not what we do, it's how we do it.'' The campaign was supported by the creation on a trial basis of a National Media Fund, which derived its money from an additional 1.5 percent monthly charge to participating MBE Centers. Because of the program's success, the fund was made permanent in 1996, and MBE has maintained a strong national advertising presence since that initial campaign.

The company's international expansion continued to move quickly during the next couple years. In June 1995, MBE's 100th European location was opened in Paris, and by the year's end there were 327 centers operating outside the United States. By that time, the company had sold a total of 47 national licenses for foreign countries. Development remained strong in 1996 as well. Among the international areas for which master licenses were sold that year were Israel and South Africa. Italy became the second country outside the United States (following Canada) to open its 100th center. Domestically, 287 new MBE Centers were sold in 1996, as the company surged toward its goal of 5,000 centers by the turn of the century.

Market research indicated that one in five U.S. households had used MBE by 1996. By this time, the success of the MBE concept was clear even to the U.S. Post Office, which sought to win back some of its lost business by offering its own version of ''pack and ship'' service. This attempt at vertical integration by the Post Office met with resistance on the part of the private postal service industry, which felt that the Post Office was competing unfairly by using money from its first-class mail monopoly to subsidize its Pack and Ship operation. In addition, shippers UPS (which by this time owned 15 percent of MBE) and Federal Express, both major allies of the mail centers, were infuriated by the Post Office's use of their logos and images in ads that they called misleading. In spite of the Post Office's counterattack, MBE remained a strong leader in the industry.

New Management, New Ownership: 1996–97

In 1996, James H. Amos, Jr., joined the company. DeSio, recovering from quadruple-bypass surgery, named Amos as his predecessor and decided to sell the business. One year later, U.S. Office Products (USOP), a company catering to the SOHO market, acquired MBE. USOP, a firm that had spent the last three years acquiring nearly 200 companies, planned to use MBE's outlets to sell its office products and services. In a November 1997 issue of *Discount Store News,* Jon Ledecky, chairman and CEO of USOP, stated, ''We want to make Mail Boxes Etc. a one-stop shop for the small business person. Think about all the different things that we can provide.''

Under new leadership, MBE continued to grow rapidly. The firm developed a new marketing slogan, ''Making Business Easier. Worldwide'' and its 500th international outlet opened in Italy. In 1998, MBE began working with IBM Corp. and Infoseek Corp. to create MBE Online, an Internet site catering to small business owners. The new venture, officially launched in 1999 as www.mbebiz.com, offered many services designed to entice business owners to use MBE for all of their professional needs.

MBE also made a strategic move in 1998 by partnering with long-time competitor United States Postal Service. The two firms began to develop a program in which MBE outlets would offer postal products and services and eventually become U.S. Postal Service Authorized Retail Outlets. The company also made important strides in the Asian market by obtaining a master franchise license in Japan. By the end of this year, more than 3,000 MBE outlets were operating in the United States.

As e-commerce became increasingly popular in the late 1990s, MBE began to forge key relationships with web-based companies. A partnership was formed with popular web auction-house eBay and iShip.com in 1999 to provide shipping and delivery options to its members. The company also began utilizing a new point-of-sale computer system in its domestic outlets that would allow for the integration of e-commerce operations. MBE's franchise locations also received a new look as MBE 2000 was introduced to franchisers offering new in-store design and marketing tools.

Continued Growth in the New Millennium

MBE entered the new millennium with more than 4,000 outlets across the globe, making it two times the size of its next five competitors combined. The company continued to see strong growth in all aspects of its business interests. The firm's pilot program with the U.S. Postal Service expanded in markets across the United States and was well received by consumers. In May 2000, MBE and Innotrac Corp. announced their investment in Return.com, a full-service on-line return service that would allow consumers to return items purchased on-line or through catalogs to participating MBE outlets for packaging and shipping. The company also began its foray into Internet banking by teaming up with National InterBank and Juniper Financial. Under the terms of the partnership, bank customers were able to deposit checks at MBE locations.

While MBE continued to prosper, its parent USOP began to feel the financial pains of rapid expansion. In August 2000, the firm announced plans to spin off MBE. Its uncertain future did not hinder MBE expansion plans, however, and the company continued to pursue growth options. In January 2001, the firm landed master license agreements in the Dominican Republic and the Caribbean. MBE also continued to look for Internet partnerships in hopes of capitalizing on e-commerce growth. *Entrepreneur* magazine named MBE the number two franchiser in its Franchise 500 list, recognizing the firm as one of the fastest-growing business opportunities available. As its future with its parent company remained up in the air, MBE's success and growth appeared to remain a constant in the upcoming years.

Principal Competitors

Kinko's Inc.; Office Depot Inc.; U.S. Postal Service.

Further Reading

Adler, Carlye, ''The Man Who Launched 4,000 Businesses,'' *Fortune,* February 5, 2001, p. 180.

Benford, Noonie, and Diane Gage, ''Out of the Woods, into the Forest,'' *Venture,* August 1988, pp. 24–25.

Byrne, Harlan S., ''Mail Boxes Etc.: It Builds Earnings Through Rapid, Global Growth,'' *Barron's,* April 5, 1993, pp. 50–52.

''Call Me Usmail,'' *Economist,* August 20, 1988, p. 59.

Gendron, George, ''A Sweet Deal,'' *Inc.,* March 1991, p. 12.

Hoover, Kent, ''Postal Service Expands Mail Boxes Etc. Program,'' *Orlando Business Journal,* February 18, 2000, p. 13.

McLeod, John A., ''Consumers Pay More But Get More at Private Postal Centers,'' *Marketing News,* October 1, 1990, p. 8.

Page, Paul, ''Retail Delivery Outlets Decry New Move by 'Customer-Friendly' Postal Service,'' *Traffic World,* June 3, 1996, p. 26.

''Reinventing the Post Office,'' *Fortune,* January 19, 1987, p. 8.

Rodrigues, Tanya, ''Promotion Ties MBE Shipping to eBay Auctions,'' *San Diego Business Journal,* November 13, 2000, p. 33.

Reosti, John, ''Banking Services Lure Mail Boxes Etc. Chain,'' *American Banker,* October 6, 2000, p. 1.

Schlax, Julie, ''Rain, Sleet, Snow and Franchising,'' *Forbes,* November 26, 1990, p. 224.

Tannenbaum, Jeffrey A., ''Mail Boxes Etc. Delivers Profits But Not to Everyone,'' *Wall Street Journal,* October 13, 1993, p. B2.

Troy, Mike, ''Growing USOP to Acquire Mail Boxes,'' *Discount Store News,* November 3, 1997, p. 6(2).

Zion, Lee, ''Mail Boxes Etc. Predicts Expansive Growth in 2000,'' *San Diego Business Journal,* March 20, 2000, p. 28.

——, ''Stamp-Edge to the Top,'' *San Diego Business Journal,* February 5, 2001, p. 41.

—Robert R. Jacobson
—update: Christina M. Stansell

Maple Leaf Foods Inc.

30 St. Clair Avenue West, Suite 1500
Toronto, Ontario M4V 3A2
Canada
Telephone: (416) 926-2000
Fax: (416) 926-2018
Web site: http://www.mapleleaf.ca

Public Company
Incorporated: 1995
Employees: 13,000
Sales: C$3.94 billion ($2.63 billion)(2000)
Stock Exchanges: Toronto
Ticker Symbol: MFI
NAIC: 31111 Animal Food Manufacturing; 31101 Manufacturing Lard; 3116 Meat Product Manufacturing; 31161 Animal Slaughtering and Processing; 311614 Rendering and Meat Processing from Carcasses; 311615 Poultry Processing, 31181 Bread and Bakery Product Manufacturing

Maple Leaf Foods Inc. is Canada's largest food processor and is one of Canada's largest rendering operations. The company employs more than 13,000 people at operations across Canada, in the United States, Europe, and Asia. Maple Leaf Foods produces fresh and processed pork and poultry products for retail and wholesale sales, as well as pet and livestock foods. The company also produces frozen dough for bakers and fresh and frozen baked goods and fresh pasta and pasta sauces.

The Early Years: Mergers and Acquisitions

Maple Leaf's origins stem back to 1836, and its history covers more than a century of mergers and acquisitions. The completion of the Welland Canal in 1833 initiated the beginning of industrial-scale milling in Canada. In 1896, Grantham Mills, the forerunner of Maple Leaf Mills Limited, was built in St. Catherines, Ontario. The Maple Leaf Brand first appeared in 1898.

In 1901, Grantham Mills and Thorold Mills merged to form the Hedley Shaw Milling Company. The Maple Leaf Mills Company was incorporated under the Dominion of Canada letters patent in 1904. In 1907, the Maple Leaf Flour Mills Company acquired the Hedley Shaw Milling Company and Grantham Mills, and the Maple Leaf Milling Company Limited was formed to take over the assets of the Maple Leaf Flour Milling Company. The Canada Bread Company Limited—later to play a major role in Maple Leaf's History—was founded in 1911 through the amalgamation of five companies.

The 1920s were a time of consolidation for Canadian meat packers who, increasingly, were relying on the export market to survive. In the latter years of the 19th century, miners and settlers had provided an expanding market for packers, but this demand leveled off around the turn of the century. However, worldwide demand for meat increased, and Canadian production increased correspondingly. Meat production grew yet again to meet the demand created during World War I. Unfortunately, at war's end, the demand for Canadian meat dropped when Canada was cut off from the European Market. Demand dropped again in 1921 when the United States imposed a tariff on Canadian beef. Within a few years, Canada was facing severe competition for the market in the United States from such countries as Argentina and Australia. The decreased demand for Canadian meat lead to a decrease in the number of meat-processing plants in the country.

Meanwhile, the Harris Abattoir Company of Toronto had succeeded during the 1920s by lowering production costs. In 1927, Canada Packers Limited was formed as a holding company when Harris purchased Gunns Limited and Canadian Packing Company Limited and then merged with William Davies Limited. J. Stanley McLean, secretary-treasurer of the Harris Abattoir Company McLean became the first president of Canada Packers Limited and held the post for 30 years. Canada Packers realized a profit of more than C$1 million during its first year of operation.

After the merger, the four companies that made up Canada Packers remained as separate operating units and continued to compete with each other until the Great Depression forced a change in their operations. Meat prices were high, and a drought in the prairies resulted in high unemployment and a decreased demand for meat. The William Davies Toronto plant closed in

Company Perspectives:

The Maple Leaf Foods management team is committed to a vision of becoming a global leader in the pork and poultry value chains, and a North American leader in the bakery business.

1931, and the four companies formed a single company in 1932. By 1933, operating expenses had been cut by C$7 million annually.

The company revived during the mid-1930s, largely due to the Ottawa Agreements that allowed Canadian packers to export 280 million pounds of bacon a year to England. At the same time that production was increasing for the meat-packing side of the business, the by-product division began to sell a mixture of scraps as a feed concentrate for animal food. This was a new venture and one that was to prove extremely profitable. Animal feed consistently remained a reliable division of the company.

Canada Packers began expanding in 1936 with the building of a meat-processing plant in Alberta and the acquisition of a tannery in Ontario. In 1938, the company opened an additional packing house and renovated other plants. The capital investment between 1935 and 1938 came to more than C$2.5 million.

During World War II, Canada continued to supply meat to England, doubling the export of bacon. Despite a labor shortage, the number of people employed by Canada Packers doubled to more than 11,000. The war years and those that followed heralded two significant events for Canada Packers. First, driven by a need for increased efficiency during wartime, the company established a research laboratory, which lead them into the production of synthetic vitamins, gelatin, synthetic detergents, and dairy products. By 1946, the chemical application of animal by-products was playing such a significant role that it was awarded the status of a separate division.

Second, in 1943 and 1944, workers at Canada Packers were organized by the United Packinghouse Works of America, later to become the Canadian Food and Allied Workers Union. This event was to have an impact on earnings for years to come. In 1947, a nationwide strike involved 16,000 meat packing workers across the country. Canada Packers negotiated new contracts two months later.

Anticipating a recession, Canada Packers stepped up its diversification efforts. The expected recession, however, did not materialize. Population growth coupled with an era of prosperity led to an increased demand for meat and meat products. The research laboratory began to focus on improved production methods, and automated slaughtering operations replaced the manual process. Similarly, the company applied new technology to the mass production of poultry. Canada Packers' sales were greater than those of its two closest competitors combined.

In the 1950s, per capita consumption of poultry doubled and continued to increase in each decade. Through investments, acquisitions, and the development of a feather-cleaning company, Canada Packers began to expand its operations in the poultry industry. In 1954, William McLean became president of the company.

In 1955, the company purchased two packers, initiating a dispute with the Restrictive Trade Commission. However, Canada Packers was able to make the case that industry-wide competition had increased and that the purchase would have no restraining effect.

Also in the 1950s, Canada Packers reorganized its many interests into separate divisions—feed and fertilizer, consumer products, and canned and frozen vegetables. By 1958, only 55 percent of sales were from meat.

Dramatic Changes in the 1960s–70s

In 1961, Maple Leaf Mills Limited was officially formed from the amalgamation of the Maple Leaf Milling Company Limited, Toronto Elevators Limited, and Purity Flour Mills Limited. Maple Leaf Mills Limited grew to be a prominent force in the production and distribution of flour-based products in Canada.

Withing Canada Packers, expansion and diversification continued. The company built two poultry plants in New Brunswick and Quebec, expanded operations in Ontario and Manitoba, and purchased a plant in Alberta. By 1963, livestock production accounted for only 36 percent of the company's assets.

The 1960s brought about the most dramatic changes that Canada Packers had seen to date. International distribution became more commonplace, and production became more specialized. North American beef was spending more time in transit than any other meat, due to the specialized processes of raising and producing beef. During this decade, Canada Packers created the largest private-food research facility in Canada, including new data processing centers in Edmonton, Winnipeg, Toronto, and Montreal. Also, Canada Packers sold its fertilizer sector, and the feed operation became known as the Shur-Gain division.

The 1960s were a time of international expansion. Canada Packers purchased meat packers in England, West Germany, and Australia. It set up trading companies in London and Hamburg and increased trading operations with the United States and Southeast Asia. At the end of the decade, exports accounted for C$145 million, or 16.5 percent of sales.

Labor disputes arose again, with a national strike in 1966 that hit Canada Packers the hardest of all the packing companies. A second strike followed in 1969. The strikes had an impact on earnings, but Canada Packers continued to increase capital spending throughout the 1970s.

In this decade, the meat packer expanded its facilities at a cost of C$137 million and purchased two additional Australian meat processors. The subsidiaries did not perform well for several years, but were expected to ultimately fill the growing demand in Asia.

Canada Packers continued to diversify during the 1970s. It separated the management of its meat packing from its other food-production groups. The fruit and vegetable segment was

Key Dates:

1898: The Maple Leaf Brand first appears.
1904: Maple Leaf Flour Mills Company Limited is incorporated.
1907: The Maple Leaf Flour Mills Company acquires the Hedley Shaw Milling Company and Grantham Mills.
1910: The Maple Leaf Milling Company Limited is formed to take over the assets of the Maple Leaf Flour Milling Company.
1911: The Canada Bread Company Limited is founded.
1927: Canada Packers Limited is formed through a merger of other companies.
1961: Maple Leaf Mills Limited is formed from the amalgamation of the Maple Leaf Milling Company Limited, Toronto Elevators Limited, and Purity Flour Mills Limited.
1990: Maple Leaf Mills and Canada Packers merge to form Maple Leaf Foods.
1995: McCain Capital Corporation and the Ontario Teachers Pension Plan Board acquire controlling interest.
1997: Maple Leaf Foods divests the last of its flour-milling operations.
1999: Company establishes a leadership academy in partnership with the Richard Ivey School of Business.

given division status in 1970, poultry in 1971, and edible oils and dairy in 1975. In 1975, Harris Laboratories was established to develop pharmaceuticals for human use. This enhanced the operations of the chemical division. The division also created MTC Pharmaceuticals for the veterinary-product industry.

Although the economic climate was not the best during this decade, Canada Packers continued to maintain acceptable earnings. The nonfood sector was the only one to show significant increases in the early 1970s. Animal feeds grew steadily, but the meat division was experiencing an earnings drain.

In 1978, Valentine N. Stock became president of Canada Packers. By the time of his death in 1987, the company had experienced a continued decline in beef demand and completed a ten-year consolidation. Stock turned Canada Packers towards the more profitable areas of fish farming, processed foods, salad oils, and pharmaceuticals.

1979 was a bad year for food packers in Canada. Costs increased and a seven-week labor dispute affected the industry, closing some plants. At the same time, McCain Foods, Canada Packers' major competitor, increased its holdings in Canada Packers to 10.3 percent. Fearing a takeover, Canada Packers repurchased 3.5 percent of its shares. No takeover occurred.

Canada Packers strengthened its nonfood exports when it acquired Delmar Chemicals Limited for C$18.2 million. Delmar joined the existing pharmaceutical division. Also in 1979, the Ontario government gave Canada Packers a C$4 million grant to construct a canola processing plant.

As the decade came to a close, profit margins were less than 1 percent for the third year in a row. Sales values had increased, adding to higher-cost inventories. Because the company had C$34.7 million in long-term debt, it grew through acquisitions and through higher profit margins through packaged meats. As consumer demand rose for convenience foods, meat processing was the only growth area.

The Troubled 1980s

For a variety of economic reasons, the 1980s were the most difficult time for the company since 1927. Thanks to geographic and product diversification, Canada Packers was able to withstand the serious blow to its beef business that occurred during this decade.

The year 1981 looked promising—profits had reached a record C$30 million. However, the industry is cyclical. Pork operations were disappointing, carcass prices rose, consumer demand lowered, and industry competition eroded earnings.

In 1983, scandal touched Canada Packers when the Canadian government investigated five companies, including Canada Packers, for price fixing. Although some companies pleaded guilty, Canada Packers was eventually exonerated.

In that same year, profits plunged, while sales continued to grow. Expenses associated with plant closings, poor performances in fresh meat operations, and foreign subsidiaries eroded the bottom line. Processed meat remained profitable, but the packing house division performed the worst in its history. Canada Packers responded by cutting hundreds of jobs in the fresh meat division and earmarking C$50 million for structural improvements in the profitable areas.

Surprisingly, nonfood products showed a profit decrease in 1983. The company realized that meats were its core products. Despite fiercely competitive profit margins, meat realized a proven cash flow.

Another labor strike occurred in 1984. Involving 3,700 employees in the company's 12 plants, the labor action cost the company C$7.5 million. The strike prevented the Maple Leaf Brand from appearing in retail markets and effectively strengthened the competitor's products. Earnings declined.

Between 1984 and 1985, the company undertook the largest and most costly reorganization of its history. Canada Packers sold a number of unprofitable businesses, while purchasing meat plants and oil refineries. Over the next four years, earnings climbed at record rates to more than C$38 million. A joint venture with SEA Farm of Norway brought the company into fish farming. By decade's end, Canada Packers had fish production facilities on both coasts and was optimistic about the future of its fish farming activities.

Another strike loomed in 1986 but was prevented by reducing the scope of nationwide bargaining. The company managed to keep negotiations on a provincial and single-plant level. Two years after Valentine Stock's death in 1987, A. Roger Perretti became CEO. Perretti planned further acquisitions beyond the meat industry, and as Canada Packers approached the new decade it had exited the beef businesses and was focusing on pork and poultry.

The 1990s: Maple Leaf Foods, Inc.

An economic recession was on its way. Market sluggishness contributed to a drop in net income to C$12.59 million from sales of over C$3 billion. To counteract these losses, the company again reorganized. The majority owner, Hillsdown Holdings, consolidated its consumer-foods division by closing plants and updating existing equipment. Hillsdown merged Canada Packers with Maple Leaf Mills to form Maple Leaf Foods, Inc. in 1990. Nonperforming divisions were closed, and the company entered a period of top-to-bottom reorganizing.

When the North American Free Trade Agreement (NAFTA) was signed with the United States, Maple Leaf increased its focus on international operations. The company followed a strategy termed ''in-filling''—buying strategically placed companies that fill holes in the core business of processed meats and baked goods. By 1994, Maple Leaf generated 8 percent of its sales from the United States, while subsidiaries in Britain, Germany, and Japan were showing promising results.

Margins were lean during the early 1990s, but the company continued to show a profit and maintained a market share of almost half of all Canadian meat packing. Despite sluggish sales, the company realized profits through cost cutting.

In 1995, the McCain Capital Corporation and the Ontario Teachers Pension Plan Board acquired controlling interest in the company from Hillsdown PLC.

Following a contentious fight for control of the family business (Maple Leaf's rival, McCain Foods), Wallace McCain was expelled from joint command of the family empire, but remained as vice-chairman. Stating he saw no conflict of interest in the arrangement, McCain then launched a billion-dollar debt-propelled bid for Maple Leaf Foods. Backed by the Ontario Teachers Pension Plan Board, the McCain bid offered a combined stock-and-cash offer for Maple Leaf. In a deal referred to as a leveraged buyout, Maple Leaf Foods would go from holding over C$100 million in cash to owing about C$575 million in long-term bank debt. The British owned Hillsdown PLC announced its interest in selling its 56 percent of shares, hoping to raise cash for European investments. Hillsdown stated it would sell to McCain if no better offers came along. After looking fruitlessly for better offers, Maple Leaf's shareholders voted to accept Wallace McCain's takeover bid.

Wallace McCain assumed the position of chief executive officer of Maple Leaf. The CEO believed that he could wring more profits from Maple Leaf Foods than had previously been realized. His strategy was to turn Maple Leaf into a lean, low-cost maker of high-value top market foods.

Richard Foot, writing for Chatham Newspapers, quoted Julian Den Tandt of the Ontario Pork Board as saying, ''The first thing we saw when the McCains took over Maple Leaf was a very strong switch from a production-driven company to a market-driven company.''

Michael McCain succeeded his father as CEO. Under the McCains's leadership, the company continued to expand in the United States. Initiating a strategic thrust into the specialty bread-and-roll market in the United States, Maple Leaf built a C$30-million bakery in Virginia, bought bakeries in New Jersey and California, and purchased a bagel plant in Brooklyn, New York. Michael McCain indicated that the bakery business in the United States was to be the most significant growth area.

In 1997, following a strategy of focusing on core business categories, Maple Leaf divested the last of its flour-milling operations. The bakery products group remains, including majority ownership in the Canada Bread Company and Maple Leaf Bakery USA.

McCain's strategy of keeping profits high by reducing operating expenses lent to a period of bitter labor disputes. In 1997, the workers at Gainers, a 91-year old slaughtering plant in Edmonton, went on strike. Michael McCain followed through on his promise to shut the doors of the old plant if a strike occurred, stating his intent to build a massive new production complex in Brandon, Manitoba. About the same time, two meat-cutting plants in Ontario struck, while 200 butchers in Saskatchewan were locked out over a wage and benefit dispute.

Also in 1997, McCain attempted a hostile takeover bid to gain control of rival company, the Schneider Corporation. In 1998, Maple Leaf Foods formally abandoned its bid and announced an intent to sell its controlling stake in the Ontario company to Smithfield, a hog producer in the United States. Later, in 2001, Maple Leaf acquired Schneider's fresh pork operations in Manitoba.

1998 proved to be Maple Leaf's worst year since the McCain takeover. Weak earnings in the bread division, combined with labor disputes at Maple Leaf Meats and expenses associated with firing staff, led to the worst annual performance since 1995. However, in May of 1999, the shareholders were told that the company was back on track, posting its best first-quarter profit and announcing the sale of a coffee shop chain. CFO Tom Muir said that Country Style operations had shown consistent profitability, but did not fit in with Maple Leaf's core business strategy.

Maple Leaf initiated efforts to recruit, train, and motivate managers and others with executive capabilities. In 1999, it launched the Maple Leaf Leadership Academy, conducted in alliance with the Richard Ivey School of Business.

Nevertheless, in 2000, profits fell to C$36.8 million compared to C$77.2 million in 1999. McCain attributed the reduction to the decline in the pork business itself. The Brandon plant, opened in 1999, lost C$20 million in the first quarter of 2000, but was expected to show a profit once it passed the startup stage.

Faced with considerable debt, a long history of labor disputes, and in a slow economic market, Maple Leaf faced potentially tough years. However, some divisions remained profitable, and once the operating costs of the Brandon plant were covered, the company profited from this area.

Principal Subsidiaries

Canada Bread Company Ltd. (68%); Maple Leaf Bakery (U.S.A.).

Principal Operating Units

The Meat Products Group; The Bakery Products Group; The Agribusiness Group.

Principal Divisions

Maple Leaf Pork; Maple Leaf Consumer Foods; Maple Leaf Poultry; Maple Leaf Foods International; Shur-Gain; Landmark Feeds; Rothsay Rendering.

Principal Competitors

ConAgra Foods, IBP, Tyson Foods.

Further Reading

Bertin, Oliver, "Maple Leaf Looks at Expansion," *Globe & Mail,* May 21, 1992.

——, "Maple Leaf Seeks Major Food Role," *Globe & Mail,* April 7, 1992, p. B3.

——, "Meat Packers Abandon Plan," *Globe & Mail,* December 24, 1992, p. B5.

——, "No Meat, No $700,000, Maple Leaf Lament," *Globe & Mail,* February 11, 1995, pp. B1, B4.

——, "President to Leave Maple Leaf," *Globe & Mail,* June 18, 1993.

Bourette, Susan, "Executive Predicts Second Bid for Maple Leaf," *Globe & Mail,* April 6, 1995.

——, "Maple Leaf Backs McCain bid," *Globe & Mail,* April 8, 1995, pp. B1, B2.

——, "Maple Leaf Boosts Bid for Schneider," *Globe & Mail,* December 13, 1997.

——, "McCain Takes Helm at Maple Leaf," *Globe & Mail,* April 20, 1995.

Foot, Richard, "Young McCain Faces New Kind of Fight," *Vancouver Sun,* December 12, 1997.

Heinrich, Kim, "Maple Leaf Takeover New Incentive for Bakery," *Vancouver Sun,* July 14, 1992, p. D2.

Jang, Brent, "Stage Set for Strike at Maple Leaf," *Globe & Mail,* August 28, 1997.

Laghi, Brian, "When the Maple Leaf Isn't Forever," *Globe & Mail,* December 5, 1997.

"Maple Leaf Says It's Back on Profit Track," *Vancouver Sun,* May 4, 1999, p. D4.

"Michael McCain to Add Title of Chief Executive at Maple Leaf Foods," *Vancouver Sun,* September 15, 1998.

Saunders, John, "Wallace McCain Foresees Maple Leaf as Grade A Prize," *Globe & Mail,* March 5, 1995, p. B1.

——, "Wallace McCain Seeks New Food Empire," *Globe & Mail,* March 7, 1995.

"Secret Talks Preceded Maple Leaf Strike," *Globe & Mail,* December 4, 1997.

Shecter, Barbara, "Maple Leaf Farms Out Bacon Production," *Financial Post,* October 8, 1997.

Valorzi, John, "Maple Leaf Seen Bound for Strike," *Globe & Mail,* November 12, 1997.

—June Campbell

M A Y O R S™

Mayor's Jewelers, Inc.

14051 Northwest 14th Street
Sunrise, Florida 33323
U.S.A.
Telephone: (954) 846-2709
Fax: (954) 846-2887
Web site: http://www.mayors.com

Public Company
Incorporated: 1983 as Jan Bell Marketing, Inc.
Employees: 3,295
Sales: $181.3 million
Stock Exchanges: American
Ticker Symbol: MYR
NAIC: 421940 Jewelry, Watch, Precious Stones, and Precious Metal Wholesalers

Mayor's Jewelers, Inc. is a chain of luxury jewelry stores that has become the name of a retooled corporation formerly known as Jan Bell Marketing, Inc. After independently running the full-service jewelry departments in 469 Sam's Clubs warehouse stores, which accounted for approximately 60 percent of its business, Jan Bell has been forced to alter its business plan. The 1998 acquisition of Mayor's provided Jan Bell with the opportunity to transform itself from a discount mass-market jewelry operation into a national retailer of luxury jewelry and timepieces. To better reflect its new emphasis, Jan Bell decided to adopt the name of Mayor's Jewelry. Amid uncertainty about its future success, the Sunrise, Florida company also has come under pressure from disgruntled shareholders, who have urged management to consider selling the business.

Establishing Jan Bell in 1983

Jan Bell was founded in Fort Lauderdale, Florida, in 1983 by Alan H. Lipton and Isaac Arguetty. The two men named the company after their wives. Jan Bell found a niche in jewelry by catering to the fast-growing wholesale membership club chains, and it quickly gained a dominant share of the business. Whereas retail jewelers generally marked up items by 200 percent, Jan Bell marked up just 17 percent to 20 percent. By manufacturing some jewelry and buying direct from other makers, eliminating middlemen to be more efficient, Jan Bell was able to offer high-quality merchandise at a reasonable price. The selection was somewhat limited, in keeping with the wholesale club philosophy. Aided by computerized inventory control, Jan Bell focused on high volume and quick turnover to control expenses.

Looking to fuel expansion, in August 1987 Jan Bell made an initial public offering of its stock and began trading on the American Stock Exchange. As wholesale clubs expanded their outlets by approximately 20 percent in 1987, Jan Bell prospered in kind. It added a line of watches to the gold and diamonds that had been its mainstay and made plans to sell through direct-mail marketing. In the late 1980s the company's earnings grew at a rate of 86 percent per year. After posting revenues of $46.7 million in 1986, Jan Bell grew to $72.5 million in 1987 and $120 million in 1988. With the wholesale clubs anticipating even further growth, investors fell in love with Jan Bell.

In 1988 Jan Bell enjoyed the fourth highest gain on the American Stock Exchange. It continued its climb in 1989, reaching more than $30 per share. From late 1987 until September 1989, Jan Bell's stock grew by an impressive 427 percent. The company completed its third secondary offering in October 1989, at which point several of its executives sold a number of shares, thus locking in some profit. The stock stalled, but it did not slip radically. Nevertheless, some analysts began to express doubts about Jan Bell. Its stock was trading at a level that was 38 times its earnings, which was considered far too high, especially with worries of a recession on the horizon. Furthermore, the company was overly dependent on the wholesale clubs and would likely begin to face stiffer competition in the jewelry segment. Management, however, expressed continued confidence in the company's long-term prospects and undertook initiatives to support that growth. In May 1990 Jan Bell acquired a controlling interest in watch distributor Big Ben '90 for $10 million. The deal was intended to assure Jan Bell of an adequate supply of watches as well as providing personnel with expertise in the wholesale watch business. Also in 1990 Jan Bell spent $3 million to buy Exclusive Diamonds International Ltd.

Despite the company's optimism and acquisitions, Jan Bell suffered a reversal of fortune in 1990. Two of the wholesale clubs, Price Club and Costco, announced in March of that year

Company Perspectives:

The Mayors experience is consistent at each store, from the elegant setting to the unparalleled client service. With deep green italian marble and plush carpeting, the décor of Mayors' spacious stores is true to its heritage while adopting a contemporary luxurious feel. For privacy and comfort, most of the stores also have spacious VIP lounges and dedicated bridal boutiques.

that they were either reconsidering the jewelry business or intended to set up their own buying and distribution operation. Jan Bell faced the prospect of losing $40 million to $50 million in sales after generating $181.3 million in revenues for 1989. The reaction from investors was harsh. From a high of $26 per share earlier in the year, Jan Bell's stock quickly tumbled to $6. The company made efforts to diversify its customer base, adding such retailers as Charming Shoppes, and thereby recovered a good portion of its stock's value. By June 1992 Jan Bell again traded above the $14 level. Rather than just acting as a jewelry wholesaler to the wholesale clubs, with its merchandise competing against others, Jan Bell began looking to lease space to sell the merchandise itself. This effort culminated in a May 1993 deal with Sam's Clubs that would restore a great deal of lost luster for Jan Bell. Sam's agreed not to buy jewelry from other sources and Jan Bell no longer had to reserve 20 percent of its counter space for competitors. Also under the terms of the deal, Jan Bell provided its own sales staff, agreed to buy out Sam's existing jewelry inventory, and paid Sam's $7 million up front and an annual tenancy fee of 9 percent of net sales. As Jan Bell made the transition to retailer, Sam's acquired 117 Pace locations in November 1993, adding significantly to the number of Sam's outlets that would have to be served.

Bringing in Retail Experience in 1994

In 1994 Jan Bell brought in a management team with more retail experience. First, it hired Peter Hayes to serve as president and chief operating officer. Hayes had almost 20 years of senior management experience in the discount store industry. After 16 years with Hills, he became the president and chief operating officer at Family Dollar before joining Jan Bell. Lipton, who had been the company's chief executive officer since 1987, then stepped down. He became co-chairman of the board along with Arguetty, who returned to the company after three years with Delheim and Worchester PLC, an international finance company. Lipton was replaced by Joseph Pennacchio, whose background centered around New York City department stores. He spent eight years at Macy's, working his way up to Merchandise Vice-President. He then became Senior Vice-President of Merchandising for the Abraham & Straus Division in Brooklyn before eventually becoming president of Jordan Marsh in 1992.

The transition from jewelry wholesaler to jewelry retailer proved difficult for Pennacchio and Jan Bell. Although operating more than 400 Sam's jewelry counters was potentially lucrative, which attracted renewed interest in the company's stock, it also came with complications. Jan Bell was now extremely reliant on the Sam's franchise, deriving from it about 85 percent of its business, but it was not allowed to advertise its jewelry counters. The company also had difficulty selling high-margin items, jewelry costing more than $1,000, because of Sam's policy of accepting only Discover among major credit cards. Jan Bell began to post a string of unprofitable quarters, and again investors were disappointed, driving down the price of the company's stock to less than $3 per share. By the end of 1995 the company saw a number of departures in management: Hayes, plus the chief financial officer and an investor relations executive. One of the founders, Lipton, also resigned, leaving Arguetty as chairman.

Pennacchio undertook a number of cost-cutting measures to place Jan Bell on firmer footing. He closed the company's manufacturing operations in Florida, relying on outsourcing to Israel, and even considered selling off the headquarters building and moving into the nearby warehouse and distribution center. In a move that was projected to save $10 million, he laid off 200 workers. He also closed down the company's wholesale operations, which were mostly devoted to selling watches. After acquiring Big Ben, Jan Bell experienced significant increases in its watch business, only to have sales fall off in 1993 and 1994. By the time it closed the division, the company estimated that it lost money on each watch it sold. Pennacchio also had difficulties with debt payment. After four months of unsuccessful negotiations with note holders, the company expressed publicly that there were doubts about the company's ability to continue as a going concern. Pennacchio insisted that the company was never close to bankruptcy, and in June 1995 he reached an agreement with creditors.

Pennacchio considered the task of turning around Jan Bell as a three- to five-year effort. He talked about expanding overseas, establishing a Jan Bell credit card, as well as opening ''Jewelry Depots'' and outlet stores. He also expressed a desire to start a direct-mail operation, a possibility that Jan Bell executives had considered since the late 1980s. In November 1995, the company opened its first jewelry depot in Framingham, Massachusetts, followed by two more units in Worchester, Massachusetts, and Vero Beach, Florida. After the company posted a $74.7 million loss for 1995, however, Pennacchio would not enjoy the luxury of three years at the helm, let alone five. In May 1996 his employment was terminated and Arquetty now took over as chief executive officer.

When Arquetty stepped in, Jan Bell was more dependent on Sam's than ever. Some 91 percent of sales came from the Sam's franchise. Approximately 8 percent was wholesale revenues from department stores, supermarkets, discount stores, and jewelry chains. Only 1 percent of sales, or $2.5 million, was realized from the three Jewelry Depots owned directly by Jan Bell. Overall, the company lost as much money in the previous four years as it had made in all the years prior to that. Nevertheless, the company was worth more than its stock price, because the value of its assets was much higher than the company's capitalization. In October 1996 Miami-based Ocean Reef Management Inc. offered $100 million for the company, but nothing ever materialized from the proposal.

Acquiring Mayor's Jewelers in 1998

Jan Bell lost another $3.3 million in 1996 before finally returning to profitability in 1997 when it earned $915,000. Late in 1996 Jan Bell expanded its efforts to diversify its retail operations

Key Dates:

1910: Mayor's Jewelry is established in Cincinnati, Ohio.
1937: Mayor's relocates to Miami, Florida.
1983: Jan Bell Marketing is incorporated.
1987: Jan Bell makes public offering of stock.
1983: Jan Bell signs franchise agreement with Sam's Clubs.
1998: Jan Bell acquires Mayor's.
1999: Sam's decides not to renew agreement; Jan Bell changes its name to Mayor's Jewelers.

by acquiring three Manhattan Diamond outlets located in shopping malls, but early in 1997 it also closed its two Massachusetts Jewelry Depots, which had not been performing up to expectations. Overall, the company appeared to have finally succeeded in making the transition from wholesale to retail. Rather than continuing to expand into the discount market, Jan Bell made a radical shift in direction in 1998 when it acquired the 24 luxury stores of Mayor's Jewelers for $92.8 million.

The third generation, family-run Mayor's was originally founded in Cincinnati in 1910 by Samuel Mayor Getz. Due to health concerns, Getz moved his family and business to Florida, opening a jewelry store in downtown Miami. His son, Irving Getz, began working at the store after returning from service during World War II, and he took over the business in 1947. In the 1960s he would open additional Mayor's stores in area shopping malls. Irving's son, Samuel A. Getz, began working with the company full-time in 1980, as Mayor's continued to add to its presence in South Florida. In 1990 Mayor's was looking to fuel greater expansion by making an initial public offering of its stock, but the IPO was canceled when the stock market fell drastically after Iraq invaded Kuwait. Mayor's would add no new stores until a 1994 merger with Atlanta-based Maier & Berkele, founded in the late 1800s, which brought four units located in the Atlanta metropolitan area. By 1997 Mayor's had 25 stores located in Florida and Atlanta, generating $142.2 million in sales, and ranking as the 28th largest jewelry retailer in the country. Other than Tiffany, there were no true national chains of upscale jewelry stores, so that the acquisition of Mayor's was the chance for Jan Bell to expand into an open niche. A year later, however, that opportunity would become almost a necessity.

The concession agreement between Jan Bell and Sam's was scheduled to expire in February 2001, and the parties entered into talks to negotiate an extension. A deal seemed likely, but Sam's surprised both Jan Bell management and investors when it announced in April 1999 that it would discontinue its relationship with Jan Bell in favor of taking over the jewelry franchise itself. With Sam's accounting for approximately 60 percent of its revenues, Jan Bell had less than two years to make up for that loss as well as sell off inventory and close up its hundreds of Sam's operations. Management tried to put on a good face, but clearly the task was daunting. Jan Bell had made some forays in selling jewelry via the internet, which accounted for less than $500,000 in sales in 1999, but the only real near-term possibility of replacing the revenues from Sam's was in an accelerated expansion of Mayor's.

Jan Bell added ten stores to its Mayor's chain in 2000, for a total of 36 located in Florida, Georgia, Virginia, Illinois, Texas, California, Nevada, and Michigan. Jan Bell also decided in 2000 to change its name to Mayor's Jewelers, a move that would not only reflect the company's change of focus but also its commitment to the luxury jewelry business. Pursuing that business on a national level, however, was not without complications. For instance, Mayor's had regional distribution agreements on a number of items, such as new Rolex watches, which it could only sell in Florida and Georgia. Moreover, other companies also sought to establish national chains of luxury jewelry stores, including Tiffany; Cartier; Zales's upscale division of Bailey, Banks & Biddle; and a concept from the Neiman Marcus department stores called The Galleries of Neiman Marcus. Upscale jewelry sales, fueled by aging baby boomers, were driving the expansion. Unlike in other industries, however, local mom-and-pop jewelry stores were quite viable competitors. Not only were the independents established in their territory with local name recognition that could rival a Tiffany, the chains' ability to use volume buying power to offer low prices brought little advantage in the luxury jewelry business, where price was not as important as the unique nature of the piece being purchased. Mayor's had a prestigious reputation in Florida, and Maier & Berkele in Atlanta, but transplanting it to new regions would not come easily.

In 2001 Mayor's closed its Sam's operations and continued to pursue its luxury jewelry business. The company came under fire from unhappy shareholders, in particular a former Jan Bell executive named Eliahu Ben-Schmuel who owned 9.56 percent of Mayor's stock, an amount that made him the company's second largest shareholder. He told the press that he was worried that Mayor's rapid expansion would result in debilitating debt. He also argued that the company lacked the proper personnel to guide such an expansion in luxury retail and that it should "sell to a big retailer who has big pockets to take it to the next stage." In March 2001 the company also would lose an experienced executive in Samuel A. Getz, who had continued to serve as president after Jan Bell acquired the company. A news release maintained that Getz resigned to pursue "other business interests and investments," but he did agree to act as a consultant to Mayor's for 18 months. That period of time would likely reveal the prospects for the company's success on a national basis, or perhaps even see a change in ownership. In April 2001, management hired New York-based investment bank TM Capital Corp. to help the company enhance stockholder value by either selling the business or merging it with another company.

Principal Subsidiaries

Ultimate Fine Jewelry and Watches, Inc.; JBM Retail Company; Regal Diamonds International, Ltd.; Exclusive Diamonds International, Ltd.; Mayor's Jewelers, Inc.

Principal Competitors

Tiffany & Co.; Cartier; Bailey, Banks & Biddle; The Galleries of Neiman Marcus.

Further Reading

Altaner, David, "Florida-Based Jewelry Company Won't Renew Contract with Sam's," *Sun Sentinel,* April 8, 1999.

——, ''Jan Bell Glitter Is Fading,'' *Sun Sentinel,* July 2, 1995, p. 1D.

——, ''Sunrise, Fla.-Based Jewelry Company to Open Luxury Stores,'' *Sun Sentinel,* March 26, 1999.

Craig, David, ''Jan Bell a Gem of a Small Stock,'' *USA Today,* January 17, 1989, p. 3B.

Danner, Patrick, ''Shareholder of Sunrise, Fla.-Based Jewelry Firm Wants Company Sold,'' *Miami Herald,* February 13, 2001.

Hackney, Holt, ''Jan Bell Marketing: The Sam's Solution,'' *Financial World,* July 6, 1993, p. 13.

Hale, Sarah, and Kevin Helliker, ''Drawing a Bead: Celebrated Jewelers Go National, But thc Locals Won't Be Pushovers,'' *Wall Street Journal,* August 5, 1999, p. A1.

''Jan Bell: On the Cutting Edge in Wholesale Jewelry,'' *Business Week,* May 29, 1989, p. 61.

Marcial, G.G., ''Flaws in a Jeweler's Future?,'' *Business Week,* December 4, 1989, p. 106.

Stieghorst, Tom, ''Jan Bell to Acquire Mayor's, Create Two-Tier Florida Jeweler,'' *Sun-Sentinel,* February 24, 1998.

Walker, Elaine, ''Miami Jeweler Aims to Shine Nationally,'' *Miami Herald,* April 5, 1999.

——, ''Sam's Club Cancels Sunrise, Fla.-Based Jewelry Firm's Concession,'' *Miami Herald,* April 7, 1999.

—Ed Dinger

MCSi

MCSi, Inc.

4750 Hempstead Station Drive
Dayton, Ohio 45429
U.S.A.
Telephone: (937) 291-8282
Fax: (937) 291-8288
Web site: http://www.mcsinet.com

Public Company
Incorporated: 1981 as Miami Computer Supply Corporation
Employees: 1,887 (1999)
Sales: $686.7 million (1999)
Stock Exchange: NASDAQ
Ticker Symbol: MCSI
NAIC: 421420 Office Equipment Wholesalers; 421430 Computer and Computer Peripheral Equipment and Software Wholesalers; 422120 Stationery and Office Supplies Wholesalers

MCSi, Inc., formerly known as Miami Computer Supply Corporation (MCSC), spent its first 15 years as a privately held computer and office automation supply company. Founded in 1981, the Ohio-based distributor services a wide range of corporate, governmental, and institutional customers.

Growth through Acquisitions, 1996–99

MCSC became a public company in November 1996. At the time of its initial public offering (IPO) the company had only 53 employees. Following its IPO, MCSC embarked on an aggressive acquisitions program. From November 1996 to the end of 1999, MCSC acquired ten regional computer and office automation supply companies and 12 audio-visual/broadcast presentation products and systems integration companies. The company's annual revenue grew from $63.4 million in 1996 to $686.7 million in 1999.

In 1998 MCSC made several acquisitions, including Axidata Inc., a Toronto-based computer supply company with annual sales of about $150 million. It was MCSC's first Canadian acquisition. Toward the end of 1998 MCSC acquired Dreher Business Products of Strongsville, Ohio, located near Cleveland. The company had annual sales of $80 million and more than 200 employees. It sold computer hardware and software, a variety of office supplies, and offered computer training, network design, and hardware configuration services. The acquisition of Axidata and Dreher would increase MCSC's annual sales from around $320 million to more than $550 million.

Around this time MCSC implemented an electronic commerce solution with two online catalogs: one for its traditional corporate customers and one for the small office/home office (SOHO) marketplace. MCSC turned to an outsourcing company, Information Engineering Corp., to plan and manage all phases of its e-business implementation, which would run on MCSC's IBM AS/400 mainframes that formed MCSC's information technology backbone. With the new e-business solution, MCSC's static web site was transformed into a dynamic e-commerce site. Orders placed at the web site could be seamlessly processed by the company's existing inventory systems.

In January 1999 MCSC launched an Internet subsidiary, Zengine, Inc., whose mission was to run Internet web sites for companies and portals that wanted to sell products and services through their own Internet storefronts. Internet portals such as Microsoft Network, America Online, and GeoCities typically sent visitors to other sites to make purchases. Zengine would combine its own Internet expertise with MCSC's expertise in merchandising and shipping to run the back end for companies and portals that wanted to sell over the Internet.

Zengine was based in Fremont, California, and started with 20 employees, plus 10 MCSC workers assigned there. Joe Savarino, who formerly worked for an online advertising technology company, was hired to be Zengine's president. Two former employees of Excite@Home, Lalit Dhadphale and Chris Feaver, were also hired. Feaver became Zengine's 22-year-old chief technology officer. Later in the year Zengine announced a multiyear contract with Excite@Home for Zengine to create an online shopping area for audio-visual products on Excite@ Home's recently launched Work.com business-to-business por-

Company Perspectives:

MCSi is a premier reseller and advanced systems integrator of computer technology and visual communications products, technologies and technical support services. Serving more than 50,000 corporate, governmental, medical, educational and institutional clients, MCSi is the nation's largest computer technology and visual communications reseller, with more than $850 million in sales and 126 locations throughout the U.S. and Canada.

tal. Excite@Home and investment banking firm William Blair & Co. took minority stakes in Zengine.

In August 1999 MCSC made its 18th acquisition since going public by purchasing Technical Industries Inc. of Atlanta, Georgia. Technical Industries was an integrator of audio-visual products and had annual sales of about $33 million. Earlier in the year MCSC had acquired another presentation products integrator, AVS of Dayton, Ohio.

In October 1999 MCSC announced it would change its name to MCSi, Inc., an acronym for the company's Media Consultants and Systems Integration business unit, which accounted for about one-third of the company's revenue. The multimedia unit designed, installed, and supported audio-visual, videoconferencing, and other multimedia equipment and systems. The name change became official in June 2000.

MCSC had a good year in 1999. Net sales increased 119 percent to $686.7 million from $313.8 million in 1998. Earnings per share increased 43 percent, while operating income grew 109 percent to $28.6 million from $13.7 million in 1998. The company's workforce of nearly 1,900 included more than 400 technical resources professionals and 600 sales representatives. At the end of 1999 MCSC was reselling more than 1,800 core products manufactured by some 500 OEMs, primarily to corporations and governmental, educational, and institutional customers.

Recognized as a Fast-Growing Company, 2000

Three previously announced acquisitions were completed in January and February 2000. The first was Video Images Inc. of Milwaukee, Wisconsin, which had annual sales of about $16 million and sold primarily in the Milwaukee and Chicago markets. The second involved Fairview-AFX, Inc., an audio-visual integrator and provider of professional video systems. Fairfax-AFX was based in Tulsa, Oklahoma, and had annual revenue of about $15 million. Also in February MCSC completed its acquisition of Duo-Communications of Canada Ltd. (DuoCom). DuoCom sold audio-visual products and had $25 million in sales through locations in Montreal, Toronto, Ottawa, Quebec City, Moncton, and Vancouver.

In February 2000 president and CEO Michael Peppel succeeded Anthony Liberati as chairman of MCSC. Liberati, who had served as chairman since 1996 and was instrumental in taking the company public, would remain a director of MCSC's Internet subsidiary, Zengine. Around this time the company changed its NASDAQ stock symbol to MCSI. In announcing the change, Michael Peppel said, ''We are now the largest advanced systems integrator of visual communications products and services in North America. MCSi, Inc. is beginning a new brand identity campaign using our trademarked logo MCSi and thus, listing under the symbol MCSI will help us accomplish this very important goal.'' In June 2000 the company officially changed its name to MCSi, Inc., with the corporate tagline, ''Media Consultants, Systems Integrators.''

The pace of acquisitions slowed somewhat in the second half of 2000, when MCSi's acquisitions focused on audio-visual products integrators. Companies acquired by MCSi included Midwest Visual Communications, Inc., which strengthened MCSi's position in Chicago and the midwestern states of Illinois, Wisconsin, Indiana, and Michigan. Midwest Visual was a 60-year-old audio-visual products integrator with about $45 million in annual sales. MCSi also acquired Westek Presentation Systems, Inc. of San Diego. This audio-visual products integrator had annual revenue of some $14 million.

MCSi also acquired audio-visual products integrator Intellisys, Inc. as part of a proposed Chapter 11 reorganization of Intellisys. Intellisys was headquartered in Westlake Village, California, and had annual revenue of $150 million. The acquisition of Intellisys was completed in January 2001. Before the end of 2000 MCSi announced it would acquire AV Associates, Inc., an audio-visual products integrator based in Storrs, Connecticut, with $18 million in annual revenue. To help finance its acquisition of AV Associates Inc., MCSi raised some $5 million through a private placement of common stock in January 2001.

In June 2000 MCSi divested its Azerty Canada business to United Stationers Supply Co., a subsidiary of United Stationers Inc., which had acquired Azerty's U.S. and Mexican businesses in 1998. Azerty Canada was MCSi's wholesale operation and generated about $115 million in annual sales. The divestiture was part of MCSi's strategy to focus on its core competencies, which Michael Peppel characterized as ''bringing computer and communications technology together. Our focus is on value-added convergent technology solutions that combine the power of data, voice and visual communications products in useful, flexible and integrated systems.''

That MCSi was a fast-growing company was confirmed by *Fortune* magazine, which ranked the company second on its 2000 list of ''100 Fastest-Growing Companies.'' The ranking was based on the company's revenue growth of 134 percent for the past three years. MCSi's revenue growth was attributed to growth in the systems integration business, increased sales penetration, increased product offerings, and the impact of acquisitions.

Toward the end of 2000 MCSi was again on track for a record year. For the first nine months of 2000 net sales were up 34 percent, operating income rose 42 percent, and net income increased 42 percent. Earnings per share also rose 29 percent. Contributing to the company's strong performance was the ongoing convergence of data, voice, and video communications products.

The year 2000 was also a significant year for MCSi's Internet subsidiary Zengine. Zengine's business involved providing a comprehensive suite of technology-based solutions to

Key Dates:

1981: Company is founded as Miami Computer Supply Corporation (MCSC).
1996: MCSC goes public with an initial public offering (IPO) on the NASDAQ exchange.
1999: MCSC launches its Internet subsidiary, Zengine, Inc.
2000: MCSC officially changes its name to MCSi, Inc.

companies that wanted to conduct electronic commerce, both for business-to-business and business-to-consumer e-commerce. Services provided included web site user interface design, product content and merchandising, personalization and customer relationship management, advertising and sponsorship management, order management, inventory management and order fulfillment, end-user customer service, and reporting and analysis. Zengine was able to provide these services as part of a complete turnkey package as well as individually. At the end of August, Zengine opened an office in Tokyo, Japan, to market its technology-based solutions in the Asia-Pacific region.

In September Zengine completed its initial public offering (IPO), selling 4.29 million shares at $13 per share. The stock began selling on the NASDAQ National Market under the symbol ZNGN on September 21, 2000. Following the IPO MCSi owned about 70 percent of Zengine's stock.

In January 2001 MCSi received an interesting offer from Anthony Liberati, MCSi's former chairman and currently a director of Zengine. Liberati offered to purchase all of the outstanding common stock of MCSi for $22 a share in cash. Following a meeting of its board of directors, MCSi announced it had hired investment banking firm William Blair & Co. of Chicago to investigate strategic alternatives. It remained to be seen whether MCSi would accept Liberati's offer.

Principal Subsidiaries

Diversified Data Products, Inc.; Consolidated Media Systems, Inc.; Axidata Inc. (Canada); Central Audio Visual, Inc.; C & G Video Systems; Duo Communications, Inc. (Canada); Audio Visual Systems, Inc.; Technical Industries, Inc.; Video Images, Inc.; Fairview AFX; Zengine, Inc. (69.5%).

Principal Competitors

CompUSA Inc.; Ingram Micro Inc.; Tech Data Corp.

Further Reading

Bischoff, Laura A., ''Kettering, Ohio-Based Miami Computer Supply Corp. Buys Atlanta Firm,'' *Knight-Ridder/Tribune Business News,* August 9, 1999.

——, ''Kettering, Ohio-Based Technology Supplier Forms E-Commerce Subsidiary,'' *Knight-Ridder/Tribune Business News,* September 2, 1999.

——, ''MCSI Targeted for Takeover Bid,'' *Dayton Daily News,* January 23, 2001, Bus. Sec.

Dillon, Jim, ''Kettering, Ohio, Computer Supplier Continues to See Record Earnings,'' *Knight-Ridder/Tribune Business News,* October 21, 1999.

''MCSi Inc.,'' *Private Equity Week,* January 22, 2001, p. 7.

''Miami Computer Supply Corp.,'' *Business First-Columbus,* February 18, 2000, p. 15.

''Miami Computer Supply Corp.,'' *Business First-Columbus,* June 23, 2000, p. 18.

Suttell, Scott, ''Sale to Dayton Distributor to Drive Dreher's Growth,'' *Crain's Cleveland Business,* November 30, 1998, p. 1.

Swoyer, Stephen, ''Miami Supply Opens up for E-Business,'' *Midrange Systems,* April 5, 1999, p. 26.

Tresslar, Tim, ''MCSI Panel Explores Equity Groups' Offers,'' *Dayton Daily News,* April 27, 2001, Bus. Sec.

——, ''Ohio-Based Computer Supply Company to Buy Canadian Firm,'' *Knight-Ridder/Tribune Business News,* December 15, 1999.

''Video Images Inc.,'' *Business Journal-Milwaukee,* December 17, 1999, p. 35.

—David P. Bianco

Meade Instruments Corporation

6001 Oak Canyon
Irvine, California 92618
U.S.A.
Telephone: (949) 451-1450
Fax: (949) 451-1460
Web site: http://www.meade.com

Public Company
Incorporated: 1972
Employees: 455
Sales: $126.8 million (2000)
Stock Exchanges: NASDAQ
Ticker Symbol: MEAD
NAIC: 333314 Optical Instrument and Lens Manufacturing

Meade Instruments Corporation is the world's largest manufacturer of telescopes for serious amateurs and academic astronomers. It designs, manufactures, imports, and distributes a full line of telescopes, telescope accessories, binoculars and other optical products. Its telescope line includes over 50 models in a wide variety of sizes and designs, which include refracting, reflecting and the state-of-the-art Schmidt-Cassegrain telescopes, which range in price from less than $100 to over $15,000. Meade's computer-controlled telescopes, which are able to locate thousands of celestial objects automatically, have changed the face of amateur astronomy. Meade manufactures its products in two facilities. One is located at its headquarters in Irvine, California, and the other in Tijuana, Mexico. Some telescopes are also produced for Meade by firms under contract in Taiwan. Meade products are sold by over 3000 dealers in the Unites States and Canada, and are further available in more than 30 countries the world over. Meade also produces optical components for fiber optic networks manufactured by TeraBeam Networks Inc.

Modest Beginnings in the Early 1970s

Meade Instruments Corp. was the brainchild of John C. Diebel, an electrical engineer who was trained at the California Institute of Technology and the University of Southern California. In the early 1970s, Diebel was a late twenty-something engineer employed by the Hughes Aircraft Company in a job he quickly grew to dislike. ''I was miserable,'' he later told *Sky & Telescope*'s David H. Levy in July 2000. ''I'd never held a job before, and I hated working for someone else.'' In the fall of 1971, he began browsing the periodicals at the Los Angeles Public Library for business opportunities, and sent out letters to companies that seemed to be good potential candidates. Months passed before Diebel finally received a single response. The Towa Optical Manufacturing Company—a Japanese maker of telescopes—agreed to let Diebel distribute their products in the United States.

The telescope business was a natural match for Diebel. His fervent interest in astronomy dated back to a science class he had taken in the eighth grade. Afterwards, he had read everything he could about the subject, and even built his own 6-inch telescope as a science project. ''I ground the mirrors myself,'' Diebel recalled to Jerry Hirsch in the September 14, 1997 edition of the *Orange County Register*. ''They were pretty crude, but they worked.'' Although the idea of an astronomy-related career had not entered Diebel's mind at the time, his interest in the topic drew him to astronomy courses offered in college by cosmologist Jesse Greenstein at Cal Tech.

In 1972, armed with his agreement with Towa, the 29-year-old would-be entrepreneur managed to get a loan of $2500 from the credit union at Hughes Aircraft—the bank he asked for $500 credit flatly refused. He ordered $2000 worth of Towa telescopes, got a post office box, and set up business in the kitchen of his small apartment. The name Meade occurred to him after a vacation trip to Lake Mead in Nevada—he added the ''e'' because he thought it looked better. Finally, he took out an ad in the July 1972 issue of *Sky & Telescope*—then the only mass magazine targeted at amateur astronomers—offering his line of refracting telescopes at prices ranging in cost from $49 to $235. ''It was very slow at first, but within six months I was making about $300 a month,'' Diebel told Hirsch. ''It was enough to live off of so I quit Hughes Aircraft.'' By the end of his first year in business, that little ad had netted Meade Instruments $8000 in sales.

The following year, Diebel moved the company to a warehouse in Costa Mesa, California, where his parents lived. There,

Company Perspectives:

Meade Instruments, the world's largest manufacturer of telescopes for the amateur astronomer, makes over 50 telescope models in a wide range of prices and sizes. Whether you are new to stargazing or an advanced observer looking to do serious astronomical research, Meade has a telescope that is right for you. From the smallest introductory model to the largest computer-controlled observatory instrument, every Meade telescope is made with one purpose in mind: to maximize your long-term enjoyment in the exploration of space and worlds beyond your own.

his father—a retired furniture store owner—joined Meade to help with the rapidly expanding product line. The elder Diebel was far more than just additional manpower, however. ''I didn't know anything about running a business,'' Diebel told Hirsch. ''He taught me everything, from preparing financial statements to talking to the bank.'' His father remained with Meade until his death in 1988.

Entering his second year of business, Diebel realized that he had tapped into a huge market, not only for telescopes but also for telescope accessories. In 1973 Meade began distributing Orthoscopic and Kellner eyepieces, and then added a line of precision rack and pinion focusers, viewfinders, filters, and camera adapters. The company had uncovered a sizable body of amateur astronomers in the United States whose demands were going unmet. Through Meade, they could purchase items that were difficult to find anywhere else. Meade products were attractive to these buyers because of custom features not usually available in models from other companies. Such features included spring-loaded gearboxes for smoother resolution, and viewfinder eyepieces with wider fields. Astronomy buffs soon flocked to Meade. In 1975, the firm turned a profit of $55,000 on $259,000 in sales, up nearly eight-fold from its first year.

Meanwhile, as Meade handled more and more Towa Optical products, the relationship between the two firms grew closer and closer. In the late 1970s, Diebel actually married the daughter of Towa's founder.

Astronomical Revolutions at Meade

In 1976, as the result of an unexpectedly high demand for tube assemblies for reflecting telescopes, Diebel shifted the direction of his young company away from distribution and began manufacturing the assemblies at Meade. ''We were selling them by the hundreds overnight,'' he told Levy.

Later in 1977, Meade released the first telescopes of its own production—the model 628 and 826 six-inch and eight-inch reflecting telescopes. Meade's product quality and prompt, dependable delivery enabled it to win a large portion of the market in a very short period of time. In 1978, its sales topped $2 million. Success came with a price, however. Although it promised delivery within six to eight weeks, the flood of orders suddenly confronted the firm with a six month backlog. Each customer was written a personal letter explaining the problem and offered a full refund if they wished—an offer few actually took Meade up on. Overtime shifts and extra workers eventually enabled the company to cut the waiting time in half.

By the late 1970s, amateur astronomy was undergoing a remarkable transformation. A radical new type of telescope was introduced—the so-called Schmidt-Cassegrain model, which utilized both mirrors and lenses to produce remarkably high resolution images. Meade threw all of its resources into the development of a Schmidt-Cassegrain for serious amateurs. Three years later, in September 1980, the company announced its first Schmidt-Cassegrain model, the eight-inch 2080.

In 1984 Meade released the LX3, an innovative telescope equipped with an electronic drive system that automatically adjusted the telescope for celestial motion. The company continued to release new models and new accessories, and by 1985, it had surpassed competitor Celestron International as the number one telescope manufacturer in the world. The news came the same year that the famous Halley's Comet was about to return, an event which unleashed an unprecedented wave of interest in amateur astronomy among the general public and boosted sales even more.

Cataclysmic Days at Meade: The Late 1980s

By 1986 John Diebel and his company were the main stars in the telescope industry. The company employed a staff of about 100 people, and had achieved approximately $13 million in sales. After fourteen years, though, Diebel was ready for a change. ''I personally guaranteed all of the company's notes with the bank, and being a financially conservative person by nature, it grew on me over the years that one mistake and all this work, 14 years, was for nothing,'' he told Tim Stevens in the January 15, 2001 edition of *Industry Week*. ''I thought it was time to take on a larger partner.'' Thus, he sold Meade for $6.5 million to the Harbor Group, a holding company based in St. Louis, Missouri.

Diebel remained involved as the company president; however, almost from the first day, the new arrangement seemed doomed. No longer his own boss, Diebel felt straitjacketed by the additional paperwork, meetings, and marketing studies required by Harbor. He and Harbor disagreed on how growth at Meade should be managed. Meade R&D suffered under the new bureaucratic management style, as well, and under Harbor new product development soon ceased almost entirely. Finally, in 1988, Diebel left the company. He moved to Hawaii, played golf, consulted Meade a day or two every week, and watched as the fortunes of the company he had founded dipped lower and lower.

By the end of the 1980s, the telescope market had reached a saturation point and Meade's sales were plummeting. In response to the crisis, the Harbor Group decided Meade's survival depended on a merger with another telescope manufacturer. In July 1990, it announced that Meade would join together with its main competitor, Celestron International—a Torrance, California-based company—to form a new firm which would enjoy about $21 million in annual sales. The next October, however, the Federal Trade Commission (FTC) sought a court injunction to block the merger, which it maintained would create a virtual monopoly in the manufacture and sale of mid-sized Schmidt-Cassegrain telescopes. Eventually in late 1990, the FTC was

Key Dates:

1972: John C. Diebel founds Meade Instrument Corp. to import telescopes from Towa Optical Manufacturing Company in Japan.
1973: Meade expands its product line and moves to a larger facility in Costa Mesa, California.
1977: Meade begins manufacturing its own products.
1980: Meade introduces the Model 2080, its first Schmidt-Cassegrain model telescope.
1984: Meade brings the LX3 series of telescopes to market; features include electronic tracking.
1986: Diebel sells Meade to the St. Louis-based Harbor Group.
1988: Meade introduces the LX6 series, with a microprocessor control system; Diebel resigns as president of Meade.
1990: FTC blocks merger of Meade with competitor Celestron International.
1991: Diebel and three partners buy Meade from the Harbor Group for $1000.
1996: ETX—Everyone's Telescope—series introduced; within a year, the ETX-90RA is the largest-selling modern telescope in the world; introduction of the Meade Autostar Computer Controller; Meade initiates Employee Stock Ownership Plan.
1997: Meade goes public.
2000: Meade engaged by TeraBeam Networks Inc. to provide optical components for its fiber optic networks.

able to prevent the merger entirely. By the time it did, Meade Instruments was hemorrhaging money—$2 million annually—a full fifth of its revenues. The firm was sliding rapidly toward bankruptcy while John Diebel watched from the sidelines.

In February 1991 the crisis came to a head. Meade's creditors called in their loans and the company, which was $2 million in the red, was unable to pay. Diebel stepped in and loaned Meade $65,000 of his own money to meet the weekly payroll while he negotiated a buyout of the company with three partners. In the end, Harbor sold all of Meade's stock along with all its assets and liabilities to the group of partners for just $1000. $510 of that came from John Diebel, who took over majority ownership of Meade once again.

Accepting an annual salary of only one dollar at first, Diebel set about to rebuild his old company. He put up $1.8 million of his own money; his three partners, all Meade employees, mortgaged their homes and came up with $250,000 in cash. That money was put toward revitalizing Meade's R&D program, which had become completely dormant under Harbor. ''Harbor hadn't moved on any of the new products we left on the burners for them,'' Meade COO Steven Murdock told Stevens, ''so we had the luxury of having engineering and proof-of-concept waiting for us.''

One project was the ETX, which stood for Everyone's Telescope, a quality instrument that anyone, regardless of his or her level of experience, could enjoy. Another project was the LX200 telescope. Planned as one of the most advanced instruments ever built for the amateur astronomer, a full $1 million was spent on its development. It came equipped with computer controls to automatically locate 64,000 various celestial objects. At about $2000—half the price of similar products then on the market—the LX200 was the first computer-controlled telescope priced for the average consumer. In the early 1990s, the company also contracted with a Taiwanese company to manufacture a line of less-expensive telescopes built to Meade's exacting specifications.

On the Road to Recovery in the Mid-1990s

Within two years of Diebel's return, Meade was in solid financial shape again. By 1995, Meade telescopes were outselling all competitors combined throughout the world. In 1996, Meade's sales rose to $29.8 million. Sales would again double by 1998, and yet again by the end of the 2000 fiscal year.

In 1996, Meade introduced the Autostar Computer Controller, which could be attached to various Meade telescope models to locate 1400 celestial objects. Diebel told *Business Week*'s Ronald Grover on May 29, 2000, that seeing Bill Gates on television inspired the development of the Autostar. ''I thought to myself, why can't we do something really revolutionary in this industry the way he did in his.'' Two years later, Meade engineers worked out a way to build the attachment at an affordable price.

In July 1996 Meade's 170 employees were given a share of the company's ownership. The Employee Stock Ownership Plan was developed by the firm's four owners to raise money, to enable employees to take part in Meade's growth, and to provide them with an incentive for remaining with the firm. Every year, employees were given stock in the firm equal to about 20 percent of their salaries. The stock was placed in a retirement account. Once workers were vested for three years in the plan, they could sell up to 50 percent of their accumulated stock. The arrangement did not directly affect the structure of the company, but employees received enough votes to elect one of Meade's five directors.

An IPO to End the 20th Century

The following year, Meade announced that it was going public. Wall Street was cautiously optimistic about the offer. Meade earnings had risen 50 percent over the previous nine months, however, about half of Meade's sales were concentrated among only seven customers. In the end, the offering on NASDAQ raised $18 million, which was somewhat less than had been hoped. $11 million was used to repay outstanding debt, and $6.8 million was used to buy out a venture capital investor. ''What a wonderful feeling to be rid of debt,'' Diebel told Roger Yu in the May 4, 1998 edition of the *Orange County Business Journal*. ''I hate debts.''

In 1998 Meade's sales increased by 27 percent, despite a 40 percent reduction in shipments to the large Japanese market. Around that time, Meade became the first telescope maker to use plastic mounting instead of traditional aluminum parts—a decision which further lowered the price of Meade products, without any loss in quality. It moved to a new production facility in Irvine, California, which was three times as large and had its own observatory. The new plant helped relieve Meade's ongoing backlog of orders.

In late 1998, the company began production in a brand new 26,000 square foot factory in Tijuana, Mexico that employed 40 people. The new facility enabled Meade to take advantage of the lower cost of Mexican labor, coupled with Tijuana's proximity to the Irvine main plant, where testing, complex assembly operations, final assembly, and shipping continued to be handled. In September 1999, Meade acquired Bresser Optik, a German distributor of optical products for $5 million in cash and 101,000 shares of Meade stock. The purchase was intended to provide a basis for broader distribution of Meade products in Europe.

By the end of 1999, Meade was on a roll. It boasted a 70 percent share of the high-end telescope market and 40 percent of the low-end market. The firm's inexpensive computer-guided telescopes had proved to be a hit with consumers. Much to the surprise of experts on Wall Street, the value of its stock doubled in a six month period, and some analysts were predicting a rise of another five points during the coming year. Instead, in March 2000, the value of its shares leapt 77 percent overnight—the result of rumors that Meade had made some kind of deal with TeraBeam Networks Inc., a Seattle-based manufacturer of fiber optic communications equipment. Speculation that Meade was considering entering the lucrative fiber optic field on some level set off frenzied trading in its shares. By the close of trading on March 15, 2000, its stock had risen to $53 with five million shares being traded—60 times Meade's daily average.

At the same time, however, there was no confirmation that the two companies had actually made any deal. The next day though, following inquiries from NASDAQ, Meade announced officially that it had been engaged by TeraBeam to manufacture optical components for TeraBeam's fiber optic networks. A month and a half later, in early May of 2000, Meade made public a 2-for-1 stock split. As 2000 came to an end, the value of Meade stock leveled out and then began to fall. The fall was a result of a convergence of factors. First, the chain of ''Natural Wonder'' stores, following a merger with ''World of Science'', stopped carrying Meade's products. The slight downturn in the economy also led to a highly disappointing 2000 Christmas season, despite the introduction into Wal-Mart and JC Penney of Meade's ETX-60, a computerized telescope selling for $295. At the end of the first quarter of 2001, the company reported a loss of $4.7 million.

Principal Subsidiaries

Bresser Optik GmbH & Co KG (Germany); Bresser Optik Geschäftsführung- und Verwaltungs- GmbH (Germany).

Principal Operating Units

Meade International; Meade Europe; Bresser Optik.

Principal Competitors

Canon Inc. Celestron International; Bushnell Optical Company; Synta Technology.

Further Reading

Berkman, Leslie, ''FTC Has Eyes on Telescope Firm Merger Monopoly,'' *Los Angeles Times,* October 10, 1990.

Berry, Kate, ''Meade's Telescope Sales Make It an Industry Star,'' *Orange County Register,* October 17, 1999.

''Federal Trade Commission Moves to Block Telescope Venture,'' *Dow Jones News Service-Ticker,* October 9, 1990.

Fields, Robin, ''Meade Shares Soar 77% On Terabeam Deal,'' *Los Angeles Times,* March 16, 2000, p. C8.

''FTC Opposes Telescope Merger,'' *Los Angeles Times,* October 9, 1990, p. P3.

Grover, Ronald, ''Back from a Black Hole,'' *Business Week,* May 29, 2000.

Hirsch, Jerry, ''Irvine Telescope Builder Proved to be Farsighted,'' *Orange County Register,* September 14, 1997.

——, ''Telescope Firm Focuses on Stock Sale,'' *Orange County Register,* February 6, 1997.

Johnson, Greg, ''Irvine Telescope Manufacturer Meade Plans IPO,'' *Los Angeles Times,* February 6, 1997, p. D5.

Kafka, Peter, ''In Focus,'' *Forbes,* November 15, 1999, p. 210.

Kelleher, James B., ''Meade Instruments is Soaring,'' *Orange County Register,* March 13, 2000.

——, ''Meade Shares Fall Back a Bit,'' *Orange County Register,* March 17, 2000.

Levy, David H., ''The Man Behind Meade,'' *Sky & Telescope,* July 2000, p. 80.

Lindquist, Diane, ''Irvine Telescope Firm Looks to Tijuana,'' *San Diego Union-Tribune,* November 28, 1998, p. C1.

''Meade Instruments CEO Says R&D Investment Paying Off,'' *Dow Jones Business News,* December 30, 1999.

Meade Instruments Corp., ''Comments on OEM Agreement,'' *Business Wire,* March 29, 2000.

''Meade Instruments Posts Earnings Well Below Analysts' Reduced Estimates,'' *Dow Jones Business News,* December 19, 2000.

''Meade Instruments Shares Soar on Word of Alliance With TeraBeam,'' *Dow Jones Business News,* March 15, 2000.

''Meade Stock Will Split 2-For-1,'' *Los Angeles Times,* May 6, 2000, p. C2.

''Missouri Holding Company Acquires Meade Instruments,'' *Los Angeles Times,* January 9, 1987, p. D3.

O'Dell, John, ''Workers Acquire a Stake in Meade,'' *Los Angeles Times,* July 20, 1996, p. D4,

Stevens, Tim, ''Master of His Universe,'' *Industry Week,* January 15, 2001, p. 76.

Yu, Roger, ''Telescope Maker Seeks to Expand Its Small Universe,'' *Orange County Business Journal,* May 4, 1998.

—Gerald E. Brennan

Metrocall, Inc.

6677 Richmond Highway
Alexandria, Virginia 22306
U.S.A.
Telephone: (703) 660-6677
Fax: (703) 768-9622
Web site: http://www.metrocall.com

Public Company
Incorporated: 1965 as Advanced Communications Inc.
Employees: 3,800
Sales: $610.2 million (1999)
Stock Exchange: NASDAQ
Ticker Symbol: MCLL
NAIC: 513321 Paging; 513322 Cellular and Other Wireless Telecommunications

With more than six million subscribers, Metrocall, Inc. ranks as the second largest paging company in the United States behind industry leader Arch Wireless, Inc.. Originally a regional paging company that served the mid-Atlantic states, Metrocall grew to provide services nationwide and is one of the largest wireless data and messaging companies in the United States. Metrocall offers advanced wireless messaging services, including two-way messaging and Internet-based content delivery.

From Regional to National Paging Company: 1965–95

Advanced Communications Inc., the predecessor company to Metrocall, Inc., was established by Harry L. Brock, Jr., in 1965. Brock incorporated Metrocall as a privately held company in 1982. When Metrocall went public in July 1993, it had about 200,000 pagers in service and operated mainly along the eastern seaboard, from New York through the Carolinas. Following its initial public offering (IPO), Metrocall completed its acquisition of FirstPage USA Inc.. Approximately 47 percent of FirstPage was owned by Pittsburgh real estate tycoon and billionaire industrialist Henry Hillman and Hillman family trusts. The Hillman interest in FirstPage resulted in a 12.6 percent ownership stake in Metrocall following the acquisition.

In 1993 the paging industry had about $2.5 billion in sales. It was enjoying annual growth of about 20 percent, due to such factors as product enhancements, affordability, and the growing acceptance of pagers by the general public. For 1993 Metrocall reported a net loss of $2.2 million on revenue of nearly $38 million, compared with net income of $3 million on $35 million in revenue in 1992. The 1993 loss was attributed to a one-time charge of $4.8 million related to the company's IPO.

Late in 1993 Metrocall acquired a paging company in California, and in 1994–95 the company added operations in Boston, Pittsburgh, San Diego, Phoenix, Las Vegas, and several Florida locations. In the process Metrocall increased its customer base to about one million, but the company felt it needed 2.5 million to 3.5 million subscribers to survive consolidation in the paging industry and become a long-term player.

After two solid years of growth through acquisitions, Metrocall ran into some difficulties in 1995. Founder and chairman Harry L. Brock, Jr., became involved in a power struggle with Metrocall's board and vice-chairman William L. Collins III. Collins, former head of FirstPage USA, became a major shareholder in Metrocall when FirstPage was acquired by Metrocall. Collins and other board members from FirstPage teamed up with outside directors to force out Brock, charging that Brock was not pursuing acquisitions aggressively enough. Brock resigned and was replaced as chairman by Richard M. Johnston. CEO Christopher Kidd also resigned and was replaced by Collins.

Another setback involved a failed bid to acquire another large paging firm, which resulted in about 100 layoffs. Institutional investors became disillusioned with the company, and Metrocall's stock fell from a high of $29 in September 1995—when the company issued four million new shares at $28.25 a share—to $16.50 in January 1996. Also affecting the stock price was concern over a pricing war among paging companies and a reported shortage of pagers for new customers. However, the stock was still trading above its 1993 IPO price of $13.

Aggressively Acquired Companies: 1996–98

With new executive leadership, Metrocall embarked on a wave of acquisitions to increase its customer base and expand its paging network. Metrocall was the sixth-largest paging com-

Company Perspectives:

During the last year, Metrocall introduced My2Way and MyeLink, the latest in interactive messaging. As our subscriber base continued to grow in 2000, an increasing number of subscribers have chosen two-way service and are now realizing the remarkable efficiencies, and peace of mind, resulting from interactive wireless messaging. Together with our PCS phone services, Metrocall offers unsurpassed coverage, and communications options, for peer-to-peer messaging, wireless e-mail, Internet connectivity and mobile phone connectivity.

pany in the United States with about 944,000 subscribers at the end of 1995. During 1995 Metrocall had raised capital for acquisitions through stock and debt offerings, leaving it with $123 million in cash on hand at the end of 1995. For the year it reported a loss of $20.1 million on revenue of $110.9 million. During 1995 the number of Metrocall pagers in service grew by 25 percent.

Metrocall's first announced acquisition for 1996 was Parkway Paging Inc. for $28 million. Based in Plano, Texas, Parkway had about 140,000 subscribers in Dallas, Fort Worth, and other Texas cities. Around this time Metrocall also acquired Satellite Paging, which had about 60,000 subscribers in New York and New Jersey, and Message Network, which had 50,000 customers in Florida.

Additional acquisitions included Page America Group Inc. of Hackensack, New Jersey, for $78.5 million, and Source One Wireless Inc., which served the Chicago area. Although Metrocall reported a loss of $7.7 million for the first quarter of 1996, president and CEO William L. Collins III confidently stated, ''We are successfully executing our stated strategy to grow, build and acquire.''

Metrocall's sixth acquisition of the year involved A+ Network, a paging company based in Nashville, Tennessee. A+ Network had about 675,000 customers in ten southern states and was the largest independent paging service in the Southeast. When the deal closed in November 1996, the transaction was valued at $341 million. To help finance the transaction, Metrocall was able to obtain a loan of $350 million from a group of banks led by Toronto Dominion and Bank of Boston Corp.

By mid-1996 Metrocall's stock was trading for less than $10 a share, more than 25 percent below its 1993 IPO price of $13 and less than one-third of the September 1995 offering price of $28.25 a share. Wall Street appeared to be reacting to Metrocall's widening quarterly losses and not to the company's revenue growth. Also affecting Metrocall's stock price was Wall Street's disillusionment at the time with telecommunications stocks in general, and paging companies in particular. Collins indicated to *The Washington Post* that as a result of depressed stock prices for Metrocall and other paging companies, Metrocall was not aggressively looking for more acquisitions for the time being. Pending acquisitions involving A+ Network, Page America Inc., Satellite Paging, and Message Network would give Metrocall some 2.2 million subscribers and make it the fourth largest U.S. paging company.

By the end of 1996 Metrocall's stock had dropped to around $5 a share, an 80 percent drop since June. Collins, Johnston, and other insiders took this as an opportunity to acquire more shares, indicating confidence that Metrocall's stock would rebound. It was a difficult year for the paging industry in general, with pricing pressures, problems with integrating acquisitions, and violations of debt contracts affecting the overall industry. For the year Metrocall posted a loss of $49.1 million on revenue of $150 million.

With investor support weakening for the paging industry, Metrocall was able to complete only four acquisitions in 1996, with the purchase of Page America closing in 1997. The company's quarterly losses continued to widen in 1997, reaching $11.7 million in the first quarter and $12.3 million in the second. Quarterly revenue more than doubled, however, rising 140 percent in the first quarter to $60.6 million and 119 percent in the second quarter to $70.3 million.

In the second half of 1997 Metrocall signed a definitive merger agreement with rival paging company ProNet, Inc. of Dallas, Texas. Under terms of the agreement Metrocall would pay $73.8 million for ProNet and assume about $170.3 million of ProNet's debt. The acquisition would give Metrocall more than four million subscribers, making it the second largest U.S. paging company behind Paging Network Inc. (PageNet) of Dallas, Texas, which had about nine million subscribers. Overall, the paging industry had about 43 million subscribers at this time.

The acquisition of ProNet increased Metrocall's workforce from 2,000 to 3,000 employees. For 1997 the company reported revenue of $289.4 million and a net loss of $60.3 million. In 1998 Metrocall acquired AT&T Wireless Services' Advanced Messaging Division for $205 million in stock and cash. The acquisition of AT&T's paging division resulted in 1.2 million new paging subscribers and a five-year distribution agreement with AT&T Wireless's retail stores, which would sell Metrocall paging products exclusively.

Also included in the acquisition of AT&T's paging division was a narrowband PCS license. To comply with Federal Communications Commission (FCC) regulations regarding the license, Metrocall was required to build out narrowband PCS infrastructure by September 29, 1999. The infrastructure would have to serve either a composite area of 750,000 square kilometers or 37.5 percent of the U.S. population. Those requirements would double over the next five years, and Metrocall reported that it expected to incur significant capital expenditures to comply with the FCC's requirements.

For 1998 Metrocall's revenue increased to $464.7 million, while its net loss widened to $129.1 million. The company ended the year with 5.75 million subscribers.

Advanced Messaging Services, 1999–2001

In 1999 Metrocall began to prepare for two-way messaging and new Internet applications. Midyear it contracted with Glenayre Technologies Inc. to upgrade its nationwide wireless network of more than 150 switches. Glenayre was a Charlotte, North Carolina-based company that specialized in building wireless platforms and manufacturing paging units. The upgrade would allow Metrocall to offer its subscribers enhanced

Key Dates:

1965: Advanced Communications Inc., the predecessor company to Metrocall, Inc., is formed by Harry L. Brock, Jr.
1982: Metrocall is incorporated as a privately held company.
1993: Metrocall goes public, with shares trading on the NASDAQ; company acquires FirstPage USA Inc.
1995: Vice-chairman William L. Collins III leads a boardroom coup, forcing the resignation of company founder Harry L. Brock, Jr., as chairman.
1997: Metrocall acquires ProNet, Inc.
1998: Metrocall acquires AT&T Wireless Services' Advanced Messaging Division for $205 million.
1999: Metrocall launches wireless Internet-based content delivery service, OnTheGoInfo.
2000: Metrocall forms Inciscent, a joint venture to provide Internet access and other technology services to small businesses.

voicemail, wireless e-mail, and Internet-based information services in addition to traditional paging services.

During 1999 Metrocall launched a wireless Internet-based content delivery service under the service mark OnTheGoInfo, using Motorola's "i Kno!" information architecture platform. OnTheGoInfo was introduced in the Washington-Baltimore area, then rolled out nationally. It included information packages that customers could select from a menu of "InfoChannels," including news, business and finance, sports, weather, entertainment, health and medicine, and others. Customers could personalize their content over the web, without having to take their wireless devices to a retail outlet. Content providers with whom Motorola had partnered for the service included The Weather Channel, SportsTicker, Etak Inc., *Billboard*, InfoBeat, OnHealth.com, The Associated Press, and others.

In mid-1999 Metrocall completed its national rollout of assured delivery messaging in the top 100 markets, which covered some 90 percent of the U.S. population. Marketed under the service mark MessageTrack, the wireless service enabled customers to receive Internet e-mail messages and have them stored for up to 96 hours. Toward the end of 1999 Metrocall strengthened its focus on Internet-based wireless services by forming a new strategic business unit, Metrocall.net, to offer bundled service solutions to the small office/home office (SOHO) market and to small and midsized enterprises. Included among the services Metrocall.net would market nationally were broadband Internet access, wireless e-mail, filtered content, and other applications and services. Through an agreement with DSL (digital subscriber line) broadband services provider Covad Communications, Metrocall would be able to resell Covad DSL services to its customers through Metrocall.net, which was later renamed Inciscent.

For 1999 Metrocall reported revenue of $610.2 million and a net loss of $172.5 million, which was attributed to noncash, acquisitions-related amortization costs. At the end of the year the company had 5.9 million subscribers and had completed the integration of the Advanced Messaging Division of AT&T Wireless. In early 2000 Metrocall announced it would acquire NationPage from AT&T Wireless Services for $13 million in cash. NationPage, a subsidiary of a company that AT&T Wireless had acquired, was a leading regional paging and wireless messaging provider in eastern Pennsylvania, New Jersey, and upstate New York. It had about 80,000 billable pagers and was already a large reseller of Metrocall services in Pennsylvania.

In February 2000 Metrocall gained $51 million in equity financing from three new investors: PSINet Inc., a global e-commerce company; investment firm Hicks, Muse, Tate & Furst, Inc.; and Aether Systems, Inc., a leading wireless application service provider (ASP). Each firm would invest about $17 million, and each would own about 10 percent of Metrocall's common stock. News of the investment sent Metrocall's stock up from around $2 a share to close around $6 a share after peaking at $7. The stock subsequently rose to more than $11 a share.

In addition to investing in Metrocall, the three firms agreed to form a high-tech joint venture with Metrocall's new business unit, Metrocall.net. The name of the venture was changed from Metrocall.net to Inciscent. As an ASP, it would provide a suite of technology services to the SOHO and small business markets. Included among the services to be offered were broadband Internet access, wireless messaging, two-way data solutions, and e-mail hosting. Metrocall owned 50 percent of Inciscent, Aether Systems owned 33 percent, and PSINet and Hicks, Muse each took a 6.33 percent interest, with other investors accounting for the rest.

In March 2000 Metrocall introduced My2Way, a new two-way wireless data and messaging service. The service enabled subscribers to send and receive wireless messages and e-mails and access Internet information from a wireless device. It also included address book, notepad, and calendar functions. My2Way would be marketed through Metrocall's 127 corporate-owned retail stores, through the company's exclusive interactive marketing agreement with America Online, and elsewhere. My2Way was also featured at Metrocall's Internet storefront on its newly designed web site. In addition, Metrocall supported the launch of My2Way with an eight-week business-to-business advertising campaign that included ads on national cable television network programming—including CNBC's *MarketWatch*—and in periodicals such as *The Wall Street Journal, Fortune,* and *Business Week.*

In May 2000 William L. Collins III, Metrocall's president and CEO, succeeded Richard M. Johnston as the company's chairman. Within a couple of months, Metrocall attempted to challenge rival Arch Wireless, Inc.'s takeover bid for Paging Network Inc. (PageNet) of Dallas, Texas. PageNet, the largest paging company in the United States, was in trouble financially. With backing from Hicks, Muse, Tate & Furst, Metrocall submitted a bid worth $1.57 billion, including $100 million in cash from Hicks, Muse, $727.5 million in stock, and the assumption of $746 million of PageNet's debt. Arch Wireless had offered stock and debt-assumption worth $1.36 billion. PageNet responded to Metrocall's offer by filing a voluntary Chapter 11 bankruptcy petition and rejecting Metrocall's bid. Subsequent litigation and backing from other investors revived Metrocall's offer, but PageNet's board of directors favored Arch Wireless. When Arch Wireless completed its acquisition of PageNet in November 2000, it became the largest paging company in the United States, with Metrocall ranking second. During the takeover bid Metrocall's stock fell from around $6 a share to just over $3 a share.

Meanwhile, Metrocall's losses were mounting and revenue was declining when compared with the previous year. For the first six months of 2000 revenue declined from $310.7 million in 1999 to $280.7 million, while losses rose from $86.7 million in 1999 to $88 million. For the third quarter revenue declined from $143 million in 1999 to $132.5 million, and losses increased from $48 million in 1999 to $60.2 million. Metrocall's stock continued to plummet through the end of 2000 and into 2001, when it was trading at less than $1 a share. NASDAQ officials notified the company at the end of 2000 that it would remove Metrocall's listing on the NASDAQ National Market System for failing to maintain a minimum bid price of $5. Metrocal had the option of relisting its stock on the NASDAQ SmallCap Market System, where it had traded in the past before being upgraded to the National Market System.

While Metrocall in particular and the paging industry in general appeared out of favor with Wall Street investors in 2000 and 2001, the company enjoyed strong financial backing from investment firm Hicks, Muse. In addition, the company's reported losses were often the result of noncash charges associated with acquisitions. Other positive developments in 2000 included the completion of Metrocall's corporate ATM (Asynchronous Transfer Mode) network. Originally intended as a virtual private network (VPN) to support internal operations, the ATM network would be made available to Metrocall's six million subscribers later in 2001. The ATM network, together with the completion of the upgrade of all of Metrocall's Glenayre messaging switches, enabled the company to allow all of its voice, data, and wireless messaging traffic to coexist on the same circuits. As a result, Metrocall would soon be able to send Internet protocol (IP) traffic through its ATM network. That would give it the competitive advantage in the wireless marketplace by being able to control the quality of its converging voice, data, video, and fax services.

Principal Subsidiaries

Inciscent (50%).

Principal Divisions

Advanced Messaging; Cellular and PCS Services; System Applications; Wireless Content and Advanced Applications.

Principal Competitors

Arch Wireless, Inc.; WebLink Wireless Inc.; SkyTel Communications Inc.; Sprint PCS; Verizon Wireless.

Further Reading

Bajaj, Vikas, "Addison, Texas-Based Paging Company Files for Bankruptcy to Speed up Merger," *Knight-Ridder/Tribune Business News,* July 26, 2000.

Behr, Peter, "Metrocall Acquires Texas Paging Firm for $28 Million," *Washington Post,* February 28, 1996, p. C1.

——, and Anthony Faiola, "Metrocall Writes a Few New Pages," *Washington Post,* March 4, 1996, p. F3.

Bredemeier, Kenneth, "Metrocall Gets Cash Infusion; Stock Soars," *Washington Post,* February 4, 2000, p. E1.

"Digest," *The Washington Post,* May 18, 1996, p. D1.

Dunaief, Daniel, "Toronto Dominion and Bank of Boston Lead Loan to Paging Company," *American Banker,* November 20, 1996, p. 29.

Files, Jennifer, "Paging Giant Challenges Rival's Bid for Troubled Addison, Texas, Firm," *Knight-Ridder/Tribune Business News,* July 20, 2000.

Irwin, Neil, "Metrocall Launches Bid for Bankrupt Paging Rival," *Washington Post,* July 20, 2000, p. E3.

——, "Metrocall Raises Bid for PageNet," *Washington Post,* September 21, 2000, p. E3.

Jones, Jennifer, "Metrocall Prepares to Fight the Two-Way Paging War," *Washington Business Journal,* July 9, 1999, p. 11.

Kady, Martin, II, "Tech Giants Team up on Wireless Venture," *Washington Business Journal,* February 25, 2000, p. 3.

Knight, Jerry, "Metrocall's Stock Needs a Wake-Up Call," *Washington Post,* July 29, 1996, p. F27.

——, "Washington Investing; Metrocall Shareholders May Reap Rich Rewards," *Washington Post,* February 7, 2000, p. F28.

"Metrocall," *CDA-Investnet Insiders' Chronicle,* January 6, 1997, p. 1.

"Metrocall Draws Near to Closing Deal for AT&T Messaging Division," *Communications Today,* October 1, 1998, p. 4.

"Metrocall Inc.," *Washington Post,* April 28, 1997, p. F36.

"Metrocall Inc.," *Washington Post,* April 22, 1996, p. F31.

"Metrocall Posts $40 Million Loss," *Washington Post,* August 10, 2000, p. E3.

"Metrocall Posts Loss of $12.3 Million in 2nd Quarter," *Washington Post,* August 6, 1997, p. D11.

"Metrocall Posts $7.7 Million Quarterly Loss," *Washington Post,* May 8, 1996, p. F3.

"Metrocall Reports Loss in Quarter," *Washington Post,* February 19, 1997, p. D13.

"Metrocall Stokes Existing Market While Acquisition Flame Cools," *Communications Today,* October 13, 2000.

"Metrocall Ups Ante for PageNet," *Washington Business Journal,* September 22, 2000, p. 99.

"Metrocall's Loss Widens," *Washington Post,* November 3, 2000, p. E5.

"Metrocall's Losses Widen in 1st Quarter," *Washington Post,* May 7, 1997, p. C12.

Mills, Mike, "Metrocall to Acquire 2 More Paging Firms," *Washington Post,* April 24, 1996, p. F1.

——, "Metrocall to Purchase Rival ProNet," *Washington Post,* August 12, 1997, p. C1.

Mulqueen, John T., "AT&T Sells Paging Division," *InternetWeek,* July 6, 1998, p. 45.

"Nashville, Tenn.-Based A+ Network Closes $341 Million Union with Metrocall," *Knight-Ridder/Tribune Business News,* November 18, 1996.

Olson, Thomas, "Hillman Takes Paging Firm Stake, Signals Interest in Beeper Merger," *Pittsburgh Business Times,* October 17, 1994, p. 1.

—David P. Bianco

Mexican Restaurants, Inc.

1135 Edgebrook
Houston, Texas 77034-1899
U.S.A.
Telephone: (713) 943-7574
Fax: (713) 943-9554
Web site: http://www.mexicanrestaurantsinc.com

Public Company
Incorporated: 1973 as Casa Ole
Employees: 2,350
Sales: $63.20 million (2000)
Stock Exchanges: NASDAQ
Ticker Symbol: CASA
NAIC: 72211 Full-Service Restaurants

Mexican Restaurants, Inc. operates nearly 90 Mexican-style restaurants in six states, almost two-thirds of which are company owned. The firm has five different restaurant concepts, which range from the moderately priced, family-oriented Casa Ole, Monterey's Little Mexico, Monterey's Tex-Mex Cafe, and La Senorita, to the more upscale Tortuga's Coastal Cantina. Many of the company's sites are in its home state of Texas, with the rest located in Louisiana, Oklahoma, Idaho, and Michigan. Nearly a fifth of the publicly owned company is controlled by founder Larry Forehand and members of his family.

Beginnings

Mexican Restaurants, Inc. traces its origins to Larry Forehand, who grew up in Texas during the late 1940s and 1950s. While he was in high school he began working as a busboy at the chain-affiliated Monterey House Mexican Restaurant in his home town of Pasadena, where he worked his way up to manager. After a two-year stint in the army, he returned to Pasadena and his job at Monterey. He soon advanced in the organization, eventually attaining the position of director of store operations for 55 of the company's locations. By the early 1970s Forehand decided he wanted to run a restaurant of his own, and he sought to buy a franchise from Monterey House. The company was just then preparing for a public offering, however, and had temporarily suspended franchise sales. With three children to support, Forehand decided to use the experience he had gained working for Monterey to open a moderately priced, family-friendly Mexican-style restaurant of his own.

On December 1, 1973 Forehand's new Casa Ole restaurant debuted in Pasadena. Its first month in operation netted $350 in profits, and sales grew steadily from there. A partner, Mike Domec, opened a second restaurant in Houston in 1976, and two years later the pair formed Casa Ole Franchise Services, Inc. to capitalize on the restaurants' popularity. One of the first franchisees to sign on was Tom Harken, a Beaumont, Texas man who earlier had sold vacuum cleaners and recreational vehicles. Harken, who had suffered from polio as a child, never finished school or learned to read but nonetheless had become a successful businessman with the help of his wife Melba. Over the next 15 years Harken opened seven Casa Ole restaurants, becoming the company's largest individual franchisee.

Forehand and Domec themselves also opened a number of new sites in the Houston metro area and in several smaller towns in Texas. By the mid-1980s there were more than 20 Casa Ole restaurants, about half built by the company and half by franchisees. A surge in growth took place beginning in 1984, when the company renovated all of its older locations and opened 12 new restaurants in an 18-month period. By 1988 Casa Ole's systemwide sales stood at $36.1 million.

The Casa Ole formula of reasonably priced, ''gringo''-friendly Mexican-style food served in a sit-down restaurant setting was well received in the marketplace. At a time when most restaurants were seeing declining sales figures, Casa Ole was reporting 10 percent annual per-store sales growth. Speaking to the *Houston Chronicle,* Forehand attributed this to the firm's careful growth strategy, its strict quality standards, its low overhead, and adherence to a Tex-Mex menu. The company employed five supervisors who continually inspected the chain's restaurants, and each Casa Ole gave out customer comment cards with every table check. Forehand or Domec personally reviewed each card and mailed letters, including gift certificates worth $5, to any unhappy patrons. In addition to keeping a close watch on the restaurant chain, Forehand participated in

Company Perspectives:

The Company's objective is to be perceived as the national value leader in the Mexican segment of the full-service casual dining marketplace. To accomplish this objective, the Company has developed strategies designed to achieve and maintain high levels of customer loyalty, frequent patronage and profitability. The key strategic elements are: Offering consistent, high-quality, original recipe Mexican menu items that reflect both national and local taste preferences; pricing menu offerings at levels below many family and casual-dining restaurant concepts; selecting, training and motivating its employees to enhance customer dining experiences and the friendly casual atmosphere of its restaurants; providing customers with the friendly, attentive service typically associated with more expensive casual-dining experiences; and reinforcing the perceived value of the dining experience with a comfortable and inviting Mexican decor.

numerous community organizations and sponsored anti-drug and educational achievement programs in the Pasadena schools.

New Investors, Expansion, and an IPO in the Mid-1990s

The firm's growth slowed during the early 1990s as the U.S. economy faltered. By 1995 there were a total of 39 Casa Ole restaurants in operation, with the last company-funded site having opened in 1989. In the fall of 1995 an agreement was reached with Tex-Mex Partners L.C. to fund renewed expansion of the chain. Tex-Mex principal Louis Neeb became chairman and CEO of Casa Ole and Patrick Morris of Tex-Mex was named president. Forehand stayed on as vice-chairman, and Domec took a seat on the company's board. Shortly after this realignment, Casa Ole went public, selling two million shares of stock on the NASDAQ exchange. The money was earmarked for buying out Mike Domec's stake in the company and for funding further expansion.

Following the IPO Casa Ole reached an agreement with Ronald Sacks, a former executive with several restaurant chains, to become a ''market partner.'' Sacks would oversee company-funded expansion into Idaho, where as many as ten restaurants were planned. The joint venture was given the name Casa Ole Mountain States LLC. Another deal was made to open sites in Louisiana, and later in the year a new company-owned restaurant opened in Copperas Cove, Texas. A franchised outlet was bought back by the company as well.

A visitor to a Casa Ole restaurant at this time would find a Southwestern-style facade that gave way to a bright and upbeat Mexican-themed interior. Free chips and two types of salsa were delivered when customers arrived. The menu included a wide range of Mexican and Tex-Mex dishes, but some American choices were available, mainly aimed at children. A typical lunch entree cost about $5, with dinner around $7, and portions were generous. Casa Ole also served beer and wine, but sales of alcohol were not emphasized. The average 4,300-square-foot restaurant seated 160 to 180.

Acquisition of Monterey's in 1997

In the spring of 1997 Casa Ole announced that it would acquire Monterey's Acquisition Corp. for $11.6 million. Monterey's Acquisition was the successor to Monterey Mexican House, where Larry Forehand had gotten his start in 1959. Monterey's now operated 26 Mexican restaurants in Texas and Oklahoma under the names Monterey's Tex-Mex Cafe, Monterey's Little Mexico, and Tortuga's Coastal Cantina. The first two concepts, 21 of them Tex-Mex Cafes and two of them Little Mexicos, were similar in format to Casa Ole, but the company's three Tortuga's outlets were more upscale. Casa Ole announced plans to convert several of the Monterey's restaurants into Casa Ole restaurants, but most would be left as they were. Monterey's, which had been founded in 1954, had struggled through bankruptcy and several changes of ownership before Casa Ole stepped in.

A few months after the Monterey's purchase, Casa Ole President Pat Morris resigned, citing strategic differences with the company's board. His replacement was Curt Glowacki, who had come to the company via Monterey's. Founder Larry Forehand now increased his involvement with Casa Ole, following a period of reduced activity while he led the Texas Restaurant Association. He took the position of Director of Franchising, in addition to serving as vice-chairman.

The company's sales had been sluggish in the months following the acquisition of Monterey's, and several steps were soon taken to improve Casa Ole's financial picture. The most prominent move was a ''sale-leaseback'' transaction in which Franchise Finance Corporation of America purchased 13 of the company's sites for $11.5 million, and then leased them back to Casa Ole. This gave the company a needed infusion of capital, which it used to pay down debt.

Shortly after this agreement was reached, Casa Ole made a deal to buy the Michigan-based La Senorita Restaurant chain for $4 million. The purchase gave Casa Ole five of the firm's nine Mexican-style restaurants and partial interest in a sixth, along with all rights to the concept and name. During 1998 Casa Ole also closed or sold several underperforming restaurants, opened two new sites, and bought another one of its franchised locations.

A New Name in 1998

Following completion of the La Senorita acquisition in early 1999, the company effected a name change to Mexican Restaurants, Inc. CEO Neeb stated that this would ''more fully reflect the Company's ongoing strategy of growing by careful new restaurant development in existing markets, coupled with opportunistic acquisitions of proven Mexican restaurant companies.'' Neeb and the company's board also decided that future expansion plans would concentrate on the Tortuga's Coastal Cantina concept. Tortuga's, which was likened to a Mexican version of the casual dining chain Denny's, had substantially higher per-check averages than the company's other concepts, and it offered a full-service bar. Overall sales volumes were also significantly higher than at the average Casa Ole. During 1999 five Tortuga's locations were opened or converted from Casa Ole restaurants. At the end of the year Mexican Restaurants owned 55 out of a systemwide total of 92 sites.

Key Dates:

1973: Larry Forehand opens the first Casa Ole restaurant in Pasadena, Texas.
1976: Mike Domec opens a second restaurant in Houston.
1978: Forehand and Domec combine forces to franchise the Casa Ole concept.
1984: Firm upgrades its older restaurants and begins to add more company-owned sites.
1996: Casa Ole goes public on the NASDAQ exchange; new round of expansion begins.
1997: Purchase of Monterey's Acquisitions, Inc. adds 26 new restaurants.
1999: La Senorita chain is acquired; Casa Ole changes its name to Mexican Restaurants, Inc.
2000: First Tennessee Securities Corp. is hired to look at the company's strategic options.

Since the public offering Mexican Restaurants had been generally managing a small profit, but with an intensely competitive marketplace and rising prices from suppliers, it was getting tougher and tougher to stay in the black. A new effort was implemented to improve food quality, service, and ambience at the chain's locations. The result was an increase in foot traffic, but Wall Street was indifferent to the company's fortunes and the stock price generally stayed below the $4 mark. Seeking to improve shareholder value, in late 2000 the company's board voted to seek advice on corporate strategy from First Tennessee Securities Corp. Several options were under consideration, included selling the company. During the summer Louis Neeb also handed his CEO duties to President Glowacki, though he continued to act as board chairman.

In early 2001 a former Mexican Restaurants director, John Textor, announced his intentions to seek control of the company, which Neeb characterized as a friendly bid. Textor headed an investor group that had acquired 16 percent of the outstanding stock. At this same time Mexican Restaurants' principal lender, Bank of America, informed the company that it would end its relationship with the chain. The bank had recently tightened its loan rules, and Mexican Restaurants could no longer meet the requirements. The company was in the process of selling two of its restaurants, but the money would not be available quickly enough to meet the Bank of America obligation.

Mexican Restaurants, Inc. was in a period of transition, which its management hoped would end in a way that would strengthen the company over the long term. While it waited for the changes to come, the firm would continue on its daily mission of providing customers with reasonably priced Mexican-style cuisine in a southwestern-themed setting.

Principal Subsidiaries

Monterey's Acquisition Corp.; La Senorita Restaurants.

Principal Competitors

Atomic Burrito, Inc.; Avado Brands, Inc.; Brinker International, Inc.; Del Taco, Inc.; El Chico Restaurants, Inc.; Pancho's Mexican Buffet, Inc.; Prandium, Inc.; Taco Cabana, Inc.

Further Reading

Carlino, Bill, ''Casa Ole Seals Monterey's Deal: Uses $s to Test Concepts,'' *Nation's Restaurant News,* July 21, 1997, p. 11.
Guerrero, Kevin, ''Mexican Restaurants Chairman Neeb Says Bidders Welcome,'' *Federal Filings Newswires,* March 13, 2001.
Levinson, Brian, ''Casa Ole Embarks on Ambitious Expansion,'' *Houston Chronicle,* September 29, 1986, p. 1.
'' 'Mexican' Earnings Up 4%, But Firm Faces Bid for Control,'' *Nation's Restaurant News,* April 9, 2001, p. 12.
Robinson, Kathy, ''It's a Whole Different Scene—Casa Ole Plays Tex-Mex Theme to the Hilt in Music, Decor and Menu Selections,'' *Idaho Statesman,* April 17, 1998, p. 14S.
Ruggless, Ron, ''Casa Ole Broadens Tex-Mex Horizon with Monterey's Purchase,'' *Nation's Restaurant News,* May 19, 1997, p. 258.
——, ''Casa Ole Chief Neeb Plots Strategy to Sidestep Stalled Sales,'' *Nation's Restaurant News,* January 19, 1998, p. 3.
——, ''Casa Ole Reports Store-Sales Increase After IPO Offering,'' *Nation's Restaurant News,* September 9, 1996, p. 11.
——, ''Mexican Restaurants Seeks to Shed Profit Drag with Focus on Its Tortuga Chain,'' *Nation's Restaurant News,* April 24, 2000, p. 11.
Silverman, Dwight, ''Casa Ole Eateries to Buy Monterey's,'' *Houston Chronicle,* May 3, 1997, p. 1.
Woodard, Tracey Taylor, ''Casa Ole Prexy Reaps Rewards from Community Involvement,'' *Nation's Restaurant News,* May 1, 1989, p. 3.

—Frank Uhle

MULTIMEDIA GAMES™

Multimedia Games, Inc.

8900 Shoal Creek Boulevard
Building 3, Suite 300
Austin, Texas 78757
U.S.A.
Telephone: (512) 371-7100
Fax: (512) 371-7114
Web site: http://www.multimediagames.com

Public Company
Incorporated: 1991
Employees: 152
Sales: $96.8 million (2000)
Stock Exchanges: NASDAQ
Ticker Symbol: MGAM
NAIC: 339999 All Other Miscellaneous Manufacturing; 513220 Cable and Other Program Distribution; 514191 Online Information Access Services; 713290 Other Gambling Industries

Multimedia Games, Inc. provides high-stakes bingo gaming and video lottery gaming systems to Native American-owned gaming centers and charity bingo halls nationwide. The company produces MegaBingo and MegaCash, live bingo games that link players at various bingo halls via satellite. Individual electronic player stations at gaming centers provide high-speed bingo gaming by connecting participants at numerous locations via private intranet. Games include MegaMania Bingo, BigCash Bingo, Flash21 Bingo, Super FlashCash, and MegaNanza. Multimedia Games also designs and manufactures video lottery games for the Native American market, including the popular Meltdown, Filthy Rich, and Reel 'Em In games.

Bingo Gaming via Satellite in the Early 1990s

Multimedia Games originated as two companies, Gamma International, Ltd., and TV Bingo Network, Inc. (TBN). Gordon Graves cofounded both companies to provide technology and services for the gaming industry, undergoing dramatic growth with federal approval of gaming on Native American land. Gamma International, established in 1988, produced MegaBingo, a high stakes bingo game transmitted daily via closed-circuit satellite television and, simultaneously, over a data telecommunications network and an audio conference call network.

Gamma designed MegaBingo to provide a low-cost operation for high-stakes bingo at charity bingo halls and Native American gaming centers. By linking several facilities into one game, hosted by Creek Nation Tulsa Bingo in Tulsa, Oklahoma, MegaBingo allowed participating bingo halls to offer larger jackpots, thus increasing the incentive to play. In addition to large cash jackpots and other prizes, MegaBingo provided the opportunity to win a $1 million jackpot. When a player made "bingo" within a specific number of balls drawn or covered all 24 numbers on the card within 50 balls drawn, that player won an opportunity to spin the Super Jackpot Wheel, with the lowest prize being a $50,000 jackpot and two slots marking a $1 million jackpot.

By early 1994 the company provided bingo games to 54 bingo halls on Native American reservations in 17 states. The 12-minute show generated $16 million in gaming revenue each year from 1991 to 1994 and revenues of about $3 million per year for each game hall. Gamma awarded more than $50 million in prizes between 1989 and 1994. The success of MegaBingo led to the development of a similar show, MegaCash, broadcast during Saturday and Sunday matinee gaming.

Graves formed TBN (originally Graves International, Inc.) in 1991 to provide multimedia communications, data processing systems, and interactive games for network television and cable television, as well as the gaming industry. Graves intended TBN to operate games specifically for the home television market. Its first game versions, however, were unprofitable. The company licensed a bingo game to Bingo McLaughlin, Inc. to produce the game at the reservation of the Pawnee Tribe of Oklahoma, which connected with other bingo halls in Oklahoma by satellite, and to provide electronic player stations for bingo play linked by computer. Bingo McLaughlin went bankrupt, however, leaving TBN with a write-off of $700,000 in 1992 and 1993. TBN also handled management and marketing for Gamma's MegaBingo operation.

Company Perspectives:

Multimedia Games is a company with more than just "games, player stations, and networks." With the advent of networked-type games, hall and casino operators have scrambled for ways to manage game delivery, monitor play, and compile data so that they may better respond to customer needs and playing patterns. Multimedia Games is now beta testing systems that fulfill these new demands.

The merger of TBN and Gamma began with an April 1994 agreement that arranged for TBN to produce MegaBingo for Gamma and to purchase the necessary equipment and assets from Gamma. TBN financed the acquisition with secured notes and warrants and formed a subsidiary, MegaBingo, Inc., to operate the game.

The arrangement allowed TBN to extend MegaBingo game play through an interactive TV game show, Million Dollar TV MegaBingo, its first profitable game for the home television market. Launched in May 1994, the show allowed viewers to hire a proxy to participate in the Sunday night MegaBingo game; each of the six participating bingo halls provided proxy players. The customer arranged for a surrogate player by mail, telephone, or in-person registration at the bingo hall. For $5.00, each player received two bingo cards for the proxy player and two copies for home monitoring. In early July TBN began offering in-person registration through more than 100 authorized retail stores, with sales averaging 60 proxy plays per outlet during the first week. The Million Dollar TV MegaBingo show, introduced in the Tulsa and Oklahoma City markets, included a trivia game with contestant participation, Native American news, and a rebroadcast of the MegaBingo game played earlier that evening, so that participating viewers could see if they won.

At the end of 1994, TBN completed the acquisition of Gamma, renamed American Gaming & Entertainment (AGE), for $1.8 million plus debt liabilities. AGE became a subsidiary of the company and TBN took the name Multimedia Games (MGAM) to reflect the new direction of the company, toward electronic game cards on individual playing stations and Internet gaming services. MGAM developed two proprietary technologies, MegaMania, a game software, and Betnet, a communications infrastructure designed for business-to-business applications. Using these new technologies, the company sought to change the dynamic of bingo gaming.

In early 1995 MGAM began to offer bingo faces on handheld, electronic bingo machines as an option to paper cards for the MegaBingo game. The machine displayed bingo faces on an LED flat screen, which a player marked from a keyboard. On the electronic system, a customer can play more cards simultaneously than with paper cards, resulting in higher level of play and increased revenues at bingo halls. The electronic game also attracted younger players to bingo. In an agreement with Power Bingo Corporation (PBC), MGAM arranged for the distribution of the electronic bingo faces and provided maintenance and repair on PBC machines at participating bingo halls. PBC received a percentage of MGAM's net revenue and MGAM received exclusive rights to distribute Power Bingo machines at Oklahoma reservations, plus a fee for machine service and maintenance. MGAM expected net revenue of $10 per machine per month.

MGAM used its association with gaming organizations to market Interlott pulltab/breakopen cards and vending machines at Native American and charity gaming markets. In a distribution contract with International Lottery, Inc., MGAM agreed to sell and distribute 1,500 machines the first year and 2,500 machines the second and third years in order to maintain exclusive rights, with the option for up to nine one-year extensions of the contract.

In June 1995 MGAM launched the Indian Gaming Network of Oklahoma (IGN-OK) to provide a bingo game to smaller bingo halls via satellite. MegaBingo Lite allowed the smaller halls an opportunity to link into one bingo game and to entice new player participation with larger jackpots. Nine halls participated in the 15 minute show, offering a $25,000 jackpot that increased $250 per game until a player won. MGAM presented MegaBingo Lite on Thursday, Friday, and Saturday evenings from the MegaBingo Studio at Creek Nation Tulsa Bingo.

MGAM also expanded gaming services with a two-hour bingo show, called Mega MegaBingo. The company held its first two-hour MegaBingo extravaganza on Labor Day and garnered gross revenue from wagers of $1.8 million. MGAM gave away two $500,000 annuity prizes and an additional $500,000 in prizes—in increments of $33,333; $25,000; $12,000; and $5,000—for a gross margin after prize giveaways of $191,000. The session involved 28 bingo halls in eight states, earning $567,000 combined.

The combination of Gamma and TBN proved successful. Within the first year of operating MegaBingo, MGAM added eight gaming halls to the MegaBingo network, including Pascua Yaqui Tribe's Casino of the Sun in Tucson and the Prairie Band Potawatomi Hall in Mayetta, Kansas. Wagering revenues for participating bingo halls increased more than 20 percent. MGAM earned a $0.5 million profit on $17.1 million in revenue at the end of fiscal September 30, 1995, compared with a $1.5 million loss on $1.4 million revenues the previous year.

Proprietary Technologies Yielding Positive Results in 1995

In October 1995 MGAM introduced MegaMania, a high-speed bingo game that allowed players to participate in the MegaBingo games on an individual electronic station. The company's Betnet technology provided the communications network that linked stations at participating gaming centers, allowing players to compete for larger jackpots through a greater number of participants. In addition, MegaMania involved strategic decisions to increase the players' chances of winning, with prizes available every 20 seconds. At 25 cents per card, odds for the progressive jackpot made $100 or more available to win every 15 minutes, and a jackpot of approximately $20,000 available every few days. MGAM installed 330 MegaMania machines in five bingo halls on the network.

The game proved to be quite popular, with more than 70 percent of the machines being played at any time. The rate of

Key Dates:

1989: MegaBingo is launched via satellite from Indian gaming hall.
1994: Gamma International and TV Bingo Network merge; company is renamed Multimedia Games.
1995: Electronic player stations are introduced with MegaMania bingo game.
1997: MegaBingo super jackpot prize is doubled to $2 million.
1998: Revenues increase 81 percent, to $70.5 million.
1999: MGAM enters Class III gaming with video lottery systems for tribes in Washington.
2000: The company begins testing software for translating remote telecast via Internet.

play, or "handle," per machine averaged $110 per hour and the net revenue after player prizes, or "hold," averaged $15.00 per hour per machine. MGAM received ten percent to 30 percent of the hold, and bingo halls garnered a net revenue of $50 per machine per day. The electronic playing stations, manufactured by Video King, were designed to allow machines from other manufacturers to network with the system. The popularity of the MegaMania game resulted in a backlog of orders for the electronic play stations.

A dramatic increase in revenues during fiscal 1996 was attributed to the success of MegaMania. Although the game did not have a significant installed base until April, MegaMania contributed $6.1 million to the 40 percent increase in total revenues of $23 million that year. At the end of fiscal 1996, 1,000 electronic player stations operated at 24 Native American gaming facilities in six states.

In December MGAM began to offer proxy players via the Internet for game play at participating Native American bingo halls. Customers used a proxy at any of 51 bingo halls in 13 states in order to compete against about 15,000 players for jackpots of up to $5,000. Players joined the American Gaming Network at betnet.com, with a payment of $29.95 and a one-time fee of $4.95. Payments were made on the web site with either a credit card or bank account, by telephone credit card payment, or check by mail. The customer had an account that MGAM debited $5.50 for each proxy play of three bingo cards. The game was not available for viewing in realtime, but could be downloaded immediately afterward. Participation was open to residents of all states except Hawaii, Arkansas, and Utah, where bingo gaming was illegal. MGAM hoped to introduce faster-paced versions of bingo to the Internet to attract younger players.

The U.S. Attorney's office challenged MegaMania's status as a Class II game, considering it to be too different from bingo. In April 1997 MGAM signed a memorandum of agreement to make certain changes to maintain its Class II status. Changes included interactive daubing bingo faces on a touch screen, and to lower the cost and prize pattern of the game. The low-cost version, at ten cents per card, provided average jackpots of $7,000, with a maximum prize of $22,000. MGAM expected the low-cost version to stimulate greater interest in MegaMania.

Throughout 1997 the company continued to receive orders for the MegaMania games, resulting in record sales. Once again MegaMania was responsible for a dramatic rise in revenues, a 70 percent increase to $39 million, and net income of $1.3 million.

In October MGAM upgraded the super jackpot wheel of the MegaBingo game, raising the top prize to $2 million and replacing the two $1 million slots on the wheel. The prize was available in $100,000 cash and a 24-year annuity. The company also added bonus prizes such as cars and trips to Las Vegas. The MegaCash game, played on Saturday and Sunday matinees, offered a $1 million jackpot.

Introducing New Gaming Opportunities in the Late 1990s

MGAM introduced several gaming systems in 1998. In February the company installed 350 of the fast-action, FlashCash electronic player stations, available for 24-hour play. During the first three weeks in operation, game play averaged $65 per machine per day. Comparatively, MegaMania took eight months to reach the same level of play. MegaRacing, a simulcast off-track betting system, opened at three native American gaming sites in Oklahoma, handling $275,000 in wagers in the first 17 days and becoming profitable for participating tribes in that time. MGAM supplied the tribes with the signal for the broadcast and related services. The company also launched BigCash Bingo, offering linked bingo with jackpots starting at $10,000, sometimes reaching $30,000 to $40,000 before a player won.

MGAM recorded another dramatic increase in revenue for fiscal year ending September 30, 1998. Revenues increased 81 percent, to $70.5 million in 1998, while net income rose 69 percent, to $2.2 million. MGAM began to see a shift in revenue sources, however, as the paper-based MegaBingo game yielded to the popularity of electronic bingo-style games. In addition, some halls discontinued MGAM's services as they began to produce their own in-house high stakes bingo games and to utilize more profitable Class II interactive or Class III games. The number of bingo halls served dropped from 61 in 1996 to 47 in 1998, while interactive, electronic playing increased from 1,000 machines in 20 gaming centers in 1996 to 3,270 machines in 64 facilities in 1998.

In 1999 MGAM began to offer direct bingo play via the Internet, launching its first interactive Internet bingo game in March. Available free at gamebay.com, FlashCash operated like a tournament sweepstakes, with cash and merchandise prizes, including a $100 prize for the player with the most points during a week of playing of two-minute games. A special 90-minute session on Sundays offered a $100 prize and the ten players with the most points played a special session for an additional $100. During the first week FlashCash averaged 25 players per game and 54 players per tournament. MGAM distributed 100,000 cards and the web site received more than one million hits. By August the FlashCash averaged 400 players per game, with 850 involved in tournament play and the web site received 13.8 million hits per week. The introduction of FlashCash quadrupled membership of the on-line player's club.

MGAM funded the site with targeted advertisements based on preference data during game play.

After national legislation defined the terms of Internet gaming, MGAM planned to offer FlashCash with a $10,000 prize; a wager of 50 cents per card won 50 cents to $100 per game. The $10,000 prize went to any player who covered a straight bingo pattern in the first four balls drawn. For an additional 25 cents per card, the jackpot rose to $25,000.

In April MGAM received approval from the Washington State Gambling Commission to develop, manufacture, and distribute Class III interactive video lottery games for the Tribal Video Lottery System (TVLS), being one of two companies to receive a license. The games imitated scratch-off lottery tickets, but with the look and feel of a slot machine. In June the company introduced several game styles, including Fruit Cocktail Deluxe, Spin & Shout, Cherries Royale, and Meltdown, as well as High Noon Poker. MGAM estimated net revenue per machine at $200 per day, with MGAM garnering 15 percent net for revenue of $30 per day per machine. MGAM offered the machines as rentals initially, with the expectation that once clients saw the profitability of the machines, that purchase or lease-purchase agreements would follow. MGAM installed the first 100 units for the Washington (State) Squaxin Island Tribe at the Little Creek Casino. By the end of fiscal 1999, the company installed more than 700 TVLS games at seven casinos. The system involved a casino management system, individual video lottery terminals, and a cashless wagering system.

As individual electronic player machines became more popular, revenues from MegaBingo continued to decline in 1999. Although electronic interactive bingo expanded to 80 clients with 4,420 playing stations, MegaBingo revenues decreased 22 percent, as participation declined to 32 halls. MGAM restructured its MegaBingo satellite television game, improving both the potential revenues at participating halls and improving the odds for winning. Renewed marketing efforts resulted in four bingo halls joining the network in October 1999, two in Oklahoma and one in Washington, at tribal gaming centers, and one charity bingo hall at Hollywood Park Racetrack in California.

In December MGAM sold a majority interest in its Gamebay.com subsidiary, selling 65 percent in a private sale of common stock and raising $4.7 million. Licensing agreements were established between MGAM and Gamebay. Gamebay obtained use of existing intellectual property to apply to nongambling Internet sweepstakes for a $1 million fee and five percent of Gamebay's revenues. If Gamebay is taken public in the future, MGAM has the option to retain a 20 percent ownership position and reduce the fee by three percent.

MGAM's efforts to extend Internet bingo play to overseas markets came to fruition in May 2000. The Republic of Liberia selected MGAM to provide high-speed interactive bingo for the Liberia International Lottery via the Internet. MGAM launched the game in July 2000.

The company's TVLS proved to be successful for MGAM, which installed three systems at casinos in Washington in May. In addition, five existing clients ordered an additional 400 terminals, a $3.5 million value. Meltdown, a slot-style game with bars and the nuclear symbol, and High Noon Poker proved to be the most popular of the video lottery games. MGAM signed a licensing agreement with WMS Gaming to adapt its casino video slot gaming devices to Native American video lottery in Washington State. The agreement involved nine WMS games, including the popular ''Filthy Rich'' and ''Reel 'Em In'' games. MGAM had the game ready in September for introduction into the Washington State Native American casino market. The seven casinos with TVLS new software allowed for cashless account wagering.

MGAM introduced new technology in the hope of expanding participation in MegaBingo by providing a less expensive broadcast system with new Internet software. In June MGAM installed and began to test the VC-2000 video clone software, which translated data received on the Internet into a telecast. Thus participating MegaBingo bingo halls no longer needed a satellite receiver to broadcast the game; the new system employed personal computers instead. If tests succeeded, the MegaBingo television game would become inexpensive to install, saving costs of production, transmission, and reception. In addition, the technology allowed the show to originate from multiple locations, using digital cameras to present the winner over the air.

While trying to maintain its traditional base of business, electronic player stations continued to be the main focus of development. By October 2000, more than 5,000 machines were interconnected in 92 Class II, Class III, and charity gaming facilities nationwide. In November the company launched the MegaNanza bingo game, a Class II game with the excitement of a Class III game. In April 2001 MGAM signed a licensing agreement with Alliance Gaming Corp. to distribute Bally Gaming & Systems products in Washington's Indian casino market. Under the agreement Bally Gaming received a royalty and a guarantee that MGAM would purchase a minimum number of units during the first two years.

Principal Subsidiaries

American Gaming Network LLC; MegaBingo, Inc.; Multimedia Creative Services, Inc.; TV Games, Inc.

Principal Competitors

GameTech International, Inc.; Littlefield Corporation; Online Gaming Systems, Ltd.

Further Reading

Busch, Melanie, ''Tulsa, Okla., Firm Explores Internet Gaming with Bingo Service,'' *Knight-Ridder/Tribune Business News,* August 1, 1996.

''Circuit Courts' Rulings Stand on MGAM's MegaMania Game,'' *Business Wire,* January 29, 2001.

''MGAM Becomes a Leading Supplier of Interactive Video Lottery Systems in Washington State,'' *PR Newswire,* June 23, 1999.

''MGAM Reports Gaming Site Performance,'' *PR Newswire,* April 5, 1999.

''Multimedia Games Adds Contracts with 10 New Bingo Halls,'' *PR Newswire,* February 25, 1999.

''Multimedia Games Announces Launch of Interactive Internet Bingo Game,'' *PR Newswire,* March 24, 1999.

''Multimedia Games, Inc. Announces New Electronic Bingo Card Product,'' *PR Newswire,* January 26, 1995.

''Multimedia Games, Inc. Introduces New Product,'' *Business Wire,* June 12, 2000.

''Multimedia Games, Inc. Premiers New Indian Gaming Network,'' *PR Newswire,* June 28, 1995.

''Multimeda Games Records $227,000 Profit,'' *Journal Record,* May 8, 1997.

''Multimedia Games Sells $1.4 Million in Electronic Stations in 3rd Fiscal Period,'' *Journal Record,* July 21, 1998.

''Multimedia Games to Launch Internet Gaming Product,'' *PR Newswire,* December 28, 1998.

''TV Bingo Network Changes Name to Multimedia Games, Inc.; Completes Acquisition of MegaBingo,'' *PR Newswire,* December 27, 1994.

—Mary Tradii

National Bank of Greece

86 Eolou Street
Athens 102 32
Greece
Telephone: 30 1 334 1000
Fax: 30 1 321 9696
Web Site: http://www.ethniki.gr

Public Company
Incorporated: 1841
Employees: 15,984
Total Assets: GRD 16.51 billion ($46 million) (2000)
Stock Exchanges: Athens New York
Ticker Symbol: NBG
NAIC: 52211 Commercial Banking, 522292 Real Estate Credit, 52239 Other Activities Related to Credit Intermediation, 52392 Portfolio Management, 52393 Investment Advice, 524128 Other Direct Insurance (Except Life, Health, and Medical) Carriers

National Bank of Greece (NBG) has been a focal point of Greek business and financial life almost from the time it opened in the spring of 1841. Beginning as a private discount and mortgage bank, it soon gained prominence and became the sole issuer of bank notes. It was forced to relinquish that role in 1928 with the establishment of the Bank of Greece, but it has remained Greece's largest financial institution. Currently NBG operates more than 600 branches in 16 countries on four continents; it also has some 35 subsidiaries. At the end of the 20th century, NBG began a push to dominate the banking market in the Balkans, including Yugoslavia, Albania, and Bulgaria. By the end of 2000, the bank estimated that it controlled roughly 40 percent of all deposits and an equal percentage of loans outstanding to Greek households.

19th Century Origins

When NBG was founded in March 1841, Greece had only been a free state for about a dozen years. For nearly four centuries, Greece had been part of the Ottoman Empire, but in 1821 the Greeks began a fight for independence that lasted until 1829. After Greece won its independence, it set about creating government and administrative institutions. Although NBG was not created as the nation's central bank, it grew steadily after its founding and played a prominent role in Greek finance throughout the 19th century.

Within a short time after its founding in 1841, NBG began to expand its services beyond basic commercial banking. Eventually, NBG became involved with agriculture, transportation, and real estate. It developed an agrarian credit program and was given the right to invest capital in Greek industries. Occasionally, the bank would issue public loans and even participate in various public works. Most important to NBG's influence, however, was that it was the only bank in Greece authorized to issue bank notes.

Greece during the 19th century was not a particularly calm and stable place. Greece borders the Aegean Sea, the outlet for the Black Sea that is Russia's only link to the Mediterranean. Although the country became a constitutional monarchy in 1845, the king, Otto I (son of Bavaria's Ludwig I) was hardly popular. His rule was despotic, and he involved Greece in the Crimean War during the 1850s. Eventually he was deposed and the crown was offered to the Danish Prince William, who would become George I. There were other clashes with the Ottoman Turks during these years, and the British Empire and France in particular still held considerable sway over the country's politics. Institutions like the National Bank of Greece were important to the country not only for the obvious services they performed but because they also had a stabilizing effect.

Through the 19th and early 20th centuries NBG continued to grow. In 1880, the Athens Stock Exchange was established, and NBG was one of the first companies listed. NBG also began to acquire other banks, such as the Privileged Bank of Epirothessaly in 1899 and the Bank of Crete in 1919.

The World Wars Shape Greece

Since gaining independence, Greece had gradually been gaining territory through a series of uprisings culminating with the Balkan wars that occurred just before the outbreak of World War I. Greece, one of the Allied nations, benefitted considera-

Company Perspectives:

National Bank of Greece, the oldest and largest among Greek banks, heads the strongest financial group in the country. It boasts a dynamic profile internationally, particularly in Southeastern Europe and the Eastern Mediterranean.

bly when the war ended; when the boundaries of Europe were redrawn, Greece had nearly twice as much land as it did before the war. Some of those gains were reversed when Turkish nationalist forces under Mustafa Kemal recaptured parts of Asia Minor, including the port city of Izmir (Smyrna). The boundaries of modern Greece were established definitively by the Treaty of Lausanne, signed in 1923. By now, NBG was a powerful force in Greek life, both political and financial.

The League of Nations, which had been formed after World War I, believed that NBG's position as both a commercial and state bank was untenable. In fact, the League said, this arrangement left open too many possibilities for conflicts of interest. In accordance with the League's policies as outlined under the Geneva Protocol, Greece agreed to establish a new state bank. The Bank of Greece was thus established on May 15, 1928. Assets in the form of gold and government debt were transferred to the new bank, as were liabilities, primarily in the form of government deposits.

Events of the 1930s had a profound effect in every corner of the world, beginning with the Great Depression and continuing with the unrest that led to World War II. By 1939, war seemed inevitable, and even established institutions such as NBG were subject to the fears of Greek citizens. A run on commercial banks began in the summer of that year; between July and September notes in circulation increased from eight to ten million drachmas. The Bank of Greece acted by making more cash available to the commercial banks to meet their obligations. This calmed the public and the bank run subsided.

In October 1940, Italy attacked Greece after the Greeks refused to cede parts of the country over to Mussolini's Fascist dictatorship. Thanks in part to the British government, which honored an earlier commitment and made significant loans to Greece, the economy managed to remain relatively stable. Moreover, the Greeks were doing quite well in keeping Italian forces at bay. Overall, 1940 proved to be a year of relative financial calm for Greece.

All that changed in April 1941, when Germany decided to attack Greece. Within a month, the Germans had taken Athens. At that point NBG had just turned 100 years old. The Greek government, including the royal family and the Governor of the Bank of Greece, went into exile. The Bank's gold and foreign exchange reserves were taken to Egypt and transferred to the South African Reserve Bank in Pretoria for the duration of the war.

The war ravaged Greece as it did all of Europe, and by its end in 1945 the economic infrastructure had to be rebuilt. The government-in-exile returned to Greece in 1946, along with the country's gold and foreign reserve supplies. International agencies such as the United Nations Relief and Rehabilitation Administration (UNRRA) and private charities helped get Greece and other countries on its feet; moreover, the British Government dropped all claims to the loans it had made to Greece in 1940. However, industrial output was roughly at one-third what it had been before the war, and bank deposits in real terms were at one-thirtieth what they had been in 1939. The Greek government created the Currency Committee, whose members included the Minister of National Economy, other government ministers, and the Governor of the Bank of Greece. All monetary, credit, and foreign exchange policy was set by the Currency Committee.

Postwar Gains and Drawbacks

Despite the Bank of Greece's prominent role, NBG was still the largest commercial bank in the country, and its role remained significant. In 1953, NBG merged with the Bank of Athens and briefly changed its name to the National Bank of Greece and Athens (the NBG name was restored in 1958). By the mid-1960s, NBG accounted for roughly two-thirds of all commercial bank deposits, as well as industry and trade financing.

In the years following World War II, however, the Greek government had been unstable. Communist forces had tried to overthrow the monarchy in the late 1940s but were defeated. All through the 1950s and 1960s, the government was divided into factions supporting communism, royalism, and the growing right wing. This right wing, in the form of a military junta, overthrew the monarchy in April 1967 and established a dictatorship led by Colonel George Papadopoulos. Although some would later suggest that the dictatorship was actually beneficial to the economy, in fact it served to divide the various factions even more sharply. Although the junta established Greece as a republic in 1973, it continued to rule until July 1974 when it was forced out and democratic civilian government (though not the monarchy) was returned.

Reaching from Past to Future

In 1977, NBG formed a committee to work on a project not commonly embarked upon by banks: the creation of a comprehensive Historical Archives Unit. From its founding, NBG had kept historical archives. Realizing the historical and research value of these archives, NBG had begun to compile historic documents for a central archives department years before, in 1938. The outbreak of war in 1941 suspended activity on the archives project, and it was revived in 1962, only to be suspended once again when Papadopoulos seized power in 1967.

This time, NBG created a committee including senior bank officials and historians to create and maintain its archives, as well as to establish a Historical Research Program on Economic History. The goal of this committee was to acquire, compile, and preserve all historical documents from NBG's founding, the records of banks and other companies that were merged with or acquired by NBG, and the personal archives of NBG's top officials. The original documents continued to be both preserved and microfilmed.

Building the Modern Bank

In the 1970s and 1980s Greece went through a transition to mainstream democratic government. The conservative New

Key Dates:

1841: National Bank of Greece (NBG)is founded as a commercial bank.
1880: NBG gains listing on newly formed Athens Stock Exchange.
1928: A new bank, The Bank of Greece, is established as nation's central bank in accordance with Geneva Protocol.
1938: First efforts are made to consolidate NBG's historical archives.
1941: Nazi occupation of Greece begins and lasts for four years.
1953: NBG merges with Bank of Athens, becoming National Bank of Greece and Athens.
1958: National Bank of Greece and Athens officially adopts name National Bank of Greece.
1962: Historical archives project (suspended from 1967–77) resumes.
1998: NBG merges with National Mortgage Bank of Greece; new bank retains NBG name.
1999: NBG becomes first Greek bank to list on New York Stock Exchange.

Democracy party held control until 1981, when the Panhellenic Socialist Movement (Pasok) gained control and elected Andreas Papandreou prime minister. Papandreou, an economist, favored a strong socialist agenda including universal health care and a pension system. The government borrowed heavily to finance its goals and inflation rose dramatically. By the end of the decade the Pasok government had fallen out of favor and the New Democrats were voted back in.

One of the most important decisions Greece had to make during this period was whether it wanted to be part of the European Monetary Union (EMU). To do this would mean that the Greek government would have to put its economic house in order.

During this time NBG continued to pursue a strategy of growth and diversification. It purchased several companies, established others, and consolidated its holdings. The company also embarked on a restructuring and modernization program. This included merging the bank's two mortgage companies, absorbing the National Mortgage Bank of Greece, merging the bank's four insurance companies into one unit, and divesting itself of assets it deemed non-core. NBG also worked to reduce the number of nonperforming loans; the number of new nonperforming loans was down to 0.19 percent by the end of 2000.

In addition, NBG enhanced its technological infrastructure, thereby streamlining operations and making it easier for the bank to be a truly global presence. NBG was one of the first Greek banks to offer its customers Internet banking. In October 1999, NBG became the first Greek bank (and only the second Greek company) to list on the prestigious New York Stock Exchange.

NBG, viewing the Balkans as an important strategic market, began acquiring stakes in regional banks. In the words of the bank, it wanted to take ''a decisive step toward transforming itself from the Bank of 11 million Greeks to the Bank of 60 million inhabitants of the Balkans.'' In 2000 it acquired a 65 percent stake in Stopanska Bank A.D., the largest commercial bank of the former Yugoslav republic of Macedonia; as well as an 89.89 percent stake in United Bulgarian Bank, one of that country's largest. By the beginning of the 21st century, NBG had established a presence in 16 countries on four continents, including offices in major internal banking centers such as New York, London, and Frankfurt. Domestically, the bank had more than 600 branches by the end of 2000, as well as more than 840 ATM machines.

Entry into the European Monetary Union meant a greater global presence for NBG, but it also meant more competition from other banks in Europe. NBG's push toward modernization, greater profitability, and improved customer service was designed both to bring in new customers and to maintain the seven million deposit accounts and one million lending accounts the bank had as of early 2001.

Principal Subsidiaries

Atlantic Bank of New York (U.S.; 99.92%), Banque Nationale de Grece (France), National Bank of Greece (Canada), NBG Balkan Fund, NBC Finance PLC (U.K.), Ethniki Mutual Fund Management, S.A., NBG Venture Capital, Ethniki Leasing, Stopanska Banka A.D.-Skopje (65%), United Bulgarian Bank (89.89%).

Principal Competitors

Alpha Bank, Commercial Bank of Greece, Credit Agricole.

Further Reading

Canadis, Wray O., *The Economy of Greece, 1944–66.* New York: Praeger, 1966.

Country Profile 2000: Greece. London: The Economist Intelligence Unit, 2000.

''From the Bank's Standpoint: 125 Years in the Service of the Nation,'' *Greece Today,* January 1966, p. 4.

Kouzos, Nick, ''The Greek Banking Industry,'' speech given at the Greek-Turkish Information Society Forum, *invgr.com,* May 27, 2000.

''National Bank of Greece Becomes First Greek Bank to List on NYSE,'' *New York Stock Exchange press release,* November 12, 1998.

Pantelakis, Nikos, ''Business Archives in Greece: The Example of the Historical Archives of the National Bank of Greece,'' presented at the CLIR/Library of Congress Conference, April 1999.

—George A. Milite

National TechTeam, Inc.

27335 West Eleven Mile Road
Southfield, Michigan 48034
U.S.A.
Telephone: (248) 357-2866
Toll Free: (800) 276-8524
Fax: (248) 357-2570
Web site: http://www.techteam.com

Public Company
Incorporated: 1979 as Computer Trade Development Corp.
Employees: 1,500
Sales: $124.16 million (2000)
Stock Exchanges: NASDAQ
Ticker Symbol: TEAM
NAIC: 541519 Other Computer Related Services; 541512 Computer Systems Design Services; 61142 Computer Training

National TechTeam, Inc. provides computer services for Fortune 1000 companies in North America and Europe. A large portion of the company's revenues come from its help-desk centers, where TechTeam staffers answer technical questions for clients' customers over the telephone and via the Internet. TechTeam also provides corporate computer training and other computer consulting services. The company's clients include automakers Ford and DaimlerChrysler, Liberty Mutual Insurance, the European Commission, and many others. After a period of explosive growth during the mid-1990s TechTeam saw its revenues drop, and the company recently has been working hard to streamline operations and refocus on its core strengths.

Beginnings

National TechTeam was founded by a Michigan dentist named William Coyro, Jr., in 1979. Coyro, who was born in Detroit in 1943, attended the University of Michigan and then the University of Detroit Dental School, where he graduated in 1969. Following service as a dentist in the U.S. Navy, he opened an office in the Detroit area. An active investor in technology stocks, in 1979 Coyro decided to become directly involved in the field by forming a company called Computer Trade Development Corp. The new company was not active initially, but in 1982 Coyro sought out investors to back a plan to market personal computers built by Solid State Technology, a firm in which he had invested. A number of his friends put $10,000 each into the endeavor. Computer Trade Development Corp. soon began marketing Solid State computers to local customers, including Ford and Chrysler, but the computer maker went out of business not long after. By this time, however, Coyro also had linked up with Fortune Systems of California and had taken an order for 5,000 of its Unix-based personal computers from Ford.

Computer Trade Development Corp. continued selling computers throughout the mid-1980s, and in 1987 the company's directors decided to offer training and support services for corporate PC users as well, much as Electronic Data Systems did for mainframe computer users. A merger with the publicly traded MegaVest Industries was effected, and the company's name became National TechTeam, Inc. Calvin Fox, an experienced investment banker from Los Angeles, had facilitated the deal and gained 10 percent ownership of National TechTeam in the process. In 1988 a merger with Far West Ventures of Costa Mesa, California brought more experienced management on board, including former TRW executive Rowland Day, who took on the CEO and president duties from Coyro. The company's founder continued to serve as board chairman. National TechTeam gave Far West 21 percent of the company's 5.2 million shares of stock in the deal.

TechTeam's entry into the computer training field was jump-started when the firm won a contract from Ford Motor Company to perform all of the automaker's North American computer training. The magnitude of the three-year contract required TechTeam to invest $3.5 million into equipment and staff development, which forced it to operate in the red for several years. When the resultant string of quarterly losses were reported, TechTeam's stock price withered, eventually hitting a low of 59 cents. Coyro and the rest of the company's board were receiving stock options in lieu of pay, a move that would benefit them in the future, but which was less appealing in the short run. The com-

Company Perspectives:

Our Mission is: To be recognized as a premier provider of knowledge management solutions. We will achieve this by analyzing the information gathered through our services to drive process improvements that make our clients more efficient and profitable.

pany's founder was forced to continue working as a dentist evenings and weekends so that he could pay his family's bills.

Once the Ford contract was under way, other companies began to discover National TechTeam. Another early client was Uniplex Business Software, which engaged the company to train commercial end-users of that firm's Unix-based products. TechTeam subsequently opened several offices around the United States to augment its Detroit-area operations center. During this period the company also began development of what was dubbed ActionTrac, a software program that tracked computer system usage and problems. ActionTrac addressed the concerns of many companies that were implementing new, untested software systems that often failed to operate as promised or had inadequate technical support. With it, information systems managers could evaluate the long-term effectiveness of new systems they were installing. TechTeam staff helped operate the ActionTrac system.

In 1990 TechTeam announced a merger with Royalpar Industries, Inc., but this fell through prior to completion. Rowland Day also left the firm, turning the reins of power back to Coyro. The job of president was filled in the fall of 1992 by Ronald Laubert, director of business development for TechTeam. The 1992 fiscal year was the company's best ever, with profits of $766,000 on income of $10.9 million. TechTeam's revenues had shot up nearly 40 percent from the previous year, which had seen profits of only $57,000. During this period contracts were signed with a number of major companies, including Chrysler Corp., Blue Cross/Blue Shield of Michigan, and U.S. Leasing International.

Discovery of a New, and Needed, Service in 1993

In April of 1993 the company began working for software maker WordPerfect Corp. to run a supplementary telephone support center for users of that company's products. WordPerfect itself would handle 65 percent of the calls, while TechTeam took on the remainder. The company gave its employees 20 hours of WordPerfect training, after which they took a test that verified their mastery of the software. TechTeam already had supplied other services to WordPerfect as an outgrowth of its Ford work, as Ford was then WordPerfect's largest customer. The new phone center sideline proved a success, and other corporations, including software maker Corel, soon called on TechTeam for similar services.

TechTeam expanded into Europe in the fall of 1993 when it formed a subsidiary called TechTeam Europe, Ltd. The Brentwood, England-based operation was opened, in large part, to offer continuity of service to TechTeam's American clients who operated in Europe. Later in the year the company acquired a Chicago-based computer services firm called Micro Systems Group in a stock exchange transaction.

The new subsidiaries and the rapidly growing telephone call center operation helped keep National TechTeam on the fast track for growth. By the end of 1993 the company had more than 400 employees, nearly double the number of just nine months earlier. TechTeam's staff was training more than 54,000 computer users a year and handling 8,600 technical support phone calls a day. Ford Motor Company remained the company's top customer, accounting for 60 percent of revenues. Half of TechTeam's total income now came from its computer contract service division, which provided phone helpline, PC networking, database development, and other hardware and software administration services. Another 40 percent was derived from the documentation and training division, and 10 percent came from hardware and software sales. Revenues for 1993 had nearly doubled from a year earlier, topping $20 million, and net earnings were up a similar percentage.

Rapid Expansion Continuing in the Mid-1990s

The company's growth continued to soar during the mid-1990s. Customer support call centers were set up for Hewlett-Packard and Micrografx, and additional business came from established customers such as Chrysler Corp. and the Prosecuting Attorneys Association of Michigan. To avoid the potential disaster of overextending its reach, the company invested in new systems and hired new staff at a pace that anticipated, rather than reacted to, new business.

In August of 1995 TechTeam signed its biggest contract ever, a $10 million deal that called for it to double the size of Hewlett-Packard's existing customer support call centers. Revenues again increased more than 100 percent during 1995, to $42 million. The new focus on telephone support services had helped the company reduce its percentage of Ford-derived work to less than half of total revenues. Other major customers included Corel Corp., which was responsible for 12 percent, Chrysler, with nearly 11, and WordPerfect, with 7.5.

In early 1996 TechTeam purchased New Jersey-based Coup, Inc., which offered training services for major corporations like AT&T and Hewlett-Packard. Also during the year a new call center was completed in Detroit suburb Harper Woods, and the company's Southfield, Michigan center was expanded significantly. A total of 1,038 phone stations were available at these sites. TechTeam also opened a new call center in Brussels, Belgium to perform European helpline work. A joint venture with Paratel NV, called National TechTeam Europe NV, was set up to handle the anticipated multilingual/multinational calls.

The company's growth was finally getting noticed on Wall Street, and the stock price surged to $27 a share in September, up from under $5 in March. Three million new shares were soon issued, joining the 11 million already in circulation. In October, TechTeam acquired USA Computer Training Centers of Boston, which offered training services in Massachusetts. The company also acquired a Nebraska-based Internet and telecommunications firm, WebCentric Communications, Inc., for nearly $7 million in stock and cash at the end of 1996.

Key Dates:

1979: Dentist William Coyro, Jr., forms Computer Trade Development Corp.
1982: The firm begins marketing personal computers with help from new investors.
1987: Merger takes the company public and changes its name; a new focus is placed on training services.
1988: Receipt of major training contract with Ford Motor Co. launches period of growth.
1993: Telephone help-desk services are introduced and quickly become a major focus of the firm; the first European office opens in England.
1997: Expansion slows; stock price drops after allegations of accounting fraud.
1998: The company settles shareholder lawsuit for $11 million.
1999: TechTeam restructures operations and returns to profitability.

In early 1997 TechTeam announced that it would hire 100 new people a month during the year to staff its still-growing call centers. The company's 1,500 employees would nearly double in number by year's end. Call center services continued to provide nearly half the company's revenues, which climbed steeply again during 1996 to $69 million. In the late spring of 1997 yet another acquisition was made, that of Drake Technologies of Warren, Michigan. Drake was a provider of telephone voice-response services. Shortly afterward a New Jersey company, Compuflex Systems, also was purchased. It was later renamed National TechTeam of New Jersey, Inc.

The Bubble Bursting in 1997

In July of 1997 an article appeared in the investor's publication *Barron's,* which alleged that National TechTeam had used a loophole in accounting rules to overstate earnings for the end of 1996 and the first quarter of 1997. The company's stock tumbled, losing a third of its value almost immediately and continuing to decline as the year wore on. A shareholder lawsuit soon followed, charging that company executives had sold off large chunks of their own holdings while artificially inflating the price by overstating earnings figures. TechTeam denied the accusations, vowing to vigorously fight the charges in court.

The year 1997 proved to be difficult for the company. In addition to the allegations of fraud, which led the Securities and Exchange Commission to ask TechTeam to restate its quarterly earnings reports, the firm's growth curve had finally peaked, and the company posted losses of $1.9 million for the year. CEO Coyro attributed the poor showing to a number of unprofitable contracts, which he said were already being supplanted by more favorable ones.

To help right the ship, in early 1998 TechTeam brought in a new president and chief operating officer, former Chrysler Vice-President Harry Lewis, and also completed a 1.5 million share stock buyback program. TechTeam also acquired Capricorn Capital, a high-technology leasing and financing firm, and bought out its partner in the Belgian call center venture.

The year 1998 saw improvements in TechTeam's operations, and at the end of the year Lewis was moved up to CEO. Shortly after his promotion, the company settled the shareholder lawsuit for $11 million. The payment was covered by insurance, but TechTeam took a $3.3 million hit for lawsuit-related expenses, which helped put annual losses at $3.8 million. More accounting troubles surfaced in early 1999 when the company again was asked to restate an earnings report that had underreported losses. New measures were put into effect to reduce the possibility of future accounting problems.

A Return to Form in 1999

During 1999 TechTeam expanded its services overseas, forming TechTeam Europe GmbH to operate in Germany. The company also created the Network Consulting Services Group to offer a variety of network-related services, and opened a new call center in Davenport, Iowa to provide services for a maker of agricultural equipment. TechTeam reported its first profitable year since 1996, earning $1.5 million on $133 million in sales. A restructuring also increased the firm's emphasis on customer satisfaction and internal communication.

TechTeam continued to see financial improvements during 2000 and also began to focus more heavily on providing Internet-based support services. A new contract with the European Commission, the policy-making body of the European Union, saw the company's staffers answering questions posted to the Union's web site. TechTeam also hired RCG Capital Markets Group in February to help boost its sagging stock price and improve relations with investors. Shortly afterward company founder William Coyro resigned as board chairman, a move that was hailed by some as necessary for the restoration of investor confidence. Coyro planned to continue to work for the company in a lesser capacity.

A joint venture with General Electric, GE TechTeam L.P., cost the company more public relations points following the closure of its Sault Saint Marie, Michigan call center and layoffs of 213 employees. Once again the company was forced to revise its quarterly accounting statement when the written-off losses proved to be underestimated. At the end of 2000 the company named M. Anthony Tam president and CEO, replacing the retiring Harry Lewis. Tam had worked earlier for The Genix Group, a data management company.

In September of 2000 an $8.5 million lawsuit was filed against TechTeam by David Sachs, who alleged that the company had failed to split profits from a joint venture they had had together. Sachs, who had headed the recently dismantled TechTeam Capital leasing unit (formerly known as Capricorn Capital), received an out-of-court settlement. Some months later Sachs sought to take control of the company by requesting that shareholders vote on his proposal to be named CEO at the annual meeting in May. The board turned down his bid, but Sachs vowed to continue to fight for control of TechTeam. He owned 500,000 shares of company stock, slightly less than 5 percent of the total.

Although it was still dealing with some nettlesome side issues, National TechTeam appeared to be firmly on the path to recovering its stride, and it was looking to the future with renewed vigor. The company continued providing computer services to numerous major clients, with help-desk services remaining its leading revenue source. A new emphasis on web-based services also was beginning to take off.

Principal Subsidiaries

TechTeam Europe, Ltd.; TechTeam Europe, NV/SA; TechTeam Europe GmbH; National TechTeam of New Jersey, Inc.

Principal Competitors

CIBER, Inc.; Computer Sciences Corporation; Electronic Data Systems Corporation; International Business Machines Corporation; Renaissance Worldwide, Inc.; SITEL Corporation.

Further Reading

Bennett, Jeff, "Dearborn, Mich.-Based Technology Firm Faces Another Lawsuit," *KRTBN Knight-Ridder Tribune Business News,* September 7, 2000.

Brammer, Rhonda, "Media Star," *Barron's,* July 21, 1997, p. 22.

Breskin, Ira, "National TechTeam Pitches in to Help Deal with Computers," *Investor's Business Daily,* February 20, 1997, p. B14.

Bridgeforth, Arthur, Jr., "On a Six-Month Climb: TechTeam Rides Industry's Out-Sourcing Trend," *Crain's Detroit Business,* September 16, 1996, p. 2.

——, "A TechTeam Player: New CEO Continues Turnaround at Tech Firm," *Crain's Detroit Business,* December 14, 1998, p. 2.

"CEO Interview—National TechTeam, Inc.," *Wall Street Transcript,* May 16, 1994.

Child, Charles, "Looking Out for No. 1: Nat'l TechTeam Wants to Be the EDS of PCs," *Crain's Detroit Business,* June 27, 1988, p. 6.

Henderson, Tom, "How TechTeam Made It," *Crain's Detroit Business,* February 1, 1994, p. 16.

Mathews, Melanie S., "A Job Is Waiting: Company Seeks Computer Techs," *Detroit News,* January 26, 1997, p. K1.

Maurer, Michael, "Outgrowing Its Stocks," *Crain's Detroit Business,* May 29, 1995, p. 2.

——, "TechTeam Helps Itself Helping with Computers," *Crain's Detroit Business,* December 13, 1993, p. 3.

Mercer, Tenisha, "National TechTeam Sued: Timing of Stock Sell-Offs Questioned by Shareholders," *Crain's Detroit Business,* September 15, 1997, p. 3.

——, "TechTeam Settles Suit for $11M: Shareholders Were Upset at Accounting," *Crain's Detroit Business,* January 4, 1999, p. 3.

——, "TechTeam's Wild Week: Stock Dives, Stabilizes after Barron's Story," *Crain's Detroit Business,* July 28, 1997, p. 2.

——, "TechTeam's Woes Persist: Annual Meeting Comes Amid SEC Inquiry," *Crain's Detroit Business,* May 25, 1998, p. 2.

——, "Troubles for TechTeam: Accounting Errors Cited in 4th Quarter Report," *Crain's Detroit Business,* March 1, 1999, p. 2.

Roush, Matt, "Tenacious: Computer-Service Company Is Shining Superstar of Stocks," *Crain's Detroit Business,* July 26, 1993, p. 8.

Snavely, Brent, "Disgruntled Shareholder Looks to Take Reins at National TechTeam," *Crain's Detroit Business,* March 12, 2001, p. 4.

——, "National TechTeam Seeks to Build Faith," *Crain's Detroit Business,* March 6, 2000, p. 4.

——, "National TechTeam Unveils Deal with European Commission: Shareholders Challenge CEO," *Crain's Detroit Business,* May 15, 2000, p. 34.

—Frank Uhle

NYMAGIC, Inc.

330 Madison Avenue
New York, New York 10017
U.S.A.
Telephone (212) 551-0600
Fax: (212) 986-1310
Web site: http://www.nymagic.com

Public Company
Incorporated: 1998
Employees: 97
Sales: $100.7 million (2000)
Stock Exchanges: New York
Ticker Symbol: NYM
NAIC: 524130 Reinsurance Carriers; 524126 Direct Property and Casualty Insurance Carriers

With headquarters in New York City, NYMAGIC, Inc. is a holding company for two insurance subsidiaries, New York Marine & General Insurance Company and Gotham Insurance Company, which are primarily engaged in the underwriting of ocean marine, commercial aviation, and cargo insurance. The companies also handle so-called ''surplus lines'' of insurance, which are the type of one-of-a-kind, unregulated, high-risk, high-rate policies underwritten by Lloyds of London. NYMAGIC also owns several insurance pools that underwrite the policies of New York Marine and Gotham Insurance, the oldest of which is Mutual Marine Office (MMO) established by NYMAGIC's founder, John N. Blackman, Sr. More than 60 percent of NYMAGIC is still owned by Blackman's two sons and their mother.

1960s Origins

After being employed in the marine insurance industry for more than a decade, Blackman decided to go it alone, starting MMO in 1964 to act as an agent for a pool of marine insurance companies. Although it was less regulated than other forms of insurance and held great potential for profits, marine insurance was also extremely risky. Blackman had both the necessary experience and willingness to take risks to write coverage for marine cargo traversing through war zones such as the Persian Gulf and for oil-drilling rigs and other types of excess-liability businesses. Blackman was also cautious, looking to spread the risk among multiple insurers. He established relationships with several partners who would remain in his pool for 30 years, mostly because Blackman made them money from the start. For managing the pool, MMO received a fee based on premium payments and profits, while members of the pool shared profits based upon their participation. Blackman and his staff of underwriters, however, were more than insurance pool managers. They developed sources to gather intelligence and screen gossip to determine what policies to gamble on. They were also smart about making policies extremely specific, carving out the kind of exceptions that can only result from a thorough understanding of the risks involved.

MMO was so profitable that in 1972, to avoid paying a stiff tax on dividends, Blackman decided to start his own insurance company, New York Marine & General Insurance. Essentially, it was a new company in the paperwork only, because it used both MMO's staff and offices. Funded with only $500,000, New York Marine at first engaged in reinsurance, another way for direct insurers to spread their risk. After building up reserves, in 1979 New York Marine was able to become directly involved in the MMO pool. In this way, Blackman, through MMO and New York Marine, would be able to derive a management fee from the pool as well as share in pool profits. Between 1979 and 1983, revenues for New York Marine doubled, reaching $9.15 million, while net income grew at an even greater pace to $1.8 million.

In 1983 Blackman began to provide coverage for the aviation industry, which had been hit hard by a number of worldwide accidents and hundreds of fatalities. Insurers paid out $350 million in damages in 1982, although premiums totaled only $280 million. Damages in 1983 would rise to $450 million, prompting a number of reinsurers to leave the business and inevitably resulted in much higher premiums, which were what attracted Blackman to the segment. MMO was willing to assume as much 3.5 percent of some airline insurance contracts.

Company Perspectives:

NYMAGIC believes it can successfully compete against other companies in the insurance market due to its philosophy of underwriting quality insurance, its reputation as a conservative well-capitalized insurer, and its willingness to forgo unprofitable business. NYMAGIC is a true underwriting company. Our underwriters aren't wed to underwriting manuals, pricing guidelines, and forms. Instead, they have a deep understanding of the nature of risk and are practiced in the art of underwriting. This translates to a level of expertise, insight and creativity you will be hard-pressed to find elsewhere.

New York Marine Goes Public in 1984

New York Marine was doing so well by then that Blackman decided to make it a ''real company'' by taking it public in 1984. It made a further offer of stock in 1985. Flush with new capital, the company was then able to increase its share in the MMO pool from 15 percent to 50 percent, a situation made palatable to pool members by the doubling of gross premiums between 1984 and 1986. Although the other pool members did not see their income drop off, New York Marine, with its increased share, watched its revenues soar, reaching $24 million in 1984 and $47.9 million in 1985. The next year, without increasing its participation in the pool, New York Marine increased revenues another 32 percent to $63.1 million. Profits also jumped 74 percent to $11.4 million. One spot of trouble came in 1985 when Mutual Fire, Marine & Inland Insurance Company was dropped from MMO. A year later, the company went bankrupt, leaving the other pool members to honor its obligations. New York Marine wrote off $569,000 after taxes, but the loss had little impact on the company's bottom line. Nevertheless, the situation caused Blackman to maintain a closer watch on MMO's four other outside pool members.

Blackman was able to achieve such impressive growth by remaining flexible. After moving into aviation coverage in 1983, for instance, MMO increased its participation in that segment to 16 percent of total premiums in 1985 and 29 percent in 1986. When rates came down, Blackman pulled back and once again adjusted his mix of business. In October 1986 he formed a subsidiary to New York Marine called Gotham Insurance Company to engage in the surplus line marketplace, providing esoteric casualty insurance for what Blackman called, ''weird risks.'' For example, Gotham Insurance wrote coverage for a Korean condom manufacturer and for a blood bank. Because of the high risk involved, Gotham Insurance could charge a high premium, but as always it was also careful to write in a number of exclusions. In the case of the blood bank, that meant precluding claims related to the AIDS virus, HIV. The company also reinsured its risk, making sure its liability never exceeded $1 million. As with New York Marine, Gotham Insurance was run by the MMO staff in the same Manhattan offices.

New York Marine had accumulated enough of a surplus to assume a larger stake in the MMO pool without having to resort to raising new capital. Like other insurers that started out as pool managers, such as industry giants Chubb Corp. and AIG (American International Group), New York Marine was in a position to take over the entire pool. Aside from stretching the company's finances, Blackman expressed reluctance to assume complete control because of loyalty to the people who had helped him launch MMO some 20 years earlier. It was a decision he never made, however, because in September 1988 Blackman died at the age of 64. He left the company in the hands of his two sons, who for some years had served as executive vice-presidents for New York Marine. Each controlled 21.3 percent of New York Marine's stock, while Blackman's ex-wife, Louise B. Tollefson, controlled 20 percent, either directly or through trusts. John N. Blackman, Jr., first went to work for his father in 1973, followed by brother Mark in 1977. John, at 41 years old, was now elected chairman of the board of New York Marine, and Mark, age 37, was named president. In October 1988, NYMAGIC was formed to serve as a holding company for New York Marine and Gotham Insurance to provide greater flexibility in the financial market.

Under the leadership of a second generation of the Blackman family, NYMAGIC officially acquired MMO in January 1991, issuing 5.8 million shares of common stock for all of the outstanding common stock of MMO. Later in 1991, NYMAGIC added new insurance pools. The company acquired a pool originally founded in 1978 to underwrite business in the Midwest, folding it into a subsidiary it named Mutual Marine Office of the Midwest, Inc. NYMAGIC also acquired a West Coast pool, which became Pacific Mutual Marine Office, Inc. Further changes occurred in MMO. Long-time pool member Utica Mutual Insurance Company dropped out of MMO in 1994, followed by Arkwright Mutual Insurance Company in 1996. By 1997 NYMAGIC controlled 100 percent of MMO.

Although taking over MMO appeared to be the route to a dramatic increase in revenues and profits, the actual results for NYMAGIC in the 1990s was less than spectacular. Revenues neared $110 million in 1992 with profits of $15.2 million, but fell off in 1993 to $92.2 million and profits of $14.6 million. In 1994 revenues rebounded somewhat, totaling more than $103 million, but the company also suffered the heaviest payout in its history with the Northridge earthquake, which cost it $5.8 million. Furthermore, NYMAGIC suffered severe losses in the aviation segment. The result to the bottom line was a fall in net profits to $9.6 million. Despite the losses caused by Hurricane Luis in 1995, NYMAGIC posted record revenues, exceeding $133 million, and profits of $20 million. In 1996, revenues dipped to $125.6 million, but MYMAGIC increased its profits to $22.6 million. In 1997, revenues again fell, to just over $121 million, yet once again the company generated record net profits of $26.4 million.

NYMAGIC Turns to London in 1997

In 1997 NYMAGIC, already with offices in New York, San Francisco, and Chicago, looked to penetrate the London marine market, whose brokers placed close to one third of the world's commercial marine business. A number of Lloyd's ''names'' had suffered major losses in the early 1990s, resulting in a many bankruptcies. Because of uncertainty in London, many customers turned to the U.S. marine markets, but as Lloyds rebounded, its agencies began to recapture lost business. NYMAGIC was eager to follow the business and participate in

Key Dates:

1964: John N. Blackman, Sr., founds Mutual Marine Office (MMO).
1972: The New York Marine & General Insurance Company is established.
1984: New York Marine goes public.
1986: Gotham Insurance Company formed as a subsidiary to New York Marine.
1988: Upon Blackman's death, his two sons assume control of New York Marine and Gotham Insurance, which become part of holding company NYMAGIC.
1991: NYMAGIC acquires the Mutual Marine Office.
1998: John N. Blackman, Jr., is forced out as chairman of board; Mark W. Blackman resigns as president and CEO.

the London market. It formed a subsidiary called MMO UK, Ltd. to engage in underwriting with Lloyd's through an entity called Syndicate 1265, for which it provided all the capital. The history of Syndicate 1265 dates back to the Chester syndicate of the 1800s, a world-famous marine hull underwriter and pioneer in drilling rig underwriting. In December 1997, NYMAGIC also acquired a Lloyd's affiliated company, Highgate Managing Agencies, Ltd., then changed its name to MMO Underwriting Agency Ltd. MMO Underwriting was subsequently granted permission in February 1998 to commence underwriting in conjunction with Syndicate 1265.

The two Blackman brothers disagreed over the direction that MYMAGIC was taking, and their differences became so irreconcilable that in September 1998 the company's board of directors voted to dismiss John Blackman as chairman. Mark Blackman also resigned as president and chief executive officer. Although acknowledging that the move was highly unusual, especially since the Blackman family held a controlling interest in NYMAGIC, the board maintained that it acted thus to preserve the integrity of the company for all of its shareholders and that the disagreements between the brothers prevented NYMAGIC from operating effectively. Two board members were selected to fill in on an interim basis: Sergio Tobia as chairman and Jean H. Goulding as president.

After searching several months for a new chief executive officer, NYMAGIC settled on Vincent T. Papa in March 1999. He had almost 20 years of experience with Orion Capital Corporation, and since 1995 had served as CEO of Orion's marine and property insurance subsidiary, Wm. H. McGee Company. Although Papa appeared to be the perfect fit for MYMAGIC, he lasted only four months. Because he disagreed with the board about the direction to take the company, he exercised an option to leave. When NYMAGIC refused to pay a severance package contained in Papa's employment contract, Papa filed suit. The matter was eventually resolved out of court in the fourth quarter of fiscal 2000.

With unstable management, NYMAGIC saw its revenues drop from $106.4 million in 1998 to $89.5 million in 1999 and profits shrink from $18.5 million to $16.4 million. Papa was officially replaced by Robert W. Bailey in January 2000. Bailey had joined the NYMAGIC board in June 1999 and was then appointed chairman in July. When Papa decided to leave the company, Bailey had stepped in as acting chief executive. He boasted more than 40 years of experience in marine and aviation insurance, coming to NYMAGIC from Aon Group, where he served as a senior vice-president of subsidiary Aon Insurance Inc. Both marine and aviation segments had experienced depressed rates in recent years, but Bailey expressed a belief that the situation had bottomed out, and NYMAGIC would be able to take advantage of a market that had fewer players. He did not, however, see an immediate improvement.

In 2000 NYMAGIC generated $100.7 million in revenues but posted an unprecedented loss in net profits, totaling more than $5.5 million. The loss was essentially caused by MMO UK, due in large part to the runoff of Syndicate 1265, which ceased underwriting in the third quarter of the year. As a consequence, NYMAGIC elected to sell Syndicate 1265. It also sold MMO Underwriting Agency in exchange for a minority interest in Cathedral Capital plc, involved in the U.K. insurance market. Early results in 2001 were also disappointing, showing few areas of strength. More than a dozen years since the death of its founder, NYMAGIC was clearly in need of the kind of vision and leadership that John N. Blackman, Sr., provided. Whether Bailey would display that and be able to revitalize the firm could only be answered with time.

Principal Subsidiaries

New York Marine & General Insurance Company; Gotham Insurance Company; Mutual Marine Office, Inc.; Pacific Mutual Marine Office, Inc.; Mutual Marine Office of the Midwest, Inc.

Principal Competitors

Allianz Insurance; HCC Insurance; Navigators.

Further Reading

Belsky, Gary, "Leading Marine Insurer Charts Riskier Waters," *Crain's New York Business,* May 23, 1988, p. 3.

Eaton, Leslie, "Full Speed Ahead: A Specialty Insurer Sets a Fast Pace," *Barron's National Business and Financial Weekly,* October 5, 1987, p. 14.

"Insurer Holding Company Replaces Top Two Executives," *Business Insurance,* September 14, 1998, p. 1.

King, Resa W., "A Catastrophic Year Had Airline Insurance Rocketing," *Business Week,* January 20, 1986.

"Nymagic Inc. Name Change," *The Wall Street Journal,* October 3, 1989, p.1.

"Nymagic Loses Two Chiefs," *The New York Times,* September 11, 1998, p. B10.

"NYMAGIC Names New CEO," *Best's Review,* February 2000, p. 165.

"Ocean Cargo Carriers," *Insurance Advocate,* September 20, 1997, p. 30.

"Soaring Insurance Costs Jolt the Airlines," *Business Week,* August 27, 1984, p. 78.

"Two Blackmans Leave Top NYMAGIC Posts Amid Strategic Dispute," *The Wall Street Journal,* September 10, 1998, p. B7.

—Ed Dinger

Octel Messaging

1001 Murphy Ranch Road
Milpitas, California 95035-7912
U.S.A.
Telephone: (408) 321-2000
Fax: (408) 321-2100
Web site: http://www.octel.com

Wholly Owned Division of Avaya Inc.
Founded: 1982
Employees: 3,000
Sales: $564 million (1996)
NAIC: 33421 Telephone Manufacturing Apparatus; 334418 Printed Circuit Assembly (Electronic Assembly) Manufacturing; 33429 Other Communications Equipment Manufacturing

Octel Messaging, formerly known as Octel Communications Corporation, is a voice-messaging service company that became a division of Lucent Technologies Inc. in September 1997, and was then spun off as part of Avaya Inc. in September 2000. Along with Octel's messaging products and services, Avaya offers voice, converged voice and data, customer relationship management, multi-service networking, and structured cabling products and services. Avaya operates as a global leader in messaging and cabling systems, and holds a strong portion of the U.S. market for enterprise voice communications and call center systems. Octel, which was established in 1982, grew quickly as the voice mail market rapidly expanded during the 1980s and 1990s. In 2001, the division served over 100,000 customers in 90 countries, catering to all types of businesses, governments, education institutions, wireless service providers, and telecom vendors.

Octel's Beginnings in the Early 1980s

Octel was founded by Robert Cohen, a product manager for a computerized instrumentation equipment company, and Peter Olson, an engineer. They met in 1981, when Cohen called Olson to fix a problem with a piece of electronic equipment that worked in the lab but not in the field. Cohen was so impressed with Olson's abilities that he suggested they start a company together.

The duo drew up a list of possible areas of specialization in the technology field and settled on voice mail because they thought it was a good market niche. At the time, most voice mail systems were made by giants like International Business Machines (IBM), whose products were large, expensive, and unpopular. Some smaller companies existed, but Olson and Cohen felt that these other small companies were not geared toward dealing with businesses in a professional manner. Therefore, Olson and Cohen designed a product to fit this niche.

Their business plan called for a voice mail machine that would cost $10,000 to make and $50,000 to sell. They wanted it to take up no more space than a closet and to be compatible with the top ten telephone systems being used at the time. Competing voice mail systems generally worked only with the manufacturer's telephone system, and none worked with all 80 PBX systems on the market. Therefore, whereas AT&T could sell its voice mail system only to businesses owning an AT&T phone system, the Octel system could be sold to anybody.

With this business plan, Octel raised about $2 million in venture capital, effectively selling half of the company to various investors in the process. When finished, the firm's system took up as much room as a large suitcase and sold for $55,000. A competing system from IBM was the size of a small room and cost $250,000. Despite its small size, the Octel system was powerful; Olson had used advanced microprocessors made by Intel and Zilog.

After spending another $4 million, Octel had the system ready in early 1984. However, corporate purchasing departments usually took about a year to order new systems—something that was overlooked when Octel's business plan was written. By fall of that year, the company had sold only about ten systems. The firm had to cut costs and raise another $7 million in venture capital. By 1985, however, orders for Octel's system began arriving. Voice mail was becoming more popular in corporate America, and thanks to its universal compatibility the Octel system sold very well for a first product by a new company.

Company Perspectives:

Avaya's Octel Messaging Division is committed to connecting people throughout the world via messaging, freeing them to communicate unconstrained by time, place, and space.

Voice mail machines were essentially computers dedicated to the purpose of answering telephones and recording the human voice. Voice mail systems translated voices into digital information and then stored it. To keep file sizes small, much of the information was stripped out, which sometimes led to a tinny quality that some users found objectionable. Also, telephone answering machines were relatively new, and many people were reluctant to leave messages with machines. Voice mail, however, offered many advantages. Because the information recorded was digital, messages could be copied or manipulated like other computer data. Thus, an executive could send ten messages simultaneously or forward a message to someone else. Also, using touch-tone telephones, callers could select from menu options and route their calls without using a human operator. Octel's system also offered options such as slowing down or speeding up a message during playback and automatic call-forwarding. Corporations were first beginning to evaluate the benefits of such systems when Octel's system came to market, and its low price tag generated interest and orders.

Rapid Growth in the late 1980s and Early 1990s

The firm became profitable in 1986, which was considered a fast takeoff for a start-up technology firm. Then, a 1987 court ruling changed telecommunications regulations to allow the regional Bell telephone companies to begin offering telecommunications services like voice mail. They were, however, not allowed to manufacture their own equipment, and therefore Octel benefited when several decided to use its equipment in their systems.

Propelled by its sales to the Bells, Octel became the country's largest manufacturer of voice mail systems in 1988, just four years after offering its first product. In just one year, its sales grew from $19 million in 1986 to $48 million in 1987. The voice mail market was booming, growing 50 percent a year by some estimates, to reach $270 million in 1987.

In February 1988 Octel went public, raising $7 million by selling 15 percent of the company. The firm was looked over carefully by the financial community because it was one of the first high-technology companies to go public after the stock market crash of October 1987. Later that year, in a sign of the growing importance of both Octel and the voice-processing industry, electronics giant Hewlett-Packard bought 10 percent of Octel. Its new link with H-P gave the young company a marketing boost and a quick presence in Europe, where its products were to be sold under the Hewlett-Packard name. It also led to increased integration of Octel's products with Hewlett-Packard's electronic-mail and computer systems.

At the time, Octel was offering two voice mail systems: Aspen systems were designed for large businesses and could contain up to 7,500 mailboxes; the VPC 100, which was engineered for smaller customers, contained up to 100 mailboxes.

In 1990, Cohen resigned as Octel's chief executive officer, citing the need to spend more time with his family. He remained on Octel's board, however. Douglas Chance, a 24-year veteran of Hewlett-Packard who had previously served on Octel's board, became the company's new CEO. Octel earned $18 million on sales of $160 million for 1990; voice mail sales for its nearest competitor—industry giant AT&T—were $140 million.

With computer technology constantly improving, Octel's systems were rapidly becoming more sophisticated, providing the link between employees (who could be at a touch-tone telephone anywhere in the world) and their employer's computer systems. Universities were also beginning to use the firm's PowerCall system for student registration. With it, the schools recorded course descriptions for students, who could then check whether a particular class was available and register for it right over the phone. In 1991, Octel introduced a device that attached to voice-processing systems and turned telephones into terminals, allowing users to interact with computers through the number pads on their telephones. The system, called the Voice Information Processing Server, let callers access databases, voice messages, and electronic mail. The system also carried caller data throughout the call so that information—an identification number, for instance—did not have to be reentered.

The Tigon Purchase: 1992

By 1992, Octel not only held a 20 percent share of the voice mail market, but also had 36 percent of the market for voice-information services (in which telephone service providers buy voice mail systems, then rent voice mail services to customers). In fact, Octel was the first company to enter this business, which had exacting standards because of the high volume of calls that were processed and because the systems themselves were attached to equipment located in the central office of a telephone company. The quickly growing cellular telephone market accounted for many of the firm's voice information services sales. The firm had installed 6,500 voice-mail machines, many at Fortune 500 companies. The firm also announced plans to introduce a universal mail box—a system that would collect messages from many sources: voice mail from a subscriber's business, home, and cellular telephones, as well as paper mail. It would also receive data, like faxes, to be printed out or viewed later.

Later that year, Octel bought Tigon, Ameritech Corp.'s Dallas-based voice messaging subsidiary. Ameritech had bought Tigon in 1988, but could not operate it to achieve a big enough profit to make it a worthwhile holding. Following the sale of Tigon to Octel, Ameritech agreed to buy voice-processing services from Tigon. Octel made Tigon a wholly owned subsidiary and renamed it Octel Network Services. At the time of Octel's purchase, Tigon had large corporate customers in most major U.S. cities, as well as some in Japan, Taiwan, Britain, Australia, and Canada. Because of the purchase, Octel quickly became the world's largest voice mail outsourcing company. Octel Network Services managed clients' voice mail networks and engaged in disaster recovery, operations management, systems administration, and project management. These

Key Dates:

1982: Robert Cohen and Peter Olsen establish Octel.
1986: The firm records its first profit.
1988: Octel goes public and becomes the largest manufacturer of voice mail systems.
1992: Octel acquires Tigon Corporation and becomes the world's largest voice mail outsourcing company.
1994: Company merges with VMX Inc. and new corporate headquarters are established in Milpitas, California.
1996: Octel forms partnerships with Qualcomm Inc. and Brooks Fiber Communications.
1997: Lucent Technologies acquires the firm.
1998: Company signs a multi-million dollar contract with Ameritech Services Inc.
2000: Octel becomes part of Lucent's spin-off, Avaya Inc.

operations brought Octel a large source of recurring revenue to help balance the one-time profit of selling a voice mail system.

Ameritech became one of the most important clients for Octel Network Services, which operated the voice mail services that Ameritech offered to residential and small-business customers. By 1994, 400,000 Ameritech residential customers were using the system, with thousands of new customers joining up every month.

Acquisitions and International Growth in the Mid-1990s

In 1993, with the use of faxes proliferating in corporate America, Octel released three products for its Voice Information Processor: Faxagent, Faxbroadcast, and Faxstation. Each consisted of a card and software. The same year, the firm began a joint venture in Israel, hoping to gain access to some of that country's technical specialists. Also in 1993, Robert Cohen rejoined the firm as president and CEO, to fill what the company had come to feel was a gap in its management. Total revenue for the year came to $338.5 million.

Octel saw an opportunity in operating voice mail systems in developing countries, and by the mid-1990s it had major installations operating in Brazil and China. In these countries, millions of customers wanted their own telephones but could not get them; thus many simply bought their own mailbox and checked messages from pay phones. The firm hoped this system would catch on in developing countries and become a major source of revenue.

In early 1994, Octel took over the industry's first voice mail company when it merged with VMX Inc. in a stock swap valued at about $150 million. Octel's first move was to write software allowing the two systems to network and to port VMXworks, a software application, to Octel's systems. Several VMX vice-presidents took similar titles in related areas at Octel.

Octel now possessed the two most popular user interfaces for voice mail. Analysts expected the acquisition to help Octel as voice processing became based less on the telephone and more on the personal computer. The purchase also brought with it VMX's Rhetorex subsidiary, which designed and manufactured voice-processing components.

At that point, Octel had an installed base of 37,000 systems, including those that came with the VMX deal. With new applications like fax products, the firm hoped to capitalize on this market to make secondary sales. Meanwhile, Octel continued to win customers. In 1994, data-processing giant Electronic Data Systems, which had purchased voice mail systems from Octel in the past, chose to use Octel's voice-processing services. The seven-year contract called for Octel to provide facilities management and services for over 100 Octel systems at Electronic Data Systems locations. Octel also signed long-term contracts with Kodak, Blockbuster Entertainment, and Texas Instruments.

In 1994, Octel finished its new corporate headquarters, a five-building complex in Milpitas, California, with 368,000 square feet of space. VMX employees also moved into the space.

With the increasing prevalence of electronic mail and the increasing power of personal computers, the creation of voice mail products for the personal computer became more important. In 1994, Octel released Visual Mailbox, a software program that allowed users on local area networks to use personal computers to access voice mail and faxes. The computers did not need built-in multimedia support, although the software required users to be on a system using Octel's VMX 200/300 voice mail system. Octel believed that voice mail would likely be provided on local area networks as they became more powerful and considered the moves an important way to prepare for future market changes.

In 1995, Octel demonstrated add-ons for Microsoft's Exchange messaging server that enabled users to integrate voice, fax, and e-mail. Also in 1995, Bell Atlantic signed a three-year agreement to use Octel's OptiMail, which permitted the outsourcing of voice and fax messaging services.

OcteLink, a network service that could integrate messages from any voice-mail system, was also developed in 1995. By the following year, both Bell Canada and Inland Steel Company and its subsidiaries had signed on for its services. In 1996, Octel also teamed up with Qualcomm Inc. in a marketing agreement that would allow Qualcomm to sell Octel's Sierra voice processing platform and applications to global wireless customers. Octel's PC division also launched Smooth Operator Ultra Lite, a product that was attractive to the small office market because of its lower price point and diverse capabilities.

Octel also continued to expand internationally, and in November of 1996, Brazil's Telesp—the largest telephone company in the country—began using Octel's Sierra product. Octel also signed contracts worth over $28 million in Japan and China.

Perhaps the most remarkable event in 1996, however, was the passing of the Federal Telecommunications Act of 1996, which allowed competitive local exchange carriers (CLECs) into regional markets. In order to be competitive in these markets, the CLECs had to offer customers a wide range of telecommunications services, opening up a new customer base for Octel. Sure enough, after the act was passed, Octel signed a multi-million dollar agreement with Brooks Fiber Communications, a national provider of competitive local exchange services.

The Lucent Technologies Purchase: 1997

Octel's expertise in voice mail services and messaging systems made it attractive to telecom industry giant Lucent Technologies, a firm looking to gain market edge in the growing global messaging services industry. In September of 1997, Lucent Technologies acquired Octel for $1.8 billion—$31 per share. Bill O'Shea, president of Lucent's business communications unit, stated in a July 1997 *Telephony* article, ''Lucent is looking at ways to support the expansion of its core business, and Octel has the capabilities to get us where we want to be in the messaging industry.'' At the time of the deal, the voice mail services industry was securing $2.3 billion in sales and was anticipated to continue growing by 20 percent per year.

In a company press release, Octel CEO Cohn stated, ''the Lucent/Octel combination will allow us to do many more things for our customers. And Lucent's commitment to messaging means that we will be an important part of its future.'' The deal also brought leadership to Octel, who over the past few years had missed product deadlines, and—with the exception of Cohen—was lacking a strong executive staff.

After the acquisition, Octel operated as Lucent's Octel Messaging Division. Just months after the integration, the division landed its largest contract in its history—a five-year multimillion deal with Ameritech Services Inc. Under the terms of the contract, Octel Messaging would manage over 1.2 million voice mailboxes for Ameritech, as well as provide its voice messaging services. The division also formed the Lucent Messaging Integrator channel, aimed at the $2 billion unified messaging market. Building upon Octel's Unified Messenger—which was developed in 1997 and allowed a user to review, reply to, forward, and delete, voice mail and email messages using a telephone or personal computer—the channel supported the product by allowing members of the channel to sell the unified system. Members of the channel included Digital Equipment Corporation, Software Spectrum Inc., and XLConnect Solutions Inc.

The Creation of Avaya Inc.

By 1999, market research firm Frost & Sullivan ranked Lucent as the leading provider of unified messaging software in the U.S., with a 24 percent share of the market. The future of the Octel division however, became uncertain as Lucent began to falter in the new millennium. In January 2000, stock fell by 30 percent after the firm announced that revenues for the period ending December 31, 1999, would fall short of expectations by $1 billion. In fact, revenues for the remainder of the year disappointed shareholders. In October, Henry Schacht, former Lucent CEO, came out of retirement to take over the firm. After drastic errors in fourth quarter reporting in 2000, stock fell by 80 percent to $13 on December 27, 2000—a $216 billion market capitalization loss.

Problems related to Lucent's inadequate launch into the optical networking market, and its shortcomings in the packet switches market, were targeted as causes for its financial problems. In response to these issues, the company began consolidating operations and cutting jobs. In order to focus on its core businesses—optical, data, and wireless networking—Lucent spun off its microelectronics interests and enterprise networks businesses to its shareholders, creating two separate entities. Octel, which was a division of Lucent's enterprise networks group, became part of Avaya Inc. The spin off was complete in September 2000. Avaya was comprised of Octel's operations as well as other Lucent properties that were part of its enterprise networks group. It operated as a leading provider of communications systems and software to businesses around the world. The company provided services to nearly 80 percent of the Fortune 500 companies, and secured $7.6 billion in sales in fiscal 2000.

Principal Competitors

Aspect Communications Corp.; Cisco Systems Inc.; Nortel Networks Corporation.

Further Reading

Borrus, Amy, and Steve Rosenbush, ''Lucent's Dark Days,'' *BusinessWeek Online,* May 7, 2001.

Burger, Dale, ''Octel Pumps Up Voice Messaging Platform But Likely to Face Stiff Lucent Competition,'' *Computing Canada,* March 17, 1997, p. 29.

Bylinsky, Gene, ''How to Shoulder Aside the Titans,'' *Fortune,* May 18, 1992, pp. 87–88.

DiLorenzo, Jim, ''Octel to Acquire VMX,'' *Telephony,* February 7, 1994, pp. 14–16.

Edwards, Mike, ''Octel Brings Phones, Computers Closer Together with Voice Processing System,'' *Computing Canada,* May 9, 1991, pp. 43, 49.

Flanagan, Patrick, ''Lucent Acquires Octel to Round Out its Product Line,'' *Telecommunications,* October 1997, p. 17.

Lee, Paula Munier, ''Going Public After the Crash,'' *Small Business Reports,* October 1989, pp. 32–36.

Levine, Shira, ''High-Octane Octel,'' *Telephony,* July 21, 1997, p. 7.

''Octel Communications Corporation,'' *Wall Street Transcript,* July 17, 1989, p. 94, 284.

''Octel Communications Names New President and Chief Executive,'' *Wall Street Journal,* October 9, 1990, p. B13.

Pitta, Julie, ''Panic!'' *Forbes,* October 28, 1991, pp. 102–103.

Pollack, Andrew, ''Hewlett-Packard Sets 10% Purchase of Octel,'' *New York Times,* August 12, 1988, p. D4.

''Voice Processing: Octel Communications Corp. Signs Multi-Million Dollar Agreement With Brooks Fiber Communications,'' *Edge: On & About AT&T,* July 8, 1996, p. 17.

''Voice Processing: Octel Debuts First Deployments of OcteLink Messaging Service,'' *Edge: On & About AT&T,* January 29, 996, p. 35.

Wahl, Andrew, ''The Lessons of Lucent,'' *Canadian Business,* February 19, 2001, p. 39.

—Scott M. Lewis
—update: Christina M. Stansell

Perry Ellis International, Inc.

3000 Northwest 107th Avenue
Miami, Florida 33172
U.S.A.
Telephone: (305) 592-2830
Fax: (305) 594-2307
Web site: http://www.perryellis.com

Public Company
Incorporated: 1967 as Supreme International Corporation
Employees: 440
Sales: $287.4 million (2001 est.)
Stock Exchanges: NASDAQ
Ticker Symbol: PERY
NAIC: 315211 Men's and Boys' Cut and Sew Apparel Contractors; 315224 Men's and Boys' Cut and Sew Trouser, Slack, and Jean Manufacturing

Originally founded by the acclaimed fashion designer Perry Ellis to manage the licensing of his name, Perry Ellis International, Inc. is now the assumed name of the licensing and marketing group of Miami, Florida-based Supreme International, which purchased Perry Ellis in 1999. In addition to a number of Perry Ellis trademark lines of clothing, the new Perry Ellis also markets Supreme International's other labels, including Crossings, Natural Issue, Munsingwear, Andrew Fezza, Ping, John Henry, Manhattan Shirts, and Grand Slam. After dropping out of the womenswear market in the early 1990s, Perry Ellis relaunched the line in 2000 after reaching a licensing agreement with Kellwood Company. Supreme International is a family-run business, established by immigrant George Feldenkreis. His son Oscar has played a major role in expanding the company beyond the import business to now designing its own products. The assumption of the Perry Ellis name has elevated Supreme International from the middle ranks of apparel makers to major worldwide brand status.

Origins as a Fashion Merchandiser in the 1960s

Perry Ellis never intended to become a designer. He was born in 1940 to a wealthy family in Portsmouth, Virginia, and after majoring in business at the College of William and Mary he earned a master's degree at New York University's School of Retailing. In 1963 he became a management trainee at the upscale Richmond, Virginia, department store of Miller & Rhodes, where he quickly proved to be a brilliant fashion merchandiser. Ellis would become one of the top customers of John Meyer of Norwich, Connecticut, a women's sportswear company, which would hire him away in 1967. For Meyer it was a chance to revitalize a slipping line; for Ellis it was a chance to work in the fashion industry of New York. At John Meyer, Ellis learned about the production and manufacture of clothes, as well as the publicity and marketing side of the business. Although he did not design, he became involved in the styling of the John Meyer lines. When owner John Meyer, diagnosed with cancer, was forced to sell the company, Ellis, in 1974, went to work for The Vera Companies as vice-president and merchandise manager of its sportswear division.

As he had done with John Meyer, Ellis provided a great deal of input on fabrics, colors, and styles at Vera Sportswear. When a new executive, Frank Rockman, took over the division, it became apparent to him that Ellis was providing more ideas than the designer, who, in any case, was about to retire. Rockman asked Ellis if he would design the line. Although he refused at first, Ellis finally accepted the position, taking over in January 1975. Within a year, Rockman was approaching the executives at Vera's parent corporation, Manhattan Industries, pressing them to allow him to start a contemporary fashion line of womenswear designed by Ellis. The result would be the Portfolio collection in the fall of 1976 and Ellis's quick ascent as a premier fashion designer. He lacked the technical skills to be considered a designer in the traditional sense, but he supplied the ideas that his assistants were then able to render as a sketch or construct into a prototype from which a pattern could be made.

Negotiations with Manhattan Industries for a contract began in 1977 and lasted until August 1978 when Ellis became president and designer of Perry Ellis Sportswear, Inc., at a salary of $150,000 a year. As part of the agreement, Ellis retained control over his own name and would be able to license it to other companies in any category of apparel outside of women's sportswear that did not directly compete with Manhattan Industries. Perry Ellis International was subsequently created to man-

Company Perspectives:

Our excellent track record over the past decade—especially since going public in 1993—has enabled us to be positioned among the leaders in menswear in the United States. The strengths and strategies that produced this excellent growth will continue to drive our progress as we go forward.

age these license deals, the first of which was with Alixandre, a fur company. Ellis was 38 years old.

As he became a celebrity designer, Ellis ran Perry Ellis International in an offhand manner, albeit with the help of his assistants. In 1981 he asked his companion, Laughlin Barker, to take over as president and legal counsel. After resigning from the New York law firm of Patterson, Belknap, Webb, and Tyler, Barker assumed his new role at the end of June 1982. At this point, Perry Ellis had nine licensees that generated some $60 million at wholesale prices and paid a 7.5 percent designer fee. Manhattan Industries received 25 percent of the company's net earnings. In 1982 Perry Ellis signed another seven licensing deals. Among other products that Barker would license were Perry Ellis fragrances and cosmetics, Japanese menswear, and a footwear line. All of the apparel was designed in Ellis's Manhattan studio.

Perry Ellis Dies in 1986

Perry Ellis was at the peak of his career when AIDS had a tragic effect on Perry Ellis International and the fashion industry in general. In January 1986 Barker died of an unspecified illness, then on May 30 Ellis died, reportedly from viral encephalitis, commonly known as sleeping sickness. Although no one would confirm that either man died from complications caused by AIDS, some newspaper accounts reported rumors that Ellis had contracted AIDS, or the stories were written in a manner to suggest that Ellis was a victim of the disease. At the time, the fashion industry was engaged in a complex form of denial. A large number of single men between the ages of 25 and 45 who worked on Seventh Avenue were dying from an assortment of ailments that were either rare or not generally considered life-threatening, yet any suggestion that AIDS might be involved was expressed only in whispers or innuendo. The issue was further complicated by the public's general fear and misunderstanding about the nature of the disease. The *Daily News Record,* a menswear trade publication, reported that talk of Ellis's AIDS diagnosis had hurt sales because some consumers were afraid they might contract the disease by simply touching Perry Ellis clothing.

Perry Ellis left Perry Ellis International to his heirs, primarily a daughter, Tyler Alexandra Gallagher Ellis, and her mother Barbara Gallagher. Ellis and Gallagher, a screenwriter and producer, had been friends for a number of years. By 1984 he was probably aware of his precarious health, while she was nearing 40 and feared that she would soon be beyond childbearing years. Both expressed a desire to have children and, according to friends, they agreed at a dinner party to conceive a child. When Ellis died Tyler was 18 months old. Ellis had previously asked another former companion, Robert McDonald, to serve as executor and trustee of his estate and to take over as president of Perry Ellis International.

Although McDonald was a former film producer with no background in the fashion industry, he agreed to Ellis's request and kept the company functioning despite the pall cast over the studio by the untimely death of its founder. Licensees in 1986 would generate more than $300 million wholesale, resulting in approximately $22.5 million for Perry Ellis International. In terms of retail volume, the company was generating some $750 million a year. The clear challenge was to keep Perry Ellis International alive despite the loss of Perry Ellis himself. In many respects a fashion designer's name had simply become a brand that actually represented the efforts of many: from design and marketing teams to the licensees themselves. Quoted in the *New York Times* shortly after Ellis's death, Jack Hyde, chairman of the Menswear Department at the Fashion Institute of Technology, said, "Let's face it, Christian Dior has been dead for a number of years, Chanel is dead, Anne Klein is dead. Business can go on. . . . There are people who think that Christian Dior is still alive because they see his label."

Longtime Ellis assistants took over the design responsibilities for the menswear and womenswear lines, but business soon began to fall off. To complicate matters, Manhattan Industries had been bought out by more profit-conscious Salant Corporation. A young designer named Marc Jacobs was then hired to oversee womenswear, and another designer, Roger Forsythe, was hired to oversee menswear. In addition, in 1988 McDonald hired Claudia Thomas, another longtime friend of Perry Ellis, who had experience as a marketer of home furnishings. In effect, he was grooming her to take over the company, because in March 1990 he too died from an AIDS-related illness, and she became president. The company was further diminished in October 1991 when Forsythe died from HIV-related causes (at the time of death his immune system was not depressed enough to be diagnosed as AIDS). The designer had gone public about his illness in a way that stood as a stark departure from the shame and secrecy that surrounded the subject of AIDS in the fashion industry of the mid-1980s. He wrote an open letter to the Perry Ellis staff as well as granting a candid interview with the *Daily News Record* to discuss his health.

To many in the fashion industry Perry Ellis International lacked focus at this stage. Even after Forsythe's death, the mass market, high-volume menswear business was doing well, but the company's signature womenswear collection, normally regarded as a loss leader, failed to provide synergy with the more mundane licensed products, where the major profits were actually realized. Although Jacobs garnered a certain amount of critical acclaim for his extreme fashion, in particular a notorious "grunge" collection, Thomas decided in 1993 to discontinue manufacturing a womenswear line. In reality, she was answering to the trustees of the estate of Tyler Ellis. Her mandate was to retain value rather than bankroll an idiosyncratic artistic vision. Perry Ellis, in effect, became just a design and licensing operation, leaving others to assume the manufacturing and distribution risks.

Thomas decided to leave Perry Ellis when her contract expired in 1994. She was replaced by Max J. Garelick, who had

Key Dates:

1967: Supreme International is founded.
1978: Perry Ellis International is founded.
1986: Perry Ellis dies.
1989: Supreme International establishes Natural Issue label.
1993: Supreme International goes public.
1999: Supreme International acquires Perry Ellis and assumes the Perry Ellis International name.

been the chief executive officer of a North American subsidiary of Rodier Paris. Perry Ellis did fairly well under Garelick, ranking number four among menswear brands, trailing only Polo, Tommy Hilfiger, and Nautica. Its only business in womenswear was a coat license. The company expanded into licensing such areas as watches, luggage, and home fashions. By the end of 1998 Perry Ellis brands generated an estimated $900 million a year in retail sales across 39 categories in 60 countries, but Salant, holders of one of its most important licenses, was forced to file for Chapter 11 bankruptcy protection. In January 1999 the trustees of the Perry Ellis estate decided to sell the company to Supreme International for $75 million in an all-cash transaction. For the trustees, given the situation with Salant, it was simply their fiduciary responsibility to protect the value of the estate by realizing $75 million, which could then be invested in a diversified portfolio for the heir of Perry Ellis. For Supreme International it was a deal that George Feldenkreis hoped would elevate his company to a new level.

Feldenkreis' family were Russian Jews who had fled to Cuba after World War II to escape communism. While his father made a living by importing electric equipment into Cuba, Feldenkreis became a lawyer. After Fidel Castro assumed power in 1959, and Cuba also became a communist country, Feldenkreis in 1961 fled to Miami with his pregnant wife, one-year-old son, Oscar, and only $700. Unable to practice law in his new country, Feldenkreis used his father's overseas contacts to start importing such diverse products as automotive parts from Asia and window glass for doors from Portugal. He also began to import guayaberas, the popular Caribbean straight-bottom men's shirt with four pockets. In 1967 he and his brother created Supreme International for their burgeoning clothing business. In addition to importing on a commission basis, Feldenkreis wanted to manufacture his own goods.

Supreme International was still quite small in 1980, with sales of $5 million and profits around $50,000, when Oscar turned 20, joined the company, and set about establishing Supreme's own brands. For several years he had limited success, but learned valuable lessons about merchandising. In 1989 he and his designers coined the Natural Issue brand. It was a simple but powerful concept that captured a prevailing desire to use environmentally friendly materials for casual clothing.

Natural Issue proved so successful for Supreme International that the company made an initial offering of stock in May 1993, raising almost $14 million, to fund expansion. It invested $500,000 in computer design equipment to quickly produce new styles. By August 1993, Supreme International acquired two companies: Alexander Martin for $460,000 and Publix Brands for $425,000. Martin brought with it the King Size Catalog, Eagelson, and the Daube clothing lines, while Publix added Albert Nipon, Adolfo, Monte Carlo, Career Club, C.C. Sport, and the Cotton Mill labels. After assimilating the new brands into its operations, Supreme International saw its annual sales reach $50 million in 1994.

Supreme International was now involved in a full range of apparel activities. It still imported guayaberas, but now designed and manufactured clothing as well as licensing its labels to others. In 1996 the company cast its net wider when for approximately $3.7 million it purchased Jolem and its labels aimed at Hispanic and African American men, including Tipo's, Cross Gear, Monte Fino, and New Step. Later in the year Supreme International made its most important acquisition to that point when it purchased Munsingwear and related brands for some $18 million. A year later the company added sweater manufacturer Crossings. Sales reached $90.6 million in 1995, $121.1 million in 1996, $155.7 million in 1997, and $190.7 million in 1998.

Late 1990s: Supreme International Assumes the Perry Ellis Name

The 1999 acquisition of Perry Ellis International for $75 million was a major move for Supreme International. It elevated the Miami company to major status in the international fashion industry. (At the same time, Supreme International also bought the Manhattan and John Henry clothing lines for $35 million from troubled Salant.) To take full advantage of the Perry Ellis deal, Supreme International decided to change its name to Perry Ellis International. Although the company's stock would trade under the new name, the Supreme International name was retained for the operating division. The Perry Ellis International Division would handle the licensing and marketing for all of the corporation's labels.

George and Oscar Feldenkreis then set about raising the profile of Perry Ellis that, although still alive in the minds of many consumers, had clearly slipped in the 15 years since the death of the designer. The company returned to womenswear, signing a licensing agreement with Kellwood to produce a high-end line. Overall, the goal was to make Perry Ellis into a lifestyle brand to compete with the likes of Ralph Lauren and Calvin Klein, from producing children's clothing to housewares. Perry Ellis took a page from Calvin Klein in early 2000 when, as a part of a $10 million marketing plan, it launched a controversial outdoor advertising campaign that featured images of nude and seminude models. When one outdoor company decided the ads were not appropriate for posting in Times Square, Perry Ellis received a bonanza of free advertising—and the kind of cachet coveted by a clothing line trying to establish itself as trendy.

The aggressive pattern of acquisitions continued for Supreme International under the Perry Ellis name. In July 2000 it paid $1.3 million for the Pro-Player, Artex, Fun Gear, and Salem Sportswear labels. In November 2000 it paid $1.75 million for the Mondo trademarks. Sales approached $230 million in 2000 and exceeded $287 million in 2001. George and Oscar Feldenkreis had clearly made tremendous strides in the previous decade. Whether they could successfully assume the mantle of Perry Ellis and build a mega-business remained to be seen.

Principal Operating Units

Perry Ellis; Munsingwear; Andrew Fezza; Ping Collection; John Henry; Crossings; Romani; Pro Player; Penguin Sport; Natural Issue; Havana Shirt Co.; Grand Slam; Manhattan; Cubavera.

Principal Competitors

Liz Claiborne, Inc.; Nautica Enterprises Inc.; Polo Ralph Lauren Corporation; Tommy Hilfiger Corporation.

Further Reading

Belkin, Lisa, ''Will Ellis Company Go On?,'' *New York Times,* June 24, 1986, p. C8.

Berman, Phyllis, ''Grunge Is Out, Licensing Is In,'' *Forbes,* May 23, 1994, p. 45.

Cardona, Mercedes M., ''Perry Ellis Strives to Refashion Itself Under New Owner,'' *Advertising Age,* October 11, 1999, p. 24.

Gibbons, William, and Peter Fressola, ''The Remaking of Perry Ellis (Matching Design House Prestigue With Mass Market Salant Corp.,'' *Daily News Record,* January 16, 1989, p. 16.

Lohrer, Robert, ''Supreme to Acquire Perry Ellis,'' *Women's Wear Daily,* January 29, 1999, p. 2.

——, ''The Supreme Example of Building On,'' *Daily News Record,* March 16, 1998, p. 1.

Lubanko, Matthew, ''Supreme International: Fashionable Growth,'' *Equities,* April 1994, p. 16.

Mayer, Barbara, ''Perry Ellis: His Design Legacy Remains,'' *Houston Chronicle,* June 11, 1986, p. 2.

Moor, Jonathan, *Perry Ellis,* New York: St. Martin's Press, 1988.

Shaw, Dan, ''Fashion's 'Comeback Kid' Moves on,'' *San Francisco Chronicle,* March 5, 1993, p. B3.

Walsh, Matt, ''Winning Team,'' *Forbes,* March 27, 1995, p. 66.

—Ed Dinger

PETsMART, Inc.

19601 North 27th Avenue
Phoenix, Arizona 85027
U.S.A.
Telephone: (623) 580-6100
Fax: (623) 580-6502
Web site: http://www.petsmart.com

Public Company
Incorporated: 1986 as The Pet Food Warehouse
Employees: 19,825
Sales: $2.2 billion (2000)
Stock Exchanges: NASDAQ
Ticker Symbol: PETM
NAIC: 45391 Pet and Pet Supplies Stores; 54194 Veterinary Services

The largest operator of pet food, pet supplies, and pet services superstores in the United States, PETsMART, Inc., stands atop a roughly $29 billion industry it helped to create. With nearly 530 mammoth stores scattered throughout the United States and Canada in 2001, PETsMART was recognized as an industry leader and pioneer, having originated the concept of a pet food and supply superstore. By aggressively pursuing expansion and stocking substantially more products in considerably larger stores than its competition, PETsMART quickly emerged as the dominant company of its kind. Although much of the chain's success was attributed to the size of its stores (all were larger than 18,000 square feet) and its vast selection of products (more than 12,000 items), PETsMART became the dominant force it represented during the mid-1990s through the astute leadership of Samuel J. Parker, the company's chairman of the board and chief executive officer. Under Parker's stewardship, PETsMART evolved into a one-stop pet shopping center offering pet grooming, adoption, and veterinary services, as well as sundry food and accessory products. In 1999, PETsMart.com, in which the firm owns an 81 percent stake, was launched and quickly became the leading provider of pet products and information available on-line. Through its subsidiaries, PETsMart, Inc. is also the largest direct marketer of pet supplies and equine products.

Company Origins

In 1987, a new concept in retailing pet food was born when Jim and Janice Dougherty opened the first store of their new company, The Pet Food Warehouse. As its corporate title suggested, The Pet Food Warehouse sold huge bags of pet food in a large, sparsely decorated, cement-floored store, giving consumers the opportunity to purchase food for their pets in bulk at discount prices. The warehouse retail concept was not new at the time, but it was the first time the high-volume, low-priced approach of retailing products to consumers had carried over to the pet industry, a roughly $7 billion-a-year industry during the mid-1980s that was dominated by supermarkets and mass merchandisers, with myriad small pet stores snatching what little was left. The Doughertys, however, were intent on adding a new type of competitor to the industry, one that could take advantage of a burgeoning trend among consumers during the 1980s and fuel the growth of their fledgling enterprise.

Jim and Janice Dougherty incorporated their company in August 1986, using $1 million in start-up investment from Phillips-Van Heusen Corporation and other investors to open their first two stores in Phoenix, Arizona, the following year. Venture capitalists continued to fund the company's expansion after the first two stores were established, providing the financial support to establish five additional stores by 1988 in Arizona, Colorado, and Texas, as The Pet Food Warehouse began to take on the qualities of a retail chain. Although there was evidence that The Pet Food Warehouse was performing well—seven stores had been established in less than two years, and annual sales had risen to nearly $16 million—there was one important financial statistic that tinctured its success, particularly in the minds of the company's all-important investors: the regional chain was losing money. In 1989, The Pet Food Warehouse lost $1.8 million, prompting the group of investors supporting the company to make a dramatic change. That year, the board of investors voted for the removal of the Doughertys, retaining the two founders as consultants but excluding them from direct control over the company they had started less than two years earlier.

Company Perspectives:

PETsMart Inc. strives to offer services and solutions to help you be a responsible pet owner by fulfilling the total lifetime needs of your pet.

Samuel J. Parker Heading Up Expansion Efforts: Early 1990s

Although the Doughertys were gone, the concept of selling pet supplies in a large retail store at discount prices remained alive, at least in the hearts of the investors who still hoped The Pet Food Warehouse approach could yield a return on their investments. To replace the Doughertys, the company's financial supporters wanted someone with more retail management experience, and in Samuel J. Parker they gained a leader with considerable experience. A 19-year veteran of the Jewel supermarket chain, Parker also had served as president of Frame-N-Lens Optical and the GEMCO division of Lucky Stores, accruing sufficient executive management experience to attract the attention of The Pet Food Warehouse's anxious controlling investors.

Parker was hired as chairman of the company shortly after the removal of the Doughertys in 1989, and he immediately began to exert his managerial control over the seven-unit chain. Although the Doughertys had originated the warehouse retail concept in the pet supply industry, Parker's refinement of the concept would produce the results for which antsy investors hoped, and he soon transformed the money-losing Pet Food Warehouse into PETsMART, Inc., one of the fastest growing companies of any kind in the United States during the early 1990s.

Once Parker was brought on board, sweeping changes were made: cement floors were replaced with tile floors, aisles were widened, and in-store lighting was brightened, creating a more hospitable environment for customers. Instead of merely selling pet food, Parker stocked the company's stores with a full array of pet accessories and supplies, attempting to beat the competition by offering a far greater selection of products at substantially reduced prices. What emerged early under Parker's reign was a hybrid version of the concept first developed by the Doughertys, a retail approach that incorporated the design of a warehouse store with the more conventional trappings of a retail store. In the rear of a PETsMART store, pet food was sold in austere surroundings; pet accessories were displayed on retail racking in the front, giving the customers who frequented each location the benefits of both worlds. In addition, Parker established grooming and veterinary centers at PETsMART stores and then set up a pet adoption service called ''Luv-a-Pet,'' creating a one-stop pet store that offered services and supplies even the largest mass merchandiser or supermarket could not match.

As these important changes were being made, engendering an entirely different type of retail competitor, the need to add additional stores became paramount for Parker. Aggressive expansion across the nation would become an integral component of the success PETsMART enjoyed during the early 1990s, enabling the chain to saturate markets before competitors could establish a foothold and also positioning the Phoenix-based company as the strongest acquisitive force in an industry that would begin to consolidate in earnest between 1993 and 1994. To finance this expansion Parker relied on the same financial source as the Doughertys, urging the venture capitalists backing PETsMART to provide the capital for the establishment of PETsMART stores throughout the southwestern United States. By the end of 1989, five additional units had been opened, giving PETsMART a total of 12; by the end of 1990, the chain comprised 29 stores, averaging 25,000 square feet and stocking roughly 7,500 products.

As the number of stores increased, so did PETsMART's annual sales, recording prodigious leaps that testified to the public's willingness to frequent a pet supply superstore. During the first five years of Parker's stewardship, PETsMART recorded annual sales growth of 85 percent, quickly securing the company's ranking as the largest operator in its industry. From 1989's total of $15.9 million, annual sales surged to $29.3 million in 1990, and nearly doubled in 1991, when the company operated 48 stores by year's end, reaching $58.2 million. That the company demonstrated such robust growth during the economically recessive early 1990s was most impressive. While the PETsMART chain blossomed many businesses, particularly retail businesses, suffered mightily in the anemic economic climate. Thus PETsMART's surge during the early 1990s testified to the soundness of the entire concept and encouraged Parker to continue his strategic expansion across the country and bolster the chain's market position.

Going Public: 1993

In 1992, annual sales jumped to $106.6 million and for the first time the company registered a profit, generating $400,000 in net income after recording a series of financial losses. PETsMART's net income leaped to $2.4 million the following year on sales of $188 million, but when these financial figures were announced they were applauded by a considerably larger group of people than PETsMART employees, management, and the company's controlling investors. In July 1993, PETsMART made its first public offering, opting to become a public company after years of relying on investors to shoulder the burden of financing the company's expansion. At the time, plans for the development of additional stores were ambitious, dwarfing the rate of expansion recorded during the previous years, as Parker and PETsMART management set sights on establishing a host of new PETsMART stores in new locations. In mid-1993 the company operated 71 stores in 13 states; by the end of the year Parker hoped to operate a total of 106 stores and broaden the chain's geographic coverage to include 20 states, then add 40 additional stores in 1994, as the race to blanket the country with PETsMART stores accelerated.

To finance this prodigious expansion the company needed capital, which the public offering would provide. Becoming a public company also would enable PETsMART to pay down its debt and give the company's controlling financiers a return on their investments, which had fueled PETsMART's expansion throughout its existence. The initial public offering yielded $125 million, giving the company the financial means to forge ahead and grab a larger share of the pet food and supplies industry.

By the time PETsMART went public in mid-1993, U.S. consumers were spending $8.5 billion annually on pet food and

Key Dates:

1987: The Doughertys open two stores under the name The Pet Food Warehouse.
1988: Five additional stores are established in Arizona, Colorado, and Texas.
1989: Samuel J. Parker joins the firm and pet grooming services are offered for the first time in its Colorado store.
1990: A total of 29 stores are now in operation under the new name, PETsMART.
1991: Sales reach $106.6 million and the firm records its first profit.
1993: The company goes public.
1994: The company acquires the PetZazz chain of stores and PETsMart Charities Inc. is established.
1995: The company purchases Petstuff Inc., ten of The Pet Food Giant's superstores, Sporting Dog Specialties Inc., and State Line Tack Inc.
1997: The company reports a loss of $34.4 million and stock price falters.
1999: A national campaign is launched and PETsMart.com begins operation.
2000: The firm sells its U.K. operations.
2001: The company begins a new advertising campaign entitled ''PETsMART: All You Need for the Life of Your Pet.''

supplies, mostly in large supermarkets and mass-merchandising outlets. This had been true when The Pet Food Warehouse first emerged in Phoenix in 1987, and continued to characterize the industry as PETsMART battled to maintain supremacy, but the company had secured its place in the vast market by stocking products the industry's largest competitors did not. Nearly 50 percent of PETsMART's food sales were derived from items such as Science Diet and Iams, brands previously available only through veterinarians and small pet shops. Although this move alone distinguished the company from its competition, that distinction began to blur as the pet food industry entered the mid-1990s.

PETsMART's success had spawned a host of imitators across the country, each trying to capture a share of the pet food and supplies market with an approach similar to that pioneered by the Doughertys and refined by Parker. During the early 1990s, each of these companies had broadened their geographic reaches, establishing new stores in new locations much like PETsMART, but as the mid-1990s neared, these companies and their respective expansion plans began to collide, creating a contentious environment within the industry that pitted one company against another. It was either acquire or be acquired in the pet food and supplies industry, with only the strongest competitors likely to withstand the ensuing battle for dominance.

Growth Through Acquisition: Mid-1990s

As the largest operator of superstores specializing in pet food, supplies, and services, PETsMART occupied an enviable position for the acquisitive years ahead. Parker had pursued a plan of rapid expansion from the beginning of his tenure at PETsMART. Now, as competition became more intense in the wake of the company's initial public offering, his plans for growth would include swallowing competing companies as well as establishing PETsMART stores in new locations. Succinctly framing the company's attitude for the future, Parker informed *Forbes* at the end of 1993, ''We're in a race,'' but even as he uttered those words the fix was in.

The company opened 41 stores in 1993, lifting annual sales from $106.6 million to $187.9 million, and acquired Phoenix-based Pet Food & Supply and its five superstores. PETsMART subsequently folded the Pet Food & Supply chain, retaining one store, then entered 1994 looking to expand wherever the best real estate deals could be had. In January 1994, PETsMART announced its intentions to acquire the 31-unit Petzazz chain from the Weisheimer Companies through an $81.3 million stock swap, an acquisition expected to add $50 million in new business and facilitate PETsMART's entry into the Chicago market, where Petzazz already operated.

In 1995, PETsMART continued to make pivotal acquisitions, including the May purchase of Sporting Dog Specialties, Inc., the world's largest catalog retailer of pet and animal supplies and accessories, and State Line Tack, Inc., a global catalog retailer of equine supplies. The year's most important acquisition, however, was the purchase of the company's closest rival, Atlanta-based Petstuff, Inc., and its 56 superstores. Announced in February, the acquisition of Petstuff further solidified PETsMART's commanding lead in the industry, giving the company control over much of the nation's pet food and supply market. Later that year, Parker retired as CEO, naming Mark Hansen as his predecessor; Parker remained chairman of the firm.

Having successfully secured a leading position in both the retail and catalog sectors of the industry, the company began to focus on internal growth. In 1996, management planned to open 50 new stores, each with a pet hospital attached to it. Operating under the name VetSmart, the pet hospitals ranged from 1,850 to 3,500 square feet and offered services from pet grooming, shots, spaying, neutering, and a variety of other services.

Financial Woes in the Late 1990s

The firm's aggressive growth strategy began to catch up with it however, and in 1997, financial problems arose. Costs related to the recent acquisitions, restructuring costs, problems with a new merchandising system, dropping sales in the flea-and-tick control products market, and a lackluster advertising campaign, all factored into a dismal financial performance. Hansen left the firm that year, and Parker returned to the CEO position. After reporting a $35.72 million loss in the second quarter of 1997, stock price languished. In August, the company initiated a poison pill plan—one that would make them less attractive to potential takeover bids by issuing a new series of preferred stock—in response to its faltering stock price.

Despite its net loss of $34.4 million in 1997, PETsMART continued to aggressively pursue internal expansion. The firm planned to open 75 new stores in 1998, and under the leadership of Parker, the firm restructured its management team as well as its corporate strategy. Philip Francis was hired to take over the CEO position and a new focus on employee training and providing high levels of customer service was initiated along with a new inventory strategy that would ensure that key products would remain in stock while slower-moving items would be discontinued.

Francis became chairman of the firm in 1999 upon Parker's retirement. In March of that year, a new $20 million national ad campaign was launched that spotlighted the firm as a one-stop shop offering pet supplies, pet adoption, and vet services. The company also opened its 500th store in Washington as well as a new distribution center in Texas.

Launching PETsMART.com in 1999

In June 1999, PETsMART.com began operation. Owned by PETsMart Inc., idealab! Capital Partners, and Global Retail Partners, the web site offered the largest assortment of pet-related products on the Internet, customer service, and expert pet advice. Tom McGovern, the CEO of the new venture, stated in a company press release, ''Not only will our product selection, customer value, and service be unmatched, but through our compelling content, expert advice, and entertaining feature articles, PETsMART.com will deliver an overall superior consumer experience.'' Sales for the year reached $2.11 billion, a small increase over 1998 sales results of $2.10 billion.

PETsMART entered the new millennium with a strong focus on expanding its North American growth. The firm sold its U.K. operations, which had posted a loss of $10.3 million in 1999. The company also changed the VetSmart name to Banfield, The Pet Hospital. It purchased a controlling interest—81 percent—of PETsMART.com. Stock price continued to remain low, however, and the company continued to post losses due to a general slowdown in consumer spending, increased competition from discounters and grocery stores, and high costs related to warehousing and distribution. Although sales were up by 5.4 percent in fiscal 2000, the firm recorded a $30.9 million loss for the year.

PETsMART started a new ad campaign in 2001 that replaced the tagline ''Where pets are family'' with ''PETsMART: All you need for the life of your pet.'' The company also outlined a three-year plan that focused on providing a high level of service to customers and pet enthusiasts by expanding its product and services offerings. With a secure position as the United States' largest retail supplier of pet-related products and services, management remained hopeful that the company was on the right track to securing financial gains.

Principal Subsidiaries

PETsMART Direct Inc.; PETsMART Charities Inc.

Principal Competitors

Kroger Co.; Petco Animal Supplies Inc.; Wal-Mart Stores Inc.

Further Reading

Dawson, Angela, ''PETsMART Breaks a National TV Effort,'' *Adweek Western Advertising News,* March 29, 1999, p. 2.

Gonderinger, Lisa, ''PETsMART Chain Barks at Suitors with Poison Pill,'' *Business Journal,* August 29, 1997, p. 1.

——, ''PETsMART to Sniff Out New Ad Shop,'' *Business Journal,* June 6, 1997, p. 4.

Helverson, Richard, ''PETsMART Seeks Growth from Within, Delves into New Lines, Services,'' *Discount Store News,* April 15, 1996, p. 19.

——, ''PETsMART: Teaching an Old Pet Care Business New Tricks,'' *Discount Store News,* December 6, 1993, p. 81.

Hooper, Amy, ''Retailers Greet Petstuff Demise with Mixed Feelings,'' *Pet Product News,* August 1995, p. 22.

Lewis, David, ''As Rivals Perish, PETsMART Increases Online Investment,'' *Internet Week,* December 4, 2000, p. 104.

Miller, Paul, ''Galloping Giant: Two Recent Deals Have Positioned PETsMART As a Leading Equine and Pet Supplies Cataloger,'' *Catalog Age,* February 1996, p. 7.

''No. 1 Still Leads Pack, Despite Flat Sales,'' *DSN Retailing Today,* August 7, 2000, p. 44.

Perez, Janet, ''Phoenix-Based PetSmart's Superstores Offer One-Stop Shopping for Pets,'' *Phoenix Gazette,* September 9, 1993, p. 9.

''Pet Consolidation in Offing: PETsMART Buys Petzazz; Enters Chicago, Portland, Ore.,'' *Discount Store News,* March 21, 1994, p. 3.

''PETsMART Inc.,'' *Wall Street Journal,* February 8, 1995, p. B4.

Reagor, Catherine, ''PetSmart Will Survive Attack on Pet Food Line by Wal-Mart,'' *Business Journal—Serving Phoenix and the Valley of the Sun,* September 30, 1994, p. 7.

Roth, Steve, ''PETsMART Plans to Open String of Metroplex Stores,'' *Dallas Business Journal,* August 24, 1990, p. 11.

Roush, Chris, ''Cash Squeeze Forced Petstuff to Sell Out to Petsmart,'' *Knight-Ridder/Tribune Business News,* May 3, 1995, p. 50.

Scalley, Robert, ''PETsMART Plans 75 Openings,'' *Discount Store News,* April 10, 1998, p. 6.

Shepherd, Kim, ''Huge Pet Stores Cater to Booming Number of Animal Owners,'' *Knight-Ridder/Tribune Business News,* September 12, 1994.

Sullivan, R. Lee, ''Puppy Love,'' *Forbes,* December 20, 1993, p. 138.

Swenson, Steve E., ''Bakersfield, Calif. Pet Supply Store Sues PETsMART for Deceptive Ads,'' *Knight-Ridder/Tribunes Business News,* September 20, 1995.

Taub, Stephen, ''Diamond in the Ruff,'' *Financial World,* September 1, 1993, p. 16.

—Jeffrey L. Covell
—update: Christina M. Stansell

Pillowtex Corporation

4111 Mint Way
Dallas, Texas 75237
U.S.A.
Telephone: (214) 333-3225
Fax: (214) 330-6016
Web site: http://www.pillowtex.com

Public Company
Incorporated: 1954
Employees: 12,000
Sales: $1.35 billion (2000)
Stock Exchanges: New York
Ticker Symbol: PTEXQ
NAIC: 31321 Broadwoven Fabric Mills; 314129 Other Household Textile Product Mills

Pillowtex Corporation is one of the three biggest producers of bedding and bath textiles in the United States. It is the leading manufacturer of what is known in the industry as "top-of-the-bed" products, including blankets, pillows, mattress pads, and comforters. Through its subsidiary, Fieldcrest Cannon Inc., Pillowtex is also the leading U.S. manufacturer of towels, and it sells many well-known home textile brands, including Royal Velvet, Cannon, and Charisma. Pillowtex's customers include practically every major North American retailer, from department stores and mass merchandisers to catalogs to large institutional organizations such as the U.S. Postal Service. The company offers more than 10,000 products, which are manufactured in plants throughout the United States and Canada. Its Dallas facilities include what is arguably North America's biggest feather and down processing plant. The company grew rapidly through acquisition, culminating in the merger in 1997 with Fieldcrest Cannon, a firm even larger than itself. Heavy debt sent the company into Chapter 11 in 2000.

Postwar Origins

Pillowtex was founded in 1954 by John H. Silverthorne to manufacture bed pillows in Dallas. The company soon began acquiring manufacturing plants in Atlanta, Chicago, Connecticut, and Los Angeles, forming the basis of what would become a "hub and spoke" manufacturing and distribution network, one of the most sophisticated systems in the industry. Sales mounted slowly but steadily from 1958 on, reaching $4 million by 1965 and $7.5 million in the early 1970s.

Notwithstanding its relatively modest growth in the early years, Pillowtex developed a reputation as a potent competitor. According to a 1990 article in trade journal *HFD-The Weekly Home Furnishings Newspaper,* one customer went so far as to nickname it "the gorilla." Rivals had no choice but to concede the company's preeminence in pillows. One unidentified competitor told *HFD*'s Sharyn Bernard, "They're an excellent company. . . . Everyone thinks of Pillowtex [when they want bed pillows]." The firm also garnered a reputation for having a creative sales force and for establishing, rather than following, product trends.

John Silverthorne continued to own and operate Pillowtex throughout much of its first four decades in business. In 1973, the founder established a long-range succession scheme by promoting Charles "Chuck" Hansen, Jr., to president. Hansen had joined the company in 1965 at the age of 25 and quickly advanced from the ranks of sales representatives to the executive offices. Although he had not originally expected to make a lifetime career at Pillowtex, he told the *Dallas Business Journal*'s Sean Wood that he hoped to make it "the largest and most profitable maker and seller of pillows, comforters and bed pads."

Hansen and Silverthorne believed that the best way to achieve that goal was to "buy" market share. The company averaged one acquisition about every four years from 1970 to 1981, adding Perl Pillow, Synthetic Pillows, Inc., and Globe Feather & Down during the period. By 1982, organic growth and acquisitions had boosted the pillow company's sales to about $56 million and made it the leader of the industry.

Diversification into Other "Top-of-the-Bed" Goods in the 1980s

Having achieved dominance in its core business, Pillowtex sought growth through other avenues in the 1980s. Acquisitions

Company Perspectives:

At Pillowtex, our entire history is dedicated to helping people sleep well. Since 1954, we've been producing the best line of bedding materials. We've grown into the largest manufacturer of bed pillows, mattress pads, down comforters, and blankets; as well as a leading provider of comforter covers. Every night, we help millions of people rest. And every morning, we make sure they get out on the right side of the bed.

throughout the decade both supplemented Pillowtex's pillow making operations and added mattress pads to the product line. The company purchased two mattress pad companies—Los Angeles-based Bedcovers, Inc. and Acme Quilting Co., Inc., America's oldest mattress pad producer—in 1983 alone. The Acme purchase also gave Pillowtex the capacity to manufacture comforters, throw pillows, moving van pads, and such decorative goods as dust ruffles and pillow shams.

Hansen noted that these additions not only boosted Pillowtex's sales volume, but also helped to shield it from downturns in individual categories. A desire to gain manufacturing and marketing synergies was another motivation behind the acquisition strategy.

Pillowtex grew so fast in the late 1980s that one competitor filed suit against it, charging that the company had violated antitrust laws and was becoming a monopoly. The lawsuit arose from Pillowtex's 1987 acquisition of Sumergrade Corporation, a North Carolina manufacturer. The $9.3 million purchase of this bankrupt business made Pillowtex the nation's leading producer of down comforters and boosted its capacity in decorative throw pillows, a fast-growing, high-margin segment. (The Texas company would further augment its decorative pillow business with the 1991 acquisition of Nettle Creek Corporation.) Sumergrade also gave its new parent a valuable Ralph Lauren Home Furnishings license and enhanced its presence on the East Coast. The antitrust suit was unsuccessful, and Pillowtex's growth continued unabated.

Some competitors speculated that Pillowtex's rapid expansion would be its downfall, making it a slow-moving giant. The company combated that tendency with a quick response (QR) program that incorporated electronic data interchange (EDI). QR coordinated information shared by the merchandiser and the manufacturer such that when a sales clerk scanned the inventory number of a given product, the network automatically reordered the item from Pillowtex. The system reduced paperwork and lead time, thereby cutting costs for both parties and creating a "just-in-time-like" operation. By the mid-1990s, all but about 10 percent of the company's customers placed their orders through EDI, leading analysts with Wheat, First Securities to call Pillowtex "one of the most technologically integrated and advanced" of pillow and blanket manufacturers.

Rapid Growth in the Early 1990s

Chuck Hansen advanced to chief executive officer and chairman when the founder died of cancer in December 1992. The new leader quickly prepared Pillowtex for an initial public offering (IPO) in 1993. The floatation offered about one-third of the company's equity to the public, while Hansen and Silverthorne's widow, Mary R. Silverthorne, split most of the remaining interest. This arrangement permitted the company to raise funds for both the Silverthorne estate and Pillowtex's growth, while maintaining control among corporate insiders.

Pillowtex moved boldly into the blanket segment in the ensuing 30 months, using part of the $53 million proceeds of the IPO to bankroll the acquisition of three blanket companies and two pillow/comforter manufacturers. The growth-hungry firm bought two old-line blanket manufacturers, Tennessee Woolen Mills, Inc. and Manetta Mills, Inc., in 1993 at a total cost of $20.9 million in cash. A year later, Pillowtex shelled out a whopping $112 million ($101 million cash and $11 million debt) for Beacon Manufacturing Company, then the largest player in the blanket segment.

Other acquisitions diversified Pillowtex internationally. Torfeaco Industries Limited, a well-established producer of pillows, mattress pads, and decorative bedding, came on board in 1993. In 1994, the growing firm paid $3.6 million for Imperial Feather Company, a pillow and comforter manufacturer. With overseas sales totaling about 10 percent of total revenues in 1995, Pillowtex laid plans to launch production and distribution operations in Europe and South America.

Pillowtex's pro forma sales nearly doubled in the early 1990s, from $259 million in 1991 to $474.9 million in 1995. Operating income increased from $19.1 million to $36.5 million during the same period, due in part to rising productivity. The company's selling, general, and administrative expenses (already ranked among the industry's lowest) declined from nearly 13 percent of sales in 1991 to 9 percent of sales by 1995. Nevertheless, net income declined from $13.2 million to a low of $7.7 million in 1994. The decreases in bottom-line profitability were attributed to debt service from Pillowtex's mid-decade acquisition spree, rising raw materials costs, and difficulties in reconciling its new affiliates. The decline in net earnings pushed Pillowtex's stock, which had risen from an introductory price of $14 per share in 1993 to a high of more than $21 early in 1994, down to less than $9 by the end of the year.

The company tried to alleviate some of its raw materials problems with the $6 million acquisition of Newton Yarn Mills, a North Carolina cotton yarn spinning factory, from Dixie Yarns Inc. in 1995. In addition, a savvy acquisition in 1996 gave Pillowtex Fieldcrest Cannon's $71 million blanket and throw business at a cost of $30 million.

Pillowtex's revenues rose to $490.7 million in 1996, and its net climbed to more than $14 million. Although in 1995 Hansen had told the *Dallas Business Journal's* Wayne Carter, "We don't control the stock price; I just try to run the company," by the end of 1996 he took a more considered approach to shareholders' concerns, noting in that year's annual report that "the heart of Pillowtex's mission is the commitment to provide a superior investment return to our shareholders." Buoyed in part by the late 1995 institution of a dividend, the stock rose from less than $12 to $18 over the course of 1996.

Key Dates:

1954: The company is founded in Dallas.
1973: Chuck Hansen becomes president.
1987: Sumergrade Corporation is acquired, making Pillowtex the nation's leading producer of down comforters.
1993: Initial public offering.
1997: Massive Fieldcrest Cannon acquisition vaults company to one of top home textile producers in the country.
2000: The company files for Chapter 11 bankruptcy protection.

The Mid-1990s and Beyond

A major management shift that started in 1995 reflected Pillowtex's transition from an "entrepreneurial" firm into a diversified corporation and telegraphed possible management succession scenarios. That year, the company reorganized into two operating segments, the Pillowtex division, in charge of pillows, mattress pads, and comforters, and the Beacon division, manufacturing woven blankets. This transitional phase soon yielded to a second shuffling. In 1997, the company reorganized along functional lines, appointing former Chief Financial Officer and Executive Vice-President Jeffrey Cordes as president and chief operating officer, former Pillowtex division President Christopher Baker as president of the manufacturing division, and hiring Kevin Finlay away from Fieldcrest Cannon Inc. to serve as president of the sales and marketing division.

Wheat, First Securities' late 1996 analysis of Pillowtex forecast earnings growth of 22 percent in 1997, as efficiencies from its earlier acquisitions began to take effect and the company paid down substantial amounts of debt. In 1995, CEO Hansen told *Dallas Business Journal's* Wayne Carter, "We're not obsessed with the need to grow. We're obsessed with being the most profitable." Nonetheless, he affirmed that the company would continue to pursue growth through acquisition in the waning years of the 20th century, noting in Pillowtex's 1996 annual report the firm's "next major milestone: $1 billion in annual sales." Pillowtex intended to achieve that goal through internal development as well as its ongoing acquisition strategy. Organic growth strategies included a plan to leverage brand equity, especially among its own labels like Health Horizons antibacterial pillows and mattress pads, to boost sales in the late 1990s. The company also boldly mounted a challenge to Sunbeam's utter domination of the electric blanket category in early 1997, hoping to capture 20 percent of this $150 million market.

Doubling Size, Going Bankrupt in the Late 1990s

In 1996, Pillowtex had snapped up the blanket and throw manufacturing business of giant towel-maker Fieldcrest Cannon Inc. In September 1997, Pillowtex announced that it had agreed to acquire the whole of Fieldcrest Cannon, a Kannapolis, North Carolina-based company that was the first name in bed and bath products. Fieldcrest was to be run as a subsidiary of Pillowtex, keeping its North Carolina base. The combined company would have sales of $1.6 billion, and 15,000 employees, making it either the second or third largest home textile manufacturer in the United States. Pillowtex paid $410 million to buy Fieldcrest and assumed $315 million of Fieldcrest's debt. The deal accomplished several of Pillowtex's stated goals: it easily pushed it into the billion-dollar-company category, and it gave the firm a complete array of home textiles, including Fieldcrest's top brands Royal Velvet, Cannon, and Charisma. Pillowtex announced that it would work to upgrade Fieldcrest's technology, budgeting $80 million in 1998 for capital improvements at the new subsidiary. Although this was the biggest acquisition the company had made yet, it was not the last. In under a year, Pillowtex again made the news with its announcement that it had acquired The Leshner Corp., a maker of terrycloth kitchen and bath products. Leshner had sales of $105 million, and its inclusion in the Pillowtex stable bumped total company revenue up to $1.7 billion.

Integrating the parts of the new, mammoth Pillowtex did not go smoothly. When it acquired Fieldcrest Cannon, Pillowtex also took on a long-running labor dispute at the towel-maker's North Carolina factories. After a struggle dating back to the 1970s, the Union of Needletrades, Textile and Industrial Employees finally won the right to organize Fieldcrest's six plants in Kannapolis in 1999. The Kannapolis workers had been paid about $2 an hour less than workers at Pillowtex's other unionized plants, and other issues in the union elections were sick pay, overtime, and pensions. Pillowtex also had poured millions of dollars into updating Fieldcrest's computer system, but did not come up with a satisfactory result. Problems with the computer system depressed sales at the division. Starting with the second quarter of 1999, Pillowtex began to lose money. Over the next 15 months, the company lost more than $67 million. Sales continued to shrink, and the company was oppressed with the debt it had taken on. Key players began to leave the company, including the president of sales and marketing, vice-president of international sales and marketing, and, eventually, the chief financial officer and the president/chief operating officer. By the second quarter of 2000, the company had to own up to a quarterly loss of more than $8 million, while interest rates rose, and total debt was more than $1 billion. CEO Hansen continued in an optimistic vein, announcing that although business in some categories fell, sales were up 5 percent with Pillowtex's top ten customers. When asked about the possibility of a bankruptcy filing, Hansen told industry journal *Home Textiles Today* (July 31, 2000), "No way in hell. That's sure as hell not on my agenda." One day after again posting dismal losses for the third quarter, Hansen resigned. Within weeks, the company filed for Chapter 11, which allowed it protection from its creditors while it reorganized its business.

Pillowtex pinned its hopes on its new president and chief operating officer, Tony Williams. Williams announced that he would simplify the company, trimming its product lines, reorganizing its manufacturing processes, and shortening cycle times to eliminate excess inventory. He also hired brand management consultants to help market Pillowtex's many leading brands. Williams predicted that Pillowtex would recover quickly and emerge from bankruptcy in 2002.

Principal Subsidiaries

Fieldcrest Cannon Inc.

Principal Competitors

WestPoint Stevens Inc.; Dan River Inc.; Springs Industries, Inc.

Further Reading

''Bedding Manufacturer Files for Bankruptcy Protection,'' *Wall Street Journal,* November 15, 2000, p. B17.

Bernard, Sharyn K., ''Pillowtex Prestige: 36-Year-Old Company Builds Strength Through Diversification,'' *HFD-The Weekly Home Furnishings Newspaper,* December 3, 1990, pp. 40–41.

Burkins, Glenn, ''Union Claims Victory at Pillowtex Plants,'' *Wall Street Journal,* June 25, 1999, p. A2.

Carter, Wayne, ''Pillowtex Straightens Out Lumps,'' *Dallas Business Journal,* September 22, 1995, pp. 8, 22.

Eckhouse, Kim, ''Brands Boom in Basics: Adding Names to Pillows and Pads,'' *HFN-The Weekly Newspaper for the Home Furnishing Network,* April 21, 1997, pp. 27–28.

Frinton, Sandra, ''At Home in Bed; Pillowtex's Growth Stays Close to Basics,'' *HFN-The Weekly Newspaper for the Home Furnishing Network,* September 11, 1995, pp. 23–24.

——, ''Buy, Pay, Diversify: Companies Map Out '96 Strategies,'' *HFN-The Weekly Newspaper for the Home Furnishing Network,* December 11, 1995, pp. 21–22.

——, ''Health Push in Pillows and Pads,'' *HFN-The Weekly Newspaper for the Home Furnishing Network,* April 22, 1996, pp. 35–36.

——, ''Pillowtex '95 Results Up,'' *HFN-The Weekly Newspaper for the Home Furnishing Network,* February 19, 1996, p. 32.

Hitchcock, Nancy A., ''Business Strategy Speeds Flow of Goods and Data,'' *Modern Materials Handling,* March 1993, pp. 54D5–54D7.

Hogsett, Don, ''New Pillowtex Sheriff Takes Aim,'' *Home Textiles Today,* January 1, 2001, p. 1.

——, ''Pillowtex Done in by Aggressive Growth,'' *Home Textiles Today,* November 20, 2000, p. 23.

——, ''Pillowtex Forced to File Chapter 11,'' *Home Textiles Today,* November 20, 2000, p. 1.

——, ''Pillowtex Posts $8.1 Mil. 2Q Loss,'' *Home Textiles Today,* July 31, 2000, p. 1.

''Home Textiles Today Top 15,'' *Home Textiles Today,* January 13, 1977, pp. 6–9.

Johnson, Sarah, ''Finlay to Pillowtex,'' *HFN-The Weekly Newspaper for the Home Furnishing Network,* March 10, 1997, pp. 27–28.

Kinter, Kim, and Donna Boyle Schwartz, ''Pillowtex Aims to Expand,'' *HFD-The Weekly Home Furnishings Newspaper,* February 2, 1987, pp. 29–30.

Lazaro, Marvin, ''Pillowtex Has It in the Bag,'' *Home Textiles Today,* March 19, 2001, p. 1.

McCurry, John W., ''Pillowtex Buys Fieldcrest Cannon,'' *Textile World,* October 1997, p. 21.

Palmeri, Christopher, ''Southern Comfort,'' *Forbes,* April 25, 1994, p. 191.

''Pillowtex Inks Deal for Leshner,'' *HFN,* June 15, 1998, p. 14.

Rush, Amy Joyce, and Sarah Johnson, ''Pillowtex Going Electric in Blankets,'' *HFN-The Weekly Newspaper for the Home Furnishing Network,* February 17, 1997, p. 4.

Schwartz, Donna Boyle, ''User-Friendly Basic Bedding: Technical Jargon Yields to Lifestyle Marketing,'' *HFN-The Weekly Newspaper for the Home Furnishing Network,* October 21, 1996, pp. 41–42.

Slott, Mira, ''Finlay Out as P'Tex Honcho,'' *Home Textiles Today,* March 13, 2000, p. 1.

——, ''Sumergrade Acquisition Brings Pillowtex Decorative Pillow Gains,'' *HFD-The Weekly Home Furnishings Newspaper,* January 18, 1988, pp. 43–44.

Stringer, Kortney, ''Pillowtex CEO Resigns, Board Member Takes Over After Disappointing Results,'' *Wall Street Journal,* October 30, 2000, p. B10.

Troy, Colleen, and Schwartz, Donna Boyle, ''Purofied Antitrust Suit Fails,'' *HFD-The Weekly Home Furnishings Newspaper,* July 13, 1987, pp. 59–60.

Wattman, Karla, ''Duties, China Quota Roil Industry,'' *HFD-The Weekly Home Furnishings Newspaper,* May 2, 1994, pp. 40–41.

——, ''In the Public Eye: Cash Infusion Puts Pillowtex into High Growth Mode,'' *HFD-The Weekly Home Furnishings Newspaper,* April 26, 1993, pp. 33–34.

——, ''Pillowtex Gains Northern Exposure,'' *HFD-The Weekly Home Furnishings Newspaper,* November 15, 1993, p. 48.

Wood, Sean, ''Pillowtex Tries to Keep from Getting Comfortable,'' *Dallas Business Journal,* June 25, 1993, p. S23.

—April Dougal Gasbarre
—update: A. Woodward

Pioneer Hi-Bred International, Inc.

400 Locust Street
700 Capital Square
Des Moines, Iowa 50309
U.S.A.
Telephone: (515) 248-4800
Fax: (515) 248-4999
Web site: http://www.pioneer.com

Wholly Owned Subsidiary of E.I. du Pont de Nemours and Company
Incorporated: 1926 as the Hi-Bred Corn Company
Employees: 5,000
Sales: $1.9 billion (2000)
NAIC: 11115 Corn Farming; 11111 Soybean Farming; 32532 Pesticide and Other Agricultural Chemical Manufacturing

Pioneer Hi-Bred International, Inc. is one of the world's largest seed companies. Pioneer develops, produces, and markets hybrid corn, sorghum, sunflower, soybean, alfalfa, wheat, canola, and vegetable seeds. The company dominates most of the markets in which it participates, holding more than a 40 percent share of the North American seed corn market, and even higher shares in European markets. The company was instrumental in one of the most important genetic accomplishments of American agriculture, the development of hybrid corn. Pioneer has in recent years become increasingly involved in the use of biotechnology. Always known as a very independent company, Pioneer agreed to be purchased by chemical giant Dupont in 1999 to stay competitive in a rapidly changing industry.

Creation of the First Company for the Development and Marketing of Hybrid Seed Corn in 1926

Pioneer was established in 1926 as the Hi-Bred Corn Company under the leadership of Henry Agard Wallace. Before the company was created, it was commonly assumed that a farmer's best-looking corn yielded the highest-producing seeds. Farmers took their handsomest ears to university-sponsored countywide and statewide contests to be judged and used as the following season's seed. But a select group of people questioned the efficacy of this seed-choosing process. One of those forward-looking people was young Henry A. Wallace. At 16, he conducted a field test pitting one of the area's best-looking ears of seed corn against one of the ugliest, and the ugliest ear outyielded the pretty one. The tassels of corn grown in test fields were removed to isolate a hybrid's desirable characteristics. ''Detassling'' continued throughout the 20th century, requiring massive numbers of seasonal laborers at Pioneer's seed corn fields.

Studies made during the first two decades of the 20th century revealed that yield varied greatly with the quality of seed: the seed yielding in the top 10 percent outproduced that in the bottom 10 percent by an average of 25 bushels per acre. At a time when farmers generally expected to yield about 40 bushels per acre, the disparity was astounding. Unfortunately, the results of these tests would have seriously undermined the university-sponsored ''pretty corn'' contests and many researchers' findings were not published.

Henry Wallace had an advantage over many researchers, however: his father, Henry C. Wallace, owned a progressive farming newspaper, *Wallace's Farmer.* The Wallace family provided a heritage of farming leadership that helped launch Pioneer: young Henry's uncle had served on President Theodore Roosevelt's first Commission on Life in Rural America, and in 1921, his father was appointed to be U.S. Secretary of Agriculture. Henry A. Wallace inherited the editor's chair at *Wallace's Farmer* that year and got both a forum for his studies and an advertising medium for his seed.

When Henry, his brother Jim, and several partners founded the Hi-Bred Corn Company in Johnstown, Iowa in 1926, it was the first business created for the specific purpose of developing and marketing hybrid seed corn. The joint stock company was established with 200 shares and a $5,000 capitalization. Hi-Bred's first seed crop consisted of 40 acres of hand-planted, hand-picked corn. The company's seed was sold by mail order through advertising in the family newspaper and profited $33.62 in the first year of sales, 1928. Sales doubled in 1929, prompting Hi-Bred to purchase 80 additional acres and create a Parent Seed Department. Soon, Pioneer's hybrid seeds domi-

Company Perspectives:

Producing the best products is the key to our success. We believe that there is no better selling aid than good performance by the product. We spend much more on research to improve our products than we spend to advertise them in the conventional ways.

nated Iowa corn yield contests. The majority of farmers, who still relied on open-pollinated seed, complained that hybrid corn was too costly and unrealistic to produce and use, so the contests were split into two separate divisions.

Surviving the Great Depression and World War II

The 1930s brought depression to the world economy and drought, erosion, and pestilence to the fields of the Midwest. The brutal growing conditions were both a blessing and a curse for Hi-Bred. Several breeds of corn failed during the harsh drought of 1934, but other lines endured the weather long enough to produce a crop. In comparison with open-pollinated fields, which performed miserably, Hi-Bred was able to show a significant advantage in hybrid corn.

As word of Hi-Bred's relative success spread, demand for the seed increased. To market the product, the company instituted the ''farmer-salesman concept,'' where farmers worked part-time for Hi-Bred and full-time on their own farms. This sales method became an industry standard and was continued throughout the century. These local representatives were familiar to their customers and had firsthand knowledge of the product and its performance. Farmer-salesmen often used eight-pound samples of seed to graphically illustrate Hi-Bred seed's advantages versus open-pollinated seed. Skeptics soon learned that the commercial seed produced heartier, stronger, more uniform plants and yielded about 20 bushels more per acre. Hi-Bred's first distributorship was established in the 1930s in the southwest.

Growing competition in the hybrid field prompted the company to distinguish itself from its rivals, and the Pioneer Hi-Bred name was instituted. Even though the company lost money throughout the depression years, remote research operations were expanded to several areas in the Midwest to test seed under varying climactic conditions. Founder Henry A. Wallace left Pioneer in 1933 to follow his father as Secretary of Agriculture. In 1941, he was elected vice-president of the United States under Franklin D. Roosevelt. Fred Lehman, Jr., a founding partner in Pioneer, succeeded Wallace as president of the company.

World War II's profound technological and workforce changes affected Pioneer as well as the rest of the world. While ''Rosie the Riveter'' took her husband's place in the factories, ''Marge the Detassler'' roamed Pioneer's corn fields. Pioneer even brought German prisoners of war into the process when labor was scarce. Wartime rationing slowed Pioneer's growth somewhat, but the company was able to expand into Canada and to expand research into cold germination and increased mechanization. Pioneer's eggs and broiler hens became a more significant part of the business during the 1940s as well. By the end of the decade, nearly all farmers had made the transition to hybrid corn seed. With much of the world engaged in war, the United States became the world's granary.

Adapting to Changes in Farming in the 1950s and 1960s

Pioneer chalked up several ''firsts'' during the prosperous 1950s: the first electronic analysis of research and sales data, the first sorghum hybrid breeding program, and the first attempts at alternative packaging. Research facilities were expanded to Florida and South America, and Pioneer entered into a joint venture with the Arnold Thomas Company to produce alfalfa hybrids. By the end of the decade, corn sales rose to 400,000 bushels per year. The company's upper management clarified the company's four guiding principles in a 1952 booklet titled, ''The Long Look.'' Executive Vice-President Jim Wallace and Sales Director Nelson Earvin noted that Pioneer had always tried to provide quality products, honest product information, strong product promotion, and advice to customers.

Farming in America had changed dramatically since Pioneer was created. The number of farms had decreased from 6.5 million to four million, and the number of farmers had shrunk from one-fourth of the population to just 5 percent. When Pioneer first sold corn seed, the average family farm consisted of 150 acres producing a variety of livestock and crops for subsistence and commercial use; by the 1960s, most farmers devoted their 300-acre farms to a single crop. Technological improvements in corn harvesters in the 1960s permitted farmers to shell corn as it was mechanically ''picked'' and dry and store it on the farm, saving time and money. These advances made new demands on hybrid corn: it had to shell easier and dry faster. Farmers averaged three hours of work per bushel of corn in 1929, but advances in equipment, pesticides, fertilizers, and especially hybridization had shortened that time to six minutes. Higher yields meant higher profits and a better standard of living for many farm families.

Pioneer concentrated on overseas development during the 1960s, establishing joint ventures in Australia, Argentina, and South Africa. As concerns about overpopulation and global hunger mounted, Pioneer strove for ever higher yields and worked to lengthen the company's growing season by creating its first winter nursery, in Hawaii. The 50th state's year-round growing season permitted three crops of seed per year. In 1972 the company added ''International'' to its name to reflect the growing importance of overseas operations. But with its eyes on foreign development, Pioneer lost market share in America.

Reorganizing and Concentrating on Research and Development, Increasing Sales and Profits, and Dealing with a Grain Embargo: 1960s–80s

By the 1960s, the U.S. hybrid seed corn market was saturated and had little unit growth, forcing a higher level of competition. DeKalb AgResearch Inc., a rival since the 1930s, pulled ahead of Pioneer in terms of market share. The rival company introduced a revolutionary hybrid that gave it a slender lead in the industry by the end of the decade. But by 1972, each of the seed corn producers held 22 percent of the hybrid seed corn market.

Key Dates:

1926: Hi-Bred Corn Company is established.
1933: Company founder, Henry A. Wallace, resigns to become Secretary of Agriculture.
1973: The company is incorporated as Pioneer Hi-Bred International, Inc.
1997: DuPont acquires 20 percent of company in a joint venture arrangement.
1999: The company becomes a wholly owned subsidiary of DuPont.

In 1973, Pioneer went public and reorganized its operations. Prior to this time, Pioneer was a federation of geographically based companies. Each independent dealer purchased its seed from Pioneer's centralized research division, but was responsible for its own operations. The incorporation and reorganization also brought about the formation of the Cereal Seed Division to breed wheat. Pioneer made acquisitions to diversify primarily within the hybrid seed business. The company expanded its alfalfa and soybean seed research with the purchase of the Arnold Thomas Co. and Peterson Soybean Seed Co. The acquisition of NORAND, a computer company, put Pioneer in debt for the first time since 1926, but the parent applied the new subsidiary's hand-held computer technology to field research and sales programs. Pioneer also acquired New Labs, a developer of microbial products that encouraged the formation of silage (feed that is fermented in a silo) and aided animal digestion. Pioneer was reorganized so that central management could assess the company's total value and consolidate its competitive efforts against DeKalb and new entrants into the market by bringing uniformity to policies, pricing, and promotion.

By the mid-1970s, the company faced new competition from chemical and pharmaceutical companies like Ciba-Geigy, Sandoz, Union Carbide, Upjohn, and Pfizer, who all applied their research expertise to the development of new hybrids. But Pioneer's decades of experience in the industry set it far ahead of these new rivals.

Over the course of the 1970s, Pioneer and its primary rival, DeKalb, applied divergent business strategies: DeKalb diversified into oil and gas exploration, mining, irrigation, and other industries, while Pioneer concentrated on developing seed with ever-higher yields. Pioneer's concentration on research and new product development paid off with the development of 3780, a corn hybrid that broke yield records and soon became the company's and the industry's best-seller. Pioneer's timing could not have been better: from 1970 to 1980, unit sales in the overall seed corn industry grew by one-third, and dollar volume tripled. Farmers were willing to pay Pioneer's premium prices for higher yields. At the same time, the United States' seed exports nearly doubled, fueled by technological improvements and increased global demand for food. By the end of the decade, Pioneer had regained the top share of the seed corn market, with 34 percent, and DeKalb's share had diminished to 14 percent. Pioneer's sales multiplied five times from 1972 to 1980, to $400 million, and profits grew eightfold, to $53 million.

The United States' 16-month grain embargo in protest of the Soviet Union's invasion of Afghanistan marked the beginning of a difficult decade for American farmers. The 1980–81 embargo caused grain prices to fall sharply, which precipitated a farm crisis in the United States. Grain surpluses from the embargo combined with a recession to force many farmers into bankruptcy. Others stuck with farming, but reduced their corn acreage to take advantage of government subsidies. A drought in 1983 deepened the downward spiral: corn acreage decreased by 27 percent over the course of the decade, and the U.S. seed corn market was diminished by one-fourth.

On the other hand, however, the Soviet grain embargo encouraged production in the affected countries, creating new markets where there were none before. After the embargo, Pioneer worked to capture these new global customers. By the end of the 1980s, Pioneer had expanded to 32 countries abroad.

Protecting Intellectual Property and Expanding into Biotechnology in the 1980s and 1990s

Rivals in the seed corn industry introduced hybrids that closely resembled some of Pioneer's best-selling products in the early 1980s. These low-priced knock-offs were so similar to Pioneer's most popular hybrids that company officials became suspicious of their origin and development. When genetic mapping proved that Holden Foundation Seeds had illegally used Pioneer's proprietary germ plasm to develop their seeds, Pioneer brought suit against the rival company and won. Pioneer instituted stricter controls to protect the company's intellectual property as a result and has worked to patent many of its products.

Pioneer expanded into biotechnological research in the late 1980s and early 1990s. Biotechnology is a genetic science that seeks to add new traits through gene manipulation rather than the slower process of traditional breeding. This emphasis on research helped Pioneer claim ''the best-performing product lineup in the seed industry,'' as well as more than 39 percent of the U.S. seed corn market by 1992. The company posted record results in the early years of the decade. Earnings rose more than 40 percent in 1991 and again in 1992 to $152.16 million in the latter year. By 1995 Pioneer would command 45 percent of the country's seed corn market.

As the greater claims of biotechnology came closer to realization, however, Pioneer and the seed industry in general would undergo some fundamental changes. It became imperative that companies reach consumers first with the latest genetically engineered seed. Because Pioneer was a year behind the competition in introducing corn that was immune to corn borer, and tardy in bringing to market a variety of seed to grow high-oil corn that would lower the cost of feeding livestock, the company saw its share of the U.S. seed corn market fall two straight years, dipping from 45 percent to 42 percent.

New players, major chemical companies, were also entering the industry, which was clearly on the cusp of a revolution. Within a few years it was expected that seeds could be bioengineered to resist drought, produce corn with a higher protein content, or lead to a lower amount of saturated fat in the eggs of chickens that ate a special strain of corn. The applications were widespread and the rewards enormous, but also as a result of biotechnology a number of companies would be forced out of business. Because the chemical companies that provided pesticides and herbicides were likely losers, giants such as Monsanto and DuPont became extremely aggressive in acquiring biotechnology assets.

After Monsanto acquired a 40 percent stake in DeKalb, Pioneer in 1997 agreed to sell 20 percent of its stock at the cost of $1.7 billion to Dupont as part of a deal to form a crop biotechnology joint venture called Optimum Quality Grains. Pioneer, long known for its independence, insisted on a 16-year agreement that would prevent DuPont from purchasing more of the company without Pioneer's approval. For DuPont, the Pioneer alliance was a major part of an overall strategy to invest in what it called the ''life sciences''—the intersection of food, farm products, drugs, and biotechnology. Although the life sciences contributed less than 20 percent of its earnings, DuPont hoped that the number would increase to 30 percent by the time the company reached its 200th birthday in 2002.

The new technology created other changes in the seed industry. Instead of being a simple commodity, genetically engineered seeds were proprietary products that had to be protected from infringement. In 1998 Pioneer sued DeKalb, Cargill, and Monsanto's Asgrow Seed Co., alleging that the three companies wrongfully obtained and used genetic material that was the property of Pioneer. In order to sell to farmers year after year, hybrid seeds are intended to be good for planting but poor at reproducing. Stray ''inbred seeds,'' however, can be found in the bags of seeds and have the potential of jump-starting a research project. Pioneer's suit contended that Cargill and DeKalb regularly purchased Pioneer seeds to engage in a practice called ''chasing the selfs.''

The seed industry continued to consolidate at a rapid pace, with DuPont and Monsanto emerging as the two most dominant entities. When Pioneer management learned that the two chemical giants were discussing a possible merger it decided that it would be at risk in a future where all that was certain was that only companies that could command the necessary research and development dollars would be able to compete. Pioneer began to negotiate a transaction with DuPont and in 1999 agreed to sell the remaining 80 percent of the company's stock for $7.7 billion. DuPont hoped that by acquiring Pioneer it could gain ground in biotech research, no longer having two units trying to balance the interests of their corporate parents.

In 2000 Pioneer was successful in two court cases. A U.S. federal district court of appeals upheld a 1985 U.S. Patent and Trademark Office decision that crops grown from genetically modified seeds could be patented. The company also settled out of court when Cargill admitted that some of its hybrid seed corn lines contained genetic material proprietary to Pioneer. Cargill agreed to pay $100 million and no longer engage in the practice of chasing the selfs.

Pioneer, as a part of DuPont, was clearly well positioned for a future that would be as rapidly changing as it would be uncertain. Resistance to biotech foods had to be overcome and the question of safety reviews and mandatory labeling still had to be addressed. In December 2000 Pioneer announced that it would postpone selling to farmers six lines of genetically modified corn because they had not yet been approved by the European Union. Concerns also were being raised about unforeseen problems with the brave new world of bioengineered crops. Because the new seeds were so genetically uniform, if one plant proved vulnerable to a new disease they all faced an epidemic. Economically, the result could be catastrophic. At the very least, the cost of production to safeguard against such doomsday scenarios would likely increase, to the detriment of revenues. One thing was certain for Pioneer and all the others engaged in biotechnology: there was no turning back.

Principal Operating Units

North American Seed Division; Research and Product Development; Supply Management.

Principal Competitors

Cargill, Inc.; DeKalb AgResearch Inc.

Further Reading

Culver, John C., and John Hyde, *American Dreamer: The Life and Times of Henry A. Wallace,* New York: Norton, 2000.

Davenport, Caroline H. ''Sowing the Seeds: Research, Development Flourish at DeKalb, Pioneer Hi-Bred,'' *Barron's,* March 2, 1981, pp. 9–10, 33.

Kilman, Scott, ''Scientists Find New Way to Manipulate Plant Genes and Modify Crop Traits,'' *Wall Street Journal,* July 20, 1999, p. B6.

Lerner, Matthew, ''DuPont is Making Life Science Move With Pioneer Stake,'' *Chemical Market Reporter,* August 11, 1997, p. 3.

Miller, James P., ''Cargill Agrees to $100 Million Settlement with Pioneer Over Genetic-Seed Traits,'' May 17, 2000, p. A3.

Pioneer: A History (videocassette), Des Moines, Ia.: Pioneer Hi-Bred International, Inc., 1992.

Raeburn, Paul, ''The Catastrophe Lurking in America's Farmlands,'' *Business Week,* May 20, 1996, p. 84.

Rudnitsky, Howard, ''Another Agricultural Revolution,'' *Forbes,* May 20, 1996, p. 159.

''Seed Corn's Long, Hot, Bruising Summer,'' *Business Week,* August 25, 1980, pp. 52, 54, 56.

''A Sustained Harvest,'' *Forbes,* October 15, 1979, pp. 120, 122.

—April S. Dougal
—update: Ed Dinger

Planet Hollywood International, Inc.

8669 Commodity Circle
Orlando, Florida 32819
U.S.A.
Telephone: (407) 363-7827
Fax: (407) 363-4862
Web site: http://www.planethollywood.com

Public Company
Incorporated: 1991
Employees: 3,970
Sales: $281 million (1999)
Stock Exchanges: New York
Ticker Symbol: PHWD
NAIC: 72211 Full-Service Restaurants; 45299 All Other General Merchandise Stores; 53311 Lessors of Nonfinancial Intangible Assets (Except Copyrighted Works)

Planet Hollywood International, Inc.—undergoing a major corporate restructuring in 2001—operates as the controlling body for entertainment-based theme restaurants located throughout the world. The company's name reflects its most well-known venture, a chain of approximately 60 company-owned and franchised ''Planet Hollywood'' restaurants that offer patrons a chance to dine in the midst of various film and television props and memorabilia. Planet Hollywood International also runs five Official All Star Café restaurants, a chain that centers on professional sports and follows a sports-bar theme, and several Cool Planet Ice Cream shops. Under the reorganization plan, management is focusing on its core business of operating Planet Hollywood restaurants.

Origins

The first Planet Hollywood restaurant opened in New York City in 1991, but the events leading to its inception can be traced back almost 20 years before that date. In 1972, a young man named Robert Earl opened a dinner theater in London called ''The Beefeater,'' which offered customers—mainly tourists—a medieval-theme dining experience. Earl, who had graduated with a degree in hotel and restaurant management from the University of Surrey, possessed a talent for creating entertainment-based restaurant concepts that drew large numbers of customers. He soon developed The Beefeater into a popular local success, which prompted him to open other theme-restaurants nearby. In the late 1970s, he created ''Talk of London,'' ''Shakespeare's Tavern,'' and ''The Cockney Club.''

Although successful in London, Earl saw greater growth potential in the American market, and therefore came to the United States in the early 1980s to sell his concepts to the developers of a then-new Disney World attraction called EPCOT Center. The deal fell through, but Earl decided to stay in Florida anyway and try his luck in the Orlando restaurant business. He opened several theme-restaurants using medieval and Wild West ideas, nurturing his new restaurant group until he sold it to a larger holding company in the mid-1980s.

After changing hands again numerous times, his enterprise landed in the lap of Mecca Leisure, which had just purchased rights to Hard Rock International's eastern region. Hard Rock International was the controlling body for the ''Hard Rock Café'' chain of music industry-based theme restaurants. In 1989, Mecca appointed Earl as the new chief executive of their portion of the Hard Rock operation and put him in charge of expanding the chain in the eastern United States.

Within two years, Earl had helped the eastern-region Hard Rock Café chain grow from 7 units to 20. During that time, Earl met film producer Keith Barish, who soon became his business partner and the cofounder of Planet Hollywood International, Inc. Earl and Barish shared a belief that music, movies, and sports could transcend all barriers, language and otherwise, that separated the people of the world. The two men decided to capitalize on the worldwide appeal of the film and television entertainment industry by opening a restaurant based on that theme. Dubbing their creation ''Planet Hollywood,'' Earl and Barish opened the restaurant in New York City in late 1991.

Quick Success in the Early 1990s

Planet Hollywood was immediately successful, drawing crowds of people who often lined up outside the restaurant for

Company Perspectives:

Planet Hollywood International, Inc. strives to act as a creator and developer of consumer brands that capitalize on the universal appeal of movies, sports, and other entertainment-based themes.

hours to get tables. Part of the restaurant's appeal lay in its museum-like quality; its decor consisted of a multitude of real film and television costumes, props, and memorabilia. The genius marketing strategy used by the restaurant's founders accounted for the rest of the attraction. They asked celebrities such as Arnold Schwarzenegger, Sylvester Stallone, Bruce Willis, Demi Moore, and Whoopi Goldberg to act as the restaurant's investor/owners. Every once in a while, these celebrities would stop by ''their restaurant'' to check in and mingle briefly with their fans. Although this did not occur all that often, customers still flocked to the restaurant in hopes that they would be one of the lucky few to dine with the stars.

A year after launching Planet Hollywood, Earl left behind his post at Hard Rock and also severed ties to his original theme-restaurant group in Orlando. He and Barish began planning the worldwide introduction of additional Planet Hollywood restaurants and started by recruiting more celebrity investors for the new locations. Climbing on board were film actors Don Johnson and his then wife Melanie Griffith, director John Hughes, comedienne Roseanne, and actors Tom Arnold, Wesley Snipes, and Danny Glover. By mid-1993, Planet Hollywood International had opened new restaurants in London and southern California and was completing the construction of a fourth unit in Chicago.

Earl and Barish hired the New York City architect David Rockwell to design the new units, each of which typically seated over 200 people and contained film props and floor layouts that were unique to their locations. Different items on display throughout the chain included Dorothy's dress from ''The Wizard of Oz,'' the pottery wheel used by Demi Moore and Patrick Swayze in ''Ghost,'' a replica of the castle from ''Dracula,'' the Batmobile, the Flintstone buggy, and a plastic model of the meat slab that was pulverized by Stallone in the film ''Rocky.'' Customers were also treated to celebrity hand print walls and big-screen televisions, which played promotional clips for upcoming movies.

Meanwhile, a Hard Rock International executive, Peter Morton, filed suit against Earl and Planet Hollywood, alleging that Earl had engaged in the appropriation of trade secrets. Morton, a cofounder of Hard Rock International and the CEO of its western region, believed that Earl's Planet Hollywood chain was a rip-off of the Hard Rock concept. Earl nonchalantly dismissed the charges, however, and the case against Planet Hollywood never amounted to much in court. Furthermore, Morton's complaint did little to deter Planet Hollywood from expanding further, nor did it curb the public's desire to patronize the new and rapidly blossoming chain. Soon Planet Hollywood was known as a worldwide leader in the theme restaurant business.

By the end of 1993, Planet Hollywood had not only opened two new restaurants in Washington, D.C., and Cancun, Mexico, but it had also signed leases for five new units in Phoenix, Arizona; New Orleans, Louisiana; Aspen, Colorado; Maui, Hawaii; and Minneapolis's ''Mall of America'' (the largest shopping mall in the United States). Each opening was a gala event, drawing enormous crowds of people to catch a glimpse of the many media personalities who made appearances and celebrated the new successes. However, the true test of a new location occurred the day after the ''official'' opening, when a restaurant actually opened its doors to the general public. Without fail, each new Planet Hollywood passed these tests with ease, and in the first year of operation, most were generating revenues of almost $15 million per unit.

A strong asset of the Planet Hollywood concept was that each unit sold licensed Planet Hollywood merchandise as well as serving food and drinks. Items of all kinds were sold, from key rings and T-shirts, to sweatshirts, watches, and leather coats. Sales of this merchandise helped boost Planet Hollywood's profit margins considerably above those achieved at other restaurants that relied solely on food to bring in profits. Merchandise became so popular that within a few years, the company began to open separate retail stores called ''Planet Hollywood Superstores,'' a move that further increased yearly profits.

Expansion in the mid-1990s

In 1994, Planet Hollywood continued its aggressive expansion program, and units continued to open worldwide. The company also began developing additional theme-restaurant ideas, including the concept for the Official All Star Café. Acknowledging the success that Planet Hollywood had achieved from drawing upon the public's interest in celebrity life, Earl and Barish decided that the Official All Star Café would be the perfect sports-based equivalent. They began recruiting professional sports figures to invest in the concept, drawing in people such as hockey great Wayne Gretzky, football icon Joe Montana, and basketball superstar Shaquille O'Neal. Plans for the new restaurants included a menu of ''stadium cuisine'' supplemented by home cooking and sales of professional sports merchandise and souvenirs.

Also in 1994, the company opened what would soon become its highest-grossing Planet Hollywood unit, in Las Vegas. Unlike most previous units, which seated approximately 250 people, the Las Vegas restaurant was designed to seat 500 and was planned by Rockwell so that there would be no ''bad'' seats. The unit's opening rivaled a sporting event or the Academy Awards in magnitude, in that it drew a crowd of more than 10,000 people who packed themselves into stadium-like bleachers nearby to witness the stars' arrivals at the event. Even former President and First Lady George and Barbara Bush were on hand to celebrate. Later that year, the entrepreneurs opened another 500-seater in Orlando's Disney World, which made Earl and Barish owners of the two highest-grossing restaurants in the United States.

At that point, Planet Hollywood was composed of 18 units around the world, and the company was projecting the addition of 17 more during 1995. The Planet Hollywood chain was expanding almost on its own, so Earl decided to begin focusing his attention and energy on other avenues of growth while the chain took care of itself. In August 1995, ground was broken in

Key Dates:

1991: Planet Hollywood is established.
1993: Famous actors begin promoting and investing in the firm.
1994: The company expands with 18 locations in operation.
1995: The development begins on the Official All Star Café concept.
1996: Planet Hollywood goes public.
1997: The company begins to lose money and stock price falters.
1998: Robert Earl takes over as chairman and CEO.
1999: The firm files for Chapter 11 bankruptcy.
2000: The company emerges from Chapter 11 under a new reorganization plan.

New York City near the original Planet Hollywood, and construction of the first Official All Star Café began. Meanwhile, plans were in the works to develop a theme-restaurant chain based on characters from the Marvel Comics series. Also, television game-show producer King World began working with Roseanne Barr's production company on a ''Planet Hollywood Squares'' television game show, which was to be a revival of the original ''Hollywood Squares'' from decades past with a new Planet Hollywood twist.

With Planet Hollywood quickly becoming a household name, the company decided to go public in 1996. Not only was stock offered to the public, but the company also convinced MBNA to issue Planet Hollywood VISA credit cards, which gave cardholders priority seating at the restaurants. A joint venture with ITT Corporation was also formed to develop Planet Hollywood casinos in Las Vegas and Atlantic City in the future. Furthermore, Marvel Entertainment Group, Inc. and Planet Hollywood International decided to move ahead with the comic book character-based restaurant concept, calling it ''Marvel Mania.'' Ideas for a new concept called ''Chefs of the World,'' which was to feature a ''star-studded'' culinary staff, also began to arise.

Some began to wonder whether Planet Hollywood was spreading its resources too thin, and speculations surfaced as to whether the company would be able to continue the growth trend that it had been experiencing for the past five years. Earl maintained ambitious goals to keep the company expanding by 30 to 40 percent each year, in both the number of restaurant locations and in annual revenues. Criticisms of that plan, however, focused on the idea that the more units that were opened, the less novel a customer's experience in patronizing the restaurant chain, which could lead to a drop in sales. Furthermore, theme restaurants were popping up all over the country, providing Earl and Barish with intense competition. The Harley-Davidson Café was gaining popularity, as were other concepts such as Robert DeNiro's Tribeca Grill, the Country Star chain (backed by Wynonna Judd, Vince Gill, and Reba McEntire), and the Thunder Roadhouse (backed by Dennis Hopper, Dwight Yoakam, and Peter Fonda).

However, Planet Hollywood and the Official All Star Café did possess one major advantage over their competition, which was the celebrity endorsement received through stars' ownership and investment in the chains. Many customers thus viewed these restaurants as the ''originals.'' As for continued growth potential, Earl dismissed skepticism with easy confidence, given that in only five years the company had grown from one $3.5 million restaurant in New York to an almost $300 million operation with approximately 50 units throughout the world.

Financial Woes in the late 1990s

Nevertheless, stock price began to falter as scepticism about the future of the company increased. Despite a rise in profits and revenues in 1996, an aggressive growth strategy fueled speculation that Planet Hollywood would not be able to finance its rapid expansion. One year later, those doubts became certainties as the firm reported a $40 million loss in the fourth quarter. Management's narrow focus on diversification became apparent as the firm's core business—the Planet Hollywood restaurants—began to show signs of neglect; menu prices were high, food was mediocre, and service was below average.

In 1998, cofounder Barish resigned, leaving Earl chairman and CEO. William Baumhauer was then hired as president, and the management looked to his turnaround skills to have a positive impact on the company's finances. In August of that year, Planet Hollywood had to deal with yet another problem when a bomb exploded in one of its franchise restaurants in Cape Town, Africa. It seemed that a black cloud had settled over the firm as a loss of $244 million was recorded that year.

Bankruptcy and Restructuring in the New Millennium

In June 1999, Baumhauer resigned after having little effect on Planet Hollywood's bottom line. The company's once bright future was tarnished as it lay under $359 million in debt. Left with few options, the company declared Chapter 11 bankruptcy on October 12, 1999. The management placed blame on a loss in revenues, increasing costs, including those related to expansion, a decrease in customers, and an increase in competition.

Planet Hollywood set out to restructure itself. Its efforts included closing and selling poorly performing Planet Hollywood restaurants and Official All Star Cafes. The management also began to put into effect a strategy to focus on its core operation, its original restaurant theme. The company stopped operation of its Planet Movies by AMC—created in July 1999—and sold its Sound Republic units. It also cut costs, eliminated jobs, and halted any ventures not closely related to its core focus.

On May 9, 2000, Planet Hollywood emerged from Chapter 11 after receiving approval for its reorganization plan. The restructuring left the firm with a cash infusion, allowing it to rebuild itself without the burden of major debt. Improvements in the restaurants included new menus, updated décor, and new products. The firms's managers also set out to capture celebrity relationships, including those of Bruce Willis, Shaquille O'Neal, and musical group N'Snyc. The firm also launched its Web site, which featured live celebrity chats, coverage of celebrity events, entertainment news, and merchandise.

Planet Hollywood entered 2001 with an uncertain future. In a Securities and Exchange Commission filing, the company stated that it had substantial assets to keep it afloat for the year. Although management kept a positive outlook on the future of the company, it recognized the financial burdens and obstacles it would have to overcome in order to remain a player in the entertainment industry in the new millennium.

Principal Operating Units

Planet Hollywood Restaurants; Official All Star Café.

Principal Competitors

Dave & Buster's, Inc.; Hard Rock Café International, Inc.; Rainforest Café, Inc.

Further Reading

Ball, Aimee Lee, ''Mr. Universe,'' *New York,* July 15, 1991, p. 38.

''Can Planet Hollywood Survive its Own Disaster Flick as Rough Year Nears End,'' *Nation's Restaurant News,* December 7, 1998, p. 29.

Greenberg, Herb, ''Earth to Planet Hollywood,'' *Fortune,* December 23, 1996.

Guttman, Monika, ''Why the Stars Orbit Planet Hollywood: With Meteoric Growth, the Eateries May Go Public,'' *U.S. News & World Report,* November 27, 1995, p. 60.

Hayes, Jack, ''Robert Earl: The King of Planet Hollywood Promises the Stars—and He Delivers,'' *Nation's Restaurant News,* October 9, 1995, p. 164.

Jackson, Jerry W., ''Planet Hollywood Eatery Chain Can Stay in Business Until Year's End,'' Knight Ridder/Tribune Business News, February 15, 2001.

Kapner, Suzanne, '' 'Starry' Vegas Night Shines on New Planet,'' *Nation's Restaurant News,* August 8, 1994, p. 7.

Levine, Joshua, ''Hamburgers and Tennis Socks,'' *Forbes,* November 20, 1995, p. 184.

Martin, Richard, ''Hard Rock Hits Planet Hollywood with Copycat Suit,'' *Nation's Restaurant News,* March 16, 1992, p. 3.

McClellan, Steve, ''King World Developing 'Planet Hollywood Squares',' ' *Broadcasting & Cable,* September 25, 1995, p. 11.

Miracle, Barbara, ''Beyond Planet Hollywood,'' *Florida Trend,* December 1993, p. 10.

''Planet Hollywood Launches New Web Site,'' *Newsbytes,* July 30, 2000.

''O'Neal Signs to Endorse Planet Hollywood Chain,'' *Nation's Restaurant News,* July 17, 2000, p. 30.

Papiernik, Richard L., ''All Quiet on the Hollywood Front After 'Picture Perfect' IPO,'' *Nation's Restaurant News,* May 13, 1996, p. 11.

''Planet Hollywood, Marvel Comics Team for Themer,'' *Nation's Restaurant News,* June 6, 1994, p. 2.

''Planet Hollywood Successfully Emerges From Chapter 11 Reorganization,'' *PR Newswire,* May 9, 2000.

''Planet H'wood, All-Star Units End AMC Venture,'' *Nation's* Restaurant News, January 22, 2001, p. 50.

Prewitt, Milford, ''Planet Hollywood Eyes New Concepts, Profits Up 82% in '96,'' *Nation's Restaurant News,* February 24, 1997, p. 11.

——, ''Robert Earl: CEO Planet Hollywood Inc., Orlando, Florida,'' *Nation's Restaurant News,* January 1995, p. 54.

Selinger, Iris Cohen, ''Lights! Camera! But Can We Get a Table?'' *Advertising Age,* April 17, 1995, p. 48.

St. Onge, Jeff, ''You Heard it Here First: DJ Planet Hollywood CEO Sees Co. Returning to Past Glory,'' *Bankruptcy Newswire,* January 25, 2000.

''That's Eatertainment: Baumhauer Out at Planet Hollywood,'' *Nation's* Restaurant News, July 5, 1999, p. 3.

Walkup, Carolyn, ''Planet Hollywood Gears to Launch Unit in Chicago,'' *Nation's Restaurant News,* July 15, 1993, p. 94.

—Laura E. Whiteley
—update: Christina M. Stansell

Popular, Inc.

209 Avenida Munoz Rivera
Hato Rey, Puerto Rico 00918
U.S.A.
Telephone: (787) 765-9800
Toll Free: (888) 724-3650
Fax: (787) 751-2137
Web site: http://www.popularinc.com

Public Company
Incorporated: 1893 as Sociedad Anomina de Economias y Prestamos: Banco Popular
Employees: 10,651
Total Assets: $1.45 billion (2000)
Stock Exchanges: NASDAQ
Ticker Symbol: BPOP
NAIC: 52211 Commercial Banking; 52231 Mortgage and Other Loan Business; 522291 Consumer Lending; 52311 Investment Banking and Securities Dealing; 52312 Securities Brokerage; 52421 Insurance Agencies and Brokerages

Popular, Inc. is a bank holding company whose principal subsidiary is Banco Popular, Puerto Rico's largest bank. This bank also operates branches in the U.S. and British Virgin Islands, and in New York City. Through subsidiaries, it also operates Puerto Rico's largest vehicle-leasing and daily-rental company, and makes mortgage and other loans. Another subsidiary of the parent holding company operates bank branches in six U.S. states, offers services such as check cashing and money transfers, makes loans, provides small ticket-equipment leasing, and engages in automatic teller-machine (ATM) switching and driving services in Costa Rica. A third subsidiary is a securities broker-dealer in Puerto Rico. The fourth provides electronic data-processing and consulting services, sale and rental of such equipment, and sale and maintenance of computer software to clients in ten countries. While most of Popular's assets remain in Puerto Rico, it greatly expanded its mainland U.S. operations in the 1990s to serve the burgeoning Hispanic population there.

The First Century For a Major Puerto Rican Financial Institution

Popular, Inc. was founded in 1893 in Puerto Rico's capital, San Juan, as the Sociedad Anonima de Economias y Prestamos: Banco Popular (Savings and Loan Corporation: The People's Bank). Its goal, as set forth in the first article of incorporation, was to ''foster the spirit of economy in all social classes, and especially in that of the poor, by means of savings.'' Fifty-two stockholders provided the initial capital of 5,000 Mexican silver pesos. The number of shareholders tripled in the first four years, and the institution prospered by making loans, including mortgage loans. With regard to savings, however, fewer than 5 percent of the depositors belonged to the working class.

Five years later, the United States occupied and annexed Puerto Rico in the Spanish-American War of 1898. Banco Popular's deposits dropped by two-thirds in that year, and a hurricane devastated the island in 1899. The following year, Congress declared the Puerto Rican peso worth only 60 cents (rather than a dollar), reducing the bank's capital funds to only $18,000.

In 1906 the bank introduced checking accounts, and in 1912 it circulated piggy banks for savings accounts; only the bank could open them with a key. Representatives of Spanish-import trading houses were the main stockholders and customers in this period (and still among the bank's largest customers 35 years later). Deposits of $921,090.98 in 1913 set a record not surpassed for more than a decade thereafter. Banco Popular was the first, and for many years the only, bank to make loans to the Puerto Rican government and to many island municipalities.

In order to conform to the island's first banking law, Banco Popular de Puerto Rico was founded again as a commercial bank (rather than a savings bank) in 1923. Rafael Carrion Pacheco became the majority stockholder in 1927. Personal loans were made available without collateral the following year. Banco Popular survived the banking crisis of the Great Depression while many other banks fell into receivership; in fact, it purchased Banco Comercial de Puerto Rico, the oldest and most respected banking institution on the island. In 1937 Banco Popular became the biggest bank in Puerto Rico, taking in

Company Perspectives:

Banco Popular is a local institution dedicating its efforts exclusively to the enhancement of the social and economic conditions in Puerto Rico and inspired by the most sound principles and fundamental practices of good banking. Banco Popular pledges its efforts and resources to the development of a banking service for Puerto Rico within strict commercial practices and so efficient that it could meet the requirements of the most progressive community of the world.

$8.82 million in deposits that year. Work began on an Art Deco headquarters building that was completed in 1939.

Banco Popular established its first branch in 1934, and had eight on the island by 1942. In 1951 it established a mobile bank-on-wheels at Fort Buchanan. This format was adopted to serve much of Puerto Rico, including even remote mountain villages, between 1957 and 1974. The number of fixed branches reached 20 in 1954. Auto loans were introduced in 1957.

By this time, a vast post-World War II migration had created a large Puerto Rican community in New York City. In 1961 Banco Popular opened its first U.S. mainland branch, in the city's borough of the Bronx. A second one, in Manhattan's Rockefeller Center, was established in 1964. That year the bank also established its first foreign branch, in the Dominican Republic. Rafael Carrion, Jr., succeeded his father as president of Banco Popular in 1965. Also that year, the bank moved its headquarters to a newly constructed building in Hato Rey, a suburb of San Juan.

Banco Popular established its first U.S. branch outside New York City in 1973, and its first outside the metropolitan area—in Los Angeles—in 1975. It joined the Visa credit-card system in 1975. The bank acquired the insolvent Banco Credito y Ahorro Ponceno (Ponce Credit and Savings Bank) in 1978, including 36 of that bank's 50 branches. With $1.7 billion in deposits, Banco Popular had grown to be included among the list of the 60 largest U.S. banks.

There were 110 branches in 1980. The following year, the company opened a branch in Saint Croix, which was the capital of the U.S. Virgin Islands. It entered Chicago in 1984 by purchasing a locally owned failed Hispanic bank there from federal regulators. Richard L. Carrion, son of Rafael Carrion, Jr., became the chief executive of Banco Popular in 1985.

Rapid Growth in Puerto Rico and on the Mainland: 1989–2001

Banco Popular had grown to 125 branches in 1989, including 10 on the U.S. mainland and three in the Virgin Islands. That year, it purchased BanPonce Corporation for cash and stock valued at between $278 and $324 million. Founded in 1971 as Banco de Ponce, BanPonce was the fourth-largest Puerto Rican bank, with 40 branches on the island and 14 in New York—where it was the pioneering Puerto Rican bank. The acquired branches took the Banco Popular name, but a new holding company was established bearing the BanPonce Corp. name until 1997, when this parent firm was renamed Popular, Inc.

Banco Popular enhanced its position as the leading choice for New York City's growing Hispanic population in 1991, when it purchased the failed Bronx-based New York Capital Bank. New York Capital was an institution with five New York branches. The following year, Banco Popular acquired seven American Savings Bank branches in Manhattan and Brooklyn, bringing its number of New York branches to 28. At that point, Banco Popular had $1.5 billion in deposits in New York and had, in addition to making mortgage loans, become the city's top originator of federal Small Business Administration loans. These small business loans were made primarily to taxi owners, but also to importers, distributors, and wholesalers seeking to borrow less than $500,000.

In order to continue to thrive, the New York operation was looking beyond Hispanic customers after commissioning a study that showed more than one-fourth of its depositors were born in the United States. Furthermore, the study showed that fewer than one-third were from Puerto Rico. Also in 1992, BanPonce became a publicly traded stock, on the Nasdaq exchange.

Banco Popular began selling mutual funds and annuities in its New York branches in 1994. By the fall of 1997, it had six branches in neighboring New Jersey as well as 29 in New York. That fall, it also made its Texas debut by purchasing Citizens National Bank, which had been serving Houston's blue-collar Hispanic population. The bank also entered Florida that year by acquiring Seminole National Bank in Sanford, and by the spring of 1999 held eight branches in that state. It opened its first Miami branch in 2001 and announced plans to establish at least 20 more in south Florida.

Meanwhile, Popular had purchased Chicago's Pioneer Bank in 1993 and soon added two others, enhancing its presence in the city to 13 locations. It also chose Chicago as its official U.S. headquarters in 1997. In 1998, Banco Popular began offering a check-cashing service in the United States which was named Popular Cash Express. A mainland-U.S. credit-card operation based in Orlando, Florida was already in existence, with nearly 200,000 customers.

In 1999 Banco Popular launched a nationwide mortgage-loan program aimed at the Hispanic market. It was supported by a national advertising campaign featuring the bank's existing national spokesman, Don Francisco. Francisco was well known, having also served at the time as the master of ceremonies of the popular Saturday-night variety show, "Sabado Gigante," telecast on Univision, the leading Spanish-language network in the United States.

Banco Popular's U.S. credit-card operation was sold to Metris Companies Inc. in 2000. That year, the North American subsidiary—by then headquartered in Melrose Park, Illinois, a suburb of Chicago—was cited for providing payday loans at triple-digit interest rates to people who could not obtain funds through conventional loans. These payday loans were available in California, Florida, and Texas through the bank's Cash Express outlets. In Texas, it was purportedly charging an annual rate of 456 percent. A spokesman for the bank told Julie Johnsson of *Crain's Chicago Business* that its Texas payday lending was a pilot program that the bank was "not at liberty to discuss."

Key Dates:

1893: Banco Popular is founded as a savings bank.
1923: Banco Popular is founded again as a commercial bank.
1937: Banco Popular becomes the largest bank in Puerto Rico.
1961: Banco Popular opens its first mainland U.S. branch, in New York City.
1989: Banco Popular acquires Banco de Ponce, Puerto Rico's fourth-largest bank.
1992: The parent company makes its initial public offering of common stock.
2000: Popular has 302 bank branches and 382 non-bank offices.

Popular in the New Millennium

Popular, Inc. was the 35th largest bank-holding company in the United States at the end of 2000, with consolidated assets of $28.1 billion and total deposits of $14.8 billion. Its income that year of $1.45 billion and net income of $276.1 million were both company records. By geographical area, Puerto Rico accounted for 72 percent of its assets, and the continental United States for 26 percent (compared to only 4 percent in 1980). Of the company's 302 banking branches, 199 were in Puerto Rico, 95 in the continental United States, and 8 in the Virgin Islands. Of the 382 non-banking offices, Equity One had 136; Popular Cash Express, 132; Popular Finance, 61; Popular Mortgage, 21; Popular Leasing & Rental, 12; and Popular Leasing, U.S.A., 11 (during 2000 a subsidiary sold its investment in Banco Fiduciario, S.A., a commercial bank in the Dominican Republic with 31 branches in 1999).

Banco Popular de Puerto Rico, Popular, Inc.'s principal subsidiary, was operating seven branches in the U.S. Virgin Islands, one branch in the British Virgin Islands, and one branch in New York, as well as its 199 branches in Puerto Rico. It included as its subsidiaries both Popular Leasing & Rental and Popular Finance, incorporated in 1989, and Popular Mortgage, incorporated in 1995. Popular Leasing & Rental was Puerto Rico's largest vehicle-leasing and daily-rental company. Popular Finance offered small loans and second mortgages. Popular Mortgage offered mortgage loans.

Popular Securities, a subsidiary of the parent company, was a securities broker-dealer in Puerto Rico with financial advisory, investment, and security brokerage operations for institutional and retail customers. GM Group, incorporated in 1989, was providing electronic data processing and consulting services, sale and rental of electronic data-processing equipment, and sale and maintenance of computer software to clients in 10 countries. Popular, Inc. also held an 85 percent interest in Newco Mortgage Holding Corp., a mortgage-banking organization with operations in Puerto Rico.

The other subsidiary of the parent—Popular International Bank, incorporated in 1992—held as its main subsidiary Popular North America. This was a holding company incorporated in 1991 for Banco Popular North America, a full-service commercial bank with branches in six states. Banco Popular North America, incorporated in 1998, held, in turn, as its subsidiary Popular Leasing U.S.A., which was incorporated in 1997 and was providing small-ticket-equipment leasing in offices in eight states. The other direct subsidiaries of Popular North America were Equity One, incorporated in 1980, which was granting personal and mortgage loans and providing dealer financing through offices in 30 states; Popular Cash Express, incorporated in 1997 and offering services such as check cashing, money transfers to other countries, money-order sales and processing of payments through offices and units in five states and the District of Columbia; Popular Insurance, incorporated in 2000 to offer insurance products in Puerto Rico; and Banco Popular National Association, a full-service commercial bank chartered in Orlando, Florida, that commenced operations in 2000. Popular International Bank also owned ATH Costa Rica and Crest, which were providing ATM switching and driving services in San Jose, Costa Rica.

Popular, Inc.'s largest shareholder in 2001 consisted of the employee retirement and profit-sharing plans that owned 8.1 percent of the common stock. Next largest was State Farm Mutual Automobile Insurance Co., which owned 6.4 percent of the common stock. Of the company's offices, branch premises, and other facilities, the majority were leased rather than owned.

Principal Subsidiaries

Banco Popular de Puerto Rico (including Popular Finance, Inc.; Popular Leasing & Rental, Inc.; and Popular Mortgage, Inc.); GM Group, Inc.; Popular International Bank, Inc. (including Banco Popular North America,; Equity One, Inc.; and Popular Cash Express, Inc.); Popular Securities, Inc.

Principal Competitors

Banco Bilbao Vizcaya Argentaria Puerto Rico, S.A.; First BanCorp; Banco Santander Central Hispano, S.A.

Further Reading

Baralt, Guillermo A., *Tradition into the Future: The First Century of the Banco Popular de Puerto Rico: 1893–1993,* San Juan: Banco Popular de Puerto Rico, 1993.

Flynn, Barry, "Puerto Rico's Banco Popular Adds Florida Operations in Manageable Pieces," *Knight-Ridder/Tribune Business News,* April 5, 1999.

Hemlock, Doreen, "Puerto Rican Banking Firm Opens First Branch in Miami," *Knight-Ridder/Tribune Business News,* January 24, 2001.

Johnsson, Julie, "Bank's Bid for Payday Loan Riches," *Crain's Chicago Business,* February 14, 2000, pp. 1, 60.

Leuchter, Miriam, "A Bank's Popular Moves," *Crain's New York Business,* May 24, 1993, pp. 3, 37.

Penn, Monica, "Hispanic Banks Go Head to Head," *Houston Business Journal,* March 12, 1999, pp. A1+.

Quint, Michael, "Generosity Leads To a Bank Merger," *New York Times,* October 26, 1989, p. D2.

Rose, Barbara, "Pioneer Buy a Foothold for Puerto Rico Bank," *Crain's Chicago Business,* September 20, 1993, p. 44.

Wahl, Melissa, "Banco Popular Becoming Just That," *Chicago Tribune,* June 24, 1999, Sec. 3, pp. 1, 4.

——, "San Juan Bank Picks Chicago as U.S. Base," *Chicago Tribune,* June 11, 1998, Sec. 3, pp. 1, 3.

—Robert Halasz

PPL Corporation

Two North Ninth Street
Allentown, Pennsylvania 18101-1179
U.S.A.
Telephone: (610) 774-5151
Toll Free: (800) 345-3085
Fax: (610) 774-4198
Web site: http://www.pplweb.com

Public Company
Incorporated: 1920 as Pennsylvania Power & Light Co.
Employees: 9,166
Sales: $5.6 billion (2000)
Stock Exchanges: New York Philadelphia
Ticker Symbol: PPL
NAIC: 221111 Hydroelectric Power Generation; 221112 Fossil Fuel Electric Power Generation; 221113 Nuclear Electric Power Generation; 221119 Other Electric Power Generation; 221121 Electric Bulk Power Transmission and Control; 221122 Electric Power Distribution

PPL Corporation operates as an international energy company providing electricity and natural gas to more than 1.4 million consumers in Pennsylvania. With power plants in Pennsylvania, Maine, and Montana, the firm also provides wholesale and retail energy to 42 states as well as Canada. PPL Corp.'s international customer base includes 4.4 million consumers in Chile, Bolivia, Brazil, El Salvador, and the United Kingdom. The company's major operating units include PPL Utilities, PPL EnergyPlus, PPL Generation, and PPL Global.

Industry and Company Origins in the Early 20th Century

Pennsylvania Power & Light Company (PP&L) grew out of the consolidation of eight small Pennsylvania electric utilities in the first two decades of the 20th century. The utilities included several small electric lighting companies formed in the 1880s in eastern Pennsylvania and the Edison Electric Illuminating Company of Sunbury, used by Thomas Edison to perfect central-station incandescent lighting in small cities and towns in Pennsylvania. Small electric companies proliferated at this time, and by 1900, 64 companies served 88 communities in the area PP&L later would serve.

As consolidation began to sweep through the electric utilities industry in the 1920s, it became commonplace for electric utility firms to merge into small regional companies. Pennsylvania Power & Light Company was formed as a result in June 1920 as a holding company for eight such utilities. The new company operated 62 steam electric and hydroelectric generating plants. PP&L, backed by another holding company called the Lehigh Power Securities Corporation, sold stocks and bonds to the public, but kept control of voting common stock of the utilities.

Like many other U.S. utilities, PP&L went through an important growth period in the 1920s, buying out other utilities, which in turn already had bought smaller utilities. It continued to expand its territory in this way, acquiring five utilities in 1923, 34 in 1928, and 21 in 1930, including the Edison Electric Company of Lancaster, Pennsylvania, one of the earliest U.S. electric companies. The early PP&L primarily supplied power for industry in Pennsylvania's coal mining and steel producing region, concentrated in the Lehigh River valley. By 1930, 70 percent of its power was used by industrial customers, and 45 percent of that went to coal mining operations. PP&L also supplied small industry and agriculture in the Susquehanna River valley north of Harrisburg, capital of Pennsylvania. Allentown and Bethlehem were the largest cities in its territory, with populations of 90,000 and 60,000, respectively, in 1930. At this time PP&L's system consisted of a large territory with widely dispersed power plants, each with a relatively small network of transmission lines, and interconnections between the various systems.

While much of the United States began to feel the effects of the Great Depression, PP&L and most other electric utilities remained somewhat shielded from financial ruin because of their status as protected, regulated monopolies. Increasing residential sales made up most sales that were lost to declining industry. PP&L added hundreds of miles of high-voltage transmission lines to its system in the 1920s and 1930s, also building a 220,000-volt interconnection with two urban utilities, Philadel-

Company Perspectives:

PPL Corporation's integrated business strategy—as well as its commitment to its customers and the communities it serves—is making the company one of the most successful generation-owning marketers of electricity in the evolving U.S. market, a premier energy delivery company in the Mid-Atlantic region, and a leading international energy company.

phia Electric Company and Public Service Electric & Gas Company of New Jersey. PP&L's industrial customers caused the company's load to peak in the morning, while the urban utilities' loads peaked in the late afternoon, when workers returned home. This led to an ideal power-sharing arrangement, although it required complex contracts to spell out which company would supply how much power under what circumstances. The firm also entered the natural gas industry during this time period.

Mid-1930s–Early 1970s: Expansion and Growth

PP&L continued to look for ways to expand and began to shift its emphasis from regions that had mined out their coal to regions with fresh coal seams. To encourage industrial use of power, the company charged industrial customers far lower rates than it charged residential and farm customers. Some political pressure was put on PP&L to change this practice, but it resisted, pointing out that it already encouraged rural electrification in other ways. PP&L had begun hooking up farmers rapidly in 1936, the year the U.S. government established the Rural Electrification Administration to make loans to farmers to create their own electric cooperatives. By 1939, 57 percent of farms in PP&L territory had electricity, compared with a U.S. average of 28 percent.

In 1947, PP&L acquired two electric utilities and the Allentown, Pennsylvania, operations of another. The firm also restructured its ownership, leaving it with more than 70,000 stockholders. By the following year, the company had 487,000 customers, and revenue of $62 million. In 1949 and 1951, PP&L sold all of its gas operations. It also sold its steam heating operations in Wilkes-Barre, Pennsylvania, in 1951, leaving it with steam operations in Harrisburg and Scranton, Pennsylvania. In 1953, it acquired Scranton Electric Company and in 1955, it laid claim to the Pennsylvania Water & Power Company. At this time, it had nearly 7,000 employees and operated in about 10,000 square miles of east central Pennsylvania. The firm supplied a population of 2.1 million people in a large number of communities including Allentown, Wilkes-Barre, Harrisburg, Lancaster, Bethlehem, Williamsport, Hazelton, Pottsville, Shenandoah, Shamokin, Mt. Carmel, Sunbury, and Scranton. PP&L owned one hydroelectric and eight steam power-generating stations and had 29,000 miles of transmission lines. Its principal fuel supply was purchased under 50-year contracts with coal companies based in Philadelphia and Reading, Pennsylvania.

The company's growth efforts continued. PP&L spent roughly $142 million on new construction between 1954 and 1959, including the building of two new power-generating stations. It also spent about $4 million between 1958 and 1962 as its share of a joint project with Philadelphia Electric Company to develop a prototype nuclear power station. In 1961, the company built a new conventionally fueled power station at Brunner Island, Pennsylvania, with a capacity of 302,000 kilowatts. Between 1961 and 1965 the company reduced rates seven times. By 1964, 29 percent of the company's electric revenue came from industrial customers. The firm also had began pooling power with other companies in Pennsylvania, New Jersey, and Maryland. This interconnection grew into one of the world's largest power pools, including many other electric utilities in a 48,700-square-mile area with a population of 18.4 million. In addition, PP&L planned $315 million in construction between 1965 and 1969, including two new power plants. It was at this time that female engineers first began to work on company crews.

By 1972, PP&L owned seven steam, two hydroelectric, 11 combustion turbine, and five diesel-engine generating stations with a total capacity of about four million kilowatts. It announced plans to build a 2.2-million kilowatt nuclear generating station on the Susquehanna River between Wilkes-Barre and Bloomsburg, Pennsylvania, in the late 1970s. PP&L began operating its own coal mines when commercial coal companies proved unable to meet the terms of PP&L's contracts. PP&L's ownership of mines protected the company from runaway fuel costs as well as interruptions in fuel supplies.

The power-sharing arrangement with Pennsylvania, New Jersey, and Maryland companies also was proving financially beneficial since PP&L was putting more electricity into the pool than it took out. In 1973, it sold 6.5 billion kilowatt-hours to other companies in the pool and earned $67 million on revenue of $385 million. Escalating fuel prices and an economic recession following the oil embargos in 1973 and 1974, however, sharply cut the growth of power utilities. PP&L used coal for 96 percent of its fossil fuel needs. Much of that coal came from PP&L's own mines at below-market costs, helping to insulate the company from oil price increases. Even so, PP&L's sales growth dropped to three percent in 1974 from seven percent in 1973. In response, the firm developed energy conservation programs for its residential consumers as well as an advisory panel to deal with the energy crisis. In 1977, PP&L appointed an outsider as president when it named Robert K. Campbell, formerly with Western Electric, to the position. By the end of the decade, PP&L was considered one of the best-managed utilities in the United States, with a profit margin of 17 percent, compared with a U.S. industry average of 12 percent. Net income for 1978 was $149 million.

1980s: Battling a National Recession

In 1980, Standard Oil Company of Ohio signed an agreement with a PP&L subsidiary under which Standard mined coal on certain PP&L properties. One year later, the firm secured more than one million customers and the Pennsylvania Public Utility Commission (PUC) approved a $101 million annual rate increase for PP&L that went into effect in 1982. The company's Susquehanna nuclear power plant, delayed for years, was finally completed at a cost of more than $4 billion in 1982.

A dip in sales in the mid-1980s was caused by a weakening national economy. In response, PP&L began the first of a series of

Key Dates:

1920: Pennsylvania Power & Light Co. is formed in Allentown, Pennsylvania.
1936: Government establishes the Rural Electrification Administration.
1947: The company takes on a new ownership structure.
1955: The company acquires Pennsylvania Water & Power Company.
1961: The company constructs a new, conventionally fueled power station at Brunner Island, Pennsylvania.
1968: Female engineers join company crews for the first time.
1977: Outsider Robert K. Campbell is appointed company president.
1981: Customer base exceeds one million.
1983: Construction on the Susquehanna nuclear power plant is complete.
1989: The company posts record sales and earnings.
1990: Campbell dies and John T. Kauffman is named president.
1994: PP&L Resources Inc. is formed as a holding company.
1997: Subsidiary Power Markets Development Co. purchases a 25.2 percent stake in Empresas Emel S.A., a Chile-based electrical holding company.
1998: The company acquires 13 Montana power plants—the largest acquisition in company history.
2000: The company restructures under the name PPL Corporation.

incentive rates designed to increase usage and attract new industry. The central effort focused on pricing schemes that would sell more power during off-peak hours, increasing company revenue without requiring the construction of new power plants. The company also began consulting with industrial customers to enhance their uses for electricity. Encouraged by the initial response, PP&L expanded the program in 1987. PP&L also began testing new lighting systems designed to use light more efficiently. The firm developed a lightweight steel transmission pole to replace its wooden poles, which were becoming expensive and scarce. In 1985, the Pennsylvania PUC approved only $121 million of a $330 million rate increase requested by the utility, boosting electricity prices about eight percent. PP&L spent about $850 million on construction between 1987 and 1989.

PP&L efforts seemed to pay off with record sales and earnings in 1989, despite rate decreases and a softening economy in the northeastern United States. The company implemented a strategy that stressed aggressive marketing, cost management, and increased sensitivity to customers. By 1990, PP&L's total generating capacity was 7.9 million kilowatts.

Growth and Restructuring in the 1990s

The firm started the 1990s under new management. Robert Campbell died and John T. Kauffman was named company president. PP&L decided to phase out its affiliated mining companies beginning in 1991, instead buying its coal through contract and on the open market. Mining its own coal had become more expensive than buying it on the open market and many of the company's mines were depleted. PP&L began working on plans to reduce its sulfur dioxide emissions by about 50 percent by 2000 because of pollution provisions in the 1990 Clean Air Act amendments. The firm also began a $22 million renovation of two of the four coal-fired generating units at its Sunbury power plant. In addition, the company discovered that fuel oil was leaking into groundwater at its Brunner Island generating station and that filters from that plant contained enough cadmium to be considered hazardous waste. Cleaning up these problems proved costly over the next several years.

At the same time, the electric utilities industry experienced another wave of consolidation prompted by deregulation. PP&L restructured to reflect industry changes and began to operate as a competitive power supplier. The firm began aggressive marketing to homeowners and new homebuilders, urging them to use electric heat. As a result, 18 fuel dealers brought suit against the firm in 1991 claiming that PP&L's use of $25 million in cash grants and advertising subsidies to lower rates and lure new customers violated antitrust laws. The suit was finally settled in 1997.

The company's business dealings continued to grow and diversify, and in 1994 management decided to form a holding company called PP&L Resources Inc. to oversee the electric utility firm's operations. Power Markets Development Co., an unregulated subsidiary, also was formed to handle domestic and international power ventures. In 1995, subsidiary Spectrum Energy Services Corporation was created to manage new business opportunities. The Energy Marketing Center also was established to buy and sell wholesale electricity.

PP&L Resources continued to experience a growth spurt in the mid-1990s. Its subsidiary, Power Markets Development Co., began a joint venture with an Austria-based company to manage hydroelectric plants in several Latin American countries. It also bought a 25 percent stake in British firm South Western Electricity plc. In 1997, the subsidiary acquired a 25.2 percent interest in Empresas Emel S.A., fostering its international presence in Chile and Bolivia.

The year 1997 proved to be a banner year for the company. Pennsylvania's electric and energy market became fully deregulated and the Pennsylvania Public Utility Commission granted PP&L Resources a license to sell its services in the state—PP&L was the first utility in the state to be granted such a license. As a result, the firm formed the Retail Energy Supply unit to provide consumers with its services in the new markets. The parent company also restructured its units. Utility operations were now called PP&L Inc., Spectrum Energy Services Corp. changed its name to PP&L Spectrum, and Power Markets Development Co. took the name PP&L Global. That year PP&L Resources also acquired H.T. Lyons, Inc., a mechanical and contracting and engineering firm. By this time, the company's Energy Marketing Center was servicing 18 states.

In 1998, PP&L Global and Empresas Emel bought a 75 percent stake in Distributidora de Electricidad del Sur S.A. de C.V., an electrical distribution company in El Salvador. The firm also increased its interest in South Western Electricity plc to 49 percent. On the domestic home front, PP&L Resources continued to purchase local companies based in Pennsylvania, including Penn Fuel Gas, which expanded its business interests into the natural gas storage and delivery markets. It also acquired 13 Montana power plants for $1.6 billion—the largest deal in company history. Subsidiary PP&L EnergyPlus Co. was created later that year.

In 1999, the firm continued to grow at a rapid pace. The purchase of local companies continued and the firm also acquired the majority of assets from Bangor Hydro-Electric Company based in Maine. A Massachusetts-based mechanical and engineering company was also purchased. PP&L Global also continued to increase its interest in Empresas Emel. The company's aggressive growth strategy paid off and PP&L Resources secured the highest annual earnings in the firm's history. Sales in 1999 reached $4.59 billion.

A New Name in the New Era of the 21st Century

Sales and earnings continued to climb as the company entered the new millennium. The Y2K issues that threatened utility firms throughout the world were nonexistent for PP&L Resources. The firm ushered in the new era by changing its corporate structure once again. PP&L Resources became PPL Corporation, a holding company with four business units including PPL Utilities, PPL EnergyPlus, PPL Global, and PPL Generation.

PPL Global continued to embark on international endeavors and purchased an 84.7 percent stake in Companhia Energitica do Maranhco (CEMAR), Brazil-based electric distributions firm. PPL also set plans in motion to develop power plants in Washington and Arizona as part of its strategic move to double its operating capacity in the Western region of the United States. Paul T. Champagne, president of PPL Global, stated in a December 2000 press release, ''PPL is expanding in regions where there is an urgent need for new energy supply and where we feel that we can work well with the local community. We are concentrating our efforts in the East, where we already are one of the largest suppliers, and in the West, where we established a base of operations in Montana last year.''

PPL Corp. ended fiscal 2000 with $5.68 billion in sales, a 23.8 percent increase over the past year. The firm operated seven coal-fired plants, one nuclear plant, two oil-fired plants, ten natural gas plants, 19 hydro plants, and 23 combustion turbine power plants. Company plans included increased expansion with a concentration on wholesale sales of electricity. Its past performance and strategic initiatives led management to believe that the firm's good fortune would last well into the new millennium.

Principal Subsidiaries

PPL EnergyPlus LLC; PPL Electric Utilities Corp.; PPL Gas Utilities Corp.; PPL Generation LLC; PPL Global LLC; PPL Service Corp.

Principal Competitors

Allegheny Energy Inc.; Exelon Corp.; GPU Inc.

Further Reading

Chambers, Ann, ''PP&L Reap Benefits of OT Conversions,'' *Power Engineering,* February 1997, p. 55.

''Chile: PP&L Global to Strengthen Position,'' *South American Business Information,* May 22, 2000.

DeKok, David, ''Electricity Sales Boost Allentown, Pa.-Based Utility Company Earnings,'' *Knight-Ridder/Tribune Business News,* January 29, 2001.

Hansen, Teresa, ''Software, Training Reduce Energy Consumption,'' *Electric Light and Power,* June 1996, p. 18.

Hughes, Thomas P., *Networks of Power: Electrification in Western Society, 1880–1930,* Baltimore, Md.: Johns Hopkins University Press, 1983.

Mahoney, Thomas A., ''Electric Utility Settles with Oil Dealers After Years of Buying Share of Market,'' *Air Conditioning, Heating & Refrigeration News,* March 10, 1997, p. 1.

''PP&L Global to Buy 13 Montana Plants in 2,600 MW Deal,'' *Power Generation Technology and Markets,* November 6, 1998, p. 1.

—Scott M. Lewis
—update: Christina M. Stansell

The Professional Golfers' Association of America

100 Avenue of the Champions
Palm Beach Gardens, Florida 33418
U.S.A.
Telephone: (561) 624-8400
Fax: (561) 624-8448
Web site: http://www.pga.com

Professional Association
Incorporated: 1916
Employees: 160
Sales: $192.73 million
NAIC: 813920 Professional Organizations; 711310 Promoters of Performing Arts, Sports, and Similar Events with Facilities; 611430 Professional and Management Development Training; 511120 Periodical Publishers; 713910 Golf Courses and Country Clubs

The Professional Golfers' Association (PGA) of America is an organization that trains, certifies, and advocates for professional golfers. It also organizes tournaments and promotes the sport of golf throughout the world. The PGA conducts approximately 40 tournaments, the best-known of which are the Ryder Cup, the PGA Championship, the Senior PGA Championship, the Oldsmobile Scramble, and the Grand Slam of Golf. The PGA also owns and runs several golf courses and training facilities, and operates a merchandising company. The PGA has more than 26,000 members.

The Early Years

The Professional Golfers' Association of America got its start in 1916, just before the United States entered World War I. The sport of golf was then relatively new to America, having first been played in an organized fashion only in the late 1880s. Golf had long been popular in the British Isles, however—particularly in Scotland, where it was thought to have originated prior to 1400.

In 1894 the first American golfing organization, the Amateur Golf Association of the United States (later the U.S. Golf Association) was formed. The first American championship tournament was held a year later. At that time, professional golfers—those who made their living from the game as teachers or exhibition players—were a low-status group. Conversely, the amateur, or so-called ''gentleman golfer,'' was the one who was best known and who primarily competed in tournaments. Regional associations of professionals were formed in 1907 and 1914, but there was no national body to represent the interests of the growing number of golf pros.

In January of 1916, a Philadelphia department store owner named Rodman Wanamaker gathered a group of professional golfers for a meeting in New York, where he suggested they form a national organization and hold a championship match. Wanamaker pledged to donate $2,580 in prize money and a trophy and medals for the top finalists, in hopes of gaining publicity for his store in the bargain. The group, which also included some top amateur players, endorsed the idea, and the Professional Golfers' Association of America was born.

It was decided that the PGA would be run by an executive committee, and this was specified in its newly-written constitution. The new organization quickly signed up 82 members, and held its first tournament in October of 1916 in Bronxville, New York. When word of the new association spread, membership quickly grew to 200.

The PGA's Efforts in the Mid-1900s

In 1917 the United States entered World War I. During the war, the PGA contacted golf clubs to ask them to reserve positions for professionals who were serving their country. The PGA also purchased an ambulance for the Red Cross, and sent $1,000 to the British PGA for war relief. The organization also cancelled its tournaments while the country was at war.

In May of 1920, the PGA began publishing a magazine, *The Professional Golfer of America.* The following year, the legendary Walter Hagen became the first American-born player to win a PGA championship. The PGA also began sanctioning certain brands of golf clubs during this time. By the end of its first decade of existence, the PGA's membership had grown to 1,548.

Company Perspectives:

In 1916, The PGA founders established the following seven objectives for the Association: promote interest in the game of golf; elevate the standards of the golf professional's vocation; protect the mutual interests of its members; hold meetings and tournaments for the benefit of members; assist deserving unemployed members to obtain positions; establish a benevolent relief fund for deserving members; accomplish any other objective which may be determined by the Association from time to time.

1927 saw the creation of the Ryder Cup, which was a match between teams of British and American players. The inaugural tournament was won by the Americans, who soon came to dominate it over the years. As the PGA began to organize more activities, its membership dues were raised, jumping from $5 to $50 by the end of the 1920s. In 1930, PGA headquarters were moved from New York to Chicago, and the organization hired a business administrator and legal advisor. The PGA also established its name as a legal trademark.

During the Great Depression, work for professional golfers naturally declined significantly. The PGA created an Unemployment Relief Committee in 1933, and the organization's business administrator took a salary cut. In 1937 the PGA established a Senior's Championship for older players, and in 1941 formed the Golf Hall of Fame to recognize the legends of the game.

As the country entered World War II, the 25-year old PGA had 2,000 members. As it had done once before, the organization donated funds and two ambulances to the war effort, and supplied golf equipment to military bases. The Ryder Cup and PGA Championships were again both suspended during the hostilities.

In 1944 the PGA, desiring a golf course of its own, leased a site in Dunedin, Florida to serve as the PGA National Golf Club. The PGA also began a campaign to encourage young people to play golf by sponsoring PGA Junior Golf Week starting in 1948. In the first year, 20,000 PGA Junior Golfers' Association membership cards were given out. During the late 1940s, the organization also raised its membership standards, requiring 5 years as an apprentice prior to applying for professional certification.

Discriminatory Policies Draw Fire: 1940s–1960s

Having been formed in an era when civil rights were not well-recognized, the PGA had originally been chartered as a "Caucasians-only" organization. In the late 1940s, inspired by Jackie Robinson's groundbreaking entrance into professional baseball, three black golfers sued the association for the right to play in PGA tournaments. Up to that point, the PGA did not admit African-Americans into its tournaments, whether they were PGA members or not. The three argued that the PGA was denying them employment opportunities because of their race. The organization subsequently agreed not to discriminate against blacks in tournament play, but the "Caucasians-only" membership clause in its constitution was left intact. This partial victory did not open the field very far, however, as PGA tournaments quickly became "invitationals," rather than open tournaments, and invitations were seldom offered to nonwhites.

In 1956 PGA headquarters were officially moved from Chicago to Dunedin, Florida, where offices were established on the second floor of a bank building. The organization's 40th anniversary saw the PGA with a record 3,800 members, who were organized into 31 sections. The PGA had by this time also started an annual merchandise show for vendors to display their products to members. Many golf pros operated shops at courses where they sold golf clubs, shoes, and other merchandise, and the show performed a useful service for them. During the late 1950s, a new generation of tournament stars was emerging, including Arnold Palmer, Gary Player, and Jack Nicklaus.

In November of 1961 the PGA, bowing to continued pressure, finally changed its constitution to remove the "Caucasians-only" clause. The organization's ranks, however, would remain largely white for some time to come. When it celebrated its 50th anniversary in 1966, the PGA's membership stood at 5,837. The following year, the PGA added another new requirement for membership—a degree from business school.

Late 1960s: Tour Players Break From the PGA

In 1968 the top touring pros, unhappy with several PGA policies, split off to form their own organization. Playing on the tournament circuit had emerged as a livelihood only in the late 1940s, when a year-round match schedule was first achieved. By the 1960s, though, income from television contracts was a growing source of the PGA's revenue, and touring golfers wanted a piece of this pie in the form of larger purses. The PGA, however, voted to add the money to the organization's general fund, which incensed its top golfers.

The final straw came when the PGA vetoed plans for a new tournament sponsored by Frank Sinatra, which was scheduled to be held within two weeks of the long-running Bob Hope Desert Classic. Both were planned for courses in the same part of California, and the PGA felt the region would not support two tournaments back to back. Chafing at PGA rulings that affected their livelihoods, most of the top touring PGA players, including Nicklaus and Palmer, formed a breakaway organization—the Association of Professional Golfers. After a partial reconciliation was later reached, the group was reconstituted as the Tournament Players Division, which would come to be an autonomous body run by a 10-member policy board. It later became known simply as the PGA Tour, Inc.

Continuing in its efforts to improve members' skills, in 1970 the PGA formalized its apprenticeship program. The number of sanctioned apprentices soon grew into the thousands. The organization also added a new major tournament in 1973—the PGA Cup. Similar to the Ryder Cup, the PGA Cup pitted British and American golfers against each other, but was played at a club in North Carolina. The PGA also held its inaugural Junior Tournament at Walt Disney World Golf Resort in Orlando, Florida several years later. The organization subsequently formed the PGA Junior Golf Foundation to help fund programs for younger golfers. The PGA Grand Slam of Golf was established in 1979

Key Dates:

1916: Professional Golfers' Association of America is formed; first tournament held.
1927: Debut of the Ryder Cup—a match between American and British teams.
1930: PGA headquarters are moved to Chicago.
1937: PGA Senior's Championship established for older golf pros.
1944: Golf course at Dunedin, Florida leased for use by the PGA.
1954: PGA's first trade show is held.
1956: PGA headquarters moved to Florida.
1961: The PGA's constitution is amended to allow non-white members.
1968: Top touring golfers break away from the PGA to form their own organization.
1979: Grand Slam of Golf debuts as a benefit for PGA Junior Golf Foundation.
1984: Oldsmobile Scramble pro/am tournament introduced.
1990: Shoal Creek Country Club's whites-only policy causes furor at PGA Championship.
1994: Golf Professional Training Program is launched.
2001: PGA Training Center in Port St. Lucie, Florida, is completed.

as a fundraiser for this organization. The Grand Slam, which matched the winners of four top tournaments, would become one of the PGA's marquee events.

After several moves to different offices in Florida during the 1960s and 1970s, the PGA found a site in Palm Beach Gardens, Florida to build a permanent headquarters facility, and relocated its operations there in 1981. That same year the PGA and the PGA Tour established a joint merchandising venture.

Growth During the 1980s and 1990s

The PGA, and golf in general, underwent a period of dramatic growth in the 1980s. The organization's membership ranks increased by almost half, and several U.S. colleges also established golf management programs. During the same decade, a popular new pro/am tournament—the Oldsmobile Scramble—was launched. In 1988 the PGA reorganized its national office. The late 1980s and early 1990s saw growing revenues from television licenses for the PGA, which signed lucrative contracts with a number of major cable and broadcast networks. The PGA Seniors tour was also now becoming a big draw as legends such as Arnold Palmer, Jack Nicklaus, Gary Player and Lee Trevino joined its ranks and boosted public interest.

The PGA's historically woeful record regarding blacks was tarnished again in 1990, however, by an incident at the Shoal Creek Country Club in Birmingham, Alabama, where the PGA Championship was being held. The incident began when a black city councilman questioned the funding of an advertisement in the tournament program, noting that Shoal Creek did not admit black members. Shoal Creek founder Hal Thompson then commented, "That's just not done in Birmingham," and a furor arose. A number of corporations dropped their television advertising for the tournament broadcast, while the PGA quickly declared that it would no longer sponsor events at clubs that discriminated. Unfortunately, the PGA had in fact already sponsored several earlier tournaments at Shoal Creek before the club's whites-only policy was publicized. After initially refusing to do so, Shoal Creek admitted a single black member in time for the tournament to take place. Nevertheless, the controversy highlighted the fact that many of the leading golfing organizations, including the PGA, were still "old boys' networks" with few leadership positions or tour members drawn from the ranks of minority groups or women. Even though the official face of the sport had long been white, the number of black golfers was growing, with one estimate citing an increase in African-American players from 384,000 in 1981 to 692,000 in 1989.

In 1994 the PGA revamped its education system, which would thereafter be known as the Golf Professional Training Program (GPTP). The GPTP, which required Class A PGA members to receive more than 600 hours of training to gain certification, was offered at a number of sites around the country. The move came after PGA members had expressed concerns that it was too easy to join the organization, with the mushrooming number of apprentices meaning that too many people had a leg up to professional status. They felt that opportunities for PGA members were decreasing and their salary figures were dropping. Members were also concerned that sales of golf equipment at pro shops was shrinking due to outside competition, which further cut into their earnings.

In addition to strengthening its training program, the PGA created a job placement service to assist members who were seeking work. Benefits extended to PGA members at this time included medical and property insurance plans, a credit union, and discounts from a range of PGA-affiliated corporations. Retirement benefits were added in 1997. Membership dues remained steady at $100 per year during the 1990s, which saw the organization's revenues from tournaments, television licensing agreements, corporate marketing deals, golf course consulting and licensing fees, and investments continuing to grow.

The mid-1990s saw the PGA enter cyberspace, with the launch of a public web site. The organization also created a second members-only Internet portal, through which professionals could look at job postings, register for tournaments, access their PGA Credit Union account, and communicate with other members. The PGA also had a home video division as well, and began producing television programs in association with the cable television Golf Channel. Around this time, the organization also sold its trade show business, which operated shows in Florida and Las Vegas, to Reed Exhibition Companies for $122 million.

A Goal For the New Millennium: Diversity

The biggest excitement in golf since the heyday of Nicklaus and Palmer was the arrival of Tiger Woods in the late 1990s. The first African-American athlete to become widely known in the sport, Woods attracted intense fan and media interest. Woods' highly visible success also boosted interest in golf among African-Americans to a greater level than ever before. Recognizing that the sport's next generation of players would come from a wider range of ethnic groups than it had originally anticipated, the PGA's outreach to minorities began to grow. CEO Jim Awtrey, who had run the association since 1988, became a vocal advocate of expanding its membership ranks to include more minorities, women, juniors, and physically challenged players. The PGA Diversity program and PGA Community Relations Program were created to bring a wider range of Americans into contact with the sport.

The year 2001 saw the PGA applying the finishing touches to construction of a new training center in Florida that would serve as the primary education center for future PGA members. It was located adjacent to the new PGA Learning Center, which was a 35 acre site at which golfers could receive instruction from PGA pros on all types of play. The organization now operated a number of other facilities as well, including the PGA Golf Club, PGA Country Club and PGA Village in Florida, and the Valhalla Golf Club of Louisville, Kentucky.

As it celebrated 85 years in operation, the Professional Golfers' Association of America continued to function as the leading organization for promoting the welfare of golf professionals in the United States. Through the championship tournaments it coordinated, its professional training programs, and its outreach campaigns, the PGA remained a prime mover in the world of golf.

Principal Subsidiaries

PGA Properties, Inc.

Principal Competitors

Augusta National, Inc.; The Royal and Ancient Golf Club of St. Andrew's; The Ladies Professional Golf Association; PGA Tour, Inc.; United States Golf Association.

Further Reading

Chambers, Marcia, *The Unplayable Lie,* New York: Pocket Books, 1995.

Grimsley, Will, *Golf: Its History, People & Events,* Englewood Cliffs, N.J.: Prentice-Hall, 1966.

Kramer, Scott, ''Follow-Up: How's the PGA Doing,'' *Golf Pro*, October 1, 1995, p. 28.

Newberry, Paul, ''PGA Still Called Racist 12 Months after Shoal Creek,'' *Los Angeles Daily News*, August 4, 1991, p. SB7.

Official Guide of the PGA Championships, Chicago: Triumph Books, 1994.

Purkey, Mike, ''The Revolt of '68,'' *Golf Magazine*, February 1, 1996, p. 48.

Shapiro, Leonard, ''The 'Other' PGA,'' *Golf Magazine*, August 1, 1998, p. 52.

Williams, Jeff, ''Shoal Creek/The Aftermath—Has Anything Really Changed?,'' *Newsday*, August 4, 1991, p. 16.

—Frank Uhle

Ramsay Youth Services, Inc.

Columbus Center
1 Alhambra Plaza, Suite 750
Coral Gables, Florida 33134
U.S.A.
Telephone: (305) 569-6993
Fax: (305) 569-4647
Web site: http://www.ramsay.com

Public Company
Incorporated: 1983 as Healthcare Services of America, Inc.
Employees: 2,455
Sales: $108.4 million (2000)
Stock Exchanges: NASDAQ
Ticker Symbol: RYOU
NAIC: 622210 Psychiatric and Substance Abuse Hospitals; 541611 Administrative Management and General Management Consulting Services

Based in Coral Gables, Florida, Ramsay Youth Services, Inc. provides education and treatment programs for at-risk, troubled, and special needs youth, either on an inpatient or outpatient basis, in a range of settings: from secure detention facilities and juvenile justice commitment facilities to residential treatment facilities, group homes, schools, and community centers. Ramsay Youth operates in nine states and the Commonwealth of Puerto Rico. The types of youth the company serves include juvenile offenders as well as those with learning and development disabilities, substance abuse problems, and mental health issues. Youth services that were traditionally run directly by local governments have become increasingly privatized, prompting a number of companies to enter the business or, in the case of Ramsay Youth, to transform a subsidiary into a company mainstay.

Formation of Predecessor Healthcare Services of America in 1983

Ramsay Youth Services was originally a subsidiary of a corporation that operated a chain of psychiatric hospitals. Healthcare Services of America, Inc. was incorporated in Delaware in 1983 and based in Birmingham, Alabama. It was founded by Charles A. Speir and Kerry G. Teel. Speir became the company's chief executive officer and chairman, and Teel served as president and chief operating officer. Healthcare Services did well at first, acquiring a number of hospitals and making an initial public offering of its stock in August 1985 to fuel further growth. For the year the company would earn $3.5 million on revenues of $69.7 million. The psychiatric hospital industry in general was in an expansive mood. For-profit companies opened up new facilities to the point of oversupply, then spent heavily on advertising to fill their beds, but the landscape was changing and care providers were not quick to adjust. They were trained to think of mental health treatment as an inpatient, hospital-related practice. Third-party payers—insurance companies and health maintenance organizations—were becoming increasingly more cost conscious and shying away from inpatient treatment, looking instead to outpatient treatment or ''partial hospitalization,'' in which patients spent the day in a structured setting but were sent home at night. By capping the amount that they would pay for psychiatric care, insurers hoped to control costs and force caregivers to forego what was seen as unnecessary treatment. The result would be a lengthy and difficult transition period for companies that continued to pursue the old paradigm in which the more beds they controlled the more revenue they could generate.

Healthcare Services was forced to face the changing realities sooner than most of its competitors. Although revenues continued to grow in 1986, reaching $109.4 million, the company posted a loss of $17.1 million. By May 1986 Keel was out. Speir would leave two years later after Healthcare Services lost an additional $27 million in 1987 despite another gain in revenues, which now totaled $132 million. The company had tried to sell off unprofitable assets to stabilize its position, but it was still forced to default on some of its loans. When Speir stepped down, the company was on the verge of bankruptcy, and brokerage firm Smith Barney was hired to help sell the business.

Acquisition by Paul Ramsay Group in 1987

In August 1987, a controlling interest in the 19 hospitals owned by Healthcare Services was acquired by the Australian

Company Perspectives:

Ramsay focuses on the types of services and programs that address the needs of youth with multiple challenges and provides the opportunity for their successful integration back into their communities as effective individuals and productive citizens.

Paul Ramsay Group for $22.5 million in cash and a $5 million commitment in further loans. Entrepreneur Paul Ramsay had been involved in the healthcare business since the mid-1970s, as well as other Australian ventures. The Paul Ramsay Group operated 16 psychiatric and other hospitals in Australia, Hong Kong, and the United States. Ramsay-HMO already was established in southern Florida, primarily serving the Cuban population.

Early in 1988 Ramsay hired Ralph J. Watts to serve as the new chief executive officer for Healthcare Services. Watts had been a senior vice-president of Community Psychiatric Centers. Although Ramsay had announced plans to move the headquarters of Healthcare Services to Florida, in order to secure Watts's service it agreed to move the company to New Orleans, where Watts lived. Later in 1988 Healthcare Services also would change its name, becoming Ramsay Health Care, Inc.

Watts quickly began to address Ramsay Health Care's many problems. First, he worked with lenders to avoid bankruptcy, then he proceeded to cut the workforce and sell off poorly-performing assets. The company earned a profit of $5 million in 1990, followed by $8.9 million in 1990. In 1991 the company posted a $9 million profit on just $104.5 million in revenues. By early 1992, however, Watts resigned over a disagreement with the board of directors over its desire to accelerate the pace at which Ramsay Health Care moved toward the outpatient business. He was replaced by Australian Gregory Browne, who had been running Ramsay-HMO.

After three years under Watt, Ramsay Health Care appeared to be better situated than most of its competitors and was optimistic about its potential for growth. Brown hoped to increase outpatient revenues from between three and 4 percent to as much as 15 percent within two years. He looked to support that growth by expanding on the company's building of satellite clinics in rural areas, as well as developing day-treatment mental health centers that fell somewhere in between a satellite clinic and an inpatient psychiatric hospital. Browne also hoped to establish more joint ventures with universities, such as the company had launched with the University of West Virginia when it built the school's psychiatric hospital, then took over the operating responsibilities and shared the profits with the department of psychiatry. Not only would such relationships lend credibility to Ramsay Health Care, they would keep it on the cutting edge of research. Investors were beginning to notice Ramsay Health Care, with some industry analysts predicting an extremely bright future for the company.

As had been the case with the company after it went public in 1985, the promising future failed to materialize. Results for the industry overall and Ramsay Health Care in particular were disappointing in 1992. For the fiscal year ending June 30, 1992, the company's net income fell to $1.97 million on $137 million in revenues. Ramsay Health Care continued to move toward providing more of an outpatient business, but the trend only accelerated faster, still leaving the company with too many unused beds and too many fixed costs. According to the National Association of Psychiatric Health Systems, the average hospital stay in 1993 was 16 days. Three years later that number would shrink to 12 days. To adjust to the changing realities, Ramsay Health Care formed a managed care division in October 1993. A year later it decided to spin off the division to create Ramsay Managed Care, with Browne also named as chairman and CEO. The hope was that as two separate companies they would be better able to pursue their own patterns of growth. Reynold Jennings, a former executive with National Medical Enterprises who had originally joined Ramsay Health Care to be groomed to replace Browne, ran the psychiatric hospitals while Browne ran the new company.

The split in operations, however, did not have the desired effect. Shortly after Ramsay Health Care reported a $17 million loss for 1995, Browne stepped down in favor of Jennings. The company lost another $16 million in 1996 before posting $3.4 million in earnings in 1997. By then it was clear that Ramsay Managed Care as a separate publicly traded company provided little advantage and that the similar name simply caused confusion. Thus, in August 1997 Ramsay Health Care reacquired Ramsay Managed Care, with management expressing optimism over the ''tremendous potential'' of returning the spin-off to the company.

In 1996 Ramsay Health Care moved to Coral Gables, Florida. The move from Birmingham, Alabama to New Orleans had been an accommodation for Watts, and no longer made sense for the company. The other Ramsay Group company in the United States, Ramsay-HMO, already had provided a number of executives for Ramsay Health Care. Ramsay-HMO had been sold to United HealthCare Corp. in 1994, but ties with Ramsay Health Care remained strong. It was easier to recruit executives from the HMO if the two companies were located in the same area and new hires would not have to relocate to New Orleans.

One of those former Ramsay-HMO executives, Luis E. Lamela, replaced Jennings in January 1998, becoming the new president and chief executive officer. Starting in a pharmacy position Lamela rose through the ranks to become the chief executive officer at Ramsay-HMO. After United HealthCare bought the company, Lamela served as CEO of the CAC Medical Centers division from May 1994 until December 1997. Under Lamela, Ramsay Health Care would embark on a radical change of focus.

Emergence of Ramsay Youth Services in 1998

In February 1998 Lamela announced that Ramsay Health Care would concentrate on expanding the business of one of its subsidiaries, Ramsay Youth Services, which had been established four years earlier with the acquisition of a Utah residential center that treated juvenile sex offenders. The unit had then expanded and posted excellent results. In connection with its shift in strategy, Ramsay Health Care engaged SunTrust Equitable Securities to help in assessing possible acquisition targets as well as divesting the company of nonyouth services assets. The

Key Dates:

1983: Healthcare Services of America is incorporated.
1985: Company makes an initial public offering of stock.
1987: Paul Ramsay Group acquires company.
1988: Name is changed to Ramsay Health Care.
1994: Company enters youth services business.
1998: Youth services becomes focus of company.
1999: Company name is changed to Ramsay Youth Services.

case for pursuing the at-risk and troubled youth business was certainly compelling. It generated between $50 billion and $65 billion a year; with local governments turning increasingly to private companies to run its youth programs it was clearly a growth area, especially in light of the fact that juvenile crime was up 60 percent over the 1980 level and that the juvenile population was expected to grow 21 percent by the year 2010. In Florida, according to state Juvenile Justice statistics, around 85 percent of the services provided in juvenile prisons were contracted out, totaling more than $320 million a year. Furthermore, almost 90 percent of Florida's residential centers for troubled youth were privately run. Ramsay Health Care also would be able to secure funding from government programs, both state and federal. Unlike contracts with insurers, which regularly knocked down rates, government agencies paid a fixed rate for an extended period of time, providing more of a predictable revenue stream. Moreover, the youth services industry was highly fragmented, with some 10,000 independent companies providing services. Consolidation in the industry was already beginning, and Ramsay Health Care was eager to position itself as a major player. Because more than half of the money spent on at-risk and troubled youth was dedicated to education, Ramsay Health Care also would look to expand in that direction as well.

As expected, the transition was expensive. The company lost more than $54 million in 1998, due mostly to restructuring costs. Ramsay Health Care sold off half of its 12 psychiatric hospitals and converted the others into residential youth-only treatment centers. It added a seventh with the opening of a facility in Alabama. In April the company acquired two youth services facilities, one located in Florida and the other in Alabama. In August the Ramsay Educational Services division took over the management of a Florida charter school in Brevard County. Charter schools, privately run but government-funded, included many devoted to children with special education needs, a good fit for Ramsay Health Care, which already possessed much of the necessary expertise. By the end of 1998 there were some 1,200 charter schools in America, a number expected to grow to 2,000 soon. To solidify its position in education, Ramsay Health Care purchased The Rader Group, which operated four Florida charter schools. With limited experience as a juvenile services provider, Ramsay Health Care made a concerted effort to gain a share of that market as well.

To better reflect the company's shift in focus, Ramsay Health Care officially changed its name to Ramsay Youth Services in January 1999. The financial strain of restructuring the business began to ease as the company rebuilt its revenues to $81 million and earned more than $3 million for the year. Ramsay Youth was especially successful in gaining new business in Puerto Rico, where it won educational and mental health contracts as well as juvenile justice contracts. In April 2000 Ramsay Youth signed a major contract with the Florida Department of Juvenile Justice to operate a 102-bed Youth Development Center for high-risk boys, ages 14 to 18. The $9.7 million contract was for a term of three years. Many of the company's government contracts were for even longer terms, thus providing the level of predictable revenues essential in raising sufficient capital to allow Ramsay Youth Services to penetrate new markets and develop compatible lines of new business. For 2000 the company reported $108 million in revenues and a net profit of more than $2.8 million. After 15 years of uncertainty, and relocations from Birmingham, Alabama to New Orleans to south Florida, the corporation that was known as Healthcare Services of America, then Ramsay Health Care, and now Ramsay Youth Services, appeared to have finally found a viable business niche.

Principal Subsidiaries

Ramsay Educational Services, Inc.; Ramsay Managed Care, Inc.; Ramsay Youth Services of Alabama, Inc.; Ramsay Youth Services of Florida, Inc.; Ramsay Youth Services of Puerto Rico, Inc.

Principal Competitors

PHC Inc.; Children's Comprehensive Services, Inc.; Res-Care, Inc.

Further Reading

Chandler, Michele, "Florida Health Care Firm Remakes Itself to Aid At-Risk Juveniles," *Miami Herald,* November 30, 1998.

Lutz, Sandy, "Bad News, Falling Profits Hamper Psych Providers," *Modern Healthcare,* May 24, 1993, p. 54.

——, "Psych Chains Had Another Tough Year," *Modern Healthcare,* May 22, 1995, p. 64.

——, "Ramsay CEO Resigns; Firm Posts Loss," *Modern Healthcare,* September 25, 1993, p. 12.

Perry, Linda, "Pressure from Payers Continues to Slow Growth of Psychiatric Hospitals," *Modern Healthcare,* May 20, 1991, pp. 70–73.

Riegel, Stephanie, "Ramsay Remains Healthy While Competitors Falter," *CityBusiness (New Orleans),* July 6, 1992, p. 1.

Snow, Charlotte, "Ramsay to Reacquire Managed-Care Spinoff," *Modern Healthcare,* April 28, 1997, p. 12.

Wallace, Cynthia, "Ramsay Is Trimming Overhead in Effort to Revive HSA Profits," *Modern Healthcare,* February 12, 1988, p. 36.

—Ed Dinger

Reno de Medici S.p.A.

Via Tucidide, 56 Torre 6
20121 Milan
Italy
Telephone: (+39) 297 960 441
Fax: (+39) 275 288 555
Web site: http://www.renodemedici.it

Public Company
Incorporated: 1967 as Cartiera del Reno SpA
Employees: 2,259
Sales: EUR 525 million ($490 million) (2000)
Stock Exchanges: Milan Madrid
Ticker Symbol: RDM.MI; RDM.MC
NAIC: 32221 Paperboard Container Manufacturing; 32212 Paperboard Mills; 32213 Paperboard Mills

Milan-based Reno de Medici S.p.A. is the leading manufacturer of recycled cardboard and foldable cartonboard in Italy and Spain and the second largest after potential merger partner Meyr Melnhof Karton of Austria. The company's main products include boxes for the packaging industry and greeting cards, a segment in which the company is one of the European market's top producers. Reno de Medici also owns a majority stake in energy production facility Cogeneracion Prat SA, located near its El Prat de Llobregat (close to Barcelona) production plant. Cogeneracion provides energy at reduced cost to Reno de Medici and the company also sells back excess energy production on the open market. Reno de Medici is active as well in the production of matches and related products, including sulfur. Cardboard production remains the company's central activity, however, accounting for more than 90 percent of the group's total sales. The company markets a wide range of paper and cardboard products under three core brand names: RDM, Ovaro, and Sarriò. The later brands come as a result of a number of major acquisitions, most notably that of Spain's Sarriò and its Italian subsidiary Saffa beginning in 1997. Reno de Medici operates six production plants in Italy and two more in Spain, selling more than 800,000 tons in the year 2000. Traded on both the Milan and Madrid stock exchanges, Reno de Medici posted EUR 525 million in sales in 2000. The company is headed by founder Giovanni Dell'Aria Burani who, together with his family, remains Reno de Medici's primary stockholder.

Founding a Carton Producer in the 1960s

Reno de Medici was founded as Cartiera del Reno SpA in 1967, with headquarters in Milan and a production facility in the Bologna-region town of Marzabotto. Already specialized in the production of cardboard, the company's initial output was just 8,000 tons. Founder Giovanni Dell'Aria Burani was to lead the company from these modest beginnings to becoming one of Europe's primary cardboard and foldable cartonboard products manufacturers in only 30 years.

Cartiera del Reno SpA prospered enough to begin adding capacity in the mid-1970s. The company added a new paper producing unit in 1975, boosting its total production output past 50,000 tons. Italy's papermaking industry remained highly fragmented throughout this period, with top paper producers accounting for only 60 percent of total national production. The remaining producers, like Cartiera del Reno, were primarily small-scale, family-owned enterprises.

Italy's lack of natural resources—such as a lack of forests—acted as a barrier to full development of the paper producing industry. Nonetheless, there were several niches available, such as the production of high-quality tissue-based writing papers, offering better growth prospects. Another niche was that of cardboard and foldable paper board manufactured from recycled materials—a more available resource in wood pulp-poor Italy. Giovanni Dell'Aria Burani steered his company toward this niche. While developing other products, such as matches, Burani's company's success was to come from its focus on the recycled cardboard market.

Growth in the 1980s

A series of acquisitions helped Burani boost his company's production to capture a leading share of cardboard production. The first of these came in 1985, when the company acquired Ovaro SpA, and that company's Ovaro-branded product range. Ovaro added some 32,000 tons of production output per year.

Company Perspectives:

The corporate purpose shall be: a) to perform industrial, commercial and service activities, in Italy and overseas, relative to, instrumental for or connected with the following sectors: paper-making and paper-transformation, including any and all complementary and intermediate production processes; chemicals in general and match-making, including any and all complementary and intermediate production processes; farming, forestry, zootechnics, transformation of relative products and foodstuffs; b) real estate, including leasing; c) acquisition of equity holdings in firms, companies, organisations, consortia and associations in Italy and overseas, the funding and technical and financial coordination thereof, the trading, exchange, possession, management and placement of public and private securities.

One year later, Cariera del Reno acquired the cardboard production division, including a 60,000-ton annual output capacity plant in Turin, from Cartiera Binda de Medici. Burani then changed his company's name to reflect the new scope of operations to Reno de Medici SpA.

Throughout the rest of the 1980s, Reno de Medici continuously updated its production facilities, adding not only state-of-the-art equipment but also stepping up the company's total output. The company returned to acquisitions in 1992, buying a strong shareholding position in Grafiche Capretta SpA. Reno de Medici later raised its position in Grafiche Capretta almost to full control, to 70 percent in 1995 and then to 91 percent in the Europoligrafico SpA subsidiary created through the 1999 merger of Bianchi Saffapack and Grafiche Capretta.

By the early 1990s, Reno de Medici's output had risen to 240,000 tons. The company credited its strong output levels and its commitment to continued modernization of its production park for enabling it to weather the deep recession of the 1990s and particularly the near-collapse of paper prices in 1993. Reno de Medici managed to maintain its profitability during this difficult period, posting a net income of L 0.4 billion on total sales of L 208 billion in 1994. A year later, the company's revenues had risen to L 284 billion, with profits jumping to L 6.6 billion.

By the mid-1990s Reno de Medici began to prepare for a public offering that would enable it to step up its capital investments and look for new acquisitions in an industry that remained somewhat stubborn and resistant to consolidation. In 1995, the company formally brought Ovaro SpA into Reno de Medici's operation, merging the two companies' activities. Reno de Medici maintained Ovaro's strong brand-name and product list, alongside its own RDM brand. The following year, Reno de Medici went public with a listing on the Milan stock exchange. Founder Burani and family maintained their majority control of the company.

Potential Merger Partners for the New Century

Reno de Medici's public offering gave it the capital backing to begin an even more ambitious expansion. After having boosted its position in Grafiche Capretta to 70 percent, which added that company's 15,000 tons of production capacity, the company looked for an even bigger partner with which to confront the growing consolidation of the European paper manufacturing industry and the buildup to the single-currency zone at the turn of the century. In 1997, Reno de Medici announced that it had agreed to merge with fellow Italian company Saffa SpA.

The merger brought a number of important new subsidiary operations, including Saffa's majority control of paper transformation division Bianchi Saffapack SA, its match-making unit Italmatch, a real estate development arm, Saffa Immobiliare, and—not least—Saffa's controlling share of Spanish cardboard manufacturer Sarriò S.A. The new company, however, retained the Reno de Medici name and remained under Burani family control.

Sarriò S.A. had, in fact, been created in 1990 when Saffa and Sarriò had agreed to combine their paperboard manufacturing operations under the Sarriò S.A. name, with Saffa retaining majority control of the newly enlarged Spanish company. The merger of Saffa and Reno de Medici created Italy's largest and Europe's second largest recycled cardboard manufacturer, behind Austria's Meyr Melnhof, with combined sales of more than L 1,100 billion and production capacity of close to 800,000 tons.

Soon after its merger with Saffa, Reno de Medici acted to take full control of Sarriò as well, merging that company's entire operation into its own, yet keeping the Sarriò brand name. The company also maintained a second listing on the Madrid stock exchange. Reno de Medici's park of production facilities now included six sites in Italy, two plants in Spain, and a ninth plant in Slovenia. The expanded company now controlled annual output volumes of up to 950,000 tons.

In late 1998, Reno de Medici sold its Slovenian carton subsidiary to Meyr Melnhof. Following the sale, Reno de Medici acknowledged its interest in a potential merger with its Austrian counterpart—with the creation of the world's largest manufacturer of greeting cards and one of the global leaders in recycled foldable carton as a result. In the meantime, Reno de Medici began reorganizing its own growing operations. The company announced that it was selling off its real estate subsidiary in 2000. Later that year the company reached a cooperation agreement with Spain's Barneda 2000 SL to form the 50–50 joint venture Barneda Carton SA, taking over Barneda's carton production while retaining the Barneda brand name. The company reached a separate agreement with ABB of Sweden to form the full-service joint venture ABB RDM Service, a company expected to reach sales of some L 35 billion.

After acquiring remaining control of Bianchi Saffapack from France's La Rochette, Reno de Medici created the Europoligrafico SpA subsidiary through the combination of Bianchi Saffapack and Grafiche Capretta in 1999. The new subsidiary, with four production units and 60,000 tons in annual output, became Italy's top paper transformation company. In that year, the company announced its intention to boost its production capacity in Spain by some 50 percent with the addition of a new coated cardboard machine at its El Prat de Llobregat factory. That expansion prompted the company to increase its shareholding in nearby power generation facility

Key Dates:

1967: Giovanni Dell'Aria Burani founds Cartiera del Reno SpA.
1975: The company adds second paper machine.
1985: The company acquires Ovaro SpA.
1986: The company acquires de Medici carton division; changes name to Reno de Medici.
1992: The company acquires shareholding in Grafiche Capretta.
1995: Ovaro is merged into Reno de Medici.
1996: The company is listed on the Milan stock exchange.
1997: The company merges with Saffa SpA.
1998: The company merges with Sarriò SA.
1999: Europoligrafico SpA is created.
2000: Joint venture Barneda Carton SA is created.
2001: The company acquires majority share of Cogeneracion Prat SA.

Cogeneracion Prat SA in February 2001, ensuring itself at reduced cost energy and additional revenues from sales of excess energy on the open market.

Reno de Medici headed into the new century with continued revenue gains, as it annual sales topped EUR 525 million in 2000. In barely more than 30 years the company had succeeded in imposing itself as a leader not only in the Italian market but across the European market as well. Nonetheless, as analysts criticized the European papermaking company for the slow speed of what was viewed as an inevitable and necessary consolidation, Reno de Medici began to look more closely at the possibility of uniting with Austrian counterpart Meyr Melnhof.

Principal Subsidiaries

Beobarna S.A. (Spain); Berneda Carton SA (Spain; 50%); Ceres Prat S.A. (Spain); Cogeneration Prat S.A. (Spain); Emmaus Pack S.r.l. (51.39%); Europoligrafico S.p.A. (91.05%); RDM RE S.A. (Luxembourg; 99.99%); Red. IM S.r.l.; Reno De Medici International S.A. (Luxembourg; 99.99%); Saffapack Sud S.r.l; Saffafrance SARL. (France; 99.58%); Sarriò GmbH (Germany); VALLI MARINE & GENERAL S.r.l.

Principal Competitors

Amcor Limited; International Paper Company; Meyr Melnhof Karton AG; Stora Enso Oyj; Svenska Cellulosa Aktiebolaget SCA; UPM-Kymmene Corporation; Van Gennecten Biermans N.V.

Further Reading

''Carton Company Acquisitions High in Europe,'' *Paperboard Packaging,* March 1998.

Patrick, Ken, ''Medici Rebuilding Board Machine at Italian Mill,'' *Pulp and Paper Online,* December 14, 2000.

''Reno de Medici Inches Closer to Startup at Spanish Site,'' *Pulp and Paper Online,* November 20, 2000.

''Sarriò Merges with Reno de Medici,'' *PPI This Week,* March 9, 1998.

—M.L. Cohen

Rica Foods, Inc.

240 Crandon Boulevard, Suite 115
Key Biscayne, Florida
U.S.A.
Telephone: (305) 365-9694
Fax: (305) 365-9399
Web site: http://www.ricafoods.com

Public Company
Incorporated: 1986 as CCR, Inc.
Employees: 3,500
Sales: $123.6 million (2000)
Stock Exchanges: American
Ticker Symbol: RCF
NAIC: 311615 Poultry Processing

Rica Foods, Inc. is the U.S. parent company of what is essentially a poultry business located in Costa Rica. With corporate headquarters in Key Biscayne, Florida, Rica Foods is composed of two subsidiaries, both operating in Costa Rica. Rica Foods is the largest producer of poultry products in Costa Rica and quickly becoming one of the largest in all of Central America and the Caribbean. The company has also gained a toehold in South America with the acquisition of a Brazilian poultry business. Rica Foods produces and markets some 600 products in three general categories. Broiler chicken is sold under a number of labels to institutional customers: schools, hospitals, grocery stores, and restaurants. In Costa Rica, the company supplies such major restaurant franchises as Burger King, Subway, Kentucky Fried Chicken, Pizza Hut, and Taco Bell. Furthermore, McDonald's has selected Rica Foods to supply chicken to all of its Central America operations. The most profitable category for the company, however, is chicken byproducts, which include sausages, bologna, chicken nuggets and patties, frankfurters, salami, and pate. These products are sold under multiple brand names to supermarkets. The Kimby brand is Costa Rica's top seller of chicken byproducts. Rica Foods also mixes unused portions of chickens with other products to produce animal feed for cows, pigs, and horses, as well as domestic pets. The company's animal feed brands are targeted both to the high-scale breeder market and pet stores and supermarkets in Costa Rica. Rica Foods is the country's leading supplier of animal feed, with 28 percent of the market. Rica Foods has also operated a restaurant chain in Costa Rica, but in 2000 elected to sell off the operation, although it retained the restaurants as customers. Finally, Rica Foods exports its chicken products, primarily to nearby countries in Central America. Exports are the means by which Rica Foods hopes to build itself into a major corporation.

Corporate Ancestor Dates to 1986

The corporation that became Rica Foods existed for ten years under a variety of names and was involved in a myriad of businesses. The company was originally incorporated in Utah in 1986 as CCR, Inc. for the general purpose of "investing in any and all types of assets, properties, and businesses." CCR made a public offering of stock in 1987. It became a holding company for three subsidiaries in 1988: W.T. Young Construction Company, Inc.; Young Trucking, Inc.; and C.C. Crane Corporation. In 1989 CCR would expand into other areas. It became involved in education with the acquisition of Direct Communications, Inc., an Oklahoma business that was licensed to market and distribute voice communications to U.S. colleges and universities. CCR formed a subsidiary, Colortex Industries, after purchasing O'Ryan Carpets for $7.9 million.

In 1991 CCR sold C.C. Crane and liquidated the Colortex operation. In October the company completed the acquisition of Cambridge Academy, Inc. in an exchange of stock. Cambridge was a nationally accredited home study high school. Its president, James K. Isenhour, now became the chief executive officer and chairman of the board of CCR. Trained as an electrician, he had worked in the electrical contracting business since the age of 23. In 1979 he was one of the founders of Cambridge Academy and in 1981 became president of the organization while simultaneously serving as the chief executive officer of Sea Coast Electric, Inc., a private family corporation. His wife, Tanzee Nahas, also served as a director of Cambridge Academy and would eventually replace him as president of the organization.

Company Perspectives:

Rica Foods, Inc. is the parent corporation of the largest producers of poultry products in Costa Rica and becoming among the largest in Central America and the Caribbean.

Under Isenhour, CCR augmented its educational business in July 1992 when it acquired Quantum Learning Systems Inc. for $7.2 million in stock. Quantum was a Florida corporation that developed and produced educational programs. A month later, CCR used stock to acquire Current Concept Seminars, Inc., which developed and produced educational programs. By the end of 1992 CCR would sell Direct Communications to Gulf Ventures, Inc. for $300,000.

In 1994 CCR sold off its trucking and construction subsidiaries for $2 million, electing to focus on its education business, as well as some real estate ventures. The company was reincorporated in 1994 in Nevada and changed its name to Quantum Learning Systems. Whatever mix of businesses this enterprise focused on, however, failed to prove successful. The company posted a net loss of $671,534 in fiscal 1995, followed by a net loss of $856,554 in fiscal 1996.

Pipasa Acquires Quantum Learning Systems in 1996

In April 1996 Quantum Learning Systems reached an agreement with the Costa Rican Pipasa corporation. First the Quantum subsidiaries were sold to the Isenhour controlled InterCoastal Financial Corporation in exchange for 50,000 shares of common stock. In effect, the original CCR corporation, since reincorporated in Utah and renamed, was now just a shell entity that Pipasa acquired to gain America legal standing and access to the U.S. capital markets. For their trouble, Isenhour and the other shareholders of Quantum gained a stake in the new corporation, renamed Costa Rica International, Inc., and its wholly owned subsidiary involved in the Costa Rican poultry industry. Costa Rica International then established a nominal headquarters in Miami, Florida, which had become a financial capital for many Latin American and Caribbean companies, and began trading its stock on the NASDAQ SmallCap Market.

Calixto Chaves, who founded Pipasa in 1969, became president and chief executive officer of Costa Rica International, with his family holding a controlling interest in the company's stock. A 1991 merger with eight other companies made Pipasa the largest poultry company in Costa Rica, with a 50 percent market share. Chaves was politically connected and a well-respected businessman in the country. He founded and served as president of Aero Costa Rica, a private Costa Rican airline. He also sat on the board of a number of Latin American companies. From 1982 to 1986 he served in the Costa Rican Ministry of Industry, Energy and Mines, and was then named Minister of Natural Resources. In 1994 he served as an advisor to the President of Costa Rica and the Ministry of Economic Business Affairs.

The establishment of Costa Rico International in the United States was in many ways a testament to the progress made by Costa Rica in the previous 50 years. Unlike many of its neighbors, Nicaragua to the north and Panama to the south, troubled by revolution and political corruption, Costa Rico had established a stable democracy, the result of the country's adoption of a modern constitution in 1948. At that time, Costa Rica also abolished the army, which in Latin America had all too often become a disruptive political force. Rather then investing in arms, the country spent its money on social services and development, and made efforts to lessen the reliance of its economy on the export of coffee and bananas. With a literacy rate of 94 percent, Costa Rica was attracting foreign investors by the mid-1990s. A major breakthrough came in 1996 when Intel chose Costa Rica over Mexico as the site for a $500 million semiconductor assembly and testing facility. Although hardly a threat to Silicon Valley, Costa Rica embraced high technology. Its businessmen began to use the Internet to sell coffee and promote tourism and other products. Some 150 small companies sprang up and began exporting software programs. Moreover, the country's liberal immigration laws and desirable lifestyle were attracting a large number of Americans and others nationalities, who also established businesses that helped drive the economy. Also unlike its neighbors, Costa Rica was posting large gains in its gross national product and enjoying low unemployment rates.

For Chaves and Costa Rica International, the move to tap the U.S. equity market was a way to grow the company's poultry business into a regional concern. Advantageously located in Central America, Costa Rica was in a perfect location to efficiently serve neighboring countries as well as the Carribean. Chicken consumption worldwide was on the rise, but there appeared to be even more opportunity in Central America. Whereas, on average Costa Ricans ate 19 kiligrams of chicken a year, the neighboring countries of El Salvador, Guatemala, Nicaragua, and Honduras consumed just 8.25 kiligrams per person. The demand for chicken would surely grow and Chaves wanted to be in a position to take advantage of it.

Costa Rica International Becomes Rica Foods, Inc. in 1998

In 1997 Costa Rica International purchased the poultry and animal feed businesses of Coopemntecillos R.L. The following year it acquired As De Oros, Costa Rica's second largest poultry producer, controlling 19 percent of the market. Costa Rica International then now controlled almost 70 percent of the country's poultry business. Several months later, Costa Rica International announced that it would change its name to Rica Foods, Inc., a move that management felt would better reflect its core business. Pipasa and As de Oros would function as two subsidiaries of the company. Also in 1998, Rica Foods announced that Pipasa reached an agreement to export some poultry products to Hong Kong for a five month period, a move that the company hope would lead to further exports to Asia. For the fiscal year 1998, Rica Foods would generate $98.97 million in revenues and post a $1.1 million profit.

In 1999 Rica Foods began trading its stock on the American Stock Exchange, a further effort to gain prestige in order to raise capital to fuel growth. The price of its stock opened at $10.50. In July 1999, As de Oros joined Pipasa in exporting products by signing an agreement to supply pet food to a major Dominican Republic supermarket chain. For the year, Rica Foods would see its 1999 sales reach $118.55 million, resulting in a $3 million net profit.

Key Dates:

1986: CCR, Inc. is incorporated in Utah.
1994: The corporate name is changed to Quantum Learning Systems.
1996: In a transfer of assets, the corporation becomes Costa Rica International with one subsidiary: Corporacion Pipasa, S.A.
1998: The company acquires Corporacion As de Oros, S.A. and changes its name to Rica Foods, Inc.
1999: Stock begins trading on American Stock Exchange.
2000: Company acquires Brazilian poultry company, Avicola Core Etuba, SRL.

Rica Foods began the year 2000 with great hopes. The company dominated its home territory and was using that success as a way to expand into emerging markets. In a forward-looking move, Rica Foods announced it would develop a poultry biotech research division, which would establish joint venture agreements with universities in the hopes of creating new revenue streams. In this vein, Pipasa acquired Karpatos S.A., a company that treated chicken manure in order to lessen the ecological effect on chicken farms, producing six types of products, including fertilizer to the Costa Rican banana industry. Combined, Pipasa and As de Oros generated 500 metric tons of manure waste each year that could thus be treated. Rica Foods also continued to search for potential takeover targets in other countries to gain market share. In May 2000 it acquired Indavinsa, a Nicaraguan poultry and animal feed concentrate company. At the same time, Chaves announced that Rica Foods was eager to enter the large Brazilian market, which held tremendous growth potential. Rica Foods also looked to the Internet in 2000. It announced that it would invest in PoultryFirst.com, a business-to-business Web site that would provide a catalog and auction environment for both buyers and sellers of poultry products. The company was owned by Chaves' son, Jose Pablo Chaves. In November 2000, Rica Foods announced that it planned to acquire 60 percent of Bounty Fresh, a company that marketed and sold fresh produce in the United States. With more than 13 years experience in exporting to Asia, Bounty Fresh provided Rica Foods with resources complimentary to its own distribution network. Then in December 2000, Rica Foods announced the acquisition of Core Etuba, SRL, a fully integrated poultry company.

By the end of 2000, however, Rica Foods had to reevaluate its position. Its stock, which had traded in the neighborhood of $30 in June, began to slide. By September it was trading around $15. When the company announced in December that its earnings for 2000 would be flat over the previous year, the stock quickly fell to the $6 range. Chaves attributed the decline to a depressed U.S. stock market in general, maintaining that the fundamentals of Rica Foods remained sound and that investors would eventually recognize the company's potential. For fiscal year 2000, Rica Foods announced that it generated revenues of $123.6 million, up 4.28 percent over the previous year, with a profit of $2.9 million. The U.S. economy, and in turn the economy of Costa Rica, were clearly not experiencing the heady growth of the late 1990s. When the company announced poor first quarter results for 2001, its stock took a further hit, falling to the $3.50 range. It had acquired an American corporate identity to gain access to the U.S. stock market, and now it had to accept the uncertainties of being a publicly traded U.S. company. Clearly, Rica Foods had to put some of its more ambitious plans on hold. It backed out of the PoultryFirst.com and Bounty Fresh deals. It did decide, however, to complete its Brazilian acquisition. Rica Food's core business remained strong, and any effort to expanded the company's market base still appeared to be a sound strategy.

Principal Subsidiaries

Corporacion Pipasa, S.A.; Corporacion As de Oros, S.A.

Principal Competitors

Industrias Bochoco SA de CV; ConAgra Foods Inc.; Pilgrim's Pride Corporation; Tyson Foods Inc.

Further Reading

Ayala, Diego, ''Costa Rica Stabilizes,'' *Global Finance,* July 2000, p. 71.

''Costa Rica International Announces Name Change and 62% Revenue Increase,'' *PR Newswire,* August 24, 1998.

''Costa Rica International, Inc. Acquires Corporacion As De Oros, S.A., The Second Largest Poultry Producer in Costa Rica,'' *PR Newswire,* March 6, 1998.

''Costa Rica Remakes Itself,'' *USA Today,* May 11, 2000, p. 15A.

Duggan, Ed, ''Rica Foods to Buy Poultry Producer,'' *South Florida Business Journal,* December 8, 2000, p. 16A.

——, ''Rica Foods Warns 2000 Earnings Flat,'' *South Florida Business Journal,* January 5, 2001, p. 14.

Fakler, John T., ''Chaves Can't Explain Rica Foods Decline,'' *South Florida Business Journal,* December 29, 2000, p. 16.

Muellner, Alexis, and John T. Fakler, ''Rica to Acquire Nicaraguan Company,'' *South Florida Business Journal,* October 27, 2000, p. 26A.

''Rica Foods Expresses Concern Over Stock Price,'' *Daily Business Review (Miami),* December 22, 2000, p. A14.

''Rica Foods' Subsidiary, Corp. PIPASA, Begins Exports to Asia,'' *PR Newswire,* October 19, 1998.

''Rica Foods Transfers to AMEX From Nasdaq Small Cap Market,'' *PR Newswire,* May 13, 1999.

Smith, Rod, ''Rica to Acquire Firm in Nicaragua, Expand Into Brazil,'' *Foodstuffs,* May 15, 2000, p. 6.

Williams, Mike, ''Costa Rica is Paradise Found For Expatriates,'' *The Atlanta Journal-Constitution,* August 20, 2000, p. C7.

—Ed Dinger

Ritchie Bros. Auctioneers Inc.

9200 Bridgeport Road
Richmond, British Columbia, V6X 1S1
Canada
Telephone: (604) 273-7564
Fax: (604) 273-6873
Web site: http://www.rbauction.com

Public Company
Incorporated: 1963
Employees: 500
Operating Revenues: $106.1 million (2000)
Stock Exchanges: New York
Ticker Symbol: RBA
NAIC: 453999 Auctioneering, with Own Facilities, Open to the General Public; 561990 Auctioneering Service, on a Commission or Fee Basis, Not Done on Own Facilities (Except Currency and Tobacco)

Ritchie Bros. Auctioneers Inc. is the world's leading auctioneer of industrial equipment. With 80 locations around the globe, the company has over 300,000 customers from 190 countries in the world. Ritchie Bros. sells an array of used industrial equipment including equipment utilized in the construction, transportation, mining, forestry, petroleum, and agricultural industries. All auctions are unreserved, public auctions.

Colorful 1960s Beginnings

The modern day Ritchie Bros. bears little resemblance to its predecessor operation of humble and colorful beginnings. It all started in Kelowna, British Columbia, in 1958. Three brothers, Dave, Ken, and John Ritchie had a history of dabbling in sales. Entrepreneurs at heart, the brothers would spare no effort to finalize the deal. Brother Dave is said to have once driven 17 hours straight through to San Diego to bring a boat back to a customer.

In time, the brothers ended up running their family's small furniture store, selling new and used furniture. One day, they complained to a friend that they were short of cash and didn't know where to find the thousand dollars needed to pay the bank. The friend suggested an auction sale. Since they had excess in their furniture inventory, the brothers held their first auction sale. The event was a success; the money was raised, and the bank was paid.

The Ritchie brothers soon began running an auction every Thursday night. It was hard work, as the furniture was heavy, and the new furniture had to be moved upstairs every Thursday to make room for the sale items. After the sale was over, the brothers would open a case of beer and begin moving the new furniture downstairs again. In the beginning, the brothers hired an auctioneer. However, the time came when the auctioneer was unavailable, so Ken Ritchie decided to do the auctioning himself. Before long, the brothers were not only organizing the auctions but doing the auctioning as well.

As their reputation grew, the Ritchies received invitations to hold sales throughout the district, and thereby moved into the disposal of forest industry plants and equipment. In turn, that brought them in contact with heavy equipment used in road building. In 1962, the Ritchie brothers noticed a void in the industrial end of the auction business and decided to try their hand in that area. They had to put up $50,000 for their first industrial auction. For years, they remembered how hard they worked in Canada's north country to get equipment to market. That first equipment auction realized a $250,000 profit.

A new milestone was reached in 1963 when the Ritchies held a highly successful industrial auction in Radium Hot Springs, British Columbia, selling over $600,000 worth of equipment. That year, the Ritchie's incorporated their thriving business. The following year, Dave Ritchie moved to the Lower Mainland to open an office in Vancouver. Ken and John remained in Kelowna and continued to play an active role in the business.

The early Canadian auctions were fraught with hazards that made for good stories. For example, there was the time Dave Ritchie went to Watson Lake in the Yukon and had to "walk out the big cats" (get the large equipment out) by building a makeshift ice bridge. On another occasion, he drove a truck for 250 miles at ten miles an hour during the frigid, Canadian winter.

Company Perspectives:

We've shown the world our innovative auction methods, our attention to detail, and our total commitment to the unreserved auction. This reputation for fair and honest auctions has instilled a confidence in our customers that they can count on Ritchie Bros. to deliver the results that they have come to expect.

The auctions themselves were events. A summertime auction held at Watson Lake was the social event of the year. Everyone in town attended, along with some 500 people from other areas. After the auction, the Ritchies rented the bridal suite of the local hotel and hosted what the *Vancouver Province* described as a ''rafter-rousing party.'' At another auction, held during a heavy snowstorm, bidders sat in their cars and honked their horns to indicate a bid. An auction held (with permission) in Kootenay National Park to auction road-building equipment ended with a steak barbecue for 300 bidders.

The earliest auctions had a ''show-biz'' flavor. The auctioneers, wearing orange hunting caps, kept up a steady patter of chatter while pieces of heavy equipment were sold. Speakers blared forth bouncy tunes and marches to energize the crowd while vendors circulated, selling drinks and snacks. After the auctions ended, the brothers packed up, like a circus, and moved the equipment out. As time passed, the auctions took on a more businesslike atmosphere, the ''show biz'' elements were abandoned.

Items typically sold at a Ritchie auction included tractors, hydraulic cranes, rock crushers, trailers, cars, trucks, aircraft, and camping equipment. Ritchie auctions were always unreserved auctions. The *Vancouver Province* quoted John Ritchie as explaining, ''No reserves. No limits. No buybacks. You buy as is. Only guarantee is a clear title.''

These early auctions were held in British Columbia, and there were only a few a year. However, following the success of the Radium Hot Springs auction, the Ritchie brothers began expanding their operations eastward. They operated sales in Alberta in 1964, Saskatchewan in 1965, Manitoba in 1966, and eastern Canada thereafter. Breaking into French speaking Quebec was a challenge, but one that was soon overcome.

The Corporate 1970s

By the early 1970s, Ritchie Bros. Auctioneers employed 25 people and was handling sales approaching C$1.5 million. Major sales were carefully planned. Ritchie employees visited the site two months ahead of the sale; they carefully cataloged the equipment, inspected it, and prepared advertising and brochures that guaranteed that the items offered were as described. The sales also featured on-spot financing for those who needed it. Remarking on the increasing organizational expertise at a Ritchie Bros. sale, one spokesperson noted in the *Vancouver Province* that ''All the major finance companies set up trailers on the site, and there is real competition for business.'' The sales began attracting bidders from Canada, the United States, and Central and South America.

In 1970, the Ritchies held their first auction sale in the United States in Beaverton, Oregon. Some C$110,000 worth of equipment was sold at the auction, marking the beginning of an expansion in North America that lasted for two decades.

By 1975, the economy in British Columbia was in a slump. Construction had slowed down severely and little road building was taking place. Many businesses were closing shop or leaving the province for greener pastures. In an interview with *BC Business Magazine,* Dave Ritchie said, ''What saves our company is, we don't rely on the buyers in BC to support us any more. We rely on the guys from Phoenix, Toronto and Edmonton. The bulk of BC contractors are working out of Alberta, now. More and more of them are moving over there. In every sale we've had here, better than 50% of the equipment has gone out of the province, 20–30% to the States, 20–30% to the rest of Canada.''

1980s–90s: International Expansion

For the next two decades, Ritchie Bros. continued to expand, forging into Europe, Asia, Australia, and the Middle East. The company opened sales offices in the Netherlands, Sweden, England, Germany, France, the Philippines, Australia, and the United Arab Emirates.

At home, in 1981, the company held a record-breaking sale of C$8 million in Edmonton, Alberta. The *Vancouver Province* reported that the company's sales had risen from $1 million a year in 1963 to a projected $100 million. Ritchie Bros. was ranked first in Canada based on volume of sales and at about fourth in North America. By that time, the company was handling about 50 percent of the auctioning of mining, forestry, oil, and machine shop equipment in Canada. Moreover, the company maintained permanent auction sites in Kamloops, British Columbia; Edmonton, Alberta; and Montreal, Quebec, as well as an operation in Portland, Oregon.

During this time, Ritchie Bros. received some of its first unfavorable press, when critics noted that the auction company thrived only when somebody somewhere went out of business. A company spokesperson, quoted in the *Globe and Mail,* admitted that ''When times are good, we do well. When times are tough, we do better.'' However, he noted, ''Ritchie Brothers helps bankrupt companies realize some money for their debtors.''

In 1987, the company held its first Ritchie Bros. auction in Europe. The sale, held in Liverpool, England, sold off equipment that had been used to rebuild the infrastructure of the Falkland Islands following the war there. Later that year, the company held its first auction in The Netherlands.

The 1990s brought several interesting auctions, along with further international expansion. In 1990, Ritchie Bros. began conducting unreserved auctions throughout the Asia-Pacific region. Ritchie auctions were held in Australia, New Zealand, the Philippines, Hong Kong, Japan, and Thailand. Moreover, Ritchie Bros. auctioned more than 20 hectares of new and used equipment accumulated by Exxon during the cleanup of the Exxon Valdez oil spill in Prince William Sound. Exxon sold most of its equipment to Ritchie Bros. for an undisclosed price, and over 8,000 bidders from around the world registered for this sale held

Key Dates:

1962: The Ritchie brothers hold their first auction.
1963: Company is incorporated.
1987: Company's first auction abroad is held in Liverpool, England.
1990: Company expands to the Asia-Pacific region.
1991: The 1,000th auction milestone is reached.
1998: Ritchie Bros. goes public on the New York Stock Exchange and celebrates its 35th anniversary.
1999: Company opens offices in Nova Scotia, South Africa, Australia, and Panama; holds first auction broadcast live on the Internet.
2000: Ritchie Bros. holds its 2,000th auction and opens a facility in Chicago.

in Anchorage, Alaska. Bidders were given a 335-page catalogue to keep track of the items, while auctioneers used a rolling, elevated, glass-enclosed booth to move through the crowds.

In 1991, Ritchie Bros. held its 1000th auction. Some of the more memorable auctions held over the next few years included the 1993 auction in Nyborg, Denmark, at which Ritchie Bros. auctioned the equipment used to build the Storebaelt Western Channel Crossing. In Hong Kong in 1996, the company auctioned the equipment used in the platform construction of the Chek Lap Kok Airport, and in 1997, Ritchie Bros. conducted Australia's largest auction to sell off mining equipment from Leo & Green Pty. Ltd. in Brisbane.

The year 1997 was particularly active for the company. In June, the auctioneers conducted a sale in Prince Edward Island, Canada, to auction the equipment used in the building of the Confederation Bridge, the bridge linking the island to the mainland of Canada. Also that month, the company held its first auction in Yokusuka City, Japan, followed, in October, by its first auction in the Middle East in Dubai, United Arab Emirates.

December 1997 marked another first for Ritchie Bros, when the company held its first videolink auction. This three-way auction allowed bidders at St. Paul, Minnesota, Beloit, Illinois and Kansas City, Missouri, to bid on equipment at any of the locations via live video conferencing. Each location provided 52-inch video screens featuring the Sony TriniCom 5100 video conferencing system. Regional manager Will Marsh said in a press release, "This is an industry first, and we're proud to make that first step in bringing industrial auctions into the high tech world. It's been years in the making."

Embracing a high-tech approach to the auction business, in late 1997 the company launched what they described as a new and improved user-friendly web page. The new site allowed visitors to enter a profile of equipment that interested them, then, on their next visit, they could instantly see where and when that equipment would be auctioned in the future. The site also offered full color brochures, an up-to-date auction calendar, and the ability to print out a "sale day" catalog.

In March 1998, Ritchie Bros. went public with an offering on the New York Stock Exchange. The offering was a success and the capital raised went towards expanding the network of facilities and to upgrade existing facilities. The next month, the company opened a new facility in Atlanta, Georgia. In September, Ritchie Bros. expanded in Canada, opening a 65-acre site at Bolton, Ontario. The new site, replacing a former Ritchie site a few minutes away, was said to be a state-of-the-art facility and the first of its kind in Canada. The facility featured 40 acres for equipment display, a 2,000-car parking lot, and seating capacity for 1,000 people. The Bolton grand opening was held in conjunction with Ritchie Bros. 35-year anniversary.

During the third quarter of 1998, the Ritchie team held its largest auction in its history. Held in Olympia, Washington, the sale grossed over $21 million. Shortly afterwards, in November, the company broke its own record, this time in Rotterdam, The Netherlands, with a sale garnering over $59 million.

In February 1999, the company purchased Forke Auctioneers, a major auctioneer of industrial equipment with headquarters in Lincoln, Nebraska. This was the first acquisition in Ritchie Bros.'s 36-year history. The Forke acquisition added sites in Florida, North Carolina, and New Mexico to the company's existing 21 sites and also provided it with the option to assume leases held by Forke on a number of auction sites.

In March 1999 the company broadcast an auction live on the Internet for the first time. The event took place during ConExpo, the Las Vegas-based premier construction and construction materials exposition. During the first two days of the show, Ritchie Bros. broadcast an auction live from Olympia, Washington, which was followed, on the third day, by broadcast of an auction in Las Vegas.

During ConExpo, Ritchie Bros. launched another update to their web site. The new site featured on-line absentee bidding. Absentee bidding had been possible previously by phone or fax, but now bidders could place their absentee bids on the web site. With live Internet broadcasting, the bidders could watch the auctions on the web and know immediately whether the bid was successful. Ritchie Bros. reported its first successful absentee bid placed over the Internet during the ConExpo auction. A buyer from Oregon placed an absentee bid on Ritchie Bros.' new web page and ended up being the successful buyer.

Also in 1999, Ritchie Bros. expanded to new markets in South America and Asia. It opened new offices in Panama and Singapore and held first-ever auctions in these locations.

The 21st Century

In 2000, Ritchie Bros. continued expansion, opening sales offices in South Africa, Jordan, and Saudi Arabia. New sites in the United States were under development in Los Angeles, Chicago, Baltimore, and Phoenix, while in Canada new sites were projected in Montreal and Edmonton. Further afield, the company hoped to establish new presences in Dubai and Singapore. In a press release to *Business Wire*, CEO David Ritchie said "Since 1997, we have invested over $100 million in our network of auction sites and increased our infrastructure in order to take Ritchie Bros. to the next level. We are about two-thirds the way through our current aggressive expansion program and I believe we are better positioned than ever to take advantage of future opportunities in the used equipment market."

In December 2000, the company experienced a new record-breaking auction at its site in Bolton, Ontario. There Ritchie Bros. realized gross auction sales of $30 million, making it the largest sale ever held by the company in Canada. Shortly thereafter, Ritchie Brothers conducted its largest agricultural sale in company history in Stratford, Ontario. After completing its final auction for 2000, the company had achieved record gross auction sales just over $1.23 billion for the year.

With 20 permanent auction sites, five regional auction units, and over 80 sales offices, Ritchie Bros. planned to continue expanding its operations globally while remaining committed to the quality of service that has worked effectively over the years. All Ritchie auctions were unreserved, meaning that the company guaranteed there would be no reserve bids, no minimums, and no owner buy-backs. Additionally, the company planned to continue offering comprehensive services covering all consignment details, including inspection and appraisals, marketing and advertising, repair or refurbish plans, lien searches, and the collection of sale day proceeds for the seller.

Principal Competitors

Neff Corporation; FreeMarkets, Inc.; Western Power and Equipment Corporation.

Further Reading

''Bruce, Alex, ''Ritchie Auctions Pull in Millions,'' *Globe & Mail*, December 8, 1984.

Ford, Ashley, ''Going Once, Going Twice,'' *Vancouver Province*, May 10, 1981.

Hays, Walt, ''BC Auctioneer Gets Big Spill-Cleanup Job,'' *Los Angeles Times*, October 11, 1990.

Moir, Nikki, ''Nothing's Too Big For Them,'' *Vancouver Province*, January 5, 1972.

Nutt, Rod, ''Ritchie Bros. to Acquire Forke Auctioneers in U.S.,'' *Vancouver Sun*, February 23, 1999.

——, ''Tough Times for Many Boon to Auction,'' *Vancouver Sun*, November 12, 1998.

''Ritchie Bros. Auctions Increase As Companies Leave,'' *BC Business*, September 1975, p. 23.

''Ritchie Bros. to Celebrate 35th Anniversary Year,'' press release, March 4, 1998.

''Ritchie IPO Makes Splash on NYSE'', *Vancouver Sun*, March 11, 1998.

Taylor, Len, ''Auction Kings Started Small,'' *Vancouver Province*, July 3, 1974, p. 13.

—June Campbell

Royal Nepal Airline Corporation

RNAC Building
P.O. Box 401
Kanti Path, Kathmandu
Nepal
Telephone: 977 1 220757
Toll Free: (800) 26NEPAL
Fax: 977 1 225348
Web sites: http://www.royalnepal.com or http://www.catmando.com/com/rnachold/rnac.htm

State-Owned Company
Founded: 1958
Employees: 2500
Sales: $110 million (2000 est.)
NAIC: 481111 Scheduled Passenger Air Transportation; 481112 Scheduled Freight Air Transportation; 481211 Nonscheduled Chartered Passenger Air Transportation; 481212 Nonscheduled Chartered Freight Air Transportation; 48799 Scenic and Sightseeing Transportation, Other; 488111 Air Traffic Control; 488119 Other Airport Operations; 48819 Other Support Activities for Air Transportation; 56172 Janitorial Services

Royal Nepal Airline Corporation (RNAC) is the state airline of Nepal, and one of the driving forces behind the country's tourist industry. Thousands arrive every year to visit the birthplace of Bhudda or to see Mount Everest, the tallest mountain in the world. Royal Nepal maintains international branches in Hong Kong, Shanghai, Singapore, Bangkok, Dubai, Frankfort, London, Osaka, Calcutta, Delhi, Bombay, and Patna. Infrastructure in the closed kingdom was very primitive at the time of RNAC's formation, and in many cases, the new air routes provided an alternative to weeks of walking between destinations. The airline has had to operate at the most rudimentary airports and has had to contend with a high local cost of fuel, which must be carried through land routes controlled by India.

Elevated Origins in the Late 1950s

To say Nepal's topography is unique would be a profound understatement. In fact, the mountainous terrain has never been traversed by railroad. Even paved roads are rare. While the elevation at the Kathmandu Airport is some 4,300 feet, some of RNAC's flights start at 12,300 feet (from Syangboche), and another runway at 9,300 feet features a 1,000-foot drop from one end to the other, making it the ultimate ski jump.

To add to the adverse flying conditions, most of RNAC's airports lack communications equipment and navigational aids. Lack of VFR (visual flying rules) meant that weather would cancel many flights. For example, in his 1991 book *Glimpses of Tourism, Airlines, and Management in Nepal,* B.R. Singh reported that 24 of the 34 airports served by Royal Nepal Airline Corporation were actually inoperative during the Monsoon season.

In the 1950s, Indian airlines were permitted to fly to Nepal's capital city, Kathmandu, as King Tribhubana Bir Bikran effected a modernization of the country's government and infrastructure. Tourists, however, were not even allowed in Nepal until 1951 (early climbers of Mt. Everest entered from Tibet); the tourism industry in Nepal only began to develop after 1960, according to P.N. Vaidya's 1987 book *Air Transport in Nepalese Perspective: A Case Study of RNAC*. By the 1980s, though, tourism would be second only to foreign aid as a source of foreign currency.

The Nepali government and private sector joined to form the Royal Nepal Airline Corporation (RNAC) on July 1, 1958 (it was formally incorporated four years later). The government's partner was a managing agent from India who held the minority share in the airline. RNAC was obliged not only to provide aviation services, but also to construct its own landing fields (the term ''airports'' would be an exaggeration for most of them).

On July 3, 1958, staffed by 97 employees, the new airline began flying a single Douglas DC-3 Dakota aircraft on several routes formerly operated by the Indian Airlines Corporation. The first towns connected were Simra, Biratnager, Pokhara, and Bhairahawa. Nepal's government was eager to accelerate the airline's expansion, and became its sole owner in October 1959.

Company Perspectives:

The company's mission is to manage the concerned air transport service inside or outside the Kingdom of Nepal in a safe, efficient, well-managed, economical and proper manner. The Corporation may exercise its power to developing air transport services so as to ensure maximum profitability and make available such services at cheap fare as far as possible.

Three months later, RNAC took over a route to Patna, India, which connected to Delhi and Calcutta.

Compilation of a Diverse Air Fleet in the 1960s

Nepal's geopolitical situation produced a strange, politically mixed fleet, which was typically financed through aid programs from the country of manufacture. Seven more DC-3s were added to the fleet between 1959 and 1964. Furthermore, China supplied a couple of AN-2 Fong Shee aircraft which did not enter scheduled service. Bell Helicopters that had been made in the United States and leased from Singapore were also used for charters. Two Russian Mi-4 helicopters also flew on scheduled routes to remote points. The route network was expanded internally and externally, soon reaching Dhaka in what was then East Pakistan.

With the arrival of a more advanced turboprop plane in 1966—the 40-passenger Dutch Fokker F-27 Friendship—RNAC commenced aerial sightseeing tours of five of the world's eight tallest mountains. Unfortunately, this plane was lost in a crash in January 1970. Despite the setback, the airline still expanded its services both internationally and domestically, soon linking some otherwise very isolated villages. A pair of Avro 748 aircraft took over the trunk routes in 1970. The next year, RNAC dispatched a handful of Canadian DHC-6 Twin Otters—a specialized STOL (short take-off and landing) plane—to airports at higher elevations. These were augmented by the even higher-performance Pilatus Porter for fields above 12,000 feet.

RNAC carried nearly 197,000 passengers in 1970–71. In 1970, Nepal reported the arrival of 46,000 tourists (not including Indian nationals, who were treated as locals in RNAC's two-tiered pricing system). Arrivals, including Indian tourists, exceeded 105,000 in 1976 and approached 163,000 by 1980.

First Jet in 1972

In 1972 RNAC acquired its first jet airliner—a Boeing 727—in cooperation with Air France. It was soon flying to Delhi, Calcutta, and Bangkok, marking the airline's first foray beyond South Asia. Nepal's increased accessibility fostered further development of a tourism industry. In January 1977, RNAC launched helicopter service to Tiger Tops National Park near the Indian border. Later that year, RNAC added jet service to Sri Lanka and Frankfurt, using leased Lufthansa jets for the Frankfurt route.

RNAC was not just bringing tourists to the country, however. It also ferried 58-ton bulldozers to Pokhara, which was inaccessible by road, for infrastructure projects there. Air mail was another important civil responsibility. RNAC carried more than 250,000 passengers and 1,700 tons of cargo in 1975–76. By the end of the 1970s, the annual passenger count had reached 400,000. Cargo traffic was virtually unchanged, held in place by equipment limitations.

RNAC's revenues were Rs 385 million in 1980–81, but the company earned just under a 1 percent return on capital. By 1983–84, however, RNAC was posting revenues of Rs 577 million and a return of 27 percent. Revenues were Rs 793.1 million for the fiscal year 1985–86. Charter traffic had grown to account for 16.4 percent of revenues, up from just 1.1 percent 15 years earlier.

Competition in the Mid-1980s

Nepal had 181,000 tourist visitors in 1985, of which 80 percent arrived by air. RNAC carried 38 percent of these tourist passengers, but that number was down from the company's peak market share of 50 percent in 1979. Indian Airlines Corporation was RNAC's main competitor, but newer entrants in the business were also competing with RNAC for market share. These companies included Singapore Airlines and Lufthansa, which started direct Kathmandu-Frankfurt service in cooperation with RNAC in October 1987.

At the time, Royal Nepal's network connected 38 domestic and 10 international destinations. RNAC was flying directly from Nepal to Hong Kong (home to many Gurkhas employed by the British Army) by 1988 via Boeing 757. In April 1988, RNAC and the CAAC (Civil Aviation Administration of China) cooperated to provide scheduled service between Kathmandu and Lhasa in the autonomous province of Tibet.

At that time, the company's fleet of 19 planes included eight Twin Otters, three Boeing 727s, and one state-of-the-art Boeing 757. The 757 was purchased in September of 1987 (Singapore Airlines and Royal Brunei were the only others also operating this advanced 757–200 variant at the time). A second 757 soon followed. The $110 million order for these two planes was Nepal's largest trade deal at the time, as reported in *Air Transport World.*

Nepal's air traffic infrastructure did not quite keep pace with its new aircraft acquisitions, though. The company's future managing director—Bali Ram Singh—would later lament that in the mid-1960s, the country was building three asphalt airports for its old DC-3s even as newer turboprop aircraft were being delivered. Furthermore, these runways were not extended for the turboprops until the early 1970s, when RNAC had already acquired its first jet aircraft.

RNAC reported revenues of $54.3 million in 1988–89, producing an operating profit of $17 million. With a workforce of 2,200, RNAC had become the country's largest employer and largest earner of foreign currency, bringing in roughly $15 million a year from abroad. Seventy-five percent of the company's passengers were foreign tourists. London, Dubai, Dhaka, Karachi, and Bombay were added to the route network in 1989.

Struggles in the 1990s

After the start of the Gulf War in 1990, RNAC helped retrieve a couple hundred countrymen who had escaped Kuwait

Key Dates:

1958: The Nepali government creates RNAC.
1966: Aerial sightseeing tours commence.
1972: RNAC begins operating its first jet airliner.
1992: Nepal's domestic market opens to competition.
1997: RNAC begins to suffer shortages of cash and planes.
2000: Aircraft leasing scandal draws protests and resignations.

for Jordan. At home, RNAC was paying $10 a gallon for fuel, which had to be trucked in through India. The airline's turnover represented one-tenth of Nepal's national budget, according to *Air Transport World.*

RNAC suffered a strike by pilots demanding more pay in February 1991. Dozens of domestic and international flights were affected. Prime Minister Krishna Prasad Bhattarai urged them to postpone their wage demands until after general elections to be held that May.

Political unrest delayed a much-needed upgrading of facilities and equipment at the airline, as well. One BAe 748 aircraft was reportedly parked at Kathmandu Airport for three years, according to *Air Transport World.* Managers longed to acquire Boeing 767s to update the aging fleet and enable nonstop service to Japan. The airline, however, was burdened with $4 million-a-month payments for its existing Boeing 757s, which accounted for nearly all of its earnings.

Half of RNAC's 645,000 passengers carried in 1990–91 were on domestic flights. Within Nepal, RNAC served 35 airfields—11 of them at tourist destinations. Due to the nature of the terrain, some of RNAC's flights had durations of less than ten minutes. Annual revenues exceeded $110 million in 1991–92. Then, the airline suffered more labor strikes in February 1992. A year later, the company terminated employees with more than 30 years seniority in order to make room for the new generation of workers.

The domestic market was liberalized in 1992, and a handful of new competitors emerged: Necon Air, Nepal Airways, Everest Air, and Himalayan Helicopters. According to R.E.G. Davies in the book *Airlines of Asia Since 1920,* by 1997 these four competitors accounted for 70 percent of Nepal's domestic air traffic.

Scheduled service to Japan was inaugurated in October 1994 with a Boeing 757 aircraft—a 15-hour trip requiring a refueling stop in Shanghai. Prior to that, RNAC had been bringing in Japanese tourists with charter flights.

The positive trend that came from inauguration of the Japan route, though, seemed to end just a few months later when a Twin Otter crashed in January 1995, killing its pilot. RNAC lost another plane, a Pilatus Porter, in November 1998. Economic constraints soon frustrated RNAC's efforts in maintaining enough jet aircraft in its fleet. Finance ministry officials declined to subsidize two new Airbus A330s worth $100 million each for the airline in April 1997. RNAC had by this time begun to post losses.

In October 1998, at the height of the tourist season, RNAC had to return a Boeing 727 when it went off lease. The scenario was repeated three months later: when management attempted to lease a Boeing 757, complete with crew, from China Southwest Airlines, RNAC's pilots launched an eleven-day strike in March and April 1999 that resulted in the lease being cancelled. RNAC went through four chief executive officers in 1998–99, while the airline's board sought a solution to the aircraft shortage and debt problem. Swirling coalition alliances in national politics likely played a hand in the high turnover at the top.

RNAC was overwhelmed when Indian Airlines suddenly suspended its operations into Nepal in December 1999 following a hijacking. Indian Airlines had typically carried 1,000 passengers to and from Kathmandu during the height of the tourist season. Thus, RNAC added its own service to Bangalore in the south of India within a year.

Adding to RNAC's struggles as the millennium approached were allegations of corruption which periodically surfaced. One case involved Dinesh Dhamija, who later founded the Ebookers Internet travel site. Dhamija had been accused of receiving his post as director of RNAC's European operations in the early 1990s on account of cronyism with Prime Minister Girija Prasad Koirala. Dhamija won a substantial settlement with the airline after a bitter court battle over these charges.

An even larger scandal revolved around the lease of a Boeing 767 aircraft from Austria's Lauda Air, which entered service in December 2000 over protests from employees and government officials. The latter claimed the deal was unnecessary since RNAC was not getting enough usage from its two existing Boeing 757s; further, the actual cost per flight hour of the Lauda jet ended up being $5,000 ($1,150 above the cost specified in the contract). RNAC chairman Haribhakta Shrestha was suspended during an investigation, along with other RNAC executives; Nepal's tourism and civil aviation minister Tarani Dutt Chataut resigned soon after.

Then another Twin Otter crashed into a hill in July 2000, killing all 25 people aboard. To add insult to injury, in October 2000 a bird strike at Tribhuvan International Airport in Kathmandu knocked out an engine on a Boeing 757, causing $60 million worth of damage. This was the second such incident in a month. Airport authorities in Nepal began hiring hunters to keep birds away by shooting them down or scaring them off with firecrackers. They blamed the presence of garbage dumps around the airport for exacerbating the problem.

As the company entered the new millennium, and its struggles seemed to continue, the topic of privatization continued to come up regularly at planning meetings—just as it had for the past twenty years. Some felt that the airline would be better equipped to deal with its obstacles if it could operate as a private corporate entity, instead of being restrained by the necessity of answering to the Nepalese government.

Principal Competitors

Asian Airlines; Bhudda Air; Everest Air; Lumbini Airways; Necon Air; Nepal Airways.

Further Reading

Adhikari, Pushpa, "Top Nepal Leaders Probed in Aviation Scam," *Times of India,* January 16, 2001.

"Airbus Could Enable RNAC to Make Non-Stop Europe Flight," *The Rising Nepal,* June 21, 2000.

"Bangalore-Kathmandu Flight Will Take Off," *Times of India,* May 27, 2000.

Chhabra, Rahul, "Thousands Stranded in Nepal," *Times of India,* December 31, 1999.

Davies, R.E.G., "Nepal's Airlines of the Himalayas," *Airlines of Asia Since 1920,* London: Putnam, 1997, pp. 89–94.

"India: Mount Everest Now Just a Flight Away," *The Hindu,* November 3, 2000.

"India: Nepal Mulls Airlines Revamp," *Business Line,* April 30, 2001.

Ionides, Nicholas, "Royal Nepal Gets Fourth New Boss in One Year," *Air Transport Intelligence,* January 14, 1999.

Kang Siew Li, "Nepal Steps Up Marketing Drive to Woo Tourists," *Business Times (Malaysia),* Nation Sec., July 15, 1996, p. 3.

Lester, Valerie, "Bhakus and Saris," *Airways,* July 1998, pp. 48–52.

McMillan, Ben, "Aircraft Shortage Hits Royal Nepal Airlines," *Air Transport Intelligence,* November 2, 1998.

——, "Nepal Examines Privatization of National Carrier," *Air Transport Intelligence,* November 18, 1998.

Mathews, Neelam, "Nepal Optimistic Over Air Service," *Travel Trade Gazette Asia,* November 17, 2000.

"Nepal Deploys Hunters to Avoid Air Crashes," *United Press International,* October 3, 2000.

"Nepali Minister Resigns Over Airline Lease Scam," *Times of India,* January 26, 2001.

Phadnis, Ashwini, "Royal Nepal's Bangalore Flight Plan Hits Snag," *Business Line,* May 10, 2000.

Proctor, Paul, "Royal Nepal Primes for Tourism Growth," *Aviation Week & Space Technology,* November 9, 1992, pp. 40.

"RNAC Angers Nepal Trade," *Travel Trade Gazette Asia,* October 23, 1998.

Shrestha, Ganga B., "Restructuring and Privatization of RNAC," June 2000, http://www.privat.gov.np/comments/comm11.html.

Singh, B.R., *Glimpses of Tourism, Airlines, and Management in Nepal,* New Delhi: Nirala Publications, 1991.

Vaidya, P.N., *Air Transport in Nepalese Perspective: A Case Study of RNAC,* Kathmandu: Bina Vaidya, 1987.

Vandyk, Anthony, "Neglect in Nepal," *Air Transport World,* January 1992, p. 96.

——, "Room (For Growth) at the Top of the World," *Air Transport World,* March 1990, pp. 100–105.

"Visit Nepal '98 Garners Mixed Accolades," *Travel Trade Gazette Asia,* January 15, 1999.

Walsh, Conal, "How Ebookers' Boss Won Cronyism Row in Nepal," *Sunday Business,* July 16, 2000, p. 9.

—Frederick C. Ingram

Royal Vopak NV

Blaak 333
3011 GB Rotterdam
The Netherlands
Telephone: (+31) 10 400-2911
Fax: (+31) 10-413-9829
Web Site: http://www.vopak.com

Public Company
Incorporated: 1999
Employees: 12,500
Sales: EUR 4.15 billion ($3.91 billion) (2000)
Stock Exchanges: Euronext Amsterdam
Ticker Symbol: VPK
NAIC: 541614 Process, Physical Distribution, and Logistics Consulting Services

Created from the merger of Dutch logistics specialists Van Ommeren and Pakhoed NV in 1999, Royal Vopak NV is the world's leading provider of logistics and distribution services to the global chemicals and oil industries. Based in Rotterdam, one of the world's busiest ports, the company's operations include a fleet of nearly 250 ships, 3,000 tank containers, 240 chemical distribution terminals, and storage capacity of nearly 24 million cubic meters available through its network of 70 terminals worldwide. The company's major divisions include Oil and Gas Logistics, which provides storage and logistics services not only for mineral oils and gas, but also for vegetable oils, animal fats, and chemical gases. Vopak's shipping fleet ranges from its 50-vessel strong barge fleet, to short sea and deep sea vessels. The company's Chemicals Logistics division is the world leader in that market, providing total capacity of more than 7.1 million cubic meters, as well as specialized shipping vessels for barging, short sea and deep sea shipping. Related to this division is the Vopak Logistics Services division, which specializes in providing services to the chemicals industry. The final major Vopak division is its Chemical Distribution wing, which is the market leader in the United States and in Western Europe. The creation of Royal Vopak was an important step toward the consolidation of the still highly fragmented chemical and oil logistics industry at the end of the 20th century.

Porter's Association in the 17th Century

The origins of Royal Vopak lay in the early 17th century, at the height of the golden era of Dutch trading activities. The most famous of the great Dutch trading houses established during this time was the Oost-Indische Compagnie (East India Company). That company also helped create Amsterdam as one of Europe's major port cities. In 1616, a group of porters, who carried goods between Oost-Indische vessels and Amsterdam's weighing house, joined together to form the Blauwhoed (''blue hat'') company. Over the next three centuries Blauwhoed added to its activities by offering storage facilities, before establishing itself as one of the Netherlands's major stevedoring, port services, and cargo agents. Blauwhoed also built up a strong real estate portfolio—an activity that continued to be carried out under the Blauwhoed name into the 21st century.

If the Dutch trading houses lost out to the rise of the United Kingdom as the world's shipping leader, the Netherlands remained a key player in worldwide trade. A number of other companies joined Blauwhoed in the port services, storage, and related markets—particularly as the country's port activity slowly shifted to the more modern Rotterdam port. A newcomer to the industry was Pakhuismeesteren (''warehouse masters''), which was formed in Rotterdam in 1818. Pakhuismeesteren originally focused on loading and unloading ships, as well as on offering storage facilities for tea, coffee, spices and other goods arriving from the Dutch colonies. Later in that century, Pakhuismeesteren began offering storage services for the rising oil industry. By 1888, propelled by the invention of the internal combustion engine, that industry began to take off, and Pakhuismeesteren began storing oil and oil products in bulk tanks.

By then, another company had joined the Dutch port services industry. Set up in 1839, Van Ommeren operated as a shipping and forwarding agent. Throughout that century and into the next, Van Ommeren expanded steadily, building up its own deep sea shipping and inland barging fleet. It also became one of the Netherlands' leading stevedoring and distribution

Company Perspectives:

Vopak aims to be the global supplier of logistics and distribution services to the chemical and oil industry. This requires the capability to provide efficient, high-quality, integrated services worldwide, with the highest safety and environmental standards. In chemicals, Vopak sets out to be the interface between producers and end-users, both as a logistics service provider and as a distributor.

companies. At the beginning of the 20th century, Van Ommeren also began tank storage operations, a market in which it quickly became a leading force. Further south in Europe, Lambert Rivière was founded in 1880, beginning its own chemical distribution activities that were to make it one of Southern Europe's leaders.

Merging Interests in the 20th Century

Another important element of the eventual Royal Vopak was founded in 1924 in Seattle, Washington, when George Van Waters and Nat Rogers began a brokerage operation in the Pacific Northwest region of the United States. This company—Van Waters & Rogers—started out handling products such as paint, naval stores and various raw materials, before turning to chemical distribution. The Van Waters & Rogers business spread quickly throughout the western United States before expanding into the eastern part of the country. By the time it entered the Canadian market in the 1950s, Van Waters & Rogers had already gained a leading position in the North American chemical distribution market.

The destruction of Rotterdam at the beginning of World War II and its subsequent reconstruction after the war, created Rotterdam not only as the Netherlands' major port, but also as one of the world's most modern and busiest ports. The rise of the oil and chemicals industries during the postwar years gave new opportunities to companies such as Blauwhoed, Pakhuismeesteren and Van Ommeren to provide extensive storage, shipping and other logistics services to these industries.

Increasing competition around the world led Blauwhoed and Pakhuismeesteren to join forces in 1967, creating Pakhoed NV. The newly expanded company combined its predecessors' strengths in storage facilities, including warehouse storage and oil and chemical storage, stevedoring, and other port support services. Pakhoed's interests in developing a full-fledged chemicals distribution wing coincided with its plan to expand its operations into the North American market. In the mid-1980s, Pakhoed took a step toward these objectives when it acquired the option to buy up the United States' distribution specialist—McKesson Corporation. Rather than exercise the option to buy McKesson, in 1986 Pakhoed instead sold the purchase option to Van Waters & Rogers in exchange for a 35 percent share in the enlarged U.S. company. By then, Van Waters & Rogers had established itself as North America's leading chemicals distribution company. Van Waters & Rogers' acquisition of McKesson set the stage for the creation of a larger holding company, Univar Corporation.

Univar had decided to enter the European market at the beginning of the 1990s. Joining with Pakhoed, Univar's partners acquired Sweden's Beyer, and formed Univar Europe NV. Pakhoed's share in that company was 49 percent, to Univar Corporation's 51 percent—while Pakhoed's share in Univar Corporation itself was reduced to 28 percent. Soon after, Pakhoed sold its share of Univar Europe back to Univar Corporation. The proceeds of this sale gave Pakhoed the capital to make a new attempt at entering the European chemicals distribution arena. In 1995, Pakhoed acquired France's Lambert Rivière, which—through its acquisitions of such rivals as Italy's UCE in 1989—had established a leading position in the southern European market, with sales of more than FFr 1 billion per year.

More Restructuring at the Approach of the New Millennium

Univar's attempts to consolidate and centralize its operations through the first half of the 1990s brought its profits into a slide. The resulting weak price in Univar's shares finally gave Pakhoed the opportunity to acquire full control of Univar Corporation in 1996. This move gave Pakhoed not only a leading share of the chemicals distribution industry in the North American market, but also a strong position across much of western Europe.

Van Ommeren, meanwhile, had attempted its own diversification in the late 1970s and early 1980s, in an attempt to counter the fluctuations in its core shipping and tank storage operations. But the company's diversification moves—notably through investments in various trading companies—proved to be unsatisfactory, and at the beginning of the 1990s the company decided to restructure and return to its main shipping and tank storage operations. As Van Ommeren divested its newly non-core operations throughout the 1990s, it also expanded its shipping operations into new areas. One such new area was an entrance into liquid cargo transportation activities, which complemented its tank storage facilities.

Consolidation within the oil and chemicals industries in the 1990s—and a wider trend toward the creation of growing numbers of globally operating companies—sparked interest in the consolidation of the related logistics, storage and distribution industries. Van Ommeren and Pakhoed first began merger talks in 1998, but that merger was soon called off when the two companies could not decide on a divestment program needed to comply with a European Commission anti-monopoly directive.

By 1999, however, Van Ommeren and Pakhoed were back together again—as continued mergers among both companies' customers had begun leading to a shrinking client base throughout the industry. Van Ommeren and Pakhoed completed their merger in 1999, adopting the name Royal Vopak. The company immediately launched a divestment and restructuring plan, including the sale of a number of the company's Rotterdam, Antwerp and other storage facilities.

At the same time, Royal Vopak began a new acquisition campaign, buying up such companies as Roland NV of Belgium (chemicals distributors) and Dystrybucja of Poland in 1999. Royal Vopak also completed ownership deals in other companies, such as the acquisition of full control of Chemgas Holding BV and Van Ommeren Gas Shipping Holding Singapore Pte.

Key Dates:

1616: Formation of Blauwhoed (''Blue Hat'') storage and transportation company.
1818: Creation of Pakhuismeesteren (''warehouse masters'') concern to load and unload ships.
1839: Launch of Van Ommeren concern, a shipping agent.
1880: Founding of chemical distributor Lambert Rivière.
1888: Pakhuismeesteren begins offering bulk tank storage facilities.
1924: Founding of Van Waters & Rogers, a Seattle-based brokerage for the Pacific Coast.
1967: Blauwhoed and Pakhuismeesteren merge to form Pakhoed.
1986: Pakhoed acquires 35 percent of Van Waters & Rogers/Univar.
1991: Pakhoed and Univar acquire Beyer (Sweden) and form Univar Europe.
1995: Pakhoed exits Univar Europe, acquires Lambert Rivière.
1996: Pakhoed acquires full control of Univar.
1998: Van Ommeren and Pakhoed call off first merger attempt.
1999: Van Ommeren and Pakhoed merge and form Royal Vopak NV.
2001: Royal Vopak acquires Ellis & Everard.

Ltd.—also known as Vogas—in 2000. The company also began buying up terminals and storage facilities, including terminals in Brazil, Mexico, Peru and elsewhere.

The newly combined company reported strong sales after its first full year. With revenues of more than EUR 4 billion, Royal Vopak maintained its leading position in its core markets. Nevertheless, Royal Vopak's market share of only some 5 percent in the highly fragmented oil and chemicals logistics segments meant plenty of room for the company to grow in the new century.

Immediately, Royal Vopak attempted to do just that. The company started the 21st century strongly, with the acquisition of the United Kingdom's Ellis & Everard. This boosted its chemical distribution capacity both in Europe and in North America. Then, duking it out with main rivals Ashland Inc. and Stinnes AG, Royal Vopak continued to make plans for acquisitions to maintain its lead. The company planned on especially targeting its chemical distribution operations over the years to come.

Principal Subsidiaries

Vopak USA Inc.; Vopak Canada Ltd.

Principal Operating Units

Oil and Gas Logistics; Chemical Logistics; Chemical Distribution North America; Chemical Distribution Europe.

Principal Competitors

Ashland Inc.; BT Shipping Limited; CHEMCENTRAL Corporation; Chemical Logistics Corporation; Croda International Plc; GATX Corporation; Helm AG; Odfjell ASA; Stinnes AG; Stolt-Nielsen S.A.

Further Reading

Change, Chang, ''Vopak Leads Consolidation in Chemical Distribution,'' *Chemical Market Reporter*, November 20, 2000.

Daily, Matt, ''Vopak Profits Rise, Sees Stronger 2001,'' *Reuters*, March 7, 2001.

Markarian, Jennifer, ''Vopak (Statistical Data Included),'' *Chemical Market Reporter*, November 20, 2000.

Milmo, Sean, ''Van Ommeren and Pakhoed Plan to Merge: Creation of World's Largest Distributor Could Trigger More Consolidation,'' *Chemical Market Reporter*, March 9, 1998.

Morris, Gregory, et. al., ''Dutch Treat in Distribution,'' *Chemical Week*, September 25, 1996.

Onstad, Eric, ''Dutch Shippers Pakhoed, Van Ommeren to Merge,'' *Reuters*, July 5, 1999.

''Vopak Launch Seals Long-Awaited Link,'' *Reuters*, November 4, 1999.

Young, Ian, ''Second Time Lucky for Vopak,'' *Chemical Week*, December 1, 1999.

—M.L. Cohen

Saks Inc.

750 Lakeshore Parkway
Birmingham, Alabama 35211
U.S.A.
Telephone: (205) 940-4000
Fax: (205) 940-4987
Web site: http://www.saksincorporated.com

Public Company
Incorporated: 1919
Employees: 55,000
Sales: $6.58 billion (2000)
Stock Exchanges: New York
Ticker Symbol: SKS
NAIC: 45211 Department Stores

Saks Inc., formerly Proffitt's, Inc., is one of the largest operators of department stores in the United States. Aside from its namesake Saks Fifth Avenue stores, the company also runs the Proffitt's chain, with close to 30 stores; the 50-store Younkers chain; Carson Pirie Scott, with more than 30 stores; the 40-store Herberger's chain; 40 specialty department stores called Parisian; the smaller chains Boston Store and Bergner's, as well as approximately 50 outlet stores under the name Off 5th. The company also has a mail-order and e-business division. This handles two catalogs, *Folio* and *Bullock & Jones,* and sells over the Internet at www.saks.com. As Proffitt's, Inc., the company grew from a small chain of Tennessee retailers into a complex of department store chains with markets across much of the Southeast and Midwest. The company acquired Saks Holdings in 1998, and changed its name that year.

Under the Proffitt Family: 1919–84

Proffitt's was founded in 1919 by David W. Proffitt. It was a department store in Maryville, Tennessee (near Knoxville) selling everything from clothing and bedding to furniture and farm implements. Evidently no place for sophisticates, it attracted customers to anniversary sales during the 1920s and 1930s by hurling live poultry from its second floor windows. Another Proffitt's was opened later in Athens, Tennessee.

D.W.'s son Harwell took charge of Proffitt's in 1958. He closed the Maryville store in 1962, moving to a strip shopping center his family had developed a mile away in suburban Alcoa. ''My father thought that was awful,'' he told a (Norfolk) *Virginian-Pilot* reporter in 1993. ''Then, after we doubled our sales, he thought it was just great.''

Proffitt's opened a store in Knoxville's first mall in 1972 and a store in Oak Ridge two years later. In 1984, when a fifth store opened in another Knoxville mall, D.W.'s heirs, including another son and daughter, began looking for a buyer who would keep the family on as managers. They found their man in Brad Martin, who, at the age of 21, became in 1972 the youngest state legislator in Tennessee history. While serving in the state assembly for ten years he earned two degrees, pieced together deals to build shopping centers in three states, and became a venture capitalist. Martin and his partners bought Proffitt's in October 1984 for $14 million. At this time the company had annual sales of about $40 million.

First Expansion Moves: 1987–93

After Martin pulled out of a planned race for governor in 1986, he began to take a more active role in his investment. He succeeded Harwell Proffitt as chairman of the company in 1987 and Harwell's son, Fred, as chief executive officer in 1989. Proffitt's went public in 1987, offering 28 percent of its common stock at $8 a share. The company had record net sales of $43.5 million and net income of $1.4 million in fiscal 1987 (the year ended January 31, 1987) but also had a long-term debt of $18.4 million.

The $8 million or so raised by public subscription enabled Proffitt's to buy the Loveman's, Inc. five-unit chain, based in nearby Chattanooga, in 1988 for $9.3 million in cash and notes. Proffitt's thereby doubled in size overnight but also assumed Loveman's considerable debt, weakening earnings in 1989 and 1990. During 1990 Proffitt's also opened stores in Chattanooga and Asheville, North Carolina, but closed an unprofitable store in Chattanooga.

By selling more stock at $12 a share in 1992, Martin raised an added $29 million. He then bought eight stores from Hess

Company Perspectives:

Saks Inc. is one of the country's premier retail enterprises, operating 354 stores in 39 states, with over $6.5 billion in annual revenues and 55,000 associates.

Department Stores Inc.—seven in eastern Tennessee and the eighth in Bristol, Virginia. In April 1993 Proffitt's bought eight more stores from Hess—five in the Hampton Roads area of Virginia, two in Kentucky, and one in Georgia—for $7.4 million, selling more stock to finance the purchase and to pay for store renovations. Two months later Proffitt's bought two more Hess stores in Richmond, Virginia, for about $1.6 million.

This acquisition proved to be one of Martin's few mistakes because Hess's unprofitable stores cut into company income. Revenues rose from $128 million in fiscal 1993 to $201 million in fiscal 1994, but net income dropped from $6.7 million to $5.7 million. In December 1996 Dillard Department Stores agreed to buy the Hampton Roads and Richmond stores for an undisclosed sum, and Proffitt's took a $2 million aftertax charge on the sale.

McRae's Acquisition: 1994

Martin's next move was bolder. In March 1994 he purchased McRae's, Inc., a retailer about twice Proffitt's size, for $176 million in cash and $32 million in notes. Founded in 1902 by Samuel P. McRae in Jackson, Mississippi as a dry goods store, McRae's was a privately held chain with 28 stores (compared with Proffitt's 25) in Mississippi, Alabama, Louisiana, and Florida with $419 million in sales in 1993. It was strong in home furnishings, men's apparel, and cosmetics. Thirteen of its 14 Alabama stores had been purchased from Pizitz, Inc. in 1987. In acquiring McRae's, Proffitt's assumed about $109 million in long-term debt and other financing and also paid $18 million to purchase four regional mall stores owned by McRae family partnerships. The McRae's stores retained their name and operated as a subsidiary.

Despite the high price Proffitt's paid, investor reaction was favorable. McRae's was regarded as one of the most successful family-owned businesses in the United States, its sales having grown from only $1 million in 1955 to $10 million in 1970. Just months before the sale, Richard McRae, Jr., president and chief executive officer, told the *Daily News Record,* "Our debt-to-equity ratio is the lowest it's been since the early 1970s, yet all of our growth has been from internal financing. We are sound. No one has ever lost a dollar by selling McRae's. . . . In fact, we have a higher Dun & Bradstreet rating than any of our competitors."

Younkers Acquisition: 1996

With the acquisition of McRae's, Proffitt's revenues swelled to $617 million in fiscal 1995, and its net income grew to $16.1 million. In April 1995 Proffitt's acquired a majority interest in Parks-Belk Co., owner and operator of four Tennessee department stores. But this transaction paled in relation to Proffitt's purchase, in February 1996, of Younkers, Inc., a Midwestern 53-store chain with annual sales slightly larger than Proffitt's own.

Based in Des Moines, Iowa, Younkers had a history even longer than Proffitt's or McRae's, dating back to 1856. Acquired by Equitable of Iowa in 1979, it became an independent company again in 1992 but soon found itself the object of a takeover bid by Carson, Pirie Scott & Co. Younkers's management turned down Carson's offer of about $163 million for the company, but succumbed to Proffitt's bid of $216 million. Like McRae's, Younkers continued to operate under its own name as both a division and a subsidiary of Proffitt's. Counting Younkers, Proffitt's revenues for fiscal 1996 surpassed $1.3 billion. Younkers was described by Martin as a "fashion-driven" business. Proffitt's converted its shoe departments from leased to in-house, and Martin said there were opportunities for the chain to grow in cosmetics and accessories.

Parisian Acquisition: 1996

Hardly had Martin completed the Younkers acquisition when he purchased Parisian, Inc., a 38-store chain in the Southeast and Midwest with annual sales of $675 million, for $110 million in cash, $100 million in stock, and assumption of $243 million in debt. Well regarded for quality and customer service, Parisian began as a Birmingham, Alabama fabric store in 1887. It was acquired by the Hess and Hollner families in 1920. Until 1963 Parisian was a single store, but over the next 14 years it built a network of a half-dozen stores, all in Alabama.

Parisian sold stock to the public for the first time in 1983. It was acquired in a leveraged buyout by Australia-based Hooker Corp. in 1988, but after Hooker filed for bankruptcy the following year, Birmingham's Hess and Abroms families bought it back, with investment from Lehman Merchant Bank Partners. The new owners opened stores in Atlanta, Indianapolis, Cincinnati, suburban Detroit, Nashville, and Orlando. Because of the large debts inherited from Hooker and disappointing 1994 results, Standard & Poor's placed $125 million in notes issued by the company on its CreditWatch. The company lost $5.5 million in 1994 but returned to profitability the next year, earning $8.8 million.

Like Younkers and McRae's, Parisian became a division and subsidiary of Proffitt's, but its corporate offices were moved to Jackson. Martin indicated that Parisian would be the company's upscale division and that home furnishings might be added to what had been almost purely an apparel chain. Interviewed by *WWD* in 1997, he said, "We see it as the premier specialty store, with many resources that aren't in traditional department stores." Parisian President and Chief Executive Officer Donald Hess remained president and joined Proffitt's board of directors.

Herberger's and Carson Pirie Scott: 1996–97

Proffitt's topped off 1996 by agreeing, in November, to acquire G.R. Herberger's for $153 million. Based in St. Cloud, Minnesota, Herberger's was a chain of 40 department stores in ten Midwestern and Western states that became Proffitt's fifth division. Strong in women's, children's, and moderately priced men's apparel, Herberger's was scheduled to develop lines in shoes and cosmetics. Martin indicated that it would focus on branded businesses, adding name brands such as Nautica, Ralph Lauren, and Tommy Hilfiger.

Key Dates:

1919: David Proffitt founds first store in Maryville, Tennessee.
1987: Brad Martin buys five-store Proffitt's chain.
1988: Firm makes first major acquisition, buying Loveman's, Inc.
1996: Proffitt's buys Younkers chain, moving the company into the Midwest for first time.
1998: In its biggest acquisition yet, the firm acquires Saks Holdings, and changes its name to Saks Inc.

Founded in 1927, the chain was sold by the Herberger family in 1972, a year in which it consisted of 11 department stores and six fabric stores with $17 million in sales. In subsequent years it made a transition from downtown locations to anchor tenant in regional malls. In 1993, when the company had sales of $265 million and income of $5.5 million, it was about 55 percent owned by an employee stock option plan. About 450 employees, including officers and directors, owned the rest of the stock. Herberger's had revenues of $327 million in 1995. The acquisition was ratified as Proffitt's ended its 1997 fiscal year in early February 1997. Because of its acquisitions, Proffitt's in fiscal 1996 more than doubled its revenues. The company lost $6.4 million after special charges of $31.4 million, including merger, restructuring, and integration costs of $20.8 million. During fiscal 1997 Proffitt's had net income of $37.4 million on sales of $1.89 billion. Its long-term debt was $510.8 million in November 1996.

As fiscal 1997 ended on February 3 of the calendar year, Proffitt's had 19 stores in its Proffitt's division (12 in Tennessee), 29 in the McRae's division (14 in Alabama and 12 in Mississippi), 48 in the Younkers division (18 in Iowa and 17 in Wisconsin), 40 in the Parisian division (15 in Alabama), and 39 in the Herberger's division (14 in Minnesota). A Proffitt's Merchandising Group had recently been formed to coordinate merchandising planning and execution, as well as visual, marketing, and advertising activities between the merchandising divisions. Certain departments in Proffitt's stores were being leased to independent companies and included fine jewelry, beauty salon, and maternity departments. During fiscal 1997 women's apparel was the leading sales category in all five Proffitt's divisions. Men's apparel ranked second in all but the Proffitt's division, where it trailed cosmetics. The other categories, in order of overall sales, were home furnishings, cosmetics, children's apparel, accessories, shoes, and lingerie.

Next the company went for another Midwestern retailer, the Chicago-based Carson Pirie Scott chain. In November 1997 Proffitt's offered $790 million in stock for Carson's, which had 52 stores in Illinois, Wisconsin, Indiana, and Minnesota. Carson's was a regional chain, much like the other Southern and Midwestern department store chains Proffitt's had picked up earlier. Carson's was a big retailer, with 1997 sales of $1.1 billion, and its acquisition vaulted Proffitt's into the number four spot in department store retailing, behind Federated, May Department Stores, and Dillard's Inc.

Saks Inc. in the Late 1990s and After

Proffitt's growth had been tremendous after Brad Martin took over the company. Starting with the acquisition of Loveman's in 1988, Proffitt's had been growing nonstop. Barely a year separated the Herberger's deal from the buyout of Carson's, and about a month after the Carson's transaction was finalized in February 1998, Proffitt's bought up the small North Carolina retail chain Brody's. But the biggest deal of all came later in 1998, with the acquisition of the preeminent New York retailer Saks Fifth Avenue. Saks Fifth Avenue was a storied New York store, with a high fashion pedigree that Proffitt's previous acquisitions lacked. Saks had been owned since 1990 by an investment group based in Bahrain, Investcorp. Investcorp. had previously owned the luxury retailers Gucci and Tiffany, and it expected to handle Saks like it had these others: run it for a few years, then cash out. But Saks apparently lacked retail focus, and it was not consistently profitable. It went public in 1996, but its stock did not do well. It had grown to close to 100 stores, including more than 40 outlet stores called Off 5th, when its owners decided to put it up for sale. Proffitt's was quick to offer a stock swap estimated at about $2.1 billion for the chain. The deal was consummated in a matter of months, and in late 1998 Proffitt's changed its corporate name to Saks Incorporated. Industry analysts were divided about the wisdom of the merger. On the one hand, Saks was wildly different from Proffitt's previous acquisitions, which had filled the moderate-to-better niche. Saks offered cutting-edge couture, with almost no merchandise overlap with any other Proffitt's chains. On the other hand, Saks had been run by bankers since 1990, and perhaps it would prosper even more under the guidance of an experienced retailer like Proffitt's. Proffitt's Brad Martin promised he could save Saks around $65 million by combining some financial and management functions with his other chains.

But the Saks Fifth Avenue acquisition did not go as smoothly as most of the company's others. A year after the merger, Saks Inc.'s stock had fallen 55 percent. Problems with Saks Fifth Avenue merchandise led the company to post lower than expected earnings. The company admitted that it was having trouble integrating the luxury retailer with its other operations. Although same-store growth increased overall by 4 percent in 1999, the rate was lower than Saks Inc.'s management expected or desired. In August 2000, Saks Inc. announced that it would spin off Saks Fifth Avenue into a separate, publicly owned company with New York headquarters. The new entity would include the Saks Fifth Avenue stores, the Off 5th outlet stores, and the chain's e-business and catalog division. But this plan was short-lived. In early 2000 Saks Fifth Avenue sales were growing, while other chains such as Younkers and Carson's were declining. The fourth quarter of 2000 told a different story, with 1.3 percent same-store sales growth at the regional chains and a drop of 3.4 percent for the upscale Saks. With the luxury goods sector in general declining, and with the Saks.com web site pulling in losses of around $7 million, the spin-off no longer seemed a safe bet. Saks Inc. canceled the split-up in early 2001. At the same time, it sold nine of its Southern regional stores, including five Proffitt's, three Parisians, and one McRae's, to the May Department Stores Co. for $310 million.

Principal Subsidiaries

Parisian, Inc.; Younkers, Inc.; G.R. Herberger's Department Stores; McRae's, Inc.; Proffitt's, Inc.; Boston Store; Boston Store Department Stores; Carson Pirie Scott & Co.; Saks Fifth Avenue.

Principal Competitors

May Department Stores Co.; Dillard's Inc.; Federated Department Stores, Inc.

Further Reading

''Accord Is Signed to Acquire Herberger's for $153 Million,'' *Wall Street Journal,* November 11, 1996, p. B4.

Barr, Elizabeth, ''Proffitt's Signs Agreement to Buy Loveman's,'' *Daily News Record,* March 10, 1988, p. 11.

Carey, Susan, ''Saks Backs Away from Spinning Off Fifth Avenue Stores,'' *Wall Street Journal,* February 9, 2001, p. B7.

Clark, Ken, ''Dept. Stores Unite: Carson's Said to Fit Well with Proffitt's,'' *HFN,* November 3, 1997, p. 1.

Diel, Stan, ''Chain Buys Parisian,'' *Birmingham News,* July 9, 1996, pp. 1A-2A.

Dinsmore, Christopher, ''Brad Martin: Pushing Proffitt's to the Max,'' *Virginian-Pilot,* Bus. Sec., June 13, 1993.

Faircloth, Anne, ''Confederates Take Fifth Avenue,'' *Fortune,* October 12, 1998, p. 152.

Hazel, Debra, ''Man with a Mission,'' *Chain Store Age,* August 1996, pp. 41–43.

Hierlmaier, Christine, ''Herberger's Legacy Lives, Thanks to CEO,'' *St. Cloud Times,* January 30, 1997, pp. C6+.

Kaufman, Leslie, ''New Owners of Saks Acknowledge Rough Spots,'' *New York Times,* August 19, 1999, pp. C1, C6.

Lawson, Skippy, ''Keeping It Friendly,'' *Women's Wear Daily (WWD),* March 26, 1991, pp. 6–7.

Lee, Georgia, ''Dillard's to Acquire 7 Proffitt's,'' *WWD,* December 16, 1996, pp. 2–3.

——, ''Proffitt's Power Play,'' *WWD,* February 3, 1997, pp. 8–9.

Lloyd, Brenda, ''McRae's Plans to Acquire Pizitz,'' *Daily News Record,* December 11, 1986, p. 2.

Moin, David, ''Proffitt's Offers $2.1B in Stock to Acquire Saks,'' *WWD,* July 6, 1998, p. 1.

Palmieri, Jean E., ''Men's Wear a Bigger Part of McRae's Overall Sales,'' *DNR,* September 15, 1993, p. 3.

——, ''Proffitt's Takes Unorthodox Road to Bigger Profits,'' *DNR,* February 17, 1997, pp. 24, 26, 48–50.

''Proffitt's To Acquire 8 Units in Tenn., Va. from Hess's,'' *WWD,* October 27, 1992, p. 12.

''Saks Inc. Appoints Christina Johnson CEO and President,'' *Wall Street Journal,* November 10, 1999, p. B19.

''Saks Inc. Says Daniel Resigned from Post as Top Merchandiser,'' *Wall Street Journal,* September 23, 1998, p. B18.

''Saks Inc. Spinning Off Saks Fifth Avenue,'' *Marketing News,* August 14, 2000, p. 21.

''Saks Profit Falls 54%, Hurt by Weak Sales at Its Flagship Stores,'' *Wall Street Journal,* March 14, 2001, p. B7.

Setton, Dolly, ''Saks Alabama,'' *Forbes,* November 1, 1999, p. 460.

Strom, Stephanie, ''Proffitt's Department Stores to Buy McRae's Retail Chain,'' *New York Times,* March 4, 1994, p. D4.

Underwood, Jerry, '' 'Class Retailer' Built on 'Good Name, Reputation,' '' *Birmingham News,* July 9, 1996, pp. 1A-2A.

Wieffering, Eric J., ''The Wealthiest Minnesotans,'' *Corporate Report Minnesota,* August 1994, pp. 34+.

Williams, Roy, ''Parisian Looks on Bright Side,'' *Birmingham News,* January 22, 1995, p. D1.

Zissu, Alexandra, ''Proffitt's Sees Payoff on Money Spent,'' *WWD,* February 19, 1997, p. 30.

—Robert Halasz
—update: A. Woodward

Samsung Electronics Co., Ltd.

250-2 ga, Taepyung-ro Chung-gu
Seoul 100-742
South Korea
Telephone: (82) 2 727-7114
Fax: (82) 2 727-7985
Web site: http://www.samsungelectronics.com

Wholly Owned Subsidiary of Samsung Group (South Korea)
Founded: 1969
Employees: 55,000
Sales: $26 billion (2000)
Stock Exchanges: Seoul
Ticker Symbol: SEC
NAIC: 333295 Semiconductor Machinery Manufacturing; 333911 Pumps and Pumping Equipment Manufacturing; 334111 Electronic Computer Manufacturing; 334119 Other Computer Peripheral Equipment Manufacturing; 333313 Office Machinery Manufacturing; 334419 Other Electronic Component Manufacturing; 333415 Air-Conditioning and Warm Air Heating Equipment and Commercial and Industrial Refrigeration Equipment Manufacturing; 333996 Fluid Power Pump and Motor Manufacturing; 333999 Other Miscellaneous General Purpose Machinery Manufacturing

Samsung Electronics Co., Ltd. is the chief subsidiary of South Korea's giant Samsung Group and the largest electronics producer in Asia. Samsung Electronics operates four main divisions including Digital Media, Semiconductors, Information & Communications, and Home Appliances. The company sells televisions, video, and audio equipment; computers and related products; phones, cellular phones, and fax machines; home appliances; semiconductors; network-related products; factory automation products; fiberoptics products; closed circuit security products; motors and compressors; and solar energy systems. In 2000, Samsung Electronics held the leading market position in the code division multiple access (CDMA) Handset, DRAM, SRAM, and color monitor markets.

Early History of Samsung Group

Samsung Electronics was created in 1969 as a division of the mammoth Korean chaebol Samsung Group. The unit was established as a means of getting Samsung into the burgeoning television and consumer electronics industry. The division's first product was a small and simple black-and-white television that it began selling in the early 1970s. From that product, Samsung Electronics gradually developed a diverse line of consumer electronics that it first sold domestically, and later began exporting. The company also began branching out into color televisions, and later into a variety of consumer electronics and appliances. By the 1980s, Samsung was manufacturing, shipping, and selling a wide range of appliances and electronic products throughout the world.

Although the rapid growth of Samsung Electronics during the 1970s and early 1980s was impressive, it did not surprise observers who were familiar with the Samsung Group, which was founded in 1938 by Byung-Chull Lee, a celebrated Korean entrepreneur. Lee started a small trading company with a $2,000 nest egg and 40 employees. He called it Samsung, which means "three stars" in Korean. The company enjoyed moderate growth before the Communist invasion in 1950 forced Lee to abandon his operations in Seoul. Looting soldiers and politicians on both sides of the conflict diminished his inventories to almost nothing. With savings contributed by one of his managers, Lee started over in 1951 and within one year had grown his company's assets 20-fold.

Lee established a sugar refinery in 1953, a move that was criticized at the time because sugar could be easily obtained through American aid. But for Lee, the act was important because it was the first manufacturing facility built in South Korea after the Korean War. From sugar, wool, and other commodity businesses, Lee moved into heavier manufacturing. The company prospered under Lee's philosophy of making Samsung the leader in each industry he entered.

From manufacturing, Samsung moved into various service businesses during the 1960s, including insurance, broadcasting, securities, and even a department store. Lee experienced several major setbacks during the period. For example, in the late

Company Perspectives:

We strive to devote our people and technology to create superior products and services, thereby contributing to a better global society. Working closely together with customers, building strong ties to the local communities we serve, and responding creatively to future challenges, are principles deeply instilled in the minds of our employees.

1960s, shortly before Samsung Electronics was created, Lee was charged with an illegal sale of about $50,000 worth of goods. The charges turned out to be the fabrication of a disgruntled government official to whom Lee had refused to pay a bribe. Nevertheless, one of Lee's sons was arrested and Lee was forced to donate a fertilizer plant to the government to win his release. Despite that and other problems, Samsung continued to flourish. Indeed, by the end of the 1960s the conglomerate was generating more than $100 million in annual revenues.

Shortly after Lee's son was arrested, Lee decided to break into the mass communication industry by launching a radio and television station, as well as by manufacturing televisions and electronic components through the Samsung Electronics division. The industry was dominated at the time by several U.S. and European manufacturers, and some Japanese companies were beginning to enter the industry. Nevertheless, Lee was confident that Samsung could stake its claim on the local market and eventually become a global contender. During the early 1970s, the company invested heavily, borrowed and coaxed technology from foreign competitors, and drew on its business and political connections to begin carving out a niche in the consumer electronics industry. In addition to televisions, Samsung branched out into other consumer electronics products and appliances.

Government Involvement During the 1970s

Samsung Electronics' gains during the 1970s were achieved with the assistance of the national government. During the 1950s and 1960s, Samsung and other Korean conglomerates struggled as the Rhee Sungman administration increasingly resorted to favoritism and corruption to maintain power. Student revolts in the 1960s finally forced Rhee into exile. The ruling party that emerged from the ensuing political fray was headed by military leader Park Chung-Hee. His regime during the 1960s and 1970s was characterized by increasing centralization of power, both political and industrial, as his government was obsessed with economic growth and development. So, while Park was widely criticized for his authoritarian style, his government is credited with laying the foundation for South Korea's economic renaissance.

To develop the economy rapidly, Park identified key industries and large, profitable companies within them. The government worked with the companies, providing protection from competition and financial assistance as part of a series of five-year national economic growth plans. By concentrating power in the hands of a few giant companies (the chaebols), Park reasoned, roadblocks would be minimized and efficiencies would result. Between 1960 and 1980, South Korea's annual exports surged from $33 million to more than $17 billion.

Samsung Electronics and the entire Samsung chaebol were beneficiaries of Rhee's policies. Several countries, including Japan, were barred from selling consumer electronics in South Korea, eliminating significant competition for Samsung. Furthermore, although Samsung Electronics was free to invest in overseas companies, foreign investors were forbidden to buy into Samsung. As a result, Samsung was able to quickly develop a thriving television and electronics division that controlled niches of the domestic market and even had an edge in some export arenas.

During the 1970s and 1980s, Samsung Group created a number of electronics-related divisions, several of which were later grouped into a single entity known as Samsung Electronics Co., Ltd. Samsung Electron Devices Co. manufactured picture tubes, display monitors, and related parts. Samsung Electro-Mechanics Co. made VHF and UHF tuners, condensers, speakers, and other gear. Samsung Corning Co. produced television glass bulbs, computer displays, and other components. Finally, Samsung Semiconductor & Telecommunications Co. represented Samsung in the high-tech microchip industry. Rapid growth in those industries, combined with savvy management, allowed the combined Samsung Electronics Co., Ltd., to become Samsung Group's chief subsidiary by the end of the 1980s.

Entering the Semiconductor Market: Late 1970s to Early 1980s

Samsung's entry into the semiconductor business was pivotal for the company. Lee had determined in the mid-1970s that high-tech electronics was the growth industry of the future, and that Samsung was to be a major player. To that end, he formed Samsung Semiconductor and Telecommunications Co. in 1978. To make up for a lack of technological expertise in South Korea, the South Korean government effectively required foreign telecommunications equipment manufacturers to hand over advanced semiconductor technology in return for access to the Korean market. This proved crucial for Samsung, which obtained proprietary technology from Micron of the United States and Sharp of Japan in 1983. Utilizing its newly acquired knowledge, Samsung became the first Korean manufacturer of low-cost, relatively low-tech, 64-kilobit dynamic random access memory (DRAM) chips.

Shortly after introducing its 64K chip, Samsung teamed up with some Korean competitors in a research project that was coordinated by the government Electronics and Telecommunications Research Institute. The result was a 1-megabit DRAM (and later a 4-megabit DRAM) chip. During the middle and late 1980s, Samsung parlayed knowledge from the venture to become a significant supplier of low-cost, commodity-like DRAM chips to computer and electronics manufacturers throughout the world. Meanwhile, its other electronics operations continued to grow, both domestically and abroad. Samsung opened a television assembly plant in Portugal in 1982 to supply the European market with 300,000 units annually. In 1984, it built a $25 million plant in New York that could manufacture one million televisions and 400,000 microwave ovens per year. Then, in 1987, it opened another $25 million facility in England with

Key Dates:

1969: Samsung Electronics is established.
1971: The company exports its first black-and-white television to Panama.
1978: Samsung Group enters the semiconductor market by forming Samsung Semiconductor and Telecommunications Co.
1983: The company enters the personal computer market.
1984: The firm officially adopts the name Samsung Electronics Co., Ltd.
1988: Samsung Electronics and Samsung Semiconductor merge.
1992: The company develops the world's first 64M DRAM.
1994: Sales increase after the 4-megabit DRAM chip is developed.
1995: Exports reach $10 billion.
1997: The company battles the Asian economic crisis.
1999: The firm undergoes a major restructuring, and profits reach $2.4 billion.
2000: Sales reach $26 billion and net profits climb to $4.7 billion.

capacity for 400,000 color televisions, 300,000 VCRs, and 300,000 microwave ovens.

Between 1977 and 1987, Samsung Group's annual revenues surged from $1.3 billion to $24 billion (or about 20 percent of South Korea's entire gross domestic product). Much of that growth was attributable to Samsung Electronics. Byung-Chull Lee died in 1987 and was succeeded by his son, Kun-Hee Lee. Kun-Hee Lee recognized the importance of the electronics division and moved quickly to make it the centerpiece of the Samsung Group. To that end, he consolidated many of the Group's divisions and eliminated some operations. He also introduced various initiatives designed to improve employee motivation and product quality. Kun-Hee Lee was credited with stepping up Samsung Electronics's partnering efforts with foreign companies as part of his goal to put Samsung at the forefront of semiconductor technology.

Focus on Electronics and Research and Development: Late 1980s to Early 1990s

Sales at Samsung Group grew more than 2.5 times between 1987 and 1992. More important, Samsung drew from potential profit gains to more than double research and development investments as part of Kun-Hee Lee's aggressive bid to make Samsung a technological leader in the electronics, semiconductor, and communications industries. Besides partnering with U.S. and Japanese electronics companies, Samsung Electronics acquired firms that possessed important technology, including Harris Microwave Semiconductors and Integrated Telecom Technologies. In 1993, Kun-Hee Lee sold off ten of Samsung Group's subsidiaries, downsized the company, and merged other operations to concentrate on three industries: electronics, engineering, and chemicals.

Under the leadership of chief executive Kim Kwang-Ho, Samsung Electronics took the microchip world by storm when it introduced its 4-megabit DRAM chip in 1994. Sales of that chip helped to push Samsung's sales from $10.77 billion in 1993 to $14.94 billion in 1994. Profits, moreover, spiraled from $173,000 to nearly $1.3 billion. In addition, Samsung had staged a bold grab for domestic market share in 1995 by slashing prices for consumer electronics and home appliances by as much as 16 percent and had wowed industry insiders when it unveiled an advanced thin-film-transistor liquid-crystal display (TFT-LCD) screen—used for laptop computers—at a world trade show in Japan.

Samsung Electronics' rapid rise and technical achievements put the company in the spotlight in the semiconductor industry. Its 4-megabit chip, in fact, had made it the leading global producer of DRAM chips by early 1995. Furthermore, Samsung Electronics was increasing its investment in development still further, as evidenced by a $2.5 billion outlay to develop a 64-megabit DRAM chip by 1998. In December of 1995, development on the world's first 1-gigabit synchronous DRAM chip was also in the works. Exports for the year increased to more than $10 billion.

Restructuring Under the Leadership of Yun Jong-Yong: Late 1990s

In just one short year, however, the market for the company's largest revenue producer became unstable. In 1996, DRAM prices fell drastically because of oversupply in the industry. While the company's telecommunications equipment and computer segment showed substantial growth, Samsung's semiconductor-related sales fell by 31.8 percent. In response, the firm implemented a new management structure that focused on increasing efficiency by implementing a new business strategy. The initiative included reforming price management to better recognize growth markets, improving communication between company managers, increasing overseas management support, implementing a new marketing strategy, and focusing on growth in telecommunications, microprocessors, and other non-memory products. Yun Jong-Yong was named CEO in January 1997 to oversee the new strategy.

As part of the firm's new focus, Samsung continued to pare down its dependency on memory chips. It developed new technologies and quickly made a name for itself in the telecommunications and cellular phone market. In May 1997, the company was named the official Olympic partner for wireless communications equipment for the 1998 Winter Games and the 2000 Sydney Games. The firm also established a telephone switching system in Ecuador, entered the Chinese wireless market by teaming up with Shanghai Great Wall Mobile Communications Co., and began selling its cellular phones to AT&T in the United States.

A crisis hit the Asian economy in the fall of 1997, and by early 1998, the Korean won—the nation's currency—was valued at 1,800 won to the dollar, which was less than half of its value just one year earlier. Samsung was forced to drastically change the way it had operated in the past and it began selling off segments that were not related to its core business. In addition, it cut 26 percent of its domestic workforce and 33 percent of its international workforce, and it slowed production.

While many Asian-based companies faltered, Samsung continued to forge ahead. The company established U.S.-based subsidiary Alpha Processor Inc. to oversee sales and marketing for its 64-bit Alpha processor product line. The firm also secured the top position in the TFT-LCD global market by capturing 18 percent of the market. In August of 1998, the firm developed a flat-screen television. Despite the trying economic times, Samsung recorded a greater than eight percent increase in gross sales. In January 1999, *Forbes Global Business & Finance* recognized the firm as the world's premiere consumer goods and services company.

Under the leadership of Yun, Samsung had successfully diversified its product line from dependence on memory chips despite the trying economic times. By the end of 1999, the chips accounted for 20 percent of sales—in 1995 they had secured 90 percent of profits and half of total sales. The company divested more than 57 of its businesses and decreased long-term debt by $10.8 billion. In addition, all of its product groups were able to secure profits during the year. Samsung also held a strong share of the cellular phone market and was one of the six top manufacturers of wireless phones and the leading producer of computer monitors. Sales for the year increased 24 percent to $22 billion while profits reached $2.4 billion. The firm's stock also rose dramatically, increasing by 233 percent to $227 a share.

Alliances for the New Millennium

Yun's successful leadership of the company during its restructuring and the Asian crisis was noted throughout the industry. In January 2000, *Fortune* magazine named Yun Asia's Businessman of the Year. The firm, which had adopted the phrase ''Leading the Digital Convergence Revolution'' for the new millennium, continued to develop new technologies and seek growth in high-margin markets. The company partnered with Yahoo! to utilize its network to sell its products on-line. It also teamed up with Microsoft to design and develop a line of cellular phones. At the same time, Samsung's exports of cellular phones increased in Kazakhstan, Mexico, Central Asia, and Central and South America. By this time, it was operating as the fourth largest producer of such phones.

Samsung's positive results continued in 2000 as the firm secured $26 billion in sales and $4.7 billion in net profits. Memory chips accounted for 38 percent of sales, information and telecommunications equipment secured 22 percent, digital media took 27 percent, and home appliances accounted for 8 percent of sales. The company looked to strategic partnerships, research and development, and growth, to maintain its positive financial record. In March 2001, it teamed up with Dell Computer Corporation in a $16 billion technology and research and development agreement. In addition, the company was selected by China to provide CDMA cellular phone networks in its four major cities.

Sales figures did decrease slightly in the first part of 2001, however, due to a slowdown in the personal computer market, an oversupply of LCDs, and a slowdown in the cellular market. Nevertheless, Samsung management continued to focus on remaining a leader in the electronics industry.

Principal Subsidiaries

Samsung Electronics America Inc.; Alpha Processor Inc.

Principal Competitors

LG Group; Matsushita Electric Industrial Co. Ltd.; NEC Corporation.

Further Reading

''Dell, Samsung Electronics Enter $16 Billion Alliance Agreement,'' *Business Wire,* March 21, 2001.

Engardio, Pete, and Moon Ihlwan, ''How a Korean Electronics Giant Came Out of the Crisis Stronger Than Ever,'' *Businessweek Online,* December 20, 1999.

''A Giant with Wings?,'' *Business Korea,* December 1994, pp. 21–23.

Jameson, Sam, ''Samsung Isn't Content to Be a Mere Giant,'' *Los Angeles Times,* July 5, 1990, p. D1.

Kraar, Louis, ''The Man Who Shook Up Samsung,'' *Fortune,* January 24, 2000, p. 28.

Nakarmi, Laxmi, with Kevin Kelly and Larry Armstrong, ''Look Out, World—Samsung Is Coming,'' *Business Week,* July 10, 1995, pp. 52–53.

Ota, Alan K., ''Samsung Expands Overseas in Drive to Transform Itself,'' *Oregonian,* July 2, 1995, p. F9.

''Samsung and Microsoft Announce Strategic Alliance,'' *AsiaPulse News,* June 14, 2000.

''Samsung Chairman Lee Kun-Hee: A Modern Day Fortuneteller?,'' *Business Korea,* August 1993, pp. 18–19.

''Samsung Electronics Records $26 BLN in Sales in 2000,'' *AsiaPulse News,* January 19, 2001.

''Samsung Electronics Records US$6.54 BLN in Q1 Sales,'' *AsiaPulse News,* April 23, 2001.

''Samsung Electronics to Expand Overseas Market for Mobile Phones,'' *AsiaPulse News,* March 23, 2000.

''Samsung Group: Lee Kun-Hee's First Five Years,'' *Business Korea,* December 1992, p. 37.

''Samsung Ranks World's 4th Largest Mobile Phone Maker,'' *Korea Herald,* February 10, 2000.

''Samsung: Steering a New Course,'' *Business Korea,* February 1992, p. 26.

''Samsung to Raise Profit to 10% of Sales or Higher by 2005,'' *Korea Herald,* December 21, 1999.

Selwyn, Michael, and Erwin Shrader, ''Samsung Takes on the Giant,'' *Asian Business,* October 1990, pp. 28–34.

Sohn, Jie-Ae, ''Samsung Group Embracing Breathtaking Changes,'' *Business Korea,* August 1993, pp. 15–18.

Steers, Richard M., with Yoo Keun Shin and Gerardo R. Ungson, *The Chaebol,* New York: Harper & Row, 1989.

Tanzer, Andrew, ''Samsung of South Korea Marches to Its Own Drummer,'' *Forbes,* May 16, 1988, pp. 84–89.

—Dave Mote
—update: Christina M. Stansell

Scottish Radio Holding plc

Clydebank Business Park
Clydebank, Glasgow G81 2RX
United Kingdom
Telephone: (44) 1565 2200
Fax: (44) 1565 2322
Web site: http://www.srh.org.uk

Public Company
Incorporated: 1973 as Radio Clyde
Employees: 1,034
Sales: £40 million ($104.9 million)(2000)
Stock Exchanges: London
Ticker Symbol: SRH
NAIC: 5131 Radio and Television Broadcasting

Scottish Radio Holding plc (SRH) is holding steady in the growing consolidation of the United Kingdom's radio industry. The Glasgow-based group is one of the United Kingdom's largest radio station operators, with stations including Radio Clyde, Radio Forth, Radio Borders, the Irish national station Today FM, and others, for a total of 16 radio licenses. The company's operations are primarily in Scotland and Ireland, with some also in northern England. SRH is also entering the digital radio market, having been awarded a national digital license in 2000. Formed in 1973, Scottish Radio has expanded its interests at the turn of the century to include publishing, focusing on the local weekly newspaper market. Through its SCORE Press publishing subsidiary, the company has 43 titles, including both paid and free publications. Another area of strong growth for SRH is billboard advertising, a market it entered in 1999. SCORE Outdoor has seen quick growth since its formation, notably through the acquisition of six outdoor billboard advertising companies. SCORE Outdoor gives SRH a network of more than 4,000 billboards throughout Scotland and into England. Coming changes in the British government's radio ownership rules is expected to lead to a shake-out in the sector; already in 2001, SRH has fought off a hostile takeover attempt from rival SMG (formerly known as the Scottish Media Group), which built up a 29.4 percent holding in SRH. Yet SRH may have found a white knight in privately owned DC Thomson, based in Dundee, the publishing group behind comics ''Beano'' and ''Dandy,'' as well as the owner of a number of newspaper titles. Merger talks among the various parties were called off in May 2001, after sharp drops in advertising revenues caused falling profits—and share prices—throughout the radio sector. With an immediate takeover averted, SRH announced its intention to remain independent and to step up its own acquisitions, pointing to a war chest worth more than £160 million. SRH is led by Richard Findlay, CEO, and cofounder and chairman James Gordon. Traded on the London Stock Exchange, the company reported revenues of £40 million.

Scottish Radio Pioneer

When Radio Clyde began broadcasting shortly before midnight on New Year's Eve 1973, it marked a turning point in U.K. radio history. Until then, radio—like television—had been the exclusive realm of government-owned British Broadcasting Corporation (BBC) Radio. The opening up of the United Kingdom's airwaves to private radio stations, made in part to thwart the growing numbers of offshore and otherwise pirate radio stations, became a fact in 1972. Radio Clyde became the first independent radio station in Scotland and quickly captured a leading share of its local Glasgow and west central Scotland audience, a position it maintained into the next century.

Although they offered the choice of listening to something other than the BBC, the United Kingdom's local radio stations were often criticized as being amateurish, a reputation that did little to help Clyde and its competitors to raise advertising revenues. Ownership rules limited the number of stations any single group might own, and the small size of most radio companies made it difficult for them to raise the capital needed for investing in new broadcasting equipment and technology. Radio owners faced other severe restrictions, such as a requirement to duplicate their programming on both AM and FM bands.

Led by founder Ian Chapman as chairman and cofounder James Gordon as CEO, Radio Clyde began taking steps to lead Radio Clyde into becoming a more mature operation. The company made an important move when it took a partial listing on

Company Perspectives:

SRH is successfully focused within the media sector: Our approach to serving local audiences, in both commercial radio and weekly newspapers, has delivered an impressive track record. All our radio services are ranked first and second in terms of their market share of listening within their broadcast areas. Similarly, all our local weekly newspapers are the most popular in the areas in which they are sold.

the London Stock Exchange in 1984, helping it fund future growth. Meanwhile, the radio market had grown steadily since the beginning of the decade, with more than 200 local radio licenses issued. The publication of the *Peacock Review of Broadcasting* in the mid-1980s gave new impetus to the growing independent radio industry; among the concessions that the government made was that it gave stations the right to split programming for the their AM and FM licenses. This allowed broadcasters to double their programming formats.

Another move toward a more mature organization came in 1986 when Radio Clyde led other independent radio station owners in Scotland and Ireland in forming an advertising booking service, Scottish & Irish Radio Sales Ltd., which became known as SIRS. The new entity gave SRH representation in London to compete for the slowly rising levels of radio advertising spending.

Acquiring Growth in the 1990s

Further relaxation of radio license ownership rules at the start of the 1990s opened the way to a growing shake down among the many independent groups operating within the United Kingdom's independent radio industry. The passage of the Broadcasting Act of 1990 not only created a number of new radio licenses, it also helped remove more ownership restrictions governing the country's body of radio licenses. These changes gave the signal for a renewed consolidation of the U.K. radio market.

After obtaining a full listing on the London Stock Exchange, Radio Clyde began to build up its own position. The company's first acquisition was a friendly takeover of Northsound Radio in 1988. Serving the Aberdeen and northeast Scotland area, Northsound had been set up in 1981 and had quickly achieved a strong listener base in its area—reaching 60 percent of its target population, giving it one of the highest scores in the U.K. market.

Radio Clyde continued to target expansion within its Scotland base. In 1991, the company launched another takeover bid, this time through a recommended share offer directed at the shareholders in Radio Forth. That station, which had begun broadcasting in 1975, brought not only its own audience, but those of Radio Tay and Radio Borders. Radio Tay had begun broadcasting in 1980, reaching an audience in northeast Fife, Tayside, Perth, and Kinross. The station's success among listeners had even led some to dub the rather diverse listening area as ''Tay Territory.'' Radio Borders was at the time one of the youngest of the United Kingdom's radio stations, having begun broadcasting only at the start of the 1990s and broadcasting to Scotland's Borders and England's North Northumberland areas. Radio Forth, Radio Tay, and Radio Borders became part of Radio Clyde in April 1991.

The newly enlarged group changed its name to Radio Clyde Holdings plc shortly after the acquisition of Radio Forth. By 1994, however, the company decided to emphasize its larger focus, changing its name to Scottish Radio Holdings plc. As the decade proceeded, Scottish Radio had managed to gain a place for itself among the leading U.K. broadcasting groups, which had begun to narrow to a small number, including Emap, GWR, Capital Radio, and its closest rival, Scottish Media Group.

Scottish Radio—or, as it increasingly preferred to be called, SRH—began to diversify its activities during the mid-1990s. The company's move into newspaper publishing—which, like radio, relied heavily on advertising revenues—came in 1995, when SRH set up its SCORE Press subsidiary. SCORE immediately acquired a base of operations when it bought Morton Newspapers for £11.2 million. Morton's collection of local weekly newspapers targeted at the Northern Ireland community gave SRH its first entry into that market.

In 1996, SRH added to its Northern Ireland activity with the acquisition of Downtown Radio. That station had been launched in 1976 and was the first independent, commercially based station to broadcast in Northern Ireland. Downtown Radio had established a sister station, Cool FM, in 1990. Meanwhile, back in Scotland, SRH added new West Sound Radio, which had been broadcasting to its Ayrshire and southwest Scotland region since 1981. West Sound was to take advantage of the splitting up of AM and FM broadcasting requirements, developing two distinct radio formats, an AM West Sound station, West FM for the Ayrshire region. When SRH acquired South West Sound that same year, the West Sound subsidiary also received a third format, that of West Sound FM, broadcasting to the Dumfries and Galloway markets. The two purchases cost SRH £1.6 million. When Ian Chapman retired as chairman that year, Peter Gordon took over his position, while the company named former Radio Forth chief Richard Findlay as CEO.

Merger Dance for the 21st Century

SRH continued to look for new acquisitions. In 1997, the company acquired majority control of Moray Firth Radio. Based in Iverness and founded in 1982, Moray Firth had originally come into SRH's sphere of operations through Radio Forth's minority share. SRH later acquired full control of Moray Firth, an acquisition that gave it the United Kingdom's largest single geographic broadcasting area. The company also added to its publishing wing with the acquisition of *Montrose Review Press* for £480,000 and *The Buteman,* located on the Isle of Bute, for £300,000.

Findlay and SRH made no secret of their interest in expanding their media interests through acquisitions, pledging as much as £100 million to the effort. Not all of their targets succumbed to SRH's charms, however. Such was the case with the company's attempt to acquire Border TV, which would have not only boosted SRH's radio operations on the Scottish and English borders, but also have brought it one of the United King-

Key Dates:

1973: Radio Clyde begins broadcasting.
1975: Radio Forth begins broadcasting.
1976: Downtown Radio begins broadcasting.
1980: Radio Tay is launched.
1981: Northsound Radio and West Sound Radio begin broadcasting.
1982: Moray Firth is established.
1988: Radio Clyde acquires Northsound Radio.
1990: The company has a full listing on the London Stock Exchange.
1991: The company acquires Radio Forth and changes its name to Radio Clyde Holding.
1994: The company changes its name to Scottish Radio Holding.
1995: The company sets up SCORE Press and acquires Morton Newspapers.
1996: The firm acquires West Sound Radio and South West Sound and also acquires Downtown Radio.
1999: The company sets up SCORE Outdoor.

dom's rare independent television licenses. Border Television rejected SRH's offer in 1998.

The following year, SRH struck out into new media territory, laying bare its advertising-driven base with the establishment of SCORE Outdoor, a subsidiary set up to handle the company's foray into billboard and other outdoor advertising. SRH literally acquired the number four spot in the United Kingdom in that market segment, making six acquisitions before the end of the decade. The first of these came in March 1999 when SRH paid £27 million for Trainer Ltd. A new acquisition followed in April, when the company bought Parkin Advertising, based in Bristol, for £9 million. A month later, SRH added operations in Birmingham, through the acquisition of Visions Posters, for £15 million.

SRH was also building up its publishing side, acquiring Angus County Press, based in Forfar for £4.2 million in 1999, and then Title Media, which published Ireland on Sunday, and Kilpenny People Holdings, giving the company its first operations in the Republic of Ireland. SRH had not abandoned growth in its core radio business, however, as it fought for one of the new digital radio licenses. The company won its license bid in 2000 and launched its 3C digital radio service by 2001.

As the dust settled on the U.K. radio industry, the consolidation frenzy of the past decade had reduced the number of major players to a select few. SRH remained an independent player, yet analysts criticized the group for its lack of size against its larger competitors. The company attempted a second time to acquire Border Television, upping its offer to £116 million. Once again, however, SRH's bid was rejected.

By the end of 2000, SRH, which had no single major shareholder to help it ward off a hostile takeover, had come into rival Scottish Media Group's line of sight. As that company sought to enhance its own largely television- and newspaper-based media holdings, it began to buy up a position in SRH. By spring of 2001, Scottish Media had acquired more than 28 percent of SRH's stock—near to the cutoff point at which, under U.K. law, a full-fledged takeover offer became mandatory.

SRH fought back however, and it was saved by DC Thomson, a Scotland-based publisher of comic books and newspapers. DC Thomson began increasing its own shareholder position in SRH, nearing the 29 percent mark by April 2001. Yet a collapse in the U.K. market's radio advertising spending had crippled share prices across most of the U.K. radio community. In May 2001, SRH announced that it had ended its merger talks with DC Thomson. At the same time, SRH, which had initially seemed interested in the idea of joining into a larger group, now affirmed its desire to remain independent and promised to spend up to £180 million on the acquisitions that would give it the critical mass to do just that.

Principal Divisions

SCORE Outdoor; Angus County Press; Black Country Bugle (England); Bute Newspapers (Scotland); Ireland on Sunday; Kilkenny People Holdings (Ireland); Leitrim Observer (Ireland); Morton Newspapers (Northern Ireland); Downtown Radio (Northern Ireland); Moray Firth Radio; Northsound Radio; Radio Borders; Radio Clyde; Radio Forth; Radio Tay; Score Digital; South West Sound (85%); West Sound Radio; Score Interactive; SRH Radio Sales.

Principal Competitors

BBC Corporation; Capital Radio plc; SMG plc; Chrysalis Group plc; GWR Group plc; Virgin Group Ltd; Emap plc.

Further Reading

Calder, Colin, ''We've Ad a Bad Spell,'' *Daily Record*, May 19, 2001, p. 43.
Dandy, Emma, and Bill McIntosh, ''Scottish Radio Pulls Out of Takeover Talks,'' *Independent*, May 17, 2001, p. 18.
Higham, Nick, ''Commercial Radio Grasps Trend for Consolidation,'' *Marketing Week*, March 30, 2000.
''Scottish Radio Record Loud and Clear,'' *Birmingham Post*, November 16, 2000, p. 29.
Yoon, Jean, ''Scottish Radio Hit by Falling Ad Spend,'' *Reuters*, May 18, 2001.

—M.L. Cohen

Seigle's Home and Building Centers, Inc.

1331 Davis Road
Elgin, Illinois 60123
U.S.A.
Telephone: (847) 742-2000
Fax: (847) 697-6521
Web site: http://www.seigles.com

Private Company
Incorporated: 1952
Employees: 700
Sales: $196 million (2000 est.)
NAIC: 444110 Home Centers; 444190 Other Building Material Dealers

Seigle's Home and Building Centers, Inc.—with six retail showrooms, four lumberyards, three manufacturing plants, and five distribution centers—is ranked among the top 50 building suppliers in the United States. The company is based in Elgin, Illinois, some 40 miles west of Chicago, where it was founded over 100 years ago as a lumberyard. Serving the Chicagoland area, Seigle's attributes its success to working with homebuilders and remodelers to ensure their success as well as to the ongoing relationships the Seigle's sales force develops with contractors.

19th Century Origins

Although not incorporated until 1952, the history of Seigle's may be traced to 1881, when the Elgin Lumber Company started up as a supplier to the building and carpentry trades. The company was founded by an assortment of leading businessmen in the Elgin, Illinois, area, led by the Borden family of dairy renown. At the time, a lumber company in Elgin stood to prosper, as the city's population boomed, property values escalated, and the building of brick structures to replace the wooden ones commenced.

During the depression era of the 1930s, Elgin Lumber suffered downturns along with many other businesses. As recovery began, at the onset of World War II, lifelong Elgin resident Harold T. Seigle and a partner pooled their money in order to purchase what was then known as the Elgin Lumber & Supply Company in 1942. The partnership incorporated as Seigle's in 1952 in a postwar period favorable to building and home improvements.

As a supplier to the construction industry, the company prospered, and in 1961 Seigle's opened its first retail center, Elgin Wholesale (later renamed Seigle's McBride Street Center). The outlet was intended to serve the growing do-it-yourself market, and toward that end the company offered cabinets, fixtures, garage doors, and plumbing and electrical supplies, as well as lumber. The growing demand for such components as pre-hung doors led Seigle's to open its own Millwork Center in 1967 for the manufacture of components.

Seigle family leadership at the company was bolstered in 1974, when Harry J. Seigle joined his father's business. The younger Seigle had spent summers during his youth working for his father at the lumberyard, loading and unloading boxcars and doing other labor-intensive duties. After high school, he attended college, ultimately earning a degree in law and setting out to practice as an attorney in Chicago. Soon, however, he returned to Elgin, deciding he was better suited for a career in business, specifically in sales at Seigle's. His arrival at Seigle's would mark the beginning of a period of remarkable changes for the company.

Increased Competition in the 1970s–80s

In the early 1970s, though it had begun to offer a more diverse product line, Seigle's was still best known as a traditional lumberyard, and competition was beginning to heat up from a new concept in the industry: the home center. Given the escalating costs of having professionals build or remodel a home, hardware stores had begun to target a do-it-yourself market more intent on larger construction projects. The resultant home center offered modern showroom facilities stocked with windows, doors, cabinetry, and other necessities for home-building, along with the tools with which to accomplish the job. Since profit margins on the sale of lumber and building materials alone were very low, Seigle's future was seriously threat-

Company Perspectives:

Our corporate purpose is to serve professional contractors and homeowners as Chicagoland's preeminent quality source for a broad variety of building products and services provided by specialists.

ened. To remain a traditional lumberyard in the competitive climate might just be the ruin of the company. Thus, Seigle's prepared to enter the home center market.

In 1975, Seigle's moved outside of Elgin for the first time, opening a retail outlet in nearby St. Charles, Illinois. The new 30,000-square-foot facility was a building center and showroom serving contractors and do-it-yourselfers alike.

Throughout many sectors of the retail industry, the 1980s gave rise to the superstore; suddenly lumberyards and home centers began losing business as contractors and homeowners did their one-stop shopping at such national chains as Home Depot and Builders Square, companies that could realize large economies of scale.

At Seigle's, the early 1980s were characterized by expansion and an aggressive attempt to be the region's premier superstore, or ''category killer'' as the retail concept was known. In 1983, Seigle's Millwork Center manufacturing operation moved into larger facilities in Elgin. Adjacent to the Millwork Center a new corporate headquarters was built, allowing Seigle's to centralize its financial, advertising, human resources, and executive staff. Also that year the company made its first acquisition, purchasing the Globe Building Materials Company of Aurora, Illinois, and renaming it Seigle's Aurora Center.

Harry Seigle's younger brother Mark joined the business during this time. The company was now completely family-owned, as the Seigles revised the partnership agreement and acquired all Seigle's stock. In 1984 the company was renamed Seigle's Home & Building Centers to more accurately reflect its commitment to both contractors and homeowners, as well as its intentions of competing with the superstore chains. The company's third retail store was opened two years later, serving the west side of Elgin, where land development was burgeoning. During this time, Harold Seigle retired, leaving the day-to-day operations of a growing chain to his sons.

Building a Future: 1990s and Beyond

By 1990, Seigle's was reporting record growth. In Mundelein, northwest of Chicago, the company opened a new Seigle's Center. In Chicago proper, Seigle's made another acquisition, purchasing the Anzalone Building Center and converting it into a Seigle's Center. Sales at Seigle's continued to meet or exceed expectations.

The age difference between Harry and Mark Seigle (11 years) allowed both brothers a turn at running the company. In 1995, Mark stepped up from his roles as vice-president and secretary to take over as president, while brother Harry became the company's chairman. Mark focused on the overall operation of Seigle's, while Harry concentrated on contractor relationships and developing new business. The management team was rounded out by a vice-president of operations and directors for the manufacturing and sales arms. The family business in 1994 realized about $151 million in annual sales, an increase of ten percent over 1993 figures.

Expansion continued apace. In order to liquidate damaged items and obsolete product lines, Seigle's opened an Outlet Center in Aurora. Soon thereafter another retail center was opened in Chicago. This Seigle's Building Center, well placed in a popular north side shopping district, offered the successful lines of Aristokraft cabinetry and Seigle's own millwork. The company also built a new component manufacturing facility in Hampshire during this time.

Having successfully widened its scope to include the do-it-yourselfer (even reportedly remodeling some stores to appeal more to women), but facing the very real market dominance of Home Depot and Lowe's in the mid- and late 1990s, Seigle's began to shift its focus to its original core customer, the professional builder. With the shift, however, the company left itself more vulnerable to the building boom/bust cycle. To counteract that challenge, Seigle's continued to expand its territory in Illinois and also enhanced the value of services it offered professionals.

Toward that end, Seigle's initiated several programs and traditions. In addition to annual holiday parties and golf outings for customers, Seigle's developed the Level Express program, aimed at helping builders save time and money. Specifically, Level Express allowed builders use of in-store phones, faxes, and copiers, to facilitate their business; moreover builders could pre-order materials, receive special discounts, and attend seminars at which they could learn more about products and industry innovations.

In order to attract and retain remodelers' business, Seigle's began the Level Express II program, which offered many of the same services to remodelers that were offered to homebuilders. For these smaller contractors, Seigle's offered general educational seminars on such topics as business management, to help them with sales, finances, marketing, and legal issues. Finally, Seigle's provided smaller contractors easy credit terms of 30 days with no interest, an offer unique in the industry.

Seigle's continued expanding through acquisitions in the late 1990s, its growth driven by a good economy and the subsequent increase in demands for new housing and remodeling. The company purchased another millworks, DuPage Millwork, in 1999, and by the year 2000 had opened another showroom Naperville/Aurora, while also doubling the size of both its Hampshire manufacturing plant and its Millwork Distribution center.

The company also began pioneering efforts to bring greater numbers from the building industry into the computer age. Through software designed by its Enterprise Computer Systems company, Seigle's offered vendors and builders the opportunity to process their transactions electronically. Confidant that the industry would more fully embrace technology and e-commerce, Seigle's worked toward offering vendors and builders the opportunity to send blueprints and specs electroni-

Key Dates:

1881: The Elgin Lumber Company is founded.
1942: Harold T. Seigle, along with a partner, buys Elgin Lumber Company.
1952: Seigle's is incorporated.
1961: Seigle's opens its first retail center.
1977: Son Harry Seigle becomes company president.
1980: Seigle family buys all company stock.
1984: Company is renamed Seigle's Home & Building Centers.
1995: Son Mark Seigle becomes president of the company.
2001: Company opens its sixth kitchen and millwork center.

cally and thereby help the company meet the customers' needs more quickly.

In the late 1990s, Seigle's reorganized its growing enterprise. Under the new plan, the company maintained five retail home centers, three manufacturing plants, and five distribution facilities. The manufacturing and distribution plants—for Seigle's pre-hung doors, trusses, windows, and cabinets—hired and trained their own sales forces. While this involved considerable time and work, it also allowed Seigle's to send specially-trained, knowledgeable salespeople to work directly with contractors and homebuilders. Selling directly to builders from the centers, instead of through the retail centers, gained market share in the Chicago area for Seigle's.

In 1998, company founder Harold Seigle died at the age of 89 after suffering a stroke. According to his obituary in the *Chicago Daily Herald,* Harry Seigle regarded his father's major business strength as his emphasis on customer service as well as his having created a corporate culture based on professionalism and respect. Indeed, Seigle's had invested heavily in developing a sales force that maintained excellent customer relations via expertise in Seigle products as well as building design in general. Seigle's Chicago Sales Group, for example, focused on the unique problems and challenges of building and rehabbing in an urban environment. Knowledge of building codes, tastes of city dwellers, and what was selling well in which neighborhoods marked the group's success.

In 2000, Seigle's purchased EVCO Windows, the largest supplier of wood windows in the Chicago area. In February of the following year, the company opened it's sixth kitchen and millwork showroom store, in Morton Grove, Illinois. The company felt that with that opening it had gained complete coverage of Chicago and the surrounding suburbs. Sales in 2000 reached \$196 million, an increase of 3 percent over the previous year and an impressive figure given intensifying competition for market share in the Chicago area.

Looking to the future, Seigle's management acknowledged that remaining privately-held did limit the company's financial resources somewhat. However, it maintained, by staying small, the company could better connect with the customers and thereby develop more valuable long-term relationships. In 2001 Seigle's celebrated its 120th year in business, and its plans to grow through acquisition lived on.

Principal Operating Units

Components; Millwork; Sales; Cabinets; Windows; Lumber.

Principal Competitors

The Home Depot Inc.; Lowe's Companies Inc.

Further Reading

Hahn, Brad, ''Elgin Entrepreneur Harold Seigle Dies at 89,'' *Chicago Daily Herald,* July 18, 1998, p. 1.
Kirkland, Vicki, ''What's Happening at Seigle's?,'' *Midwest Homebuilder,*'' Fall 2000.
''Mark Seigle Takes the Helm at Seigle's,'' *Building Supply Home Centers,* March 1995, p.1M.
Patterson, Jennifer, ''There's More to Harry Seigle than Building Supplies,'' *Chicago Daily Herald,* March 23, 2000, p. 29.
Pecen, Michael, and Walter E. Johnson, ''Chicago Face-Off; Who Will the Retail Winners be When the Final Bell Sounds?,'' *Do-It-Yourself Retailing,* August 1995, p. 239.
''Seigle's Building Centers,'' *Do-It-Yourself Retailing,* March 1999, p.73.
''Seigle's Building Ctrs. Buys W. Chicago Rival,'' *Crain's Chicago Business,* April 26, 1999, p. 32.
''Seigle's Makes the Best of a Challenging Year,'' *National Home Center News,* February 5, 2001, p. 8.
Shuster, Laurie, ''A Category-Killer for Chicago Builders,'' *Chilton's Hardware Age,* November 1999, p. 38.
Spak, Kara, ''Seigle's Moving Billing Offices Out of St. Charles, Elgin,'' *Chicago Daily Herald,* November 11, 2000, p. 4.

—Lisa Musolf Karl

Shell Oil Company

One Shell Plaza
Houston, Texas 77002
U.S.A.
Telephone: (713) 241-6161
Fax: (713) 241-4044
Web site: http://www.countonshell.com

Wholly Owned Subsidiary of Royal Dutch/Shell Petroleum Inc.
Incorporated: 1922 as Shell Union Oil Corporation
Employees: 12,750
Sales: $19.2 billion
NAIC: 211111 Crude Petroleum & Natural Gas Extraction; 32411 Petroleum Refineries

One of North America's leading producers of oil, gas, and petrochemicals, Shell Oil Company has distinguished itself through its commitment to industry innovation. It operates as the leading oil and gas producer in the deep-water Gulf of Mexico and its four major operating segments include Oil and Gas Exploration and Production, Downstream Gas, Oil Products, and Chemical Products. Shell Oil operates as a subsidiary of Royal Dutch/Shell Group, the second largest oil company in the world. In 1999, Shell Oil and its U.S.-based counterparts secured 22 percent of the Group's income.

Company Beginnings in the Early 20th Century

The Royal Dutch/Shell Group began selling gasoline imported from Sumatra in the United States in 1912, to capitalize on the growth of the country's automobile industry and to compete with the Standard Oil Company. Starting with the formation of the Seattle-based American Gasoline Company, Royal Dutch/Shell Group also founded Roxana Petroleum Company in 1912 in Oklahoma to locate and produce crude oil. This was followed by the opening of refineries in New Orleans, Louisiana in 1916 and in Wood River, Illinois, in 1918.

It soon became clear to Royal Dutch/Shell Group that with so much gasoline already available in nearby California, it was impractical to continue importing the product for sale in the Pacific Northwest. Therefore, it acquired California Oilfields, Ltd. in 1913, which, when coupled with a new refinery built two years later in Martinez, California, gave the company the ability to fully integrate its operations. To reflect this new capability, the name of American Gasoline was changed to Shell Company of California in 1915. At this time, the company designed and built its first gasoline service station. Dubbed ''the crackerbox,'' the station was originally constructed of wood. This structure was later replaced by a model made of prefabricated steel that required only a few days to erect.

Rapid Expansion During the 1920s

The oil boom of the early 1920s, particularly at Shell's Signal Hill, California site, provided the company with an opportunity to penetrate the Los Angeles area with sales of Shell gasoline and petroleum products manufactured in its new refineries nearby. In 1922, Shell Company of California and Roxana Petroleum merged with Union Oil Company of Delaware to form a holding company called Shell Union Oil Corporation. Approximately 65 percent of the holding company's shares was held by Royal Dutch/Shell Group.

By the late 1920s, the company was actively laying pipeline across the country to transport oil from its Texas fields to the Wood River refinery. Shell Pipe Line Corporation, established in 1927 upon the acquisition of Ozark Pipe Line Corporation, also connected these fields to a new refinery built in Houston in 1929. This refinery was dedicated to manufacturing products destined for sale on the east coast of the United States and overseas. In 1929, Shell Petroleum Corporation, a forerunner of Shell Oil Company, purchased the New Orleans Refining Company, which later became one of Shell's largest manufacturing facilities.

Shell Development Company was formed in 1928 to conduct petrochemical research. The following year, after the discovery of chemicals that could be made from refinery byproducts, the Shell Chemical Company began its manufacturing operation. By 1929, Shell gasoline was being sold throughout the United States. Although the economic problems of the early

Company Perspectives:

Shell Oil follows the Royal Dutch/Shell Group's "Blueprint for Success" and strives to be passionate in taking care of customers; to become the model of diversity for corporate America; to be an organization where people can achieve their full potential; to achieve the leading-edge in financial performance, health, safety, and environmental performance; and strives to have a strong national profile and identity.

1930s forced the company, along with the entire oil industry, to reassess and curtail its operations to some degree, Shell continued its chemical research. This resulted in the opening of two plants for manufacturing synthetic ammonia in 1931 and for making synthetic glycerin in 1937.

Continued Growth: 1930s–70s

Upon developing the ability to synthesize 100-octane gasoline, Shell began supplying this fuel to the U.S. Air Corps in 1934, and gradually became one of the largest producers of aviation fuel. Because of the increased demands of the military during World War II, Shell shared this technology with the rest of the industry. It also helped the country overcome its wartime loss of natural rubber supplied by Java and Singapore by providing butadiene, a chemical required for the production of synthetic rubber products.

In 1939, Shell Oil Company of California merged with Shell Petroleum Corporation, whose name was subsequently changed to Shell Oil Company, Inc. Ten years later, the name was changed again to Shell Oil Company.

Until 1939, the company had offices in San Francisco, California; St. Louis, Missouri; and New York City. The St. Louis office was closed in 1939, and San Francisco operations continued until 1949, when New York became the sole headquarters. Shell increased its oil exploration activities and expanded production to satisfy the growing fuel needs created by U.S. drivers' passion for big cars. New chemical plants were built that enabled Shell to become a leading producer of epoxy resins, ethylene, synthetic rubber, detergent alcohols, and other chemicals. Shell also pioneered the development of new fuel products during the 1950s, including jet fuel and high-octane, unleaded gasoline for automobiles.

In 1958, the company redesigned its service stations in an attempt to make them more compatible with surrounding areas. The ranch-style station was introduced at this time and continued as the company's primary retail outlet until the introduction of the self-service station in 1971. Shell provided additional retail support by launching several payment alternatives, including an offer to honor all other oil company credit cards and a travel-and-entertainment card bearing the Shell name. These developments helped Shell gain a significant share of the U.S. market for automobile gasoline.

By the 1960s, growing environmental concerns led Shell to invest heavily in systems intended to reduce pollution and to conserve energy in its plants. In the following decade, the company began publishing a series of consumer-oriented booklets on such topics as car maintenance and energy conservation.

At the same time, the company turned its attention offshore and began drilling for oil and natural gas deposits in Alaska and the Gulf of Mexico. It soon became expert in using enhanced techniques to find and recover oil from U.S. fields. One of its biggest successes was the 1983 strike at the Bullwinkle prospect in the Gulf of Mexico. This recovery operation was expected to produce 100 million barrels of oil.

In 1970, Shell moved its headquarters to Houston. The company expanded into coal production in 1974 with the formation of Shell Mining Company. This business unit eventually operated mines in Wyoming, Illinois, Ohio, Kentucky, and West Virginia.

John F. Bookout assumed the presidency of the company in 1976, after the mandatory retirement of his predecessor, Harry Bridges. Bookout, a 25-year Shell veteran, had risen through the ranks of the company's oil and gas exploration and production division. Bookout took over during a period when high oil prices and flattening demand led other petroleum producers into ill-fated diversification attempts outside the oil industry. Rather than follow this path, Bookout elected to penetrate the oil industry more deeply and to emphasize increased efficiency in the company's ongoing operations. Beginning in 1978, for example, the company upgraded a number of its refineries and closed many of its less profitable service stations to concentrate on those in metropolitan areas with higher sales volume.

In 1979, Shell outbid several competitors to purchase California's Belridge Oil Company. The firm, which was subsequently renamed Kernridge Oil Company, gave Shell badly needed crude oil reserves at a time when opportunities for successful drilling ventures were declining. The company's technological expertise in steam-injected oil recovery enabled Shell to boost Kernridge's domestic production and reduce its reliance on more expensive foreign sources.

Beginning in January 1984, Royal Dutch/Shell Group launched a bid to acquire the remaining shares of Shell Oil Company. Attracted by Shell's U.S. oil reserves, the country's stable political situation, and a low corporate tax structure, cash-rich Royal Dutch/Shell viewed Shell as an increasingly worthy investment. The attempted buyout soon developed into a hostile battle over the amount that Royal Dutch/Shell had offered Shell shareholders. Its original offer of $55 a share was perceived as inadequate by Shell's directors and financial advisers, who placed the company's worth at closer to $75 a share, even though the offer represented a 25 percent premium over the stock's current selling price. By May, however, John Bookout and four other Shell executives agreed to tender their shares in exchange for Royal Dutch's sweetened offer of $60 a share. This agreement paved the way for the eventual completion of the takeover in June 1985.

Problems in the Mid-1980s to Early 1990s

In the following year, Shell came under the attack of an anti-apartheid coalition in the United States consisting of union representatives, activists, and members of various church

Key Dates:

1912: The company begins selling gasoline in the United States.
1913: California Oilfields, Ltd. is acquired.
1915: American Gasoline Company changes its name to Shell Company of California.
1922: The company merges with Union Oil Company to form Shell Union Oil Corporation.
1929: By now, Shell gasoline is being sold throughout the United States.
1939: Shell Oil Company of California merges with Shell Petroleum Corporation.
1949: The firm officially adopts the name Shell Oil Company.
1970: Company headquarters is moved to Houston, Texas.
1971: Shell introduces the self-service gas station.
1979: The firm acquires Belridge Oil Company.
1985: Royal Dutch/Shell Group acquires the remaining shares of Shell Oil.
1989: Shell is forced to pay cleanup costs related to the Rocky Mountain Arsenal in Colorado.
1994: Production begins at the Auger platform.
1996: The Mars platform is installed in the Gulf of Mexico.
1998: Shell and Texaco Inc. form Equilon Enterprises LLC; Motiva Enterprises LLC is formed by Shell, Texaco, and Saudi Aramco.
1999: Shell begins to restructure operations due to poor financial results.

groups that protested against Royal Dutch/Shell's involvement in South Africa. Through picketing in 13 cities, the coalition hoped to exert a negative impact on Shell's gasoline sales while also making the U.S. public aware of the parent company's coal, oil, and chemical operations in South Africa. A boycott launched by the AFL-CIO, United Mineworkers, and National Education Association in cooperation with the Free South Africa Movement was initiated to protest both alleged mistreatment of South African workers by Royal Dutch/Shell and the company's inaction against apartheid. Although Royal Dutch/Shell officials contended that the company was a strong anti-apartheid voice, by the end of 1988, Berkeley, California and Boston, Massachusetts had joined the fray trying to ban purchases of Shell products within city limits.

Shell encountered additional problems in 1989, over the cleanup of the Rocky Mountain Arsenal in Colorado. It was there that Shell had manufactured pesticides between the early 1950s and 1982, allegedly dumping carcinogens on the grounds. Also under scrutiny was the U.S. Army, which had used the Rocky Mountain plant to make nerve gas during World War II. Sued in 1983 by the state of Colorado under the federal superfund law, both the Army and Shell offered a plan to pay for cleaning up the site. The state subsequently deemed the proposal unsatisfactory. A California superior court ruled that insurance companies covering the company were not liable. Shell appealed that decision, but eventually reached an agreement with the U.S. government whereby Shell would pay 50 percent of the cleanup costs up to $500 million, 35 percent of costs between $500 million and $700 million, and 20 percent of costs in excess of $700 million. Through 1994, Shell had incurred $240 million in expenditures on the cleanup effort.

Led by President and Chief Executive Officer Frank H. Richardson, who succeeded John Bookout upon his retirement in 1988, Shell boasted strong cash flow and a decreasing level of long-term debt in the late 1980s. Underlying this rosy situation, however, were problems for Shell on the production side. In 1988, Shell was able to produce 531,000 barrels of oil a day, but by 1994, that figure had fallen to 398,000 a day. Shell had settled on the Gulf of Mexico as its prime area of exploration and development, an area that was disappointing during the period. The recession of the early 1990s compounded Shell's difficulties by causing a decline in demand for petroleum products and pushing prices down. Like other U.S. oil companies, Shell saw its revenues steadily decline throughout the early 1990s—from $24.79 billion in 1990 to $21.09 billion in 1993.

In 1991, Shell decided that it had to cut operating costs to generate enough money to boost its production. The company announced that it would cut ten to 15 percent of its workforce as part of a corporate restructuring. Over the next two years more than 7,000 jobs were eliminated, reducing Shell's workforce from 29,437 in 1991 to 22,212 in 1993.

Meanwhile, Shell engineers and workers were hard at work designing and constructing a $1.2 billion Auger platform in the deep waters of the Gulf of Mexico. With ten to 15 billion barrels of oil and gas lying under these waters, the question was not whether there was oil and gas to be found, but whether it could be extracted profitably. Located 135 miles offshore and in water of record depth of 2,860 feet, production began at the Auger platform in April 1994 and quickly reached 55,000 barrels a day, more than the anticipated peak of 46,000 barrels. Shell was the acknowledged leader in deep-sea drilling and its commitment to the Gulf had begun to pay off. Shell already had two more platforms in the works, which were scheduled to begin production by 1997. The three projects were expected to generate 150,000 barrels a day, creating oil and gas worth $1 billion annually.

On the retail side, by 1994, Shell had 8,600 stations operating in 40 states and the District of Columbia and had strengthened its position as the top gasoline marketer in the United States. Shell's refinery activities in the early 1990s were highlighted by the beginning of construction of a $1 billion clean fuels project in Martinez, California, to be completed by 1997. Meanwhile, Richardson had retired in 1993 and was succeeded by Philip J. Carroll.

Focus on Exploration and Production: Mid-1990s

Shell's position in the mid-1990s was much healthier than earlier in the decade, due in large part to the success of its deepwater operations in the Gulf of Mexico. In July 1996, the company launched its Mars Platform, a $2.1 billion oil and gas project in the Gulf of Mexico. Standing 3,250 feet high from the seafloor, Shell expected Mars to recover more than 700 million barrels of oil and gas equivalent.

The company also formed Shell Midstream Enterprises (SME), a business unit designed to market the firm's expertise and pipeline infrastructure in the Gulf of Mexico to oil companies with no pipelines of their own. By now, Shell was operating as the largest producer in the Gulf of Mexico and had three major pipeline projects under way in that region. The Mississippi Canyon Gathering System was being developed to transport natural gas from Shell-owned Mars, Ursa, and Mensa fields. The Garden Banks Gathering System project included new construction on another pipeline platform in the Gulf, and the Nautilus/Manta Ray project included development of a natural gas pipeline system in the Green Canyon area of the Central Gulf. Shell's net income reached $2 billion in 1996, an increase of 33 percent over the previous year.

Amidst Shell's successes that year, the company did come under fire when Ken Saro-Wiwa, a Nobel Peace Prize nominee, was put to death after leading a campaign against Shell's operations in Nigeria. In 1994, the activist had been arrested as part of a military program designed to protect Shell operations in that region—Shell operations accounted for 40 percent of Nigerian government revenue. His plight to end pollution in the area ultimately led to his death, which created an outpouring of protest and a worldwide boycott against Royal Dutch/Shell and its affiliates from human rights groups and activists.

In 1997, the company acquired Tejas Gas, a large southwestern pipeline company, and obtained full ownership of Coral Energy, a partnership developed between the two to market natural gas output in North America. Shell also teamed up with Texaco Inc. to combine both companies' Western and Midwestern U.S. downstream operations, including refining, transportation, marketing, and lubricants, in an effort to cut costs. The formation of Equilon Enterprises LLC was completed in early 1998 and secured a 13 percent share of the domestic refining market, and 14.6 percent of the U.S. gasoline market. Shell owned 56 percent of the venture, and Texaco retained 44 percent.

Motiva Enterprises LLC was created shortly after Equilon and included the East and Gulf Coast downstream operations of Shell, Texaco, and Saudi Aramco. The formation of the two new ventures was anticipated to save $800 million and secure $45 billion in revenues.

The firm also made some key partnerships in 1997 relating to production and exploration. Shell and BP Amoco announced the formation of Altura Energy Ltd., which combined production assets of both firms in the Permain basin of West Texas and Southeast New Mexico. Aera Energy LLC also was formed and included the California-based production and exploration assets of Shell and Mobil Corp.

Restructuring During the Late 1990s

In June 1998, Jack E. Little took over as president and CEO of Shell after Carroll retired. By that time, the firm had restructured its business operations into four new segments, including Oil and Gas Exploration and Production, Downstream Gas, Oil Products, and Chemical Products.

In 1999, the financial strains related to the firm's expansion and low oil prices forced Shell to rethink its current strategies. Operating profits had sunk to such low levels that the company announced plans to sell its interest in the Altura venture as well as the majority of the Tejas Gas Co.'s downstream gas assets. It also planned to divest a number of its chemicals businesses and restructure the Aera Energy venture.

As oil and gas prices remained low in 1999, Shell continued to cut jobs. By March, more than 1,000 jobs had been cut in its exploration and production business segment. In April, Little retired and Steven L. Miller, managing director of Royal Dutch Petroleum Company, was named president and CEO. At the same time, Shell's parent took over full control of the subsidiary—which in the past had acted completely autonomously and filed separate quarterly financial results—in an attempt to centralize and control operations.

Although Shell entered the new millennium under the tighter reins of Royal Dutch/Shell, it continued to focus on exploration and production. The firm began development of its Na Kika project in the Gulf of Mexico, which was projected to recover more than 300 million barrels. Shell also announced plans to develop two other deep-water projects, entitled Serrano and Oregano. In October 2000, through its affiliate Coral Energy, Shell also opened a pipeline linking natural gas between the United States and Mexico. That same month, Texaco and Chevron announced plans to merge. As part of the deal, Texaco eventually would have to divest its portions of Equilon and Motiva, leaving Shell with an option to purchase a greater interest in the venture.

To boost production levels, Shell launched a hostile $1.8 billion bid in 2001 for Barrett Resources Corp., a natural gas producer. Its holdings in the Rocky Mountains, the second largest natural gas basin in the United States, made it extremely attractive to Shell, whose gas output would increase by 20 percent with the purchase. Shell was unsuccessful in its attempts, however, and in May, withdrew its offer after Barrett accepted a deal from Williams Cos. Inc. Nevertheless, Shell's focus on increasing exploration and production efforts left no doubt in the industry that the firm would remain a key player among oil companies.

Principal Subsidiaries

Coral Energy; Equilon Enterprises LLC; Motiva Enterprises LLC; Pecten Arabian Company; Shell Finance Co.; Shell Leasing Co.; Shell Pipe Line Corp.

Principal Competitors

BP plc; Chevron Corporation; Exxon Mobil Corporation.

Further Reading

Beaton, Kendall, *Enterprise in Oil: A History of Shell in the United States,* New York: Appleton-Century-Crofts, 1957.

Bridges, Harry, *The Americanization of Shell: The Beginnings and Early Years of Shell Oil Company in the United States,* New York: Newcomen Society in North America, 1972.

Clewes, Bill, "How Shell Plans to Provide E & P Services on the Open Market," *Offshore,* September, 2000, p. 142.

Culbertson, Katherine, "Exxon, Shell Oil Log Record Years Despite Weak Downstream Results," *Oil Daily,* January 22, 1997, p. 1.

Kupfer, David, ''Worldwide Shell Boycott,'' *Progressive,* January 1996, p. 13.

McWilliams, Gary, ''The Undersea World of Shell Oil,'' *Business Week,* May 15, 1995, pp. 74–78.

Merolli, Paul, ''Motiva Cost Savings Face Analyst Skepticism,'' *Oil Daily,* June 1, 1998.

——, ''Shackling of Shell Was a Long Time Coming,'' *Oil Daily,* March 17, 1999.

——, ''Shell Oil Poised for Wholesale Changes,'' *Oil Daily,* February 22, 1999.

Miller, William H., ''Last of a Breed,'' *Industry Week,* July 18, 1988.

''Mobil, Shell, Conoco Watch Earnings Sink,'' *Oil Daily,* April 23, 1998.

Rouffignac, Ann de, ''Shell, Texaco Sign Major Deal to Combine Refining Assets,'' *Houston Business Journal,* March 21, 1997.

Sampson, Anthony, *The Seven Sisters: The Great Oil Companies and the World They Shaped,* 4th ed., New York: Bantam Books, 1991.

Shell Oil Company: A Story of Achievement, Houston: Shell Oil Company, 1984.

''Shell Oil Launches Hostile Bid for Barrett Resources,'' *Futures World News,* May 1, 2001.

''Shell Pays $1.45 Billion in Gas Deal,'' *Energy Report,* October, 1997, p. 11.

Shell: 75 Years Serving America, Houston: Shell Oil Company, 1987.

Smith, Gene, ''Even First-Class Shell Must Change to Stay Competitive,'' *Oil Daily,* July 15, 1991, p. 2.

Tubb, Maretta, ''Shell's New Business Segment Sparks Pipeline Construction,'' *Pipeline & Gas Journal,* August 1996, p. 18.

Wells, Barbara, *Shell at Deer Park: The Story of the First Fifty Years,* Houston: Shell Oil Company, 1979.

—updates: David E. Salamie, Christina M. Stansell

Sierra On-Line, Inc.

3060 139th Avenue Southeast
Suite 500
Bellevue, Washington 98005-4097
U.S.A.
Telephone: (425) 649-9800
Fax: (425) 641-7617
Web site: http://www.sierra.com

Wholly Owned Subsidiary of Vivendi Universal Publishing
Incorporated: 1979 as On-Line Systems
Employees: 685
Sales: $69.5 million (1999)
NAIC: 51121 Software Publishers; 334611 Software Reproducing

Sierra On-Line, Inc., a subsidiary of Vivendi Universal Publishing (formerly known as Havas Interactive), operates as one of the original developers and largest publishers of interactive entertainment and productivity software worldwide. The firm's four major brands include Sierra Attractions, Sierra Home, Sierra Sports, and Sierra Studios. The company's popular software titles include Hoyle, You Don't Know Jack, the Print Artist Series, the Hallmark Card Studio series, Grand Prix Legends, Nascar Racing 3, Football Pro 99, King's Quest, and Homeworld.

Late 1970s Origins and Growth

Sierra's story began when personal computers were a novelty. In 1979, Los Angeles computer programmer Ken Williams bought an Apple for Christmas. His wife Roberta, a real estate speculator, soon found herself hooked on an early text-only, interactive game called Colossal Cave. She was intrigued by the possibilities of incorporating graphics into such a narrative adventure game. Ken Williams had himself previously stumbled upon these games while logged onto a remote mainframe computer during a tax software programming session. In 1980, Roberta Williams wrote a murder mystery and her husband wrote the computer code for the game in less than a month. Mystery House, the resulting product, immediately sparked incredible demand as the first computer adventure game to combine text and graphics. In the first six months, more than 3,000 copies were sold, worth a retail value of $75,000. These impressive sales came in spite of low-tech packaging involving Ziploc bags and text clipped from magazines.

The company, first known as On-Line Systems, moved in 1980 to Oakhurst, California, at the foot of the Sierra Mountains, and was renamed Sierra On-Line. Its second product, also authored by Roberta Williams, was The Wizard and the Princess; it sold more than 60,000 copies and offered color graphics. Within three years the company's sales reached $10 million. Roberta Williams's attention to story made her games stand out among the industry's first games, which had been developed by programmers, students, and hackers. This was ironic, since the innovation in her first adventure game was the graphics.

Although Ken and Roberta Williams believed their venture to have lucrative possibilities from the beginning, their success was limited by the growth of the personal computer industry. At first, computers were simply too expensive for the mass market. At the urging of investors, in 1983 the company began producing cartridges for the early Atari video game machines, which were about to fall out of fashion. The resulting disaster forced Sierra to cut its number of employees from 120 to 30. Sierra later agreed to produce a version of its Red Baron game, to be released in 1996, for Nintendo's cartridge-based video game system.

A major break for the company came in 1987, when IBM hired the company to develop a game to highlight its XT line of PCs. King's Quest, conceived by Roberta Williams, proved Sierra could continue to ride the crest of innovation and lead a new generation of video games. Aside from garnering international awards, King's Quest spawned as many sequels as a Hollywood blockbuster. By the mid-1990s, series sales had reached three million copies, with each sequel selling better than its predecessor.

Sierra On-Line featured female heroines in later versions of King's Quest and in the 1995 release Phantasmagoria, a development in which Roberta Williams took pride. Realizing that most buyers of computer software were male, she dared to make

Company Perspectives:

Sierra On-Line Inc.'s goal is to develop and bring to market the most creative and technologically advanced products available. Sierra strives to deliver high-quality interactive products that are fun, exciting and innovative in design to appeal to a wide variety of consumers.

a female character, Princess Rosella, the protagonist for King's Quest IV. The gambit worked, and the game sold twice as well as its predecessors. In 1994, Roberta Williams estimated that women made up 15 percent (growing 2 percent yearly) of Sierra On-Line's customers.

In 1989, the company started its own games-only network, another first, which fared poorly out of the gate in spite of a $1 million investment. The ImagiNation Network, originally known as the Sierra Network, formed an alliance with Prodigy in 1993, and added CUC International's Shopper's Advantage on-line shopping service. Although the network reached 45,000 subscribers, high development costs consumed its increasing revenues ($20 million in 1994). The company's poor performance at this time prompted layoffs of 60 employees. The network was taken over by AT&T in 1994, which agreed to pay royalties to Sierra for its software used on the network, as well as certain development costs.

In 1990, Sierra acquired Eugene, Oregon-based Dynamix, a specialist in flight simulation games founded in 1984 by Jeff Tunnell and Damon Slye. Bright Star Technologies, an educational software firm founded by programmer Elon Gasper, was added in 1992 just as the educational software market was becoming the fastest-growing segment of the software industry. The timing was perfect for Sierra: according to Software Publishers of America, annual home educational software sales rose from $146 million to $243 million in 1993. Bright Star benefited from improved distribution and marketing, and Sierra was able to build on Bright Star's HyperAnimation, Talking Tiles, and Alphabet Blocks offerings. The success of this enterprise resulted in 19 new employees being hired at Bright Star in the first year, quadrupling the workforce.

The company went public in 1989, and a second offering followed in 1992, when sales were $41.7 million. The year 1993 proved to be a bleak one and losses were reported in 1994 as well. Sierra relocated its headquarters and moved to the Seattle area in 1993. Ken Williams cited difficulties convincing senior executives to move to rural Oakhurst, California as the prime reason for the move. In the same year, Sierra bought Coktel Vision, headquartered in Paris, which published both education and entertainment software. Ken Williams stated that Sierra's goal was to become the leader in educational software. To this end, Sierra and Western Publishing Group Inc., a leading publisher of children's books, joined in developing interactive software for children aged three to eight under Western's "Golden Step Ahead" brand. Children's Television Workshop, producers of "Sesame Street," announced plans to create a show based on Sierra's Dr. Brain math and science series. Sierra Education also marketed and developed such titles as Berlitz Live! and Talking Tutors. A 1995 joint venture with Pioneer Electronic Corp. established a presence in Japan through Sierra Pioneer, Inc. European sales were worth $15.7 million in 1995 and American sales hit $60.7 million. Other exports, including Canada and Asia, were worth $5.0 million.

Expansion in the Mid-1990s

With $90 million in cash available in 1995, Sierra shopped for underdeveloped companies in fields beyond the highly seasonal entertainment and educational software markets. To round out its strategy games, Sierra bought Cambridge, Massachusetts-based Impressions Software. Sports, auto racing, and flight simulation offerings were beefed up with the purchase of Papyrus Design Group (Watertown, Massachusetts) and SubLogic (Champaign, Illinois), respectively. Home productivity, however, was the focus of Sierra's 1995 acquisitions. The rights to Print Artist, a desktop publishing program for producing greeting cards and banners, were acquired from The Pixellite Group, a group of ten California developers. Green Thumb Software and Arion added gardening and cooking titles to the Sierra line. P.F. Collier embarked on a joint venture with Sierra to produce a multimedia encyclopedia. Sierra breezed into the kitchen with its 1995 purchase of Arion Software's MasterCook series. The series offered a way to manage a database of recipes, as well as scale down the ingredients to produce differing numbers of servings. Although the adventure category's share of Sierra's sales fell to 36 percent in 1995 from 47.4 percent the previous year, education sales hovered around 14 percent. Most of the growth came in the simulation category, nearly doubling from 15.2 percent to 27.9 percent.

With the coursing growth of computer technology, Sierra On-Line came into its own. Multimedia systems and the compact disc added the capacity for full-motion video and high fidelity audio to the gaming scene. Mixed-Up Mother Goose, touted as the first true PC multimedia game, was released in 1990. Sierra On-Line spent lavishly to make the game-playing experience live up to its potential; development efforts occupied more than 75 percent of its staff, and scores of writers, musicians, and actors were employed. The company developed a special computer language, Sierra Creative Interpreter, to allow artists and musicians to contribute without being mired in programming details.

After months of delays, Phantasmagoria finally was released in 1995. A true multimedia product, the game was contained on seven CD-ROMs and featured live actors, three-dimensional backgrounds, and high-fidelity sound effects. CD-ROM products, with their capacity to hold tremendous amounts of sound and picture data, grew increasingly important to Sierra, accounting for 36 percent of game sales in 1994 and 65 percent in 1995. Phantasmagoria was too violent for retailer CompUSA Inc., which refused to carry it. The company included a password protection option with the game to let concerned parents limit their children's access to explicit scenes. The Leisure Suit Larry series had earlier made certain critics groan because of suggestive themes. Nevertheless, by 1995 it had sold more than one million copies.

Sierra pushed the envelope of gaming again in 1995 when it applied IBM VoiceType speech recognition technology to its

Key Dates:

1980: Sierra On-Line begins operating in Oakhurst, California.
1983: Sales reach $10 million.
1987: A partnership with IBM is formed and King's Quest is developed.
1989: The firm goes public.
1990: The company acquires Dynamix.
1992: Bright Star Technologies, an educational software firm, is acquired.
1993: Company headquarters moves to the Seattle, Washington area; Paris-based Coktel Vision is purchased.
1995: The company acquires Print Artist, Green Thumb Software, and Arion Software.
1996: Sierra is acquired by CUC International.
1997: The company acquires Berkeley Systems and Books That Work.
1999: Havas S.A. acquires Sierra.

Command U-boat simulation. Allowing players to merely speak commands rather than enter them through a keyboard or mouse, the CD-ROM included a video orientation featuring historical footage of World War II U-boat commanders. To operate, the game required up-to-date hardware and Windows 95.

Changes in Ownership in the Late 1990s

The company's products were distributed in at least 50 countries in the mid-1990s. Sierra's recent acquisition spree left it with a plethora of software offerings, allowing it to compete with the likes of Microsoft and Broderbund Software. At the same time, the firm's diverse content brought it to the attention of consumer services company CUC International. Sierra agreed to be acquired by CUC in a $1.06 billion stock swap. The deal, announced in February 1996, gave Sierra access to CUC's powerful marketing abilities and its outreach of more than 40 million customers. Sierra eventually operated as part of Cendant Software—after a CUC name change to Cendant Corporation—along with Knowledge Adventure, Davidson & Associates Inc., and Blizzard Entertainment. The Cendant Software unit was touted as one of the largest PC consumer software groups in the world.

Under new ownership, Sierra continued to grow and develop new software. In April 1997, the firm purchased Berkeley Systems, a publisher known for its You Don't Know Jack series, its After Dark screen saver series, and the bezerk network. Sierra also acquired Books That Work, a software developer dedicated to home-related projects. The company continued to focus on introducing new software. Some of its offerings included the Mission Force: Cyberstorm game; a new version of its Print Artist; Print Artist 4.0 Platinum; and the Software Companion for PalmPilot.

As consolidation continued to sweep through the retail software market, Cendant's arsenal of companies anchored its position as a top player in the market. In August 1998, it secured 16.8 percent of the retail market, just ahead of The Learning Company's 16.2 percent, and Microsoft's 10.7 percent. Although Sierra flourished under Cendant Software, parent company Cendant Corp. was faltering under a mountain of debt. As part of its plan to restructure and sell off its noncore assets, Cendant Corp. sold its software publishing arm to Paris-based Havas S.A. for roughly $800 million. In January 1999, Cendant Software became Havas Interactive and operated as worldwide leader of interactive content with Sierra among its holdings.

Restructuring and Significant Product Development for the New Millennium

Yet again under new ownership, Sierra began to reorganize its operating structure. It formed four divisions, separating its diverse offerings into Sierra Attractions, Sierra Home, Sierra Sports, and Sierra Studios. The firm continued to take advantage of the Internet and its vast opportunities for creating Internet interfaces for its games. When Starsiege, a science fiction combat game, became available in March 1999, an Internet interface was made available for game players where they could join a game in progress, talk to other players, read information on the game, and get tips and hints for playing the game.

Sierra continued to introduce new software throughout the year. The firm released The Complete Web Studio, catering to home users who needed a simple way to create web sites. The program offered everything from templates to an upload wizard. Sierra also launched its newest version of Hoyle Casino, a CD-ROM game that was named the best-selling casino game of 1999 by PC Data. The company ended 1999 by releasing three new home and garden software products and MasterCook Food & Wine, a venture with *Food & Wine* magazine.

The Sierra Home division continued to release new products as the company entered the new millennium. The Generations Family Tree Millennium Collection was launched with more than 200 years of immigration records. With the software package, a user had access to 60,000 web links, immigration content, Ellis Island information, and family tree clip art. In May 2000, Sierra teamed up with Hallmark Cards Inc. to create Hallmark Card Studio, a personal expression software package. The firm also continued to build upon its popular Hoyle CD-ROM series.

Sierra management continued to pursue avenues that would allow its software products to develop into easy-to-use and informative Internet interfaces. Its games continued to have a cult-like following among game players and new releases were eagerly anticipated. Under the leadership of Havas International, which was renamed Vivendi Universal Publishing early in 2001, Sierra was poised to remain a leader in software entertainment for years to come. New leadership at Sierra was named in May 2001 and consisted of Thomas Hernquist as president and CEO, and Michael Ryder as COO and senior vice-president of product development. Both men were big names in the industry and reportedly looked forward to their mission as stated in a company press release: "expanding Sierra's success across platforms, toward what is increasingly a mass market, and internationally."

Principal Divisions

Sierra Attractions; Sierra Home; Sierra Sports; Sierra Studios.

Principal Competitors

The Learning Company; Microsoft Corp.

Further Reading

Baker, M. Sharon, ''CFO's Sharp Pencil Puts Sierra On-Line on Track,'' *Puget Sound Business Journal,* November 18, 1994, p. 9.

——, ''Sierra Buy Speeds Software Consolidation,'' *Puget Sound Business Journal,* February 23, 1996, p. 1.

——, ''Sierra Buying Spree Lifts It into Top Ranks,'' *Puget Sound Business Journal,* January 5, 1996, p. 1.

——, ''Sierra On-Line Goes Shopping for Smaller Software Firms,'' *Puget Sound Business Journal,* June 9, 1995, p. 4.

——, ''Sierra On-Line Moving HQ to Seattle Area,'' *Puget Sound Business Journal,* May 21, 1993, pp. 1, 39.

——, '' 'Visionary' Workaholic Leads Game-Maker Sierra,'' *Puget Sound Business Journal,* October 22, 1993, pp. 1, 49.

Brandt, Richard, ''Serious Money from the Games PCs Play,'' *Business Week,* May 21, 1990, p. 112.

Brenesal, Barry, ''Journey to the Dark Side with Gabriel Knight,'' *PC Magazine,* May 31, 1994.

Champion, Jill, ''Redesigning the Classics,'' *Compute,* January, 1992, p. 8.

Eng, Paul M., and Evan I. Schwartz, ''The Games People Play in the Office,'' *Business Week,* October 11, 1993, p. 40.

Greenman, Catherine, ''Phantasmagoria Retailers Wait,'' *HFN: The Weekly Newspaper for the Home Furnishing Network,* July 10, 1995, p. 85.

——, ''The Teaching Game: Big Bucks Lure Software Makers to Mix Education and Entertainment,'' *HFD: The Weekly Home Furnishings Newspaper,* June 20, 1994, p. C14.

Kenedy, Kristen, ''Sierra President on CUC Merger,'' *Computer Retail Week,* March 4, 1996, p. 24.

Khalaf, Roula, ''Accounting Adventure,'' *Forbes,* September 28, 1992, pp. 116–18.

Khermouch, Gerry, ''IBM, Sierra Set Campus Disk Drive,'' *Brandweek,* August 30, 1993, p. 3.

Kramer, Farrell, ''Game Designer Touts Story: Woman Has Seen Some Controversy with Career Choice,'' *The State* (Columbia, S. Car.), November 5, 1995, p. H3.

LaPlante, Alice, ''The Other Half,'' *PC Week,* March 21, 1994, p. A1.

Lasky, Michael S., ''PalmPilot Goodies,'' *PC World,* May 1998, p. 76.

Linderholm, Owen, ''Build a Web Site in a Day,'' *Network World,* September 13, 1999.

Losee, Stephanie, ''Fortune Visits 25 Cool Companies: Sierra On-Line,'' *Fortune,* Autumn 1993, p. 82.

Manly, Lorne, ''Titles Try Hybrid Online Options,'' *Folio: The Magazine for Magazine Management,* May 1, 1994, p. 22.

''Next He Does Robo-Cop?,'' *Time,* October 4, 1993, p. 93.

Nicholls, Paul, ''Multimedia Personal Computing: A Guide to the New MPC,'' *CD-ROM Professional,* September 1992, pp. 113–17.

Rooney, Paula, ''Consolidation Shifts Power in Retail Software Market,'' *Computer Retail Week,* October 26, 1998, p. 6.

Rubenking, Neil J., ''Leisure Suit Larry Shapes Up,'' *PC Magazine,* March 29, 1994, p. 408.

Sandberg, Jared, ''AT&T Corp. Agrees to Pay $40 Million for Remaining 80% of ImagiNation,'' *Wall Street Journal,* November 16, 1994, p. 6.

Sanner, Matt, ''Strategy for the Thinking Gamer,'' *PC World,* October 1996, p. M12.

Schiff, David, ''The Dangers of Creative Accounting,'' *Worth,* March 1993.

Schwartz, Steven A., ''Space Quest 1: Roger Wilco in the Sarien Encounter,'' *Macworld,* April 1993, p. 171.

Shaw, Simon, ''Games War,'' *Management Today,* December 1994, pp. 76–80.

''Sierra Home Releases Genealogy CD-ROM Suite,'' *Information Today,* April 2000, p. 43.

''Sierra Intros Voice-Controlled Game,'' *Newsbytes,* September 18, 1995.

''Sierra On-Line Inc.,'' *Television Digest,* February 13, 1995, p. 14.

Spector, Lincoln, ''Recipe Software—It Isn't All Out to Lunch,'' *PC World,* January 1996.

Trivette, Donald B., ''The Top 100 CD-ROMs: Entertainment,'' *PC Magazine,* September 13, 1994.

—Frederick C. Ingram
—update: Christina M. Stansell

SIFCO Industries, Inc.

970 East 64th Street
Cleveland, Ohio 44103
U.S.A.
Telephone: (216) 881-8600
Fax: (216) 432-6281
Web site: http://www.sifco.com

Public Company
Incorporated: 1913 as the Steel Improvement Company
Employees: 800
Sales: $106.14 million (2000)
Stock Exchanges: American
Ticker Symbol: SIF
NAIC: 331221 Rolled Steel Shape Manufacturing; 331316 Aluminum Extruded Product Manufacturing; 332313 Plate Work Manufacturing; 332111 Iron and Steel Forging; 332112 Nonferrous Forging; 332813 Electroplating, Plating, Polishing, Anodizing, and Coloring; 333319 All Other Miscellaneous Fabricated Metal Product Manufacturing

SIFCO Industries, Inc. specializes in repairing jet turbine components and supplying parts to the aerospace market. The company is half-owned by descendants of C.H. Smith, who took over the company in the 1920s. Although dwarfed by rivals AAR Corp. and Goodrich Corporation, SIFCO has played a pioneering role in the aerospace industry, being the first to successfully forge alloys of titanium and other space age metals. By 2000, two-thirds of SIFCO's business was repair work; aircraft parts accounted for the rest.

Early 20th Century Origins

The Steel Improvement Company was founded in Cleveland, Ohio in 1913. Its five principals formed the company to market new scientific principles in the 4,000 year-old art of heat-treating metals. Three years later, Steel Improvement merged with an adjacent business—the Forest City Machine Company—which was a supplier of hardware for power lines. The new entity was called the Steel Improvement and Forge Company.

The new automobile and aircraft industries, as well as ships and military armaments, provided a ready market for the company during World War I. Peacetime profits, however, were scarce.

In 1920, the company's bankers encouraged C.H. Smith to leave Alcoa's pioneering aluminum forge to work as Steel Improvement's sales manager. Upon his arrival at the company, Smith attempted to make the company less dependent on the highly competitive auto industry. He found new business as a supplier to makers of valves, air compressors, and forklifts. But his greatest success came in improving high-stress components (specifically, still-plugs) for the oil industry. Steel Improvement used a new forging, rather than casting, process with nickel-based alloys to create still-plugs that could withstand the heat, pressure, and corrosion in oil refining equipment. This created a hugely successful new line of business.

Smith was promoted to the position of company president in 1925. One of his first tasks was to relocate the growing company's facilities to a site near downtown Cleveland—a site that the company would occupy for more than 70 years. The new plant opened in 1928.

New Lines of Business in the Depression Years

Steel Improvement nonetheless suffered in the Great Depression. It did pick up two new lines of business, though: forging mass-produced golf club heads, and creating specialized parts for the nascent aircraft industry. This latter area of endeavor took off, so to speak, during World War II. In 1939, the Thompson Products Company (later a part of TRW) contracted Steel Improvement to make forgings for its British client, the Bristol Aeroplane Company (later a part of Rolls-Royce plc).

Meanwhile, Steel Improvement had already been making parts for military equipment, including high-strength torpedo propellers. By the end of the war, the company was also producing turbine wheels for aircraft turbosuperchargers and jet engines.

Charles Smith, Jr. (''Charlie'') was named as the company's president and chief officer at the age of twenty-two, following the sudden death of his father in December 1942. At the time,

Company Perspectives:

SIFCO Industries, Inc. is dedicated to serving the technical needs of the aerospace industry in the production, repair, coating, machining and marketing of jet engines and aerospace components. We are committed to the absolute satisfaction of our customers worldwide through competitive pricing, total service, comprehensive technology and superior quality.

Charles Jr. had been attending the Massachusetts Institute of Technology and had already previously worked in various departments at Steel Improvement—apparently being groomed for a leadership position.

Postwar Pioneering

Steel Improvement was involved in pioneering metallurgy research projects after World War II. The company became the first to successfully forge titanium in 1949. Six years later, it was forging molybdenum alloys, which were used in rocket nozzles. Both projects were arranged by GE. At the same time, Steel Improvement was also supplying parts for the Canadian firm A.V. Roe Ltd.—a subsidiary of Britain's Hawker Siddely, Ltd.—who was developing a jet fighter for the Canadian military.

Steel Improvement sold its Canadian operations in 1954 and bought the neighboring Champion Forge Co.—a company which acted as supplier to the Cleveland Pneumatic Tool Company, a leader in landing gear for large planes. Some of the equipment obtained from Champion Forge was used to start plants in South America. The first was created in 1958 in cooperation with Industrias Kaiser Argentina; Steel Improvement only took a 5 percent equity share in this venture. SIFCO do Brasil, launched the next year in partnership with Cia Mechanica e Importadoro, S.A., would become the Southern Hemisphere's largest producer of forgings. In 1961, Steel Improvement helped design a large forge in India, earning a two and a half percent holding in Bharat Forge Company, Ltd. as a commission.

Steel Improvement bought Minneapolis-based Custom Tool and Manufacturing Company in 1957, whose machining capabilities extended the new parent company's opportunities for state-of-the-art aerospace engineering. Steel Improvement's research and development extended to new methods of titanium fabrication, electroplating, and electrochemical machining (ECM).

Steel Improvement was privately and closely owned until December 1956, when some shareholders sold a portion of their holdings. Additional new shares were issued in August 1957.

A New Name and New Opportunities: 1969 Through the 1980s

At the beginning of the year 1969, Steel Improvement changed its name to SIFCO Industries, Inc. The company then ventured into the aluminum forging business through the 1969 acquisition of Schick Products on the West Coast. Schick produced aluminum hand tools in addition to aircraft forgings; however, the company was ultimately unable to find a market for them. A more successful venture, also launched in 1969, was the purchase of an Avon, Ohio plant that would become SIFCO Bearings. Another enduring line of business begun in the late 1960s was the repair of jet turbine components for airlines—beginning with Northwest in Minneapolis—where SIFCO located its turbine component repair facilities.

The company began listing on the American Stock Exchange in September 1969, seven months after changing its name. Leadership was restructured soon after. Executive vice president Toby Milnes became president and chief operating officer, while Smith became chairman of the board and chief executive officer.

SIFCO built a high volume forge (Presforge) in 1979. The same year, it bought a small Michigan company specializing in cold forging. In 1980, a dedicated facility was built in Tampa, Florida to handle turbine blade repair work. SIFCO Turbine Component Services (STCS) was spun off as a separate company, with Westinghouse Electric Corporation taking a 35 percent share. Work on a facility in Cork, Ireland began in 1983.

Tough Times in the Mid- and Late 1980s

Kevin O'Donnell, who had become SIFCO's president and chief operating officer in 1976 and was a company veteran since 1947, was named CEO in February 1983. Eventually, upon his shoulders fell the job of dismantling the company's high-volume automotive forging operations, which the company shed in the late 1980s due to lowered demand and competition from abroad and from alternate materials. *Crain's* noted that forging had accounted for 75 percent of revenue and 84 percent of operating income in 1982; four years later, it accounted for only about 50 percent of revenue and just 3 percent of profits. SIFCO's total revenues were $72 million in 1982 and just $61 million in 1986. An acrimonious, four-week strike at SIFCO's Cleveland forge accompanied the downsizing, which left SIFCO with a total of 550 employees in 1990.

The company also closed or sold all of its interests in Brazil and India, as well as the cold forge (Coldforge) and bearings operations. SIFCO then looked to its aerospace business for growth, expanding its subassembly and replacement parts manufacturing. It also continued to contribute to advanced aerospace programs, such as the Space Shuttle.

SIFCO posted a $2.4 million loss in fiscal 1988 but boasted a $4.5 million profit the next year. Its stock price more than doubled during the year.

Jeffrey P. Gotschall, a grandson of the company founder, was named president in 1989, and CEO the next year upon Kevin O'Donnell's retirement. At that point, the Smith family owned about half of SIFCO's stock.

Recovery in the 1990s

The recession that crippled the airline industry in the early 1990s affected SIFCO as well. Defense orders continued to fall after the end of the Cold War; more layoffs followed. The company did seek to capitalize on its areas of expertise during that time. SIFCO launched a new forging joint venture with the

Key Dates:

1913: Steel Improvement formed to exploit metalworking science.
1920: C.H. Smith joins Steel Improvement.
1939: Steel Improvement begins production of airplane parts.
1949: Titanium forging pioneered.
1958: Brazilian venture is begun.
1969: Company changes name to SIFCO Industries, Inc.; lists on American stock exchange.
1980: New turbine repair center built in Tampa.
1991: Industry-wide recession affects revenues.
1996: Restructured SIFCO posts record sales.

People's Republic of China in January 1990. In June 1992, SIFCO acquired Selectrons Ltd. of Waterbury Connecticut, a competitor in metal-plating equipment. SIFCO later sued this company's former owner for fraud, alleging he sold his customer list to another competitor before the transaction.

SIFCO lost $440,000 on sales of $57.6 million for the 1992 fiscal year, after earning $2.8 million on $65.3 million in 1991 revenues. There was clearly a need for further restructuring. Uniquely, a 10-member commission of employees was created in 1994 to decide where cuts needed to be made at SIFCO's Ohio forge. A consulting firm was also brought in. By the end of the year, 35 jobs had been eliminated while the company worked on increasing efficiency, thus putting the company in the black again. SIFCO also benefited from its customers reducing the number of suppliers on their vendor lists.

A number of smaller competitors went out of business during the downturn; SIFCO had survived. In 1995, SIFCO took over some forgings work from Wyman-Gordon Co., which was closing an outdated plant in Massachusetts. The $400 million company had a reputation for technological leadership.

The recovery of the commercial airline business in the mid-1990s was good for SIFCO, which benefited from new orders at Boeing Co. By 1996, SIFCO was reporting record sales, which surpassed $100 million in fiscal 1997. Aerospace components sales rose 46 percent.

SIFCO in the New Millennium

SIFCO then expanded its facilities in Ireland and Florida, but did not realize expected sales growth. Income for the fiscal year ending September 30, 2000 was $2.4 million, down from 1999's $3.8 million; sales fell to $106.1 million from $115.5 million.

A $7.5 million turbine blade repair joint venture with Rolls-Royce plc, a leading jet engine producer, was announced in March 2001. Aimed at clients in the Americas, work was to initially be completed at SIFCO's Tampa facilities.

Principal Subsidiaries

SIFCO Custom Machine; SIFCO Holdings Inc.; SIFCO Irish Holdings Ltd.; SIFCO Selective Plating (France); SIFCO Selective Plating, Ltd. (U.K.).

Principal Divisions

SIFCO Selective Plating; Turbine Component Services and Repair; Aerospace Component Manufacturing.

Principal Operating Units

Turbine Component Services and Repair; Aerospace Component Manufacturing.

Principal Competitors

AAR Corp.; Goodrich Corporation; Kellstrom Industries, Inc.; LDC Inc.

Further Reading

Ashyk, Loretta, "With its Downsizing Complete, SIFCO Turns Away from Forging," *Crain's Cleveland Business,* April 6, 1987, p. 3.
Gaw, Jonathan, "Park-0hio, SIFCO Discussed Merging," *Plain Dealer (Cleveland),* December 8, 1994, p. 1C.
Gerdel, Thomas W., "Concessions Kept SIFCO From Default; Forgings Firm Reports Loss, Hints at Job Cuts," *Plain Dealer (Cleveland),* November 16, 1993, p. 1.
——, "Ohio Suppliers Try to Keep Up with New Orders," *Plain Dealer (Cleveland),* November 1, 1997, p. 1C.
McKenna, Joseph F., "SIFCO Is 'Positioned,' But Now the Race Starts," *Industry Week,* June 18, 1990, p. 26.
Prizinsky, David, "Aerospace Parts Orders in a Dive," *Crain's Cleveland Business,* August 5, 1991, p. 3.
——, "Defense Cuts, Airline Woes Squeeze SIFCO," *Crain's Cleveland Business,* January 4, 1993, p. 3F.
——, "Forging a Turnaround," *Crain's Cleveland Business,* September 5, 1994, p. 1.
——, "SIFCO's CEO-to-Be Continues Leadership Tradition," *Crain's Cleveland Business,* June 4, 1990, p. 4.
Sabath, Donald, "Executive Forging Ahead at SIFCO; Founder's Grandson to Lead Forge Group," *Plain Dealer (Cleveland),* January 20, 1998, p. 3C.
——, "Ohio Suppliers to Benefit from Boeing Plane Orders," *Plain Dealer (Cleveland),* September 14, 1996, p. 1C.
——, "SIFCO Industries Forging Ahead," *Plain Dealer (Cleveland),* January 12, 1997, p. 2I.
——, "SIFCO to Take Over Work from Mass. Forging Plant," *Plain Dealer (Cleveland),* June 2, 1995, p. 2C.
Smith, Charles H., *SIFCO Industries, Inc.: 'Forging Ahead',* New York: Newcomen Society of the United States, 1983.
Suttell, Scott, "Stampeding Market Brings Lofty Returns," *Crain's Cleveland Business, Special Section,* May 25, 1998, p. S21.
Thompson, Chris, "SIFCO Lawsuit Alleges Fraud in Asset Sale," *Crain's Cleveland Business,* October 4, 1993, p. 3F.
Valenti, Michael, "Sensors Unite for Process Improvement," *Mechanical Engineering,* September 1992, p. 54.

—Frederick C. Ingram

Simula, Inc.

2700 North Central Avenue, Suite 1000
Phoenix, Arizona 85004
U.S.A.
Telephone: (602) 631-4005
Fax: (602) 631-9005
Web site: http://www.simula.com

Public Company
Incorporated: 1975
Employees: 750
Sales: $97.3 million (2000)
Stock Exchanges: American
Ticker Symbol: SMU
NAIC: 54171 Research and Development in the Physical, Engineering, and Life Sciences; 33636 Motor Vehicle Seating and Interior Trim Manufacturing; 336399 All Other Motor Vehicle Parts Manufacturing; 336413 Other Aircraft Parts and Auxiliary Equipment Manufacturing; 551112 Offices of Other Holding Companies

Simula, Inc. makes high-tech products designed to protect people in vehicles. As a research firm, Simula helps draft safety requirements for civil and military air transports; as a manufacturing firm, the company designs products to meet the new requirements. The company's business is split evenly between the military and commercial sectors. About half the seats in new US military helicopters are made by Simula. Headquartered in Phoenix, Arizona, Simula operates eight divisions and subsidiaries located throughout the United States and the United Kingdom, with more than 700 employees worldwide.

Company Origins: 1970s–80s

Simula, Inc. was founded by Stanley Desjardins in 1975 to bring crash safety research results into production. Years before, Desjardins was born in a farm town in northern Minnesota, and his family followed his father to an Army base in Idaho during World War II. Desjardins later joined the National Guard himself, and served active duty in the Korean War. There, he may have seen the need for better protective equipment in military helicopters.

The GI Bill put Desjardins into college, and he studied mechanical engineering at the University of Idaho. There, he developed an interest in solid-propellant rocketry. As a result, in 1958 he took a job at Thiokol Chemical Corp. in Utah, working on nozzle design for the Minuteman program—the first solid-propellant intercontinental ballistic missiles (ICBMs). After ten years at Thiokol, Desjardins accepted a job offer from a friend at a tiny Arizona company (later part of Ultrasystems Inc.) studying crash safety. Soon thereafter, in 1975 Desjardins founded Simula, Inc. to bring this research—and the results gathered from it—into production.

Simula had no shop facilities of its own, and its first big break was supplying seats for Sikorsky Aircraft Corporation's bid for a military utility helicopter contract. Desjardins developed the energy-absorbing, ''crashworthy'' seats himself—seats which helped Sikorsky's design beat out a Boeing offering for the contract. Desjardins later told *The Business Journal (Phoenix)* that the design work for those seats started on a drawing board that a friend kept in his bedroom.

In 1981, federal regulators contracted Simula to study jet airliner crashes. One of the firm's recommendations was stronger seats, which would later become a key line of business for the company. Within a decade, the company soon grew to employ 185 people by the 1990s.

Growth and Expansion Into the 1990s

The company earned a net income of $1.7 million on revenues of $15.1 million in 1991, up from earnings of $94,000 on 1990's $12.3 million in revenues. Thus, Simula decided to launch its initial public offering in April 1992 at $5 a share. The company was hoping to raise money to enter the commercial aircraft market, which would be a vital strategic move, given post-*perestroika* defense cutbacks.

In August 1993, Simula bought San Diego-based Airline Interiors Inc. for $4 million, gaining access to aircraft manufac-

Company Perspectives:

Simula makes a life saving difference every day. For over 25 years we have developed and supplied equipment and systems designed to safeguard human lives. Our technologies and products are sold around the world for a wide range of applications in various markets and industries.

turers. Simula's sales rose by a third for the year to $24.8 million, though earnings declined 11 percent to $1.1 million.

In July 1994, Simula bought Coach and Car Equipment Corp., a $12 million a year company based in Elk Grove, Illinois, that produced railway seating systems. Simula also began developing side airbags for automobiles. Airbags were also being designed for use inside the Army's UH-60 Blackhawk helicopter. About half of Simula's business at the time involved defense contractors.

Bulkhead airbag systems for commercial aircraft was another potential new market. Simula also had an offering for the relatively small armored car market: a cheap, portable $10,000 kit that included armored panels and a secondary bulletproof windshield.

By the end of 1994, Simula's share price had exceeded $25, and the company was being touted as the darling of Arizona's high tech sector. The company then landed a deal to put Inflatable Tubular Structure (ITS) side-airbags in BMWs beginning in 1997. Informally dubbed *weisswurst,* (''white sausage''), these were to be produced in Scotland in collaboration with Autoliv AB, a Swedish airbag manufacturer. Simula chose to work with Autoliv because it felt it needed a partner acquainted with the mass volumes required by the automotive industry, where production was measured in millions—not hundreds—of units.

Tough Financial Times in the Mid- and Late 1990s

Donald W. Townsend, the company's chief financial officer since 1986, received the titles of president and chief operating officer of Simula in November 1994. The founder and former president, Desjardins, remained as the company's chairman and CEO (though Townsend would later become CEO as well).

The company's profits doubled to $2.1 million in 1994 on sales of $41.2 million. An additional public offering in March 1995, however, failed to garner the desired response. Simula had hoped to net $25 million from the sale, which was earmarked towards reducing debt and expanding manufacturing facilities. But the company ended up with only $22 million from the sale. It was thought that the high share price in relation to earnings (36 times 1994 earnings) and a relatively high debt level ($20 million) may have discouraged investors. Desjardins personally owned 45 percent after the offering; he had planned to sell some of his shares, but changed his mind.

Simula's earnings grew at a 90 percent clip throughout 1995, but its share price fell more than 20 percent one week in November. It was then that enraged analysts learned the company's third quarter profits were derived largely from a tax benefit related to a previous acquisition.

On a positive note, Simula picked up new armoring business early in 1996 due to the United States military's peacekeeping deployment in Bosnia. The company then announced plans to relocate from Tempe to downtown Phoenix in May 1996. By that time, Simula had 730 full-time employees working in several plants around the country.

In 1996, Simula formed a UK subsidiary to supply BMW's side airbags from a plant in Newcastle, after beginning the production in Phoenix. At the same time elsewhere in northern England, the Manchester-based Airtours tour operator ordered seats for its Airbus A320 aircraft from Simula's San Diego-based Airline Interiors unit.

After 12 consecutive quarters of income growth, Simula finally announced a loss for the third quarter of 1996. The loss was attributed to more conservative accounting practices. In fact, Simula would post a loss for the year, and that was just the beginning of the bad news. Production problems in 1997 kept its airliner seat business unprofitable, as inexperienced workers had trouble meeting demand.

A joint venture with leading automotive airbag supplier TRW Vehicle Safety Systems Inc. was announced in June 1998, and helped to reassure investors. The losses continued, however, even though sales rose 33 percent in 1998 to $100.7 million. The company's share price fell to $5 by mid-1999. Complaints of low stock ownership among board members prompted one director, Tom Emerson, to pledge to invest $50,000 in the company; but it was a promise that had not yet been kept by May 2000.

The company's Coach and Car Equipment division was sold at a $4 million loss in November 1999, in an attempt to pay off debt that amounted to 70 percent of capitalization. Simula received $10 million in the controversial sale to a group of investors, but the deal was written so that Simula would receive only interest payments until 2004. Simula shareholders and Coach & Car employees doubted the buyers' ability to pay, and in April 2000 Simula wrote off the $10 million note, though it still expected to eventually be paid ''something'' from the money-losing enterprise.

In January 2000, Simula also announced the sale of its Airline Interiors Inc. unit to Weber Aircraft Inc., a Texas-based subsidiary of Zodiac SA of France. The sale went through for $11.4 million in cash and $9.4 million in assumed liabilities.

Meanwhile, Simula had supplied seating and parachutes, free, for the Team Re/Max attempt to circumnavigate the world in a hot-air balloon in 1998–99. Its share price did not prove as buoyant as the balloon, however, falling to an all-time low in May 2000 of about $2. This dip in price came alongside news of a first-quarter loss resulting largely from divestments in the previous year.

New Direction in 2000 and Beyond

Bradley P. Forst, a Phoenix lawyer, was named CEO on October 1, 2000 after Donald Townsend resigned. Simula's

Key Dates:

1975: Simula, Inc. is founded to produce crashworthy helicopter seating.
1981: US Government commissions Simula to study airliner crashes.
1992: Simula goes public.
1995: The company begins five years of losses, even as revenues grow.
1997: BMW Inc. begins offering Simula's side airbags in certain automobile models.
2000: New officers, new strategies attempt to satisfy shareholders.

heavily depressed share price rose 40 percent on the news, once again reaching $2. Soon after taking office, Forst announced plans to add more outsiders to the board of directors, as well as review the sales-based executive bonuses that had irked minority shareholders for so long. Strategically, the company would focus on making air bags as well as body armor and armor for military vehicles.

De-listed from the Big Board, Simula began trading on the American (AMEX) Stock Exchange in November 2000. After losing money every year since 1995, Simula lost $6 million in 2000, mostly due to write-offs and restructuring charges. Auditors warned of Simula's ability to remain a going concern after one of its lenders, a Beverly Hills investment bank, refused to grant waivers for non-monetary violations of a loan agreement. Simula officials stated this investment bank had asked $2 million for such waivers. Forst was optimistic of buying back the $20 million note with help from another financier, though.

Principal Subsidiaries

Airline Interiors, Inc.; Artcraft Industries Corp.; International Center for Safety Education, Inc.; Simula Automotive Safety Devices, Inc.; Simula Automotive Safety Devices, Ltd. (UK); Simula Composites Corporation; Simula Polymer Systems, Inc.; Simula Protective Systems, Limited (UK); Simula Safety Systems, Inc.; Simula Technologies, Inc.; Simula Transportation Equipment Corporation.

Principal Divisions

Automotive Safety Systems; Aerospace & Defense Systems; Advanced Polymer Materials; Technology Development & Testing.

Principal Operating Units

Commercial Products; Aerospace and Defense.

Principal Competitors

Autoliv AB; Israeli Aircraft Industries Ltd.; Martin-Baker Aircraft Co. Ltd.; Mexican Industries in Michigan Inc. Safety Components International, Inc.; TRW Vehicle Safety Systems Inc.

Further Reading

''Auditors Question Viability of Troubled Simula,'' *Associated Press State & Local Wire,* April 19, 2001.
Davis, Riccardo A., ''Simula Bows to Its Critics,'' *Arizona Republic,* October 17, 2000, p. D10.
——, ''Simula Stock Falls Hard,'' *Arizona Republic,* May 12, 2000, p. D1.
Fehr-Snyder, Kerry, ''Phoenix-Based Simula Sees Stock Rise on News of Air Bag Deal,'' *Arizona Republic,* June 10, 1998.
Foster, Ed, ''Simula, Inc. Loss Attributed to Accounting Change,'' *Arizona Republic,* November 15, 1996.
——, ''Tempe Firm's 'Sausage' Could Save You; Auto Safety Device Shields Head in Crash,'' *Arizona Republic,* August 4, 1995, p. C1.
Gilbertson, Dawn, ''Ford's News Gives Simula Another Boost,'' *Arizona Republic,* April 12, 1998, p. D1.
——, ''Shareholders Underwhelmed by Simula Vows,'' *Arizona Republic,* June 20, 1999, p. D1.
——, ''Simula Director Yet to Keep Promise,'' *Arizona Republic,* May 12, 2000, p. D1.
——, ''Simula Shares Crash in Rough Week,'' *Arizona Republic,* November 19, 1995, p. D2.
——, ''Simula Stock Jumps 39 Percent as CEO Retires,'' *Arizona Republic,* October 3, 2000, p. D1.
——, ''Simula Writes Off Note for $10 Million,'' *Arizona Republic,* April 18, 2000, p. D1.
Gilbertson, Dawn and Russ Wiles, ''Phoenix Firm to Divest Train-Seat Unit in Hopes of Paying Off Debt,'' *Arizona Republic,* November 8, 1999.
Golfen, Bob, ''Endurance Testers; Simula Pushes Gear's Limits to Improve Safety,'' *Arizona Republic,* December 21, 2000, p. D1.
Hart, Dan, ''Simula Loss Wider Than Expected,'' *Arizona Republic,* March 31, 1999, p. E3.
Luebke, Cathy, ''Stan Desjardins: Simula Founder Is Well-Versed in Every Aspect of His Business,'' *Business Journal (Phoenix),* October 12, 1992, p. 12.
Maio, Patrick J., ''Sit Tight,'' *Investor's Business Daily,* July 18, 1995, p. A4.
Mencke, Claire, ''Rebound,'' *Investor's Business Daily,* September 27, 1994, p. A6.
Reagor, Catherine, ''Simula Stock Jumps as It Crashes Into New Markets,'' *The Business Journal (Phoenix),* October 7, 1994, p. 24.
——, ''Simula to Expand, Files $35 Million Offering,'' *Business Journal (Phoenix),* February 10, 1995, p. 1.
Rolwing, Rebecca, ''Tempe, Ariz. Firm Built Equipment for US-Australian Balloon Quest,'' *Arizona Republic,* January 4, 1999.
——, ''Valley Firms Rush to Fill Bosnian Orders,'' *Business Journal (Phoenix),* February 9, 1996, pp. 1F.
Rundle, Rhonda L., ''Do You Envy Clinton His Limo? This Kit Could Be for You,'' *Wall Street Journal,* September 25, 1995, p. B1.
Schneider, Paul, ''Longtime CFO Wins Key Post at Surging Firm,'' *Arizona Business Gazette,* November 17, 1994, p. 9.
——, ''Rise in Stock Price Follows Simula Growth,'' *Arizona Business Gazette,* June 9, 1994, p. 9.
——, ''Simula, Founder to Sell Shares of Growing Business,'' *Arizona Business Gazette,* March 23, 1995, p. 6.
Waxler, Caroline, ''Injury-Proof,'' *Forbes,* June 16, 1997, p. 270.
Weinstein, Randi, ''Reinventing a Firm,'' *Business Journal (Phoenix),* April 27, 2001, p. 20B.
Wiles, Russ, ''Simula Doubled Take in '94,'' *Arizona Republic,* March 3, 1995, p. D1.
——, ''Simula Offering Falls Short; $22 Million Net Below Firm's Goal,'' *Arizona Republic,* March 31, 1995, p. E1.

—Frederick C. Ingram

Singer & Friedlander Group plc

21 New Street
Bishopsgate
London EC2M 4HR
United Kingdom
Telephone: (+44) 20-7623-3000
Fax: (+44) 20-7623-2122
Web site: http://www.singer-friedlander.com

Public Company
Incorporated: 1920
Employees: 1,409
Sales: £585.76 million ($874.4 million) (2000)
Stock Exchanges: London
Ticker Symbol: SFL
NAIC: 523110 Investment Banking and Securities Dealing; 522293 International Trade Financing

Singer & Friedlander Group plc is one of the United Kingdom's last remaining independent merchant banks, providing investment banking services to an essentially private clientele. The firm offers a wide range of services, such as asset management and independent savings accounts, including offshore banking facilities, unit trusts, and financing facilities. In the late 1990s, Singer & Friedlander's forecast of an extended bear market led it to separate from its Collins Stewart brokerage subsidiary, which was sold back to its founders in 2000. The company also has moved to liquidate its 55 percent share of Sweden's Carnegie Group, spun off in a public offering in June 2001. Singer & Friedlander's stake dropped to just 32 percent after the IPO. Although these two units represented the largest part of the firm's net profits, Singer & Friedlander's moves have enabled the company to streamline its activity and focus on its core investment banking services. The company also has suggested an interest in stepping up its venture capital investments. Singer & Friedlander is led by chairman and CEO John Hodson. The firm, one of the top 250 listed on the London stock exchange, posted more than £585 million in 2000.

Stockbroker Origins at the Turn of the Century

Julius Singer founded a stockbroking firm in London in 1907. Singer was joined soon after by Ernst Friedlander, a native of Germany, whose family had been a prominent name in Berlin banking since the middle of the previous century. Friedlander himself had been the founder of the first merchant bank to open in South Africa, and he had been named as chairman of the Johannesburg stock exchange. Friedlander's background gave the young firm a strong boost into the growing London exchange.

World War I disrupted trading, and the company, possibly because of its ties with Germany, was forced to withdraw from the London exchange. Instead, Singer and Friedlander entered the banking industry. After taking on two new partners, Julius Stern and Max Ullman, in 1920, the company incorporated as a partnership under the Singer & Friedlander name.

Singer & Friedlander established itself as one of the most prominent merchant banks in London's City. By 1957, the firm was able to go public. The public offering helped make the bank an attractive takeover target, however. Over the next 30 years, Singer & Friedlander was to find itself under a number of new owners.

Yet losing its independence did not stop Singer & Friedlander from continuing to grow and develop its product portfolio. The bank was one of the first British merchant banks to invest in the booming Japanese market in the 1960s, as that economy shifted from a developing market to that of one of the world's economic drivers. Singer & Friedlander also became interested in the Spanish market, which, while languishing under the Franco dictatorship, was to see a renaissance after Franco's death in the mid-1970s. Back at home, Singer & Friedlander was expanding from its London bank, targeting the United Kingdom's regional markets with satellite office operations, such as an office opened in Birmingham in 1963. Other locations included offices in Bristol and Nottingham.

In 1971, Singer & Friedlander opened its own offshore banking facility. Taking advantage of liberalized tax policies

Company Perspectives:

We are an independent financial services group, involved in merchant banking, investment management, stockbroking and property. We provide a speedy, skillful and innovative service to our clients in all areas of business, via our extensive network of offices throughout the UK and overseas. We constantly look to improve our services to customers, whilst making strategic advances into new product areas. Our aim is that our client service should be second to none.

and other opportunities for financial secrecy, Singer & Friedlander launched a subsidiary operation on the Isle of Man. Geared toward overseas residents seeking to shelter from the often crushing tax burdens of their home countries, Singer & Friedlander (Isle of Man) Ltd. became the first of London's merchant banks to open facilities on the island. Another diversification for the bank came in the 1980s, when Singer & Friedlander became involved in the international trade of third world debt.

Last of the Independents for the 21st Century

Singer & Friedlander regained its independence in 1987—and soon found itself one of the few remaining independent merchant banks in a rapidly consolidating British banking sector. At the start of the 1990s, Singer & Friedlander returned to its roots, setting up a new stockbroking arm through the 1991 acquisition of Collins Stewart. That firm specialized in both corporate financing and brokerage services and came to represent a major share of Singer & Friedlander's operating profits, particularly with the stock market boom in the late 1990s. Singer & Friedlander initially bought majority share in Collins Stewart, before acquiring full control in 1998. The brokerage maintained, in large part, autonomous operations throughout the decade, however.

Singer & Friedlander made a number of investments and acquisitions in the 1990s, including that of a dog racing track and a participation in Peoples Phone, an early entrant in the United Kingdom's mobile telephone market. The company stepped up its acquisition activities in the mid-1990s, with the objective of entering markets that were being left behind in the fast-building consolidation of the country's financial sector, such as car leasing and other financing operations.

An important acquisition came in 1994 when Singer & Friedlander acquired a 55 percent controlling interest in Swedish brokerage Carnegie Group. That firm had its roots in Scotland, when George Carnegie, a member of Scotland's noble class, came to Sweden. Carnegie's son David established D. Carnegie & Co in 1803, building the business into one of the region's largest trading houses. In the 1930s, Carnegie ventured into banking with the acquisition of Langenskiöld, which was placed under the Carnegie name. The company also developed a brokerage division. By the 1950s, as the world's trading houses faced new competitions from the rise of air-based cargo, Carnegie shifted entirely to banking activities. The deregulation of the European financial market in the 1980s led Carnegie to begin its international expansion, opening offices in Luxembourg, London, New York, and in Southern Europe, while also becoming one of the leading investment banks and brokerage firms in the Nordic market.

Key Dates:

1907: Julius Singer founds London brokerage.
1920: The company is incorporated as Singer & Friedlander.
1957: The company is listed on the London stock exchange.
1963: Regional expansion occurs; a Birmingham office is opened.
1971: Singer & Friedlander (Isle of Man) Ltd. is launched.
1987: Singer & Friedlander becomes an independent bank.
1991: Collins Stewart is acquired.
1994: Carnegie Group (Sweden) is acquired.
1998: The company exits from capital markets operations.
2000: The company spins off Collins Stewart.
2001: Carnegie Group is listed on the Swedish stock exchange.

Toward the end of the decade, Singer & Friedlander, now led by Chairman and CEO John Hodson, began to reorient its operations. In 1998 the company sold off its capital markets operations in a management buyout, in a deal worth nearly £1 million. Two years later, as the stock market boom, driven by the growth of Internet and other high-technology stocks, appeared to be reaching a plateau, Singer & Friedlander decided to begin an exit of this market. In 2000, the company released Collins Stewart in a management buyout, netting the company some £120 million. At the same time, Singer & Friedlander announced its intention to separate itself from the Carnegie Group—despite that subsidiary's strong profits.

Nonetheless, Singer & Friedlander, recognizing the onset of a bear market, stuck firm to its decision to spin off the Carnegie Group in an initial public offering on the Swedish stock exchange, which reduced Singer & Friedlander's holding to slightly more than 30 percent. The IPO, which valued Carnegie at up to $750 million, was scheduled for June 2001. Singer & Friedlander then announced its intention to concentrate on its core investment banking and merchant banking operations.

At the same time, the bank began a £64 million property disposal program, enabling it to build a war chest with which to pursue acquisitions to boost its new core operations, a move begun in February 2001. The new direction was meant to make the bank less vulnerable to the volatile markets. Yet, as one of the last remaining independent merchant banks in London, Singer & Friedlander itself remained an attractive takeover target in the quickly consolidating global banking industry.

Principal Subsidiaries

S&F Isle of Man; S&F Investment Funds; S&F Investment Management; S&F Banking Division; The Carnegie Group (Sweden; 32%).

Principal Competitors

3i Group plc; Aberdeen Asset Management plc; AMVESCAP plc; Barclays Plc; Close Brothers Plc; Durlacher Corporation plc; Old Mutual plc; Schroders plc; St. James's Place Capital; UBS Warburg.

Further Reading

Bennett, Neil, ''Singer in Pounds 500m Takeover Talks,'' *Sunday Telegraph,* February 13, 2000.

Brown-Humes, Christopher, ''Carnegie Decides to Brave IPO Fray,'' *Financial Times,* May 14, 2001.

Hughes, Chris, ''Singer & Friedlander to Sell Property Arm,'' *Independent,* February 27, 2001, p. 21.

Orr, Robert, ''S&F Bolstered by Carnegie,'' *Financial Times,* February 26, 2001.

Yoon, Jean, ''Singer & Friedlander Profit Up, Cautions Downturn,'' *Reuters,* February 26, 2001.

—M.L. Cohen

Smith+Nephew

First Choice in Medical Devices

Smith & Nephew plc

Heron House, 15 Adam Street
London WC2N 6LA
United Kingdom
Telephone: +44 (0) 207 401 7646
Fax: +44 (0) 207 930 3353
Web site: http://www.smith-nephew.com

Public Company
Incorporated: 1937 as Smith & Nephew Associated Companies Limited
Employees: 11,213
Sales: $1.8 billion (1999)
Stock Exchanges: London New York
Ticker Symbol: SNN
NAIC: 339111 Laboratory Apparatus and Furniture Manufacturing; 339112 Surgical and Medical Instrument Manufacturing; 339113 Surgical Appliance and Supplies Manufacturing; 326199 All Other Plastics Product Manufacturing; 333314 Optical Instrument and Lens Manufacturing; 42145 Medical, Dental, and Hospital Equipment and Supplies Wholesalers

Smith & Nephew plc operates as a medical device provider in more than 35 countries. Its products are related to orthopaedics, endoscopy, advanced wound management, and rehabilitation. The firm also operates BSN Medical, a 50/50 joint venture, along with Beiersdorf AG. Since 1998, Smith & Nephew has been restructuring business operations and divesting its consumer businesses to improve earnings and focus on medical devices. In 2001, the firm was a leader in wound management and was among the top four orthopaedic companies in the industry.

Victorian Origins

Thomas James Smith was born in 1827. He trained as a pharmacist, first as an apprentice in Grantham, Lincolnshire and then, in 1854 and 1855, at London's University College, where Lord Lister, the antiseptic innovator, also studied. In 1856 he was admitted into the newly formed Royal Pharmaceutical Society and in August he bought his first shop at 71 Whitefriargate, Hull.

Smith soon became involved in the wholesale trade of bandages and related materials. Smith took advantage of his proximity to the docks and fishermen of Hull and began supplying hospitals with cod liver oil, valued for its therapeutic value in cases of rickets, tuberculosis, and rheumatism (vitamins had not yet been identified). At the time, doctors' visits were expensive and pharmacists were often the first ones consulted. Most medicines did not require a prescription, and factory-made pills were only beginning to displace concoctions produced by doctors and pharmacists.

Smith's father loaned him £500 in 1860 so he could convert two cottages on North Church Street into a warehouse. It was such a good year that he sought even larger accommodations in 1861, renting some buildings at 10 North Churchside, which he bought in 1880 with the help of another £500 loan from his father. Business was so good because he had traveled to Norway on a Norwegian gunboat to buy 750 gallons of cod liver oil. It was a shrewd business deal, as the Norwegian product was both cheaper and better tasting than the previous supply from Newfoundland; the solid fat (stearine) had been processed out of it. At the same time, Smith's marketing efforts generated many new accounts among the hospitals of London. By 1880, he had even shipped once to Cairo. At the encouragement of a correspondent, Smith registered his oil under the brand name Paragon Cod Liver Oil, to punctuate its outstanding qualities. Two larger competitors established factories in Norway after medical opinion swung decidedly in favor of the Norwegian product.

T.J. Smith never married; in 1896, a few months before his death, his 22-year-old nephew Horatio Nelson Smith (named after T.J.'s father) became a partner. H.N. was known for his long hours and direct, inquisitive manner. H.N. had apprenticed for six years making draperies. The firm, now known as T.J. Smith & Nephew, shifted its production away from cod liver oil in favor of bandages. In 1907, it was registered as a limited liability company. When H.N. joined the company in 1896, staff numbered three. But when he signed a contract with the Turkish government in 1911 after the outbreak of the war with

Company Perspectives:

Smith & Nephew aims to be the first choice for patients, customers, investors, and employees, by establishing and meeting clear performance targets, developing innovative new products, and earning the trust of all with whom we deal.

Bulgaria, employment reached 54. Soon thereafter a small local competitor, Lambert & Lambert, was acquired.

Smith & Nephew bought sanitary towel manufacturer SASHENA Limited in 1912 (the name an acronym for ''Sanitary Absorbent Safe Hygienic Every Nurse Advocates''). The line was later known as, ''Lilia,'' which had originally referred to an industrial cellulose towel product. The line also incorporated the 1925 acquisition of a half share of a German mill for producing cellulose sanitary towels, which had been developed to cope with the scarcity of cotton. As James Foreman-Peck records in his book *Smith & Nephew in the Health Care Industry,* the materials and methods for their manufacture were similar to surgical dressings, and women, buoyed by suffrage and a heightened role in the workforce, were becoming more affluent. In 1954, the line continued with the introduction of the Lil-lets brand of tampons.

Configuring for Modern Times

World War I provided a huge demand for bandages. Smith & Nephew staff increased to 1,200 as the company obtained contracts with several of the Allied governments as well as the American Red Cross. The firm's textile capacity also was used for producing certain military paraphernalia, such as weapons belts. In addition, legislation in the early 1920s, which stipulated that miners and factory workers have access to first aid kits in the workplace, offered Smith & Nephew a natural opportunity. Nevertheless, after the Great War, production was scaled down considerably, to 183 employees. Furthermore, the Great Depression spurred many administrative changes that helped shape the company into a modern manufacturing corporation. Marketing efforts became more specialized. The company was incorporated as Smith & Nephew Associated Companies Ltd. (SANACO) in 1937.

Smith & Nephew often looked to Germany for technological innovations; H.N. Smith's knowledge of the German language appears to have served him well. In 1930, the company obtained the British rights to Elastoplast bandages, made from a specially woven cloth coated with adhesive, from Lohmann AG. The bandage, though more expensive than others, provided a quick and very effective fix for varicose ulcers in particular, noted various journals.

Smith & Nephew introduced a similar bandage called the Cellona plaster of Paris bandage in 1930. Although it seemed more expensive than the materials it would replace, the effort saved from making messy casts offset the costs and the bandage's light weight made patients more comfortable and healed them faster. Concerns over industrial accidents made the product's introduction timely. The bandages were later named Gypsona.

Much of Gypsona's complex manufacturing process originated with German companies. Several other types of bandages soaked in various types of medicines were co-opted from Germany and the United States. In 1946, a waterproof version was developed, and a new line known as Ultraplast (which later earned a Royal Warrant) came with the 1958 purchase of the Scottish company Wallace Cameron. In 1961, Elastoplast bandages controlled three-quarters of the market.

Cold War Diversification

In the 1950s, Smith & Nephew had to decide whether to modernize its textile operations in Britain or buy textiles from the Far East. It and the unions agreed to the former, although a media campaign to enlist the support of other employers was necessary. The firm's mills subsequently earned a great reputation for efficiency. Interestingly, its mills in England and France were poised to produce denim when the enduring blue jeans fashion trend arrived from America. The automation of the company's mills included the purchase of one of the earliest commercially available computers in the 1950s, called the Leo. Its 1963 replacement was so large that the company leased processing time until the 1970s.

Before its 1951 purchase of Herts Pharmaceuticals, Smith & Nephew had been dependent on technology developed outside the company. Herts, which before World War II was the U.K. subsidiary of Beiersdorf, was best known for PAS and other of the earliest oral treatments for tuberculosis. Like other research firms the company was to acquire later, however, Herts lacked the resources to develop and promote them properly on its own. After the merger, Herts also worked on psychotropic drugs and, closer to Smith & Nephew's core business, breathable membranes for covering wounds, the first of which was called Airstrip and was introduced in 1952. In addition to guaranteeing itself a supply of these types of films, the company was able to license these processes to other firms.

Smith & Nephew entered the hypodermic syringe market in 1954 with the purchase of S. & R.J. Everett & Co. The firm set up a recycling service to provide a more thorough sterilization than the boiling the hospitals had been doing, but disposable syringes made this obsolete.

Through Lilia Limited, the company formed a joint selling company with Arthur Berton Ltd., makers of the Dr. White's Brand, in 1955. Three years later both Arthur Berton and Southalls (Birmingham) Ltd. were acquired, making Lilia-White (Sales) Ltd. the leader of the sanitary protection market. To bolster its position, Smith & Nephew bought Johnson & Johnson's Wrexham sanitary protection factory in 1962. This line contributed the second largest turnover to Smith & Nephew; healthcare products remained first. Sanitary protection products made up the second largest portion of the firm's profits after healthcare products. The company also sold cosmetics and children's clothing.

The group bought No. 2 Temple Place in 1962 to house its headquarters. New products of the 1960s included disposable products and washable cotton blankets to prevent the spread of infection in hospitals. It introduced a standardized nurse's uniform, which was more efficient to produce than the myriad

Key Dates:

1856: Smith opens his first shop in England.
1896: Nephew Horatio Nelson Smith partners with his uncle and the firm changes its name to T.J. Smith & Nephew.
1912: The firm acquires sanitary towel manufacturer SASHENA Limited.
1918: Demand during the war increases staff levels to 1,200 employees.
1937: The firm incorporates as Smith & Nephew Associated Companies Ltd.
1951: The company purchases Herts Pharmaceuticals.
1958: Arthur Berton and Southalls (Birmingham) Ltd. are acquired.
1968: Smith & Nephew fends off a takeover attempt by Unilever.
1986: Richards Medical Company of Memphis, Tennessee is purchased.
1995: The firm makes several key acquisitions including Homecraft Holdings Ltd., Acufex, and Professional Care Products Inc.
1997: Dermagraft is launched in the United Kingdom.
1998: The company begins to restructure, focusing on orthopaedics, endoscopy, and wound management.
1999: The firm's stock begins trading on the New York Stock Exchange.
2000: The company sells its consumer products business.
2001: Joint venture BSN Medical begins operations.

styles then existing among hospitals. A huge leap in efficiency was realized by a joint venture with Johnson & Johnson and a regional Scottish hospital board to develop individually wrapped sterilized dressings, which saved the hospitals the considerable expense of installing and running sterilizing equipment. Total group sales in 1964 was £28.3 million.

In 1968, the giant Unilever conglomerate tried unsuccessfully to purchase Smith & Nephew in an emotional contest with its management, who initiated a campaign for the hearts and minds of its shareholders, touting the company's family tradition as well as its superior financial performance. The tactic worked well when Unilever's plan to slash dividends came to light.

The 1970s were characterized by pressures on margins and volume. The National Health Service, which accounted for much of the firm's U.K. business, became more demanding and cost-conscious; international competitive pressure also increased. This resulted in increased resources for research and development in the next decade. New buildings at the company's venerable Hull site were constructed in 1981 and 1986. Marketing and sales operations for the Health Care division were brought to Hull in 1982, joining the rest of the company's functions.

In the mid-1980s, Smith & Nephew began licensing OpSite, a skin covering, through Johnson & Johnson. The 1985 purchase of the American company Affiliated Hospital extended the firm's product line into rubber gloves and steel trolleys. 3 Sigma Inc., another U.S. company, also was purchased. In 1987, sports injury specialist Donjoy Inc. and Sigma Inc., which made peristaltic infusion pumps, were added. Phizer Hospital Products Inc.'s United Medical Division, which made special surgical dressings in Florida, was acquired in 1988. In 1986, the company bought Richards of Memphis, Tennessee, which specialized in trauma and orthopedics, for £192.7 million.

Smith & Nephew's 1989 purchase of Ioptex Inc. for $230 million suffered from bad timing: soon thereafter, prices for the company's cataract replacement lenses fell by nearly two-thirds, thanks to U.S. government intervention. Smith & Nephew sold the company to Allergan for £11 million in 1994, pulverizing the company's profit that year.

But an example of the company's good fortune was illustrated by Nivea brand moisturizing cream. Overseas rights for the Nivea brand of moisturizing cream passed to Smith & Nephew with the acquisition of Herts Pharmaceuticals Ltd. in 1951. Soon it contributed almost as much as Elastoplast bandages to the firm's consumer sales. In 1992, Beiersdorf paid £46.5 million to buy back U.K. and Commonwealth rights for what was estimated to be the largest toiletry brand in the world. Smith & Nephew continued to earn a 17 percent royalty on U.K. Nivea sales without having to spend any money on advertising. In the 1960s, the brand was extended with "Nivea Lotions" and an upscale skin care line known as "Nivea Visage" competed with L'Oreal in the 1990s.

Searching for 21st-Century Markets

The transformation of Smith & Nephew into a modern multinational corporation occurred under Chief Executive Eric Kinder in the 1980s. S&N's international trade dated back to T.J. Smith's early days; companies had been established in Canada in 1921 and in Australia and New Zealand in the early 1950s. Kinder felt the company needed to extend its export markets beyond post-Imperial Commonwealth countries. By the late 1990s, Smith & Nephew had substantial holdings in Europe and Asia. Sales in the United Kingdom accounted for 54.1 percent of the group's total in 1980; ten years later, that figure had dropped to 23.6 percent, with the United States as the company's biggest market.

The company broadened its European reach. In 1987, it bought the Spanish firm Alberto Fernandez S.A., which made latex products such as gloves and prophylactics. In France, the company bought Cogemo S.A., makers of continuous passive motion machines, and Sanortho S.A., which made orthopedic implants. A German distribution venture with B. Braun GmbH was set up in 1985 and expanded to include Switzerland in 1988. But newly developing countries in Asia seemed to offer the best opportunities for growth. Smith & Nephew's division in Japan, established in 1990, achieved sales of more than £30 million in five years. In the 1990s, the company forecast that China and India would be among the ten largest healthcare markets within 30 years. By 1995, the firm had three offices in China, with plans to manufacture bandages there eventually. Sales in Africa, Asia, Australia, and the Pacific were worth £151 million in 1994, still quite less than the £239 million garnered in the United Kingdom. The United States remained the largest market, providing Smith & Nephew with 40 percent of its sales, or £470 million. Continental Europe accounted for £205 million in sales, up from £37 million in 1984.

At the same time as the geographic range was expanded, the commodity status of certain product lines had to be redressed to improve the company's profit margins. In 1991, John Robinson took over as chief executive, succeeding Kinder, who then served as chairman. Under Robinson, the company specialized in products for tissue repair and protection (''wound management''), rather than the grab bag of medical supplies it once offered. Its research goals have been progressing, an executive told *Management Today,* ''from replacement to repair to regeneration.'' In 1993, Smith & Nephew moved its research center from an Essex mansion to a new site in York Science Park, convenient to York University, an esteemed research institution.

Sacramento-based Cedaron Medical Inc. licensed its Dexter computerized physical therapy system in 1994 to Smith & Nephew, which hoped to succeed by offering a high-tech solution at a lower than average price. The rehabilitation equipment market was growing at least five percent a year at the time of the acquisition, and industrial hand injuries such as carpal tunnel syndrome, which was then beginning to get its share of press attention, seemed a precipitous omen for the Dexter.

Smith and Nephew committed at least $10 million to a 1994 joint venture with California's Advanced Tissue Sciences Inc. (ATS) to culture cartilage cells for joint replacement applications. This project held the potential to open a vast new market and save patients from expensive and painful surgery. ATS benefited from Smith & Nephew's ability to fund the project through years of testing.

The firm continued its growth into the mid-1990s. In 1995, the firm made a series of key acquisitions, including Homecraft Holdings Ltd., a U.K.-based manufacturer of daily living aids; Acufex, a leading manufacturer of surgical instruments and related devices; and Professional Care Products Inc., an orthopaedic accessories firm. The following year, Smith & Nephew continued on its buying spree as well as focusing on product development. That year, the firm announced another joint venture with ATS that would produce bio-engineered human skin replacement called Dermagraft. The new product was targeted at the $2.5 billion chronic diabetic foot ulcer market and eventually became available in 1997 to the U.K. market.

Smith & Nephew also teamed up with the University of Massachusetts in 1996 to establish a research center that was dedicated to the development of endoscopic procedures and instrumentation. The Human Tissue Repair Research Laboratory also was opened in the biology department of the University of York and was fully funded by the firm.

Restructuring During the Late 1990s and into the New Millennium

In 1997, the company began to restructure operations. A Health Care division was formed, integrating the operations of orthopaedic and endoscopy businesses. The new division, based in Memphis, Tennessee, was ultimately formed as a means of consolidating all U.S. sales and distribution functions. The restructuring continued into the following year when Smith & Nephew adopted a new management structure as well as a new strategy that focused on core operations in orthopaedics, endoscopy, and wound management.

Exogen Inc, a U.S.-based manufacturer of ultrasound fracture healing devices, and 3M Corp.'s shoulder and hip implant and instrumentation segment, were acquired in 1999, as part of the firm's new focus. The company continued to look for strategic partnerships that fit into its new plan and began divesting operations that were no longer suitable, including its Bracing & Support business.

In November 1999, Smith & Nephew's stock began trading on the New York Stock Exchange. At the time of the listing, nearly one-third of company employees were based in the United States and more than 40 percent of company sales originated in the United States. In a November 1999 *Memphis Business Journal* article, Larry Papasan, president of the firm's Memphis operations, stated the listing ''will boost the company's visibility and help its quest for more acquisitions. Our objective is to significantly expand employee ownership, to hopefully attract more customers and general owners of our shares, and make our shares much more visible to the investment community and institutional investors.''

The firm continued with its restructuring strategy into the new millennium. In June 2000, its consumer products business, including its feminine hygiene and toiletry products, first aid dressings, and the Nivea distribution business, was sold. In November, Orthopaedic Biosystems Ltd. Inc., a U.S.-based surgical device firm, was purchased as part of its focus on endoscopy. Operating profit for fiscal 2000 increased by 24 percent.

In 2001, Smith & Nephew sold its Ear, Nose, and Throat (ENT) business to Gyrus Group plc. In April of the same year, a joint venture with Beiersdorf AG, entitled BSN Medical, began operation. The venture included the woundcare, casting, bandaging, and phlebology businesses of both firms, and each parent owned 50 percent of BSN. Smith & Nephew CEO Chris O'Donnell stated in a company press release, ''We believe that the creation of the joint venture is the best way to maximize the value of these businesses for the parent companies and their shareholders. The parents have appointed a first class management team as BSN Medical, and are confident that they will achieve a successful future for the new company.''

Smith & Nephew management remained confident that the firm was on the track to achieving future growth and profits. The company continued to focus on research and development as well as broadening its core products and services by forming strategic alliances and making key acquisitions.

Principal Subsidiaries

Exogen Inc.; Orthopaedic Biosystems Ltd. Inc.

Principal Divisions

Orthopaedics; Endoscopy; Wound Management; Rehabilitation; BSN Medical.

Principal Competitors

Biomet Inc.; Stryker Corporation; DePuy Inc.

Further Reading

''Advertorial Blitz Pushes S&N's Simple Skincare,'' *Marketing Week,* March 31, 1995, p. 15.

Auguston, Karen, ''Giving Customers What They Want, When They Want It,'' *Modern Materials Handling,* September 1995.

Beresford, Philip, ''Winners & Losers: MT250,'' *Management Today,* June 1991, pp. 32–42.

Borzo, Greg, ''Glove Shortage Creates Anxiety,'' *Health Industry Today,* November 1991, pp. 1, 14–15.

Braly, Damon, ''Traditional Burn Dressings Market Slowed by Growing Synthetics Usage,'' *Health Industry Today,* December 1993.

Ferguson, Anne, ''Smith & Nephew's Specialty,'' *Management Today,* April 1986, p. 64.

Foreman-Peck, James, *Smith & Nephew in the Health Care Industry,* Aldershot, Hants: Edward Elgar, 1995.

Heller, Robert, et. al., ''Britain's Best Managed Eight,'' *Management Today,* April 1986, pp. 58–67.

Hoggan, Karen, ''Nivea: Smooth Operator,'' *Marketing,* August 30, 1990, pp. 18–19.

Larson, Mark, ''Cedaron Signs Licensing Deal with British Firm,'' *Business Journal Serving Greater Sacramento,* February 21, 1994.

Latham, Valerie, ''Nivea Spreads Range,'' *Marketing,* April 1, 1993, p. 5.

Lorenz, Andrew, ''Why Focus Favors Smith & Nephew,'' *Management Today,* January 1996, pp. 32–36.

Lucas, Spencer, ''Driven to Success: Ken Harvey Relied on Enthusiasm—Not Experience—To Get Ahead at Smith & Nephew Richards,'' *Memphis Business Journal,* December 18, 1995, p. 1A.

Robertshaw, Nicky, ''Smith & Nephew Heads to NYSE,'' *Memphis Business Journal,* November 5, 1999, p. 1.

''Sanitary Protection Products,'' *EIU Retail Business,* No. 437, July 1994.

Sewell, Tim, ''An Investment Pays Off,'' *Memphis Business Journal,* May 15, 1995.

Silverman, Suzann D., ''A Joint Effort,'' *International Business,* August 1994, pp. 68–70.

''Smith & Nephew in Good Health,'' *Management Today,* June 1991, p. 36.

Smith & Nephew plc, ''Company History,'' London, U.K.: Smith & Nephew plc, 2001.

Upton, Richard, ''The Bottom Line: Smith & Nephew Sticks to the Well-Tried Remedies,'' *Personnel Management,* July 1987, pp. 37–39.

Werner, Curt, ''Smith & Nephew Take Global Viewpoint,'' *Health Industry Today,* April 1997, p. 9.

—Frederick C. Ingram
—update: Christina M. Stansell

Sound Advice, Inc.

1901 Tigertail Boulevard
Dania Beach, Florida 33004
U.S.A.
Telephone: (954) 922-4434
Toll Free: (800) 749-1897
Fax: (954) 926-4389
Web site: http://www.wegivesoundadvice.com

Public Company
Incorporated: 1974
Employees: 850
Sales: $198.4 million (2000)
Stock Exchanges: NASDAQ
Ticker Symbol: SUND
NAIC: 443112 Radio, Television and Other Electronic Stores

Sound Advice, Inc., headquartered in Dania Beach, Florida, owns and operates a chain of stores that retail high-quality electronic products. Its holdings consist of 24 Sound Advice outlets in Florida;. five Bang & Olufsen specialty stores, also in Florida; two Showcase Home Entertainment centers in Scottsdale and Chandler, Arizona, plus a home-theater showroom in the Great Indoors store in Scottsdale; and an Electronics Interiors store in Palm Beach Gardens, Florida. Founded in 1974, Sound Advice has grown into Florida's largest specialty retailer of upscale, higher-end home entertainment and consumer electronic products, including home and car audio systems, large-screen televisions, home theater systems, video equipment, and personal electronic devices and accessories, excluding computers and computer-related items. In June 2001, the company agreed to be bought by Tweeter Home Entertainment Group Inc., leaving its fate as a continuing entity in its own name uncertain.

1974–85: From Questionable Start-Up to Solid Retailer

Sound Advice Inc. started up under something of a cloud, as Peter Beshouri, the company's CEO and chairman, has never had any qualms about admitting. In 1974, a group of three investors, including Thomas D. Powell, put up $100,000 in cash to fund the enterprise. As was later divulged, the problem was that most of the cash came out of a drug-traffic suitcase carried into the deal by Powell, who later admitted that it was raised from smuggling marijuana.

The partners convinced four former University of Michigan students who worked with Beshouri at a Tech Hi-Fi store in Detroit to get the enterprise up and running. Beshouri, just 18 and barely out of high school, already had electronic sales experience and had become manager of the Detroit store when he was just 17. He joined the others in Florida a few months after Sound Advice's founding in Fort Lauderdale, and two years later he opened and managed the company's first Tampa store. That was just the initial step in his mercurial rise in the company's chain of command, which, in 1982, saw him, at a youthful 27, become both Sound Advice's CEO and chairman. In 1985, he also became the company's president.

At the time they were hired, Beshouri and the others from Michigan had no knowledge of the source of the startup funds, though one of Powell's partners, Michael Blumberg, later confirmed that he had been suspicious. Powell even provided Sound Advice with another $95,000 in 1975, helping the fledgling company stay on its feet. The truth about the source of Powell's investment money finally came out in 1984, when the federal government indicted him on drug charges and income tax evasion. Because the only tainted money in Sound Advice was in Powell's stock, in 1985 the government sold that stock back to the company and exonerated it of any complicity in the illegalities of Powell. Meanwhile, Powell began a ten-year jail sentence at Florida's Eglin Air Force Base.

Before the disclosure of Powell's felonious activities, Sound Advice grew apace on both Florida coasts. The company's first focus was on high-quality stereo equipment, though it gradually extended its line to encompass a broad range of home entertainment equipment. Unlike the growing number of deep-discount, power-merchandising giants that set a new trend in the 1980s, Sound Advice courted a fairly narrow customer base made up of people who wanted only the best quality merchandise regardless of price. For a few years, the company's upscale appeal con-

Company Perspectives:

Sound Advice is a retailer of high-quality consumer electronics products with 24 Sound Advice stores in Florida, five Bang & Olufsen specialty stores, two Showcase Home Entertainment stores in Arizona, and an Electronics Interiors store in Palm Beach Gardens. By offering our customers the best products and the best service in an upscale, hands-on environment, Sound Advice has created a unique and enviable position in the market. The loyalty of our customers says it all.

cerned Beshouri and his associates, but the venture's success eventually allayed fears of its being too elitist. As reported in a January 1988 article in *General Merchandise Trends*, Beshouri said, "We used to worry that customers thought we were high falutin'. Then we found out we were and it's okay to be."

1986–90: Going Public and Facing the Competition

In 1986, Sound Advice went public, raising further questions about the source of its seed money. Attorneys with Oppenheimer & Co., which was handling the company's initial stock offering, recommended full public disclosure of the circumstances, with a note explaining that questions had been raised regarding the source of the funds. Beshouri, without argument, agreed to the note's inclusion.

The disclosure had no real adverse effect on the company. In 1987, its sales grew by almost 44 percent, up to $36.8 million, an increase of $11.2 million over its 1986 revenue of $25.6 million. Because Sound Advice added two new stores, expanded four, and relocated another, in the same period the company increased its retail space by 68 percent.

At the beginning of 1988, the company's projections called for an expansion of two to three new stores each year, an ambitious pace. Continued enlargement of existing stores was also planned, largely because store enlargement had already contributed to impressive same-store sales growth.

Despite a recession that was cooling down the nation's economy in the late 1980s, Sound Advice fared well. By the end of 1988, it owned and operated 17 stores in Florida, with gross sales of $55 million, which earned it the 40th ranking on *Forbes'* list of the 200 best small companies in the United States. The company was also on its growth target, having opened the year with just 14 stores in operation.

Furthermore, still bucking the national trend towards deeper discounts on lower-end-of-the-line items, the company was achieving success with its upscale policy intact. In 1988, its smallest television sets were major brand, 25-inch models. Its least expensive stereo receivers sold at prices starting at about $150, considerably more than lower-quality stereo receivers were selling for in the big discount outlets.

By 1990, Sound Advice's sales had risen to $91.5 million, but there was a net income drop over the previous year. The growth pace had also slowed somewhat. Although the expansion of some of its existing stores increased the retail chain's total square footage, the company opened no new stores between 1988 and 1990. Sound Advice still operated just 17 stores but plans did call for the opening of two more stores plus the expansion of three others before the end of the calendar year. The company attributed the drop in net income to a non-recurring inventory shrinkage and expenses incurred in conjunction with future expansion.

While Sound Advice also began to experience some competitive pressures from Circuit City, which entered the South Florida market in 1990, the company initially tried to stick to its strategy guns rather than wage a price war with that retail giant. Tentatively, Sound Advice did start moving lower on the price spectrum and added four new suppliers in hopes of expanding its customer base by attracting more lower and mid-range price tag shoppers. The company also changed its displays, taking items out of their glass showcases, giving them hands-on accessibility for customers.

1991–95: Challenges on Several Fronts

In the summer of 1991, Sound Advice attempted to negotiate a merger with Image Entertainment, the parent company of Audio King, a Minnesota-based chain of electronic stores. The two companies had signed a letter of intent just prior to the early June Consumer Electronics Show, but the deal collapsed in July. Spokesman for Sound Advice, Roy Casey, the company's CFO, indicated that the company would refocus its expansion energies towards opening new stores in its home market of Florida, where, the company's managers believed, sales could be increased efficiently without a major rise in cost.

In April 1992, the company became embroiled in an investigation prompted by Robert Jarkow, a former employee who charged that Sound Advice had made intentional misstatements to its auditors in its financial reports for the year ending on June 30, 1991. As a result of a 1992 internal investigation resulting from the charge, six shareholders brought suit against the company, and while Sound Advice denied any deliberate wrongdoing, it admitted that it had unintentionally misrepresented its earnings on statements made between 1988 and 1991. It corrected the errors through a series of balance sheet adjustments totaling $3.5 million. Meanwhile, the stockholders' suit continued, resulting in a $2.8 million settlement in their favor in November 1993.

Embarrassed by the investigation and suit, the company was relieved to put the matter behind it. The affair had driven its per share stock price from an all time high of $15 in 1991 to a low of $2.75 in 1992 and led to an ongoing SEC investigation. Peter Beshouri hoped to bolster the company's reputation by impressing Wall Street with growth and strong earnings. According to a May 1994 article in *Florida Trend*, Beshouri wanted to grow the company by as much as 50 percent within the year, expanding the chain to 30 stores. Plans for 1995 called for opening seven to ten stores outside Florida, in Washington, D.C., northern Virginia, and southern Maryland. At the same time, plans for entering markets in Texas, Georgia, North Carolina, and Pennsylvania were also on the drawing board.

However, because Sound Advice had made some other decisions that turned out badly, the company's expansion plans had

Key Dates:

1974: Company is founded in Fort Lauderdale, Florida.
1976: Peter Beshouri becomes manager of company's first store in Tampa.
1982: Beshouri becomes Sound Advice's chairman and CEO.
1984: Founding partner Thomas Powell is indicted for tax evasion and drug trafficking.
1986: Sound Advice goes public.
1992: Reported misrepresentations in the company's financial statements lead to shareholders' suit and SEC investigation.
1998: Sound Advice opens its first two Bang & Olufsen stores.
2000: Company acquires Showcase Home Entertainment.
2001: Sound Advice agrees to sale of company to Tweeter Home Entertainment Group Inc.

to be put on the back burner if not altogether shoved off the stove. For one thing, by 1992 the company had started trying to compete more aggressively with much larger, national chains like Circuit City, Best Buy, and BrandsMart USA by broadening its product line to include additional lower-cost television, VCR, and audio equipment brands and models. Also, in 1994, because the larger competitors sold personal computers and accessories, Sound Advice joined the ranks, adding these to its merchandise line. The result was that the company was almost beaten into extinction. It lost money in 1994 and 1995, and though it escaped the fate of some of the other small companies, including Incredible Universe, Standard Brands, Buy Wise, and Kaufman & Roberts—all of which went out of business—it was badly reeling.

1996–98: A Return to the Tried and True

In 1996, surrendering to marketplace realities, Sound Advice discontinued selling computers and basically returned to its original strategy of selling high-end home entertainment equipment requiring professional installation. Still, the company was slow to recover. In 1996, it again posted a net loss, $4.2 million, and its bottom-line woes continued through 1997 and 1998, though by that last year the loss was limited to $1 million. Although it had not expanded into the *terra incognita* beyond Florida, where it still operated just 25 stores, the enterprise had begun to show signs of financial health. By 1998, it was getting help from the new digital technology that had started to invade the market in the form of higher-end products that seemed tailor-made for Sound Advice and its typical customers—those who wanted quality regardless of price. Of particular appeal to Beshouri were the new, very pricey high-definition television (HDTV) sets and the necessary and equally expensive accouterments to go with them: digital processors, DVD players, surround-sound speakers, high quality cabling, and even a whole satellite system.

In 1998, Sound Advice opened two new full-size stores, one in Tallahassee and one in North Palm Beach. It also opened its first two mall-based Bang & Olufsen stores, which sold that Danish company's audio products and accessories and featured selected products set in discrete display areas.

1999–2001: Imminent Merger with Tweeter Home Entertainment

As the century closed, what James McNair in his 1998 article ''Florida-Based Sound Advice Takes the High Ground'' described as the company's ''tortoise-paced'' expansion began gaining some ground. Between June 1999 and October 2000, it opened three more Bang & Olufsen stores. Also in October 2000, Sound Advice completed the acquisition of Showcase Home Entertainment, a Scottsdale, Arizona-based retailer of high-end electronics and custom design services. That company's holdings included two upscale stores in Scottsdale and Chandler, Arizona. Showcase also operated the home entertainment centers of The Great Indoors home design centers in Dallas and in Scottsdale. Importantly, the acquisition was Sound Advice's first venture outside Florida.

Next, in November, Sound Advice announced the debut of Electronic Interiors, a center based on its new concept in the design, integration, and installation of audio, video, and home-theater technology. Located at Florida's Palm Beach Gardens Mall, the center employed the Bang & Olufsen nested-store configuration as well as other automated and customized showrooms. Features included a small movie theater suggestive of early cinemas, electronics for bedrooms and bathrooms, and customized rooms housing home-entertainment systems.

In February 2001, Sound Advice announced that it had been notified that Tweeter Home Entertainment Group might seek a merger of the two companies. Tweeter, a national, 95-store audio and video retail chain, informed Sound Advice that it had a Schedule 13D filing with the SEC stating that it and the family of Samuel Bloomberg, Tweeter's chairman, owned 336,000 shares, or about 8.5 percent, of Sound Advice's common stock and that it might seek to purchase more. Tweeter sought to begin talks with Sound Advice about a possible merger; however, in a press release February 27, 2000, Peter Beshouri indicated that, given the trading value of Sound Advice's stock, no proposals would be likely to appeal to the company's shareholders. The message seemed to be that Sound Advice was going to continue hoeing its own row. However, in June 2001, Sound Advice relented, and agreed to be sold to Tweeter Home Entertainment for stock with a value of about $150 million. It remained to be seen whether Sound Advice would be merged into Tweeter or become a wholly-owned subsidiary continuing to do business under its established name.

Principal Competitors

Best Buy Co., Inc.; Circuit City Stores, Inc.; Radio Shack Corporation; Service Merchandise Company, Inc.; Wal-Mart Stores, Inc.

Further Reading

Byrne, Harlan S., ''Sound Advice Inc.: Electronics Retailer Steps Lightly on Mass-Merchandisers' Turf,'' *Barron's*, August 26, 1991, p. 38.

''Choosing Upscale Audio and Television IS Sound Advice,'' *Chain Store Age-General Merchandise Trends*, January 1988, p. 33.

Greenberg, Manning, ''Branching Out: Florida Based Sound Advice Plans to Establish New Stores in Other States,'' *HFD-The Weekly Home Furnishings Newspaper*, November 14, 1994, p. 74.
Grieves, Robert T. ''Drug Smuggler's Startup,'' *Forbes*, December 26, 1988, p. 136.
McNair, James, ''Florida-Based Sound Advice Takes High Ground in Retailing,'' *Knight-Ridder/Tribune Business News*, November 30, 1998.
Parks, Kyle, ''Sound Management?,'' *Florida Trend*, May 1994, p. 26.
''Retail Deals Collapse,'' *Television Digest*, July 22, 1991, p. 15.
''Sound Advice and Tweeter Home Entertain Group Announce the Signing of a Definitive Merger Agreement,'' *PR Newswire*, June 4, 2001.
''Sound Advice Expanding,'' *Television Digest*, July 30, 1990, p. 16.
''Sound Advice Settles Suit,'' *Television Digest*, November 15, 1993, p. 19.

—John W. Fiero

Spanish Broadcasting System, Inc.

2601 South Bayshore Drive
Coconut Grove, Florida 33133
U.S.A.
Telephone: (305) 441-6901
Fax: (305) 446-5148
Web site: http://www.spanishbroadcasting.com

Public Company
Incorporated: 1983
Employees: 568
Sales: $122.7 million (2000)
Stock Exchanges: NASDAQ
Ticker Symbol: SBSA
NAIC: 513112 Radio Stations

The Florida-based Spanish Broadcasting System, Inc. (SBS) is the nation's second largest Spanish-language broadcasting company, behind Hispanic Broadcasting, and the largest one principally owned by Hispanic Americans. The company operates 19 Spanish-language radio stations serving the New York, Puerto Rico, Miami, Chicago, Dallas, San Antonio, and Los Angeles area markets through its numerous wholly-owned subsidiaries. Among its best-known stations are KLAX-FM in Los Angeles, WSKQ-FM and WXLA-AM in New York, and WXDJ-FM in Miami. The company's New York WSKQ-FM station is the number one station in its target demographic group (Hispanic adults between 18 and 49). Altogether, SBS's stations reach over 61 percent of the country's Hispanic population and offer a wide variety of formats: Spanish Tropical, Regional Mexican, Tejano, Spanish Adult Contemporary, American Contemporary Hits, American 80's Hits, Spanish Adult Top 40, Spanish Oldies, and Dance. JuJu Media, 80 percent of which SBS owns, operates LaMusica.com, a bilingual Spanish-English Web site dedicated to Latin music, news, and other forms of Latin American entertainment and culture. Raul Alarcon, Jr., son of SBS founder Pablo Raul Alarcon, Sr., owns 41 percent of the company's shares and is the current chairman, CEO, and president.

1983–89: From Radio Station to Broadcast System

Pablo Raul Alarcon, Sr., a native of Camaguey Province, Cuba, immigrated to the United States when Fidel Castro was leading his insurgent forces to power. Before that, in the early 1950s, Alarcon had begun his career in radio as an announcer and soon established a three-station chain in Camaguey. He moved to New York as a political refugee in 1960 and took a job as a deejay at a Spanish-language station in Manhattan. Alarcon was eventually promoted to station programming director. He eventually purchased and operated a recording studio and an advertising agency and by 1983 was in a sound enough financial position to purchase his first radio station, WSKQ-AM, the initial station in what would become the Spanish Broadcasting System. He was joined in the business by his son, Raul Alarcon, Jr., who took on the job of sales manager.

By 1989, Alarcon had built SBS into the largest Hispanic radio company in the United States. The company's revenues by the end of 1988 had reached $21.1 million, and its network consisted of six stations. Alarcon was not timid about paying high prices for SBS's acquisitions. In the fall of 1988, the company paid $55.5 million for a New York City FM station, and, in a 1989 column in *Fortune*, Alarcon defended the purchase: ''Some people call me a crazy Cuban. . . . But if you don't take calculated risks, you can't make huge gains.'' Indeed, any skepticism from analysts failed to slow Alarcon and his company down; he noted that the seminal Spanish-language AM station in New York and AM and FM stations purchased in Los Angeles and Miami were ''extremely profitable.''

1990–93: Recession Forces Adjustments but Does Not Halt Expansion

The broadcasting industry hit some hard times during the recession of the early 1990s. Like other companies, SBS had to make some changes just to survive. Hispanic network operators made adjustments in programming and marketing techniques, and they also made a united effort to sell the radio medium in the face of tough competition from television and print media. Along with mainstream broadcast companies, the Spanish-language radio operators had to trim their costs in order to maintain a healthy cash flow. Still, through the worst of it, SBS continued to expand into new sectors. For example, in 1991 it negotiated a

Company Perspectives:

Our strategy is to maximize the profitability of our radio station portfolio and to expand in our existing markets and into additional markets that have a significant Hispanic population. We believe that the favorable demographics of the U.S. Hispanic population and the rapid increase in advertising targeting Hispanics provide us with significant opportunities for growth. We also believe that we have competitive advantages in the radio industry due to our focus on formats targeting U.S. Hispanic audiences and our skill in programming and marketing to these audiences.

deal with Telemundo Group, a Florida-based television broadcaster, under which SBS leased transponder space from Telemundo for satellite broadcasts of news, primarily originating in Miami, to the company's stations and other affiliates.

Fortunately for SBS and other Hispanic networks, their audience base continued to expand at a solid pace and their Spanish-language radio audience tended to be heavier users of the medium than was the population at large. Because television was so completely dominated by English-language programming, native Spanish-speaking citizens and émigrés also had far fewer media entertainment choices.

As a group, that audience was rapidly becoming an important consumer group. In Los Angeles, in Arbitron's fall 1992 fall survey, SBS's KLAX-FM was named the top-ranked radio station in the area. That fact surprised many, especially since the station had changed its call letters and switched its format to Mexican ranchera, a blend of folk and banda dance-style music. With the changes the station made, spearheaded by Alfredo Rodriguez, KLAX-FM's general manager, in just three months the station vaulted into the top spot from a distant 23rd ranking. As a result, because it was able to command much greater rates for advertising time, the station became very profitable, almost overnight. In 1992, it billed around $2.2 million for air time; in 1993 the figure approached $15 million.

By 1993, SBS's stations numbered seven: KLAX-FM and KXED-AM in Los Angeles; WSKQ-AM and WSKQ-FM in New York; and WCMQ-AM, WCMQ-FM, and WZMQ-FM in the Miami-Florida Keys area. These were, of course, principal Spanish-language broadcasting markets. Essentially, among the solid and growing Hispanic markets, this left only the markets in Texas to penetrate, something SBS would eventually do. First, though, the company would continue to expand in its three areas in New York, California, and Florida.

1994–96: Going Public Under a New Generation of Leadership

In 1994, on the eve of some important changes for the company, Pablo Raul Alarcon, Sr., turned over operational control of SBS to his son, Raul Alarcon, Jr. The economic recovery, in full swing, prompted the company to undertake further growth, as did the financial condition of the company. In fiscal 1995, SBS's revenues reached $55 million, giving the company some investment clout and furthering its investment plans.

To help those plans, SBS also went public in 1996, hoping to raise $50 million from its 7.5 million share offering to finance its purchase of WPAT-AM, a New York area (Patterson, New Jersey), English-language station. At the time, SBS already operated WSKQ-FM (Mexican oriented) and WXLA-AM (salsa music) in the same market. The company also undertook further expansion in Miami in 1996, when, from New Age Communications, it purchased WRMA-FM (Romance 106.7) and WXDJ-FM (El Zol 95), respectively, the first and third ranked Spanish-language stations in South Florida. The $110 million deal also installed New Age's president Russ Oasis on SBS's executive team as executive vice-president and chief operating officer. Oasis, who owned 50 percent of New Age, had acquired El Zol in 1987 for $8.1 million and Romance in 1994 for about $21.3 million, then managed both into very profitable and popular enterprises.

The company's national expansion plans were helped with the 1996 federal deregulation of rules that prohibited a single company from owning more than two AM and FM stations in a single market or commanding more than a 25 percent audience share. SBS also benefitted from the fact that by 1995 Hispanic purchasing power had climbed to $220.3 billion, encouraging a rapid rise in media advertising to that population segment. Analysts estimated that of the $1 billion spent on ads targeted to that segment, about $321 million was spent on radio advertising.

1997–2001: New Radio Markets and the Internet

SBS's 1996 expansion in the Florida market led to the 1997 relocation of its headquarters to Miami, a move that put it at the heart of another one of the principal Hispanic-American population centers in the United States. The move also positioned the company somewhat closer to its other developing markets in Puerto Rico and Texas.

In September 1999, SBS entered a definitive agreement with AMFM, Inc. to purchase eight FM radio stations in Puerto Rico. The $90 million acquisition included WIOA-FM, WIOB-FM, WIOC-FM, WCOM-FM, WZMT-FM, WZNT-FM, WOYE-FM, and WCTA-FM. AMFM had purchased the stations the year before, from Primedia Broadcast Group, for $75 million. Collectively, in 1998 these stations ranked first in audience and sales in the Puerto Rico market. The arrangement with AMFM, Inc. also included a time-brokerage agreement that would allow SBS to sell advertising time on the stations following the expiration of the waiting period mandated by the Hart-Scott-Rodino Act.

Also in 1999, in part to help finance its expansion efforts, SBS undertook recapitalization. Management planned to achieve its goal through a $200 million secured credit facility arranged by Lehman Brothers, $235 million raised in the high-yield bond market, and another $280 million generated from a new public offering of stock. Besides providing the capital for the Puerto Rico acquisitions, proceeds from the offering and the debt issues were slated to be used for restructuring the company's whole capitalization, both refinancing existing unsecured debts and redeeming preferred stock. The stock offering, made in November, exceeded expectations, selling 21.8 million shares of stock at $20 per share for a total of $435.8 million.

Key Dates:

1983: Pablo Raul Alarcon, Sr., purchases WSKQ-AM in New York and founds Spanish Broadcasting.
1994: Spanish Broadcasting System Inc. is incorporated in Delaware; Raul Alarcon, Jr., succeeds his father as president and CEO.
1996: Company goes public; it acquires WRMA-FM and WXDJ-FM from New Age Communications.
1997: SBS moves headquarters from New York to Miami.
1999: Raul Alarcon, Jr., succeeds his father as SBS's chairman; company buys 80 percent of New York-based LaMusica.com and recapitalizes.
2000: SBS continues its expansion with the acquisition of several stations.

In the same year, SBS also diversified by tapping into the nation's newest craze—the Internet. SBS jumped onto the electronic superhighway when it purchased 80 percent of the issued and outstanding capital stock of JuJu Media, Inc., owner of LaMusica.com, a bilingual Spanish-English Internet Web site focused on the U.S. Hispanic market. The New York-based LaMusica.com, created in 1995, offered a wide variety of content, including concert listings, an international club directory, articles on popular Latin personalities, reviews of CDS, and record charts. It also afforded visitors the opportunity to view new music videos, hear CD-quality audio, and purchase CDS. With monthly site hits of over three million, LaMusica.com was the most frequently visited Latino-music Internet site in the United States. Its appeal for SBS was the rapidly growing number of people listening to radio on the Internet. By 1999, the estimated purchasing power of the 26 million people in the Hispanic media market had reached $279 billion, and Ray Alarcon, Jr., and his managing team were certain that LaMusica.com would provide advertisers a new and efficient means of reaching those people plus a way of providing SBS's own listeners with a premier Internet service.

Radio was still the company's bread and butter business, however, and its expansion included the acquisition of more stations in both old and new markets. Early in 2000, for $75 million, SBS purchased KACE-FM, one of the last two radio stations in Los Angeles with African American-oriented programming. SBS acquired KACE from Cox Radio, Inc., which had five years earlier bought the station from former professional football standout, Willie Davis.

SBS next acquired six stations from Rodriguez Communications, Inc (RCI) and its affiliate, New World Broadcasting. SBS bought all of RCI's outstanding capital stock and the assets of New World, paying $165.2 million, which consisted of $121.7 million in cash and $43.5 million in SBS's class A common stock. The deal opened two new markets for SBS—Dallas and San Francisco—and expanded its operations in Los Angeles and San Antonio. Format flips turned Korean programming stations KFOX-FM and KREA-FM in Los Angeles into Spanish-language stations, while the two Dallas stations, KTCY-FM and KXEB-AM, were already designated Spanish-language formats. These were placed under the management of RCI's president and COO, who went onboard SBS as western regional vice-president. In Spanish, too, was KSAH-AM in San Antonio; its Regional Mexican programming complemented SBS's FM station, KLEY, in that same city. The station in San Francisco, KXJO-FM, was among a string of California rock simulcast stations and was also to be reformatted.

In August 2000, SBS also teamed up with America Online in a strategic promotional alliance. Under the terms of the agreement, SBS's LaMusica.com became an anchor tenant on AOL and began providing music and other entertainment programming across selected AOL brands. In exchange for its coverage on AOL, SBS began promoting AOL in radio spots.

Early in 2001, SBS announced its agreement with the International Church of the Foursquare Gospel (ICFG) to purchase ICFG's Los Angeles radio station, KFSG-FM. In what was seen as SBS's calculated effort to replace Hispanic Broadcasting as the nation's number one Spanish-language radio network, SBS agreed to pay a hefty $250 million to the nonprofit religious group. This would be the highest price ever paid for a Los Angeles radio station and would require a total overhaul in programming. The acquisition would, in brief, be a risky venture, one that would involve deficit operating until at least 2003, but one that SBS believed would also greatly enhance the company's competitive presence in the number one Hispanic radio market in the United States.

Principal Subsidiaries

SBS of Greater New York, Inc.; Spanish Broadcasting System of Florida, Inc.; Spanish Broadcasting System of California, Inc.; Spanish Broadcasting System of Greater Miami, Inc.; Spanish Broadcasting System of San Antonio, Inc.; Spanish Broadcasting System of Illinois, Inc.; Spanish Broadcasting System of Puerto Rico, Inc. (incorporated in Puerto Rico); Spanish Broadcasting System, Inc. of New Jersey; Spanish Broadcasting System of Puerto Rico, Inc. (incorporated in Delaware); SBS Funding, Inc., JuJu Media, Inc.; Alarcon Holdings, Inc.; Spanish Broadcasting System Network, Inc.; SBS Promotions, Inc.

Principal Competitors

Clear Channel Communications, Inc.; Grupo Radio Centro, S.A. de C.V.; Hispanic Broadcasting Corporation; Infinity Broadcasting Corporation; Radio Unica Communications Corporation.

Further Reading

''AMFM Inc. to Sell Eight Radio Stations in Puerto Rico to Spanish Broadcasting System, Inc. for $90 Million,'' *Business Wire*, September 22, 1999.

Arrarte, Anne Moncreiff, ''Spanish Radio Stations Fetching Premium Prices in Miami,'' *Knight-Ridder/Tribune Business News*, September 19, 1996.

Bachman, Katy, ''SBS Expands West,'' *MediaWeek*, May 22, 2000, p.18.

Cobo, Lucia, ''Hispanic Groups Make the Most of Tough Times,'' *Broadcasting*, May 20, 1991, p. 40.

Davenport, Carol, ''On the Rise: Paul Alarcon Jr., 33,'' *Fortune*, July 3, 1989, p. 138.

''Hispanic Company Buys One of Los Angeles' Last Black Radio Stations,'' *Jet,* January 10, 2000.

Lacey, Stephen, ''Loan Helps Spanish Broadcasting for IPO,'' *Bank Loan Report*, November 22, 1999.

Phadungchai, Naruth, ''Lehman Airs Spanish Broadcasting Deal,'' *Bank Loan Report*, October 25, 1999.

Pulley, Brett, ''Latin Lover,'' *Forbes*, January 24, 2000, p. 92.

''Spanish Broadcasting Announces Acquisition of Six Radio Stations in the Top U.S. Hispanic Markets of Los Angeles, San Francisco, San Antonio and Dallas,'' *PR Newswire*, May 8, 2000.

''Spanish Broadcasting System Acquires Majority Interest in LaMusica.com; Deal Creates Latino Radio and Internet Powerhouse,'' *PR Newswire*, April 29, 1999.

Torpey-Kemph, Anne, ''SBS Teams with LaMusica.com,'' *Mediaweek,* May 10, 1999, p. 37.

Viles, Peter, ''Spanish KLAX Cruising in Los Angeles,'' *Broadcasting & Cable*, April 12, 1993, p. 58.

Whitefield, Mini, ''New York-Based Spanish Broadcasting System Pans IPO,'' *Knight-Ridder/Tribune Business News*, January 4, 1996.

—John W. Fiero

The Steak n Shake Company

500 Century Building
36 South Pennsylvania Street
Indianapolis, Indiana 46204
U.S.A.
Telephone: (317) 633-4100
Fax: (317) 633-4105
Web site: http://www.steaknshake.com

Public Company
Founded: 1934
Employees: 18,000
Sales: $408.7 million (2000)
Stock Exchanges: New York
Ticker Symbol: SNS
NAIC: 72211 Full-Service Restaurants; 53311 Lessors of Nonfinancial Intangible Assets (Except Copyrighted Works)

One of the oldest restaurant chains in the United States, The Steak n Shake Company operates more than 370 Steak n Shake restaurants throughout 17 midwestern and southeastern states. Of the 370 restaurants in operation, approximately 50 are franchised, with the remainder company-owned. The Indianapolis, Indiana-based chain is best known for its burgers (which are referred to as ''steakburgers'') and milkshakes, but also serves a range of other sandwiches, salads, soups, and side dishes. The restaurants, which are open around the clock, cater to a mid-range, casual dining market, with the average meal costing approximately $5.60. They offer full-service dining areas, counter service, and drive-through options.

1930s: A ''Normal'' Beginning

The business that would grow into the Steak n Shake chain began in the early 1930s in Normal, Illinois, in a Shell gas station. The station's owner was Gus Belt, an Illinois native who had owned a tire distributorship before going into the service station business. In 1932, looking for a way to make his station more attractive to motorists, as well as to supplement his income, Belt hit upon the idea of running a small restaurant in conjunction with the gas business. He began offering customers all the chicken they could eat, along with french fries and cole slaw, for 45 cents. For an additional small charge, thirsty travelers could wash their chicken down with a glass of beer.

Soon, however, the nearby Illinois Normal State Teachers College began objecting to beer being served so close to campus. When the college threatened to shut down Belt's small operation, he and his wife secured a $300 loan and used it to turn their gas station into a real restaurant. In February of 1934, the Belts opened their new eatery, renamed Steak n Shake. The ''steak'' in the name referred to the restaurant's hallmark sandwich, the steakburger—made with real cuts of T-bone, strip steak, and sirloin, ground up, formed into patties, and grilled. The ''shake'' referred to thick vanilla, chocolate, and strawberry flavored milkshakes, prepared with ice cream the Belts made themselves.

Belt was a stickler for quality in virtually every aspect of his business. In a time when Board of Health standards for restaurants varied widely from county to county, and most roadside eateries were run in a careless, slapdash way, Belt turned scrupulous sanitation into a marketing advantage. He designed the new Steak n Shake to look reassuringly clean, with a stark stainless steel and black-and-white decor that was kept shiny with frequent scrubbings. Belt's standards for the food he served were likewise stringent. He developed a formula for what he believed would be the perfect burger, which started with the best meat available in Illinois, ground fresh and mixed according to a precise ratio of lean to fat. Belt then grilled the burgers in a unique, carefully choreographed method that seared in the juices and crisped the exterior, and served them on a fresh, custom-designed bun. Even condiments did not escape his attention; he soon began slicing his pickles lengthwise so that diners got a taste of pickle with every bite of burger.

A savvy marketer, Belt did not let his customers overlook the care and quality that went into their meals. He often wheeled in a barrel of steaks during the restaurant's busiest times and ground them up while the diners watched. This practice of allowing the customers to watch while the food was prepared extended to the cooking phase as well. The Belts' new building

Company Perspectives:

What is Steak n Shake? A restaurant. And by that we mean a place where, instead of standing in line to order, you sit down. We serve you from a full menu including chili, melts, salads, soups, and club sandwiches. But we are most famous for Steakburgers. Why do we call them Steakburgers? Because we can. Steakburgers are made from real steak cuts—sirloin, t-bone and strip steak—and grilled a special way to sear in the flavor. Our real-milk Milk Shakes are hand dipped the old fashioned way as we have done it from our start. These are our core items: Steakburgers and Milk Shakes–good enough to name a restaurant after.

had an open layout that allowed customers to watch the cooks prepare their meals, which gave rise to the Steak n Shake slogan, "In sight, it must be right."

In addition to its dine-in business, the original Steak n Shake offered curb service. This proved to be highly successful, and soon the restaurant had all the business it could handle. In a July 2000 interview with the *Chicago Sun-Times,* Mel Tulle, a former curbside waiter at the original Steak n Shake, recalled that customers were "driving circles around the restaurant because there was no place to park." Tulle went on to say that the Belts even had a Normal police officer directing traffic around the restaurant.

With his Normal Steak n Shake thriving, Gus Belt began expanding. In 1936, he opened a second restaurant in Bloomington, Illinois. A third and a fourth soon followed, in Bloomington and Decatur, Illinois, respectively. Near the end of the 1930s, the Belts acquired an existing restaurant in Champaign, Illinois and converted it into a Steak n Shake. Soon after that, they purchased two restaurants operating under the name "Goal Post"—one in Champaign and one in East Peoria, Illinois—and turned them into Steak n Shakes as well. By 1939, still another Steak n Shake had opened, in Danville, Illinois, giving the Belts a chain of eight locations.

1940s–60s: Expansion and Ownership Changes

By 1943, there were 15 Steak n Shakes. Most were located in Illinois, but at least one was doing a booming business in Hot Springs, Arkansas. Most of the sites were company owned, although Belt had allowed for a few franchisees. In the late 1940s, Steak n Shake expanded into St. Louis—an area that was to become a major market for the chain. Between 1948, when the first St. Louis store opened, and 1954, the Belts opened ten highly successful restaurants in the city, making it the location most heavily populated with Steak n Shakes. Belt financed the St. Louis growth by making a public offering of the company's stock, but the Belts themselves continued to own a controlling interest.

In 1954, Belt died of a heart attack. He left the Steak n Shake chain—consisting of 24 restaurants in Illinois and St. Louis, and one restaurant each in Daytona Beach, Florida and Hot Springs, Arkansas—in his wife's hands. Edith Belt ran the business exactly as her husband had, adhering carefully to the standards and practices he had established. During the 15 years under her leadership, Steak n Shake gradually expanded to include 51 locations in Illinois, Missouri, Florida, and Indiana, but little else changed.

In early 1969, Edith sold her controlling interest in Steak n Shake to Longchamps, Inc., a chain of steakhouses headquartered on the east coast. The sale price was approximately $17 million. During the two and one-half years Longchamps controlled Steak n Shake, it saw sales increase from $17 million to $23.5 million. Because of some managerial missteps, however, the company found itself facing a lawsuit filed by stockholders and pressure from its bankers. In the fall of 1971, Longchamps sold its controlling interest in Steak n Shake to the Indiana-based Franklin Corporation.

1970s–80s: Changing Hands Again

With the ownership change, Robert Cronin became the chairman of Steak n Shake. After making a detail-level assessment of the operation, Cronin began making a few cautious changes to the restaurant's menu. Some of his changes were simply designed to return Steak n Shake to its roots. For example, during Longchamps's tenure, management had replaced the chain's traditional, real ice cream milkshakes with shakes made from a mix. Cronin immediately reverted to the old method, using the real ingredients. He also reduced the cost of a cup of coffee—then 15 cents—to its pre-Longchamps price of ten cents. Other of Cronin's changes, however, were innovations. He contracted with Sara Lee to add an array of desserts to the menu—the first non-milkshake desserts ever served at Steak n Shake. He also added such side dishes as cottage cheese, pineapple salad, and baked beans.

Most of Cronin's attention, however, was focused not on tinkering with the menu, but with growing the chain. Launching an aggressive expansion campaign, he more than doubled the number of restaurants in just a few years. By 1975, the number of Steak n Shakes had grown to 130.

The 1970s brought with them some difficulties for the company, however. Fast-food restaurants were becoming ubiquitous on the American landscape, and the popularity of Steak n Shake's curb service was overshadowed by the ease and speed of these new eateries' drive-through windows. The increased competition, in tandem with the challenges inherent in running a more geographically dispersed operation, took its toll on Steak n Shake. Cronin responded by eliminating curb service at most of the chain's locations and closing several restaurants. It was during this time of realignment that the company's headquarters was relocated from Illinois to Indianapolis, Indiana.

In 1981, the Franklin Corporation sold its interest in Steak n Shake to Ed W. Kelley, a veteran in the restaurant business. Since 1974, Kelley had been the principal shareholder and managing general partner of Kelley & Partners, Ltd., a Florida company with investments in snack food distribution companies and restaurants. In 1982, Kelley formed a new holding company—Consolidated Products—to serve as the parent company for Steak n Shake. According to a November 1995 issue of *Indiana Business Magazine,* Kelley and his associates chose the nonspecific name "Consolidated" because they intended to acquire and manage other restaurants aside from Steak n Shake.

Key Dates:

1934: Gus Belt opens the first Steak n Shake in Normal, Illinois.
1939: Steak n Shake has eight locations.
1948: Steak n Shake moves into St. Louis, which will prove to be one of its largest markets.
1954: Belt dies, leaving restaurant chain to his wife Edith.
1969: Edith Belt sells the 51-unit Steak n Shake chain to Longchamps, Inc.
1971: Longchamps sells its interest in Steak n Shake to the Franklin Corporation.
1975: There are 130 Steak n Shake locations.
1981: The Franklin Corporation sells Steak n Shake to Ed Kelly, who forms Consolidated Products.
1986: Consolidated forms a Specialty Restaurants Division.
2000: Consolidated Products discontinues its Specialty Restaurants group; changes its name to The Steak n Shake Company.

By the mid-1980s, Steak n Shake again was facing difficulties. The company's earnings had flattened, and its growth had stalled. In 1985, James Williamson, Jr., was hired as president and CEO of Consolidated Products, inheriting a company that had posted five quarters of losses. Williamson, like Cronin before him, took a hard look at what was going on at the restaurants. He scrutinized the menu, eliminating infrequently ordered items that required a great deal of preparation. He also reviewed the appearance of the restaurants and, feeling that some had strayed too far, brought them back into alignment with the prototypical black-and-white, visible-kitchen look.

In a more dramatic effort to bolster its sagging bottom line, Consolidated began a program of diversification. Forming a specialty restaurants division, the company began acquiring and/or opening a variety of casual dining steakhouses and other specialty restaurants.

By the late 1980s, the Steak n Shake chain was again on solid ground, posting record profits. The Specialty Division, however, had yet to earn a profit. In 1990, Consolidated appointed Stephen Huse as president, at the same time acquiring two of his specialty restaurants located in Bloomington and Indianapolis, Indiana. Although Huse's mission was to turn the Specialty Division around, he did not stay with the company long enough to make much of an impact. He resigned in 1991, eventually to be replaced by Alan Gilman.

1990s: Rapid Growth

The 1990s ushered in a new era of growth for Steak n Shake. The chain, which contained slightly more than 100 units at the beginning of the decade, was to more than triple in size over the next ten years.

Part of the growth stemmed from a franchise campaign, which the company launched in 1991. Between late spring and fall of that year, the company signed franchise agreements for 15 restaurants in the Charlotte, North Carolina and Atlanta markets; four restaurants in the Louisville and Bowling Green, Kentucky markets; and five restaurants in the cities of Jonesboro and Little Rock, Arkansas.

As the mid-1990s approached, Steak n Shake was truly thriving. The company had seen steady growth since the mid-1980s and had posted record earnings every quarter for six years. With such a strong position, management believed the chain was ideally poised for rapid growth; in 1994, the company announced that it planned to double the number of Steak n Shakes by 1998. Its expansion strategy was to ''cluster'' its locations, adding units in markets that already had a Steak n Shake presence, and then eventually expanding out into contiguous metropolitan markets, in order to benefit from existing name recognition.

Steak n Shake lost no time. In 1995, the chain had 171 restaurants in 12 states, including 34 franchised units; by the end of 1997, the company had added 57 company-owned stores and 21 franchised units, bringing the total restaurants in the chain to 249. In 1998 and 1999, 85 new units were added to the Steak n Shake stable, and the expansion was still going strong. The company had shown remarkably consistent growth, as well, in its sales and profits. Between 1994 and 1999, total sales grew from $185 million to $387 million; earnings grew from $7.2 million to $19.7 million, and Consolidated's stock appreciated 372 percent.

By the middle of 2000, Consolidated Products decided to expend all of its energies on the Steak n Shake brand. The company announced that it planned to discontinued its Specialty Restaurants division, closing or selling its remaining non-Steak n Shake locations. ''Steak n Shake has been our vehicle for growth and that's where we intend to focus our attention,'' explained company spokesperson Victor Yeandel in a September 2000 interview with the *Indianapolis Business Journal.* The company also announced that it was changing its name to more accurately reflect its new focus; therefore, in early 2001, Consolidated Products formally became The Steak n Shake Company.

Looking to the Future: Still More Expansion

Steak n Shake continued to have ambitious plans for growth as it moved into the new millennium. The company's goal was to have 600 Steak n Shake restaurants by 2004, with more than 500 of them company-owned. It was likely that the company's growth strategy would continue to emphasize gradual geographic expansion, moving from one metropolitan area into adjacent markets. Beyond becoming bigger, it seemed unlikely that Steak n Shake would exhibit many changes throughout the coming years. As various generations of management had discovered, the fundamentals of Gus Belt's restaurant concept were virtually timeless—and there was no good reason to tinker with a proven formula for success.

Principal Competitors

Advantica Restaurant Group, Inc.; Burger King Corporation; Checkers Drive-In Restaurants, Inc.; CKE Restaurants, Inc.; Frisch's Restaurants, Inc.; McDonald's Corporation; Sonic Corp.; Triarc Companies, Inc.; TRICON Global Restaurants, Inc.; Wendy's International, Inc.; White Castle System, Inc.

Further Reading

Cronin, Robert, *Selling Steakburgers,* Carmel, Ind.: Guild Press of Indiana, 2000.

Culbertson, Katie, ''Steak n Shake to Get Parent's Full Attention,'' *Indianapolis Business Journal,* September 25, 2000, p. 6.

Hoekstra, Dave, ''Still Shaking,'' *Chicago Sun-Times,* July 16, 2000, p. 1.

Johnson, Douglas, ''What's for Dinner?,'' *Indiana Business Magazine,* November 1995, p. 8.

Luciano, Phil, ''Steaks and Shakes,'' *Peoria Journal Star,* October 17, 1993, p. B1.

Miller, Susan, ''Steak n Shake Serves Nostalgia with Burgers,'' *Indianapolis Star/News,* February 10, 1999, p. C1.

Partington, Martha, ''Steak n Shake: 'Famous for Steakburgers' for 56 Years,'' *Indiana Business Magazine,* April 1, 1990, p. 37.

—Shawna Brynildssen

Texaco Inc.

2000 Westchester Avenue
White Plains, New York 10650
U.S.A.
Telephone: (914) 253-4000
Fax: (914) 253-7753
Web site: http://www.texaco.com

Public Company
Incorporated: 1926 as The Texas Corporation
Employees: 18,000
Sales: $50.1 billion
Stock Exchanges: New York Toronto London Zurich Brussels Geneva
Ticker Symbol: TX
NAIC: 212111 Bituminous Coal and Lignite Surface Mining; 211111 Crude Petroleum and Natural Gas Extraction; 32411 Petroleum Refineries; 44711 Gasoline Stations with Convenience Store

Texaco Inc. operates in more than 150 countries and, upon completion of its merger with Chevron Corporation, will stand as the world's fourth largest publicly traded energy firm. Texaco explores, discovers, and produces oil and natural gas; manufactures and markets fuels and lubricant products; operates trading, transportation, and distribution facilities; and manufactures alternate forms of energy for the power, manufacturing, and chemical markets. Texaco has expanded with the growth of the U.S. automobile industry in the early 20th century and quickly developed international production and marketing interests. By the 1960s, it had established the largest sales network of any U.S. oil company, with operations concentrated in refining and marketing. The oil crisis of the 1970s cut off many of its international sources of crude oil and left it with limited reserves. Texaco was poised for recovery in 1984, when it entered into a court battle with Pennzoil Company over the acquisition of Getty Oil. Since settling with Pennzoil in 1988, Texaco has pursued an almost constant restructuring effort in an attempt to recapture its former profitability and prominence in the oil industry. On October 16, 2000, Texaco announced its intention to merge with Chevron, forming ChevronTexaco. While the deal was expected to be completed by summer 2001, some issues concerning the divestment of some of Texaco's joint ventures stood to delay the merger.

Early Beginnings at the Start of the Century

Texaco was founded during the early boom years of the Texas oil industry. In 1901, a gusher at the Spindletop oil field sent hundreds of entrepreneurs into Beaumont, Texas. Among them was Joseph S. ''Buckskin Joe'' Cullinan, an oilman who had begun his career working for Standard Oil Company in Pennsylvania. The Spindletop wells led to the rapid establishment of more than 200 oil companies, pumping out as much as 100,000 barrels a day. Cullinan saw an opportunity in purchasing that crude for resale to refineries. With the help of New York investment manager Arnold Schlaet, he formed The Texas Fuel Company with an initial stock of $50,000. Cullinan and Schlaet began soliciting additional investments in New York and Chicago. After raising $3 million, they reorganized their venture as The Texas Company.

Cullinan immediately began constructing a pipeline between Spindletop and the gulf coast of Texas. He built a refinery at the Texas coastal city of Port Arthur, and from there the company shipped its oil to Louisiana sugar planters, who used it to heat their boilers. In the fall of 1902, salt water leaked into the Spindletop wells and ruined many of the companies based there. The Texas Company survived with a timely discovery of oil at Sour Lake, 20 miles northwest of Spindletop. Other strikes soon followed in Oklahoma and Louisiana.

With Cullinan's oil expertise and the financing of his New York backers, The Texas Company soon became one of the nation's most prominent oil companies. Cullinan continued to drill wells in the southwest region, building more pipelines to connect them with Port Arthur. By 1908, the company was selling to all but five western states, and by 1913, its assets were worth $60 million. The nickname Texaco came from the cable address of the company's New York offices. Texaco gained popularity as a product name and, in 1906, the company registered it as a trademark. The well-known logo first appeared in

Company Perspectives:

Texaco is a company that has captured hearts and minds. Our employees' vision, their daring and their determination shaped the character of our company for nearly a century, and these are the same attributes we will carry into the century to come.

1909, as a red star with a green ''T'' in the center. The company formally changed its name to Texaco Inc. in 1959.

Continued Growth and Production Expansion: 1910 to the 1920s

At the time of Texaco's founding, oil was used primarily for lighting and as fuel for factories and locomotives. Texaco met this demand with its first consumer product, Familylite Illuminating Oil, introduced in 1907. After 1910, however, the automobile revolutionized the oil industry. Demand for gasoline, formerly considered a waste by-product of kerosene, expanded rapidly. Texaco followed this trend, and by 1914, its gasoline production surpassed that of kerosene. The company went from distributing gasoline in barrels to underground tanks to curbside pumps and, in 1911, it opened its first filling station in Brooklyn, New York. By 1916, 57 such stations were in operation across the country. Powered by the growth of the automobile industry and the high demand for petroleum created by World War I, Texaco quadrupled its assets between 1914 and 1920.

After World War I, Texaco continued to concentrate on its automotive gasoline and oil production, introducing new products and expanding its national sales network. In 1920, two researchers at its Port Arthur refinery developed the oil industry's first continuous thermal cracking process for making gasoline. Named after its founders, the Holmes-Manley process greatly increased the speed of the refining process as well as the amount of gasoline that could be refined from a barrel of crude. Texaco marketed this gasoline through its retail network, pushing into the Rocky Mountain region between 1920 and 1926, and into West Coast markets with the acquisition of California Petroleum Company in 1928.

Products introduced during the 1920s included the company's first premium gasoline, as well as Texaco Aviation Gasoline and automobile motor oils. To market the lighter oils it refined from Texas crude, Texaco launched its first nationwide advertising campaign. The slogan ''Clean, Clear, Golden'' appeared at Texaco's filling stations, which displayed its motor oils in glass bottles. By 1928, Texaco owned or leased more than 4,000 stations in all 48 states.

The company's growth also was reflected in its corporate structure. Finding Texas's corporation laws too restrictive for doing business on such a large scale, Texaco decided to move its legal home. In 1926, it formed The Texas Corporation in Delaware, which then bought out the stock of The Texas Company and reorganized it as a subsidiary called The Texas Company of Delaware. The company also moved its headquarters from Houston to New York. The Texas Corporation acted as a holding company for The Texas Company of Delaware and The Texas Company of California—formerly The California Petroleum Company—until 1941, when it merged with both and formed a single company known as The Texas Company.

The Texas Corporation's earnings reached an all-time high in 1929, but then dropped precipitously after the stock market crash. Overproduction, economic recession, and low prices plagued the oil industry in the early 1930s. The company embarked on a strategy of introducing new products to stimulate demand. Texaco Fire Chief Gasoline was launched in 1932, and the company advertised it by sponsoring a nationwide Ed Wynn radio program. Havoline Wax Free Motor Oil, developed after the acquisition of the Indiana Refining Company in 1931, followed two years later, halting its losses by 1934. In 1938, The Texas Corporation, still nicknamed Texaco, introduced Texaco Sky Chief premium gasoline and also began promoting its Registered Rest Rooms program, assuring motorists that their service stations were ''Clean across the Country.'' In 1940, Texaco began its landmark sponsorship of the New York Metropolitan Opera's Saturday afternoon radio broadcasts. This program, which is still running, is the oldest association between a U.S. company and an arts program.

International Expansion Beginning in the 1930s

While The Texas Corporation promoted its products and services at home, it undertook vigorous expansion abroad. During the 1930s it began exploration and production in Colombia and Venezuela. In 1936, it joined with the Standard Oil Company of California to create the Caltex group of companies, a 50–50 venture in the Middle East. The Caltex group consolidated the operations of both of these companies east of the Suez Canal. Texaco also purchased a 50 percent interest from Standard Oil of California in the California Arabian Standard Oil Company, later renamed the Arabian American Oil Company (Aramco). The Caltex and Aramco ventures vastly expanded Texaco's sources of crude and also enabled it to integrate its operations in the Eastern Hemisphere.

The entry of the United States into World War II brought dramatic changes for The Texas Corporation. About 30 percent of its wartime production went to the war effort, primarily in the form of aviation fuels, gasoline, and petrochemicals. The company worked closely with Harold L. Ickes, federal petroleum administrator for the war effort, who organized the nation's oil companies into several nonprofit operations. The Texas Pipe Line Company, a subsidiary, oversaw the completion of two federally sponsored pipelines from Texas to the East Coast.

Texaco also joined War Emergency Tankers Inc., which operated a collective tanker fleet for the War Shipping Administration. Another such venture was The Neches Butane Products Company, which manufactured butadiene, an essential ingredient in synthetic rubber. This enterprise gave Texaco its start in the infant petrochemicals industry, and after the war it purchased a 25 percent interest from the Federal Government in the Neches Butane plant. Texaco acquired full ownership of this operation in 1980. The company furthered its interests in petrochemicals in 1944, when it formed the Jefferson Chemical Company with the American Cyanamid Company. Texaco later bought out American Cyanamid's interest in this venture and then merged it with its newly formed Texaco Chemical Company in 1980.

Key Dates:

1901: The Texas Fuel Company is formed.
1911: The company opens its first filling station in Brooklyn, New York.
1913: Company assets are worth $60 million.
1920: The Holmes-Manley process is developed to speed up the refining process.
1926: The firm incorporates as the Texas Corporation in Delaware.
1936: The company joins with the Standard Oil Company of California to create the Caltex group of companies.
1944: The Jefferson Chemical Company is formed in partnership with the American Cyanamid Company.
1959: The firm officially adopts the name Texaco Inc.
1966: The German oil company Deutsch Erdol A.G. is purchased.
1969: The trans-Andean pipeline is built.
1975: Revenues begin falling because of the Arab-Israeli War, the OPEC embargo, and the nationalization of foreign oil assets in many overseas nations.
1980: Texaco restructures, decentralizing its operations into three major geographic oil and gas divisions.
1984: The company purchases the Getty Oil Company.
1987: Texaco files Chapter 11 bankruptcy after the court upholds a $10.5 billion suit brought on by the Pennzoil Company; the firm eventually settles for $3 billion.
1988: The company fends off takeover attempts made by Carl Icahn.
1993: The firm restructures itself once again.
1995: Texaco re-enters the Canadian market by repurchasing Texaco Canada Petroleum Inc.
1996: The company settles a racial discrimination lawsuit amidst negative publicity.
1998: Shell Oil Company and Texaco form Equilon Enterprises LLC; Motiva Enterprises LLC is created by Texaco, Shell, and Saudi Aramco.
2000: Company announces plans to merge with Chevron Corporation.

With the end of World War II, Texaco faced renewed customer demand at home. U.S. consumption of oil exceeded its production for the first time in 1947, and Texaco reacted by tapping new foreign sources for its crude oil. In 1945, Texaco's jointly owned Caltex companies increased their refining capacity on Bahrain, reaching 180,000 barrels per day by 1951. Texaco also formed the Trans-Arabian Pipe Line Company with three other oil companies to build a pipeline connecting Saudi Arabia's oil fields with the eastern Mediterranean. At home, Texaco increased its refining capacity with the Eagle Point Works near Camden, New Jersey. It also introduced several new automotive products, including Texaco Anti-Freeze and Texamatic Fluid for automatic transmissions.

Aggressive Expansion During the 1950s and 1960s

During the 1950s and 1960s, Texaco concentrated on expanding its global refining and marketing operations. The acquisition of the Trinidad Oil Company in 1956 and the Seaboard Oil Company in 1958, both of which held proven reserves in South America, expanded its interests in the Western Hemisphere. To increase its production in the Amazon Basin, the company built a jointly owned trans-Andean pipeline in 1969 and a trans-Ecuadorian pipeline in 1972. To increase its production in Europe, moreover, Texaco purchased the majority interest in the West German oil company Deutsch Erdol A.G. in 1966. It also reorganized the Caltex group in 1967, taking over one-half of the group's interest in 12 European countries that it had been serving from Saudi Arabia. This move allowed the company to expand its marketing operations in Europe, while leaving the Caltex companies free to concentrate east of the Suez Canal, where they enjoyed their greatest market penetration. Texaco brought its petrochemical business to Europe in 1966 with a plant in Ghent, Belgium, and to Japan three years later.

In the United States, Texaco expanded its interests by acquiring regional companies and increasing its refining capacity. The company strengthened its position on the East Coast by buying the Paragon group of companies in 1959 and the White Fuel Corporation in 1962. In 1962, it also acquired mineral rights to two million undeveloped acres in West Texas from the TXL Oil Corporation. The company's petrochemical production grew rapidly during this period, with the addition of a new unit at the Eagle Point works in 1960, and one of the world's largest benzene plants in Port Arthur in 1961. Texaco's operating volumes doubled between 1960 and 1970, with gross production surpassing three billion barrels per day in 1970.

Problems in the 1970s

Texaco's tremendous growth came to an abrupt halt in the 1970s. The Arab-Israeli War, the OPEC embargo, and the nationalization of foreign oil assets in many overseas nations cut Texaco's profit margins and endangered its sources of crude. Furthermore, federal price controls and mandatory allocation regulations restricted Texaco's ability to raise prices or withdraw from unprofitable markets. Its net income dropped from $1.6 billion in 1974 to $830.6 million a year later and remained at that level for the rest of the decade.

Tensions in the Middle East prompted a wave of nationalizations in the oil industry. In 1972, Saudi Arabia began to nationalize the assets of Aramco, in which Texaco owned a 50 percent interest, and took over all of its operations in 1980. Between 1973 and 1974, Libya nationalized the Texas Overseas Petroleum Company, a Texaco subsidiary. The decade ended with the Iranian revolution displacing Texaco's interests there and the Caltex group selling off part of its operations to the Bahrain government.

Texaco increased its exploration efforts and reorganized its marketing operations at home. Drilling activities increased both onshore and offshore in the southwest, as well as in new areas such as the North Sea and eastern Atlantic. The company also modernized its refineries to maximize the yield from each barrel of crude. Texaco made its most dramatic alterations in its retail network, abandoning the 50-state plan that had made it the United States's largest seller of oil. It began to withdraw from unprofitable markets, cutting operations in all or parts of 19 states in the Rocky Mountain, Midwest, and Great Lakes regions. It also reduced its number of service stations and opened more modern outlets in high-volume areas.

The 1980s began with the U.S. economy still suffering from recession, but the deregulation of the oil industry offered Texaco new flexibility in trying to recoup its fortunes. Under the direction of its new chairman, John K. McKinley, Texaco undertook a major restructuring plan in 1980. It decentralized its operations into three major geographic oil and gas divisions representing the United States, Europe and Latin America, and West Africa, as well as one worldwide chemical organization called the Texaco Chemical Company. The company expanded its exploration program and it also committed more resources to projects for developing alternative fuels, such as coal gasification and shale oil.

Retrenchment in its refining and marketing operations continued with the closing of six inefficient refineries by 1982, and the reduction of its retail outlets from 35,500 in 1974 to 27,000 in 1980. Texaco introduced a new logo in 1981, a red "T" inside a white star and red circle, to promote its high-volume System 2000 stations. These stations were a quick success, with more than 1,200 in the United States by 1987. The company also added a new operating division in 1982, Texaco Middle East/Far East, and made several important acquisitions to bolster its reserve base. By 1985, Texaco's net income was once again more than $1 billion.

The Getty Purchase: 1984

In the middle of this comeback, Texaco became involved in a legal battle. The 1984 purchase of the Getty Oil Company had promised to speed Texaco's recovery by adding an estimated 1.9 billion barrels of proven reserves to its assets. Pennzoil Company filed suit, however, claiming that Texaco had interfered with its plans to acquire three-sevenths of Getty's shares. In the resulting court case, a Texas State District Court in Houston ordered Texaco to pay Pennzoil $10.5 billion in damages. Arguing that important New York and Delaware state laws had been ignored in the case, Texaco obtained an injunction from a federal court in New York that temporarily halted the payment of damages while it appealed the decision.

In February 1987, the Texas Court of Appeals upheld the decision. To protect its assets while continuing its appeals, the company filed for protection under Chapter 11 of the United States Bankruptcy Code. Texaco spent most of 1987 in Chapter 11 while continuing its litigation. As a result, it incurred its first operating losses since the Great Depression, finishing the year $4.4 billion in the red. After the Texas Supreme Court refused to hear an appeal, New York financier Carl Icahn began buying Texaco's rapidly depreciating stock in an attempt to force it to settle with Pennzoil. A few weeks later Texaco agreed to pay Pennzoil $3 billion rather than appeal the decision to the Supreme Court, allowing it to begin planning for its emergence from Chapter 11.

Icahn continued to buy the company's stock, however, and in early 1988, he began a takeover bid. Texaco's board of directors had submitted a restructuring plan to the shareholders for meeting the company's debt obligations. Icahn favored, instead, the sale of the company. He launched the biggest proxy battle in business history when he tried to gain control of five seats on the board of directors, but he was ultimately defeated in a June 1988 shareholders' election. The board of directors then agreed to buy out Icahn's interest in Texaco.

With the Pennzoil case and the takeover attempt behind it, Texaco rebuilt its market position under the leadership of chairman and CEO James Kinnear by selling off assets and undertaking new joint ventures. From 1987 to 1989, it sold its operations in Germany and Canada, as well as fixed assets in the United States (including 2,500 gas stations) and the Middle East, raising $7 billion in the process. It also expanded drilling operations in the North Sea and offshore California, while continuing its exploration efforts in Asia, Africa, and South America.

In 1988, Texaco U.S.A. transferred approximately two-thirds of its refining and marketing operations to Star Enterprise, a joint venture established with Saudi Arabia's Aramco. Other moves have included the acquisition of Chevron's marketing operations in six European countries and the company's first commercial application of its coal gasification technology in an electric plant in the Los Angeles basin.

The recession of 1991–92 depressed demand for petroleum products and forced prices lower. As a result, Texaco's revenue dropped from $40.51 billion in 1990, to $37.16 billion in 1991, to $36.53 billion in 1992, while net income fell from $1.41 billion in 1990, to $1.29 billion in 1991, to $1.04 billion in 1992. By 1993, net income had improved to $1.07 billion, but revenue continued to fall, dropping to $34.07 billion. That same year Kinnear retired and was succeeded by Alfred C. DeCrane, Jr.

Restructuring and Focusing on Exploration and Production: Early to Middle 1990s

Starting in 1993, DeCrane guided Texaco through yet another restructuring intended to improve its competitiveness. Like almost every other U.S. oil company going through restructuring at the time, Texaco reduced its workforce. A cut of 2,500 workers, or 8 percent, over a one-year period contributed to a $200 million reduction in overhead in 1994. DeCrane also wanted Texaco to focus on its core oil and gas operations, so he divested the company of its chemical business. In 1994, Texaco sold the Texaco Chemical Company to the Huntsman Corporation for $850 million. That year the company also sold more than 300 scattered, unprofitable oil- and gas-producing properties to Apache Corporation for $600 million.

With the funds generated through these moves, Texaco could increase its budget for overseas exploration and production. Seeking to increase production by 125,000 barrels a day by the end of the decade, Texaco began to pursue opportunities in Russia, China, and Colombia. To minimize its exposure in such risky areas of operation as Russia, Texaco, like other oil companies, turned to joint ventures with its competitors. For instance, Texaco formed the Timan Pechora Company L.L.C. with Exxon, Amoco, and Norsk Hydro to negotiate a production-sharing agreement with Russia for the Timan Pechora Basin, which may hold more than two billion barrels of oil.

The much leaner Texaco of the mid-1990s had yet to return to its former prominence, but was in better shape than in many years. One positive sign was Texaco's reentry into the Canadian market in 1995, with its $30 million reacquisition of Texaco Canada Petroleum Inc. With the company committed to increasing its capital spending overseas from 45 percent of total capital spending to 55 percent by 1998, Texaco seemed determined to get its share of the oil available outside the United States.

In 1996, the firm budgeted $2.1 billion for international development. The firm delineated gas finds in the deep water of the Gulf of Mexico and developed new projects in the North Sea, Nigeria, Angola, Australia, and Southeast Asia. Production also was increased in Kuwait and Saudi Arabia. In July of that year, Peter Bijur was elected Texaco CEO and began to restructure its corporate management, forming three business units, including Worldwide Upstream, International Downstream, and Global Business.

Facing Problems During the Late 1990s

Amidst the positive changes occurring at Texaco, the firm fell subject to negative publicity in late 1996, when a tape recorded by a Texaco executive surfaced that caught corporate officials making racial slurs and planning to destroy documents related to a discrimination suit brought against the firm in 1994. Eleven days after the tape became public, the company settled the suit, paying $154 million to more than 1,500 black employees, with an additional $35 million in raises over a period of five years. The firm also adopted a new diversity training program in response to the suit.

Texaco continued to forge ahead, however, and in 1997, the company purchased California-based oil producer Monterey Resources Inc. for $1.4 billion, in the largest acquisition since the 1984 Getty purchase. The firm also completed its work on the Texaco Exploration Multispectral Spectrometer (TEEMS), a device used for locating oil and gas. Net income for the year rose by 32 percent over the previous year to $2.67 billion.

In early 1998, Texaco teamed up with Shell Oil Company to create Equilon Enterprises LLC, which combined the refining and marketing units of both companies, as well as their trading, transportation, and lubricants businesses, in the West and Midwest sections of the United States. Texaco and Shell also formed Motiva Enterprises LLC along with Saudi Aramco, which combined the eastern and Gulf Coast U.S. refining and marketing businesses of the three firms. These two new companies were created to cut costs and secure profits.

Crude oil prices fell in 1998, due to decreased demand related to the Asian economic crisis, economic conditions in Russian and Latin America, and warm weather in many regions. Texaco's aggressive expansion efforts of the past were curtailed as the firm was forced to cut capital spending and implement a $650 million cost-cutting program that included laying off more than 1,000 workers. The industry felt relief, however, when OPEC responded to the collapse in oil prices by cutting production. By the second half of 1999, prices became stable and the Asian economy began its turnaround.

Meanwhile, Texaco's downstream operations were faltering. Its Equilon and Motiva ventures were securing unremarkable profit margins. As a result, Texaco began focusing on its upstream operations in 1999 and also began selling off segments that did not fit with its business strategy. The firm made a wildcat discovery in Nigeria as well as offshore in Western Australia. The firm also acquired a 45 percent stake in the Philippine Malampaya gas project and increased its stake in the Venezuelan Hamaca project.

By the end of the decade, the company was once again facing lawsuits. In early 1999, the company settled a $3.1 million suit concerning a sex discrimination lawsuit filed by 186 female employees who claimed Texaco did not pay them fairly. A group of Ecuador Indians also brought suit against the firm claiming the company had ruined their rainforest and increased the risk of cancer in the area because of oil contamination.

Changes for the New Millennium

Texaco entered the new millennium focused on remaining a strong leader in the industry. As part of its growth strategy, the firm partnered with Tyumen Oil Company to market lubricants in open stores in Russia and Ukraine. The firm also purchased an interest in Prista Oil A.D., a Bulgarian-based lubricant company, and secured a lubricant supply agreement with AB Volvo.

The company once again resumed merger talks with Chevron Corporation in 2000—original merger negotiations had fallen through in 1999. Bijur wrote in the 2000 Texaco Annual Report, ''2000 was a year in which the fundamental changes in our industry became more apparent then ever before. It was the year Texaco chose to take a dramatic step forward to ensure that, in this new world of energy, we can continue to deliver superior value to shareholders, not just for one year but for many years to come.'' The dramatic step referred to in the report was the October 2000 announcement of the planned merger that would create ChevronTexaco Corporation. The proposed combination would form the third largest producer of oil and gas in the United States, with assets of $77 billion. The terms of the deal included Texaco shareholders receiving .77 shares of Chevron common stock for each share of Texaco common stock they owned, with Chevron shareholders keeping existing shares. Upon completion of the deal, company headquarters would be moved to San Francisco, California.

Bijur announced his departure from Texaco in February 2001. The *Oil Daily* reported, ''In his five years at the helm of Texaco, Bijur had a rough ride that ended with the sale of the company. Bijur abandoned Texaco's course of aggressive expansion by cutting capital expenditures. In 1998, he led Texaco in disappointing downstream deals by merging US assets with Royal Dutch/Shell and Saudi Aramco to create Equilon and Motiva, two companies Texaco now will have to sell in order to get antitrust approval for the Chevron merger.'' The February 2001 article also reported that Texaco had not performed well under Bijur's leadership in comparison to other oil companies, ultimately leading to its sale to Chevron. Dave O'Reilly was slated to be chairman and CEO of the combined firm.

The European Union approved the Chevron purchase in March 2001, and the Federal Trade Commission was expected to give its go-ahead in spring 2001. Both companies planned to begin operation as ChevronTexaco in the summer of that year, although some details concerning the divestment of joint ventures threatened to stall the completion. Upon final completion of the deal, ChevronTexaco's position as the fourth largest integrated oil company in the world—behind Exxon Mobil Corporation, Royal Dutch/Shell Group, and BP plc—would be secured.

Principal Subsidiaries

Caltex Petroleum Corp. (50%); Equilon Enterprises LLC (44%); Four Star Oil & Gas Co.; Hydro-Texaco Holdings; Motiva Enterprises LLC (31%); Saudi Arabian Texaco Inc.; Star Enterprise (50%); TEPI Holdings Inc.; Texaco Cogeneration Co.; Texaco Exploration & Production Inc.; Texaco International Trader Inc.; Texaco Overseas Holdings Inc.; Texaco Pipeline Co.; Texaco Refining & Marketing Inc.; Texaco Trading & Transportation Inc.; TRMI Holdings Inc.; Texaco Brasil S.A. Produtos de Petroleo; Texaco Canada Petroleum Inc.; Texaco Denmark Inc.; Texaco Investments (Netherlands), Inc.; Texaco Overseas (Nigeria) Petroleum Co.; Texaco Panama Inc.; Texaco Britain Limited (U.K.); Texaco Limited (U.K.); Texaco North Sea U.K. Co.

Principal Competitors

BP plc; Exxon Mobil Corporation; Royal Dutch/Shell Group.

Further Reading

Abcede, Angel, ''Texaco Remakes Itself into New Global Image,'' *National Petroleum News,* April 1996, p. 17.

''Corporate Restructuring '90s Style: Merge and Purge, Lean and Mean,'' *National Petroleum News,* September 1994, pp. 16–18.

de Rouffignac, Ann, ''Shell, Texaco Sign Major Deal to Combine Refining Assets,'' *Houston Business Journal,* March 21, 1997.

''EU Oks Chevron, Texaco Merger,'' *Oil Daily,* March 2, 2001.

Folmer, L. W., *Reaching for a Star: Experiences in the International Oil Business,* Austin, Tex.: L.W. Folmer, 1993.

James, Marquis, *The Texaco Story: The First Fifty Years 1902–1952,* New York: The Texas Company, 1953.

Melcher, Richard A., Peter Burrows, and Tim Smart, ''Remaking Big Oil: The Desperate Rush to Slash Costs,'' *Business Week,* August 8, 1994, pp. 20–21.

Petzinger, Thomas, *Oil & Honor: The Texaco-Pennzoil Wars,* New York: Putnam, 1987.

''Powerless Bijur Decides to Leave Texaco,'' *Oil Daily,* February 6, 2001.

''Sales Should Seal Chevron, Texaco Deal,'' *Oil Daily,* January 26, 2001.

''Scandal at Texaco,'' *Maclean's,* November 18, 1996, p. 43.

Shannon, James, *Texaco and the $10 Billion Jury,* Englewood Cliffs, N.J.: Prentice Hall, 1988.

Shook, Barbara, ''Texaco to Acquire Monterey for $1.4 billion,'' *Oil Daily,* August 19, 1997, p. 1.

Smart, Tim, ''Pumping Up at Texaco,'' *Business Week,* June 7, 1993, pp. 112–13.

Texaco Inc., ''Texaco Highlights,'' White Plains, N.Y.: Texaco Inc., 2001. Available from http://www.texaco.com.

''Texaco Makes Find Off Nigeria,'' *Oil Daily,* January 7, 1999.

Texaco Today: The Spirit of the Star, 1902–1992, White Plains, N.Y.: Texaco Inc., 1992.

Toal, Brian A., ''The Man Behind the Star,'' *Oil & Gas Investor,* February 1994, pp. 42–45.

—updates: David E. Salamie, Christina M. Stansell

Trailer Bridge, Inc.

10405 New Berlin Road East
Jacksonville, Florida 32226
U.S.A.
Telephone: (904) 751-7100
Toll Free: (800) 554-1589
Fax: (904) 751-7444
Web site: http://www.trailerbridge.com

Public Company
Incorporated: 1991
Employees: 282
Sales: $91.7 million (2000)
Stock Exchanges: NASDAQ
Ticker Symbol: TRBR
NAIC: 48832 Marine Cargo Handling; 484121 General Freight Trucking, Long-Distance, Truckload

Jacksonville, Florida-headquartered Trailer Bridge, Inc., describes itself as ''an integrated trucking and marine freight carrier.'' Its main business is the transportation of freight via a truck and tug-drawn barge system, principally between the continental United States and Puerto Rico. Its trucks operate throughout the lower 48 states, taking freight containers to the company's marine facilities in Jacksonville or Newark, New Jersey, where they are loaded on company-owned vessels and shipped overseas, usually to San Juan, Puerto Rico. Trailer Bridge owns and operates over 140 tractors and 1,300 trailers and uses its own drivers and equipment. It also owns five Triplestack Box Carriers, which were delivered in 1998. These specially-designed vessels, with their larger freight capacity, were the first ones in 15 years to be fabricated for use in the Puerto Rican trade. They accommodate the company's comparatively-larger, signature 53-foot long and 102-inch wide freight containers, and when completed joined two of the world's largest roll-on/roll-off barges already in use. Trailer Bridge is a primary beneficiary of the Merchant Marine Act (1920), or Jones Act, which stipulates that all vessels carrying cargo between two ports in the United States or its possessions must have been built in the United States, be owned by U.S. citizens, and be crewed by U.S. mariners. Until his death in June 2001, the company's majority stock holder was Malcom P. McLean, the inventor of freight containerization and Trailer Bridge's founder.

1956–91: Malcom McLean and the ''Intermodal Revolution''

Trailer Bridge, a relative newcomer on the transportation block, only goes back to 1991, though its founder, Malcom Purcell McLean, carried with him long-established industry credentials that had made him legendary long before he started up Trailer Bridge. McLean started out in the business world as the manager of a service station in his home state of North Carolina, but in 1935 switched to driving a truck on that state's back roads, where he learned that success depended on the ability to move freight on time at competitive prices.

It was McLean, once described by *Fortune* as one of the ten most important innovators of the century according to company literature, who initially came up with the idea of shipping freight in containers that could be transported by truck and then stacked or piggybacked on railway cars or ships for further freighting. The idea eventually won him a distinguished place in the International Maritime Hall of Fame.

McLean began this ''intermodal revolution'' in 1956, when his company, McLean Trucking, started experimenting by loading, intact, 35-foot highway trailers onto a freighter, the *Ideal X*, for shipping by sea. It was a simple but brilliant alternative to the dockside unloading of trailer freight, the reloading of it into cargo holds of ships, and then the reversing of the process when the cargo vessels arrived at their unloading destinations. For some industry observers, McLean had introduced an industrial innovation almost as significant as Henry Ford's Model T assembly line.

Still, the idea met considerable resistance, especially from longshoremen and carriers who had a lot at stake in the old ''break-bulk'' methods of handling cargo. McLean had to put up his own money to make container vessels from retrofitted oil tankers. Initially, these went only from New Jersey to Houston and back, but eventually they began transporting containers overseas.

Company Perspectives:

Trailer Bridge's mission is to provide cost and service effective transportation that contributes to the success of both the customers and the company. The mission will be achieved through commitment to a continual improvement process that best matches customers' needs with the company's strength. Attainment of the mission will result in financial strengths needed for sustained growth, overall product improvement and ongoing achievement of customer, employee and shareholder objectives.

In order to fully implement the new system, McLean wanted to set up a new shipping company using barges for carrying the containers. However, because Interstate Commerce Commission regulations prohibited a single company from operating carriers on both surface and water, when he bought Pan-Atlantic Steamship Company, he had to divest his ownership of McLean Trucking. He then reorganized Pan-Atlantic, and what emerged was Sea-Land Service Inc., a company that proved that the container system of handling cargo was very efficient and cost effective. Among other things, it lessened fuel and cargo-handling expenses and, thanks to drastically reduced pilferage, also sent insurance rates spiraling downward.

In 1969, for $500 million, McLean sold Sea-Land to R.J. Reynolds, though he did not leave the business. He stayed on as a Reynolds director, but after becoming frustrated with corporate rigidity in the face of new ideas, he resigned. In 1978, he bought U.S. Lines, which at the time was ailing financially. Five years later, in 1983, at age 69, he set out to take the container system into Pacific waters, and commenced the manufacture of 12 container ships in South Korea. At the time, they were the largest container ships in the world and were designed to circumnavigate the globe. The venture did not go well, however. The U.S. Lines' Econoships, designed to keep fuel consumption as low as possible, were fuel efficient, yes, but very slow, and they lost their appeal when the oil boom ended with the market glut of the mid 1980s. McLean's company went bankrupt in 1986.

Indefatigable and undaunted, McLean started up his new venture, Trailer Bridge, when he was closing in on 80, a time of life when most would simply lack the energy for such an undertaking. Officially, Trailer Bridge started up in 1991, but it did not begin operations until 1992.

1992: Company Begins Full Scale, Profitable Operations

Trailer Bridge set out to transport stacked containers to embarkation points in the United States and then ship them via barges to Puerto Rico, and began actively offering the service in 1992.

After it recorded a net loss that partial business year, it made a profitable run for the next four years, despite the fact that its revenue dropped off in 1995 and remained basically level through 1997.

The company's "differentiated" service soon garnered the acceptance of companies shipping goods to Puerto Rico from the U.S. mainland, and in 1993, its first full year of operation, the company achieved a 93 percent outbound (shipments from continental U.S. to Puerto Rico) vessel utilization rate, capturing about 5 percent of that particular market.

By 1996, Trailer Bridge's success prompted the company to modify both of its triple-deck barges. It contracted a New Orleans shipyard to add a section to each, increasing the barges' length from 450 feet to 736 feet, turning them into what at the time were the biggest trailer barges in the world. The additional length increased their capacity by 56 percent, allowing them to transport 416 containers, 150 more than they had previously been able to carry. Still, the company needed to do more. By 1997, Trailer Bridge controlled only about 8 percent of the country's southbound, Puerto Rico container-barge transport business, way behind its chief competitors, Navieras, which claimed about 33 percent, and Crowley American Transport, with a 29 percent share. Ranking fourth, Trailer Bridge also ran behind Sea-Land, which had about a 19 percent wedge of the market pie.

That the company needed a greater volume of trade was evident by the start of 1997. Despite its early success, Trailer Bridge faced the problem that its annual revenues were leveling out. In 1995, the company earned a net income of $4.4 million on revenue of $62.5 million, but it showed only a slight increase in 1996, when its revenues increased by just $0.6 million and resulted in a net income that dropped to $2 million.

In order to command a bigger market share, Trailer Bridge took additional steps to increase its freight-carrying capacity. In March 1997, it ordered two new, specially made, 408-foot ocean-going container barges, which, when completed, would double the company's cargo hauling capacity. The low-draft barges were designed specifically for the company's integrated cargo system and were able to accommodate 213 53-foot containers stacked three-high on the vessels' decks.

In the meantime, Trailer Bridge opted to go public, and in mid-1997 filed plans for an initial public stock offering of $31 million to be underwritten by Alex, Brown & Sons Inc. The company planned to use the funds generated by the offering for the purchase of new equipment, as well as to reduce its debt, garner some working capital, and pay a dividend to its private stockholders.

It was also in 1997 that the company started its New York–Florida service, between the ports of Newark, New Jersey, and Jacksonville. For this coastal run, which put the company in competition with trucking and rail carriers, Trailer Bridge planned to build another three Triplestack Box Carriers. Initially, the company scheduled two runs per week from New York to Florida. At the time, as it indicated in its SEC filing, Trailer Bridge's growth strategy called for initializing marine service to additional destinations protected under the Jones Act, including Hawaii and Alaska. Such ambitious plans had to be put on hold, however, for, starting in 1997, despite annual increases in revenue, Trailer Bridge's bottom line went into the red. Its loss of $2 million in 1997 was its first recorded loss since its initial year of operation.

1998 and Beyond: Fierce Market Competition and Rising Costs

The losses continued in 1998 and 1999, when, respectively, the company inked red figures of $2.5 million and $2.1 million.

Key Dates:

1956: Malcom P. McLean starts "intermodal" container shipping.
1991: McLean founds Trailer Bridge. Inc.
1993: Company begins first full-year of operation.
1996: Trailer Bridge increases vessel capacity by 56 percent with insertion of midsections in its two barges.
1997: Company goes public.
1998: Trailer Bridge completes the addition of five Triplestack Box Carriers to its fleet.
2001: Founder McLean dies at the age of 87.

Still, in the same period, revenues rose, up to $77.2 million in 1998 and $88.6 million in 1999. The company continued to get a good share of the business, and it was devising strategies designed to make it even more competitive. For example, in February 1999, Trailer Bridge put a web site on the Internet, highlighting its "Advantage" theme. In addition to stressing its dedication to providing each customer with "more value, service, and growth," the site provided shipping information and sailing schedules, with daily updates for both its Atlantic Highway and Puerto Rico services.

As the century drew to a close, Trailer Bridge also continued to land major shipping contracts, insuring its continued revenue growth. In September 2000, it signed a multi-year agreement with Sensormatic Electronics Corporation, the world's leading supplier of security systems. Although based in Boca Raton, Florida, Sensormatic operated a large plant in Aguadilla, Puerto Rico, and the company contracted Trailer Bridge to transport hundreds of 53-foot high container loads from Puerto Rico to various destinations in the United States. Yet later in the year, Trailer Bridge also won a multi-year contract with DaimlerChrysler Corp., becoming the exclusive carrier for that company's new vehicles shipped to Puerto Rico from the U.S. mainland.

Despite the new business, Trailer Bridge's net loss reached $10.3 million in 2000. According to an April 9, 2001 *Journal of Commerce* piece online, a contributing cause was what CEO John McCown termed a "brutal price war" that was "producing extraordinary losses in the endgame of the long overdue market shakeout." Other factors contributing to the inflated net loss were increased fuel costs, shipment cancellations due to inclement weather, and unexpected increases in trucking costs as well as a $3.7 million non-cash charge against income necessitated by reversing tax credits taken in previous years. A plus factor for Trailer Bridge that could help it down the line was the disclosure in 2000 that the company's vessels, burning cleaner fuel than those of its competitors, offered distinct air quality advantages over its competitors. Conceivably, the company's growing environmental-friendly reputation could draw additional business in a difficult and contentious market.

The heated price war of the late 1990s led to Trailer Bridge's accusations that one of its main competitors, Sea Star, was offering noncompensatory rates for shipments to and from Puerto Rico in a predatory pricing strategy designed to win new shipping contracts and dominate the U.S. mainland-Puerto Rico maritime shipping trade. In its complaint to the Surface Transportation Board, Trailer Bridge charged that Sea Star, majority-owned by Matson Navigation Inc. and Totem Express, was illicitly receiving federal subsidies from Matson's joint service agreement with APL Ltd. in the Pacific. APL was collecting federal subsidies of $2.1 million annually for each of the nine ships in its international service, subsidies for which ships under the Jones Act were ineligible.

Trailer Bridge and other container shippers taking advantage of the exclusionary protection of the Jones Act faced some risks. There were some pressures to open a Jones Act window to allow the use of foreign-built and owned and operated vessels to transport freight between U.S. ports, including those in its possessions. Also, although the independence movement in Puerto Rico was not supported by the majority of the people in the early 2000s, attitudes were subject to change. Yet as long as the law remained in effect, and the political situation in Puerto Rico remained the same, Trailer Bridge would easily hold its own against its competition. It will not, however, have the guiding spirit of Malcom McLean: he died of pneumonia on May 25, 2001.

Principal Competitors

Crowley Maritime Corporation; CSX Corporation; Navieras de Puerto Rico; Sea Star Line; Sea-Land.

Further Reading

Bonney, Joseph, "Malcom McLean Dead at 87," *JoC Online (Journal of Commerce),* May 30, 2001.

——, "Return of the Trucker," *American Shipper,* March 1992, p. 16.

Brennan, Terry, "Trailer Bridge Inc.," *Journal of Commerce,* June 15, 1999, p. 1.

Burrows, Gary, "Return of Malcolm McLean," *American Shipper,* August 1991, p. 12.

Dupin, Chris, "No Changes for Trailer Bridge," *JoC Online (Journal of Commerce),* June 27, 2001.

——, "Trailer Bridge Posts 2000 Loss," *JoC Online (Journal of Commerce),* April 9, 2001.

Finotti, John, "Florida's Trailer Bridge Inc. Plans Stock Offering," *Knight-Ridder/Tribune Business News*, June 3, 1997.

——, "Trailer Bridge Inc. Stretches Florida-Puerto Rico Barge to 736 Feet," *Knight-Ridder/Tribune Business News*, May 10, 1996.

Lyons, Claire, "Uncontained Visionary," *Seatrade Review,* December/January 2001.

"New Study Highlights Environmental Benefits of Using Trailer Bridge Over Competitors," *Business Wire*, October 16, 2000.

Sherrid, Pamela, "Captain Courageous," *Forbes*, October 24, 1983, p. 40.

"Trailer Bridge Announces MEMPHIS BRIDGE," *PR Newswire*, November 13, 1998.

"Trailer Bridge Christens Puente Valiente," *PR Newswire*, March 30, 1999.

"Trailer Bridge Expands Service Between Northeast and Puerto Rico," *Business Wire*, September 11, 2000.

"Trailer Bridge, Inc.: Interview with John D. McCown," *Wall Street Transcript,* January 8, 2000.

"Trailer Bridge Plans NY/Florida Service," *American Shipper*, July 1997, p. 46.

"Trailer Bridge Signs Multi-Year Agreement with Sensormatic Electronics Corporation," *Business Wire*, September 8, 2000.

Wilner, Frank N., "Predation or Competition?," *Journal of Commerce*, June 21, 1999, p. 17.

—John W. Fiero

Transamerica–An AEGON Company

600 Montgomery Street
San Francisco, California 94111
U.S.A.
Telephone: (415) 983-4000
Fax: (415) 983-4400
Web site: http://www.transamerica.com

Wholly Owned Subsidiary of AEGON N.V.
Incorporated: 1928
Employees: 5,700
Total Assets: $13 billion (1999)
NAIC: 524113 Direct Life Insurance Carriers; 52413 Reinsurance Carriers; 53249 Other Commercial and Industrial Machinery and Equipment Rental and Leasing

Transamerica—An AEGON Company, purchased by AEGON N.V. in July 1999, operates as the third largest U.S. life insurer along with AEGON USA. The firm is involved in life insurance, financial services, and real estate services. Its commercial products and services include life insurance and employee benefits, structured settlements, commercial lending, leasing, real estate information, reinsurance, and institutional investment products. Transamerica's personal financial products and services include investment products, mutual funds, life insurance, long-term care insurance, annuities, variable products, and retirement services. After the merger, its operations were integrated with AEGON USA, part of the AEGON Insurance Group—one of the top ten life insurance and financial services organizations in the world.

Early History: 1900s to 1930

When Peter Amadeo Giannini, the son of Italian immigrants, began dreaming of his career in turn-of-the-century San Francisco, he had not set his heart on building a banking empire. Instead, at the age of 12 he was sneaking out of his home at night to work in his stepfather's produce business and, by the age of 19, was a full partner. His early success at this business allowed him to retire at the age of 31 with a modest, but comfortable, fortune. His foray into the banking world did not begin until several years later when he received a legacy from his father-in-law, Joseph Cuneo, who had made Giannini a director of his Columbus Savings and Loan Society, a building and loan association in San Francisco. Giannini's career in banking lasted more than 40 years, and during this time he established the Transamerica Corporation.

After Giannini was appointed a director of Columbus Savings and Loan he became immersed in a number of disagreements with other directors of the bank over policy issues. He consequently left the Savings and Loan Society and established his own banking business, which was located directly across the street from Columbus Savings and Loan. Giannini organized the Bank of Italy with $150,000 in capital contributed by his stepfather and ten friends. He envisioned the bank as an institution for the "little fellow," and the bank subsequently made loans to merchants, farmers, and laborers who were mostly of Italian descent.

Ironically, the San Francisco fire and earthquake of 1906 established Giannini's reputation in the banking world. As he stood amid the rubble of his bank on the morning of the earthquake, he was able to salvage more than $2 million in gold and securities. To avoid the looters who were running through the city, he hid his bank's resources under piles of vegetables in a horse-drawn cart borrowed from his former produce business. Giannini immediately alerted his depositors that their savings were safe and began making loans to businessmen who had lost their savings and their companies.

Giannini's success as a banker is also clearly evidenced by his anticipation of the 1907 stock market crash, and his accumulation of gold before the crash. When the crash came Giannini was able to pay his depositors in cash while other banks were using certificates for cash. From this experience, Giannini realized that only larger banks would ensure security and, therefore, he began purchasing small banks and converting them into branches of the Bank of Italy. With these acquisitions Giannini established the first branch banking policy in California.

The Bank of Italy grew so rapidly that by 1919 Giannini was able to form Bancitaly Corporation to organize the expansion.

Company Perspectives:

Transamerica Corporation strives to meet the needs of today's businesses through its commercial products and services division—from commercial lending, group life insurance, leasing and structured settlements, to real estate. The firm also is dedicated to helping families secure their financial future—from life insurance to investments.

In 1928, Bancitaly Corporation was followed by Transamerica Corporation, which was formed as a holding company for all of Giannini's banking, insurance, and industrial concerns.

Giannini's expansion into other areas of the financial services had established him as a leader in the financial services field. By 1929, he had moved into the New York banking scene and purchased the solidly established Bank of America. The following year after this important acquisition, all of Giannini's banks were consolidated into Bank of America National Trust and Savings Association. Transamerica played the role of parent company throughout this period.

Problems in the 1930s–40s

In 1931, just a year after the consolidation of his banks under Bank of America, Giannini retired and left the top post to Elisha Walker, a Wall Street investment banker. Walker did his best to break up this ''empire'' created by Giannini. Not surprisingly, Giannini forced Walker out in what was called a ''furious proxy battle'' at the 1932 annual meeting.

During the previous few decades Giannini's operations had been closely observed by both Wall Street and regulatory branches of the U.S. government; Giannini's success had found critics within both these institutions. Throughout the 1930s, Transamerica experienced problems with regulatory procedures and changes enacted by the government. In 1937, Transamerica sold 58 percent of its stock in Bank of America, although it still controlled the board of directors. At the time of his death in 1949, Giannini was embroiled in a fight with the Federal Reserve Board as to whether or not Transamerica had violated the Clayton Anti-Trust Act in creating a ''credit monopoly'' by placing directors on the boards of banks in the huge chain owned by Bank of America. It was the Reserve Board's belief that Transamerica still controlled the bank even after the 1937 split.

Focus on Occidental Life Following the Bank Holding Company Act of 1956

The split between Bank of America and Transamerica was present throughout World War II until 1956, when Congress passed the Bank Holding Company Act, which did not allow bank holding companies the right to involve themselves in industrial activities. By this time, Transamerica was a holding company for several industrial concerns as well as the successful Occidental Life Insurance Company. As a result of the passage of this Act, Transamerica sold its banks, forming Western Bancorporation, and was left with Occidental Life and other smaller concerns under its direction.

While the litigation continued over Bank of America, Transamerica was resourcefully building up its life insurance business through Occidental Life. By the early 1960s, Occidental Life had assets of $751 million. The success of Occidental Life was, in large part, due to its ability to make the most of a sale. In the postwar 1930s, Occidental was selling term life insurance to California families. Since term life insurance carried lower premiums than full life insurance, other insurance companies dismissed this type of sale as a trivial pursuit, but Occidental banked on high-volume sales that would eventually be converted into full life insurance as the policyholder's income increased, thus making up for the initially low profit. This method worked. Occidental's insurance sales increased from $1 billion in 1945 to $6 billion in 1955 to $16 billion in 1965.

Because of the success of Occidental Life it is not surprising that in 1959 President Horace W. Brower was interested in expanding the company's financial services and moving toward ''modern merchandising techniques.'' When Brower rose to the chairman's seat, he looked outside the company to find a ''hard-nose financial man'' who could successfully run the company as president. The man Transamerica found was John R. Beckett, a 42-year-old investment banker and vice-president of Blyth and Company's San Francisco office. Beckett was considered to be extremely conversant with the world of finance and negotiations, an important quality since Brower was ready to begin a major acquisition program for Transamerica Corporation.

The plan at Transamerica during this time was to create a financial institution where people could do all their business, something of a ''department store of finances.'' It was Beckett's belief that people wanted ''convenience and service,'' and he was willing to provide such banking. Beckett's concern centered on the fact the financial service industry changed quickly, and he was determined to stay ahead of his competitors.

Occidental Life was used as a base for changing Transamerica into a holding company not only for insurance but also for other companies within the service field. Beckett was interested in companies that would ''work in harmony with one another in the market place.'' The first major acquisition after Beckett became president was Pacific Finance Corporation in 1961, and additional acquisitions focused on land, title insurance, and mortgage banking companies. New credit card, leasing, and life insurance operations also were started during the 1960s. By 1969, Transamerica was considered a large service conglomerate. To his credit, Beckett changed the dependency on Occidental from 75 percent of the company's profits to slightly more than 50 percent by 1966.

Growth Through Acquisition: Late 1960s

Beckett saw the transformation of Transamerica not only as a chance for consumers to do business with a ''friendly'' full-service bank, but also as a way to impress upon customers the importance of using these services over and over again. Beckett compared Transamerica to General Electric: ''We hope it will be like the family that buys a refrigerator from G.E. If they like the product and the price, and they get good service, they'll go back to G.E. when they need a new stove. . . . That's exactly what we're trying to do in financial services.''

Key Dates:

1928: A.P. Giannini establishes the Transamerica Corporation, as a holding company for his businesses.
1929: The company acquires the Bank of America.
1956: Congress passes the Bank Holding Company Act; Transamerica sells its banks, forming Western Bancorporation, and is left with Occidental Life and other smaller concerns under its direction.
1960: John R. Beckett is named president.
1965: Insurance sales increase to $16 billion.
1967: The company acquires United Artists.
1968: The company purchases Trans International Airlines and Budget Rent-a-Car.
1981: James R. Harvey is elected president and begins divesting operations not related to financial services and insurance.
1986: Trans International Airlines and Budget Rent-a-Car are sold.
1991: By now, Frank C. Herringer has taken over as president and CEO.
1993: The company exits the property and casualty insurance market.
1994: The company sells Transamerica Fund Management Company.
1995: The company acquires a $1 billion portfolio of home equity loans from the ITT Corporation.
1997: The company sells its consumer finance business for more than $1.1 billion.
1999: AEGON N.V. acquires Transamerica for $10.8 billion.

Beckett's attempts to enlarge Transamerica resulted in the company being labeled a conglomerate, but Beckett strongly disagreed with this image. Beckett saw managers of conglomerates as ''opportunists, people who make acquisitions strictly on an ad hoc basis. They move too quickly, pay too much, use funny accounting, and don't look for long-range values. Eventually their bubbles will burst.'' In contrast, Beckett believed that he was acquiring companies slowly and in concert with a plan to provide a full-line financial services company.

According to Beckett's plan, financial services also included leisure time services for consumers, such as movies and travel. In 1967, Transamerica acquired United Artists and in 1968, Trans International Airlines and Budget Rent-a-Car. United Artists would prove to be the acquisition of the 1960s that resulted in financial difficulties for Transamerica.

United Artists, created in 1919 by such movie stars and directors as Douglas Fairbanks, Sr., Mary Pickford, Charlie Chaplin, and D.W. Griffith, looked like a profitable acquisition in 1968, but in 1970, two years after Beckett became chairman, Transamerica's earnings dropped by half because of an $18 million loss due to several unsuccessful films. Beckett, although caught by surprise by the large loss at United Artists, eventually saw the film company turn into a very profitable business by the late 1970s with successful films such as *Rocky, Coming Home,* and *One Flew over the Cuckoo's Nest.*

Along with these successes, however, there was also unrest within United Artists; the management who had initially sold the film company to Transamerica was now interested in buying it back. Beckett fought back, telling *Fortune* magazine that if ''the people at United Artists don't like it, they can quit and go off on their own.'' That is exactly what they did.

Restructuring: 1980s–90s

Beckett claimed that he would never sell United Artists, but in 1981 it was sold for $380 million under the direction of President James R. Harvey, who took over in January 1981 when Beckett became chairman. Harvey was an executive vice-president under Beckett and had been with the company since 1965. Harvey's goal for Transamerica was to concentrate primarily on financial services and insurance. Over the next several years, Harvey would pursue this goal by making an enormous number of acquisitions ($1.7 billion worth) while at the same time divesting Transamerica of a host of operations that fell outside the newly defined operational area ($1.5 billion worth).

Trans International Airlines and Budget Rent-a-Car were both sold in 1986, and Transamerica Title was sold in 1990. By 1991, Harvey was chairman of Transamerica, and Frank C. Herringer had taken over as president and CEO. Herringer continued Harvey's program to remake Transamerica with the 1993 divestiture of the firm's property and casualty insurance operations. Initially, the company attempted to find a private buyer for the unit, which was in a segment of the insurance industry that had been performing poorly, but there were no takers. So the firm spun off the operation early in 1993 through an initial public offering. Transamerica retained a 26 percent stake in the new company, known as TIG Holdings Inc., which it then sold through a second public offering later in the year, marking its complete exit from the business. Transamerica used the money generated by the offering—about $1 billion—to pay down its debt and invest in its remaining operations.

The company suffered a setback in the financial services area in 1994 when it decided to sell its mutual funds business, Transamerica Fund Management Company. The operation was not as effective as some other mutual funds companies in that it was unable to develop methods to sell the funds other than through Transamerica's own insurance agents. The buyer of Transamerica's mutual funds business, John Hancock Mutual Life Insurance Co., in fact sold two-thirds of its funds through channels other than its own agents. The unit sold for $100 million.

More than offsetting this development, however, was Transamerica's 1995 purchase of a $1 billion portfolio of home equity loans from the ITT Corporation. Transamerica's leasing operations also received a major boost in 1994 with the acquisition of a British counterpart, Tiphook PLC, for more than $1 billion in cash. The acquisition strengthened Transamerica's position in the international transportation equipment leasing market, as well as making it number two in the industry worldwide. Overall, the company's success in its latest transformation was evident in the record gross revenues of $5.35 billion and record net income of $427.2 million in 1994.

Transamerica continued to restructure its operations into the mid-1990s. The firm moved its real estate tax service division, which had seen a decrease in 1995 earnings due to a reduction in home mortgage refinancing, to Dallas, Texas, in an effort to cut costs. By now, its financial and insurance divisions also were operating out of Los Angeles, California, and Chicago, Illinois, leaving only its realty operations and corporate headquarters in the famed Transamerica Pyramid building in San Francisco.

In 1997, the firm took its divestment operations one step further with the sale of its consumer finance business to Household International for $1.1 billion. Transamerica Financial had posted losses of $45 million in 1996, while the consumer finance industry was hit by a wave of consolidation. The deal was part of Transamerica's strategy to centralize its consumer lending operations. According to a *Mergers & Acquisitions* article, the strategy included selling ''almost all of its existing businesses and redeploying capital while building a centralized real estate-secured lending business.''

While divesting certain operations, Transamerica continued to look for strategic alliances that would be beneficial. In early 1998, the company acquired the retail finance business of Whirlpool Financial Corporation for $1.3 billion. The firm also recorded solid financial results for the year; its stock was priced below average, however, which made it a prime takeover target.

The AEGON Merger: 1999

Sure enough, in February 1999, Transamerica announced that it was going to be acquired by Dutch insurance company AEGON N.V., who was attracted to the firm's strong position in the U.S. insurance, reinsurance, and annuities market. The deal included $9.7 billion in stock and cash and the assumption of $1.1 billion in Transamerica debt. ''In a rapidly consolidating and globalizing financial services industry, this transaction unites Transamerica and its shareholders with one of the most financially strong and successful companies in the worldwide insurance industry,'' stated CEO Herringer in a *Business Insurance* article.

At the time of the announcement, Transamerica's life insurance businesses—collectively held under the name Transamerica Life Companies—operated in the United States, Puerto Rico, the Virgin Islands, Guam, Canada, Taiwan, Bermuda, and Hong Kong. Its commercial lending business had lending offices in the United States, Canada, and Europe. The firm's leasing operations included more than 826,000 units that were leased to 380 depots across the globe. Its real estate services included information businesses as well as Transamerica Real Estate Tax Service, the largest business in the division.

The merger, completed in July 1999, combined the operations of AEGON USA and Transamerica to form the third largest U.S. life insurer. The two, operating among the AEGON Americas Companies division along with Seguros Afore Banamex AEGON, had combined assets of $131.6 billion. The focus of the combined companies was life insurance, annuities, and money management services, leaving much speculation as to whether or not AEGON was going to sell Transamerica's commercial financing, global container leasing, and real estate tax service businesses.

Under the leadership of AEGON, Transamerica entered the new millennium as an industry leader. Although its parent decided not to sell its other businesses for the time being, the firm's focus was strongly set upon its insurance and related services. The company's reinsurance group began expanding in Latin America and Asia, and in 2001, Transamerica set plans in motion to sell insurance in China. As one of North America's best-known insurance brands, Transamerica was positioned along with AEGON to see continued success in the years to come.

Principal Operating Units

Commercial Financial Services; Intermodal Leasing; Life Insurance; Mutual Funds; Real Estate Tax and Flood Services Reinsurance.

Principal Competitors

AXA Financial Inc.; Northwestern Mutual; The Prudential Insurance Company of America.

Further Reading

''Aegon-Transamerica to Form Third-Largest U.S. Life Insurer,'' *Business Insurance,* February 22, 1999, p. 1.

Bary, Andrew, ''San Francisco Giant: There's a Lot More to Transamerica Than Its Striking Headquarters,'' *Barron's,* August 10, 1998.

Carlsen, Clifford, ''Transamerica Set to Shed Unprofitable Unit,'' *Insurance,* January 22, 1993, p. 4A.

Dolan, Carrie, ''Transamerica Unit Fetches About $1 Billion,'' *Wall Street Journal,* April 20, 1993, p. A3.

Feuerstein, Adam, ''Transamerica Exodus Continues,'' *San Francisco Business Times,* February 16, 1996, p. 1.

Gilpin, Kenneth N., ''ITT Reported in $1 Billion Loan Sale to Transamerica,'' *New York Times,* April 1, 1995, pp. 35, 37.

Koster, George H., *The Transamerica Story: 50 Years of Service and Looking Forward,* San Francisco: Transamerica Corporation, 1978.

Leuty, Ron, ''CEO Reshapes the Pyramid,'' *San Francisco Business Times,* December 10, 1999, p. 1.

McGough, Robert, ''John Hancock Is Planning to Acquire Transamerica Corp.'s Mutual Funds,'' *Wall Street Journal,* October 18, 1994, p. C18.

Proctor, Lisa Steen, ''Transamerica to Sell Its 420-Branch Consumer Finance Business,'' *Los Angeles Business Journal,* March 17, 1997, p. 12.

''Transamerica Sheds a Finance Unit,'' *Mergers & Acquisitions,* July-August, 1997, p. 9.

—updates: David E. Salamie, Christina M. Stansell

Tubos de Acero de Mexico, S.A. (TAMSA)

Edificio Parque Reforma
Campos Eliseos 400, Piso 17
Mexico City, D.F. 11560
Mexico
Telephone: (52) 5 282 9900
Fax: (52) 5 282 9962
Web site: http://www.tamsa.com.mx

Public Company
Incorporated: 1952
Employees: 2,731
Sales: 4.24 billion pesos (US$443.91 million) (1999)
Stock Exchanges: Mexico City American
Ticker Symbols: TAMSA TAM
NAIC: 331111 Iron and Steel Mills; 33121 Iron and Steel Pipes and Tubes Manufacturing from Purchased Steel

Tubos de Acero de Mexico, S.A., which is generally referred to by its acronym TAMSA, is one of the world's leading producers of seamless steel pipes and the only one in Mexico, manufacturing them at a plant in Tejeria, Veracruz. This product, widely used in the petroleum and natural-gas industries, is manufactured in a wide range of widths, lengths, thicknesses, finishings, and grades. The company also produces steel ingots and bars as the material used to make the pipe. The raw materials to make the ingots and bars are purchased from domestic and foreign sources. A controlling share of TAMSA is held by a group that also controls producers of steel pipe in Argentina and Italy.

Prospering with PEMEX: 1952–83

TAMSA was founded in 1952 by Bruno Paglia, an Italian-born entrepreneur who emigrated to Mexico after first living in the United States. Some 50 million pesos (US$4.32 million) was originally pledged to the enterprise by Mexicans of Italian origin and foreign investors. Paglia received one-fifth of the shares. Another fifth went to Axel Wenner Gren, a Swedish industrialist. It was later learned that Miguel Aleman Valdes, president of Mexico (1946–52), also received shares, as did the widow of the previous president, Manuel Avila Camacho. Nacional Financiera, a government agency, provided 20 percent of the capital and took 30 percent of the shares in 1954. Government backing was essential to the enterprise, because it needed a secure market in the form of Petroleos Mexicanos (PEMEX), the government monopoly responsible for all oil production in Mexico. PEMEX also supplied TAMSA with its energy needs. In return, TAMSA became the chief source of seamless steel pipes for PEMEX, which previously had to import this product.

TAMSA began production during 1954 and made its initial public offering on the Mexican stock exchange in 1956. Exports to the United States began after the pipe received approval from the American Petroleum Institute in 1955. The company's pipes were also used for irrigation and by installations of electric power. Originally, pipe was purchased semifinished from other firms. In 1959 TAMSA began to make its own steel ingots in an electric furnace, using imported scrap iron as the raw material. Production reached 42,352 metric tons of pipe in 1956, with a value of 50.86 million pesos (US$4.07 million). The company took a stake in 1961 in Metales de Veracruz, S.A., which made reinforced pipe and high-pressure bottles and tanks.

In 1963 TAMSA produced 195,740 metric tons of pipe but was still importing 85 percent of its scrap iron. To free itself from such dependence, the company began making its own raw material in 1966, after signing a pact with the Mexican steelmaker Hojalata y Laminas, S.A. (HYLSA), giving it the right to use HYLSA's direct-reduction HyL process to convert iron ore into a substance (sponge iron) suitable for steelmaking. TAMSA took a one-sixth share the following year in a consortium to mine iron ore in the states of Colima and Jalisco for this purpose. The company added to its facilities in 1973–74 a mill to make special round and square steel bars. Company sales came to 1.71 billion pesos (US$136.8 million) in 1975. The sales figure was 5.96 billion pesos (about US$260 million) in 1980, when TAMSA's output came to 241,820 tons. TAMSA took a 48-percent share in 1982 of Aerramientas y Tricones, S.A. de C.V., a producer of drill bits. The following year—shortly after a precipitous fall in oil prices touched off an economic crisis—TAMSA suffered its first strike, which, according to the company, cost it 600 million pesos (perhaps

Company Perspectives:

Our common mission is to continue being world leaders in the manufacture of seamless steel pipes, extending to our clients excellent service, keeping our costs at low levels, and seeking technological advances that allow us to remain in the vanguard of our industry.

US$5 million). An internal union dispute paralyzed the company's operations for 14 days in 1984.

Seeking New Customers: 1984–92

TAMSA opened its second plant, for manufacturing flat steel, in 1983. This raised its annual production capacity to 760,000 metric tons of pipe a year, but production in 1984 rose only to 325,810 tons a year, roughly one-third above the 1980 level. The following year, production dropped to only 296,740 tons. Sales of 128.38 billion pesos (about US$210 million) in 1986 compared poorly with the company's debt of $550 million. Consequently, TAMSA was employing 1,200 fewer workers than the 6,500 in 1983. Because of the economic crisis, PEMEX had cut back on its orders, and exports became a major factor for TAMSA for the first time. In 1982 the company sold only 2,975 metric tons abroad to two countries, but its exports reached 25 percent of sales in 1984 and 1985. However, this gave rise in the United States to antidumping charges that resulted in a ''voluntary'' limit on exports of tubular goods until 1992.

Despite these problems, TAMSA registered a profit every year in this period except 1986 and 1987. The debt, however, had reached at least $734 million by the time creditor banks reduced it to $280 million in late 1989. The company was now placing its hopes on the international markets, exporting, in 1990, 70 percent of its output to 42 countries. This was an impressive performance considering that, as TAMSA's export director explained to the *Wall Street Journal,* ''Customers didn't think such a technical product could come out of Mexico.'' However, the typical overseas sale was at a price inferior to that paid by PEMEX. Another hurdle to overcome was corruption at the port of Veracruz, raising costs so high that shippers were routing cargo to sites as distant as Houston. Seeking new sources of profit, the company even took a 20-percent stake in a cellular phone venture that held the franchise in two Mexican states.

After a profitable 1991, TAMSA's sales fell 37 percent the following year, and extraordinary charges led to a net loss despite an operating profit. PEMEX cut its purchases by 30 percent, and foreign orders fell by 49 percent in 1992. The recent demise of the Soviet Union was a particular blow, since this country—now broken into fragments and in desperate economic straits—had been TAMSA's chief customer abroad. And ominously, steel pipes were being replaced in some cases by plastic ones of high density and resistance. TAMSA closed the older of its two plants in 1992, reducing its labor force from 4,516 to 2,023.

Under New Management: 1993–99

TAMSA's stock, once trading as high as $25 a share, was selling at little more than $5 a share—less than half book value—in 1993, when the Rocca family of Milan, who were among the original investors in the enterprise, took a controlling share by paying the company's managers $67.1 million in cash. The Roccas also controlled Siderca S.A.I.C., an Argentine company, that, combined with TAMSA, held about one-fourth of the world's seamless steel-pipe market. But the two were selling their products at or near a loss, and TAMSA again lost money in 1993 (before a tax-related one-time gain) on sales that dropped 24 percent in value. In order to make ends meet, the company sold mining interests, land, and offices, withdrew from the cellular phone consortium, and dismissed another 5 percent of its labor force. Nearly half its debt of $492 million was short-term. In order to market a $65-million, five-year bond offering in 1994, it had to extend investors an annual interest rate of 13.5 percent—a junk-bond level. Almost immediately after TAMSA floated this loan, capital flight forced Mexico to devalue its peso, resulting in a new economic crisis.

Paolo Rocca, TAMSA's new chairman, and his team of Italian managers sought to change some of the company's business practices. For example, TAMSA was importing narrow-diameter pipe rather than producing it because the company was still gearing its production to PEMEX's needs, and PEMEX generally bought only large-diameter pipe. TAMSA also was importing rather than producing high-resistance pipe because of its own technical limitations. No immediate solution was found for these shortcomings, but the company formed a useful alliance with PEMEX—still its chief customer—to cut the costs of both by converting to just-in-time shipping. This required TAMSA to build three distribution centers near PEMEX exploration and drilling operations, but it strengthened the links between the two enterprises. The new management also reduced expenses by cutting its staff in Mexico City, the site of corporate headquarters, and selling the company airplane.

On an international level, the Roccas were seeking global synergy, employing TAMSA, Siderca, and Dalmine, S.p.A., an Italian company they founded in 1996 to specialize in industrial pipe. Each would seek business on its own but would be linked by communications satellite and the Internet, complementing periodic face-to-face meetings between the technicians and sales representatives of the three units, whose initials formed the letters of a parent organization named Grupo DST.

TAMSA's pipe production rose each year, peaking at 618,000 metric tons in 1997 as Venezuela became a major customer, purchasing more than 200,000 tons and employing TAMSA's just-in-time expertise. Meanwhile, TAMSA's production per employee rose from 101 tons in 1992 to 260 in 1997. Net sales rose to a peak of 7.84 billion pesos (about US$827 million) and net income to 2.57 billion pesos (about US$270 million) in 1996. Profits partially accrued from tax benefits arising from the company's losses in prior years. Long-term debt fell from 3.27 billion pesos (about US$345 million) in 1995 to 554.01 million pesos (about US$58 million) in 1998. (Peso figures for 1995–98 are in constant pesos with purchasing power at the end of 1999.) The company was even able to pay an annual dividend.

In 1997 the Venezuelan government decided to sell CVG Siderurgica del Orinoco, C.A. (Sidor), its steel company. Among the five companies that paid $1.2 billion for a 70-

Key Dates:

1952: TAMSA is founded to furnish seamless steel pipes for PEMEX, Mexico's oil monopoly.
1966: TAMSA begins making sponge iron to convert into steel products.
1983: A second TAMSA steel plant opens just as Mexico falls into an economic crisis.
1989: An agreement with creditor banks reduces TAMSA's crushing debt.
1992: Again in difficulty, TAMSA closes the older of its two plants.
1993: TAMSA comes under the control of investors who also control an Argentine competitor.
1997: TAMSA's pipe production reaches a record 618,000 metric tons.

percent share of Sidor (through Consorcio Siderurgia Amazonia, Ltd.) were Siderca and TAMSA. It was a questionable decision, for the sudden decline in world oil prices in 1998 to a level as low as $7 a barrel impacted TAMSA's sales to both of its chief markets, PEMEX and the Venezuelan oil industry. Sales to the United States were again being restrained by an antidumping ruling in 1995 that imposed an annual review for five years. As a result, TAMSA's pipe production fell to 565,000 metric tons in 1998 and 406,000 tons in 1999. The percentage of production exported fell from 80 percent in 1995 to 62 percent in 1999. Production of steel ingots and bars for use in making pipe fell from 744,000 metric tons in 1997 to 500,000 tons in 1999. Sidor was reported in 1998 to be about $40 million behind in payments to its creditors because of low world prices for steel and a deep recession in Venezuela. Nevertheless, that year TAMSA and a state-owned Venezuelan company, Cia. Venezolana de Guayana, entered an alliance to form CVG Tubos Industriales y Petroleros, in which TAMSA took a 70-percent stake. Renamed Complejo Siderurgico de Guayana C.A., this enterprise met TAMSA's requirements for hot briquetted iron—a raw material for the production of steel—in 1999.

TAMSA had net sales of 6.88 billion pesos (about US$726 million) in 1998 and 4.24 billion pesos (US$443.91 million) in 1999. It had net income of 1.63 billion pesos (about US$171 million) in 1998 but lost 77.23 million pesos (US$8.08 million) in 1999. The company eliminated its long-term debt, however, in the latter year. Siderca held a 41-percent stake in TAMSA through a Dutch-based affiliate.

Because of the prior closing of its older plant, TAMSA was obtaining its requirements for steel scrap, pig iron, sponge iron, and ferroalloys in both national and international markets. These raw materials were converted into the steel ingots and bars needed to make seamless steel pipe. The petroleum industry was using TAMSA's coated pipe to support the walls of oil and gas wells during and after drilling. Production pipe was then used to extract crude oil and natural gas. Conduction pipe was employed to transport oil and gas from the wells to refineries and storage tanks, and then to loading and distribution centers. The company also had the capacity to produce 7,500 metric tons of cold-drawn pipe with the diameter and wall thickness required for use in boilers, superheaters, condensers, heat exchanges, automobile production, and several other industrial applications.

TAMSA's engineers were, in 1999, working on the development of nonconventional pipes of high capacity with diverse applications, such as used by the auto industry and for the conduction of energy. The purpose was to find profitable business segments, such as the supply of special pipe—hard or flexible, as required by circumstances—and of different sizes. It was calculated that industrial pipe not related to energy could provide the company with 20 percent of its sales in the near future. The company even felt it could employ the technical and commercial resources of Grupo DST to aid companies seeking to drill wells in geologically difficult maritime zones where high-resistance but flexible pipe would be needed to make corrections in the route of evacuation. Experts said that the Gulf of Mexico contained zones with these characteristics, and that sooner or later they would be exploited.

Principal Competitors

Maverick Tube Corp.; Nippon Steel Corp.; Oregon Steel Mills Inc.

Further Reading

Barragan, Maria Antonieta, "El acero, por un tubo," *Expansion,* November 27, 1991, pp. 69, 71, 74, 76–77.

"Como caminar sobre un tubo," *Expansion,* April 14, 1999, pp. 34–39, 41–43.

La politica siderurgica de Mexico, Mexico City: Impremento Nuevo Mundo, 1976.

Martinez Staines, Javier, "Colgada de un tubo," *Expansion,* January 13, 1993, pp. 54, 56.

Ortiz Echavarria, Joaquin, "Las deudas por un tubo," *Expansion,* November 22, 1989, pp. 76, 79.

Solis, Dianna, "Mexico's Tubos De Acero Grows Robust by Making Itself a Pipeline for Exports," *Wall Street Journal,* July 17, 1991, p. A6.

"TAMSA Stands by Venezuela Investment," *American Metal Market,* March 31, 1999, p. 16.

Toledo Beltran, Daniel, and Francisco Zapata, *Acero y Estado,* Mexico City: Universidad Autonoma Metropolitana, 2 vols., 1999.

Torres, Craig, "Mexican Pipe Maker TAMSA Boosts Emphasis on Exports," *Wall Street Journal,* June 22, 1994, p. B3.

—Robert Halasz

Ubi Soft Entertainment S.A.

28, rue Armand Carrel
93108 Montreuil sous Bois
France
Telephone: (+33) 1 48-18-50-00
Fax: (+33) 1 48-57-07-41
Web site: http://www.ubisoft.com

Public Company
Incorporated: 1986
Employees: 1,700
Sales: EUR 259.8 million ($239 million) (2000)
Stock Exchanges: Euronext Paris
Ticker Symbol: UBI
NAIC: 5112 Software Publishers

France's Ubi Soft Entertainment S.A. is aiming for pole position in the world's video gaming industry. The Montreuil-based company is a producer, publisher, and distributor of video games for every gaming platform—from Gameboys, to PCs, to next-generation platforms including the Playstation2, Xbox, Dolphin, and Game Cube. Ubi Soft has grown rapidly since the mid-1990s to capture one of the top 20 spots in the world's gaming industry. Not content to rest, the company is gunning for a position in the global top five by the year 2005. Ubi Soft is already France's number two games maker—behind Infogrames—and one of the top three European publishers. The company develops its own games with one of the world's largest in-house production studios, publishes games developed by third-party producers, and acts as a distributor for other game publishers. Ubi Soft has more than 1,200 titles in print, and continues to develop new titles each year. The company's software is generally grouped under the educational, cultural, and entertainment categories. The company's early growth was fueled by the worldwide success of its Rayman character, which was launched in 1995 and which has helped the company sell more than six million copies of games under that title alone. The Guillemot family continues to own 30 percent of Ubi Soft, which is traded on the Euronext Paris stock exchange.

Brotherly Beginnings in the Mid-1980s

The five Guillemot Brothers—Yves, Michel, Christian, Gerard and Claude—were in their twenties when they took over their parents mail-order business in 1984 and formed Guillemot Informatique. The brothers originally oriented the business toward the distribution of hardware and accessories for the growing computer market in France. By the mid-1980s, however, the Guillemot family had recognized the importance of computer software—particularly as the computer industry neared full standardization of computer hardware platforms.

In 1986, the Guillemots set up a second company dedicated to the distribution of computer software. The young Brittany-based company had already become interested in entertainment software long before anyone ever dreamed that the video gaming industry would one day become larger than the motion picture industry. The Guillemots established Ubi Soft Entertainment S.A. in 1986. The company set out building up a distribution business, acting as a middle-man to bring foreign software titles to French retailers.

Expansion in the Late-1980s

By 1988, Ubi Soft had succeeded in attracting a number of important customers. Electronics Arts, Sierra, Microprose, Novalogic, and other early entertainment software leaders granted Ubi Soft the French distribution license for their titles. Soon, these companies had rapidly expanded their relationship with the young French company by extending their agreements to include international distribution contracts, as well. Ubi Soft not only imported and distributed games and software, but also began taking responsibility for adapting the software to specific language markets.

Ubi Soft established its first international subsidiary in England in 1989, launching Ubi Soft Entertainment Ltd. The company then quickly opened offices in the United States and Germany. The computer gaming market, however, remained restrained to a small but growing hard-core audience. While technology had come a long way from the original text-based computer games of the early 1980s, computers still were not powerful enough to offer the graphics, sounds, and music

Company Perspectives:

Ubi Soft's aim: be part of the top 5 worldwide publishers in 2005; make Rayman one of the 10 most popular cartoon characters in the world in 2005. Ubi Soft's ambition: spark your curiosity and desire to learn, take you beyond your dreams into these imaginary and yet incredibly realistic worlds . . . Invite you into this 360 degree-free world, which will quickly become yours. Ubi Soft strategic choices: the creation of innovative, quality software; creation and exploitation of strong brand names; the development of a major international production structure; the continuous deployment of a sales and marketing organization; exploration of the wide possibilities for expansion within the interactive entertainment market.

needed to help computer gaming take off with the general population.

Ubi Soft, however, was quick to recognize opportunities coming from other areas. The birth of a new generation of gaming consoles, taking over from such former game systems as the computer-like Atari and Commodore systems, sparked new industry in home video gaming. The new consoles by Sega and Nintendo needed a new array of software titles, and Ubi Soft quickly added such titles as ''Star Wars: The Empire Strikes Back'' and ''Street Racer'' to its distribution lists.

A Game Developer for the 1990s

A number of events marked the beginning of a mature video game industry in the early 1990s. An important step forward came with the birth of the Soundblaster computer sound card standard that opened new possibilities of music and sound on the formerly silent computer. The Guillemot brother's hardware distribution business was to become a chief factor in the success of the Soundblaster standard, which in turn produced benefits for Ubi Soft. Another significant event was the release of the computer game ''Myst'', which produced the first great hit for the video game industry and attracted an entirely new audience to computer games and video games in general.

Ubi Soft profited from the growing interest for the products it distributed. By then, the company was already preparing to transform itself from a simple distributor into a software production house. In 1993, Ubi Soft made a first step toward its goal when it acquired licenses from Sony and Sega to produce software for their video game platforms. By the following year, Ubi Soft had set up its own production house. The production house operated as a collection of studios, each of which were in charge of a specialized production area. In this way, Ubi Soft was able to keep up with the fast-pace of technological developments, while also developing strong characters for its games. The company also continued pursuing its international growth, opening distribution subsidiaries in Spain and Italy.

The Launch of Rayman in the Mid-1990s

Ubi Soft's big break came in 1995 when it launched ''Rayman'', its first company-produced title. Based around the title character's mission to save the world, Rayman became an international hit, and also set the company's tone for the next several years as a specialist in family and children's software. Rayman and its sequels, developed for the full panoply of video game platforms, proved to be a lasting success for Ubi Soft. Rayman titles topped 6.5 million copies sold by 2001, and even formed the basis for the character's own television cartoon series.

The success of Rayman enabled Ubi Soft to restructure its operations around its three areas of operations: distribution, publishing, and production. Ubi Soft also created a new organization for its software titles, grouping them under four principal lines: games, educational, artistic, and children's. The company then took a leap onto the stock market, taking a listing on the Paris bourse' secondary market in 1996.

1996 also saw the company achieve a new publicity coup. The widely publicized launch of a new Intel processor featuring so-called MMX Technology—which was supposed to enhance a computer's graphics performance—was accompanied by a Ubi Soft title, ''POD'', the first game to highlight the new technology's capabilities. Ubi Soft achieved international recognition through POD, which would go on to sell more than two million copies for the company. Ubi Soft also produced another hit that year, the ''F1 Racing'' simulation.

Meanwhile, Ubi Soft continued to develop its international network, opening production and distribution offices in Canada, Australia, and, significantly in Shanghai, China—where the company soon captured some 30 percent of that country's growing and potentially enormous market for video games. The company won another important license from Playmobil, releasing its first title under that brand name in 1998.

Ambitious Growth in the New Century

1998 saw an acceleration in Ubi Soft's activity. The company opened a new string of production studios in New York, Casablanca, Barcelona, Milan, and Tokyo. It also launched distribution subsidiaries in the Netherlands, Denmark, and Belgium. The company signed a number of important new distribution and licensing agreements with such companies as 3DO and Criterion. Meanwhile, the huge success of Sony's Playstation, the Nintendo 64, and the latest Sega, was helping to boost the company's revenues. The company's console-specific titles, including Rayman, Monaco Grand Prix and SCARS, came to represent nearly 50 percent of its annual sales.

Ubi Soft was also an increasingly international company—by 1999, nearly 70 percent of its sales came from outside of France. The North American market was also becoming more and more important for the company. By 2000, the United States market alone topped 30 percent of the company's sales. By then, Ubi Soft had won another important round of licenses, including those for Batman from Warner Bros., Donald Duck and Jungle Book from Disney Interactive, and others. In that year, the company also launched a children's television cartoon series based on its Rayman character. Adding to its international activities were the opening of a new production studio in Beijing, China, and a distribution subsidiary in Brazil.

Ubi Soft's growth enabled the company to move its stock listing to the Euronext Paris main board in 2000. By then, the

Key Dates:

1986: Guillemot brothers create Ubi Soft Entertainment S.A.
1988: Ubi Soft wins international distribution agreement from Sierra, Microprose, Electronic Arts, etc.
1989: Company opens subsidiary in United Kingdom.
1994: Company launches in-house production studios.
1995: Rayman is launched.
1996: Ubi Soft is listed on Paris stock exchange.
1997: Ubi Soft releases POD and opens production studios in Shanghai and Montreal.
1998: Production studios are opened in New York, Barcelona, Milan, Tokyo, and Casablanca.
1999: Production studios are opened in Beijing.
2000: Company acquires Red Storm (USA), Sinister Games (USA), and Grolier Interactive (UK); Ubi Ventures S.A. is launched.
2001: Blue Byte (Germany) and Learning Company entertainment division (U.S.A.) are acquired.

company's sales topped the FFr 1 billion mark, and Ubi Soft could claim a position among the world's top 20 video game companies—an achievement made almost entirely through internal growth, as opposed to through acquisitions, etc. Yet Ubi Soft now set even higher goals for itself, becoming determined to top EUR 1.5 million in sales and to crack into the top five of the world's gaming companies by 2005. In order to meet this goal, Ubi Soft finally set out on an aggressive—yet selective—acquisition drive, targeting companies to fill out its lists of titles.

In 2000, Ubi Soft made several important acquisitions—most notably, that of Red Storm, the games producer co-founded by Tom Clancy and a successful developer of titles based on Clancy's written works. The Red Storm acquisition, which cost Ubi Soft US $45 million, also gave the company a strong new online gaming component. Other acquisitions followed, with the purchases of U.S.-based production studios Sinister Games, and role-playing game specialist Grolier Interactive, based in England. The company also developed its distribution network through the purchases of Italy's 3D Planet SpA and Austria's Gamebusters.

At the beginning of the new millennium, online gaming became widely tipped as the next major trend in video game entertainment, and Ubi Soft rushed to boost its own presence in that market. In 2000 the company launched a new subsidiary, Ubi Ventures S.A., with its mission being to provide capital and aid in the development of start-ups related to online gaming. The company, together with Guillemot Corporation, acquired a position in the online gaming platform Gameloft.com. Another investment was in Ludi Wap S.A., a company specialized in providing games for the growing number of internet-access-capable mobile phones. The company expected online gaming to provide as much as 40 percent of its total revenues by 2005.

Ubi Soft started the new century with two more important acquisitions—those of Germany's Blue Byte, the country's leading gaming software producer, and the entertainment division of the Learning Company, which brought Ubi Soft a strong list of some 80 software titles (including the rights to the Myst series). Ubi Soft's sales topped EUR 250 million for its 2000 year. The company's selective approach to acquisitions had given it a series of strong brand names, while also extending its catalog to include game titles targeted at every segment of the increasingly diverse video game market.

Still led by CEO and founder Yves Guillemot and his four brothers in 2001, Ubi Soft seemed likely to meet its ambitious goals for gaming dominance. By 2005, Ubi Soft hoped to boost its revenues past EUR 1.5 billion.

Principal Subsidiaries

Ubi Soft Divertissements Inc. (Canada); Ubi Soft Entertainment Ltda (Brazil); Ubi Soft Entertainment Inc. (USA); Ubi Soft Entertainment Ltd (UK); Ubi Soft Entertainment GmbH (Germany); Ubi Soft SpA (Italy); Ubi Studios Srl (Italy); Ubi Soft Entertainment S.A. (Spain); Ubi Studios Sl. (Spain); Ubi Soft Entertainment (Belgium); Ubi Soft Entertainment B.V. (Netherlands); Ubi Soft Entertainment A/S (Denmark); Ubi Soft Srl (Romania); Ubi Soft Entertainment SARL (Morocco); Ubi Computer Software Co., Ltd (China); Ubi Soft KK (Japan); Ubi Studios KK (Japan); Ubi Soft Entertainment Pty Ltd (Australia); Ubi Ventures S.A.

Principal Competitors

The 3DO Company; Acclaim Entertainment, Inc.; Activision, Inc; Eidos plc; Electronic Arts Inc.; Hasbro, Inc.; Infogrames Entertainment S.A; LucasArts Entertainment Company LLC; Microsoft Corporation; Nintendo Co., Ltd.; SEGA Corporation; Sony Corporation; THQ, Inc; Vivendi Universal Publishing.

Further Reading

Dubois, Guillaume, ''Yves Guillemot, Breton 32 bits,'' *L'Expansion*, June 13, 1996.

Gurgand, Nicolas, ''Ubi Soft croque Red Storm,'' *Transfert*, August 29, 2000.

Mathiot, Cedric, ''Achat gagnant pour Ubisoft,'' *Liberation*, September 11, 2000.

Soula, Claude, ''Naissance d'un héros très moche,'' *Nouvel Observateur*, May 1998.

—M.L. Cohen

Vosper Thornycroft Holding plc

Victoria Road
Woolston
Southampton SO19 9RR
United Kingdom
Telephone: (+44) 023-8042-6000
Fax: (+44) 023-8042-6010
Web Site: http://www.vosperthornycroft.co.uk

Public Company
Incorporated: 1966
Employees: 3,882
Sales: £379 million ($606.0 million) (2001)
Stock Exchanges: London
Ticker Symbol: VSP
NAIC: 3366 Ship and Boat Building; 488390 Other Support Activities for Water Transportation

Vosper Thornycroft Holding plc is one of the world's major builders of warships and other marine ships, and the second-largest military and paramilitary shipbuilder in the United Kingdom, behind BAE Systems. During the 1990s, however, Vosper Thornycroft took strong steps to counter the highly cyclical and unstable shipbuilding market—particularly given the economic difficulties among many countries in the Asian market—by diversifying into related areas. As such, Vosper Thornycroft is now composed of three primary business divisions: Shipbuilding, Engineering & Composites; Support Services & Integrated Logistics; and Marine Products. Support Services & Integrated Logistics provides the engineering, logistics, and facilities management services to both domestic and foreign naval training programs, as well as its own training and employment services activities. Marine Products has concentrated in such naval and commercial vessel components as electronic control systems, motion control and stabilization systems, navigation and propulsion equipment and gas turbine fuel systems. Vosper Thornycroft's successful diversification has enabled it to generate more than 64 percent of its annual turnover through its non-shipbuilding operations. Nonetheless, the company continues to compete for and win contracts to design and build new ships for the British and other navies. The company is led by CEO Matin Jay, and shares are traded on the London Stock Exchange.

Two Companies With Late 19th Century Beginnings

Vosper Thornycroft was created in a merger between two prominent British shipbuilders in the mid-1960s. Both Vosper, based in Portsmouth, and Thornycroft, located in Southampton, had been established toward the end of the 19th century. The companies followed different directions, however, with Thornycroft gaining a reputation for its large-scale warships and Vosper developing smaller patrol-type craft. Thus, the eventual 20th century merger meant that the combined Vosper Thornycroft Holding plc featured highly complementary operations.

Thornycroft was established in 1864 by John I Thornycroft, who, at just 19 years of age, built his first steam launch ship. Thornycroft's original shipyard was at Chiswick, on the River Thames near London. Through the remaining years of that century, Thornycroft was responsible for building a number of the mainstays of the British Royal Navy, including the HM Destroyer Albatross, the HM Gunboat Melik, and the Launch Nautilus. At the beginning of the 20th century, however, Thornycroft transferred its operations to a larger yard at Southampton, which was the site of some of the United Kingdom's oldest working shipyards. The new quarters allowed Thornycroft to produce more modern warships, including the Tribal Class destroyer HMS Tartar, capable of speeds of 35 knots and more. At the same time, Thornycroft produced commercial class vessels, such as the cruise ships used by the Thomas Cook agency for its Nile River cruises.

Meanwhile, nearby Portsmouth saw the development of Vosper & Co. during this same period. Established in 1871 by Herbert E. Vosper, who was only 21 years old at the time, Vosper & Co. initially built boats for the local fishing and whaling industries. Soon, though, the company was also building commercial shipping vessels, tugboats, and barges. Vosper also developed its own engines, winning a reputation for its paraffin-driven engines at the beginning of the 20th century. The company also adapted its engines to other fuel types, such as steam and crude oil.

Company Perspectives:

A strategy is firmly in place which will enable Vosper Thornycroft to exploit its market leadership position and grow both organically and through acquisitions. Our mission is to maximize shareholder value. We will deliver this by building competitive advantage through working in partnership with our clients and anticipating market changes.

The period leading up to and including World War I gave both Vosper and Thornycroft a boost. Thornycroft's production turned toward destroyers—the company-built HMS Lance was credited with the first naval shot of the war—and submarines, while also helping to develop depth-charge systems. During the war, Thornycroft's HMS Teazer set a world speed record for destroyer-class ships, topping 40 knots in 1917. During this time Vosper had also turned its production toward support for the British war effort, producing work boats, dingies, and tenders, while also expanding into the production of shells.

The post-war years proved difficult for both companies, though, as the end of hostilities naturally slowed new ship orders. A major project for Vosper during this time was the refitting of the famous Discovery, used by Captain Scott on his explorations of Antarctica. After Herbert Vosper retired in 1919, the company began to shift its direction toward building up its design and engineering operations, and particularly to developing new engine designs.

Meanwhile, Thornycroft had diversified its production in order to compensate for the reduction in orders from the British Navy. The Southampton yard produced a number of vessel types, ranging from tugboats to cattle barges. Yet Thornycroft continued to take orders for military craft, completing a new-generation destroyer, the HMS Amazon, and also building six destroyers for the Chilean navy. John Thornycroft, by then known as Sir John, died in 1928. The company remained in the family, as his son John E. Thornycroft took over the company's direction upon his death.

Wartime Recovery in the 1940s

The depression years led Vosper to develop a new specialty—that of high-speed boats. The company's V8 engine quickly became a driving force behind a new growth period for Vosper, and the company became an important supplier to the British Navy, adding such ship designs as seaplane tenders. Vosper also helped develop a new class of motor-torpedo boats (MTB), capable of speeds of up to 48 knots. While the British government remained Vosper's main MTB customer, the company also began selling to foreign navies. During World War II itself, Vosper produced hundreds of MTBs, gaining international renown while also developing new types of rescue craft.

Thornycroft also benefited from the massive buildup toward World War II. The company launched two new D Class Destroyers—the Daring and the Decoy—both capable of reaching speeds of over 38 knots. The company also designed aircraft carriers to support the growing importance of airplanes in military strategy. Thornycroft became a part of the backbone of the British naval war effort, producing destroyers, mine layers, landing craft, and torpedo boats throughout the duration of the war.

The end of World War II forced both companies to once again turn to commercial construction to fill in the gaps left by the drop in military orders. During the 1950s, Vosper began developing a new class of air-sea rescue ships—the Brave Class series—capable of reaching speeds of more than 50 knots. Thornycroft continued to produce large-scale vessels, ranging from cruise ships to ferries and other passenger ships, while also picking up a number of yacht commissions. Destroyers remained a mainstay of Thornycroft's activities, though, including the 390-foot-long HMS Duchess. Still larger was the completion of the Sechura oil tanker, which had a displacement of 6,000 tons.

Mid-1960s: Vosper and Thornycroft Merge

The death of John E. Thornycroft in 1960 precipitated the merger between Thornycroft and Vosper at mid-decade. By then, both companies were enjoying strong international sales, each in their own specialized areas. With Thornycroft covering large-scale ships and Vosper supplying world-class patrol boats, the combined Vosper Thornycroft Holding plc—created in 1966—became one of the world's leading shipbuilders. Throughout the end of the decade and into the next, international orders became particularly strong for the company, arriving from the Middle East and Asia, as well as from Africa.

Vosper Thornycroft was buoyed by a number of important orders throughout the 1970s, including one from the British Royal Navy for Type 21 frigates, and another even larger order for Mark 10 frigates from the Brazilian government. The company also began development of reinforced plastic vessels, including the *HMS Wilton*, the first glass-reinforced plastic mine-counter-measures ship. The rise of a Socialist government in Great Britain brought the company under government control in 1977. The nationalization of Vosper Thornycroft proved brief, and in 1985 the company was taken private again through a management buyout led by the company's president, Peter Usher. Vosper Thornycroft listed on the London stock exchange soon thereafter.

A Shipbuilding Leader in the Late 20th Century

Throughout the 1980s, the waning Cold War years continued to provide strong orders for the company. Tensions in the Middle East, particularly in the Persian Gulf region, brought Vosper Thornycroft many orders from that part of the world. The end of the Cold War, however, cut deeply into the company's military-related orders throughout much of the world. Thus, in the 1990s Vosper Thornycroft put into place a diversification strategy to provide a buffer for its more cyclical shipbuilding operations.

By the late 1990s, Vosper Thornycroft had successfully reduced its reliance on military and other shipbuilding orders by extending its operations into two related areas—those of Marine Products and Support Services and Integrated Logistics. Marine Products included systems development, such as navigational, stabilization, and other control systems; and Support Services and Integrated Logistics focused especially on providing support services for both the company's own and other

Key Dates:

1864: Thornycroft is founded.
1871: Vosper & Co. is founded.
1919: Thornycroft delivers six destroyers to Chile.
1954: Vosper launches Brave Class boats.
1966: Vosper and Thornycroft merge.
1977: Company is nationalized by British government.
1985: Management buyout occurs and company gains listing on London Stock Exchange.
1998: Company acquires Brisco Engineering and Koop Nautic Holland.
1999: Company wins order for three fast-attack vessels for Greek navy.
2000: Acquisition of Bombadier Defence Services UK is completed.
2001: Company wins order for three offshore patrol boats for British navy; controversy over order soon ensues.

vessels, as well as related services such as training programs and employee placement.

Much of the company's diversification effort was completed by a series of acquisitions. Among the first of these was its purchase of HSDE in 1994, which added manufacturing facilities for the production of electronic controls. The company boosted its Marine Products division again in 1998 when it acquired Koop Nautic Holland, a small designer and manufacturer of stabilization systems based in the Netherlands. That same year, the company also added Brisco Engineering, which was acquired from Industrial Controls Services Group.

Vosper Thornycroft also developed its support services division during the mid-1990s. It acquired a 37 percent share of Flagship Training; it formed a 50–50 joint venture called FSL with GEC Marine; and it won a £300 million contract to take over the administration, training, and information systems of the Naval Recruiting and Training Agency. Another significant acquisition came in 2000, when the company acquired Bombadier Defence Services UK, adding that company's aircraft and equipment maintenance operations to its own. By the end of the decade, the company's diversified activities accounted for more than 60 percent of total sales.

Vosper Thornycroft in the New Millennium

In 1999, Vosper Thornycroft proved it had remained a key player in the worldwide shipbuilding industry when it won a contract to supply three fast-attack vessels to the Greek navy. The poor economic climate among the Asian and other markets at the end of the 1990s, however, caused a number of potential customers to defer the awarding of new shipbuilding contracts. By the end of 2000, Vosper Thornycroft was faced with an 18-month gap in its shipbuilding order book. The company, threatened with the possibility of being forced to close down its Southampton yard (which would have ended some 500 years of shipbuilding activity in that city), was rescued by an order from the Royal Navy for three new offshore patrol vessels.

At the same time, the company was awarded a contract to build three of 12 new Type 45 destroyers for the British Military. Yet that contract was soon embroiled in controversy. The deal was threatened when Vosper Thornycroft's larger rival, BAE Systems, tendered a bid to build all 12 destroyers. Such a move would effectively have given BAE Systems a domestic monopoly on all future destroyer production, since without the order, Vosper Thornycroft would not have been able to afford necessary upgrades to its production capacity. The dispute, which centered as much around maintaining a competitive domestic market, prompted the British government to hire the Rand Corporation to examine the Royal Navy's procurement program. The outcome of the investigation remained pending in 2001.

Principal Subsidiaries

Brisco Engineering Ltd.; Careers Enterprise Ltd (50%); Careers Management Ltd; Flagship Training Ltd. (37%); Halmatic Limited; Jiig-Cal Progressions Ltd.; Koop Nautic Holland BV; Maritime Dynamics Inc. (U.S.); Saudi Vosper Thornycroft Company Ltd (49%)(Saudi Arabia); Surrey Career Services Ltd.; TSS (UK) Ltd; Vosper Thornycroft (UK) Ltd; Vosper Thornycroft Controls Ltd; Vosper Thornycroft Controls Inc. (U.S.); Vosper Thornycroft, Inc. (USA); Vosper Thornycroft International Ltd.; Vosper Thornycroft International Services Ltd.; Vosper Thornycroft (Malaysia) Sdn. Bhd.; Vosper Thornycroft Marine Products Ltd.; VT Services Ltd.; VT Southern Careers Ltd. (75.1%); VT West Sussex Careers Ltd. (80.1%); Van Dusen & Meyer Inc. (U.S.); Vosper-ManTech Ltd. (60%).

Principal Divisions

Shipbuilding, Engineering & Composites; Support Services & Integrated Logistics; Marine Products.

Principal Competitors

BAE Systems Ltd.; Conrad Industries, Inc.; Harland and Wolff Holdings plc; Hyundai Corporation; Kvaerner ASA; Litton Industries, Inc.; Mitsubishi Heavy Industries, Ltd.; Mitsui Engineering & Shipbuilding Co., Ltd.; Montedison S.p.A.; National Steel and Shipbuilding Company; Newport News Shipbuilding Inc.; Niigata Engineering Co., Ltd.; ThyssenKrupp AG.

Further Reading

Harrison, Michael, "Vosper Secures Jobs with Pounds 60mn Order for RN Patrol Vessels," *Independent*, March 17, 2001, p. 19.

——, "Vosper Urges MoD to Speed Up Shipbuilding Order," *Independent*, November 15, 2000, p. 20.

Jay, Adam, "Vosper Prepares 650 Layoffs at Southampton," *Daily Telegraph*, October 4, 2000.

Nicoll, Alexander, "US Consultants Called into Vosper Thornycroft Dispute," *Financial Times*, May 3, 2001.

"Vosper Thornycroft Wins British Offshore Patrol Vessel Competition," *Defense Daily*, March 24, 2001.

—M.L. Cohen

Waste Holdings, Inc.

3301 Benson Drive, Suite 601
Raleigh, North Carolina 27609
U.S.A.
Telephone: (919) 325-3000
Toll Free: (800) 647-9946
Fax: (919) 325-3013
Web site: http://www.waste-ind.com

Public Company
Incorporated: 1970 as Waste Industries, Inc.
Employees: 2,100
Sales: $242.43 million (2000)
Stock Exchanges: NASDAQ
Ticker Symbol: WWIN
NAIC: 562111 Solid Waste Collection; 562212 Solid Waste Landfill; 562219 Other Nonhazardous Waste Treatment and Disposal

Waste Holdings, Inc., called Waste Industries, Inc. until April 2001, is one of the top ten waste companies in the United States. It boasts 42 collection operations, 24 transfer stations, 100 county convenience centers, nine landfills, and eight recycling facilities serving 360,000 municipal, residential, commercial, and industrial locations in the Carolinas, Virginia, Tennessee, Mississippi, Alabama, Georgia, and Florida. Unglamorous though it may be, trash equals cash in the heavily regulated world of solid waste management. Not many companies can count back more 100 consecutive quarters without a loss. The company is 60 percent owned by the Poole family.

Origins

Before starting Waste Industries, Inc. in 1970, Lonnie C. Poole, Jr., earned a civil engineering degree from North Carolina State University and an M.B.A. from UNC-Chapel Hill. After serving as an aviator in the Army, he worked as an engineer at two corporations. At one of these, the construction equipment producer Koehring in Springfield, Ohio, he conducted market research on a new mobile landfill compactor. Although the product did not test successfully, the experience introduced Poole to the world of trash at an opportune time: the federal government was beginning to mandate more sanitary disposal of garbage.

Thus Poole discovered his niche. He returned to his hometown of Raleigh in 1970 to start his business and to avoid moving his new family to yet another new town. At the age of 33, Poole founded Waste Industries, Inc. later in the year with $10,000 in start-up capital, derived from the sale of his home in Ohio, while the family moved in with his parents. Poole convinced his father to let him run the family store as well.

Poole then applied for another job at a local Caterpillar dealer, writes *Waste Age,* whose owner, Gregory Poole (no relation), provided additional start-up money. This allowed Waste Industries to begin serving several locations at once.

Jim W. Perry, who earned an engineering degree from North Carolina State before becoming a missile launch officer for the Air Force, joined the company in 1971 as its first employee. The company had a tough year convincing communities to operate landfills on a fee basis; private operators were rare. Increasingly stringent government regulations, however, would make the idea seem more plausible in coming years.

In 1972, Waste Industries started collecting corrugated cardboard for recycling. Eventually the managers learned how to price collection services to reduce risk in the volatile recycled commodity markets. This area would provide only a tiny fraction of revenues.

Waste Industries formed a waste equipment sales company, KABCO, in 1973, both to raise cash and to ensure access to good equipment prices. By then, Waste Industries was active in the counties of Wake, New Hanover, and Vance. Smaller towns and counties proliferated throughout the Southeastern countryside. Waste Industries offered these smaller communities a convenient solution to the heavily regulated problem of waste management. The company ran transfer stations for those counties that chose to export their waste.

The industry began to consolidate somewhat in the 1970s. At the same time, the public sector began to transfer more

Company Perspectives:

Throughout its 30 year history, Waste Industries has provided its customers with responsive, cost effective and environmentally sound solutions to their solid waste disposal and recycling needs and currently operates 43 collections operations in the Carolinas, Virginia, Tennessee, Mississippi, Georgia, Alabama, and Florida. Waste Industries, Inc. is a recognized leader in the industry and continues to be one of the fastest growing Waste and Recycling service companies in the Southeast.

responsibility for day-to-day waste management operations to private companies like Waste Industries, though the South lagged behind the rest of the nation in this trend.

Writes *Waste Age,* profits were low due to low acceptance from the public, who was not accustomed to paying fees to dump trash. Waste Industries exited the landfill business by 1979, instead concentrating on its trash pickup business. It had much better luck obtaining this type of contract from municipalities.

Branching Out in the 1980s and 1990s

As Waste Industries established branch operations in the mid-1980s, the company adopted a decentralized structure, because of the predominance of local issues affecting the business. It also installed a sophisticated computerized data collection system. After 16 years with the company, Jim Perry was named president and chief operating officer in 1987.

Waste Industries went on an acquisition binge in 1990. In the next seven years, it acquired 19 solid waste collection operations in a bid to become the Southeastern market leader.

A Houston-based firm with a similar name, TransAmerican Waste Industries Inc., offered to buy Waste Industries, Inc. for $209 million in stock in July 1996. Poole rejected the offer when TransAmerican modified it to a combination of $150 million in cash and stock, plus the possibility of a $50 million bonus if earnings targets were met. TransAmerican focused more on waste processing and disposal, compared with Waste Industries's strength in waste collection.

By 1997, Waste Industries had 20 branch collection operations, 11 transfer stations, and four recycling facilities serving 150,000 municipal, residential, commercial, and industrial locations, reported *World Wastes.* It operated 100 ''county convenience sites'' in rural areas of North Carolina. The company competed against as many as 9,000 smaller garbage collecting operations.

Public in 1997

The company launched its initial public offering (IPO) on May 14, 1997. The Poole family owned about 54 percent of shares after the offering, worth $135 million in 1998. Earnings for 1997 were $6 million on revenues of $116 million. After thereby raising funds for expansion, it examined more than 50 collection companies and landfills for purchase. Waste Industries owned few landfills of its own at the time. It relied on 60 public and five private dumps. Landfills and transfer stations were the focus of its expansion strategy in the late 1990s.

Annual revenues were about $160 million after the IPO. The company would increase employment by half, adding 600 new workers, and would acquire 34 companies in the next three years.

Waste Industries had a 25 percent market share in the Carolinas as it expanded in Georgia, Tennessee, Virginia, and Alabama. The Southeastern economy and population were growing a third faster than that of the rest of the country, said Poole. Commercial and industrial customers accounted for more than two-thirds of volume, noted *Barron's.* Waste Industries issued more shares to finance other purchases. It continued to expand in North Carolina and Georgia in 1999. In addition, the company acquired a landfill in Decatur County, Tennessee, a partnership with Liberty Waste Services.

In 1999, the company's CEO forsook his usual $400,000 a year compensation package, pocketing only a $4,200 car allowance and $50,000 in stock options (he already owned 48 percent of the company). Poole used the opportunity to cash in on tax credits; he also had won $442,000 for winning a blue marlin fishing tournament, ''enough to keep the lights on,'' he told the local *Triangle Business Journal.*

Waste Industries signed a lease for the top floor of a new Raleigh office building in October 1999. Soon after, the company traded a $60 million credit line with BB&T for a $200 million one with a BankBoston-led group of eight banks. Waste Industries had approached its credit limit with BB&T as it acquired ten companies in the first nine months of the year. (In so doing, it entered new markets in Mississippi, Alabama, and Virginia.) At an 8.25 percent average interest rate, the new financing was about two points more expensive, but the flexibility it offered seemed worth it to the company. A low share price ($13 a share at the time) prevented it from financing acquisitions by issuing new shares. Waste Industries's debt load of $130 million was two-thirds its total capitalization, reported *Triangle Business Journal,* and its interest payments were approaching net earnings.

Damage by two hurricanes pushed down earnings and share price in the second half of 1999. A record 22-inch snowfall followed in January. The company reported improved profits and sales for the fourth quarter, but warned of the pending impact of rising diesel costs. Waste Industries used acquisitions to expand its facilities in the Greenville, South Carolina area. In 2000, the company also bolstered its operations in Atlanta.

Even after buying 15 companies in one year and 58 in the 1990s as a whole, Waste Industries was still growing too slowly to suit some analysts, noted *Waste Treatment Technology News.* The industry was consolidating rapidly and they felt the company was at risk of being forced to sell out to a rival. Waste Industries continued its buying spree, moving into Kentucky, West Virginia, and Washington, DC in 2000.

High Tech in 2000

Waste Industries used the Internet for branch communications and speedier customer service. In 2000, the company

Key Dates:

1970: Lonnie Poole, Jr., launches Waste Industries with $10,000.
1990: Waste Industries begins buying up other companies left and right.
1997: An initial public offering fuels even more takeovers.
2000: The company shifts much of its communications to the Internet.

completed a project that replaced its satellite-based network with web-based e-mail and data transmission. It also redesigned its web site to allow customers to pay bills on-line, the first trash collection company on the East Coast to do so. These on-line payments were expected to cost half as much to process. Waste Industries also was using laptop computers to electronically govern the engines of its trucks. In 2000, it was beginning to plan its pickup routes using sophisticated planning software.

Waste Industries's share price fell nearly to $8 in April 2000. In June, the company announced its first stock repurchase plan. The slump was in large part due to changes in the weather—hurricanes and record snow—and to the downturn that had affected most publicly traded waste management companies.

In June 2000, Waste Industries traded two of its collections operations in Tennessee and Georgia, as well as an interest in an Alabama landfill, for a landfill and collection operation in eastern North Carolina from Allied Waste Industries. Waste Industires had begun buying landfills again in 1999, mostly to prevent other private companies from controlling the rates it paid.

As the company turned 30 in 2000, Poole told *Waste Age* that one of the keys to its success was employees who could do ''extraordinary work in a very ordinary business.'' He also acknowledged the particular effort required to make garbage haulers feel good about their jobs. The company nevertheless had an annual turnover rate exceeding 40 percent—not atypical for the industry.

Waste Industries merged with the newly created Waste Industries MergeCo to form a new holding company, Waste Holdings, Inc., in April 2001.

Principal Divisions

Central; East; Georgia; Mississippi Valley; South.

Principal Operating Units

Collection Operations; Disposal Operations.

Principal Competitors

Allied Waste Industries, Inc.; Casella Waste Systems, Inc.; Republic Services, Inc.; Waste Connections, Inc.; Waste Management, Inc.

Further Reading

Burns, Matthew, ''Waste King Poole Puts a Lid on His Paycheck,'' *Triangle Business Journal* (Raleigh, N.C.), May 21, 1999, p. 50.

——, ''Waste Loading on Debt to Spur Deals,'' *Triangle Business Journal* (Raleigh, N.C.), November 19, 1999, p. 1.

Byrne, Harlan S., ''A Prize Catch,'' *Barron's,* October 26, 1998, p. 20.

Fickes, Michael, ''Nothing But 'Net,'' *Waste Age,* WasteExpo 2001 Supplement, March 2001, pp. 174–77.

Rosser, Jenny, ''Its Stock Wastes Away,'' *Triangle Business Journal* (Raleigh, N.C.), June 23, 2000, p. 1.

Southerland, Randy, ''A Hometown Boy's Dream,'' *Waste Age,* November 2000, pp. SS8–SS18.

——, ''Life at 30,'' *Waste Age,* November 2000, pp. SS3–SS6.

''Waste Industries Plans Spending Spree,'' *Waste Treatment Technology News,* March 2000.

''Waste Industries Swaps with Allied Waste,'' *Waste Treatment Technology News,* July 2000.

Wolpin, Bill, ''Waste Industries Comes of Age,'' *World Wastes,* August 1997, pp. 16–20.

Youden, Pat, ''Innovative Trash,'' *Triangle Business Journal* (Raleigh, N.C.), June 23, 2000, p. 21.

——, ''Techie Talks Trash,'' *Triangle Business Journal* (Raleigh, N.C.), June 23, 2000, p. 28.

—Frederick C. Ingram

Wegmans

Wegmans Food Markets, Inc.

1500 Brooks Avenue
Rochester, New York 14603-0844
U.S.A.
Telephone: (716) 328-2550
Fax: (716) 464-4664
Web site: http://www.wegmans.com

Private Company
Incorporated: 1931
Employees: 28,500
Sales: $2.75 billion (1999)
NAIC: 44511 Supermarkets and Other Grocery (Except Convenience) Stores

Wegmans Food Markets, Inc. is a privately held, family-run corporation that operates a regional supermarket chain of approximately 60 Wegmans stores, in addition to 17 Chase-Pitkin Home and Garden stores. Known for its innovative approach to grocery retailing, Wegmans is consistently cited as one of the nation's top retailers and best places to work. With headquarters in Rochester, New York, Wegmans operates primarily in the central and western parts of New York. In the 1990s the chain expanded into Pennsylvania and New Jersey.

Starting Small in 1916

Wegmans was founded as the Rochester Fruit and Vegetable Company in 1916, a small food store run out of the front of the Wegman family's house in Rochester. After six years of selling groceries from home, brothers Walter and John Wegman moved their enterprise to a small, full-scale grocery store featuring canned goods, produce, a bakery, and even a cafeteria.

The two brothers became known as innovators in the grocery business, and in the early 1930s, they opened a self-service grocery, a new concept that would revolutionize food shopping. The new store was incorporated in 1931 as Wegmans Food Markets, Inc. The Wegmans store became a successful operation as well as a tourist attraction, featuring self-service and several other innovations, including vaporized water spray for vegetables and fruits, refrigerated food display windows, homemade candy, and a cafeteria that seated 300 people.

In 1950, Robert Wegman, son and nephew of the founders, became president of Wegmans stores, and the company began to invest in businesses that would enhance its central focus. Wegman acquired an egg farm and developed an on-site meat processing center and a central bakery. He also formed Wegmans Enterprises, Inc. to handle real estate development, leasing, and property management for the company. In 1969 he was named chairman and CEO of Wegmans, and the company expanded outside of Monroe County, building stores in Syracuse, New York.

1970s: Broadening Wegmans' Scope

The 1970s brought new 40,000-square-foot stores that were intended to incorporate the ''mall in a store'' concept. These new stores included gift cards, floral products, and pharmaceutical departments and were open 24 hours. Wegmans also became only the third chain in the country to use electronic cash registers, installing an optical scanner system in a Rochester store in 1972.

In 1973, Robert Wegman capitalized on the growing demand for do-it-yourself home improvement products, opening his Home Improvement Center next to one of the company's Rochester groceries. The following year, Wegmans purchased Bilt-Rite Chase-Pitkin, Inc., a retail operation that sold lumber, hardware, millwork, garden and landscape materials, and building supplies. Wegmans soon began expanding this chain, building Chase-Pitkin stores next to existing Wegmans stores. Robert Wegman's son Danny assumed the presidency of Wegmans in 1976.

The company began carrying its own store brand items in 1979, and the line became so popular that by the early 1990s, Wegmans was carrying 1,000 items under its own brand name, including a line of soda. In 1983 Wegmans became one of the first chains to install automated teller machines connected to local banks. The ATMs were profitable for the store because Wegmans owned the machines and charged fees to the bank for providing all the front-line services, including replenishing cash and receipt forms. Other developments included the 1986 establishment of the Wegmans Federal Credit Union for company

> **Company Perspectives:**
>
> *At Wegmans, we believe that good people, working toward a common goal, can accomplish anything they set out to do. In this spirit, we set our goal to be the very best at serving the needs of our customers. Every action we take should be made with this in mind. We also believe that we can achieve our goal only if we fulfill the needs of our own people. To our customers and our people we pledge continuous improvement, and we make the commitment: ''Every day you get our best.''*

employees. Four years later, the company opened one of the first child care services offered by a private company with its Wegmans Child Development Center in the town of Greece, New York.

Civic Contributions

Wegmans prided itself on its contributions to the communities in which it operated, noting its donations of damaged packaged goods and perishables to local food banks as well as its sponsorship of local events, donations of foods to charitable activities, and contributions to community projects. Wegmans has been nationally recognized several times throughout its history.

In 1987, *Fortune* magazine named Wegmans the best U.S. supermarket in terms of customer service. In 1991, Wegmans' Work-Scholarship program was awarded a ''Points of Light Award'' by President George Bush. The company, one of only two supermarket businesses, was also listed in the 1993 publication of *The 100 Best Companies to Work for in America.* Wegmans' entry in this list was based on the company's child and development center, medical and vacation benefits for part-time workers, scholarship program and Work-Scholarship Connection, job security, and opportunities for promotion.

Wegmans received the American Business Press competition, ''Points of Light,'' for its community service through its Work-Scholarship Connection program. Started in 1987, the program helped mostly 14- and 15-year-old children at risk of dropping out of school. The store gave these participating students part-time jobs and assigned a mentor to each of them. The mentor, an adult co-worker, helped the student on the job and with schoolwork. Students who stayed on the job and stayed in school to graduate from high school also earned a $5,000 college scholarship to the school of his or her choice.

Nevertheless, Wegmans has had its share of controversy and critics. The company came under attack from consumer groups as well as the New York State Attorney General's office for its alleged refusal to adhere to the state's item pricing laws. Wegmans' violations of state item pricing laws dated back to 1986, but the company argued that item pricing increased consumer costs because of the expense of pricing each item. Wegmans continued to stand by its electronic scanner pricing, claiming it was more accurate than price stickers and refused to pay fines levied against it for violations of the unit pricing regulations. Wegmans won the Attorney General's lawsuit, and the item pricing law in question subsequently expired in 1991.

Wegmans also faced protests from environmental groups when it launched a campaign to decrease paper bag use in favor of plastic. Environmentalists claimed that Wegmans was misleading the public with its claim that plastic bags were better for the environment than paper bags. The critics argued that for Wegmans the main issue was cost: paper bags cost $41 per thousand while plastic cost $18.50 per thousand. According to Wegmans, however, paper bags did not disintegrate in modern dumps any more quickly than plastic, and production of plastic was more energy and resource efficient. Wegmans finally responded to protests by letting each customer decide how he or she wanted purchases bagged. Furthermore, the company established bins for customers to deposit plastic bags for recycling, as part of a trial program with Mobil Chemical Company for recycling plastic. Wegmans also began using paper bags made from recycled paper.

Wegmans also felt criticism commonly directed at companies that experience periods of growth and operation expansion. The needs of the company, it was felt, in some cases conflicted with the needs and interests of local residents when Wegmans sought to enlarge existing stores, requiring the purchase of surrounding properties and development of new traffic control patterns.

By 1993, the largest Wegmans stores were 120,000 square feet, three times the size of the ''mall-in-a-store'' facilities established 20 years earlier. New Wegmans superstores included cafes with Chinese food, pizza and pasta bars, as well as cappucino and coffee bars. Wegmans promoted itself as a strong advocate of health and nutrition, launching a series of bulletins called ''Strive for Five,'' prepared by a registered dietician and featuring information and recipes for fruits and vegetables. Furthermore, in the early 1990s, Wegmans launched a line of diet foods, called ''Just Help Yourself,'' featuring frozen, prepackaged meals comparable to those offered by diet centers.

Expansion beyond New York

In 1993 Wegmans opened its first store outside of New York State, choosing nearby Erie, Pennsylvania. Over the next five years the chain would move eastward, adding five more stores, the last of which was located in Allentown, Pennsylvania. Wegmans appeared as if it was poised to enter the affluent suburbs of Philadelphia. Instead, the chain moved into the New Jersey market, opening a store in West Windsor Township just south of Princeton in 1999. The following year, the chain opened a store in Bridgewater, New Jersey. It also announced plans for a third unit, this one to be located in the upscale Monmouth County bedroom community of Manalapan, an hour-and-a-half south of Manhattan. Monmouth and Ocean counties, with their populations in excess of one million and annual household income of more than $48,000, appeared to be the perfect market in which to spread the Wegmans' concept.

During the 1990s Wegmans replaced older stores with new facilities and constantly adjusted their offerings in accordance to customer feedback. Wkids Fun Center opened in stores to provide supervised child care while parents shopped. The chain added to their list of private label products, offering phone cards, packaged bread, cereal, frozen family meals, as well as

Key Dates:

1916: Wegman family establishes the Rochester Fruit and Vegetable Company.
1931: Wegmans is incorporated.
1949: Stores are converted to self-service format.
1974: Company acquires Bilt-Rite Chase-Pitkin building and garden supply stores.
1999: First New Jersey store is opened.

vitamins, minerals, and herbs. Wegmans was especially responsive to the baby boomer market that was becoming more health conscious, bolstering not only its offering of product lines but health-related books, magazines, and yoga videos as well. Wegmans also introduced sushi bars to many of the Market Cafes in its stores. In 1999 it opened a highly popular French patisserie in its flagship store, created in large measure by president Danny Wegman's daughter, Nicole.

Wegmans and its efforts were recognized by major publications. In 1998 it was ranked number 16 by *Fortune* magazine (using the authors of the 1993 book) as one of the ''100 Best Companies to Work for in America.'' While the industry average employee turnover rate was 16.7 percent a year, Wegmans' turnover was only 9 percent. The company would continue to make the top employer list through 2001. According to customers, in a 2000 *Consumer Reports* survey of supermarket chains, Wegmans ranked second.

However, Wegmans suffered some setbacks in the 1990s. Because of competition from home improvement chains such as Home Depot, the Buffalo-area Chase-Pitkin stores were closed. Wegmans endured a public relations embarrassment in 1997 when it, along with several manufacturers, were sued by the New York State Attorney General's office for colluding to eliminate manufacturers' coupons in Upstate New York, where coupons are more heavily used than in other regions of the country, at great expense to both retailers and manufacturers. Without admitting guilt, Wegmans agreed to settle by paying $500,000.

Wegmans, with its loyal base of customers and unique blend of ambiance, products, and services, has been somewhat immune to competition. Loathe to become so large a chain that management can't keep close tabs on individual stores, Wegmans faced a number of challenges. Mergers in the supermarket industry were creating superchains that commanded tremendous benefits from their economies of scale. Furthermore, grocery products were becoming increasingly more available at drugstore chains and big box discounters like Kmart and Target, which were opening supercenters that included full lines of groceries. In late 2000, the trade journal *Supermarket News* suggested that Wegmans might be an acquisition target for Kroger or Safeway, or even part of a three-way merger between Virginia-based Ukrop's Supermarkets and North Carolina-based Harris Teeter. Wegmans dismissed all such speculation, intent on remaining independent. Whether the sheer economics of contemporary grocery retailing forecloses that option, however, remained to be seen.

Principal Competitors

Great Atlantic & Pacific Tea Company (A&P); Penn Traffic Company; Safeway Inc.; Wal-Mart Stores Inc.

Further Reading

Khermouch, Gerry, ''Wegmans Builds Its Local Base with Private Label,'' *Brandweek,* March 8, 1993, p. 23.

Linstedt, Sharon, ''Supermarkets Brace for a Good, Old-Fashioned Food Fight,'' *Buffalo News,* January 28, 2001, p. P50.

——, ''Wegmans May Get Buyout Offer Journal Says,'' *Buffalo News,* September 21, 2000, p. E1.

——, ''Wegmans, Tops Rated Among Nation's Best Supermarkets,'' *Buffalo News,* August 18, 2000, p. C7.

Narisetti, Raju, ''P&G Settles with New York over Coupons—Firm, Nine Others Agree to Provide $4.2 Million in Cents-Off Squabble,'' September 10, 1997, p. A4.

Uttal, Bro, Bill Saporito, and Monci Jo Williams, ''Companies That Serve You Best,'' *Fortune,* December 7, 1987, p. 98.

''A Winning Day at the White House,'' *Supermarket Business,* November 1991, p. 9.

—Wendy J. Stein
—updated by Ed Dinger

Whitman Education Group, Inc.

4400 Biscayne Boulevard
Miami, Florida 33137
U.S.A.
Telephone: (305) 575-6510
Fax: (305) 575-6537
Web site: http://www.whitmaneducation.com

Public Company
Incorporated: 1979 as Whitman Medical Corporation
Employees: 1,099
Sales: $77.6 million (2000)
Stock Exchanges: American
Ticker Symbol: WIX
NAIC: 611519 Other Technical and Trade Schools

Whitman Education Group, Inc. operates more than 20 for-profit, postsecondary schools in 13 states, offering both nondegree certificate programs as well as undergraduate and graduate degree programs. Originally devoted to training ultrasound technicians, Whitman's Ultrasound Diagnostic School also now offers short-term programs in a variety of healthcare fields at its 15 locations in nine states. The five campuses that comprise Whitman's Sanford-Brown College offer professional certificate programs in computer technology and business in addition to programs in the healthcare field. Like other Whitman schools, Colorado Tech University is geared toward working adults, but unlike the others it also offers degree programs. Students can earn bachelor's degrees in computer science, management, engineering, and education; and master's degrees in computer science, computer engineering, electrical engineering, management, and business administration. Colorado Tech also offers doctorate degrees in computer science and management. The chairman of Whitman's board is well-known Miami entrepreneur Dr. Phillip Frost, who owns more than a third of the company's stock.

Founding Whitman Medical Corp. in 1979

The original name of the company was Whitman Medical Corp. when it was first organized in 1979. Operating out of Clark, New Jersey, Whitman Medical made medical products, albeit with little success. In 1984 the company entered the education field by acquiring Ultrasound Technical Services, Inc. for $1,000 and 50,000 shares of stock, thereby gaining two New York schools that trained ultrasound technicians. Combined enrollment totaled just 50 students. Over the next nine years the company would add eight more schools, boosting enrollment to some 400 students. By 1991 the company posted revenues of $3.4 million, attracting the attention of Frost, who in April 1992 led an investment group that purchased 980,000 new shares of Whitman Medical stock for $1.5 million. A trust associated with Frost bought an additional 19 percent of the company. He was soon named chairman of Whitman; its stock nearly doubled in price, mostly due to the strength of his name.

Frost took an unusual path to becoming an acclaimed entrepreneur and eventually cited by *Forbes* magazine as one of America's wealthiest people. His formative years in Philadelphia provided what he described as ''a meager background.'' He learned about business by working in his father's shoe store, yet he would attend an Ivy League college, The University of Pennsylvania, where he majored in French literature. Unsure of his future plans during his senior year, he turned to medicine, mostly because a scholarship was available for graduates of his old high school at the Albert Einstein College of Medicine in New York. He then distinguished himself during his residency at the University of Miami and was named to the school's faculty. In 1970 he joined the Mt. Sinai Medical Center in Miami Beach and established the dermatology department, which he would chair until 1990. Aside from his medical practice and administrative duties, Frost found time to become involved in business. He started a fish farm in the everglades, and when a drought dried up his ponds and killed off his stock, Frost displayed a talent for dealmaking that would later serve him well, as he salvaged the venture by selling off the land at a profit. Frost also invented several medical-related devices, including a disposable instrument for doing biopsies. In 1972 he and his partner Michael Jaharis bought a small drug manufacturer, Key Pharmaceuticals, that was on the verge of collapse. Key was intended to market Frost's inventions, but with Jaharis running the company's day-to-day affairs, Frost again showed off his talent for making shrewd deals, building the company through a number of acquisitions. He also demonstrated a keen instinct for adaptability. Key found a niche by developing and marketing new delivery systems for already proven drugs. The culmination for Frost at

Company Perspectives:

Whitman is a proprietary provider of career-oriented post-secondary education. Our students are predominantly adults seeking graduate, undergraduate and non-degree certificate and diploma programs to facilitate their success in the high-demand job fields of information technology, healthcare and business.

Key came in 1986 when he was able to sell the business to Schering-Plough for a staggering $835 million, pocketing $150 million for both himself and his partner. Frost then bought Diamedix, a diagnostics kit company, and Pharmedix, a pharmaceutical company, both of which were small and losing money. In December 1987 he combined them with a chemical company named Ivaco to create IVAX Corp. By the mid-1990s, IVAX would be America's largest generic drug maker.

Compared with his previous ventures, Frost's involvement with Whitman Medical was from a major transaction. As chairman of the Department of Dermatology at Mt. Sinai Medical Center of Greater Miami from 1972 to 1990, as well as serving as a trustee of the University of Miami, Frost had shown a commitment to education, but he also recognized the business potential of Whitman Medical's proprietary schools. Although business schools and technical schools had operated in America for more than a century, proprietary schools generally suffered from an unsavory reputation, considered in higher education circles as little more than diploma mills, whose graduates had an unusually high default rate on student loans. Both the federal government and a number of states cracked down on the industry. In 1989 federal regulations on student loans were tightened so that schools were dropped from the program if student default rates exceeded 40 percent in one year or 25 percent in three consecutive years. States also took steps to make sure that programs were providing a legitimate education. As a result, many of the less reputable schools were forced to close their doors. At the same time, the demand for training, especially among adults already in the workforce, was growing. Downsized workers looked to find new areas of employment, while other students simply wanted to move to higher paying jobs. Furthermore, as businesses became computerized, many established workers also required new training in order to perform their work. The initial public offering of stock made by technical school giant De Vry in 1991 reflected the rising prospects for proprietary schools. A highly fragmented industry overall, postsecondary, proprietary education was poised for consolidation by companies with the necessary financial backing.

Concentrating on Education in 1993

After Frost became chair of Whitman, Randy S. Proto continued to serve as president. Until Frost bought into the company Proto had been the chief executive officer for seven years, with an ownership stake in a number of Whitman Medical's proprietary schools. Before that he had worked for Computer Processing Institute, serving in a number of executive capacities before becoming vice-president and school director. In 1993, Whitman Medical discontinued its manufacturing operations in order to devote all of its resources to its education business. In 1994 the company added five new Ultrasound Diagnostic School locations, bringing the total to 15. It also made its first major acquisition, the $9 million combined cash and stock purchase of Sanford-Brown College. The history of Sanford-Brown dated back to 1868 when the school was established in St. Louis to train Civil War veterans. For fiscal 1994 Whitman generated more than $12 million in revenues and posted a profit of $352,819. With the Sanford-Brown acquisition adversely impacting the bottom line in 1995, Whitman Medical would lose almost $150,000, although revenues would increase to approximately $17.5 million.

Whitman Medical undertook a number of changes in 1996. To better reflect the new focus of the business the company changed its name from Whitman Medical Corp. to Whitman Education Group, Inc. It also relocated from New Jersey to Miami, setting up shop in IVAX's office building. Not only did the move bring the business closer to Frost, the company's largest shareholder, Whitman also was interested in Florida's growing population, looking to expand upon the schools it already operated in Pompano Beach, Tampa, and Jacksonville.

In March 1996 Whitman made its second major acquisition, taking over Colorado Technical College and its advertising agency, Concept Communications, in an all-stock transaction. The school was established in 1965 in Manitou Springs, Colorado, with the goal of training ex-military personnel in such fields as television and radio repair. It went through a number of owners before ex-Marine and former mattress salesman David O'Donnell took over in 1986. He inherited one building with a condemned roof, $1.8 million in debt, and just 240 students. He moved the trade school to Colorado Springs and began the process of turning around the business before eventually selling out to Whitman. Because Colorado Tech had been accredited by the North Central Association of Colleges and Schools in 1986, it formed the basis of Whitman's University Degree Division. As the result of the merger with Whitman, however, the school lost its eligibility for federally funded student financial aid programs. Nevertheless, Colorado Tech continued to grow under O'Donnell and its new parent corporation. The school opened a new campus in Denver in the Denver Tech Center, then acquired Huron University and its two South Dakota campuses. Having lost its accreditation, Huron, which was founded in 1883, was on the verge of collapse when Colorado Tech purchased the school for $2.25 million. The Sioux Falls campus would serve as a new location for Colorado Tech, while the main Huron campus would take Whitman into the residential institution business, serving more traditional college-age students. Also in 1996, Ultrasound Diagnostic Services added to its curriculum. Beginning with seven of its schools, it offered a Cardiovascular Technology program, which trained medical personnel in noninvasive cardiac procedures, including EKG, echocardiography, and stress testing. The new Medical Assisting program provided training in basic healthcare administrative functions such as scheduling, insurance billing, and medical computer systems, as well as training for basic on-site laboratory tests, vital signs, sterile procedures, diet, and medication. Overall in 1996 Whitman saw its revenues more than double, exceeding $36 million, but again the company posted a loss, which amounted to $100,000.

Suffering a Downturn in 1996

Although Frost made the 1996 *Forbes* 400 list of the nation's wealthiest people, attributed with a personal fortune of

Key Dates:

1979: Whitman Medical Corp. established.
1984: The company acquires Ultrasound Technical Services.
1992: Dr. Phillip Frost becomes chairman of the board.
1993: Manufacturing operations are discontinued.
1994: Sanford-Brown College is acquired.
1996: The name is changed to Whitman Education Group; Colorado Technical University is acquired.

$490 million, his reputation for a Midas touch was coming under question. IVAX went through two failed merger attempts, and poor financial results led to a 64 percent drop in the company's stock in 1996, forcing a sell-off of nondrug assets. The price of Whitman stock, which had risen from $3 a share in 1995 to almost $10 a share by July 1996, also would begin to suffer, as investors became less enamoured by the so-called "Frost factor" and began looking for more tangible evidence that Whitman was ever going to be profitable. In 1997 the company would again see increased revenues, nearly $47 million, yet it lost more than $4.3 million.

In March 1997, Frost brought in one of his IVAX executives to run Whitman, installing Richard C. Pfenniger in the newly created position of chief executive officer and vice-chairman. An attorney, Pfenniger had served in a number of positions at IVAX, including chief operating officer and secretary of the corporation. He had also been a member of Whitman's board since 1992. As the company digested its acquisitions and Pfenniger made efforts to control costs, Whitman returned to modest profitability in 1998. Revenues continued to grow, exceeding $60 million, and Whitman reported a net profit of $143,000. During 1998, the company also decided to unload its Huron acquisition, selling the university to a group of investors led by the school's chancellor. Despite increased enrollment Huron was losing money, and Whitman recognized that the growth area in the proprietary education industry was working adults who attended part-time, rather than recent high school graduates who attended a residential institution. The proprietary education business continued to look promising, accounting for $3.5 billion in 1995, according to the most recent numbers. Moreover, that figure was just 2 percent of the $211 billion a year spent on higher education, indicating that there was still considerable upside for companies like Whitman.

It appeared that Whitman finally had turned the corner in fiscal 1999. The company earned more than $3 million on revenues that now approached $74 million, yet the company stumbled early in fiscal 2000. A change in advertising strategy, turning to radio and television instead of print, proved ineffective. Enrollment was down, first quarter results revealed a significant loss, and the price of Whitman stock began to slide. In response Pfenniger instituted a $1.5 million cost reduction program for the remainder of the year. Perhaps more troubling was the bad publicity the company received over a lawsuit that originally began in 1997 and achieved class action status in 1998.

The suit, initiated by former students of Ultrasound Diagnostic Schools, alleged that the school did not meet the minimal standards of an ultrasound program because it lacked meaningful admission standards, instructors were not qualified, and students were allowed to graduate without demonstrating proficiency. In essence, the suit alleged that the ultrasound school perpetuated fraud, using students to secure money through the federal government student loan program. Pfenniger vehemently denied the charges, contending that Whitman was the victim of opportunists. Nevertheless, the company settled the suit for $7.3 million in October 2000. Although some of the amount was covered by insurance, Whitman would have to take a one-time, after-tax charge of $932,000. Pfenniger continued to deny the charges and insisted that the company simply settled to avoid further litigation costs.

In part due to the settlement, Whitman lost $500,000 in 2000 on revenues of $77.6 million. The company's stock also dipped as low as $1. Whitman continued to show promise, however, in that it was well established in a business marked by tremendous opportunity. The number of potential students in coming years was a statistical reality, and the increasing need for postsecondary school training in the modern world was not in dispute. Moreover, the business seemed recession-proof, with bad economic times simply increasing the need for training. The likelihood was high that Whitman would eventually find its feet. Whether it would become another $1 billion business to add to the mystique of Phillip Frost, however, seemed far less certain.

Principal Subsidiaries

Ultrasound Technical College, Inc.; Sanford-Brown College, Inc.; CTU Corporation; Colorado Technical University, Inc.

Principal Competitors

Corinthian Colleges, Inc.; De Vry Inc.; ITT Educational Services Inc.

Further Reading

Guinta, Peterm, "Frost Is Building Another Drug Firm," *South Florida Business Journal,* December 7, 1987, p. 1.
Hick, Virginia Baldwin, "Trade Schools Pick Up Business," *St. Louis Post-Dispatch,* April 29, 1996, p. 10.
Hosford, Christopher, "Following Frost's Footsteps," *South Florida Business Journal,* November 23, 1992, Sec. 1, p. 1A.
Jaffe, Thomas, "The Patient Recovered," *Forbes,* August 23, 1999, p. 66.
Millar, Susan R., "Making the Grade with Whitman," *South Florida Business Journal,* July 8, 1996.
Miracle, Barbara, and Janice G. Sharp, "The Florida CEO: Who Delivers—and Who Doesn't," *Florida Trend,* June 1994, Sec. 1, p. 39.
Narvaes, Emily, "Colorado Tech Earning High Grades," *Denver Post,* July 7, 1997, p. E1.
Reingold, Jennifer, "Play It Again, Sam," *Financial World,* March 11, 1996, p. 24.
Strosnider, Kim, "For-Profit Higher Education Sees Booming Enrollments and Revenues," *Chronicle of Higher Education,* January 23, 1998, pp. A36–A38.

—Ed Dinger

Wild Oats Markets, Inc.

3375 Mitchell Lane
Boulder, Colorado 80301
U.S.A.
Telephone: (303) 440-5220
Fax: (303) 928-0022
Web site: http://www.wildoats.com

Public Company
Incorporated: 1987
Employees: 9,080
Sales: $838.1 million (2000)
Stock Exchanges: NASDAQ
Ticker Symbol: OATS
NAIC: Supermarkets and Other Grocery (Except Convenience) Stores

Wild Oats Markets, Inc., is the third largest natural foods grocery chain in the United States. With over 9,000 employees, the company provides organic produce, steroid- and hormone-free meats, bulk foods, vitamins and herbal supplements, and other products in its 110 full-service grocery stores across the nation. Riding a wave of growth in the natural and health foods market, Wild Oats has expanded rapidly since its founding in 1984. Although the company has opened a significant number of new stores, its growth has come mainly through the acquisition of single health food stores or small grocery chains. Its stores, in 23 states, are run under the names Wild Oats Market, Henry's Marketplace, Sun Harvest, and Nature's Fresh; in Canada, the company runs a chain known as Capers. The health food market is a small but profitable niche, dominated by only three significant chains: Wild Oats; market leader Whole Foods Inc.; and Trader Joe's Co., which sells primarily on the East and West Coasts. Hoping to bolster profits, Wild Oats named a new president and chief executive officer in 2001 and announced plans to sell off unprofitable stores and revamp some store formats.

Strong Growth from the Start in the 1980s

The history of Wild Oats Markets can be traced to 1984, when Michael Gilliland and his wife, Elizabeth Cook, entered the food retail business. While most natural or health food stores are based on the owners' dedication to health foods and a commitment to the environment, Gilliland and Cook got started by purchasing a convenience store, which they bought with cash advances on 17 credit cards and a second mortgage on Gilliland's mother's house. After the purchase of two other convenience stores, the pair decided to buy a natural foods market, Crystal Market, which they felt would prosper in health-conscious Boulder, Colorado. The $300,000 purchase, completed in 1987, thrust the couple into an environment quite different from the junk-food focus of convenience stores, an environment that gradually persuaded Gilliland and Cook to become healthy eaters themselves. In that first store, Gilliland worked the counter, while Cook worked the deli. Soon, the couple had opened another natural foods store, on the south side of Boulder, called Wild Oats Community Market. As the Wild Oats business expanded, a holding company was formed, and Gilliland became chief executive officer and president, while Cook became vice-president and in-house attorney.

The store grew steadily the first few years. By the end of 1991, Gilliland and Cook had opened two other Wild Oats stores in Colorado as well as two in Santa Fe, New Mexico. Another was opened in Albuquerque in early 1992. The company had a stable base in the early 1990s that enabled it to take advantage of a boom in the consumption of natural and organic products. ''It's happening everywhere,'' said Elizabeth Bertani, marketing director for New Hope Communications, a publisher of trade magazines for the industry. ''There's been a phenomenal upswing in natural foods consumption.'' With $2 million in investor funds, Wild Oats expanded into Arizona and Missouri in 1992 and into California in 1993. With 650 employees and 1993 sales of $50 million, Wild Oats had become the third largest natural foods chain in the United States.

Wild Oats continued to exploit the phenomenal growth in what used to be considered a tiny niche. The *Natural Foods Merchandiser* reported that sales for the industry were up 18 percent in 1993, to more than $6 billion. And they continued to accelerate. By 1995, industry sales were at $9.17 billion, up 21.5 percent from the previous year. In comparison, food sales as a whole grew only 2.5 percent between 1993 and 1994. (With total food sales at $416 billion, however, natural foods still had

Company Perspectives:

We promise to provide our customers with the best selection of natural foods and health care products in an atmosphere of friendliness, eagerness to serve and readiness to educate. We are committed to making our stores a pleasant and exciting place to shop and work, and to be active, responsible contributors to the lives of our staff, customers and community.

plenty of room to grow.) Wild Oats paralleled this industry boom, growing at a rate of 544 percent between 1989 and 1993. In 1994, *Inc.* magazine included Wild Oats on its list of the 500 fastest growing small companies. As if to underscore the point, the company bought two Kathy's Ranch Markets in Las Vegas in July of that year, for a total of 16 stores in five states.

Wild Oats benefited not only from rapid growth in the industry, but also from the business savvy of Gilliland. Never a slave to one vegetarian ideology, Gilliland designed each store to cater to local tastes. For example, the market in Boulder was completely vegetarian and fostered a down-to-earth image, whereas the Santa Fe store sold meat and high-end, specialty items. In some places Wild Oats was advertised as a gourmet market rather than a natural foods market. ''I'm a great believer in figuring out where customers are and walking with them,'' Gilliland said to Michele Conklin of the *Rocky Mountain News.* ''It doesn't do you any good to put a hard-core vegetarian market in the middle of Pasadena because you're going to go out of business.''

Despite its rapid expansion, Wild Oats in 1994 was still far behind the nation's top-selling natural foods grocery chain, Austin, Texas-based Whole Foods Markets. With sales of $300 million, Whole Foods also surpassed the next largest competitor, Fresh Fields, based in Rockville, Maryland. Wild Oats' most intense competition, however, challenged it much closer to home: Boulder, Colorado-based Alfalfa's Markets. After years of head-to-head competition, Wild Oats acquired Alfalfa's in 1996.

History and Acquisition of Alfalfa

Founded roughly the same time as Wild Oats, Alfalfa's had followed a similarly rapid growth curve. Mark Retzloff and Sahid Hass Hassan had cobbled together funds from investors, the Small Business Association, and themselves to open Alfalfa's Market in 1983. Retzloff told Claudia Ventura-Abbott that he ''wanted to deliver high-quality, natural foods to people. . . . I was very environmentally conscious. It always seemed right to me to be involved in this business. It was a conscious type of work; it was making changes.'' The store shelved only products with no artificial additives, then looked for pesticide-free produce and steroid-free beef. The company worked directly with farmers and ranchers to encourage the production of and provide a market for natural products. This commitment led Alfalfa's to work with 1,000 suppliers, compared with the supermarket average of 60 suppliers. Not the usual tiny health food store, Alfalfa's became a full-service grocery store. ''When we started out,'' Retzloff said to Ventura-Abbott, ''we wanted to be a transition-type of market. We didn't want to be classified as a health-food store. We wanted to provide an atmosphere that people would feel comfortable in. We knew we'd have to carry a full line of products—produce, fish, meat, deli, and bakery, as well as convenience products, paper goods, and cleaning supplies.'' The company added an in-store café in 1985 and hosted a cooking school with professional cooks and guest chefs. By 1989 Alfalfa's was one of the top five natural food retail stores in the United States and had annual sales of $19 million.

In late the 1980s and early 1990s, Whole Foods tried to take over Alfalfa's Markets several times, culminating in a bid in July 1991 that was on the verge of acceptance when Alfalfa's stockholders balked at a condition that 51 percent of Alfalfa's stock be converted to Whole Foods. The company continued to grow, taking advantage of the same market wave that Wild Oats was riding. ''There is a window here. You can't grow if the demand is not there, and now seems to be the time,'' Hass Hassan said to Jim Sheeler of the *Boulder Daily Camera,* ''There is an opportunity now and within the next two years. Five years ago, there were few communities that would support a concept like this. Now there are hundreds.'' Alfalfa's reached sales of $30 million in 1991, with 500 employees; it then reached $48 million in sales in 1993. The company arranged additional financing to expand further, adding several stores in Colorado, including stores in Denver, Littleton, Fort Collins, and Vail. By 1994 Alfalfa's had six stores in Colorado and had acquired Vancouver, Canada-based Capers, with two stores and two more soon to open. Alfalfa's competition with Wild Oats then grew more fierce as it opened a store in Santa Fe, New Mexico, in 1995, where Wild Oats already had a store.

In addition to being based in Boulder, Colorado, Alfalfa's and Wild Oats had much in common. Their commitment to providing wholesome, natural foods was joined with their commitment to their employees and the community. Both stores had profit-sharing plans; at Wild Oats this took the form of bonuses if the employee's store hit its financial goals. Wild Oats also paid $200 annually to each employee toward a ''wellness purchase,'' such as massages or a bike. Both companies were involved in the community: Wild Oats paid for one hour out of 40 of employee volunteering and gave 7.5 percent of pretax profits to environmental and social causes.

Despite their similarities, the two companies took pains to distinguish themselves, particularly in Boulder. Gilliland explained to Tammy Tierney of *Denver Business Journal,* ''They take the high end; we take the low end. We have lower prices, are more low key, and are not so inclined to gourmet items.'' Elizabeth Cook expanded on the difference to Tierney, ''We're a hard-core natural foods store. They concentrate on food service. We concentrate on bulk and mainstream grocery.'' In addition to competing for customers head-to-head in several cities in the West, the companies competed in their acquisitions. Both reportedly bid for the Kathy's Ranch stores in Las Vegas. ''I think we both learn from each other,'' Gilliland said to Sheeler. ''There's a certain amount of competitiveness that has kept us going, and if it were just us or them, I don't think we would have expanded so quickly.''

However much Gilliland appreciated the competition, he was willing to forego it. In 1995 he began negotiations to acquire

Key Dates:

1984: Gilliland and Cook buy their first food store.
1987: The couple buys the Crystal Market in Boulder, Colorado, and renames it Wild Oats.
1993: Wild Oats becomes the third largest natural foods chain in the United States.
1996: Wild Oats acquires competitor Alfalfa's Markets; company goes public.
2000: Chain has more than 100 stores.

Alfalfa's. That year, Wild Oats had expanded to 21 stores and had reached sales of $100 million. Although Alfalfa's had only 11 stores that year, it reportedly had also reached $100 million in sales in 1995. The merger would make Wild Oats the second largest natural food chain, outpacing Fresh Fields. The potential merger ran into a couple of problems. New Mexico raised questions about whether the merger would violate antitrust regulations. It eventually recommended that Wild Oats sell one of its stores in New Mexico but did not actively challenge the merger. In addition, Whole Foods Markets reportedly renewed its own efforts to buy Alfalfa's, leading to rumors of a bidding war. Although Whole Foods had lost its previous three bids to buy Alfalfa's, it had the money to make a sweet offer. With 42 stores across the United States and sales of $500 million in 1995, it had the resources to out-muscle Wild Oats.

Wild Oats prevailed, however, and the merger went through. The final agreement stipulated that the company would be based in Boulder and take the name Wild Oats, although existing stores would operate under their original names. The merger created a company with $200 million in sales and 3,600 employees in 39 stores in the United States and Canada. Gilliland remained CEO and Hassan served as president of the new company. The merger was completed in July 1996, with Gilliland and Cook owners of 30 percent, investors owning approximately 50 percent, and Wild Oats and Alfalfa's officers owning the other 20 percent.

Going Public in 1996

After the acquisition of Alfalfa's, Wild Oats concentrated on its next major goal, that of offering shares of the company on the public market. On October 23, 1996, the company achieved that goal, offering 1.69 million shares of stock on the NASDAQ. Speculation had been high that the stock would soar at the initial public offering(IPO), but with an offer price of $25, trading was low and the stock closed the first day at only $25.38. Jon Lieber, a broker at A.G. Edwards, considered the initial price too high, but also speculated that New York's biggest brokers did not understand Wild Oats' philosophy. ''I'm from Manhattan,'' he said to John Accola of the *Rocky Mountain News,* ''and, believe me, health food is definitely few and far between. You walk out of any exchange at noon, and they are inhaling hot dogs, pizzas, and gyros.'' Gilliland had expressed some concern about this to Conklin at the *Rocky Mountain News* before the IPO: ''The biggest challenge will be balancing Wall Street but staying true to our mission. Is Wall Street going to appreciate that we have guest practitioners (such as nutritionists) on staff that we're not making money off of?''

The stock slipped after the IPO, coming to rest for the next few months around $17 to $18 a share. Then, in mid-January 1997, an analyst downgraded her rating of the company two notches based on information that Whole Foods intended to challenge Wild Oats by opening stores in Boulder, Denver, Santa Fe, and Salt Lake City—traditional Wild Oats territory. The stock fell 26 percent in one day, to $13.13.

Wild Oats ended 1996 with strong growth figures. Sales had risen to $192.5 million, largely because of the opening of seven new stores and the acquisition of 13 stores in 1996. The company did report a net loss for the year, however, of $4.5 million. The company attributed the loss to nonrecurring charges related to acquisitions, the closing of some stores, and the consolidation of corporate headquarters after the Alfalfa's acquisition. Without these nonrecurring charges of $7 million, company profits would have been $2.5 million, up from $779,000 in 1995. In addition, same-store sales, which only measure sales from stores the company has owned for at least a full year, rose 3.8 percent, almost double the figure predicted by analysts.

These figures did not raise market confidence, however. The day Wild Oats announced its final quarter numbers, its stock actually fell $.25, to $13.88. Gilliland responded to continued concern about Whole Foods' proposed new stores by citing the double-digit gains in the natural foods market, which he felt assured Wild Oats room for continued growth, even in a more crowded marketplace. In addition, he was quoted by Lisa Greim in the *Rocky Mountain News* as saying, ''We do very well against them in California. I think Whole Foods is going to be disappointed.''

Despite the apparent lukewarm confidence of the stock market and the specter of increased competition from Whole Foods, Wild Oats continued its aggressive pattern of growth through acquisitions. The company completed a deal with Wholly Harvest in Florida in early 1997, trading stock for two stores. Wild Oats also moved into the Northwest, purchasing two natural food supermarkets in Eugene, Oregon, in March 1997. With the purchase of two stores in Memphis, Tennessee, the number of stores owned by Wild Oats rose to 47, a number the company planned to raise even higher in the coming years.

Competitive Landscape in the Late 1990s and After

Competition between Wild Oats and Whole Foods intensified in the late 1990s. Whole Foods opened its Boulder store in early 1998, and Whole Foods' chairman John Mackey announced (as reported in *Supermarket News*, March 30, 1998) that his firm was ''seeking head-to-head competition.'' Not only were both stores in many of the same markets, but they both stocked almost all the same things. Whole Foods made its mark by being bigger. Its stores on average were 24,000 square feet, with a mix of jumbo stores, like the Boulder branch, which was 39,000 square feet. Whole Foods commanded an estimated eight percent of the natural foods market by 1998, while Wild Oats had captured about two percent. Wild Oats distinguished itself from Whole Foods by aiming for a less traditional consumer. It wanted to be perceived as a natural foods store, not a specialty supermarket. Its stores generally followed two formats, a medium and a small. Most of its stores were around 15,000 square feet, and the small-format stores were only about 8,000 square feet. Chain-wide, Wild Oats's most profitable area was its Natural Living department, which sold herbs, vitamins, and personal care products. This one department accounted for almost one-quarter of the company's sales. After Whole Foods opened its huge Boulder store in 1998, Wild Oats announced it would open new, larger stores, of about 25,000 square feet, while also continuing to build small-format stores in certain markets. Meanwhile, by the end of 1998, rumors appeared in the business press that Whole Foods was ready to acquire Wild Oats. While Wild Oats executives refused to comment, Whole Foods CEO Mackey told *Supermarket News* (November 16, 1998) that it had no plans to buy its rival.

Wild Oats continued to make its own acquisitions, buying up two smaller chains in 1999. It paid $21.5 million for a Texas chain of nine Sun Harvest Farms, and then took over the San Diego chain of farmer's market-type stores called Henry's Marketplace. All told, Wild Oats merged with or acquired 41 stores in 1999. By 2000, Wild Oats had grown to over 100 stores. And the natural foods category continued to boom, keeping up a growth rate of close to 20 percent annually. Wild Oats's sales growth outdid the industry. Sales hit $721 million in 1999, a 36 percent rise over the year previous, and profits too grew 23 percent, to $17.8 million. A growing customer base and high mark-ups in the profitable niche seemed to promise great things for Wild Oats. Yet in some ways the chain was clearly not doing as well as Whole Foods. In terms of sales per square foot, the average traditional supermarket brought in $487. Wild Oats topped this easily, bringing in $538 per square foot, but Whole Foods was managing to make $826 per square foot.

By mid-2000, Wild Oats began to talk about adopting a new strategy, planning first to increase the average size of its stores, bringing them up to between 28,000 and 30,000 square feet. The company also decided to stock a different mix of products, bringing in more of the gourmet items the consumers were demanding as well as fresh bakery items and flowers. Also among the company's early growth plans was the expansion of the Henry's Markets chain, from 12 units to 18 by the end of 2001.

By the end of 2000, however, financial results were less than impressive, and Wild Oats management decided to close eight stores and take a $14–$15 million write-down. The company also said it would move to discount more items, while increasing its advertising budget. Speculation arose again that the chain was up for sale. Wild Oats reported a fourth quarter loss in 2000 and predicted flat sales for 2001 because of the store closings. The firm ended 2000 with sales of over $838 million, but it posted a net loss of $15 million. Comparable store sales, a measure of sales at stores that have been open for at least a year, also fell off, dipping 2.6 percent for 2000. Without fanfare, Wild Oats named a new president and CEO in March 2001. The company chose Perry D. Odak, who had previously held the same post at Ben & Jerry's Homemade Inc., the well-known ice cream company. The company continued its expansion, with plans to open ten new stores in 2001. One of these was a new prototype, a 26,000-square-foot store that would devote 20 percent of its floor space to made-to-order food.

Principal Subsidiaries

Wild Oats of Texas, Inc.

Principal Competitors

Whole Foods Market Inc.; Trader Joe's Co.

Further Reading

Accola, John, "On Wall Street, It's Mild Oats," *Rocky Mountain News*, October 24, 1996, pp. 1B, 16B.

Brown, Adrienne, "Real Deals," *Colorado Business*, March 1997, pp. 20–25.

Conklin, Michele, "Growing His Oats," *Rocky Mountain News*, July 7, 1996, pp. 1–2, 11–14.

Gonzalez, Erika, "Food Stores Merger Gets Scrutiny," *Boulder Daily Camera*, March 15, 1996.

——, "New Suitor in Grocery Merger," *Boulder Daily Camera*, January 18, 1996, p. 1B.

Greim, Lisa, "Wild Oats Gains, Stock Falls," *Rocky Mountain News*, January 25, 1997.

"Integration Woes Lead to Losses at Wild Oats," *Supermarket News*, February 26, 2001, p. 44.

Kelly, Erin, "Health-Food Chains Spar for Baby-Boomers," *Fortune*, April 3, 2000, p. 56.

Lopez, Christopher, "Alfalfa's Natural Up North," *Denver Post*, July 24, 1994.

Parker, Penny, "Wild Oats Sowing New Seeds," *Denver Post*, November 18, 1994, pp. 1C, 5C.

Sheeler, Jim, "Wild Oats, Alfalfa's Become Power Players with Acquisition," *Boulder Daily Camera*, July 26, 1994.

Smith, Jerd, "Alfalfa's, Wild Oats Expanding Rapidly with Venture Funds," *Denver Business Journal*, January 24, 1992.

Smith, Kerri S., "Wild Oats Jarred," *Denver Post*, January 15, 1997, pp. 1E, 8E.

Springer, Jon, "Food for Thought Workers Vote for Union," *Supermarket News*, April 10, 2000, p. 4.

Sutton, David, and Jennifer Lindsey, "Specialty Food Partners Make Profit," *Denver Post*, November 23, 1985, p. 2E.

Tierney, Tammy, "Markets Cash in on Buyers' Health Kick," *Denver Business Journal*, April 10, 1992.

Ventura-Abbott, Claudia, "Alfalfa's Laying Plans for Healthful Expansion," *Boulder County Business Report*, October 1989, pp. 18, 36.

"Whole Foods, Wild Oats Rivalry Intensifying," *Supermarket News*, March 30, 1998, p. 1.

"Wild Oats: It May Be Time to Reap," *Business Week*, November 16, 1998, p. 190.

Zwiebach, Elliot, "Whole Foods: No Talks with Wild Oats," *Supermarket News*, November 16, 1998, p. 4.

——, "Wild Oats CEO Sees Potential for Growth," *Supermarket News*, May 11, 1998, p. 4.

—Susan Windisch Brown
—update: A. Woodward

INDEX TO COMPANIES

Index to Companies

Listings in this index are arranged in alphabetical order under the company name. Company names beginning with a letter or proper name such as Eli Lilly & Co. will be found under the first letter of the company name. Definite articles (The, Le, La) are ignored for alphabetical purposes as are forms of incorporation that precede the company name (AB, NV). Company names printed in bold type have full, historical essays on the page numbers appearing in bold. Updates to entries that appeared in earlier volumes are signified by the notation **(upd.)**. Company names in light type are references within an essay to that company, not full historical essays. This index is cumulative with volume numbers printed in bold type.

INDEX TO INDUSTRIES

Index to Industries

ACCOUNTING

ADVERTISING & OTHER BUSINESS SERVICES

AEROSPACE

AIRLINES

AUTOMOTIVE

BEVERAGES

BIOTECHNOLOGY

CHEMICALS

CONGLOMERATES

CONSTRUCTION

CONTAINERS

DRUGS/PHARMACEUTICALS

ELECTRICAL & ELECTRONICS

ENGINEERING & MANAGEMENT SERVICES

ENTERTAINMENT & LEISURE

FINANCIAL SERVICES: BANKS

FINANCIAL SERVICES: NON-BANKS

FOOD PRODUCTS

FOOD SERVICES & RETAILERS

HEALTH & PERSONAL CARE PRODUCTS

HEALTH CARE SERVICES

HOTELS

INFORMATION TECHNOLOGY

INSURANCE

LEGAL SERVICES

MANUFACTURING

MATERIALS

MINING & METALS

PAPER & FORESTRY

PERSONAL SERVICES

PETROLEUM

PUBLISHING & PRINTING

REAL ESTATE

RETAIL & WHOLESALE

RUBBER & TIRE

TELECOMMUNICATIONS

TEXTILES & APPAREL

TOBACCO

TRANSPORT SERVICES

UTILITIES

WASTE SERVICES

GEOGRAPHIC INDEX

Geographic Index

Germany

Greece

Hong Kong

Hungary

India

India *(continued)*

Indonesia

Iran

Ireland

Israel

Italy

Japan

Korea

Kuwait

Luxembourg

Lybia

Malaysia

Mexico

Nepal

New Zealand

Nigeria

Norway

Oman

Peru

Philippines

Poland

Portugal

Qatar

Russia

Saudi Arabia

Scotland

Singapore

South Africa

South Korea

Spain

Sweden

Switzerland

Taiwan

Thailand

The Netherlands

Turkey

U.S.A

United Arab Emirates

United Kingdom

United States *(continued)*

United States *(continued)*

United States *(continued)*

Venezuela

Wales

Zambia

NOTES ON CONTRIBUTORS

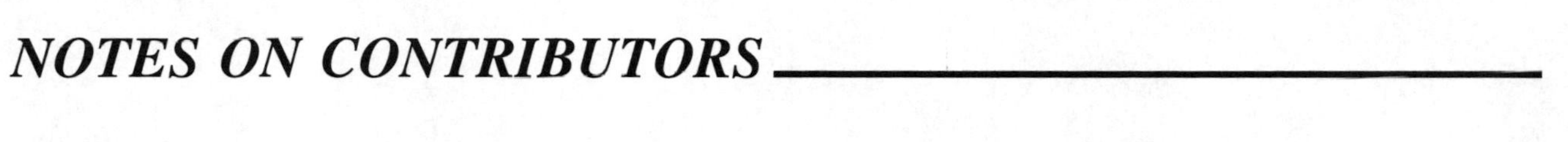

Notes on Contributors

BIANCO, David. Freelance writer, editor, and publishing consultant.

BRENNAN, Gerald E. Freelance writer based in California.

BRYNILDSSEN, Shawna. Freelance writer and editor based in Bloomington, Indiana.

CAMPBELL, June. Freelance writer and Internet marketer living in Vancouver, Canada.

COHEN, M. L. Novelist and freelance writer living in Paris.

DINGER, Ed. Brooklyn-based freelance writer and editor.

FIERO, Jane W. Freelance writer and editor.

FIERO, John W. Freelance writer, researcher, and consultant.

HALASZ, Robert. Former editor in chief of *World Progress and Funk & Wagnalls New Encyclopedia Yearbook*; author, *The U.S. Marines* (Millbrook Press, 1993).

HAUSER, Evelyn. Researcher, writer and marketing specialist based in Arcata, California; expertise includes historical and trend research in such topics as globalization, emerging industries and lifestyles, future scenarios, biographies, and the history of organizations.

INGRAM, Frederick C. South Carolina-based business writer who has contributed to *GSA Business, Appalachian Trailway News,* the *Encyclopedia of Business,* the *Encyclopedia of Global Industries,* the *Encyclopedia of Consumer Brands,* and other regional and trade publications.

LEMIEUX, Gloria A. Freelance writer living in Nashua, New Hampshire.

MEYER, Stephen. Freelance writer based in Missoula, Montana.

MILITE, George A. Philadelphia-based writer specializing in business management issues.

ROTHBURD, Carrie. Freelance technical writer and editor, specializing in corporate profiles, academic texts, and academic journal articles.

STANSELL, Christina M. Freelance writer and editor based in Farmington Hills, Michigan.

TRADII, Mary. Freelance writer based in Denver, Colorado.

UHLE, Frank. Ann Arbor-based freelance writer; movie projectionist, disc jockey, and staff member of *Psychotronic Video* magazine.

WALDEN, David M. Freelance writer and historian in Salt Lake City; adjunct history instructor at Salt Lake City Community College.

WERNICK, Ellen. Freelance writer and editor.

WOODWARD, A. Freelance writer.